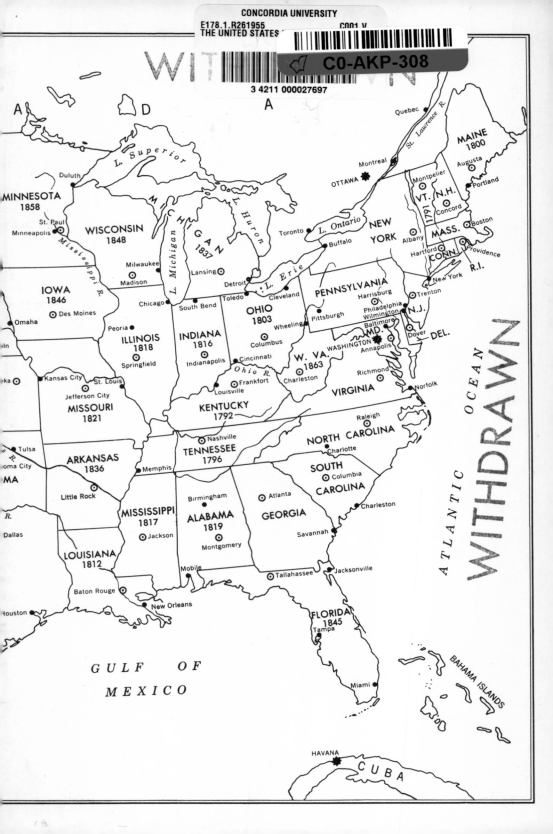

WITHDRAWN

A   D   A

Quebec

MAINE
1800

L. Superior

Montreal   Augusta
Duluth   St. Lawrence R.
OTTAWA   Montpelier   Portland

MINNESOTA
1858   VT. N.H.
          Concord
St. Paul   Toronto   L. Ontario   **NEW**   Albany   **MASS.**   Boston
Minneapolis   **WISCONSIN**   Buffalo   **YORK**   Hartford   **CONN.**   Providence
          1848   **R.I.**
          L. Michigan   New York
Milwaukee   Lansing   Detroit   L. Erie   **PENNSYLVANIA**   Trenton
Madison   Cleveland   Harrisburg   **N.J.**
IOWA   Chicago   Toledo   Pittsburgh   Philadelphia   **DEL.**
1846   South Bend   **OHIO**   Wheeling   Wilmington   Dover
Omaha   Peoria   1803   Columbus   Baltimore   **MD.**
          INDIANA   Cincinnati   WASHINGTON   Annapolis
ln   **ILLINOIS**   1816   **W. VA.**   Richmond
          1818   Indianapolis   Ohio R.   1863
Kansas City   Springfield   Frankfort   Charleston   **VIRGINIA**   Norfolk
ka   St. Louis   Louisville
          Jefferson City   **KENTUCKY**
MISSOURI   1792
1821   Raleigh
          Nashville   **NORTH CAROLINA**
Tulsa   **TENNESSEE**   Charlotte
oma City   **ARKANSAS**   1796   **SOUTH**   Charleston
MA   1836   Memphis   Columbia
          Little Rock   **CAROLINA**
R.   Birmingham   Atlanta
Dallas   **MISSISSIPPI**   **ALABAMA**   **GEORGIA**   Charleston
          1817   1819   Savannah
          Jackson   Montgomery
LOUISIANA
1812   Mobile   Tallahassee   Jacksonville
Houston   Baton Rouge
          New Orleans   **FLORIDA**
                    1845
                    Tampa

GULF   OF

MEXICO   Miami

ATLANTIC   OCEAN   **WITHDRAWN**

BAHAMA ISLANDS

HAVANA   **CUBA**

McGRAW-HILL SERIES IN HISTORY

The United States in World History

FROM ITS BEGINNINGS TO WORLD LEADERSHIP

McGRAW-HILL SERIES IN HISTORY

Albjerg & Albjerg   Europe from 1914 to the Present

Bannon   History of the Americas
VOLUME I: The Colonial Americas
VOLUME II: The American Nations

Blake   A Short History of American Life

Eckles & Hale   Britain, Her Peoples and the Commonwealth

Gustavson   A Preface to History

Lucas   A Short History of Civilization

Rae & Mahoney   The United States in World History

Riegel & Long   The American Story
VOLUME I: Youth
VOLUME II: Maturity

Schapiro   The World in Crisis

Turner   The Great Cultural Traditions
VOLUME I: The Ancient Cities
VOLUME II: The Classical Empires

Yanaga   Japan since Perry

The United States
in World History

FROM ITS BEGINNINGS TO
WORLD LEADERSHIP

John B. Rae, Ph.D.
Associate Professor of History
Massachusetts Institute of Technology

Thomas H. D. Mahoney, Ph.D.
Associate Professor of History
Massachusetts Institute of Technology

SECOND EDITION

1955   McGRAW-HILL BOOK COMPANY, INC.
New York   Toronto   London

THE UNITED STATES IN WORLD HISTORY

Library of Congress Catalog Card Number 54-12257

II

THE MAPLE PRESS COMPANY, YORK, PA.

To Our Parents: James B. Rae and Agnes MacNaught Rae
Thomas H. Mahoney, Jr. and Frances Lucy Mahoney

PREFACE

The reception given to the first edition of this work has encouraged us in our belief that the history of the United States ought to be presented in its setting as part of a broader Western civilization and, in modern days particularly, of a world civilization. In an age when the whole world is more closely knit in terms of ease of communication than were the states of the Union at the time the Constitution was adopted, and when the United States has become the mainstay of the free peoples, most Americans have come to realize that their lives can be profoundly affected by what happens to strange people in distant lands. It is equally important to realize that this interrelationship is nothing new. It is closer and more obvious now than it used to be; nevertheless, the fact remains that the development of the United States has always been an integral part of the development of a larger civilization. An understanding of this point is essential to an appreciation of the real meaning of our country's history.

It should be emphasized that this book is not intended to be a general history of the world since 1492. It is a history of the United States in its world setting. Our purpose has been to show how the major historical forces of modern times—political, economic, cultural, technological, intellectual—have contributed to the growth of the United States, and how the United States in turn has generated forces which have affected the development of present-day civilization.

While we have, therefore, retained the basic approach of the first edition, we have sought to improve upon it as far as possible. We have received many excellent suggestions from a number of those who have used the book in their classes. We have followed them wherever possible and regret only that limitations of space and cost prevented us from incorporating them all. For such advice we wish particularly to express our indebtedness to Professors Dorothy G. Fowler of Hunter College, Henry L. Rofinot of Villanova College, Gaston N. Buron of the United States Coast Guard Academy, Clive M. Warner of Santa Monica City

College, and Edwin T. Force of Santa Ana Junior College. The author of the chapters on Modern Imperialism is indebted to Professor Lowell J. Ragatz, Chairman of the Department of History, Ohio State University, for valuable ideas on the subject which he imparted in class lectures while the author was a student at George Washington University where Professor Ragatz was then teaching. The authors also appreciate the helpful comments that have been made by students at M.I.T. and at other colleges. In addition, we have done our utmost to correct the mistakes that have appeared in the volume. Our colleagues have been zealous and cooperative in pointing them out to us; for whatever errors appear in the present text, however, the responsibility is ours alone.

We have had generous assistance in the preparation of the revised manuscript. Dr. Vernon D. Tate, director of libraries at M.I.T., and Mr. Robert E. Booth, associate librarian, made indispensable contributions to the illustrative material. Much helpful criticism has been offered by our colleagues, especially Professors Leslie H. Fishel, Jr., James G. Kelso, and Lawrence W. Towner. The considerable amount of typing that has been required has been done willingly and competently by the secretarial staff of the department of humanities at M.I.T.: Miss Virginia M. Butler, Mrs. Arthur S. Chivers, Miss Bernice M. Bianchi, and Miss Nancy P. Randall. Mrs. John B. Rae has again been responsible for the index. And, as with the first edition, our thanks are due to Professor Howard M. Bartlett, head of the department of humanities, for extending whatever aid and encouragement lay within his power.

JOHN B. RAE

THOMAS H. D. MAHONEY

CONTENTS

Preface   vii

List of Maps   xv

List of Illustrations and Charts   xvi

**PART ONE. THE EMERGENCE OF
THE MODERN WORLD**   1

1. *Economic Life*   3

    Agriculture—Industry—Commercial Expansion—Mercantilism and
Colonial Policy

2. *Intellectual Progress*   22

    The Reformation—The Rise of Science—The Influence of Science on
Thought—The Age of Reason

3. *Government and Society*   39

    The Social Pyramid—Absolute Monarchy—The Development of Consti-
tutional Government in Great Britain

4. *The Evolution of the European State System*   54

    Europe at the End of the Thirty Years' War—The Eighteenth-century
Revisions of the European State System—The World Wars of the
Eighteenth Century

5. *The American Colonies*   67

    The Spanish Empire—New France—The English Settlements—Colonial
Government—Economic and Social Organization—Imperial Relationships

**PART TWO. THE AMERICAN REVOLUTION
AND THE ORGANIZATION OF A NEW
NATION**   91

6. *Immediate Causes of the Revolution*   93

    The Revision of British Imperial Policy—The Organization of American
Opposition—The Coming of the Revolution

7. The Revolutionary War   107

The Balance of Forces—The War: First Phase—The Declaration of
Independence—The Saratoga Campaign—Revolution to World War—
The Closing Campaigns

8. The Aftermath of the American Revolution   122

The Peace Settlement—Effects of the American Revolution in Europe—
The Revolution in American Society—The Confederation

9. The Constitution   136

The Federal Convention—Ratification—The Federalist Period—Judicial
Interpretation

PART THREE. THE ERA OF THE FRENCH REVOLUTION AND NAPOLEON   157

10. The French Revolution   159

The Critics of the Old Regime—The National Assembly—The Overthrow of the Monarchy—The Radical Republic—The Directory

11. America's Foreign Relations, 1789–1800   177

Washington's Proclamation of Neutrality—Maritime Difficulties with
England—Washington's Farewell Address—The French War Scare,
1796–1800

12. Napoleon   191

The French Imperial Expansion—The Road to Moscow—The War of
Liberation—The Hundred Days

13. Neutral Rights and the War of 1812   207

The Barbary Pirates—The Purchase of Louisiana—The United States as
a Neutral, 1803–1812—The Causes of the War of 1812—The War of
1812—The Treaty of Ghent

14. The Congress of Vienna and Its Aftermath   219

Leading Personalities—Problems—The Division of Spoils—The Concert
of Europe—The Monroe Doctrine and the Independence of Latin
America

PART FOUR. THE INDUSTRIAL REVOLUTION   233

15. The Revolution in Production   235

The Introduction of Power Machinery—The Textile Industry—Iron and
Steel—The New Industrial Society—The Beginnings of Labor Unionism
and Social Reform

16. The Revolution in Transportation 249

Roads and Canals—The Coming of the Railroad—Ocean Transportation—Communications

17. New Economic Doctrines 261

The Classical School—Utopian Socialism—Scientific Socialism—Anarchism and Syndicalism

PART FIVE. LIBERALISM AND NATIONALISM IN EUROPE AND AMERICA 273

18. Liberalism and Nationalism in Europe 275

Austria—Russia—The Return of the Bourbons in France—England under the Tories—Straws in the Wind—The Revolutions of 1830—The Great Reform Bill—France under Louis Philippe—The Revolutions of 1848—The Tide Turns—The Revolutions of 1848 Assessed

19. Liberalism and Nationalism in the United States 290

Jacksonian Democracy—Democratic Influences in American Society—Reform Movements—The West and the Public Domain—Manifest Destiny—Cultural Trends

20. The Second Empire and the Unifications of Germany and Italy 311

The Crimean War—The Second Empire—The Unification of Italy—The Unification of Germany: Background—Bismarck—The Schleswig-Holstein Episode—The Seven Weeks' War—The Franco-Prussian War.

21. Nationalism and Sectionalism in the United States 325

Bases of Sectional Conflict—The Missouri Compromise—The Nullification Controversy—The Compromise of 1850—Irrepressible Conflict—The Election of 1860

22. The Civil War 341

Secession and the Outbreak of War—The Balance of Forces—Military Operations—Naval Operations—Europe and the Civil War—Confederation in Canada—The Home Fronts—Reconstruction

PART SIX. MODERN TECHNOLOGY AND ITS PROBLEMS 365

23. The Expansion of Industrialism 367

The Rise of Big Business in the United States—The Growth of the Trusts—American Railroad Expansion—Industrial Expansion in Europe

24. Industrial Society 386

Urbanization and Social Change—Trends in Social and Economic Thought—Labor Unionism in Europe—Labor Organization in the United States—American Culture in an Industrial Era

25. *The Industrializing of Agriculture* 403

Science and Technology in Agriculture—The Settlement of the American West—Agrarian Discontent—European Agriculture under Overseas Competition

26. *Political and Social Trends in Europe, 1870–1914* 416

The Advance of Democracy in Great Britain—Social Unrest in Germany—The Troubles of the Third Republic—Unrest in Russia—Italy, Spain, and the Dual Monarchy

27. *The Progressive Movement in the United States* 431

The Currency and the Tariff—The Election of 1896—The Rise of the Progressives—The Administration of Theodore Roosevelt—The Progressive Revolt—The New Freedom

PART SEVEN. THE NEW IMPERIALISM 453

28. *The Rise of Modern Imperialism: The Partition of Africa* 455

The Principal Advocates of Imperialism—The British in South Africa—The British Occupation of Egypt—Other British African Holdings—The French in Africa—Germany and the Dark Continent—The Italians in Africa—The Lesser Powers in Africa

29. *European Imperialism in Asia and the Pacific* 470

The Opening of China—The Emergence of Japan—The Scramble for Concessions in China—The Russo-Japanese War—India—Southeast Asia—Penetration into Central Asia—Turkey and the Bagdad Railway

30. *American Imperialism* 484

The United States and Latin America—Background of the Spanish-American War—Course of the War—Results of the War—The Annexation of Hawaii—The Panama Canal—Other American Possessions—The Evolution of a Colonial Policy—Reassertion and Enlargement of the Monroe Doctrine—"Dollar Diplomacy"—Woodrow Wilson and Latin America

PART EIGHT. THE FIRST WORLD WAR AND THE PEACE SETTLEMENT 509

31. *The Coming of the War* 511

Power Politics and the Alliance System—Militarism—The Absence of International Machinery to Prevent War—Crises Caused by Nationalistic and Imperialistic Clashes—The Balkan Wars, 1912–1913—War between Triple Alliance and Triple Entente

32. The First World War   525

The Opening Campaigns—The Military Deadlock—Organization for Total War—The Entry of the United States—The End of the War

33. The Postwar Peace Settlements   547

The Versailles Conference—Principal Problems—Fate of the Fourteen Points—The Treaties—Wilson, The Treaty of Versailles, and the United States Senate

34. Liquidating The Peace Settlement   561

The League of Nations—The League in Operation—The Reparations Problem—Inter-Allied Debts—Multipower Pacts—Disarmament

PART NINE. INTERNAL PROBLEMS, 1919–1939   575

35. Totalitarianism in Europe   577

The Russian Revolution—The Organization of the Soviet State—Soviet Economic Policies—Fascism in Italy—The German Republic—The Nazi Dictatorship

36. The European Democracies   594

Economic Complications in Great Britain—The Commonwealth of Nations—Trouble Spots in the Empire—Domestic Problems of the French Republic—The Smaller Democracies of Europe

37. Reaction and Depression in the United States   609

"Back to Normalcy"—The Boom Period—Weak Points in the Economy—Prohibition—The Depression—The Maturing of American Culture

38. The New Deal   627

"The Hundred Days"—The Currency Question and Foreign Trade—Industry—Labor—Relief and Social Security—Agriculture—Conservation and Electric Power—Politics and the Judiciary—New Deal Foreign Policy

39. The Far East between World Wars   648

The Chinese Revolution—The Washington Conference, 1921–1922—China's Civil War—Japan—The Manchurian "Incident"—The Sino-Japanese Conflict—Soviet Russia and the Far East

PART TEN. THE SECOND WORLD WAR AND AFTER   659

40. The Causes of the Second World War   661

The Revival of the Alliance System—The Civil War in Austria—The Assassination of King Alexander of Yugoslavia—The Rearmament of

Germany—The Ethiopian Adventure—The Spanish Civil War—*Anschluss*—"Who Holds Bohemia Is Master of Europe"—The Outbreak of War

41. The Second World War: European Phase   678

The Early Blitzkriegs—The Fall of France—The Battle of Britain—The Mediterranean and the Balkans—The Invasion of Russia—The United States and the War

42. The Second World War: Global Conflict   697

Mobilizing America for War—The High Tide of the Axis—The United Nations Counteroffensive—The Invasion Year—The End of the War

43. International Cooperation   714

The United Nations—The San Francisco Conference—The United Nations in Operation—Policy Making through Conferences—Liquidating the War

44. The World since the War   732

The Iron Curtain—Western Europe—Asia—Africa—The American Republics—The United States

45. The Cold War   750

The Marshall Plan—The North Atlantic Treaty Organization (NATO) —The European Defense Community—The Near and Middle East— South Asia—The Far East and Southeast Asia—Africa—Latin America —The Point Four Program—The Problem of the Atom

Appendix A.   The Declaration of Independence   771

Appendix B.   The Constitution of the United States   775

Bibliography   791

Index   809

LIST OF MAPS

Front End Paper: The United States

Back End Paper: The United States as a World Power

1.	The Colonial World in the Eighteenth Century	9
2.	The Reformation	24
3.	Eighteenth-century Europe	55
4.	Mainland Colonies in North America (1655)	73
5.	The Revolutionary War and the Peace Settlement (1783)	117
6.	The United States under the Articles of Confederation	131
7.	Napoleonic Europe (1809)	197
8.	Europe after the Congress of Vienna	224
9.	The Chesapeake and Ohio Canal	252
10.	Territorial Expansion of the United States	302
11.	The Civil War (1861–1865)	342
12.	Railroad Land Grants in the United States	377
13.	The Partition of Africa (1870–1914)	458
14.	Imperialism in Asia (1914)	475
15.	Central America and the Caribbean Region	494
16.	Europe during the First World War	527
17.	Europe between the First and Second World Wars	584
18.	United States and European Possessions in the Western Hemisphere	644
19.	A Decade of Japanese Expansion in East Asia	653
20.	The World in 1940	667
21.	The Nazi March across the Continent	683
22.	The Pacific Area (1941)	704
23.	The NATO Countries	735
24.	The Cold War	762

LIST OF ILLUSTRATIONS
AND CHARTS

1. The Battle of Lexington   103
2. The Cotton Gin   239
3. The *Monitor* and the *Merrimac*   353
4. The Rise and Fall of Homesteading in the West   406
5. The Tariff—"A Hydra That Must Be Crushed"   435
6. Organs of the United Nations   719
7. Relationship of Regional Organizations in Europe   752

PART ONE

The Emergence of the Modern World

Selecting the point at which a study of modern history should begin is necessarily an arbitrary process, since history does not divide itself automatically into neat and easily recognizable compartments. The period between the discovery of the New World and the coming of the American Revolution can, however, be identified with reasonable accuracy as the era in which the institutions of medievalism perceptibly decayed and the basic elements of modern civilization became dominant in Western society. During these years European life underwent a series of radical transformations. The religious unity of the Middle Ages was disrupted by the Reformation, and a new intellectual force appeared with the rise of modern science. Economic activity expanded greatly in scope and began to be affected by technological improvements, with the result that capitalist forms of organization became paramount in the Western world. Politically, feudalism broke down and the nation-state emerged as the characteristic political unit.

Since these changes were taking place simultaneously with the discovery and colonization of the New World, they form an integral part of American as well as European history. The people who settled America were, after all, Europeans, who brought with them the laws, the religious faiths, the economic systems, the social institutions, and the cultural standards of their homelands. Much of this heritage had to be modified to suit their new environment, but none of it was ever entirely abandoned. It may be noted that America was peculiarly a product of the forces of the modern world. Commercial capitalism and religious ferment played the most important parts in its settlement, and while some efforts were made, especially by the Spaniards, to establish feudal institutions in the New World, they did not by and large survive transplanting.

America itself was a modernizing influence of the first magnitude.

1

The discovery of an unsuspected continent contributed substantially to the broadening of intellectual horizons. More directly, the products of the New World profoundly affected Europe's standard of living and swelled the flow of commerce, and the gradual development in America of a society differing noticeably in some respects from that of Europe had an unavoidable reaction on European thought.

There are, moreover, indirect influences to be considered. The emerging world of science, capitalism, and nationalism was the world of which the United States would eventually become an important member. Consequently, many of the trends and events of this period must be regarded as having great future significance even if they had no obvious bearing on American development at the time. To give one illustration, the evolution of Russia and Prussia during the seventeenth and eighteenth centuries was undoubtedly of remote concern to most contemporary Americans; to the twentieth century it appears in a rather different light.

1

Economic Life

Among the developments which marked the emergence of modern civilization, those which affected economic life had the most direct and immediate significance for the great mass of the people in the Western world. The economic pattern of this era presents a picture of old systems of agriculture, industry, and commerce continuing to function but steadily being undermined by the pressure of the new forces represented in the advance of capitalism. Capitalism may be defined as the form of economic organization in which wealth—using the term in its broadest sense to include not only money but means of production, goods, and other types of property—is for the most part privately owned, either by individuals or groups of individuals, and is employed by them to create additional wealth for the sake of profit. This incentive to produce new wealth makes capitalism dynamic and distinguishes it from the relatively static economies that preceded it. Capitalistic enterprise existed in the ancient world, and it developed to respectable proportions during the later Middle Ages, but in both eras the prevailing economic pattern was one of production for subsistence and little more.

Historically, capitalism has developed in three overlapping phases: commercial capitalism, in which large-scale enterprise was concentrated in trading and associated banking operations; industrial capitalism, which witnessed a tremendous forward step in productive capacity through the introduction of machine power; and finance capitalism, in which direction over the utilization of capital was largely in the hands of those who controlled money and credit. For the period under consideration commercial capitalism was the dominating variety. Industrialism was just making its appearance toward the end, and finance capitalism was a much later development.

AGRICULTURE

Down to the close of the eighteenth century, the great majority of the people in every country of Europe lived by farming, and most of them continued to cultivate the soil by methods that had changed very little in several centuries. Agricultural life was focused largely around the medieval manor, a self-contained, closely regulated unit in which the economic status of the individual members usually approximated their social status, and in which rights and duties were carefully prescribed and passed along unchanged from one generation to the next. A brief description of the manorial system will suffice to show its character. A typical manor would extend over about fifteen hundred acres and house a community ranging in status from the lord of the manor, its political and social head and also its largest landholder, down to several varieties of peasants, whose holdings might vary from fifty acres to one. This is not the place to discuss medieval land tenure; for practical purposes, each member of the community had the right to cultivate a prescribed area of land, the amount varying in accordance with his hereditary social status. Almost without exception, farming was carried on by the "open-field" system, whereby the arable land was divided into two, three, or four large fields, with three the most common arrangement, and cultivated according to a planned rotation which left one of the fields fallow each year— an arrangement made necessary because letting the soil rest periodically was the only effective way known to preserve its fertility.

In order to have the land distributed as equitably as possible—that is, so that no one individual would have all the best soil, and so that each would have some land in the cultivated fields every year—landholdings were made up of small strips scattered over the entire open-field area. Thus, a peasant with thirty acres on a three-field manor might have ten separate strips in each field. This intermingling, plus the fact that only the wealthier inhabitants of the manor were likely to own implements such as plows, meant that farming operations had to be closely controlled community rather than individual enterprises, a condition which inevitably handicapped experimentation. Outside the open fields was the common: wasteland where the entire community shared such rights as grazing live-stock and collecting fuel. The stock on the manor was generally bred indiscriminately and was of poor quality. Since winter feed was not available, most of the animals were slaughtered in the fall and the meat salted down to preserve it—an uninspiring contribution to an already limited diet.

Decline of the Manorial System. As a means of production, the manor was inefficient. The three-field rotation meant that one-third of the fertile area was always idle, and although improved methods could be and sometimes were adopted without disturbing the basic organization of the manor, on the whole it was difficult to introduce innovations into a system governed chiefly by custom and tradition. The system owed its long survival essentially to the fact that it served well enough in a relatively static society, where trade was limited and each community provided most of its own needs. It was not suited to an expanding economy, and consequently, in those countries of Europe where the growth of commerce and industry created a market for foodstuffs, the manor began to decline as an economic unit fairly early in the modern period. The growing of crops for market rather than for mere subsistence brought agriculture into the pattern of money economy, one very important result being that the complicated obligations and services by which manorial peasants held their land were gradually abandoned in favor of cash rents.

The Agricultural Revolution. Moreover, the demand for greater farm production stimulated the development of modern scientific agriculture. Quite naturally, the countries which were farthest advanced commercially pioneered in this field. As early as the sixteenth century some English landlords were "enclosing" their open fields in order to turn their manors into sheep pastures, wool being England's great export staple at this time, while others were copying improved methods of tillage evolved by the Dutch, who, living on land reclaimed from the sea, had to develop something better than the wasteful techniques of open-field cultivation. By the end of the next century what has been termed the Agricultural Revolution was well under way.

The most radical transformation in agriculture during this period took place in England, where the manor lost its importance as a social institution earlier than in continental Europe and where a thriving commerce and growing industry offered greater incentive to farming for profit. By the eighteenth century enthusiasm for scientific agriculture in Great Britain was at a high pitch. Jethro Tull, adopting ideas which he had seen used in French vineyards, introduced improved methods of planting, described in his widely read book, *Horse Hoeing Husbandry*. Lord Charles Townshend, grandfather of another Charles Townshend much more closely associated with American history, experimented with the scientific use of fertilizer and with crop rotations which would introduce soil-enriching crops such as turnips and thus eliminate the need for leaving part of the land uncultivated—achieving such success as to win for himself the cognomen of "Turnip" Townshend. Robert Coke of Holkham operated a model farm where his neighbors could witness the application of the new agriculture. Scientific stockbreeding is usually credited to Robert Bakewell, although there are grounds for suspecting that Bakewell's reputation rests on other people's ideas. Among their disciples was George III, who reveled in the title of "Farmer George" and whose devotion to agricultural progress was probably of more lasting benefit than his dabbling in statecraft, since the royal patronage served to make scientific farming fashionable.

Enclosures. The result of all this activity was an accretion of knowledge about the chemistry of soils, rotation of crops, and techniques of cultivation sufficient to guarantee that farm output could meet the demand—but not under the open-field system. The constant experimentation and meticulous care needed for scientific farming could not be carried on where each man's holdings were intermingled with everyone else's and where deviation from community routine was virtually impossible. To reap the full benefit of the new methods, farms had to be in compact blocks, preferably fenced off so that each individual could do as he saw fit without interference from his neighbors. Agitation for enclosures consequently grew in intensity as improved farming techniques became more and more profitable and common, and by the close of the eighteenth century had made such headway in Great Britain that Parliament authorized enclosure in any rural community where the majority of the landholders desired it. By this process the land was redistributed so that each individual was given the same acreage as before, but in a compact holding rather than scattered strips. Theoretically, everyone was as well off as before; practically, the small landholders were almost driven out of existence. In most cases the lead in enclosing was taken by the large landholders, usually the county gentry, who were likely to get their own way because they enjoyed social prestige as well as economic power. Moreover, the common land was included in the redistribution, since it could now be cultivated by the use of the improved methods, with the result that the small farmer, who seldom had the capital to engage in scientific agriculture, lost rights of considerable value and got in exchange an allotment of land which he could not use. All too often he was compelled to sell out and either become a landless farm laborer or move to some city and join the growing mass of factory workers. Thus, while the enclosure movement undoubtedly stimulated agricultural production in Great Britain, it had unfortunate social effects in the destruction of almost the entire class of independent farmers and the concentration of land ownership in the hands of a comparatively small group.

INDUSTRY

Industrial life in the Western world during the beginning of the modern era was marked by the stirrings of what was to become the Industrial Revolution. The craft guilds in which medieval industrial production had been concentrated began to break down. Like the manorial system, the guilds proved inadequate to the needs of an expanding world, less, perhaps, because they were inherently unsound than because they had become closed corporations inaccessible to new talent and ideas. When the demands of commerce called for greater output of goods to trade with, the guilds could not meet the call, and production migrated from the towns to the country districts, where guild restrictions did not apply.

The Domestic System. Thus, the seventeenth and eighteenth centuries became the age of the "domestic" or "putting-out" system, whereby production was carried on by artisans working in their own homes. The textile industry in England offers the clearest example of how the system worked. Cloth was turned out by weavers scattered throughout the rural areas, from yarn spun on spinning wheels, usually by the women of the weaver's family. The tools were owned by the workers and the power was human power. Sometimes the artisan carried his own goods to market; more often, he bought his raw materials from and sold his finished products to a traveling merchant-clothier.

This individual gradually evolved into the key figure in the industry. Since marketing was in his hands, he was in a position to dominate the operations of the workers with whom he dealt, until the bulk of the artisans became, in practice if not in theory, workers for wages, with the traveling merchant functioning as a capitalist employer, determining not only the prices he would pay for cloth—or whatever commodity he was dealing in—but also establishing standards and exercising supervision over the work done. One of the roots of the modern factory system, indeed, is the practice adopted by many of these merchant-capitalists of concentrating their employees in one place so that their work could be more effectively supervised.

It should be understood that the putting-out system was never the sole means of industrial production. During its heyday it competed with both its predecessor and its successor. The craft guilds of the towns continued to account for a considerable, although steadily declining, share of the industrial output, while in such fields as iron manufacturing fairly large-scale and centralized operation was required by the nature of the work. No rural artisan could smelt ore or cast cannon in his own cottage. Nor was the system the idyllic combination of independent craftsmanship and farming that has sometimes been depicted. It is doubtful whether the average craftsman owned enough land to make him appreciably independent of his earnings.

In general, industry during this period occupied a distinctly less important place in the economic life of the Western world than either agriculture or commerce. It was in the process of outgrowing the medieval craft system and passing into some form of capitalist organization and control, but until the latter part of the eighteenth century its expansion was restricted by lack of mechanical power and the limitation of markets imposed by poor transportation. The overcoming of these handicaps represents a large part of what is commonly referred to as the Industrial Revolution, which will be discussed separately later (see Part Four).

COMMERCIAL EXPANSION

Up to the time of the American and French revolutions, the expansion of commerce was easily the most important factor in the economic life of the Western world, much more far reaching in its effects than contemporary developments in either agriculture or industry. It involved a great physical expansion of European civilization, the establishment of European settlements in the Western Hemisphere and the Far East, the introduction to Europe of a host of new commodities, the development of modern forms of business organization, and the founding of modern banking systems. As commerce grew in importance, commercial policies became matters of vital concern to national governments, and wars were fought for real or fancied trade advantages. More than that, the mercantile class, in western Europe at least, grew in wealth and power until it was in a position to challenge the political and social leadership of the old landed aristocracy.

All this was no sudden upheaval, but the flowering of an evolutionary process dating well back into the Middle Ages, to the time when the chaos which followed the collapse of the Roman Empire moderated sufficiently to permit a limited volume of trade to be carried on. The Crusades provided an impetus to commerce by giving Europe closer contacts with the East, and in due course a thriving trade in luxury goods grew up, centering principally in the Italian cities of Venice and Genoa.

Overseas Expansion. But the overland route to the Orient was difficult and costly and the nations of western Europe resented the virtual monopolization of this traffic by the Italian states. These factors, coupled with a growing knowledge of both geography and navigation, led the Western countries to look for direct sea routes to the Far East and resulted in the voyages of discovery which mark the real beginning of the modern era. Portugal was the pioneer. In the half-century before Columbus's voyage Portuguese navigators reached out to the Azores and pushed all the way down the African coast, until in 1497 Vasco da Gama rounded the Cape of Good Hope to reach India and founded a prosperous but short-lived Portuguese Empire in the East Indies. In the meantime Christopher Columbus managed after much effort to interest the Spanish government in his plan to reach the Orient by striking directly west across the Atlantic and thus, in 1492, stumbled upon a hitherto unsuspected continent. (While Norse voyagers probably had reached the

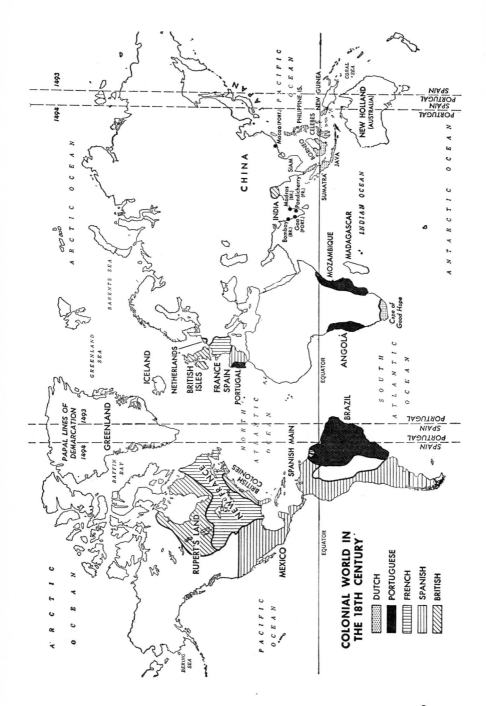

COLONIAL WORLD IN THE 18TH CENTURY

Legend:
- DUTCH
- PORTUGUESE
- FRENCH
- SPANISH
- BRITISH

9

American mainland some five-hundred years before, their discoveries had no lasting results and were unknown to the rest of Europe in any event.)

By virtue of being the first arrivals, Spain and Portugal found themselves in possession of extensive, if somewhat vague, claims to most of the American continent and a considerable part of the Far East. Indeed, as early as 1493 they went so far as to secure papal approval for an agreement dividing all newly discovered territories, present and prospective, between themselves.[1] They were not, however, left long in undisputed possession of their property. Other countries, especially England, France, and Holland, refused to recognize the right of Spain and Portugal to monopolize the New World and the ocean trade routes and subjected their commerce and colonies to vigorous attacks, both authorized and unauthorized. Spain's hope of stamping out these attacks at their source evaporated with the defeat of the Armada in 1588 by the English and Dutch; from then on the right to overseas empire rested solely on ability to take and hold it.

Portugal proved too weak to stand the ruthless competition that developed. In the seventeenth century its East Indian possessions were lost to the Dutch and most of its position in India to the English and French, who thereupon embarked on a century-long duel with each other for control of India's wealth. The Dutch also took Brazil but were unable to hold it. Spain came off somewhat better. A tremendous surge of expansion in the century following Columbus's voyage gave her an empire covering all of South and Central America, except for Brazil, and extending across the Pacific to the Philippines. The disaster to the Armada marked the beginning of a long decline for Spain, but she remained strong enough to hold what she had and even to push north into the future territory of the United States in Florida, Texas, New Mexico, and California. The momentum of Spanish expansion lasted until the middle of the eighteenth century. The rival nations succeeded in taking some of the West Indian islands, but otherwise their colonizing efforts were forced into the still unoccupied parts of the American continent. The French moved into Canada, where the St. Lawrence River offered an attractive route into the interior, while the English settled in the coastal regions between French and Spanish territory. Adventurers of both nations, in addition, made repeated but futile attempts to find a northern sea route to the East. Holland, a trading rather than a colonizing power, was not greatly interested

---

[1] The original line of demarcation was moved farther west in 1494, and it thus gave Portugal possession of Brazil, which was reached in 1500 by the Portuguese Admiral Cabral while he was following an extreme westerly course on his way through the South Atlantic to the Cape of Good Hope and India. In the Far East, the Philippines were subsequently claimed by Spain on the basis of Magellan's discovery of the islands and were colonized by that country, although they were actually on the Portuguese side of the line.

in establishing itself on the American mainland. Its colony of New Netherlands on the Hudson River, neglected and badly governed, fell into English hands in 1664 virtually without resistance.

Effects of the Discoveries. The impact of the discoveries on European life, and on commerce in particular, can scarcely be exaggerated. With the opening of an all-water route to the East, commodities which previously had been rare luxuries could now be brought to Europe in quantities that made them available to a much broader market. In addition, both the Orient and the New World became sources of products which were completely new to European civilization. A partial list would include tea, coffee, tobacco, potatoes, and cotton. Commercial activity expanded tremendously under the impetus of the opportunities that were opening up for it, and it was further stimulated by the influx of gold and silver from America, which greatly increased the volume of money in circulation and caused a general rise in European price levels.

As the scale of commercial activity increased, new forms of business organization had to be devised to meet unprecedented conditions. Particularly in enterprises involving long overseas voyages, the task of financing trading ventures was likely to be beyond the resources of any one individual. Even if all went well, the length of time required for the slow sailing ships of the day to reach their destination and return imposed a severe strain on a merchant's credit, and the problems of trade were seldom that simple. Allowance had to be made for the risk of loss through shipwreck, or piracy, or the attacks of rivals who might decide to eliminate competition by force. Once away from his own country, a merchant had to look out for himself. If he got into trouble, appealing to his government was useless; governments of this period were not equipped to assert their authority at a distance, and even if one tried, its action would normally be much too late to do any good.

Chartered Companies. The need to pool resources and share risks brought the chartered company to the fore as the dominant mechanism of this period for conducting overseas commerce. These companies were organizations given a monopoly of trade with specified areas by their governments; in view of the risks the companies assumed, it seemed only fair that their members should have an exclusive right to the profits. Thus, England had, for example, the Muscovy Company to trade with Russia, the East India Company to trade with the Orient, and the Hudson's Bay Company—still functioning today under its charter issued in 1670—to compete with France for the resources of Canada. Besides commercial operations, it was common custom for a chartered company to act as representative of its government within its allotted area, the outstanding example being the British East India Company, which maintained its own army, contracted alliances and fought wars with Indian princes, and, although shorn of much of its power at the end of the eighteenth century, remained the official agency of British government in India until 1857.

There were two principal types of chartered companies, the "regulated" and the "joint-stock" company. In the former, the members shared in the privileges of the charter and were entitled to whatever protection and assistance the organization could provide, but they traded as individuals. The joint-stock company had more lasting significance as the predecessor of the modern business corporation. Its members held shares in the organization, which carried on business in its own name and as a corporate unit. The customary administrative arrangement was to have the affairs of the company managed by a governor and a board of assistants, subject to the approval of the general body of stockholders, who met at regular intervals.

The joint-stock companies have a peculiar importance in the history of the United States in that the most important of the early English colonies in America were settled by such companies, and the joint-stock form of organization consequently had a considerable influence on the pattern of colonial governments. The Virginia Company of London founded Jamestown and helped to send the Pilgrim Fathers to New England. The Massachusetts Bay Company not only established a colony but moved itself and its charter over there, so that the joint-stock company became the government of Massachusetts, with the stockholders' meeting becoming the General Court of the colony. Rhode Island and Connecticut sought the security of charters as soon as they could, and the documents they received organized the colonies very much as if they had been trading companies, with a governor, board of assistants, and an assembly of the "freemen," the equivalent in the colony of stockholders. However, colonial self-government, even in New England, cannot be attributed solely to the joint-stock company. Local governments were established in all the English colonies, regardless of how they originated, and the pattern of a single executive, with a small council to advise and assist him, and a representative assembly, was virtually universal. It was, after all, substantially the system with which Englishmen were familiar in their own country.

Banking and Credit. An adequate system of banking and credit was just as necessary to the expanding world of commerce as improvements in business organization. In some respects such a system was already in existence. The Venetians and other Italian merchants of the later Middle Ages conducted banking operations as an essential adjunct to their commerce, developing bills of exchange and foreign credits to a high degree of efficiency in order to reduce to a minimum the need to ship gold and silver around Europe, an expensive and risky task. Lombard Street in London still commemorates the Italian merchants who were among the first to make that city a financial center. In addition, as money economy became more and more important in European life, demands for substantial amounts of capital arose not only from business, but from monarchs who needed funds to maintain standing armies and fight wars, with the result that wealthy mercantile houses like the Medici of Florence and the Fuggers of Augsburg became heavily involved in moneylending in spite of the church's disapproval of the taking of interest. Eventually, as the demand for capital and credit increased, full-fledged banks began to appear in some of the important commercial centers, such as the Bank of Amsterdam, which was founded in 1609 and for over a century was easily the strongest financial institution in Europe. These early banks were for the most part deposit banks which invested their clients' funds chiefly in commercial ventures, occasionally in government loans, and very seldom in industry.

However, in spite of these achievements, it can hardly be said that business during the early modern era functioned in a satisfactory financial medium. The worst deficiency unquestionably was the relationship of government to currency and credit. Coinage was crude, lacking in uniformity, and, what was more important, subject to arbitrary manipulation by the issuing authorities, whether they were heads of states or the bewildering profusion of lesser individuals who possessed the right to coin money. Even as comparatively modern and enlightened a king as Frederick the Great of Prussia resorted to systematic debasement of his currency in order to ease the financial strain of his protracted wars. Public finances in general were poorly organized. The embryonic tax systems which were replacing the personal services and obligations of feudal society were inefficient and unproductive; indeed, the practice of farming out the revenue—that is, selling the right to collect taxes to private contractors —was commonplace until the era of the French Revolution.

Meanwhile, governments were facing financial problems of increasing complexity, mainly because of progress in the art of war. The replacement of feudal levies by the more efficient and dependable professional armies cost money. Soldiers had to be paid with some degree of regularity if they were not to transfer their services en masse to some other prince with a better treasury, quantities of munitions and supplies had to be accumulated, and weapons, especially firearms, of steadily growing efficiency and correspondingly higher cost had to be provided. The same story applied to naval warfare. The day when any merchantman could be a warship was passing. Naval vessels had to be specially built for the purpose and manned by at least a nucleus of professional naval men. Thus, with uncertain revenues and mounting expenses, the governments of this period were constantly in the market for loans, a situation which helped to stimulate the development of banking and credit institutions but which was also attended by a good deal of risk. A ruler who found himself hard pressed financially could always simply repudiate his debts, and in a day of absolute monarchy there was no redress open to the creditor. The Fugger fortune, estimated at about $50,000,000 in present-day terms, was wiped out when the Austrian Hapsburgs defaulted, and the suspension of debt payments by Charles II of England in 1673 toppled the London goldsmiths from the dominant position they had achieved in English banking. Public loans, in consequence, were usually made at interest rates which reflected the lender's uncertainty that he would ever see his money again.

The only country to find a reasonably adequate solution for its financial problems was Great Britain, and its success came only after a bitter struggle for power between King and Parliament, in which the question of who should control the nation's funds had been a vital factor. The victory of Parliament in 1688 was an essential preliminary to the stabilization of finance because it meant that the moneyed classes could be asked to invest in a government over which they had a considerable degree of control.

The Bank of England. The most important single step was taken in 1694. In that year the British government, involved in a general European war and hard pressed for funds, adopted the proposal of a Scotsman, William Paterson. A group of financiers loaned the government the money it needed and in return were chartered as the Bank of England, with power to conduct a general banking business and also to issue notes up to the amount of the institution's capital, which consisted of the loan to the government. The Bank also functioned as a depository for public funds and general fiscal agent for the Treasury. It was not a monopoly, but its intimate relationship with the government enabled it eventually to become the controlling influence in British finance. Moreover, since the note issues of the Bank of England were based on its loans to the government, they were, in effect, guaranteed by the credit of the nation and thus could circulate as a secure paper currency. It was a mutually advantageous arrangement. The promoters of the Bank of England received an obviously valuable privilege; in return, their financial stake in the stability of the existing government would assure their support for it, a welcome strengthening of a regime established by revolution only five years before. Just a century later Alexander Hamilton would follow an almost identical policy in order to secure the backing of the moneyed classes for the newborn Federal government of the United States.

For a time the success of Paterson's plan was an isolated phenomenon. The European world was dazzled by the potentialities of such relatively new mechanisms as banks and joint-stock companies; that there were limitations too had to be learned by trial and error—mostly error.

Some twenty-five years after the founding of the Bank of England, Britain was lured into a project for paying the national debt by chartering a company which would assume the debt in exchange for a monopoly of trade with Spanish America. The South Sea Company was a speculative enterprise from the start, with far more political influence than economic strength, and its only achievement was to plunge the country into a wild orgy of stock gambling, the "South Sea Bubble," which terminated inevitably in a wholesale crash. France promptly duplicated Britain's experience. Another Scots financier, John Law, interested the French government in a plan for establishing a central bank similar to the Bank of England. Law's plan, in fact, was modeled on Paterson's and was sound enough in its inception, but it became mixed up with a Company of the Indies which was going to pay France's national debt by exploiting, among other things, the resources of French Louisiana. The "Mississippi Bubble" burst in 1721, leaving France with disorganized finances and a suspicion of national banks, neither one remedied until the days of the Napoleonic Empire. Even the traditionally thrifty and cautious Dutch were not immune. The powerful Bank of Amsterdam folded up late in the eighteenth century because of ill-advised efforts to prop up the Dutch East India Company. Thus, in spite of the very considerable progress that had been made, banking and credit in the Western world were still on a far from satisfactory footing when the period of the American and French revolutions was reached.

MERCANTILISM AND COLONIAL POLICY

This process of economic growth had important repercussions in political policy. Kings and statesmen were fully aware of the growing importance of industry and commerce. It took no great discernment to perceive that a nation's military and political power had come to depend very largely on its economic power. How, then, was such power to be attained? The answer generally accepted throughout Western civilization in the period from 1500 to 1800 was the somewhat ill-defined body of theory known as mercantilism, which may be summed up as the belief that a nation's economic life should be regulated in such a way as to strengthen the state—strengthen it, that is, against other states. Mercantilism was never a philosophy of internal social reform.

Mercantilism was not so much a well-organized body of economic doctrine as a concrete expression of public policy, varying considerably in detail from one country to another, although the basic objective was always the same. The earlier mercantilists were marked by an almost fanatical preoccupation with the accumulation of gold and silver. To them specie was the sole measure of national wealth, and economic policy was to be directed at building up the supply of precious metals within the state by exporting as much and importing as little as possible. This thesis was faulty in its overemphasis on possession of bullion and its assumption that commerce could be made to flow in one direction only, but it did have a reasonably practical foundation in contemporary conditions. In an age when soldiers fought for pay rather than patriotism, no state could afford to be caught without an adequate supply of specie in time of war. A king with a well-filled treasury, no matter what other resources he lacked, could always hire an army to fight for him. King George III's use of Hessians against the American colonists was an example. The preoccupation with gold and silver was thus natural enough under the circumstances.

Later mercantilist thinkers were more liberal in their concept of wealth. While they continued to rate gold and silver highly, they realized that productive capacity and commercial activity were at least equally important factors in national power, so that the objective of mercantilist policy broadened to become the attainment of national self-sufficiency instead of simply coin-collecting. Thus, to the securing of a favorable balance of trade was added the encouragement of new industries by bounties and subsidies, control of prices and quality of goods in the hope of gaining a competitive advantage in foreign trade, and, above all, provision as far as it could be made for having everything needed to wage war produced within the country. Maritime commerce and fisheries were highly regarded not only for the income they yielded but because, in building ships and training seamen, they contributed to the potential naval power of the state.

Advantages of Colonies. Colonies occupied a very important place in the mercantilist scheme of things. They could supply commodities not produced by the mother country itself and thereby eliminate the undesirable necessity of buying such goods from foreigners. They were especially valuable if they were sources of precious metals or of the tropical and subtropical products which the world-wide expansion of commerce had made essential items in European economy. Colonies also offered a market where the manufacturers of the home country could enjoy a privileged position, extending if necessary to the complete exclusion of foreign competition. Moreover, a distinctive feature of mercantilist theory was that colonies were needed as an outlet for surplus population. It is very doubtful whether Europe was actually overpopulated in relation to its resources, limited as they were, but the mercantilists assumed the existence of a surplus population because it was the only explanation they could find for the phenomena of unemployment and poverty. So, national greatness demanded the acquisition of colonies and then rigorous control to insure that the colonies would function exclusively for the benefit of the mother country.

Mercantilism was definitely not a doctrine of international good will. It never seems to have occurred to the mercantilists that an exchange of goods and services could benefit everyone concerned. They regarded all countries as rivals and assumed that, if any one secured an additional share of the world's commerce, some other necessarily lost. Trade advantages thus became objects of keen competition between nations, to be fought for if other methods of gaining them failed. England and Holland waged three wars between 1654 and 1678 solely because of business rivalry, and the long duel between Great Britain and France in the eighteenth century, while not purely commercial in character, was predominantly a contest for colonies and maritime supremacy.

Colbert. The greatest exponent of mercantilism was Jean-Baptiste Colbert, finance minister of Louis XIV of France from 1661 to 1683. He himself, a middle-class administrator, owing his position solely to his ability, was a personification of the growing importance of commerce and industry in the life of the state. During his twenty-two years in office he worked with single-minded devotion to increase the revenues of his king by making France prosperous. He reformed the administration of the finances so that a larger proportion of the revenue collected reached the treasury; he stimulated industry by tariffs and subsidies; he built roads and canals to facilitate the flow of goods; he imposed stringent regulations to guarantee that French products would be superior to others; he chartered companies to get a greater share of overseas trade for France; and he tried to build up a colonial empire. In the end he failed. Louis XIV squandered Colbert's revenues on his extravagant palace at Versailles and in fruitless wars. Colbert would not have objected to the wars if they had been directed at winning trade and colonies for France; but they were not. They were fought to increase the prestige of the French monarchy in Europe. Efficient as Colbert was, he was unable to touch fundamental weaknesses in France's economic structure, such as the inequitable distribution of taxes which left much of the wealth of the nobility and clergy unburdened. Nor could he interfere with Louis XIV's intolerant religious policy, which drove from France the most industrious and productive element of its population. What was worse, the exiled Huguenots—the French Protestants—made substantial contributions to the prosperity of France's rivals, notably Great Britain and Prussia. Finally, after his death, Colbert's system fell into less capable hands, and its restrictions proved to be a serious handicap to French industry. Nevertheless, the superficial brilliance of Louis XIV's reign led to widespread imitation of Colbert's methods.

Spanish Colonial Policy. For the New World, the significant aspect of mercantilism was the systems established by the colonizing powers of Europe to reserve to themselves the resources of their overseas possessions. Spain, first in the field and therefore first to formulate a colonial policy, set up a monopoly, the *Casa de Contratación* at Seville, through which all trade with Spanish America was funneled. European goods were carried across the Atlantic by vessels sailing from Cadiz in closely organized fleets, and each year the "plate fleet" was assembled at Havana to carry the output of the New World's mines back to Spain. The practice of grouping the ships into fleets gave some security against pirates or raiders from other countries with a somewhat casual attitude toward international law; it also made supervision of colonial trade easier.

The Spanish colonial policy functioned for about three hundred years; beyond that little can be said for it. The constriction of commerce into limited channels and excessive emphasis on the production of minerals, especially gold and silver, stultified the economic development of the Spanish colonies and, in fact, made them financial liabilities to their mother country. Perhaps the system would have worked more successfully if Spain had furnished an adequate industrial and commercial base for its empire. As it was, the steady economic decay of Spain, induced by religious bigotry, a fantastically reactionary aristocracy, and general misgovernment,[2] eventually made the whole Spanish Empire dependent on outside resources and threw the profits of its commerce into other hands, principally Dutch. By the eighteenth century the plate fleet still sailed under Spanish colors, but most of its cargo was destined for the pockets of Amsterdam burghers, to pay for the foodstuffs, and the manufactured goods which Spain had to import in order to live. And if the Spanish government received little benefit from its enormous empire, the Spanish people received even less. Since most of Spanish America already had a substantial native population, there was little incentive for the poorer classes of Spain to emigrate. Exploiting colonial resources could be done more cheaply by enslaving the natives or importing Negroes when the Indians died off, than by trying to use white labor, which in any event would find unfavorable climatic conditions. So the Spanish population in America was never more than a thin layer at the top of colonial society: public officials, military and naval personnel, members of the clergy, owners of great estates, and a sprinkling of merchants.

French Colonial Policy. The French colonial system was not as elaborate as the Spanish, but it was just as restrictive. Because of internal difficulties France did not undertake seriously to become a colonial power until the reign of Louis XIV, so that the formulation of colonial policy fell largely into the hands of Colbert, who simply extended to France's overseas possessions the same detailed control of economic life as he had established at home. In the West Indies, where conditions were the same for

[2] A major contributor to the impoverishment of Spain was the *Mesta,* a great sheep-raising monopoly the operations of which discouraged agriculture and badly damaged the soil by overgrazing.

all countries, the French possessions were neither better nor worse off than anyone else's. In Canada, however, French experience offers an interesting comparison with the development of the English colonies to the south. While conditions were not quite so favorable, there was nevertheless an opportunity for building up a strong and populous French settlement, an opportunity which France signally failed to utilize. Part of the reason was physical; the ease of access into the interior offered by the St. Lawrence and the Great Lakes tempted the French to disperse their energies, despite Colbert's disapproval, in fur trading over a wide area. The rest of the explanation lies in the rigidity of French policy. The regulation from Paris of every detail of political and economic life in Canada and a land system which attempted to reproduce European feudalism were not conditions calculated to attract settlers, and France's refusal to tolerate religious dissent in any part of its empire deprived Canada of the type of immigration which was so important a factor in building up the English colonies in America. If their government had been a little less shortsighted, French Huguenots could have contributed just as much to Canada as they did to South Carolina.

The British Colonial System. The British colonial system, the one which most directly affected the future United States, was a peculiar mixture of restraint and liberality. Britain accepted the tenets of mercantilism as wholeheartedly as its neighbors but put them into practice with substantial modifications. For one thing, the fact that Britain was developing as a constitutional rather than an absolute monarchy meant that the British government could not exercise the arbitrary authority over its colonies that France and Spain applied to theirs. British colonists were Englishmen, with rights under English law which could not be casually set aside. Moreover, since the British colonies in America, stretching as they did from Nova Scotia to the West Indies, were a heterogeneous collection, founded by a variety of methods and highly diversified in resources, it was all but impossible to formulate a coordinated system of control for them.

Britain's economic policy for its colonies was based on the Acts of Trade and Navigation, passed at intervals between 1651 and 1696. As it finally evolved, the system established by the Navigation Acts had three ~~~~eral features. First, commerce between Great Britain[3] and foreign nations could be carried only in British ships or in vessels belonging to the country with which the trade was being conducted. This requirement was aimed at the Dutch, who at this time dominated maritime commerce.

---

[3] The term "Great Britain" is not quite accurate for the whole period covered by the Navigation Acts. Scotland was originally excluded from their benefits but was placed on an equal footing with England in 1707. Ireland, on the other hand, was originally included but was barred from colonial trade in 1663.

Second, no foreign vessels were permitted to trade with British colonies. Third, Britain was to be made the focal point of traffic between Europe and the colonies. All European-manufactured goods destined for the colonies had to be sent to Britain for transshipment, and the colonial products which were on the list of "enumerated goods" also had to be sent to Britain for reexport. Thus British merchants would be assured the middlemen's profits, and, since some tax had to be paid in Britain on most of the commodities, the British Treasury would benefit also. At first the enumerated goods were limited to such distinctly overseas products as sugar, molasses, tobacco, cotton, and dyewoods, but eventually the list was extended to cover virtually everything the colonies exported except fish, which could be sent directly to the Catholic countries of southern Europe.

Restraints on Colonial Economy. There were two important extensions of this system. One was the enactment of legislation restricting manufacturing within the colonies that competed with home industries: woolen goods (1699), hats (1732), and finished iron products (1750). The manufacture of these goods was not prohibited, but they were not supposed to be sold outside the colony in which they were made. The other was the Molasses Act of 1733, especially interesting because it affected only intercolonial trade and not commerce between America and Europe. The merchants of the New England and middle colonies had built up a thriving commerce with the West Indies, sending foodstuffs and lumber to the islands and bringing back sugar and molasses, chiefly for conversion into rum. Besides this direct exchange there was the "triangular trade," in which vessels, usually laden with rum, sailed from the mainland colonies to West Africa, there picked up cargoes of slaves for the "middle passage" to the West Indies, and then returned home with sugar and molasses.

This commerce extended to the entire West Indies area, regardless of national ownership, and was generally profitable to all the parties involved. The plantations of the West Indies did not produce their own food and were always in need of additions to their labor supply. For the mainland colonies this trade was particularly welcome as one of their few sources of specie, of which they were chronically short because their money was continually being drawn off to pay for British manufactured goods. However, the planters of the British islands felt that they were entitled to preferential treatment. It was obviously to their advantage to compel the merchants of the mainland colonies to buy from them instead of from French, Dutch, or Spanish plantations. It was equally obviously to the advantage of the merchants to be free to make their purchases wherever conditions were most favorable, but the planters had the stronger influence in Parliament. The Molasses Act, passed for their benefit, imposed a tax of sixpence a gallon on foreign sugar and molasses products imported into the British colonies on the American mainland, while admitting such products duty-free if they came from British possessions.

Influence of Navigation Acts. The effect of this body of legislation on colonial economic life is not easy to appraise. Colonial commerce was certainly restricted to a considerable degree, but there were compensating advantages. Colonial ships were counted as British under the Navigation Acts and could, therefore, participate freely in the considerable volume of trade within the British Empire from which foreigners were excluded. In addition, the British government paid bounties to stimulate the production of some colonial goods, notably naval stores, and it tried to help the overseas plantations by suppressing the cultivation of tobacco in England. Most important of all, the whole system was laxly administered and loosely enforced. The fundamental difficulty was physical; the area to be covered was far too big for the slow sailing ships and poor communications of the period. It was simply impossible to watch every inlet on the American coast where illicit trade might be carried on—as a matter of fact, it was impossible to do it in Britain itself. To make matters worse, eighteenth-century Britain lacked the efficient civil service necessary for the proper administration of this complicated body of legislation. Public officials were political appointees, sometimes able but more often mediocre, usually underpaid, and occasionally dishonest.

Under these conditions the Acts of Trade rested lightly on the American colonists. It is impossible to say just how extensively these laws were evaded, since those who were engaged in illegal commerce naturally did not publicize their activities, but it is quite evident that a very considerable volume of colonial commerce contributed nothing to the King's revenues. Probably not as much of this traffic was conducted by smuggling as has been generally supposed. It was much easier, after all, to falsify ships' papers or secure the connivance of customs officials. Also, there was a good deal of variation in the colonial attitude toward the British regulations. The Navigation Acts themselves appear to have been reasonably well observed, the Molasses Act, which was unpopular, was generally violated, and the restrictions on colonial manufacturing were simply ignored altogether. And while colonial opinion occasionally protested against specific pieces of legislation, there was not, until just before the Revolution, any widespread opposition to the colonial system as a whole. It was true that in theory the economic life of the colonies was at the mercy of Parliament, but the colonists seem to have been perfectly willing to accept the theory as long as no serious attempt was made to put it into practice.

2

Intellectual Progress

Important as the economic developments described in the preceding chapter were, their influence on the emergence of modern Western civilization was matched and probably overshadowed by the intellectual forces which made their appearance during the same period of history. The freeing of the human mind from the restraints imposed by medieval tradition and established authority and the steady increase of knowledge were essential prerequisites to the creation of the world as we know it today. This process is still far from complete, and, as is frequently the case with significant historical developments, it cannot be given any definite point of origin. It was, however, becoming clearly discernible at the time of the discovery of America and was markedly stimulated by the broadening of man's physical horizons which came from that event.

In its earlier stages this intellectual development followed two main trends. One was the religious upheaval known as the Reformation, in which the authority of the Catholic Church was successfully challenged in a large part of the Western world and a variety of denominations emerged, each asserting the validity of its own views on theology and church organization. The other was the evolution of modern science, which in due course not only revolutionized man's concept of the physical world but also affected profoundly virtually every field of human thought. These two movements were largely independent of each other. In general, scientists were seldom theologians, and theologians were almost invariably wrong in their judgments on scientific discoveries.

Nevertheless, there was some relationship. The impetus for both developments came principally from the general stimulation of the European intellect known as the Renaissance. The characteristics of the Renaissance cover too broad a field to permit concise definition, unless one is to say that they represent the stirring of all the forces that were to bring the modern world into existence. The term itself refers to the revival of learning which became discernible in Italy late in the thirteenth century and spread from there to the rest of Europe during the next three hundred years. There was more to the Renaissance, however, than an intense interest in the classics and a flowering of literature and the arts. It marked a change in the intellectual climate of Europe, a lessening of the medieval attitude that the human race was on this earth merely to prepare for the hereafter in favor of a lively curiosity regarding this world and man's place in it. Speculation of this kind inevitably led to scientific investigation and, in northern Europe especially, to movements for the reform of existing religious and social institutions.

In one vital matter both the Reformation and the rise of science moved in the same direction. The scientist could not accept any ideas or facts as valid merely because they had been officially approved by some traditional authority, whether it was the church or a Greek philosopher; he could accept only what had been subjected to ascertainable proof by observation or experiment. In other words, the individual had to judge for himself. Protestantism rested on the same foundation, even though its early leaders would have been horrified at the thought. It was a revolt against a long-established authority, and it appealed fundamentally to the right of any man to read and interpret the Scriptures for himself. It was a long, painful process, but the combined forces of religious dissent and the scientific method eventually led to the principle of freedom of thought.

THE REFORMATION

The Reformation, like all great historical movements, was a composite of many factors. It was an upsurge of protest against abuses in the Catholic Church; it was influenced by the beginnings of nationalism in Europe; it was aided by the desire of some kings and nobles to annex the properties of the Church within their dominions; it was a reflection of the growing importance of commerce and the middle class, which was attracted to theological doctrines sanctioning the acquisition of wealth. But above all it was a religious phenomenon. What gave it its tremendous impact on Western civilization was the fact that human beings in the sixteenth and seventeenth centuries were genuinely and intensely concerned with theological problems.

Prior to this time there had been some incipient Protestant movements, such as those of Wycliffe (1324–1384) in England and Huss (1369–1415) in Bohemia, but they had been suppressed. Just before Martin Luther appeared on the scene, the low state into which the Church had fallen was under severe criticism by the Humanists of northern

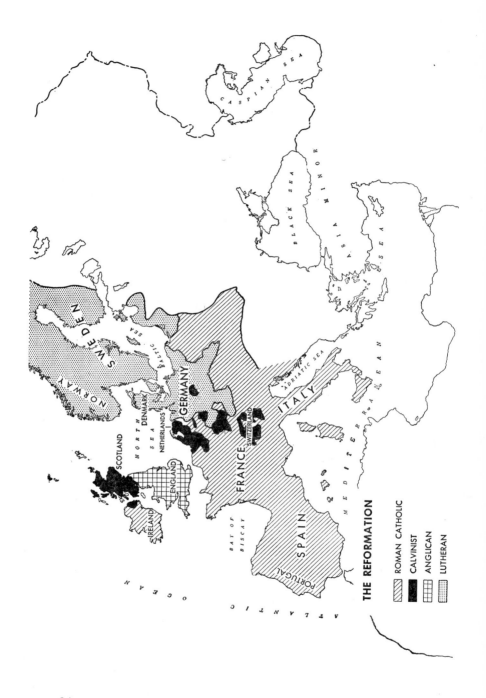

THE REFORMATION

ROMAN CATHOLIC
CALVINIST
ANGLICAN
LUTHERAN

24

Europe, a group of intellectuals infected with the spirit of Renaissance, the most prominent of whom was the great Dutch scholar Erasmus (1466–1536). The Humanists, however, had no desire to break with the Church.

Martin Luther. The man who first successfully challenged the authority of the Catholic Church was Martin Luther. Son of a family of peasant miners, Luther started to study law but became a monk to try to settle his deep conviction of sin, which he finally did settle by discovering in the Scriptures the doctrine of salvation by faith; that is, that man is saved by faith in God's grace and not by good works or observance of ritualistic formalities. Like the Humanists, Luther was disturbed by the obvious evils in the Church, and, being an emotional rather than an intellectual individual, he was finally brought to the point of explosion. The specific incident which touched off his revolt was the sale of indulgences, documents issued by the Pope granting remission of the temporal punishment for sin. The flagrant irreverence of the methods employed in this practice aroused Luther's wrath, and on 31 October 1517, he voiced his protest in ninety-five theses posted on the door of the Castle Church in Wittenberg.

At this point Luther had no intention of separating from the Church, but he was carried on by his own fervent zeal and the wave of discontent with religious and economic conditions in Germany which his action set in motion. In a surprisingly short time much of Germany and all of Scandinavia fell away from the Church of Rome and accepted the doctrines of Luther. As elaborated by Luther himself and Philip Melanchthon, these doctrines reaffirmed salvation by faith, rejected the authority of the Pope and made the church a national institution, abolished monastic orders and the celibacy of the clergy, and cut the sacraments to two, baptism and the Lord's Supper. Drastic as these changes appeared, Lutheranism was essentially conservative. It retained the hierarchial organization and much of the ritual of the Catholic Church, and, while it enjoyed widespread popular support, its survival during its early days rested on the adherence of powerful German princes and the kings of Sweden and Denmark. Their motive was genuine conviction in most cases, but it was strengthened by the prospect of acquiring for themselves the power and possessions of the Church. The assistance of the princes was fully acceptable to Luther. Although he had some sympathy for the miserable condition of the German peasantry, when the peasants revolted in 1525 he unhesitatingly ranged himself on the side of "law and order," which in this case meant savage and brutal suppression of the rebellion.

But once the first break from Catholicism had been made, others of a more far-reaching character were bound to follow. Only two years after Luther's protest against the sale of indulgences, Ulrich Zwingli repeated the action in Zurich, Switzerland, and went on to effect sweeping religious changes, abolishing all the traditional ritual of the Catholic creed. Zwingli's career was brief; in 1533 he was killed in a war between Protestant and Catholic cantons in Switzerland, one of the earliest of the long series of religious wars which convulsed Europe until from sheer exhaustion the rival faiths reluctantly consented to let each other live. His greatest significance is that he prepared the way for John Calvin, the Frenchman whose place in the Protestant movement is at least coequal with Luther's. The circumstances of Calvin's change of faith are obscure, except that it had taken place by 1534. Two years later he published *The Institutes of the Christian Religion,* expounding doctrines that proved to be revolutionary in their import.

Calvin and Calvinism. Calvin's beliefs coincided on the whole with Luther's, the chief difference being that, in interpreting the Bible, Calvin was a "strict constructionist" while Luther was a "loose constructionist," a reflection, unquestionably, of the fact that Calvin was logical where Luther was emotional. The distinctive feature of Calvinism was its doctrine of predestination, which taught that God had determined from the beginning of time who was to be saved and who was not, and that man could do nothing about it. On the face of it this doctrine would seem to imply that an individual could live as he pleased, since nothing he did could affect his fate in the hereafter, but Calvin went on to explain that the elect were bound to lead righteous lives and try to do the will of God according to the Scriptures, because that was the visible evidence of their salvation. In other words, good works and devoutness were not a means to salvation but a consequence of it. Calvinism was a stern and harsh but incalculably strong faith. Since its adherents were convinced that they were carrying out the unchangeable will of God, they were quite prepared to defy any earthly power that got in their way.

A second factor which gave Calvinism both strength and significance was its system of church government. In contrast to both Catholicism and Lutheranism, authority was vested in the whole body of members of the church instead of the pope or the head of the state. There were no bishops, and while the clergy were regarded as the final judges of what the Bible taught, they shared their administrative powers with lay elders or deacons. Moreover, each congregation usually exercised the right to choose its own minister. Calvinism was thus democratic in tendency, even though Calvin himself ruled Geneva with all the highhanded arbitrariness of an absolute monarch.

Calvinism spread widely. It became the dominating creed in the Protestant cantons of Switzerland, Holland, Scotland, and some of the German states. French Protestantism, a minority movement but an aggressive one, was almost entirely Calvinistic. In England it produced Puritanism in the Church of England and various independent groups (Separatists) outside it. From all these sources Calvinism passed over the Atlantic to the future United States. The Pilgrims were English Separatists; the Puritans founded and controlled Massachusetts and Connecticut; the Dutchmen who settled in New Netherlands, later to become New York, belonged to the Dutch Reformed Church; Scotch-Irish and German Calvinists moved in numbers into Pennsylvania and the western sections of Maryland, Virginia and the Carolinas; and the French Huguenots were an influential element in the southern colonies. With all due allowance, therefore, for the contributions of the Catholics in Maryland and the Quakers in Pennsylvania, and for the strong position of the Anglican church as the established church in many of the colonies, American religious thinking up to the Revolution and for many years afterward was overwhelmingly Calvinist in character. Wherever Calvinism spread, it was particularly strong among the middle classes. It appealed to them because Calvin held that all occupations were equally sacred in the sight of God, emphasized the virtue of hard work and thrift, and regarded worldly prosperity as a sign of divine blessing.

The Reformation in England. England had its own peculiar religious development. The specific cause for that country's break with the Roman Church was the refusal of the Pope to annul the marriage of Henry VIII. (This was his first marriage. Five others followed.) To settle the controversy Henry took matters into his own hands and had Parliament pass a series of acts terminating the authority of the Papacy in England and making the King the official head of the church, but without any major doctrinal change at the moment. Subsequently, both Lutheran and Calvinistic ideas became more influential in England, and a conflict developed between those who wanted to stay as close as possible to the old faith, or even to return to it altogether, and those who wanted the Anglican church to be more definitely Protestant. After temporary victories by both sides, religious peace was restored on the accession of Queen Elizabeth in 1558 by a settlement which kept the Church of England separate from the Catholic Church but made its creed broad enough to include a considerable variety of religious opinion. There were some irreconcilable Catholics on one side and some irreconcilable Protestants, mainly Calvinist, on the other, but the Elizabethan compromise won the approval of the great majority of Englishmen.

Under Elizabeth's wise rule there was no serious controversy, but after her death in 1603 the reform movement known as Puritanism became much more active. The Puritans, as stated above, were strongly Calvinistic in their thinking, and what they wanted in religion was to reform the Church of England according to their ideas, and especially to eliminate all traces of Catholicism. On the left wing of Puritanism were the Separatists, also known as Nonconformists or Dissenters, who rejected the authority of the Church of England altogether. Puritanism in the present day has an unfortunate connotation of narrow-minded intolerance which is quite inaccurate. The Puritans of the seventeenth century included a remarkable variety of individual types, including such outstanding figures as John Milton, Oliver Cromwell, John Winthrop, and Roger Williams. They made distinctive contributions to government and intellectual life as well as to religion, and their influence on both British and American history has been profound.

The Counter Reformation. It should not be assumed that the Catholic Church was standing idly by while these attacks were being made on its authority. It launched a vigorous countermovement which purged the organization of most of the abuses condemned by the reformers, checked the spread of Protestantism, and even recovered some territory that had been lost. The principal manifestations of this Counter Reformation were, in the order in which they appeared: the founding of the Society of Jesus by Ignatius Loyola in 1540, giving the Church an aggressive, rigidly disciplined monastic order with a steadfast devotion to the propagation of the Catholic faith; the reorganization in 1542 of the Inquisition, an ecclesiastical court for the suppression of heresy, the influence of which was felt chiefly in the Spanish Empire and to a lesser extent in Italy; and the meeting of the Council of Trent between 1545 and 1563, which clarified Catholic doctrine and strengthened the organization of the Church.

Religious Conflict. A dispassionate contemporary observer, if any such individual had existed, would probably have deplored the Reformation because its immediate consequences appeared to be mostly strife and persecution. Religious dissension flared up into civil and international wars. Protestants and Catholics in Germany, after a preliminary and inconclusive trial of strength in the War of the League of Schmalkalden (1546–1555), fought out their differences in the bitter Thirty Years' War (1618–1648), with most of Europe becoming involved before the conflict was over. Religious antagonism plunged France into a series of civil wars between 1560 and 1589, and it was an important factor in precipitating the English Civil War in 1642, as well as an additional irritant in relations between England and Ireland. Religious toleration was conspicuously absent. Wherever any creed became dominant, it persecuted every other, not necessarily with any spirit of vindictiveness, but with the serene assurance that it alone was right, and that those who disagreed should be punished for their own good, much in the "this-hurts-me-more-than-it-hurts-you" attitude of the parent who has to discipline an unruly child.

But to attribute all this ill feeling to religion would be inaccurate oversimplification. The so-called wars of religion were not so much a product of the Reformation as of the general restlessness in European life which caused the Reformation. In one form or another they would have broken out anyway. The greatest of them, the Thirty Years' War, is an excellent case in point. While it was precipitated by religious rivalry, the battle lines were never clearly drawn on that issue. The conflict between Catholic and Protestant was mixed with and at times overshadowed by a struggle for power between the Hapsburg dynasty and the lesser German princes; the intervention of Gustavus Adolphus of Sweden was motivated as much by desire for personal glory and the expansion of his kingdom as by zeal for Protestantism; and during the last half of the war both Swedes and Germans were virtually spectators of a straightforward contest for power between Catholic France and Catholic Austria.

The political implications of religious persecution must be understood also. In every European country the church, whatever its denomination, was closely identified with the machinery of the state, so that religious policy was normally dictated by political considerations. Where religious uniformity was regarded as essential to political unity, it was enforced, and much of what passed for religious bigotry should be charged to this factor.

On the other hand, where domestic harmony was more likely to be secured by some degree of toleration, monarchs and statesmen were likely to ignore their own theological preferences. In France, when the leader of the Huguenots, Henry of Navarre, succeeded to the throne in 1589 as Henry IV, he became a Catholic because that was the faith of the great majority of his subjects and his conversion was the most direct way to bring the country's civil wars to an end. He provided for his former associates by the Edict of Nantes (1598), granting the Huguenots the right to practice their religion and giving them control of a number of French towns as security. After Henry's death Cardinal Richelieu followed much the same policy. He did, it is true, attack the Huguenots and destroy their political privileges, but he left their religious rights unmolested. He would certainly have regarded Louis XIV's revocation of the Edict of Nantes in 1685 as a retrograde step.

The Growth of Toleration. Even the Thirty Years' War, regrettable as it was, led to some degree of toleration. Since none of the warring sects, Catholicism, Lutheranism, and Calvinism, could destroy each other, the peace settlement agreed that each prince could determine the creed of his own subjects, and those people who could not accept their ruler's decision were to be given an opportunity to emigrate. It was not much of a concession to religious freedom, but it recognized a limited right of dissent.

So the turmoil of the Reformation in the end led to toleration. For that we have to thank an uncounted multitude of ordinary men and women of all creeds whose faith meant more to them than anything else.

Most of them, by present-day standards, would be considered narrow-minded and bigoted, but their faults were also their virtues. The intensity of conviction which caused them to persecute others also caused them to defy exile, imprisonment, and death in defense of their own beliefs. They simply refused to be suppressed, and ultimately their stubborn faith proved to be stronger than either governmental or ecclesiastical authority.

Toleration came at first as a matter of expediency rather than principle, but once it had gained a foothold, liberty of worship as a recognized right was bound to follow in due course. This concept was not generally accepted until the fires of religious controversy had died down and theological problems had ceased to be the focal point of the intellectual life of the Western world, a period which may be regarded as beginning with the rationalistic eighteenth century, but it had made its appearance earlier. Holland, which experienced its full share of persecution during its struggle for independence, permitted a degree of religious freedom unequaled in any contemporary European state. In America Roger Williams not only preached the doctrine that the civil authority had no right whatsoever to interfere with the individual in religious matters but founded in Rhode Island a community where this doctrine was practiced. Freedom of conscience was also preached by minority groups such as the Quakers and the Anabaptists.

Other Effects of the Reformation. Outside the field of religion the Reformation had two very important consequences. One, to which reference has already been made, was its economic influence. The rise of Protestantism was closely associated with the rise of commercial capitalism, although it would be impossible to say which was cause and which was effect. Protestantism held that holy living did not require withdrawal from the affairs of this world; on the contrary, it emphasized that it was a solemn obligation to God for everyone to work earnestly at whatever occupation he was engaged in, and if this earnest labor produced wealth, that was a sign of God's approval. Calvinism in particular, by stressing the importance of sobriety and thrift and condemning luxury and extravagance, encouraged the traits that made for the accumulation of capital. In addition, the confiscation of Church property in the Protestant countries released a considerable amount of wealth, much of which found its way into business channels and, therefore, increased the supply of available capital.

The second important by-product of the Reformation was its effect on the spread of education. Since the Protestant sects all maintained the supreme authority of the Bible, they naturally wanted their communicants to be able to read and understand the Scriptures, and they also had to meet the problem of training their own clergy. Once they had established themselves, therefore, practically all the Protestant groups became active in founding colleges and seminaries and in trying to provide at least elementary education for the mass of the people. Ideals normally ran ahead of achievement, but considerable progress was made, and that devotion to the ideal was genuine is well illustrated by the action of the Puritans of Massachusetts in founding Harvard College only six years after their arrival. On the Catholic side the Jesuits were equally appreciative of the value of education and matched their Protestant rivals in establishing schools and colleges. Admittedly most of the education of the Reformation period was limited in content and dogmatic in objective, but it did bring the learning process to a greater number of people than had ever been reached before.

THE RISE OF SCIENCE

The impact of the Reformation on Western civilization was immediate and dramatic; it shook European society from top to bottom. In sharp contrast, the rise of science was a slow, comparatively obscure process. It began in the same period as the Reformation, but scientific thought had no pronounced effect on intellectual life until the eighteenth century, and even then it scarcely touched the great mass of the people. What happened was that, as the Reformation spent its force and interest in theological problems declined, thinking men turned more and more to science or to the application of scientific methods to other fields of knowledge. This change is not necessarily evidence of a fundamental conflict between science and religion. It might be, but it can be more simply interpreted as showing that the human mind even at its best is limited to concentration on one thing at a time.

This book will not attempt to decide who was the father of modern science, if anybody was. Some scientific curiosity existed during the Middle Ages, and the insatiable genius of Leonardo da Vinci produced a number of remarkable scientific discoveries. But the medievalists worked in an unsympathetic atmosphere, with wholly inadequate facilities for acquiring or exchanging information, and Leonardo's knowledge died with him. The development of science as a cumulative process begins with Nikolaus Copernicus (1473–1543). As the formulator of the theory that the earth revolves around the sun, Copernicus is one of those historical figures of whom practically everyone has heard but about whom very few people know anything. Because his idea was so revolutionary, he hesitated to publicize it, and it did not appear in print until the year of his death. The motive which induced Copernicus to undertake his investigations is almost as significant as the heliocentric theory itself. He rejected the concept of the earth as the center of the universe—named the Ptolemaic system after its principal exponent, the Greek philosopher

Ptolemy—simply because the proofs offered to support it were cumbersome and complicated, while Copernicus believed that nature was simple, uniform, and orderly, a point of view which sums up the whole philosophy of the new science.

While Copernicus was right in his basic assumption, he did not leave a finished product behind him. His proofs were incomplete, and some of his concepts were erroneous. For example, he thought that the motion of the planets was circular. It took a succession of scientists to establish his theory completely and correctly. First came the Danish astronomer Tycho Brahe (1546–1601) and the German Johannes Kepler (1571–1630). Brahe, peculiarly enough, rejected the ideas of Copernicus but did much to confirm them by exhaustive and carefully recorded astronomical observations. Brahe's pupil, Kepler, used the data thus collected to show the real nature of the solar system. Further work on the Copernican hypothesis was done by the great Italian mathematician and scientist Galileo Galilei (1564–1642), although the Inquisition compelled him officially to disavow his belief that the earth moved. Galileo was able to add to the evidence compiled by his predecessors by using a telescope, which he built himself after hearing about the construction of a similar instrument in Holland. In addition to his astronomical work Galileo contributed to the growing body of scientific knowledge the law of the pendulum, the law of falling bodies, and a good deal of information on dynamics.

The Newtonian System. The culmination of this unfolding of the true nature of the physical universe was reached with Isaac Newton. Besides offering further mathematical proof for the theories of Copernicus and Galileo, Newton made the very vital addition of the law of gravity. He also rounded out Galileo's work on the laws of motion, formulated one of the theories of the composition of light, and shares with the German Leibnitz the credit for inventing calculus. Perhaps the most remarkable feature of this remarkable performance is that it all occurred during the first half of Newton's life. The *Principia,* published in 1687, contains all of his major achievements in science and mathematics, and the system of physics developed in this work lasted without substantial modification until the twentieth century. Most of the remaining forty years of Newton's life were spent supervising British coinage as warden of the mint, and he served twice as Member of Parliament for Oxford. His achievements in the field of physics were supplemented by the accomplishments of others, among them the discovery of the barometer by Torricelli (1645), the invention of the air pump by von Guericke (1654), the two together making possible study of the properties of air, and substantial advances in the investigation of electricity, in which the name of Benjamin Franklin figures prominently.

Newton's contribution to mathematics was one of a number of developments in that field which constituted a necessary adjunct to the rise of science. Logarithms made their appearance in 1614, the invention of a Scotsman, John Napier, and modern algebra began with the work of the French philosopher-mathematician Descartes some twenty years later.

Chemistry and Medicine. Chemistry as distinguished from alchemy can be traced to Robert Boyle (1627–1691), who first defined a chemical element accurately, in addition to formulating the law of the expansion of gases. In the century after his death, oxygen and hydrogen were identified, and the greatest of all the chemists of this era, Antoine Lavoisier (1743–1794), discovered the law of the conservation of matter. Lavoisier, like Newton, became a government official, but he had the misfortune to enter the service of the French monarchy just before the outbreak of the Revolution, with the result that the guillotine brought his career to an abrupt end.

The point at which the new science made its most direct contact with ordinary people was its effect on medicine. Accurate understanding of the functioning of the human body was ushered in by Andreas Vesalius (1515–1564), a Flemish physician teaching in Italy, who introduced the radical innovation of teaching anatomy by direct observation and dissection. The next major step was William Harvey's discovery of the circulation of the blood (1628), confirmed by the researches of Marcello Malpighi (1628–1694), one of the first scientists to use a microscope. Investigations in this field progressed favorably, and an important step in the control of epidemic diseases was taken with the development of inoculation for smallpox, superseded in the 1790's when Edward Jenner introduced the superior method of vaccination.

THE INFLUENCE OF SCIENCE ON THOUGHT

No catalogue of discoveries, however important, can convey by itself any adequate impression of the impact of the new science on the intellectual life of the Western world. The findings of the scientists had a cumulative effect amounting to a new revelation, the influence of which penetrated deeply into every field of thought. Three major considerations emerged from the expansion of scientific knowledge. The first was that long-established authorities were not to be relied on merely because they were long established. Aristotle, Ptolemy, and the medieval Schoolmen had all been proved to be in error about the nature of the physical universe. The second was that the physical universe, as far as it had been possible to examine it, was everywhere governed by immutable natural laws, functioning with mathematical precision. The third was that these natural laws could be ascertained through the medium of human reason, by observation, experiment, and calculation. In fact, it appeared that any problem would yield to the application of reason by the methods of science.

Rationalism. From these considerations an entire body of philosophy emerged, built upon the twin pillars of Reason and Natural Law, and defined by the term rationalism. What was known to be true of the physical world was assumed to be true of human relations as well—namely, that they were regulated by natural laws. True happiness, it was believed, lay in man's using his powers of reason to find out what those laws were and then consenting to be governed by them. So the thinkers of the eighteenth century searched for rational and natural systems of religion, government, and economics.

The concept of a natural religion was first presented in systematic form by Descartes and the brilliant Dutch Jew Spinoza (1632–1677). From their doctrines the creed known as Deism evolved. Its tenets were simple. The entire universe was regarded as a great machine operating in accordance with fixed principles. God became, instead of a highly personal Deity, the Supreme Being who had created the machine and kept it operating. Man's function was simply to justify his place in this natural order by living a good and useful life. Deism, therefore, involved a rejection of many of the accepted doctrines of Christianity. It had no place for miracles or any other supernatural intervention in human affairs, since it was completely illogical that an impersonal Creator who had built the universe as a perfect mechanism would arbitrarily interfere with his own fixed laws. For this reason Deists were frequently assailed as atheists by spokesmen of the more orthodox faiths. Most of the intellectuals of the eighteenth century were Deists: a list of its adherents includes Voltaire, Franklin, Jefferson, and Thomas Paine. Deism was fairly important in advancing the idea of religious freedom, since the Deists regarded the bitter theological controversies of the Reformation period as meaningless, but beyond that its influence was limited. It was confined to a comparatively small group of intellectuals and never filtered down to the mass of the people. It could, indeed, have no appeal for anyone but an intellectual, since it possessed no emotional satisfaction.

The achievements of the rationalists in the social sciences had a broader and more far-reaching influence. The rationalists, in fact, created the social sciences for the modern world through their firm conviction that social processes such as government and economics were subject to fundamental laws just like the natural sciences. They went looking for these fundamental laws and, of course, found what they wanted. Some of their conclusions may be regarded critically by a later age, but they did pioneer in making systematic investigations of the problems of human society. What was of more immediate significance was that the findings of the rationalists coincided with the aspirations of the rising middle class for a more important place in the social order. This result could hardly be called accidental; the principal exponents of the natural-law philosophy came from the middle class and were predisposed to accept its ideals as standards of judgment. The new doctrines, therefore, found ready acceptance in those quarters where strong discontent with the established order of things was developing. Rationalism supplied the intellectual basis for both the American and French revolutions.

John Locke. Of the political philosophies evolved by the rationalists, the most significant for Americans is that of John Locke (1632–1704). His ideas on government were based on two theses, both rooted in the concept of natural law. First, he asserted that all men possessed certain natural rights, the most important of which, in Locke's opinion, was the right to acquire and hold property. Second, he held that in man's natural state there was no governmental authority, but that in the course of time men had banded together by mutual agreement and instituted governments in order to safeguard their natural rights. Governments, in other words, owed their existence to a "social contract," under which their powers were closely defined. According to Locke the proper function of government was limited to securing its subjects in their natural rights. When any government became arbitrary or tyrannical, then the contract was dissolved; the people had the right to overthrow the old regime and substitute a new one which would abide by its obligations. These doctrines were something more than abstract political theories. Locke developed them while he was an active member of the Whig opposition to the later Stuarts, and they were used to provide a philosophical justification for the Glorious Revolution of 1688. American students should also feel at home with Locke's ideas. The classic exposition of them in practice is the Declaration of Independence:

> We hold these truths to be self-evident, that all men are created equal, that they are endowed by their Creator with certain inalienable Rights, that among these are Life, Liberty and the pursuit of Happiness. That to secure these rights, Governments are instituted among Men, deriving their just powers from the consent of the governed. That whenever any form of Government becomes destructive of these ends, it is the Right of the People to alter or to abolish it. . . .

Locke was a constitutionalist. While his theories were principally a reaction against the belief in the divine right of kings, he would have disapproved of any political system in which the powers of government were not strictly limited. Both he and the Americans who were to follow his principles a century later distrusted the tyranny of the mass just as much as the tyranny of the individual.

Natural Law in Economic Thought. In the field of political economy, or economics, the concept of natural law was slower in taking effect, so that its full influence on Western thought was deferred until the nineteenth century. The French Physiocrats, who were the first important exponents of rationalism in economics, did not develop their ideas until late in the eighteenth century. Their doctrines were simple and clear. Since, they argued, economic life was governed by irrevocable natural laws, then all attempts at human regulation were bound to be useless at best, harmful at worst. The Physiocrats were probably responsible for the expression *laissez faire*. For all their devotion to natural law, they never succeeded in defining clearly what the natural laws of economics were. They believed that agriculture and mining were the true source of national wealth and were skeptical of the value of manufacturing and commerce, but their energies were devoted mostly to attacking the cumbersome system of regulation which France had inherited from Colbert. The principal figures of this school were Dr. François Quesnay, physician at the court of Louis XVI, Turgot, occasionally finance minister under the same monarch, and E. I. du Pont de Nemours.

Contemporary with the Physiocrats and strongly influenced by them was Adam Smith, professor at Glasgow University. His work, *An Inquiry into the Nature and Causes of the Wealth of Nations,* published in the eventful year 1776, is one of the great books of world history, although it is unfortunately one of those classics more often referred to than read. Smith accepted the main body of Physiocratic doctrine, except that he regarded labor as the real source of wealth and gave industry and trade at least equal status with agriculture. He went beyond the French thinkers in postulating the law of supply and demand as the controlling factor in economic activity. He also pointed out the relationship between the size of the market and the division of labor (specialization) and exploded the mercantilist theory that international trade could benefit only one party. While he was a devotee of *laissez faire,* believing that national prosperity was best achieved by letting each individual follow his enlightened self-interest, Smith could see some practical limitations to his doctrines, and he should not be held responsible for the deification of human greed attained by his nineteenth-century disciples.

In emphasizing the worth and dignity of men as individuals, possessed of inalienable natural rights, rationalism contributed substantially to the rise of humanitarianism in the late eighteenth century, although the results achieved in this field were due at least as much to the revival of evangelical Christianity. The great Italian jurist Beccaria (1738–1794) pointed the way to substituting reasonable punishments for crime for the inhuman but ineffective practices employed by even the most enlightened European states. John Howard (1726–1790), an English Quaker, devoted his life to the amelioration of prison conditions. Other reformers attacked slavery and the slave trade with considerable success.

THE AGE OF REASON

All these intellectual developments appeared to the thinkers of the eighteenth century to have inaugurated a new era of civilization. They proudly referred to it as the Age of Reason, or the Enlightenment. All the outworn traditions of the past, all the evils with which humanity was afflicted, were going to crumble before the pure and unfettered exercise of reason. This new gospel was preached with a conviction and an intensity worthy of the orthodox religious creeds which the rationalists despised as emotional and illogical.

While the movement was international in its scope, it reached its height in France during the middle of the eighteenth century, where its advocates were known as the *philosophes*. Since their greatest achievement was to prepare the way for the French Revolution, they will be discussed later in connection with that event. Before that, however, their teachings were influential enough to convert a number of the ruling princes of Europe, so that the Age of Reason was also the era of Enlightened Despotism. The enlightened despots were a group of monarchs who conceived it their duty to govern their realms for the welfare of their subjects, in accordance with the principles of the new philosophy but without sacrificing any of their own powers. With this objective most of the rationalist thinkers heartily agreed, for, with all their devotion to the doctrine of natural rights, few of them had any faith in the ability of the common people to rule themselves. They believed that reforms would have to be imposed from above, by rulers who would embody Plato's conception of the philosopher-king.

The Enlightened Despots. The most important of the enlightened despots were Frederick the Great of Prussia, Catherine the Great of Russia, and Joseph II of Austria. Others appeared in Spain, Portugal, Tuscany, Sweden, and Denmark. Of the whole group the only one who was really successful was Frederick of Prussia. After the series of wars by which he made Prussia a major power, Frederick devoted the rest of his life to the internal welfare of his country. He accomplished much because, in addition to his own outstanding ability, he enjoyed the advantages of a homogeneous, well-disciplined people and an efficient civil service, the only one of its kind in Europe. Yet Frederick's career illustrates admirably the fundamental defect in the principle of Enlightened Despotism. Everything depended on the will of one man. When that one man was a Frederick the Great, the system would work reasonably well, but no human agency could guarantee that Prussia or any other state would be governed by a constant succession of Fredericks. Once the guiding spirit was withdrawn, his reforms invariably collapsed.

Joseph of Austria was a more sincere idealist than Frederick, but he had none of his Prussian rival's advantages. The Hapsburg dominions were a polyglot collection extending from Belgium to Hungary, and Joseph's well-meaning but tactless attempts to impose a uniform and efficient administration upon them merely aroused resentment, strong enough frequently to flare into revolt. His establishment of religious toleration antagonized the dominant Catholic Church, and his effort to help the peasants brought the landed aristocracy down on his head. So Joseph died a disappointed man, although some of his work did survive. Catherine of Russia also was probably genuinely devoted to the principles of Enlightened Despotism, but in practice she accomplished little, largely because her position as Empress was not strong enough to permit antagonizing the Russian nobility.

The lesser exponents of the creed ran into similar difficulties. The privileged classes of Europe did not propose to give up their favored position merely because it was not in accord with the dictates of reason. Gustavus III of Sweden was assassinated and Count Struensee of Denmark executed for the crime of trying to improve the condition of the common people. The common people themselves frequently objected to being reformed without their consent, a quirk of human nature which the philosophers had overlooked. Enlightened Despotism was a short-lived and, on the whole, an unsuccessful experiment.

The Age of Reason was coming to an end at about the time of the American and French revolutions. It contributed much to modern civilization. It introduced a tolerant spirit and a willingness to investigate and analyze facts which the Western world badly needed. Its adoption of the scientific method for the study of the institutions of human society laid the foundation for future progress in this field, even though in the hands of the rationalists themselves the scientific approach led to a dogmatic insistence on distinctly hypothetical natural laws. With all its substantial achievements, the Age of Reason nevertheless fell short of the optimistic hopes entertained for it. The new era of reasonableness, simplicity, and order did not materialize, principally because ordinary people are not governed exclusively by reason. Even at its height rationalism had a very limited appeal. While the philosophers were speculating about the world of reason, the mass of the people were responding to emotional religious movements as Methodism in England and Pietism in Germany. By the end of the eighteenth century even the intellectuals were turning away from the gospel of reason. Rousseau heralded the rise of Romanticism, which appealed to the emotions, and the German philosopher Kant restored faith to a position of intellectual respectability. It should be understood that there never was a complete repudiation of rationalism; reason merely ceased to be regarded as the only factor that mattered.

3

Government and Society

In spite of the various new influences that were at work in the Western world after 1500, the general structure of European society underwent little obvious change before the outbreak of the French Revolution. Until then it retained the outward characteristics of feudalism, with modifications depending upon the degree to which each country had been affected by the developing forces of modern civilization. The dominant feature of this social system was its division of people into fairly well-defined classes, each differing in the extent of its political and legal rights. As a matter of fact the stratification was so complex that it would be safe to say that no two individuals had exactly the same status in the social order. However, for purposes of discussion the broad classification recognized in the organization of the States-General in France will be used: two privileged groups, the clergy and the nobility, and the unprivileged mass of commoners. Since French society was the pattern for the rest of Europe during the greater part of this period, its structure may be taken as typical.

THE SOCIAL PYRAMID

The first estate consisted of the clergy, a term which in this connection is restricted to the Catholic clergy in France and the clergy of whatever the official state-supported church was in other countries. As a group it enjoyed a favored position. The established churches were usually well endowed—the Catholic Church owned an estimated one-fifth of all the property in France at the time of the Revolution—and most of them received income from special ecclesiastical taxes as well. Members of the clergy frequently were only partially subject to the ordinary civil laws, and they were exempted from most taxes, although in France the church organization periodically made voluntary contributions to the government.

However, the clergy were by no means a uniform group. Stratification within their ranks was as well marked as it was among the population in general. The higher clergy, the bishops and archbishops, were almost invariably drawn from the nobility, to whom the church offered one of the suitable careers for younger sons. Too often their appointments were due to family influence or royal favor, their incomes high, and their duties light. The lower clergy on the other hand, the parish priests and the curates, came from the common people, did practically all the hard work, and were so badly paid that not infrequently they had to till the soil along with their peasant parishioners in order to live. This description may be applied to almost any European state in the seventeenth and eighteenth centuries; it fits Catholic France, Anglican England, and Lutheran Prussia equally well.

Along with the clergy, the nobility, the second estate in France, held a privileged status in the social order. As a group it was also wealthy, about as numerous as its clerical counterpart, and on the whole less useful. In France and most other continental European countries the members of the aristocracy were entitled to special treatment at the hands of the law; they monopolized the highest offices of the state, church, and army; they were exempt from some taxes and underassessed for others; if they enjoyed favor at court, their incomes were likely to be supplemented by sinecure appointments in government or by straightforward pensions from the public treasury; they held considerable legal and economic power over the peasants who worked their estates. Whether these privileges were earned or not was becoming debatable by the eighteenth century. The rise of centralized national states was steadily undermining the political power of the landed aristocracy, and the institution of the professional standing army had almost completely destroyed its former position as the warrior class. The increasing complexity of both public administration and the art of war called for a degree of training and ability not necessarily conferred by heredity, with the result that there was an increasing proportion of middle-class officials in government and middle-class officers in the military establishments, although such men were seldom permitted to rise to the higher posts.

The members of the aristocracy were all conscious of their superiority to the rest of humanity, but among themselves wide gradation in status existed. The court nobility, enjoying the favor of the king and spending their time and money in luxurious idleness, looked down on the country nobility, who from lack of funds or just from preference remained on their estates. The greater country nobles, fairly well off and possessing some authority in local government, were distinct from their lesser brethren who had nothing but pride of rank to set them apart from the mass of the people. And all noble families of long standing despised new-comers to their ranks. For, in France and England at least, the aristocracy was not a closed corporation. In England there was no real line of demar-cation between the nobility and the upper middle class. Intermarriage was fairly common; there was no social stigma attached to an aristocrat marry-ing a commoner as long as the commoner had enough money. Titles could be acquired by royal favor, by service to the nation, or by outright pur-chase. In France the caste line was more rigidly drawn, but there the influx of bourgeois officials into government service created a *noblesse de robe* existing alongside the older *noblesse d'épée,* and with the passage of time the distinction between the two tended to become fainter.

The Commoners. The population of France toward the close of the eighteenth century has been estimated at about twenty million. Of these about 250,000 were divided between the two privileged classes; all the rest were the commoners who cultivated the land, conducted the nation's busi-ness, and paid most of its taxes. The same proportion may be assumed to be reasonably accurate for the rest of Europe. The commoners were no-where nearly as distinct a group as the two privileged orders; and in the nature of things they could not have been. There were simply too many of them, and their class constituted a complicated social pyramid by itself.

At the top was what can best be termed the upper *bourgeoisie:* the great merchants, the bankers, the successful professional men, all repre-senting the growing power of commercial capitalism. Individuals in this group were likely to be far wealthier than any landed aristocrat and even more likely to be abler and better educated. This class was conscious of its position and eager to translate its economic and intellectual power into political power. It succeeded in doing so in England and Holland during the seventeenth century and became an integral part of the governing class. In France it was unable to break down social discrimination to any-thing like the same degree. Some members of the French *bourgeoisie,* as we have stated, made their way into the nobility through government service, but this route was open to only a few and no other existed. The French aristocracy, with less practical wisdom than its English counter-part, was unwilling to share its position and ally itself with the rising power of capital. The French state needed the economic support of the *bourgeoisie,* and it had to turn to this class for its financial administrators —Colbert in the seventeenth century, Turgot and Necker in the eighteenth. But none of these men was permitted to institute any reforms that touched the privileges of the nobility, and the middle class as a whole was refused any real share in the conduct of government. So it became, quite naturally, the focal point of discontent with and criticism of the Old Regime.

Next on the social and economic scale was the large and heterogeneous lower middle class, a group which included the retail merchants, shopkeepers, skilled craftsmen, independent freeholding farmers—the "yeomen" in England—and the more prosperous tenant farmers or peasants. It was hardly a distinctive class. For one thing, it was fluid; its successful members moved out of it into the upper *bourgeoisie,* and the unsuccessful went down into the "masses." In addition, it was too far down in the scale to have political significance. While those of its members who belonged to merchant or craft guilds had some say in town government, the lower middle class as a whole could expect little recognition until the existing order had been violently shaken. Nevertheless, it was showing some signs of ferment. It leaned heavily to nonconformist religious creeds and from them gradually acquired the habit of independent thought. However, this group had little opportunity to express itself politically until the era of the great revolutions.

The Base of the Pyramid. At the bottom of the social pyramid, despised and feared by privileged classes and *bourgeoisie* alike, was the mass which, for want of a better term, has to be called the proletarians— the propertyless workers in the towns and the bulk of the peasants in the country. They had few rights of any sort, and those that they possessed were quite likely to be ignored. The masses in England were perhaps a little better off than elsewhere in Europe, because they were at least free in the eyes of the law, while serfdom was still prevalent on the Continent. Everywhere their economic and social position was incredibly bad. Nobody regarded them as fit for even the rudiments of education, and certainly nobody dreamed of permitting them to have any voice in their own destinies. A few fortunate individuals might occasionally work their way up into the middle class, but for most of the group the only prospect was a lifetime of poverty with no hope of improvement.

Why, it may be asked, did not these people revolt? Occasionally they tried, as in the German Peasants' War of 1525, but isolated and sporadic uprisings by leaderless and unorganized mobs were easy to suppress. The great majority of the unprivileged were too ignorant and too close to the animal level of existence to be more than vaguely aware that things might be better. The inert conservatism of the mass smothered the aspirations of the few who did have some vision of a better world, and any moves that these few might make were certain to be ruthlessly suppressed. The ruling classes might squabble among themselves, but they could always close ranks against a threat from below. Once the settlement of America opened up an avenue of escape through emigration, it is not surprising that increasing numbers of common people in western Europe decided that the uncertain hazards of the New World were preferable to the certain misery of the Old, or that many of them were willing to enter temporary slavery as indentured servants in order to pay for their passage.

ABSOLUTE MONARCHY

At the time of the discovery of America the political pattern of Europe was changing from feudalism, with its decentralization of authority and its dissipation of power through a complex hierarchy of nobles, to absolutism, in which the state became a centralized organization with power concentrated in the hands of a single individual. In the course of the next century the transition was virtually completed, and absolute monarchy became the prevalent form of government in Europe until it, in turn, collapsed in revolution. The only exceptions of note were England, Holland, and Switzerland.

Absolutism replaced feudalism because it was a better system of government. Making the king the supreme authority in the state involved the risk of tyranny, but, in an age when popular control of government was a visionary concept, it was the only alternative to the anarchy and lawlessness of the feudal aristocracy. Consequently, in their struggles for power against the nobility, the dynasties of Europe could generally count on the support of the common people, especially the middle class, who needed political stability in order to conduct trade. The increasing complexity of warfare was another important factor. The political strength of feudalism rested on the military supremacy of the mailclad knight on horseback, but the invention of gunpowder and the development of firearms reduced that overromanticized figure to an anachronism and substituted the highly trained professional army as the instrument both for enforcing internal order and securing the state from invasion. Such an army could not be created on short notice. It had to be maintained on a permanent basis, and it also had to be under the unrestricted control of the head of the state if it was to function efficiently. The standing army thus became a bulwark of royal authority. It was a formidable bulwark too; one of the most difficult problems British and American constitutionalists had to solve was that of providing the state with adequate military security and, at the same time, preventing the armed forces from becoming a weapon of tyranny.

Divine Right of Kings. After it had gained a solid foothold, royal absolutism acquired a philosophy of its own in the doctrine of the divine right of kings. This theory started with the convenient assumption that God must approve of kings or He would not have placed them in their exalted stations. Therefore, it followed that kings derived their authority from God, and opposition to royal authority was the same thing as opposition to the will of God—in short, sacrilege. The popularity of this doctrine among reigning monarchs is readily understandable.

While examples of absolutism could be taken from any country in Europe, the institution reached its highest development in France and can best be studied there. It took centuries of struggle for the French monarchy to establish effective authority over the country, and at the beginning of the modern era its position was still none too secure. A succession of weak kings in the middle of the sixteenth century proved unable to prevent France from being torn apart in the series of civil wars between Catholics and Huguenots. The accession of Henry IV in 1589 found most Frenchmen willing to accept a king strong enough to keep order; Henry, in fact, owed his throne largely to the support of the moderate Catholic party, the *Politiques,* who wanted above all to restore order and keep France from foreign domination. Henry fulfilled their expectations. He was an enlightened despot almost two centuries ahead of his time, and, until his assassination by a religious fanatic in 1610, he and his great minister, the Duc de Sully, did much to repair the ravages of civil war and rehabilitate France as a major power.

Henry's untimely death left the nine-year-old Louis XIII on the throne, and an incompetent regency almost lost all the ground the monarchy had gained. The outstanding event of this period was the meeting of the States-General in 1614 in an attempt to straighten out the affairs of the kingdom. However, the clergy and the nobles refused to listen to proposals of reform introduced by the commoners, and after an exhibition of complete futility, the States dissolved, not to assemble again until 1789. France was saved from another descent into disorder by the emergence of Cardinal Richelieu as chief minister of state from 1624 to 1642. Able and ruthless, Richelieu was the real founder of absolutism in France. Every factor in French life which threatened to weaken the authority of the monarchy was systematically attacked. The destruction of the special political privileges of the Huguenots has already been mentioned. The power of the nobility was undermined by entrusting the administration of local government to middle-class officials, the *intendants,* appointed by and completely responsible to the crown.

Louis XIV. With Louis XIV (1643–1715), royal absolutism reached the apex of its development. Louis believed implicitly that he ruled by divine right. His concept of monarchy was just the converse of Enlightened Despotism; instead of regarding the king as existing to promote the welfare of his subjects, he regarded his subjects as existing to promote the welfare of their king, with the king the sole judge of what his welfare was. He summed up his doctrine in the expression, *"l'état, c'est moi,"* and he was remarkably successful in making this concept a reality. Some of his success he owed to the work of his predecessors in destroying the political power of possible rivals to the crown. Louis finished this process by encouraging his nobles to become courtiers in immediate attendance upon him, and by officially outlawing Protestantism through the revocation of the Edict of Nantes. He also strengthened his authority by being willing to work hard at the task of being king. While he had a structure of councils to advise him on matters of public policy, he made the decisions—big and small—himself. In addition, he had the good fortune to be surrounded by extremely able helpers. The career of Colbert as minister of finance has already been discussed. Colbert's rival and eventual successor, Louvois, distinguished himself as minister of war by organizing an army which, for a time at least, had no equal in Europe. To command this force Louis had as generals Turenne, one of the acknowledged masters of the art of war, and Vauban, the greatest military engineer of his time.

With all these assets, the reign of Louis XIV, which lasted until 1715, became the most brilliant in the history of the French monarchy. His armies—for a while—marched almost unhindered through the territories of his neighbors. Holland saved itself in 1672 only by the desperate expedient of opening the dikes and flooding the country. Louis' great palace at Versailles and his glittering court were the envy of every prince in Europe. Literature and the arts flourished under the king's patronage; his reign witnessed the golden age of French drama, the era of Molière, Racine, and Corneille.

The cost of all this grandeur to France is another matter. Louis XIV's insistence on concentrating the entire management of his kingdom in his own hands may have satisfied his conception of the importance of his position, but it made for bad government. Rather than risk incurring the king's displeasure, subordinate officials simply refused to assume responsibility. Decisions which should have been made by local authorities on the spot were passed up through the hierarchy of officialdom until they reached the king; it was ridiculous, for example, that the question of repairing a church belfry in Quebec should have had to be referred to Paris. Louis himself worked hard and conscientiously, but no man could possibly have kept up with the mass of detail which came before him. Under successors who had all his prerogatives but little of his industry, the system resulted in governmental paralysis. Louis' religious bigotry was equally unfortunate. The Huguenots were no menace to him, and they were an asset to France because they included a large proportion of the nation's merchants and skilled craftsmen. By driving them out Louis dealt a serious blow to his own country's prosperity and contributed heavily to the power of its rivals.

The Cost of Absolutism. Moreover, the splendor of Versailles and the interminable wars were expensive. The political and social structure of France being what it was, the bill was footed mainly by the already overburdened peasantry, as well as by reckless borrowing from the *bour-*

geoisie. The exactions from the common people might have been borne a little more cheerfully if the king had ever shown the slightest interest in their welfare, but he never did. To him the masses of the French people existed only to provide the wherewithal to gratify his wishes.

The wars themselves produced no benefits great enough to justify their drain on the resources of France. Like many another autocrat, royal and otherwise, Louis XIV did not know when to stop. The early successes of his magnificent army fired his ambition to the point where he would not let his neighbors live in peace. He produced flimsy claims to adjoining territory, and he made each acquisition the basis for further demands. He ignored treaty obligations when it suited him, and he pounced on his victims without warning. Eventually, as he might have foreseen, he brought a united Europe down on his head. The climax was reached with the War of the Spanish Succession (1701–1713). This conflict broke out when one of Louis XIV's grandsons inherited the throne of Spain. It might have been averted if Louis had been willing to guarantee that the two countries would never be united under the same king, but he would not. Although his opponents were ultimately unable to alter the Spanish succession, they did shatter the armies of Louis XIV. Turenne had been killed in the Dutch War, and no commander of equal ability rose to take his place. On the allied side, Britain produced an outstanding military genius in John Churchill, Duke of Marlborough, while the forces of the sluggish Hapsburg Empire reached an unusual height of military effectiveness under Prince Eugene of Savoy (born, incidentally, in Paris but turned down by the French Army, to which he had first offered his services). The crushing victory of Marlborough and Eugene at Blenheim in 1704 put France on the defensive for the rest of the war.

An additional factor of long-term importance was that Louis XIV, in his absorption with conquests in Europe, neglected the French Navy. A force which was able to meet the navies of Britain and Holland on equal terms as late as 1692 declined to a position of definite inferiority ten years later. By the end of the War of the Spanish Succession, Britannia ruled the waves pretty effectively. So the reign of Louis XIV terminated for France in military disaster, naval decay, and general impoverishment. It is hardly surprising that his death evoked no particular manifestation of sorrow from his people.

THE DEVELOPMENT OF CONSTITUTIONAL GOVERNMENT IN GREAT BRITAIN

It is a matter of paramount importance for the United States that England, instead of following the trend of the rest of Europe toward autocracy, successfully resisted the attempts of its monarchs to make themselves absolute and established a working system of constitutional government, because Americans drew their political ideas and institutions predominantly from the mother country. Furthermore, the extension of the British constitutional system to the colonies gave the inhabitants of the colonies invaluable training in self-government, with the result that when they became independent they were mature enough politically to avoid the blunders commonly made by people who are managing their own affairs for the first time.

Modern English history is generally regarded as starting with the accession of the Tudor dynasty in 1485. The Tudors, the most important of whom were Henry VIII and Elizabeth, were an able family who contrived to have their own way without making an issue of the extent or nature of royal authority. They had, on most occasions, a judicious sense of how far the English people were willing to go in support of a given policy, and they were careful to have their wishes legalized by the established constitutional methods. Most Tudor Parliaments were "rubber-stamp" assemblies, meekly carrying out the desires of the reigning monarch with only an occasional protest. Nevertheless, it was of considerable significance for the future that Parliament continued to meet, that its authority was officially acknowledged, and that England was governed by Act of Parliament even if those acts, for the time being, were royal decrees in disguise.

Parliament and the Stuarts. Elizabeth was the last of the Tudors. Upon her death in 1603 the English crown passed to the Stuart dynasty in the person of James VI of Scotland, who became James I of England. James, supposed to have been described by the Duc de Sully as "the wisest fool in Europe," was a firm believer in the divine right of kings, but he lacked the political acumen of his predecessors. Through most of his reign he was wrangling with his Parliaments, chiefly over religion and money. The religious difficulty was that James preferred the "High Church" wing of the Church of England and, consequently, came into conflict with the growing force of Puritanism, which was strongly represented in the House of Commons.

The financial difficulty was not entirely the king's fault. The general rise of prices caused by the influx of gold and silver had left the fixed revenues of the crown insufficient to meet the ordinary expenses of carrying on the government. James made matters worse by extravagance, so that he was repeatedly compelled to ask Parliament for additional funds, and, since Parliament naturally tried to take advantage of its favorable bargaining position, friction between the two increased.

James's successor, Charles I, was even more devoted to political and religious authoritarianism than his father. At the beginning of his reign, mismanaged wars with France and Spain forced him to appeal to Parliament for money; in return, Parliament in 1628 compelled the king to sign the Petition of Right, which forbade taxation without the consent of Parliament, arbitrary arrest, billeting of troops in private houses, and the imposition of martial law in peacetime. Charles signed this document because of his financial difficulties, but he had no intention of keeping his obligation any longer than was necessary. A year later he dissolved Parliament and attempted to rule England by himself.

This experiment lasted until 1640. Charles tried to raise revenue by a variety of expedients, such as the revival of old, forgotten laws and the sale of monopolies, but the one method which would have made him permanently independent of Parliament, the imposition of new taxes by royal decree, was closed to him because he lacked an army to enforce it. The most celebrated of his devices was his resort to "ship money," a tax sometimes levied on seaport towns as a substitute for their obligation to provide ships for the navy in times of danger. Charles extended the tax to the entire country, a reasonable enough procedure if done by proper authority, since naval defense was a responsibility of the whole nation. However, the legality of the king's action was challenged by John Hampden, and when five out of the twelve judges who heard the case voted in Hampden's favor, the king's prestige suffered, since the judges were his appointees.

While Charles was trying to make himself supreme in the political sphere, he was also carrying on an anti-Puritan crusade in religion through the instrumentality of Archbishop William Laud. Laud's persecutions, plus the prospect that the king might succeed in making himself absolute, led to the emigration of about twenty thousand Puritans to New England between 1630 and 1640. The position of Catholics under Charles I and Laud was somewhat better, since Charles was married to a French princess, but it was still uncertain enough to induce the Calvert family to establish Maryland as a Catholic refuge in 1632.

If Charles I had been able to maintain his personal rule long enough, it is quite possible that Parliament might have become a forgotten relic like the French States-General. Charles, however, made an irretrievable blunder when he attempted to impose Anglicanism on Presbyterian Scotland. (England and Scotland were governed separately although they had the same king.) The Scots promptly rose in revolt to defend their religion. Charles, faced with a war for which he was completely unprepared, was forced to summon a new Parliament in 1640; and his discontented English subjects once again had an outlet for their grievances.

The Long Parliament. When Parliament assembled, in fact, its members were much more interested in trimming the king's powers than they were in giving him the means to defeat the Scots, so much so that Charles angrily dissolved it after it had been in session less than three months. This step may have satisfied his feelings but it did nothing for his finances, and so before the end of the year the Short Parliament was succeeded by the Long Parliament, which was to remain officially in existence until 1660. Its leaders when it first met were John Pym—"King" Pym to his opponents—and John Hampden. Among its rank-and-file members was an unobtrusive Puritan country gentleman called Oliver Cromwell.

The Long Parliament did nothing to end the Scottish War, for the simple reason that it did not want to give Charles exclusive control over an army which might be turned against Parliament, and also because the continued existence of the Scottish army kept the king in a convenient state of insolvency. The Scots understood this situation clearly and conducted themselves accordingly, maneuvering so as to maintain pressure on Charles but not to antagonize the English people. Parliament turned its energies to thoroughgoing reforms of both state and church, all of them unacceptable to the king. The result was inevitable; both sides began raising forces and in 1642 open hostilities broke out.

The Civil Wars. The ensuing Civil War lasted intermittently until 1649. The Royalists, or Cavaliers, consisted mainly of the landed gentry and their dependents in the rural districts where Puritanism was weak. The Parliamentary party, or Roundheads (so-called from the Puritan fashion of wearing short-cropped hair), contained the Puritan gentry and the great majority of the townspeople. It made an open alliance with the Scots after the war started. The king, having the support of the traditionally military class, had a slight advantage in the early encounters, but this was soon overcome when Cromwell began to organize an army of earnest Puritans, with religious zeal added to strict military discipline. The "Ironsides," commanded by one of the most brilliant generals England has ever produced, made short work of the royal forces. Eventually Charles gave himself up in despair. He then started a series of blundering intrigues, trying to play off the English against the Scots, and the English Presbyterians—who controlled Parliament and wanted to make their creed the established church in England—against the Independents, who were led by Cromwell, controlled the army, and favored the Congregational type of church organization. All he succeeded in doing was convincing his enemies that there could be no peace in England while he lived; in 1649 he was tried by a special court, convicted of treason, and executed. The doctrine of the divine right of kings carried considerably less weight in England after that.

The Rule of Cromwell. For the next ten years England experimented unsuccessfully with new forms of government. A Commonwealth, with Parliament as the supreme authority, failed because of the intolerance of the age. The Independents found their existence threatened, but their control of the army enabled them to overthrow the Commonwealth and set up a military dictatorship with Cromwell as Lord Protector. Cromwell, to his credit, did not want to be a dictator. He tried to find some alternative, and the short-lived Instrument of Government drafted by some of his followers stands unique as the only written constitution ever adopted in England. Cromwell, however, found little support outside the army. His death left the English people sick of Puritanism and military rule; by almost unanimous consent they restored the monarchy in the person of Charles II, son of Charles I, who had been living in exile most of the time since his father's death.

The Restoration. The new king cleared the way for his recall by promising to respect the position of Parliament and to grant an amnesty, with some exceptions, to his former opponents. The enthusiastic welcome which he received upon his return to England in 1660 did not deceive him about the realities of his position. He had the Stuart love of autocracy and he leaned toward Catholicism in religion, but he was shrewd enough to sense the limits beyond which he could not push his people, and he had no desire either to share his father's fate or, as he put it himself, to "go on his travels again." For the twenty-five years of his reign he worked quietly to strengthen his position, and he succeeded in making himself virtually absolute for the two or three years before his death. He enjoyed the affection of his subjects to the last, an affection in no way diminished by the king's notoriously loose living. Subsidies from Louis XIV, in return for which Charles was briefly and somewhat discreditably involved in war with Holland, relieved his financial dependence on Parliament temporarily, but his victory over his Parliamentary opponents was due chiefly to their blunders in trying to exclude the king's Catholic brother and heir, James, Duke of York, from the succession to the throne. This controversy marked the origin of the party system in English politics. Those who supported the king became known as Tories; those who opposed him, as Whigs. They represented, in general, the same elements of the population as the Cavaliers and the Roundheads.

The Revolution of 1688. Charles II died in 1685; his successor, James II, took just three years to lose everything his brother had gained. James was no more determined to be absolute and probably no more staunchly Catholic than Charles had been, but he pursued his objectives with a complete lack of tact or finesse. His heavy hand was felt in the American colonies as well as at home. One rebellion against James in England was crushed in 1685, but his arbitrary government soon alienated even the loyal Tories, with the result that, when the birth of a son to James in 1688 opened up the prospect of indefinite continuation of his dynasty, both parties combined to drive James out and invite his son-in-law, William of Orange, the Stadtholder of Holland, to become king.

This "Glorious Revolution" is a focal point in the evolution of constitutional government in Great Britain. Divine right had nothing to do with this change of monarchs. James was deposed, and William and his wife Mary were made joint sovereigns by Act of Parliament. Three other pieces of legislation, all passed in 1689, completed what is known as the Revolution Settlement. The Bill of Rights confirmed the exclusive authority of Parliament to levy taxes, required frequent meetings of Parliament, asserted the right of freedom of speech in Parliament, excluded Catholics from the throne, and prohibited the maintenance of a standing army in peacetime without consent of Parliament. Since an army was needed in view of the troubled state of Europe (as Stadtholder of Holland, William was already engaged in the War of the League of Augsburg against Louis XIV), authority to maintain it was granted by the Mutiny Act, whose time limit of six months, later extended to a year, guaranteed that the power given to the crown could be easily revoked if necessary. The Toleration Act gave freedom of worship to all Protestant sects except the Unitarians.

While the Glorious Revolution did not definitely establish Parliament as the supreme authority in government, it gave British constitutional development an irresistible impetus in that direction, and subsequent events accelerated the trend. The fact that William and Mary were childless and that Mary's sister Anne, who became queen in 1702, had survived all her fourteen children, compelled Parliament to intervene in the succession again. An act of 1701 provided that after Anne's death the crown should pass to the nearest Protestant relatives of the royal family, the ruling house of Hanover in Germany. The succession problem also was responsible for the union of England and Scotland in 1707. Friction between the two countries, arising mainly from English economic discrimination against the Scots, was creating a situation in which Scotland might well refuse to accept the Hanoverian dynasty, restore the Stuarts, and become completely independent again. The Act of Union eliminated this danger. It created the United Kingdom of Great Britain, with a single Parliament for both countries; although Scotland retained its separate legal system, educational system, and established church. The Scots accepted the Hanoverian succession and were given complete equality with the English in economic matters. It was certainly a wise solution of the problem; it was extremely unfortunate that an equally wise solution could not have been found at the time for Ireland.

Development of Parliamentary Government. The beginning of the eighteenth century, therefore, saw Parliament's authority as a legislative body established beyond the possibility of serious challenge. It not only controlled the nation's finances; it could alter the succession to the throne and revise the structure of the state. The next and culminating stage in the evolution of British constitutionalism, the extension of Parliamentary control to the executive branch of the government through the agency of the Cabinet, was substantially completed during the next fifty years. Up to this period the reigning monarch was, in fact as well as in theory, the administrative head of the state, and his ministers were his own appointees, responsible to him alone. Both William of Orange and Anne regarded themselves as having the same power in this field as their predecessors (Anne was the last British monarch to exercise the royal veto), but both discovered that, in order to secure legislative approval of their policies, it was necessary to defer to the wishes of Parliament in selecting ministers. The growth of the party system still further limited the sovereign's freedom of choice. William at first thought that he could secure harmony by keeping an even balance between Whigs and Tories in his administration; experience demonstrated, however, that government worked most smoothly when all the principal ministers of state belonged to the party which controlled Parliament. By the time Anne came to the throne, it was fairly well recognized that a shift in party strength in the House of Commons would produce at least some changes in the personnel of the Cabinet. (Because of its hereditary character, the House of Lords was much less subject to changes in party alignment. In any event, even at this time the House of Commons was somewhat more important because of its right to initiate all financial legislation.)

When Anne died in 1715, the Elector of Hanover became king as George I. Neither he nor his son, George II, had any particular knowledge of British political problems, and both found their authority so limited as to furnish little incentive for them to take a strong interest in the affairs of their new kingdom. This situation had a threefold result: (1) decisions on matters of public policy were made by the king's Cabinet, a body consisting of the principal ministers of state, rather than by the king himself; (2) the members of the Cabinet came to regard the approval of Parliament as more important than the approval of the monarch, the more so because they were invariably members of Parliament, either Lords or Commons, themselves; and (3) the individual who inevitably emerged as leader of the Cabinet, or prime minister, gradually became the real head of the government. The first recognized prime minister was Sir Robert Walpole, who held that post from 1721 to 1741. While the confidence which both George I and George II gave to him was highly useful, Walpole's power rested on the support of the Whig party, then dominant in Parliament, and it was the withdrawal of this support that eventually caused his resignation, thereby confirming the principle that the prime minister and his Cabinet colleagues were responsible to Parliament and not to the king.

By the time the third George came to the throne in 1760, full of ideas about the proper functions of a monarch, the system of parliamentary government was too firmly rooted for him to have any hope of attacking it directly. The only method open to him to secure the power he desired was to use the considerable prestige and influence inherent in his position to build up his own party in Parliament, an experiment which achieved a limited success but collapsed largely because of the fiasco which George III's ministerial selections made of their relations with the American colonies.

As it had evolved up to the end of the eighteenth century, Britain's political structure was still far from making the nation a democracy. Property qualifications and other restrictions on the suffrage kept the electorate down to a very small proportion of the population, certainly not over three per cent. The landed aristocrats dominated the House of Lords completely and the House of Commons almost as completely. Nevertheless, Britain did have a government of law, in which the rights of the individual were respected to a degree unknown in the absolute monarchies of continental Europe; and Parliament, with all its limitations, was responsive to public opinion.

The British colonies in America grew up in this atmosphere. Their inhabitants responded to the long struggle with the Stuarts just as their compatriots at home did, and they considered themselves entitled to all the rights won by the Civil War and the Glorious Revolution. Colonial self-government was stimulated indirectly also. From 1640 to 1660 England was too absorbed in its internal conflicts to devote much attention to its scanty colonies in America. They were left to shift for themselves, and they did so quite successfully. After the Restoration another twenty years elapsed before Charles II and James II moved to strengthen royal authority in the colonies by creating the Dominion of New England, and that experiment had scarcely been started when it was swept away by the Glorious Revolution. Consequently, by the time Britain had settled its own governmental problems and was in a position to think about a comprehensive colonial policy, the colonial assemblies had acquired through long usage considerable powers which could not readily be disturbed.

4

The Evolution of the European
State System

The problems of internal political organization which England and France settled in such contrasting ways were symbolic of a trend which would become increasingly important in the life of Europe and eventually of the rest of the world: namely, the creation of an international society composed of independent sovereign states, in which a nascent sense of nationhood was gradually replacing personal loyalty to a prince as a bond of union. The establishment of a strong central government was an obvious preliminary step in the creation of such a state. After internal stability had been achieved, then the state in question could defend its rights or assert its claims against its neighbors.

The process of nationalization was far from uniform. France, Spain, and England could be clearly identified as nation-states as early as 1500, although all three still had serious internal difficulties to encounter. Elsewhere in Europe the concept of the national state was either just beginning to appear or was still nonexistent. The conclusion of the Thirty Years' War in 1648 found Europe in widely varying stages of national development, but since that peace settlement embodied some recognition of the principle of state sovereignty, it makes a convenient point at which to survey the developing political organization of Europe.

EUROPE AT THE END OF THE THIRTY YEARS' WAR

By the time the Treaties of Westphalia were signed in 1648, nationalism was firmly rooted in western Europe. The existence of three power-

54

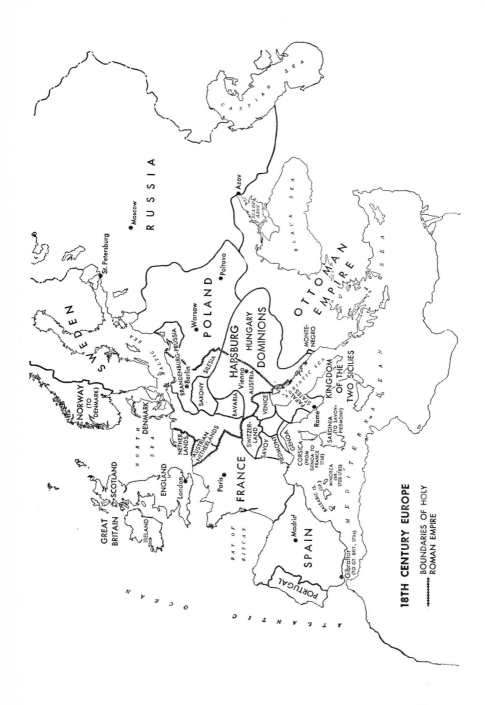

18TH CENTURY EUROPE

—————— BOUNDARIES OF HOLY
╬╬╬╬╬╬╬ ROMAN EMPIRE

55

ful states on the Atlantic seaboard has already been referred to. France emerged from the Thirty Years' War as nearly the victor as anyone was, and well on its way to becoming the foremost military power of Europe. Spain had passed the crest of its greatness and was at the beginning of a long period of decay, but it was nevertheless a strong nation, still in control of a great colonial empire as well as Belgium and other European territories outside its own borders. England's civil wars did not affect its national unity; they were conflicts for control of the machinery of government and involved no threat of national disintegration.

Other national states had also come into existence. The independence of Holland and Switzerland, both fused into nationhood by a long struggle for freedom, was formally acknowledged in 1648, and eight years earlier Portugal had taken advantage of the Thirty Years' War to terminate a forced and unpopular union with Spain. In northern Europe Denmark, which then included Norway, and Sweden were strong states.

Central Europe possessed virtually nothing that resembled national organization. Italy was a hodgepodge of petty states, some of them independent but most of them dominated at various times by Austria, Spain, or France. Germany was nominally organized as the Holy Roman Empire, a political entity forever characterized by Voltaire's classic observation that it was neither holy nor Roman nor an empire. The position of emperor was theoretically elective (hence the title of elector held by the various German princes who possessed the right to take part in an imperial election), but in practice it had become hereditary in the Hapsburg dynasty. The imperial office was an empty dignity; the larger German states like Brandenburg, Bavaria, and Saxony conducted themselves pretty much as they pleased. The emperor, however, was the most powerful prince in Germany and one of the most powerful in Europe because he was also the ruler of the extensive Hapsburg territories, a sprawling collection centering upon Austria, Hungary, and Bohemia, which no one ever quite succeeded in making into a nation. As a matter of convenience the Hapsburg dominions will be referred to simply as Austria.

Farther to the east Poland was a large and populous state, but already suffering from misgovernment by the most incompetent aristocracy in Europe. The Polish nobility devised the preposterous *liberum veto,* the provision whereby any single member of the Polish Diet could not only veto any action by that assembly but could dissolve it and annul all its previous decisions. Poland was in poor condition to enter an era of highly competitive international politics. Russia, geographically isolated from the rest of Europe, was still regarded as an Asiatic power. It had, however, a strong autocratic government and in the near future would be able to take advantage of Poland's political chaos and Sweden's physical inability to maintain itself as a great power. The Balkan area was part of the Ottoman Empire, which had just about exhausted its expansive force and was on the threshold of decay. Placed outside the orbit of European civilization by their religion, the Turks were nevertheless an important factor in European politics because of the strategic position they occupied, notably their possession of the straits leading into the Black Sea and their contiguity to both Austria and Russia. Even that most Catholic king, Louis XIV, had no scruples about invoking the aid of the infidels against his Hapsburg rival.

THE EIGHTEENTH-CENTURY REVISIONS OF THE EUROPEAN STATE SYSTEM

The relative position of each of these states in the European order was never constant, and as the nation-state became more and more the basic unit of political organization, their rivalries tended to become more intense and fluctuations in importance to become more rapid and radical. The period between the end of the Thirty Years' War and the outbreak of the French Revolution witnessed a marked transformation in the European alignment. Two new first-class powers arose in Russia and Prussia; several older states declined noticeably, and one, Poland, disappeared altogether. The friction generated by this process was largely responsible for a long series of wars, most of which spread to the New World as the colonial powers found their overseas rivalries interlocked with international politics in Europe.

Rise of Russia. The rise of Russia to the rank of a great European power is customarily dated from the reign of Peter the Great (1689–1725), although some spadework had been done by Czar Ivan the Terrible (1547–1584). Peter came to the throne with a passionate desire to "westernize" his country. To accomplish this aim, two steps were necessary: one, to reform Russian society, at least at the top, by eliminating its Asiatic characteristics and introducing some of the manners and customs of European civilization; the other, to break Russia's isolation by securing direct access to the Western world, which meant securing seaports on the Baltic or, less desirable, on the Black Sea.

Peter carried out the first step by a direct and ruthless application of autocratic power. The Russian nobles were compelled, whether they liked it or not, to accept the conventions of contemporary European society; the army and navy were reorganized on Western standards; technicians and artisans were imported to introduce European industrial methods; the Orthodox Church was converted into an instrument of the state. Few of Peter's reforms did much more than impose a veneer on the surface of Russian life, but he did give Russian development an impetus in the direction of Europeanization which it never again lost.

The acquisition of satisfactory outlets to the West was a problem which could not be solved by the mere exercise of the Czar's will. When Peter came to the throne, Russia's only major seaport was Archangel, remote from the center of the country and open only a short part of each year. Access to the Baltic was blocked by the Swedes and to the Black Sea by the Turks. The port of Azov was wrested from the latter early in Peter's reign, but the only adequate solution to his problem lay in the Baltic, which meant a conflict with a nation whose military prestige had declined little since the great days of Gustavus Adolphus. For such a conflict, however, Russia had two great advantages. One was that Sweden had jealous neighbors, including Poland, who were blind to the menace to their own security in the growing power of Russia; the other was that Sweden was fundamentally too weak in population and resources to outlast the tremendous latent strength of its eastern neighbor.

The conflict which enabled Peter to realize his desires was the Northern War (1700–1721), between Sweden on one side and Russia, Poland, and Denmark on the other. It opened with brilliant Swedish victories over all their opponents in turn, but in 1708 Charles XII of Sweden committed the fatal blunder of undertaking an invasion of Russia. Like Napoleon's Grand Army a century later, the Swedish army was ruined by the Russian winter, and in 1709 its remnants were annihilated by the Russians at Poltava in the Ukraine. Although Charles escaped to keep the war going another decade, Sweden's military power was broken. The peace settlements gave Russia the Baltic seaboard from Poland to Finland.

After Peter's death Russia stagnated until the reign of the Empress Elizabeth (1741–1761), who introduced French culture to the Russian court and made Russia a major factor in European affairs by taking part in the Seven Years' War. Then Catherine the Great (1762–1796) completed the work of making Russia a recognized European power. A would-be enlightened despot, Catherine's grandiose schemes of internal reform had few practical results. If anything, she left the Russian peasantry worse off than it had been before. Her contribution to Russian greatness was the conquest of the northern coast of the Black Sea from the Turks, and, more important, the partitioning of Poland in conjunction with Austria and Prussia.

Partition of Poland. The dismemberment of the Polish state was perhaps inevitable in view of the irresponsibility and selfishness of its ruling class, but it still reflected little credit on either Catherine or Frederick the Great of Prussia, who saw to it that nothing should be done to reform the chaotic government of Poland. Maria Theresa of Austria was an unwilling partner, entering the combination because she could not afford to let her rivals be the sole beneficiaries of Polish disintegration. The first partition took place in 1772; Russia and Prussia helped themselves to more territory in 1793; and then, after a brief outburst of Polish resistance under Thaddeus Kosciusko, the three powers took what was left in 1795.

Rise of Prussia. The other newcomer to the ranks of the great powers, Prussia, had an even more spectacular climb to prominence. This state got its start early in the seventeenth century when the Hohenzollern dynasty added to its electorate of Brandenburg the duchy of East Prussia and some minor principalities in western Germany. The immediate result was hardly impressive. Brandenburg-Prussia consisted of three widely separated blocks of territory, none of them wealthy, and lacking in natural defenses against hostile neighbors. Survival, to say nothing of expansion, called for efficient utilization of such resources as the state possessed and the creation of a strong military force.

The first positive steps in this direction were taken by the "Great Elector," Frederick William (1640–1688). By judicious politics in the closing phase of the Thirty Years' War he made some valuable additions to his dominions, and after the conflict was over he enlarged his army until it was second only to that of Austria among the German states. In order to raise the revenues needed to pay for his military machine, Frederick William organized his government so as to secure the utmost efficiency and economy in public administration, and he made every effort to introduce new industries into his territories, his most successful stroke in this direction being the settlement of a large number of exiled French Huguenots in Brandenburg.

Frederick William's successor is notable for only one thing. In return for services he rendered to the emperor, he was permitted to assume the title of king for the part of his dominions which lay outside the Holy Roman Empire, namely, Prussia, so that the scattered Hohenzollern possessions now became the Kingdom of Prussia. The next king, Frederick William I (1713–1740) was a miserly tyrant with an almost insane passion for building up his army. At the time of his death Prussia, the thirteenth state of Europe in population, had the fourth largest army, a condition which necessarily made for an abnormal emphasis on militarism in Prussian life. Frederick William himself seldom used his impressive military machine, although he did get into the Northern War in time to share in the spoils of fallen Sweden. His principal contribution to the rise of Prussia was to create the instrument used by his son, Frederick II, or Frederick the Great.

Frederick the Great. Of Frederick the Great's character it is necessary to say only that he was a military and political genius with a profitable lack of moral scruples. He continued the opportunistic policies of his predecessors on a more audacious and ambitious scale, and he raised the Prussian army to heights of proficiency by adding inspiration to its already excellent training and organization. He wasted little time in impressing himself on Europe. The year of his accession, 1740, also witnessed the death of the Emperor Charles VI. Charles, having no male heirs, had spent his last years getting the states of Europe to recognize the rights of his daughter, Maria Theresa, through an agreement called the Pragmatic Sanction, to which Prussia was a party. The treaty obligation meant nothing to Frederick; before 1740 was over, Prussian troops, unprovoked and without warning, marched into the Austrian province of Silesia, thereby plunging Europe into the War of the Austrian Succession. Once Frederick had shown the way, the rest of Maria Theresa's neighbors, including France and Spain, joined him in attempting to dismember Austria. Great Britain, already at war with Spain and the bitter colonial rival of France, was the only major power to support the Empress. During the war Frederick played fast and loose with his allies as well as his opponents, and at its conclusion in 1748 he emerged with the only clear-cut gain—he retained possession of Silesia.

Since the outcome of the war was unsatisfactory to everyone else, the next eight years were spent in preparations for renewing the struggle. As part of these preparations, everybody changed sides. France came to the conclusion that aggressive Prussia was more dangerous than sluggish Austria and concluded an alliance with Maria Theresa. Russia and some of the smaller German states also joined the combination against Frederick. Prussia and Britain, left without their former partners, took the obvious step of joining forces; Britain, after all, was fundamentally uninterested in who controlled Germany but was very much interested in preventing an increase of French power, while Frederick needed whatever help he could get.

When the European phase of this conflict was resumed in 1756, Frederick again was responsible for touching off hostilities by invading Saxony, a step somewhat more justified than his invasion of Silesia, since he was the intended victim of a powerful combination and it was sound policy for him to strike before his opponents could complete their concentration. Nevertheless, the odds against him were so great that, in spite of his brilliant generalship, he was saved only by the timely defection of Russia. He came out of the Seven Years' War with his country exhausted, but still in possession of Silesia.

For the remainder of his reign Frederick devoted most of his energy to the rebuilding of his devastated country, a task which won him recognition as the foremost of the enlightened despots. He made only one more territorial acquisition, but it was a very important one. Prussia's share in the first partition of Poland was the area known in the twentieth century as the Polish Corridor. Its annexation united East Prussia physically to the Hohenzollern possessions in central Germany and made

Prussia for the first time a reasonably compact state. When Frederick the Great died in 1786, his country had become one of the foremost military powers of Europe.

THE WORLD WARS OF THE EIGHTEENTH CENTURY

While frequent wars were nothing new in Western civilization, those which accompanied the evolution of the sovereign state as the basic unit of government have a particular significance because they originated in the forces that were creating the modern world. From the end of the Thirty Years' War until the outbreak of the French Revolution the conflicts into which Europe was periodically plunged were concerned predominantly with rivalries between states. The points at which the interests of the various states clashed were bewildering in their variety, but certain broad factors can be discerned. One governing consideration was the problem of balance of power, a much-misunderstood phrase which means simply that no state wished to be dominated by any other and each consequently tried to conduct its foreign policy in such a way as to prevent its rivals from becoming too strong. The apparent inconsistencies in the policies of the great powers can almost all be accounted for by the constant shifting of forces necessary to maintain such a balance in a period when drastic changes were taking place in Europe's political pattern. In addition, the maritime nations (chiefly Great Britain, France, Spain, and Holland) clashed repeatedly over colonial claims and commercial privileges. The alignment on these issues was simple; Great Britain and France fought a century-long duel for colonial and naval supremacy, with Holland and Spain playing increasingly minor roles.

These two factors interlocked because the position of the colonizing states in Europe had a direct bearing on their ability to compete with each other overseas. France and Spain were enemies until the decline of Spain eliminated it as a menace to France and both found their colonial possessions threatened by the rise of British sea power. French policy from the reign of Louis XIV on was torn between the desire to dominate Europe and the desire to build up a colonial empire, with the result that it accomplished neither. British policy, on the other hand, was directed consistently at supporting resistance to the expansion of French power on the European continent as the most effective method of reducing France's ability to fight in other parts of the world. This interrelationship between the European balance and the competition for overseas empire meant that any major war would be world-wide in scope. No European conflict of any importance could fail to involve the colonial powers, and they were certain to fight wherever their interests clashed.

Wars of Louis XIV. The first in this series of world wars were the two waged by a coalition of European states against Louis XIV, the War of the League of Augsburg (1688–1697) and the War of the Spanish Succession (1701–1713), known in American history as King William's War and Queen Anne's War respectively. The two should really be regarded as one continuous struggle with an uneasy armistice in between, because both were fought for the same reason: the limitless ambition of Louis XIV and the tremendous military strength of France constituted so great a threat to the other nations of western and central Europe that they were compelled to subordinate whatever differences they had among themselves and unite for mutual protection. While armies marched and countermarched across Europe, France and Great Britain began their long struggle for empire by extending the conflict to North America. There the French occupation of Canada and Louisiana, the latter including both the Ohio and Mississippi valleys, presented a barrier to future English expansion, although the French were never sufficiently numerous in any of their North American possessions to hold them against a determined and well-organized attack. The Comte de Frontenac, the capable governor of New France, launched a series of destructive Indian attacks on the New England frontier. The British colonists, superior in numbers but badly handicapped by a lack of unity among their colonial governments, struck back unsuccessfully against Quebec and successfully against the French holdings in Nova Scotia.

The wars of Louis XIV were terminated by the Treaty of Utrecht in 1713. Although the French king's hopes of being master of Europe had been shattered, the victors were too exhausted by their long struggle to impose a harsh peace on him. France gave up Nova Scotia to the British, the European balance was adjusted by an agreement that the crowns of France and Spain (both of them now held by members of the Bourbon family) should never be united, and by Spain's ceding to Austria the Spanish Netherlands (Belgium) and sundry territory in Italy. Spain also yielded the naval bases of Gibraltar and Minorca to Great Britain and agreed to permit a limited amount of British trade with the Spanish colonies.

This setttlement kept the major powers of Europe in relative peace for a quarter of a century. The next world-wide conflict had two distinct points of origin: a colonial squabble between Britain and Spain, which burst into war in 1739, and Frederick the Great's invasion of Silesia a year later. The Anglo-Spanish quarrel arose from the commercial concessions made by Spain in the Treaty of Utrecht. The Spaniards claimed that British merchants were brazenly taking advantage of these privileges to engage in virtually unlimited trade with the Spanish colonies, an accusation undoubtedly true enough, except that it ignored the fact that the evasions of the Spanish trade regulations were carried out with the connivance of the Spanish colonists, who could hardly have existed if they had complied with their mother country's stringent restrictions. At any rate, Spanish attempts to suppress this illegal commerce resulted in clashes of growing intensity, until they finally flared out in 1739 into the War of Jenkins' Ear, so called because a certain Captain Jenkins testified before Parliament that he had been brutally set upon by Spanish coast guards and deprived of an ear while he was peacefully pursuing his illicit business. He even produced a box containing what he asserted was the ear in question.

Anglo-French Conflict. Underlying this conflict was an increasingly bitter antagonism between Great Britain and France over colonial problems. In North America the French had embarked on an ambitious project for hemming in the British colonies by a chain of forts extending from Canada to the mouth of the Mississippi, and their great fortress of Louisburg on Cape Breton Island stood as a threat to the Newfoundland fisheries, which were vital to the welfare of New England. In India, where previously the British and French East India Companies had operated under a gentleman's agreement to do business peacefully and ignore any outbreak of war in Europe, trouble was developing from the schemes of François Dupleix, who hoped to build a French empire in India by forming a network of alliances with native princes. To protect their interests the British had to do the same thing and so started reluctantly along the road that led them eventually to mastery of India.

Under these conditions a showdown was bound to come sooner or later. The peaceful proclivities of Sir Robert Walpole in England and Cardinal Fleury in France kept the two nations from an open break until the Prussian invasion of Silesia. Then all Europe flared into war, Walpole and Fleury were swept aside, and, in the picturesque words of Macaulay, "Because Frederick wished to rob a neighbor whom he had promised to defend, black men fought each other on the coasts of Coromandel and red men scalped each other by the Great Lakes of North America." However, considering the importance of the issues that were at stake, the War of the Austrian Succession proved singularly indecisive. The inconclusiveness of its European phase has already been mentioned, and in the colonial struggle the war parties in both France and Great Britain failed to match their ardor with efficiency. The French took Madras in India, and in North America an expedition from the British colonies captured Louisburg. It was all wasted effort; Madras and Louisburg were returned to their original owners when peace was concluded in 1748.

The next eight years, as we have seen, were spent in a general reshuffling of alliances preparatory to renewing the contest. That, at least, was the case in Europe; in the overseas areas preparations went far beyond the stage of diplomatic negotiations. As early as 1751 one of Dupleix' Indian allies opened a new attack on the British, but this time the able Frenchman found himself checked by the superior genius of Robert Clive. Three years later the directors of the French East India Company decided that Dupleix' activities were bad for business and recalled him. If they hoped by this move to restore the former live-and-let-live situation in India, they were too late; both sides were now too deeply involved in Indian politics to withdraw. In this same year (1754) hostilities broke out again in America as the result of the establishment of a French post at Fort Duquesne, on the present site of Pittsburgh. Virginian forces under George Washington were promptly sent to drive the French out but were defeated. The British government thereupon dispatched General Braddock and a force of regulars in 1755 to reestablish Britain's claims to the Northwest, still without declaring open war on France. Everything went wrong with this operation. Braddock and the colonial governments could not get along together, and, if it had not been for Benjamin Franklin's ability to soothe ruffled feelings and secure the needed transport and supplies, the expedition might never have started at all. Then, when it was almost in sight of its goal, it suffered a disastrous defeat.

Seven Years' War. These scattered conflicts were absorbed into the greater struggle when the Seven Years' War, the French and Indian War of American history, began in 1756. The combination of France, Austria, and Russia had a crushing superiority in numbers but a complete absence of inspired leadership and a fatal inability to coordinate its forces. On the other side, at the start of the war, the visible assets were British sea power and Frederick's military genius. Although cooperation between the British and Prussians was not much better than among their opponents, they contrived to supplement each other's efforts at the critical points. During the first two years, while the British government was fumbling uncertainly, Frederick fought with a brilliance which gave him a place among the great commanders of history. Then, when Prussian resistance began to weaken in the face of overwhelming force, William Pitt became prime minister of Great Britain and galvanized that country into effective action.

Pitt saw to it that Prussia received the material and military aid it needed to remain in the war, because Prussia performed an essential function in Pitt's strategy—that of pinning as much French military power as possible to the European continent. In the meantime, British forces assaulted the French empire from one end to the other. Louisburg fell to Jeffrey Amherst in 1758. A year later James Wolfe took Quebec and John Forbes took Duquesne, renaming it Fort Pitt. A British reverse at Ticonderoga merely staved off the finish; in 1760 Amherst fought his way up Lake Champlain to Montreal, and French resistance in North America was over. In the West Indies, Martinique and Guadeloupe were scooped up by British sea power, and in India Britain's supremacy was established beyond question by 1760. Spain's belated entry into the war in 1762 proved to be an ill-judged step; before the year was out, Havana and Manila had been added to the British trophies.

By this time everyone was ready for peace. France and Spain had obvious reasons for wishing to terminate hostilities, and in Britain the young king George III, jealous of Pitt's power, forced him to resign and brought a peace party into office. The peace settlement of 1763 restored the *status quo* in Europe to the extent that there were no important transfers of territory. The balance of power, nevertheless, was permanently affected by the demonstrated strength of Russia and Prussia. In the colonial areas, as one would expect, far-reaching changes did take place. Britain returned Martinique and Guadeloupe to France but annexed Canada and all French territory as far west as the Mississippi. Since Louisiana was transferred to Spain at the same time, France no longer possessed even a foothold on the North American continent. Spain also managed to get back Manila and Havana by exchanging Florida for them. French holdings in India were reduced to a few innocuous trading posts. In view of the completeness of the British victory, these terms were not unduly harsh, especially for Spain; there was, however, no question about maritime supremacy being firmly in Britain's hands.

Social Effects of Eighteenth-century Wars. Quite apart from the political changes involved, this long series of wars had profound effects on the development of Western civilization. Military organization was naturally affected most directly. These prolonged and far-flung conflicts could not be fought with improvised forces, hastily raised and armed, such as had been used as recently as the Thirty Years' War. They required long-term, professional armies and navies, permanently maintained in peace as well as war, and these in due course appeared in every important European state. They were recruited normally by voluntary enlistment, but, since service in the lower ranks was not especially attractive, impressment usually had to be resorted to in wartime. Another common practice was the hiring of foreigners. Prussia was notorious for the way in which it scoured Europe for likely recruits, and even populous France employed both Swiss and German mercenaries as integral parts of its army.

The existence of large-scale military establishments was a powerful stimulus to commerce and industry. Armies and navies had to be fed, clothed, and munitioned in wholesale quantities, a highly profitable function which naturally devolved upon the business community. The same group had to be called upon to help finance the wars, because wars, then as now, required considerably more money than could be raised by taxation—particularly by the inefficient tax systems of the eighteenth century.

Raising funds by borrowing was nothing new in European political practice, but the demands of this series of world conflicts began the transformation of what had usually been a matter of haphazard and individual arrangement into a systematic relationship between the government and the money market. The general effect, in western Europe at least, was to increase the economic and political importance of the *bourgeoisie* as the class which alone could provide the money and materials needed for the conduct of war.

The economic strain of these wars had other significant consequences. Triumphant Britain, with a flourishing business life which had enabled it to outlast its enemies through a century of struggle, nevertheless found itself in 1763 with a national debt big enough to alarm British statesmen, and their attempts to pass some of the burden on to their colonies started the chain of events that led directly to the American Revolution. France, potentially at least as wealthy as her great rival, found the burden of prolonged warfare too great for her antiquated governmental machinery, and her financial distresses likewise culminated in revolution.

Growth of Nationalism. Finally, the organization of Europe into a collection of sovereign states stimulated the growth of nationalism, one of the most potent forces of modern civilization. The development of national feeling was a slow, essentially unconscious process. It was not a motive in the formation of nation-states prior to the end of the eighteenth century. That was the work of strong-minded monarchs solely desirous of concentrating authority in their own hands and unconcerned with the national characteristics of the people over whom they ruled. Yet among peoples who were reasonably homogeneous in race and language the creation of powerful central governments led inevitably to the breaking down of provincial loyalties, and the sense of allegiance to the person of the monarch was gradually transformed into one of allegiance to the state of which he was the symbol. Nationalism was firmly rooted in England by Elizabeth's reign, and it was further strengthened by pride in the victory over Spain. Holland and Switzerland, as we have said, acquired national solidarity by virtue of their long struggles for independence. National consciousness was also visible in France and Spain, although in both countries it was somewhat diluted by regionalism, class divisions, and, in France, religious differences.

5

The American Colonies

Throughout the period covered by this section, the ties between the New World and the Old were very close. Quite apart from their direct political relationship with Europe, the early colonists naturally clung as closely as they could to the customs and modes of living with which they were familiar, and this cultural bond was intensified by a continuing dependence on Europe as a market for colonial products and a source of supply for manufactured goods. Nevertheless, American life rapidly acquired its own distinctive characteristics, compounded from the necessary adjustment to existence in a new environment, the motives which drew settlers across the Atlantic, and the particular conditions surrounding the founding and development of the individual colonies.

THE SPANISH EMPIRE

In a study of the rise of the United States in the modern world, the phase of the extension of European civilization to America represented by British colonization must naturally receive the major share of attention. The fact remains, nevertheless, that Spain was first in the field. It had brought practically all of South and Central America under its control before the first English colonies were founded,[1] and its dominions covered a good three-fourths of the entire American continent when the United States became an independent nation. Since the Spanish Empire had a pronounced influence on the future of the United States, both because

[1] Portuguese Brazil was part of the Spanish Empire during the period (1580–1648) when Portugal was ruled by Spain, and the Portuguese colonial system resembled the Spanish.

substantial parts of it eventually were absorbed into American territory and because it produced most of the American republics with which the United States is now closely associated, its principal characteristics need to be understood.

Some features of Spanish colonization have been described in Chapter 1. As suggested there, the creation of the Spanish Empire was an outstanding feat. In an incredibly short time, the *conquistadores* swept over an enormous area, overthrowing in the process the well-organized empires of the Aztecs in Mexico and the Incas in Peru, until it seemed that Spain would make good its claim to the whole of America. That prospect disappeared with the decline of Spanish power in Europe. At the end of the sixteenth century, the successful revolt of the Dutch, the rise of English sea power, and the restoration of internal order in France made it impossible for Spain to exclude her rivals from the unoccupied parts of the American continent but did not stop the momentum of her own expansion. The high-water mark of Spanish colonization was reached only with the peaceful acquisition of French Louisiana in 1763 and the founding of a mission and *presidio* on San Francisco Bay in 1776.

When these last steps were taken Spanish expansion into North America had become defensive in purpose. Its objective was not so much to colonize as to keep other claimants out of areas where they might become a menace to the heart of the empire. Louisiana was to be a barrier against the British, just as Texas had previously been occupied to check the French. California's function was to keep the Russians in Alaska from pushing farther south along the Pacific coast. These provinces, in consequence, were never settled intensively, but the influence of their founders has left a lasting impress of Spanish culture on southwestern United States, principally in architecture and place names, but also in a considerable residue of Spanish-speaking people.

Government. The organization of the Spanish Empire reflected, as all colonial empires did, the political and social characteristics of the mother country. Unlike the competitors who later challenged her position on the American continent, Spain was comparatively little affected by the forces which were changing the medieval into the modern world. Neither the rising power of commercial capitalism nor the Reformation made any serious impression on Spanish life. Her greatest rival, England, became capitalistic and Protestant; Spain remained essentially feudal and Catholic. The colonial institutions of the two countries, in consequence, developed along radically different lines.

At the apex of the Spanish imperial structure was the Council of the Indies, a body formally established in 1524 with complete power, subject to the approval of the king, to rule Spanish America. It enacted laws; it acted as a court of final appeal on colonial cases; it advised the crown on the appointment of administrative officers and defined their functions; and it supervised the operations of the *Casa de Contratación*. In America, the authority of the Spanish crown was vested in two viceroys, the Viceroy of New Spain, governing all the Spanish possessions in Central and North America from his capital at Mexico City, and the Viceroy of Peru, who governed South America from Lima. As the personal representatives of the king, the viceroys were given complete authority over their territories, although the general lines of policy they were expected to follow were laid down by the Council of the Indies.

As Spanish imperial policy developed, other officials and agencies came into existence, partly to assist the viceroys, partly to act as a check on them. The viceroyalties were gradually divided into districts, ruled by a complicated hierarchy of captains-general, presidents, and governors, and occasionally removed from the authority of the viceroy altogether. In the eighteenth century, the increasing administrative burden resulted in the creation of new viceroyalties for New Granada (Colombia and Venezuela) and La Plata (Argentina, Uruguay, and Paraguay). Superimposed on this hierarchy of executive officials, were the *audiencias,* which were originally judicial bodies but eventually acquired considerable administrative powers and even some control over ecclesiastical matters. Finally, in the late eighteenth century the Bourbon dynasty in Spain introduced into America the French system of *intendants*. These officers were given independent authority over colonial finance and commerce.

The Church. In addition, the Catholic Church occupied a very important place in the Spanish colonial system. Missionary zeal to convert the native population played a vital part in Spanish expansion in America. The only other nation to match Spain's efforts in this direction was France. In the long run, the monastic orders which founded missions throughout Spanish America undoubtedly did more to plant Spanish civilization in the New World than the mailclad *conquistadores* like Cortés and Pizarro. The Church was in effect an organ of the Spanish state, since the king alone had the right to appoint ecclesiastical officials. It had complete control over education, and the welfare of the Indians was its special province. Its legal position should not be taken to mean that the Church was simply a passive instrument of the Spanish crown; it exercised a positive and considerable influence on the determination of imperial policy, particularly in attempting to humanize the treatment of the conquered peoples.

Nowhere in all this structure was there any provision for giving the Spanish colonists a voice in the management of their own affairs. True, the complexity of officials with overlapping duties and independent responsibility to an authority in faraway Spain made for inefficiency, and the inhabitants of colonies were frequently able to ignore regulations they strongly disliked. But evading the authority of an autocratic government is not the same thing as learning the art of self-government. When the United States became independent, its people already had ample experience in governing themselves and thus were able to erect a stable political structure in a very short time. The republics which grew out of the Spanish Empire lacked the political maturity of their northern neighbor and had to acquire it by a long process of trial and error, with frequent lapses into the authoritarianism to which they were accustomed.

The Indians in Spanish America. As it happened, the Spaniards founded their empire in a part of America admirably suited to their political system. The English colonies were established on what was for practical purposes an empty continent. The scattered Indian tribes of North America, with their primitive social organization, were an annoyance rather than an obstacle to European settlement, and were too few in number and too intractable to be of use as a labor supply. They were simply driven out to make room for Europeans. The Spaniards, on the other hand, occupied a well-populated region, most of whose inhabitants had already been reduced to servitude by the Aztecs and Incas and were indifferent to the substitution of one set of masters for another. Spanish colonization accordingly took the form of a small group of conquerors exploiting the forced labor of the conquered, a situation which lent itself to autocratic control and harsh treatment of the subject peoples.

It may be questioned, however, whether the Indians of Spanish America were worse off than they would have been under the rule of any other European state of the period, or than other native populations have been under European domination in later and presumably more enlightened times. The Spanish government itself, under the inspiration of Bartolomé de las Casas, the Franciscan monk who devoted his life to the Indians, regarded the Indians as its wards and was genuinely concerned with promoting their welfare. If its good intentions were not always translated into fact, it was because of the difference between formulating a policy in Madrid and having it carried out by unsympathetic colonists in America. The United States was to have a similar experience with its own Indian policy. Spain's efforts, moreover, were far from fruitless; after all, the bulk of the population of Spanish America is still of Indian descent.

Society in the Spanish colonies was as rigidly stratified as in Europe. The European-born Spaniards formed a privileged aristocracy; below them came the creoles, the American-born Spaniards, then the mixed bloods, and finally the Indians and the Negro slaves. When independence came to Spanish America, this caste structure was one of the most formidable obstacles in the way of forming genuine popular governments.

NEW FRANCE

Along with Britain and Spain, France was a major contender for empire in North America; there was, indeed, a period of almost a century when France had a fair prospect of being the most successful contender, largely through her good fortune in finding a convenient route into the interior of the continent. French claims to the St. Lawrence were established early by the explorations of Jacques Cartier in 1534. However, eighty years elapsed before permanent settlements were founded at Port Royal, Nova Scotia, in 1603, and Quebec in 1608 by the great Samuel de Champlain. After that, expansion was rapid. French explorers and missionaries pushed westward through the Great Lakes and then southward until the mouth of the Mississippi was reached by La Salle in 1682. French settlement in Louisiana followed, the most important step being the founding of New Orleans in 1718. Thus the opening of the eighteenth century saw France in control of the "heartland" of North America.

To govern this great domain France simply extended the autocratic system of the mother country. The French colonists, like the Spanish, had virtually no voice in the management of their own affairs; all authority was vested in three individuals: a governor, who had both civil and military powers; an intendant, who was both a judicial and a fiscal officer; and a bishop, who was the ecclesiastical authority. These three officials, each independent of the others, were supposed to act as a supreme council. However, as could have been expected, they were just as likely to quarrel with each other as to cooperate.

The Church, the Indians, and the Fur Trade. As in the Spanish Empire, the Catholic Church was a powerful influence in New France —indeed, there were no more devoted missionaries to the Indians than the French Jesuits and Recollets. In their dealings with the Indians, the French present an interesting comparison to their Spanish and English rivals. The Spaniards enslaved the natives; the English drove them out; the French mixed with them. In general, during the colonial wars the North American Indians showed a preference for France, with one vital exception. The Iroquois Confederacy was anti-French from the time that Champlain quite understandably took the side of his Algonquin hosts in a tribal clash on the shores of the lake that now bears his name. This initial conflict was perpetuated by rivalry for the fur trade, since the Iroquois could enjoy a profitable position as middlemen if this trade was routed to Albany and New York rather than to Montreal and Quebec.

The weaknesses of the French colonial system have been described previously. To restate them, ease of access to the interior and the attraction of the fur trade tempted the French to spread themselves thinly over a vast area; the rigorous climate of Quebec and a shortsighted colonizing policy discouraged migration to New France; and excessive control from Paris stifled the development of a healthy and self-sustaining political and social structure. Finally, too much of France's energy was spent on European wars to leave enough to spare for building a strong colonial empire.

As we have seen, France lost her North American possessions in the Seven Years' War. French influence, however, survived. In the United States, the state of Louisiana retains pronounced characteristics of French culture to this day, and place names scattered widely over the rest of the country—Detroit, Marquette, Duluth, Des Moines—attest to the prowess of the explorers of New France. In Canada, the French population has retained its distinctive identity, its language and customs, and has played a major role in the history of the Dominion, and consequently in the history of North America.

THE ENGLISH SETTLEMENTS

The story of the early English settlements in America scarcely requires detailed repetition; Jamestown and Plymouth Rock are part of American folklore, although, as is usual with folklore, the core of fact has been heavily encrusted with legend. The basic characteristics of the movement still need to be studied, however, if one is to understand how the forces at work in contemporary Europe influenced the colonization of America and what each of the colonies contributed toward the eventual development of a distinctive American society.

One outstanding feature of the British colonies in America is their remarkable diversity. No two of them started in exactly the same way or followed exactly the same pattern of growth. Some of this variation was a natural consequence of the wide geographical area covered by the colonies, but not all of it. What can best be defined as the human element was conspicuously present as the factor responsible for the differences between colonies so closely related physically as Virginia and Maryland or Massachusetts and Rhode Island.

Virginia. Virginia, where the English established their first permanent settlement in North America, furnishes an excellent example of the economic motive for colonization. It was founded by the Virginia Company of London in 1607 as a straightforward business venture—not an especially successful one for the company. It lost money consistently as the expected flow of overseas products failed to materialize; it soon ran into political troubles and finally had its charter revoked in 1624. The colony itself, however, was on its way to economic security by the time the com-

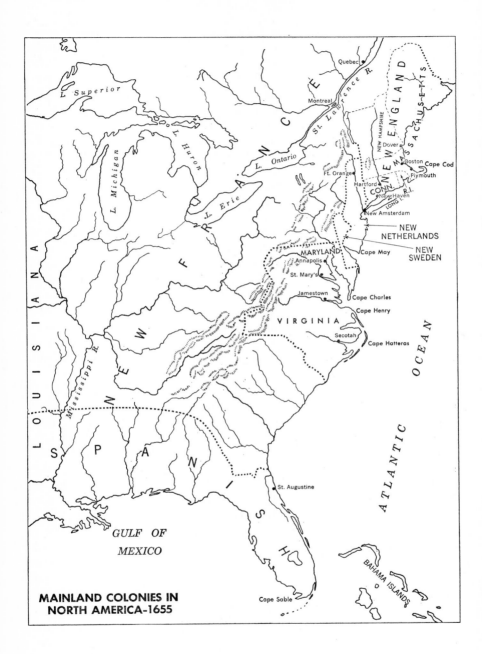

MAINLAND COLONIES IN
NORTH AMERICA-1655

73

pany was dissolved. After an initial period of extreme hardship, in which it owed its existence largely to the efforts of Captain John Smith, seaman, explorer, warrior, and chronicler (with an occasional tendency to emphasize his own prowess), Virginia found prosperity in the cultivation of tobacco, after an improved method of curing the leaf had been devised by John Rolfe, better known as the husband of Pocahontas.

From then on Virginia's growth was steady and assured. The profits of tobacco planting furnished all the incentive that was needed to attract a continuous stream of settlers from Great Britain, some to take up land immediately, others to work as indentured servants in the hope of eventually becoming landowners. Some of the immigrants arrived unwillingly, either transported by the government for various offenses or simply kidnapped, but not enough to be an important factor in the life of the colony. Despite this influx of white settlers, the chronic shortage of labor led to the importation of Negro slaves, beginning as early as 1619. Virginia was in no sense a political or religious experiment. After the dissolution of the Virginia Company, the colony was governed directly by the British crown, although the House of Burgesses established by the company in 1619 remained in existence as the first representative assembly in the New World. The Church of England was the only officially recognized religious body, with its position rigorously enough enforced so that large numbers of Puritans who tried to settle in Virginia were compelled to move to neighboring Maryland.

The Pilgrims. The New England colonies had a combined religious and economic origin. The earliest arrivals, the Pilgrims of Plymouth, were a group of English Separatists—that is, Protestant dissenters who rejected the authority of the Church of England—who had fled to Holland to escape persecution at home. While they found freedom of worship among the tolerant Dutch, their opportunities for earning a living were limited, and they were concerned about the prospect of their children being absorbed into an alien community. Some of the congregation, therefore, decided to emigrate to America, and in 1620 they set sail in the *Mayflower,* with financial backing from English merchants who were interested in possible profits from the venture and an informal assurance from King James I that they would not be molested in the exercise of their religion. The mixed character of the enterprise is attested by the fact that at least half the *Mayflower's* passengers were not Pilgrims at all, but ordinary emigrants hoping to find a better life in America.

The avowed destination of the Pilgrims was northern Virginia; why they settled where they did, well to the north of the Virginia Company's grant, has remained an unsolved mystery. They must have known approximately where they were, because Captain John Smith had explored the New England coast only a few years before, and the leaders of the

Pilgrim group had consulted him when they were drawing up their plans. It is quite possible that, navigation in the early seventeenth century being what it was, they made their landfall on the New England coast accidentally and simply decided to forgo the discomforts of further voyaging. It is equally possible that they had decided from the beginning to stay out of the jurisdiction of Anglican Virginia.

Whatever the motive for it, their choice involved problems of its own. The Pilgrims succeeded, after some difficulty, in getting a satisfactory title to their land from the English authorities, but they never did secure a clear right to exercise governmental powers, although they did so as a matter of plain necessity. Consciousness of their dubious position was one reason for the drafting of the Mayflower Compact, which was essentially an effort to provide some sanction for the authority of the colony's leaders. On the economic side, Plymouth was on the whole a poor location. It was not well situated to become a commercial center, and the immediate hinterland had few resources to offer. Except for some minor fur-trading ventures, Plymouth Colony developed into a self-sustaining agricultural community. In later years Governor William Bradford and his associates must often have regretted that, in their very natural eagerness to get ashore and provide themselves with shelter before winter came, they had failed to explore the coast a little more thoroughly and so had missed the much better site of Massachusetts Bay.

The Puritans in Massachusetts. That location fell to the Puritans, who appeared in New England about ten years after the Pilgrims, in a migration much larger in scope and much more adequately financed. The Puritans were not far from the Separatists in doctrine and ritual; the major distinction was that the Puritans believed in a state church and so, instead of breaking away from the Church of England, they hoped to reform it from within. In the face of the persistent hostility of the Stuart kings, many Puritans became discouraged with their prospects in England and turned to the idea of emigration. They were attracted to Massachusetts Bay when some of their number in 1623 established a fishing and trading post on Cape Ann, later moved to Salem.

In contrast to the Pilgrims, practically all of whom were plain artisans or farmers, the Puritan colonists included a number of men of wealth and social standing, a matter of considerable importance in an age of sharp class distinctions. The influence of these men was used to good advantage in England by securing for the new colony a charter of incorporation as the Massachusetts Bay Company, thereby giving it an unimpeachable legal foundation. The charter omitted, apparently by design, to stipulate where the meetings of the company should be held; in 1630 the document was taken to Massachusetts by John Winthrop and became the constitution of the colony.

Massachusetts prospered from the start. Between 1630 and 1640 immigration was heavy, with economic depression in the eastern counties of England, the stronghold of Puritanism, accentuating discontent with political and religious conditions. Moreover, Winthrop proved to be an excellent governor for a community of strong-willed colonists. He had, it is true, the Puritan tendency to be intolerant and occasionally ruthless toward opponents, but he was more moderate in this respect than most of his associates, and he was gifted with judgment and ability. He carried Massachusetts safely through controversies which might have caused serious trouble, either by producing internal conflict or by attracting the unwanted intervention of the English authorities.

Although the founders of Massachusetts had themselves been the victims of persecution, they set up a system of government in which no dissent from their own ideas was permitted. Control of the colony was in the hands of an oligarchy composed of the wealthier inhabitants and the clergy of the established Congregational Church. The power of this group was somewhat modified by the admission of representatives of the freemen of the colony to the General Court in 1634, but since new freemen could be admitted only by the governing group and had to be church members, this concession had little effect on the general policy of the colony. The discontent created by this arbitrary regime, together with the pressure resulting from the influx of new settlers, led to Massachusetts' sending out offshoots to other parts of New England.

Offshoots of Massachusetts. The first of these was Connecticut, founded in 1633 by a group of settlers under the leadership of the Reverend Thomas Hooker, although the Dutch from New Amsterdam and the Pilgrims from Plymouth were actually first on the scene with trading posts at Hartford and Windsor respectively. The fertile lands of the Connecticut valley formed the chief attraction for the Hooker migration, which therefore ranks as one of the earliest phases of the great westward movement which constitutes a vital part of American history. The government organized by the Massachusetts settlers, who eventually absorbed the Pilgrims and expelled the Dutch, was modeled on that of the parent colony. It functioned without formal legal sanction until 1662, when Connecticut was granted a charter by Charles II, largely through the efforts of John Winthrop, Jr. This document, through what seems to have been a piece of sharp practice on Winthrop's part, incorporated into Connecticut the neighboring colony of New Haven, founded in 1638 by a group of English Puritans as an independent commercial venture.

Rhode Island also grew out of emigration from Massachusetts, distinguished from the movement into Connecticut by the fact that it was involuntary. The founder of the colony was a Puritan clergyman, Roger Williams, who shook both the religious and political foundations of Massachusetts by preaching first that the civil government had no authority over religious matters, and second that land titles in America granted by the English crown were worthless because the Indians were the legitimate owners of the soil. The horror-stricken General Court ordered Williams arrested and sent back to England, but, warned apparently by Governor Winthrop himself, he escaped and in 1636 made his way, with some of his followers, to the head of Narragansett Bay, where he established Providence as a community in which his doctrines could be put into operation. A year later another theological squabble in Massachusetts led to the exiling of the adherents of Mrs. Anne Hutchinson. Most of them, including Mrs. Hutchinson herself, settled on the island of Rhode Island. These outcasts naturally banded together for mutual protection against further oppression from Massachusetts and, in spite of Williams' views on land titles, deemed it advisable to secure legal recognition from England. A charter was issued by Parliament in 1644, during the English Civil War, but after the restoration of the monarchy it was replaced by a new document in 1663. This charter embodied the principle of freedom of worship, unusual for the seventeenth century but probably fully acceptable to King Charles II.

Some of Mrs. Hutchinson's followers left Massachusetts for New Hampshire, which, together with Maine, originated as a royal grant to Captain John Mason and Sir Ferdinando Gorges. Both areas were also claimed by Massachusetts. After a long controversy the rights of the proprietors were sustained, but Massachusetts acquired jurisdiction over Maine by buying out the Gorges heirs.

Maine and New Hampshire were exceptions to the general New England pattern of colonies organized on the lines of the joint-stock company. The proprietary system—that is, the method of establishing colonies by grants of land to favored individuals—never took root in that section. The first successful example of this method was Maryland, founded in 1632 by a royal grant to Sir George Calvert, later Lord Baltimore, who was given complete jurisdiction over his prospective colony, subject to the qualification that his government had to conform to the laws of England. Sir George Calvert died before he could take advantage of his grant, but his plans were carried out by his son, Cecilius.

Maryland. The Calverts, who belonged to the English Catholic nobility, had two objectives. They wanted a prosperous estate for themselves, and they hoped to establish a refuge for their coreligionists in England. Neither objective was fully achieved. The proprietary rights of the Calverts suffered from time to time because of conflicts within the colony and also because of changes in the family's political fortunes in England, although these rights remained in existence until the Revolution. On the religious side fewer Catholics than Protestants settled in Maryland.

Calvert's remedy for this situation was the passage of a Toleration Act by the Maryland assembly in 1649, a measure which turned out to be too far in advance of its time. The Protestant majority shortly afterward deprived the Catholics of their political privileges.

New York and New Jersey. The disturbed political conditions in England during the 1640's and 1650's retarded colonization somewhat. No new colonies were founded during this period; in fact, the Puritan victory in the Civil Wars resulted in a number of New England settlers returning to the homeland. The restoration of the Stuarts brought with it a new outburst of activity, this time with the proprietary system in the ascendant. In 1664 the English holdings on the American continent were extended by the conquest of New Netherlands. This settlement had been founded in 1624 by the Dutch West India Company, but since the company was more interested in trade than colonization, it had taken no very firm root. The land policy, giving great estates in the Hudson valley to a few favored individuals, the "patroons," was calculated to repel rather than attract settlers, and the dictatorial rule of the Dutch governors made their regime generally unpopular. The entire colony fell without firing a shot to a naval force commanded by James, Duke of York, brother of King Charles II and later king himself as the unpopular James II. He was given his conquest, renamed New York in his honor, as a proprietary grant with boundaries originally extending from Maryland to the Connecticut River. Dutch institutions and property rights, including the patroon system, were not disturbed, but pressure from English settlers compelled the duke to establish a colonial assembly. The proprietorship lasted until James became king, at which time New York automatically became a royal province.

New Jersey came as a by-product of the acquisition of New York. James gave this part of his domain to two of his friends, who in turn sold their rights to other parties, including a group of Quakers. The confusion of claims resulting from these transactions led to the various proprietors' surrendering their powers of government to the crown in 1702.

The Carolinas. In the meantime, other proprietary colonies were coming into existence. Early in Charles II's reign a group of eight favored courtiers received an extensive grant which they named Carolina in honor of the king. The Carolina proprietors planned on an ambitious scale, including a fantastic constitution drafted by John Locke, fortunately never put into effect, but their colony nevertheless grew slowly. In 1712 its two distinct areas of settlement were formally separated into North and South Carolina, and a few years after that the proprietors surrendered their rights to the crown.

Pennsylvania. The most successful of the proprietary colonies was Pennsylvania, founded in 1681 by William Penn as an asylum for

Quakers and, for that matter, for virtually everyone else who was dissatisfied with the Old World. The son of an English admiral, Penn inherited from his father the friendship of both Charles II and the Duke of York, as well as a debt owed by the duke. Combining friendship and the debt, Penn secured a generous grant from the duke's proprietorship, named Pennsylvania by the donor. A liberal land policy, complete religious freedom, and a humane legal system made Pennsylvania the focus of immigration into the American colonies during the eighteenth century. Natural advantages aided this process; the colony had a more fertile soil than New England, and at the same time it had a climate more suitable to white settlement than the South. Delaware, also part of the Duke of York's grant, was sold to Penn in 1682, but while it was subject to the authority of the Governor of Pennsylvania, it had, except for a short period, its own separate assembly.

Georgia. Georgia, the last of the continental colonies to be established, owed its origin to the desire of a group of English philanthropists, headed by General James Oglethorpe, to provide an opportunity for paupers and poor debtors in England to make a fresh start in life. Their project was supported by the British authorities because a colony in that region would serve as a check to Spanish expansion from Florida; and in 1733 Oglethorpe and his associates were incorporated as trustees of the new colony for a period of twenty years, after which control was to revert to the crown, in accordance with the new British policy of keeping the colonies under more direct political control. Settlement progressed very slowly, partly because the trustees imposed restrictions, such as the prohibition of slavery, which irritated those who did settle in Georgia, but mainly because the new colony, located in what was very much a raw frontier area, was simply not as attractive to immigrants as its well-established neighbors. One of the sponsors of the Georgia scheme, Captain Thomas Coram, disapproved of the location and was largely instrumental in persuading the British government to establish a new colony at Halifax, Nova Scotia, in 1749. This experiment proved so successful that Nova Scotia remained loyal to the crown when the Revolution came.

COLONIAL GOVERNMENT

The most conspicuous feature of governmental organization within the American colonies is the surprising degree of uniformity it attained among units of such varied origins. Each colony sooner or later fell into the pattern of having a single executive, elected in New England (in Massachusetts until 1684), appointed in the others, either by the crown or the proprietors; a council, also elected in New England and usually appointed elsewhere, which functioned as an upper house of the legislature; and a representative assembly, chosen by a restricted suffrage normally based on landholding. None of these governments was democratic in the modern sense of the word. All were dominated by the upper classes which emerged in colonial life—in general, the merchants of the seaboard towns in the north and the planters of the tidewater area in the south. In each, as settlement gradually pushed westward, there was a tendency for conflict to develop between the newer and the older areas. Nevertheless, they were much more representative than any government in contemporary Europe. In a country where land was plentiful and cheap, the restrictions on suffrage excluded a much smaller proportion of the whole people than was the case in eighteenth-century England; the colonial assemblies, therefore, were likely to reflect popular opinion reasonably accurately.

The respective powers of the various elements in the colonial governments were never well defined and were usually settled by a trial of strength, in which the assemblies by and large acquired much more authority than British officialdom really approved of. Acts of the assemblies were nominally subject to veto by the governors, but since the assemblies early assumed complete control of finances in their separate colonies, including payment of the governor's salary, it was not always expedient for that individual to insist on his point of view. The political history of most of the colonies is studded with conflicts between governors trying to carry out their instructions and assemblies seeking to maintain or expand their rights. Long before the Revolution, American political leaders were thoroughly versed in the techniques of legislative resistance to what they considered executive usurpation.

The Zenger Case. One of these contests produced a historic victory for freedom of the press. In the course of opposition to the administration of the unpopular Governor Cosby in New York, John Peter Zenger, publisher of a New York newspaper, was indicted for libel in 1734 for a series of articles attacking the governor. In accordance with English law of that day, the jury in a libel case was supposed to pass only upon the fact of publication; if the jury decided that the defendant had actually published the material in question, then it was up to the judges to rule whether it was libelous or not. Zenger's attorney, Andrew Hamilton, persuaded his jury to pass on the truth of Zenger's statements and had his client triumphantly acquitted. Hamilton's position was not immediately recognized as good legal doctrine, but after the Zenger case it was inordinately difficult to use the libel laws in the American colonies as a means of suppressing criticism of the government.

Early Efforts at Colonial Unity. Attempts to coordinate the colonial governments, either by spontaneous action on the part of the colonists or under the direction of the British authorities, were made sporadically, but without lasting success. The longest-lived experiment in colonial unity was the New England Confederation, formed in 1643 by Massachusetts, Plymouth, Connecticut, and New Haven. New Hampshire was left out because Massachusetts claimed jurisdiction over it and Rhode Island because it was not considered quite respectable by its neighbors. The organization was created chiefly to provide for common defense when the outbreak of civil war in England threw the colonies on their own resources. It was not a very strong union. Commissioners from each of the members met at intervals to discuss their mutual problems, but they had no power to make binding decisions. Nevertheless, the Confederation lasted for forty years and helped to see New England through the crisis caused by the dangerous Indian outbreak of the 1670's known as King Philip's War.

The New England Confederation was dissolved when Charles II moved to strengthen his authority in his overseas possessions. The king's first step was to attack the charters of the New England colonies, which were the least amenable to royal control but which at the same time were legally vulnerable because they had, as a matter of simple necessity in meeting unforeseen conditions, interpreted their charter powers liberally. The Massachusetts charter was annulled by judicial proceedings in 1684. Although Connecticut and Rhode Island succeeded in keeping their documents out of the hands of the law, it appeared that the royal policy had gained its objective when, under James II, the New England colonies were consolidated with New York and the Jerseys to form the Dominion of New England. It was an unpopular arrangement, which could have won acceptance only if it had been tactfully handled and had been given time to take root. But James's governor, Sir Edmund Andros, was arbitrary, although capable, and James himself did not keep his throne long enough to make his policy stick. The Revolution of 1688 in Great Britain was echoed in the colonies by an enthusiastic expulsion of the fallen monarch's officials.

While the Dominion of New England disappeared in the reaction against Stuart rule, the desire on the part of the British government to strengthen its control over the colonies did not. It was, it is true, pursued rather more circumspectly after 1689. Vested interests were given due consideration, and the idea of consolidation was abandoned, but whenever the opportunity offered, chartered and proprietary colonies were converted into royal provinces—that is, colonies whose governors were appointed directly by the crown. In New England, Connecticut and Rhode Island were allowed to resume their original charters, and they continued to be governed under these documents until well after the Revolution. Massachusetts received a new charter in 1691 making it a royal colony, with the pill sweetened by provisions for an elective council, the incorporation of Plymouth, and confirmation of jurisdiction over Maine. Elsewhere,

New York and Virginia were already under royal control. The others were gradually brought into line as their proprietors tired of fruitless squabbles with their settlers and surrendered their rights, until by the middle of the eighteenth century only Pennsylvania and Maryland remained in proprietary hands.

In the end, this policy did not achieve its objective of strengthening the authority of the crown in the colonies, principally because the British governments of the early eighteenth century neglected to implement it properly. There were two glaring weaknesses in the administration of the royal colonies. One, already mentioned, was the practice of leaving the governors completely dependent on their assemblies for funds. The other was in the selection of the governors themselves. A few, like Spotswood of Virginia, Eden of North Carolina, and Shirley of Massachusetts, were able men who won the confidence of the people in their colonies; some, like Sloughter and Cosby of New York, were incompetent or worse; most were honest but uninspiring mediocrities, completely unfitted to handle the delicate task of getting British policies accepted by a highly individualistic people, most of whom had come to America to get away from the restrictions of European society. Curiously enough, although Americans were frequently appointed to colonial governorships, they were in general less popular than the men who were sent over from Britain.

Albany Plan of Union. The only gesture made toward colonial unity after the collapse of the Dominion of New England was the Albany Congress of 1754, a body of delegates from seven colonies assembled on the initiative of the British Board of Trade in an attempt to devise some effective means of cooperation against the French menace. The Congress adopted a Plan of Union drafted by Benjamin Franklin, providing for a president-general of all the colonies appointed by the crown, and a council in which each colony would be represented in proportion to its contribution to the general treasury. This government was to have jurisdiction over all intercolonial affairs and to be subordinate to Parliament only in matters concerning the whole empire. Franklin's plan, embodying as it did the first practical suggestion for a federal system, failed of acceptance because neither the British government nor the colonial assemblies were willing to surrender any of their powers to this proposed new organization.

ECONOMIC AND SOCIAL ORGANIZATION

Once the initial trials of settlement were over, life in the American colonies rapidly developed distinctive characteristics of its own. Its most conspicuous common feature was the predominance of agriculture as the basic economic activity. Colonial agriculture, however, diverged sharply from the contemporary European pattern. The manorial system simply would not flourish in a country where land in limitless quantities was to be had for the taking. Efforts to establish something resembling the European land system were made, especially by the holders of proprietary grants, and some vestiges of Old World land tenure lasted until the Revolution, but in most colonies the agrarian population was made up of what, for practical purposes, can be classed as independent freeholders. The principal exceptions were New York, where the patroon system persisted, and the plantation areas of the South where tobacco and rice were cultivated on large estates by slaves and white indentured servants, although even in these colonies small-scale farming was predominant outside the coastal area.

The abundance of land in the colonies had one unfortunate result in that the developments of the eighteenth century in scientific farming were almost entirely ignored in America. There was little pressure on an American farmer to expend time and effort in conserving his land when fresh soil was so readily available. Colonial agriculture, in consequence, too often took the form of "mining" rather than cultivation. This condition was especially bad in the tobacco-planting regions, where production of the same crop year after year created a serious problem of soil exhaustion. Some enlightened landowners, among them George Washington and Thomas Jefferson, experimented with the new agriculture, but their example was not generally followed. In addition, the constant flow of settlers into new territory tended to make American landowners more interested in the quick profits of speculation than in the slower income of pure farming.

Most colonial agriculture was conducted on a subsistence basis, the occupants of each farm living largely on what they produced themselves. The Southern plantations again constituted the principal exception. Their staples were grown to be sold in the European market, with commodities to supply their needs coming back in exchange. By the beginning of the eighteenth century the farms of the middle colonies—Pennsylvania, Maryland, New Jersey—had also developed a thriving export trade, sending grain to the West Indies, where concentration on sugar planting was so great that the islands had to import practically all their foodstuffs.

Colonial Commerce. Although enough of it existed to draw restrictive legislation from Parliament, manufacturing was an insignificant item in colonial economy. Commerce was another matter altogether. New England's situation, with its poor soil but its abundant good harbors, its ample supplies of lumber readily available for shipbuilding, and its proximity to the Newfoundland fisheries, practically invited its people to turn to the sea for their livelihood. And turn to the sea they did. Their fisheries found a good market in the Catholic countries of southern Europe, but for the most part the merchants of New England, having little of their own to export, had to make their money by carrying other people's goods. Their most profitable trade was the West Indian commerce described in the first chapter of this book.

Philadelphia and New York were also important commercial centers. Farther south, trade was largely in the hands of British merchants, who functioned as agents for the planters in the shipment and sale of their crops. This arrangement seldom worked to the advantage of the planters. Most of them habitually bought what they wanted from Great Britain through these same merchants, on credit, and if the planter was a careless businessman, as he frequently was, or if the merchant was unscrupulous, as he sometimes was, then the planter found himself getting deeper and deeper into debt. Since the planters came to believe that they were being systematically victimized, this situation became a factor in straining relations between the colonies and the mother country.

The British colonists were not as successful as the French in tapping the fur trade. New York had some of it, through the friendly relations between the Iroquois Confederacy and both the Dutch and the English. South Carolina also had a substantial fur trade, since its access to the west was not as badly impeded by the Appalachian barrier as was the case in other colonies, and its hinterland was less subject to French or Spanish interference.

Population and Immigration. The population of the colonies early acquired the heterogeneity that has been characteristic of America ever since. German and Polish artisans were among the first settlers of Jamestown, and from then on, as a general rule, immigrants from any quarter were welcomed and readily absorbed. Swiss, Frenchmen, and Scots Highlanders formed important elements in the Carolinas; Swedes and Dutchmen were living on the Delaware when Penn arrived and were left undisturbed; and New York never lost the traces of its Dutch origin. New England had the least infiltration of non-English stock, but it had some— Scots and Irish, some of them transported by Cromwell in the course of his rise to power, and French immigrants who gave to Boston such figures as Peter Faneuil and Paul Revere. Tolerant Rhode Island acquired a considerable Jewish community at Newport, which contributed much to that city's prosperity, and similar groups appeared in New York and Philadelphia.

In the first half of the eighteenth century two great waves of immigration arrived, apart from the normal and continuous influx of settlers from England. One was Scotch-Irish, forced out of northern Ireland by British economic discrimination and by discontent with their political subordination; the other was German, coming largely from the areas of western Germany devastated by the wars of Louis XIV. So many of them, in fact, came from the Rhenish Palatinate that German immigrants were referred to indiscriminately as Palatines. Most of this immigration flowed through Philadelphia into the section of Pennsylvania where the descendants of the Germans are still to be found as the Pennsylvania Dutch, then southwest along the fringes of the Appalachians into the back country of Maryland, Virginia, and the Carolinas. For the time being the mountains themselves, and still more the French and Indian menace beyond them, barred further expansion to the west.

The preference for this area is simple enough to explain. Since these immigrants were mainly interested in farming, New England had little to offer them. New York's best land, the Hudson valley, was preempted by patroon estates, and, while some Germans settled along the Mohawk, their opportunities were limited by the presence of the Iroquois, who were both too powerful and too valuable as allies to be disturbed. In the coastal areas of the South, the plantation system was too firmly rooted to make the region attractive to newcomers unless they had the resources to become planters themselves.

Social Classes. Of equal importance with this racial diversity as a factor in colonial life was the social stratification which existed. Each colony acquired a clearly defined upper class, consisting principally of the wealthy merchants in the North and the large-scale planters of the South. To these groups could be added the higher officials of the government, the most successful professional men—chiefly lawyers—and, within limits, the clergy. The New England clergy were definitely part of the ruling class in the seventeenth century, but their power declined noticeably during the eighteenth, in spite of the influence of the revival known as the Great Awakening. In other colonies the clergy ranked somewhat lower in the social scale. Most of the population fell into what by contemporary European standards was the "lower middle class." It included, besides the bulk of the clergymen as stated above, the independent farmers, the small merchants and retail tradesmen, the skilled artisans, and the majority of the professional men. In the colonies the class was in a reasonably comfortable economic position and had some political power. Below it was the unprivileged group of town laborers and ordinary seamen, tenant farmers, and, still further down, the white indentured servants and the slaves.

The indentured servants constituted an important part of the labor supply in this period. They were mostly immigrants who paid their passage to America by selling their services for a period of years. During this term of servitude they had few rights of any sort, but once it was over they were free citizens with the same status as anyone else. Sometimes paupers and orphans were shipped to America to be indentured servants, and the demand for labor on the plantations made kidnapping a fairly profitable trade; the great majority of the indentured servants, however, came over of their own free will, believing that the opportunity of getting to America was worth a few years of semislavery. The system gradually died out, since planters came to prefer Negro slaves as being cheaper, better adapted to outdoor labor in a hot climate, and easier to handle.

Caste lines in the colonies were nowhere nearly as rigid as in Europe. Social distinctions were based fundamentally on wealth, and there was nothing to prevent an enterprising individual from moving up in the scale. There was, nevertheless, some class conflict, which tended to become sharper as the Revolution approached. In virtually every colony the dominant upper class was faced periodically with pressure from the middle group for a greater share in political power. The position of the ruling oligarchy was maintained partly by property qualifications on suffrage, and partly by geographical discrimination—that is, as colonies expanded, the newly settled areas were given representation in their assemblies under conditions which guaranteed their subordination to the seacoast regions, where the oligarchy was strongest.

At times this internal friction broke out into open violence. As early as 1676 Virginia was convulsed by Bacon's Rebellion, largely an outburst of discontent by the small landowners, their grievances inflamed by falling prices for tobacco, against their royal governor and his ruling clique of tidewater planters. The leader of the rebellion, Nathaniel Bacon, was himself a member of the ruling class—a phenomenon not too infrequent in history. His sudden death ruined the movement after a promising start, and it was savagely repressed by Governor Berkeley, for which Berkeley was recalled and censured by Charles II. The overthrow of James II in 1689 brought an open clash between the aristocracy and the common people of New York, with the upper class remaining in control because, in the confusion over the change of government, the leader of the popular party, Jacob Leisler, allowed himself to get into a position where his enemies could successfully charge him with treason and have him executed. Finally, in the Carolinas the back-country farmers organized themselves as the Regulators and broke into open rebellion in North Carolina in 1771—against their colonial government, not Britain. The Regulators were defeated, and this internal conflict was presently absorbed into the greater conflict of the Revolution.

IMPERIAL RELATIONSHIPS

All the American colonies had one vital common interest in the fact that all were members of the British Empire and were intimately concerned with the development of imperial policy. The relationship between Great Britain and her colonies rested principally on the system of commercial regulation created by the Navigation Acts, which has already been described in Chapter 1. Along with this economic policy the British built up, or at least attempted to build up, a system of political control intended to provide some sort of effective coordination for their rather loose-jointed imperial structure. Their failure to create an efficient and well-integrated mechanism for this purpose was due in large part to the accidental circumstance that colonial policy was formulated during the period when Britain itself was undergoing a series of major constitutional changes, so that the relative powers of the various branches of the government were none too clearly defined. On the eve of the Revolution, Americans could and did argue that the colonies were subject to the crown but not to Parliament, although for a century they had unquestioningly accepted the right of Parliament to pass laws regulating their trade.

Administrative Bodies. General supervision over colonial affairs was exercised by the Privy Council, an appointive body theoretically composed of the king's immediate advisers. It was destined to be overshadowed by the cabinet, but at this time it still possessed considerable executive authority. As far as the colonies were concerned, its powers included the appointment of governors and other crown officials, and the right to veto acts of the colonial assemblies, as well as to function as a court of final appeal. Gradually, as the empire grew and colonial problems became more complicated, the Council was compelled to delegate most of the work of colonial administration to another agency, the Board of Trade and Plantations, which was established in 1696. Officially, the Board of Trade was simply an advisory body, but, since its recommendations were usually accepted by the Privy Council, it became for practical purposes the principal administrative authority over the colonies.

It was not, however, the only administrative authority. Political problems involving the colonies also fell within the jurisdiction of the Secretary of State for the Southern Department, an individual who combined approximately the present-day positions of Foreign and Colonial Secretary. The rise of the cabinet as the supreme executive authority increased the Secretary of State's importance in colonial administration, but his diplomatic duties seldom left him time, even if he had the inclination, to pay much attention to colonial matters. The increasing complexity of colonial affairs led to the creation of a separate colonial secretaryship shortly after the Seven Years' War. Enforcement of the customs and navigation laws was shared by the Treasury and the Admiralty, while colonial defense fell naturally within the province of the War Department. Finally, the Church of England in the colonies was under the supervision of the Bishop of London. This division of responsibility was to some extent unavoidable and need not have been a handicap if the government as a whole had been efficient and well coordinated. Few British governments of the eighteenth century, however, could meet these qualifications, with the result that the machinery for political control of the American colonies usually worked either badly or not at all.

Paper Money. In only one respect, indeed, did the supervisory power of Britain prove genuinely irksome to the American colonists prior to the French and Indian War. That was the vetoing of colonial laws for the issuance of paper money. The currency problem in the colonies was serious and perplexing. They had no internal source of gold and silver, as the Spanish colonies had; their entire supply of specie came from trade, chiefly with the West Indies, and what was secured in this way was immediately drained off to pay for purchases in Great Britain, leaving the people of the colonies with insufficient hard money for their everyday needs. (This was one problem which independence did not solve; it continued to plague the United States until the twentieth century.) The attempts of colonial governments to remedy this deficiency included a number of experiments with "bills of credit," sometimes based on land, sometimes simply promises to pay in coin at some future date. Since paper money was a new device in Western civilization, these issues occasionally got out of hand, although colonial experience was certainly no worse than that of other governments in later years. However, merchants who had to make payments in Britain could not use paper currency, and pressure was brought to bear on the British authorities. In consequence, most paper-money laws were vetoed either by governors or by the Privy Council. This policy satisfied the advocates of "sound" money, but contributed nothing whatever to solving the problem of providing an adequate circulating medium for the colonies.

The paper-money question illustrates neatly the outstanding feature of British political control over the colonies; it functioned well enough to prevent them from doing things of which the British government disapproved, but it was almost useless as a means of getting them to take positive action in concurrence with British imperial policy. This lack of affirmative authority was brought out still more sharply in the relationships between Britain and the American colonies during the world wars of the eighteenth century.

Colonial Wars. The problem was not a matter of Britain dragging unwilling colonials into the consequences of her European and imperial involvements; the Americans themselves were eager enough to use the resources of the British Empire to weaken or destroy French and Spanish influence in North America. The trouble was that joint action by Britain and her colonies depended, in the last analysis, on purely voluntary cooperation. If the colonial governments chose to give it, well and good; if they did not, there was little Britain could do about it. What happened in practice was that each colony assisted the mother country roughly in proportion to its own exposure to danger. Massachusetts, with its Maine frontier exposed to attack from Canada and its fisheries threatened by French occupation of Nova Scotia; Virginia, with claims to the Ohio valley disputed by the encircling French; Georgia and South Carolina, exposed to Spanish attack from Florida or Cuba: all these participated in the struggle for empire with a zeal equal to that of Britain itself. On the other hand New York, relatively safe behind the barrier of the Iroquois, and Pennsylvania, with the merchants of Philadelphia unwilling to violate their principles or spend their money, did less than they could have. The contribution of the other colonies was sporadic and limited, except that the seaport towns found that these wars provided profitable opportunities for trading with the French and Spanish West Indies.

Under these conditions British efforts in North America were necessarily cumbersome. For almost eighty years they made little headway against the French, and a decision was reached only when the genius of William Pitt did succeed temporarily in getting the home country and the colonies to cooperate with reasonable enthusiasm. A good deal of mutual recrimination was an inevitable consequence of this protracted struggle. The British accused the colonials of refusing to carry their proper share of the burden. The Americans on their side taxed the British with bungling leadership and with sacrificing American interests to the needs of British diplomacy in Europe.

Both parties had some justification for their attitude, but neither was completely in the right. Even when it had the best of intentions the British government could not possibly avoid stepping on colonial toes, for the simple reason that policies which appeared in London to be desirable for the empire as a whole might run counter to the immediate interest of some particular colony. Until Pitt's time the conduct of military operations in America was generally uninspiring, but the British commanders were badly handicapped by the reluctance of colonial assemblies to provide supplies for them. On the other hand, while the total colonial effort was admittedly less than it could have been, it was nevertheless substantial, and those colonies which did exert themselves vigorously were entitled to resent the belittling of their contribution by British officialdom.

The British triumph in the Seven Years' War should have eliminated most of this mutual irritation, since Britons and Americans alike felt an intense patriotic pride in the magnitude of their joint victory. But they found, as others have found before and since, that a successful war may solve one set of problems but is likely to substitute another. For the Americans, the removal of the French from Canada and the Spaniards from Florida loosened one of the bonds of empire, in that they were no longer so heavily dependent on Britain for protection. For the British, the acquisition of vast new territories seemed to demand a recasting of imperial policy and, as a necessary adjunct, an overhauling of the machinery of imperial government. If this situation had arisen fifty years earlier, the British government would probably have had its way. By 1763, however, the American colonies had grown physically to the point where they felt fully able to take care of themselves, and the long period of "salutary neglect," in which British authority had been exercised only negatively when it had been exercised at all, had resulted in the colonial governments becoming not only thoroughly accustomed to managing their own affairs but completely convinced that they had an unqualified right to do so without outside interference.

PART TWO

The American Revolution and the Organization of a New Nation

The preceding chapters have endeavored to describe the emergence of the forces that have created the modern world. The winning of American independence marks the point at which these forces began to attain visible maturity. For a people to stage a successful revolt was not in itself original; what made the American Revolution so important in the evolution of Western civilization was the fact that it came at the time when Western thought was thoroughly permeated with the philosophy of natural rights and offered what was in effect a laboratory demonstration of this philosophy in action. As a secondary, but none the less important feature, the Revolutionary War became another episode in the struggle for empire between Great Britain and France, with somewhat drastic and unforeseen consequences to both powers.

Nor was the American Revolution confined to the actual attaining of independence by the United States. It remained to be seen whether the American people could make a republican government work. There were sectional and class divisions to be overcome, and there was the still more fundamental problem of avoiding the errors which had wrecked republican experiments in the past: political power in the hands either of a privileged few or of an unrestricted and irresponsible majority.

The United States responded to this challenge by a federal constitution whose provisions kept these forces satisfactorily under control. It permitted local autonomy while at the same time it created an effective central government, and it made the rule of the majority subject to restraints that would safeguard the rights of minorities. Moreover, in operation the American constitutional system showed that it was flexible enough to be adapted by usage and interpretation to changing conditions. It had its imperfections, but it came closer to solving the problems of popular government than anything the world had seen up to that time.

6

Immediate Causes of the Revolution

Historians are usually very cautious about designating any specific date as pivotal in history; yet there are dates to which that term can be accurately applied, and 1763 is one of them. The Peace of Paris in that year saw the British Empire at what seemed to be an unchallengeable peak of prestige, its most dangerous rival virtually eliminated as a colonial power, and mother country and colonies apparently bound closer than ever. Twenty years later the empire had been torn apart, and a new nation had come into being which presented to the world the first concrete embodiment of the political philosophy of natural rights.

It is possible to go behind the Seven Years' War and point to various factors which might be rated as symptoms of a coming breach between Great Britain and her American colonies—the constant bickering between the colonial assemblies and the royal authorities, for example, or the growing political unrest within the colonies. Nevertheless, in 1763, the British colonial system had been functioning for a century without producing any major crisis suggestive of a general desire on the part of the Americans for independence. Admittedly, the system had functioned inefficiently and had been accepted by the colonists without serious protest largely for that reason. An eventual separation was doubtless inevitable, since it is not reasonable to suppose that a rapidly expanding America would have submitted to British control indefinitely. The fact remains, however, that the sequence of events which caused the Revolution to occur when it did had its immediate origin in the outcome of the Seven Years' War.

THE REVISION OF BRITISH IMPERIAL POLICY

Unfortunately for Britain, her political leadership at this juncture was poorly qualified for the delicate task of reorienting colonial policy to

93

meet the conditions which arose after 1763. With the supremacy of Parliament an assured feature of her constitutional system, the old distinction between Whig and Tory had become meaningless, and new lines of cleavage had still to develop. Politics had become little more than a struggle for office among factions consisting of the followers of various prominent individuals. Cabinets were formed by combining enough of these factions to provide a Parliamentary majority, but these alliances were usually short-lived. The development of systematic policies under these conditions was impossible; ministerial changes were too frequent, and in any case it was better to adopt temporary expedients than try to solve basic issues and upset the unstable equilibrium of a government.

The king himself fitted into this general pattern. If George III had been an abler man, his efforts to control Parliament by using his patronage and influence to build a party of his own might have permitted him to give a more positive direction to British policy; but while George was well-meaning and earnest, far from the unscrupulous tyrant of American Revolutionary legend, he was too dull and obstinate to succeed in his self-appointed role of "Patriot King." In practice, he was essentially just one of a group of factional leaders, with enough authority to block policies he disliked and keep his opponents out of office, but with none of the qualities of a genuine statesman.

Few among his supporters or his opponents could qualify as great statesmen either. A political system which put a premium on patronage and factional intrigue was not conducive to the rise of outstanding leaders, and none appeared during the critical years preceding the American Revolution. Britain was governed at the time by men who were honest, reasonably competent, but totally lacking in vision and imagination, as witness their consistent miscalculation of American reactions to their measures. Pitt (now Lord Chatham) might conceivably have kept the empire together, since he enjoyed the confidence of the Americans even though he believed firmly that the colonies should be subordinate to the mother country, but Pitt was handicapped both by ill-health and the persistent animosity of George III.

Imperial Problems. In justice to British statesmanship, it must be admitted that the problems it was called upon to face had no easy solutions. Whatever disposition was made of the newly acquired territory in the Ohio and Mississippi valleys was bound to antagonize someone. Fur traders wanted the whole area closed to settlement in order to preserve their business; on the other hand, land companies involving both British and American interests had been organized to develop this region well before the Seven Years' War and were now pressing their claims vigorously. The right of the crown to administer the territory at all was disputed by several colonies, Virginia in particular, on the ground that this western land had originally been given to them by charter or royal grant. Finally, the Indians had to be considered, a fact brought sharply to the attention of the British government by Pontiac's War in 1763, an outbreak brought on by a combination of bungling diplomacy, unscrupulous fur traders, and Indian apprehensions of loss of their land. The British were almost driven back east of the mountains and had to use considerable forces of regular troops to suppress the rising.

Consequently, in 1763 Lord Shelburne, then in charge of colonial affairs, issued a royal proclamation prohibiting settlement west of a line drawn along the crests of the Appalachians. Shelburne, who had a better grasp of the colonial problem than any of his contemporaries in British public life, intended the Proclamation Line as a temporary measure to preserve peace until an orderly land policy could be worked out, but the instability of domestic politics drove him from office shortly afterward. His successors permitted the whole matter to rest for ten years, greatly to the annoyance of prospective settlers and speculators alike, since they assumed that they were to be perpetually excluded from these rich western lands for the benefit of a small coterie of British fur traders.

Financial Difficulties. The question of imperial finance held still more explosive possibilities. When the Seven Years' War ended, Great Britain had a national debt of £130,000,000, staggering for those days, and an unprecedentedly heavy tax load. It seemed only fair to British statesmen that part of this burden should be carried by the colonies, since the war had been fought largely for their defense. In British eyes, moreover, the colonies had failed to contribute their fair share of the actual costs of the war. While this belief had a substantial foundation in fact, it was also true that some colonies had supported the war to the best of their ability. The total colonial contribution to the imperial effort was less than the Americans claimed it to be, but certainly greater than the British were willing to admit. The colonies could reasonably feel that their alleged lack of cooperation provided insufficient grounds for a radical extension of British control over them. An additional element in the British calculations was the government's estimate that a force of ten thousand men would be needed to protect the American frontier, at an annual cost of £350,000. This expenditure, too, appeared to be one which should be borne by the colonists rather than the British taxpayer. The Americans might conceivably have agreed if they had been convinced that this force was really to be used for frontier defense, but, when most of it was stationed in seaboard towns, they became not unreasonably suspicious of the purpose for which the troops were intended.

The most obvious method of raising money from the colonies was to increase the revenue from duties on colonial commerce. In the past, the customs laws had been so poorly enforced that the income from them was less than the cost of administration. During the Seven Years' War, however, Britain had adopted more stringent measures to try to stop the widespread traffic carried on by American merchants with enemy islands in the West Indies. One of the new techniques was the use of "writs of assistance," or general search warrants, to enable customs officers to search houses and ships for smuggled goods on suspicion. These writs became the object of an eloquent attack by James Otis of Massachusetts, who challenged their legality with the historic assertion that Parliament did not have the authority to deprive British subjects in America of their constitutional rights.

With the coming of peace George Grenville, Chancellor of the Exchequer, undertook a comprehensive revision of the financial relationship between Great Britain and the colonies. As an administrator Grenville was honest and efficient, but unimaginative; he seems to have had no suspicion that his plans might not be cordially received in America. First of all, he sought to increase the customs revenues by better administration and by imposing new taxes on colonial commerce in the Sugar Act of 1764. The most important change was the reduction of the sixpence a gallon duty on foreign molasses provided in the Molasses Act of 1733 to threepence a gallon—but with provision for rigorous enforcement. If Grenville had expected American merchants to welcome the lower tax, he was mistaken. To them it was no concession; it was a new burden on an important item of their trade, since the Molasses Act had been largely ignored in the colonies.

The Stamp Act. Since the customs duties alone would not produce enough revenue for Grenville's purposes, he added two other pieces of legislation in 1765: the Quartering Act, requiring colonial governments to house and supply British troops stationed within their borders; and, most important of all, the Stamp Act. This law was Grenville's answer to the problem of raising revenue in the colonies. It required stamps to be placed on practically every variety of document used in America—birth and marriage certificates, legal papers of all types, college diplomas, and newspapers and almanacs. It was, from the point of view of a financial expert, a well-devised plan; as a piece of statesmanship it was an atrocious blunder. The Proclamation Line had affected only a small group of land speculators and the Sugar Act only the northern merchants, but the Stamp Act touched practically every individual in the colonies and was, therefore, the first British measure to arouse united American opposition. If it had been accepted, its effect on any one individual would, it is true, have been slight, but it would have been a severe strain on colonial economy as a whole, since the sum total of all the cash payments required by the act would have aggravated the chronic shortage of currency in America.

Although other British statesmen, including Grenville's brother-in-law, William Pitt, had previously weighed the advisability of imposing a stamp tax on the colonies and decided against it, British officialdom in 1765 was so far from anticipating what the American reaction would be that the act passed Parliament with only slight opposition.

A storm of protest greeted the Stamp Act in the colonies. It was impossible to sell the stamps, because the unwary Americans who had applied for posts as distributors were intimidated into resigning. The authority of Parliament to pass such an act was vigorously denied, on the ground that, as British subjects, the American colonists could not be constitutionally taxed without their consent, and since they were not represented in Parliament, only their own assemblies had power to tax them. If this contention was somewhat weak in view of the fact that the colonies had accepted British customs laws without question, the British rejoinder that the Americans were "virtually represented" in Parliament was no stronger. This point of view held that the colonies were in the same position as those communities in Britain itself which had no members of Parliament of their own but were considered to be represented by members from districts with similar interests.

However, the British government was not likely to be moved from its position by an appeal to constitutional theory. Economic pressure was a different matter. On the initiative of Massachusetts, an intercolonial congress, the Stamp Act Congress, met in New York and adopted an agreement calling for a boycott on British goods. It was so effectively observed and enforced that within a year British merchants were appealing to Parliament for repeal of the Stamp Act. Faced with this situation at home and the practical impossibility of enforcing the law in the colonies, the government reluctantly gave way. Grenville fell from power, and in 1766 Parliament repealed the Stamp Act, but, as a face-saving gesture, appended to the repeal a Declaratory Act, asserting the right of Parliament to legislate for the colonies in all matters whatsoever. American opinion chose to celebrate its victory in getting rid of the Stamp Act and to ignore the Declaratory Act.

Internal Conflicts in the Colonies. The conservative elements in the colonies, as a matter of fact, were more anxious to see the agitation quiet down than to keep it alive by arguing over an abstract constitutional issue. The debate over Grenville's measures had not only crystallized American opposition to British authority; it had intensified the internal conflicts in the colonies as well. The mass of the people, disfranchised or underrepresented in their colonial assemblies, displayed an alarming tendency to assume that "no taxation without representation" applied to their own legislatures as well as to Parliament. The upper classes had to face an awkward dilemma: to protect their economic interests against Britain they needed the political support of the common people, which would have to be paid for by extension of political privileges; on the other hand, to preserve their domination of colonial government they needed the military support of the mother country, which would have to be paid for by acceptance of British financial policy.

The Townshend Acts. Britain could have resolved this difficulty by lettings things stay as they were after the repeal of the Stamp Act, but British statesmen were still obsessed with the idea of raising a colonial revenue. Charles Townshend, who became Chancellor of the Exchequer in 1766, believed that he had found a painless method of extracting money from the Americans. Observing that American protests against the Stamp Act had emphasized the illegality of Parliament's imposing *internal* taxes on the colonies, and that no question had been raised about the validity of the laws for the regulation of imperial commerce, Townshend came to the too facile conclusion that the colonists would accept *external* taxes without objection. The Townshend Acts of 1767, consequently, imposed duties on paints, painter's colors, lead, glass, and tea imported into the colonies from Great Britain. They also authorized the use of writs of assistance, created an American Customs Board to supervise enforcement of the revenue laws, and struck at the power of colonial assemblies by providing that the income from these taxes was to be used to pay the salaries of royal officials in the colonies as well as to help support the garrison. As if to emphasize its determination to reduce the colonial governments to nonentities, Parliament in this same year suspended the rights of the New York Assembly for failure to meet its obligations under the Quartering Act.

This political issue destroyed whatever chance the Townshend Acts had of being accepted without protest. The colonists would probably have objected to the new duties in any event; they were certain to be violently opposed to a tax program which earmarked the revenues for the purpose of strengthening the authority of the crown at the expense of the colonial legislatures. Townshend's distinction between external and internal taxes was successfully refuted, in American eyes at least, by John Dickinson, in his *Letters from a Farmer in Pennsylvania*. Dickinson acknowledged the right of Parliament to pass laws for regulating the trade of the empire, but, he pointed out, tariffs on goods shipped from Britain to British colonies were obviously designed to raise money rather than regulate trade. They were, therefore, just as much taxes on the American colonies as the Stamp Act had been and just as unconstitutional.

Once again American resistance took the form of nonimportation agreements. There was no colonial congress this time, and the agreements were not as well observed as they had been two years before, but they served their purpose. In 1770 a new Cabinet in Britain decided that it was poor policy for the country to burden its own exports and repealed all the Townshend duties except the tax on tea, which was retained as a symbol of Parliament's right to tax the colonies. As with the repeal of the Stamp Act, the concession was enough to quiet the agitation in America —at least in its more obvious manifestations. Indeed, it appeared that peaceful relations might be completely restored. Parliament, after the failure of its two attempts to raise a colonial revenue, was disposed to let the question rest for the time being, and the colonial conservatives were more than ever anxious to avoid stirring up further popular outbursts. However, the disturbances of the 1760's had set in motion forces that could not readily be halted. As a result of the long controversy the various elements in American society which objected to the new British colonial policies found themselves drawing together into a compact body, with a political philosophy whose basic principles were agreed upon but whose ultimate objective was still uncertain.

THE ORGANIZATION OF AMERICAN OPPOSITION

The intellectual foundation of American opposition to British intervention in colonial affairs has already been suggested. Beginning with James Otis's attack on writs of assistance, colonial leaders took the position that Americans, as subjects of the British crown, were entitled to all the rights enjoyed by Englishmen at home—theoretically enjoyed, to be strictly accurate, since the rights claimed by the colonists were certainly not enjoyed by the common people of England at this time. American political thinkers of this period quite obviously regarded the "rights of Englishmen" as being synonymous with the "natural rights" of eighteenth-century philosophy. At first, the American claims were distinctly modest. During the controversy over the Stamp Act, colonial opinion was more accurately represented by the conservative Daniel Dulany than by radicals like Patrick Henry and James Otis. Dulany insisted that the colonists could legally be taxed only by legislative bodies in which they were represented—that is, by their own assemblies. He rejected the British doctrine of "virtual representation," but he still was willing to acknowledge Parliament as the supreme legislature for the empire as a whole. However, as the British government continued to assert its power to rule the colonies directly, American claims of colonial autonomy increased in proportion, until just before the outbreak of hostilities they had reached the point of declaring that the empire was really a federation under a common sovereign, with Parliament only one among several legislatures, each supreme in its own sphere—a concept with a striking resemblance to the present British Commonwealth of Nations.

These views were held with varying degrees of intensity by a substantial majority of the people of the colonies, including many who subsequently became loyalists during the Revolution. While it is true that the controversy with Britain had the effect of stimulating the political consciousness of the common people of America and raising the question of who should rule *in* the colonies as well as who should rule *over* them, the American Revolution was not a "class struggle" in the present-day meaning of that term. The movement affected and divided every level of American society.

Divisions of Opinion. In the northern and middle colonies the merchant class provided much of the initial impetus for resistance to the new policies of the mother country, since it was adversely affected by such measures as the Sugar and Townshend Acts and the improved enforcement of the navigation laws. Some members of this class, like John Hancock, stayed on to become leaders of the Revolution; others became alarmed at the democratizing tendencies of the movement they had started and eventually drifted into loyalism. The lawyers as a group followed the lead of the merchants, with rather more radical leanings on the whole. The clergy of the dissenting churches were almost to a man on the colonial side; the Anglican clergy, as one would expect, felt that their first allegiance was to the crown. The common people for the most part were anti-British, from motives compounded of specific grievances such as the Stamp Act and the British refusal to permit issues of paper money, and a general consciousness that weakening the authority of the home government would improve their own chances of gaining political power.

Similar conditions prevailed in the South. The small-scale farmers of the Piedmont, long resentful of the domination of the planters of the Tidewater, identified resistance to Britain with their own democratic aspirations, although in North Carolina the bitterness of many of the former Regulators was still so strong that they chose to support the crown simply because their seaboard rivals opposed it. The planters themselves occupied the peculiar position of being the one aristocratic group in the colonies which was virtually unanimous in its resistance to British authority. Their Northern counterparts, the patroons of New York, divided sharply, mainly along the lines of their own factional quarrels, with the majority on the conservative side. The Southern planters were antagonized by the mother country's western land policy, and they felt themselves to be victimized by a commercial system which kept many of them in debt to British merchants, but neither consideration accounts satisfactorily for their attitude. The best explanation seems to be that they were unwilling to be governed by anyone but themselves.

In fact, with the exception of a small minority consisting largely of those who held office under the crown, most Americans in the 1760's agreed on opposition to the revised British policy toward the colonies. Where they disagreed was on the extent to which opposition should be carried. The variety of shades of opinion was bewildering, but two main currents can be identified. The conservative position, supported strongly by the upper classes, wanted the withdrawal of specific items of Parliamentary legislation, without any vital change either in the structure of the empire or the existing political organization of the colonies. What the advocates of this point of view really wanted was a return to pre-1763 conditions, and many of them proved unwilling to carry their resistance to the point of an open break with the mother country. The radicals wanted both a change in imperial relationships which would give the colonies complete control of their own affairs and a shift of political power inside the colonies in favor of the common people. Even among this group, however, the idea of independence had made little perceptible headway by 1770. Some of the leaders may have regarded it as the ultimate solution for their problems, but it was still at best a vague and remote possibility.

Intercolonial Organization. In spite of the community of interest which Americans displayed in their response to the attempted extension of British authority, it took time for anything resembling an effective intercolonial organization to emerge. The Stamp Act Congress met, passed its resolutions, and disbanded without attempting to set up any permanent machinery for coordinating the action of the colonies. The "Sons of Liberty" were local societies without any general organization, and they soon fell into disrepute because of their propensity to rowdyism and violence. The Townshend Acts produced "Associations" to enforce the nonimportation agreements, but they were also local in character, and they disappeared as soon as they had achieved, or seemed to have achieved, their purpose.

With the repeal of the Townshend Acts the conservatives in America, anxious for internal peace and satisfied that Parliament would now leave them alone, made no further effort to organize or control colonial opinion. It was a tactical error on their part, because the function they so complacently abandoned passed into the hands of the radicals. The task of keeping opposition to British authority alive was taken over by men like Patrick Henry, Christopher Gadsden of South Carolina, and, most important of all, Samuel Adams of Massachusetts.

Samuel Adams. A master of political organization and propaganda, Adams was given an object lesson early in his life on the effect of Parliamentary intervention in colonial affairs. His father had been a participant in the Land Bank of 1741, a paper-money scheme, and was ruined when Parliament killed the project by extending to Massachusetts the Bubble

Act of 1720, an act originally aimed at the speculative excesses of the South Sea Bubble. With the aid of James Otis and Joseph Warren and the financial backing of John Hancock, Adams created a well-disciplined political machine in Boston, which dominated both the Boston town meeting and the General Court of the colony and used both bodies as forums for continued denunciation of British policy. He was also responsible for organizing the Committees of Correspondence, first of all in Massachusetts and then throughout the colonies. These groups of like-minded individuals exchanged information and ideas, with the result that when the next crisis developed, the radicals were in substantial agreement on the policies they wished to pursue, and the Committees also constituted an intercolonial organization sufficiently cohesive to guarantee adoption of the radical program.

In addition, the Adams faction tried to keep their fellow-countrymen aroused against Britain by publicizing incidents which seemed well adapted to this purpose. Their greatest opportunity was provided by the "Boston Massacre" of 1770. Two British regiments had been sent to Boston in 1768 to protect the members of the Customs Board after a riotous outbreak involving, interestingly enough, one of John Hancock's ships, and troops and townspeople had developed a cordially reciprocated dislike for each other. The "Massacre" started with the snowballing of a British sentry but degenerated into a less innocent pastime as a larger and larger crowd gathered. The sentry summoned help, and finally the soldiers, either goaded beyond endurance or mistakenly assuming in the uproar that the order had been given, fired into the crowd and killed four people. Respectable Bostonians deplored the affair as a regrettable outbreak of mob violence; when the soldiers involved were tried for murder, they were successfully defended by John Adams (Sam's cousin) and Josiah Quincy. Nevertheless, it was the Sam Adams version, presenting the incident as an unprovoked assault by the brutal soldiery on a group of peaceful citizens, which reached the American people first and was most generally accepted at the time.

THE COMING OF THE REVOLUTION

In spite of their skill and vigor, the radicals faced a discouraging prospect after the repeal of the Townshend Acts. Since this conciliatory gesture coincided with a period of rising prosperity, most Americans lost interest in troublesome political questions and preferred to let imperial relationships remain as they were. There were, it is true, occasional incidents such as the burning of the British revenue cutter *Gaspée* in Narragansett Bay, but they failed to arouse any widespread popular excitement. The radicals, in fact, owed much of their ultimate success to the wholehearted cooperation of the British government, unwitting, of course, but none the less effective.

The final crisis was precipitated by the financial troubles of the great East India Company. Between mismanagement and a falling market for tea, the company was sliding into bankruptcy in the early 1770's. Since it was virtually a public institution, Parliament, in 1773, intervened in its behalf with a scheme which, it was hoped, would serve the dual pur-

The Battle of Lexington. From Rev. C. A. Goodrich, *History of the United States* (Hartford, Conn., 1823). This is distinctly an American version of the historic Nineteenth of April, indicating that the British started the shooting. The mounted officer is Major Pitcairn of the Royal Marines, who did his best on this occasion to prevent the clash and was later killed at Bunker Hill.

pose of saving the company and propitiating colonial opinion. The plan was simple; all taxes collected in Britain on tea transshipped to America were canceled, and the company was permitted to carry its tea directly from the Orient to the colonies. The effect would be to cut the price of tea in America drastically and thereby give the company a monopoly of the colonial market.

The American response was not quite what had been anticipated. The unrepealed Townshend tax on tea had stimulated a considerable smuggling trade in that commodity, but no colonial merchant was going to be able to compete, legally or illegally, with the East India Company. The mercantile community was driven into the arms of the radicals, not only because of the prospective loss of their tea business, but because of the valid apprehension that, if Parliament by manipulating taxes could create a colonial monopoly in tea, it could do it for all other commodities as well.

Thanks to the work of Adams and his associates, the opposition to this latest British move was well organized and efficient. In most colonial seaports the ships carrying the East India Company's tea were simply sent back without being allowed to discharge their cargoes. One consignment was landed in Charleston and remained there in storage until the State of South Carolina sold it in the middle of the Revolutionary War. In Boston, however, a band of men disguised as Indians boarded three tea ships on the night of December 16, 1773, and dumped their cargoes into the harbor.

The Boston Tea Party and the Intolerable Acts. For the British government the Boston Tea Party was an unpardonable provocation. George III and his current prime minister, Lord North, felt that they had been patient and conciliatory long enough toward the center of sedition on Massachusetts Bay, and in this attitude they were supported by most factions in Parliament. Arguments over abstract constitutional rights or even attacks on the king's troops might be tolerated, but wanton destruction of property was going too far. Punishment took the form of the Coercive or Intolerable Acts of 1774, which closed the port of Boston until the destroyed tea should be paid for, reorganized the government of Massachusetts, reinforced the Quartering Act, and provided for sending political offenders to England for trial.

Another measure, the Quebec Act, was classed by the Americans among the Intolerable Acts, although it did not really belong there. It was the result of ten years of rumination on two problems: how to govern the French of Quebec and what to do with the territory in the Ohio valley taken from France in 1763. Its passage at this time was simply coincidence. The law confirmed to the French population of Canada the exercise of their Catholic faith and the right to be governed by their own laws rather than the English common law, and it extended the boundaries of Quebec to include the entire Ohio valley, apparently in order to keep this territory under strict control of the crown and dispose of the conflicting claims of the American colonies. On the whole, the Quebec Act was a wise piece of statesmanship, but in American eyes it was obnoxious because it appeared to perpetuate their exclusion from the West. Their attitude on this point was natural enough; it was, however, ridiculous for the New England clergy to allege that the grant of religious toleration was the beginning of a British plot to impose Catholicism on the colonies. It was not only ridiculous; it was bad policy. When the crisis came, the position of the French Canadians was largely determined by the contrast between Britain's liberality and the intolerance of their immediate neighbors to the south.

The British authorities seem to have assumed that singling out Boston for punishment would not produce any general American reaction. Colonial provincialism being what it was, this calculation might have been shrewd enough under ordinary conditions, but it failed to take into account the effectiveness with which the Committees of Correspondence had been organized. It also failed to allow for the fact that Americans were not quite so parochial in their outlook as to be oblivious to the point that what had happened to Boston could happen to any other locality that incurred the displeasure of the crown. Far from regarding the situation as a private argument between Massachusetts and the home government, the other colonies united to resist this latest threat to their liberties, and at the instigation of Virginia convened another colonial congress, the First Continental Congress, at Philadelphia, in September, 1774.

The First Continental Congress. The work of this Congress suggests strongly that Lord North's ministry blundered badly in overestimating the force of sectional rivalry in the colonies and ignoring the opportunities offered by factional dissension. When the Congress assembled, the balance between the conservatives, seeking only repeal of the Coercive Acts and withdrawal of the tea monopoly, and the radicals, determined to secure complete colonial self-government, was extremely close. The more aggressive and better organized radicals managed to have the Congress adopt the Suffolk Resolves, a series of resolutions introduced by the Massachusetts delegates calling upon the colonies to refuse to obey the Coercive Acts, and then went on to defeat by one vote the compromise offered by the conservative Joseph Galloway of Philadelphia. Galloway's Plan was based on Franklin's Albany Plan of Union. It envisaged the creation of an intercolonial legislature which would be an American branch of Parliament. Laws concerning the colonies would require the assent of both bodies. Unfortunately for Galloway and his friends, they received no support from across the Atlantic. American opinion was still wavering, and a timely gesture of conciliation from Britain could very well have tipped the balance in favor of the conservatives. But George III was determined that the authority of the crown should be conclusively acknowledged, so that although North, who sincerely wanted to preserve peace, was able to win the king's contest to some proposals for compromise, they were invariably "too little, too late."

After the defeat of the Galloway Plan, the First Continental Congress completed its work by reviving the boycott of British goods, a policy enforced by local committees, whose lack of legal sanction did not handicap them in the least. Then the Congress adjourned after issuing a call for a second congress to meet in the following spring and take such steps as current conditions might require. Meanwhile, preparations were begun, more intensively in New England than elsewhere, for a resort to force if it became necessary.

By the time the Second Continental Congress met in May, 1775, the break had already come with General Gage's expedition to Lexington and Concord on the 19th of April, in search of military stores being collected by the Massachusetts patriots. To this day no one knows who fired the first shot on Lexington Green, although each side naturally accused the other. The outcome of the day's events was that the British troops found themselves besieged in Boston, and Congress had a full-fledged war on its hands, with no very clear notion whether the objective to be realized was the establishment of a new nation or simply the effecting of a change of policy in London.

7

The Revolutionary War

THE BALANCE OF FORCES

In an appraisal of the position and prospects of the rival combatants at the beginning of the Revolutionary War, the liabilities on the American side stand out rather more conspicuously than the assets. Against the revolting colonies was the British Empire, mistress of the seas, possessed of a small but excellent army, and equipped with the commercial, financial, and industrial resources necessary for war to a degree unmatched by any contemporary state. To face this concentration of power the Americans could offer thirteen chronically unharmonious colonies, united by a Congress which was a national government by default—it had assumed the functions of government because it was the only body in existence in a position to do so, and the functions were not accompanied by authority. There was no organized military force except the militia, and while colonial economy was prosperous enough, it was predominantly agrarian. It was weak in industrial and weaker still in financial resources.

The defects in the American governmental and economic structure accentuated each other. Congress, having no power to raise funds by taxation, had to finance the war by borrowing and by issuing paper money based on little more than promises for an uncertain future. Meanwhile, the individual states (as they became in 1776) were issuing paper currency of their own to meet their war expenses and fill the long-standing shortage of an adequate circulating medium. Toward the end of the war an influx of loans from abroad and the administrative reforms carried out by Robert Morris as Superintendent of Finance introduced some order into the national finances, but neither provided any lasting remedy

107

for the defects inherent in a faulty political organization. Morris finally had to resign after only two years in office, thoroughly discouraged and considerably poorer than he had been when he took office.

The procurement of men and materials for prosecuting the war encountered similar handicaps. Requisitions from Congress were treated by state legislatures much as requisitions from the British government had been treated by colonial assemblies in the past—they were more often ignored than honored. Recruiting for the Continental forces was difficult, because most men preferred the easier militia service or the profitable opportunities offered by privateering. Shipments from abroad and considerable ingenuity at home provided enough arms and munitions, but otherwise the supply system was grossly defective. It is much too easy to overlook the fact that the suffering of Washington's army at Valley Forge was entirely unnecessary. There was plenty of food and clothing available; while Washington's men starved, ten miles away in Philadelphia Howe's troops were living in plenty, on supplies drawn from the neighboring countryside. The trouble was that Congress had neither the power nor the funds to get what it needed, and the state governments were unwilling, except in acute emergencies, to compel their citizens to make sacrifices.

The Loyalists. The most serious weakness of all in the American position was that they were a divided people. The Revolution was a civil war as well as a war for independence. The precise extent of loyalist sentiment is impossible to determine accurately, but it has been estimated that of the two million inhabitants of the colonies at the outbreak of war, a third were actively or passively loyalist in sympathy. Many of the active loyalists served in the British army or formed their own military units; in fact, since personal grievances were involved, some of the bitterest fighting of the war was between rival American forces. After the Declaration of Independence, loyalty to the crown became treason to the United States, and, since a people engaged in a life-and-death struggle cannot be expected to tolerate internal dissent, no matter how reasonable, the treatment of the loyalists forms one of the less pleasant aspects of the American Revolution. It may be said, however, that the patriots had considerable provocation, and their persecution of the loyalists fell far short of the mass extermination which has frequently been the fate of dissident groups elsewhere.

American Assets. Among the American assets, the most important was physical possession of a vast extent of territory. When the war began there was no British force between Canada and Florida, except the garrison besieged in Boston. To recover its colonies, Britain would have to reconquer the entire area, and do it all from a distance of three thousand miles with slow and cumbersome transportation. Canada and Florida might be useful as staging bases, but nothing more. The men and materials would have to come from Britain itself. The Americans, on the other hand, could win their war merely by holding what they had. Furthermore, the territory to be conquered was more effectively defended than the lack of organized American military forces would suggest. The militia of the Revolution had serious drawbacks. They were poorly trained, undependable, and almost always unwilling to serve for long periods of time or at any distance from their homes. Nevertheless, they were always available for a few weeks' service in their own localities, and when properly led they gave a good account of themselves. British generals discovered by experience that their armies could move nowhere in America without the countryside's turning out against them.

The British task would have been difficult enough if it had been efficiently handled, but it most decidedly was not. The conduct of the war came under the direction of Lord George Germain, the Colonial Secretary, an individual who had been cashiered from the British army for cowardice at the Battle of Minden in 1759 but who had risen in politics through the favoritism of George III. Germain's performance of his duties should win him the gratitude of every American; few men did more to make the United States independent. In addition, British public opinion was almost as sharply divided as American. An influential minority in Parliament, led by some of Britain's ablest political figures, opposed the war, although it had no satisfactory solution to offer for the problems which had precipitated the conflict.

This political opposition may have been reflected in the reluctance of men to enlist for service against the "rebels," but any such conclusion has to be qualified by the fact that low pay and harsh discipline made the British forces unattractive anyway. The lack of volunteers, however, did play an important part in the war, since Germain decided to make up his shortage of man power by hiring German mercenaries. It was perfectly routine practice for eighteenth-century Europe, but it was politically inept in that it gave the Americans an excellent point for propaganda. In any event, the German troops, most of them unwilling conscripts, were poorly equipped and trained for fighting under American conditions. If the same amount of money and material had been invested in organizing loyalist forces, the returns would have been considerably greater.

The Attitude of Europe. The attitude of Britain's European neighbors was a factor of commanding importance to both parties from the beginning of hostilities. To Britain it was a serious handicap; since her rivals, France in particular, were certain to take advantage of her trouble if a favorable opportunity arose, she could not afford to strip the home islands and the rest of the empire of their defenses and concentrate on crushing the rebellious colonies in North America. The Americans, conversely, were encouraged by the knowledge that Britain's enemies would give them some assistance, certainly with money and materials and possibly by open intervention. As it turned out, both sides were to see their expectations fully realized. At the outset foreign aid to the Americans was limited, mainly because France, the power most interested in seeing Britain weakened, preferred to follow a cautious "wait-and-see" policy. Her foreign minister, the Comte de Vergennes, was perfectly willing to embarrass the British as much as possible, but he had no desire to involve his country in another unsuccessful war.

However, if French officialdom was cautious, French idealists were enthusiastic about this struggle for freedom. The most effective of these idealists was Pierre Caron de Beaumarchais, author of *The Barber of Seville* and *The Marriage of Figaro*. Beaumarchais, with the connivance of Vergennes, organized a bogus trading company, Hortalez et Cie., for the shipment of arms and munitions to the Americans—the material being supplied by the French royal arsenals and paid for by loans from the French treasury. Other sympathizers, like the Marquis de Lafayette, crossed the Atlantic to serve in the American army. Along with them came a stream of European soldiers of fortune, few of whom contributed anything of value to the American cause. Conspicuous among the exceptions was the German Baron von Steuben, who drilled Washington's soldiers during the terrible winter at Valley Forge, using the Prussian discipline in which he had been trained but adapting it to American conditions. By the following spring Washington's Continentals were, man for man, the equal of any European regulars.

George Washington. Finally, it can be said that the Americans had the advantage in leadership. No one on the British side approached George Washington in stature. A wealthy Virginian aristocrat, he had nothing to gain and much to lose by supporting the Revolution; his motive was patriotism pure and simple. His selection to command the Continental forces was logical on military grounds in view of his distinguished record in the French and Indian War. It was also a shrewd political move, initiated by the astute political mind of John Adams of Massachusetts. At a time when all the fighting was taking place in New England, the appointment of a Northerner as commander in chief might well have left the Southern colonies feeling that the Yankees had got themselves into this mess and could now get themselves out of it. It was a fortunate choice for the United States. Washington had some defects as a general, but lack of character was not among them. His faith and determination never faltered, and it is no exaggeration to say that Washington alone carried his country through the darkest moments of the Revolutionary War.

THE WAR: FIRST PHASE

Since both parties had drifted into hostilities, and neither was quite sure what it was fighting for, the opening stages of the war were devoid of any systematic plan of campaign. The siege of Boston occurred simply because the only British garrison in the colonies was stationed there. As a base for reconquering the colonies the town was too far to the north and east; the proper policy for the British was to abandon it at once and begin again from a more favorable location. Instead, they hung on passively for almost a year, suffering a check at the Battle of Bunker Hill and finally undergoing the humiliation of being driven out by Washington's seizure of Dorchester Heights, from which eminence the town and harbor were commanded by British cannon taken at Ticonderoga.

Meanwhile, the Americans were engaged in their only important offensive operation of the war. This was a two-pronged invasion of Canada, with one army under Richard Montgomery proceeding up Lake Champlain to Montreal and then Quebec, while the other, under Benedict Arnold, crossed the wilderness of Maine in a march of incredible difficulty. The French Canadians gave their prospective liberators a cool reception, and an assault on Quebec, undertaken on 31 December 1775 because the enlistments of most of the troops expired on the following day, was repulsed, Montgomery being killed and Arnold wounded. In spite of its failure, this expedition produced unexpected benefits, because a large force of British troops destined for operations farther south was diverted to Canada. The immediate effect was to delay the contemplated attack on New York; later, the presence of this army in Canada inspired the directors of British strategy with the idea which led to Saratoga.

Capture of New York. In 1776, the British came closer to winning the war than they ever did again. They failed to win a foothold in the South, it is true, but they offset that by capturing New York. If they had taken the opportunity presented to them of destroying Washington's army as well, it is doubtful whether American resistance could have continued. After the evacuation of Boston, the British troops proceeded to Halifax, where they were strongly reinforced and then, under the command of General Sir William Howe, sent to New York. If they had arrived a little earlier, they could have taken the city without opposition. As it was, Washington, judging correctly where his adversary would strike, reached New York first. Howe's expedition, accompanied by a naval force under his brother, Admiral Lord Howe, did not appear in the New York area until early in July, and another month elapsed before active operations were begun.

Even so, the defense of New York came close to being an irretrievable disaster for the American cause. Washington's army was badly beaten on

Long Island late in August and narrowly escaped annihilation. After more delay, Washington was driven out of Manhattan and finally retreated across New Jersey to the comparative security of the Pennsylvania side of the Delaware. Howe followed in leisurely pursuit as far as the river and then, believing that his opponent was now harmless, returned to the comforts of New York, leaving a chain of garrisons behind him to secure New Jersey.

Trenton and Princeton. He was wrong. Washington's army was not out of the war; it was just close to it. Like Arnold and Montgomery before him, Washington was faced with expiring enlistments at the end of the year and had to do something to restore American morale while he still had an organized military force. Calculating that the Hessian troops in Trenton would be celebrating Christmas with more enthusiasm than discretion, he recrossed the Delaware, struck at the town on Christmas Day, 1776, and captured the entire garrison. Then he successfully evaded a British relief force, defeated part of it at Princeton, and withdrew to a strong position at Morristown. Trenton and Princeton were minor affairs as battles go, but they came at a most opportune time. The American cause never looked quite so hopeless again.

THE DECLARATION OF INDEPENDENCE

Just before Admiral Howe's warships dropped anchor in New York harbor, Congress reached the momentous decision on what the object of the war was to be and transformed the United Colonies into the United States. This movement was a comparatively recent development. As late as the autumn of 1775 sentiment for independence was still confined to a radical minority. The colonies continued to profess allegiance to George III and insisted that they were in arms merely to resist the tyrannical acts of his ministers. The course of events made this position increasingly untenable. The antagonisms generated by prolonged conflict pushed the prospect of eventual reconciliation further and further into the background, and the unyielding attitude of the king himself gradually drove most moderate Americans to the reluctant conclusion that independence was the only solution to their problem. Moreover, as long as their status remained uncertain, the colonies were handicapped in securing aid from abroad and suppressing loyalism at home.

Parliament itself forced the issue by an act of December, 1775, prohibiting all trade with the rebellious colonies. Then, less than a month later, the case for independence was convincingly presented in Thomas Paine's pamphlet *Common Sense*. Paine, himself an Englishman whose radical political ideas had made him unacceptable in his own country, did an amazingly effective job of crystallizing American public opinion.

In clear and forceful language he attacked the institution of monarchy, ridiculed the idea of a small island governing a continent, and pointed out the economic and political benefits which would accrue from independence.

Opposition to independence at this time came mainly from the upper classes, still facing the awkward choice between submission to British authority and submission to the rising forces of American democracy. The climax of the struggle was reached when Richard Henry Lee of Virginia introduced a resolution into Congress on 7 June 1776, declaring that "these United Colonies are, and of right ought to be, free and independent states." After a vigorous debate, with John Adams as the most effective spokesman for independence and John Dickinson leading the opposition, Lee's resolution passed on 2 July, and two days later the Declaration itself was adopted.

The preparation of this document had been entrusted to a special committee of Congress headed by Thomas Jefferson, and the actual drafting was done by Jefferson himself. The Declaration is divided into two parts: the first is a justification of independence by the broad principles of natural rights of eighteenth-century philosophy; the second is a list of the specific grievances of the Americans against George III. Some of the grievances appear unconvincing today, but they were genuine enough to the Americans of 1776.

The immediate effect of the Declaration of Independence was to compel the American people to make up their minds. There was no longer a middle-of-the-road position to occupy; Americans either gave their allegiance to the United States or to Great Britain. It also encouraged Britain's enemies in Europe to provide more support, since they now had definite assurance that they were contributing to the disruption of the British Empire.

The long-term effects of the Declaration are incalculable. Its forthright assertion of the "inalienable" rights of man has been ingrained into the pattern of American thought as the classic exposition of what the American way of life ought to be, so that even though Jefferson's ideals have not always been attained in practice, they have invariably been accepted by most Americans as the goal toward which their civilization must move. Beyond the United States, the principles of the Declaration of Independence have inspired liberalism throughout the world. Its "self-evident truths" are as self-evident to lovers of freedom now as they were in 1776, and they have continued to be the final appeal of humanity against oppression of any kind. Americans of the present day would do well to remember also that the Declaration was drawn up out of "decent respect for the opinions of mankind." The men who established the United States were perfectly aware that their country was part of a world community and took it for granted that what the United States did was properly a matter of concern to the entire community.

THE SARATOGA CAMPAIGN

For some time after its promulgation, the Declaration of Independence had somewhat uncertain prospects of survival as anything more than an abstract expression of lofty sentiments. While Washington was being driven out of New York and across New Jersey, the remnants of Arnold's army in the north were fighting a desperate rear-guard action against the strong British force which had been sent against them. The climax was reached with a battle between two makeshift fleets at Valcour Island on Lake Champlain in October, 1776. Arnold's fleet was annihilated, but before it was destroyed it inflicted so much damage on its opponents that they had to abandon further operations on the lake until the following spring.

This action was easily the most important American naval operation of the war, for the delay won by Arnold was to have far-reaching consequences. During the winter, Lord George Germain in London evolved an elaborate plan for concentrating the principal British forces in America by having the 7,000 troops in Canada move to New York by way of Lake Champlain and the Hudson River. The alternative possibility of sending these troops to New York by sea was rejected because it would leave Canada exposed to another American invasion. Part of Howe's army in New York was to provide support by pushing up the Hudson to Albany, and a third detachment, composed mainly of loyalists and Indians, was to distract the American defenders still further by marching from Oswego down the Mohawk valley to the same point. Howe himself, with the rest of his army, was authorized to go ahead with his own project of attacking Philadelphia.

On the map, and at a distance of three thousand miles, it was an attractive prospect. The worst defect of the scheme was that it required coordination of three armies separated from each other by wilderness and enemy-held territory, but even so it might have worked if it had been in abler hands. To begin with, command of the forces in Canada was taken from Sir Guy Carleton, the governor of Canada, and given to "Gentleman Johnny" Burgoyne, a friend of the king and Germain and a competent enough officer, but distinctly not in Carleton's class either in ability or in his knowledge of American conditions. Worse still, Germain neglected to send Howe clear instructions about his part in the plan.

Howe's Capture of Philadelphia. The result was that Howe went off to Philadelphia, and, since he believed that the fall of the American capital would end the war, he took the bulk of his army with him. The subsequent capture of Philadelphia turned out to be a profitless victory. American resistance did not collapse, and in the following spring the British decided, in view of the entry of France into the war, that holding the city was a waste of men who were more urgently needed elsewhere. Meanwhile, Sir Henry Clinton was left in New York with insufficient strength to drive up the Hudson and effect the intended junction with Burgoyne.

The expedition down the Mohawk valley, under the command of Colonel St. Leger, likewise failed to operate "according to plan." In its case, Germain seems to have overlooked the possibility of opposition. St. Leger's Indians became discouraged after a bloody battle with the New York militia at Oriskany in August, 1777, and shortly afterward the approach of American reinforcements under Benedict Arnold induced St. Leger to abandon his siege of Fort Stanwix and return to Canada. As happened frequently with irregular forces in the Revolutionary War, retreat was synonymous with distintegration.

Burgoyne's Expedition. That left Burgoyne's army to carry on by itself. For a time, it appeared quite capable of reaching New York unaided. There was no American fleet to oppose its progress on Lake Champlain, Ticonderoga fell without a struggle, and by the end of July Burgoyne had reached the Hudson at Fort Edward. After that his troubles began to accumulate. Indeed, once he left Lake Champlain his progress was slowed appreciably by skillful American delaying tactics and by his own enormous difficulties of supply and transport.

Burgoyne also made the error common to most British generals in the Revolutionary War, of believing overoptimistic assurances of loyalist support. There were plenty of loyalist sympathizers in most parts of the country, but as a general rule they preferred to remain passive rather than expose themselves to future reprisals by their neighbors. There were not enough British troops in America to conduct military operations and occupy any considerable extent of territory at the same time, and the loyalists discovered early that as soon as the exigencies of war sent British forces out of a given area, the patriots simply moved back in, with unpleasant consequences for those who had shown open devotion to King George. However, Burgoyne's assumption that the countryside would be friendly led him to send a detachment of his slow-moving German troops on a foraging expedition into southern Vermont. It was cut to pieces at Bennington, and a relief force sent to its rescue narrowly escaped the same fate.

This disaster delayed Burgoyne still more, so that it was not until September that he resumed his advance from Fort Edward. By then Howe and St. Leger were both out of the picture; Washington, whose desire to hold Philadelphia did not blind him to the real danger, had sent reinforcements from his own command to the northern army, now under General Horatio Gates; and the New England militia were gathering in strength, their zeal to fight intensified by the fact that Burgoyne's Indians had got out of hand and had staged an indiscriminate massacre along the upper Hudson. In front of Burgoyne was Gates's army in a strong position at Bemis Heights, fortified under the direction of Thaddeus Kosciusko; behind him other American forces were harassing his communications with his base in Canada.

In a matter of days the situation of the British army became critical. It made two tentative probes at Gates's lines and was sharply repulsed both times. Then, with supplies running low and immediate retreat to Canada the only chance of saving his army, Burgoyne displayed a fatal indecision and finally capitulated to Gates at Saratoga on 17 October 1777.

REVOLUTION TO WORLD WAR

For the historian the American Revolution is a very satisfactory war because its decisive turning point is so clearly and indisputably marked by the surrender at Saratoga. The repercussions of that event changed the whole course and character of the struggle by dispelling France's reluctance to take sides openly. The actual conversion of Vergennes to a policy of outright intervention was accomplished by Benjamin Franklin, at this time American Minister to France and one of the most successful diplomats the United States has ever had.

When the news of Saratoga reached him, Franklin immediately pointed out to Vergennes that the British government would probably respond to the disaster by offering very conciliatory peace terms, and that the Americans would undoubtedly accept unless they were guaranteed active military aid from abroad, since even their victory over Burgoyne gave them no assurance of being able to win independence by their own efforts. Franklin played on Vergennes' fears of a reunited British Empire, with the mother country resentful of the aid France had already given to the colonial rebels, and in contrast dangled before him the prospect of a flourishing French trade with an independent United States, no longer subject to the restraints of the Navigation Acts.

Franklin's estimate of the British reaction to Saratoga was perfectly accurate. Upon receipt of the news Lord North tried to resign—in fact, he was to keep on trying at frequent intervals until the end of the war— but the king would not consent, since the only alternative was a government willing to recognize the independence of the United States. North did get royal approval for a measure which would have given the Americans everything they wanted short of independence. However, because

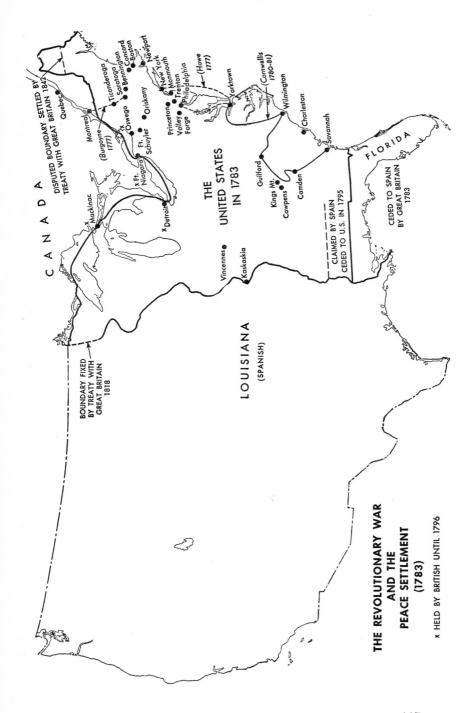

CANADA

DISPUTED BOUNDARY SETTLED BY
GREAT BRITAIN 1842
TREATY WITH

Quebec

Ticonderoga
Saratoga
Bennington
Concord
Boston
Newport

Montreal
Oswego
Oriskany
New York
Monmouth
Trenton
Princeton
Valley Philadelphia
Forge

(Burgoyne
1777)

Ft.
Schuyler

x Ft.
Niagara

Mackinac

x Detroit

THE
UNITED STATES
IN 1783

(Howe
1777)

Yorktown

(Cornwallis
1780-81)

Wilmington

Charleston

Savannah

FLORIDA

Guilford

Kings Mt.

Cowpens

Camden

CLAIMED BY SPAIN
CEDED TO U.S. IN 1795

CEDED TO SPAIN
BY GREAT BRITAIN
1783

Vincennes

Kaskaskia

LOUISIANA
(SPANISH)

BOUNDARY FIXED
BY TREATY WITH
GREAT BRITAIN
1818

**THE REVOLUTIONARY WAR
AND THE
PEACE SETTLEMENT
(1783)**

x HELD BY BRITISH UNTIL 1796

Parliament had to have its customary Christmas holiday, this proposal did not pass until early in March, 1778, a month after Franklin and Vergennes had signed a treaty of alliance in Paris.

The French Alliance. Vergennes and Louis XVI were thoroughly convinced by Franklin and the news from London that they must act at once or lose forever their opportunity of splitting the British Empire. In their eagerness, indeed, they threw away France's excellent bargaining position. After all, it was the United States which needed help and France alone which could provide it, but so skillfully did Franklin play on the possibility of American acceptance of the North concessions that the treaty was exceptionally favorable to the United States. In this agreement, until 1949 the only formal alliance to which the United States had ever been a party, the two signatories pledged themselves to mutual support until the independence of the United States was acknowledged. France renounced all claims to territory on the mainland of North America, a stipulation necessary to secure American approval of the treaty, since memories of the French and Indian War were still fresh and the American people would certainly have preferred a settlement with Britain to the reestablishment of French power on their frontiers. In return, the United States gave a vague promise to protect French possessions in the West Indies.

War between France and Britain followed as a matter of course. As additional insurance against defeat, Vergennes wanted to bring Spain into the Franco-American combination, but the response from Madrid was unenthusiastic. Although the Spaniards were willing enough to injure Britain and had been giving some covert assistance to the Americans, the Spanish government was unwilling to take any step which would imply open approval of a colonial revolt—it had, after all, an extensive colonial empire of its own, whose inhabitants might be inspired to follow the American example. It also had an uneasy and, as it turned out, accurate premonition of what kind of neighbor an independent United States would be. After a year of negotiating, Vergennes finally persuaded Spain to enter the war, as the ally of France but not of the United States, by invoking the Family Compact of 1761 between the two Bourbon dynasties and promising to remain in arms against Britain until Spain had recovered Gibraltar. Vergennes, it will be observed, had maneuvered himself into a situation not uncommon among statesmen anxious to win a war—he had made commitments the future redemption of which might easily prove embarrassing. He was pledged to the United States to fight until independence was won and to Spain to fight until Gibraltar was captured, and neither of his allies was interested in the other's objective.

The only other power to become directly involved in the war was Holland. The Dutch had developed a thriving commerce with the

United States through their island possessions in the West Indies, particularly St. Eustatius, and at the end of 1780 the British came to the conclusion that the simplest way to stop this traffic was to declare war on Holland. Like practically everything else Britain did in this war, this decision, sound enough in theory, proved unfortunate in practice. Admiral Rodney in the West Indies promptly descended on St. Eustatius and became so engrossed in the division of spoils that he let his French opponent sail north unhampered to take part in the Yorktown operation.

The Strain on British Sea Power. Besides the active belligerents, Britain had to count on potential hostility elsewhere. Catherine of Russia at one time contemplated renting twenty thousand Russian troops to the British but changed her mind. Later, irritated by British interference with neutral commerce, she organized the Baltic states into a League of Armed Neutrality, which imposed an added burden on the British navy.

Except perhaps for financial aid, sea power was the most important tangible asset secured by the United States from European intervention. With due allowance for the valiant efforts of the small Continental navy and the useful activities of the swarm of American privateers, America's own naval resources were inadequate to offer any serious challenge to Britain's command of the sea. The appearance of France as a belligerent changed conditions radically. The French navy at this time was in a high state of efficiency, while the British fleet had deteriorated, partly because of mismanagement and partly because the war had cut off its supply of ship timbers from America. In addition, from 1778 on, British naval strength had to be spread out to protect the home islands, the West Indies, Gibraltar, and India.

THE CLOSING CAMPAIGNS

The benefits of the French Alliance did not become immediately obvious to the American public. A French fleet crossed the Atlantic in 1778 to operate halfheartedly in American waters. It took part in a badly coordinated attack on Newport, Rhode Island, and then sailed off to the West Indies, where France's real military interests lay. Not until 1780 did a French army arrive in the United States, and it was sent only at the urgent insistence of Lafayette. For their part, the British forces in America, now under the command of Sir Henry Clinton, Howe having gone home, seemed little affected either by the Saratoga disaster or the potential menace of France. Their evacuation of Philadelphia in the middle of 1778, a move which gave the Steuben-drilled Continentals of Washington's army a chance to display their worth in the disappointing Battle of Monmouth, was simply a prelude to the opening of a new theater of operations in the South.

In reality, the British position was much weaker than it appeared on the surface. Even when the United States had been its only opponent, Britain had been unable to provide enough man power to secure a decision, and after the intervention of France and Spain no more troops could be spared for the American war. The British commanders in America had to get along with what they had. If they wished to strike in a new area, they could assemble the necessary forces only by giving up some of their existing holdings. Thus, the invasion of the Southern states compelled the abandonment first of Philadelphia and then of Newport. Moreover, the operations in the South were undertaken with no stronger motive than the vague hope that something would turn up—specifically, the elusive will-o'-the-wisp of loyalist support.

The Southern campaign started promisingly enough. Savannah and Charleston fell, a Franco-American attempt to retake the former failed, and an American army under Horatio Gates was routed at Camden. But then this campaign bogged down just as its predecessors had. The majority of the Southern loyalists followed the example of their Northern counterparts and held back until they could be sure that the British were there to stay. When it moved inland, Lord Cornwallis's army was lost in a hostile countryside. It could win battles, but it could not win the war, and it was eventually fought to a standstill by Gates's successor, Nathaniel Greene. With the help of Southern partisan bands, Greene kept up a constant harassing warfare, fighting whenever the opportunity offered, and gradually wearing down his opponent by keeping him marching all over Georgia and the Carolinas.

The Virginia Campaign. The only remedy Clinton and Cornwallis could devise was to try again somewhere else, this time in Virginia. Some British forces had already been operating there, including a contingent of loyalists under Benedict Arnold, now a British major general as a reward for his attempt to sell out West Point, and in 1781 Cornwallis joined them, with instructions to establish a naval base on Hampton Roads. Accordingly, after some preliminary sparring with Lafayette, he made his way to Yorktown. It was his misfortune to arrive there just as the French and Americans at last completed arrangements for an effective combination of their forces.

The three elements in the combination were the Comte de Rochambeau's expeditionary force, which had been spending a year in comfortable inactivity at Newport, Washington's army, engaged in watching Clinton in New York, and De Grasse's fleet. The three in concert stood an excellent chance of capturing either New York or Yorktown. Washington would have preferred to attack New York, but since sea power was the indispensable factor in whatever enterprise was attempted, he left the decision to De Grasse, and the French admiral picked Yorktown. It was not only the easier objective; it had the advantage of being somewhat closer to his West Indian sphere of operations.

Yorktown. Considering the slow and uncertain communications at their disposal, the French and American commanders achieved a masterpiece of coordination. Rochambeau's army marched overland from Newport to join Washington outside New York, their concentration here convincing Clinton that he and not Cornwallis was in danger, and the two then proceeded southward, reaching the head of Chesapeake Bay less than a week after De Grasse arrived at its entrance. The British had less luck with their communications. The dispatch vessels sent from the West Indies to warn Admiral Graves in New York of De Grasse's voyage were captured, so that Graves had no way of knowing what was happening until Admiral Hood appeared in New York with most of Rodney's fleet.

The combined British force then headed for the Chesapeake, and on 2 September 1781, Cornwallis's fate was settled by an indecisive naval battle off the Virginia Capes. Because signals were misunderstood, half the British fleet never got into action at all; the other half suffered considerable damage, although only one ship was sunk. De Grasse made no effort to press his advantage beyond keeping contact for a few days in order to insure the safe arrival of the French squadron which was bringing Rochambeau's siege artillery from Newport, and Graves returned to New York to refit. That was enough. Before the British fleet could be made ready for sea again, Cornwallis's situation had become hopeless. He surrendered his army on 18 October 1781, almost four years to the day after Burgoyne's capitulation at Saratoga.

8

The Aftermath of the American Revolution

As far as the two original combatants in the Revolutionary War were concerned, Yorktown settled the issue over which they were fighting. In Great Britain the news of Cornwallis's surrender convinced both government and people that their colonies were irrevocably lost. Lord North fell from power, much to his relief, and a new ministry took office, dominated by Lord Shelburne and Charles James Fox and prepared to discuss peace on the basis of American independence. The Americans on their side were more than willing to terminate their six years of wearing struggle. Negotiations between the two began early in 1782, but the treaty of peace was not concluded until September, 1783. Anglo-American differences were all settled within a few months; the long delay in ending the war was due entirely to the tangled relationships between the United States, France, and Spain.

Vergennes had landed squarely in the diplomatic dilemma which he had prepared for himself. One of his allies had got what it wanted and the other had not. Since 1779 a French and Spanish army had been besieging Gibraltar without giving the slightest indication that it was ever likely to capture the place, but nevertheless Spain was matching its reluctance to get into the war with an equal reluctance to get out until it had secured something for its efforts. Vergennes himself wanted peace. The war was proving a severe strain on the French treasury, and there was little likelihood that France would emerge with any substantial territorial gains as compensation, especially after her temporary naval superiority had been dissipated by Rodney's victory over De Grasse at the Saints'

122

Passage in April, 1782. However, the French statesman believed that his obligations to Spain required him, since he could not deliver Gibraltar, to support Spanish claims to territory in North America, claims which in their most extreme form would have confined the United States east of the Appalachians. On the other hand, with British diplomacy ready to take advantage of any rift among its opponents, Vergennes could hardly afford to antagonize the United States by open disregard of American interests.

Diplomatic Complications. It was an awkward position to be in, and it is not in the least surprising that Vergennes' efforts to extricate himself convinced the American peace commissioners that he was not to be trusted. The three of them, Franklin, John Jay, and John Adams, were instructed by Congress to do nothing without the approval of the French government. Franklin, who was in a position to appreciate Vergennes' difficulties, was somewhat more inclined than the other two to comply with these instructions. Jay, however, arrived in Paris fresh from an unhappy experience as American Minister in Madrid. He had never been officially recognized by the Spanish government, and he had developed a pronounced hostility toward Spain, which made him more than ready to be suspicious of Spain's ally. In Paris, he came to the conclusion that Vergennes was trying to sell out the United States for the benefit of Spain and decided that the only remedy was to disregard his instructions and negotiate independently with the British. When John Adams arrived from his diplomatic post in the Netherlands, he concurred wholeheartedly with Jay's action, and Franklin followed the lead of his colleagues without any very strong objection.

The result was that the United States and Great Britain signed a preliminary treaty of peace on 30 November 1782; in deference to the French alliance, the agreement was not to take effect until Great Britain and France had come to terms. Vergennes complained about the failure of the Americans to consult him, but his protest seems to have been designed principally to keep his record straight for the benefit of his other ally. Jay's recalcitrance, in fact, was of considerable value to France. Coming as it did on the heels of a catastrophic failure to storm Gibraltar, the threat that the United States would make a separate peace convinced the Spanish government that it would be useless to continue fighting. The Spaniards accordingly consented to accept Florida instead of Gibraltar and end the war.

The Treaty of Paris. The sole beneficiary of all this diplomatic complication was the United States. Considering that British garrisons still held New York, Charleston, Savannah, and several posts in the Northwest Territory, the Americans won the peace rather more emphatically than they won the war. It was to be expected that Great Britain would acknowledge the independence of the United States, but at the start of the negotiations neither Congress nor the American peace commissioners had quite dared to hope for as liberal treatment as they received in the matter of boundaries. As defined by the Treaty of 1783, the new nation was to extend westward to the Mississippi, between the Great Lakes on the north and Florida in the south. The Great Lakes boundary was a compromise between American hopes of annexing Canada and British hopes of establishing the line at the Ohio River. The southern frontier was fixed by a secret agreement providing that if Spain held West Florida at the end of the war, the line would be the 31st parallel, while if Britain recovered this area, the boundary would be farther north at the mouth of the Yazoo—an arrangement of which Spain thoroughly disapproved when it came to light.

Britain's motives in agreeing to such a generous territorial settlement are to be found in her difficulties with France and Spain. Although George Rogers Clark had occupied much of the area between the Ohio and the Lakes for the state of Virginia, there is little evidence to show that his achievement influenced the negotiations in Paris. Britain had to have peace; and since she could not hope to hold the American West against Spain, whose claims would be backed by France, she preferred to give the territory to the United States rather than let a European rival have it. A secondary, but nevertheless important, consideration was that Shelburne, who was both thoroughly conversant with the Western problem and friendly toward the Americans, hoped that giving the United States ample room for expansion would remove the ill feeling caused by the war and lay the foundation for future Anglo-American friendship.

Boundary Adjustments. At the insistence of John Adams, speaking for the maritime interests of New England, the right of Americans to share in the Newfoundland fisheries was recognized, although in such ambiguous language that it remained a matter of dispute between the two countries until 1911. Some of the boundary provisions also had to be revised afterward because of the limited geographical knowledge available to the peacemakers of 1783. The boundary between Maine and New Brunswick remained a source of acrimonious controversy until 1842, when it was settled by a healthy application of common sense on the part of Daniel Webster, then Secretary of State, and Lord Ashburton, the special envoy appointed by the British government to solve the problem. They divided the territory in dispute, with the United States getting the larger share.[1] At what was originally the northwest corner of the United States,

[1] The Webster-Ashburton negotiations were enlivened by the "battle of the maps." Webster had come into possession of a map found in Paris which he believed was the one referred to by Franklin as having been used by the peace commissioners. It had the boundaries of the United States marked in red and showed

the treaty stipulated that the boundary should run from the Lake of the Woods "due west to the Mississippi," a provision made completely impractical by the subsequent discovery that the headwaters of the Mississippi were almost due south of the Lake of the Woods. Since neither country considered the region in question to be of any great value, this difficulty was quietly settled in 1818 by fixing the boundary at the 49th parallel.

The only concessions made by the United States in the Treaty of 1783 were face-saving gestures to satisfy the British. Britain wanted a guarantee that debts owed by Americans to British merchants before the outbreak of the Revolutionary War would be paid, and it also wanted restitution of confiscated loyalist property. Jay, Franklin, and Adams were willing to concede the first point but were faced with the difficulty that no guarantee given by Congress could be enforced on the individual states. All they could agree to was a clause stipulating that merchants of both countries should "meet with no lawful impediment" in trying to collect their debts. On the matter of loyalist property the Americans were much less conciliatory, a reflection of the bitterness of the civil conflict which had accompanied the War of Independence. They finally consented to a provision that Congress should recommend to the several states that they restore loyalist property. Both parties knew that it was a meaningless gesture, but the British negotiators had to have it to get the treaty approved by Parliament.

None of the other participants in the Revolutionary War emerged from it with anything of value. Spain, as stated above, received Florida as a consolation prize instead of Gibraltar and held it uneasily for less than forty years before selling it to the United States. Holland, which had never wanted to be involved in the conflict at all, was content simply to make peace. France, the most vitally concerned of the trio, had to take her reward chiefly in the moral satisfaction of seeing her great rival defeated; the annexation of St. Lucia in the West Indies and Senegal in West Africa did not begin to offset the cost of the war.

EFFECTS OF THE AMERICAN REVOLUTION IN EUROPE

The indirect influences of the American Revolution on the Western world extended well beyond the immediate terms of the peace settlement

---

the British claims to be correct. The British Foreign Office, on the other hand, had found a red-line map in London which it believed to be authentic and which upheld the American claims. Production of this adverse evidence materially facilitated ratification of the Webster-Ashburton Treaty on both sides of the Atlantic.

of 1783. Liberals everywhere saw in the American victory a promise that the rights of man would eventually triumph in their own countries. This reaction was, as one would expect, especially strong in France. Although their government had intervened in the war for purely practical reasons and without any desire to encourage republicanism, French idealists had all along identified themselves with the American cause, and its victory stimulated their ardor for reform in their own country. Lafayette and others who had served in the American army returned home with glowing accounts of American life, and at least some of the men who marched from Newport to Yorktown with Rochambeau must have formed their own impressions of the contrast between the condition of the common people in the United States and in France. Inspiration is not a measurable commodity, but it can be said with assurance that, if the American bid for independence had failed, the third estate in France would have been less determined to assert its rights in 1789. A more direct connection between the American and French revolutions is that the War of Independence wrecked the already shaky finances of the French monarchy, and it was impending bankruptcy which drove Louis XVI to the radical expedient of summoning the States General.

In Great Britain, the immediate effect of the loss of the American colonies was to discredit the king's political leadership. British liberals were able to console themselves with the thought that their principles had won even if their country had lost, since the fall of the North ministry compelled George III to accept a cabinet unsympathetic to his ideas of personal government. While George's influence remained substantial, at least until insanity claimed him in his later years, the point had been clearly established that the king's own preferences must yield to parliamentary and public opinion. Indeed, if the upheaval in France had not come along so rapidly, with the dual effect of diverting attention from domestic problems and producing a strong conservative reaction, some of the reforms which materialized in nineteenth-century Britain might have followed directly in the wake of the American Revolution. The redistribution of membership in the House of Commons so as to give it some resemblance to the distribution of the population as a whole was seriously considered at this time—an interesting commentary on the doctrine of "virtual representation" which defenders of the Stamp Act had used twenty years before. An Irish nationalist movement, ably led by Henry Grattan, was able to use the pressure of the American War to win a considerable measure of legislative independence in 1782. Unfortunately, since this step did not go as far as to extend political equality to Catholics and, therefore, left the Irish Parliament in the hands of a minority of Protestant landowners, it was not a success, and the experiment was abandoned in 1801 in favor of absorbing Ireland into the United Kingdom. Again because of the religious difficulty, the union of Great Britain and Ireland failed to produce the same happy results as the earlier union of England and Scotland.

American Independence and the British Empire. The gloomy anticipation of many Englishmen that losing their American colonies would lead to collapse of the empire proved to be unfounded. The British position in India remained secure, their losses in the West Indies were trivial, and, thanks to the emigration of loyalists from the United States, their hold on Canada was firmer than it had been before. The number of these exiles is estimated to have been between sixty and eighty thousand. Some went to Europe, but the majority settled in New Brunswick and Ontario, to give the English in Canada numerical equality with the French for the first time.

It used to be widely believed, both in the United States and Great Britain, that the American Revolution caused the liberalization of British colonial policy. If it did, it was a long-term influence, because there was no substantial change in colonial policy for over fifty years. During the period immediately after the Revolution, Britain was, if anything, inclined to be stricter in controlling her empire and enforcing the Navigation Acts, because most contemporary British statesmen attributed the American revolt to the fact that previous governments had allowed those colonies altogether too much of a free hand. Modernization of British colonial policy really began with an unsuccessful rebellion in Canada in 1837. The authorities in London at that time were not satisfied with merely suppressing the uprising; they sent Lord Durham to Canada to find out what had caused it, and the Durham Report, recommending autonomy in internal affairs as the best remedy for colonial grievances, laid the foundation for the present Commonwealth of Nations.

THE REVOLUTION IN AMERICAN SOCIETY

For the United States, the Revolutionary War brought about internal changes which were scarcely less important than the winning of independence. The revolt from Great Britain crystallized the political rivalries of colonial days and resolved them largely in favor of the radicals. The power of the old colonial aristocracy was broken, and the new nation started off on a distinct if still incomplete democratic trend.

During the course of the war, eleven of the thirteen states replaced their colonial governments with new written constitutions. The exceptions were Connecticut and Rhode Island, whose people were content to keep their charters in effect with a few changes in wording. The new constitutions all recognized the sovereignty of the people, although they uniformly restricted the right of suffrage to owners of property or taxpayers. However, the franchise was considerably extended, and, in the Northern states at least, the inequalities in representation which had existed during the colonial period were removed. In the South, the planter aristocracy was able to retain most of its political monopoly.

Along with these changes in the structure of government went a movement to eliminate from American life those customs and institutions which appeared to be vestiges of the aristocratic society of Europe and therefore unsuited to republican America. The features of feudal land tenure which had been transplanted to the colonies were abolished—the quitrents paid by landowners to the crown or the proprietors, the system of entail, whereby the property rights of a family could be made inalienable, and the practice of primogeniture, by which estates passed from eldest son to eldest son. The disappearance of these practices encouraged dispersal rather than concentration of landownership. Small-scale landholding was further encouraged by the sale of confiscated loyalist property. The Pepperell estates in Maine, which extended thirty miles along the coast, the DeLancey holdings in New York and New Jersey, the great Fairfax estate in Virginia, the proprietary lands of the Penns and the Calverts—these and many others were broken up and distributed among a multitude of new owners.

Church and State. The most important of the internal changes emanating from the Revolution was the separation of church and state. Where the Church of England had been the established religious body, it lost its privileged position, partly on grounds of principle and partly because it was regarded as a representative of British authority. Its adherents reorganized after the war as the Protestant Episcopal Church of America. Most of the state constitutions guaranteed religious freedom and prohibited the support of any ecclesiastical body with public funds. In Massachusetts, Connecticut, and New Hampshire, the Congregational Church, whose clergy had been actively favorable to the Revolution, was not disestablished until early in the nineteenth century, but members of other denominations could have their taxes used for their own churches. Except for the Catholics, American religious groups which had old-world ties followed the example of the Episcopalians by breaking them and forming independent organizations. The Catholic Church in the United States was given an increased dignity by the appointment of its first American bishop, John Carroll, Bishop of Baltimore, in 1788.

The enthusiasm for the rights of man generated by the Revolution also expressed itself in various humanitarian activities, the most conspicuous of which was a strong antislavery agitation. The two decades after the War of Independence saw slavery abolished north of the Mason and Dixon line—the line separating Pennsylvania from Maryland, named for the two otherwise obscure English surveyors who ran it in the middle

of the eighteenth century. The most striking feature of this movement is
that it extended to the South. Enlightened Southern opinion of this period
regarded slavery as an evil for which there was unfortunately no visible
remedy, since the consequences of emancipating a mass of illiterate and
semisavage Negroes were unforeseeable and frightening. However, if
slavery could not be abolished, its growth could be curbed and some of
its worst aspects ameliorated by attacking the African slave trade. Virginia and Maryland prohibited this traffic altogether, the other Southern
states restricted it, and all supported the clause in the Federal Constitution providing for its ultimate elimination. A Virginian, Thomas Jefferson, was also primarily responsible for the exclusion of slavery from the
Northwest Territory.

Economic Consequences. The economic pattern of American life
was not fundamentally altered by the Revolutionary War. The population continued to be overwhelmingly agricultural, and an agricultural
society is less likely to be disturbed by war than a more complex economic
organization. Much of the United States, indeed, had been affected either
slightly or not at all by military operations. There was little fighting in
New England after the evacuation of Boston, Pennsylvania was a theater
of conflict for less than a year, and then only in the vicinity of Philadelphia, and Virginia was scarcely touched until the Yorktown campaign.
For most people, consequently, the war brought little interruption in their
ordinary pursuits; the men of a community might turn out occasionally
for militia duty, but then they would return to their farms. Thus, although
the strain was felt in a severe postwar depression, the United States
emerged from its long struggle for independence with its productive
capacity virtually unimpaired.

The most obvious aftereffect of the war on the nation's economy was
financial chaos, and that was due chiefly to the inability of the central
government to raise funds by taxation or to exercise any real control over
coinage and the issuance of paper currency. The policies of the states
varied and in their variation added to the general confusion. Massachusetts, for example, followed a stringent "sound-money" policy, while
neighboring Rhode Island went to a wild extreme of legal-tender paper
issues. This monetary instability served to intensify the unsettled business
conditions of the immediate postwar period.

Manufacturing received some stimulus when the normal flow of supplies from Great Britain was cut off, but the coming of peace brought a
renewed influx of British goods to the American market which retarded
the growth of domestic industry. Maritime commerce was, for the time
being at least, the hardest hit branch of American economy. With the
attainment of independence, American merchants found themselves freed
from the restrictions of the Navigation Acts, but also deprived of their

former privileges in trading within the British Empire. The severest blow was the exclusion of American ships from the British West Indies. It was hoped that this loss would be offset by concessions from France and Spain, but although both countries did open some of their colonial ports to American commerce, they did not replace the West Indian traffic of colonial days. American merchants had to solve their problems by their own enterprise; by far the most important result of their efforts in the 1780's to find new outlets was the establishing of direct contacts between the United States and the Far East.[2]

THE CONFEDERATION

The most serious difficulty confronting the United States at the close of the War of Independence was the organization of its national government, and it was here that the prospects of the new nation were poorest. The Revolution had been fought because the authority claimed by a central government clashed with the rights asserted by a number of local governments, but it had not solved the problem of how to reconcile the two; it had merely transferred the responsibility for finding a solution, as far as the thirteen American states were concerned, from the British Parliament to the American people. For a time it appeared that the Americans would prove unequal to the task. Even the friends of the United States in Europe doubted its ability to survive, and its enemies gleefully predicted speedy disintegration in the face of particularism and exaggerated local pride.

The task of creating a national government had been taken up by the Second Continental Congress as a natural corollary to the Declaration of Independence and had been entrusted to a special committee under the chairmanship of John Dickinson, who had accepted the decision of the majority after his initial opposition to independence. This body drafted the Articles of Confederation and Perpetual Union, which were completed in 1778 and submitted to the states for ratification.

That process took three years because of a disagreement over the disposition of the West. Seven states had claims to Western land, the best being that of Virginia, which could not only assert extensive rights under its charter but was also in physical possession of much of the territory in question. The six "have-not" states naturally felt that they were being discriminated against, and Maryland refused to ratify the Articles until the West was acknowledged to be the common property of the whole nation. Finally, in 1780 and 1781, the states claiming territory

[2] In the very year following the conclusion of the Revolutionary War, the first American vessel, the appropriately named *Empress of China,* inaugurated American Far Eastern trade.

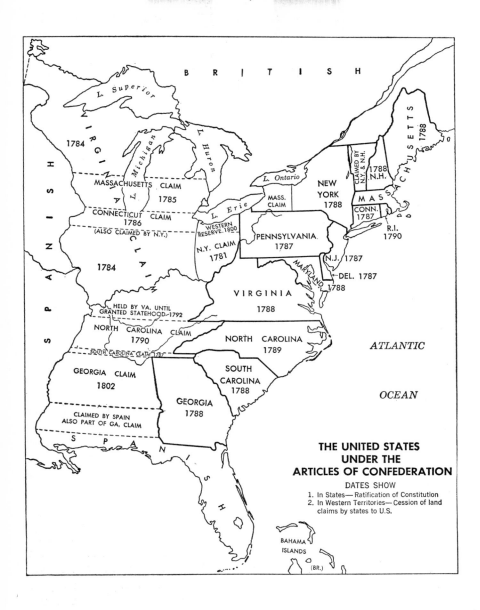

THE UNITED STATES
UNDER THE
ARTICLES OF CONFEDERATION

DATES SHOW
1. In States— Ratification of Constitution
2. In Western Territories— Cession of land
claims by states to U.S.

northwest of the Ohio agreed to relinquish their rights to the United States, except for the Connecticut Western Reserve on the southern shore of Lake Erie, which was kept until 1800, and an area retained by Virginia to satisfy the land bounties given to Virginian veterans of the Revolutionary War. The territory south of the Ohio, except for Kentucky and Tennessee, was ceded soon afterward. By its insistence that the West should belong to the whole people of the United States, Maryland made a vital contribution to national unity at a critical time.

The Articles of Confederation. In considering the Articles of Confederation, it should be borne in mind that Dickinson and his colleagues could not have created a stronger national government if they had wanted to. The individual states were not as yet prepared to surrender any consequential portion of their newly acquired sovereignty. Furthermore, the Articles were drafted during the heat of the Revolutionary War, when their framers were acutely conscious of the oppressive features of the British imperial system, and an obvious effort was made to prevent those features from being duplicated in the new framework of government. In American eyes George III was a tyrant; therefore, there would be no American executive who might conceivably acquire the same authority. The intervention of the Privy Council in colonial affairs had been disliked; the Articles provided no national judiciary to overrule state courts. British prohibition of colonial issues of paper money had been resented; each state retained the right to issue its own currency. British commercial regulations had restricted colonial trade; under the Articles the imposition of tariff duties and other measures for controlling commerce were left to the states. Finally and most important of all, the war had been precipitated by British attempts to tax the colonies; the Articles gave the states alone the right to levy taxes. The funds needed by the national government were to be raised by requisitions on the states.

The only agency of central authority created by the Articles was a Congress, essentially nothing more than a legitimatized version of the Second Continental Congress. Each state could have two to seven delegates but only one vote. Unanimity was necessary to amend the Articles and the assent of nine states for major decisions. Since the states paid their own delegates, Congress was an assembly of diplomats rather than a national legislature. In theory, it had fairly extensive powers. It was authorized to make war and peace, to maintain an army and navy, to conduct foreign relations, to supervise Indian affairs, to coin money and regulate the value of currency, and to adjudicate disputes between states.

In practice, these powers were largely illusory because Congress had no way of enforcing its decisions. It could send requisitions to the states for money, but it could not compel the states to honor them. The states generally fell far short of their quotas, if indeed they paid any attention to the requisitions at all. Congress seldom collected enough to meet the ordinary running expenses of the government. Lack of funds made it impossible to maintain military forces. It was equally impossible to pay either principal or interest on the debt incurred during the war. The conduct of foreign affairs also proved unsatisfactory. Foreign nations were reluctant to negotiate commercial treaties with the United States because they were aware that promises made by Congress could be disregarded with impunity by the states.

The Northwest Ordinance. Congress had undisputed jurisdiction only over the Western territory ceded to it by the states, and its provision for the governing and settling of this area constitutes the one great achievement of the Confederation. The incentive to act came from the desire of two land companies, the Scioto Company and the Ohio Company, to acquire parts of the Northwest Territory. The former was a speculative venture which proved a failure, but the Ohio Company was well financed by New England capital and had an astute agent in the Reverend Manasseh Cutler. With Congress in urgent need of money, it was not difficult to reach an agreement for the purchase of several million acres by the two companies at bargain prices, part of which was paid in bounty warrants and certificates of indebtedness. If land was to be sold, it would have to be surveyed. To meet this need Congress passed the Land Ordinance of 1785, establishing the method of rectangular survey which was subsequently applied to the entire public domain of the United States. The land was to be laid out in townships six miles square, subdivided into thirty-six sections of 640 acres each. Four sections in each township were reserved for the United States and one for the support of public schools.

In organizing a government for the Northwest Territory, Congress established principles which became fundamental in the growth of the United States. Its policy was foreshadowed in a resolution of 1780 pledging that any Western territory ceded to the United States would be made into new states, on an equal footing with the old. Four years later, Jefferson put this idea into concrete form in an Ordinance providing for the creation of ten states in the Northwest. This Ordinance was adopted by Congress but never put into effect, and the definitive formulation of governmental policy for the West was left to the Northwest Ordinance of 1787.

This document, which appears to have been drafted mainly by three members of the Ohio Company, Nathan Dane, Manasseh Cutler, and Rufus King, was a detailed revision of the plan developed by Jefferson in 1784. It provided that the region should be administered at first by a governor, a secretary, and three judges appointed by Congress. When the population had reached five thousand free adult males, the territory was to be given a legislature, consisting of an assembly elected by the people and a council appointed by Congress, and a nonvoting delegate in Congress. In due time, the area between the Ohio and Mississippi rivers was to be divided into not less than three or more than five states, each to be admitted to the Union when it had acquired sixty thousand free inhabitants. Eventually five states were created in the Northwest Territory —Ohio, Indiana, Illinois, Michigan, and Wisconsin. The Ordinance gave generous guarantees of civil liberty and stipulated that "religion, morality, and knowledge, being necessary to good government and the happiness of mankind, schools and the means of education shall forever be encouraged." It specified that "the utmost good faith" should be observed toward the Indians, a promise too frequently ignored, and, as stated before, it prohibited slavery in the Northwest Territory.

As a contribution to the future development of the United States, the Northwest Ordinance ranks close to the Constitution and the Declaration of Independence. It established the pattern for absorbing new areas into the Union by systematic progression from territory to statehood and thereby made possible the orderly expansion of the United States. The only feasible alternative would have been to treat the West as a colonial area and try to keep it in political and economic subjection to the eastern seaboard. A little reflection will suggest that the prospects for such a policy were distinctly poor. The rapidly growing West would never have accepted a status of permanent inferiority, and any attempt to maintain such a relationship would inevitably have ended in disaster.

Decline of the Confederation. It was eloquent testimony to the decay of the Confederation that Congress was barely able to muster a quorum to pass the Northwest Ordinance. There was little incentive for men to devote their time and energies to the hopeless task of trying to run an impotent government. With the unpaid interest on the public debt steadily accumulating, the credit of the United States was fast disappearing, and there was no remedy in sight. An attempt to provide the government with a revenue by amending the Articles of Confederation so as to permit Congress to levy a 5 per cent duty on imports was vetoed once by Rhode Island and a second time by New York. Settlement of the West was retarded by the lack of military power to keep the Indians under control. Merchants were handicapped by the confusion of thirteen separate currency and tariff systems and by the inability of the national government to command respect abroad. States squabbled with each other freely—New York with Connecticut and New Jersey over alleged commercial discrimination and with New Hampshire over title to Vermont; Pennsylvania and Connecticut over land along the upper Susquehanna—and Congress was helpless to settle their disputes.

Dissatisfaction with the Articles of Confederation was brought to a head in 1786 by the outbreak of Shays' Rebellion in Massachusetts. This was an uprising of debt-ridden farmers in the western part of the state against the eastern conservatives who dominated its government. Under the leadership of Daniel Shays, a veteran of the Revolutionary War, the rebels prevented the courts in their area from foreclosing mortgages and demanded that the legislature issue paper money and enact stay laws to postpone the collection of debts. As it turned out, the revolt was easily suppressed by the state authorities, but the complete inability of Congress to give any assistance served to arouse concern over the defenseless condition of the country against either foreign invasion or domestic insurrection.

Conservative elements in particular deemed it imperative to establish a national government capable of maintaining security and order and restoring economic stability. It should not be assumed, however, that the movement for the Constitution arose purely from a desire to safeguard the interests of property. It was much more a product of sincere patriotism, alarmed by the prospect that, unless something was done to strengthen the Union, disintegration and internal chaos were inevitable. If that should happen, the separate states would be at the mercy of foreign powers and all the gains of the Revolution would be lost. Most Americans accepted the need for some improvement in their national government; where they differed was on the question of how much additional power ought to be given to it. Too little would defeat the purpose of obtaining security; too much might imperil individual freedom.

9

The Constitution

THE FEDERAL CONVENTION

The history of the world contains few examples of political genius equal to the framing of the Constitution of the United States. It was the work of men who combined vision with sagacity, who could take advantage of the opportunities offered to them, and who were aware of the distinction between what was theoretically desirable and what was practically acceptable. The first step in the formation of a new government grew out of discussions between Maryland and Virginia over the navigation of the Potomac River. Since this matter was closely associated with broader questions of commercial policy, the two states, at the instigation of James Madison, sponsored an interstate convention to consider adopting uniform standards for the regulation of commerce. This convention met at Annapolis, Maryland, in 1786. Since only five states sent representatives, it could do nothing to achieve its immediate purpose, but its members, under the skillful direction of Madison and Alexander Hamilton, recommended to Congress that another general convention be called, with authority to consider the whole problem of strengthening the central government. Congress, helpless to remedy matters by itself, accepted the suggestion and requested the states to send delegates to a convention in Philadelphia in May, 1787. All that this body was specifically empowered to do was amend the Articles of Confederation.

Twelve states complied, Rhode Island being the sole dissenter, and the caliber of the delegates who were chosen shows that the gravity of the occasion was fully recognized. Virginia sent a conspicuously able group, including George Washington, who became president of the convention as a matter of course and whose tremendous prestige was of in-

136

calculable value, and James Madison, who more than anyone deserves the title of "Father of the Constitution." The Pennsylvania delegation included Benjamin Franklin, now too old to play an active part in the proceedings but still capable of giving sound advice to his colleagues, James Wilson, a keen legal scholar and student of government, and Robert Morris, whose experience in trying to manage the finances of the Revolutionary War made him acutely aware of the existing government's deficiencies. From Delaware came John Dickinson to revise his own handiwork. Alexander Hamilton represented New York, but his value to the convention was reduced both because his own views on the powers a central government should have were so extreme as to be completely impractical and because his two associates on the New York delegation decided that the convention was going too far and withdrew, leaving Hamilton unable to vote. An enumeration of the rest of the membership of the Federal Convention is needless; it was virtually a roster of the distinguished figures of American public life. Of the notable absentees, Thomas Jefferson and John Adams were abroad on diplomatic missions, and John Jay was busy with his duties as Secretary of Foreign Affairs.

The Constitution of the United States materialized as an "open covenant," but it was definitely not "openly arrived at." The convention decided to conduct its meetings in secret, mainly because its members felt that it would be extremely difficult to compromise disagreements if each controversial point became a subject of public dispute. In addition, those who had made up their minds from the beginning that the Articles of Confederation would have to be scrapped preferred to have their new frame of government seen by the people as a whole. In that way judgment could be passed on the general structure rather than on isolated details, and the chances of acceptance would be greater.

The Virginia and New Jersey Plans. This group, of which Madison and Wilson were the guiding spirits, had its proposals ready for discussion, when the convention assembled, in the form of the Virginia or large-state plan. It contained the elements of the Constitution as it finally emerged, providing for a national executive, judiciary, and two-house legislature, with, in addition to the powers of the existing Congress, authority to legislate on all matters "to which the separate states are incompetent." It could also disallow state laws violating the articles of union, and it could summon the forces of the Union to deal with refractory states.

The objectionable feature of this plan, as far as the small states were concerned, was that representation in both branches of the national legislature was to be based either on population or contribution to the support of the government. William Paterson of New Jersey drew up a counterproposal, also providing for a national executive and judiciary but retaining Congress as it was, with one vote for each state. Congress's powers were to be increased by permitting it to raise money through import duties and, of all things, a stamp tax, and, as in the Virginia plan, the central government would be exercised on the states rather than on the individual citizens, a system fortunately abandoned in subsequent discussion. The New Jersey plan would simply have patched up a few of the worst weaknesses in the Articles of Confederation, but it did make a signal contribution to the Constitution in its clause stipulating that "all Acts of the United States in Congress—and all Treaties made and ratified under the authority of the United States, shall be the supreme law of the respective States—and that the Judiciary of the several states shall be bound thereby in their decisions, anything in the respective laws of the Individual States to the contrary notwithstanding."

The main point at issue between the two plans was the method of representation in the national legislature, and on this question the convention threatened to deadlock completely. Finally, a special committee worked out a compromise, for which the Connecticut delegation was chiefly responsible, establishing a bicameral legislature in which the states would be represented equally in one branch and according to population in the other. It was modified by the "federal ratio," also a compromise, whereby the basis of representation in the House was to be the free population plus three-fifths of the slaves.

Character of the Constitution. With this decision accepted, the convention was quite definitely committed to substitute a new form of government for the Articles of Confederation. In devising this government, the members of the convention followed in general the principles of eighteenth-century political philosophy by creating an organism with carefully defined functions and with three branches independent of and acting as checks upon each other. The delegates, however, were not primarily interested in political theories. They were dealing with a concrete situation, and they preferred to find remedies which had stood the test of experience. They borrowed heavily from their own state and colonial governments, from the British political system, under which most of them had been brought up, and from the Articles of Confederation.

There was substantial agreement that the new Federal government should have the power to levy taxes, to regulate interstate and foreign commerce, and to control the currency, and that the states should be forbidden to impose export or import duties and to issue currency of their own. On these points the Articles had been clearly defective. On other matters conflicts of interest or opinion had to be settled by compromise or, in some cases, by an intentional vagueness of wording which left future generations free to interpret those points to suit their needs. The framers of the Constitution were not trying to solve all problems for all time; they were trying to establish a government which would work more effectively than the Confederation and which the American people of 1787 would be willing to accept.

The Presidency. The provisions of the Constitution regarding the presidency offer an excellent illustration of this technique. A strong executive was needed, and yet there had to be some limitation on the power of the President. In view of the importance of the office, the method of election and the length of tenure demanded careful consideration. The result is that what the Constitution leaves unsaid about the presidency is at least as important as what it says. The President is given broad powers, but no attempt is made to specify how he shall exercise them. He is charged with executing the laws of the United States; he appoints the principal administrative and judicial officers of the Federal government, subject to confirmation by the Senate; and he is responsible for the conduct of foreign affairs, subject to the limitation that treaties must be approved by a two-thirds majority in the Senate. His veto power gives him a share in the legislative process. He is also Commander in Chief of the armed forces of the United States, a function originally given him to insure subordination of the military to the civil authority, but which has frequently been used by vigorous executives to permit acting in situations not otherwise covered by the President's powers.

The President's term of office represents a compromise between those who, like Hamilton, felt that the Chief Executive should have life tenure, and those who believed that a limit should be imposed on the length of time any one man might serve. It appeared desirable to permit a good President to remain in office and equally desirable to make provision for getting rid of a poor one without undue delay. Both objectives were achieved by the four-year term, without restriction on the number of terms a President might have.[1]

The method of election worked out by the convention proved to be the least successful feature of the Constitution. A conservative group, distinctly representative of the classes rather than the masses, the delegates realized that some participation in the government by the common people was essential, but they wished to hold it to a minimum. In determining how members of Congress should be elected, they evaded this problem altogether by providing that Senators should be chosen by state legislatures and Representatives by those who were qualified to vote in each state for the most numerous branch of the state legislature. To men with this point of view it was unthinkable that as important an office as the presidency should be filled by popular election, and yet to have the choice made by Congress or by state governments would impair the

[1] The Twenty-second Amendment, adopted in 1951, now restricts Presidents to two terms.

President's independence. The attempted solution was the electoral college. Each state was to choose, in whatever manner it saw fit, as many electors as it had Senators and Representatives, and these electors in turn chose the President. Originally, each elector voted for two candidates, the second highest on the list becoming Vice-President. However, after the elections of 1796, in which Jefferson, the defeated candidate, became Vice-President and would, therefore, have assumed control of the government if John Adams had died in office, and of 1800, in which the two Republican candidates, Jefferson and Burr, received an equal number of electoral votes, the system was changed in 1805 by the Twelfth Amendment, so that each elector voted separately for President and Vice-President. Of still greater importance is the fact that the rise of political parties has eliminated the freedom of choice intended by the framers of the Constitution, since electors are pledged to their party's candidates. The electoral college has become largely a meaningless formality.

The Federal Judiciary. The judicial branch of the Federal government also has its powers defined in general terms. The Constitution states: "The judicial power of the United States, shall be vested in one Supreme Court, and in such inferior courts as the Congress may from time to time ordain and establish." It gives these courts jurisdiction in "all cases, in law and equity, arising under this Constitution, the laws of the United States, and treaties made . . . under their authority," as well as in cases coming under certain specified categories. The most interesting feature of this Article is that no specific mention is made of the authority of Federal courts to pass on the constitutionality of acts of Congress or of state legislatures, although this power is clearly implied in the statement quoted above and in the provision of Article VI making the Constitution the supreme law of the land. Moreover, the debates in the convention itself and on ratification of the Constitution afterward make it manifest that the framers of the document understood it to contain the power of judicial review.

The great achievement of the Federal Convention was to design the Constitution so that the authority of the national government is exercised directly upon the individual citizens and not upon the states. That superficially simple device turned out to be the key to successful federalism. The Confederation had demonstrated the futility of trying to have the United States government depend upon the voluntary cooperation of the individual states to execute its functions. The most obvious remedy, suggested in both the Virginia and the New Jersey plans, of having the national authority enforced upon the states would inevitably have produced a series of civil wars, with dissolution of the Union in a very short period of time. The system which was adopted permits the nation and the states to operate side by side, each in its own sphere. It has not, of course, worked without friction; perfection in government has still to be attained. Disputes over the proper boundaries between Federal and state power have been commonplace in American politics, and on occasion states have defied the national government, once to the extent of civil war. Nevertheless, the fact that there has been only one civil war and that its outcome vindicated the authority of the Union is in itself sufficient tribute to the men who drafted the Constitution.

RATIFICATION

If the Federal Convention had interpreted its duties literally, it should have presented the Constitution to Congress as a rather sweeping amendment of the Articles of Confederation, and Congress in turn should have submitted it to the states for the unanimous consent required by the Articles. As a matter of practical politics, this procedure would have meant rejection of the Constitution, a circumstance of which its framers were fully aware. Rhode Island, controlled by an agrarian faction, was certain to refuse ratification, and the attitude of several of the states represented at the convention was extremely doubtful. As the first step toward meeting this difficulty, a special method of adoption was written into the document. It was to be submitted in each state to a convention called for this particular purpose, and it was to go into operation when nine states had accepted it. Congress might normally have been expected to resent this somewhat highhanded overriding of its instructions and its rights, but by 1787 it had recognized the futility of its own position and was content to pass the Constitution along to the states for their action.

The struggle for ratification was one of the most ably conducted political campaigns in American history. Considering what was at stake, it was fortunate for the United States that the balance of skill lay with the Federalists, as the proponents of the Constitution called themselves. They were probably a minority of the whole people of the United States in 1788. They had the support of the business classes and a large segment of the planter aristocracy, but the farming population in general was inclined to feel that the document went too far in centralizing authority and contained no adequate guarantees of the rights either of the states or of individuals.

The fate of the Constitution rested with the four large states— Virginia, Pennsylvania, New York, and Massachusetts. If all four accepted it, the other states would have little choice but to follow them. If any of them rejected it, the new government would start off under a serious handicap. In Pennsylvania, the local situation favored prompt action on the part of the Federalists, since they were a compact group, concentrated in and about Philadelphia, while the opposition would need time to muster its strength among the farmers scattered through the interior of the state. The call for the ratifying convention was accordingly rushed through the state legislature, and Pennsylvania accepted the Constitution before the end of 1787.

The Critical States. Similar tactics were out of the question in the other three states. When the Massachusetts convention met, the Federalists were in the minority. Consequently, they played for time until they could convert some of the doubtful members. The influential support of John Hancock, governor of the commonwealth and chairman of the convention, was won by a deft suggestion of high office in the new government. At the time the suggestion was made, Hancock was in bed with an attack of gout, which his old friend Sam Adams, now a staunch Federalist, predicted would clear up as soon as the sense of the convention became evident. Other votes were secured by an agreement to propose amendments to the Constitution safeguarding individual liberties, and in the end Massachusetts ratified by a vote of 187 to 168. In Virginia, there was a long and brilliant debate, with such outstanding figures as Washington, Madison, and John Marshall arguing the case for the Constitution and Patrick Henry, James Monroe, and Richard Henry Lee opposing it. As in Massachusetts, the winning over of an influential individual, Governor Edmund Randolph, and the prospect that some of the objections to the Constitution would be removed by amendment, played an important part in winning the decision for the Federalists. New York witnessed a bitter but familiar division of opinion: New York City for ratification, the upstate region against. One is tempted to suggest that, if New York City had opposed the Constitution, the upstate counties would have been for it. The New York convention was treated to the persuasive influence of the *Federalist* papers, the work of Hamilton, Jay, and Madison, and also to the threat that the city would secede and ratify the Constitution by itself in the event of an adverse vote. Virginia's action also had its effect, since Virginia was the tenth state to ratify and the Constitution was, therefore, certain to go into operation. In July, 1788, the New York convention fell into line by a vote of 30 to 27.

North Carolina and Rhode Island were still holding out, but their absence, which was certain to be temporary, could be endured. The Congress of the Confederation formally declared the Constitution adopted, arranged for the first elections, and then passed unobtrusively out of existence. As everyone had expected, George Washington became the first President, the only President ever to receive a unanimous electoral vote. The new government officially began its existence on 4 March 1789, although it was not until 30 April that Washington reached New York to be inaugurated.

Two features of the contest for ratification deserve comment. One is that it produced the first ten amendments to the Constitution, commonly called the Bill of Rights. They were approved almost as soon as the Constitution went into operation, in redemption of the pledges made to secure its adoption. The other is that the opponents of ratification acquiesced in the decision that had been reached. That was a sign of political maturity. The test of a people's ability to govern themselves is not so much whether they can design a system of government as whether they can agree to cooperate in making it work. The United States was not to be plagued, as other experiments in constitutionalism have been, by the refusal of a powerful minority to assent to the principles underlying its political structure. By way of comparison, France in 1791, Germany in 1920, and Spain in 1931 all drafted excellent constitutions, only to see them collapse, a result in some measure of the irreconcilable hostility of strong groups within each country.

THE FEDERALIST PERIOD

The Constitution provided a framework; the details were still to be filled in by interpretation and adaptation of the terms of the document to the practical needs of government. In 1789, these needs were considerable. The new Federal government inherited from its predecessor little but a land system and a collection of unpaid debts. The United States had to set its house in order, and it was about to be faced with international complications of unforeseen magnitude because of the outbreak of revolution in France. The process of dealing with these problems resulted in establishing a political pattern which has been constant in the United States ever since and has become an integral part of its constitutional structure.

During the first formative years of its existence the national government was controlled by much the same group of men as had been responsible for drafting and adopting the Constitution. At the beginning of Washington's administration, this group coalesced as the Federalist party. Few political organizations have enjoyed more outstanding leadership. Dominated by Alexander Hamilton, who became Washington's Secretary of the Treasury, the party included John Adams, John Marshall, John Jay, Thomas and C. C. Pinckney, and President Washington himself, although he tried earnestly to avoid partisanship in the conduct of his office. This galaxy of talent explains the early predominance of the Federalists and also their sudden and irretrievable collapse. The party was top-heavy. Its members subscribed to Hamilton's thesis that government should be vested in "the rich, the wise, and the good" and were inclined to assume that anyone who possessed the first of these attributes necessarily possessed the other two also. They distrusted the common people, with the result that their party was doomed to extinction once the growing forces of American democracy had acquired organization and leadership. Nevertheless, the Federalist party governed the United States ably during the period required for the Constitution to take root. Indeed, it is one of the ironies of history that the Federalists, who hated and feared democracy, contributed substantially to its success in the United States by giving it a firm foundation on which to develop. The initial task facing the first Congress was the organization of the necessary machinery of government, which was accomplished by creating five executive departments (State, Treasury, War, Justice, Post Office) and establishing the Federal judicial system by the Judiciary Act of 1789. After that, the problem demanding most immediate attention was finance. Congress provided a revenue by passing a tariff act and then called on Secretary of the Treasury Hamilton for advice. Hamilton was ready. In a series of able reports he laid out a financial program embodying three principal steps: (1) funding the national debt at its face value, (2) assumption by the Federal government of the debts incurred by the states during the War of Independence, and (3) chartering a national bank.

Hamilton's Program. This program had a dual purpose. One was to put the credit of the United States on a solid footing. The other was to implement Hamilton's political philosophy, whose general character has already been described. Hamilton himself was no aristocrat, except through his marriage into the Schuyler family, but few men in the history of the United States have held a more aristocratic concept of government. He believed that men were motivated solely by material considerations and that only those who had a substantial interest in the community through possession of property were fit for political responsibility. Regarding the Constitution as weak and unsatisfactory, he hoped to strengthen the national government by tying it financially to the upper classes in American society. The new securities issued to fund the national and state debts and stock in the Bank of the United States would provide attractive investments for wealthy citizens and give them an incentive to maintain the government.

Hamilton's operations provided faster profits for his select group in a way which he may or may not have anticipated. During the depression of the 1780's, many of the original purchasers of Revolutionary securities had sold their holdings at prices as low as fifteen cents on the dollar to men with the means to buy them up and keep them in the hope of ultimate redemption. In addition, news of Hamilton's intentions leaked out and precipitated a wild flurry of speculation. Hamilton's own honesty has never been in question, but he was certainly indiscreet about telling his friends what he proposed to do. Hamilton's opponents made the most of the point that a favored few were being enriched at the expense of those who had made the actual sacrifices during the Revolutionary War, but they could offer no satisfactory alternative to his program because it was, after all, financially if not politically sound. However inequitable the effects might be upon individuals, the credit of the United States could be established only by redeeming their obligations in accordance with their terms.

A policy whose benefits apparently went entirely to Eastern capital was certain to be viewed with misgiving in the South and West, but the opposition had to find organization and a program of its own if it was to make any headway against the well-integrated Federalists. These elements were supplied by Thomas Jefferson and James Madison. Jefferson, as Secretary of State, was Hamilton's cabinet colleague, and Madison, now in Congress, had been closely associated with him in the drafting and adoption of the Constitution, but both came to view his course with increasing suspicion, not only on economic grounds but because of Hamilton's obvious desire to create a privileged ruling class in the United States. Jefferson believed that the whole people could be more safely trusted with political power than any select groups, although he preferred the actual governing to be done by a "natural aristocracy" based on talent rather than wealth or birth. He also felt that republicanism flourished best in an agrarian society and therefore disapproved of Hamilton's desire to encourage commerce and manufacturing.

There was no serious objection to the funding of the national debt, for the simple reason that there was nothing else to do. The assumption of the state debts was less acceptable, because Jefferson and his followers were afraid of making the states financially dependent on the Federal government. Jefferson's attitude, however, was still uncertain, and he was induced to make a deal, which he afterward regretted, whereby he gave his support to the Assumption bill in return for having the national capital located on the Potomac.

The Bank and States Rights. The open break came on Hamilton's proposal to charter a national bank. To Jefferson, this project represented a dangerous concentration of economic power. Since, however, he was not equipped to challenge Hamilton on financial grounds, he chose to raise the constitutional issue instead, arguing that because the Constitution made no mention of a national bank, Congress had no right to create such an institution. According to Jefferson, the Constitution was to be interpreted literally; the Federal government could exercise only such powers as were granted by the specific language of the document. If it attempted to go further, it was invading the rights reserved to the states. Thus the "states-rights" argument was injected into American politics in a form which has characterized it subsequently, as a cover for other and weaker objections to a proposed measure and a favorite resort of the party which happens to be out of power in the national government at the moment.

When the Bank charter came before him for signature, President Washington was in so much doubt about its constitutionality that he asked both Jefferson and Hamilton to submit written opinions. Jefferson expounded the states-rights, strict construction view of the Constitution. Hamilton, on his side, developed the doctrine of "implied powers." He took the position that the Federal government, within the limits of its delegated powers, possessed the customary attributes of sovereignty, including the privilege of choosing appropriate methods to carry out its functions. As authority for his stand he cited the clause in Article I of the Constitution authorizing Congress "to make all Laws which shall be necessary and proper for carrying into Execution the foregoing Powers." Hamilton contended that, since Congress had been given the right to regulate the currency and since a national bank was the most advantageous means of achieving this objective, Congress had full power to charter such a bank. Jefferson also referred to the "necessary and proper" clause but emphasized the word "necessary." He argued that, while a bank might be a convenient means of regulating the currency, it was not an indispensable one and therefore could not be considered as authorized by the language of the Constitution. Washington, however, accepted Hamilton's interpretation and signed the bank bill.

The First Bank of the United States was patterned on the Bank of England. It had an authorized capital of $10,000,000, one-fifth of which was subscribed by the government. It could issue notes up to the amount of its capital, and since these were receivable for obligations to the United States, they were expected to provide a stable and acceptable circulating medium. The Bank also functioned as a depository and disbursing agent for government funds. Its main office was in Philadelphia, then the financial as well as the political capital of the nation, and it established branches, as permitted by its charter, in the other important commercial centers.

Jefferson and the Republican Party. His rival's victory stimulated Jefferson to undertake seriously the organization of a political party in opposition to the Federalists. It was a lengthy operation, because the bulk of his support had to be drawn from the agrarian population, people who were not in constant contact with each other as were the business and professional men who were the main strength of Federalism. In this task, Jefferson showed a talent for practical politics as least equal to his ability as a political theorist. His most important achievement was to add to his Southern and Western adherents the well-oiled New York machine headed by George Clinton and Aaron Burr and including the Society of Tammany.

Jefferson's party called itself Republican; the name Democratic was originally applied to it by the Federalists as a term of opprobrium, since upper-class opinion of the period regarded a democrat as a very low type of individual who wished to destroy the foundations of society by letting the common people govern themselves, and it did not become the official title of the party until the days of Andrew Jackson. The party made no serious effort to contest the election of 1792. Its organization was still incomplete, and in any event Jefferson was both too shrewd a politician and too wise a statesman to oppose President Washington's reelection.

After 1792, the serious foreign problems created by the revolution in France and the outbreak of a general European war diverted the attention of American political leaders from domestic issues without in the least abating party rivalry. On the contrary, the alignment already formed by the dispute over Hamilton's financial program was solidified by a divergence of opinion on foreign policy. American opinion was uniformly sympathetic to the French Revolution in its early stages, since the French people appeared to be doing just what the American people had done a few years before, but when the radicals took control in France and all Europe burst into flame, the conservative-minded Federalists were horrified. They saw in these newest developments just what they had feared would be the consequences of entrusting power to the masses—a wanton attack on property and religion. They dreaded the spread of French ideas to America, and, since French ideas and French military power were obviously going hand in hand, the Federalists developed a strongly pro-British attitude, regarding Great Britain as the champion of Christian civilization against anarchy. The Republicans, on the other hand, retained their enthusiasm for France. They felt that the revolutionists were fighting for liberty against long-established tyrannies and could hardly be expected to achieve their aims without violence, regrettable as it might be. Economic factors influenced this alignment also. The Federalist merchants of the Northeast had strong commercial ties with Britain, while to the average Southern planter any businessman, Yankee or British, was an object of distrust.

Retirement of Washington. In 1796, George Washington decided to retire from public life to a well-earned rest at his beloved Mount Vernon. Few men have ever served their country with more unselfish devotion. Washington much preferred the life of a country gentleman to either military or political glory; he took the presidency as he had taken the post of commander in chief in the War of Independence, because he conceived it to be his duty. He was not a "popular" President in the sense that he inspired affection among the great masses of people; he was aloof and reserved in public, although he could unbend among his intimate friends. He did, however, command a deserved respect. In his eight years as President he carried the United States through the delicate period of adjustment to its new Constitution with the same resolution he had displayed during the trying days of the Revolution. His boundless common sense and forbearance provided a salutary check on Hamilton's disposition to go to extremes and kept factional disputes from developing their full intensity until the government was secure enough to stand them. When he had to encounter unforeseen and dangerous foreign complications, he faced them with patience and tact, refusing to be swayed either by pressure from abroad or public excitement at home.

With Washington out of the picture, the Federalists and Republicans could give free rein to their antagonism. The election of 1796 was closely contested between John Adams on one side and Thomas Jefferson on the other. Since the Federalists were still somewhat better organized and had Washington's prestige in their favor, Adams won by the narrow margin of 71 electoral votes to 68. He was destined to have an unhappy four years as President. Although an able statesman and a staunch patriot, he was completely lacking in popular appeal and given to the belief that his merits were unappreciated. At home, he had to face not only Republican opposition, but hostility from Hamilton and his followers within his own party. Abroad, he had the continued problems of the European war to meet.

The growing strength of republicanism provoked the Federalists into an ill-advised effort to maintain themselves in power by repression, which, in turn, drew from the Jeffersonians a radical restatement of their constitutional doctrine. Taking advantage of the critical condition of Franco-American relations, which had precipitated an undeclared naval war between the two countries, the Adams administration passed a series of four acts in 1798, known collectively as the Alien and Sedition Acts. The Alien Acts, which extended the time required for naturalization from five to fourteen years and authorized the President to deport undesirable aliens by executive order, were aimed at foreign liberals who had been dislodged by the European upheaval and had sought refuge in the United States, where their political philosophy steered them into the Republican fold. Among these "subversive" individuals were Albert Gallatin, the Swiss-born financier who had been a moderating influence during the Whisky Rebellion in Pennsylvania and who was to become Jefferson's Secretary of the Treasury, Dr. Joseph Priestley, the English chemist, and P. S. duPont de Nemours. The Sedition Act was directed against internal enemies. It included among its offenses any speech or writing "with intent to defame" the President or Congress, and this section was enforced with undue zeal on Republican editors.

The Virginia and Kentucky Resolutions. The Republican rejoinder came in the form of the Virginia and Kentucky Resolutions, passed by the legislatures of those states and written by Madison and Jefferson respectively. On the somewhat dubious thesis that aliens were under the protection of the states in which they resided and the more substantial one that the Sedition Acts violated the Bill of Rights, these resolves declared that Congress had exceeded its constitutional powers in passing the Alien and Sedition Acts and called upon the other states to join in declaring the acts null and void. This appeal was based on the "compact" theory of the Constitution. This theory held that the Federal Union was formed by a compact among the several states, each acting in its sovereign capacity, whereby limited powers were granted to a central authority. As the parties to the compact, the states were the proper judges of whether its terms were being observed and were entitled to declare inoperative any act of Congress which they deemed to be beyond the powers delegated to the Federal government.

These resolves were intended simply as campaign material for the election of 1800, and neither of the authors seems to have sensed the future implications of his arguments, although each, as President of the United States, was destined to have them flung back at him by embittered Federalists. In later years, the compact theory was elaborated into the doctrine of nullification, that any one state could nullify a Federal act which it deemed unconstitutional, and, much more ominous, into the doctrine of secession, that a state, as a last resort, could resume its sovereign powers and withdraw from the Union.

That a major crisis did not develop immediately was due chiefly to John Adam's sturdy refusal to be stampeded into reckless decisions by the Hamiltonians. He made little use of the powers given to him by the Alien and Sedition Acts, and he terminated hostilities with France as soon as he saw a favorable opportunity. The latter step was the most creditable act of a long and honorable career. Although their attack on civil liberties had cost the Federalists heavily in public support, if Adams had let the quarrel with France grow into open war, he would undoubtedly have been reelected in a wave of patriotic enthusiasm. But he believed that the United States needed peace more than John Adams needed a second term. His decision not only deprived him of the one issue which could have beaten the Republicans; it intensified the dissension in his own party.

Election of Jefferson. The election of 1800 was a sweeping Republican victory. The party won control of both Houses of Congress, and its Presidential candidates, Jefferson and Aaron Burr, received 73 electoral votes each, to 65 for Adams and 64 for C. C. Pinckney. This tie, as was described previously, resulted from the original provisions of the Constitution for the electoral college, whereby each elector voted for two candidates for President. One Republican elector should have voted by arrangement for someone other than Burr—anyone would have done—but this precaution was overlooked. In consequence, the choice between the two was thrown into the outgoing House of Representatives, still controlled by the Federalists, and an attempt developed to give the presidency to Burr, a machine politician who might be won over to Federalism. This time it was Alexander Hamilton's turn to put country above party. Much as he disapproved of Jefferson, he preferred him to Burr, and he also felt that the people had clearly intended Jefferson to be President. Finally, after a long deadlock, Hamilton's influence swung the election to Jefferson.

Thomas Jefferson himself always believed that the Republican victory in 1800 had saved popular government in the United States. His opponents, on the other hand, regarded his election as a national disaster. Pious old ladies in New England buried their Bibles to prevent the "atheist" Jefferson from burning them, and men who should have known better bemoaned the inevitable collapse of their country into anarchy and Jacobinism. Actually, the election affected the United States very slightly. The pomp with which Washington and Adams had surrounded the presidency was replaced by an easygoing simplicity, some Federalist officeholders were removed in favor of Republicans, and that was about all. Its mild impact on American life is, in fact, the significant feature of the election. It demonstrated that the Constitution would function successfully under the conditions of party rivalry which are a normal feature of free government and that control of the Federal machinery could change hands in an orderly and peaceful manner.

JUDICIAL INTERPRETATION

The judiciary was the one part of the national government to remain outside Republican control after the election of 1800, but it proved to be an extremely important exception. During the first ten years of their existence, the Federal courts had operated in relative obscurity. Although they had clearly established their right to pass on the constitutionality of Federal and state legislation, they had not utilized this power to any great extent. The elaboration of judicial review into an instrument for making the Supreme Court of the United States the final authority on the Constitution came after 1801, or, to state it accurately, after the appointment of John Marshall as Chief Justice.

Marshall, a Virginian and a distant relative of Thomas Jefferson, was given his post by John Adams in the last few weeks of Adam's presidential term. An ardent Federalist, he took a broad view of the powers of the national government and considered it his duty to protect the rights of property against the encroachments of Republicanism. He was not a legal scholar, but he had an incisive analytical mind which could go to the heart of a problem and grasp the basic issues involved and an ability to express his opinions in clear and forceful language. His normal procedure was to make his decision and assign one of his colleagues to provide the legal support for the verdict—"Brother Story will add the citations." The measure of his personality is revealed in the fact that he dominated the Supreme Court until his death in 1835, although all during that period a succession of Republican Presidents appointed a succession of Republican justices in the hope of building up an anti-Marshall majority. Almost invariably the new appointees fell under Marshall's spell, including "Brother Story," or Justice Joseph Story of Massachusetts, who was one of the brightest Republican legal lights when Jefferson placed him on the Supreme Court but who became Marshall's most devoted adherent.

Marbury v. Madison. Marshall's first objective upon becoming Chief Justice was to assert the authority of the Federal judiciary in unmistakable fashion. He found his opportunity in the case of *Marbury v. Madison.* In February, 1801, just before the incoming Republicans took over the national government, the Adams administration passed a new Judiciary Act greatly expanding the Federal courts. The act was admittedly needed, but the defeated Federalists might properly have left the task to their successors, and they clouded their motives by displaying an indecent haste to fill the new judicial positions with good Federalists. According to legend, as midnight on 3 March 1801 approached, John Marshall, who was serving as Secretary of State although he had already been appointed Chief Justice, was busy signing commissions with James Madison, the incoming Secretary, standing over him watch in hand.

William Marbury was one of these "midnight justices" whose commission had been signed and sealed but not delivered. Madison refused to give it to him, whereupon Marbury applied to the Supreme Court, under the provision of a section of the Judiciary Act of 1789, for a writ of mandamus to compel Madison to deliver the commission. In his decision, Marshall held that, as the law stood, Marbury was entitled to his commission but that the Supreme Court could not issue his writ because the law under which he had brought suit was unconstitutional. He maintained that, since the Constitution had specifically given the Supreme Court original jurisdiction in certain cases and appellate jurisdiction in all others, Congress could not enlarge the Court's original jurisdiction by legislation. It was the first time the Supreme Court had held an Act of Congress unconstitutional, and, in doing so, Marshall emphatically asserted the right of the judiciary to function as interpreters of the Constitution. He concluded his opinion:

> The particular phraseology of the Constitution of the United States confirms and strengthens the principle, supposed to be essential to all

written constitutions, that a law repugnant to the constitution is void, and that courts, as well as other departments, are bound by that instrument.

Obviously, if the courts were obligated to determine whether Federal and state laws conformed to the Constitution, they would have to exercise the power of deciding what the Constitution meant.

Marshall and American Nationalism. In Marshall's hands, this power became an instrument for giving judicial sanction to the nationalistic concept of the Constitution as opposed to the compact theory expounded in the Virginia and Kentucky Resolutions—in other words, to the concept that the Federal government was a national government, possessing sovereignty in its own right within the sphere of its authority, and not merely the agent of a group of sovereign states. The decisions by which this doctrine was imbedded in the American system of government can be divided into three general categories: (1) those which increased the authority of Federal courts; (2) those which restricted the powers of the states; and (3) those which expanded the powers of the Federal government.

Marbury v. Madison is the most important case in the first class, with *Cohens v. Virginia* (1821) ranking next. The Cohens case involved two men convicted by Virginia courts for selling lottery tickets, in violation of Virginia law but under the presumed protection of an Act of Congress. Marshall upheld their conviction, but the important part of his decision was his assertion of the right of the Supreme Court to take cognizance of an appeal from a state court where the validity of a Federal statute was in question, even if the parties involved were the state itself and one of its own citizens. He held that such an appeal was not a suit against a state within the meaning of the Eleventh Amendment, which prohibits a state from being sued in the Federal courts. In support of this ruling Marshall declared:

> America has chosen to be, in many respects, and to many purposes, a nation; and for all these purposes her government is complete; to all these objects it is competent. The people have declared that in the exercise of all the powers given for these objects it is supreme. It can, then, in effecting these objects, legitimately control all individuals or governments within the American territory.

The Sanctity of Contract. Of the major decisions restricting the power of states, two were based on the clause in the Constitution forbidding states to impair the right of contract. The first, *Fletcher v. Peck* (1810), arose from an effort by the Georgia legislature to rescind a land grant made by its predecessors under conditions of acknowledged fraud. Marshall held that the courts could not go into the motives behind the passage of a legislative act. The original grant was valid and constituted a contract between the state and the grantees; the subsequent act revoking the grant was an impairment of contract and, therefore, unconstitutional. The second case, *Dartmouth College v. Woodward* (1819), involved an attempt by the state of New Hampshire to revise the charter of Dartmouth College so as to bring the institution under control of the state. The fact that the legislature was Republican and the trustees of the college were Federalists was at least partly responsible for this action. Whether it affected Marshall's decision or not is another matter. He maintained, at any rate, that the charter issued to Dartmouth College by George III in 1769 was a contract, binding on the state of New Hampshire as successor to the rights and obligations of the British crown, and that the state could not constitutionally alter the charter without the consent of the college authorities. This decision has been of paramount importance in protecting religious and educational institutions operating under charter from arbitrary political interference. It also had some influence in restricting the regulation of business corporations by the states, until later courts modified Marshall's doctrine by allowing the states to use their "police power" to safeguard the public interest.

The Commerce Clause. Marshall's nationalism appears most prominently in the two great cases of the third category, *Gibbons v. Ogden* (1824) and *McCulloch v. Maryland* (1819). The first developed because the State of New York had conferred a monopoly of steamboat traffic in New York waters on Robert Fulton and his politically powerful relatives, the Livingstons. Ogden, a licensee of the monopoly, had tried to restrain Gibbons from operating a steamboat between New York and New Jersey under a Federal coasting license. The question at issue was the extent of the power given to the national government by the commerce clause of the Constitution. Did it include the control of navigation, could it be exercised inside a state, and did the states have a concurrent and possibly conflicting jurisdiction within their own borders? Marshall's ruling on these points declared:

> The word used in the constitution, then, comprehends, and has always been understood to comprehend, navigation within its meaning; and a power to regulate navigation is as expressly granted as if that term had been added to the word "commerce." . . .
>
> Commerce among the states cannot stop at the external boundary-line of each state, but may be introduced into the interior. . . . If Congress has the power to regulate it, that power must be exercised where the subject exists. . . .
>
> . . . In exercising the power of regulating their own internal affairs, whether of trading or police, the states may sometimes enact laws the validity of which depends on their interfering with, and being

contrary to, an act of Congress passed in pursuance of the constitution. . . . In every such case the act of Congress, or treaty, is supreme; and the law of the state, though enacted in the exercise of powers not controverted, must yield to it.

The New York monopoly was accordingly held unconstitutional. Marshall's decision opened a wide field for the exercise of Federal power through the agency of the commerce clause and also prevented American commerce from being strangled by a mass of local restrictions.

Implied Powers. *McCulloch v. Maryland* was the greatest of all Marshall's constitutional decisions. It was repetition, in almost exactly the same terms, of the controversy between Hamilton and Jefferson over the right of Congress to charter a national bank, this time with the Supreme Court as arbiter instead of the President. Hamilton's Bank of the United States had been permitted to go out of existence upon the expiration of its charter in 1811, but the financial confusion which developed during the War of 1812 compelled the Republicans themselves to establish a Second Bank of the United States in 1816, modeled on the first and with power to establish branches in various parts of the country. The state of Maryland, adhering to the pure Jeffersonian doctrine, moved to attack the "monster" by imposing a tax on its Baltimore branch, which McCulloch, the cashier of the branch, refused to pay on the ground that the bank was an agency of the United States government and not subject to the jurisdiction of the state. In his decision, Marshall went exhaustively into the character of the Federal Union and not only gave judicial sanction to Hamilton's doctrine of implied powers but expressly rejected the compact theory as untenable. Pointing out that the Constitution had been ratified, not by the state governments, but by the people of each state in their conventions, he said,

> The government of the Union is emphatically and truly a government of the people. In form and substance it emanates from them, its powers are granted by them, and are to be exercised directly on them, and for their benefit.

Then he went on to state the principle of implied powers in its classic form:

> We think the sound construction of the constitution must allow to the national legislature that discretion, with respect to the means by which powers it confers are to be carried into execution, which will enable that body to perform the high duties assigned to it, in the manner most beneficial to the people. Let the end be legitimate, let it be within the scope of the constitution, and all means which are appropriate, which are plainly adapted to that end, which are not prohibited, but consist with the letter and spirit of the constitution, are constitutional.

The Bank, according to Marshall, came within the scope of this definition as a "necessary and proper" means of enabling Congress to perform its constitutional functions of regulating the currency and collecting taxes. It was, therefore, an instrumentality of the Federal government and, as such, could not be taxed by a state. The power to tax, Marshall pointed out, included the power the destroy; if a state could tax a Federal agency at all, it could tax it so heavily as to render its proper functioning impossible. Since the Constitution and laws of the United States had been declared to be "the Supreme law of the land," then the agencies employed to execute them could not be subjected to the authority of the states.

While the doctrines expounded by Marshall have been modified in detail from time to time, his fundamental principles have remained unchanged. No other one man has influenced American government quite so profoundly. His bold assertion of the right of judicial review was mainly responsible for giving the Supreme Court its unique position in the political structure of the United States, a position which makes it by far the most powerful judicial body in the world. More important, by placing the power of the courts behind a broad construction of the Constitution, Marshall gave the concept of the nature of the Federal Union an advantage which the states-rights doctrine was never afterward able to overcome, and he thereby did much to make the Constitution an instrument capable of being adapted to the changing needs of an expanding nation. He also—and this was certainly inadvertent on Marshall's part— helped to make the Federal Union a rallying point for the democratic ideal, because, in order to refute the thesis that the Union was a creation of the states and that they were the ultimate repositories of sovereignty, he emphasized the doctrine that the Union was created by the whole people of the United States and from them derived its own independent sovereignty.

PART THREE

The Era of the French Revolution and Napoleon

Few events of modern times have been as far-reaching in their effects as the revolution which broke out in France in 1789. The French Revolution has been called "the great turning point of modern civilization" for many reasons, among the most important being the emphasis which it put upon individualism, a characteristic of Western civilization ever since. Originally intended merely to correct existing legal and financial abuses, it was destined to sweep away the Old Regime in France, bring almost a quarter of a century of war to Europe and other continents as well, and transform Europe, and hence the world, into a radically different state of affairs than existed almost universally in 1789. The Revolution was profoundly affected by the philosophy of the eighteenth century with its emphasis upon man and his individualism and perhaps would never have taken place except for this prevalent ideology. This stress upon freedom was matched by an equal insistence on the principle of equality of opportunity or "career open to the talents."

At the outset, the Revolution was the product of the French aristocracy which resented its subordination by the court. It was this class (the aristocrats) who alone had sufficient legal standing to force the king to summon the States General. The increasingly powerful *bourgeoisie* was in no such position. But it was the middle class which quickly wrested the initiative from the aristocracy and took over control, only to lose it temporarily to a popular movement in 1793 to 1794, during the Terror. This interruption was brief but telling, and, while the *bourgeoisie* regained its leadership and maintained it henceforth, the Terror markedly influenced subsequent events. As Chateaubriand so well put it: "The patricians began the Revolution; the plebeians finished it."

The effects of the Revolution on the world have been very extensive —not the least of which has been to make war something which directly touches the lives of all the citizens of a country engaged in it. Furthermore, it commenced the destruction of all the old ties which characterized the Old Regime everywhere. Its influence upon modern nationalism has been especially great. As a result of the wars of the French Revolution and Napoleon, people everywhere have come to feel that they possess in their own nation peculiar characteristics which set them above others. This persistent feeling was destined to make the promotion of a universal world order based on the brotherhood of man most difficult of attainment. On the other hand, "Liberty, Equality, and Fraternity," which became the slogan of the French Revolution, are words emblazoned forever throughout the world. They were words which encouraged the liberals of the nineteenth century as they sought by revolution to make them meaningful in their own lands.

10

The French Revolution

The eighteenth century had witnessed a remarkable criticism of the order of things in France. The absolute monarchy of Louis XIV (1643–1715) had brought the French people only a series of disastrous wars and defeats, oppression, and unhappiness, while England, a land of relatively free thought and political freedom, had prospered and grown powerful. Only in the realm of literature had France attained preeminence during the reign of Louis. This success was attributed to the fact that the great writers of this period had followed the dictates of reason. Consequently, it came to be taken for granted that neither the traditional religion of France nor her government could pass the tests demanded by reason. Already during the reign of the Sun King, religious skepticism had become manifest and had been accelerated during the reign of his successor, Louis XV. A number of writers commissioned themselves to lead the people in a fight against the institutions of government and religion as they then existed. These men called themselves the *philosophes*.

Chief among their mediums of action were the *salons*, the learned societies, and the Masonic lodges. In these places, the spirit of the Enlightenment spread until it had made inroads even among members of the clergy, not to mention high financial circles and the aristocracy. In the cafés and elsewhere, public and semipublic discussions were numerous. There were even reading and thinking societies which met to discuss the latest works of the *philosophes*.

These men helped the middle class appreciate more fully its grievances and also its strength. The success of the American Revolution greatly aided their work. They could point to the example of a people which had dared to invoke the right to rebel against those who ruled them

159

contrary to the theory of the natural rights of man. The Declaration of Independence and the Articles of Confederation were widely studied and admired.

In the earlier part of the century, the Marquis de Montesquieu (1689–1755) mocked French religion and institutions in his *Persian Letters.* This clearly recognized, albeit indirect, attack on the Old Regime was highly successful. Montesquieu's best-known work was his *Spirit of the Laws,* published in 1748. He manifested a preference for a constitutional monarchy, but it was his advocacy of separation of the various branches of government which gave the book its chief fame and later had an influence on the American and French revolutions.

Voltaire. The outstanding champion of the Age of Reason was Voltaire (Jean François Marie Arouet), who lived from 1694 to 1778. As a young man, he achieved fame in the aristocratic *salons* of Paris but was thrown into prison by a young nobleman whom he had offended, and was freed only on the condition he would leave France. Three years of exile in England won him some attention through the publication of his *Letters on the English,* which appeared in French in 1734. His praise of the English way of life contrasted with the lack of similar virtues in France. He managed to return home for some years and then spent three years at the court of Frederick the Great in Prussia. After a violent quarrel with Frederick, Voltaire returned home and, in 1760, settled down in a small town near the Swiss border where, rich and independent, he devoted his remaining years to a fierce fight against the Catholic Church. Newspaperman, historian, poet, militant conversationalist, this cynical man became the idol of an age which resembled him. He was sometimes even called "King" Voltaire, so widely was he known and so great was his influence. With his driving energy and devastating personality he contributed much toward destroying for many people their respect for established authority.

His contemporary and opponent, Jean Jacques Rousseau (1712–1778), a Swiss, first achieved fame in Paris when he won a prize for an essay in 1749. He maintained that the wickedness of man was due to what he saw in society. His ideas were developed in such works as *The New Héloïse* (1761), sometimes regarded as an attack on the institutions of marriage and the family, *Émile* (1762), where he outlined his ideas on education, and the *Social Contract* (1762).

Rousseau. Actually, Rousseau was not one of the *philosophes* as such. In fact, he deplored their shortcomings. Yet his influence in causing the downfall of the Old Regime, especially in the years following his death, was very great. Looking about for something on which to base an attack against the age in which he lived, he hit upon nature. All that a man required to attain happiness was to follow nature and abandon himself to the dictates of his heart. It is not amiss to point out here that this philosopher of sentimentality and the natural failed to distinguish between what is natural and what is primitive and, to a considerable extent, was guilty of escapism. His *Social Contract* preached the untrammeled sovereignty of the people, to be exercised in accordance with what Rousseau called the "general will," an abstraction referring to the desire of the people as a whole to do what is best for themselves. Normally this general will would be expressed by the will of the majority, but not always since majorities can be wrong. In the absence of any satisfactory method of determining the general will, Rousseau held that the will of the majority must be supreme.

His claim that sovereignty resides in the people and that governments derive their power from the consent of those who are governed combined with the attacks on the Old Regime by the *philosophes* to act in an incendiary fashion upon the minds of Frenchmen of the day. Before passing to a consideration of the concrete results of the attacks on church and state, it is necessary briefly to make mention of the *Encyclopedia,* a monumental undertaking consisting of thirty-five volumes. Directed by Denis Diderot (1713–1784), it was completed in 1765, and almost all the *philosophes* were contributors. Instrumental in making its publication possible despite the strong attempts at suppression was Madame de Pompadour, one of the king's mistresses.

It endeavored to show to what point human reason had caused science and literature to progress and also to demonstrate that mankind could do perfectly well without religion. Diderot, the editor, was as much of an anticlerical as was Voltaire. The work had a great success since it was recognized as a propaganda vehicle for the dissemination of the aims and spirit of the *philosophes*.

Thus, from the brief foregoing description, it can be seen that in the field of ideas the ground for a revolution in France had been carefully cultivated throughout the eighteenth century. Yet the student must not conclude that the French Revolution was the product of the *philosophes* alone. The causes of this titanic event may be found in financial and agrarian conditions, the rise of a strong middle class, the general inefficiency of the government, and a widespread impatience to improve the nation's condition. The big contribution of the *philosophes* lies in their success in weakening respect for the authority on which the Old Regime was based.

THE NATIONAL ASSEMBLY

Mention has already been made in the text of the conditions under which society lived under the Old Regime throughout Europe. Suffice it to say here that by 1788 in France both the middle class and large segments of the masses were eager for improvement of their government, which was faced with bankruptcy. It might be noted again that part of France's financial embarrassment could be traced to the aid given to the American colonies during the revolution. At any rate, the French people greeted with great joy the announcement of the king that elections were to be held to choose the members for a meeting of the States General, to open 1 May 1789. This body had not met since 1614, and the hopes which people previously had were now increased. Yet almost immediately a controversy arose over the manner in which the States General should meet and also vote. The First and Second Estates, the clergy and nobles, respectively, maintained that each body should meet separately and that voting should be by Estates rather than individuals. The people pointed out the inconsistency here involved in that their representatives, chosen by approximately ninety per cent of the nation's population, could be outvoted by the representatives of such a small minority. They insisted that the number of seats allotted to the Third Estate be doubled in order to give equality of representation. The government yielded to this demand late in December, 1788, but remained adamant in refusing to grant voting by head instead of by order.

Elections to choose the members of the various Estates were held in the spring of 1789. It was a time when conditions, owing to a hard winter, were very bad. The Third Estate elected over five hundred members, over half of whom were lawyers, and an equal number of alternates who also went to Versailles for the session and so augmented the ranks of the commoners.

All over the land, lists of grievances and suggestions for remedying conditions were drawn up and sent with the representatives to the meeting of the estates. These lists, called *cahiers,* revealed a remarkable agreement on the need for reducing the power of the monarchy to a limited one with a responsible ministry, a representative legislative body, tax redress, improvement of land conditions, and the establishment of guarantees of personal civic liberties for the citizens.

The States General. After some preliminaries, the formal opening of the States General took place on 4 May 1789. As yet, no concession to the wishes of the Third Estate for equality of voting had been granted, a fact which charged the atmosphere. After more than a month of quarreling over this point, the commoners decided to act. On 12 June under the inspiration of the Abbé Siéyès, who had deserted the First Estate and joined the Third, they adopted the attitude that they were the representatives not of a class but of the *nation.* This step attracted a number of members of the lower clergy who felt closer to the commoners than to their own body. Thus strengthened, the Third Estate proclaimed itself on 17 June to be the National Assembly. In this announcement may be seen the first real step of the revolution. The 19th of June saw the First Estate, following a close contest, vote to join the Third and thereby sanction its action.

The following day when the members came to their chamber for deliberation, they found it closed, ostensibly for repairs. Instead of being coerced, they repaired to a nearby indoor tennis court where they took the "Tennis Court Oath," swearing not to separate until they secured for the French people a constitution. Within one week, enough new recruits from the two upper bodies had gone over to their ranks to warrant their taking the name of the National Constituent Assembly. Subsequently, on the 27th, Louis XVI recognized their victory and ordered the remaining members of the upper groups to join this body.

Meanwhile, conditions throughout the country had failed to improve. There was an acute food shortage and prices were extremely high. So important is this point that one French historian has said, "If bread had been cheap, the brutal intervention of the people, which was indispensable to assure the destruction of the Old Regime, would perhaps not have occurred, and the *bourgeoisie* would have triumphed less easily." Added to this was the difficulty that the king's acceptance of the situation in the States General was not what it seemed. A strong concentration of troops around Paris and Versailles had begun to take place early in July. In the city itself, flotsam and jetsam from all over the land had gathered. Many of the new arrivals were desperate adventurers ready to risk anything. In such an atmosphere of unrest, excitement, and suspicion, a rumor spread that the troops had arrived to quell the National Assembly.

Mirabeau, a member of that body, raised the question in the Assembly, and the king replied that the troops were merely for the purpose of protecting the Assembly. But his actions belied his words and on 11 July he dismissed Necker, the liberal minister who served as a check on those close to the king who were urging him to stage a royal *coup d'état* against the Assembly. News of Necker's dismissal the next day brought a great public demonstration on his behalf in Paris, which at times reached serious proportions and caused considerable damage and looting. On the 13th the electors of Paris took it upon themselves to reorganize the local government. They also formed a middle-class police force to maintain order and protect lives and property. This body marked the beginning of the National Guard. Thus was the old system of local government changed at the outset of the revolution. Other large cities quickly followed the example of Paris.

Storming of the Bastille. The situation grew worse by the morning of 14 July, with the result that a mob began collecting outside the Bastille, an old prison where according to popular legend many victims of an unjust government were incarcerated. More important was the fact that the building symbolized the Old Regime. The commander of the garrison, one De Launay, had only about a hundred men at his disposal, including some Swiss mercenaries. After hours of indecision, it appears that someone among the defenders fired on the crowd. An exchange resulted and the mob laid siege to the fortress. Aware of the helplessness of the situation, the commander of the Bastille surrendered on an agreement that he and his men would be given a safe passage. As a result perhaps of the losses the attackers had suffered, the promise was treacherously broken, and De Launay and his men were slaughtered and mutilated. The cells were emptied and yielded the sum total of seven prisoners, all of whom seem deservedly to have been there, although two of the wretches were insane. Symbolically, the fall of the Bastille was so important that its anniversary has become the French Fourth of July. Immediately, the events of that day had effects. The king announced the next day that he had ordered the troops from Versailles, and, on the 16th, recalled the popular but incompetent Necker. Publicly the king visited Paris and openly appeared to accept with good grace the whole series of swiftly moving events.

Already, in the provinces July had produced violence owing to famine conditions that were rather widespread. This real suffering was made worse by the spread of fantastic rumors concerning what would happen next as a result of events in Paris. This combination of the real and the imaginary produced a state of near rebellion. In the grip of a wild fear—the "Great Fear" it was called—acts of violence and lawlessness took place. Not only did the agrarian people rise up in many sections of the land but the townsfolk attacked those they deemed to be their oppressors. When word came of the fall of the Bastille, the chaos was increased. Out of this welter of confusion, there emerges quite clearly the fact that the peasants were determined to secure the abolition of feudal dues. The new National Guard was soon able to quell these peasant uprisings. Their services had been brought into play by the leaders of the municipalities, who were men of property, frightened by the trend of events.

Reports from the country began pouring into the Assembly and produced quite a degree of concern in that body. Being essentially a bourgeois body, its sympathies did not go out to the peasants. Yet it was obvious that the Assembly had done little to help the peasants, whose *cahiers* showed quite clearly what their grievances were.

Abolition of Feudal Privileges. On the night of 4 August, such liberal nobles as the Vicomte de Noailles, who had nothing to give himself, and the Duc d'Aiguillon spoke in favor of voluntarily abolishing feudal dues. These speeches touched off a veritable orgy of self-sacrifice which lasted well into the morning. Privilege after privilege, including some of a clerical nature, was freely abandoned by the suddenly magnanimous Assembly, some of whose members were astute enough to recognize the value of such an act voluntarily performed before it might be forcibly required. Later, in the cool, calm light of reason, some financial modifications were made. Nonetheless, the significance of the events of that night was great. It meant the end of the feudal system and the guilds and the appearance of equality of taxation, opportunity, and civil privilege.

In the remaining days of August, the deputies resumed their discussion of a proposed bill of rights, which news of the "Great Fear" had interrupted. The result of their work was announced under the title of the Declaration of the Rights of Man and the Citizen. It was largely based on English and American models but also bore the strong imprint of the philosophy of Rousseau.

Every citizen was said to be born free and to possess rights older than any existing society. These included liberty, property, security, and resistance to oppression. The nation was sovereign, and law was defined as "the expression of the general will." Religious liberty (provided it did not "derange the public order established by law") and freedom of speech and the press were privileges guaranteed the citizens. All public officials were servants of the people, who were entitled to protection from arbitrary action on the part of such persons. Equality of taxation was pledged also. A careful reading of the Declaration will reveal that its intent was to level the aristocracy to a state of equality with the middle class, but not to raise the masses. Yet this statement was to serve later as the model for the constitution framers of a number of European countries.

A new crisis developed on 5 and 6 October when the march of the Parisian women to Versailles took place. This event was caused by a combination of an acute shortage of bread in Paris and the king's delay in signing the legislation implementing the work of the night of 4 August and the recent Declaration of the Rights of Man. During the confusion on the morning of the 6th, some of the women managed to enter the queen's chambers, and Marie-Antoinette narrowly escaped with her life. General Lafayette, who had been sent from Paris with the National Guard to protect the royal family, prevailed upon the monarchs to appear before the people a little later. At that time, a cry of "On to Paris!" arose, and the king agreed to return with the people and to see to it that Paris was properly provisioned. That evening, the royal family was ensconced in the Tuileries. Since "the baker, the baker's wife, and the baker's boy" were now in Paris, the Assembly followed suit by shortly moving to the capital from Versailles.

Confiscation of Church Property. Because of the need for funds to conduct the expenses of the government and owing to the general confusion which made the collection of taxes an impossibility, the Assembly decided on a far-reaching step 2 November 1789. It was voted to appropriate the lands of the church and to issue paper currency, called the *assignats,* based on this confiscated property. The Assembly now assumed the task of the support of the clergy, payment of expenses involved in holding services, and such former functions of the church as education, poor relief, and care of the sick and aged. At first, the *assignats* were not legal tender but merely notes bearing 4 per cent interest and granting certain privileges relative to purchase of church lands. By August, 1790, they had become legal tender, still supported by the expropriated church lands. These notes operated in such a fashion that they aided the revolution by tying to its fortunes a whole class of people whose stake in life depended on the government. This seizure of church property and the assumption of the Catholic Church's financial obligations left the Assembly with a number of difficult problems.

Prior to the expropriation of these lands and property, the Assembly had passed a provisional law in October, 1789, suspending monastic orders. On 13 February 1790, all monastic vows were suppressed, and religious orders which required vows were abolished. The members of such disbanded groups were strongly urged to become civilians on a pension but were permitted, if they so desired, to enter one of the monastic houses which the government designated to be set aside for this purpose.

On 12 July 1790 came the passage of a law dealing with the secular clergy, who had earlier suffered the loss of their lands and property. The measures embodied in this day's legislation are called the Civil Constitution of the Clergy. Provision was made for the election of priests and bishops by the electorate regardless of their religious affiliations, according to a view that the ecclesiastics were public servants. Clergymen were later forced to swear an oath to support this legislation. Those who refused were to be dropped by the state from the rolls and given pensions. Continuation of one's priestly duties without taking the oath would mean persecution. Louis XVI agreed 26 December 1790 to approve this legislation but acted under duress. Only seven bishops in the country agreed to the oath, among them being Talleyrand; over fifty per cent of the lower clergy likewise refused.

Clash between Catholic Church and Revolution. Then, in March and April, 1791, Pope Pius VI condemned officially this French legislation together with various earlier acts such as the abolition of the tithes. Even more dynamic was his condemnation of the principles of the French Revolution itself, a logical step if one recalls that the revolution was so largely the outcome of eighteenth-century rationalism.

In the light of future events, it is difficult to overestimate the significance of this anticlerical legislation by the Assembly. It meant, for ex-

ample, that the king was faced with choosing between his faith, in which
he sincerely believed, and the revolution, which he hoped to control. Not
only the king but all Catholics were now in conscience forced to reject
the revolution. The consequence was a divided nation. Obviously, the
government reasoned that it must stand behind the "juring" clergy and
take strong steps to punish the "nonjurors," or refractory priests. Concretely, this decision led to more measures aimed against such churchmen.
This persecution was a very patent interference with freedom of religion
but was justified on the grounds of the wording in the Declaration of
the Rights of Man. Whatever the reasons behind such legislation, the
results could not fail to be harmful to France. It precipitated a veritable
counterrevolution of a very sanguinary nature.

At this juncture, the royal family determined upon a desperate step.
On 20 June 1791, they set out from the Tuileries, bound for the eastern
border where there were loyal troops. Beyond in Luxembourg waited the
Austrians of the queen's brother, Emperor Leopold. The hapless family
was apprehended almost within sight of safety and forced to return to
Paris. However, the king was forgiven through the invention of a fiction
by those in the Assembly who feared for the safety of the constitutional
monarchy they were bent on establishing. Nonetheless, the capture at
Varennes played into the hands of those who favored a republic, and they
strove the harder to realize their hopes.

At present, the strength of the republicans was insufficient, and on
30 September 1791, the Assembly was dissolved after having voted its
members ineligible for election to the new legislature, which would operate under the constitution drawn up by the Assembly and accepted by
the king on 14 September.

THE OVERTHROW OF THE MONARCHY

This body, known as the Legislative Assembly, held its inauguration
1 October. The membership numbered 745, elected by what were
euphemistically called the "active citizens," *i.e.,* the middle class. In its
ranks were groupings which bore a faint resemblance to political parties
but which lacked unity and discipline and were highly individualistic.
The Right, firm believers in a constitutional monarchy, was chiefly made
up of a faction called the Feuillants. On the Left sat the Girondins, so
named because their chief leaders were from the department of Gironde
(Bordeaux). This group ardently advocated the abolition of the monarchy in favor of a republic. Between these two extremes sat the majority
of the legislators torn between the sentiments of these opposing groups.
The greater verve and drive of the Girondins slowly but surely won most
of this group over to their way of thinking.

Most of the members of the Legislative Assembly were newcomers to parliamentary procedure. They were local lights whose work in the provinces had closely followed that of the National Assembly. Their religious and financial policy was based on that of their predecessors at Paris. Their unique achievement was the plunging of France into foreign war at a time when a Girondin ministry was in power, headed by Roland and Dumouriez. This group seem to have had a complex which made them feel that France was chosen to lead a people's crusade against the Old Regime in Europe. Incidentally, they felt as many before and since them have felt, that war would entrench them in power.

Outbreak of War. They defended their action on the grounds, first, that many prominent French *émigrés* were intriguing against the government in the courts of Europe, and, second, that many German princes who owned lands in Alsace were refusing to give up their feudal dues. Moreover, on 27 August, the Prussian King, Frederick William II (1786–1797), and the Austrian Emperor, Leopold II (1790–1792), had issued the Declaration of Pillnitz, which stated that they would interfere in France if the powers, including England, gave their unanimous consent. On 7 February 1792, these two nations signed an alliance against France. This statement at Pillnitz was given a different connotation in France and helped rally popular support to the government. Consequently, on 20 April 1792, the Legislative Assembly declared war on Austria, which was immediately joined by Prussia. Thus commenced nearly a quarter of a century of warfare, which was to spread throughout Europe and much of the rest of the world. The Girondins who had pushed through the war declaration claimed it was "the just defense of a just people against the unjust aggression of a king." France's powerful opponents were convinced of her military unpreparedness and were confident of an easy victory. It was true that the French officer corps had suffered numerous defections since the revolution began and that the remaining aristocratic officers were not trusted. Moreover, there was too great a spirit of equalitarianism abroad in the ranks to make for efficiency. The French seemed to offer proof of the justification of their adversaries' confidence, because the war opened with a series of reverses, which tended to heighten a revolutionary spirit of unrest which was pervading Paris.

Excitement grew apace, and rumors spread like wildfire in Paris. It was bruited about that Louis XVI was guilty of treason against the nation. On 20 June a wild mob attacked the Tuileries, but the coolness of the monarch stemmed them. As the war continued to fare badly, the Assembly announced in July that the country was in mortal danger and called for the formation of a volunteer army. At this point, the Prussian commander, the old Duke of Brunswick, issued a manifesto, which said that the allies intended to restore Louis XVI to his full power and threatened vengeance on Paris if anything happened to the king or his family.

Then came what appears to have been a carefully formulated plot by Parisian extremists to overthrow the monarchy once and for all. On the night of 9 August, the legal Paris Commune (municipal government) was overthrown by a revolutionary group, and there then ensued a well-planned attack on the Tuileries led by the National Guard and other armed men. The palace, defended only by the Swiss guard and the king's personal noble retainers, was ordered surrendered by Louis, who took refuge with the members of the Assembly. The attackers butchered the Swiss and ransacked the palace.

The September Massacres. The king was then ordered suspended from his functions and placed under arrest. In its fright, the Assembly arranged for a temporary executive and called for the election by universal manhood suffrage of a new assembly to draw up a constitution for the country. Meantime, the Paris Commune and the Jacobin clubs were virtually supreme when news came that Verdun had fallen. A call went out for more volunteers to defend the country, but first an outlet was given to primitive emotions. From 2 to 7 September, there took place the infamous September Massacres in Paris. Many prisoners, including a large number of "refractory" priests, were in some cases given mock trials and then summarily executed. In other instances, they were simply brutally slaughtered on the grounds that a royalist plot to surrender Paris to the foreigners had been conceived. Elsewhere in France similar episodes took place.

THE RADICAL REPUBLIC

The elections for the new assembly, the National Convention, coincided with a veritable wave of hatred against the Old Regime and the king, cleverly stirred up. Highhanded methods were employed to prevent any royalist sympathizers from voting in the contests, which were run off in August and September. Just the day before the new revolutionary assembly formally opened, the French under Dumouriez and Kellermann turned back the Prussians at Valmy in a rather quaint battle. The moral uplift which came with this news was enormous. Valmy proved to be a dominant influence in keeping Paris from occupation and in turning the tide of the war.

In theory but not in practice elected by universal manhood suffrage, the new legislative body was composed entirely of republicans. The Girondins, led by Brissot, Condorcet, and Roland, sat on the Right. The Center was to be held down by the Plain (or the Marsh as it was scornfully called), headed by Abbé Sieyès. This body possessed a majority. On the Left was the Mountain[1] led by Robespierre, Danton, the artful Duke of Orleans, Philippe Égalité, cousin of the king, Marat, Desmoulins, and many others, including the "orator of all mankind," Anacharsis Klootz, a renegade Prussian baron. These groups were not political parties in the real sense, it must be remembered; they were collections of people who felt that for the most part they were among kindred spirits. People were free to come and go from one group to another and to vote as they desired.

The first important act of the new body was its abolition of the monarchy 21 September 1792. The following day was then designated as the first day of the Year I of the French Republic.

The war continued to go well, and by the end of September the reorganized French volunteers were actually on German soil. On 19 November, intoxicated with success, the French proclaimed through their legislature their desire to aid all peoples who wished to rid themselves of their tyrannical governments and enjoy the blessings of liberty.

Execution of the King. A quarrel within the Convention developed between the Girondins and the Mountain. The Girondins now considered themselves the opponents of violence, whereas the Mountain, largely responsible for the September massacres, justified and praised its use. The trial of the king widened the breach between the two, since the Girondins sought to save him out of a fear that his death might seriously endanger the revolution, whereas the Mountain desired to execute him for treason. The vote, which saw Égalité voting for execution, was narrowly in favor of conviction. The unfortunate monarch was guillotined 21 January 1793 and met his death with the greatest personal courage.

The execution of Louis immediately brought England and Spain into the ranks of those arrayed against the French Republic, with the result that by the summer of 1793 France was opposed by Austria, Prussia, England, Holland, Spain, Sardinia, and Tuscany.[2] In the field of ideological opposition to the revolution was Edmund Burke's famous *Reflections on the French Revolution,* which brought about numerous replies in a war of words in England. Most able of those who dueled with Burke in this battle was Tom Paine.

The powerful opposition which faced France would appear to have been too much for any nation to withstand. However, although most of Europe was in the field, the allies lacked unity of any kind. Moreover, the second partition of Poland, arranged in the summer of 1792, occupied

---

[1] So called from their seats in the chamber, which were the top rows of the left side. They drew strong support from such clubs as the Jacobins (who originally met in a former Dominican convent in the Rue St. Jacques) and the Cordeliers (who first met in a former Franciscan monastery).

[2] The following year the Holy Roman Empire declared war on the French.

Russia and prevented Austria and Prussia from using their full strength against France. There is also the important point that the French were fighting in defense of their homeland and in behalf of a cause a sufficient number of Frenchmen believed to be just. Their forces were not professionals but citizen zealots, whose enthusiasm proved a great advantage.

Domestic opposition was still vocal, and in March a royalist revolt broke out in the Vendée, a part of western France. Furthermore, the desperate financial situation was made worse when food riots were added to it. As if France did not have enough to contend with, military reverses occurred, and France's best general, Dumouriez, deserted in disgust to the Austrians.

Rise of the Jacobins. Gradually, the Convention began to be dominated by the Mountain because of the inability of the Girondins to improve conditions. Emergency decrees were passed in March and April which gave proof of the steady rise of Danton and the Mountain. These energetic measures amounted to the establishment of a virtual dictatorship, under a Committee of Public Safety led by Danton.

Steadily, the tempo of attack against the Girondins was stepped up, but they retaliated by stirring up trouble in the departments. Accordingly, on 2 June, the Mountain revealed its great strength by effecting the arrest of a host of Girondin deputies, including a number of well-known persons. This event gave the Mountain undisputed control, although about a score of the Girondins escaped and precipitated a series of uprisings, called the Federalist revolts, so that by June a large part of the country was in revolt against the Convention. Royalists took advantage of the situation, and their armies in the Vendée considerably extended the territory under their sway. Toulon was besieged by the British fleet under Admiral Hood.

Despite its desperate plight, the Convention managed to find time to write a constitution, which was the original purpose for its being. It proved to be a rather democratic document, yet designedly it appealed to property owners. Wisely, the Mountain decided to have it ratified by the people before it became operative. The voting, held in July, was conclusively in its favor. However, Danton was not returned to the Committee of Public Safety by the members of the Convention because they were sensitive to criticism directed against the failures in both the civil and foreign wars.

At this point, one of the more prominent members of the Mountain, Marat, was assassinated by a young provincial Girondin sympathizer, Charlotte Corday. The death of the "Friend of the People" and the setback dealt to Danton combined to bring to the fore the so-called "Incorruptible," Robespierre, who now dominated the Convention although checked in theory by the other members of the Committee on Public Safety.

An effective reorganization in the summer of 1793 saw the collapse of the Girondin-inspired uprisings owing to lack of unity and direction. Only two cities of importance remained opposed to the Convention. They were Toulon, where the British had been welcomed, and Lyons, which went under a formidable republican attack in August.

The 10th of August, anniversary of the overthrow of the monarchy, was set as the date for the promulgation of the new constitution, but it was never applied because of the dangers inherent in holding elections at such a critical time. Accordingly, the actual operation of the constitution was postponed, and it was made clear that the Convention would govern until peace was declared.

The Nation in Arms. On 23 August, the members decreed the levy of the entire male population capable of bearing arms. All other citizens of both sexes were made liable for national service in whatever way the government deemed desirable, *e.g.,* work in the munitions factories, nursing, etc. The direction of this task was given to Lazare Carnot, whose work was destined to win him the name of the "Organizer of Victory" and, later, to enable one of his descendants to become a President of the Third Republic. The immediate result of this decree was the formation and equipping of fourteen new and hastily trained armies; the long-range result was the new commonly accepted principle of the nation in arms. In September in an attempt to control inflation, maximum prices were imposed on a large number of items and wages were fixed by law.

The following month the capture of Lyons was followed by the slaughter of many inhabitants. The blood which flowed seemed to loose a passion for more, with the result that the queen was guillotined on 16 October. Shortly thereafter, victories were scored over the Vendéens, and thousands of them were put to death over a period of several months. The sanguinary month of October ended with the execution of a score of Girondins. After that the dispatch of Philippe Égalité on the ground of his aristocratic birth followed.

Robespierre and the Terror. These events were part of the Terror which accompanied the victory of the revolutionary government, justified on the grounds of the need for national unity. In the provinces, it took a macabre form, and over ten thousand suspects were slain without the formality of a trial. The real power during this period was the Committee of Public Safety. Despite its successes in 1793, it was under the fire of two opposing factions in the Convention. These were the Hébertists and the Dantonists or *ultras* (extremists) and *citras* (moderates). The former contained a number of men who can best be described as a lunatic fringe. They demanded the rigorous repression of all opponents of the revolution, were merciless opponents of the Catholic Church, and led the way in the movement which abolished the worship of God and substituted for it the cult of Reason. The other group was a collection of individuals with grudges against the Committee of Public Safety. They felt that the revolution had gone far enough in the direction of the left and wished to check it at this point. Danton himself even desired to make peace with the enemy. The existence of these two formidable groups only encouraged Robespierre, who dreamed of crushing them and then welding the forces of the revolution into his ideal, the Republic of Virtue and Equality.

The war itself was vigorously prosecuted and successes won by such young revolutionary generals as Hoche, Pichegru, and Jourdan. It was well for them they were victorious, for the Committee of Public Safety would tolerate no failures from its commanders. It was victory or death, a fact which motivated frequent gambling and the use of unorthodox tactics which often threw the unimaginative professional generals of the opposition into confusion. Toulon was freed from the British in December by a brilliant young artillery expert, Napoleon Bonaparte, a man who had fairly close connections with Robespierre.

Through the simple device of playing off one group against the other, Robespierre and the Committee of Public Safety got rid of their domestic enemies in the spring of 1794. First, the Hébertists were arrested, and on 24 March the chief ones guillotined, including Hébert himself and many of the foreign adherents such as Baron Klootz. Next came the turn of the *citras*. On 5 April, Danton, Desmoulins, *et al.*, were executed. Thus, with the formidable opposition gone, Robespierre was now free to work out his dream, the Republic of Virtue.

The Republic of Virtue. To supplement the civic virtues he so admired, Robespierre realized the need of a religion. Late in 1793, the government had remade the calendar and introduced new names for the months, eliminated the saints' days, and replaced the Sabbath with an arrangement whereby every tenth day would be a holiday, a fact obviously not to the workingman's delight. On 8 June, Robespierre launched his new religion, which he had busily improvised, at a ceremony called the Festival of the Supreme Being.

But he was not long mooning. On 10 June, the powers of the Terror were augmented through the passage of a law granting juries power to convict without evidence suspected opponents of the Republic of Virtue. The consequences of such a law are patent: innocent victims by the drove were herded to the guillotine, and many a grudge was repaid in grisly fashion. The number executed in less than two months exceeded the total number during the past year.

Since Robespierre was popularly identified with this carnage, a reaction against him set in, and he fell victim to a conspiracy. On 27 July, he was arrested along with several close followers, but friends managed his release. Early the next morning, he was again captured, and that night he was guillotined along with many of his closest friends. In this manner the Republic of Virtue ended, to the great delight of the Parisians, whose nerves were at the breaking point. The extremists were now pretty well gone, and in the Convention were more moderate individuals whose only thought was self-preservation. Correctly reading public sentiment, they set out to chart a new course for the revolution. Thus, on 27 July, or the Ninth *Thermidor* (according to the revolutionary calendar), a reaction commenced against the excesses of the immediate past.

THE DIRECTORY

Success in the war, resulting first in the checking of the Prussians and then of the Austrians, was somewhat offset by a series of domestic troubles which were due to bread riots, the revival of monarchist sentiment, the return of various *émigrés,* and other difficulties. The Convention settled down and, by way of reply, demonstrated its conservative trend in the formulation and promulgation of a new constitution, 22 August 1795. This Constitution of the Year III was designed to guarantee the continuance of middle-class control. It vested executive authority in a committee of five Directors who were required to be at least forty years of age. The term of office was five years, and each year a new Director would be chosen. The Directory, as it was called, was to be elected by the legislators and was empowered to appoint ministers and to supervise law enforcement. In an effort to provide some separation of powers, the legislative branch of the government was entrusted to a bicameral body to be elected indirectly. The two houses were, respectively, the Council of Five Hundred, whose duty it was to propose legislation, and the Council of Ancients, which numbered 250 and was authorized to study and pass legislation.

A few days after the constitution was enacted, the Convention passed a law which made mandatory the retention in the new body of two-thirds of the members of the Convention for the first year and one-third for the second year. This unenlightened act provoked immediate reaction. A well-organized Parisian insurrection broke out against the hated Convention, whose name was synonymous with the Terror. However, on 5 October, Napoleon Bonaparte, to whom command of the Convention's troops had been given, ended this uprising with the famous "whiff of grapeshot."

On 26 October, the Convention dissolved itself, and France was launched upon a history of several years of corruption, plots, and intrigues. Within both the Directory and the Councils, there was a split into two main parties, the Constitutional and the Revolutionary. The former did not favor a constitutional monarchy as the reader might suspect from the name but rather was the party of peace, pledged to putting the constitution into full operation. On the other hand, the Revolutionaries sought a continuation of the war and the perpetuation of the revolutionary policies. Basically, their motive was to maintain themselves in office at any cost.

Continuation of War. The big and burning issue of the moment was war or peace. Only England and Austria of the members of the First Coalition were still left in the field. Since the latter had lost Belgium (the Austrian Netherlands) to France through the incorporation of these provinces into the French Republic, 1 October 1795, she desired to keep fighting. Although England hoped for peace, she stood by her ally. Thus, to the satisfaction of the Revolutionary party, the war continued. Meanwhile, the domestic opposition in the Vendée was finally liquidated by the competent young General Lazare Hoche.

Through the brilliant work of Napoleon, Austria was overcome in the First Italian Campaign and forced to sign the Treaty of Campo Formio, 17 October 1797, wherein Bonaparte showed himself a statesman of the first rank as well as a military hero.

At home, a serious domestic difficulty had been encountered with the discovery of a leftist plot against the Directory. Led by one Babeuf, this intrigue was based on a plan to overthrow the Directory by violence and substitute for it a state founded on economic equality for all. Quickly crushed, this conspiracy ended in disaster for its leaders. Then, a projected *coup d'état* by the Constitutional party was overwhelmed on 4 September 1797, when the party in power cracked down on the plotters, whose leaders were mostly shipped to French Guiana and the horrors of the "dry guillotine."

In sole control of the government for the moment, the Revolutionaries now took stock. They were more than ever eager for more foreign war. This is perhaps understandable, if not excusable, when one bears in mind that the armies of France were of little expense to the government. They lived off the land in the occupied countries and shipped wealth in various forms constantly into France. Moreover, continued warfare meant postponement of the serious problems of demobilization with the attendant danger of a military overthrow of the government. In such circumstances, it is no wonder that Napoleon's projected invasion of Egypt to cut Britain's communications with India was enthusiastically supported.

Despite the success of French arms and the gains achieved thereby, the financial condition grew precarious. So, on 30 September 1797, a partial bankruptcy was declared and interest payments were suspended on two-thirds of the public debt. From this time forward, the corrupt Directory was supreme once more, but its troubles mounted. The result was virtually domestic ruin and the constant threat of foreign disaster. The following year saw the passage of the Conscription Law, so desperate had the Directory become. This introduction of the age-class system of military service was destined to become the European standard afterward, but the Directory had great difficulty in making it operative at first because of the war weariness of the populace. Desertions, self-inflicted mutilations, and a sudden real or alleged attachment for the married state became evident.

Fall of the Directory. In such circumstances, the French had to face the Second Coalition of Great Britain, Austria, and Russia, which was formed in late December, 1798. Lesser lights among the opposition included the Ottoman Empire, Portugal, and Naples. As usual, the war opened badly for the French during 1799, and this time it began to look as if all were certain to be lost. The Directory stood discredited through its inability to prosecute the war with the great power at its disposal. Conversely, and perhaps more important from the public view, it had not achieved peace.

The Directory pinned its last hopes for survival on a military man. The general originally chosen was Joubert, but he was killed in battle. There was now but one man left, Napoleon. Negotiations were begun with him by the Abbé Sieyès, now one of the Directors. The general was in Egypt, where he had just won a victory over the Turks. However, his fleet had been defeated by the English under Nelson in the great Battle of the Nile, 1 August 1798, and his supplies were thereby cut off, although the French in Egypt did not surrender until 1801. The evidence is quite conclusive that Napoleon deserted his army, but the brilliance and daring of his safe trip home would have been enough to cause the public to forget this fact even if it had been understood. He arrived as a conqueror at exactly the opportune moment and, by an astute *coup d'état* on 9–10 November (18th and 19th *Brumaire*), he surrounded the Councils with his loyal troops and won for himself the post of supreme commander. Shortly thereafter, a new constitution was promulgated whereby Napoleon became First Consul of the French Republic, and the period of military dictatorship formally began.

Napoleon's rise to power did not mean an end to the French Revolution. It signified its inheritance by a man who perpetuated many of its reforms and changes. He warmly praised the revolution and sought to create the impression that he would see to it that Liberty, Equality, and Fraternity became vital things and not abstract concepts.

11

America's Foreign Relations, 1789–1800

In the eventful year of 1789, George Washington commenced his first administration. In choosing his cabinet, he was setting a precedent for others to follow. Consequently, he exerted considerable care. Thomas Jefferson was a wise choice for the important position in the State Department. He had been abroad, from 1782 to 1783, as one of the American Peace Commissioners, although he had arrived in France too late to take part in the negotiations, and he had been commissioned to negotiate various treaties of commerce with European states willing to do business with the United States. After this service, in 1785, he became minister to France. In this post he served with distinction, following his modest introduction of himself to Vergennes by the observation that he had merely succeeded Dr. Franklin; no one could replace him.

It was while serving at Versailles that Jefferson formed the convictions which became the basis for his foreign policy. He became more fiercely American in his outlook than he had ever been. He felt that America was infinitely better off than Europe and should stay that way by jealously preserving its hard-won democracy. He was convinced that the solution lay in a policy of isolation, in which conclusion he merely shared the prevailing sentiment among the top American statesmen of the day. As an alternative, should isolation prove impossible, he thought that the United States ought to be ready to profit from the distresses of Europe. It might easily prove possible for America to achieve gains for itself when Europe was engaged in a dynastic war or other conflict.

As Secretary of State, Jefferson faced several difficult problems, chief

177

among which were troubles connected with commerce and American relations with Great Britain. France was proving herself quite helpful in the matter of trade. She accorded various favors to Americans in her ports and, in addition, took about two-thirds of the important fisheries products of New England. Most significant, however, for American merchants and shipping interests was the fact that France had opened her West Indian ports to American vessels and thereby provided a profitable market.

Anglo-American Problems. On the other hand, the British government, influenced by its shipping interests, refused for over ten years following recognition of American independence to sign a commercial treaty with its former colonies. American ships fell under the direful provisions of the Navigation Acts, and the lucrative British West Indian trade was firmly closed to Americans. Furthermore, the British had refused to send a minister to this country and were rather nasty about the problems of the fisheries and evacuation of the Northwest fur-trading posts.

Accordingly, President Washington and his Secretary of State, appreciating the gravity of the situation with England, decided to sound out the British in an effort to discover what terms they wanted met before sending a diplomatic representative to the United States. Gouverneur Morris was chosen for the mission; partly because he happened to be in France at the moment, selling Virginia tobacco and trying to buy up the American debt to France at a pretty discount, and partly because of his reputation for shrewdness. The astute Morris was instructed to endeavor to negotiate a commercial treaty and also to seek settlement of the vexing questions of the fisheries and the Northwest. He was soon in contact with the younger Pitt, Britain's Prime Minister, who lost no time in bringing up the touchy question of the unpaid debts owed to British merchants by Americans. Thus, an impasse was reached, but Morris noted that the chances of breaking it seemed to improve at moments when the foreign situation was not too satisfactory to the British. He observed this fact particularly in connection with the Nootka Sound controversy, a war scare between England and Spain. Spanish officers from Mexico had seized several British ships which were in the act of establishing fur-trading settlements on Nootka Sound near what is now Vancouver, British Columbia.

Since such a war would have extended to the colonies of the disputants, Washington became concerned. He was afraid that Great Britain might seek to conquer Louisiana, then Spanish territory, from bases in Canada and in the process march over American territory. If the British should request permission for such a march, what should his answer be? Adams advised him that the policy of the United States should be to refuse permission for such a march but not to resist forcibly if the British proved determined to make it. Hamilton, a strong Anglophile, favored giving consent rather than risking war with Britain. Jefferson proposed that the President avoid a direct answer, since he thought that the situation might offer a profitable opportunity for bargaining. While the crisis lasted, Morris seemed in a fair way to succeed in his negotiations, but when Spain backed down the attitude of the British Foreign Office toward the United States stiffened appreciably.

Appointment of a British Minister. This incident confirmed Jefferson in his belief that Great Britain would not voluntarily make concessions to the United States. Throughout 1789 and 1790 he and his friend James Madison, at this time a member of Congress, agitated for some form of discrimination against British trade in the hope that such action would compel Britain to change her policy. This threat finally induced the British government to send an observer, Major Beckwith, to the United States to study the situation, and he promptly advised the appointment of a regular minister. The post went to George Hammond, who arrived in October, 1791, and was soon in close personal contact with Hamilton. His primary mission was to prevent the imposition of restrictions on British trade with the United States. He was instructed to employ delaying tactics and was not authorized to sign anything, but merely to discuss matters. When Jefferson discovered these instructions, he protested in a note submitted to Hammond in May, 1792, but the British minister was advised by Hamilton that Jefferson did not reflect the policy of the administration. As it happened, Hamilton was wrong; nevertheless Hammond transmitted his information to London and Jefferson's note went unheeded.

WASHINGTON'S PROCLAMATION OF NEUTRALITY

Although the French Revolution had broken out in 1789, the United States did not become much concerned until 1793, when France went to war not only with Austria and Prussia, which had attacked her in 1792, but also with Great Britain and others. Those who shared Jefferson's thesis of the United States' taking advantage of the distresses of Europe felt that here was a golden opportunity to gain valuable trade concessions. As a neutral, America's volume of business was bound to expand. The chief difficulty in the way of a policy of neutrality was the public sympathy for America's old friend and ally, France. There was a widespread sentiment in the United States which favored the principles of the French Revolution. People joyously sang the *Marseillaise* at the theater in many cities, and in Philadelphia the wax works did a big business reproducing the execution of the unfortunate Louis XVI. It needed also to be borne in mind that the United States was bound by the terms of the Alliance of 1778 with France. This agreement pledged the United States to guarantee to France the protection of her North American island possessions. The commercial treaty of the same date contained two articles which gave French privateers and prizes of war the exclusive right of being received in American ports whenever France was a belligerent.

The President and his two chief cabinet ministers were agreed on the wisdom of American neutrality in the European conflict, but there was disagreement on how to proceed to insure it. The idea of a presidential neutrality proclamation was opposed by Jefferson, who suggested a policy of watchful waiting. This procedure, he argued, would have the advantage of forcing England to grant concessions. If, however, a proclamation had to be issued, he felt that it ought to be done not by the President alone but by Congress. Washington, on the other hand, supported by Hamilton, felt that it was entirely proper for him to make such an announcement. Accordingly, 22 April 1793, what has come to be known as Washington's Proclamation of Neutrality was issued. It simply declared that American conduct toward both belligerents would be "friendly and impartial." It forbade American citizens to aid any of the belligerents and declared that any found guilty would be punished. The importance of the announcement is that it indicated a policy of independent procedure on the part of the United States. Jefferson, it might be added, was greatly disappointed in the President's course of action. Nor was he alone. The Francophiles of the nation were loud in their condemnation of this "betrayal" of the "sister republic."

Jefferson's Recognition Policy. There remained the question of recognition of the new French government of the Revolution, now that the monarchy had been dissolved. This time Jefferson's views carried the day. He held that every nation had a right to govern itself as it pleased and pointed to the American Revolution as an example. America could not deny to others what it had sought for itself. Washington agreed and promised to receive a diplomatic emissary of the new French government, an act tantamount to recognition. Incidentally, this act of recognition was destined to serve as a precedent to be followed with few exceptions down to the administration of Woodrow Wilson.

France, for its part, was not disappointed in American neutrality. It was wise enough to recognize America's military deficiencies. Of no considerable aid as a military factor, the United States would be more useful to French policy as a neutral. In this capacity, its merchant marine might carry food to France and its West Indian possessions. Satisfied, then, for the time being, the new French government sent its first diplomatic representative to the United States to further France's interests. The choice proved to be the high-spirited and rather boisterous Edmond-Charles Genêt, a former infant prodigy. Now thirty and experienced in diplomacy through service at the court of Catherine the Great, where he represented the Bourbons, Genêt arrived in Charleston, South Carolina, amidst the enthusiastic greetings of a yelling mob of French sympathizers. Wherever he went in America, the reaction was the same. The result was that he erroneously concluded that America was wild over both him and his country. The set of secret instructions which he brought with him from Paris was fantastic. It included such points as planting the seeds of liberty in Louisiana and other provinces adjacent to the United States. Kentucky was also described as a region where he might employ his talents for stirring up excitement. He was ordered to see to it that French privateers were allowed in American ports and all others excluded and was commissioned to fit out as many French privateers in American ports as possible. He also was armed with a number of captains' commissions in the French army, which were to go to Indians of the Northwest in return for stirring up the tribes against Canada. Further blank commissions were to be used to win over persons willing to operate against Spain's possessions, since Spain was no longer allied with France. One of these commissions made George Rogers Clark a brigadier-general, with instructions to capture New Orleans. In no time, the main American ports along the Atlantic from Boston south were alive with French privateers. George Hammond, the British minister, strenuously protested. Actually, the provisions of the 1778 agreements merely gave France the privilege of sheltering her privateers and prizes in American waters. Nothing had been said about fitting out such ships. The administration decided as a result of this activity to strengthen neutrality, and in 1794 Congress passed a Neutrality Act which ordered out of American waters all privateers fitted out in them together with their prizes; forbade such fitting out in the future; banned foreign courts within American sovereignty (Genêt had set up prize courts); and provided machinery for the prosecution of American citizens enlisting in the United States for service under a foreign government.

Meanwhile, Genêt had become obnoxious to the administration, and it had proved necessary for the government to reprove him for his activities. Genêt's reaction to this rebuke was a threat to go over the President's head and appeal to the American people. Of course, this foolish threat proved too much to endure, and a special courier was sent to Paris in August, 1793, asking for Genêt's recall. His overstepping himself in the United States had caused him to lose favor at home. Were he to return, it undoubtedly meant his execution. Washington generously agreed to allow him to remain in America. Since his first wife had died, he was remarried to an American, the daughter of Governor Clinton of New York. He settled down quietly in Jamaica, Long Island, and later became interested in the Erie Canal. To make amends to the French for the feelings about their representative, the administration sent James Monroe, publicly known for his admiration of France, to Paris as the American emissary.

MARITIME DIFFICULTIES WITH ENGLAND

By the summer of 1793, the United States was getting quite involved with Great Britain over the question of neutral trade. Maintaining neutrality in a domestic sense was, as we have seen, something of a problem, but to achieve the protection of neutral rights on the high seas in the face of the formidable power of the Royal Navy was a far more difficult undertaking. Americans were trading at as furious a clip as the times permitted, but Britain was in the process of seizing enemy property wherever it could be found. The United States held to the doctrine of "free ships, free goods," except for contraband. Foodstuffs and naval stores did not strike the Americans as being contraband, but Britain did not see it this way. American ships loaded with grain for France were hauled into English ports. Great Britain passed an order in council on 8 June 1793, the so-called "Provision Order," which commanded the British fleet to bring into English ports all neutral ships destined for France with cargoes of corn, meal, and flour. Such cargoes were not to be confiscated but purchased by the British at a fair price, or arrangements could be made to sell the cargo to a neutral nation friendly to Britain.

On 6 November 1793 came another order in council stating that the British fleet was to bring in all ships involved in trading with French colonies. This order was contrary to the Rule of 1756, which stated that trade closed to neutrals in time of peace could not be opened to them in time of war. Conversely, if such ports were open in peacetime, they were to remain so in time of war. Britain herself had accepted this practice and was now vitiating it. Chiefly affected from the American viewpoint was the trade with the French West Indian ports. In rather short order some three hundred American ships engaged in this trade were captured. Feeling in the United States against Britain ran very high as a result.

Shortly thereafter, on 31 December 1793, the resignation of Jefferson as Secretary of State took effect. He had become sick and tired of Hamilton's meddling in foreign policy. Hamilton had effectively wrecked Jefferson's opposition to these British acts through his assurance to Hammond that nothing serious was contemplated and that the opposition publicly voiced was only for local consumption.

The news of Jefferson's resignation, which had been relayed to Britain in advance, undoubtedly had a lot to do with the passage of a new order in council on 8 January 1794. Combined with the Jefferson matter was, of course, the aroused state of American public opinion. The new order restored the Rule of 1756, and American shipping was allowed direct trade with the French West Indies, provided that no contraband was involved. Nonetheless, the desired effect was not produced. Feeling in the United States continued to run high, and Jefferson spoke of it as an intolerable situation. None of the proposed discriminatory resolutions secured congressional approval, but an embargo on all American shipping for one month was voted 25 April 1794 and, upon its expiration, renewed for another month.

The Canadian Frontier Problem. Meanwhile, in the fall of 1793, the frontier crisis had become acute. This difficulty was due to the fact that the Indian tribes were holding out for the Ohio River as the boundary between their territory and the United States. An American commission had unsuccessfully endeavored to treat with them in 1793. The Indians, confident of British backing and reveling in their victory over General St. Clair a short time before, proved quite truculent. Warfare seemed imminent, especially as Governor Simcoe of Lower Canada was determined to bring about the creation of an Indian barrier state. His activities led Lord Dorchester, the General Carleton of the American War of Independence, now governor-general of Canada, to urge caution. Simcoe, however, was too exuberant a spirit. On their side, the Americans under General "Mad Anthony" Wayne were drilling for another attempt at the Indians. Simcoe now converted Dorchester to his views and began arming the Indians. This news, coming about the same time as the Caribbean ship captures, intensified the prevailing Anglophobe feeling. At this point, the Battle of Fallen Timbers between the Indians and the Americans under Wayne was fought on 20 August 1794 and ended in a convincing American victory.

The British authorities in Canada now felt that the Americans would try to take by force one of the important Northwest posts still held by the British, contrary to their pledge at the Treaty of Paris in 1783, namely Detroit. The Washington administration, however, did not desire a war with Britain. Federalist senators urged the President to send a special envoy to England in an effort to straighten things out at the last moment. Meantime, being patriotic Americans, they advocated the strengthening of the national defense and even proposed increasing the army to fifty thousand men. Alexander Hamilton was suggested as the man most likely to undertake the special mission, but his unpopularity at the moment was too great to risk this venture. Hence, he requested Washington to send John Jay instead. Since Jay was Chief Justice of the Supreme Court, there was immediate opposition on this ground. His extremely pro-British sympathies were also recalled, but the President was adamant, and Jay embarked for England.

Jay's Treaty. Jay was instructed not to enter any agreement with Britain which was contrary to the existing treaty with France; secondly, there was to be no commercial treaty signed which failed to open the

British West Indies to American shipping. The British Foreign Minister, Baron Grenville, was quite apprehensive about the possibility of a revival of an armed neutrality similar to that formed during the American Revolution against Britain and was inclined to be reasonable. Once again, Alexander Hamilton entered the picture by informing George Hammond that the United States entertained no intention of joining such an enterprise. Hammond forwarded this information to Grenville, whose position was considerably strengthened. Negotiations were concluded with the signing of what is called Jay's Treaty, 19 November 1794.

He did achieve the surrender of the Northwest posts by the British, to take effect in 1796. The problems of claims arising out of British interference with American commerce, the uncollected British debts in the United States, and the disputed Maine-New Brunswick border were referred to mixed commissions for arbitration. The principle involved in such an action was admirable. Less praiseworthy was Jay's failure to get anything accomplished in his treaty relative to American neutral rights. By tacit consent this was a surrender to British interpretation of these questions. Nothing was said either about impressment of American seamen, which the British had begun to practice at an alarming rate. He likewise failed to secure a satisfactory West Indian trade arrangement. In fact, his concessions here to the British were so great that the Senate struck out this article of the treaty before it was ratified.

The treaty was extremely distasteful to the people of the United States. Jay's effigy was burned, Hamilton was stoned at a public gathering, and the press was full of acrimonious comments. The Senate, meeting in special session, ratified the treaty by a bare two-thirds majority on 22 June 1795. Washington had to dismiss his Secretary of State, Edmund Randolph, for his part in seeking to defeat ratification. Hamilton had also resigned, but this was due to a desire to free Washington from embarrassment and not because of any really outstanding difference of opinion. The opposition resorted to a skillful move by attempting to block the treaty in the House of Representatives through refusing to vote the appropriations necessary to provide for the commissions set up in the terms of the treaty. The victory was achieved by the Federalists in the House by the scant margin of three votes.

Despite its unpopularity, Jay's Treaty was actually about the best that could have been achieved in the circumstances. The important thing was that it secured peace against a potentially powerful enemy and thus allowed the United States a chance to expand while Europe was embroiled in the wars of the French Revolution and Napoleon.

The Southern Frontier. With relations now more or less patched up with Britain, the administration had problems facing it in connection with Spain and France. In the Southwest, matters were in a somewhat dangerous state because of the policy of the Spanish governor of Louisiana, Carondelet, who took control in 1791. The admission of Kentucky to the Union that year had tended to shift the center of intrigues being carried on against the United States by unscrupulous individuals from this region to New Orleans. Carondelet's policy was founded on an improved system of offensive and defensive alliances with the Indians.

In 1784 the Creeks had allied themselves with Spain, but in 1790 President Washington had invited their chieftain, Alexander McGillivray, to New York to negotiate a treaty. The result was the Treaty of New York, a treaty of perpetual friendship between the United States and the Creeks, who put themselves under the protection of the United States and agreed to abandon all lands north and east of a proposed line in West Georgia in return for an annuity of $1,500. The Creeks likewise agreed to give the government advance warning of any foreign designs against the United States. McGillivray was appointed special agent of the government among the Creeks with the rank of brigadier general and $1,200 per annum.

This procedure was repeated in 1791 with the Cherokees, a fact which greatly angered Carondelet, who began to urge the Creek chieftain to repudiate the Treaty of New York. Upon the latter's refusal, the inducement offered by Spain was increased, and McGillivray agreed to incite his tribesmen again against the Georgia settlers. Still dissatisfied with the results, Carondelet, in 1793, organized a General Indian Confederation comprising Creeks, Choctaws, Chickasaws, and Cherokees. These tribes agreed to defend Louisiana and the Spanish Floridas against all attacks. Now that he had won over the Indians of the Southwest, the Spanish governor began to formulate plans for gaining the aid of the Northwestern tribes to drive back American settlers. Hence, from 1791 on Spanish policy became increasingly dangerous to the United States, and by 1794 there was an intrigue being carried on by a Spanish official in the United States aimed at the creation of a buffer state between the Appalachians and the Mississippi.

Pinckney's Treaty. At this point the European situation played into the hands of the United States. Spain had decided to desert Britain in the war against France and ally herself with the latter. Fearful of Britain's anger, the Spanish government sought to wean the Americans away from any rapprochement with Britain. At first, the Spanish tried to win the Americans over to a triple alliance with Spain and France for the joint preservation of territories in America; if this were unacceptable, Spain proposed a Spanish-American alliance for the same purpose, in return for Mississippi and boundary concessions. Thomas Pinckney, the new American negotiator in Spain, refused both proposals, with the approval of the President. While the negotiations were going on, there arrived in Madrid a copy of the Franco-Spanish peace signed at Basel. The Spanish Foreign Minister, Godoy, therefore, decided to grant America's wishes in order to conserve Spain's strength against possible British retaliation. Thus, on 27 October 1795, the treaty known as Pinckney's Treaty was signed. Spain recognized 31° north latitude as the southern boundary of the United States and granted freedom of navigation on the Mississippi to American citizens. Except for Spanish subjects, all others were excluded. To this was added the privilege of American citizens to land goods destined for oceanic shipment at New Orleans for a period of three years, tax-free. At the expiration of this time, the Spanish monarch might renew the privilege or assign some other place on the banks of the lower Mississippi for this purpose, technically called the right of deposit. Both nations agreed to restrain the Indians within their territory, a point which later proved very valuable in aiding American acquisition of East Florida. The maritime provisions of the treaty were along the lines of "free ships, free goods," and a mixed commission was provided to adjudicate spoliation claims. The treaty was quickly ratified in the Senate by a unanimous vote.

The opening of the Mississippi together with the right of deposit at New Orleans stimulated the commercial activities of the American West and aided the eastern ports as well. With the signing of the Jay and Pinckney Treaties, the Washington administration had protected the territory of the United States, achieved prestige, and displayed astuteness. The European situation had proved extremely helpful to the United States.

WASHINGTON'S FAREWELL ADDRESS

President George Washington was by now heartily sick of the whole mess. The attacks on his integrity which had taken place as a result of his acceptance of the Jay Treaty and the excesses of some of the pro-French faction had wearied and disgusted him, so he bent himself to the formation of what has gone down in American history as his Farewell Address. He had been building up to this declaration of policy for a number of years. The document owes its origin to Hamilton and Madison as well as to the first President. It was actually written by Hamilton but based upon an outline drawn up by Washington. On 15 May 1796, he handed Hamilton a group of topics entitled "hints or heads of topics"— items jotted down in no particular order but covering matters he wished to bring before the American people at some time. These ideas became the soul of the Farewell Address.

It appeared first in the public prints, 19 September 1796, and was aimed to remove all doubts as to whether the President sought reelection to a third term. Pointing out that his health was enfeebled, Washington proclaimed his intention of retiring but wished to take this opportunity to defend himself against the vituperation which had been hurled at him. He commenced by making an appeal to all who loved the country to maintain the national Union. Then, he launched into his main theme. This was an exhortation to avoid the wars of Europe together with any European alliances for the present. The United States should have as little permanent connection with Europe as possible. However, it must fulfill its present obligations, *i.e.,* the treaty with France. Europe's wars were not America's concern. The United States could remain neutral and pursue an individual course. It would not be long before the country would grow strong enough to choose between peace and war, but as an infant nation it must choose peace. Time was vital in order to give the nation a chance to settle and mature.

Too frequently, the interpretation put upon this speech has professed to see in it a policy of complete isolation, which it most certainly was not. It might better be construed as a policy of vigilant defense. Isolation comes in only when it would be to America's advantage. The first President felt that twenty years would suffice for the purpose of acquiring sufficient strength to make American wishes respected, but even in that time he did not desire to isolate commercial relations.

THE FRENCH WAR SCARE, 1796–1800

The ratification of the Jay Treaty precipitated a near war between the United States and France. The French professed to look upon the treaty as inconsistent with the Franco-American Treaty of Alliance. They were quite upset over American acceptance of British maritime practices which, of course, essentially denied "free ships, free goods" and permitted British interpretation of contraband and blockade practices. From the American point of view, France was herself guilty of vitiating the maritime provisions of the Treaty of 1778. She had followed almost the same path as the British in interfering with neutral commerce wherever she could.

In its anger over American acquiescence in British maritime practices, the French government passed a decree, 2 July 1796, which declared that all neutral vessels were henceforth to be treated by France in the same fashion as by Britain. America struck back in the instructions given C. C. Pinckney as Minister to France by Secretary of State Timothy Pickering. Dated 6 January 1797, these were virtually a Federalist party manifesto in defense of that party's attitude toward France. They called for an examination of France's claims to American gratitude and asserted that France had only promoted its own interests during the War for American Independence. Moreover, it was said that France had continued to look out for its own interests in the peace negotiations. There followed a discussion of the activities of various French ministers to the United States since America had become independent. Finally, there was a flat declaration to the effect that France's decrees injurious to American commerce must be rescinded.

Pinckney's arrival was most unceremonious. He was refused recognition by the French and, when he insisted upon a clarification of his status, was informed that he was trespassing and was liable to arrest. Accordingly, he fled to Holland, and the result was a practical rupture of diplomatic relations between France and the United States. For France followed up its treatment of Pinckney with an announcement that it would not receive any American representative until French grievances against America had been settled to France's satisfaction. A decree of 1797 effectively abrogated the Treaty of 1778 as far as maritime rights were concerned, and the French began seizing American vessels freely. In the one year, from 1 July 1796 to 30 June 1797, some three hundred and sixteen American vessels were captured by the French.

The XYZ Affair. This treatment induced Pickering to suggest to the Cabinet that the country prepare to defend its interests. Adams, however, was desirous of patching things up by resorting to negotiations and so decided to send a mission to France. The President's suggestion was warmly received by Jefferson, who, because he was Vice-President, declined the President's offer to head the commission of negotiators. As finally constituted, this body numbered three men, C. C. Pinckney, Elbridge Gerry, and John Marshall. The latter pair arrived in France in the fall of 1797 and were joined by Pinckney, who came over from Holland. Marshall served as the leader of the group, but even he could not bring about their reception by Talleyrand, who was serving as Foreign Minister under the Directory. Talleyrand, while out of favor in France, had traveled in the United States, between 1794 and 1796, and made an easy living by offering supposed French state secrets for sale and also by dabbling in Western land speculation. The net result of his American visit was to put the United States in a very low place in his esteem. Therefore, when the American commission arrived, he decided to seek bribes before offering to negotiate. This was his customary method of procedure and did not represent any special insult to the Americans. The latter were met by three representatives of Talleyrand, and informed that each member of the French group must be paid a sum of money; that the United States must promise a loan of several millions to France; pay the debts the United States owed to France immediately; pay for spoliations to French commerce by American ships; and lastly, President Adams was to apologize for the nasty language he had used in a recent speech toward France. The reaction of the stunned Americans was summed up in C. C. Pinckney's utterance, "No! No! Not a sixpence!" This phrase was improved by some bright American with an eye toward public relations and later emerged as "Millions for defense; not one cent for tribute!" The three French negotiators also underwent a transformation at the hands of Secretary of State Pickering. He substituted for their names the letters X, Y, Z, and so the "XYZ Affair" was born.

In January, 1798, Marshall sent Talleyrand a long statement of America's case and received somewhat tardily in March a reply which was quite brief and to the point. Talleyrand held that France's case, not America's, was in a very favorable light and chided the United States for its temerity in sending C. C. Pinckney to France. He concluded by observing that the French Directorate was willing to deal with someone of impartial views and suggested Elbridge Gerry, who had been worked on by a French hussy named Madame de Villette. Secretly, Talleyrand had arranged a meeting with Gerry and was convinced that the latter was on France's side. Disgusted at the way events were developing, Marshall and Pinckney left France, but Gerry remained. Finally, it was necessary for Pickering to recall him. The news of what had happened during the XYZ Affair reached the United States in a number of installments and so prolonged the bitter feeling. There was some talk of war in the capital which prompted one Dr. George Logan, a Philadelphia Quaker, to take it upon himself to remedy the situation. This busybody embarked for France on his own hook to see Talleyrand. That august personage quickly received him, and Logan became very friendly with the French government, which professed to see in him the prototype of all "good Americans," *i.e.*, pro-French. Little good, of course, came from this unauthorized trip, except the passage by Congress of the so-called Logan Act of 1799, providing for the punishment of those guilty of unauthorized negotiations with a foreign government. Such persons were liable to a fine of not more than $5,000 and a prison term not to exceed three years. Dr. Logan, as a result of all the free publicity he received, went to the Senate from Pennsylvania in 1801.

President Adams now authorized the creation of a navy department and called for ten thousand volunteers in the army. Washington was called from retirement and appointed commander in chief in the event war should come. He agreed only on condition that Hamilton be named as his next in command. This proved difficult for Adams, but as he had no alternative he accepted Washington's request.

Naval War with France. The beginnings of a navy existed in the shape of three frigates launched in 1797 through Congressional authorization in 1794 for use against the Barbary pirates. The passage of legislation in 1798 quickly provided the nucleus of a small but efficient navy. Hostilities of an undeclared nature took place with the French from 1798 to 1801, and the regular navy was implemented by American privateers. On 7 July 1798, the President declared all treaties with France abrogated. The internment of enemy aliens, in the event of war, was authorized, and under the impetus of the war hysteria the Federalists passed the notorious Alien and Sedition Acts.

Those Federalists who were bent on war, however, made the mistake of reckoning without the President. Adams again decided to resort to a commission to bring France to book without the need of war. His wisdom in this instance was deep because the French were plainly worried over the possibility of the pro-English Federalists making common cause with Britain. Indeed, the Pitt government eased the severity of its maritime practices against American shipping in just such a hope and even went so far as to permit a temporary trade for American vessels in the British West Indies. For its part, the American government further demonstrated its dislike of France by according *de facto* recognition to the Negro insurrectionist government of Toussaint L'Ouverture, which had overthrown French power in the Caribbean island of Haiti.

Despite the opposition of his own party, the President went ahead with his plans for avoiding war by choosing a commission to go to France. Napoleon, now First Consul of France, accorded a warm reception to the Americans, and negotiations began immediately. Eventually, there emerged from these discussions the Convention of 1800, as the agreement was called. It suspended all old treaties between the United States and France, thus putting an end to America's first formal alliance. Similarly, it suspended all claims for damages between the two parties. On the positive side, it provided for a commercial treaty between the two nations which embodied the most-favored-nation principle. It also restored the maritime provisions to which the United States had always adhered up to the Jay Treaty. Thus, by resort to diplomacy, Adams solved the French problem satisfactorily for the time being and ended the dangerous drift toward war.

12

Napoleon

When Napoleon became First Consul of the French Republic in December, 1799, France came under a government called the Consulate which, outwardly at any rate, preserved the name of a republic until 1804. Keenly aware of the weaknesses of the political testament he had inherited, Bonaparte felt that a synthesis of the best features of the Old Regime and the Revolution could be made to do the job of satisfying the French people, who were tired of the inefficiency and corruption which had been so prevalent during the Revolution and sick of the license which events had loosed following 1789. They did wish, however, to preserve the gains which the Revolution had brought them in the social and economic changes it had introduced.

Although none could know it at the time, the future history of Europe for years afterward was to be linked intimately with the character of this young general, then only thirty years of age. It will, therefore, be worth while to glance briefly at the personality of this famous man.

Napoleone di Buonaparte was born 15 August 1769 in Corsica, an island recently purchased by France from Genoa. In an effort to make French rule more acceptable to the proud and stubborn Corsicans, it was decided to educate some of the prominent youths in France at the expense of the French government. When he was old enough, Napoleon was so honored and received a first-rate military education. He was a rather morose and lonely individual while in school in France but managed to do quite well in such subjects as history, mathematics, and military science.

Once determined, along with another young Corsican, Pozzo di Borgo (also destined to achieve fame in a foreign land as adviser to Alexander I of Russia), to free Corsica from French rule, Bonaparte was swept to fame and power in the French Revolution. We have previously seen how he first attracted attention by his victory over the British at Toulon in 1793. Then followed in rapid succession his defense of the Convention in 1795, the first Italian campaign culminating in 1797, and finally his Middle Eastern campaigns in Syria and Egypt, from which he had come, apparently unconquered, to his present prominence.

This physically short but tireless man was a sincere believer in himself and his destiny. Clever, unscrupulous, driving, he was a very astute student of human nature and knew its weaknesses and how to capitalize on them. Although his men idolized him and on countless occasions he created the impression that it was mutual, their sufferings meant nothing to him in reality. This dramatic quality of his always served him well.[1]

The Consulate. In order to wipe out the "provisional" stigma attached to his rise to power, Napoleon lost no time in having promulgated a constitution he had quickly devised with the aid of Sieyès. This Constitution of the Year VIII went into operation 25 December 1799. On the surface, it provided for continuation of the republic but, in reality, was a military dictatorship under the First Consul (Napoleon), whose term of office was to be ten years and whose powers were virtually limitless. Assisting him in the executive branch of government were two other consuls whose duties were almost exclusively advisory. The Consul later appointed a Council of State composed of 30 (and eventually 45) members to aid him in legislative study. The three consuls together appointed a Senate of 80 members for life. This body then selected the Tribunate, numbering 100, and the Legislative Body, numbering 300, from lists arrived at in a complicated fashion starting from a basis of universal manhood suffrage. The Senate also had power to pass on the constitutionality of measures and so acted as a kind of Supreme Court. The Tribunate's power was restricted to a discussion of proposed legislation but it had no power to vote, whereas the Legislative Body could vote but was forbidden any discussion! From this description, the reader can observe the synthesis of democracy and dictatorship which the ingenious framers achieved. The constitution was a written one and provided for universal manhood suffrage, but it nullified the effect of these concessions to the Revolution through the power granted the First Consul. To further the illusion of democracy, it was submitted to the people for ratification in a plebiscite the results of which were not finally known until February, 1800, although it was placed in operation in December, 1799. The vote, incidentally, was 3,011,107 in favor, to 1,565 opposed.

Internal Reforms. With his passion for organization, Bonaparte set to work and achieved a number of lasting results. In the field of local administration, he altered the work of the Revolution through his changes in the departments. He kept the geographical arrangement of the

[1] Hegel pictured him as the "world spirit" in action.

Revolution, which had been an effort to eliminate the curse of provincialism and foster nationalism in its stead, but replaced the elective boards and councils in these units with a prefect for each. The departments were also given subprefects for each district, and each commune was given a mayor. These officials were put into office by the First Consul and were selected from names submitted by the minister of the interior. The first man to hold this important office was his brother Lucien, who had been President of the Council of Five Hundred when Napoleon's *coup d'état* against the Directory had taken place. Through a combination of wisdom and ruthlessness, he quickly achieved the domestic pacification which no government of the Revolution had been able to achieve.

Next, he set himself to the difficult work of fiscal reform through consolidating the national debt and instituting a sinking fund. In February, 1800, the Bank of France was established, likewise with a view toward centralization. Among its heaviest stockholders were members of the Bonaparte family. One of its functions was to issue bank notes up to a specified limit. Collection of taxes was taken away from local officials and entrusted to agents of the central government with considerable success. The net result of his efforts in these various activities was to restore the government's credit and to achieve relative stabilization of the nation's finances.

The Code Napoléon. "The second Justinian" was well aware that one of France's greatest dreams in the days before and since 1789 was clarification of the laws and removal of the legalistic chaos which had long plagued France. While some beginnings had been made by the Revolution, it remained for Bonaparte to achieve a success for which he will always be justly famous. This celebrated Code Napoléon, which was completed in 1804 after several years of driving by the relentless Bonaparte, has become the basis of the legal system of numerous countries throughout the world and still serves one of the American states, Louisiana. It protected the interests of people of property and at the same time maintained the principal social accomplishments of the Revolution, *e.g.,* equality of all citizens before the law and freedom of religion and opportunity.

Building where the Revolution had left off, Bonaparte zealously set out to realize a national system of education. Each commune was required to support an elementary school; grammar schools were placed under the national government; each town of sufficient importance was to have a high school staffed by teachers appointed by the state; and all special schools became subject to regulation. In 1808, there was established the Imperial University, whose functions included licensing of all schools and teachers. Patriotism and obedience to Napoleon were among the principal requirements throughout the entire educational system.

While there were no trains in Napoleon's France for him to make run on time, he did institute a huge program of public works. Roads and bridges were improved, and many new ones constructed, with emphasis placed, as Rome had before him and Mussolini and Hitler were to afterward, to those of a military nature. The network of canals and inland waterways was also made more efficient, and his engineers made worthwhile alterations in France's chief harbors. It was under Napoleon that the beautiful city of Paris began the career which was to win for it the name of the "City of Light."

The Concordat. In the interests of national unity, Napoleon put an end to the serious division among the French people on the score of the country's traditional religion, although it was no easy task for him to accomplish. Opposition to the Catholic Church was still strong among the intellectual classes and those who had profited in any way through the revolutionary activities aimed against the Church. In addition, the army was considerably affected by atheism. Napoleon had to move circumspectly, and so his first negotiations with the papacy were secret. But in 1801 a concordat was signed between the First Consul and the new Pope, Pius VII. It provided for acceptance by the pope of the loss of lands and property during the Revolution as well as the end of the tithes. The government pledged payment of the priests' salaries. Napoleon was given the right to nominate the bishops, who would be invested in office by the pope. The bishops, in their turn, would appoint the members of the lower clergy. Catholicism was declared to be "the religion of the majority of Frenchmen" and that of the three consuls as well. The signing of the concordat was an important step in Napoleon's program of national unity so well begun in other fields. It preserved freedom of religion since Protestants and Jews were similarly tolerated and aided. To the holders of former church possessions, the aura of legality was now attached to their property, and they were able to relax their fears. In general, the concordat was very well received by the people and endured until the anticlerical government of the early twentieth century repealed it.

Louisiana and Santo Domingo. In the field of empire, the First Consul hoped to reconstitute France as a colonial power. His ambition was to make Louisiana into a strong colony. His Foreign Minister, the astute Talleyrand, likewise shared his enthusiasm for the project. Spain was willing to part with what she considered wasteland. Accordingly, in October, 1800, a preliminary secret treaty was signed whereby Spain returned Louisiana to France and the Spanish king received from Napoleon a small Italian kingdom to be ruled by his son-in-law. Two years passed before Charles IV finally ratified this arrangement and then only after Napoleon assured him that France would not transfer the territory to any third power.

To complete his colonial designs for the moment, Napoleon decided to regain control of France's richest possession, the island of Santo Domingo,[2] which had fallen into the hands of the Negroes following a highly successful revolt. He sent an army of crack veterans of the European wars under the leadership of his own brother-in-law, General Leclerc, to perform the task. Although the native leader, Toussaint L'Ouverture, was tricked into an agreement with Leclerc which resulted in a treacherous seizure of the valiant black man and his subsequent death in a French prison, the combination of renewed native opposition and decimating attacks of yellow fever proved too much for the French. Louisiana had been intended as a granary for this rich sugar island, which was considered of far greater value and importance. The setback Napoleon received in Santo Domingo, combined with several other circumstances, induced him to sell Louisiana to the Americans in 1803.

Temporary Peace in Europe. The student will remember that France was at war with the Second Coalition. The members, Great Britain, Russia, and Austria, had enjoyed considerable success and appeared to be in a position to carry the war to France herself. Napoleon's first good fortune here was his detachment of Russia from the allies by means of shrewd statesmanship. The Czar Paul I now revived the League of Armed Neutrality against Britain. This consisted, through the Northern Convention of 1800, of Russia, Prussia, Sweden, and Denmark, but the destruction of the Danish fleet by Nelson following close on the heels of Paul I's assassination early in 1801 ruined the effectiveness of this diversion of British strength. Nonetheless, England had lost an ally.

Meantime, the First Consul himself had gone into action in a second Italian campaign against Austria. His great victory in this campaign was Marengo, 14 June 1800. The Austrians were ultimately forced to sign the Treaty of Lunéville, 9 February 1801, which removed them from the Second Coalition and left Britain alone.

Barring the failure of his colonial ambitions, Napoleon's career as First Consul was a succession of achievements, not the least of which was the conclusion of the Peace of Amiens, 25 March 1802, with the British. This won for him the gratitude of a war-weary French people whose joy was, unfortunately, to be short-lived, as Amiens proved to be only a temporary armistice of some sixteen months. The treaty represented real concessions by the English and amounted practically to a recognition of French control of the Continent. In their relief that the war was over, the French people ratified a life term as Consul for their leader, and he was given the right to name his successor. The vote was 3,568,885 to 8,374.

Before the consulate could be transformed into the First Empire,

[2] The western half of the island, Haiti, was French; Spain had ceded the eastern half, Santo Domingo, to France in 1795.

there remained the job of appeasing or liquidating remaining domestic opposition. The establishment of the Legion of Honor with its annuities won over sufficient discontented military men to lessen the danger from that quarter. Jacobin remnants, still dreaming of the Revolution, did not prove a serious menace. The royalists, abetted by the English, did, however, pose a real problem. A royalist conspiracy in 1803–1804 was crushed through the swift apprehension of the chief figures. This plot was made the excuse for the judicial murder of a young and well-liked member of the Bourbon house, the Duc d'Enghien, who was seized on German soil with a callous disregard for law that shocked the rest of Europe.

THE FRENCH IMPERIAL EXPANSION

The country backed Bonaparte, and on 18 May 1804 he was proclaimed Emperor of the French. His consecration took place 2 December in the presence of Pope Pius VII, but Napoleon placed the imperial crowns on his own and Josephine's head. The French people ratified the transformation by a vote of 3,577,329 to 2,569. The reasons for their action seem clear enough: Bonaparte's brilliant record of domestic reform and foreign victory, followed by his elimination of domestic opposition, had united the people of France squarely behind him.

The Emperor's main preoccupation was war. The conflict with England had been resumed in 1803 following the armed peace after Amiens. For a time, Napoleon had made menacing preparations for an invasion of England. He had massed men and barges at Boulogne, but the attempt never materialized and in August, 1805, the War of the Third Coalition had become a reality. The French encamped at Boulogne were rushed toward the Rhine to meet the Austrians. Other members of this coalition included England, of course, and Russia and Sweden. Spain allied herself with France.

On 20 October 1805, the Austrians were defeated at Ulm and three days afterward surrendered an army of 50,000. Just one day later, there took place one of the great naval battles of all time, Trafalgar, where Nelson defeated the combined French and Spanish fleets without the loss of a single British ship. Although Nelson was killed, his victory assured the British mastery of the seas throughout the long years of the war.

Although his sea power had been smashed forever, Napoleon struck back fiercely on land. On 2 December came his defeat of the combined Austrians and Russians at Austerlitz. This victory, scored on the first anniversary of his coronation, was a decisive one, for it caused Austria to capitulate to him for the third time. The Treaty of Pressburg, 26 December, recognized Napoleon as king of Italy, whose territory now embraced Venetia, Istria, and Dalmatia. Bavaria and Württemberg, two South

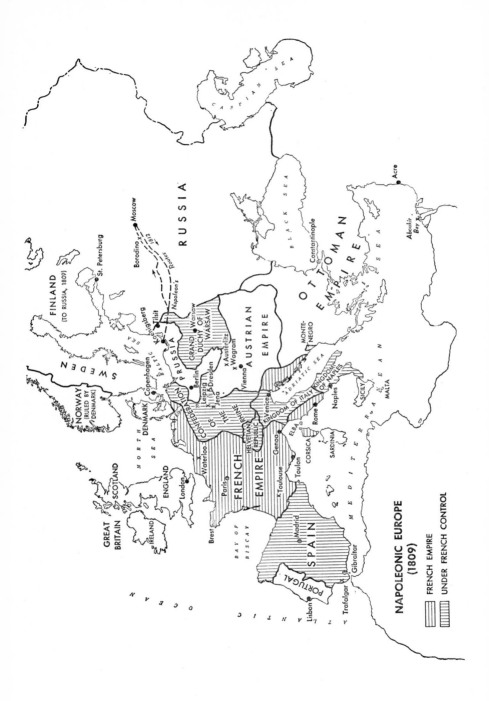

NAPOLEONIC EUROPE
(1809)

FRENCH EMPIRE

UNDER FRENCH CONTROL

German states which had helped Bonaparte, were now recognized as kingdoms, and Austria was forced to yield territory to them.

Napoleon and Germany. In 1806, Napoleon's passion for organization, together with his desire to reduce the importance of both Austria and Prussia in German affairs, led to the formation of the Confederation of the Rhine under his auspices. The net immediate result of his maneuverings in German affairs was to reduce the number of German states from over three hundred to about one hundred and to put much of Germany under French power. The long-range result was a tremendous impetus toward the unification of Germany. The following months saw the end of the thousand-year-old Holy Roman Empire. Napoleon's wishes were served by the Austrian Emperor, Francis I, who gave up his title of Holy Roman Emperor. It is quite clear that Napoleon intended the replacement of this venerable empire with his own. He is on record as having said that his ambition was the unification of Europe with uniformity of laws, courts, coinage, etc.

Prussia had been temporarily lulled by the gift of Hanover but decided not to stand idly by any longer, and so, by October of 1806, its armies stood face to face with the French in Saxony.[3] In the great double battle of Jena and Auerstadt, 14 October 1806, the Prussians were crushed, and two weeks later Napoleon was in Berlin.

The Russian allies of Frederick William III of Prussia were next met at bloody Eylau in February, 1807, where a stalemate occurred, and the respective armies went into winter quarters. In the meantime, the war had reached the Near and Middle East. Napoleon's agent, General Sebastiani, managed to get the Turks to break their alliance with England and Russia, and war between Turkey and Russia resulted in 1806.

The Treaty of Tilsit. Napoleon's forces resumed their drive east by capturing Danzig from the Russians on 26 May 1807 and then defeating them decisively at Friedland, 17 June. This setback, impelled Russia, disgusted with its allies, to seek a new alliance. Thus, on 25 June on a raft in the Niemen at Tilsit, Napoleon and Alexander I, Czar of all the Russias, began to discuss terms which meant the end of the Third Coalition. Prussia was reduced in size and strength, but Napoleon consented to allow Frederick William III to keep his throne. Prussia, however, virtually paid the cost of the war. Her loss of population was one-half, and she was stripped of some of her best holdings. Polish territory, gained by Prussia in the partitions of that unhappy country, was formed by Na-

[3] The Prussian war party had been able to win over the reluctant king by convincing him of Napoleon's duplicity. Moreover, Prussia keenly resented Napoleon's arbitrary execution of a Prussian bookseller, named Palm, for circulating a pamphlet appealing to the nation to save Germany from the French Emperor. Thus, it was a thoroughly aroused nationalistic opponent France now faced.

poleon into the Grand Duchy of Warsaw, which Alexander now recognized. A secret agreement on Turkey saw the treacherous Bonaparte consent to sell out these recently acquired allies of his, since they no longer served his purpose. Alexander agreed to mediate with England on Napoleon's behalf and, if the British refused the terms, to make common cause against them. Little time was lost in this respect. The bombardment of Copenhagen and capture of the Danish fleet by the British shortly after Tilsit forestalled potential trouble from this source but drove Russia into the arms of France. The Russians declared war on England in September.

Tilsit and the months immediately following it were the high-water mark of Napoleon's career. He now controlled territory double that under French influence when the Treaty of Amiens was concluded, and France's boundary was the Rhine, realization of an historic French dream. By 1808 there were seven kings who owed him either everything or a great deal for their titles. His victories up to this point had largely been scored over inefficient governments, but now he was about to face nations which opposed his arbitrary interference with the lives of their citizens. Here was to be the chief explanation for his downfall—nationalism. In the Iberian Peninsula, in Prussia, and in Russia, he was to meet the angry force of proud, outraged people who supported their government's efforts at overthrowing the ambitious French leader.

The Continental System. But as always England remained Napoleon's chief foe. Against Britain, his principal weapons were economic. To bring this persistent foe to her knees, the Emperor established his Continental System, which aimed at closing the Continent to the English. His first step was an order closing North German ports to British goods. On 16 May 1806 the British issued an order in council declaring the entire coast from the Elbe to Brest blockaded. This paper blockade was known as "Fox's Blockade," after the English cabinet officer. Napoleon retaliated 21 November 1806 with the Berlin Decree, which declared the British Isles blockaded, forbade any trade in British goods in countries under his influence, threatened confiscation of any British goods discovered, and prohibited the use of European ports by any ships which had put in at a British port or sailed from one of her colonies. The consequences of such a policy would hurt everyone, including France herself and the neutrals, but Napoleon felt quite sure that England would crack first. The British retaliated by issuing another order in council, 7 January 1807, forbidding neutrals to trade between French ports and those of Napoleon's allies under threat of confiscation of ship and cargo.

With the victory over the Third Coalition acknowledged at Tilsit, Napoleon included his Continental system in the treaty, and Russia and Prussia agreed to close their ports against the British. Sweden's indecision resulted in Russia's (Napoleon's ally) expulsion of the Swedes from Finland, which Alexander I seized in 1809.

More orders in council were issued in November and December, 1807, which penalized neutrals severely for compliance with Napoleon. Neutrals might, however, trade between British ports and enemy colonies, and with blockaded Continental ports if they were willing to put in first at a British port, unload the cargo, and pay various charges. On 17 December 1807, Napoleon struck back with his Milan Decree. Any ship submitting to British orders in council became legal prey. This meant, as far as he was concerned, the end of neutrals.

The Spanish Revolt. The month previous to the Milan Decree, the French occupied Portugal because of its refusal to participate in the Continental system. Early the following year, a domestic quarrel in Spain supplied Napoleon with the pretext he needed, and Spain felt the heavy boot of the French invader. By November, 1809, nearly all that unhappy country was temporarily overrun. Its weak monarch, Charles IV, and his heir Ferdinand had been expelled, paving the way for the ascension to the Spanish throne of Napoleon's brother Joseph. Marshal Murat, Napoleon's brother-in-law and the conqueror of Spain, replaced Joseph as king of Naples. Yet the Peninsular campaign (1808–1813) was to prove a long and costly one for Napoleon. Obstructive geography, the fierce nationalistic pride of the Spanish people, their hatred of Napoleon because of his offensive treatment of the Pope,[4] and the help supplied by Great Britain in arms, gold, and men were to prove too much. The British expeditionary force was led by the able Sir Arthur Wellesley (later Duke of Wellington). The Peninsular campaign was a great boon to England, for it provided both a chance to get her goods into the Continent and an opportunity to make life miserable for Napoleon by harrying him incessantly.

The setbacks which occurred here revived hope in the hearts of the Austrians and Prussians. Meanwhile, Alexander in Russia had become somewhat disgruntled. Because he now desperately needed the Czar's help, Napoleon arranged to meet him at Erfurt in September, 1808. The result was a halfhearted renewal of Tilsit, but this time it was Alexander and not Napoleon who held the trump cards.

The next year the Austrians, riding on the wave of a tremendous nationalism, felt that their reorganization following the disastrous Treaty of Pressburg was complete. Led by the Archduke Charles, brother of the young Emperor Francis I, the army was indeed formidable, and, since a

[4] Napoleon treated the Pope very cavalierly. The Pope's refusal to join the Continental system angered Napoleon and in February, 1808, French troops occupied Rome in retaliation. The following year, the Papal States were declared incorporated with France, an act which immediately led to Napoleon's excommunication, followed by the seizure and imprisonment of the Pope.

war of liberation was proclaimed, it had an impelling motivation. War was declared early in 1809. Within less than a month after the war began, the diplomatically harried but militarily still astute Napoleon had entered Vienna. Nonetheless, a week later his green recruits were defeated at Aspern and forced across the Danube. There he united his forces with those of his stepson Eugene, the Italian viceroy, who had driven the Austrians out of Italy. The augmented French under Napoleon now sought out the Archduke Charles and decisively defeated him in the great battle of Wagram, 5–6 July 1809. Austria sued for an armistice and 14 October signed the punitive Treaty of Schönbrunn, calling for the loss of over 30,000 square miles of territory and three and a half million people.

The Austrian Marriage. The following spring the Emperor, who had set aside the unfaithful and barren Josephine, was married to the Archduchess Marie Louise, daughter of Emperor Francis I of Austria. This match, facilitated by Metternich, was for Napoleon the culmination of a long-cherished hope. His family was now united with an ancient imperial house, and he could found a real dynasty. The union did result in the birth of a son and heir in March, 1811. This boy was named by the proud father the King of Rome (now second city of the empire) but is best remembered as L'Aiglon.

Hence, by the end of 1809, following the victory over Austria, in the political sphere things took on an appearance of relief for the Emperor. But the hated English had punched too many holes in the Continental System to suit him in the economic sphere. Smuggling, the compliance with British orders in council, and an inefficient customs organization were the chief defects. Even Napoleon's own brother Louis, King of Holland, had helped the British by his unwillingness to adhere to the Continental system out of fear of harming his Dutch subjects! On 1 July 1810 Louis was forced to flee into exile, and the country was made an integral part of France in order to strengthen the Continental System. Numerous "new Tyres had arisen on the waves" to serve as clearing houses for the smuggling trade. To mention but a few, there were the islands of Sicily, Sardinia, Malta, and Helgoland. The profits were high and so were the prices, but British goods were then of such standards of excellence as to be considered well worth it.

In October, 1810, Napoleon issued a new decree from Fontainebleau which called for the destruction throughout the empire of all British goods except those few which had entered by means of licenses.[5] Customs courts were set up to try nonconformers, and agents were busily engaged in seeking evidence.

---

[5] This secret licensing arrangement provided at high cost a limited opportunity for French merchants to import certain English manufactured and colonial goods provided they exported French products of an equal value.

Although the economic battle which raged between England and Napoleon hurt both sides, it was the former which suffered the least. Her troubles from the Continental System were sporadic and temporary, whereas Napoleon's were cumulative. Beginning in 1810, he resorted to the practice of annexing territories guilty of smuggling. This practice did not help France because Napoleon's fiscal policies had so disrupted the Continent's economic life that speculation was rampant. Unkind agricultural years in 1810 and 1811 made things worse and resulted in a near famine, wide unemployment, high prices, and resultant economic dislocation. The suffering brought on might be borne reluctantly by the French, but not by the allies and satellites.

THE ROAD TO MOSCOW

The years from 1810 to 1812 were the most peaceful since Amiens, but the quiet was not a restful one. The Peninsular campaign was still in progress; the Continental System, as we have seen, was producing discontent; Prussia was undergoing a renaissance; and the Russian Czar Alexander I was growing increasingly restive.

The latter had become more and more wary of Napoleon, following their conference at Erfurt. The Austrian marriage confirmed his suspicions that Napoleon intended to replace Russia with Austria. Again, Napoleon's refusal to give the Russians a free hand in Constantinople angered Alexander, as did the Emperor's incorporation of the north German coast with France, together with the deposition of Alexander's kinsman, the Duke of Oldenburg. Moreover, the Czar feared that Bonaparte had plans to restore Poland as a buffer state against Russia.

On Napoleon's side, the defeat or neutralization of Russia was essential to his dream of a European Confederation under his rule. Furthermore, Russia's refusal to cooperate fully in making the Continental System a success irritated him, as did Alexander's offer of independence to the Poles under Russian protection in 1812.

Both sides began preparations for a conflict. Napoleon signed alliances with Austria and Prussia whereby these countries agreed to supply him with 30,000 and 20,000 troops respectively. To prosecute the war, the Emperor raised his famous Grand Army, which numbered some 600,000 and included Germans, Swiss, Poles, Dutch, Austrians, Croats, Spaniards, and Italians! About one-third were French, a result of the fact that the flower of the French army was fighting in Spain.

Russia was not idle for its part. A treaty with Sweden, since 1809 led by its new Crown Prince and heir to the throne, the Napoleonic Marshal Bernadotte, who had recently broken with his old mentor, was signed in early 1812. That same spring Russia made peace with Turkey and also with England.

Following initial minor successes, the well-equipped Grand Army defeated the Russians in the sanguinary battle of Borodino, 7 September 1812. One week later, the French were in Moscow, which they found a deserted city. The following day mysterious fires began to break out and spread so that by the end of a week three-quarters of the city was destroyed. Hoping to receive a favorable reply to his request of Alexander that he surrender, Napoleon waited five weeks in Moscow in vain. Then he began 18 October the disastrous retreat. The weather proved an ally of Russia, just as space had been during the invasion. As Victor Hugo laconically remarked, "It snowed." When safety was finally reached in December, about one-sixth of the original army remained alive. A quarter of a million men had lost their lives on Russian soil. The rest were prisoners or had deserted. Thus had a fourth attempt to invade Russia ended.[6]

Despite the censorship which had characterized Napoleon's regime,[7] disconcerting news had trickled back to Paris. An abortive republican plot had been smashed and the central figures executed. Nonetheless, the situation remained critical. As far back as 1808, Talleyrand had become involved in another plot which had foreign backing. It, too, had failed, but it had established in several foreign capitals the slippery foreign minister as a man to watch and possibly utilize if the right occasion arose. Mindful of the uncertainties of his position, the Emperor early in 1813 had passed an act which set up a regency under the Empress until the young King of Rome attained his majority.

Determined to defeat England and Russia once and for all, the desperate Emperor resorted to every expedient to prepare for new campaigns in the spring of 1813. He had the necessary legislation enacted to provide new recruits, and he endeavored to pacify the Catholics by signing a new concordat with the Pope.

THE WAR OF LIBERATION

However, two of the nations which had supplied officers and men for the Grand Army felt that the time was ripe to overthrow the tyrant. Prussia had undergone a remarkable regeneration following its defeat at

[6] Since the Kievan period, there have been five attempts to conquer all of Russia militarily. The invasions of the Tartars in the thirteenth century and of the "Tushino" Poles in the early seventeenth century were successful, whereas those of Charles XII, Napoleon, and Hitler were failures.

[7] For example, news of Trafalgar was kept from the French people until after Napoleon's downfall.

Jena and Auerstadt in 1806. Prussian intellectuals had early praised the spirit of the Revolution and were eager for the same reforms to visit their country. The romantic reaction against the Age of Reason had its spokesmen in Prussia also, who preached the glories of the past and the greatness of the state. By crying down provincialism, they emphasized the importance of the German fatherland. An age of reform set in from 1807 to 1815 and was spearheaded by the work of such reformers and intellectuals as the Baron vom Stein, ably assisted by Hardenberg. They revamped the systems of local government, abolished serfdom, freed industry from grinding exactions by the state, and improved the fiscal system. The army was remodeled along the lines of universal military service by such men as Scharnhorst, Gneisenau, and Clausewitz. Despite Napoleon's limitation of the Prussian army to a size of 42,000 men, the Prussians got around this by the ingenious device of short-term training of recruits. Once they had served long enough to master the basic requirements of the soldier, they went into the reserves, new men took their place, and the process was repeated.

Patriotic literature was widely propagandized, and patriotic organizations were formed, *e.g.,* the *Tugendbund.* The University of Berlin was founded in 1810 to further educational reforms. Most effective among the intellectuals who stressed the new German nationalism was Fichte, whose *Reden an die deutsche Nation* (Addresses to the German Nation), 1807–1808, gave a great impetus to the movement.

On 3 February 1813, Frederick William III appealed to his people from Breslau to form volunteer corps. Partial mobilization of regulars quickly followed, and on 28 February Prussia signed the Treaty of Kalesch with Russia. This military alliance pledged Prussia a return to her 1806 status should victory be achieved. Shortly afterward, in March, England and Sweden also signed a military alliance aimed against Napoleon. Prussia felt ready and so declared war on France (17 March 1813). Thus began the famous War of Liberation.

Austria took advantage of Napoleon's difficulties by announcing in the spring of 1813, after the war had begun, its intention of being an "armed mediator." In other words, Metternich skillfully put his country into the position of an armed neutral while waiting to find out which way the wind would blow.

The Final Coalition. In May, Napoleon won a series of victories over the allies in Germany. At this point Metternich projected himself onto the scene and arranged a temporary armistice which lasted until August. While this was in effect, England signed treaties with Russia and Prussia pledging financial assistance to both, in return for their promise not to reach a separate peace with France.

From 5 July to 11 August, a Congress of Prague was held with

Austria as mediator, but it led to failure, and Austria issued a declaration of war against France. She, too, was given financial assistance by the British. The factor which probably dictated Metternich's action, however, was the news from Spain on the eve of the Congress. Joseph Bonaparte had been forced to flee for his life, and Wellington and the Spaniards had virtually ended the long, dreary war of attrition which had cost Napoleon several hundreds of thousands of his best men.

On 16–19 October came the great "Battle of the Nations" at Leipzig, where Napoleon was soundly beaten by the allies and driven across the Rhine. All around him his puppets began to desert. On 8 November, the allies proposed a peace to Napoleon which would leave him the Alps and the Rhine as French boundaries. His refusal left him on the defensive, vainly seeking to protect France from the conquering enemy armies.

Meanwhile, the conqueror of Spain, Wellington, had crashed into southern France and continued his successes until 10 April 1814, when he concluded the southern campaign in a blaze of glory at Toulouse.

Napoleon's brilliance was one of the few things which failed to desert him, but his common sense seems to have gone, as his refusal of the generous terms offered by the allies would indicate. His egoism and firm belief in his destiny drove this "world spirit on horseback" to fight on against hopeless odds. Setbacks continued, and on 31 March the allies entered Paris shortly before Napoleon arrived for a last-ditch defense. The refusal of his marshals to continue the fight left him no alternative, and on 6 April, the Emperor abdicated at Fontainebleau in favor of his son. This settlement proved unsatisfactory to the victors, and a few days later he made his surrender unconditional. He was given sovereignty over the island of Elba in the Mediterranean, together with an annual pension of 2 million francs. The French senate, under the influence of Talleyrand, declared the Bourbons restored in the person of Louis XVIII, brother of the executed Louis XVI. Bernadotte, incidentally, made an unsuccessful bid for the throne, but the opposition of Talleyrand was too formidable.

THE HUNDRED DAYS

The allies now turned to the important business of making a peace treaty with France. The first Treaty of Paris (30 May 1814), was a handsome one from the French point of view. She was allowed to keep her 1792 borders, which represented something of a gain over those of 1789, since parts of the papal holdings, Germany, Italy, and Belgium had been added in the first flush of the Revolution. No indemnity was required, and in the colonial field France lost only Tobago, St. Lucia, and Mauritius (all to England) and the Spanish part of Santo Domingo was restored to Spain. On the other hand, Portugal returned French Guiana. The general European settlement, owing to its numerous ramifications, was postponed for a careful consideration at Vienna. The leniency of the allies toward France was dictated by a desire to restore the Bourbons to a reasonably strong and at the same time relatively stable country. But the French were not pleased with the drab regime which had emerged from the long years of color and excitement. This fact played into the hands of Napoleon, who was informed of domestic developments, and, coupled with the disagreement among the allies which had developed at Vienna, it led him to risk everything on a gigantic gamble. He escaped from Elba and landed on the Riviera with a number of faithful followers, 1 March 1815, and set out immediately for Paris. Troops sent out to arrest him went over to him with shouts of *"Vive l'Empereur!"* On 20 March he was back in Paris in a short-lived triumph destined to last only 100 days. The Bourbons had fled, leaving him temporarily master of France. So far so good, but one of his guesses went awry. The allies quickly ended their differences at Vienna and opposed him, much to his chagrin. The Big Four (England, Austria, Prussia, Russia) formed a new alliance against him, and all other European countries were invited to join.

In June, Napoleon went into action in Belgium and scored some initial successes against the Prussians, but in Italy the Austrians defeated Murat, who had joined Napoleon. The Bourbons were restored in Naples, and Murat had to flee to France.[8]

On 18 June on the field of Waterloo, Napoleon's dream was ended forever by the united efforts of the Prussians, under Blücher and Gneisenau, and a combined British, German, and Dutch army, under the Duke of Wellington. Four days later Bonaparte abdicated for a second time. A hope of escape to America was thwarted on the Atlantic coast, and he surrendered to the English. Taken to England, he was shipped by common consent of the allies to the lonely island of St. Helena in the bleak South Atlantic. His final days were spent there writing his memoirs and paving the way for the Napoleonic legend which has had such a lasting effect in France and has produced so much romantic nonsense. The "Enemy and Disturber of the Tranquillity of the World" died 5 May 1821.

---

[8] He later made a desperate attempt in 1815 to restore himself to the throne of Naples, but it ended in his execution.

13

Neutral Rights and the War of 1812

When Thomas Jefferson became President of the United States, his principal desire was to uproot the "monarchical" tendencies of the Federalists and pursue his ideal of making America an agrarian republic. He very much wished to avoid European complications. Yet before long Jefferson was as deeply embroiled in foreign affairs as his predecessors had been. The depredations of the Barbary pirates formed a minor but annoying issue which had to be dealt with. Much more important, the convulsions of the Napoleonic Wars drew the United States irresistibly into their orbit, with the result that Jefferson and his successor, James Madison, had to devote most of their attention to protecting the rights of the United States as a neutral. In the end, their efforts to secure these rights by peaceful methods failed, and the United States became involved in war with Great Britain.

THE BARBARY PIRATES

Mediterranean waters for some time had been infested with corsairs from the North African regions of Morocco, Tripoli, Tunis, and Algiers. Rather than suffer their costly depredations, the European states were accustomed to paying tribute to these freebooters. Prior to the winning of independence, American commerce was safe in these waters, since England purchased protection which applied to her possessions as well. With the former American colonies now independent, the Barbary pirates demanded ransom in return for safe passage of American vessels. American trade in the region was of some importance, and hence it was deemed advisable to follow the lead of the European states and purchase protection. In the years 1795 to 1797 Washington and Adams made treaties with Algiers, Tripoli, and Tunis, which cost over a total of one million dollars in cash together with costly gifts to the pirate leaders. Rather than go to war, the United States continued to adhere to these treaties, which were, of course, highly unsatisfactory and always subject to the vagaries of the Barbary leaders.

In February, 1801, the Bey of Tripoli repudiated his treaty with the United States and later declared war by the accepted custom of chopping down the flag-pole of the American consul. The United States for its part did not dignify the occasion with a war declaration, but President Jefferson ordered a few ships sent to the Mediterranean under Commodore Richard Dale. His blockade of Tripoli proved ineffectual, and, in 1802, Dale was replaced by Commodore Richard V. Morris. Morocco now declared war on the United States because she claimed her trade was injured. Morris, however, also proved to be inefficient and was relieved by Commodore Edward Preble. Within a short time, he had forced Morocco to end her war with the United States. The Moroccans renewed their earlier treaty of 1786 with the United States, but this time without any presents.

While this was an event of good fortune, there was a happening on the unlucky side to offset it—the loss of the U.S.S. *Philadelphia,* which ran on a ledge in Tripoli harbor while pursuing a corsair. The ship was looted by the Tripolitanians, and Captain William Bainbridge and three hundred of its crew taken captive. Bainbridge managed to get a message to Preble suggesting that the ship be destroyed in order to prevent the pirates from floating it. The expedition for this purpose was headed by Lieutenant Stephen Decatur, who volunteered his services, and whose brilliant action in depriving the Tripolitanians of the *Philadelphia* was described by Lord Nelson as "the most bold and daring act of the age." On land, an expedition led by William Eaton, American consul in Tunis, achieved a notable victory by the capture of the city of Derne in April, 1805, following a lengthy and hazardous desert crossing from Egypt. Peace was concluded in June, 1805, and American naval forces were withdrawn from the Mediterranean in 1807 in line with the administration's policy of keeping naval forces in home waters because of the difficulties posed by impressment and the conflict over American neutral rights.

This retreat prompted the Bey of Algiers to start seizing American vessels and demanding presents from the government. It was not until after the War of 1812 that the United States was free to deal with the marauders. President Madison's recommendation to Congress that war be declared against Algiers resulted in action to bring the pirates to terms, which was achieved in 1816. The whole episode tended to reflect prestige on the young American republic, since it was the first country to resist the practice of paying tribute to these buccaneers and so encouraged several of the European maritime powers to employ force themselves to put an end to this interference with their trade.

THE PURCHASE OF LOUISIANA

As was seen in the previous chapter, Napoleon came into possession of the vast Louisiana territory owned by Spain through a secret treaty signed 1 October 1800, the Treaty of San Ildefonso. When Jefferson got wind of Napoleon's plans in 1802, he naturally became alarmed, because with mighty France as our western neighbor, American plans for this region would be seriously jeopardized. It would not be stretching the truth to hold that even American independence would have been in danger. Accordingly, Jefferson sent James Monroe to France to secure purchase of "the island of New Orleans." Lying between Florida and Louisiana, New Orleans could thus serve as an outlet for the produce of Western Americans. Should Napoleon be unwilling to sell, Monroe was to talk about the possibility of an Anglo-American alliance in an effort to convince Napoleon of the wisdom of selling.

The imminent reopening of war in Europe, following the short-lived Peace of Amiens between Britain and France, coupled with the disastrous setback dealt the French in Santo Domingo, caused Napoleon to alter his plans. He therefore decided to get rid of Louisiana, which the resumption of hostilities might make difficult to hold from the English anyway. The money he could get from the United States for the sale of Louisiana could be used to wage war against Great Britain.

Monroe had scarcely landed in France when Talleyrand amazed the American minister, Robert R. Livingston, by asking him what the United States was prepared to offer for the purchase of the entire Louisiana territory. Much as he personally would have liked to conclude the bargain there and then, Livingston had to await the arrival of Jefferson's special emissary, Monroe. Together, they finally agreed with Napoleon's finance minister, Barbé-Marbois, upon the sum of 60 million francs ($15,000,000) together with the assumption by the United States of the claims of its citizens against France not to exceed 20 million francs. The papers were signed 30 April 1803. The treaty was accepted by Jefferson, although he had serious doubts about the constitutionality of such a purchase. The significance of the acquisition of Louisiana cannot be overestimated. It provided Americans with the long-sought outlet at New Orleans for Western goods, doubled the area of the United States, and provided the country with its future breadbasket.

West Florida. Into the new lands flying the American flag, settlers began to pour by the thousands. By 1810, the population of the regions embraced by the purchase reached a million, representing a threefold increase in less than a decade. A demand was voiced by those residing in the Southwest that the government take possession of Florida. Jefferson made every effort to convince Spain that West Florida was actually included in the Louisiana Purchase but failed to win his case. The settlers, however, were determined. In 1810, the inhabitants of the region between the Mississippi and Pearl rivers, the western half of West Florida, revolted against the Spanish and captured Baton Rouge. They proclaimed their independence and applied for admission to the United States. President Madison then took military possession of the land, backed by Congress, and thus West Florida came into the United States, being incorporated in 1812 into the state of Louisiana. In that same year, the strip east of the Pearl River was taken over by the United States and made a part of the Territory of Mississippi.

Tecumseh. In the Old Northwest, there remained the problem of getting rid of the Indians if the settlers were to gain possession of the lands held by the red men. The latter formed a confederacy of tribes led by the able Shawnee chief, Tecumseh. The members pledged themselves not to sell their lands to the whites and to abstain from whisky. To the frontiersmen, this action could have but a single explanation—it was an English scheme to ruin them. In 1811, the Battle of Tippecanoe was fought between the Indians of Tecumseh's federation and the frontiersmen led by William Henry Harrison, Governor of Indiana Territory. The losses suffered by the forces under Harrison exceeded those of the Indians, but the outcome was represented as a great triumph for the settlers. Harrison's charges that the English in Canada were guilty of supplying the Indians with guns and ammunition were well substantiated.

The result of this combination of activity in the Southwest and the northern interior was a desire to annex Florida, remove the Indian menace once and for all, and even to annex Upper Canada. The off-year congressional elections of 1810 sent to Washington a number of fiery young Westerners bitten by the expansionist bug and all members of the Republican party. The Twelfth Congress convened 4 November 1811, and almost half of its membership was new. The Western and lower Southern influx mentioned above came to be known as the War Hawks. Because of their extreme youth, they were referred to as "the boys." One of their number, Henry Clay, thirty-four-year-old Kentuckian, was elected Speaker of the House. Using his privilege, he saw to it that the leading congressional committees were generously sprinkled with War Hawks. Determined upon war with England, they soon found adequate excuses for such a course of action in the commercial picture.

THE UNITED STATES AS A NEUTRAL, 1803–1812

At the time of the purchase of Louisiana, it looked as if the dream of nonentanglement with Europe might well come true. The Jay Treaty, the Convention of 1800 with France, and the acquisition of Louisiana seemed to rid the country of the danger. Unfortunately, such was not to be the case. The reason lay in the importance of American neutral trade. The naval war going on between the powers soon caused serious hindrances to this lucrative commerce.

Let us briefly examine the issues. In the first place, the Rule of 1756 stated that ports closed to neutrals in times of peace would not be open to them in war. Conversely, ports open in peace were likewise free in wartime to such traffic. As early as November, 1793, the British had issued an order in council which went beyond the Rule. However, another order in council in January, 1794, restored it by reverting to the earlier situation. Accordingly, after 1794, American trade with the French West Indies began to boom. Americans were importing the products of both these possessions and the Spanish West Indies as well. They would then reexport them not only to European ports but to British ones as well by representing them as neutral property. Moreover, American foodstuffs could be disposed of at handsome prices in ports not actually under blockade. The returns thus achieved bade fair to bring an undreamed-of prosperity to the United States. To give a semblance of legality to their action in importing West Indian products and then reexporting them, American shippers paid a tariff in the United States, but drawbacks upon reexport partially compensated them.

The "Broken-voyage" Question. In his annual message of 1804, President Jefferson announced that relations with Europe were undisturbed and that American neutrality continued. However, the British began to take steps to end this situation whereby Americans were selling foreign West Indian products in British home markets in competition with British importers who, naturally, raised a strong protest in Parliament over this anomalous situation. Despite the fact that a British court had upheld the American cause in 1802 in the case of the *Polly,* an American ship captured while engaged in carrying French West Indian products to Europe, through the decision of Sir William Scott that breaking the voyage by putting in at an American port and paying duties was a legitimate practice, this decision was now reversed. In 1805, Sir William Grant, Lord Commissioner of Appeals, ruled in the case of the *Essex,* another American ship similarly captured, that the products remained French and could, therefore, be seized by the British. In 1806, in the case of the *William,* Sir William Scott concurred with Grant despite his earlier stand in the *Polly* case. He now held that the drawback which was given constituted a return of the duty paid and was not fair. In effect, he ruled, such a voyage was not broken but actually continuous.

Impressment. Because of difficulties of acquiring sufficient crews for the manifold tasks of the Royal Navy, the English had begun to resort to the practice of stopping American vessels and taking from them members of the crew, who were thus forcibly impressed into the British service. Britain maintained that such men were British subjects. Holding to the doctrine of inalienable allegiance, she maintained that British subjects could not be naturalized elsewhere, for "once an Englishman, always an Englishman." It is true that there were frequent desertions from the ranks of the British navy, but British officers who found themselves shorthanded were often inclined to be careless about identification.

To complicate American difficulties even further came Fox's Blockade. In an effort to enforce this declaration, the British resorted to stopping ships anywhere on the high seas and even to "hovering" just off American ports. Jefferson sought to wage a diplomatic war against the English in retaliation. Unhappily the Republicans lacked the sagacity of their Federalist predecessors, who had recognized the need of a fleet to back up their diplomatic maneuvers. The Republicans scorned a navy and had even ordered a halt put upon construction of new naval vessels.

While Jefferson was rather ineffectually pursuing a diplomatic path lacking the backing of force, the Continental System and the retaliatory British measures produced further interference with American commerce.

At this pressing juncture of affairs, there occurred the *Chesapeake-Leopard* Affair in 1807. H.M.S. *Leopard* had stopped the U.S.S. *Chesapeake* and summarily taken off four "deserters," three of whom were native-born Americans. Before taking the men, the *Leopard* had fired several broadsides. The effect on public opinion in the United States was incendiary and served to heighten the already present spirit of Anglophobia.

The Embargo. Furious over the orders in council and impressment, Jefferson decided to declare an embargo on all trade out of American ports. Congress agreed and the declaration took effect in December, 1807, and lasted until March, 1809. The administration's philosophy in this action was based on a belief that American trade was so indispensable to the belligerents that they would renounce their obnoxious practices rather than suffer the loss of this commerce. It needs to be emphasized that not only was trade with Great Britain and France prohibited but trade anywhere. The effects of this action by the administration were merely to exacerbate the already strained relations with both Britain and France. The American public did not like this course of action any too well and showed its dislike in the elections of 1808, when the Republican majority in Congress was reduced. The shipping class was furious and actually would have preferred a state of war to such an intolerable situation which slowly throttled its interests. The effect upon the belligerents left much to be desired; the British government appeared to be totally unconcerned, while Napoleon seized all the American ships he could find in ports under his control on the ground that he was actually helping the American government punish its own malefactors. This action was announced in April, 1808, in his Bayonne Decree. In one year of the embargo, some ten million dollars' worth of American shipping was ruined.

The embargo having proved a miserable failure, Jefferson's successor, Madison, elected to employ economic pressure in a more persuasive way. Congress lifted the embargo and replaced it with a Nonintercourse Act of 1809 which reduced the countries affected by banning commercial relations with France and Great Britain. Furthermore, the Nonintercourse Act stipulated that it would be lifted if either country were willing to rescind its discriminatory practices against American commerce. The British minister in Washington was quick to assure Madison that his country would be only too happy to do so. Immediately, trade was reopened with England only to find that the minister had overreached himself. Thus, the legislation had to be reinstituted against Great Britain. Napoleon, meanwhile, managed to get his hands on a number of American ships now in other European ports as a result of the lifting of the embargo.

In desperation, the administration now replaced the Nonintercourse Act in 1810 with an act known as Macon's Bill Number 2, which stated that the United States would trade with the power which withdrew its decrees or orders against American shipping and would refuse to trade with the other. Napoleon was quick to seize this advantage. He saw that it would be necessary only to pretend to acquiesce, and all would go well for a while at any rate. He had one of his officials write to Madison saying that the Berlin and Milan decrees would not be enforced after 1 November 1810, if either the British orders were canceled or if the United States caused Britain to respect her rights. Madison fell for this deceit and announced that we would trade with France but not with Britain. What he neglected to take into consideration was that this pledge of Napoleon's was only a note, signed not by Napoleon but by the Duc de Cadore, and not a formal decree. In reality, the Berlin and Milan decrees remained on the books, as Napoleon was at some pains to make known in Europe. In addition to resuming nonintercourse with England, the administration broke off diplomatic relations in February, 1811.

THE CAUSES OF THE WAR OF 1812

From this time forward conditions failed to improve and, in June, 1812, President Madison's request for a declaration of war against England was approved by a small congressional majority. Since France was behaving with virtually equal disdain for American shipping, a motion to declare war against her also was defeated by the slimmest of margins.

The basic cause of the war was expansion. Ostensibly, however, it was prompted by Britain's cavalier attitude toward American neutral commerce and her impressment of American seamen. The proof that the former reason explains the vote for war may be gleaned from England's willingness to offer an armistice and to withdraw her obnoxious orders. Madison refused this offer and continued the war on the ground of impressment, despite the fact that the main source of trouble was now removed by England's offer.

It must be kept in mind that Anglophobia was rather strong in the country, especially in the frontier regions, and the President felt sure of his ground, despite the opposition of members of his own party from the North and, of course, the Federalists. That opposition proved very formidable in the election of 1812, and Madison's victory was far from an easy one. The issue was quite clear. The reelection of Madison meant that the war would be prosecuted, whereas election of his opponent, De-Witt Clinton, meant peace. The votes of the Western states with the healthy aid of the South decided the contest.

THE WAR OF 1812

The United States went to war with Great Britain at a critical period in the latter's war against Napoleon. Fortunately for Britain, the United States government and people were miserably unprepared for war and lacked everything necessary for such an undertaking, with the possible exception of the enthusiasm whipped up in the West, a poor substitute for the sinews of war and the planning and strategy necessary. Lacking also were sufficient funds for the ambitious undertaking voted by Congress. New England's pronounced opposition to the war meant that the New England capitalists would not support it.

Since the regular army amounted to a mere handful, some seven thousand, the administration had to depend upon militia to wage the war. Their reaction can best be described as apathetic. Repeatedly, these detachments would refuse to fight outside the boundaries of their own states. The difficulties inherent in invading Canada can readily be surmised when one adds to the weaknesses sketched above a woeful lack of military leadership.

In the minds of the War Hawks, Canada could be captured through a mere two months' marching expedition. This expectation failed to take into account both American weakness and the strength of the defenders, who were capably led by Isaac Brock. The first two months of the Canadian campaign ended with the Americans ingloriously thrown back on the defensive. General Hull had lost Detroit; Van Rensselaer and his successor, General Smyth, had accomplished nothing along the Niagara frontier; and General Dearborn, who was supposed to capture Montreal, got as far as the Canadian border and then discovered that his men would not leave American soil. Thus, defeat coupled with inertia characterized the grandiose talk of invading Canada in the first year of the war.

In the early stages on the high seas, the picture was far more encouraging from the American standpoint. Naval units and privateers proved devastating in their raids on British commerce. Such famous names in American naval history as David Porter, Stephen Decatur, Isaac Hull (nephew of the general who surrendered Detroit), James Lawrence, and William Bainbridge scored notable victories over ships of the Royal Navy. The most celebrated American ship of the war proved to be the invincible U.S.S. *Constitution,* conqueror of the *Guerrière* and winner of the sobriquet "Old Ironsides."

The Northern Frontier. Far more important in the strategic sense were the American naval victories on the Great Lakes, since in the absence of usable land communications, control of the Lakes was vital to military success. Oliver Hazard Perry's victory on Lake Erie on 10 September 1813 broke the British hold on the Northwest. Detroit had to be abandoned, and the retreating British and their Indian allies were overtaken and disastrously defeated by William Henry Harrison in the Battle of the Thames a month later. Tecumseh was among the slain. Earlier in the same year a temporary superiority on Lake Ontario enabled General Dearborn to raid York (now Toronto) and burn the Parliament House of Upper Canada.

In 1814, the British were able to increase the tempo of their American war now that the Napoleonic venture was drawing to a close. Fortunately for the United States there was a marked improvement in leadership by this time which proved highly important in helping to strengthen this country's position. Jacob Brown captured Fort Erie on 4 July, and Winfield Scott defeated the British at Chippewa simultaneously. Both of these engagements took place on Canadian soil. Shortly afterward, on 25 July, the forces of Brown and Scott fought a numerically superior enemy force to a standstill at Lundy's Lane before they were forced to retreat onto American territory.

The major British effort to invade the United States was made by an army of 15,000 men, many of them veterans of the Peninsular War, under the command of Sir George Prevost. This force took Burgoyne's old route down Lake Champlain but did not get as far. When his fleet was destroyed at Plattsburg, on 11 September 1814, by an American squadron under Thomas MacDonough, Prevost immediately returned to Canada. In desperation the British government offered the commmand in North

America to the Duke of Wellington, but the conqueror of Napoleon declined, pointing out that victory was impossible without control of the Lakes. His advice was to make peace.

Attack on Washington and Baltimore. That same year, with their virtually uncontested supremacy on the seas, the British landed an army in Maryland which was intended to attack the capital at Washington. Outnumbered by the American defenders, the British soon dispersed their opposition and entered the city, 24 August 1814, where they nearly succeeded in capturing the President, who had expected his defending force to turn back the attackers. The commanding officer gave orders to put the public buildings to the torch, and among the edifices which suffered were the Capitol and the White House. Moving over to Baltimore, the attackers met strong resistance and were driven off. Francis Scott Key, who had witnessed the attack on Fort McHenry, which guarded the harbor, was so moved by the events that he penned what was destined to become the American national anthem.

Jackson and New Orleans. In the Southwest, Tennessee militia under Andrew Jackson scored impressive triumphs over the Indians in the battles of Horseshoe Bend, 27 March 1814, and Fort Jackson, 9 August 1814. These victories won for Jackson command of all American troops in the entire Southwest. He anticipated British use of Pensacola as a base for attacking him and beat the enemy to the punch by invading and burning the town, although it happened to be Spanish, a legal nicety which did not bother "Old Hickory" one iota.

Although peace was actually concluded 24 December 1814, at Ghent, the news had not yet arrived before the final battle of the war was fought. Paradoxically, this Battle of New Orleans (8 January 1815) proved to be both the biggest engagement in the war and America's sole notable triumph on land. The British were led by the able General Sir Edward Pakenham and numbered ten thousand regulars. Jackson's forces were a motley collection of militia, frontiersmen, pirates under the notorious Jean Lafitte, and adventurers, but they were expert marksmen superbly commanded by a first-rate soldier who took advantage of a system of defenses which included cotton bales. During the heat of the battle, which cost the English the staggering total of almost two thousand casualties against American losses numbering thirteen men, Jackson is reputed to have uttered the inspiring words: "Elevate them guns a little lower."

THE TREATY OF GHENT

Peace negotiations had gone on throughout the war. A few days after the war began, Monroe, the American Secretary of State, had written the

American Chargé d'Affaires, Mr. Jonathan Russell, who was still in London, what the conditions were under which the United States would make peace. They were: (1) that the orders in council must be repealed and (2) that impressment must cease. As has previously been noted, the British were quite willing to call off their orders but, on the other hand, felt that they could not yield on the question of their practice of impressment.

Early in the progress of hostilities, Russia offered its good offices to mediate the dispute. To its credit, the Madison administration reacted favorably and appointed John Quincy Adams, American minister to Russia, along with James A. Bayard and Albert Gallatin, to negotiate with the British and Russians in the latter's capital. The British, however, rejected the Russian offer on the ground that the troubles were of a special character which did not permit outside interference. Yet Castlereagh announced his willingness to deal directly with the Americans, a suggestion which likewise met favor in Washington. Added to the original negotiators were Henry Clay and Jonathan Russell. By July, 1814, all five of the Americans met at Ghent, Belgium, where they were joined by a British delegation, definitely inferior to the American group. The reason for such a second-rate British team was England's preoccupation with the more important matter of the problems connected with the defeat of Napoleon. Unfortunately, the American group was by no means unified. Their instructions were quite explicit and called for no settlement unless the matter of impressment was satisfactorily resolved. The British for their part were instructed to bring up the old idea of an Indian barrier state and also to make no concessions relative to the important fisheries. Eventually the American instructions had to be altered because the British were adamant on impressment.

The Treaty of Ghent included hardly any of the subjects which had brought about the war. Not a word was said about impressment or neutral rights. Both sides agreed to return to the *status quo ante bellum,* and provision was made for mixed commissions to arbitrate boundary disputes between the United States and Great Britain along the Canadian-American frontier. In addition to impressment, the issues of neutral rights, blockade, the fisheries, and the West Indian trade were left unsolved.

Despite its weaknesses, the treaty did have the advantage of bringing the return of peace and was very well received in the United States, where the Senate gave it unanimous approval. The dissatisfaction felt in England was dissipated by the news of Jackson's victory at New Orleans, and by the revelation of Napoleon's escape from Elba.

The Hartford Convention. Even New England, whose Federalist leaders had been threatening secession, was pleased because peace meant freedom to trade without restrictions. The New England Federalists, indeed, had gone so far as to call a convention at Hartford at the end of 1814 to consider withdrawing from the Union, but the movement turned out to be a fiasco. The Hartford Convention came under the control of moderate elements and contented itself with demanding an immediate cessation of "Mr. Madison's War" and proposing amendments to the Constitution designed to protect the special interests of New England, with the implied threat of secession if these demands were not met. The most astonishing part of the performance was that this assemblage of Federalists solemnly and seriously asserted the sovereignty of the states and endorsed the compact theory of the Constitution. When the emissaries who were to present these demands reached Washington, they were greeted by the news of Jackson's victory at New Orleans and wisely decided that the occasion was inopportune for them to speak their piece.

In contradistinction to the earlier expansionist hopes, the terms of the treaty were construed in the country at large to be an American victory! This naïve inerpretation contributed largely to a new sense of nationalism and helped to pave the way for the era of good feeling.

In its wake came better relations, on the whole, with Great Britain, not the least of which was the signing of the Rush-Bagot Agreement, 28 April 1817, which provided for mutual disarmament on the Great Lakes, an agreement still in effect. Moreover, the troublesome fisheries question in the northeast was partially settled 20 October 1818, by giving to American citizens the right to take fish along the Newfoundland and Labrador coasts and to dry them on unsettled shores. Trouble over this question did not disappear and was to recur frequently, but the settlement arrived at represented a considerable improvement in the position of the American fishermen.

14

The Congress of Vienna and

Its Aftermath

On 1 March 1814, the representatives of Great Britain, Austria, Russia, and Prussia, the "Big Four" of the day, had signed a treaty of alliance at Chaumont which pledged them to achieve lasting peace for Europe once France was defeated. As the moment approached for the commencement of the Congress of Vienna, hope was at a fever pitch among the peoples of Europe. There was even talk that war might be prevented forever through a disarmament agreement. Some expected to see an international court established to which disputes among nations could be directed for arbitration. Freedom of the seas was another dream cherished by many, although the continuing war between Great Britain and the United States made it an illusory hope. Various humanitarian aspirations, such as the outlawing of slavery, were likewise being entertained.

Unfortunately, the powers had other plans for the Congress, which may be said to have begun 29 September 1814, when the plenipotentiaries held a conference.[1] These representatives of aristocracy, many of whom had been restored to power through the defeat of Napoleon, were in complete unanimity on behalf of the old order, the right of hereditary princes to rule all peoples. There were no linguistic difficulties, such as beset later peace conferences, nor were there any ideological differences of note.

Decisions were reached in committee and in the informal social gatherings which were held almost continuously throughout the more than eight months of the Congress. Balls, parties, operas, theatricals, hunts, etc., combined to keep the delegates in a merry whirl of festive activities. As

[1] Actually, there was no formal opening nor was there ever a plenary session.

one cynical observer commented, *"Le congrés danse, mais il ne marche pas."* It is generally agreed that the cost of entertainment, which was borne by Austria, the host, was in the vicinity of 30 million florins.

LEADING PERSONALITIES

The gracious host, Emperor Francis I of Austria, played his role to perfection, but his personal influence over the proceedings was not particularly advanced by his lavishness. It remained for his astute Foreign Minister, Prince Metternich (1773–1859), who acted as president of the Congress, to gather the laurels for his country.

The Russian delegation was led by its powerful Czar Alexander I, who had been so largely instrumental in the downfall of Napoleon. His personal advisers were numerous and included such influential figures as Count Nesselrode, the Grand Duke Constantine, the Corsican Pozzo di Borgo, and the Prussian Baron vom und zum Stein. The Czar disliked Metternich personally and possessed toward England what might best be described as an inferiority complex.

The English representatives were headed by Viscount Castelreagh and the Duke of Wellington. Their influence was directed chiefly toward the achievement of a return to the balance-of-power system and the maintenance of Britain's maritime and colonial supremacy.

King Frederick William III of Prussia, a second-rate man who was easily dominated by the Czar, was present with his leading statesmen, Prince von Hardenberg and Baron von Humboldt.

Defeated France was accorded a place and through its veteran survivor of the entire Revolutionary and Napoleonic periods, the slippery Talleyrand, was destined to enjoy a role of great prominence. The former Prince of Benevento was again serving as France's Foreign Minister, and he proved to be one of the dominating personalities of the Congress.

PROBLEMS

The main concerns of the assembled diplomats were the permanent return of security, the restoration of the Old Regime throughout Europe (in so far as this was possible), and a division of spoils which involved a redrawing of the map of Europe.

Among the difficult problems that plagued the architects of Vienna were the settlements to be made regarding the Kingdom of Saxony and the claims to the Grand Duchy of Warsaw. Alexander I hoped to restore Poland, grant it a liberal constitution, and ally it with Russia under his personal role. Should he succeed in his design, Russia would at last become truly a European power. His principal Polish adviser was Prince

Adam Czartoryski, who saw eye to eye with the Czar. A deal consummated in 1813 had won Prussia's support for this plan in return for Russia's promise to assist Prussian territorial claims on Saxony, whose ruler had made the error of remaining loyal to Napoleon too long. British objections to this bargain were strong because of England's fears that the balance of power would be upset by the strength which would accrue to Russia should such a plan become a reality. The Austrians were also opposed to a step which would increase the power of Prussia. This split in the "Big Four" became so marked that Talleyrand's support was enlisted by Metternich and Castlereagh, and France was arrayed on the side of Great Britain and Austria by means of a secret treaty, which was signed 3 January 1815. The addition of France was the factor which broke the deadlock and prevented the possible outbreak of war among the conquerors of Napoleon.

Talleyrand as Peacemaker. It is interesting to observe the speed with which Talleyrand immediately strengthened his country's newly gained position of importance by proclaiming France to be the champion of the small powers! At any rate, a compromise on Poland and Saxony was reached at the psychological moment when Europe appeared to be drifting dangerously close to a war which no one really wanted.

The agreement provided that Austria should be given back all of her former holdings in Poland; Prussia and Russia to secure the rest of that unhappy country. The lion's share of the important Grand Duchy of Warsaw went to Russia. Alexander I, Czar of all the Russias, became king of a newly constituted Polish kingdom and granted his subjects a liberal constitution. He craftily saw to it, however, that this document contained sufficient checks to render it rather impotent. Prussia agreed to scale down her Saxon claims and content herself with about two-fifths of that country. Saxony proved very recalcitrant but finally her ruler, King Frederick Augustus, yielded.[2]

This settlement helped to accelerate the work of the peacemakers, which was temporarily interrupted by the beginning of the Hundred Days in March, 1815. To facilitate the restoration of ancient privileges and the return of a state of equilibrium in the international situation, the powers employed as guides in their work the principles of legitimacy and compensations. Moreover, they constantly kept in mind the need for containing France in the future. This was to be done through the erection of a *cordon sanitaire*, or protective barrier, whereby France's neighbors would be strengthened in order to enable them to maintain a better check on the possibility of France's return to the path of aggression. The intro-

---

[2] On one occasion, the Czar called the Saxon king "a traitor to the common cause," which prompted Talleyrand to comment: "That, your Majesty, is a question of dates."

duction of the principle of legitimacy is generally credited to Talleyrand. It embodied the return to their thrones of all the "legitimate" rulers who had been dethroned as a result of the wars which had swept Europe. In the case of France, this concept meant that the restored Bourbons were entitled to all the territory they had ruled before the Revolution. The principle of compensations may best be described as a system of rewards and punishments whereby friends of the "Big Four" would be assisted in the territorial settlement and enemies chastised.

THE DIVISION OF SPOILS

Austria regained her former position of dominance in the affairs of Italy and the Germanies. Although her loss of the troublesome Austrian Netherlands (later Belgium) was ratified, she was compensated by the award of territory elsewhere. In addition to the return of the rest of her former possessions, she received Lombardy and Venetia, Illyria, Salzburg, the Tyrol, and Galicia. Through the restoration of the "legitimate" rulers of the duchies of Parma, Modena, and Tuscany, her dynastic influence was regained in these parts of Italy.

We have seen that Prussia won only two-fifths of Saxony, but she was given compensation through the acquisitions of Swedish Pomerania and some territory on both sides of the Rhine. Her Rhenish advances were achieved by a desire on the part of the powers to encircle France with a ring of strong states. Actually, these lands thus acquired became the means whereby Prussia was later transformed from an agricultural state to an industrial giant, since these territories contained excellent mineral resources. Posen and Danzig also fell to the lot of Prussia.

For Germany as a whole, a loose Germanic Confederation composed of thirty-eight states was formed. This arrangement was a blow to the plans of those who dreamed of the creation of a unified Germany. The defeat of this hope was due principally to Metternich, who felt that a lax German union could be more easily controlled by Austria. As actually set up, a Germanic Diet under the presidency of Austria was the instrument charged with the direction of affairs common to the Germanies. The 38 states represented some advance over the 350 of the Holy Roman Empire.

The Continental gains of Russia were perhaps the most impressive. She secured about four-fifths of Poland, Bessarabia (conquered from the Turks in 1812), and Finland (taken from the Swedes in 1809).

Great Britain was content to take its share of the spoils solely in the colonial field. The English had largely financed the wars against Napoleon, and the expense to the English taxpayer was not inconsiderable. Colonies in furtherance of trading possibilities and the continued maintenance of British maritime supremacy were deemed valuable. The list of acquisitions includes several Caribbean islands, part of Dutch Guiana, most of what is now British Honduras, Malta, the Ionian Islands, Ceylon, Mauritius, and Cape Colony.

Since the Dutch had been among the heaviest contributors to Britain's gains, it was agreed that they should be compensated. Moreover, the *cordon sanitaire* around France would be strengthened if the compensation took the form of contiguous territory. The linking of the Austrian Netherlands (later Belgium) with Holland under the restored Prince of Orange, now recognized as King of the United Netherlands, seemed to fulfill these requirements.

Sweden, forced to agree to the loss of Finland to Russia and Swedish Pomerania to Prussia, was granted Norway, which was stripped from Denmark as a punishment for the latter's connection with Napoleon. At the height of Napoleon's power the Swedes had made one of his marshals, Bernadotte, the heir to the Swedish throne. Bernadotte sensed the coming of disaster in Russia and changed sides at the right time, with the result that his descendants still retain the crown of Sweden. In furtherance of the *cordon sanitaire,* the Kingdom of Sardinia, on France's southern border, had its position enhanced through the return of Savoy and Piedmont and the addition of Genoa.

About the only other accomplishments of the Congress were the declaration abolishing the slave trade, the adoption of articles relative to the free navigation of international rivers, and the acceptance of some rules relative to diplomatic precedence. As an additional check against France, the neutralization of Switzerland was agreed upon.

Defects of Vienna Settlement. This, then, was the sum total of accomplishment of what was destined to be the last all-European and none-but-European peace conference at the close of a world-wide conflict. Its defects are obvious although their source may not be so patent to the student. It was the common necessity for the defeat of Napoleon which had given birth to the alliance of Austria, England, Prussia, and Russia. To enlist the support of their peoples, these countries had either openly or tacitly pledged liberal reforms that would go into effect when peace was attained. The one goal common to all the partners was the overthrow of the common enemy. Once that was achieved, it was easy to forget domestic promises. Inertia set in and the people, sick to the death of war, avidly clutched at the prospect of peace—peace at any price. Dominating both the domestic and foreign scenes was the all-powerful desire on the part of the ruling classes to return to the *status quo ante bellum*—an understandable enough wish to do what we now know to be impossible, *i.e.,* to turn back "the clock of history." Anything which threatened that return must be annihilated.

Nationalism. And yet the disregard for a force which had already shown itself potent and which was destined to loom increasingly larger

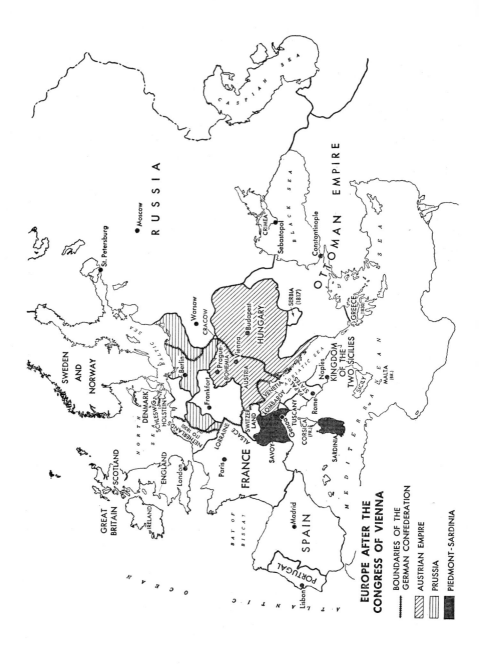

**EUROPE AFTER THE
CONGRESS OF VIENNA**

BOUNDARIES OF THE
GERMAN CONFEDERATION

AUSTRIAN EMPIRE

PRUSSIA

PIEDMONT-SARDINIA

throughout the nineteenth and twentieth centuries was both callous and injudicious. That force was nationalism. The failure of the peacemakers in this instance is amply demonstrated by the quick collapse of their settlement in the Netherlands in 1830. Here they had united two peoples long separated in both religion and economics. The Catholic Flemings and Walloons who constituted the southern provinces of the United Netherlands successfully broke the unnatural union and achieved their independence as the Kingdom of Belgium. Both Italy and Germany were the victims of a flagrant violation of the principle of nationalism, and, a little over half a century after Vienna, both finally realized their postponed unification. The hapless Poles, so often the victims of partitioning by their greedy and more powerful neighbors, had to wait over a century before they could be reunited. The union of Sweden and Norway, long unsatisfactory, was finally terminated in 1905.

If nationalism, destined to be one of the most powerful forces of the new century, had been violated, so, too, was its twin force in importance, liberalism. Everywhere power was in the hands of those whose sympathies certainly cannot be described as liberal. The "legitimate" monarchs were now all back in power once more, and democracy was looked upon with disfavor and suspicion.

But if the Congress of Vienna neglected nationalism and liberalism, it did succeed in reconstructing the framework of the European family of nations in such a fashion that despite localized, albeit sanguinary, wars and political tumults of great import, it stood fast for a century. In those one hundred years, the mother continent of Western civilization was destined to grow in influence, wealth, and prestige to such a degree that the world became indebted to it spiritually, culturally, and, of course, financially. Imperfect as was their work, in comparison with that of their opposite numbers at Versailles in 1919, the men of Vienna have undergone a rehabilitation in the eyes of many.

THE CONCERT OF EUROPE

With Napoleon successfully banished once and for all, France under a "legitimate" monarch and surrounded for good measure by strengthened and watchful neighbors, and the peace terms written, the victors were eager to make their gains permanent. Metternich earnestly desired peace, but a peace resting on the foundation of a system of collective security firmly in the hands of the allied sovereigns. The Treaty of Paris, signed in November, 1815, called for the "Big Four" or Quadruple Alliance to meet periodically in congresses to discuss the problem of maintenance of the peace, to take whatever steps might be necessary to ensure this goal, and to prevent revolutionary tendencies from reappearing. Thus the

Quadruple Alliance was to be the machinery for the preservation of the *status quo* through a system of collective security at the highest level. This arrangement was also looked upon as adequate to prevent a threat to the peace from the individual action of any particular country. A further advantage to the congress system was thought to be its ability to prevent international misunderstandings through the presence of this medium of discussing matters.

For his part, the Russian Czar had devised a mystical and none too clear arrangement called the Holy Alliance, which most of his fellow sovereigns signed. A notable exception was England, where the prince regent pleaded lack of authority. The Pope was not invited to be a signatory. Although meaningless in practice, it was confused by contemporaries with the Quadruple Alliance. In reality, the Holy Alliance was simply a pledge on the part of the various monarchs to be guided by Christian principles in their dealings with one another and toward their subjects. In 1818, the French, having fulfilled the obligations required of them by the Treaty of Paris, were admitted to membership, and the Quadruple Alliance was broadened to become the Quintuple Alliance temporarily. It can be seen that this arrangement was not a League of Nations but a very exclusive group of the big powers dedicated to the keeping of the peace by force.

The ever-present fear of the outbreak of revolutionary activity prompted the conservative "legitimate" governments, including that of Great Britain, to restore reaction in the year following Vienna. Numerous suspects were seized, and many "dangerous" individuals placed under arrest. Liberal newspapers were frequently the victims of confiscation by the authorities. Yet Britain's Castlereagh disagreed with Metternich. The former felt that to establish a police rule over Europe was neither possible nor in the best interests of Great Britain. Metternich, on the other hand, was more than ever convinced that it was the only effective means whereby maintenance of the *status quo* could be guaranteed. In this connection, Metternich was strongly supported by Alexander I. A possible explanation for this stand by the former openly professed advocate of liberal tendencies, *e.g.*, the Polish constitution, may well be his realization that policing Europe would enable him to send Russian armies marching through Europe with impunity, a point which Castlereagh doubtless well comprehended.

Revolutions of 1820. At any rate, the fears of the reactionaries were real enough, as the wave of revolutions which broke out in 1820 and 1821 in Spain, Portugal, Naples, Sardinia, and Greece[3] amply dem-

[3] The Greek War of Liberation against Turkey (1821–1829) was extremely popular in the United States, where the revolutionaries were looked upon as the virtual reincarnation of the ancient Greeks. A veritable "Greek fever" resulted. Among its lasting results are the names of such places as Ypsilanti, Michigan, and

onstrated. In each of the first four instances, constitutions were forced upon unwilling rulers by the revolutionaries. Thoroughly alarmed, Metternich, now the personification of reaction, a role he was destined to hold until 1848, dominated congresses of the powers at Troppau in 1820, Laibach in 1821, and Verona in 1822. He managed to secure adoption of his demands that the powers intervene wherever necessary in the affairs of even friendly states in order to crush by force revolutionary constitutions and to restore any "legitimate" rulers who might have been dethroned as a result of revolutionary activity. The sole dissenter to this proposition was Great Britain, for reasons to be described below. Employing the "right of intervention," Austrian forces overwhelmed the Neapolitan and Sardinian revolutions, while French troops were, ironically enough, deployed to crush the Spanish uprising and restore the miserable Ferdinand VII to his throne.

Great Britain's coldness stemmed from the fact that the British were not very keen on the idea of any permanent alliances. They preferred to go their own way by keeping the balance of power. They saw the increased power and prestige which could accrue to the state which crushed a revolution and recognized the danger such action represented to international equilibrium. For example, they did not like the thought of French influence increasing in Spain. Despite the reactionary Tories, there existed in England at this time a strong liberal movement which was appalled over the ruthless manner in which those democratic uprisings had been defeated. As important as the above reasons are to explain Britain's aloofness to the idea of the "fire brigade of Europe," it would be difficult to underestimate the significance of the fact that, were Spanish absolutism to be restored at home, there was grave danger of the loss to the British of the rich Latin-American markets, so long coveted by England and only recently opened up to British trade as a result of the liberal revolutions waged throughout Spain's New World empire against Spanish rule.

THE MONROE DOCTRINE AND THE INDEPENDENCE OF LATIN AMERICA

The United States, where the concert of Europe was popularly called the Holy Alliance, had early developed a strong dislike for this instrument of reaction. There was some fear that the "fire brigade" might actually

---

a greater emphasis on Greek architecture which was so popular in the nineteenth century. A number of Americans actually enlisted in the Greek ranks during the struggle for Greek independence. There is a tomb in Athens near the ancient temple of Olympus and Zeus which commemorates the "American Friends of Greece."

turn to Latin America in an attempt to restore Spain's colonies to their "legitimate" ruler. Should such be the case, the possibility of a conflict then with the United States was considered as highly probable. There had been widespread popular sympathy in the United States for the Latin-American revolts engineered by such intrepid men as Bolívar, San Martín, and Bernardo O'Higgins, which had succeeded in overthrowing the authority of Spain and in replacing it with a number of republics based on the American model. The American people were quite flattered, and there was a good deal of sentiment prevailing that the government accord official recognition to our "sister" republics. The leader in this drive was Henry Clay. Because of the delicate negotiations then hanging fire with Spain over the purchase of Florida, the competent Secretary of State, John Quincy Adams, wisely insisted that we move with circumspection in order not to give offense to Spain and thereby jeopardize our prospects of acquiring Florida. When that treaty was safely ratified in 1819, we swiftly accorded recognition and commenced diplomatic relations with our neighbors. In so acting, the United States showed courage, because it was done in the face of powerful European disapproval.

By the fall of 1823, following the French invasion of Spain, the popular fear of European intervention in the affairs of our southern neighbors had even reached the high level of the Monroe administration. The President himself and Secretary of War Calhoun were deeply concerned over this dire prospect.

Alaska and Oregon. A further disconcerting element was Russia's action relative to the Pacific coast of North America. In September, 1821, Alexander I issued an imperial ukase (edict) prohibiting foreign vessels from approaching within one hundred Italian miles[4] of the coast of Russian America (Alaska) north of the 51st parallel.

This was at once a rather highhanded action from the point of view of international law and an announcement that Russia had an interest in the Oregon country, then claimed by both the United States and Great Britain. These governments were quick to send notes of protest to Russia. The American note was memorable in that it contained a sentence which apparently served as the model for the noncolonization principle of the Monroe Doctrine a few months later.

George Canning, who became British foreign minister after the suicide of Viscount Castlereagh, now appeared upon the scene in August, 1823, with a proposal to the United States minister, Richard Rush, that the two countries issue a joint declaration against any European intervention in the affairs of Latin America.

President Monroe, upon receipt of this suggestion, decided to seek the advice of two living former Presidents, Madison and Jefferson, both

---

[4] An Italian mile measures 6,085.2 feet.

of whom had long been none too well disposed toward England. These elder statesmen were each in favor of the British proposal, as was Monroe himself. Adams, quite to the contrary, stood firmly opposed to such a procedure and strongly advised unilateral American action. He took a long-range view of the proviso Canning had slipped into his offer, to the effect that both parties should pledge themselves never to acquire any part of Spanish America. Adams realized that the day might well come when such action would be an imperative necessity for the United States, and he suspected that Canning was seeking to prevent us from what he, too, recognized as undoubtedly inevitable. Furthermore, Adams was convinced that the danger of European intervention was actually more apparent than real. It also seems highly probable that so sagacious an individual as Adams could deduce that the British would use their fleet in any event to prevent the restoration of Spanish power in America, in order to protect the rich market the South American republics would offer the British merchants. Adams managed to gain approval of his views in the cabinet. Indeed his role was so prominent that he has often been considered the author of Monroe's pronouncement.

Monroe's Message to Congress. The medium ultimately selected for the issuance of the unilateral American warning to the powers not to intervene in Latin America was the President's annual message to Congress, 2 December 1823. Very briefly, Monroe made known his opposition to southward expansion along the Pacific coast by Russia. He stated clearly that "the American continents, by the free and independent condition which they have assumed and maintain, are henceforth not to be considered as subjects for future colonization by any European powers." This constitutes his remarks on what has come to be known as the noncolonization principle.

After a lengthy intermission in his message devoted to other matters, the concert of Europe was informed that its "political system" was "essentially different from that of America" and that "candor" and "amicable relations" decreed that he announce to them that America would consider "dangerous to our peace and safety" any effort "to extend their system to any portion of this hemisphere." He declared that the United States had not interfered with "the existing colonies or dependencies of any European power" in the past nor would it do so in the future. Conversely, any attempt to interfere with "the Governments who have declared their independence," *i.e.*, all of Spanish America except Cuba and Puerto Rico, would be treated "as the manifestation of an unfriendly disposition toward the United States."

In conclusion, he wound up the doctrine of the two spheres by promising adherence to the traditional policy of the United States of not interfering in the domestic affairs of any European power. In other words,

Europe was to stay out of American affairs, except in the case of those powers which still had colonies in the New World, and they would be expected to limit their activities solely to these possessions. In return, the United States would refrain from any involvement in European concerns.

In reality, there was nothing new about Monroe's pronouncement. He had merely given expression to traditional American policy dating back to the Founding Fathers. Yet it was of tremendous importance in that it clearly stated what was to become one of the bulwarks of American foreign policy for over a century. American policy since the beginning of the country's independence was now crystallized and presented to the world for future reference as a clear and forthright pronouncement of America's plans for the Western Hemisphere. This was its true significance.

It received the warm support of the vast majority of the informed portion of the American public of that day, which was basking in a mistaken belief in its own power. It was (and long remained) conveniently forgotten that the main obstacle to the restoration of Spain's colonies was not the pronouncement of the United States but rather the formidable British fleet.

The British Reaction. Canning did not in the least like the American announcement, particularly since he had already taken steps to ensure that there would be no intervention on the part of the only European power which might be sufficiently interested to make the attempt, France. In October, 1823, he had received a signed memorandum from the Prince de Polignac, French ambassador to England, disclaiming any intention on France's part to send troops to Spanish America. This declaration removed the most formidable threat, since neither Austria nor Russia was sufficiently interested to undertake such a risky venture. In a petulant mood, Canning published the Polignac memorandum the following year in order that he and not Monroe would receive credit. The South American states which had greeted the Doctrine with approval now knew to whom they were really indebted. Nonetheless, the importance of the Monroe Doctrine was in no sense altered by this revelation. Monroe and Adams had performed a great service, whose importance would grow with the years.

Early Movements for Latin-American Independence. Spanish America's struggle for emancipation was the product of many causes, not the least of which were the ideas stemming from such upheavals as the Glorious Revolution, the American Revolution, and the French Revolution. As in the American Revolution, the liberators were faced by both apathy and positive opposition from many of their fellow residents in the Spanish colonies. Unlike the Americans, the Spanish liberators had few sympathetic ears in the mother country, nor did they receive any aid from the enemies of Spain comparable with that which came to the American colonists from England's powerful rivals. Perhaps the greatest foreign contribution to the work of the liberators was the one already discussed above, *i.e.,* the unofficial and even unconscious British-American unity of opposition to the concert of Europe.

Revolutionary agents frequently sought British assistance on the plausible grounds that Spain had helped the Americans win their freedom from England and, thus, England should have no compunction in assisting the Spanish colonists achieve their independence. A very enticing bit of bait constantly held before English eyes was the prospect of lucrative trade arrangements with the new countries once they became independent. Francisco Miranda, a Spanish army officer, had become quite interested in the cause of the liberators and, prior to playing the active role he later did in their behalf, had as early as 1783 sought to interest such prominent Americans as Alexander Hamilton in the cause of Latin-American freedom. In 1806, Miranda and his "Immortals" abortively began their attempt to free Venezuela by sailing from New York, which they had used to some extent as a haven for their conspiracy.

The first success scored in the long struggle for Latin-American freedom from their European masters (France and Portugal as well as Spain) was at the expense of the French in what is now the Republic of Haiti. By 1803 the French had been cleared from the island of Española, which the French called Saint-Domingue, and 1 January 1804 the independence of Haiti was proclaimed.

Effects of Napoleonic Wars. It was not, however, until Napoleon's invasion of Spain in 1808 that events played into the hands of the Spanish-American revolutionaries. Joseph Bonaparte's usurpation of the Spanish throne precipitated a veritable rash of nationalism in Spain, characterized by a wave of juntas (committees) in the provinces, culminating in the establishment of a Supreme Central Junta in Madrid. This body before dissolving itself created a regency which, in turn, summoned a Cortes (parliament).

The regency in sending out a call for the Cortes invited the colonists to send representatives, in language that was most encouraging to the liberals in the colonies. They responded with alacrity and played a part in the sweeping changes proclaimed (but impossible of fulfillment at the time) by the Cortes which touched upon conditions in the New World. Such revolutionary pronouncements as freedom of the press, the equality of colonists with Spaniards, and other equally liberal sentiments were proclaimed. In 1812, the Cortes promulgated a constitution for Spain. Unfortunately, something had happened to its liberalism. The colonists were given inadequate representation in the Cortes, and the Council of the Regency even refused to abandon Spain's preeminent rights in her American colonies.

The Winning of Independence. The defeat of Napoleon and the return of Ferdinand to the Spanish throne served to restore the old order at the expense of the liberals. The reaction in Spain gave vitality to Spanish-American aspirations for independence. Prior to 1816 sentiment for a complete break with the mother country had been uncertain at best, and only La Plata (modern Argentina, Uruguay, and Paraguay) had succeeded in throwing off the Spanish yoke. Then, however, the prospective loss of the comparative freedom enjoyed while the authority of the Spanish crown was in abeyance resulted in revolt spreading from province to province. From Argentina San Martín and O'Higgins crossed the Andes to liberate Chile and then turned north to Peru, escorted by a fleet under the British Admiral Thomas Cochrane, temporarily in the service of Chile. Meanwhile Simón Bolívar, originally a follower of Miranda, was freeing the area now included in Venezuela, Colombia, Ecuador, and Panama and was descending on Peru from the north. San Martín unselfishly gave way to Bolívar, and the final blow to Spanish power on the American continent was the victory of Bolívar's lieutenant Sucre at Ayacucho in Peru in 1824. A year later Cuba and Puerto Rico were all that was left of the once great Spanish empire in America.

Curiously enough, the brief revival of Spanish liberalism in 1820 served to strengthen the movement for colonial independence, since the upper classes in the colonies became reconciled to separation rather than risk coming under the authority of an equalitarian and anticlerical regime in Spain. This factor was especially important in Mexico, where during the 1820's a conservative faction overthrew the Spanish viceroy, O'Donoju, and sponsored the "empire" of Augustín Iturbide. This conservative influence accounts in part for the fact that the aspirations of the liberators were not fully realized. Independence was won, but, to the great disappointment of Bolívar, the new states refused to unite; moreover, for the mass of the people, "freedom" was too often a mockery which meant only the replacement of Spanish rule by a local oligarchy of great landowners. Yet the underlying liberalism of the revolt from Spain was never completely lost. If progress toward genuine democracy in most of Hispanic America has been slow and painful, it has nevertheless been persistent.

Portuguese Brazil likewise won its freedom (1822) but differed from its Spanish neighbors in that it did not adopt a republican form of government but rather an imperial one under Dom Pedro, the son of the former prince regent of Portugal. Dom Pedro, not too willingly it must be noted, granted his subjects a liberal constitution, and Brazil quickly achieved recognition from the United States, Great Britain, and even Portugal itself.

PART FOUR

The Industrial Revolution

As Western civilization entered the nineteenth century, it had to face not only the political and intellectual ferment stirred up by the American and French revolutions but also a comprehensive and accelerating transformation of its economic life as the result of the process customarily referred to as the Industrial Revolution. This term embraces a considerable variety of technological and economic developments, but its essential characteristics are two: (1) the application of machine power to production and communication and (2) the concentration of production into factory units. It was not a revolution in the sense that it represented a sudden violent upheaval. The roots of industrialization go far back into the past, and it has continued without interruption to the present. But if it is understood as meaning a prolonged but nonetheless radical change in the economic structure of modern civilization, with correspondingly pronounced effects on every other aspect of human society, the term Industrial Revolution is perfectly accurate.

The simplest explanation of the coming of industrialism is that it was a logical outcome of the rise of capitalism. In a period of rapidly expanding economic activity, with a corresponding steady increase in the demand for goods, business enterprise was naturally attracted to the opportunities for profit offered in devising methods of achieving large-scale production. But economic pressures alone could not have produced the Industrial Revolution if the Western world had not developed the degree of technological skill requisite to substitute machinery for human power. The origins of this technological advance lay fundamentally in the progress of science, which made available both a knowledge of basic mechanical principles and the techniques for making exact measurements. Science, moreover, created a demand for highly skilled craftsmanship in the making of instruments.

233

Another important factor in the process of industrialization was an increase of population in the Western world, which operated both as cause and effect of economic advance—cause in that more people created a greater demand for goods and services; effect in that better methods of production and distribution made it possible for a given society to support a larger population. This phenomenon became pronounced during the eighteenth century, largely because the progress of medicine and the general improvement in the European standard of living resulting from commercial expansion were combining to reduce the rate of infant mortality. During the early stages of the Industrial Revolution population growth became still more rapid and has continued, with slightly diminishing tempo, into the twentieth century. The process has been repeated in each society that has become industrialized.

The first country to become industrialized was Great Britain, for reasons that will be described later. From there industrialism spread with the resistless progress of a glacier. In the first half of the nineteenth century it penetrated into Belgium, France, Germany, and the United States. Thereafter its progress accelerated; by the end of the century it extended to the entire world. Each country in turn encountered identical problems: cities mushroomed, extremes of wealth and poverty were accentuated, and the question of the extent to which the state should intervene in economic matters became acutely controversial.

American experience followed a somewhat divergent course at the outset. The rapid territorial expansion of the United States made it possible to absorb many of the initial effects of industrialization without the same degree of economic upheaval as the more congested nations of Europe felt. Lack of capital and skilled labor made American industry both qualitatively and quantitatively inferior to that of Great Britain and France until after the Civil War, although individual Americans early displayed the technical ingenuity which seems to be a national characteristic and contributed many important inventions to industrial progress.

15

The Revolution in Production

The first phase of the Industrial Revolution falls into the period between 1700 and 1860. During the eighteenth century industrialism emerged as a conspicuous feature of British economic life, and by the end of the Napoleonic Wars Great Britain had become a highly industrialized state. The movement then began to spread to the rest of the Western world, until in the latter part of the nineteenth century the industrial expansion of the United States and Germany ended Britain's long primacy.

The reasons for Britain's early lead in industrialization lie chiefly in the relatively advanced stage of economic and political development which she had attained in the eighteenth century. Her extensive worldwide commerce created a demand for goods for export in quantities which could not be satisfied by the old handicraft methods of production, and it also enabled British businessmen to accumulate a surplus of capital which was available for investment in new enterprises. In disposing of their capital, British investors were considerably freer than their European counterparts. After the achievement of Parliamentary supremacy the British middle class was able to exert a strong enough influence on the government to see to it that national economic policy was designed for their benefit. The labor situation was equally favorable. The medieval guild system broke down in England in the sixteenth and seventeenth centuries, thereby removing restrictions which might otherwise have hampered the development of new industries and the organization of factories. And just as the industrial process was getting itself firmly established, the labor supply was considerably increased by the displacement of the rural population as the result of enclosures.

There were natural advantages also. The early Industrial Revolution was based on coal and iron, and Britain had ample and easily accessible deposits of both. The damp climate of the British Isles was favorable to textile manufacturing. In addition, the country's insular position gave its businessmen a degree of security not enjoyed elsewhere. Throughout the long series of world wars in the eighteenth century, culminating in the struggle against Napoleon, England herself was never a theater of military operations, except for one abortive uprising in favor of the exiled Stuarts in 1745. These wars, in fact, were a powerful stimulus to British industry, because with their own economic activities handicapped by armies marching and countermarching across their territory, Britain's allies—and not infrequently her enemies—had to depend on British manufacturers to supply them with the materials of war.

THE INTRODUCTION OF POWER MACHINERY

The substitution of mechanical for human power was, as has been stated, the primary characteristic of the Industrial Revolution. It was, quite obviously, the only way in which the demand for a progressively greater volume of goods could be met. The earliest factories utilized water power, which was satisfactory where it could be conveniently employed but was subject to the serious drawback that the best locations were likely to be mountainous districts remote from markets, materials, or labor. The full-fledged expansion of industry required a source of power which could be used wherever it was economically desirable. The first and for a long time the only solution to this problem was found in the steam engine.

Acquaintanceship with the properties of steam goes back to the days of classical Greek civilization, but, as has frequently happened in the development of inventions and industrial processes, knowing the underlying scientific principles was something very different from possessing the technological skill necessary to give them practical application. The first steam engine to be used industrially was the Newcomen engine, designed in England about 1705 by Thomas Newcomen. It was an atmospheric rather than a true steam engine. Its essential mechanism consisted of a piston and a cylinder open at one end. Steam was used to push the piston to the open end, then the cylinder was cooled, and the vacuum resulting from the condensation of the steam brought the piston back. A mechanism for operating the steam valves automatically was reputedly added by an unknown boy who was employed to do this work on a Newcomen engine by hand; he became bored by the monotony of his job and rigged up a device which let him sleep while the engine worked. Because of the loss of heat involved in cooling and reheating the cylinder for each stroke, the Newcomen engine was extremely inefficient and wasteful of fuel. It was used chiefly to provide power for pumping out coal mines.

James Watt. Early in the 1760's the deficiencies of the Newcomen engine came to the attention of James Watt, the man whose career strikingly illustrates the marriage of capitalism to technology which produced the Industrial Revolution. A trained maker of scientific instruments, Watt had worked for the University of Glasgow and while there had done considerable research on the properties of latent heat. When he was asked to repair a Newcomen engine, Watt saw its enormous waste of energy and developed a more efficient machine by providing a separate condensing chamber and by closing the cylinder so as to rely on steam pressure alone as the source of power. Later he added the automatic governor and the crank-and-shaft arrangement to transform the thrust of the piston into rotary motion. Watt, in short, worked out all the essential principles of the reciprocating steam engine and was fortunate enough, after some distressing experiences, to find associates who could make it commercially practicable. One was his eventual partner Matthew Boulton, a Birmingham ironmaster who supplied the capital and the business experience for the firm of Boulton and Watt; the other was John Wilkinson, another English ironmaster who just at this time had devised techniques for boring cylinders with reasonable accuracy.

Watt patented his invention in 1769. The importance of his achievement should be measured by the fact that for a hundred years afterward the reciprocating steam engine had no serious competition as a source of power, either in industry or transportation. The internal combustion engine, the electric motor, and the steam turbine were all innovations of the late nineteenth or early twentieth century.

THE TEXTILE INDUSTRY

The textile industry was among the first to feel the impact of mechanization, and its experience offers perhaps the clearest example of how each new process created demands for further improvements. The industry was, as we have seen, well organized for production by means of the putting-out system and under capitalist control. Even so, its output was restricted by the amount of human power which could be applied to spinning and weaving, and, since cloth was one of England's staple items of export, superior methods of production were urgently desired. Both the government and private organizations offered prizes for inventions which would increase output.

The earliest mechanical improvement was the flying shuttle, perfected by James Kay in 1738. It was a hand-operated device which increased the productivity of the individual weaver, with the result that cloth could be woven much faster than yarn could be spun. The attack on this bottleneck brought about the industrialization of cloth manufacturing. First of all came James Hargreaves's spinning jenny in 1764, an elaboration of the old-fashioned spinning wheel, with the wheel turning several spindles. The yarn produced by the spinning jenny was coarse and required the mixing of flax with the cotton. To overcome this defect Richard Arkwright patented the "water frame," apparently based on the designs of other inventors with less capital and business acumen. This machine was a bulky contrivance which had to be operated by water power—hence its name. Its appearance meant that spinning had to move from the household to the factory, because no artisan could accommodate a water frame in his cottage, much less buy one. Arkwright himself went on to become a highly successful textile manufacturer, less because of his inventive genius, whose existence can be questioned, than because of his ability as an organizer and financier.

In 1779 Samuel Crompton produced the "mule," so called because it combined the best features of the spinning jenny and the water frame, and with his invention the mechanization of spinning was substantially complete. The weaving process was now the bottleneck, since it was still carried on by individual craftsmen, but it took another fifty years to refine mechanical weaving to the point where it could compete with the hand loom.

The Textile Industry in the United States. Two Americans, Eli Whitney and Elias Howe, completed the structure of mechanization in the textile industry. Whitney's contribution, the cotton gin, which he perfected in 1794, made it possible to provide the new textile factories with the vast quantities of raw material they demanded. Previously, the cotton seed had to be removed from the bolls by hand, a procedure so slow that, even with slave labor, it would have prevented cotton from being produced in quantities and at prices suitable for large-scale manufacturing. Whitney's machine, like so many of these significant early inventions, was simple in design—a spiked cylinder pulling the fiber through a set of fixed spikes and thus removing the seeds. Its implications were far from simple. It made cotton growing, for the time being at least, highly profitable, helped to spread plantation agriculture in the United States from the southern seaboard into the interior as far west as Texas, and reinvigorated the institution of slavery. Howe's sewing machine, patented in 1846, made possible the rapid conversion of the finished cloth into clothing and also contributed to the industrialization of boot and shoemaking.

The textile industry spread from Great Britain to the United States with surprising rapidity when one considers the comparative immaturity of American economic development. The first successful textile mill in the United States was built at Pawtucket, Rhode Island, in 1790 under the direction of Samuel Slater, an English mechanic who reproduced Arkwright's machinery from memory. From then on progress was constant. The interruption of trade caused by the Embargo and Nonintercourse acts and the War of 1812 gave a considerable stimulus to domestic industry, both by cutting off the supply of foreign goods and by diverting capital from maritime commerce. Textile manufacturing concentrated in New England for somewhat the same reasons as had promoted its rise in Great Britain. There was surplus capital available from the profits of Yankee commerce, the climate possessed the necessary dampness, and there was ample water power. New England, in fact, relied on water power to operate its mills long after Old England had turned to the steam engine.

The cotton gin. From the original model.

The outstanding figure in the history of early American cotton manufacturing was Francis Cabot Lowell, who established his first factory at Waltham, Massachusetts, in 1813. Lowell had studied English methods extensively and was able to make some important improvements upon them. Because of the circumstances which resulted in spinning being successfully mechanized some decades before weaving, the British textile industry was organized to carry on the two processes separately. Lowell designed a power loom of his own and instituted the system of doing both spinning and weaving in the same plant. By the 1820's his associates were doing so well that they had to build the city of Lowell to accommodate their expanding enterprises. Lowell also distinguished himself as an industrialist with a rather more humane attitude toward labor than was customary at this time.

Elsewhere in the Western world there was little serious competition with the British textile industry until the last half of the nineteenth century. The sole exception was Belgium, whose progress in industrialization was almost as rapid as that of its cross-channel neighbor. France was handicapped by the turmoil of the Revolution, and after internal stability had been restored, its textile industry continued to place strong emphasis on small-scale production of high-quality goods, although the Jacquard loom, invented in 1801, was a notable French contribution to mechanical weaving. Germany suffered from lack of capital and political disunity.

IRON AND STEEL

Progress in the manufacturing of iron and steel was perhaps the most important single element in the early Industrial Revolution, since the economic practicability of the new machines, both in production and transportation, depended on these metals being available in adequate quantities, at low cost, and with a sufficiently high standard of quality to meet the demands of an expanding technology.

Like textiles, the iron and steel industry shows a step-by-step development from one improved process to another. The beginning of modern methods can be identified with the substitution of coal for charcoal as the fuel used for smelting iron ore. Some experiments in this direction had been carried on during the seventeenth century, but a workable technique, based on using coke rather than ordinary coal, was first discovered about 1710. It was a valuable contribution to Britain's industrial progress, since the country had limited timber resources but ample supplies of bituminous coal.

Smelting is, of course, only the preliminary step in making iron and steel. There was still no good method of turning out a finished product which would be both dependable in quality and low in cost. The development in the 1780's of the "puddling" process for making wrought iron was a major advance; in fact, wrought iron was to remain the basic metal of industrialism for another sixty years. The first process for making cheap steel on a large scale had to wait until the middle of the 1850's, when it was discovered almost simultaneously by two men working independently of each other, William Kelly in the United States and Henry Bessemer in Great Britain. Bessemer, already a wealthy man and working in a country well advanced industrially, was able to exploit his discovery more advantageously than Kelly, who operated a small ironworks in Kentucky.

The influence of armaments manufacturing on the progress of the iron and steel industry is perhaps regrettable but nevertheless impossible to ignore. Henry Cort, one of the inventors of the puddling process, made ordnance for the British navy. Bessemer initially became interested in steel because he was experimenting with projectiles for artillery. In the United

States, Eli Whitney conceived the idea of machine production of standardized parts because he wanted to manufacture firearms more cheaply. His pioneer work in this field must rate as his greatest achievement, well ahead of his invention of the cotton gin. To put his idea into operation he had to spend several years designing equipment and training workmen before he could be assured of having parts made with the necessary precision. His factory in New Haven, Connecticut, began to produce on a small scale in 1807 and eventually proved much more remunerative to Whitney than the cotton gin, since the latter suffered from the disadvantage of being so simple a device that it was much too easy for others to copy it.

Expansion of Iron and Steel Production. Industrialization in iron and steel spread from Great Britain rather more slowly than in textiles, largely because of the more complex technological problems involved. Large-scale production in Germany can be dated from the 1840's, when the Krupp works was established at Essen, but the full development of the industry was retarded by lack of high-grade iron ore, a deficiency not remedied until exploitation of the Lorraine ore fields after 1871. The United States, although it had produced iron in considerable quantities since the colonial period, lagged behind Britain in technological development until after the Civil War. Charcoal remained the principal fuel for smelting as late as the 1840's, partly because wood was plentiful and cheap, and partly because the only coal as yet discovered in America was anthracite, which was not adapted for use in blast furnaces until the late 1830's. With the discovery of soft coal and iron ore in western Pennsylvania in the 1850's, Pittsburgh became the recognized center of the industry.

One conspicuous and understandable feature of American iron production, in which it outstripped its European rivals, was the manufacturing of improved agricultural implements, for which the westward expansion of the country created an increasing demand. In the 1830's the invention of the steel plow by John Deere and the mechanical reaper by Obed Hussey and Cyrus McCormick laid the foundation for American leadership in this field. All three were able to profit from their inventions, with McCormick achieving by far the greatest success. In the middle 1840's he took the bold step of moving his business, the predecessor of the International Harvester Company, to Chicago, then well to the west of the existing industrial area in the United States but destined, as McCormick realized, to become the metropolis of a vast agricultural empire. In addition, McCormick was aware that farmers, especially pioneer farmers, would not ordinarily have the cash to buy expensive pieces of equipment, and he devised one of the earliest plans of installment payment in order to sell his products. His business sense, it should be emphasized, was accompanied by a genuine technical skill. At the International Exposition in London in 1851 his machines, greeted skeptically by Europeans who still regarded the United States as a partially cultivated wilderness, easily demonstrated their superiority to their European competitors.

THE NEW INDUSTRIAL SOCIETY

The process of industrialization which had taken place in textiles and in iron and steel gradually extended to the manufacturing of most other basic commodities. Even in those occupations where mechanization was slow to gain a foothold, such as shoemaking, the trend in the early nineteenth century was toward concentration of the workers in large plants, in which more effective supervision was possible and which offered the advantages of specialization—of having each worker perform a single operation. The effect was to bring into being a social and economic system such as the world had never seen before, with production carried on in great factories, the tools owned by a small group of industrial capitalists, and the working force a propertyless mass, with nothing to sell but their labor, a commodity easily replaceable and constantly threatened by the advance of the machine.

Urbanization. The most obvious indication of the coming of industrialism was the rapid growth of new cities. Wherever factories were located, whether because of accessibility to sources of power, markets, or materials, population necessarily gathered about them. There were, of course, important towns and cities in existence before the Industrial Revolution—national capitals like London and Paris, trading communities like Amsterdam, Bristol, and Boston, and even centers of handicraft manufacturing, such as Antwerp, Lyons in France, and Norwich in England—but most of them were small by present-day standards, and their aggregate population was a very minor fraction of the population of the Western world as a whole. The urbanization of modern life is a direct consequence of the Industrial Revolution. In eighteenth-century England the older towns, with the exception of London, saw themselves outstripped by newcomers in the north and west—Manchester, Sheffield, Birmingham —where the water power and the coal fields were located. As other countries were affected, they also produced their crop of manufacturing centers—Essen and Düsseldorf in Germany, Lowell, Fall River, Paterson, and Pittsburgh in the United States, to name only a few of the earliest arrivals.

In the main, these industrial cities were unpleasant places to live in. Most of them were small villages or simply empty fields until they were selected as factory sites strictly on grounds of economic utility, and they expanded without form or plan. The factory workers were accommodated in sprawling rows of tenements designed solely to house the largest number of people at the lowest possible cost. These conditions were substantially reproduced wherever the Industrial Revolution spread, although in the United States the humanitarianism of Francis Cabot Lowell made Waltham and Lowell exceptions for a time—but still exceptions.

· ***New Social Classes.*** The advent of the machine altered the social structure of Western civilization by raising to positions of commanding importance two classes which had hitherto occupied a relatively minor place, the industrial capitalists and the industrial laborers. The former were the chief beneficiaries of the new system of production, since the profits of successful factory operation gave them wealth on a scale completely eclipsing the commercial fortunes of the preceding era. Some of the leading industrialists of this early period were inventors like Watt and McCormick, who were able to control the exploitation of their own discoveries; others were self-made men like Arkwright, who rose from the masses by virtue of superior business ability and the ruthlessness needed to survive under fiercely competitive conditions; most were middle-class capitalists who had already made money in commerce or under the putting-out system and now invested their funds in factories because of the much greater returns they offered. For example, Samuel Slater's mill in Pawtucket was financed by the Rhode Island mercantile firm of Brown and Almy, whose wealth had been acquired principally through commerce with the West Indies. In 1750 the industrial capitalist was a somewhat rare figure; a century later he dominated the Western world economically and was reasonably close to dominating it politically.

Industrial labor presents a much less cheerful picture. While machine production has been economically beneficial to modern civilization as a whole, since the tremendously increased output of commodities at low unit cost has resulted in a general raising of standards of living, these gains have frequently been secured at the expense of the weaker members of society, among whom must be reckoned the factory workers during the initial stages of industrialization. Labor conditions were unbelievably bad. Accounts of how British factories operated at the beginning of the nineteenth century, compiled in the course of investigations by governmental authorities, read more like lurid fiction than official reports. Wages were far too low to afford a decent subsistence. The normal working day was fourteen to sixteen hours, spent in factory buildings with little provision for ventilation or sanitation, and with no safeguards whatever on the machinery.

If conditions were hard for adult male workers, they were infinitely worse for the women and children who made up a large part of the labor force because they could operate machines as well as men and did not have to be paid as much. There were plenty of them available. Wage scales were so low that every member of a laborer's family had to be put to work at the earliest possible moment as a matter of sheer necessity; for a time, also, some manufacturers made a practice of leasing pauper and orphan children from poor-relief authorities, ostensibly as "apprentices." Little children worked in factories from dawn to dusk, with half an hour off for meals, during which period they were expected to clean their machines; or sat all day in coal mines opening and closing the doors in the seams to let the coal carts pass.

Depressions and Unemployment. Accompanying these atrocious working conditions was the constant fear of unemployment. Periodic depressions were nothing new in the economy of Western civilization, but the accelerated tempo of economic life produced by industrialization resulted in their striking more frequently and with greater force. In the past, the impact of depressions had been considerably softened by the fact that the great majority of the people of Europe lived in virtually self-sufficient agrarian communities. But a factory worker had no land to cultivate; his job was his only means of livelihood. If business conditions deprived him of it, he could be sure that thousands of others would be in the same position and that he had no hope of finding employment elsewhere. With wages barely on the subsistence level, or perhaps below it, no factory worker could save enough to carry his family over until prosperity returned. He had to depend on charity or starve. In addition, the machine brought with it what is now called "technological unemployment." Each new mechanical invention benefited society as a whole by multiplying productive capacity, but it also meant, as a rule, that an older process was supplanted and the people engaged in it deprived of their occupation.

It should be borne in mind that the exploitation of human beings did not begin with the Industrial Revolution. Low wages, long hours, unhealthy working conditions all existed in previous economic systems; the factory had at least the merit of displaying these evils in such highly concentrated form that it was no longer possible to ignore their existence, and eventually public opinion was sufficiently aroused to take action. If this awakening had come earlier, some of the worst features of the arrival of industrialism might have been ameliorated, but it is doubtful whether any of them could have been avoided altogether.

The fundamental difficulty was that no one foresaw the Industrial Revolution or could have predicted the course it would take or the problems it would create. Until the consequences of industrialism had thoroughly impressed themselves on Western society, comparatively few people were even aware that they existed. It took time for the nature of the new industrial order to be understood, and more time to decide what to do about it. Meanwhile, the victims of mechanization had to fend for themselves.

THE BEGINNINGS OF LABOR UNIONISM AND SOCIAL REFORM

There were two possible methods of alleviating the plight of industrial labor short of violent overthrow of the entire economic and social system. One was for the state to use its authority; the other was for the workers themselves to try to improve matters by using whatever economic power they possessed—in other words, by forming unions. Each was a process of slow step-by-step development, contending at the outset with a public opinion which was hostile at its worst, indifferent at its best.

The launching of the trade-union movement was particularly arduous because of the formidable political and legal barriers which had to be surmounted. Since the working classes in Great Britain did not have the right to vote until the passage of the Reform Bill of 1867, they were powerless to influence legislation affecting their interests. The first important act dealing with labor organizations, the Combinations Law of 1799, was distinctly adverse. It reinforced the existing common-law doctrine that all combinations in restraint of trade were illegal by defining as criminal conspiracies all combinations aimed at raising wages, shortening working hours, or interfering in any way with industry and trade. France passed a similar act in 1791.

The Combinations Law was repealed in 1824, largely as the result of a campaign inspired by Francis Place, a remarkable individual who was by vocation a tailor but by avocation a political philosopher devoted to the advancement of human freedom. The immediate consequence was a vigorous outburst of union activity, reaching its climax in the formation of the Grand National Trades Union by Robert Owen in 1833. Owen had begun a long and colorful career by establishing a model factory at New Lanark, in Scotland, to demonstrate his belief that industry could make profits without degrading labor. Although his experiment was reasonably successful, he won many admirers but few imitators, and he was eventually forced out by partners who had no use for this humanitarian nonsense. Owen then turned to socialism and labor organization. The Grand National Trades Union was an ambitious attempt to unite all British labor into a single organization, with a program of sweeping social reform.

This first surge of union activity was short-lived. The repeal of the Combinations Law was a negative victory. It removed the worst barrier to unionization, but it still left labor organizations with an ill-defined legal status. More important, even though workers could lawfully form unions, their economic power was as yet very weak. The Grand National Trades Union collapsed in the depression of 1837. For the next ten years the energies of British working classes were absorbed by the Chartist movement, a purely political agitation directed at winning manhood suffrage. When Chartism in its turn failed, trade-unionism revived, but on a different basis than before. The labor organizations which appeared in Britain during the 1850's were unions of skilled workers, interested only in securing what benefits they could within the existing industrial system and avoiding all association with programs of radical reforms.

Factory Legislation. While the unions were fighting their way into existence, substantial progress was being made in legislating against the worst abuses of the factory system. With the workers themselves politically impotent, their cause had to be championed by others, and the leadership in the movement for factory reform in Great Britain came primarily from the landed gentry, supported by a few enlightened industrialists. This phenomenon can be explained in part on materialistic grounds. The landholders resented the growing political power of the industrial middle class and struck back at it economically by demanding that the government intervene to improve factory conditions. Party rivalry accentuated this class antagonism. The landed gentry constituted the Tory, or Conservative, party, while the middle class was the mainstay of the Whigs, or Liberals.

It would be a mistake, however, to write off the British factory legislation of this period as a by-product of class and party conflict. There were much deeper forces at work, the most important of which was the revival of evangelical Christianity in the last half of the eighteenth century, exemplified in England by the rise of Methodism. The evangelicals did not set out to be social reformers. When John and Charles Wesley first undertook to carry the gospel to the masses, they were trying to save souls and not bodies. But it became increasingly more difficult for anyone to be concerned with the religious welfare of British factory workers and remain indifferent to the urgent need of improving their material conditions. Evangelicalism led naturally to humanitarianism.

In the field of factory reform the outstanding figure was Anthony Ashley Cooper, seventh Earl of Shaftesbury. Shaftesbury, a landed aristocrat, was a profoundly religious man and was not motivated by any class feeling or material consideration. He could have done much better for himself by following a routine political career, but he refused all offers of public office in order to devote himself to his chosen task of alleviating human misery. His efforts were rewarded by a series of acts which by 1850 gave Britain the elements of a factory code for the protection of its workers. The first effective piece of legislation was the Factory Act of 1833, which prohibited the employment of children under nine and restricted the hours of labor for young people in the textile industry, and, what was equally important, provided for a force of government inspectors to see that the law was obeyed. Then followed the Mines Act of

1842, forbidding the use of women and children underground, and the Ten Hours law of 1847. Because the prevailing legal concept held that any regulation of working conditions for an adult male was an infringement of his freedom of contract, this act officially applied only to women and minors, but since they constituted so large a part of the factory labor force, its effect was to make the ten-hour day standard for all industrial laborers.

American Working Conditions. The United States, with its political and economic system both stemming from Britain's, produced a labor movement on the British pattern, but still with significant variations. Conditions in the early American factories were not good. Although Francis Cabot Lowell provided reasonably attractive surroundings for his employees to live and work in, and European visitors were much impressed by the neatly dressed factory girls and the carefully supervised dormitories of the city of Lowell, this example, like Owen's, was admired rather than followed. The "Lowell system" eventually broke down under the stress of competition, and the rise of industrialism in the United States was characterized in general by the same low wages, long hours, and exploitation of women and children which had accompanied its growth in Europe.

American workers of the early nineteenth century were nevertheless in a considerably more favorable position than their European contemporaries. To begin with, the United States was expanding so rapidly that, in spite of a high birth rate and heavy immigration, there was normally a shortage rather than an excess of labor. The open West drew off much of the surplus rural population which in Europe had no option but to crowd into the industrial centers. On the other hand, immigration played somewhat the same role in the United States as enclosures had in England, in that many of the immigrants, notably those who fled from famine-stricken Ireland in the 1830's and 40's, arrived penniless and had to take whatever work they could find in the places where they landed.

American labor, furthermore, had acquired a voice in government by the time industrialism got itself firmly rooted in their country. Under the impetus of the democratizing forces which reached their peak in the administration of Andrew Jackson, most states adopted manhood suffrage. In the 1830's a number of short-lived workingmen's parties of the Northeast helped to secure some reforms desired by labor, such as free schools and the abolition of imprisonment for debt, but they made little progress in the direction of factory legislation, mainly because the industrialization of the United States had not as yet gone far enough to make such legislation urgently necessary.

Early Labor Movements in the United States. This condition, along with the intense individualism of American life, also retarded the growth of labor unions in the United States. The first labor organizations to appear were local societies of craftsmen such as carpenters and shoe-makers, rather than of factory workers. In the early 1830's many of these groups combined into fairly substantial trade associations in the principal cities, but most of these bodies disappeared during the panic of 1837. Unionism did not revive until the 1850's, beginning with the formation of the National Typographical Union in 1852, and its full-scale development came after the Civil War. During this period the labor movement in the United States was subjected to some legal restrictions, but to a much lesser degree than in Europe. Until 1842 state courts customarily applied the English common-law doctrine of conspiracy to organizations of workers; in that year, however, the Supreme Judicial Court of Massachusetts ruled in *Commonwealth v. Hunt* that laborers had the right to organize and bargain collectively as long as their methods were lawful, and this decision, although not in any way binding on other states, was generally accepted.

As the effects of industrialism became more pronounced, some sporadic efforts were made to regulate working conditions. The most conspicuous step was President Van Buren's action in 1840 adopting the ten-hour day for Federal employees. The number of people directly affected was slight; Van Buren's order was important chiefly as an endorsement of labor's desire to make ten hours the standard working day. Three years later Massachusetts moved to restrict child labor, if limiting the employment of children under twelve to ten hours a day can be called restriction, and in 1847 and 1848 New Hampshire and Pennsylvania adopted ten-hour-day laws, with Pennsylvania also prohibiting child labor in some industries. American society was still so predominantly agrarian both in composition and outlook that leading labor reformers, such as Horace Greeley and the Englishman George Henry Evans, were disposed to seek relief for the working classes in free homesteads ("Vote yourself a farm" was the slogan of Evans' newspaper, *The Working Man's Advocate,* and Greeley's "Go West, young man" is familiar to all Americans), rather than in factory codes. It was a mistaken conception, because factory workers as a class were neither qualified for farm life nor attracted to it, but it shows how strongly the frontier influenced American thinking on economic problems.

16

The Revolution in Transportation

In the creation of modern industrial civilization the development of new methods of transportation is at least as important as the application of machine power to production. Large-scale manufacturing demands the ability to draw raw materials from an extensive area and distribute the finished products to a wide market. Both requirements can be met only if methods are available for moving large quantities of commodities cheaply and efficiently. Until the middle of the eighteenth century—only two hundred years ago—such methods did not exist. Transportation had not changed fundamentally since the beginning of civilization. Goods were carried on land by animal-drawn vehicles over poor roads, a slow and prohibitively expensive process. Water transportation met the test of cheapness, but, despite improvement in the art of navigation and the construction of sailing ships, it was still slow and uncertain.

ROADS AND CANALS

The most urgent need for improvement was in the field of inland transportation. After the fall of the Roman Empire the art of roadbuilding became almost extinct in the Western world. As a matter of fact, at the beginning of the eighteenth century the best roads in England were still those the Romans had left behind them fifteen hundred years before. The others—and this description can be applied to most of the rest of Europe— were seldom more than dirt tracks, barely passable in dry weather and completely impassable in wet. Responsibility for their upkeep was in the hands of the local parish authorities, whose efforts were usually limited to having some dirt occasionally thrown into the worst holes.

The first step taken in England to improve these conditions was the

249

chartering of turnpike companies, beginning in the 1660's, to construct roads with private capital and reimburse themselves by collecting tolls. Some useful work was done in this way, but many of the turnpike companies turned out to be purely speculative enterprises, while others neglected to keep their roads in repair after they had been built. In any event, little effective progress was possible until improved methods of highway construction were developed in the latter part of the eighteenth century. The pioneers in this field were two Scots engineers, Thomas Telford and John McAdam. Their principles were essentially the same, based on successive layers of stones with the largest at the bottom and a gravel or dust surface on the top. McAdam's system was somewhat cheaper and easier and just as effective, and so his name has been perpetuated in modern highway construction.

In spite of the work of these men, Great Britain lagged behind France in the creation of an efficient highway system, partly because France, as a continental power, needed good internal communications for military as well as commercial purposes. By the time of the Revolution France had 30,000 miles of good roads, most of them radiating from Paris and practically all built by the government. Labor was provided by the hated *corvée,* which thus performed a useful national function even if it was one of the major grievances of the peasantry against the Old Regime.

European Canals. These improved highways performed their greatest service in speeding the carriage of passengers and mails. For freight they were inadequate; the roads themselves were satisfactory, but the cost of moving heavy goods by wagon limited their usefulness. The needs of expanding industry were first effectively met by canals. The canal-building era in England began in 1760, and during the next seventy years some 3,000 miles were completed. Like the turnpike roads, the British canals were built and operated by private capital, and the success of the early projects led to a wave of speculation and needless construction. The coming of the railway put most of the British canals out of business.

On the continent of Europe canal building was undertaken even more vigorously than in Britain, again with the difference that it was usually carried out by the government rather than by private enterprise. The French canal system, in fact, originated with the Duc de Sully and Colbert, the latter being responsible for the construction of the Languedoc Canal connecting the Atlantic and the Mediterranean. Its greatest development, however, took place during the nineteenth century. Germany and the Netherlands also created extensive networks of inland waterways, both canals and improved rivers. All have continued to the present day to play an important part in the hauling of heavy goods.

For the United States, internal transportation posed problems which had to be solved in the interests of both economic expansion and political unity. There were enormous land distances to be covered, and between the eastern seaboard and the growing West was the barrier of the Appalachian Mountains, crossed at the time of the Revolution by a few primitive roads: Daniel Boone's Wilderness Road through the Cumberland Gap and the military roads built by the British in the French and Indian War. American highway development characteristically began in close conformity to the British pattern. The building of the Philadelphia and Lancaster Turnpike in the 1790's touched off a boom in turnpike construction, by private capital under state charters, which lasted until the 1830's. Most of these roads were macadamized, but toward the middle of the century the cheapness and plenitude of timber led to the building of plank roads in some parts of the South and West. Their low initial cost, however, was offset by expensive maintenance.

The National Road. The most ambitious attempt to provide highway connections between East and West during this period was the construction of the National or Cumberland Road by the United States government. When Ohio was admitted to the Union in 1802, it was agreed that, in compensation for the immunity of the public lands from taxation by the state, part of the revenue from land sales in Ohio should be applied to the building of roads to link Ohio with the Atlantic seaboard —a significant step, since it represented the first utilization of the public domain as a means of financing transportation for the West. Congress responded by appropriating funds for the National Road, fixing the eastern terminus at Cumberland, Maryland, because other highways and the Potomac River furnished access to the coast from there. Nothing much was done until the close of the War of 1812, but in 1818 the road was opened to Wheeling on the Ohio. Eventually it was extended, partly finished, to Vandalia, Illinois, and surveyed as far as Jefferson City, Missouri.

As an economic agent the National Road was an outstanding success. Until more efficient means of transportation superseded it, it was the main route to the West. It carried a heavy volume of traffic and contributed much to the development of the Northwest. Its troubles were political. Orthodox Jeffersonians were disturbed by the idea of the Federal government exercising jurisdiction within the states in order to keep the road functioning, with the result that in 1822 President Monroe vetoed a bill to impose tolls for its maintenance. The government then lost interest in the highway, and in Jackson's administration it was turned over to the states through which it ran.

The Erie Canal. Canal building in the United States was undertaken with an enthusiasm rather in excess of the capacities of a young and undeveloped country. As early as the 1780's George Washington was interested in a company for improving the Potomac River, with the hope of eventually opening a route to the Ohio, and New York was speculating on the possibilities of the Hudson-Mohawk valley. The latter project was the first to materialize when Governor DeWitt Clinton finally succeeded in persuading his state legislature to begin construction of the Erie Canal in 1817. It was a stupendous undertaking. There were no power shovels in those days and few trained engineers; the entire 300 miles from Albany to Buffalo had to be dug by hand, under the supervision of men who had to learn their art as they went along—and learned it so well that the Erie Canal became a school from which engineers went out to build other canals and sometimes railroads. When it was opened in 1825, with im-

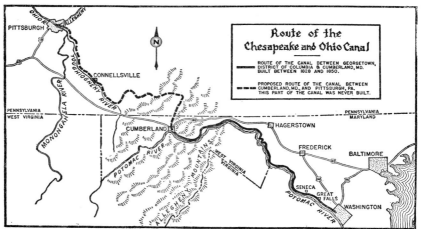

From *Chesapeake and Ohio Canal* (National Park Service, 1942, p. 6).

pressive ceremonies, it more than justified the expectations of its promoters. Freight charges between New York and Buffalo dropped to a tenth of what they had been; New York City, previously second to Philadelphia among American cities, vaulted into first place by a wide margin; and the canal tolls repaid in ten years the $10,000,000 which had been spent on construction.

The success of the Erie touched off a mania of canal building. New York's rivals tried frantically to match her route to the West. Washington's Potomac project was revived in 1828 as the Chesapeake and Ohio Canal, but topographical and financial difficulties stopped this waterway at Cumberland, Maryland, and it took until 1850 to get that far. For similar reasons Pennsylvania had to abandon the idea of building a canal from Philadelphia to Pittsburgh and substitute a system of railroads, canals, and, at the summit of the Alleghenies, inclined planes, with stationary engines at the top to pull canal boats up one side and let them down the other. This "Main Line" was never profitable and in the 1840's was sold to the predecessor of the Pennsylvania Railroad. None of the other Eastern states possessed New York's unique natural advantages; their successful canals were strictly local in character.

In the Northwest a different situation existed. There the easy natural routes between the Great Lakes and the Ohio and Mississippi rivers offered an alluring prospect of extending the advantages of the Erie Canal over a wide area. In the 1830's and 40's several ambitious canal-building projects were undertaken, with discouraging results. They suffered from being incorporated into general "internal-improvement" schemes beyond the ability of frontier states to finance, with the result that they were caught in the panic of 1837 and their completion delayed. By the time they were in full operation, the railroads were coming along to compete with them for traffic. In spite of their financial failure these canals nevertheless played a substantial part in the economic development of the Old Northwest. Just before the Civil War the state of Michigan, with the aid of a Federal land grant of 750,000 acres, built the St. Mary's Canal, subsequently taken over by the United States government and converted into the present "Soo" Canal.

Internal Improvements. The importance of internal transportation to the United States was so great that the question of how far the national government should go in promoting "internal improvements," a term referring simply to means of transportation, became one of the major political issues of the pre-Civil War period. In the country as a whole both private capital and the financial resources of the states were insufficient to meet the demand for transportation. The West in particular, with great potentialities but little ready cash, considered it imperative that the Federal government should assist in providing access to the nation's resources. There was, however, lively sectional opposition. The South, although at first favorably disposed, became increasingly hostile to a policy which would require high tariffs to provide the necessary funds and might lead to an expansion of Federal authority over the states. The Northeast disliked the growing political power of the West and was afraid that rapid expansion would drain off labor from Northern factories. By midcentury, however, Northern opinion had also undergone a reversal, as more and more Northern capital was poured into the exploitation of the West and a rising tide of immigration dispelled fears of a labor shortage.

This sectional friction made it impossible for the United States to adopt a comprehensive policy of internal improvements, although three were proposed. In 1808, Albert Gallatin drew up a plan for a nationwide network of roads and canals, to be financed by the revenue from the public domain, and in 1817 John C. Calhoun, at this period an ardent nationalist, suggested using the funds derived from chartering the Second Bank of the United States for a similar scheme. Gallatin's report was filed, and Calhoun's bonus bill was vetoed by President Madison on constitutional grounds. Henry Clay's "American System" never evolved into a concrete proposal; it was essentially a statement of general principles, aimed at promoting sectional unity by high tariffs to stimulate Eastern industry and internal improvements to accelerate the growth of the West. The tariff duties would pay for the internal improvements; the Eastern Industrial centers would provide a market for Western farm products; and the expanding West would afford an outlet for Eastern manufactures.

Federal Aid. What was done was to extend assistance in various ways to individual projects which could command enough political support. In the two decades after the War of 1812 Congress gave financial aid to some canals and subscribed to the stock of a number of turnpike companies, in the face of opposition which came to a head with Jackson's veto of the Maysville road bill in 1830. Although this road, from Maysville to Lexington, Kentucky, was intended as a link in an interstate highway, Jackson held that it was not properly an object of Federal concern because it was located within the limits of a single state. The veto did not terminate the giving of cash subsidies for internal improvements, but it was obvious that large-scale assistance of this type could no longer be counted on.

The advocates of internal improvements were more successful in getting grants of public land. The use of the public domain for this purpose appeared to be an obvious remedy for the problems of the West. The land was there in apparently limitless quantity, waiting only for transportation to make it accessible; why not, then, use the land to provide the transportation? There could be no constitutional objection, since Congress could dispose of the public domain as it saw fit, and it could be—and was—argued that it was only wise management to give away part of the nation's estate for a purpose which would enhance the value of the rest. Between 1827 and 1866 some 4,500,000 acres of land were given to aid the construction of canals, and about half that amount for the building of wagon roads. Most of these grants were in the form of alternate sections along the routes, reaching a maximum of five per mile for the major canals.

THE COMING OF THE RAILROAD

Useful as canals were, they also had limitations. They were expensive to build and required extremely favorable natural conditions. Transportation was still slow, and in northern climates all movement was likely to be stopped by ice in winter. The Industrial Revolution needed something better, and it found it in the railroads.

The railway came into existence as a combination of two separate products of industrial expansion, the tramway and the steam engine. The tramways originated in the collieries as a means of facilitating the hauling of coal from the mine to the nearest waterway. At first they were simply two rows of planks laid down to provide easier passage for wagons; later they were elaborated into wooden rails with strips of iron on the top to reduce wear and flanges to hold the wheels in place. For some reason which no one has ever been able to fathom the English mine tramways had a gauge of 4 feet 8 inches. Since the pioneer English railway builders received their training in the mining industry, they naturally used the dimensions to which they were accustomed, with an extra half inch added to allow freer play for locomotive wheels. Then, as British methods were carried to other countries by British engineers, this gauge became standard throughout most of the world.

When Watt's steam engine appeared, its possibilities as a method of locomotion were recognized, although in its existing form it was much too heavy and bulky in proportion to its power. The first major step in the evolution of the steam locomotive was taken by Richard Trevithick, an English mining engineer, in 1801. By the simple expedient of exhausting the steam from the cylinders through the smokestack, Trevithick provided a draft for the firebox which enabled him to get what was then a very high steam pressure, fifty pounds to the square inch (Watt's engines worked on pressures of five or six pounds), and thus reduce the ratio of weight to power.

George Stephenson. Other inventors followed Trevithick, and by 1815 steam locomotives, primitive and slow but workable, were pulling loads regularly on mine tramways, including an engine built by the foremost of railway pioneers, George Stephenson, a mechanical genius with unbounded faith in the future of the steam locomotive. In the early 1820's he was given the task of constructing a railway from Stockton to Darlington, two towns in Yorkshire about twenty miles apart, and was then put in charge of a much more important project, a line from Liverpool to Manchester. In spite of Stephenson's predilection for steam, the directors of the company were for some time uncertain about motive power. Their doubts were resolved by the "Rainhill trials," held in October, 1829, in which a steam engine, the "Rocket," built by Stephenson and his son Robert, won easily. Its only serious competitor was another steam locomotive, the "Novelty," designed by John Ericsson, better known to Americans as the builder of the U.S.S. *Monitor*. These engines attained the phenomenal speed of thirty miles an hour, which caused much headshaking among the medical profession, most of whose members held that the human body was not intended to be propelled through space at such velocities.

Railways in Europe. The superiority of the railway over all other existing methods of transportation was obvious. It was comparatively cheap to build; it could haul heavy loads at low cost; it could reach localities inaccessible to waterways; and it was fast and dependable. Its expansion, in consequence, was astonishingly rapid. The Liverpool and Manchester was completed in 1830; within twenty years Great Britain had 6,500 miles in operation and many more under construction. The outlines of the major systems which would eventually emerge were becoming visible, although as yet the railway network was composed of a mass of short lines, independently owned. The fact that the railway was a public utility, semimonopolistic in character, had become sufficiently evident to produce an Act of Parliament in 1844 imposing a very mild degree of regulation.

France, with its excellent system of highways and waterways, had less immediate need of railroads than Great Britain and did not undertake large-scale construction until the 1840's. By that time France had accepted the prevailing economic philosophy sufficiently to leave the operation of its railways to private enterprise, but with construction subsidized by the government and carried out in accordance with a carefully drawn plan whereby nine trunk lines were to be built, each with a monopoly in its own territory. This policy was a product of two factors: (1) that France did not have as great resources of private capital as Britain; (2) that the military importance of railways to a Continental state required closer governmental supervision than was necessary in either Great Britain or the United States. These considerations led to outright government ownership in other countries. Most of the German states built and operated their own railway systems, although Prussia and Saxony had a mixture of public and privately owned lines until the 1870's. The rest of Europe saw little major railway development until the last part of the nineteenth century. Russia's one great achievement during the period under discussion was the line between St. Petersburg (now Leningrad) and Moscow, built by the American engineer George Washington Whistler and allegedly located by the Czar Nicholas I drawing a straight line on a map and ordering the railway put there.

Early American Railroads. Nowhere in the world was the railroad adopted with greater zeal than in the United States, because it was clearly recognized as the answer to the country's problem of internal transportation. The seaboard cities whose Western commerce was being siphoned off to New York by the Erie Canal turned to railway building with particular enthusiasm. As early as 1827 Baltimore and Charleston launched projects for reaching the Mississippi Valley by rail, and a few years later Boston attempted to tap the trade of the West by a railroad to Albany. In the 1840's, as has been stated, Pennsylvania's "Main Line" was abandoned in favor of an all-rail route from Philadelphia to Pittsburgh. Yet New York, against whom all this railroad building was aimed, became after all the first Eastern seaport to make rail connection with the interior waterways. The Erie Railroad, begun in 1835 to satisfy those counties in New York State which were not helped by the canal, managed in spite of political troubles and financial mismanagement to reach Dunkirk on Lake Erie in 1851, a year before the Baltimore and Ohio was completed to Wheeling and the Pennsylvania to Pittsburgh. Shortly afterward a second route from New York to the Great Lakes was established by the consolidation of a number of small lines between Albany and Buffalo into the New York Central.

Public Aid. With the exception of the Western and Atlantic, built and operated by the state of Georgia, American railways were privately owned. The Western states, which might otherwise have indulged in railroad construction, had been convinced by their financial disasters in the 1830's that the development of transportation had better be left to private capital. Nevertheless, public aid to railroad construction was forthcoming in generous quantities. States and municipalities bid vigorously for projected lines with stock subscriptions, bond isues, and land grants. The Federal government stayed out of the picture until 1850, when Stephen A. Douglas secured a land grant for the Illinois Central and Mobile and Ohio Railroads. Within the next ten years some 32,000,000 acres of the public domain were given to aid railroad construction in the West. These grants all gave the alternate sections for six sections in width on either side of the lines. Within a wider belt of fifteen miles the grantees could select land to compensate for any tracts within the six-mile limits which had previously been disposed of. In spite of this provision, few railroads received their full quota of land. In addition, a clause taken over from the canal grants required them to carry troops and government property "free from toll," a concession eventually interpreted as entitling the government to a 50 per cent rebate in rates from land-grant railroads.

The importance of the railway in American life is reflected in the contributions Americans have made to its technical development. The swivel truck on locomotives and cars was an American innovation, devised by John B. Jervis because American trains had to negotiate sharper curves than European. The truncated-cone form of wheel was adopted for the same reason. Robert L. Stevens, builder of the Camden and Amboy in New Jersey, now part of the Pennsylvania, designed the T rail to economize on iron and accidentally discovered the virtues of the wooden tie. The first British railways had the tracks laid on granite blocks, and American engineers copied this practice, until a delay in the delivery of granite led Stevens, rather than hold up construction, to lay his rails "temporarily" on wooden ties and find to his surprise that they were much more satisfactory. The long distances to be covered in the United States produced the sleeping car just before the Civil War, and at the same time George Westinghouse was working on his air brake, although it did not come into general use until the 1870's.

OCEAN TRANSPORTATION

The steamboat preceded the steam locomotive by some years for the simple reason that it was technically much easier to mount a steam engine in a ship's hull than to put it on wheels. Credit for its development has to be shared by a number of individuals. Between 1780 and 1805 James Rumsey and John Fitch in the United States and William Symington and Henry Bell in Scotland built steamboats that were mechanically but not financially successful. It was left for Robert Fulton to demonstrate that the steamboat had commercial possibilities when his *Clermont,* powered by a Boulton and Watt engine, began operation between New York and Albany in 1807.

In spite of this promising start, steam power took much longer to become dominant on the ocean than it did on land. The early marine engines were cumbersome and prodigious consumers of fuel; until they had been refined, it was impossible to build a ship of reasonable size capable of carrying enough coal for a long voyage. The first steam-powered vessel to cross the Atlantic, the American *Savannah* in 1819, used its engines for a total of eighty hours on the entire voyage. For thirty years after Fulton, steamships were restricted to inland waterways and coastwise traffic, where frequent refueling was practical. They were especially successful on the Mississippi River system, some six hundred being in operation there by 1860.

The steamship's coming of age dates from 1838, when two British vessels crossed the Atlantic on steam power alone. Within the next few years the Cunard Line instituted regular service between Liverpool and New York. Nevertheless sailing ships more than held their own for another twenty years. They were much cheaper to operate than steamers, not appreciably slower, and about to achieve the apex of their development in the American clipper ship.

The Clipper Ships. The clippers, evolved from earlier types which American shipbuilders had designed for privateering and other purposes requiring fast ships, appeared in the 1840's to meet the demand for speed on certain ocean routes. In the China tea trade, the first cargoes to reach London from the Orient each season commanded premium prices, and the discovery of gold in California in 1849 brought with it high profit for speedy passages to San Francisco. (The revolutionary implications of the railroad for land transportation can perhaps be appreciated more thoroughly when one considers that it took less time to go by clipper around the Horn to San Francisco than to go directly overland by wagon.) When the British Navigation Acts were repealed in 1851, American clippers took over the Australian wool trade. In self-defense, the British took to building clippers of their own.

The clipper era, however, was short-lived. The necessary sacrifice of cargo capacity for speed made them expensive to operate, and they could not survive the steady improvement of the steamship. A major contribution to the victory of steam was John Ericsson's perfection of the screw propeller in the 1840's. Paddle wheels were, and still are, a satisfactory driving mechanism in smooth or shallow water, but for ocean voyages they were inefficient. The propeller also accelerated the adoption of steam power for warships, since it enabled all the machinery to be put below the waterline, where it was less exposed to enemy shot. In addition, the building of the Suez Canal in the 1860's by the French engineer Ferdinand de Lesseps opened a short route to the Orient which was much easier for steamers to negotiate than sailing vessels.

The decline of sail was disastrous for the American merchant marine. Where the United States, with its bountiful supply of timber, had an advantage in the construction of sailing ships, Great Britain, with its superior industrial plant, was better equipped to develop iron steamships. American shipowners, too, were so fascinated by the success of the clippers that they tended to ignore the possibilities of steam. Perhaps their attitude would have been different if the national government had been willing to match Great Britain in subsidizing steamship lines, but the Southern-dominated Congresses of the 1850's were unwilling to support a business whose profits would go to the North. In the absence of such encouragement, American capital began to abandon the highly competitive field of maritime commerce and turn to the more attractive opportunities offered by the internal development of the United States. The Civil War provided the final blow. The depredations of Confederate raiders virtually drove the American flag from the oceans, not so much by actual destruction as by forcing up insurance rates on American ships and causing a wholesale transfer of American tonnage to foreign registry.

The substitution of iron for wood in ship construction was, of course, another product of the Industrial Revolution. Like practically everything else, it was a slow process, but not, as is sometimes believed, because of an ignorant asumption that iron ships could not float. The chief difficulty was that a fairly effective method had been devised of keeping wooden hulls from fouling by sheathing them with copper. This process would not work with iron. Consequently, until adequate docking facilities had been provided throughout the world, iron ships could be employed only in limited service.

COMMUNICATIONS

The improvement of transportation carried with it a corresponding improvement in communications, although most of the principal developments in this field came after 1870. Better highways and the coming of the railroad made possible an expansion of postal services. In 1840 Rowland Hill persuaded the British government to adopt his proposal for a uniform postal rate for the entire country, based on his cost analysis showing that distance was a negligible factor in the expense of handling mail, and with this step modern postal systems came into existence.

The first effective mechanical method of communication was the semaphore system evolved in France and highly developed under Napoleon I. Chains of signal stations, each one within sight of the next, stretched from Paris to the principal seaports, enabling messages which previously had taken days to transmit to be passed along in a matter of hours. The working of this system is graphically described by Alexandre Dumas in *The Count of Monte Cristo*. Perhaps because of the reaction of the rest of Europe against anything savoring of the French Revolution, semaphores failed to attract support outside of France.

The most important single contribution of this period to the expediting of communications was the invention of the telegraph. Although the principal credit belongs to the American Samuel F. B. Morse, the telegraph, like most of the great advances in technology, was international in origin. It rested on the studies of electricity and magnetism made in the eighteenth century by Franklin and others, and telegraphic messages were transmitted successfully in Great Britain and Germany some years before Morse sent his historic "What hath God wrought?" from Washington to Baltimore in 1844. Morse's relation to the telegraph was much like Fulton's to the steamboat; he was the first to make it practical.

By 1860, telegraph lines covered most of western Europe and the eastern United States. Experiments in cable communication across the Atlantic began in 1857. The cable laid in that year broke, but in 1858 Queen Victoria and President Buchanan were able to exchange greetings. Then, after a few months of service the line broke again, and it was not until after the Civil War that lasting success was achieved, largely because of the unremitting efforts of Cyrus W. Field.

17

New Economic Doctrines

The coming of industrialism and its attendant problems to the Western world stimulated an interest in economic theory more intense than had ever been experienced. One group of thinkers undertook to explain industrialism and justify its consequences, mainly by relying on the concept of natural law inherited from the eighteenth century. This school held that economic processes were governed by fixed laws with which it was not only undesirable for any human agency to interfere, but impossible. This doctrine won general support from the industrial middle class because it offered employers a convincing argument against governmental regulation or control of their enterprises. On the other side was a collection of theorists seeking to find a remedy for the evils of industrialism by radical reorganization of the economic system, concentrating about the concept of socialism, which would substitute public for private ownership of the means of production.

THE CLASSICAL SCHOOL

The philosophy of economic individualism came initially from the natural-law concepts of the Physiocrats and Adam Smith. Their ideas have been discussed in an earlier chapter and can most easily be summarized by Smith's contention that if each individual were left free to pursue his own economic advantage, natural laws would operate like an "invisible hand" to direct his efforts into activities which would be for the benefit of society as a whole. This point of view was powerfully reinforced by the growth of utilitarianism, a social philosophy first expounded at the end of the eighteenth century by Jeremy Bentham, legal scholar and political philosopher.

Utilitarianism derived its name from Bentham's thesis that social institutions should be judged solely on the basis of their usefulness, a concept which he defined as whatever contributed to the greatest happiness of the greatest number. Bentham, an academic recluse more at home with abstractions than realities, even tried to work out a mathematical table for evaluating happiness. In general, he and his followers believed that their ideas could best be realized by promoting individual freedom and enlightenment. This attitude made them vigorous advocates of political and legal reforms such as the extension of suffrage and public education, but in the economic sphere it led them to an extreme laissez-faire position, although the greatest of the utilitarians, John Stuart Mill, became a champion of social reform in the later stages of his career.

While the doctrines of economic individualism gained widespread support throughout the Western world during the first half of the nineteenth century, they received their fullest elaboration and most general acceptance in Great Britain. There they were regarded as so timeless and universal in their application that they were dignified by the term "classical." Their proponents were popularly referred to as the "Manchester School," a title symbolizing the identification of the laissez-faire philosophy with the rise of British industrialism.

Since this book is not a treatise on economics, it will not attempt to analyze the classical theories in any greater detail than is necessary to understand their influence on public policies. The classical thinkers believed implicitly in the virtues of private enterprise and unrestricted competition. They regarded the function of government as limited to the preservation of order; in no circumstances should public authority attempt to interfere with the free flow of trade or to regulate wages and hours of labor. In one important respect the Manchester School differed from the eighteenth-century laissez-faire philosophies. Both the Physiocrats and Smith were convinced that permitting the natural laws of economics to operate freely would produce general prosperity, at least in the long run; their successors had no such optimism. To them economics was an exact science whose principles must be observed without regard to their consequences. In fact, as far as they could see, the laws of economics made it inevitable for the few to prosper at the expense of the many.

Malthus. The first of this school was Thomas R. Malthus, an English clergyman who in 1798 published his *Essay on Population,* expounding the thesis that population, if unchecked, always tends to increase in geometrical ratio while the food supply can be increased at best in arithmetical ratio. The only checks which Malthus could envisage were pestilence, famine, and war, as well as a possible "prudential" check in which he had little confidence—postponement of marriage and voluntary restriction of the size of families. He was thoroughly convinced that the bulk of the human race could expect nothing better than a bare subsistence. Any improvement in the condition of the laboring classes, he thought, could only be temporary, because it would simply lead to earlier marriages and a higher birth rate, until the gain was literally swallowed up. A logical corollary of this doctrine, which the opponents of social reform were not slow to discern, was that the poor must be held responsible for their own misery, since it stemmed solely from their incontinence.

Ricardo. David Ricardo was perhaps the greatest of the classical economists and certainly the most unreadable. He was a wealthy stockbroker who became interested in economic questions because of controversies over the monetary policies of the Bank of England at the close of the Napoleonic Wars. His friends, notably James Mill, a leading utilitarian philosopher and father of the more famous John Stuart Mill, persuaded him to publish his ideas in 1817. Ricardo incorporated Malthus's theory into his "Iron Law of Wages." He held that wages are stabilized at a level which permits the working classes to exist and perpetuate themselves without increase or diminution. He was, of course, speaking of "real" wages, the purchasing power of what the laborer was paid, rather than money wages. Any attempt, by legislation or otherwise, to raise the income of the workers was useless; it would result only in an increase in their numbers and a consequent decline in their standard of living to the subsistence level again. It can readily be understood why economics was termed the "dismal science."

Ricardo also formulated the law of diminishing returns: that is, that beyond a given point the successive application of further units of capital or labor to the same object will increase the total aggregate production, but the yield for each additional unit will decline. Ricardo himself used this principle only to explain the existence of rent. He argued that the steady pressure of population on the food supply necessitated the cultivation of progressively poorer land. Since, however, the price of foodstuffs was governed by competitive market conditions and not by the quality of the land, the difference between costs of production on good land and on poor was taken by the landowners in the form of rent. In other words, landowners lived at the expense of the rest of the community.

The case against limiting hours of labor was stated by Nassau Senior, first Professor of Political Economy at Oxford and frequently referred to as "Last-hour" Senior. He maintained that most of the working day was absorbed in meeting the costs of production; the manufacturer made his profit only during the last hours. Finally, the whole body of classical economic doctrine was synthesized and clarified in the works of John Stuart Mill (1806–1873), with the qualification mentioned above, that he eventually abandoned the extreme doctrine of *laissez faire* and became an advocate of social reform.

The influence of the laissez-faire doctrine during its heyday was tremendous. Among the business classes especially its principles were accepted as infallible. The coming of factory legislation was seriously retarded by a sincere belief that such legislation was bound to be useless. Employers who might otherwise have been perturbed by the conditions under which their employees lived and worked could console themselves with the thought that they themselves had no responsibility in the matter. It was too bad, but the poor were condemned to stay poor because the inexorable laws of political economy said so.

On the positive side, *laissez faire* produced a general liberalization of economic policy. Between 1815 and 1870 the restrictions of mercantilism were scrapped throughout most of Europe, and there was a general tendency to lower tariff barriers. This movement went furthest in Great Britain, which adopted free trade as a national policy. The principal impetus in this direction was given by the agitation against the corn laws, a body of legislation built up over a long period of time, but particularly during the French Revolutionary era, in order to protect domestic agriculture from foreign competition. As Britain's industrial population increased, the country became progressively less able to produce its own food supply, and the most obvious effect of the corn laws was to create artificially high prices.

The Corn Laws. The attack on the corn laws was led by the Anti-Corn-Law League, founded in 1839 by Richard Cobden. Cobden and his close associate, John Bright, personify the Manchester School at its best. Both were successful manufacturers with a reputation as good employers, prominent members of the Liberal party, and convinced devotees of *laissez faire*. They were prepared to support any humanitarian reform as long as it did not contravene the orthodox doctrines of the Manchester School. There seems to be no reason to doubt the honesty of their motives in urging repeal of the corn laws on the ground that this action would enable the laboring masses to buy the necessities of life more cheaply, but it is equally certain that some of their fellow industrialists who contributed to the Anti-Corn-Law League were not unmindful of the fact that reducing the workers' cost of living would remove a potent argument for raising wages. The prospective loss to the landowners did not disturb Cobden and Bright, since both accepted Ricardo's doctrine that the interests of landowners were adverse to those of both capital and labor.

The landowners, however, were still strongly entrenched in Parliament and indisposed to sacrifice themselves on the altar of *laissez faire*. What brought victory to the Anti-Corn-Law League was not the force of its arguments but the catastrophic failure of the Irish potato crop in the middle 1840's. The failure would not have been catastrophic but for the iniquitous land system then existing in Ireland, which compelled the peasants to sell their wheat crop in order to pay their rent and rely on their potatoes for food. The potato famine caused incredible suffering. Thousands died of starvation, and hundreds of thousands more sought relief from a hopeless situation by emigrating, some to the already congested industrial cities of England and Scotland, most to the United States.

Confronted with this situation the then prime minister, Sir Robert Peel, decided that the corn laws would have to go. Peel was a Conservative, fully aware that the majority of his party would refuse to follow him, but nevertheless with Liberal support he forced repeal of the corn laws through the House of Commons in 1846. The overwhelmingly Conservative House of Lords was brought into line by the old Duke of Wellington, who disliked Peel's policy but, good soldier that he was, recognized that circumstances had made it necessary to abandon an untenable position. Once the break had been made with the protective system, Britain moved rapidly to complete free trade, the next important step being the repeal of the historic Navigation Acts in 1851.

For a time it appeared that the British example might be generally imitated. The Walker Tariff of 1846 in the United States, the moderate duties adopted by the German *Zollverein*, and the Cobden Treaty of 1860 between Great Britain and France all reflected the influence of free-trade ideas. There were, however, dissident voices to point out that, under existing conditions, Great Britain alone was in a position really to profit from free trade. She was so far ahead of her neighbors in industrial development that she had no need to fear competition from them and every reason to desire free access to the markets of the world.

The Protectionists. The greatest European champion of protection was Friedrich List (1789–1846), an ardent German nationalist whose desire to see his country unified affected his economic thinking. Between 1825 and 1832 he lived in exile in the United States, the result of over-enthusiastic advocacy of liberal ideas in his native Württemberg, and was profoundly influenced by American thinking on protection. List was willing to agree with the orthodox economists that complete freedom of trade among nations represented the ideal system, provided the participants were competing on equal terms. But, he pointed out, nations were not at identical stages of economic development. Those whose industrial growth was still in its preliminary phases needed to have their productive capacities fostered by intelligent action on the part of their governments, not by disturbing private enterprise, but by stimulating it through protection from foreign competition, guarantees of individual freedom within the state, promotion of education, and cultivation of the arts and sciences.

List used the United States as the outstanding contemporary example of the benefits of protection, and his theories, as suggested above, came from American sources. Perhaps because individualism and freedom of enterprise were simply taken for granted in the United States, there was no important American contribution to the pure classical doctrine during the first half of the nineteenth century. What there was of original American thought was pragmatic, dealing with such problems as the tariff and the regulation of banks. List's doctrines are essentially an elaboration of the ideas expounded by Alexander Hamilton in his *Report on Manufactures* in 1791. List came into contact with Hamilton's principles through his association with the American economist Matthew Carey (1760–1839), whose son Henry Carey (1793–1879), influenced in turn by List, developed an economic philosophy holding that national wealth depended on maintaining, through governmental action, a proper balance between industry and agriculture. Neither Carey nor List, however, can be said to have had any marked influence on contemporary tariff policies. In the United States, tariffs were determined by political and sectional pressures; in Europe, protection made little headway until the period of intense nationalistic rivalry which came after 1870.

UTOPIAN SOCIALISM

The idea of organizing human society on a cooperative basis, with each member working for the good of the whole rather than for his own profit, is a very old one in the intellectual life of Western civilization, but it did not take concrete form as the doctrine of socialism until the pressure of the Industrial Revolution gave meaning to critical appraisals of the economic structure. The first body of socialist thought to have a noticeable influence on modern life has been termed "utopian," because its advocates believed that an ideal society could be brought into being by individuals voluntarily associating themselves into model communities.

Count Henri de Saint-Simon (1760–1825) is generally regarded as the earliest of the utopians. A French nobleman who saw service in the American Revolution and later narrowly escaped execution at the hands of the Jacobins, he touched only the fringes of socialism in his economic thinking. He accepted the idea of private property, but he advocated the organization of government along economic rather than political lines and the transformation of the state into a sort of vast workshop directed by leaders of industry and science so as to secure maximum productive effort for the benefit of all. Saint-Simon's followers went further than he did in attacking the institution of property and eventually converted their philosophy into a religious cult. Since their appeal was to the intellectuals rather than the masses, the influence of the Saint-Simonians took the indirect form of contributing ideas for other socialist thinkers to use.

Fourier. The utopians who attracted the greatest popular following were a French contemporary of Saint-Simon, François Charles Fourier

(1772–1835), and Robert Owen (1771–1858). Fourier gave to the world an intricate scheme for organizing humanity into self-sufficient and autonomous communities known as "Phalanges." No detail of the organization of the Phalanges was too small to Fourier to overlook. Each was to comprise four hundred acres of land and contain four hundred families, all living communally in a single large building. Monogamy was to be abolished in favor of free association between the sexes because Fourier believed that the emancipation of women was indispensable to social progress. Private property was retained in form of stock in the community, and the profits of the Phalanges—where they were to come from cannot be rationally explained—were to be divided five-twelfths to labor, four-twelfths to capital, and three-twelfths to management.

Robert Owen. Owen, the only one of the great economic thinkers of this period to have practical industrial experience, based his system of socialism on his experiment at New Lanark. He believed that man was a product of his environment and that if he were given the proper surroundings, his innate natural goodness would assert itself. He hoped at first to achieve this aim by establishing model communities, similar to Fourier's but not quite so complex. When these attempts failed, he turned to schemes for organizing the exchange of goods without profit. The central idea was that each producer, instead of being paid in money, should receive "labour notes" representing the amount of labor time required to make his product and exchangeable for commodities valued at the same amount of labor time.

This project failed also, to some extent because the participants developed an aptitude for exaggerating their own efforts. Out of it, however, came the present-day cooperative societies, which Owen, peculiarly enough, did not recognize as a development of his ideas, chiefly because they functioned within the framework of the existing monetary system. Nevertheless, the fundamental principle of the cooperative movement is to dispense with profits, generally by refunding them to the members, and the best known of the early consumers' cooperatives, the Rochdale Pioneers, established in England in 1844,[1] had six disciples of Robert Owen among its founders.

The United States possessed a strong attraction for utopians. It had plenty of cheap land available for establishing socialist communities; its people were unhampered by the weight of Old World tradition and willing to try new ideas. In 1825 Owen selected New Harmony, Indiana, as the site of his most ambitious attempt to demonstrate the soundness of his theories on environment. Fourierism was even more strongly supported by American intellectuals. Horace Greeley and Albert Brisbane were enthusiastic advocates of Fourier's principles during the 1840's, and several

[1] The Larkhall Victualling Society in Scotland, still in existence, is some twenty years older than the Rochdale organization.

Phalanges were organized, the most famous being Brook Farm on the outskirts of Boston. It was supported by most of the prominent literary figures of contemporary New England, but it was not a success and was abandoned after a few years of struggle when a fire destroyed its main building. Altogether some forty utopian communities were established in the United States before 1850. A few which were founded by religious sects have survived; the rest were short-lived. American society was too individualistic for socialism to have a chance of taking root. There was no real pressure for social reorganization in a country offering such boundless opportunities for individual enterprise.

Closely resembling the utopians in their approach to economic problems were the Christian socialists. They envisaged the coming of an ideal society, not through the organization of model communities but through the application of the principles of Christian brotherhood to economic relationships in general. They tried to express their principles by the encouragement of cooperative societies, but their chief influence was felt in stimulation of social reforms within the structure of capitalism.

SCIENTIFIC SOCIALISM

The utopian socialists were idealists who based their hopes on the perfectibility of human nature. Although their writings contained some penetrating and effective criticisms of the existing economic order, they turned for a solution of economic problems to an optimistic assumption that men could be persuaded voluntarily to abandon the profit motive and agree to work cooperatively, an assumption certainly unwarranted by historical and economic facts. Thus the utopians contributed much to socialist thought but little to practical application of socialist principles. Their appeal was to the intellectuals rather than the masses who were the logical objective of economic reformers, and in consequence their movement was soon superseded by a more realistic approach to the socialist concept.

This shift in outlook appears in the ideas of Louis Blanc (1811–1882), who has been regarded both as a utopian and as a forerunner of scientific socialism. He believed, like his predecessors, that competition should be replaced by voluntary association, but not in the form of model communities. Blanc advocated the organization of "social workshops," essentially cooperative societies composed of the workers in each industry. The initial impetus to this process was to be given by the state, which would provide the capital to launch the workshops and operate them during their formative stages. Afterward control was to be assumed by the members. Blanc believed that his workshops would function so much more efficiently than capitalist factories that eventually all capital and labor would be attracted to them. Ultimately, he felt, the altered conditions of labor would result in people losing the profit motive and accepting the idea of equality of wages.

Karl Marx. Blanc's resort to the authority of the state as the means of instituting his social workshops indicated the approach which the scientific socialists were to take. However, except for students of economic theory the early scientific socialists have been almost completely eclipsed by the figure of Karl Marx. Born in Treves, Germany, in 1818, Marx began his career as a student of philosophy, but a growing devotion to radical doctrines led to his exile from Germany in 1843. He lived in Paris for two years and then, under pressure from the French government, moved to Brussels, where he published the *Communist Manifesto* in 1848, in collaboration with Friedrich Engels. Engels, the son of a wealthy textile manufacturer, was a devotee of socialism who threw in his lot with Marx and provided him with many of his ideas and most of his financial support. They used the name "Communist" to distinguish their movement from utopian socialism. In 1848 Marx returned to Germany, but on the collapse of the revolutionary movement there he settled in London for the remainder of his life, working on his monumental study, *Das Kapital.* The first volume appeared in 1867. After Marx's death in 1883, two more were edited and published by Engels from Marx's notes.

Like the classical economic doctrines, Marx's teachings cannot be analyzed in detail in this chapter, the more so because even his own disciples have seldom been able to agree on the precise meaning of his ideas. The essential features of Marxism can be discussed under three broad headings: (1) the materialistic interpretation of history, (2) the theory of surplus value, and (3) the inevitability of communism. The first came from the thesis, not original with Marx, that the course of human history has been determined primarily by economic considerations. To this theory Marx added the contention that history can be explained in terms of a perpetual class struggle between the exploiting few and the exploited many—masters and slaves in classical times, barons and serfs in the Middle Ages, and capitalists and workers, or *bourgeoisie* and proletarians, in the modern industrial era.

The doctrine of surplus value came, interestingly enough, from the classical economists. Marx agreed with them that labor was the source of value: that is, that the real value of a product was determined by the amount of labor needed to create it. However, he maintained, in a capitalistic society the earnings of each individual worker represented only part of the value he created, because, under the "Iron Law of Wages," he was paid only enough to keep him alive. The rest of the value produced by the worker—the "surplus"—was taken by capital in the form of profit, interest, and rent. In other words, if a laborer could produce enough for his own subsistence in five hours a day, that was what he received as wages; his output during the rest of his working day went to his employer, and under the competitive conditions of capitalism he had to work on his employer's terms or lose his job.

The Doctrine of Revolution. These same competitive conditions, according to Marx, made revolution inevitable. The increasing intensity of the struggle for profits was leading to alternating periods of over-production and depression, at constantly shorter intervals and with each crisis more severe than its predecessor. Moreover, the effect of competition was that the stronger capitalists drove the weaker out of business and into the ranks of the propertyless proletariat. Eventually this growing accumulation of human misery was certain to explode. Marx believed that violence would be necessary to dispossess the exploiting classes, although he recognized a remote possibility that communism might be introduced peacefully into democratic countries. Immediately after the revolution would come a transitional period, the "dictatorship of the proletariat," needed for the education of the people in general in the principles of socialism. When that process was completed, the classless society would come into existence, and the political state would "wither away."

Marx's doctrines virtually drove all previous systems of socialism out of existence. Their tremendous influence can be attributed to the fact that Marx substituted for idealistic plans for a new society an impressive mass of evidence to demonstrate that socialism was an inevitable product of historical and economic forces. Marx, in fact, was to socialism what John Calvin was to Protestantism; the materialistic interpretation of history had much in common with predestination. Good Marxists would, of course, do all in their power to hasten the coming of the revolution, but they could ignore failures in the comfortable assurance that they were bound to win in the end.

ANARCHISM AND SYNDICALISM

Individualism and socialism represent the two major approaches to the economic problems of industrialism. In determining economic policy the people of the Western world in general turned to one concept or the other, or sometimes to a combination of the two. There were, however, some other schemes for social reorganization which, although they attracted comparatively few adherents, had a fairly marked influence on the pattern of economic thought.

The most important of these theories is anarchism, a philosophy originating chiefly in the theories of the Frenchman Pierre Joseph Proudhon (1809–1865). He is sometimes classed as a socialist because of his violent denunciation of the institution of private property—he defined property as theft—but he attacked socialism just as vigorously. He evolved little in the way of positive theory; that was done by his disciple, Michael Bakunin, an exiled Russian nobleman. The anarchist creed was that all restriction of individual freedom, particularly restraint by government of any kind, was evil. Remove these restraints, the anarchists believed, and men would voluntarily cooperate on terms of complete equality. Bakunin and his followers believed that government could be eliminated only by violence. Another group, led by Count Tolstoy, the Russian novelist, felt that the doctrines of anarchism could be spread by peaceful persuasion and example.

Toward the end of the nineteenth century anarchism became somewhat closely allied with syndicalism, a philosophy advocating the abolition of all political government and the control and operation of each industry by its own workers. The principal exponent of this doctrine was another of the radical thinkers who flourished so freely in nineteenth-century France, Georges Sorel (1847–1922). It was a theory which satisfied the anarchists' conviction that all government, autocratic or democratic, was oppressive and at the same time offered a workable plan of economic organization for an industrial society. It has had considerable influence on working-class movements in France, Spain, and Italy.

PART FIVE

Liberalism and Nationalism
in Europe and America

During the half-century following the close of the Napoleonic Wars the Western world went through a period of considerable internal turmoil. Between 1815 and 1853 peace between nations was reasonably well preserved but revolutionary outbreaks seriously disturbed European society, while between 1853 and 1871 warfare was almost constant. Beneath all this tumult was a coherent pattern. Western civilization was trying to cope with new and powerful social forces: industrialism, which we have just considered; and two others whose influence has also extended to modern times, liberalism and nationalism.

Liberalism, which may be defined as the desire for constitutional government and ultimately for complete democracy, had been entrenched in Western thought by the natural-rights philosophy of the Enlightenment and given a strong impetus by the American and French Revolutions. Nationalism, the aspiration of national groups to become sovereign units independent of any other national group, had been a slow growth in the Western world until the French Revolution transformed it into virtually a new religion—a fanatical worship of *la patrie*. Both liberalism and nationalism at first represented challenges to the order of things established at the Congress of Vienna; later, however, nationalism was seen to be a force which could as readily be employed by conservatives as by radicals. Thus while liberalism suffered a severe check in the collapse of the revolutionary movements of 1848, nationalism continued with unabated fervor and by 1870 had achieved spectacular triumphs in the unifications of Germany and Italy. Liberalism by contrast had acquired a firm foothold only in Great Britain, although by 1870 it was showing signs of revival elsewhere in Europe.

The United States also felt the impact of these forces, although in somewhat modified form because of the differences between American and European conditions. The American people had no entrenched old order to dislodge from power, and they had already established a constitutional government, so that American liberalism could take the form of an intense enthusiasm for the common man and for carrying the democratic ideal as far as possible. To reinforce their efforts, the expanding frontier proved to be a strong democratizing influence. It was also a nationalizing influence; the more fervent expressions of nationalism in Europe had an American counterpart in Manifest Destiny. American nationalism, however, had to contend with the centrifugal forces of sectionalism, and the conflict between the two finally had to be settled by civil war.

18

Liberalism and Nationalism in Europe

The birthplace of the most marked characteristic of the nineteenth century, modern nationalism, was in France, and its parents were the French Revolution and Napoleon. The events of the Revolution had been followed very closely in both Germany and Italy by the intellectual leaders in those lands. These men were originally strong believers in internationalism and in the ideals of the French Revolution. Their interest carried over into the early Napoleonic period but underwent a change after 1806 when the full realization of the oppressive features of Napoleon took root, and he was recognized precisely for what he was—a tyrant and not a liberator of men. He had freely taken the man power and money of both Italy and Germany and had taxed heavily for his own purposes. Secretly, many began to arm against him, and great cosmopolitans like Schiller now turned toward nationalism as a result of this oppression.

Schiller, Hegel, and Fichte may be taken as examples of those who tried to interpret nationalism in international terms. They made an effort to reconcile their old spirit with the new nationalism, but in so doing they tended to make Germans out to be superior people who were more civilized than others. The transition from this stage to one of an almost irrational emphasis on one's nationalism was not difficult and the nineteenth century made it quite nimbly. The stress on one's own country had its roots in the widespread revulsion toward anything French in the period immediately following 1815 and also in the swing toward conservatism which had shown itself so strong at the Vienna Congress.

Yet despite the strong anti-French feeling, the European middle class and the intellectuals favored such ideas of the Revolution as the sovereignty of the people expressed in a written constitution, religious toleration, and the equality of all before the bar of justice. Unfortunately for their hopes, they ran up against the formidable opposition of the conservatives, now solidly entrenched in power. Hence, the fruition of their dreams was destined to be delayed some years. In order to understand more clearly the strength of conservatism in the era between 1815 and the revolutions of 1830, it is advisable to glance briefly at conditions within the individual countries then ruling the international roost.

AUSTRIA

The empire of the Hapsburgs was a citadel of conservatism. The personal power of the Emperor was considerable and his chief minister, Metternich, shared that strength. So influential was the latter in European affairs that the period 1815–1848 is often called the Age of Metternich. The diverse peoples who were the subjects of the Emperor were so split linguistically, racially, and even religiously that the sole thing they possessed in common was their allegiance to the crown. They completely lacked political power, which was safely concentrated in the hands of the aristocrats. To do the work of government, there was a large bureaucracy recruited largely from the ranks of the middle class, which was otherwise unimportant and small in numbers.

To perpetuate this system called for a rigid censorship of speech, press, and assembly. Furthermore, the stronger conservatism tended to be everywhere, the easier the task became domestically. Thus, Metternich had from the first been a champion of collective action in the interests of conservatism. Any leak in the dike he considered a potential disaster which must be repaired immediately to prevent its spread.

This explains Metternich's vigilance in keeping close watch over affairs in nearby Germany and Italy. He it was who had dissuaded Frederick William III from granting his subjects a constitution. Moreover, he persistently used Austria's dominant position in the Germanic Confederation as a sounding board from which there constantly issued fulminations against even potential revolutionary activities.

The radical tendencies of the German student fraternities, or *Burschenschaften,* combined with the murder of a Russian spy, Kotzebue, by a psychopathic Prussian student, Karl Sand, led Metternich in 1819 to jam through the German Diet reactionary decrees called collectively the Karlsbad Decrees. Included in these measures were provisions for the dissolution of the *Burschenschaften,* the dismissal of any professors in German universities suspected of liberal tendencies, further strengthening of the censorship laws, and a concerted witch hunt for all radicals.

RUSSIA

Meanwhile, in Russia, the liberalism of Alexander I had shown itself to be more apparent than real. Such events as the assassination of his agent, Kotzebue, a mutiny among Russian troops, and the dissatisfaction of the Poles with the constitution he had granted them proved too much for Alexander's liberality, and his remaining years were spent in devoting himself to the furtherance of autocracy at home and reaction in foreign affairs. Censorship of what press there was proved so rigid that it resulted in a dangerous radicalism among Russian intellectual circles which expressed its criticism of the existing order in the one field left open—the novel.

Alexander's death in 1825 opened the way for his more liberal brother, the Grand Duke Constantine, to ascend the throne. His refusal to do so resulted in the coronation of another brother, Nicholas I. Constantine's decision was a blow to the hopes of a body of liberal army officers who had enjoyed a taste of the comparative freedom found in France when they were there following the defeat of Napoleon. In protest, they staged an abortive revolt at St. Petersburg. They convinced their illiterate men to support them and cries of "Constantine and Constitution" rent the cold air on 26 December 1825. The soldiers, in general, believed that "Constitutya" was the grand duke's wife. Nicholas took strong measures to curb this outburst, and the revolt of the "Decembrists" was speedily crushed.

By conviction cold to any liberal tendencies, Nicholas now inaugurated his infamous "Nicholas System," which produced, among other things, the dreaded "Third Section," a secret police organization which has remained an essential feature of the Russian government down to the present, although its name has undergone a series of changes.

THE RETURN OF THE BOURBONS IN FRANCE

With the restoration of the Bourbons in the person of Louis XVIII to rule over France, an effort was made at a compromise between the extremes of the former monarchy on the one hand and the Revolution and Napoleon on the other. Shortly after coming to the throne in 1814 before the return of Napoleon, Louis had promulgated a charter by "divine right." It guaranteed such liberties as those of religion and press and such equalities as taxation and legal status. It also satisfied those who had profited most from the events of 1789–1814 by guaranteeing the land settlement of the Revolution, the public debt, the titles of Napoleonic nobility, and war pensions. There was to be a bicameral legislature on the English model, consisting of a Chamber of Peers and an elective

Chamber of Deputies with high property qualification for both voting and holding office. A further weakness in the charter was the power granted the king to issue ordinances in times of crisis. The first elections under the charter produced such an overwhelming conservative victory that the Chamber was dubbed the "Nonesuch Chamber" (*Chambre Introuvable*). Its reactionary legislation was too much even for the king, who seems genuinely to have sought a middle road between the extreme left and the extreme right, so he dissolved the Chamber. The new elections produced a more moderate body, although it too was strongly monarchist in sympathy.

The death of Louis in 1824 resulted in the coronation of the last of the ill-fated Louis XVI's brothers. Charles X was an ultraroyalist and had succeeded to the throne as a result of the assassination of the Duke of Berry, Louis XVIII's nephew, by a fanatic in 1820. This act caused a wave of indignation which strengthened the ultraroyalists, the extreme conservatives who felt that the charter favored Louis XVIII and the revolutionaries too much. Charles quickly set about to strengthen the influence of conservatism within the limits of the charter. His heavy-handed interference with freedom of the press, his dissolution of the National Guard, his extension of the voting qualifications, and his willingness to aid in the indemnification of the aristocracy for their losses in the Revolution served to make him extremely unpopular and prepared the way for an uprising against him which will be discussed below.

ENGLAND UNDER THE TORIES

With the return of peace to Europe following Napoleon's final defeat, conditions in victorious England were immediately affected. A period of acute economic suffering set in after 1815. Her exports slumped and grave unemployment resulted. This condition was intensified by the return of the war veterans, and to make matters worse there were several poor harvests. Coupled with unemployment was the passage of a new corn law which prohibited the importation of "corn" (grain) from abroad so long as the domestic price did not exceed eighty shillings a quarter (approximately eight bushels). This proved the last straw, and the masses fell to rioting in protest against this discriminatory action in favor of the landlord class and against the interests of the people so badly beset with the problem of unemployment.

The government stubbornly resisted the opposition and struck back forcibly by suspending the Habeas Corpus Act in 1817 and then later passing the notorious Six Acts in 1819. The latter seriously interfered with freedom of the press, speech, and assembly. That same year, troops had been used to disperse a peaceful mass protest meeting in Manchester. The loss of the lives of six people and the numerous injuries caused the event to become known as the "Massacre of Peterloo."

Decline of Reaction. The death of George III in 1820 and the accession of George IV coincided with a recession of the floodwaters of reaction. Within two years, the fierce penal code which provided capital punishment for some two hundred offenses, many of them pitifully minor, was ameliorated. This change may be traced to the rise to power about this time of men possessed of humanitarian instincts—men like Peel and Huskisson. By 1830, capital crimes were reduced to about twenty.

The rapid swing away from reaction that now began saw improvements in the fields of commerce and religion as well. In 1823, the Navigation Acts were modified, bounties abolished, reductions in the rates of a number of items, including raw materials, achieved, and reciprocal trade agreements established. The removal of religious disabilities was a significant step forward. Formerly, Dissenters, Roman Catholics, and Jews had been prevented from holding legally any military or civil office, national or local. The prohibition against the Dissenters had been inoperative since 1689 but technically still existed. Together with the Catholics and Jews, they were still taxed for the support of the Established Church. Repeal of the Test and Corporation Acts (1828) formally removed the political liabilities of the Dissenters, and, in 1829, came the Catholic Emancipation Act. This legislation enabled Catholics not only to vote but to hold seats in both houses of Parliament.

STRAWS IN THE WIND

The foregoing will serve to illustrate the fact that Europe was almost solidly gripped in the vise of reaction following the defeat of Napoleon. However, there were events taking place which suggested that perhaps all was not quite so well as it appeared on the surface. Arrayed in opposition to the Metternichian system were the forces set in motion by the Industrial Revolution. These forces included individualism, free competition, and *laissez faire*—all favorable to the middle class. This division of society was determined to bring about the end of special privilege and so began to seek political control. Its resentment against the renewed strength of conservatism everywhere was great.

The first break in the power of the conservative ranks in the post-Vienna period was the liberation of Serbia in 1817. The Serbs had been in revolt against the Turks in 1804, and their ultimate victory did not cause much concern to the concert of Europe. The event which may be said to have broken the back of the concert of Europe was the Greek War of Liberation (1821–1829). Until 1825, this conflict proved to be a sanguinary stalemate which produced a good deal of fratricidal warfare among the Greeks themselves when they were not arrayed against the common enemy. For reasons of their own, several of the powers decided to intervene in 1825 on the side of the Greeks. The Russians were traditional enemies of the Turks and could use the pretext of aiding their fellow Orthodox Catholics to throw off the Turkish yoke and perhaps even drive the latter from the holy city of the Orthodox religion, Constantinople. Britain was in sympathy with the revolutionaries because the English people, influenced by such writers as Lord Byron, took the same attitude adopted by many Americans and looked upon the Hellenes as the founders of Western civilization. A more cogent reason for England's attitude was the financial interest British bankers had assumed in the Greek cause. Moreover, an independent Greece meant potential customers for British goods and services. The French, too, took a benign view of the Greeks, since a Turkish defeat meant an enhanced position in the Mediterranean for France. The net result of these various national interests brought about a decision to intervene in the strife on the side of Greece despite the fact that it meant that a revolutionary cause would benefit and a "legitimate" ruler would be opposed. On the other side, the Turks enlisted the aid of their vassal, the Pasha of Egypt, Mahomet Ali, an ex-pirate.

In 1827, the combined Turkish-Egyptian fleet was annihilated in the battle of Navarino Bay by allied sea power. Subsequently, a private war ensued between the Turks and Russians, 1828–1829, which produced additional disaster for Turkey. Having absorbed sufficient punishment, the Sultan agreed in the Treaty of Adrianople (1829) to grant the Greeks full independence. This treaty also provided for the transfer of Turkish rights in the Caucasus to Russia and the granting of autonomy to the provinces of Moldavia and Wallachia, which were later combined to form Rumania. Paradoxically then, Greece's independence resulted from the fact that she was aided in upsetting the *status quo* by several of the powers most interested in its maintenance. The only solace conservatives were able to derive from the whole affair was the satisfaction that at least Greece did not become a republic. She formed a monarchy under a Bavarian prince, Otto, who became king of the Hellenes.

THE REVOLUTIONS OF 1830

In 1829, the same year Greece won its freedom, the ultraconservative French monarch, Charles X, further enraged the French electorate, already disgusted with his policies, by appointing as premier the Prince de Polignac, a man unacceptable to the Chamber of Deputies. Refusing to abide by the voters' will as expressed in an election held in 1830 to test the popularity of this appointment in a clear-cut contest, Charles issued four ordinances (the July Ordinances) which curbed freedom of the press, dissolved the new Chamber before it assembled, disfranchised about three-quarters of the voters, and called for new elections.

The July Ordinances proved unacceptable, and familiar scenes of the Revolution were reenacted as the streets of Paris were once more barricaded. A few days of fighting convinced Charles of the inability of his forces to win. Accordingly, he fled to England, and the July Revolution was finished.

The speedy collapse of the monarchy caught the victors unprepared with a plan of government to replace it. The workers ardently hoped for a republic, but the middle class was as ill disposed to such an extreme as it was to the beaten monarchy. A compromise was reached when the Chamber of Deputies awarded the crown to Louis Philippe of the Orleanist branch of the Bourbons and son of Philippe Égalité of Revolutionary memory. For this decision two of France's elder statesmen, Talleyrand and Lafayette, were largely responsible.

The *bourgeoisie* was quite well pleased with a constitutional monarchy which was now set up, but the proletariat, whose members had made possible the victory over the forces of Charles X, was bitterly disappointed with this turn of events. The workers were further disillusioned when the franchise was carefully restricted by a property qualification so heavy that only two hundred thousand could meet it. The strong middle-class tinge left a heritage of discontent which did not augur too well for the future of the July Monarchy.

Belgian Independence. The news that another revolution had broken out in France produced great excitement throughout Europe. The Belgians, chafing under the union with Holland, rose up and successfully achieved their independence from the Dutch, although formal recognition was delayed until 1839, when Belgian independence and neutrality were guaranteed by England, France, Austria, Russia, and Prussia. Intervention in the Belgian uprising by those still adhering to the Metternichian theory would perhaps have been quick had not England once again taken a favorable view of a revolution. Moreover, the July Monarchy was sympathetic toward the Belgians, and this combination of British and French opposition was enough to make potential meddlers reflect carefully before doing anything so rash as to aid the Dutch.

An uprising took place in Poland against the Russians, but Poland was left to win its freedom by itself and was quickly overwhelmed by its far more powerful adversary. The revolt was drowned in blood, and many of the flower of young Polish manhood were sent to Siberia and certain death. The constitution granted to Poland by Alexander I was abrogated by way of further punishment.

The other revolutions of that eventful year—those in the Germanies and Italy—proved failures except for the grant of constitutions or the extension of further privileges in several small German states. In Italy, the revolts centered in Parma, Modena, and the Papal States. The failure of France to send assistance and the lack of any changes in Prussia and Austria spelled the doom of these revolutions.

THE GREAT REFORM BILL

It is necessary at this point to turn our attention back to events in Great Britain. It will be recalled that the era of reaction between 1815 and 1820 had been checked and various liberal reforms introduced in the following decade. Nonetheless, the problems created by the Industrial Revolution cried out for solution. The indifference of Parliament to the pleas of the masses and the few articulate spokesmen who championed reform finally made imperative a revamping of Parliament if any real change for the better was to result. At the close of the period of the twenties, George IV died and was succeeded by William IV, an event which produced a new election for seats in the House of Commons.

In order to appreciate better the significance of such a happening, it is advisable to consider for a moment the political machinery of the country. The upper house, the House of Lords, was the citadel of the titled aristocracy. The peers were extremely powerful and were not destined to lose their real legislative privileges until 1911. Not all peers were Lords of Parliament; only those whose title so designated. Representation of the Scottish and Irish peers was also provided, although today this source of membership is on its way to extinction. Membership included, in addition to the categories listed above, the "lords spiritual," the two archbishops and the various bishops of the Established Church, and seven "lords of appeal," jurists who are made peers for life and given seats in Lords where they serve as the "law lords" and act as Britain's Supreme Court. This latter function is one of the two special privileges still retained by the House of Lords. Its other dictinction is its power to impeach in cases brought before it by the House of Commons.

Voting Qualifications. The lower house, Commons, was chosen by highly varied methods. Through a provision dating back to 1429, men residing in a county might vote if they held freehold land which possessed a rental value of at least forty shillings a year. From this time until 1832, county membership in Commons was decided by the "forty-shilling freeholders." In the same period, the borough (corporate towns) suffrage had been, on the whole, considerably narrowed. In some towns, virtually any male could vote; in others, scarcely one in a hundred had the privilege. The situation reduced itself pretty much to this—whether a man could vote or not depended almost exclusively on where he lived.

Every county was entitled to two representatives and every borough, regardless of size, had at least one member. It had been so long since a redistribution of seats had taken place that many towns, once prosperous, had fallen into decay while others had increased considerably in population. Still others had come into existence as a result of the Industrial Revolution and had enjoyed huge growth. Those which were newcomers or had grown, like Manchester, Sheffield, and Leeds, were entitled either to no representation or their increased size went unrewarded.

"Rotten" and "Pocket" Boroughs. Meanwhile, towns whose population had shrunken or even disappeared continued to be represented. The generic term "rotten boroughs" was given such places. There are many humorous illustrations; a few will suffice. At least three completely uninhabited boroughs, Old Sarum, Corfe Castle, and Downton, the latter a salt marsh completely inundated by the sea, were duly represented by two members apiece. The constituency of Bute's lone freeman nominated and elected himself.

This condition was made to order for the wealthy, who often controlled several seats. A borough whose voters were in the pay of a rich patron came to be known as a "pocket borough." The Duke of Newcastle at one time had about a dozen seats at his disposal. In fact, it has been said that at least two-thirds of the 658 members of Commons were controlled in this fashion. This being the case, the patrons were in a position to block all proposals for parliamentary reform. Where the constituency was too large to be controlled in this fashion, votes were often sold on the open market. Since the elections were held over a period of from ten days to two weeks and the results were tabulated publicly, a shrewd voter could hold off until the market price was at its highest before selling his vote. This practice was quite open, and there were even cases of clubs whose sole reason for being was to sell the votes of the members en masse. In the words of the younger Pitt: "The House of Commons is not representative of the people of Great Britain; it is representative of nominal boroughs, of ruined and exterminated towns, of noble families, of wealthy individuals, and of foreign potentates."

In 1832, with a Whig government in power, a reform bill was introduced. Although it managed to pass Commons, it was killed in Lords. It was brought in again and once more passed the lower house only to be rejected again by the upper chamber. When it became clear that it would suffer the same fate in Lords following a third passage through Commons, the prime minister, Earl Grey, requested the king to create enough new peers to insure victory for the measure. Upon the king's refusal, Grey resigned. The king then requested Wellington, the celebrated "Iron Duke," to form a government.

At this point, the masses went into action. Rioting broke out on a frightening scale, and it seemed as if the prophecy of Macaulay that a "wreck of laws, . . . confusion of ranks, the spoliation of property, and the dissolution of social order" would come to pass. The explanation of this sudden virile activity on the part of the hitherto passive English masses is quite simple. They mistakenly believed that universal suffrage was the issue.

Passage of the First Reform Bill. With matters at such a crisis, Wellington proved unable to form a government, and William was reluctantly forced to recall Grey. The latter accepted the prime ministership on condition that His Majesty threaten to create enough new peers to pass the bill. This threat proved enough, and the measure passed Lords when about one hundred of its members absented themselves from the division rather than approve the legislation. Thus did the great Reform Bill of 1832 become the law of the land. In the first place, the act succeeded in wiping out most of the rotten and pocket boroughs. Consolidation of some of the remaining small boroughs was achieved, and others had their representation reduced from two to one. In this manner, over one hundred and forty seats were made available for redistribution among the more heavily populated cities and towns. Second, the suffrage requirements were altered but very unsatisfactorily. In the counties, several special classes were added to the "forty-shilling freeholders." In the boroughs, a uniform basis was now adopted. All who owned or rented a house whose rental value was at least ten pounds a year could now vote. This provision excluded lodgers. Third, voting was now limited to two consecutive days in an effort to reduce the flagrant corruption which had characterized the old, lengthy period of time the polls remained open.

The act almost doubled the number of voters, but it cost many who previously were entitled to vote in the boroughs their franchise. It further retained the old distinction between county and borough instead of adopting a uniform basis. The total electorate now numbered about 650,000 out of a population of almost twenty-five millions. Needless to say, it produced great disappointment among those whose hopes had risen so high. Its net result was the admission of more members of the middle class possessed of some means to a position where they could now share power with the old aristocratic landowners.

Chartism. The few halting steps toward social reform which followed the political events of 1832 encouraged the English working class to seek the realization of the hopes for which they had rioted in 1832. Accordingly, in 1838, the year following the crowning of Victoria as queen, the Chartist movement made its appearance. The People's Charter advocated six points. These were: (1) universal manhood suffrage, (2) the secret ballot, (3) annual Parliaments, (4) removal of property qualifications for members of Parliament, (5) equal electoral districts, and (6) the payment of a salary to members of Parliament. Chartism reached its peak in 1848, a year in which conditions in England were generally quite poor. The Chartists claimed to have nearly six million signatures affixed to a huge petition seeking the attainment of the six points. They prepared to present their petition to Parliament and the air became tense with excitement. To meet the expected violence the government swore in an army of special constables, whose ranks included one Louis Napoleon Bonaparte, and called upon the old Duke of Wellington to preserve order. This formidable opposition proved too much for the Chartists, who dispatched their petition to Commons in a horse-drawn conveyance and peacefully awaited the results. The Charter was found to contain less than one-third of the vaunted total of signatures, and many of the others were spurious. A typical example of the false names affixed was "Victoria, Rex." The movement ended in farce, and the return of prosperous times before the year ended served to dispel the danger of revolution. Elsewhere in Europe, the reigning governments were not so fortunate, and 1848 proved to be another great year of unrest and revolution.

FRANCE UNDER LOUIS PHILIPPE

The July Revolution in France in 1830 solidified the position of the upper middle class in that country. France now had a "citizen king" who played his part convincingly by affecting bourgeois dress and manners. He was frequently given to walking the streets unattended like any other businessman of the day.

Despite his assumption of the common touch, Louis Philippe was distrusted by those who hoped for a republic. The republicans were not alone in their dislike of the king, who was detested by the Legitimists, the Bonapartists, and the Socialists. Nor was he particularly acceptable to the Clerical group. The power of the latter among the peasants and the Catholic intellectuals like Frederick Ozanam, founder of the St. Vincent de Paul Society, Catholic lay social workers, was considerable. The country folk resented the fact that the clergy had been prohibited from teaching in the schools in a country which was nominally Catholic and grew gradually in their dislike of the July Monarchy.

For ten years, even among the ranks of the king's own supporters there was disunity. The result was ten ministries in that period. One division of the Orleanists was the Party of Progress, the other the Party of Resistance. The former advocated a program of gradual reform and favored granting aid to peoples abroad who sought to overthrow their government. The other group, the Resistance, opposed further reform at home and looked with favor on the *status quo* abroad. In 1840, this party came to the fore, and Guizot, one of their number, formed a new government whose policy was one of complete inertia in both domestic and foreign affairs.

Fall of Louis Philippe. Meanwhile, the movement for reform continued. By 1847, its chief medium of expression was through a series of banquets at which the subject of reform was broached. A particularly important banquet was scheduled for Washington's birthday, 22 February 1848. The government, upset by the spread of these affairs, foolishly prohibited the holding of the scheduled banquet. This decision was meekly accepted by those who were to have attended the meeting but not so by a combination of students and workers who commenced rioting in protest. By the 23d the rioting grew and the king dismissed Guizot in the hope of satisfying the clamor. The third day saw Louis Philippe's abdication in the face of the now serious revolt. Overjoyed by this event, the Republicans and Socialists temporarily joined forces and declared a republic on 25 February.

To satisfy the demands of their partners, the Republicans consented to establish national workshops, a project long advocated by the Socialist Louis Blanc. The system put in operation proved a farce. It called for the employment of men in the senseless task of digging ditches. This ridiculous practice tended to react to the detriment of the Socialists, as their foes hoped would be the case. When the new Assembly, which was chosen by universal manhood suffrage, decreed an end to the national workshops, there was an uprising of the workers. This was smothered by General Cavaignac, who was given full authority by the Assembly to master the situation, during three sanguinary days—the terrible June Days. With the Socialists beaten and discredited, the victors now turned to the work of implementing the Constitution of 1848 which the Assembly drew up.

THE REVOLUTIONS OF 1848

At this point, it is necessary to leave France and glance elsewhere in Europe in the period following 1830. In Germany, liberalism was effectively checked by the power of Metternich in the federal Diet, but economically, and ultimately politically, some progress was made through the spread of the Prussian-sponsored *Zollverein* (customs union) which erased internal barriers, provided tariff protection against foreign competition, and cemented good relations between the members. In Austria-Hungary, liberal opposition to the rigid tactics of Metternich gradually grew in strength. Moreover, Slav and Hungarian nationalism made their appearance. Hence, nationalism and liberalism were causing the Austrian authorities a good deal of concern.

Throughout Italy there was widespread discontent. On one thing there was agreement among the leaders of the dissatisfied people. This was the unification of the country and the expulsion of foreign rulers. Regarding the projected government when this was achieved, there were three main proposals. One was a republic; a second was a federation under the pope's presidency; and a third was a constitutional monarchy under the House of Savoy. Everywhere, there was a strong national feeling, the *risorgimento,* which created an atmosphere of great expectancy.

Expulsion of Metternich. When the news that the familiar barricades had gone up in Paris and a revolution had taken place spread through Europe, it acted as the impulse needed to charge the smoldering liberal and national sentiments into action. So powerful was its initial fury that Metternich, the champion of conservatism, was forced to flee Vienna in the wake of a liberal uprising. A constitution was won by the revolutionaries and an Imperial Parliament created. The Magyars in Hungary won the right to their own autonomous government but quickly ran into the formidable opposition of the Serbs and Croats within their country. The Czechs in Bohemia now demanded from Austria privileges similar to those given the Magyars. Feudalism was swept away by the various new governments, and glittering promises of freedom of speech and press together with real representative government were made.

In Italy, the Austrians were driven to the defensive by the enraged power of the liberals and nationalists. Charles Albert, King of Sardinia-Piedmont, voluntarily gave his subjects a constitution and commenced the Italian War of Liberation against Austria. Both Pius IX and Ferdinand II of Naples contributed soldiers and other aid for the cause. The future looked indeed promising.

In Prussia, Berlin was the scene of fierce fighting between the workers and the soldiers of Frederick William IV until the monarch called off his troops rather than cause further loss of life and personally wore the colors of the *Burschenschaften.* Elsewhere in Germany, the situation facilitated the calling of the Frankfurt Assembly, a meeting of liberals to draw up a constitution providing a unified Germany.

THE TIDE TURNS

Just when prospects appeared bright for the success of the men of 1848, the tide began to turn slowly but firmly. Within the Austro-Hungarian Empire, the victors fell to fighting among themselves. It was a combination of clashing nationalities and conflicting loyalties which produced a situation made to order for the conservatives to regroup. General Windischgrätz conquered strife-torn Prague, and the Bohemian revolt was checked. In Italy, Austria's fortunes rose when internal dissensions and suspicions divided the force facing the hated whitecoats. Under the successful generalship of Radetzky, Austria trounced the Italians at Custozza and Novara. These victories emboldened the Austrians to turn homeward. By the fall of 1848, Windischgrätz, with the aid of the South Slavs, who were promised reforms in return for their help, reentered Vienna, which was split by a quarrel among the liberals. At this juncture, the feeble-minded Ferdinand I abdicated in favor of his eighteen-year-old nephew, Francis Joseph I, who was destined to rule until 1916.

Windischgrätz was now in a position to turn to Hungary, where Louis Kossuth, Hungarian liberal and nationalist, declared the independence of his country in 1849 and set up a republic. In their determination to crush this upstart, the Austrians decided to seek help from Nicholas I, Czar of All the Russias. The Czar was receptive owing to his fear that a Hungarian success might encourage his own subject nationalities. His armies quickly turned the tide and the Hungarian revolt was ended. Hungary was punished by being reduced to the position of an Austrian province. Kossuth, however, managed to escape and finished his years in exile.

While Austria was slowly and painfully putting its house back in order following the uprisings, the Prussian king was quick to revert to his old ways because of his discovery that the loyalty of the army was his. This led to a movement of fierce repression which saw the arrest and execution of thousands of the revolutionaries. Many others left the country and sought refuge in the United States, where they contributed such outstanding persons as Carl Schurz to their adopted homeland. As a sop to those who survived in Prussia, a constitution was promulgated in 1850 which was rigged in such a fashion that control was vested in the hands of the reactionaries.

The Frankfurt Assembly. The Frankfurt Assembly, mentioned above, met in 1848 during the height of the revolutionary surge throughout Europe, and there was every indication that a unified Germany would result from its deliberations. It dealt with the question of Austrian membership by means of a compromise unacceptable to Austria, which therefore did not join but hurled a significant threat of its intentions toward the *projet d'union* when the time was ripe for such action. Undismayed, the delegates continued their work and decided to form a federal union to be headed by an hereditary emperor. The constitution drawn up was based on both the American and English models and was a remarkably liberal document. It was decided to offer the Prussian king the position of emperor, but his insulting refusal to have anything to do with the Assembly unless his fellow princes agreed marked the real end of the whole movement. It quickly collapsed as many states recalled their delegations upon Frederick William's refusal. The remaining delegates sought vainly to win the backing of the German people against the autocrats, but the response was insufficient, and troops dispersed the remnants of the Assembly by force. So ended the attempt to unite Germany in democratic fashion, and with it was left a heritage of bitterness and disappointment.

In Italy, the only lasting gain for the forces which had sought the expulsion of the Austrians and the unification of the country was the fact that Sardinia had won a constitution which was not taken away once the revolutions had proven unsuccessful. This document, the *Statuto,* was destined to be the constitution for Italy when she did achieve unification in 1870. In fact, it remained so down to the end of the Second World War, although the Fascist government of Mussolini altered it so as to make it almost unrecognizable. Another ray of hope was to be gleaned from the leadership the House of Savoy had shown in the fight against Austria. But these two factors provided scant consolation to the saddened Italian patriots and dreamers of 1848.

THE REVOLUTIONS OF 1848 ASSESSED

By 1850, it can be said the Revolutions of 1848 and 1849 were at an end. Conservatism had triumphed and nationalism, liberalism, and socialism had been beaten. The apparent results of all the strife and bloodshed were meager. A few constitutions here and there and the end of feudalism in Austria seemed to be the sum total on the credit side of the ledger. On the debit side, everywhere the "men of '48" were dead, exiled, or reduced to submission, and men of property were disposed to make common cause with the monarchies in an effort to stamp out democracy. So quickly had the situation altered from a universally favorable beginning to a dismal defeat that pessimism seemed justified. Yet within a generation the hopes so nearly achieved were destined to be realized in the field of nationalism. The uprisings of 1848–1849 had undermined the structure of the Metternich system, and by 1871 Germany and Italy were unified and the Dual Monarchy had been established in Austria-Hungary. Liberalism, too, would soon have its day; although it would progress less rapidly and would not attain its objectives as completely.

19

Liberalism and Nationalism in the United States

The people of the United States emerged from the War of 1812 with an intense pride in their country and an exuberant optimism about its future. The war itself had ended on a sufficiently victorious note to gratify patriotic feeling. Deeper than that, perhaps, was a sense of relief at the return of peace to the world as a whole and of elation that the young republic of the United States had not only survived twenty-five years of acute international crisis but had come out with its constitutional system unimpaired and its territory doubled. When Americans turned from the international scene to consider their internal affairs, the prospect seemed equally favorable. There was, on the surface at any rate, an atmosphere of political harmony. The Federalist party had disappeared as a national organization, destroyed by its inability to adapt itself to change and by the stigma of sedition attached to it during the War of 1812, but some of the doctrines of Federalism had been taken over by the dominant Republicans. The ardent nationalism of the "War Hawks" carried over after the return of peace into policies which would have delighted Alexander Hamilton. Led by Henry Clay and John C. Calhoun, the new generation of Republicans enacted a high tariff in 1816 in order to protect the country's nascent industries from the flood of British goods which poured across the Atlantic when trade relations were resumed, and in the same year they chartered the Second Bank of the United States as the most effective method of ending the financial chaos which had developed during the war. This institution was modeled closely on its Hamiltonian predecessor. Its capital was increased to \$35,000,000, and, in

290

addition to performing all the functions of the First Bank, the Second Bank was intended by its organizers to act as a restraining influence on the numerous local banks that had come into existence, particularly by policing their note issues so that adequate provision was made for redemption in specie.

Election of 1824. Political peace lasted until the end of Monroe's administration, but before this last member of the "Virginia dynasty" went into retirement, new party lines were already forming. Personal rivalries among Republican leaders created factions, and evidence that strong conflicts of interest lay close beneath the surface of national unity appeared in the fierce dispute over the admission of Missouri to the Union in 1820. The reshuffling of political forces came into the open with the election of 1824, in which no less than five candidates, all Republicans, ran for the presidency. For the second time in American history, no candidate received a majority in the electoral college, and the choice of a President was thrown into the House of Representatives. Largely through the influence of Henry Clay, himself one of the unsuccessful candidates,[1] Congress picked John Quincy Adams in preference to Andrew Jackson, and Adams in turn made Clay his Secretary of State. Each move was natural enough in the circumstances; Adams and Clay were far closer to each other in their outlook on national problems than either was to Jackson. It is doubtful whether the accusation of a "corrupt bargain" made by the disappointed Jacksonians was valid, but it was believed nevertheless, and it served to accentuate the cleavage within the Republican party.

Partisan bitterness, indeed, turned Adams's administration into four years of frustration. John Quincy Adams was an able statesman with a remarkably broad experience in public life, but, like his father before him, he could not master the art of making himself personally popular, and he would not use the office of President to build up a following for himself. In his inaugural address he presented to Congress a program of sweeping nationalism, asking Federal aid for internal improvements, the establishment of a national university, and the encouragement of scientific research. Congress made no effort to enact any of his recommendations. Clay's hopes of strengthening the ties between the United States and the new republics of Latin America met a similar fate. His opponents in Congress blocked the appointment of United States delegates to an inter-American congress at Panama in 1826. Two delegates were finally named, but one died en route and the other arrived too late. As it turned out, the

[1] Clay had finished fourth in electoral votes and was therefore constitutionally ineligible for selection by the House. The third man on the list, William C. Crawford of Georgia, was ruled out of consideration by a physical collapse. The fifth candidate, John C. Calhoun, dropped out of the presidential race and became Vice-President.

Panama Congress accomplished nothing, and Simón Bolívar, who had summoned it, was rather more friendly to Great Britain than to the United States, but it was regrettable that this first gesture at Pan-Americanism should have been turned into a factional issue in the United States.

JACKSONIAN DEMOCRACY

Little was done, indeed, during Adams's term of office but prepare for the next election. When it came in 1828, this time a straightforward contest between Adams and Jackson, the campaign degenerated into an appalling outburst of partisan rancor. Whatever issues were present were ignored in a fury of personal abuse, with completely unwarranted attacks on the character of the two candidates. The result was never seriously in doubt; Adams received little support outside of New England, and Andrew Jackson became President of the United States.

As a matter of fact, it would have been difficult for either side to define accurately what was at stake in this election. Adams was backed by the business classes who a generation before had been the mainstay of the Federalists. Jackson had the support of the Southern planters, who were alarmed by Adams's extreme nationalism. Among them was Calhoun, who took second place on the Jackson ticket under the impression that he would be the General's successor in 1832. The New York Democratic organization, which had helped to put Jefferson in the White House in 1800, now, under Martin Van Buren, gave its support to Jackson. But most important of all, Jackson was the choice of the farmers of the West and the industrial laborers of the East. He was the representative of a popular impulse which can perhaps best be described as the American manifestation of the upsurge of liberalism which produced the July Revolution in France and the first Reform Bill in Great Britain.

From this impulse grew Jacksonian Democracy, a term indicative of an optimistic and many-sided faith in the common man rather than of a systematic body of political or economic thought. Jackson himself was an unknown quantity when he arrived in the White House. He was a popular idol because of his brilliant military career, but his political views were indefinite—a fact which had made him all the more acceptable as a candidate. He was, however, far from being the uncouth and illiterate frontiersman depicted by his enemies. He was an astute judge of men and issues, and, while he was ably advised by such men as Amos Kendall, Francis P. Blair, Roger B. Taney, and Martin Van Buren, the final decisions on matters of policy were made by Old Hickory in person.

The Jacksonian creed was fundamentally an adaptation of Jefferson's philosophy to the changing conditions of American life. Jefferson, it will be recalled, had believed in entrusting government to the common people, but had felt that true democracy could be achieved only in an agrarian society, where political equality could rest on a foundation of economic independence. He also wanted the conduct of public affairs vested in a "natural aristocracy" composed of men of talent. By the 1820's Jefferson's ideal had become unattainable. The rise of industrialism in the North and the expansion of the plantation system in the South made it impossible for the United States to become exclusively a nation of free-holding farmers. The Jacksonians resolved this difficulty by preaching political equality regardless of economic condition. They accepted the economic pattern as they found it, except that they were prepared to use the authority of the state against any concentration of economic or financial power which appeared to them strong enough to constitute a menace to free government.

Jackson and the Bank. The implementing of this last feature of their doctrine involved the Jacksonians in one of the greatest political battles of the period, the attack on the Second Bank of the United States. During the 1820's the bank, under the able presidency of Nicholas Biddle, had developed into an extremely powerful institution with almost autocratic control over the country's banking system. Biddle suppressed "wild-cat" banking rigorously by presenting for immediate redemption in specie any dubious banknotes which appeared in the Bank of the United States or its branches. This practice endeared him to the business community, which desired sound banking and currency, but it antagonized the agrarian South and West, where easy bank credit was strongly desired.

To the Jacksonians the Second Bank of the United States was the "Monster," a financial monopoly incompatible with true democracy. Jackson himself regarded it both as unconstitutional, John Marshall to the contrary, and unsound, for reasons best known to himself. As it turned out, however, the friends of the Bank were responsible for bringing matters to a head. As the election of 1832 approached, an opposition party was forming under the leadership of Henry Clay and Daniel Webster. It called itself the National Republican party at first but later adopted the title "Whig," to indicate that its members were fighting "King Andrew" just as their fathers had fought George III.

The Whig leaders, in search of an issue, hit upon the question of rechartering the Bank. Their strategy called for introducing a recharter bill in the spring of 1832. Congress was certain to pass it, and it was almost equally certain that Jackson would veto it. If he did, the Whigs believed that public opinion would support them and that the Democrats would split badly on the issue. If he did not, then he could be taxed with not knowing his own mind. It took some time to persuade Biddle to cooperate. The banker was sure of his position in Congress, he had supporters in Jackson's Cabinet, and his initial judgment was that it would be wiser to let the question of recharter wait until after the election. However, his dislike of Jackson was so great that he finally consented.

It was a mistake. The scheme proceeded "according to plan" through everything but the final stage. The application for recharter was introduced into Congress, passed, returned by Jackson with a blistering veto, and then in the election Jackson scored a decisive victory over Clay. The Whigs had disastrously underestimated the President's hold on the affections of the people. The ordinary man in the street understood little of central banking and public finance; he made his decision on the ground that if Andy Jackson was against the Bank of the United States, he was against it too.

Removal of the Deposits. The existing charter would expire in 1836, but Jackson was unwilling to wait. He was still convinced that the Bank was unsound, and he was determined to remove the funds of the United States government from it while there was time. He planned to transfer the public funds to a group of selected banks operating under state charters—forthwith dubbed Jackson's "pet banks"—an arrangement which would have the additional merit of preventing financial monopoly and satisfying Democratic scruples about the constitutionality of a national bank. The execution of the plan produced one unforeseen difficulty. By the act chartering the Second Bank of the United States, control of government funds in the institution was vested in the Secretary of the Treasury and not the President, and Secretary Louis McLane was opposed to Jackson's policy. It was not enough of an obstacle to bother Andrew Jackson. If he could not change the law, he could change the Secretary of the Treasury. McLane was "promoted" to be Secretary of State, and when his successor, William Duane, likewise proved obstinate, he was in turn replaced by Attorney General Roger B. Taney, who was thoroughly in sympathy with the President's position and carried through the removal of the deposits.[2] This service undoubtedly influenced the selection of Taney as Chief Justice when John Marshall died in 1835, although the choice was fully justified by Taney's own outstanding legal ability.

It cannot be said that the Jacksonian solution of this problem was entirely a happy one. The President and his adherents were undoubtedly right in their belief that the Second Bank of the United States had too much power for a private corporation, but complete destruction of the institution was a needlessly drastic remedy. Since its charter was due to expire in 1836, it would have been a simple matter for the Democrats to make whatever changes they saw fit. As it was, the United States was

---

[2] There was no physical "removal." Beginning in September, 1833, government revenues were placed in the "pet banks," of which there were eventually eighty-nine, and expenses were paid from the account in the Bank of the United States until it was exhausted.

left for the next eighty years without the stabilizing influence of a central banking system. The "pet banks" were unsatisfactory and had to be replaced during Van Buren's administration by the Independent Treasury, a plan whereby subtreasuries were established in the principal cities to take custody of government funds. These functioned well enough for that purpose, but they afforded no control whatsoever over banking or the issue of bank credit. Such regulation as there was had to be imposed by the states, and their standards varied widely—from comparatively high in the Northeast to virtually nonexistent on the frontier.

Panic of 1837. The immediate effect of Jackson's policy was to launch a speculative boom. When the government's funds began flowing into their vaults, the "pet banks" were able to expand their loans, and to do it rather casually now that Mr. Biddle's watchful eye was no longer on them. Speculation in Western land was particularly intense. Indeed, in 1835 and 1836 the revenues from land sales rose so rapidly that the national debt was paid off and the Treasury found itself embarrassed by an accumulating surplus which it had no way to dispose of. After some debate, Congress attempted to solve this problem by adopting Henry Clay's proposal that the surplus be distributed to the states in four installments, ostensibly as a "loan." One installment was paid to the states before the panic of 1837 came along to settle the problem of the surplus more effectively than Congress had done.

The crash would have come sooner or later, but its arrival was accelerated by Jackson's "hard-money" views. As the land boom of 1835 and 1836 developed, he became profoundly disturbed at the volume of banknotes pouring into the Treasury to pay for land purchases and moved to check it by his Specie Circular of 11 July 1836, ordering public officials to accept only gold and silver coin in payment for public lands. The effect was an immediate constriction of credit and the bursting of the speculative bubble. The full force of economic collapse came just in time to greet Jackson's chosen successor, Martin Van Buren.

DEMOCRATIC INFLUENCES IN AMERICAN SOCIETY

The democratizing impulse which had put Andrew Jackson in the White House spread far beyond the immediate area of party conflict. Political life in general moved toward greater popular control of the institutions of government. Between 1810 and 1850 all states of the North and West, and some in the South, adopted manhood suffrage (for white males only). The last Northern state to fall in line was Rhode Island, where the ruling oligarchy grudgingly gave way after a "rebellion" in 1842 in which the only casualty was an innocent bystander in Massachusetts.

Distrust of secret societies as tending to create a privileged class produced a short-lived Anti-Masonic party which ran a candidate for President in the election of 1832.[3] Even the spoils system, certainly the most generally criticized feature of Jackson's administration, was defended on the ground that rotation in office was the democratic way to run a government.

Party Conventions. Party organizations themselves gave way to the democratic tide by adopting the system of having candidates nominated in conventions by delegates theoretically representing the rank and file. The Anti-Masons were the first party to hold a national convention (1831), but the Democrats were quick to take over the idea. Unfortunately, in their eagerness to demonstrate their party solidarity, the Democrats adopted a rule requiring a two-thirds majority for nomination in their national convention. Jackson, of course, had no difficulty meeting this requirement in 1832, nor did Van Buren four years later, but the two-thirds rule subsequently plagued Democratic conventions, by enabling minorities to block popular candidates, until its abrogation in 1936.

Van Buren's emergence as Jackson's successor was a political defeat for John C. Calhoun. The South Carolinian's fall from grace was principally a consequence of the widening gulf between his own intensifying sectionalism and Jackson's robust devotion to the Union. A contributing factor, however, was that Calhoun contracted a touch of the "Eaton malaria" which devastated official Washington during Jackson's first term. The source of the trouble was Peggy Eaton, née O'Neill, the wife of John Eaton, Jackson's Secretary of War. Apart from Martin Van Buren, who was Secretary of State, the other members of the Cabinet belonged to the Calhoun wing of the party, a circumstance seeming to confirm the general assumption that Calhoun was Jackson's heir apparent. However, Mrs. Eaton's reputation was sufficiently clouded—whether justifiably or not has never been established—for aristocratic Washington hostesses, led by Mrs. Calhoun, to refuse to accept her socially. Old Hickory, who had a deep respect for women and was doubly sensitive on the subject of scandal because of the slurs cast at his own wife during the campaign of 1828, immediately sprang to the lady's defense, abetted by Van Buren, who was, rather fortunately, a widower. Eventually, at Van Buren's suggestion, the President accepted the resignations of the entire Cabinet—thereby avoiding any appearance of discriminating among elements of the Democratic party. The affair securely established the "Little

[3] The anti-Masonic agitation began from the disappearance in 1826 of one William Morgan, who had written a book purporting to expose the secrets of the order. Two years later a body found in the Niagara River near the scene of the disappearance was alleged to be Morgan's. No accurate identification was ever made, but Thurlow Weed, who was trying to build the movement into a personal political machine, is reputed to have said of the corpse, "It's good enough Morgan until after the election."

Magician" in Jackson's favor and made him a certain choice for the Presidency whenever the General chose to retire.

"Tippecanoe and Tyler too." If imitation is the sincerest form of flattery, then Jacksonianism in politics was triumphantly vindicated in 1840, when the Whigs won the election by adopting their opponents' tactics of appealing to the masses. Their prospects for victory were bright in any event, since the Van Buren administration had been a period of unrelieved depression. Men like Clay and Webster, prominent enough to have made many enemies, were passed over as presidential timber in favor of General William Henry Harrison, the "Hero of Tippecanoe." To attract Southern votes, John Tyler of Virginia, an extreme states-rights Jeffersonian, was nominated for Vice-President, to give a ticket of "Tippecanoe and Tyler too." The party adopted no platform, thereby giving its spokesmen free rein to champion any issues they found convenient. An incautious Democratic editor then presented the election to Harrison by alleging that, given a log cabin, a pension, and enough hard cider to last him the rest of his life, Harrison would be glad to retire from politics. From then on issues were forgotten. Monster parades, featuring log cabins and hard cider, replaced debates on political problems, and Harrison literally floated into the presidency. Then, to the consternation of the predominantly nationalistic Whigs, the elderly general died a month after his inauguration and left the government in the hands of John Tyler.

REFORM MOVEMENTS

Beyond the field of politics, the spirit of Jacksonian Democracy was reflected in a variety of movements for social reform, stimulated by zeal for human welfare and closely related to the contemporary humanitarian crusades in Europe. The utopian experiments and the workingmen's parties described in the previous section were part of this reform movement. Both were short-lived, but the workingmen's parties did stimulate state legislation abolishing imprisonment for debt and imposing regulations on banks, and they also contributed effectively to the agitation for public education.

Public Education. The idea of free schools had existed since early colonial days, and it had been reinforced by the provision of the Northwest Ordinance allocating land for the support of public schools. Except in Puritan New England, however, little had been done to translate the ideal into practice, and even there the public-school system was scarcely adequate. During the Jacksonian era the belief that education, at least in its elementary form, should be made available to all became markedly stronger, and most states laid the foundations of public-school systems. The most conspicuous figure in this movement was Horace Mann, who gave up a promising political career to work for the cause of public education. He was made chairman of the Massachusetts Board of Education in 1837 and became a vigorous proponent of theories based on the efficient Prussian school system, but adapted to American conditions. Some public high schools were established in the Northeast in the 1830's and 40's, but secondary education in general remained in private hands. The same was true of the colleges, although fifteen state universities were founded by 1850, mostly in the public land states where grants for this purpose were made to each new state as it was admitted to the Union. National recognition of the principle that higher education was a public responsibility was first expressly indorsed in the Morrill Act of 1862, granting land to the states for the support of colleges of "agriculture and the mechanic arts."

The humanitarian impulses of the era found an outlet in the reform of prison conditions and practices and in the single-handed and effective crusade by Dorothea Lynde Dix for better treatment of the insane. A movement for international peace appeared, led by William Ladd and Elihu Burritt. More directly affecting the daily lives of Americans was a campaign for temperance which became a lively political issue in some states and produced a few rather short-lived prohibition laws. There was even a strong feeling that liberty and equality should apply to women as well as men. At the instigation of women such as Elizabeth Cady Stanton and Lucretia Mott, a woman's-rights convention was held at Seneca Falls, New York, in 1848. Ultimate success was not to be achieved until 1920, but some progress was made before the Civil War in improving women's legal status, permitting them to control their own property, and giving them fuller opportunities for securing an education.

The liberal enthusiasm of Americans extended to the aspirations of other people. Thus, Samuel Gridley Howe went off to fight in the War of Greek Independence before he took up his lifework of educating the blind, and the revolt of the Spanish colonies was warmly received by the American public. Later, when Louis Kossuth, the Hungarian patriot, visited the United States after the Revolution of 1848, he was given an almost hysterical welcome.

Abolitionism. Of these humanitarian movements, the one with the most immediate impact on American life was abolitionism. The antislavery agitation of the Revolutionary era had never died out, although it had been made to appear very ineffectual in the face of the great expansion of slave agriculture which accompanied the rise of cotton cultivation. The Quakers continued to oppose slavery with quiet perseverance, and in the 1820's there was some support for a scheme to repatriate emancipated Negroes to Africa. This plan resulted in the founding of Liberia, whose capital was named Monrovia in honor of James Monroe, but it never had enough backing either in money or in public opinion to make it anything more than a small-scale experiment. In 1831 the antislavery movement acquired an aggressive and militant character with the founding of the *Liberator* in Boston by William Lloyd Garrison. He was not by any means the sole spokesman of abolition. Benjamin Lundy, Theodore D. Weld, and the Grimke sisters of South Carolina contributed at least as much to the antislavery movement as Garrison did, but he personified the new spirit of abolitionism more effectively than anyone else —absolutely uncompromising, regarding slavery as an unpardonable moral evil.

Until the coming of the Civil War the outright abolitionists remained a small if very vociferous minority. At the beginning, indeed, Northern opinion was distinctly hostile, looking on the movement as a serious menace to sectional harmony. The ferocity of the abolitionist assault nevertheless alarmed the leaders of the South. They tried to suppress it by barring abolitionist literature from the mails and by getting Congress to refuse to accept abolitionist petitions. This latter move, however, drew down on them the wrath of doughty old John Quincy Adams, who became a member of the House of Representatives after his retirement from the presidency. No abolitionist, Adams saw in denial of the right of petition a curtailment of civil liberties and after ten years of single-handed effort forced the rescinding of the "gag rule" just before his death in 1848.

American life during the Jacksonian era was also affected by two distinct waves of immigration. During the 1830's and 40's there was a heavy influx of Irish, driven out by famine conditions in their own country. These Irish immigrants settled mainly in the industrial towns of the Northeast—few had money enough to go farther—and also constituted much of the labor force which built the canals and railroads of the period. Their coming stimulated an outburst of "native Americanism" among people who disliked this great addition to the Catholic population of the United States. Because anti-Irish feeling was most pronounced among the Whig upper classes, the Irish became, for the most part, devoted adherents of the Democratic party. Following them came a wave of Germans, many of them political exiles—especially after the failure of German liberalism in 1848. The bulk of these immigrants moved to the West either to become farmers or to congregate in St. Louis, Milwaukee, and Cincinnati. The liberal idealism which had compelled their departure from Germany aligned most of them with the antislavery forces. By 1860 they constituted an important element of Republican strength and were staunch supporters of the Union.

THE WEST AND THE PUBLIC DOMAIN

The rise of democracy in the United States had one very important stimulus not present in contemporary Europe—namely, the existence of an open and expanding frontier. The westward movement had been a continuous process since the establishment of the first colonies; with the coming of improved transportation in the nineteenth century, its pace accelerated considerably. At the end of the Revolutionary War only a few exiguous settlements existed west of the Appalachians; by the time Jackson became President two states, Louisiana and Missouri, had been created on the far side of the Mississippi, fur traders were ranging over the Great Plains and the Rockies, and commerce moved in regular caravans over the Santa Fe Trail; by mid-century, migration, leaping over the supposed "Great American Desert," had planted American settlements firmly on the Pacific coast.

The settlement of the West was materially assisted by a gradual change in the government's public land policy. The first major land act, passed in 1796, applied most of the provisions of the Northwest Ordinance to the entire public domain, but with emphasis placed on treating the land as a source of revenue and as security for the national debt. The smallest unit which could legally be sold was 640 acres and the minimum price was two dollars an acre, a combination well beyond the resources of the ordinary frontier settler. Lagging sales and the growing political power of the West led to reductions in the amount of land which could be purchased and to a liberal credit system, but this combination encouraged speculation and led to a severe Western depression in 1819. A year later a new land act lowered the minimum price to $1.25 an acre and reduced the purchasable area to 80 acres.

The Land Act of 1820, however, still did not go far enough to satisfy the desires of the West. The settlers not only wanted their land as cheaply as possible, they wanted protection against speculators. Enterprising frontiersmen had a habit of "squatting" on attractive land before it was surveyed or offered for sale, only to find their farms snapped up by speculators when the public sale was held. Led by Senator Thomas H. Benton of Missouri, spokesmen of the West in Congress succeeded in winning acknowledgment of the right of "preemption," whereby the actual settler was given priority in buying his land. A series of laws to this effect culminated in the Preemption Act of 1841, which gave a settler the right to acquire up to 160 acres at the minimum price. Even without such legislation, Western pioneers were far from helpless. In many regions "claim associations" were formed, whose members attended the land sales and, by persuasive flourishing of rifles, bowie knives, and lengths of rope, discouraged outsiders from bidding.

The next logical step was free homesteads, but, despite vigorous championship of this idea by Horace Greeley and others, Southern opposition prevented a homestead law from being passed until 1862. The act of that year permitted any bona fide settler to acquire 160 acres by living on the land and cultivating it for five years. With that the United States finally committed itself to the policy of using the public domain to promote the growth of the West rather than for revenue, a policy which had been developing for the preceding forty years through the repeated concessions to settlers and the grants of land given to and in the construction of roads, canals, and railroads.

Influence of the Westward Movement. Westward expansion was perhaps the most powerful of all the democratizing influences in American life. It is true that the movement did not follow a uniform pattern. The tide of migration tended to go due west rather than to cross sectional lines, with the result that the differences in social organization which characterized the older states were extended into the newly settled areas. The Northwest, where slavery was prohibited by law, developed the small-scale, independently owned farms typical of the Northeast; the Southwest, with soil and climate admirably suited to cotton growing, duplicated the plantation system of the older slave states. Nevertheless, there were certain common features of Western development. The individuals who migrated west were likely to be the ambitious and restless souls, without too much regard for established traditions and conventions. In addition, social distinctions carried little weight on the frontier, where ability to survive took precedence over everything else. Even in the cotton states the planters who spread over Alabama and Mississippi and eventually pushed into Texas were self-made newcomers and not the aristocrats of the seaboard states. The West therefore generated an aggressive democracy which in due course reacted upon the rest of the country. Indeed, one of the reasons for the spread of manhood suffrage during the Jacksonian era was the desire of the Eastern states to lessen the attractiveness of the West for their inhabitants.

Western life had the peculiar quality of being highly individualistic and strongly cooperative at the same time. The frontier settler had to depend principally on himself, but there were occasions when he had to have the assistance of his neighbors, and on such occasions custom demanded that the assistance should be freely and generously given. In any event the loneliness of frontier life created an incentive to make the most of any opportunity for social intercourse. Perhaps the most conspicuous result of this desire was the astonishing variety of religious sects which flourished on the frontier. Of the older churches, the strongly evangelical denominations such as the Baptists and Methodists had the greatest appeal for people whose normal existence was dull and colorless, and they were supplemented by a host of new creeds of generally similar character. Of these the one with the most pronounced influence on Western development during this period was the Latter Day Saints, or Mormons, founded by Joseph Smith in 1830. Even for the frontier the Mor-

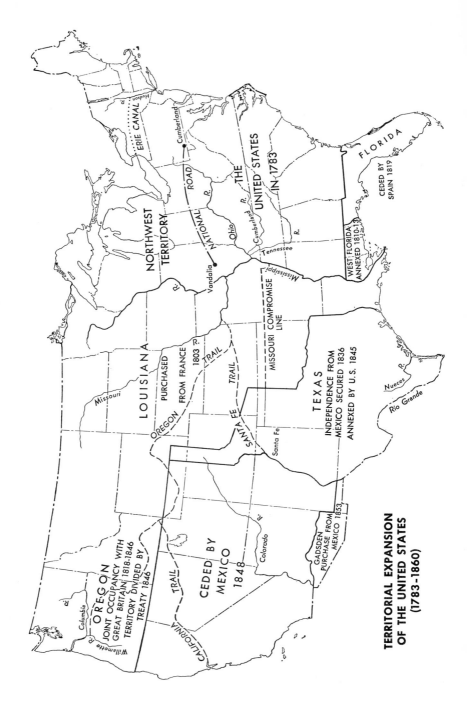

TERRITORIAL EXPANSION OF THE UNITED STATES (1783-1860)

mons were radical and were constantly in difficulties with their neighbors. From western New York, where Smith founded the church, they moved to Nauvoo, Illinois. Then, after Smith had been killed by a hostile crowd, they crossed the plains in 1846 to the Great Salt Lake under the masterful leadership of Brigham Young. The settlement of Utah stands out as one of the few examples of organized mass migration in the American westward movement, and of those few it is indubitably the greatest. To move ten thousand people into an arid desert and build a thriving community based on a carefully regulated system of irrigation was a remarkable achievement. The only part of the plan to fall through was the intention of the Mormons to leave the jurisdiction of the United States; the Mexican War thwarted that prospect.

MANIFEST DESTINY

Along with its vigorous democracy, the West bred the forceful American nationalism known as Manifest Destiny. It was a compound of an earnest belief that the United States had achieved the ideal political system, which ought to be extended as widely as possible, and an unshakable conviction that a beneficent providence had intended the American people to occupy the empty continent stretching west to the Pacific. Some of the more ardent enthusiasts of Manifest Destiny were prepared to take in everything from Panama to the North Pole, but most of them were willing to settle for less—a little less. Fulfillment of this destiny, whether in its extreme or moderate aspects, necessarily involved friction with other claimants to the same territory—with Great Britain, which had been in joint possession of the Oregon country with the United States since 1818, and still more with Mexico, inheritor of the Spanish dominions in North America which sprawled from California to Texas. It also involved a ruthless disregard of the rights of the native inhabitants. The United States government itself usually tried to treat the Indians fairly, although one of the dark spots in Jackson's administration is his acquiescence in the expulsion of the Cherokees from Georgia, but the frontier settlers usually had little respect either for the Indians or the treaties negotiated by a distant authority in Washington.

Texas and Oregon. Manifest Destiny as an important political issue began with the planting of an American colony in Texas by Stephen Austin in 1824. At first this arrangement was mutually advantageous; the American settlers got cheap land, and the Mexican government got colonists for the empty spaces of Texas. However, as the Americans increased in numbers, friction between them and the Mexican authorities developed, coming to a head when the dictator Santa Anna rescinded the right of local self-government in 1835. In the ensuing revolt the Texans made good their independence at the Battle of San Jacinto, on 21 April 1836, and established the Republic of Texas with Sam Houston, a close friend of Andrew Jackson, as president. The new nation, recognized as such by everyone except Mexico, promptly asked to be annexed by the United States but was, for the moment, refused, mainly because of bitter opposition in the North to acquisition of an area which could be made into a considerable number of slave states.

In the year that marked Texan independence Captain Benjamin Bonneville led the first wagon train over the Oregon Trail to the Willamette valley. The Oregon Territory, covering Oregon, Washington, Idaho, and British Columbia, had been occupied jointly, as stated above, by the United States and Great Britain since 1818. Offers by the United States to divide the territory at the 49th parallel had been refused by the British, who wanted to make the Columbia River the boundary. Before 1836 white settlement in Oregon had been limited to scattered posts of the Hudson's Bay Company and a few American missionaries, but after Bonneville's journey a steady influx of American immigrants both strengthened the hold of the United States on the southern half of the territory and made imperative some settlement of the question of jurisdiction.

By the early 1840's Manifest Destiny was the paramount issue facing the American people, in spite of the unwillingness of some of their political leaders to tackle problems which might have explosive internal repercussions. Besides the Oregon question, Texas had become a matter of acute concern because of the possibility that the Lone Star Republic might fall under British or French influence. Houston was, in fact, carrying on negotiations with both governments to enlist their aid in compelling Mexico to recognize Texan independence, although the underlying motive in these negotiations appears to have been to force the reluctant authorities in Washington to act. At the same time British and French activities in the Pacific generated alarm about the future of California, which, being remote from Mexico City and sparsely populated, appeared ripe for acquisition by some stronger power. There was some American settlement in California, brought there by Yankee merchantmen stopping on their way to the Orient. Even distant Hawaii came within the scope of Manifest Destiny. It was also on the route to the Far East, was a base of operations for New England whalers, and had attracted the attention of American missionaries. In 1842 Secretary of State Daniel Webster announced a special American interest in the island kingdom and warned the rest of the world to keep its hands off.

Fifty-four Forty or Fight. A treaty for the annexation of Texas failed of ratification early in 1844 because of opposition from the free states. Since, however, that was a presidential year, the decision was simply passed from the Senate on to the people. The two prospective major party candidates, Henry Clay and Martin Van Buren, came to a gentleman's agreement to omit the embarrassing Texas question from the campaign, but while Clay received the Whig nomination in due course, Van Buren stumbled over his party's two-thirds rule and lost a bitter convention battle to James K. Polk, a rabid expansionist thoroughly in sympathy with the Democratic demand for the "*re*occupation of Oregon and *re*annexation of Texas." The Democratic position was that both territories had originally belonged to the United States, Oregon by virtue of prior occupation and Texas as part of the Louisiana Purchase. Even Polk, however, paid his respects to the vexing slavery problem associated with Texas by focusing attention on Oregon with his slogan of "Fifty-four forty or fight." Faced with a groundswell of enthusiasm for Manifest Destiny, Clay belatedly tried to straddle the issue. The maneuver won him no expansionist votes and alienated the abolitionists, with the result that a third party, the Liberty party, cut into the Whig strength sufficiently to give Polk the electoral vote of New York by a narrow margin and with it the presidency.

Although James K. Polk is not ranked as one of the greatest of American Presidents, he was a man of marked industry and tenacity of purpose. Texas was taken out of his hands before his inauguration because President Tyler, anxious to have the credit for acquiring it, pushed a joint resolution for that purpose through Congress in February, 1845. In his foreign policy Polk moved cautiously, preferring to secure his ends by negotiating rather than fighting. A British change of heart about the 49th parallel opened the way for a compromise on Oregon if Polk could extricate himself gracefully from "Fifty-four forty or fight." Polk did. Since it was obviously undesirable to go to war with Great Britain and Mexico simultaneously, the President adroitly induced the Senate to advise accepting the 49th parallel as the Oregon boundary, whereupon he "reluctantly" abandoned his pugnacious slogan and concluded a treaty on 15 June 1846.

War with Mexico. Mexico was more obstreperous. She refused to acknowledge the annexation of Texas and broke off diplomatic relations with the United States. Polk, nevertheless, attempted to negotiate. He sent John Slidell to Mexico in November, 1845, to try to get Mexico to recognize the annexation in exchange for the assumption by the United States of claims of American citizens against the Mexican government, with the Rio Grande as the boundary between the two countries. The Mexicans regarded the Nueces River as the southern boundary of Texas. Slidell was also authorized to make an offer for the purchase of New Mexico (which included the present states of New Mexico, Arizona, Utah, Nevada, and parts of Colorado and Wyoming) and California.

His mission, however, failed because no Mexican government could stay in power if it showed any sign of making concessions to the United States. Early in 1846 Polk brought matters to a head by ordering General Zachary Taylor, then stationed at Corpus Christi, to advance to the Rio Grande. War was probably inevitable in any event; Polk's action simply touched off the conflict a little earlier than might otherwise have been the case. Taylor's forces naturally came into conflict with the Mexicans, who claimed that he was invading their territory, and a clash on 25 April 1846 enabled the President to inform Congress (11 May), that war existed by act of Mexico.

The Mexican War can be summed up as badly planned and well fought. Nothing had been done in advance to expand the army or to formulate any systematic strategy for winning the conflict. But the twelve-month volunteers who supplemented the regular forces were tough if undisciplined fighters, and the generalship was normally of a high order. At the start, the administration could undertake only the two most obvious moves. First, forces were sent to occupy New Mexico and California, a task easily accomplished, although in California there was a weird tangle of authority among Colonel Stephen Kearny, who had crossed the continent via Santa Fe with 500 men, the naval forces which had occupied San Francisco Bay, the American settlers who established the "Bear Flag Republic," and Captain John C. Frémont, the "Pathfinder of the West," who was in the area with an exploring party when the war broke out and took it on himself to act for the United States government, his position strengthened by the fact that he was Senator Benton's son-in-law.

Second, Taylor, with his army already on the Rio Grande, was sent on into northern Mexico. There he won victories but achieved nothing of strategic value. Indeed, his victories caused more concern in Washington than in Mexico City, since "Old Rough and Ready" was a Whig and was materializing as a national hero with excellent prospects for the presidency. Since there appeared to be a dearth of good Democrats in high military rank, Polk toyed with the idea of making Senator Benton a lieutenant-general but fortunately was dissuaded by Secretary of War William L. Marcy.

The Halls of Montezuma. Finally, the administration turned to a proposal submitted at the beginning of the war by General Winfield Scott for an expedition to strike directly at Mexico City. Scott was a Whig too, but since it was his idea and he was the senior major-general in the army, he could hardly be denied the command and there was always the chance, moreover, that two Whig heroes would cancel each other out (an unfounded hope since Taylor was elected President in 1848 anyway).

Scott's march to Mexico City was a brilliant performance. He was given less than ten thousand men where he had asked for twenty thousand, and over half of these were short-term volunteers. Nevertheless, Vera Cruz was taken on 27 March 1847, and two weeks later a formidable position at Cerro Gordo was neatly by-passed. At Puebla the army had to halt for three months while men whose enlistments had expired were sent home and replacements brought out; then on to Mexico City, where hard fighting alternated with peace negotiations. After the storming of Chapultepec on 13 September, the Mexicans gave up, and four days later American soldiers and marines marched into the ancient capital of the Aztecs, just as Hernando Cortés's *conquistadores* had done three centuries before.

Treaty of Guadalupe Hidalgo. The somewhat bewildering political conduct of the Mexican War carried over into the peace settlement in that the Treaty of Guadalupe Hidalgo was negotiated and signed in behalf of the United States by an individual who had no authority to do so. This was Nicholas P. Trist, the chief clerk of the State Department, who had been sent along with Scott to take advantage of any peace proposals that might develop. Before the final negotiations began, Polk became dissatisfied with Trist and recalled him, but Trist stayed on just the same and functioned as the official representative of his government—for which he was fired when he returned to Washington. However, the treaty which he signed on 2 February 1848 was duly ratified. In it Mexico acknowledged the annexation of Texas with the Rio Grande as the boundary and ceded California and New Mexico to the United States in exchange for $15,000,000 and the assumption by the United States of American claims against Mexico. Thus, the continental United States was completed, except for the Gadsden Purchase of 1853, bought from Mexico for $10,000,000 to provide a route for a Southern transcontinental railroad.

Clayton-Bulwer Treaty. Manifest Destiny extended beyond Mexico to Central America, where the possibilities of an isthmian canal attracted both the United States and Great Britain during the 1840's. When the United States, by treaty with New Granada (Colombia) in 1846, secured transit rights over the Isthmus of Panama, the British countered in 1848 by declaring a protectorate over the Mosquito Indians, located on the Atlantic coast of Nicaragua, thereby staking out a claim to the best alternative route across Central America. Nicaragua protested and was naturally supported by the United States. Anglo-American rivalry in this area was terminated by the Clayton-Bulwer Treaty of 1850, whereby the two powers somewhat ambiguously renounced territorial ambitions and more explicitly guaranteed the neutrality of any canal that might be constructed. The subsequent withdrawal of the British from the Mosquito Coast made this agreement a satisfactory one, for the time being, to the United States.

After 1850 Manifest Destiny, like everything else in American life, was plunged into the maelstrom of sectional conflict. It still had enough expansive force to produce Commodore Matthew C. Perry's expedition to Japan in 1853, which opened that country to American commerce. For the most part, however, its energies were dissipated in demands for the acquisition of additional slave territory in Mexico or, preferably, Cuba. This agitation reached a ludicrous climax in 1854 when the United States ministers to Great Britain, France, and Spain met in the stimulating atmosphere of Ostend, Belgium, and solemnly announced to the world that the time had come for Spain to sell Cuba to the United States or, failing Spanish acquiescence, for the United States to take the island.

CULTURAL TRENDS

It is a marked testimony to the essential unity of Western civilization that in a period when the American people were absorbed with their internal problems and had a minimum of interest in Europe, a clear community of ideas and interests persisted. The development of American nationality brought with it an emerging American culture. However, just as Jacksonian Democracy and Manifest Destiny were the American expressions of liberalism and nationalism, so the patterns of American cultural life were basically variants of the prevailing intellectual currents of the Western world. Without this external stimulus, indeed, American cultural standards must unavoidably have declined, since a pioneering agrarian society is not the most fertile soil for literature and the arts.

The predominant current of the early nineteenth century was romanticism, which can most conveniently be summarized as a reaction against the extremes of eighteenth-century rationalism. In general the romanticists emphasized emotion instead of pure reason and glorified nature in its wild state in preference to the form and order dear to the Age of Reason. American romanticism reached its peak in transcendentalism, a school of thought developed by the New England intellectuals who clustered about Ralph Waldo Emerson and deriving its name from the fact that its adherents believed man to be capable of grasping truths that "transcended" reason.

Literature. The period from 1815 to 1860 was, indeed, the great age of New England letters. Other sections of the country made their contributions to American literature: Washington Irving, James Fenimore Cooper, and Herman Melville in New York; Edgar Allan Poe, William Gilmore Simms, and Augustus Longstreet in the South. They did not, however, compare with the galaxy of talent which gave Boston the titles of "Athens of America" and "Hub of the Universe"—philosopher Emerson; poets Longfellow, Lowell, Whittier; novelists Hawthorne and Alcott; historians Parkman, Bancroft, Motley. New England had passed the pioneering stage and had the wealth and leisure to support the arts; it may be also that the New England mind was showing the effects of Calvinistic training released from the restraints of Calvinistic theology.

While some of the writers of this period, notably Hawthorne and Melville, were distinctly pessimistic, the characteristic note of American romanticism was one of optimistic idealism, in harmony with the temper of the times in the United States. This was perhaps best expressed by Emerson and at the time of the Civil War by Walt Whitman; it also appears in the devotion of most of the men of letters to reform movements —Whittier and Lowell, for example, applied much of their poetic talent to denunciation of slavery.

Fine Arts. In art and architecture the United States still depended on Europe, although some prominent Americans emerged, such as Gilbert Stuart and John Trumbull in painting and Charles Bulfinch in architecture. Architectural trends changed during the early nineteenth century from Georgian, or colonial, to classical, partly because a classical revival was one of the many aspects of romanticism and partly because Georgian architecture was regarded as a British survival and therefore unsuited to republican America. American music likewise was in an embryonic stage; apart from some religious music, the one conspicuous American composer of this period was Stephen Foster, whose beautiful Southern melodies—"My Old Kentucky Home" and "Swanee River," to name only two—were destined to become imperishable.

Science. Science, of course, has always been international, so that a close relationship between American and European scientists was nothing unusual. Indeed, two men who must be rated as leaders of American science at this time came from abroad: Louis Agassiz (1807–1873), for many years professor of natural history at Harvard and international authority on fossils, was born in Switzerland and educated in Germany; and John James Audubon (1785–1851), the great ornithologist and artist, was born in the French West Indies and educated in France.

Facilities for training scientists in the United States were limited. Rensselaer Polytechnic Institute was founded in 1824; the scientific schools at Harvard and Yale followed in the 1840's, along with the Smithsonian Institution, based on a bequest by James Smithson (1765–1829), an English scientist who admired American democracy although he had never seen the United States.

Yet despite its limitations, American science had some notable achievements to its credit. There was no lack of scientific ability in a generation which produced, among others: Asa Gray (1810–1888), regarded as the founder of American botany; Joseph Henry (1797–1878),

Princeton physicist and first director of the Smithsonian Institution, whose researches in electricity and magnetism contributed much to the development of telegraphic communication; Matthew F. Maury (1806–1873), a naval officer who was a distinguished pioneer in the field of oceanography; and Benjamin Silliman (1779–1864) professor of chemistry at Yale, who with his son and namesake (1816–1885) dominated that field for many years. In addition, the United States had to its credit the conspicuous advance in medicine represented by the development of anesthesia, for which the principal credit goes to Crawford Long of Georgia and William Morton of Massachusetts. The first operation in history in which ether was used as an anesthetic was performed at the Massachusetts General Hospital in 1846.

20

The Second Empire and the Unifications of Germany and Italy

With the suppression of the Parisian workers in the "June Days," the French National Assembly turned to the task of making and adopting a constitution for the Second French Republic. This document provided for a unicameral legislature and a President, both to be elected by universal manhood suffrage. The President's term of office was to be four years and he was ineligible for reelection.

The presidential aspirants included the Socialist Ledru Rollin; General Cavaignac, the champion of order, who was backed by the Republicans; Prince Louis Napoleon Bonaparte, a nephew of the great Napoleon; and the poet Lamartine, candidate of the Catholic party. The election proved to be a landslide for Louis Napoleon, who polled five million votes compared to the one and a half million of the runner-up, General Cavaignac. The explanation for this overwhelming victory may be illustrated by the story of the Napoleonic veteran who when asked if he would vote for Napoleon replied, "Why shouldn't I? I whose nose was frozen at Moscow." The growth of the Napoleonic legend during the days since 1815 had been impressive, and the name of Louis Napoleon seemed to be a symbol of the lost greatness of France.

Within a short time, the President and the Assembly began to differ and their enmity increased in 1850 when the Assembly passed an electoral law effectively disfranchising about one-third of the electorate. This act gave Louis Napoleon an opportunity to pose as the champion of the masses, a chance he needed to offset the adverse reaction to some of his measures which bore a conservative tinge. The fight raged for about a year, and then the President staged a *coup d'état* on 2 December 1851, the anniversary of his uncle's victory at Austerlitz.

On this day, he announced the dissolution of the Assembly, the restoration of manhood suffrage, and a proposal to be submitted to the voters by means of a plebiscite that he be empowered to revise the constitution. Opposition was ruthlessly dealt with, and the President's action was ratified in the popular vote, 7,500,000 to 645,000. The new constitution followed speedily and went into effect in January, 1852. Although it restored universal male suffrage, it extended the President's term of office to ten years and increased his powers markedly. This new instrument was based on the Constitution of the Year VIII, his uncle's handiwork.

The next step in the dissolution of the Second Republic was not long in coming. Following a triumphant tour of France in the fall of 1852, during which cries of *"Vive l'Empereur"* were obligingly raised by individuals planted in the crowd for that purpose whenever he spoke, he announced on 2 December the transformation of France into the Second Empire with himself as Emperor Napoleon III. Another plebiscite convincingly ratified this move, and so France was launched on eighteen years of another Napoleonic imperial regime.

THE CRIMEAN WAR

Scarcely had the Emperor assumed his crown when trouble broke out in the Near East. Napoleon eagerly snatched at an opportunity to pose as the defender of the Holy Places. The Turks had been forced to concede certain guarantees relative to the Holy Land but the question of whether the Orthodox Catholics or the Roman Catholics were to benefit most by these concessions led to a difference of opinion between Napoleon and Nicholas I, Czar of all the Russias. England took France's side in order to check Russian expansion toward the Mediterranean. Together they supported the Turks, who decided in favor of the Roman Catholics. Anticipated help from Austria was not forthcoming for the Russians, who bitterly denounced what they considered rank ingratitude. After all, it had been Russia which had gone to the assistance of Austria at a most critical time during the revolutions of 1848 and 1849 and had made possible the subduing of the Hungarians. The result was the Crimean War in 1853 with Britain, France, and Turkey arrayed against Russia. In 1855 Sardinia joined the allies and made a modest contribution in return for a voice at the peace table, where it might prove possible to enlist assistance in the projected plan to expel Austria from Italy and thus facilitate the
.   .   on of the peninsula.

1854, the allies laid siege to the great Crimean bastion of Sebastopol. The war was a savage one[1] and produced, despite the presence of Florence Nightingale and other nurses who for the first time in history brought the ministering "angels of mercy" into a military campaign, tremendous loss of life. The ravages of disease were especially devastating. At a crucial moment, Nicholas I died. Shortly afterward Sebastopol fell, and the war was over, since Alexander II was willing to talk peace terms.

Congress of Paris. Napoleon as the real instigator of this sanguinary conflict was the proper one to act as host to the powers and so the Congress of Paris took place in 1856. Here, the Emperor endeavored to outdo the brilliance of Vienna in 1814–1815 and reveled in his role. The terms of the treaty included: (1) a guarantee of the independence and the integrity of Turkey; (2) a promise by the Sultan to accord better treatment to all his subjects without distinction, matched by the assurance of the powers that they would not interfere in the relations between the Sultan and his subjects; (3) the neutralization of the Black Sea; (4) freedom of navigation on the Danube; and (5) the principalities of Moldavia and Wallachia (the nucleus of modern Rumania) were accorded autonomy under Turkish auspices.

The Declaration of Paris supplemented the treaty. It (1) abolished privateering; (2) proclaimed that free ships made free goods, except for contraband; (3) made neutral goods, except contraband, not liable to capture when under an enemy flag; and (4) ruled that a blockade to be legitimate had to be effective. It is interesting to note that the United States refused to become a signatory to the Declaration although its terms with the exception of the outlawing of privateering were exactly what this country had always espoused. The only explanation for this strange action is that the State Department, then presided over by William L. Marcy, felt that the United States might one day need privateers and it would represent too much of a sacrifice to give them up. The only other powers not to adhere were Spain and Mexico.

THE SECOND EMPIRE

Domestically, the Second Empire was characterized by the significant gap between theory and actuality. Manhood suffrage was continued but in practice it meant little since the Government effectively maintained its power. Freedom of press and speech were proclaimed but subtle persuasion was used to keep them safely within bounds.

A firm believer in the fact that a prosperous nation was a happy one, Napoleon encouraged big business. During his regime, Ferdinand de Lesseps built the Suez Canal, the railroad mileage was increased fourfold,

[1] One of its highlights was the charge of the Light Brigade at Balaclava, immortalized in verse by Tennyson.

new banks flourished, and very satisfactory trade agreements were worked out with England and the German *Zollverein.* In general, France enjoyed a period of great prosperity which was surprisingly well distributed among all classes of the people.

Determined to leave an enduring monument to his fame, Napoleon bent his energies to make Paris truly the "City of Light," the world's most beautiful capital. The magnificent boulevards and parks of modern Paris were built, together with an imposing array of public edifices.

Happy over the way things were progressing, the Emperor felt secure enough to grant a few liberal concessions beginning in 1859, making possible the appearance of a mild opposition group, which, although few in numbers and disunited, at least had a chance to voice occasional criticism of the regime. Constantly reminded of the brilliant foreign policy of his uncle and model and equally aware of the drab record of his own immediate predecessor in this respect, Napoleon pursued at all times an extremely active interest in foreign affairs.

THE UNIFICATION OF ITALY

For the time being, it is necessary to leave our discussion of the Second Empire and turn to the affairs first of Italy and then of Germany. Ever since the days of the Congress of Vienna, every attempt at the unification of Italy had proven unsuccessful, but the desire on the part of Italian patriots was as strong as ever. Secret societies such as the *Carbonari* (Charcoal Burners) with thousands of members and Giuseppe Mazzini's *Young Italy* were dedicated to the achievement of unification. During the Revolutions of 1848, a short-lived measure of success had been enjoyed by the liberals and nationalists. A temporary republic had been set up in Rome but had collapsed with the appearance of French troops sent by President Bonaparte, a former member of the *Carbonari,* to protect the pope. In Sardinia-Piedmont, as previously stated, Charles Albert had granted his subjects a constitution and had personally led his people in an unsuccessful attempt to drive the Austrians from northern Italy. His failure brought about his abdication in favor of his son, Victor Emmanuel II.

Cavour. In 1852, Victor Emmanuel selected for his prime minister Camillo Benso, the Conte di Cavour, who was destined to become the "Brains of Italy." A liberal and a confirmed nationalist, Cavour was convinced that the only way in which Italy's hopes could be realized was through the enlistment of outside assistance. Like Bismarck after him, he was favorably disposed toward alliances. Much to the surprise of everyone, he declared war in 1855 on Russia—a somewhat paradoxical procedure since Cavour had shown himself no friend of the Roman Catholic

Church in Sardinia—and dispatched an expeditionary force to fight with the allies in the Crimea. At the Congress of Paris, Cavour, as he had anticipated, was given an opportunity to address the notables. In a brilliant speech, he called the attention of his allies to the condition of Italy and made a most favorable impression. Two years later, a secret meeting between Cavour and Napoleon III was arranged in the French town of Plombières, where an alliance was cemented against Austria. Napoleon agreed to wage war on the side of Sardinia provided that Austria could be made to appear the aggressor. Since the Emperor had a keen eye for any desirable territorial acquisitions, Cavour dangled before him the promise of the French-speaking provinces of Nice and Savoy as compensation. Sardinia was to receive Lombardy and Venetia, the Austrian provinces in northern Italy. The plans completed, the Italians set to work to nag the Austrians into a declaration of hostilities, which occurred in 1859. True to his promise, Napoleon rushed French troops to the aid of the Sardinians.

The Emperor personally led his soldiers on the field of Solferino, where the French and the Sardinians scored an impressive victory over the whitecoats. Napoleon's experiences in this battle convinced him that war was the proper province of his generals and was not for him. In the other important engagement of the brief campaign in Lombardy, the Austrians were defeated at Magenta. With their hopes at a fever pitch, the Sardinians were preparing to invade Venetia, when the astounding and disheartening news came that Napoleon had faithlessly deserted his friends and made a unilateral peace treaty with the Austrians at Villafranca. This revelation so upset Cavour that he lost his customary equanimity and sought to continue the war single-handedly. Victor Emmanuel, however, retained his reason. Knowing that such an undertaking could only prove disastrous, he prevailed with great difficulty upon Cavour to accept the best of a bad bargain. Thus, Lombardy was annexed to Sardinia and Venetia was retained by Austria. Nice and Savoy were transferred to French control. Shortly afterward, Parma, Modena, and Tuscany were the scenes of uprisings which overthrew the petty tyrants who ruled these duchies and all voted in 1860 to annex themselves to Sardinia-Piedmont. At the same time, a revolt in the papal territory in northern Italy known as the Romagna achieved a similar result.

As to the reasons for Napoleon's desertion of Cavour, there are several which can be advanced. In the first place, his actions in aiding Italian unification were resented by the French Catholics, who realized that if Italy were to be unified it would be ultimately at the expense of the pope. Secondly, Napoleon had no desire to create a strong Italy which might eventually contest with France the supremacy of the Mediterranean. His sole objects had been the weakening of France's old rival, Austria, which had been such a thorn in the side of Napoleon I, and the acquisition of Nice and Savoy. Finally, there was the fear of possible trouble with Prussia, which might conceivably take advantage of France's preoccupation in Italy.

Garibaldi. Despite her disappointment over the fact that the task of driving Austria out of Italy was only half completed, Sardinia could find solace in the very real progress made to date. At this point, the popular Joseph Garibaldi, whose exploits were legendary and who had rendered valuable service in 1859, came to the fore. The "Sword of Italy" conceived the idea of raising a band of volunteers and with them waging war against the King of Naples. In 1860 his "redshirts" or "The Thousand," as they were also called, embarked from Genoa for an invasion of Sicily which they proceeded to conquer against tremendous odds. This done, Garibaldi, his ranks now increased fourfold, invaded the mainland to assault the rest of the kingdom of the Two Sicilies. His progress was sensational as many of the people and huge numbers of the king's troops went over to his ranks. In the only real battle of the campaign, Garibaldi was victorious. The king fled in terror, and Garibaldi was left as dictator of the entire Kingdom of Naples.

Garibaldi's success was disconcerting to Cavour, who feared lest the impetuous soldier might attack Rome, which was still defended by French troops. In order to forestall such a risky venture, which would undo all the good so far achieved, Cavour dispatched Victor Emmanuel to Naples at the head of the Sardinian army. En route, the Marches and Umbria, papal territories, were occupied. Garibaldi handed over the kingdom of the Two Sicilies to Victor Emmanuel and freely renounced his title of dictator. He hailed Victor as the king of all Italy, a proclamation which was ratified by the first Italian parliament, meeting in Turin in 1861. Plebiscites in the Two Sicilies, Umbria, and the Marches had previously resulted in an overwhelming vote in favor of joining Sardinia.

Restrained from assaulting Rome, Garibaldi modestly went into retirement. Inaction proved too much for him, and, since death had removed the restraining hand of Cavour in 1861, the old soldier made two unsuccessful attempts to capture Rome and present it to Victor Emmanuel.

During the Seven Weeks' War between Austria and Prussia in 1866, Italy acquired Venetia as a result of an alliance with Bismarck. Thus, only Rome remained outside the framework of a completely unified Italy by 1866. In 1870, with the outbreak of the Franco-Prussian War, Napoleon III, desperately in need of all the troops he could muster, withdrew the French garrison protecting the Eternal City. The Italians were quick to capitalize on this situation and sent an army into Rome, on 20 September 1870. A one-sided plebiscite approved this *fait accompli,* and

Rome became the capital of Italy. The pope refused to recognize the legality of the action which put an end to the temporal powers of the papacy and retired to the Vatican as "the prisoner of the Vatican," where his successors emulated his example until 1929. Thus, the old dream of the Italian nationalists and liberals was fulfilled, and a united Italy was ready to take her place in the councils of Europe.

THE UNIFICATION OF GERMANY: BACKGROUND

Historically, the French and Germans had long been enemies. At Vienna, in the settlement achieved there, Prussia became the protector of the Germans against France in the future when Prussia acquired provinces on the Rhine. This became all the more evident since Austria had given up the Austrian Netherlands (Belgium) and taken compensation elsewhere. Nonetheless, as we have seen, Austria continued through Metternich to be the arbiter of German affairs.

Prussia meanwhile went about its business in unspectacular fashion. By 1834, the *Zollverein*, originally a free-trade arrangement among the various provinces of Prussia, had extended its operations until it had created an economic unit of German states which could be politically united either through the acquisition of the smaller states by Prussia or through a federal union which excluded Austria. The coming of the Industrial Revolution to Germany served to dramatize the need for unification in some form. But arrayed against the idea of unification were such forces as the Austrian Hapsburgs, who so far had proved strong enough to prevent such an event, and various selfish interests, too numerous to list, which felt that unification would adversely affect them. Furthermore, sectionalism and provincialism were powerful forces in opposition to consolidation. And, finally, there was the religious division of Germany almost evenly into Protestants and Catholics, each of which feared the other might gain some special advantage which might well prove disastrous for the side not favored.

The French Revolution of 1848 had galvanized Germans into action. The Frankfurt Assembly convened in May, and the hope was widespread that it would draw up a constitution for a united Germany. Its failure has already been noted, but the hostility shown to the idea by the European powers is worth a brief mention. England, Russia, France, and later Austria for different reasons all manifested their opposition to a unified Germany. This international hostility was keenly resented by patriotic Germans, but they were helpless in the face of it. By 1851, the Germanic Confederation again held sway under the aegis of Austria. Austrian leadership now became extremely vigorous, and Prussia, whose king a few short years ago had been offered the crown of a unified Germany, was treated cavalierly. Frederick William IV in "the humiliation of Olmutz" in 1850 had been explicitly forced to give up any intentions of establishing a Germanic federal union led by Prussia.

Alarmed over Austria's new haughtiness toward her in the Confederation, Prussia commenced to adopt measures to insure military parity. The fires of unification did not die despite the setback administered but smoldered fiercely. More and more the proponents of force were heard advocating preparedness. Not only must there be a united Germany under Prussian leadership but it must be strong enough to hold its own against the powers whose disapproval in 1848 had helped to check the movement. Increasingly, it was becoming obvious that if the job of unifying Germany was to be accomplished it must be performed by Prussia. Austria had demonstrated not merely a lack of interest in such a project but had evinced positive hostility. Furthermore, Austria's own vital concerns lay elsewhere. As an ally later when the task had been performed, she would be useful. As a leader, she was not to be followed.

BISMARCK

From 1851 to 1859, the Prussian delegate to the federal diet at Frankfurt was Otto von Bismarck, one of the powerful Prussian *Junker* class. During the years he spent at Frankfurt, he reached the conclusion that if Prussia was ever to become a great power, it needed an alliance with France, an old enemy of Austria. This project was so revolutionary that it won few supporters. Undismayed, Bismarck stuck manfully to his guns. He concentrated his efforts upon converting the Prussian heir apparent, Prince William, to his way of thinking, but succeeded only in getting "kicked upstairs" for his trouble by being promoted to the post of Prussian ambassador at the Russian court in St. Petersburg.

For several years, Bismarck was allowed to cool off in the Russian "icebox" before being moved to Paris, where he now represented Prussia at Napoleon III's gay court. These unsought tours of duty actually served Bismarck well. His Russian experiences taught him the value of an alliance with the Bear. His brief sojourn in France revealed the weakness of Napoleon III to his keen eye. Napoleon, in his turn, was contemptuous of Bismarck.

Deadlocked with the lower house of the *Landtag* over a bill seeking increased army appropriations, William, now king, called Bismarck home in 1862 and made him prime minister (minister president) of Prussia. The appointment was extremely unpopular, as Bismarck was considered a dangerous ultraconservative whose influence would be used against liberalism.

He met the opposition head on in the struggle to secure the necessary appropriations for the army. He was determined that Prussia must be militarily strong for the work that lay ahead. No parliamentary body was going to stand in the way by employing constitutional methods. If the lower house of the *Landtag* would not vote the appropriations, he would give no account of how the government spent the money it collected. As he bluntly declared to the members: "The great question of the day will not be decided by speeches and majority votes—that was the great mistake of 1848 and 1849—but through blood and iron." From 1862 to 1866 the money request was refused, but Bismarck managed to find the necessary funds anyway. Driving relentlessly toward his goal—the unification of Germany under Prussian leadership with Austria expelled—he cracked down hard on the liberals. To Bismarck, the end, especially if it were a patriotic one, justified the means.

THE SCHLESWIG-HOLSTEIN EPISODE

The funds which Bismarck supplied despite the refusal of parliament provided Prussia with the desired military reforms. The army was strong, well equipped, and ably led by the military genius, Helmuth von Moltke.

In 1864 came the first of the three wars, spaced over six years, Prussia was destined to fight before Germany became unified. The Danish War came about out of difficulties arising from the incorporation of the duchy of Schleswig in 1863 by Denmark. This region was peopled partly by Danes and partly by Germans. Its neighboring duchy, Holstein, was completely German and was a member of the Germanic Confederation whereas Schleswig was not. Both had been linked with Denmark for centuries through a personal union with the Danish king. Since it was apparent that Denmark might annex the other duchy as well, Bismarck saw an excellent opportunity to make use of his army. He easily induced Austria to declare war also on Denmark, since the former could ill afford to permit Prussia to add to its strength by annexing the two provinces herself. Denmark was overcome by her powerful opponents in a matter of a few days and forced to cede Schleswig and Holstein. In the disposition of spoils (Treaty of Gastein) Austria was given Holstein (the province largely peopled by Prussians) and Prussia received Schleswig. Austria was thus neatly placed in the jaws of a pincers. Furthermore, Prussia won the right to dig a canal connecting the North Sea and the Baltic at Kiel.

THE SEVEN WEEKS' WAR

Bismarck was now in a position to make his second move in his plan for unification, the elimination of Austria even if it meant a war to accomplish his aim. The Gastein settlement made it practically inevitable, since it gave Austria the task of ruling turbulent Germans in Holstein whom

Bismarck could be called upon to defend. Before the stage was set for hostilities, it was necessary to win French neutrality. On the sands of Biarritz, Bismarck was able to get the fatuous Napoleon to agree to remain aloof should Austria and Prussia do battle. Then Italy was offered an opportunity to make an alliance with Prussia in return for the promise of Venetia. Russia could be counted upon to stand aside since she had not forgiven Austria for failing to come to her assistance in the Crimean War.

With everything in readiness, Bismarck proceeded to bait Austria in the Germanic Confederation until the Austrians were in a frenzy. An Austrian proposal in the Diet for mobilization of the troops of the various members of the Confederation against Prussia was adopted, and war broke out in 1866. With the exception of a few northern states, all the members supported Austria. The war which followed lasted exactly seven weeks. Prussia was fully prepared and was better led and equipped than her opponents. The Prussian general, Helmuth von Moltke, left little to chance. In a couple of days, Austria's satellites were eliminated and Prussian troops poured into Bohemia in clocklike fashion. There at Königgratz (or Sadowa as the battle is also called), a battle involving hundreds of thousands of troops took place on 3 July. The victory of the Prussians in this decisive engagement was in no small measure due to their new needle gun, a breechloader. Königgratz was the deciding factor and Austria was beaten.

For Bismarck, this was sufficient. He had no desire to humiliate Austria, since already he was thinking ahead to a war with France in order to solidify Germany. Furthermore, Austria might be otherwise useful in the future. Therefore, the Treaty of Prague (1866) was surprisingly moderate. Austria was compelled to drop out of Germanic affairs in that the old Diet was dissolved and Austria was not to be a member of its successor. Schleswig and Holstein were incorporated into Prussia. Lastly, Venetia was ceded to Italy. The indemnity imposed was so slight as hardly to be worth mention.

The Dual Monarchy. Both Germany and Austria now underwent reorganization as a result of the war. The dual monarchy of Austria-Hungary was formed in 1867 by the *Ausgleich,* or Compromise. Francis Joseph was now recognized as Emperor of Austria and King of Hungary. The Germans of Austria and the Magyars of Hungary each had their own autonomous government, and there was in addition an imperial parliament to discuss matters of common concern such as foreign affairs, imperial finance, and defense. This arrangement satisfied the Germans and Magyars, but left the numerous other nationalities under Hapsburg rule still in a subordinate position.

North German Confederation. Prussia annexed outright several of Austria's late Germanic allies. The rest of Germany north of the Main was reorganized as the North German Confederation, with a constitution written by Bismarck. Under its terms the king of Prussia was made hereditary president of the Confederation, governing through a chancellor responsible to him and not to the legislature. The first Chancellor, naturally, was Bismarck. The legislature consisted of a lower house, the *Reichstag,* elected by manhood suffrage, and an upper house, the *Bundesrat,* composed of delegates appointed by the rulers of the various states in the Confederation. The foreign and military affairs of the Confederation were to be managed by Prussia. Four south German states, Bavaria, Württemberg, Hesse, and Baden, remained independent. They were reluctant to accept Prussian domination, and Bismarck did not want to drive them into the arms of Napoleon III by attempting to coerce them. The French emperor played into Bismarck's hands by demanding cession of the Bavarian Palatinate as compensation to France for Prussia's gains in the Seven Weeks' War, with the result that the south German states took alarm and concluded military alliances with the North German Confederation.

THE FRANCO-PRUSSIAN WAR

Prussia's startling achievements surprised Europe considerably. Most upset was Napoleon. He had decided that the Austro-Prussian War would be a stalemate which he would mediate and from which he would gain concessions and was deeply chagrined when Prussia not only won the war in seven weeks but proceeded to form the North German Confederation. As one shrewd French observer remarked: "It is France that is defeated at Sadowa." French hostility to Bismarck increased, and she began to seek "revenge for Sadowa." This delighted Bismarck, who was of the opinion that if France could be maneuvered into attacking Germany, the southern states would make common cause with their brethren and unification would be completed.

A vacancy in the Spanish throne as a result of the Spanish Revolution of 1868 provided the occasion which led to the outbreak of the Franco-Prussian War. The Spanish offered the crown to Leopold of Hohenzollern-Sigmaringen, who oddly enough was also a relative of Napoleon! Leopold accepted the offer in July, 1870, after having received the permission of King William, head of the House of Hohenzollern. The news of his acceptance enraged the French, who did not relish being surrounded by Hohenzollerns. The result was pressure applied on King William who, in turn, let the Sigmaringen branch know he would be pleased if Leopold reconsidered, which that worthy did much to Bismarck's chagrin.

The Ems Dispatch. Unable to resist the temptation to exploit his victory, Napoleon dispatched his ambassador, Count Benedetti, to Ems, where King William was vacationing. Benedetti was instructed to require

William to promise that *never* would there be any Hohenzollern candidacy for the Spanish throne. This senseless demand was rejected, and Bismarck was informed of what had transpired by means of a telegram.

Bismarck, who happened to be in the company of his generals von Moltke and von Roon when the dispatch arrived from Ems, perceived that a golden opportunity had presented itself. Assured by them that all that was necessary was the go signal, the Iron Chancellor shaded the wording of the message in such fashion that it became "a red flag for the Gallic Bull."

The following day, 14 July 1870, Bastille Day as he well knew, Bismarck published the Ems Dispatch and before the day was over France declared war with amazing lightheartedness. Equally exuberant were the Germans, who really were prepared down to their "gaiter buttons" (as the French war minister had assured Napoleon his troops were), and the southern states quickly joined their northern brethren for the defense of the fatherland. A legend, probably apocryphal but illustrative, has it that news of France's declaration of war reached Moltke's headquarters after the general had retired for the night. When an aide awakened him, Moltke merely said, "Open my desk, take out the envelope you will find there, and follow the instructions inside," and then turned over and went back to sleep. In actuality the Germans were not as mechanically perfect in their conduct of the war as they seemed to be, but their mistakes were cancelled out by appalling mismanagement on the other side. A month after the opening of hostilities Marshal Bazaine's army of 180,000 men was shut up in Metz and when the Emperor himself, assisted by Marshal Patrice Maurice MacMahon, tried to lead France's last trained army to Bazaine's relief, he was maneuvered into a trap at Sedan and forced to surrender, 2 September 1870, with all his troops.

French resistance was kept alive after Sedan by a spontaneous impulse on the part of the people, their efforts centering on a stubborn defense of Paris. When news of the Emperor's capture reached the capital 4 September, the defenders declared an end to the Second Empire and so posed a familiar problem—what kind of a government was France to set up in lieu of the one just overthrown?

By 28 January 1871, Paris could hold out no longer (the citizens had been reduced to eating dogs, cats, and even rodents) and capitulated. The treaty of peace was signed at Frankfurt, 10 May 1871. Alsace and much of Lorraine were ceded to Germany, and an indemnity of one billion dollars was assessed on defeated France. Until such time as it should be paid in full, Germany was to occupy French territory, the occupation expenses to be borne by France. To say that the terms were strict is to put it mildly.

The German Empire Founded. To add to France's humiliation, on 18 January 1871, in the Hall of Mirrors at Versailles, the German Empire had been born. The Prussian King was recognized as German Emperor under the name of William I, and the German Empire, incorporating the previously independent southern states, replaced the North German Confederation. The latter's constitution was taken over with only minor changes. Thus was the unification of Germany finally achieved —by blood and iron.

For defeated France the task of organizing a new government was rather more perplexing. A National Assembly was chosen shortly after the surrender of Paris, the Germans granting an armistice so that the elections could be held, for the dual purpose of making peace and drawing up a constitution. In this body the monarchists held a majority over the republicans, not so much because the French people wanted a monarchy as because the republicans, led by fiery Léon Gambetta, still refused to admit defeat and were willing to continue the war. Indeed, the conservatism of the Assembly was so unacceptable to the Paris radicals that they established their own government, the Commune of Paris, with the result that, in April and May, 1871, the city underwent a second siege, this time by French troops with the German occupation forces as spectators. The Commune was finally suppressed after violent and sanguinary street fighting.

The Third Republic. The prospects of monarchy in France were shattered by dissension among the monarchists themselves. Their delegates in the Assembly were split into a Bourbon and an Orleanist faction, and there was even a small but devoted band of Bonapartists. In 1873 an agreement between the Bourbons and Orleanists was nullified by the stubborn insistence of the Bourbon claimant, the Comte de Chambord, on being accepted as a king by divine right in the best manner of Louis XIV. Meanwhile, since the government of France had to be carried on while the factions in the Assembly bickered, Adolphe Thiers was appointed "Chief of the Executive Power"—the title of President had too strong a republican connotation for the Assembly. Thiers himself was an Orleanist, but by 1873 the course of events had convinced him that "a Republic is the form of government that divides us least." His growing republican convictions led the Assembly to replace him in 1873 with Marshal MacMahon, a good Legitimist who could be depended on to step down when and if conditions became ripe to reestablish the monarchy.

The opportunity never came. MacMahon stoutly refused to have anything to do with a *coup d'état,* and French public opinion was carried along on the same tide of liberalism that had produced Britain's Second Reform Bill and made it appear advisable to Bismarck to incorporate manhood suffrage into his constitution for a united Germany. In 1875 the National Assembly reluctantly completed a republican constitution for France. The document provided for a President with only nominal powers, real executive authority being vested in a cabinet responsible to the legislature, and bicameral legislature, composed of a Chamber of Deputies chosen by manhood suffrage and a Senate chosen on a more limited basis. The first elections under this constitution were a resounding victory for Gambetta and the republicans; it was, nevertheless, to be demonstrated in the future that substantial elements in French life accepted the Third Republic without enthusiasm, and some never accepted it at all.

21

Nationalism and Sectionalism
in the United States

Ebullient democracy and aggressive expansionism promised a bright future for the United States, provided it remained united. Whether it could or not was by far the gravest problem facing its people during the half-century after 1815. Nationalism had a dual effect on the United States. In its larger sense it was a unifying influence, finding its outlet in such ways as Manifest Destiny, the nationalizing opinions of John Marshall, and the efforts of the major political parties to maintain their ascendancy by harmonizing sectional interests. In its lesser aspect, sectionalism, it threatened to split the United States into two or possibly three separate nations.

Sectionalism, it should be emphasized, was a form of nationalism. Its spokesmen customarily used the language of states' rights, but they were really thinking, whether they were aware of it or not, in terms of larger areas with a common economic and social structure. And because the United States was a country of rapid growth and constant change, allegiances shifted easily between nation and section. Daniel Webster, a representative of New England particularism in 1812, delivered the most eloquent of all pleas for the Union in his Reply to Hayne in 1830— "Liberty and Union, now and forever, one and inseparable." John C. Calhoun, the War Hawk of 1812 and champion of nationalism during the Monroe administration, by 1830 had become the great philosopher of sectionalism.

BASES OF SECTIONAL CONFLICT

The rise of sections was unavoidable in a country as large as the United States. Differences in climate, topography, and natural resources made for differences in economic and social organization and a consequent divergence of outlook on national problems. By itself this situation need not have been unduly troublesome. Every country, even the smallest, has its crop of local rivalries, and, if the United States had been a static society, it would no doubt have been able to work out a satisfactory balance of sectional interests. But the United States was not a static society. It was in a continuous process of internal growth and territorial expansion, and each fresh change brought with it a disturbance of sectional equilibrium. Repeated clashes of interest, accentuated by emotional tension, produced a cleavage which could no longer be met by the ordinary methods of political compromise.

Sectional Groupings. During the generation prior to the Civil War the United States fell into three broad sectional groups: (1) the East, the industrial and commercial area north of the Mason and Dixon Line; (2) the South, comprising the slave states; and (3) the West, the region where pioneer agriculture was still prevalent. These sections were not fixed units, nor were the boundaries between them clearly defined. The line of demarcation between East and West moved constantly westward as industry followed agriculture, and while the political division between free and slave territory was distinct enough, there was a large border-state area in which sectional influences overlapped. The major groupings were nevertheless fully recognized and understood by Americans of the period. Because of their differences in economic and social structure, the sections were jealous of each other's influence on the Federal government; each wanted to secure Federal legislation favorable to its particular interests or at least to be able to prevent the passage of adverse legislation.

The East in general favored national policies which would promote its commercial and industrial interests. It wanted especially a high tariff and a sound currency. On the matter of promoting westward expansion, the Eastern industrialists were at first decidedly cool, because they were afraid of the West's draining off their labor supply and consequently forcing up wages. Their apprehensions were unfounded, since factory laborers seldom moved to the frontier, an undertaking requiring both money and knowledge of farming, but until the mid-century point, Eastern opinion was reluctant to spend public funds for internal improvements or reduce the price of public land. Then, as immigration solved the labor problem and Eastern capital saw in the West an expanding market and a source of profitable investment, this attitude gradually changed.

The South became, of course, the most distinct of the sections, chiefly because of the existence of its "peculiar institution," slavery. At the close of the War of 1812 there seemed every reason to assume that the South would keep pace with the North in industrialization, but between the economic attraction of filling the apparently insatiable demand for raw cotton and the fact that social prestige was measured in terms of ownership of land and Negroes, Southern wealth was plowed back into more and more plantations, leaving industry, commerce, and finance almost entirely in Northern hands.

The South, as a matter of fact, was enslaved by slavery. Southern writers defended the institution on the grounds that all great civilizations of the past had been built by a leisure class supported by slave labor, and that slavery actually benefited the Negroes by introducing them to Western civilization and Christianity. They could and did draw telling contrasts between the material conditions of the slaves on the plantations and that of the "free" laborers in the factories of the North and Europe, but fundamentally the South clung to slavery because it could not get rid of it. Economically, slavery in the long run was unprofitable. Slave labor was inefficient and unreliable, one-crop agriculture exhausted the soil, the extension of the plantation area into the Southwest eventually led to falling prices for cotton, and the closing of the African slave trade forced up the price of slaves. Between 1820 and 1860 the cost of a prime field hand rose from $600 to $1,800; for this trebled investment the planter received no correspondingly higher return. Yet the South's capital was so completely tied up in slavery that it was economically impossible to abolish the institution. It was socially impossible also. No Southerner cared to consider the problems involved in emancipating four million illiterate Negroes, a great many of them not far removed from savagery. As it was, the nightmare of servile insurrection haunted Southern minds and goes far to explain their extreme sensitivity to attacks on slavery.

In national affairs the South, as an exporting section, opposed the tariff. It bought its manufactured goods outside, either in the North or in Europe, and the sole effect of the tariff was to increase the cost of these goods to the purchasers. The South therefore regarded the tariff, with considerable justification, as a bounty paid by itself to Northern industry. It also opposed reducing the price of public land, partly because it wanted as much of the West as possible held open for the plantation system rather than given away to "squatters," and partly because a lowering of land revenues might have to be compensated for by raising the tariff. Federal aid for internal improvements was disliked (in principle—Southern public-land states were perfectly willing to accept railroad grants), because it held the possibility of increasing the power of the national government over the states, and that in turn might lead to Federal meddling with the "peculiar institution."

The characteristics of the West have already been described. It was the focal point of political strategy during this period because the continuous process of westward expansion kept bringing new states into the Union and increasing the West's political power, and because its interests were at once in harmony and in conflict with those of both the older sections. As an agrarian region the West shared "cheap-money" views on banking and finance with the South; on the other hand, its hopes for future industrial development gave it some sympathy for the tariff, and between the small-scale farmers of the Northwest and the planters of the South there was an irreconcilable conflict over the possession of new land in the areas where the two systems of agriculture overlapped. The bitterest sectional conflicts were those fought over the political and economic control of the West.

THE MISSOURI COMPROMISE

The first of these quarrels exploded in the middle of the "era of good feeling" during Monroe's administration. In 1818 Missouri applied for admission to the Union as a slave state. It was the second part of the Louisiana Purchase to become eligible for statehood, Louisiana having been admitted in 1812 without the slavery question being raised. Since the Northwest Ordinance applied, naturally, only to what had been American territory at the time of its adoption, there was no legislation governing the status of slavery in the Louisiana Purchase. As matters stood in 1818, the free states had already outstripped the slave states in population and therefore had a majority in the House, but there was an equal balance in the Senate. The admission of Missouri would tip it one way or the other, and the decision might conceivably determine the future of slavery in the entire Louisiana territory.

When the bill for the admission of Missouri came before the House, James Tallmadge of New York added an amendment to it providing for the eventual abolition of slavery. The House passed the measure in this form by a sectional vote, but the Senate rejected it, and an acrimonious debate began in Congress and the country at large. To the aged Thomas Jefferson the Missouri controversy came like a "firebell in the night" and filled him with well-founded apprehensions about the future. Sectional antagonism, however, was still in its early stages, and the fact that Maine, heretofore a part of Massachusetts, was seeking separate statehood, opened the way for a settlement after two years of wrangling. The Missouri Compromise of 1820 admitted Missouri as a slave state and Maine as a free state, and established the line 36° 30′ (roughly the southern boundary of Missouri) as the boundary between free and slave territory in the Louisiana Purchase. A glance at the map suggests that the North got much the better of the bargain, but it was not so regarded in 1820. Much of the region north of the compromise line was then termed the "Great American Desert" and was considered to be unfit for settlement.

THE NULLIFICATION CONTROVERSY

The Missouri Compromise was acceptable enough to both sides to remove the slavery issue from politics for the time being, but it did not diminish in the slightest the growing clash of interest between the free-labor economy of the North and the slave-labor economy of the South. The conflict simply found another outlet in the tariff question, supplemented by a new and ominous debate on the nature of the Union.

The tariff was, of course, a product of advancing industrialism. Prior to the War of 1812 the duties averaged from 10 to 12 per cent and were intended primarily to raise revenue. The financial needs of the war resulted in an approximate doubling of rates, and the strong nationalistic spirit which followed the war led to the continuation of these rates by an act of 1816 for the express purpose of protecting domestic manufactures. A revision of the tariff eight years later revealed that sectional unity on the issue had disappeared. The South was now opposed to protection, while the East and West in general supported Henry Clay's "American system" of national self-sufficiency.

In 1828 there was still another tariff act, designed chiefly for political purposes. With an eye on the coming presidential election the low-tariff men in Congress framed the "Tariff of Abominations," designed to be as distasteful as possible to New England industrialists in the hope that a split in the protectionist ranks would result. Outspoken John Randolph of Virginia, indeed, declared, "The bill referred to manufactures of no sort or kind but the manufacture of a President of the United States." The New Englanders, however, reasoning that a poor tariff was better than none, voted for the bill anyway.

The Exposition and Protest. While the Southerners had no one but themselves to blame for the Tariff of Abominations, this fact did not allay their discontent with it in the slightest. The center of hostility to protection was South Carolina. In 1828 Calhoun embodied his state's objection to the tariff system in his *Exposition and Protest,* which advanced the compact theory of the Constitution a step beyond the position taken in the Kentucky and Virginia Resolutions. Where Jefferson and Madison had asserted that the states, as a body, could properly determine whether the central government was observing the limits of its delegated powers or not, Calhoun claimed that any *one* state could assume this authority and could declare null and void within its own borders an Act of Congress which it deemed to be unconstitutional. In Southern eyes a tariff for protection, rather than for raising revenue, was unwarranted by the Constitution.

Calhoun's doctrine of nullification drew two historic rejoinders. One was Webster's reply to Hayne, which developed out of a debate on public-land policy in which East and South both bid for the support of the West. Robert Y. Hayne, Senator from South Carolina, argued that the industrial East was using the power of the national government to exploit the agrarian sections and invoked the nullification theory as the most effective defense. Webster on his side denied the validity of the compact theory, asserted that the Constitution was the creation of the people and not the states, and denounced nullification as certain to disrupt the Union. The other was delivered by Jackson at a dinner in honor of Jefferson's birthday, 13 April 1830. The Calhoun wing of the Democratic party had planned the affair as an endorsement of nullification, but their hopes were sadly upset when Old Hickory offered as the toast of the evening: "Our Federal Union; it must be preserved."

The Ordinance of Nullification. The crisis came to a head when a new tariff act was passed in 1832. The legislature of South Carolina called a special convention which on 24 November 1832 adopted the "Ordinance of Nullification," declaring the tariff inoperative in South Carolina and threatening secession if force should be used against the state. Whatever merit this step may have had in political theory, it was certainly ill timed. Andrew Jackson was not the man to give way to threats. The President had no strong feeling on the tariff, but he was devoted to the Union and he was bound to see in South Carolina's action a challenge to his own authority as President of the United States. He very promptly denounced the nullifiers and made it abundantly clear that he would use force to execute the laws if necessary. A bill, the "Force Bill," to authorize employment of the armed forces of the United States for this purpose was introduced into Congress and became law on 1 March 1833.

On the same date, however, Jackson also signed a compromise tariff hastily pushed through Congress under the direction of Henry Clay, then Senator from Kentucky. This measure provided that the duties should be reduced gradually over a ten-year period until they reached a general level of 20 per cent. It was enough. The South Carolinians were discouraged by the unwillingness of the other Southern states to support them and had not anticipated Jackson's firm stand. There was, moreover, a strong Union party in the state led by Joel R. Poinsett. The result was that the convention reassembled on 11 March 1833, thumbed its nose at the United States government by nullifying the Force Act, and then repealed the Ordinance of Nullification.

The crisis had been safely passed, but with some disquieting after-effects. Each side felt it had won. The authority of the national government had been vigorously asserted, it is true; on the other hand, the nullifiers could claim that by their stand they had extorted a substantial concession. In addition, Southern leaders came to the conclusion that nullification did not afford a sufficient guarantee of states' rights, since no one state could successfully defy the national government in the event that compromise proposals failed, and they began to think increasingly in terms of the more drastic step of secession.

THE COMPROMISE OF 1850

Paradoxically it was Manifest Destiny, the most forceful current expression of American nationalism, that next raised the specter of disintegration of the Union. The Texan revolt was greeted unenthusiastically in the Northeast, mainly because of the fear that Texas, if annexed to the Union, would be subdivided into four or five new slave states. In the face of this opposition political leaders tried to move cautiously, but Manifest Destiny could not be restrained indefinitely; when it burst forth in the Mexican War, with California and New Mexico at stake as well as Texas, it precipitated an outburst of sectional antagonism more intense than anything previously encountered.

To the antislavery men the war was nothing but the culmination of a slaveholders' conspiracy to tip the political balance in their favor by acquiring vast areas for conversion into new slave states. Even among Northern expansionists there was some resentment over the fact that their aspirations for the whole of Oregon had been jettisoned so that the government could devote its energies to acquiring prospective slave territory from Mexico. Northern hostility to the presumed objectives of the Mexican War found an outlet when President Polk asked Congress in 1846 for funds with which to purchase territory from Mexico in the event that an opportunity arose to make peace. To the appropriation bill for this purpose David Wilmot, a Democrat from Pennsylvania, tacked a rider stipulating that slavery should be excluded from any territory so acquired.

The Wilmot Proviso. The Wilmot Proviso reopened the battle between the sections for control of the West. The House of Representatives, with its Northern majority, twice passed the Proviso, but the Senate, where the balance between free and slave states was still maintained, rejected it. Although the House was persuaded to abandon the Proviso itself, the deadlock continued on the question of organizing governments for the territory acquired from Mexico. Antislavery opinion still insisted on prohibiting slavery altogether. The more rabid Southerners, the "Southern Rights" faction as they now termed themselves, followed Calhoun's latest doctrine, which held that the Federal government could not exclude slavery from any territory, on the ground that the public domain was owned jointly by all the states and that therefore citizens of all states had the right of free access to it with their property. Between these extreme views were two compromise schools of thought. One, favored by President Polk, wished to extend the Missouri Compromise line to the Pacific; the other, advocated at first by Lewis Cass of Michigan and later more effectively by Stephen A. Douglas of Illinois, suggested "popular sovereignty," or permitting the inhabitants of the territories to decide on the slavery issue for themselves. In the acrimony of political debate the contestants chose to ignore the one concrete fact in the situation, although they were perfectly aware of its existence—to wit, that very little of the newly acquired territory was suited to slave agriculture. They were fighting over the principle of whether slavery should be permitted to expand, and ultimately to exist. Denied access to fresh soil, its own inefficiency would kill it in time, and its demise was certain to be accelerated if the free states were to win control of the entire West.

The Mexican War ended and the election of 1848 came and went with the problem still dangerously unsolved. In a reversal of what had happened in 1844, a revolt of antislavery Democrats in New York, supporting Martin Van Buren as a "Free-Soil" candidate, gave that critical state to the Whigs and caused the defeat of Lewis Cass. The Whigs were just as badly divided on the slavery question, but they were able to unite behind Zachary Taylor on his reputation as a military hero without committing themselves too deeply on issues. When Taylor took office the situation had become still more complicated by the discovery of gold in California, which created an acute need for stable and orderly government in that area. At Taylor's suggestion the residents of California elected a constitutional convention, which drafted a constitution organizing California as a free state.

Movements for Compromise. By this time the South was talking openly of secession. If California's action were approved by Congress, it might become a precedent for the rest of the Mexican Cession; at best it would eliminate the possibility of extending the Missouri Compromise line to the Pacific. Moreover Taylor, although a Southerner, was showing an alarming lack of sympathy for slavery. There was secession agitation in the North also among the more rabid abolitionists, who wanted to form a new union of free states. However, the very urgency of the crisis served to bring all the moderate elements together in an attempt to reach a settlement. Henry Clay and Daniel Webster, now at the end of their long and varied careers, made a last great effort to save their beloved Union, ably supported by Stephen A. Douglas, representing the new generation coming to the fore in American politics. Their work was made somewhat easier when Taylor's sudden death brought the less obdurate Millard Fillmore into the presidency.

Clay, "the Great Compromiser," introduced into Congress the series of resolutions which became the basis of the final settlement. Webster, rising to perhaps his greatest height of statesmanship, denied the possibility of peaceful secession but called on the North for concession, arguing cogently that the laws of nature would exclude slavery from California and New Mexico. Douglas pressed for popular sovereignty as the most satisfactory method of ending the dispute. On the other side Calhoun, already so feeble that his speech had to be read for him, accused the North of trampling on the rights of the South and insisted that Congress had no right to prevent slaveowners from taking their property into the territories. Antislavery opposition to the compromise was led by William H. Seward, who acknowledged that Congress had complete jurisdiction over the territories and could admit or exclude slavery as it saw fit, but announced that there was "a higher law than the Constitution."

Terms of the Compromise. The current of public opinion, however, was running strongly in favor of compromise. In September, 1850, the three bills incorporating Clay's proposals—the first of them dubbed the "Omnibus Bill"—became law. As it was finally worked out, the Compromise of 1850 provided the following:

1. California was admitted as a free state.

2. The rest of the Mexican Cession was organized as the territories of Utah and New Mexico, with no reference to slavery.

3. Texas relinquished some territorial claims to the United States in return for a payment of $10,000,000. The debts of the Republic of Texas were to be paid by the state and not assumed by the United States; in compensation Texas retained possession of its public lands.

4. The slave trade but not slavery was abolished in the District of Columbia. This was a delicate point with both sides. Antislavery men considered it disgraceful that slaves should be openly sold in the capital of a free nation; Southerners felt that excluding slavery from the District would be a censure of the institution.

5. A more stringent Fugitive Slave Law was enacted. This was the major concession to the South, which had complained for years that the free states were ignoring their constitutional responsibilities in the matter of capturing and returning runaways. The act, however, proved to be a boomerang to the South, since the spectacle of fugitives being forcibly returned to slavery alienated many Northerners who had previously been indifferent to slavery.

The Compromise was a ramshackle and unsteady structure, but it served its immediate purpose, mainly because the great majority of the American people, North and South, were heartily sick of quarrels over slavery and hoped in this way to be rid of them. Moreover, by postponing secession for ten years, the architects of the Compromise saved the Union, although in a manner they could not have foreseen. If the break had come in 1850, the difficulties of restoring the Union would probably have been insuperable. The North was not as yet far enough ahead of the South in man power and economic resources to give it a reasonable prospect of victory in a civil war. Nor was the North a cohesive unit in 1850. The railroad trunk lines had still to link the Atlantic seaboard with the inland waterways, and the economy of the Northwest remained heavily dependent on the Mississippi River system. It is entirely possible that in 1850 the Northwest might have thrown in its lot with the South, or perhaps formed a separate confederacy of its own—a proposal which attracted some adherents when the war finally came.

By 1860 the free states were in a much stronger position. Their economic development had continued to outstrip that of the South, and the economic interests of the industrial Northeast and the agrarian Northwest had been brought closer together by the completion of three through rail lines between Eastern seaports and Chicago and St. Louis. The South had only one such line, the collection of railroads between Charleston and Memphis. Consequently, when the break came, Northern public opinion, although far from unanimous, was firmly enough united to sustain the effort needed to restore the Union, and Northern resources were far more adequate for the task than they would have been in 1850.

IRREPRESSIBLE CONFLICT

The political truce achieved by the Compromise of 1850 was rudely and unexpectedly shattered at the end of 1853 when Stephen A. Douglas introduced into the Senate a bill for the organization of the Territory of Nebraska, with a provision that the question of slavery should be settled by popular sovereignty—this although the entire territory, which included the present states of Kansas and Nebraska and most of the Dakotas and Montana, was north of the Missouri Compromise line. It was generally assumed at the time that Douglas was simply bidding for Southern support for his presidential aspirations. Subsequent investigation has indicated two other possible motives for the Nebraska bill. First, Congress was actively discussing possible routes for a transcontinental railroad, and organizing the Nebraska Territory would improve the prospect of the railroad being so located as to make Chicago its eastern terminus. Second, the prospective opening of this area to settlement, particularly without restriction on slavery, was popular in Missouri, where Douglas's friend and ally, Senator James Atchison, was facing a difficult campaign for reelection. Before the bill had progressed very far its sponsor accepted two amendments designed to win Southern favor. Senator Archibald Dixon of Kentucky inserted a clause stating explicitly that the Missouri Compromise had been repealed by the Compromise of 1850, and the southern part of the territory, Kansas, was detached and organized separately. The presumption was that if the normal pattern of westward migration were followed, Kansas would be settled from the slave state of Missouri and under popular sovereignty would itself become a slave state.

The Kansas Conflict. With the appearance of the Kansas-Nebraska bill, antislavery opinion in the North exploded. This casual discarding of a sectional arrangement which had been accepted by both sides for a generation seemed to indicate that the slaveholders were determined to establish their institution throughout the entire West, and many Northern Democrats, as well as the remnants of the Whigs and Free-Soilers, rose in vigorous opposition. The Democratic organization was strong enough to force the bill through Congress and make it into law on 25 April 1854, but that was only the beginning of the struggle. The fate of Kansas still depended on which section could send the most settlers into the territory.

In this phase of the contest the North had the advantage, by virtue of its greater population and the fact that Kansas was not really attractive to slaveowners. Migration to Kansas from the free states was organized and financed by the New England Emigrant Aid Society, which sent out prospective settlers equipped with all they needed to establish new homes on the frontier—household goods, agricultural implements, and Sharps rifles, known as "Beecher's Bibles" after Henry Ward Beecher had asserted in a sermon that a good repeating rifle would be as valuable as a Bible in doing the work of God in Kansas. The South had no such organization; its interests had to be left to bands of armed Missourians, the "border ruffians," such as the "Doniphan Tigers," who crossed into Kansas and voted in the territorial elections. The free-state and slave-state factions elected separate governments, and while President Pierce was fumbling helplessly with the situation, Kansas received a preview of the Civil War.

On the national scene the Kansas crisis caused a momentous upheaval in political alignments. The Democrats, although managing for the moment to retain a shaky solidarity, lost a considerable number of their Northern adherents. The Whigs disintegrated completely, the Southern wing, led by Robert Y. Toombs and Alexander H. Stephens of Georgia, going over to the Democrats, while the Northern wing drifted about uncertainly looking for a new political home. For a short time it appeared that some elements of the Whig party might reunite in the American or "Know-nothing" party, one of those peculiar organizations which occasionally spring up in the United States to preach intolerance under the guise of "100 per cent Americanism." The Know-nothings originated as a secret society, the Order of the Star Spangled Banner, which was anti-Catholic and antialien and whose members were sworn to reply, "I know nothing" to any inquiries about the organization. The American party, however had no genuine appeal, and after a single flurry in the congressional elections of 1854 it too broke up over the slavery question.

The Republican Party. Antislavery opinion found its outlet in the Republican party, a combination of Northern Whigs, anti-Nebraska Democrats, and Free-Soilers organized in 1854. The name Republican, the original title of Jefferson's party, was shrewdly chosen to attract Democratic voters. The new party was not abolitionist but was emphatically opposed to the further expansion of slavery. With John C. Frémont as its candidate it contested the election of 1856 with surprising vigor for a new and untested coalition. Frémont lost to James Buchanan mainly because Northern conservatives regarded the Republicans as too radical in their views on slavery and so exclusively sectional as to be a menace to the Union.

In the meantime other events were contributing to arouse sectional antagonism to the breaking point. Two books played their part. One, the well-known *Uncle Tom's Cabin,* by Harriet Beecher Stowe, was by far the most effective antislavery treatise ever published. Published in 1853, it had a tremendous circulation in the North and Europe, but not in the South, and, since it lent itself admirably to dramatization, its message reached many thousands of people who would not have read the book. The other book, Hinton Rowan Helper's *The Impending Crisis in the South,* published in 1856, has a special interest as a violent attack on slavery by a Southerner. Helper came from the nonslaveholding whites who constituted the majority of the South's population, and he appealed to this class to abolish slavery for its own good, since he believed that slavery was bringing economic ruin to these nonslaveholders. The book had a considerable circulation in the North but was banned in many parts of the South. Further irritation was caused by the enforcement of the Fugitive Slave Law, which resulted in occasional riotous outbreaks in the North and complaints from the South that the free states were evading their legal obligations, and by the increasing activity of the "Underground Railroad," whereby abolitionist sympathizers assisted runaways to escape to Canada.

The height to which tension had risen was dramatically illustrated by threats of physical violence in Congress and finally by the attack on Senator Charles Sumner of Massachusetts by Representative Preston Brooks of South Carolina. Sumner, on 19 May 1856, delivered a speech on the Kansas question in which he definitely overstepped the bounds of good taste, particularly in personal abuse of Senator Butler of South Carolina. Brooks, who was Butler's nephew, appeared in the Senate Chamber three days later with a heavy cane and beat Sumner into unconsciousness while the latter was seated at his desk. The uproar in both sections over the incident can readily be imagined.

The Dred Scott Case. Next, the Supreme Court of the United States became involved in the slavery quarrel. People who deplored the growing violence of sectional antagonism and wanted to see everything quietly compromised had great hopes that a decision by the Supreme Court on the legal status of slavery in the territories would settle the current argument, and in his inaugural address on 4 March 1857 President Buchanan stated that this question was about to be passed on. Two days later the Court handed down its decision in *Scott v. Sandford,* without the anticipated pacifying effect.

The Dred Scott case originated when Dred Scott, a Negro slave belonging to Dr. John Emerson, an army doctor domiciled in Missouri, was taken by his master, in the course of Dr. Emerson's military duties, to the free state of Illinois and the territory of Minnesota, free under the Missouri Compromise. When the two returned to Missouri, Scott did not question his status as a slave, but after Dr. Emerson's death he brought suit (1846) to secure his freedom from Mrs. Emerson on the ground that he had automatically ceased to be a slave on being taken to free soil. The Supreme Court of Missouri held that Scott was still a slave under the laws of that state. In the meantime Mrs. Emerson was married again, this time to an abolitionist congressman from Massachusetts. In order to avoid political embarrassment to her husband and also to get the case before the Federal courts, she sold Scott to her brother, J. T. Sandford of New York. Thus, Scott, claiming to be a citizen of Missouri, was now suing a citizen of another state. The case reached the Supreme Court in 1856.

The Court at this time was composed of seven Democrats, five from slave states—including Chief Justice Taney, who was a Marylander—and two ex-Whigs, now Republicans. The seven Democrats initially agreed to rule that the laws of Missouri governed Scott's status and that he was therefore still a slave without going any further into the slavery issue. However, when it was discovered that the two Republicans, Curtis and McLean, were going to file a dissenting opinion discussing and upholding the constitutionality of the Missouri Compromise, Taney felt that the majority could not afford to give the appearance of sidestepping the issues. In consequence, he himself rewrote the decision, which, besides affirming Scott's status as a slave, laid down two startling doctrines:

1. Negroes could not be citizens. Taney argued that the Constitution had been written in the full knowledge that slavery existed, and that its guarantees of civil rights could not have been intended to apply to the Negro race.

2. Congress had no right to prohibit slavery in any territory, since such action would have the effect of depriving American citizens of their property, or at least of the right to use their property freely. The Missouri Compromise was therefore unconstitutional.

The Southern Rights group, of course, was delighted. The Republicans, on the other hand, indignantly denounced the Court as a tool of the slaveholding oligarchy, and asserted that the decision had been prearranged by the "slave power," an accusation which was not in fact true but which was given credence at the time by Buchanan's apparent foreknowledge of what was going to happen. The Northern Democrats were placed in an awkward position, since their doctrine of popular sovereignty had been shattered. Obviously, if Congress could not exclude slavery from a territory, a territorial government created by Congress could not do so either.

The Lincoln-Douglas Debates. This was the point on which Lincoln tried to impale Douglas in their Freeport debate in 1858. Lincoln posed the question whether there was any way whereby the people of a territory could legally exclude slavery. Douglas extricated himself deftly by pointing out that while a territorial government could not constitutionally prohibit slavery, it could effectively prevent establishment of the institution by simply refraining from enacting the local police regulations without which slavery could not survive. This "Freeport doctrine" was plain common sense and saved Douglas's senatorship, but it alienated the leaders of the South. The planter aristocracy had reached a state of mind in which it would accept nothing but complete endorsement of the virtues of slavery. The planters were in unwitting agreement with Lincoln's "house divided" speech of 16 June 1858, that the Union could not exist permanently half slave and half free but would have to become all one or all the other. To the Southerners, of course, there could be only one choice. They had convinced themselves that a great civilization could rest only on a foundation of slavery, and they had conjured up a beautiful vision of a gracious and cultured ruling class governing a mass of submissive and contented slaves—a vision which has been cherished by romantic writers as a genuine picture of the Old South.

Douglas was also in trouble with the Southerners about Kansas. In 1857 Buchanan endorsed a constitution drafted at Lecompton by the proslavery faction in that state and prepared to submit it to the voters, not for acceptance or rejection, but for adoption with or without slavery. Douglas denounced this move as a violation of popular sovereignty, incurring Buchanan's ill will to such an extent that administration pressure was used to try to defeat Douglas in the Illinois senatorial election of 1858. Douglas's adherents in Congress, however, were strong enough to force the passage of a compromise, the English bill, whereby the Lecompton Constitution was to be submitted as a whole to the people of Kansas, baited with a grant of public land (customary for all new states) if they accepted and indefinite postponement of statehood if they rejected it. They rejected it.

John Brown's Raid. To complete the sectional rift came John Brown's raid on Harpers Ferry, an event which appeared to confirm the South's worst fears regarding the eventual result of antislavery agitation. Brown was an abolitionist fanatic who conceived the idea of seizing the arsenal at Harpers Ferry and, with the arms thus acquired, of establishing a refuge for runaway slaves in the Virginia mountains. He was supported financially by a group of overearnest abolitionists, some of whom suffered convenient lapses of memory later. The attempt failed. Brown and his band captured Harpers Ferry (16 October 1859) but received no encouragement from the local Negroes. Ironically enough, the first man killed in this effort to aid the slaves was a free Negro. At the end of the day a company of marines commanded by Robert E. Lee stormed the engine house in which Brown and his men had fortified themselves. Brown himself was captured, tried for treason and murder, and executed.

The ease with which the coup had been suppressed did nothing to minimize the reaction it caused in the South. Here, in concrete form, was the South's nightmare, servile insurrection. Here too was convincing proof that the Northern abolitionists were prepared to encourage slave rebellions. On the other side of the picture, Brown's dignified conduct at his trial won him widespread sympathy in the North. After his death his desire to free the slaves was remembered and his method of doing it forgotten.

THE ELECTION OF 1860

It was perfectly evident that 1860 would be a critical year. The South believed that its entire social structure was in danger, the North was vigorously opposed to any further extension of slavery, and the Democratic party, the only remaining national political organization, was split between the Douglas faction and the Southerners. As it happened, the Democratic convention was the first to meet, but unfortunately for party harmony it met, as arranged in 1856, in Charleston, South Carolina. The Douglas men were in the majority, and when they refused to agree to a platform plank calling for Federal protection of slavery in the territories, the Southern Rights group, led by the noisiest of the "fire-eaters," William Lowndes Yancey of Alabama, walked out of the convention. If they could not rule the Democratic party, they would leave it; in a few months they were to demonstrate that they felt the same way about the Union.

The fragments of the party then moved north, possibly in search of a cooler atmosphere, and met again in Baltimore. This time the Douglas Democrats were able to nominate their idol; the seceders, however, assembled separately and nominated John C. Breckinridge of Kentucky on an extreme Southern Rights platform.

This Democratic split, of course, greatly enhanced the Republican prospects, and there was a lively struggle for the nomination when the Republican convention met in Chicago. The most prominent contender was William H. Seward, but Seward, although actually reasonably moderate in his views on slavery, was stamped as a radical because of his remarks about "higher law than the Constitution" and "irrepressible conflict," and in his long political career he had inevitably made many enemies. So Seward was unable to muster the necessary strength and the prize went, after some deft maneuvering, to Abraham Lincoln. The Republicans had no trouble with their platform. Their stand on slavery pledged no interference with the institution where it already existed but opposed its further extension. The real vote-getting planks were the promises of a high protective tariff, free homesteads, and support for a Pacific railway.

In the meantime still another ticket had been put into the field, that of the Constitutional Union party with Senator John Bell of Tennessee as its candidate. The party was composed mainly of former Whigs who could stomach neither the Democrats nor the Republicans and whose attitude on the slavery problem was that if nobody paid any attention to it, perhaps it would go away.

The most accurate description of what followed is that the United States held two separate presidential elections in 1860. In the free states the race was between Lincoln, Douglas, and Bell; in the slave states between Breckinridge, Douglas, and Bell. In most parts of the South, Lincoln was not even on the ballot. Lincoln, with about 40 per cent of the total popular vote, carried every free state except part of New Jersey and had a clear majority in the electoral college; Douglas was a strong second in popular votes but his support was so widely distributed that he was a poor fourth in electoral votes. Breckinridge carried the lower South and Bell the border states. The popular and electoral votes were as follows:

	Popular vote	*Electoral vote*
Lincoln	1,857,610	180
Douglas	1,365,967	12
Breckinridge	847,953	72
Bell	590,631	39

To a casual observer these figures might seem merely a peculiar example of how the American system for electing a President worked. The South saw them in another light; a President had been elected by Northern votes alone. Two days after the election the legislature of South Carolina passed an act summoning a special convention, and on 20 December 1860 that body unanimously adopted an Ordinance of Secession withdrawing South Carolina from the Union.

22

The Civil War

Between the fall of Napoleon and the outbreak of the First World War, no conflict was of greater fundamental importance to the Western World than the American Civil War. It was more than a domestic quarrel in the United States, more even than a clash between freedom and slavery. It was the nineteenth century's supreme test of whether a government based on the concept of democracy could stand. Abraham Lincoln, with his unfailing faculty for getting to the heart of a problem, saw as clearly then what was at stake as anyone has since: "now we are engaged in a great civil war, testing whether that nation, or *any nation* so conceived and so dedicated, can long endure." The friendliness of the British and French upper classes for the South and the devotion of the British masses to the North stemmed from an instinctive recognition of the underlying issue as much as from considerations of practical interest. Certainly, the English cotton spinners who were thrown out of their jobs by the cotton shortage had no immediate material incentive to support the Union, and yet the Union had no more staunch devotees. So, while we can freely and wholeheartedly admire the heroism of the Southern struggle for independence, we can hardly avoid being thankful that it ended as the "Lost Cause."

SECESSION AND THE OUTBREAK OF WAR

The secession of South Carolina plunged the whole United States into a period of bewilderment and doubt. The nation's political machinery showed a serious defect at this juncture. Lincoln would not be formally inaugurated until 4 March 1861; in the meantime he could exercise no authority except in so far as the Republicans in Congress chose to accept

341

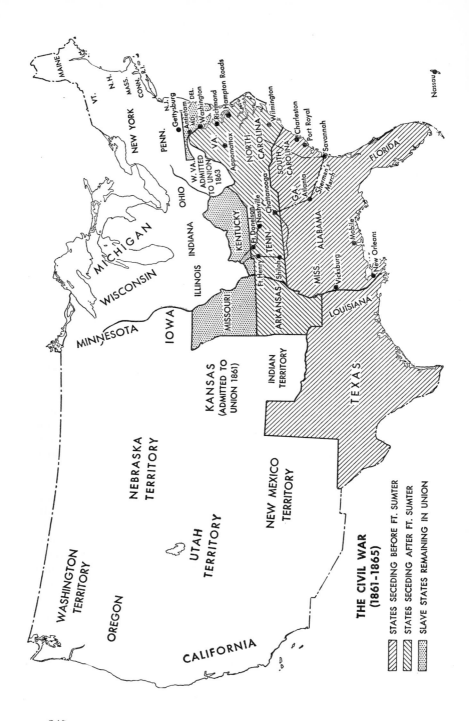

THE CIVIL WAR
(1861-1865)

▨ STATES SECEDING BEFORE FT. SUMTER

▧ STATES SECEDING AFTER FT. SUMTER

▨ SLAVE STATES REMAINING IN UNION

his advice. James Buchanan, still legally the Chief Executive but about to go out of office, was unwilling to take positive action in a confusing situation. The result was that the country was without effective leadership for a critical three months.

During that time the rest of the lower South—Georgia, Florida, Alabama, Mississippi, Louisiana, and Texas—followed South Carolina out of the Union and at a convention in Montgomery, Alabama, in February and March, 1861, organized the Confederate States of America. The Constitution of the Confederacy virtually reproduced the Federal Constitution, with such modifications to Southern taste as one would expect. The document was expressly stated to be a compact among sovereign states, the existence of slavery was guaranteed, and the Confederate government was forbidden to impose a protective tariff or spend money for internal improvements. The African slave trade was still prohibited, an apparent inconsistency in the Southern attitude toward slavery which is explained by the desire of the original seceding states to win the support of the border slave states, where the reopening of the slave trade was regarded with disapproval. Other interesting features of the Confederate Constitution were the single six-year term for the President, the provision allowing cabinet ministers to sit in Congress and take part in the debates, without the right to vote, and the power given to the President to veto individual items in appropriation bills. The convention also chose Jefferson Davis of Mississippi as provisional President of the Confederacy.

Under the stress of war, this constitution worked reasonably well. The basic weakness of the Confederacy's political structure was the attitude of the men who had to make it function. Most Southern statesmen had been talking so long in terms of states' rights that they were unable to realize that what they were now fighting for was Southern nationalism.

Compromise Efforts. While the Confederacy was being organized, frantic efforts were being made in Washington to find another compromise. Senator John J. Crittenden of Kentucky, Henry Clay's successor, came closest to a solution with a proposal to amend the Constitution so as to make 36° 30′ the boundary between free and slave territory and provide adequate guarantees for the protection of slave property. The South might have accepted the Crittenden Compromise, although that is uncertain, but Lincoln was unalterably opposed to anything that would permit the further extension of slavery, and the Republicans in Congress followed his lead. A somewhat similar proposal advanced by a peace convention called by the state of Virginia in February, 1861, was also rejected by the Republicans. Perhaps this insistence on confining slavery within its existing limits makes Lincoln and the Republicans responsible for the war, but it is difficult to argue that they were wrong. The secession issue had to be settled sooner or later. There could be no lasting internal peace for the United States if a discontented minority could get what it wanted by simply threatening to secede from the Union.

When Lincoln was inaugurated he made it perfectly clear that, while he hoped for peace, he was determined to uphold the authority of the United States government. This position meant that he must refuse to surrender the forts in Confederate territory still held by Federal garrisons. There were four of these, but only Fort Sumter, in Charleston Harbor, was in serious danger; the others, indeed, remained in Federal hands throughout the war. In order to forestall a relief expedition being sent to Sumter, Confederate batteries opened fire on 12 April 1861; the fort was taken with no loss of life on either side, and the Civil War had begun.

With the outbreak of hostilities, the slave states which had not as yet committed themselves had to come to a decision. Virginia, North Carolina, Tennessee, and Arkansas refused to be parties to coercion of their sister states and threw in their lot with the Confederacy, although Union sentiment in the western counties of Virginia was so strong as to lead to their secession from the state and admission to the Union as West Virginia in 1863. Maryland, Kentucky, and Missouri were held for the Union by vigorous action on the part of their Union sympathizers and skillful handling by Lincoln. Kentucky, as a matter of fact, at first declared itself neutral and took sides only upon the invasion of its territory by Confederate troops late in 1861.

THE BALANCE OF FORCES

In the conflict which had now begun, the balance of material resources lay distinctly with the North. In population the Union states outnumbered the Confederacy by about 23,000,000 to 9,000,000, including the Negroes, and in economic and financial strength the disparity was even greater. The South was an agrarian region; it had some factories, but nothing to compare with the well-developed industrial plant of the North, its rail system was fragmentary, and its banking was done either in the North or Europe.

Wars, however, are seldom decided by material factors alone. The imponderables in the situation were sufficiently complex to make the outcome of the war uncertain. To begin with, the Confederacy occupied a vast extent of territory, whose recovery would constitute a serious military problem, and there was no assurance that the people of the North would be willing to make the necessary sacrifices. A substantial minority in the North disapproved of secession but disapproved still more of using force to restore the Union, and there were some outright Southern sympathizers. A slightly different turn in military fortunes on one or two occasions might have given this peace party enough strength to compel the government to end the war. The Confederacy had its troubles with internal dissension also. West Virginia was symptomatic of a strong Union sentiment which, although most pronounced in the Appalachian region, existed in all parts of the South. At the other extreme were men of the stamp of Governors Joseph E. Brown of Georgia and Zebulon Vance of North Carolina, who carried states' rights to a point where it seriously impeded the prosecution of the war.

Quite apart from the dissenters, public opinion on the issues of the war was thoroughly confused. In the North, there were three distinct schools of thought among the supporters of the government. One, represented in the main by Democrats like Douglas and General George B. McClellan, wanted to restore the Union without disturbing slavery— "The Constitution as it is and the Union as it was." Another, the Radical Republicans, was determined that the conflict should result in the extinction of slavery. The third group, best personified by Lincoln himself, held that the primary objective was to restore the Union but was willing to see slavery abolished if conditions were favorable. The Confederates always insisted that they were fighting only in defense of their rights and not to preserve slavery.

Military Strength. In the matter of military strength, there was little to choose between the two combatants at the beginning. The Regular Army, only 14,000 strong and scattered over numerous frontier posts, was manifestly incapable of subjugating the South by itself, quite apart from the fact that a third of its officers resigned to go with their section. For practical purposes, both sides started on an amateur basis. In fighting qualities, they were closely matched; most battles of the Civil War were so hard fought that the victor was too exhausted to follow up his advantage. Once the war became prolonged, the greater man power of the North and its superior ability to equip an army steadily tipped the scales against the Confederacy. Both parties resorted to conscription, the South in 1862 and the North a year later, but the draft acts were neither popular nor effective.

The naval situation was somewhat more favorable to the Union. Although some Southern officers resigned, the ships themselves remained in Federal possession (except for some vessels needlessly and ineffectively scuttled in the Norfolk Navy Yard, including the steam frigate *Merrimac*). True, most of the serviceable warships were scattered on foreign stations when the war started and even when concentrated were too few in number to blockade the Confederacy, but again the industrial capacity of the North made possible an expansion which was denied to the South.

Political Leadership. On the political side of the war, Union leadership was distinctly superior. Jefferson Davis was able and conscientious, and he had to work under appalling handicaps. Perhaps no one else in the South could have done better. His principal defect was his inability to handle men. He quarreled with his Congress and with state governors; his feud with Joseph E. Johnston seriously weakened Confederate military leadership. Lincoln, on the other hand, came into his responsibilities with much less apparent qualification than his Southern rival, but he had an ability to learn by experience and a genius for human relations which Davis lacked. Lincoln had to deal with a Congress and a public sharply divided on the objectives of the war; with infinite tact and patience, he managed to keep both radicals and moderates working together in the common cause, not harmoniously, but with enough unity of purpose to make victory possible. The principal members of his cabinet were men who thought themselves better fitted to be President than he was. William H. Seward expected to be the "power behind the throne." On 1 April 1861—an appropriate date for the action—Seward made the astounding proposal that the United States declare war on France and Spain, on the assumption that a surge of patriotism would bring the seceded states back to the Union. Lincoln firmly put Seward in his place and made him an excellent Secretary of State. He displayed a similar finesse in handling the insatiable self-seeking of Salmon P. Chase, Secretary of the Treasury.

MILITARY OPERATIONS

When the Civil War began, neither Union nor Confederacy had any inkling of the magnitude of the struggle that lay ahead. In the North, the aged Winfield Scott,[1] commanding general of the United States army in 1861, was hooted at for stating that the restoration of the Union would require the enlistment of 300,000 men for three years, a strict blockade of the South, and control of the Mississippi. Newspaper editors with a profounder knowledge of warfare than Scott had been able to acquire in forty years of service made sarcastic references to "Scott's anaconda" strangling the South. The First Battle of Bull Run (21 July 1861), was brought on by the popular clamor of "On to Richmond," based on the happy assumption that the rebellion would collapse as soon as loyal troops appeared on Southern soil.

In the conduct of the war, the Confederacy enjoyed an initial advantage in strictly military leadership. It was fortunate in finding immediately such commanders as Lee, Jackson, and J. E. Johnston, while the Union had to undergo a painful process of trial and error before it discovered generals in whom it had confidence. The North had no dearth

[1] Scott, like George H. Thomas and David G. Farragut, was a Southerner who placed loyalty to the nation ahead of loyalty to a state.

of military talent, but it suffered from political interference and the natural errors of an administration which had to learn by experience where the proper boundary lay between the spheres of the civilian and the military authorities.

Once the war began in earnest, the principal land operations fell into two major theaters. In Virginia, Union and Confederate armies fought for their respective capitals, Washington and Richmond. In a strictly material sense, either side could have abandoned its capital without losing its ability to fight on; in fact, Lee's army, always inferior to its opponent, would have been better off if it had not been tied so closely to Richmond. The two cities, however, acquired a moral value which made their defense a political necessity. The war in Virginia was a stalemate. Union armies were unable to take Richmond until the final collapse of the Confederacy, and the two Confederate invasions of the North were repulsed. The Western theater presented a somewhat different set of conditions. There were strategically important points like Vicksburg and Chattanooga, but none as vital to public morale as Washington and Richmond. The Western armies, consequently, had more freedom to maneuver. Although operations in this area lacked some of the dramatic qualities of those in Virginia, it was here that the war on land was won. Instead of great armies fighting each other to a standstill, in the West the Union forces moved irresistibly, with only an occasional check, down the Mississippi until they controlled the entire river, and then eastward into the heart of the Confederacy.

McClellan's Attack on Richmond. The Virginia phase of the war had its effective beginning with George B. McClellan's attack on Richmond in the spring of 1862, an operation which affords a fascinating study in the interplay of personalities, politics, and strategy. The plan itself was sound enough—to utilize Union command of the sea to attack Richmond by way of the peninsula between the James and York Rivers. McClellan, however, was not the man to carry it out. He had a talent for organization and was popular with his troops, but he was excessively cautious in action. As a Democrat, he was unacceptable to the Radical Republicans, but this would not have been a handicap if he had taken the trouble to retain Lincoln's confidence instead of ignoring the President and indulging in grandiose visions of himself as the "savior of the Union."

The Confederates made the most of this situation. While McClellan laboriously made his way toward Richmond, "Stonewall" Jackson threatened Washington by a brilliant campaign in the Shenandoah valley and then joined Lee's forces for the Seven Days' Battles (26 June–1 July), which drove the Federals from the vicinity of the Confederate capital. The repulse cost McClellan the confidence of the North and gave his political opponents their opportunity. The peninsular campaign was abandoned, and a new attack on Richmond by land was organized under General John Pope. Lee, however, outmaneuvered Pope and defeated him in the Second Battle of Bull Run (29–30 August 1862).

The Confederates followed up their success by invading Maryland, in the hope that that state might be induced to secede. In addition, a victory on Northern soil might well persuade the people of the North that restoration of the Union was impossible and would almost certainly lead to British and French recognition of Southern independence. In this crisis Lincoln restored McClellan to command, as the only man who possessed the confidence of the Army of the Potomac, and "Little Mac," aided by the fortuitous capture of an order showing that his opponent's forces were quite widely scattered, acted with somewhat more promptitude than usual. Lee was forced to stand on the defensive at Antietam Creek, where, on 17 September 1862, one of the hardest-fought battles of the war took place. When it was over, Lee withdrew to Virginia; the invasion which had promised so much had failed.

The Emancipation Proclamation. This victory gave Lincoln the opportunity to take a step for which he believed the time had come—the issue of the Emancipation Proclamation. It was principally a military measure aimed at weakening the South by announcing that on 1 January 1863 all slaves in territory still in rebellion against the United States should be free, but it also had some effect in strengthening the North's position among the slavery-conscious nations of Europe.

McClellan's reward was removal from his post, this time for failure to pursue Lee with sufficient vigor. He was replaced by Ambrose E. Burnside, a competent corps commander who was overwhelmed by his new responsibility and whose sole accomplishment was to lose thousands of men in a futile assault on Fredericksburg (13 December 1862). His successor, "Fighting Joe" Hooker, started promisingly by driving across the Rappahannock on 29 April 1863 but then unaccountably lost his nerve and gave Lee a chance to take the initiative. Stonewall Jackson went off on a flanking march and took Hooker completely by surprise at Chancellorsville. It was the last battle for Jackson. He was mortally wounded by his own troops, and his death was a heavy price to pay for the Confederate victory.

Gettysburg. After Chancellorsville, Lee decided to try another invasion of the North, for much the same reasons as before but not quite under the same bright auspices. The military situation in the West was deteriorating, with Grant closing in on Vicksburg, and the hopes of foreign intervention were fading. A smashing victory on Northern soil seemed to offer the best prospect for restoring the Confederacy's fortunes. So "Lee's Miserables" again crossed the Potomac, with Hooker cautiously keeping between them and Washington. As the armies groped for each other, Hooker quarreled with the administration and was replaced by General George G. Meade. A chance encounter, unplanned and unwanted by either commander, brought both armies together at Gettysburg. Here, (1–3 July 1863) the best-known battle of the Civil War was fought. For three days Lee, perhaps made overconfident by his previous victories, hammered fruitlessly at a strong and stubbornly held Union position. To the climax of the battle, Pickett's charge, could be applied the remark made by the French officer who watched the charge of the Light Brigade at Balaclava—*"C'est magnifique, mais ce n'est pas la guerre."* The Confederates retired to Virginia again, without pursuit, mainly because Meade's army was also badly battered, but also in part because Union troops had to be dispatched to suppress the draft riots in New York City.

The Western War. In the meantime, the war in the West had been producing decisive results. Action here began rather earlier than in Virginia. In February, 1862, Ulysses S. Grant, just returned to the army after a series of disheartening experiences in civil life, struck at the Confederate posts of Forts Henry and Donelson, on the Tennessee and Cumberland Rivers respectively. He was given efficient cooperation by Union naval forces—in fact, Fort Henry surrendered to a naval attack before Grant's troops arrived. The fall of the two forts opened the rivers to Federal gunboats and compelled the Confederates to abandon most of central and western Tennessee. Grant then pushed down the Tennessee toward the railroad junction of Corinth, Mississippi. At Pittsburgh Landing, or Shiloh, he was surprised (6 April 1862) by a Confederate army under Albert Sidney Johnston. Grant's troops, however, recovered creditably, Johnston was killed, and when on the next day Union reinforcements arrived under Don Carlos Buell, the Confederates were driven from the field.

Both sides had suffered heavy casualties, and although the surprise was due mainly to the inexperience of officers and men alike, Grant's reputation suffered. He might have been removed altogether if Lincoln had not stood by him, on the ground that he could hardly spare a general who fought. As it was, General Henry W. Halleck assumed direct command of the army, which in six weeks laboriously dug its way from Shiloh to Corinth (20 miles). Halleck was then called to Washington as Chief of Staff, a position which made him little more than a chief clerk for Lincoln and Secretary of War Stanton. For the remainder of 1862, fighting in the West was inconclusive. A Confederate army under Braxton Bragg invaded Kentucky and came close to Louisville but was checked by Buell at Perryville (28 October). For failure to pursue vigorously, Buell was removed in favor of General W. S. Rosecrans, who at the end of the year fought an indecisive battle with Bragg at Murfreesboro, Tennessee.

Vicksburg and Chattanooga. The center of activity then moved back to the Mississippi, with Grant again in command. His objective was Vicksburg, the last great Confederate stronghold on the river (New Orleans had been taken by Admiral Farragut in April, 1862). Repeated attempts to approach the city from the north were frustrated, but Grant was persistent. Finally he swung part of his army down the west bank of the Mississippi, crossed the river south of Vicksburg, and, living off the country as he went, thrust between the Confederates in Vicksburg, commanded by John C. Pemberton, and the relief force which Joseph E. Johnston was assembling at Jackson, Mississippi. Pemberton, thoroughly bewildered by Grant's movements, was shut up in Vicksburg; Johnston was unable to raise the siege, and on 3 July, the day that Pickett's charge broke on Cemetery Ridge, the defense of Vicksburg came to an end. The formal surrender took place on the Fourth.[2] A few days later, when the smaller post of Port Hudson fell to a Union army from New Orleans, the Confederacy was split in two.

As if stimulated by these great events, the armies in eastern Tennessee began to move again. In early September the Federals captured Chattanooga but then suffered a stinging defeat at Chickamauga (19–20 September 1863), which might have been catastrophic except for a stubborn stand by the corps commanded by George H. Thomas, the "Rock of Chickamauga." Then, while the Confederates leisurely besieged Chattanooga, the Federal government took prompt and effective action. Grant was made commander of all Union forces in the West, and on 23 November 1863 he was able to drive Bragg's army from its position outside Chattanooga, in an attack featured by the unscheduled storming of Missionary Ridge by Thomas's troops.

Grant in Command. Grant was now stamped as the man to win the war. In the following spring, he was made lieutenant-general and given command of all the Union armies, with assurance from Lincoln that he would be free from political interference in military affairs. With Grant's appointment, the Union armies acquired a coordinated strategy for the first time in the war—something the Confederacy never achieved. To the end of the war, Jefferson Davis kept the detailed direction of military operations in his own hands, a function which, as Lincoln discovered by experience, can seldom be efficiently performed by a man who has the other duties of the head of a state to consider.

Grant's plan was fundamentally simple. The Union armies in Virginia were to pound Lee's forces ceaselessly and relentlessly, in order to pin them to Virginia and prevent any of them from being detached to

---

[2] Vicksburg did not celebrate Independence Day thereafter until 1947 when, with appropriate ceremonies, General Dwight Eisenhower was the city's guest of honor.

other threatened areas. Meanwhile, the Western armies, now commanded by William Tecumseh Sherman, were to break into the heart of the Confederacy and destroy its power to resist. The storm burst on Lee in May, 1864, when Grant's troops drove across the Rappahannock into the "Wilderness" near Chancellorsville, just as they had done under Hooker a year before. They were stopped again, but Grant was not Hooker. When his frontal advance was checked, he edged around Lee's right, threatening to get between the Confederates and Richmond. The two armies moved around to McClellan's old battlegrounds, and finally Grant crossed the James to attack Petersburg. Lee was barely in time to check him there, but he did, and the contending forces settled down to a long dreary siege in the winter of 1864–1865. By the time he reached Petersburg, Grant had lost as many men as Lee had in his entire army. However, in spite of mutterings in the North about "butcher" Grant, Lincoln supported his commanding general, and there were always replacements for the Union losses, while the Confederacy was exhausting its man power.

The March through Georgia. Simultaneously with Grant, Sherman launched his offensive into Georgia. After Chattanooga, Jefferson Davis had been reluctantly obliged to substitute Joseph E. Johnston for his unpopular friend Bragg. Johnston's defensive tactics, like Lee's, were admirable, but between two veteran armies, each capably led, the bigger and better equipped one was bound to win. The Confederates backed slowly along the railroad to Atlanta; as fast as they tore the line up, Sherman's engineers repaired it. By the middle of July, the contestants were in front of Atlanta, whereupon Davis dismissed Johnston and replaced him with John B. Hood. Hood switched over to the offensive, as he was patently expected to do, with no better result than to lose a large part of his army and Atlanta as well. The city fell on 2 September 1864.

Sherman was then faced with a difficult problem. His supply line, a single railroad to Chattanooga and Nashville, was long and exposed; he could not spare troops to protect it and penetrate further into Georgia at the same time. Hood, moreover, was trying to pull the Federals out of Georgia by invading Tennessee. Sherman's solution was to send Thomas back to Tennessee with part of his army to meet Hood, while he himself would cut loose from his communications with the rest, 60,000 strong, and march across Georgia to the sea. The state was both the granary of the Confederacy and the home of most of its industry. If its resources could be destroyed, the South would be fatally weakened. The famous march began on 15 November 1864. With Hood's army absent, there was no effective resistance, and Sherman's troops left a belt of devastation sixty miles wide all the way across Georgia. They reached the sea at Savannah on 10 December and made contact there with Union naval forces.

Hood's invasion of Tennessee was a fiasco. After a costly and need-less assault on one Federal force at Franklin (30 November), he settled down to a preposterous siege of a stronger army in Nashville. Thomas calmly prepared to deal with the intruder, in spite of growing impatience in Washington with his apparent inactivity. When he was satisfied that he was ready, he sallied out of Nashville and virtually destroyed Hood's army (15 December 1864).

The end was coming fast. Sherman swung north from Savannah to administer to the Carolinas the treatment he had given Georgia, again opposed by Johnston, who had all his old skill but only the scraps of an army. Meanwhile, as the spring cleared the ground in Virginia, Grant stretched the Confederate lines until they were too thin to be held. On 3 April 1865, Lee abandoned Petersburg and Richmond to take his one remaining chance—a desperate retreat to join Johnston. The starving and dispirited army was overhauled by a vigorous Union pursuit, and on 9 April Lee surrendered unconditionally at Appomattox Court House. When Johnston gave up the hopeless struggle two weeks later, the war was over. The remaining Confederate forces in Alabama, Mississippi, and Texas surrendered without further resistance.

NAVAL OPERATIONS

The naval operations of the Civil War cannot be described in detail, but it should be clearly appreciated that they were as vital a part of the Union victory as the campaigns on land. In fact, the campaigns which brought the restoration of the Union within the realm of military prac-ticability—the conquest of Tennessee and the clearing of the Mississippi —depended completely on the support of the ubiquitous Federal gun-boats on the inland waterways. This river navy had not even existed when the war started; it was a product of Northern ingenuity and tech-nical resources. The same thing took place at sea. The United States, a minor naval power when the Civil War started, created an entirely new fleet which in due course subjected the Confederacy to the slow strangula-tion of blockade.

The blockade was supplemented by operations against the major Confederate ports, the most important being Farragut's capture of New Orleans, the greatest metropolis of the South, by an audacious dash past the Confederate fortifications on the lower Mississippi (24 April 1862), and his closing of Mobile Bay in a well-planned operation which produced the largest-scale naval engagement of the war (5 August 1864). The seaports on the Atlantic were more immune to naval attack. Charleston and Savannah were held until Sherman appeared in their rear, and Wilmington, North Carolina, remained open until the capture of Fort Fisher on 15 January 1865.

The blockade, although effective enough to impose a crippling strain on Southern economy, was never absolute. Blockade running grew into a flourishing business, financed by British, Southern, and sometimes even Northern capital. The technique was to use neutral vessels for the ocean haul between Europe and some neutral point close to the Southern coast —Nassau in the Bahamas was the favorite—and then transfer the cargo to specially built blockade runners. Since these ships were difficult to in-

The *Monitor* and the *Merrimac,* from S. M. Schmucker, *History of the Civil War* (Philadelphia, 1865). The wooden vessel on the right is the U.S.S. *Minnesota,* damaged in the previous day's fighting. The identity of the one on the left is not clear, but it is probably intended to be one of the Confederate armed steamers that took part in the battle.

tercept, the Union naval authorities elaborated on the "broken-voyage" doctrine developed by the British during the Napoleonic Wars and began seizing the slower ocean carriers, on the ground that the destination of the cargo and not the vessel was what mattered, and that the carrying of contraband intended for the Confederacy must be regarded as one continuous voyage. This procedure went beyond previous British blockading practice, but the British, foreseeing potential future utility for themselves in the doctrine of "continuous voyage," judiciously said nothing.

The Confederate Navy. Although the Confederacy lacked the means to compete with Northern sea power, its naval authorities showed considerable ingenuity and resourcefulness in making the most of what they had. The idea of building a few tremendously strong ironclads was a good one for the inferior navy, and it had enough menace in it to keep the North worried. Unfortunately for the South, when it came to a competition in building ironclads, the North could make them faster and better. When the Confederates converted the *Merrimac* into the *Virginia,* the Union was able to start work on the *Monitor* three months later and still have it ready in time for the historic battle in Hampton Roads on 9 March 1862.

The Confederacy tried to offset its shipbuilding handicaps by having warships constructed abroad. This policy achieved nothing that weakened the blockade, but it did produce several raiders, the most famous of which was the *Alabama,* to prey on Northern commerce. Their activities delivered the final blow to the already decaying American merchant marine, since they stimulated a wholesale transfer of American ships to foreign registry, but their effect on the prosecution of the war was negligible. The commerce they destroyed was not essential to Union victory, and the Union navy wisely refused to let its major energies be diverted from the blockade. It managed, nevertheless, to run down virtually all the raiders in due course. The *Alabama,* after a spectacular two-year career, was sunk off Cherbourg, 19 June 1864, by the U.S.S. *Kearsarge.* Since the Confederate ships had been built in British yards, the United States subsequently claimed damages from Great Britain for failing to maintain the obligations of a neutral. By the Treaty of Washington in 1870, this claim was submitted to arbitration, and the United States was awarded $15,500,000.

EUROPE AND THE CIVIL WAR

The Confederacy's best prospect of compensating for its material deficiencies was to secure foreign aid, and its statesmen were blithesomely certain that such aid would be forthcoming. Unfortunately for themselves, they made the error, all too common for Southern political thinkers of the period, of evolving alluring theories without too much regard for cold facts. They believed implicitly in "King Cotton," assuming that if the cotton supply for the factories of Great Britain and France were cut off, the resulting economic distress would compel both countries to intervene and stop the war. They also believed that Great Britain would refuse to recognize the legality of the Union blockade on the ground that it was ineffective.

As it turned out, cotton was not King. Since the cotton crops of 1859 and 1860 had been unusually heavy, there was an oversupply on the market when the war began. A shortage developed later, but it was never complete. Britain found other sources of supply in Egypt and India, some leaked through the blockade, and some was produced in territory under Union control.

Other factors on which the Confederates had failed to calculate were present to curb the Southern sympathies of the British governing class. Whatever the upper classes thought, the common people were emphatically pro-Union, and even the aristocracy hesitated to approve of slavery. A series of poor harvests in Britain made Northern wheat rather more essential than Southern cotton. Elder statesmen like Lords Palmerston and Russell could remember the War of 1812 and had no desire to have another swarm of Yankee privateers turned loose on British commerce. As far as the blockade was concerned, the Southerners completely missed the point that Britain, as the world's leading naval power, had a long-term interest in permitting precedents to be established which would be as favorable as possible to the blockader.

British Policy. Thus, in spite of its preference for a Confederate victory, the British government had no intention of becoming unnecessarily involved in the Civil War and was prepared to recognize Southern independence only after the Confederates themselves had established it beyond reasonable doubt. The British recognition of the Confederacy as a belligerent—that is, as a group controlling territory and organized military forces and entitled to be considered as waging war in accordance with international law—was deeply resented in the North but was the only sensible procedure in the circumstances. The United States government itself, while regarding the Southerners in theory as rebels, in practice treated them as belligerents.

Britain's "wait-and-see" policy was complicated by the fact that in a war of this magnitude, with British support vital to one side and British neutrality equally vital to the other, troublesome incidents were bound to arise. The first such incident occurred on 8 November 1861 when Captain Charles Wilkes of the U.S.S. *San Jacinto* stopped the British steamer *Trent* en route from Nassau to Havana and removed two Confederate diplomats, John Slidell and James Mason, who were on their way to England. Britain, supported by most of the rest of Europe, regarded the act as a clear violation of neutral rights. Lincoln and Seward were inclined to agree, but were in an awkward position because the Northern public, badly in need of moral stimulus at the time, hailed Wilkes as a hero. After a period of tension, moderate counsels prevailed on both sides of the Atlantic. Queen Victoria's husband, Prince Albert, who wanted to preserve peace, toned down the note drafted by the British Cabinet, while Lincoln and Seward, once the public excitement had subsided a little, released the Southerners with an expression of gratification that Great Britain was now supporting the principles for which the United States had fought in 1812.

The next difficulty was caused by the construction of the *Alabama* at the Laird yard in Liverpool. British law permitted the building of such a ship, provided it was not armed in British territory, but to make matters safe a dummy contract had been arranged. The true destination of the vessel was common knowledge, and the very able American minister in London, Charles Francis Adams, finally persuaded the British foreign minister, Lord John Russell, to ask the crown's law officers whether sufficient grounds existed to detain the ship. Unfortunately, the official consulted chose that moment to go insane; the delay allowed a warning of the government's intentions to leak out, and the *Alabama* hastily slipped down the Mersey on a "trial" trip from which she never returned.

When the same yard began building two powerful rams, Adams was determined that there should be no repetition of the *Alabama's* escape. On 5 September 1863, he went so far as to use the word "war" to Russell. As it happened, Russell had already arranged for the British Admiralty to requisition the ships. The declining military fortunes of the Confederacy were making involvement in the American war increasingly unattractive to Great Britain. Events in Europe were also conducive to British neutrality. The outbreak of revolt in Poland in 1863 made Anglo-Russian relations uncertain for a while, and the Schleswig-Holstein crisis of 1864 momentarily raised the specter of a general European war.

The French in Mexico. The attitude of France was governed by Napoleon III's restless search for prestige. His active interest in Mexico began in 1859, partly because he needed something to offset the somewhat inadequate showing he had just made in Italy. In 1861 he managed to organize a joint effort by France, Spain, and Great Britain to compel payment of debts owed their citizens by Mexico, but the British and Spaniards had no sympathy with Napoleon's larger ambitions and soon withdrew. By June, 1863, French troops had reached Mexico City, and a year later they installed Maximilian of Hapsburg as Emperor. Maximilian chose to believe that the Mexican people had called him to his new station; his loyal subjects, however, displayed a distressing tendency to support the republican government of Benito Juarez and engage in guerilla activities against the French troops.

The government of Juarez also continued to be recognized by the United States. The Lincoln administration and the people of the North were vehemently opposed to Napoleon III's violation of the Monroe Doctrine, but while the Civil War lasted there was nothing they could do about it except have Secretary of State Seward file protests for the sake of the record. On his side, Napoleon was perfectly aware of what restoration of the Union would mean to his puppet empire in Mexico. He was desperately anxious to have the Confederacy win its independence. If Britain had intervened in the American war, he would have followed gladly, but his position in France was too insecure and the state of Europe too unsettled to permit him to act on his own initiative, or even to be too obviously unneutral.

The outcome of the Civil War doomed the Mexican Empire. In 1866, Seward pointedly asked when the French forces in Mexico were going to be withdrawn. The effect of this step can perhaps be overrated. The cost of keeping Mexico subjugated and the apparent impossibility of the task had made the enterprise increasingly unpopular in France, and the growing menace of Prussia made a curtailment of overseas military commitments advisable, so that Napoleon III was about ready to cut his losses in any event. The threat from the United States was probably the deciding factor. The French troops left Mexico in 1867. With their departure, Maximilian's regime collapsed, and Maximilian himself was captured by the republicans and executed.

Russia. The one European state to be ostentatiously friendly to the Union was Russia. Alexander II, a moderately liberal Czar during the first part of his reign, liked to be classed with Lincoln as a great emancipator because of his abolition of serfdom in Russia, and in 1863 he sent the Russian fleet to Northern ports in what was assumed to be a demonstration of good will. The Czar's motives, however, were not as disinterested as they seemed. When the Polish revolt of 1863 raised the possibility of war between Russia and Great Britain, the Russian government decided that its navy should be placed in a position where it could raid British commerce instead of being locked up in the Baltic, and a visit to the United States provided an effective cover for this move. Because the threatened conflict never materialized, the facts of the situation remained concealed for fifty years, and at the time the appearance of the Russian warships was taken at its face value, with excellent effects on Northern morale.

For Europe as a whole, the American Civil War was an encouragement to political liberalism. It may have been sheer historical coincidence that the Second Reform Bill in Great Britain, the adoption of manhood suffrage by the North German Confederation, and the liberalization of the Second Empire in France all came within a few years after the American people had shown that democracy and national strength were not incompatible; one may question, however, if these concessions would have been granted as readily had the South, with its aristocratic social philosophy, succeeded in winning its independence.

CONFEDERATION IN CANADA

In addition, the Civil War contributed directly to the formation of the Dominion of Canada. The creation of such a union had been urged by some Canadian leaders for several years previously, but there had been no great pressure on the various provinces to act, and the British authorities had been somewhat cool to the idea because they feared that a united Canada might be tempted to leave the empire. However, the tensions of the American conflict generated threats of war between Great Britain and the United States, which would almost certainly mean an American invasion of Canada. Furthermore, at the end of the Civil War there were some vociferous American demands that Canada be ceded to the United States in compensation for the aid given by Britain to the Confederacy.

Under these conditions sentiment for confederation grew steadily. Canada's constitutional convention met in 1864, first at Charlottetown, Prince Edward Island, and later at Quebec, and the result of its labors, after some revision, was enacted by the British Parliament in 1867 as the British North America Act. It gave Canada a government combining the British parliamentary with the American federal system. The title "Dominion" was chosen instead of "Kingdom" as a concession to republican sentiment in the United States; even so, the American House of Representatives passed a resolution denouncing the British North America Act as tending to strengthen monarchy in the Western Hemisphere.

THE HOME FRONTS

Some historians refer to the Civil War as the "Second American Revolution," mainly because of the consequences to American life of the destruction of the planter aristocracy as a political power and the resultant unchallenged domination of the United States by Northern industrialism for a full generation. The term is perhaps extreme, since industrialism was on its way to the top before the war started; its progress was simply accelerated by the conflict. Nevertheless, the war and its aftermath did have far-reaching and lasting effects on the United States.

In the North, civilian life was less obviously disrupted than the magnitude of the conflict would suggest. There was no total mobilization. Business continued to function by itself without any control by the government. Some branches of industry, particularly iron, textiles, and meat packing, were tremendously stimulated by the demands of the Union armies. Agriculture also benefited from the requirements of the military forces and a series of poor harvests in Europe, and because of the drain on man power caused by the war, turned increasingly to mechanization.

The resources of the Union made it certain that financing the war, although it would necessarily involve some strain, would not be too difficult. The tariff was increased, not merely to raise money but because the Republicans were advocates of protection, excise taxes were imposed on virtually everything, and an income tax of 2 per cent on incomes over $3,000 a year was adopted. Even so, the Federal government met most of the expenses of the war by borrowing, as well as by the issue of $450,000,000 of "Greenbacks," unsecured paper money whose value in terms of gold bobbed up and down with the fortunes of the Union armies.

Implementing the Republican Program. "Politics as usual" accompanied "business as usual." Because of the withdrawal of the Southern Democrats when their states seceded, the Republicans gained control of both houses of Congress and were thus able to carry out their program much more rapidly than they could have expected when the platform of 1860 was drafted. The raising of the tariff has already been mentioned, the principal step in this direction being the Morrill Tariff of 1861. The next year saw the passage of the Homestead Act and the Pacific Railway Act, the latter chartering the Union and Central Pacific Railroads and providing for subsidizing them by bonds and land. In 1863 and 1864, the National Bank Acts attempted to restore some order to the chaotic banking system which had developed after Federal supervision had been removed by the abolition of the Second Bank of the United States. These acts permitted banks, upon complying with specified conditions, to receive national charters and to issue banknotes, which were not legal tender but were receivable for all payments to the government except import duties. The note issues were required to be backed by government bonds for at least 90 per cent of their value—an auxiliary purpose of this legislation being to provide a new outlet for bonds. Notes issued by banks operating under state charters were subject to a 10 per cent tax, enough to drive them out of circulation. In addition, the Thirteenth Amendment, formally abolishing slavery, was added to the Constitution.

The opposition to the government occasionally went to lengths which by present-day standards would be considered seditious. The attempt to coerce states back into the Union was denounced as unconstitutional; an immediate cessation of hostilities was demanded; and Congressman Clement L. Vallandigham, spokesman for the extreme antiwar faction of the Democratic party, openly called on Union soldiers to desert. Secret societies such as the "Copperheads" sprang up whose methods of forcing an end to the war were indistinguishable from giving aid and comfort to the enemy. In the circumstances, Lincoln showed an amazing restraint. There were some arbitrary arrests and an occasional invocation of martial law, but on the whole freedom of speech and the press were left undisturbed. The peace movement was strong enough to reduce Republican strength in the congressional elections of 1862, and in 1864, taking advantage of the inevitable weariness produced by the long conflict, it made a bid for the presidency that had Lincoln worried.

However, the Democrats crippled their chances by trying to combine a peace platform (written by Vallandigham) with a win-the-war candidate in General McClellan. More important, the Union military successes in the fall of 1864—Mobile Bay, the capture of Atlanta, and the clearing of the Shenandoah—gave the people of the North confidence in early victory and assured Lincoln's reelection.

The Confederate Home Front. In contrast to the prosperity that it had brought to the North, the Civil War spelled economic catastrophe for the South. The Confederacy fought with an improvised industrial system and practically no money. Some loans were floated abroad, but the principal financial resources of the Confederate government were issues of paper money, which depreciated disastrously, and collection of taxes in kind. Apart from finance, the most serious weakness in Confederate economy was transportation. The Southern railway system was none too good when the war started, and with the blockade cutting off replacements of material, it became progressively worse. Confederate soldiers went hungry, not because there was a lack of food, but because the railroads were unable to handle the needed volume of traffic.

Since most of the military operations took place in Confederate territory, large areas of the South were devastated, and the abolition of slavery made the task of rehabilitation extraordinarily difficult. To most of the emancipated Negroes, "freedom" simply meant that they would never have to work again. Many of them left their plantations to wander around aimlessly in the expectation that the government would take care of them. It was impossible because of the lack of money in the South to restore the plantation system on a basis of wage labor, and it took some time for Southern agriculture to readjust itself to new conditions.

RECONSTRUCTION

Nevertheless, the bitterness engendered by the war would probably have disappeared rapidly if peacemaking had followed the lines of Lincoln's Second Inaugural—"with malice toward none, and charity for all." Lincoln's death was a major tragedy for the South. His program for Reconstruction called for the restoration of the Southern states to the Union as soon as their own people could form responsible governments, and with his great prestige and limitless tact, he could, in all probability, have got this policy adopted. His successor, Andrew Johnson, a Union Democrat from Tennessee, tried to carry out Lincoln's plans, but Johnson, while honest and courageous, did not have Lincoln's ability and lacked influence in the Republican party.

Reconstruction fell into the hands of the Radicals in Congress, dominated by vindictive old Thaddeus Stevens of Pennsylvania. Their motives were a combination of desire to see the South punished, sincere humanitarian zeal to protect the rights of the Negroes, and hopes of maintaining Republican domination by keeping control of the restored states, which meant that the Negroes must be allowed to vote. The clash between President and Congress on this issue began as early as 1864, when Lincoln's "10 per cent" plan, calling for the readmission of Southern states whenever 10 per cent of their population had taken an oath of allegiance to the Union, was challenged by the Wade-Davis bill, killed by pocket veto, and the subsequent Wade-Davis Manifesto, both asserting the exclusive jurisdiction of Congress over Reconstruction. It may be pointed out that both Lincoln and Johnson adhered to the theory on which the war had been fought, that the right of secession did not exist and that the Southern states had therefore continued to be states of the Union, although temporarily under the control of dissident elements—a thesis supported by the Supreme Court in *Texas v. White* (1869). The Radicals, on the other hand, were taking the position, even if they refused to admit it, that the Southern states had actually left the Union and needed congressional permission to return to it.

The South, unfortunately for itself, played into the hands of its enemies. Some of the state governments reestablished under Lincoln's plan enacted "Black Codes" to regulate the status of the freedmen. It was a necessary task, but it was done in such a way as to give the people of the North the impression that slavery was being restored in fact if not in name, a point which the Radicals exploited to the utmost. Similarly, the subsequent activities of secret societies like the Ku Klux Klan merely provided an effective argument for continuing a repressive policy.

Political Reconstruction. Political Reconstruction is a complicated story, which can only be summarized here. The Radicals were able to secure control of both houses of Congress in sufficient strength to overturn the presidential program and enact their own. First, they drastically extended the jurisdiction of the Freedmen's Bureau, an agency created toward the close of the war to help the Negroes through the difficult period of adjustment between slavery and freedom. Second, they enacted civil-rights legislation designed to enforce racial equality. Finally, the Reconstruction Acts passed in 1867 placed all the area of the former Confederacy, except Tennessee, under military rule until such time as state governments were formed which would guarantee Negro suffrage and ratify the Fourteenth Amendment. Both the Fourteenth and Fifteenth Amendments were pushed through at this time by the Radicals in order to give constitutional sanction to their principles. Neither accomplished its ostensible purpose. The Fourteenth Amendment found its principal utility as a barrier to attempts at the regulation of business by the states, while the Fifteenth, which supposedly guaranteed to the Negroes the right to vote, became a dead letter.

The "carpetbag" governments which emerged in the South have become a byword for political corruption. Actually, they were not appreciably worse than contemporary state governments in the North, and some of the things they did, such as providing liberally for public education, might well have been preserved if the reaction against them had not been so violent as to sweep out the good with the bad.

Impeachment of Andrew Johnson. Johnson fought the Radicals stubbornly, but his vetoes were monotonously overridden. Nevertheless, his opposition provoked the Radicals to extreme measures of retaliation, culminating in impeachment proceedings. The principal charge against the President was his refusal to observe the Tenure of Office Act of 1867, a law passed mainly to prevent the removal of Secretary of War Stanton, who was working heart and soul for the Radicals. If the impeachment had succeeded, the presidency, under existing law, would have devolved on "Bluff Ben" Wade of Ohio, a prominent Radical and at this time president pro tem of the Senate. Johnson, however, was saved when seven Republican senators joined the Democrats to vote for acquittal, leaving the Radicals one vote shy of the two-thirds majority required for conviction. Had the decision gone the other way, the United States might well have seen Congress become dominant over both the executive and judicial branches of the national government. Such a development would of course have produced a major change in the constitutional structure, with the emergence of some sort of parliamentary system and the reduction of the presidency to the role of figurehead as the most likely outcome.

Despite this setback, the Radicals apparently won complete control of the United States government when their candidate, General Grant, was elected President in 1868. (They had already curtailed the jurisdiction of the Supreme Court in order to prevent judicial interference with their program.) Nevertheless, they were on the way out. The people of the North were tiring of holding the South in subjection; the death of Stevens deprived the Radicals of their ablest leader; and Grant, for all his political ineptitude, was an honest man who sincerely desired sectional peace. One by one the Southern states were readmitted to the Union and the Federal garrisons withdrawn; these steps were invariably followed by the collapse of the carpetbag governments and the recovery of political power by the Southern whites.

The Disputed Election. By 1876 only three states—South Carolina, Florida, and Louisiana—were still under Federal occupation. In that year the Republicans, somewhat embarrassed by the scandals of the Grant administration, nominated the eminently respectable Governor Rutherford B. Hayes of Ohio for President, while the Democrats picked as their candidate Governor Samuel J. Tilden of New York. On election night it appeared that Tilden was the victor, but the Republicans challenged his right to the electoral votes of these three Southern states. The Democrats in turn questioned the validity of a Hayes electoral vote in Oregon.

A major political crisis ensued, since the Constitution is not clear on the subject of counting electoral votes. The Senate was Republican, the House Democratic, and neither would accept the other's interpretation. Finally an Electoral Commission was created, to consist of five members of each house and five justices of the Supreme Court. As finally constituted this body comprised eight Republicans and seven Democrats, and this was the margin by which the disputed votes were given to Hayes, to make him President by an electoral vote of 185 to 184. This decision was accepted by the Southerners in Congress in return for assurances from Republican leaders of economic and political favors to the South, including the withdrawal of the remaining troops.

So Reconstruction ended. It failed to achieve its objectives; instead it left behind a legacy of racial antagonism, since the Southern whites reacted to it by uniting in support of "white supremacy." In all fairness it should be pointed out that some extremes were avoided. There was no general proscription of Confederate leaders; the civil disabilities imposed on them were in most cases removed after a comparatively few years, and many of them became important figures in political and economic life. Jefferson Davis suffered a term of imprisonment but was released when it proved impossible to try him for treason, while General Lee was allowed to terminate his career peacefully as president of what is now Washington and Lee University.

PART SIX

Modern Technology and Its Problems

The convulsions of the 1860's marked the close of a period of drastic political change and the beginning of an era of relative stability. By the opening of the following decade the principal nations of the world had assumed the form they were to retain until the great upheavals of the twentieth century. The United States had passed through the ordeal of civil war and emerged with its national unity securely established; the German Empire and the Kingdom of Italy had taken their places among the great powers; France had finally achieved comparative internal peace under the Third Republic; and Great Britain had quietly transformed itself into a democracy. In the Far East, the Meiji Restoration of 1867 started the westernizing of Japan, and even Russia saw some concessions to the spirit of the age in the abolition of serfdom and the legal reforms of Alexander II.

As if it had been waiting for just such an atmosphere of political security, industrialism proceeded to advance on a scale and at a pace completely overshadowing anything it had done up to that time. Scientific and technological discoveries came in bewildering profusion, and entire new industries were brought into existence. The world's agriculture was merged into the pattern of industrial economy. The balance of economic power shifted radically, as Great Britain lost its formerly undisputed preeminence to fall behind the United States and Germany, and industrialization began to spread beyond the confines of the Western world.

With this expansion came problems, similar to those encountered already during the earlier stages of the Industrial Revolution, but greatly magnified. Each industrialized state found itself wrestling with economic and social forces which at times seemed incapable of being controlled. Each sought a solution in its own way, but with a basic consistency of method—the extension of governmental authority over economic processes.

23

The Expansion of Industrialism

The new developments in industry and technology during the last part of the nineteenth and the beginning of the twentieth centuries were so far reaching that they are frequently designated as the second Industrial Revolution. New industries such as petroleum, rubber, chemicals, and aluminum appeared; electricity and the internal combustion engine arose as sources of power to challenge the century-long domination of steam; and the automobile and the airplane, the telephone and the radio introduced new factors into transportation and communication.

Concurrent with this industrial expansion, and a necessary adjunct to it, was the evolution of large-scale business organization. Its forms varied in detail from country to country, but they were basically similar in that they represented methods of concentrating capital in unprecedented amounts and also of wielding tremendous economic power. While small-scale enterprise continued to flourish in many fields, by 1900 "big business" clearly dominated the key points of world economy—iron and steel, mining, oil, textiles, transportation, and communications forming a partial list.

THE RISE OF BIG BUSINESS IN THE UNITED STATES

Just as Great Britain provides the prime example of the Industrial Revolution in its early stages, so the United States affords the best example of the expansion of industrialism in modern times. Between the Civil War and the opening of the twentieth century, little more than a generation, the United States advanced from a position behind Britain and France in industrial capacity to unchallenged world leadership. By 1910 its output of steel, the key index of industrial strength, exceeded that of all the rest of the world. American technological progress was matched only by Germany, and its development of large-scale business organization was unequalled anywhere.

The conditions which made this phenomenal growth possible can be fairly readily summarized. The United States was a fertile field for big business first of all because it was a big country. American industrialists had a broad market at their disposal, with no internal tariff or other restrictions. It was an expanding market also. The open spaces of the West filled up rapidly after the Civil War, and the population of the United States as a whole increased from a little over 30,000,000 in 1860 to almost 100,000,000 in 1910. Natural resources were available in abundance. Both anthracite and bituminous coal had been mined before the Civil War, and production mounted astronomically afterward. The oil fields of Pennsylvania and Ohio were first tapped in 1859. Iron ore was found in tremendous quantities in Minnesota and northern Michigan, with the Great Lakes providing easy transportation to the industrial centers of the East, and prospectors wandering through the Rocky Mountain area in search of gold discovered rich deposits of silver, lead, and copper. Timber was plentiful until wasteful exploitation depleted the supply.

Invention. Invention also played its part. Americans, of course, have no monopoly on inventive genius, but they have contributed their fair share to technological progress. Some of the more conspicuous achievements of the 1865–1914 period were Alexander Graham Bell's telephone (1876), Thomas A. Edison's phonograph (1877), incandescent lamp (1879), and his work on the dynamo and electric power later, Ottmar Mergenthaler's linotype machine (1886), and the contributions of Samuel P. Langley, Glenn Curtiss, and the Wright brothers to the airplane in the early years of the twentieth century. American industry also profited from the discoveries of others. Large-scale production of steel in the United States began in the 1870's, using first the Bessemer and then the Siemens-Martin open-hearth process, both British in origin. German inventors did the pioneer work on the internal-combustion engine, but it was left to Americans to apply Eli Whitney's mass-production technique to the manufacture of automobiles—and, for that matter, of practically everything else. The automobile industry gave belated economic importance to Charles Goodyear's discovery of the method of vulcanizing rubber (1839).

Labor. Labor conditions in the United States during the post-Civil War period were generally favorable to the industrialists. The highly individualistic traditions of American life handicapped the growth of labor unions, and the weight of legislation and judicial opinion was on the side of the employer. The rapid increase in population provided an ample supply of labor for the demands of industry. It may be noted that this increase was only partly due to immigration. The almost 30,000,000 people who entered the United States between 1860 and 1920 account for less than half the total increase in the population of the United States during this period. There was work enough to be done; the immigrants did not saturate the labor market, but they did have an adverse effect on the development of labor organizations in that they provided a constant influx of unorganized and unskilled labor.

The political atmosphere could scarcely have been better. With the power of the Southern planters broken by the Civil War, labor weak, and the Western farmers difficult to organize and inclined to stick to the political alignment formed in 1860, the industrialists were able to do much as they pleased until the close of the nineteenth century. On the positive side, the government aided industrial expansion by continuing the high-tariff policy adopted in 1861 and by a free-and-easy disposition of natural resources. Negatively, no effective restrictions were imposed on business by the national government until early in the present century. When popular pressure induced the states from time to time to attempt to regulate economic matters, they found themselves hampered by judicial interpretation of the "due-process" clause in the Fourteenth Amendment, the provision that no state "shall deprive any person of life, liberty, or property, without due process of law." The courts held that a corporation was a person within the meaning of this clause and that "unreasonable" restriction of business enterprise—"unreasonable" being subject to judicial definition—was a violation of due process.

The Corporation. The instrumentality thus protected, the corporation, became the dominant form of business organization because it offered manifest advantages in addition to its favorable legal position. A corporation is an artificial person created by law, capable of conducting business, suing and being sued in its own name; its existence is not affected by changes in the composition of its individual members. It also normally possesses the feature of limited liability—that is, if the concern should fail, the individual stockholder is liable only for the amount of his investment. The corporation thus provides the security and permanence needed for the organization of large-scale business enterprise.

Since corporations are usually chartered by the states rather than by the national government, organizers of large enterprises early developed the practice of shopping around for the states with the most lenient incorporation laws. New Jersey and Delaware have long been favorites. The place of incorporation need have no relation to where the bulk of the business is done. In addition, the device of the holding company, which is simply a corporation authorized to own stock in other corporations, has proved highly useful in big business organization as a means of exercising central control and also of dissipating supervision by state authority. A corporation organized in one state may be controlled by a holding company chartered in another, and the possibilities of further development have resulted in occasional weird "pyramids" of corporations and holding companies.

The corporation, in short, made it possible for American business to exploit to the full the benefits of large-scale organization, and those benefits are very considerable. Only a big concern can utilize effectively the techniques of mass production, which were developed in the United States much more intensively than anywhere else in the world, or afford the expenditures for scientific and technological research which are the indispensable adjunct of present-day industrialism. The undesirable feature of big business is, of course, its tendency to evolve into monopoly, but this risk can be controlled and is probably worth accepting in order to secure the advantages of large-scale operation.

Two other problems presented by the growth of big corporations have yet to be met satisfactorily. First, in organizations where the number of security holders frequently runs into thousands, minority control is not only feasible but commonplace. It is physically impossible for all the individuals who own stock or bonds to play a direct part in running the business, and few, in fact, have any interest beyond the return on their investment or the speculative value of their holdings. As a result, control of a large corporation can be achieved with as little as 10 or 15 per cent of the voting stock. Second, as a consequence of this condition, ownership and management have a tendency to become separated. The directors and executive officers who represent a corporation to its employees and to the public are seldom its owners if the organization is a big one. This element in industrial relations is of comparatively recent origin, and its implications are as yet only partially understood.

THE GROWTH OF THE TRUSTS

The most conspicuous feature of American industrial development in the period after 1870 was the rise of the great trusts. Technically, a trust is a form of business combination whereby the stockholders of a number of independent firms vest the control of their stock in a committee of trustees. In American history, however, the word has acquired a broader connotation and has been applied to any monopolistic combination, or even to any giant business organization whether monopolistic or not.

Since every major industry in the United States produced some form of giant combination, it is impossible to describe all the trusts that came into existence. Nor is it especially necessary. The evolution of giant business organizations can be observed clearly in two of the nation's most important industries, steel and oil. The former revolves about the career of Andrew Carnegie, the Scots immigrant who was brought to Pittsburgh by his parents in 1848 (at which time "Andy" was thirteen) and had risen from bobbin boy in a cotton factory at $1.20 a week to be superintendent of the Pittsburgh Division of the Pennsylvania Railroad in 1863. Unlike most of his fellow tycoons, Carnegie did something in the Civil War besides make money; he helped to set up the field-telegraph system for the Union armies. During the war the iron business of Pittsburgh boomed, and Carnegie was drawn into it.

His first major step was the construction of the J. Edgar Thompson Steel Works in 1872, the largest Bessemer steel plant in the United States at the time, thoughtfully named for the president of the Pennsylvania Railroad, which was expected to be a major purchaser of the products. Carnegie did not introduce the Bessemer process to the United States. He was not an innovator or even an outstanding organizer; his success lay in his ability to exploit other people's ideas and in the forceful personality which made him the supersalesman for his company. A good judge of men, he showed great shrewdness in picking associates to manage the production side of the business.

Carnegie's "Vertical" Trust. The administrative genius of the Carnegie organization was Henry Clay Frick, who became general manager in 1886. Under his direction the Carnegie Steel Company evolved from a conglomeration of associated enterprises into an integrated "vertical trust" controlling the process of steelmaking from start to finish. The company owned its own ore fields at the head of Lake Superior, its own ore ships on the Great Lakes, its own railroad to Pittsburgh (Bessemer and Lake Erie), its own coal mines and coke ovens, and its own plants for making finished iron and steel. In 1900, its last year of separate existence, the profits of the Carnegie Steel Company reached $40,000,000 and, although American steel enjoyed a tariff rate of 45 per cent, Carnegie's cost of production was less than that of any foreign competitor.

Two flaws marred the picture. One was Frick's implacable hostility to organized labor, which precipitated a bitter strike at the company's Homestead plant in 1892. The company won the strike, but its public relations suffered. The other was growing jealousy between Carnegie and Frick over control of the enterprise. Since both were aggressive, dominating personalities, a clash was inevitable, and this internal friction was largely responsible for Carnegie's decision to come to terms with J. P. Morgan rather than fight for supremacy over the American steel industry.

The Carnegie organization, while easily the largest in the industry, was not a monopoly, and during the 1890's Morgan had been trying to enter the field by combining independent companies. In 1901, however, the two giants came to terms to form the United States Steel Corporation, first business organization in the United States to attain a capitalization of a billion dollars. Carnegie, having sold his interests for $450,000,000, retired to devote the rest of his life to philanthropy, in accordance with his principle that a rich man was obligated to spend his money for the benefit of society.

Rockefeller and Oil. While Carnegie was becoming the master of steel, John D. Rockefeller was building up an even greater empire in oil. Petroleum was a newcomer in American and world economy, its large-scale commercial development dating from 1859, when Edwin L. Drake sank "Drake's Folly," the first oil well in the United States, at Titusville, Pennsylvania. Northern Pennsylvania then enjoyed its counterpart of the California gold rush. New towns came into existence virtually overnight, many of them to disappear just as fast, and derricks sprouted all over the countryside, some bearing placards announcing the intention of their operators to drill to "hell or China."

As the new industry became stabilized, the principal refineries concentrated in Cleveland, Pittsburgh, and Buffalo, all convenient to the oil fields and at the same time centers of transportation to outside markets. It was in this phase of the business that John D. Rockefeller made his appearance. Already a successful commission merchant in Cleveland, he became interested in oil refining shortly after the Civil War, and by 1870 his Standard Oil Company was the largest firm in the Cleveland refining group. His first ambitious attempt at monopoly came in 1872, when he and a group of associates joined forces through a holding company, the South Improvement Company. This organization reached an agreement with the New York Central, Erie, and Pennsylvania Railroads whereby the Standard Oil interests were not only to receive a substantial rebate on their own shipments but also on the shipments of their competitors— in other words, a portion of the freight rates paid by competing refineries would be turned over by the railroad to the South Improvement Company, along with copies of the waybills. The scheme, however, leaked out and proved too much even for the easygoing business standards of the period, with the result that the railroads disavowed the arrangement and the charter of the South Improvement Company was revoked by the Pennsylvania legislature.

The Standard Oil Trust. This reverse had no appreciable effect on Rockefeller's fortunes. For the next ten years he continued to destroy or absorb competitors until the Standard Oil Company and its allies controlled 90 per cent of the oil refining in the United States. The methods employed varied according to circumstances. If a rival proved obstreperous, he was crushed, but Rockefeller was fundamentally a practitioner of the old political axiom of "If you can't fight 'em, jine 'em."

Time and again opposing combinations dissolved when their ablest leaders were persuaded of the greater advantages accruing from membership in the Standard organization.

In 1882 a second attempt at a general combination was made by the formation of the Standard Oil Trust, an arrangement whereby voting power in the stock of twenty-seven associated enterprises was placed in the hands of a committee headed by Rockefeller. In contrast to the Carnegie structure in steel, the oil combine developed as a "horizontal" trust, dominating the industry by securing a monopoly at one level—namely, the refining process. With this key position firmly in its grasp, Standard could and did extend its control without difficulty to the transportation and marketing of petroleum products. It was content to leave the production of crude oil to others, since they had little choice but to sell their oil to Standard on Standard's terms.

The trust fell foul of the growing public hostility to such combinations and was dissolved by the State of Ohio in the 1890's, only to reappear as a giant holding company, the Standard Oil Company of New Jersey. This company in turn became one of the targets of Theodore Roosevelt's trust-busting activities. In the Federal district court where suit was instituted in 1907 against the Standard Oil Company of New Jersey for violation of the Sherman Antitrust Act, Judge Kenesaw Mountain Landis achieved national prominence by fining the company $29,000,-000. The Supreme Court in 1911 ordered the monopoly dissolved but canceled the fine. Standard Oil was broken up into thirty-two separate companies, all, however, still effectively controlled by Rockefeller and his associates. Their monopoly was terminated less by legal action than by the great expansion of the oil industry from the Pennsylvania-Ohio area to other parts of the United States and opening of new fields in other areas of the world, developments which made the business so big that no one combination could hope to control it.

Similar conditions existed in every other important industry. The almost complete monopoly achieved by Rockefeller was an extreme case, but there was a general pattern of a preliminary period of bitter and chaotic struggle among a mass of small firms, followed by the rise of one or two great concerns to a commanding position. For example, although the automobile industry has always been highly competitive, unquestioned supremacy has been shared since early in the present century by Ford and General Motors. The growing domain of electricity was largely preempted by Westinghouse and Thomas A. Edison's General Electric Company.

Banking. Directly associated with this expansion of industry was the growth of great banking houses. Big business required capital in unprecedented amounts; its needs, in fact, could not be filled by the money markets of the United States, and much of the development of America was financed in Europe. Virtually every great industry, the notable exceptions being the Carnegie Steel Company and the Ford Motor Company, had to rely on the bankers to secure the necessary capital, a situation which led eventually to what is termed "finance capitalism"—that is, control of industry passed into the hands of those who were in a position to provide the funds.

At the close of the Civil War it appeared that the dominant figure in American banking would be Jay Cooke, who had acquired great prominence by promoting sales of government bonds during the war. Cooke, however, became overinvolved in building the Northern Pacific and crashed in the panic of 1873. Leadership then gradually passed into the hands of J. P. Morgan, who had the advantage of British connections to give him a good position in the London money market. Morgan's first major exploits came in the field of railroad financing, where he instituted the process known as "morganization"—meaning simply that, in order to protect himself and his clients, he insisted on having a voice in the management of the enterprises he financed and in taking steps to eliminate cutthroat rate competition and other practices of the late nineteenth century which all too frequently led to railroad bankruptcy. By 1900 he had entered the field of industry and was, as we have seen, responsible for the organization of the United States Steel Corporation. There were other great banking houses independent of Morgan, but there was business enough for all of them, and they cooperated with each other closely enough to give some color to the charge that a "money trust" existed.

The Sherman Act. The reaction of the public to the formation of the great trusts perhaps belongs with a discussion of the general social consequences of industrial expansion, but something can appropriately be said about it here. The tremendous concentration of economic power in the hands of a few individuals, and the tendency of those individuals to use their power to exploit the public, produced an increasing volume of discontent until in 1890 Congress was induced to pass the Sherman Antitrust Act, declaring combinations or conspiracies in restraint of trade between the states or with foreign nations to be illegal. The act, which simply applied to interstate and foreign commerce the existing common-law doctrine regarding conspiracy in restraint of trade, was vaguely worded. In fact, the Harrison administration did not want to pass an antitrust law at all; finding itself compelled to do so by popular pressure, it resorted to the loosely phrased Sherman Act in the hope of throwing the whole problem into the courts.

Under these conditions the Sherman Act was doomed to ineffectiveness. In its first major test, the case of *U.S. v. E. C. Knight Co.* (1895), it failed dismally. The government was somewhat languidly prosecuting the sugar trust controlled by the Havemeyer interests, but although it was proved that the trust embraced 98 per cent of the sugar refineries in the United States, the Supreme Court held that the actual process of manufacturing was not commerce, even though the products were destined to be sold through the channels of interstate commerce, and therefore sugar refining did not come within the scope of the Sherman Act. Even in the more vigorous hands of Theodore Roosevelt, the Sherman Act was at best a mild deterrent to industrial combination, especially after the courts adopted the "rule of reason," following Roosevelt's own distinction between "good" and "bad" trusts. Mere bigness was not sufficient grounds for dissolution; a monopoly adverse to the public interest had to be proved.

AMERICAN RAILROAD EXPANSION

The development of the American railway system in the period after the Civil War requires separate consideration because of the unique part the railroads played in the development of the United States as a whole. In a country of vast continental distances, internal transportation was the most vital ingredient of economic expansion, and until very recent years this transportation was provided almost exclusively by the railroads. Water competition existed only in limited areas: in the coastwise traffic and in the movement of bulk commodities such as coal and ore on the Great Lakes. The great days of Mississippi steamboating ended with the Civil War. Highway transportation by truck, bus, and private automobile became a threat to the railroads only in the 1920's, and commercial air transport is of still more recent vintage. Fundamentally it was the railroads that opened the West, brought raw materials to industry, and tied industry to its markets. In performing this function they became one of the biggest of big businesses. They were in themselves a major outlet for the products of heavy industry; their expansion and organization into great systems showed American business enterprise at its best; and the financial legerdemain and rate practices of their formative years showed the same business enterprise at its worst.

The Pacific Railways. The principal features of American railway development in the late nineteenth century were the spanning of the continent and the consolidation of the multitude of small lines into integrated and powerful systems. The building of the transcontinentals began with the Pacific Railway Act of 1862, chartering the Union Pacific Railroad to build west from the Missouri River and the Central Pacific to build east from Sacramento until the two lines met. Each was given a modest land grant of five sections to a mile, increased to ten in 1864, and a subsidy in Federal bonds of $16,000 a mile in level country, $32,000 in the hilly regions, and $48,000 in the Rocky Mountain area. This bond subsidy was a loan, not a gift, and was eventually repaid. Even with this assistance neither road was able to begin construction until 1865, after which both started to build at a furious and phenomenal speed, each striving to complete the greatest possible mileage and earn the maximum subsidy before they met. The Union Pacific made up its labor force from Irish immigrants and discharged Civil War veterans; the Central Pacific imported thousands of Chinese. Tracks were finally joined at Promontory, Utah, on 10 May 1869.

The builders of the two lines deserve high credit for their physical accomplishments in spanning an unsettled wilderness and conquering the variety of problems presented by the Sierras, the Great Plains, and the deserts. Their financial operations appear in a somewhat different light. Since through traffic was not likely to be heavy enough by itself to support the two companies, both faced a fairly long period of slender returns until the territory they traversed should be filled up with settlers; their promoters, therefore, decided to reimburse themselves by the quick profits of construction. The directors of the Union Pacific organized themselves as a construction company, the Crédit Mobilier, and duly awarded themselves the contracts for building the road, with a satisfactory margin of profit—over 300 per cent in one year. The funds were supplied by the government subsidy, a mortgage on the land grant, and the sale of Union Pacific securities. Since the Federal government had a stake in the railroad, undue curiosity on the part of Congress was restrained by a judicious distribution of Crédit Mobilier stock. It is estimated the line was built for about twice what it should have cost. In the early 1870's the scandal finally broke, and a congressional investigation led to the abrupt termination of several political careers. The Central Pacific, controlled by four remarkable individuals, Collis P. Huntington, Leland Stanford, Charles Crocker, and Mark Hopkins, also had its construction company, but the "Big Four" contrived to dissolve the organization and destroy its records before any unpleasant publicity developed.

After the first Pacific Railway Act, Congress chartered the Northern Pacific (1864), Atlantic and Pacific (1866), and Texas Pacific (1871). Of these, only the Northern Pacific reached the West Coast. The main beneficiaries of the acts incorporating the other lines were the owners of the Central Pacific, to whom they represented potential rivals for through rail traffic to California. To forestall this menace the Big Four organized the Southern Pacific and, with the consent of Congress, preempted the rail routes into California from the south.

Railroad Land Grants. None of these companies was given financial aid by the Federal government, but they were treated liberally in the matter of land grants. If the Northern Pacific had received all the

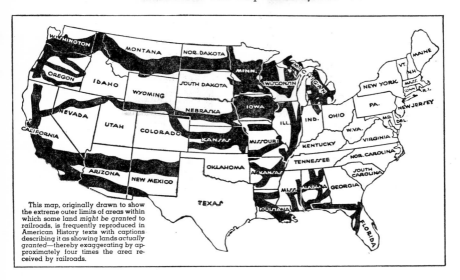

This map, originally drawn to show the extreme outer limits of areas within which some land *might be granted* to railroads, is frequently reproduced in American History texts with captions describing it as showing lands *actually granted*—thereby exaggerating by approximately four times the area received by railroads.

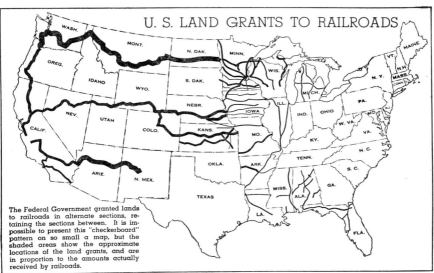

U. S. LAND GRANTS TO RAILROADS

The Federal Government granted lands to railroads in alternate sections, retaining the sections between. It is impossible to present this "checkerboard" pattern on so small a map, but the shaded areas show the approximate locations of the land grants, and are in proportion to the amounts actually received by railroads.

From R. S. Henry, "The Railroad Land Grant Legend in American History Texts," *Mississippi Valley Historical Review*, Vol. 32, No. 2. Reprinted by courtesy of the author.

land to which it was theoretically entitled by its charter, it would have had some 47,000,000 acres. At the same time Congress was extending and enlarging the pre-Civil-War railroad grants to the states. By 1871, when public opinion compelled the cessation of railroad grants, about 198,000,-000 acres had been pledged for this purpose, although forfeitures and other losses reduced the amount eventually received by the railroads to less than 130,000,000 acres. The effects of the policy are extremely difficult to estimate. The development of the American West, which depended on the provision of rail transportation, may have been accelerated by ten or fifteen years; on the other hand, the prospect of a land grant undoubtedly stimulated the construction of some rail lines which later proved economically unsound. The fact that the land grants carried an obligation to give rate concessions to government traffic proved to be an unexpected advantage to the government; by the time this privilege was rescinded in 1945, the savings to the government in reduced rates came to several times the original value of the land grants.

Some of the local lines assisted in this way grew into transcontinentals. The Atchison, Topeka, and Santa Fe started in 1863 as a project for opening the undeveloped area of southwestern Kansas, although its founder, Cyrus Holliday, dreamed of building a railway all along the old trade route of the Santa Fe Trail. The fortuitous rise of the range-cattle industry while the line was making its way across the Kansas plains gave it a financial strength unusual for Western railroads of this period, enabling it to cross into New Mexico, take over the defunct Atlantic and Pacific, and reach California in 1884.

James J. Hill. Meanwhile, a bankrupt Minnesota railroad, the St. Paul and Pacific, in the late 1870's attracted the attention of James J. Hill, a Canadian-born merchant of St. Paul. Hill's interest in the line arose at first from its possibilities as a means of tapping the resources of the Red River valley and also of providing an easier means of shipping supplies to Hudson's Bay Company posts in western Canada. In 1878 he bought the line from its discouraged Dutch bondholders. Reincarnated as the St. Paul, Minneapolis, and Manitoba, and then as the Great Northern, Hill's railroad kept pushing west until it reached Puget Sound in 1893. Hill was an excellent executive who built solidly and well, and he did so much colonizing work in the Great Northern's territory as to give it the name of "the Hill country" and himself the title of "Empire Builder." Since the Northern Pacific was a direct competitor of the Great Northern, Hill acquired control of the rival line, using the financial support of the House of Morgan in the process.

A complete account of Western railroad development must include a reference to the Canadian lines. Hill had Canadian backing for the Great Northern, and some of the men who were introduced to Western railroading in this way became the builders of the Canadian Pacific, whose story resembles that of the American transcontinentals, except that, since Canada had no Eastern rail network to start from, the Canadian Pacific became a genuine "transcontinental" in that it ran from coast to coast. Because construction of the railroad had been pledged when the Dominion of Canada was formed in 1867, the Canadian government aided it liberally with land and money. Competing lines built later proved to be financially weak and were ultimately incorporated into the Canadian National system (government owned), on the reasonable ground that it was economically better for the people of Canada to keep these lines running at a loss rather than have them cease operating altogether.

Railroad Consolidation. In the East, the numerous small lines already in existence at the time of the Civil War were extended and consolidated, a process which brought into prominence a number of colorful and occasionally notorious figures. Most colorful of all was Cornelius Vanderbilt, usually known as the Commodore because of the extensive steamship interests by which he laid the foundations of his fortune. At the close of the Civil War, when he was already seventy years old, the Commodore decided that his future lay in railroading. His first venture was the New York and Harlem, a road which in those days operated horse-drawn cars along the streets of lower Manhattan and then, under steam power, made its way north to Chatham, New York. Successful market operations with Harlem stock encouraged the Commodore to acquire control of the better located Hudson River Railroad, and from that he moved on in 1867 to take over the original New York Central. The Commodore, however, lost a fight for the competing Erie line, mainly because the fascinating triumvirate which ran the Erie—Daniel Drew, Jay Gould, and Jim Fisk—printed stock as fast as Vanderbilt bought it, to the accompaniment of a barrage of injunctions and maneuverings for the support of the New York legislature.

The Pennsylvania Railroad, major rival of the New York Central, stands almost unique among American railways in that it never fell under the domination of any one outstanding individual. It had a succession of able presidents, including Carnegie's friends, Thomas A. Scott and J. Edgar Thompson, but none of them owned the system as Vanderbilt and Hill owned theirs. This peculiarity does not appear to have handicapped the Pennsylvania. As early as 1869 it had acquired its own line to Chicago, and thereafter it expanded steadily through the heart of industrial America.

Of the remaining major Eastern trunk lines, the Baltimore and Ohio, although expanded aggressively during this period, was always overshadowed by its more powerful neighbor, the Pennsylvania. The Erie went through a period of lurid financial manipulation at the hands of the triumvirate previously mentioned. Finally, after Drew had been fleeced by his partners and Fisk had been murdered by a rival for the affections of one Josie Mansfield, J. P. Morgan intervened in the interest of European investors and forced Gould out. Included in this railway activity was the rehabilitation of the Southern lines, which had been badly wrecked by the Civil War. Recovery was necessarily a slow process, although the progressive industrialization of the South attracted Northern capital; the major Southern rail systems did not take form until the 1890's.

The Railroad Problem. Like the trusts, the railroads in their development raised problems that eventually required governmental intervention. It had originally been taken for granted that competition among rival lines would automatically regulate rates and protect the public, but experience demonstrated that this assumption was only partially correct. There was, it is true, fierce competition between points served by two or more lines, but there were also innumerable intermediate points with only one rail connection, and railway managers developed the technique of compensating for low competitive rates by raising charges to noncompetitive points. Frequently a short haul cost more than a long haul on the same line. Theoretically every railroad in the United States might have been paralleled by a rival, but attempts at such duplication of facilities were not encouraging.

There was enough overbuilding to produce a frantic struggle for traffic. A railroad represents a heavy investment of capital; since its fixed charges continue whether it does any business or not, it is always better for it to carry some traffic than none at all. As this fact became evident, competing railroads engaged in cutthroat rate wars periodically settled by the organization of "pools," arrangements whereby rates were stabilized and traffic apportioned among competing lines. These pools were not legally enforceable and were usually dissolved by one of the participants breaking the agreement. The evidence indicates that most of the pools were beneficial rather than harmful to railroads and public alike. It might have been better to give them legal sanction and permit them to remain in existence, but that was out of the question in an era when public opinion was violently opposed to monopoly in any form.

A far less justifiable practice was the granting of secret rebates to favored shippers. Business concerns capable of providing a steady volume of freight in carload or trainload lots received preferential treatment in this way, if they were in a position to bargain among rival routes. Thus, the Standard Oil Company, with three railroads bidding against each other for its traffic, benefited tremendously from rebates, while the Carnegie Steel Company, almost entirely dependent on the Pennsylvania Railroad, paid full rates on its shipments until it acquired its own rail line to Lake Erie. This power to discriminate among business concerns, or even among entire communities, by manipulating rates was strongly resented by the great mass of shippers who were not in a position to demand special favors.

Railroad Regulation. The first organized group to attack the rate-making methods of the railroads was the farm organization called the Patrons of Husbandry, or Grange. Since the farmers blamed excessive railroad rates for some of their post-Civil-War troubles, the Grangers succeeded in having several Middle Western states pass laws fixing "reasonable" rates for both railroads and grain elevators and won a historic victory when this action was challenged in the courts. In the "Granger cases" (1877) the Supreme Court held that certain forms of business enterprise were so affected with the public interest that the state could properly use its "police power" to regulate them. The court also ruled that, although the Granger laws necessarily interfered with interstate commerce, the states were within their rights as long as Congress had taken no action, and that the determination of the reasonableness of rates was a legislative and not a judicial function. These two points were subsequently reversed, the first in the Wabash case (1886), in which the Supreme Court held that a state could not infringe on the power of Congress to control interstate commerce, and the second in *Chicago, Milwaukee, and St. Paul v. Minnesota* (1889) and *Smyth v. Ames* (1898), in which the doctrine was laid down that the reasonableness of rates fixed by a regulatory body was subject to judicial review.

Regardless of judicial opinion, state regulation of railroads was bound to be ineffective. Agitation for Federal action was brought to a head by the Wabash decision, with the result that in 1887 Congress passed the Interstate Commerce Act. It prohibited pooling, rebates, and higher charges for a short haul than a long one "under substantially similar conditions," required that rates be reasonable, without defining the term, and established the Interstate Commerce Commission to administer the law. However, the Commission could enforce its authority only by taking complaints to court, and the courts were no more friendly to the Interstate Commerce Act than they were to the contemporary Sherman Act. In the first ten years of its existence the Commission was denied power to prescribe rates and so severely limited in its other functions that it became little more than a research agency.

INDUSTRIAL EXPANSION IN EUROPE

The industrial rise of Germany after 1870 was in every way as spectacular as that of the United States. From being a somewhat laggard competitor of Great Britain and France, Germany advanced in a generation to become the foremost industrial nation in Europe and the second in the world. The Franco-Prussian War had an effect on Germany similar to that of the Civil War on the United States; by assuring political unity and stability, it created an atmosphere in which businessmen could operate with confidence. It also brought direct economic benefits to Germany. The billion-dollar indemnity paid by France provided capital for industrial development, and the annexation of Lorraine gave Germany a bountiful supply of high-grade iron ore in close proximity to the coking coal of the Ruhr.

Like the Federal government of the United States at this period, the Imperial government of Germany was more than willing to aid the process of industrial expansion. A protective tariff policy was formally adopted in 1879, at the behest not only of the manufacturers but of the large landowners, who were feeling the competition of cheap foodstuffs from overseas. Industrial combination was actively encouraged in Germany, which became preeminently the home of the cartel. This term, like the American "trust," has come to be applied to monopolistic agreements in general, especially those of an international character. Technically it refers to an arrangement among independent business concerns for regulating prices, output, or markets, without the concentration of stock control provided by a trust or holding company. Germany also developed some giant industrial enterprises similar to those of the United States, conspicuous among them being the Krupp steel concern, and the A.E.G. (Allgemeine Elektrizitäts Gesellschaft).

German Industrial Organization. A factor of great importance in Germany's industrial growth was the systematic application of science to industry. Until the time of the First World War, Germany was ahead of the rest of the world in facilities for scientific and technical education, and German business organizations were keenly aware of the potentialities of organized research. The result was to give Germany a virtual world monopoly in the production of chemicals and of aniline dyes (although the process for making dyes from coal tar was actually discovered by an Englishman, W. H. Perkins, in 1856), and a very strong position in the manufacture of electrical equipment.

Several other elements in the German advance can be noted. An adequate supply of labor was provided by a rapid increase in population (from 40,000,000 in 1870 to 70,000,000 in 1914), despite heavy emigration to the United States, and to a lesser extent, to Brazil and Argentina, and the abolition of the guild system in 1869 removed cumbersome restrictions on the labor market. As far as raw materials were concerned, Germany possessed adequate deposits of coal, iron, and potash, but nothing else. Germany's late start was useful in that her factories and machines could take advantage of the most recent technical improvements while her competitors, principally Great Britain, were burdened with a considerable quantity of obsolescent plants. German industry, for example, used electric power earlier and more extensively than either British or French, and Germans did much of the pioneering work with internal-combustion engines.

Finally, transportation, as in the United States, played a vital role in industrial progress, although in this field the two countries went in opposite directions. Where the American rail network was built and operated by private enterprise, Germany turned to state ownership. Bismarck, who saw in the railway both an important military weapon and an instrument for promoting economic unity, wanted to bring the entire railway system under the control of the Imperial government, but on this point he had to yield to the particularism of the German states. However, Bismarck's objective was largely achieved by the fact that the Prussian state railways, with which were incorporated those of Alsace-Lorraine, controlled about 80 per cent of the total mileage and in particular served the major industrial areas. The Prussian system was efficiently operated and by manipulating freight rates was able, in effect, to subsidize favored industries.

The German government also fostered inland water transportation by improving its navigable rivers and building canals to connect them. Since both waterways and railways were government controlled, there was no ruinous competition between them, such as appeared in both Great Britain and the United States. Joint rates and traffic arrangements were worked out, with the result that in 1913 the waterways carried about 25 per cent of Germany's freight, their share consisting chiefly of bulky commodities such as coal and ore. A major achievement was the completion in 1895 of the Kiel Canal, connecting the Baltic and North Seas. Although built primarily for strategic reasons, it has always enjoyed a heavy commercial traffic.

Great Britain. Great Britain, with its industrial system well established by 1870, presents a picture after that date of steady progress along existing lines instead of dramatic expansion such as took place in the United States and Germany. While the country lost the virtual industrial monopoly it had acquired in the early days of the Industrial Revolution, its aggregate output continued to increase, and it even retained its leadership in certain fields. It continued to be Europe's principal coal producer and easily led the world in shipbuilding, the latter industry bolstered by the fact that Britain's merchant marine carried half of the world's ocean traffic. There were also some valuable by-products of Britain's long-standing industrial and commercial preeminence. London was the world's financial center, and a considerable surplus of capital was available for investment in the colonies and in foreign countries.

The movement toward industrial consolidation was less pronounced in Britain than in its principal rivals, partly because the law frowned on combinations in restraint of trade, and partly because the policy of free trade made it impossible to monopolize the home market. Nevertheless, under the pressure of foreign competition, there was some tendency for groups of small firms to unite in order to secure the economies of large-scale operation. This tendency appeared first in iron and steel, where

German and American pressure was heaviest, and later in textiles, where J. and P. Coats established a "thread trust" after the best American pattern.

In general, it can be said that Britain's economic position, although still strong, was becoming progressively less favorable. The country was so intensively industrialized that it normally imported four-fifths of the food supply for the 45,000,000 inhabitants, and it also had to import most of the raw materials for its industries, since the British Isles contained only coal and iron. By the beginning of the twentieth century Britain's balance of trade was unfavorable; the gap between the value of goods imported and the value of goods exported was filled by income from the maritime carrying trade, from banking and insurance services, and from foreign investments. As industrialism became world-wide, it became increasingly difficult for Britain to hold its export markets, and even its carrying trade and financial predominance were subject to vigorous competition from the new industrial powers. In addition, Britain's long term of unchallenged leadership had developed habits of mind in its businessmen which made them slow to adopt new processes and techniques. The loss of the aniline-dye industry to Germany is a case in point, and in its industrial system as a whole Britain fell behind both American and German practice in utilizing laborsaving machinery and mass-production techniques.

France. France, like Great Britain, experienced a steady industrial growth after 1870, but on nothing like the scale of its neighbors. While France recovered rapidly from the economic losses of the War of 1870, several other factors were present to restrict its industrial development. Its remaining coal and iron deposits were poorly located with respect to each other. Its population remained stationary at a little over forty million, and because of the prevalence of peasant ownership, a large proportion of the French people was content to stay on the land. French manufacturing, moreover, tended to emphasize small-scale, high-quality production. The principal exception was iron and steel, which necessarily involved large-scale operation and in which a great vertical combine, Schneider-Creusot, developed.

Russia. Russia was well behind the rest of Europe. Industrialism did not gain a real foothold there until the 1890's, when the energetic Count Witte, Minister of Finance under Nicholas II, undertook an extensive program of economic development, mainly with French capital. The greatest achievement of the Witte regime was the construction of the Trans-Siberian Railway by the Russian government. With the somewhat reluctant consent of the Chinese government the eastern section of the line was built across Manchuria as the Chinese Eastern Railway. The Pacific was reached at Port Arthur just before the outbreak of the Russo-Japanese War in 1904. The loss of Port Arthur and the general weakening of Russia's position in Manchuria which followed the Japanese victory resulted in the construction of an alternative route on Russian territory to Vladivostok.

Of the other European states, Italy developed an industrial area in Piedmont and Lombardy but was severely handicapped by a total lack of raw materials. Belgium was very highly industrialized, and Sweden, with excellent deposits of high-grade iron ore, acquired a respectable steel industry. Other industrial areas of importance existed in Catalonia, the northeastern part of Spain, and in the provinces of Austria and Bohemia in the Dual Monarchy. In other words, by the beginning of the twentieth century, industrialism extended over all western and central Europe.

Outside Europe and North America, the Industrial Revolution was still in its preliminary stages. The most advanced of the nonoccidental countries was Japan, where industrial development was part of the systematic program of westernization begun in 1868. Japanese economic life came under the monopolistic control of a few great families, whose empires included factories, banks, mines, and steamship lines. The country's chief economic asset was an abundant supply of incredibly cheap labor, which made possible the underselling of competitors' goods in their own markets in spite of tariffs. Japan, however, was a minor factor in the world market prior to 1914.

24

Industrial Society

The great expansion of industrialism brought with it an intensification of the social problems introduced into modern civilization by the Industrial Revolution. The concentration of population in great cities was accelerated, and marked changes in economic and social groupings took place. As industrial systems became more complicated, economic thinking produced numerous variations on the standard themes of capitalism and socialism. Most important of all, the industrial laboring class increased tremendously in numbers, to become a political and economic force of the first magnitude. Labor organizations became national in scope in order to match the corresponding growth in the size of industry.

URBANIZATION AND SOCIAL CHANGE

Wherever industrialism appeared, it was featured by a pronounced shift of population from country to city. Between 1870 and 1914 the proportion of people in Great Britain who lived in communities officially classified as "urban" rose from 60 to 80 per cent; in Germany, from 36 to 60 per cent; in the United States, from 16 to 40 per cent; and in France, from 31 to 44 per cent. Most of this increase occurred in the great cities rather than in the small towns. The effects of this trend on living habits have been so far reaching as to be almost impossible to describe. The concentration of masses of people in small areas gave rise to a host of problems, among them housing, the prevention of crime, public health, recreation, education, and the organization of municipal government.

Of these, the maintenance of public health was an obvious necessity for which even the most conservative were willing to accept governmental

386

intervention, and the means were at hand in the great advance of medical science which took place in the nineteenth century. Especially important in the control of contagious diseases were the bacteriological discoveries of the Frenchman Louis Pasteur and the Prussian Robert Koch. In addition, the continued growth of democratic sentiment during this period resulted in public education being reasonably well provided for. Housing was, however, another matter. Slum areas characterized the great cities of every nation, and efforts to eliminate them have met with only limited success. The need of the urban populations for recreation has also been only partially met; the most conspicuous effect of urbanization in this field has been the development of forms of mass entertainment such as professional sports and moving pictures.

The development of rapid transportation has acted to some extent as a check on concentration in urban areas by making it possible for people to live at some distance from their places of employment. The electric trolley car first appeared in Germany in the 1870's and in the next forty years enjoyed a spectacular rise. In the United States, not only were street railways built in every large city, but "interurban" lines competed actively with the railroads for local passenger traffic. In the greater metropolitan centers, subways and elevated lines were built in an attempt to relieve congestion on crowded streets. Later, the bus and the private automobile made possible a wider dispersal of city population; they were also destined to drive the trolley car out of existence in all but the larger cities and seriously reduce the passenger business of the railroads.

Emancipation of Women. Few of the social consequences of industrialism have been more sweeping in their effects than the change it produced in the status of women, a change which can also be attributed in part to the continuing influence of liberalism. Women had been employed in factories since the beginning of the Industrial Revolution, and succeeding developments enlarged their opportunities to work outside the home. The invention of the typewriter in 1867 opened a field which has been almost exclusively occupied by women, and they also became an important element in retail enterprises. As increasing numbers of women became economically independent, a demand for political and legal equality inevitably followed.

By the end of the nineteenth century most countries of the Western world had freed women from their previous subordination in the eyes of the law—in other words, they were given full rights to their property and earnings. Opportunities for higher education were opened to them, the United States being especially lavish in this respect. State universities were invariably coeducational, and the period after the Civil War saw the founding of numerous women's colleges. This development was followed by the appearance of women in professions such as medicine and law.

The demand for political equality, however, met with strong masculine resistance. The male mind recoiled from the thought of woman's tender nature being exposed to the coarse realities of politics. On the other side, the advocates of woman suffrage asserted that women would be a purifying influence in public life. As early as the 1870's John Stuart Mill was agitating in Parliament to allow women to vote, but most of his fellow members regarded the idea as ridiculous. There the matter rested until the early years of the twentieth century, when a militant suffragette movement in Great Britain reached proportions closely resembling civil insurrection, from which a harassed government was rescued only by the outbreak of war in 1914. The United States escaped Britain's trouble because woman suffrage by this time had already made some gains in state and local governments. As early as 1900 some Western states allowed women full political equality. Elsewhere the movement was ineffective, except in Norway, where women were given the franchise in 1905, and in Australia and New Zealand. The part played by women in the First World War resulted in their being given the right to vote, with some restrictions, in Great Britain in 1919, and in the United States a year later, when the Nineteenth Amendment was ratified. Germany adopted woman suffrage in the Weimar Constitution in 1920, Soviet Russia preached the equality of the sexes, but France, for all its liberal tradition, did not fall in line until 1946, partly because French politicians feared that women voters would be too responsive to the influence of the clergy.

Communications and Journalism. The combination of technological progress and the growth of cities produced another virtual social revolution in the dissemination of news and ideas. The telegraph, the cable, the telephone, and eventually the radio, first made practical by Guglielmo Marconi in the 1890's, made possible the transmission of news all over the world in a matter of hours and even minutes; inventions such as the linotype machine and the power-operated rotary press permitted mass production of newspapers; and the great cities provided a reading public in numbers sufficient to justify this mass production. Journalism became big business, developing in newspaper chains and in press associations and syndicates its own counterparts of the trusts and cartels of industry.

This change necessarily affected the techniques of journalism. In place of the newspaper designed primarily to express its editor's opinions came the newspaper designed to attract the widest possible sales, because, while advertising became the principal source of revenue, advertising value depended on circulation. The pioneer of the "new" journalism—sometimes referred to as "yellow" journalism—in the United States was Joseph Pulitzer, a German immigrant who began his career with the St. Louis *Post-Dispatch* in the late 1870's and moved into New York in the early 1890's by purchasing the *World*. Pulitzer's methods were to seek popular appeal by playing up sensational news, advocating social reforms, and using special features such as women's pages and comic strips. In these methods he was promptly outdone by William Randolph Hearst, who bought the New York *Journal* in 1896. Pulitzer, it may be said, was not a mere sensationmonger. He regarded the newspaper as an instrument of social uplift and believed that his tactics were a justifiable means of getting his ideas to the masses. And in spite of his glaring headlines, he insisted on factual accuracy in his stories. Pulitzer and Hearst had numerous imitators in the United States, and their work was duplicated in Great Britain by Alfred Harmsworth (Lord Northcliffe). Other newspapers copied the methods of mass appeal without going to the same extremes. Popular magazines also multiplied, utilizing techniques similar to those of the newspapers.

TRENDS IN SOCIAL AND ECONOMIC THOUGHT

The intellectual foundations for the defense of and attack upon the structure of industrial capitalism had been well established by 1870. The basic conflict between free enterprise and socialism remained unchanged, except that the increasing complexity of industrial society introduced a number of variations upon both themes.

The most important influence on social thought was the continued broadening of scientific knowledge. As new discoveries followed each other in bewildering profusion, ideas about the nature and functioning of the universe had to undergo a constant process of revision. Most influential of all in its impact on society as a whole was the theory of the evolution of species expounded by Charles Darwin and Alfred Wallace in 1859. Transferred to social institutions, evolution resulted in law and government being regarded as dynamic organisms rather than as fixed, unalterable structures.

Social Darwinism. In economics the initial effect of this new intellectual current was to strengthen *laissez faire*. Competition and the survival of the fittest were the basis of progress in nature; presumably they constituted the formula for social progress as well. This thesis, admirably suited to justify business methods of the late nineteenth century, was most effectively expressed by the English philosopher Herbert Spencer, whose *Social Statics* appeared in 1884, and by the American W. G. Sumner. They believed that nothing should be done by government which could possibly be done by private enterprise—Spencer even disapproved of the post office—and they opposed legislation for social reform as tending to promote survival of the unfit.

These ideas, however, were too remote from the realities of industrial society to meet with general acceptance, since they postulated absolute equality of opportunity and completely free competition. The general trend of capitalistic thought was to work out methods of preserving the benefits of free enterprise but also to extend those benefits to the mass of the people. This school of thought sought to eliminate evils and abuses in the existing system through the use of governmental action.

An American variation on this doctrine was offered by Andrew Carnegie in his "gospel of wealth." Carnegie agreed with Spencer to the extent of believing that the ideal society was competitive and that in such a society the ablest individuals would necessarily rise to the top. He also believed, however, that great fortunes should be used for the welfare of society as a whole. The decision on how to use these fortunes should be made by those who had accumulated them, since they were, as the ablest members of society, the best judges of the matter. Carnegie put his own doctrines into operation by lavish gifts for education, libraries, and the promotion of world peace, and his example was widely followed. The Rockefeller fortune has been used still more lavishly for philanthropic and humanitarian purposes. Even Daniel Drew left a promissory note (unpaid) to endow a theological seminary.

Socialism. Socialist thought of the period was predominantly Marxist, but its appeal varied considerably from country to country, and there was a sharp difference of opinion among socialists on how their aims were to be achieved. Socialism was strong in Germany and France, weak in Great Britain, and a negligible factor in the United States. Russian socialists were few in number, but energetic and usually in jail or exile. The growth of the movement was retarded by its own internal dissensions, which arose fundamentally because socialism could not separate itself from the general cultural trends of the nineteenth century. Between 1870 and 1914 the entire Western world appeared to have accepted the principle of representative government, and many socialist thinkers became convinced that the revolution preached by Marx was no longer necessary. They felt that socialism could be achieved by peaceful and orderly legislative methods, and to this end they advocated participation by socialists in "bourgeois" governments and cooperation with nonsocialist parties to promote reforms within the structure of capitalism.

Orthodox Marxists attacked this "revisionist" heresy vigorously. If the prophet said there was to be a revolution, then revolution there must be. The split between the two schools widened until it separated the socialist movement into the socialist and communist parties of the present day. Before 1914 revisionism on the whole had the better of the contest, except in Russia, where the prospect of peaceful change was remote. The Russian socialists broke apart in 1903 (at a meeting in London—it was not considered feasible for the party to hold a convention in Russia) into the Bolsheviki, or majority, led by Nicolai Lenin, who held to the necessity of revolution, and Mensheviki, or minority, led by George Plekhanov, who believed that socialism must be attained through democracy.

In Great Britain and the United States socialist thought, as would be expected, leaned heavily toward peaceful change. The first important socialist influence in Great Britain was the Fabian Society, founded in 1883 by a group of intellectuals (including George Bernard Shaw) for the purpose of spreading socialism by education. In 1893 the Independent Labour party was founded by Keir Hardie, committed to achieving socialism by legislation. It became part of the British Labour party ten years later.

The United States had a vigorous proponent of Marxism in Daniel De Leon, who formed a short-lived Social Democratic party in the 1890's, and it also had its own contribution to socialist thought in Edward Bellamy, whose book, *Looking Backward* (1887), envisaged a society which had taken advantage of the benefits of large-scale enterprise and eliminated its evils by organizing the whole community into one great trust controlled by the people. American reform sentiment, however, followed other paths than socialism.

Of the other philosophies of economic reform, syndicalism has already been mentioned as acquiring considerable influence in the Latin states of Europe. It also had some following in the United States in the Industrial Workers of the World, otherwise known as the I.W.W. or "wobblies." As a theory advocating violent revolution and expropriation of property by the workers, syndicalism had much in common with communism and has tended to be absorbed by it.

Henry George. The most unique scheme of social reform in this period came from an American, Henry George. In *Progress and Poverty* (1879), George pointed out that, although industrialism greatly increased the quantity of goods that could be produced, its advance was accompanied by intensified poverty for the masses. This evil he attributed to private ownership of land. Capital and labor both had to pay for the use of land, and as population increased, land values, and consequently rents, rose, so that landowners became wealthy at the expense of the rest of the community and with no effort on their own part. George's solution was to impose a tax on land to its full rental value and eventually to make land common property, with the government imposing a tax in the form of rent for the right to use it. This tax, he claimed, would replace all other forms of taxation and relieve both capital and labor of the burden of supporting landowners in idleness. George was not, as is sometimes assumed, a socialist; he would retain private property in everything but land. His ideas, in fact, are an obvious corollary of Ricardo's theory of rent, and he himself acknowledged his intellectual debt to the Physiocrats.

LABOR UNIONISM IN EUROPE

The growth and spread of industrialism, by increasing both the numbers and the problems of the industrial laboring class, carried with it an accompanying expansion of labor organization. The expansion was both geographical and structural; unionism followed the Industrial Revolution wherever it went, and labor organizations of necessity had to increase in size if they were to match strength with big business.

In Great Britain craft unions of skilled workers were well established by 1870, although their legal position still left much to be desired. While the repeal of the Combinations Law in 1825 had removed the legal barrier to the formation of trade-unions, the courts refused to acknowledge the right of such organizations to hold property or sue in their own name, and laws against strikes and picketing remained on the statute books. The enfranchisement of the industrial workers by the Reform Bill of 1867 cleared the way for the removal of these difficulties, since the labor vote was now a factor which politicians had to take into account. The Trade Union Act of 1871 permitted the unions to be registered as "friendly societies," and four years later work stoppages and peaceful picketing were made legally permissible.

For the next twenty-five years British unionism followed a conservative policy, working for specific improvements in labor conditions and wages and abstaining from political activity or championship of schemes of radical reform. Unrest, however, became more pronounced toward the end of the nineteenth century. Organization spread to the unskilled workers, a movement featured by the successful strike of the London dockers in 1889, and this new element was more receptive to socialism and more willing to enter politics than the old and wealthy craft organizations. In 1899 the Trades Union Congress recommended cooperation with the socialists and the cooperative societies to increase the number of representatives of labor in Parliament.

Founding of British Labour Party. Then, in 1901, came the Taff Vale decision. The Taff Vale Railway in Wales had been the scene of what would now be called a wildcat strike, in the course of which railway property had been destroyed. The company thereupon sued the Amalgamated Society of Railway Servants, to which the strikers belonged, for damages and was awarded £23,000 by the House of Lords, exercising its function as Britain's highest court. If unions were thus to be held liable for the acts of their members, even if unauthorized, their funds were in serious danger, and the craft unions, which had the most to lose, were driven to join their more militant brethren in political action to get the decision reversed. The British Labour party was formally organized in 1903. While it included the cooperative societies and the Independent Labour party, the trade-unions were and have continued to be its principal component, and in its early years it was not definitely committed to socialism.

The new party, however, was still a minor factor in British politics; the bulk of the working-class vote went to the Liberals, who had been converted to a policy of social reform, and it was the Liberals who passed a Trades Disputes Act in 1906 protecting union funds. After this, indeed, there was a decline in political activity by the unions, in spite of a flurry caused by another adverse decision of the House of Lords, the Osborne judgment (1909), which prohibited unions from using their funds to support representatives in Parliament. Since members of Parliament were unpaid, this decision would have been a severe blow to labor representation, but Parliament remedied the situation in 1911 by providing salaries for members of the House of Commons, and two years later it authorized use of union funds for political purposes provided contributions for such purposes were not compulsory.

By 1914, therefore, organized labor in Great Britain was on a firm footing. Besides the legislation mentioned above, provision had been made for arbitration of industrial disputes, and the right of collective bargaining was fully recognized. The steady growth of the Labour party and the sympathetic attitude of the Liberals made the unions politically secure. Total union membership was about 4,000,000.

Labor Unions in Germany. Since industrialization had to precede the growth of a strong labor movement, trade-unionism developed in Germany considerably later than in Britain. Not until 1902, in fact, did union membership in Germany pass the million mark. In addition to Germany's belated entry into the industrial field, other factors retarded the progress of labor organization in that country. German unionism was strongly political from the outset and suffered in consequence from ideological conflicts. Three rival groups emerged: the socialist unions, closely affiliated with the Social Democratic party and committed to the principles of Marxism; the Christian unions, sponsored by the Catholic Church in order to check the growing influence of Marxism on the workers; and the Hirsch-Duncker unions, which were organized on the model of the British craft unions and were antisocialist. The socialist unions were the strongest, but they suffered from the attempt to suppress socialism launched by Bismarck in 1878.

With the termination of the antisocialist campaign in 1890, the German labor movement grew rapidly, until in 1913 its membership exceeded 3,500,000, about two-thirds of it in the socialist organizations. This figure represented a smaller proportion of the total population than in Britain, and German unionism was not likely to attain the strength of its British counterpart until a greater degree of popular government had been secured in the Reich.

French Labor Movement. French labor had been associated with radical political movements since 1848 and made no change in its ways after the Third Republic came into existence. The movement, however, was slow to gain strength, partly because industrialism was not as important in France as in Britain or Germany, and partly because of internal dissension among various brands of socialists. Moreover, the government of the Republic, fearing a revival of the Paris Commune, was suspicious of labor organization in any form. Not until 1884 was legal sanction given to the formation of trade-unions.

The major step in the development of French unionism was the founding in 1896 of the *Confédération Générale du Travail,* which rapidly became the dominant factor in French labor. The C.G.T. was openly and avowedly syndicalist in policy; its objective was not to seek reforms for the workers but to weaken and eventually destroy capitalism by direct action—strikes, sabotage, intentionally poor work, and "slow-downs." It would appear that the radical character of this program kept most French workingmen out of the union movement, since in 1913 labor organizations in France had just over a million members. The principal challenge to the authority of the government, a railway strike in 1910, proved a fiasco. The premier, Aristide Briand, himself a socialist, broke the strike by issuing mobilization orders to the railway men and then requiring them, as soldiers, to run the trains.

LABOR ORGANIZATION IN THE UNITED STATES

In the United States as in Europe, the increased tempo of industrial expansion was reflected in the labor movement. Unions, like industry, became national in scope. Conditions of American life, however, made the acquiring of substantial economic power by the unions a slow and tedious process. Since American society had always been individualistic and fluid in character, American workers were not as class-conscious as Europeans and were slower to become aware of a need for organization; the description of the American workman as "a capitalist temporarily without capital" is a reasonably accurate picture of his state of mind. Geographical variations provided a complication; in the highly industrialized North unionism was able to get a foothold shortly after the Civil War, but in the South, where industrialism was just emerging, it was virtually nonexistent until the twentieth century. The attitude of the government and the courts, and of public opinion in general, was normally unfriendly to labor organization, and, most important of all, the tremendous influx of immigration handicapped the unions by providing industry with a constantly renewed supply of cheap labor. The restriction of immigration early became a cardinal policy of organized labor in the United States.

Immediately after the Civil War several important unions came into existence—the Brotherhood of the Footboard, which later became the Brotherhood of Locomotive Engineers, the Knights of St. Crispin, organizing the shoemakers, and the National Labor Union, the earliest attempt at a general, nationwide organization. This last group, founded in 1866 by William H. Sylvis, typifies the uncertainty with which American labor was groping for its objectives. It was a conglomeration of local unions and miscellaneous reform groups, and it was less concerned with strict collective bargaining than with promoting cooperatives and agitating for woman suffrage and the restriction of immigration. At its height the National Labor Union had some 600,000 members and could claim some credit for the passage of an act in 1868 providing an eight-hour day on government work, but it failed to survive the panic of 1873.

The Knights of Labor. Meanwhile, in 1869 Uriah S. Stephens of Philadelphia founded the Noble Order of the Knights of Labor, the original membership consisting of nine tailors, including Stephens. It was his ambition to unite all those who worked for a living, regardless of occupation, race, or sex, into one great organization. The only persons ineligible for membership, in fact, were lawyers, bankers, saloonkeepers, and professional gamblers. The Order was a secret society at first; even its name was replaced in public notices by five asterisks. In the late 1870's, however, this feature of the organization had become a handicap, partly because of the disapproval of the Catholic Church, but mainly because public opinion was identifying the Knights with the "Molly Maguires," an organization of coal miners in the Pennsylvania anthracite fields with a penchant for direct action. In 1881, therefore, the Knights of Labor abandoned secrecy. By this time Stephens had retired and Terence V. Powderly had succeeded him as Grand Master.

The Powderly regime witnessed a phenomenal rise and an equally phenomenal decline in the fortunes of the Knights of Labor. Between 1881 and 1885 its membership rose from 50,000 to over 700,000, stimulated chiefly by a successful strike on Jay Gould's railroads in the Southwest although Powderly himself disapproved of strikes. The organization's political influence was a strong factor in the passage of the Chinese Exclusion Act in 1882 and the law prohibiting the importation of contract labor in 1885. It appeared at that point to be firmly and permanently established in the American industrial scene, and yet five years later it had disappeared.

The reason for its collapse lay in its structural weakness. The "one-big-union" idea made for large membership but unwieldy organization. It was impossible to harmonize the interests of skilled and unskilled workers, and other internal conflicts appeared as membership grew. The new recruits assumed that the success of the Gould strike could be repeated indefinitely, with the result that after 1885 the Knights became involved in several industrial conflicts which brought only defeat and discredit.

The worst blow to the Knights of Labor was an incident for which they were not responsible, the Haymarket affair in Chicago in 1886, which grew out of a dispute at the McCormick Harvester Company. When four strikers were killed in a clash with the police, a protest meeting was called in Haymarket Square on the evening of 4 May, with some members of the Knights participating but chiefly under the auspices of a group of anarchists, who were fairly strong in the Chicago area at the time. After several uninspiring speeches had been delivered, the police pushed into the crowd to break up the meeting, someone threw a bomb, and several policemen were killed. The anarchist leaders were promptly arrested and eight of them convicted of murder. Although none of them was the actual culprit (he was never found), the judge who conducted the trial ruled that their doctrines had inspired the deed and made them accomplices in it. Four were executed, one committed suicide in his cell, and the others were subsequently pardoned by Governor John P. Altgeld, an act which made Altgeld the target of a furious outburst of abuse. In the public mind the Knights of Labor became identified with violence, and they never lived it down.

The A. F. of L. As the Knights declined, a better organized and better led rival arose to replace them. The craft unions, the associations of skilled workers, had never liked the "one-big-union" policy, and in 1881 they organized themselves as the Federation of Organized Trades and Labor Unions, renamed the American Federation of Labor in 1886. The leaders of this movement were two men who had entered organized labor as cigar makers, Adolph Strasser and Samuel Gompers. The latter, an immigrant born in London of Dutch-Jewish parentage, became the first president and retained the office, except for one year, until his death in 1925.

The A.F. of L. was organized almost exclusively on craft lines, although it did eventually include some industrial unions—that is, unions composed of all the workers in a given industry. The most important of these was the United Mine Workers. For the most part, however, the Federation ignored unskilled labor. Its policies were avowedly conservative. It would have nothing to do with radical reform movements but concentrated on securing for its members whatever immediate benefits it could within the capitalistic system. It sought to achieve its ends by economic action and refused to become involved in politics except to support candidates of the established parties who were deemed friendly to labor.

By these methods the Federation built itself up to become indisputably the most powerful American labor organization, with a membership approaching two million in 1914. It was by no means all-inclusive. The railroad brotherhoods refused to affiliate with it, and the radical element of American labor formed its own union, the Industrial Workers of the World, in 1904. The I.W.W., however, declined rapidly after 1918. Moreover, in an era of assembly-line production, in which most industrial workers performed operations requiring little training or skill, the craft-union principle was limited in its effectiveness.

Industrial Conflicts. Labor's struggle for recognition in the United States was punctuated by a number of violent industrial conflicts, in which labor as a rule had to contend not only with employers but also with governmental authority as well, since public officials generally made the protection of property their first concern during a strike. To some extent this attitude can be explained by the fact that these outbreaks were widely but erroneously regarded as revolutionary attacks on the structure of American society; few, in actuality, involved any deeper issue than disputes over wages and working conditions.

The first major strike occurred in 1877, when the Eastern trunk-line railways cut wages by 10 per cent. The trainmen, mostly unorganized, walked out spontaneously, and frequent clashes between strikers and militia followed. Since the country was still in the throes of the 1873 depression, hordes of unemployed were available to swell the mob when trouble started. The worst outbreaks were on the Baltimore and Ohio and Pennsylvania systems, Pittsburgh being the scene of a three-day riot with considerable loss of life and destruction of property. The intervention of Federal troops restored order and broke the strike.

The next decade witnessed the strikes associated with the rise and fall of the Knights of Labor. Then, in 1892, came the Homestead strike, already referred to in connection with the Carnegie Steel Company. The specific cause, again, was reduction in wages, imposed less from necessity than from Henry C. Frick's determination to break the Amalgamated Association of Iron and Steel Workers. When Frick hired a force of Pinkerton detectives to subdue the strikers, a bitter fight resulted which the Pinkertons lost. Public opinion was antagonized by Frick's high-handed action but veered around when an anarchist tried to assassinate him. Continued violence brought the state militia into the picture, and the strike collapsed. This defeat destroyed the Amalgamated Association; the steel industry was nonunion thereafter until 1937.

The Pullman Strike. Two years later another major conflict was precipitated by a dispute between the Pullman Company and its employees at the "model" community of Pullman, Illinois. With the depression of 1893 as the excuse, wages had been cut, but not the rent on the company-owned houses or the prices at the company stores, and when George Pullman flatly refused to discuss grievances, the strike followed. The cause of the unorganized Pullman workers was championed by the American Railway Union, led by Eugene V. Debs, and a general tie-up of rail traffic followed because the union refused to handle Pullman cars. The railroads fought back through a General Managers' Association.

The decisive factor in the Pullman strike was the intervention of the Federal government, engineered by President Cleveland's Attorney General, Richard S. Olney. Olney persuaded Cleveland that the strikers were interfering with transportation of the mails and induced him to send troops to Chicago, over the vehement protest of Governor Altgeld, who insisted that the state authorities had complete control of the situation and that the national government had no constitutional right to act unless the state called on it for assistance. There were, in fact, no serious disorders until after the troops arrived.

In addition, Olney's representative in Chicago secured from the Federal circuit court a sweeping injunction against the officers of the American Railway Union, prohibiting them from encouraging the strike in any way, on the ground that it was a conspiracy against interstate commerce and therefore a violation of the Sherman Act. Debs refused to obey and was sentenced to six months' imprisonment, his conviction being upheld by the Supreme Court in 1895. In the face of this opposition by the Federal government, the strike collapsed, and the American Railway Union presently disintegrated.

The Injunction. The major consequence of the Pullman strike was to demonstrate the value of the injunction as an antistrike weapon. An injunction is a court order, usually issued to protect property until a dispute can be adjudicated, and since violation constitutes contempt of court, the offender can be punished without a jury trial. The ease with which employers could secure injunctions from conservatively inclined judges was a major grievance of organized labor, until their use was drastically curtailed by the Norris-La Guardia Act of 1932. The invoking of the Sherman Act against labor unions was also an ominous portent, although its full potentialities were not to be realized for another decade.

The one notable victory scored by labor came in the anthracite-coal strike of 1902. In this case two factors were present to distinguish it from previous industrial conflicts: public sympathy was distinctly with the miners, and Theodore Roosevelt was President of the United States. Conditions in the coal fields were unbelievably bad. The majority of the miners lived in what can best be described as industrial feudalism. The coal companies owned the mining towns—houses, stores, public services (if any), and public officials. Low wages were aggravated by payment in scrip redeemable at company stores rather than in cash, and by deductions for tools and equipment. Unionization, although bitterly and ruthlessly fought, made steady progress after the founding of the United Mine Workers in 1890, and at the time of the strike the miners were ably led by John Mitchell, whose willingness to arbitrate contrasted sharply with the arrogant refusal of the mineowners to deal with the union on any terms. Their state of mind was immortalized in the reply made by George F. Baer, president of the Philadelphia and Reading Railroad, to an appeal for settlement of the dispute in a Christian spirit: "The rights and interests of the laboring man will be protected and cared for, not by the labor agitators, but by the Christian men to whom God in His infinite wisdom has given control of the property interests of the country."

Roosevelt's intervention came because he regarded himself as the representative of the public, who stood to suffer from a prolonged coal strike. When the President offered to mediate, the owners undertook to instruct him in his duty, which, according to them, was to use troops to break the strike. It was not exactly a tactful line to take with Theodore Roosevelt. He retorted by threatening to send the army to the anthracite fields to mine coal, whereupon the owners reluctantly gave way and, after a stormy conference in the White House, agreed to accept arbitration. The result was the granting of a substantial part of the miners' demands. This decision, however, was scarcely more than a truce in a chronic conflict; labor relations in the coal industry have continued turbulent to the present.

Labor and the Courts. Of the obstacles which organized labor in the United States had to encounter perhaps the most difficult to surmount was the persistently unfriendly attitude of the courts. Besides the ever-present threat of injunctions, the unions found that the Sherman Act was a far greater menace to them than to the manufacturers at whom it was ostensibly directed. The theory that union activity could be considered a violation of the antitrust law had been advanced during the Pullman strike, and it reached its full judicial stature with the decisions of the Supreme Court in the Danbury Hatters' case (*Loewe v. Lawlor*) of 1905 and *Gompers v. Buck Stove and Range Company* in 1907. In the former, a union boycott of the products of a nonunion plant was held to be a conspiracy against interstate commerce, and a $240,000 fine was imposed on the hatters' union and its members individually. In the latter, Gompers and other officials of the A.F. of L. were adjudged guilty of violating the Sherman Act because the organization's newspaper carried a list of nonunion firms under the heading "we don't patronize." Execution of the sentences was suspended on technicalities.

Labor Legislation. American labor did not duplicate the performance of British labor in somewhat similar circumstances by launching its own political party, but it did support the growing progressive movement which was the most marked contemporary factor of American politics. In consequence, when Woodrow Wilson was elected President, labor was rewarded by a clause in the Clayton Act of 1914 exempting farm and labor organizations from the operation of the antitrust laws and restricting the use of injunctions in labor disputes. Hailed by Gompers as "labor's Magna Carta," the Clayton Act proved somewhat of a disappointment, since the labor provisions were subsequently weakened by judicial interpretation. The Wilson administration was also responsible for the La Follette Merchant Seamen's Act of 1915, greatly improving working conditions for American sailors, and the Adamson Act of 1916, establishing an eight-hour day on the railroads.

The enactment of this legislation indicated that organized labor had at last secured a recognized position in American life, even though the position attained was not as satisfactory as could be desired. Unions in the United States were weaker in legal status and represented a smaller proportion of the total working population than in Britain; on the other hand, they had more power than French or German unions of this period and were far less subject to internal quarrels over political doctrines that had no immediate bearing on the functions of a labor organization.

AMERICAN CULTURE IN AN INDUSTRIAL ERA

The great social changes produced by expanding industrialism were accompanied by equally substantial developments in the intellectual sphere. Some were stimulated directly by industrialization and its social consequences; others stemmed from new discoveries in science; still others had no obvious direct relationship with either. An adequate description of the pattern of Western culture in modern times would require far more space than is available here, but it is possible to indicate some of the basic trends as they appeared in American culture during the period when the United States was approaching maturity.

Darwinism. The predominant intellectual influence in the United States during the half-century following the Civil War was the revised outlook on life generated by Darwinism. We have seen something of the effect of Darwinism on social and economic thought; in other areas of intellectual activity it had similar repercussions, manifested in a tendency to regard everything as being in a constant process of evolutionary change, presumably but not necessarily for the better. This attitude had little place for absolute truths, or fixed standards of right and wrong, and it was reinforced at the beginning of the twentieth century by new theories in physics, which attracted attention if not understanding because of the publicity given to Albert Einstein's work on relativity. These theories seemed to invalidate much of the Newtonian concept of a "clockwork" universe governed by unalterable laws, and they therefore contributed to the disposition to exalt relativism in other matters.

The first major impact of Darwinism was felt in the field of religion. Since the theory of evolution appeared to invalidate accepted theological doctrines, it precipitated a violent controversy whose repercussions are still occasionally felt. On one side were those who insisted that religious belief was no longer tenable in the face of scientific discovery; on the other, those who demanded that the scientific evidence for the evolutionary theory be disregarded because it conflicted with their interpretation of the Scriptures. In the end, of course, the churches survived and were able to reconcile science and faith, since, after all, religious truths are not dependent on scientific hypotheses.

Pragmatism. Of the philosophies produced by these new intellectual currents, the most widely accepted in the United States was pragmatism, popularized mainly by William James and John Dewey. Its essence was that ideas must be tested by action—in other words, whether an idea is good or not depends solely on how it works in practice. Abstract speculation was considered of little use; thought should lead to action. It was a philosophy with a strong appeal to a practical-minded people who were engaged in creating the most productive material civilization the world had ever known. Its drawbacks were that it led rather too easily to an overemphasis on material values and that it encouraged a facile assumption that moral standards and values were determined merely by custom and convenience.

For literature and the arts the generation after the Civil War was too much a period of frenzied money-making, ostentatious display of newly acquired wealth, and sheer bad taste to be genuinely encouraging. One of its outstanding literary figures, Mark Twain (Samuel L. Clemens) aptly characterized it as the "Gilded Age." Others like novelist Henry James and artists James McNeill Whistler and John Singer Sargent found the atmosphere of their native land so depressing that they chose to do most of their work in Europe.

Yet it presently became clear that American cultural life was simply readjusting itself to changed conditions rather than losing vitality. The "Gilded Age" itself witnessed a reform of higher education, led by men like Presidents Daniel C. Gilman of Johns Hopkins and Charles W. Eliot of Harvard, whereby American universities began to acquire a status comparable to that of their European counterparts. This movement was generously endowed by those same uncouth millionaires who were so distasteful to the intelligentsia. In the field of architecture this period, while predominantly one of overornate design, witnessed the development of a distinctive American form in the skyscraper.

Literature. By the turn of the century there was an outburst of literary activity which showed that the American mind was in reasonably healthy condition. Much of it was literature of protest, dealing with the various evils that had crept into American life during this era of industrial expansion, and as such it will be described in connection with the progressive movement. It may be pointed out here that it was thoroughly in keeping with the pragmatic character of American culture at this time for its leading literary figures to write on immediate and specific problems. Even those writers who were interested more in creating literature than in reforming society—like William Dean Howells, Hamlin Garland, or Winston Churchill[1]—were to be found using contemporary issues as their themes.

Art and Music. In art and music the United States still depended heavily on European talent, but Americans were nevertheless making some substantial contributions of their own. Apart from the expatriates, there was a respectable group of American painters in this period—such men as John La Farge, one of the earliest American impressionists; Winslow Homer and Thomas Eakins, who found ample inspiration in American scenes; and Frederic Remington, representative of a group that managed to capture the color and romance of the "Wild West." In sculpture, Augustus Saint-Gaudens and Daniel C. French were doing first-class work.

In general, it can be said that the United States was developing a cultural life commensurate with the growth of its national life as a whole, and within the broad structure of Western culture. Comparisons between American and European standards are likely to be misleading and useless. If the United States seemed to lag in certain areas of cultural achievement, it was not because Americans were intrinsically more materialistic than Europeans or less appreciative of intellectual and cultural values, but simply because American energies had been channeled in other directions by three centuries of settling a continent. What the United States lacked, it drew from the common cultural heritage of the West, and it was making an increasing contribution to that heritage in return.

[1] No relative of the British statesman, who in the early stages of his career was frequently confused with the then better known American novelist.

25

The Industrializing of Agriculture

The shift of population in the Western world from the country to the city was indicative of the progressive integration of agriculture into the structure of industrial economy. This process was relatively slow until 1850, but after that date it accelerated noticeably. The development of the railroad and the steamship facilitated the settlement and cultivation of new producing areas such as the American and Canadian West, Argentina, and Australia, since these areas, enjoying the advantage of fertile and cheap soil, needed only cheap and efficient transportation to enable them to compete effectively with European agriculture in its own market. Scientific and technological discoveries also increased the productivity of agriculture, with results that appeared to invalidate the predictions of Thomas Malthus. Although the population of the Western world grew rapidly, and a constantly greater proportion was engaged in occupations other than the production of food, the food supply grew even more rapidly. Farming ceased almost entirely to be conducted on a self-sufficient basis and concentrated instead on raising marketable crops.

SCIENCE AND TECHNOLOGY IN AGRICULTURE

The foundations of scientific agriculture had been laid in the eighteenth century, and progress thereafter was consistent. Research and experiment resulted in a stream of discoveries regarding better methods of cultivation and stockbreeding, improved varieties of crops, and new fertilizer. An epochal step was Baron von Liebig's pioneer work on soil chemistry (1840). Geographically, however, scientific agriculture was restricted to western Europe. The Russian peasant was too backward to be affected, and in the United States, despite the efforts of well-known figures like Washington and Jefferson and lesser known ones like Elkanah

Watson in New England and Edmund Ruffin in Virginia, the abundance of cheap land was a deterrent to scientific farming. It was much easier to "mine" the soil and then move west.

After 1860, however, the Federal government undertook active sponsorship of agricultural research and education. In 1862 the Department of Agriculture was created, although it was not given cabinet rank until 1889. The Morrill Act, also in 1862, granted land to the states for agricultural colleges, and sixty-nine of these institutions have been established, either as separate colleges or as parts of state universities. Subsequently, the Hatch Act of 1887 provided for the support of agricultural experiment stations in each state, and the Smith-Lever Act of 1914 granted funds to support agricultural extension services. The effect was to make readily available to American farmers advice and assistance on a generous scale and to counteract somewhat the wasteful practices of the past.

Mechanization. If the United States was slow to adopt scientific agriculture, it was well ahead of the rest of the world in the mechanization of farming. The vast open stretches of the prairies were peculiarly well adapted to the use of farm machinery, and the scarcity and high cost of labor in the West provided the economic incentive.[1]

The work of McCormick and Hussey before the Civil War has been described in an earlier chapter. Their machines were refined and improved, and innumerable new inventions followed, among which mention should be made of John F. Appleby's twine binder (1878), which eliminated the last manual process in harvesting grain, and Joshua Glidden's development of barbed wire (1874), which solved the problem of fencing on the treeless Great Plains. Throughout much of the "wheat belt" west of the Mississippi, harvesting came to be done by fleets of "combines," doing the whole operation mechanically and requiring only a small crew. Originally these machines were horse-drawn, but the steam engine and later the more efficient gasoline-powered tractor have brought about a reduction of the animal as well as the human labor force required for farming.

One great staple crop, cotton, long resisted mechanization. The availability of cheap agricultural labor in the South, both white and colored, was partially responsible, but a more important obstacle was the nature of the cotton crop, which required careful selection of the ripe bolls. The major change in Southern agriculture produced by the destruction of slavery and the plantation system was sociological rather than

[1] It may seem strange that there was a scarcity of labor in a period of rapid population growth, with immigration at its height and with unemployment a serious problem in the industrial areas of the United States. The explanation is that most of the increase in population, both natural and immigrant, went to the cities.

technical. The plantations were for the most part broken up into tenant farms, and because of the lack of money in the South at the end of the Civil War, sharecropping (that is, payment of a portion of the crop as rent) became widely prevalent. The system did occasionally permit a sharecropper to become an independent farmer. On the other hand, it encouraged continued concentration on one-crop agriculture—cotton or tobacco—since a landlord would insist on his tenants producing a crop that would find a ready market.

THE SETTLEMENT OF THE AMERICAN WEST

At the end of the Civil War the United States was settled as far west as a line from Minnesota to Texas, and on the Pacific coast. The vast territory in between was still the domain of fur traders, prospectors, and Indians. A single generation sufficed to occupy this area; in 1890 the Census Bureau reported that there was no longer an unbroken frontier line. There was still plenty of vacant land. The Bureau defined the frontier as the point beyond which settlement was less than two inhabitants per square mile, and two people per square mile is a long way from congestion. Indeed, more land was taken up under the Homestead Act in the thirty years after 1890 than in the thirty years prior to that date. It was, nevertheless, a matter of profound significance that the end of free land and the open West was in sight. The future development of the country would necessarily be intensive rather than extensive.

Three distinct waves of migration took part in the closing of the frontier. One was a mining advance into the Rocky Mountain area, composed mainly of prospectors moving eastward from California after the gold deposits there had been worked out. Beginning in 1860 gold and silver were found in Nevada, Colorado, Idaho, and Montana, each discovery precipitating a rush similar to the California gold rush of 1849. The richest strike was in Nevada, where the Comstock lode produced over $300,000,000 worth of silver in twenty years. The pattern was always the same. When the first influx of eager fortune seekers faded away with the exhaustion of the readily accessible deposits, it was replaced by organized mining companies, employing machine methods and requiring a substantial investment of capital. Eventually the attention of the mining companies extended from gold and silver to the less glamorous but equally profitable metals such as copper and lead, which the West possessed in abundance.

The Cattle Kingdom. The second element in the passing of the frontier came initially from Texas, in the form of the northward movement of cattle into the Great Plains which created the "cattle kingdom" and the American West of popular romance. Cattle had flourished in

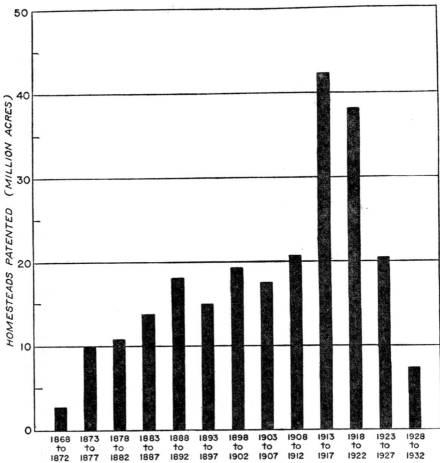

The Rise and Fall of Homesteading in the West. Homesteading east of the short-grass country had already slackened by 1868. These bars showing the acreage patented up to 1933 indicate, in the main, the sweep and decline of range-land homesteading. The sharp advance in the 1913–17 period is largely explained by the passage of the so-called Three-year Homestead Act of 1912. [From *The Western Range,* Senate Document 199 (U.S. Department of Agriculture 1936, p. 219).]

Texas since Spanish times, but their remoteness from Eastern markets limited their commercial value. The railroad changed the picture completely. The Civil War was hardly over before Texas ranchers began driving their herds north to meet the railroads pushing west, in the process making the happy discovery that cattle would flourish on the Great Plains and could even survive through the winter.

During the next twenty years the range cattle industry attained enormous proportions. Every year great herds, each numbering into the thousands, made the "long drive" from Texas along the Chisholm Trail, to fatten on the free grass of the plains until they were ready to be shipped to market. At first the cattle trail went across Oklahoma (then Indian territory) into Kansas; later, the steady advance of homesteading farmers pushed the cattlemen west into Colorado and Wyoming, whence the cow country extended north into Montana and across the Canadian border. By the early 1880's the number of cattle driven into the Great Plains was estimated at six million. "Cow towns" sprang up along the Western railroads—Abilene, Newton, Dodge City, Ogallala, Miles—to enjoy brief and unruly periods of prosperity. From there the cattle were shipped to the stockyards of Chicago and Kansas City, and then the newly devised refrigerator car took the processed meat to the Eastern markets.

At its height the cattle boom was both picturesque and profitable. Eastern and European capital flowed into stock raising, along with adventurously inclined individuals such as the young Theodore Roosevelt; and the man who tended the herds, the cowboy, became for most of the world the personification of the American West. But, as the range filled up, cattlemen found themselves confronted with problems. The public-land laws of the United States were designed for farmers and made no provision for large-scale stock raising. Barbed wire, useful as it was to the cattlemen, was even more useful to the homesteader, and the inexorable westward march of the farming frontier steadily encroached on the domain of the cattle kingdom. The farmers had the support of the national government and the public-land system; rather more important in an environment where disputes were customarily settled on the spot rather than by recourse to law, they had the advantage of superior numbers.

Much of the Great Plains region was admirably suited to cattle raising and very poorly suited to an agricultural system based on the conditions of the Mississippi valley, but Congress was extremely slow to recognize this fact. Not until 1916 was a Stock Raising Homestead Act passed, permitting the legal acquisition of 640 acres, and this was still too small a unit for ranching purposes. Grazing on the public domain remained unregulated until the passage of the Taylor Grazing Act in 1934, by which time only the least valuable parts of the public domain were left. The cattlemen, however, were responsible for the shortsighted overstocking of the range which precipitated the collapse of the cattle kingdom. By 1885 there were far more cattle on the open range than it would support, with the result that hundreds of thousands died when exceptionally severe winters struck in 1886 and 1887. The boom ended then, and stock raising was reorganized on a less ambitious scale but in more stable form.

Westward Migration. The agricultural advance into the Great Plains was the last and most rapid phase of the westward movement which had characterized American history since the founding of the first settlements. This movement was not interrupted in the least by the Civil War, and after the conflict was over its pace accelerated noticeably. Discharged veterans who were unwilling to return to their previous pursuits were attracted to the West by the prospect of free land or the lure of precious metals, as were numerous Southerners who saw no future in their devastated section. The most powerful stimulus, however, was provided by the railroads, which not only facilitated westward migration and provided access to markets for frontier products but also functioned as energetic colonizing agents.

Since the Western railroads of the United States were almost all built in advance of settlement, they had to create their own traffic by building up the areas they traversed. Some of them, notably the Great Northern, Burlington, and Santa Fe, built up extensive organizations to attract settlers. They maintained hundreds of agents in the East and Europe, sought out individuals and groups interested in moving to the American West, provided special immigrant trains and hostels, and aided settlers to secure land.

The new farming frontier had its own special problems. As settlement passed the 98th meridian, it entered a semiarid and timberless region, where agricultural technique had to be drastically revised. The lack of natural fencing material was remedied, as we have seen, by barbed wire, but human ingenuity was unequal to the task of providing an adequate supply of water. Irrigation was feasible only in limited areas. Elsewhere, deep wells pumped by windmills and the technique of "dry farming," whereby the moisture content of the soil was conserved as much as possible, alleviated the difficulty without removing it. Plains agriculture was essentially an uncertain gamble on each year's rainfall. If these conditions had been better appreciated at the start, penetration into the Great Plains might have proceeded more cautiously, but, as it happened, the first influx of settlers coincided with a succession of good seasons, which, coupled with the natural fertility of the virgin soil, raised oversanguine hopes regarding the agricultural potentialities of the region. Much of it was productive, for those with the skill and patience to cope with droughts, windstorms, and grasshoppers; much of it, on the other hand, should have been left to the cattlemen. The thin topsoil yielded bountiful crops at first, but the combination of repeated plowing and inadequate rainfall have too frequently turned it into dust.

The Land System. For the farmer as for the cattleman, a land system based on the conditions of the Middle West was unsatisfactory on the Great Plains. The 160-acre homestead was too small for dry farming and too big for irrigated land, which requires careful and intensive cultivation. Attempts were made to encourage irrigation by the Desert Lands Act of 1877, which authorized the sale of 640 acres of land at $1.25 an acre in return for an agreement to irrigate, and the Carey Act of 1894, which ceded arid lands to the states for irrigation purposes. Neither worked well, and in 1902 the Newlands Act made irrigation a direct responsibility of the Federal government. The needs of dry farming were finally recognized in 1909 by an act permitting the homesteading of 320 acres in certain states.

The Indians. One other problem had to be disposed of in settling the Great Plains. They were the last free domain of the Indians, and the plains tribes naturally resented this encroachment on their hunting grounds. From 1860 to 1880 there was almost constant warfare, which could have only one conclusion in spite of occasional incidents such as the annihilation of General Custer's command at the Little Big Horn in 1876. One after the other the Indian tribes gave up their hopeless struggle and settled down in reservations as wards of the government.

In its Indian policy the United States government has to be given credit for good intentions. It tried to deal justly with the Indians. Its good intentions, however, were marred by inept and occasionally corrupt administration of Indian affairs and by the refusal of Western settlers, whether farmers, cattlemen, or miners, to admit that the Indian had any rights whatsoever. White aggression was the usual cause of Indian wars, but it was always the Indians whom the army was called on to suppress. In the 1880's public conscience became sufficiently aroused to demand more equitable treatment for the Indians, and the Dawes Act of 1887 embodied a new policy. By it eventual dissolution of tribal organization, individual ownership of land, and admission of the Indians to citizenship were provided for. The effects of this policy have been varied, but at least the threatened extinction of the Indians was arrested, and some groups have benefited considerably. The Five Civilized Tribes of Oklahoma attained citizenship as early as 1901. They were the descendants of Eastern tribes which had been expelled from their homes in an earlier day, including the Cherokees driven out of Georgia during Andrew Jackson's administration in direct defiance of rulings of the Supreme Court, and it was poetic justice that the desolate waste to which they had been sent should turn out to be rich in deposits of oil.

AGRARIAN DISCONTENT

The technical improvements in agricultural methods and the physical expansion of the producing area were all to the good in so far as they increased the world's food supply, but they brought with them serious economic and social maladjustment for the rural population. In the United States the "farm problem" has been persistent since 1870, defying solution because of its extremely complex character.

The basis of the farmer's difficulties was the weakness of his position in a highly organized society. His operations had become integrated with industrial economy. He was dependent on railroad and steamship companies to transport his crops to market and on industrial corporations for machinery and supplies. The more extensive use of machinery and the gradual disappearance of free land meant that more capital was needed for agriculture, so that the volume of farm indebtedness was greatly increased. An incidental and important consequence was that farm tenancy, hitherto unusual in the United States, became more common.

If American agriculture had been producing only for the home market, the farmer's position might have been stronger, but the combination of improved agricultural methods and the great expansion of the producing area resulted in the supply of farm products increasing more rapidly than the demand for them. In the United States alone, the output of staple crops—wheat, corn, cotton, meat—multiplied from three to fivefold during the half century from 1860 to 1910. From a third to a half of these crops had to be sold in the world market, into which was being poured simultaneously the grains of Canada and the Ukraine and the meats of Australia and Argentina. While the farmer thus had to sell in a highly competitive market, he had to buy in the protected home market.

Agricultural Depression. The impact of these forces on American agriculture was heightened by the fact that the decade of the 1860's had been a relatively prosperous one for the farmer, with the demand for foodstuffs stimulated by the Civil War, the various European conflicts of the period, and poor harvests in Europe. After 1870 these favorable conditions disappeared, the extension of railway and steamship lines brought about a continuous opening of new agricultural areas, and a catastrophic decline in farm prices followed. In the thirty years after the Civil War, the price of wheat, corn, and cotton, the three great American staples, dropped by two-thirds. Farm income fell at the same time as productivity was rising; worse still, the declining price level made it increasingly difficult for the farmer to repay his debts.

The obvious remedy was organization for the control of output and prices, but while farm organizations were established, their effectiveness was always limited. The farm population was too numerous and too widely scattered to combine into a cohesive whole, and common grievances were frequently obscured by local interests. The Eastern farmer, for example, was more likely to regard the Westerner as a rival than a fellow sufferer. Moreover, agrarian discontent in the late nineteenth century focused on the more obvious, and on the whole superficial, aspects of the problem. The farmer of this period, believing, with some justification, that too much of the price paid by the consumer for farm products was absorbed in freight rates and storage charges and that he was the victim of a deflationary currency policy, concentrated his attention on those issues. Both, it was true, were elements in the farm problem, but neither went to the root of it.

The Granger Movement. Agrarian unrest flared up in the early 1870's in the form of the Granger movement, whose influence on railroad regulation has been discussed previously. When Oliver H. Kelley founded the Patrons of Husbandry in 1868 he had no intention of creating a political weapon. His purpose was merely to help break down the isolation of rural life. When farmers met in their local granges, however, it was inevitable that they should discuss their economic troubles and that they should use the organization ready at hand as a convenient instrument for pressing their demands. When it became a means of expressing farm discontent, the Granger movement swept the country, numbering some 800,000 members at the height of its career.

The Grange also tried to promote farmers' cooperatives in order to eliminate middlemen's profits. Few of these enterprises succeeded, mainly because farmers were inexperienced in their management and still too individualistic in outlook to give them the necessary support. The idea, nevertheless, survived and in the twentieth century made considerable progress under different auspices.

The Farmers' Alliances. When another period of poor harvests in Europe arrested the decline of American farm prices in the late 1870's the Granger movement reverted to its original social functions. The relief, however, was only temporary. Conditions became even worse in the 1880's, and the agrarian revolt acquired a greater intensity. It now found its outlet in the Farmer's Alliance, whose program of political and economic reform was much more sweeping than that of the Grangers. The Alliances favored the free coinage of silver, government ownership of the railroads, and reorganization of the banking system to provide more liberal credit. They also sponsored cooperatives on a more ambitious scale than the Grangers and engaged in widespread educational activities. Their leaders included a number of colorful figures: "Pitchfork Ben" Tillman of South Carolina, who became governor of that state and later United States senator as the champion of the "poor white" farmers of the South; Ignatius Donnelly, the Minnesota sage who "proved" the existence of the lost continent of Atlantis and the Baconian theory of Shakespeare; Mrs. Mary Lease, who urged Kansas farmers to raise "less corn and more hell." The great weakness of the Alliance movement was its inability to unite on a national basis. Latent sectional distrust and the racial issue divided it into two groups, the Northwestern Alliance and the Southern Alliance.

After 1890 the Alliances became identified with the Populist party, whose place in the American scene will be described later. The failure of Populism as an independent political force reacted unfavorably on the Alliances, and they passed out of existence shortly after the climactic election of 1896. Their disappearance was expedited by an improvement in economic conditions which, as had been the case with the Grange, caused the farmers to lose interest in organization. The long decline in farm prices was finally halted about 1900. While the farmer still had grievances, they were no longer quite so acute, and agrarian unrest became only one of several factors in the Progressive movement of the early twentieth century.

EUROPEAN AGRICULTURE UNDER OVERSEAS COMPETITION

The conditions which underlay the distress of the American farmer had a still more devastating effect on European agriculture. In crowded Europe land values and rents were high, and centuries of cultivation made extensive fertilization necessary for much of the soil. In the new producing areas, on the other hand, land was abundant and cheap, sometimes free, and the soil possessed its virgin fertility. This advantage in cost of production, combined with cheap and efficient transportation by rail and steamship, made it possible for a torrent of foodstuffs from overseas to swamp the European market. The consequent decline in farm prices affected the European farmer even more drastically than the American. Land values dropped, and in many regions the production of cereals was either drastically curtailed or abandoned altogether. Agricultural laborers, whose position throughout most of Europe was unattractive at best, were particularly hard hit by lowering of wages and unemployment.

One immediate consequence was a sharp decline in Europe's rural population. Some movement from country to city was certain to take place in any event, because of the greater appeal of city life and the increasing opportunities for employment in industry, but it would have been less pronounced if agricultural conditions had been brighter. There was also a mass exodus from the farms of Europe to the New World. From Norway and Sweden thousands of farmers, giving up the hopeless struggle to make a living in their homelands, went to establish a new Scandinavia in Minnesota and the Dakotas in the 1870's and 80's. German emigration to the United States was also heavy at this time. Later, agricultural dislocation was responsible to a large extent, although not entirely, for sending millions of southern Europeans to the United States.

In the face of these conditions agriculture in central and western Europe was forced to undergo extensive reorganization. Much of the land formerly devoted to grain crops was converted to pasturage and dairy farming or to market gardening. Production of wheat and other staples survived only in areas of high fertility or under governmental protection against outside competition. The remedies adopted varied in accordance with national conditions and requirements.

British Agriculture. British agriculture was by far the worst sufferer, since no effort was made to restrict the importation of foodstuffs from abroad. Free trade for Great Britain was a matter not only of principle but of very practical consideration. With the country so densely populated that it could not possibly produce all its own food, and with less than a fourth of the total population engaged in agriculture, it was manifestly poor policy, and poor politics, to attempt to aid the farmers by measures which would raise the price of food for the urban masses. Consequently, in spite of the agitation for "tariff reform" led by Joseph Chamberlain in the early years of the present century, the British public flatly refused to consider protection until after the First World War.

Forced to fend for itself, British agriculture displayed alarming structural weaknesses. It had stagnated since the great days of "Turnip" Townshend and Robert Coke. Although the experimental station at Rothamstead, founded in 1837, had been the first such institution in the world, agricultural education and research had since been neglected and was well below both American and German standards. Worst of all was the landholding system whereby great estates were cultivated by tenant farmers. Until the 1880's tenants had no property right in any improvements they might make on the land and, therefore, had little incentive to make any substantial capital investment. Rack-renting, the practice of raising rents because a tenant's improvements had added to the value of the land, was most prevalent in Ireland but not unknown in England and Scotland.

Apart from economic considerations, the heavy concentration of land ownership—more than half the area of the country was owned by about four thousand individuals—was considered undesirable on social grounds and persistent efforts were made to increase the number of small holdings. Little progress was made until the passage of the Small Holdings and Allotments Act of 1907, which empowered local authorities to acquire land for this purpose, and even then there was no radical change in the pattern of landholding. By this time agriculture had been largely reorganized along specialized lines and had recovered some degree of prosperity, although the food supply for the mass of the people was almost entirely imported.

German Agriculture. Although it was also strongly affected by competition abroad, Germany managed by systematic effort to preserve a substantial portion of its domestic agriculture. Scientific research was applied to farming with the same excellent results as in industry. For example, sugar beets were cultivated more intensively in Germany than anywhere else in the world, providing a crop that was not only highly profitable but extremely valuable in enriching the soil. Land unfit for cultivation, about a quarter of the total area of Germany, was devoted to forestry, under strict control by the various states to guarantee that the amount of timber cut should be matched by new planting.

Governmental policy toward agriculture was strongly influenced by the fact that the production of grain crops, which were most seriously exposed to foreign competition, was largely in the hands of the politically powerful *Junker* aristocracy of eastern Germany. It was pressure from this class, even more than from the industrialists, that led to the adoption of a high tariff by the Imperial government. Military considerations also played an important part. It was possible for Great Britain to accept dependence on outside sources for its food supply, because its naval superiority would keep those sources accessible in time of war. Germany had no such security and felt obligated to make a concerted effort to attain agricultural self-sufficiency. This goal was approached but not achieved. In 1914 Germany was producing about three-quarters of its own food.

France. In France the prevalence of small-scale peasant ownership acted as a deterrent to any general agricultural upheaval, although it also retarded the adoption of modern techniques of farming. France, like its neighbors, experienced a shift of population from country to city and a decline in the domestic production of grain, but the disturbance to its economy was much less pronounced, although it was necessary to impose a high tariff on agricultural products. Of the industrialized states of Europe, France alone was able to produce most of its own foodstuffs.

The Land Problem in Russia. Russia, and eastern Europe in general, occupied an entirely different agricultural position. This whole region was still economically a colonial area, with little industrial capacity of its own. Its broad expanses of rich soil approximated New World conditions, and although its farming methods were primitive, the low standard of living of its peasantry kept its costs of production at a level that enabled its products to compete freely in the world market.

Russia had its own farm problem as a consequence of the emancipation of the serfs by Alexander II. It had been recognized that freedom for the peasants meant little unless they were also given some land of their own, but the measures taken to achieve this end left the peasants thoroughly dissatisfied. Of the fifty million serfs in Russia in 1861, about half were on land owned by the crown and the rest were on the estates of the nobility. The first group offered no difficulty, since the Czar could do what he liked with his own property. For the others, however, the government had to purchase land from the aristocracy, under an arrange-

ment whereby the peasants were to repay the purchase price in installments over a period of forty-nine years. The peasants complained bitterly
that the allotments given them were too small and the "redemption payments" too high, and they seem to have been justified. Although about
half the land in Russia had been turned over to peasant ownership by
1905, individual holdings seldom exceeded 25 acres and were usually well
below that figure.

Moreover, since the village communities, or mirs, were made collectively responsible for the redemption payments, their individual members
were restricted from leaving in order to avoid their obligations, so that
some of the conditions of serfdom remained. When revolutionary unrest
in Russia became serious in the early years of the twentieth century, the
government deemed it advisable to conciliate the peasants. The balance
of the redemption payments was cancelled in 1904, and under Prime
Minister Stolypin land reforms were instituted, designed to give the
peasants full rights of ownership and improve their status by introducing
modern methods of agriculture. Little progress, however, had been made
by the time the First World War broke out, and none of the reforms went
to the heart of the problem—namely, the demand of the peasants for
more land. The inability of the Czarist regime to find a remedy for agrarian discontent was one of its most disastrous failures. In a country whose
population was 90 per cent rural, the attitude of the peasantry was likely
to be decisive in a crisis, and the outbreak of revolution in 1917 found this
normally conservative class disaffected.

26

Political and Social Trends
in Europe, 1870–1914

The period between the end of the Franco-Prussian War and the beginning of the First World War was in many ways a golden age in the history of Europe. European civilization had become a pattern for the entire world to copy, and during these years this civilization displayed its most favorable aspects. The phenomenal advance of industry and technology appeared to be creating a new era of plenty. No general wars disturbed the march of progress; although there were frequent conflicts in various parts of the world, all were localized and none affected the continent of Europe except in the chronically turbulent Balkans. In addition, representative government gave every indication of becoming firmly established from one end of the continent to the other.

Offsetting these hopeful developments were forces that threatened to upset the stability of European society. Nationalistic feeling grew steadily more intense, eventually generating antagonisms that made the preservation of peace impossible. Within each country were currents of unrest which caused periodic crises. It is with these internal problems that this chapter is concerned. While they differed in detail in each country, they had an underlying similarity in that they were, in the main, a combination of the continuing pressure of political liberalism and the demand for social reform produced by industrial expansion.

THE ADVANCE OF DEMOCRACY IN GREAT BRITAIN

Great Britain, with representative government securely established and thoroughly accustomed to reform by parliamentary methods, was in

416

a better position than any other major European state to deal with internal pressures. At the beginning of the period under consideration, Britain had made a great stride toward democracy in the Reform Bill of 1867, which granted manhood suffrage to most of the urban population. It had also made considerable progress in regulating industrial conditions, although the working classes still suffered from economic insecurity.

The Second Reform Bill had less immediate effect on British politics than might have been expected. The Liberal and Conservative parties maintained a steady alternation in power, with no vital cleavage on most issues. The Liberals were led until the 1890's by William Ewart Gladstone, a magnificent orator and master of finance, thoroughly imbued with the tenets of nineteenth-century individualism. He was responsible for two further advances toward complete democracy. The Forster Education Act of 1870 provided England with its first adequate system of state-supported free schools, and in 1884 the Third Reform Bill gave the rural population the right to vote on the same basis as the urban.

Gladstone's Conservative rival was the colorful Benjamin Disraeli. His domestic policy envisaged a "Tory democracy" in which the aristocracy and the masses would join forces against what he considered the selfishness and greed of the middle classes. In conformity with this ideal he sponsored the legislation of the 1870's strengthening the position of trade-unions. He did not, however, succeed in committing his party wholeheartedly to this program, and after his death in 1881 the Conservatives preferred to ignore domestic problems as much as possible and concentrate on imperial expansion.

The Irish Question. The most controversial issue was the perennial problem of Ireland. The attempt to amalgamate Ireland into the United Kingdom by the Act of Union in 1801 had not been successful; Irish nationalism persisted in spite of both coercion and concession. Until the 1880's the movement lacked unity of organization and objective. There was as much pressure for land reform as for self-government, and with good reason, since the Irish land system displayed absentee ownership at its worst. Organizations like the Irish Land League, committed to peaceful agitation, competed for public support with the openly terroristic Fenian Society.

In the early 1880's the various Irish groups were consolidated into a single Nationalist party by Charles Stewart Parnell, who was of English parentage and Protestant in religion. The Irish Nationalists introduced the American technique of filibustering into British politics and twice overthrew cabinets because they held the balance of power between the major parties. Finally, in 1886 Gladstone committed the Liberals to Home Rule and joined forces with Parnell. It was not mere opportunism on Gladstone's part. He had given much thought to the Irish problem and had been responsible for the disestablishment of the Anglican Church in Ireland in 1869 and the enactment of a land law in 1881 placing landlord-tenant relations under the supervision of a government commission.

His espousal of Home Rule touched off a political tempest of the first magnitude. Home Rule, it was asserted, would fatally weaken the British Empire. Moreover, a religious question was involved. The Protestants of Ulster objected to being placed under the control of the Catholic majority in southern Ireland, and their attitude was strongly supported in England. The Conservatives were unalterably opposed to Home Rule in any form. The Liberal party split on the issue; a minority of "Unionists" headed by Joseph Chamberlain seceded, and the Conservative-Unionist combination was strong enough to defeat the bill introduced by Gladstone. The Unionists were soon formally absorbed into the Conservative party.

The Home Rule cause suffered another disaster shortly afterward when Parnell's career was abruptly terminated by the revelation of his affair with Mrs. O'Shea. Gladstone tried again in 1894 and succeeded in pushing a Home Rule Bill through the House of Commons, but it was defeated in the House of Lords. The decision of the peers was confirmed by a Conservative victory in 1895.

The Conservatives attempted to remove the causes of Irish discontent by further land reform. The Wyndham Act of 1903 virtually eliminated absentee landlordism by providing for the purchase of land by the government for resale, on long-term credit, to the Irish peasantry. It was a statesmanlike measure; indeed, if it had been enacted about fifty years earlier, it might have made Ireland a satisfied member of the United Kingdom. By 1900, however, Ireland wanted self-government and would settle for nothing less. In retrospect, it is evident that Gladstone's judgment was far sounder than his opponents'. Given Home Rule in the 1890's, Ireland would probably have been as satisfied with its position in the British Empire as Canada or Australia. As it was, the refusal of Home Rule simply encouraged the rise of the more radical Sinn Fein organization, whose objective was complete independence for Ireland.

Social Reform. By the turn of the century economic issues were pressing to the foreground of British politics. The growing power of labor, the gradual spread of socialism, and the desire of the masses for some degree of security against unemployment and loss of earning power because of sickness or old age created a demand for sweeping social reforms, in the face of which the Liberals abandoned their historic devotion to *laissez faire* and became advocates of governmental action for the benefit of the underprivileged. The leading exponent of this new Liberalism was David Lloyd George, who represented in his own person the rising force of democracy in Britain. He was a Welshman, a commoner, a Dissenter, and he was not a "public-school" product—in short, he was the antithesis of the traditional governing class.

For a time, the attractions of imperial expansion served to divert attention from domestic issues, but after the disillusioning experience of the Boer War, enthusiasm for imperialism declined and public interest returned to internal problems. For these the Conservatives had no better solution than Joseph Chamberlain's plan for a renewal of tariff protection, with preferential rates between Britain and the Dominions. It was not enough. In 1905 the Liberals won a decisive victory at the polls and came into power with an unmistakable popular mandate for social reform.

The new administration possessed an exceptional array of talent. Sir Edward Grey, as Foreign Minister, was destined to play a leading role in a period of international crisis; John Morley, historian and philosopher, was made Secretary of State for India and sponsored the granting of a limited measure of self-government to that country; Winston Churchill, a recent convert from the Conservatives, with whom he disagreed on the tariff question, held several offices, ending as First Lord of the Admiralty. In the all-important field of social legislation, the guiding spirit was Lloyd George, operating from the strategic post of Chancellor of the Exchequer.

His first major step was an Old Age Pension Act in 1908, providing small pensions, paid entirely by the state, to all people who had reached the age of seventy, and whose income was below a specified figure. This law naturally increased the expenditures of the government, and since Britain was simultaneously involved in an expensive naval race with Germany, additional revenue had to be found. In 1909, therefore, Lloyd George introduced his "people's budget," which proposed to raise the needed funds by heavy taxes on landowners. The inspiration for this scheme came from Henry George, whose economic thinking greatly influenced his British namesake. (The two men were not related.) The budget passed the House of Commons, but the House of Lords, always predominantly Conservative and composed overwhelmingly of landowners, rejected it.

The Parliament Act. This action precipitated a constitutional crisis. The lower House indignantly asserted that it had sole jurisdiction in financial matters; the Lords retorted that this was no finance bill, but a social revolution. Parliament was dissolved in January, 1910, and the question submitted to the people. The result was that the Liberals were returned to power, but with their numbers reduced so that they were dependent on the support of the Labour party, now forty-five strong, and the still solid phalanx of Irish Nationalists. Both groups demanded a *quid pro quo* for their votes, the Labourites requiring further social legislation and the Irish a revival of Home Rule.

The popular verdict was clear enough so that the Lords submitted and passed the budget. The Liberals, however, now determined once and for all to break the upper chamber's annoying habit of functioning as a Conservative stronghold when the Liberals were in power. Another election was held in December, 1910, on the issue of curbing the House of Lords, with the Liberal-Labour-Irish coalition retaining substantially the same position as before. The government then introduced the bill which in due course became the Parliament Act of 1911. It provided that any money bill passed by the House of Commons must be passed by the House of Lords within a month; if the upper House did not give its assent within this time, the bill became law automatically. Any nonfinancial measure could become law without the approval of the House of Lords if it was passed by Commons three times over a period of two years. The Act empowered the Speaker of the House of Commons to certify a measure as a money bill, and it also fixed the maximum life of a Parliament at five years, except in emergencies. The Parliament Act is one of the landmarks of British constitutional development. It deprived the House of Lords of any real share in the legislative process, making it little more than an advisory body. It also provided for the payment of salaries to members of the House of Commons—a clear indication that the propertied classes no longer monopolized British political life. The Lords were, of course, opposed to the Parliament Act and rejected it when it first appeared before them. Prime Minister Asquith then resorted to the time-honored weapon of threatening to create enough new peers to pass the bill, whereupon the Lords, as on similar occasions in the past, gave way.

The Liberal Program. With this obstacle surmounted, the Liberals were free to carry out the remainder of their program and also pay their political debts. Prior to 1911 they had enacted, besides the Old Age Pension Law, a Workmen's Compensation Act (1906), making compensation mandatory for sickness or injury incurred in the course of employment, an eight-hour day in the mining industry (1908), and minimum wages in certain occupations (1909). Crowning this structure was the National Insurance Act of 1911, which provided for compulsory insurance against sickness and disability for all employed persons whose wages were below a specified level, and insurance against unemployment in the industries where it was most prevalent. The insurance funds were established by contributions from employers, workers, and the government. The sickness and disability provisions of the act were based on Germany's experience with similar legislation adopted there in the 1880's, but the idea of insuring against unemployment was a new experiment.

An attempt was made to reward the Irish Nationalists for their support by introducing a new Home Rule Bill. It passed the House of Commons late in 1912 and was promptly rejected by the House of Lords, so that, under the provisions of the Parliament Act, two years would have to elapse before the bill could become law. In this interval tension in Ireland mounted until civil war appeared inevitable. The people of Ulster formed a military organization, the Ulster Volunteers, to resist Home Rule by force, whereupon the people of southern Ireland countered by organizing their own Nationalist Volunteers. It was an extraordinary situation. Ulster was threatening rebellion against the British government because it wanted to remain united to Great Britain; the rest of Ireland was preparing to give armed support to the British government in order to enforce separation from Great Britain.

Just before the two-year time limit expired, however, the First World War broke out, and Parliament suspended further consideration of Home Rule. If Britain was satisfied, Ireland was not. The moderately inclined Nationalists lost their hold on the people, and the Sinn Fein movement grew rapidly, until it precipitated the Easter Rebellion of 1916. The uprising was crushed and most of its leaders executed. One of the few to escape was Eamon de Valera, whom the British preferred not to catch because he was American-born and in 1916 Great Britain did not want to alienate American public opinion.

The Dominions. Ireland's troubles stand in striking contrast to the steady and almost unobtrusive development of self-government in Britain's overseas dominions, the parts of the empire whose population was predominantly European. Following the precedent established by the creation of the Dominion of Canada, the Commonwealth of Australia was organized in 1900, the Dominion of New Zealand in 1907, and the Union of South Africa in 1910, all with complete autonomy in internal matters, although they continued to be represented by Great Britain in foreign affairs. The wisdom of this liberal colonial policy was seen in the wholehearted support given to the mother country when war came. In South Africa, it is true, some unreconciled Boers seized the opportunity to revolt, but they were put down by local forces under the leadership of two of their own former comrades-in-arms, Louis Botha and Jan Christian Smuts.

SOCIAL UNREST IN GERMANY

The German Empire began its career in 1871 with bright prospects. It had replaced France as the dominant military power of Europe, it was about to undergo a great economic expansion, and its political system, although carefully designed to keep control of essential functions in the hands of the monarchy, was sufficiently liberal to give the people a sense of having a share in the government. Nevertheless, the architect of the structure, Bismarck, now Chancellor of the Empire, was not satisfied. The German Empire was his creation, and for the remainder of his public career his policy was directed at attacking any forces, internal or external, which might threaten its integrity.

The first object of his suspicion was the Catholic Church. To Bismarck, and to rabid German nationalists in general, Catholics necessarily were divided in their loyalty, and the Chancellor in any event resented the existence in Germany of a powerful organization which he could not control. Developments within the Church gave Bismarck an opportunity to attack it. The *Syllabus of Errors* issued by Pius IX in 1864, condemning liberty of conscience, secular education, and divorce, antagonized the middle-class liberalism of the period, and the promulgation of the doctrine of papal infallibility in matters of faith and morals by the Vatican Council in 1870 aroused further opposition.

The Kulturkampf. Taking advantage of the widespread spirit of anticlericalism, Bismarck attacked Catholicism in what was termed the *Kulturkampf.* He began in 1872 by pushing a law through the Reichstag expelling the Jesuits from Germany. Then, since the Catholic states of the empire could not be expected to support his program, the rest of the campaign was waged through the Prussian legislature. Between 1873 and 1875 a series of laws known as the May laws—because the first was passed in May, 1873—or Falk laws—after the Prussian Minister of Education who was their official sponsor—placed under state control the Catholic clergy and educational institutions and suppressed a number of religious orders.

The German Catholics fought back vigorously. They refused to obey the Falk laws and counterattacked politically through the Center party, whose numbers increased considerably during this decade. By 1878 Bismarck was aware that the *Kulturkampf* had failed, and he was too shrewd a politician to persist in a hopeless cause. Furthermore, he was coming to see in the rise of socialism a more serious threat to the internal stability of the Empire than the fundamentally conservative Catholic Church. Consequently, when the accession of a new pope, Leo XIII, with more moderate views than his predecessor, offered Bismarck a chance to withdraw gracefully from his anti-Catholic position, the *Kulturkampf* was quietly abandoned.

Growth of Socialism. The growth of socialism as an effective force in Germany began with the organization of the Social Democratic party at Gotha in 1875. Bismarck found a pretext for attempting to crush the movement when two efforts were made in 1878 to assassinate the Emperor. Laws were immediately passed prohibiting socialist meetings and suppressing their publications, although Social Democrats could still be elected to the Reichstag.

Bismarck was fully aware that the German workers were attracted to socialism because they had genuine grievances and that repression would not in itself solve the problem. He decided, therefore, to eliminate working-class discontent by using the authority of the state to give the masses economic security; his hope was that they would then be grateful to the existing government and forget about revolution. Bismarck's program was carried out in three steps: (1) a Sickness Insurance Law (1883), (2) an Accident Insurance Law (1884), and (3) an Old-age Pension Act (1889). All were compulsory and were supported by contributions from employers, workers, and the government. The socialists opposed this legislation because they feared precisely the result that Bismarck desired—namely, that the workers would become satisfied with capitalism. As it turned out, they might as well have saved their energy. The German working class accepted the benefits of the social-insurance laws but continued to vote the Social Democratic ticket just the same.

The antisocialist campaign, in fact, was as dismal a failure as the *Kulturkampf.* Bismarck himself would not admit defeat, but his long career was approaching its close. The Emperor William I, whose relations with the Iron Chancellor had always been close and cordial, died in 1888. His son, Frederick III, survived him by only a few months, and was succeeded by the young, aggressive, and ambitious William II. Since the new Emperor intended to direct affairs of state in person, a clash between him and Bismarck was inevitable, and in 1890 the chancellor resigned. William, who wanted to be popular with all his subjects, then had the repressive legislation repealed.

Constitutional Problems under William II. From 1890 to 1914, Germany's internal politics consisted largely of a struggle by liberal elements to restrict the power of the crown. William II was himself largely responsible for forcing this issue. He was well meaning but emotionally unstable, perhaps because of his acute sensitiveness to the fact that he had a withered arm,[1] and he was given to tactless and blundering public observations on both domestic and foreign problems. His activities produced a demand that Germany be made a genuine constitutional monarchy with the chancellor and the other ministers responsible to the Reichstag rather than to the emperor. Other reforms, such as the abolition of the three-class system of voting in Prussia, were also desired.

This sentiment expressed itself in a phenomenal increase of Social Democratic strength. That party, although still committed in principle to the ultimate extinction of capitalism, also adopted a program of "minimum demands," including the aforementioned political reforms, which could be achieved within the existing structure of society, and these minimum demands attracted the votes of nonsocialist liberals. In the election of 1912 the Social Democrats won 35 per cent of the total vote and became the largest single party in the Reichstag, although they still did

---

[1] This handicap contributed to his Anglophobia. His mother was English, a daughter of Queen Victoria, and he blamed her and her people for his misfortune.

not have a majority. It is conceivable that a few more years of peace would have seen the German liberals achieve their objective, but the war intervened, and democracy in Germany later had to be attempted under very unfavorable conditions.

THE TROUBLES OF THE THIRD REPUBLIC

France, unlike its neighbors, had to face the problems of the new industrial era with a government whose stability was, to say the least, uncertain. The Third Republic was, as we have seen, the creation of men who really wanted a monarchy but were unable to agree on a monarch. While it was undoubtedly acceptable to a majority of the French people, it always had to encounter the hostility of substantial and irreconcilable elements, eager to capitalize on any weakness it might display. In the opposition were listed the old aristocracy, still trying to repeal the French Revolution, the army officers, largely drawn from the upper classes, the Catholic Church, distrustful of republican anticlericalism, and the wealthy businessmen, fearful of the growth of socialism.

The republican victories in the elections of 1877 and 1878 gave the new regime an apparently firm foundation. Marshal MacMahon was ousted from the presidency and a staunch but inconspicuous republican substituted. In the decade after 1878 the government, whose outstanding statesman after Gambetta's death in 1882 was Jules Ferry, engaged in vigorous colonial expansion abroad and reform of the educational system at home. The public schools were thoroughly reorganized, both because it was felt that the superiority of the German schools had been a contributing factor in the victory of 1870, and because the republicans desired to weaken clerical influence in French education.

Political Unrest. Political calm, however, was short-lived. In the late 1880's evidence of corruption in high places, particularly a spectacular scandal in connection with the bankruptcy of the Panama Canal project undertaken between 1881 and 1887 by Ferdinand de Lesseps, stimulated vigorous attacks on the Republic. There is nothing to indicate that public morality in France was any lower than in the United States at this period, and certainly it was no lower than in the France of the July Monarchy or the Second Empire. It was therefore an ominous sign that scandals which a stable regime could have shrugged off were elevated to the level of national crises.

A menace of a different kind was personified by General Boulanger, a picturesque soldier who for a time fancied himself as another Napoleon. That he lacked the necessary qualities was demonstrated by the fact that, when the government finally plucked up enough courage to charge him with conspiracy, he lost his nerve and fled to Belgium, later to commit suicide on his mistress's grave. Nevertheless his brief appearance in the limelight revealed that the "man on horseback" had a strong appeal to disturbingly large sections of French opinion—those for whom the passion for *revanche* on Germany for the humiliation of 1870 overrode all other considerations, and those who wanted a "strong man" to keep the masses in their place.

The Dreyfus Case. The disruptive factors in French life came to a head with the Dreyfus Affair of the 1890's. Captain Alfred Dreyfus was convicted by court-martial in 1894 of selling military secrets to "a foreign power" (Germany) and was banished to Devil's Island for life. Subsequently it developed that the documents pointing to his guilt were forgeries, but the officer who pointed this out, Colonel Picquart, merely succeeded in getting himself transferred to one of the remoter parts of Tunisia. Dreyfus's cause, however, was then taken up by others, including Georges Clemenceau and the novelist Emile Zola, who exposed the facts of the case in a blistering pamphlet called *J'Accuse.*

Presently the whole nation took sides. The military authorities refused to concede that a mistake might have been made, and they were supported by the royalists and a strong section of Catholic opinion. In addition, the fact that Dreyfus was Jewish served to reveal an ugly undercurrent of anti-Semitism. On the other side, the republicans took alarm at what appeared to be a conspiracy on the part of their enemies. After a second court-martial in 1899 refused to accept new evidence and reaffirmed Dreyfus's guilt, "with extenuating circumstances," the President of the Republic pardoned him. Since this action still implied guilt, the case was taken to the civil courts, and in 1906 Dreyfus's innocence was finally established. He was restored to his rank in the army, while his defender, Colonel Picquart, was brought back from the desert and made Minister of War.

Church and State. The political consequences of the Dreyfus affair were considerable. In 1899 the various republican factions joined forces in a Ministry of Republican Defense, determined to eradicate the monarchist influences in the army and the Church. The reform of the army was only partially carried out, since the danger of war was too great to permit any drastic changes in personnel. The reversal of the verdict in the Dreyfus case, however, was a clear assertion of the superiority of the civil power. The church had to face the full force of republican wrath, a situation for which the leaders of French Catholicism had only themselves to blame, since most of them had chosen to ignore Pope Leo XIII's advice, given in 1892, that the church was not committed to any one form of government and that French Catholics should accept the republic.

The first step in the anticlerical campaign was the Associations Law of 1901, which imposed stringent restrictions on religious associations—that is, monastic orders—and resulted in the dissolution of many of them. The educational activities of the surviving associations were abolished in 1904. Then, in 1905, the Separation Law repealed Napoleon I's Concordat of 1801 and withdrew state support from any form of religion. Church property was taken over by the government but was to be turned over in trust to associations of laymen. For a time a serious crisis threatened when Pope Pius X forbade Catholics to form such associations, but the government, even with Clemenceau as prime minister, moved cautiously and eventually amended the law so that religious services could be held.

Once it had weathered its various crises, the French republic began to devote some attention to questions of social reform. In this field France lagged behind her industrial neighbors. Not until 1906 did the ten-hour day become the legal standard for French industry, and the only measure of social security to be adopted was an Old-age Pension Law in 1910.

UNREST IN RUSSIA

On the other side of Europe, the sluggish Russian Empire was feeling the impulse of the forces of modern society. Alexander II's liberalism disappeared when he discovered that limited reforms merely created a demand for more. His regime gradually returned to the old ways of repression, until his disappointed liberals finally turned in desperation to terrorism and assassinated the Czar himself in 1881.

Alexander III (1881–1894) was a reactionary autocrat who intensified the suppression of revolutionary agitation and adopted a policy of extreme nationalism, which involved the persecution and attempted "Russification" of minority groups with the Empire. The guiding spirits of his reign were Pobiedonostsev, Procurator of the Holy Synod (administrative head of the Russian Church), who regarded all Western ideas with distaste, and Count Plehve, Minister of the Interior, under whom the secret police reached new heights of arbitrary power. As part of the Russification process, Plehve encouraged violent attacks on the Jews.

Alexander's successor, Nicholas II, was a vacillating individual who had the misfortune to come to the throne just as Russia began to be noticeably influenced by industrialism. Count Witte's program for encouraging the building of factories and railways increased Russia's economic resources, but politically it meant the strengthening of the Russian middle class and the appearance of an industrial proletariat which, denied any other outlet for discontent, turned to revolutionary socialism.

Unrest came to a head with the outbreak of the Russo-Japanese War in 1904. The appalling mismanagement of the war and the humiliation of defeat by a much smaller opponent raised discontent with the government to new heights. The government's only answer was given on 22 January 1905, when a great crowd marched through St. Petersburg to present a petition for reform. The marchers were led by a priest, Father Gapon, who was the head of a group of labor unions sponsored by the government, but instead of meeting the "Little Father," they were greeted by volleys of rifle fire from a battalion of Cossacks. The public reaction was immediate and sharp. Strikes broke out and spread to all classes of people until life in Russia was brought almost to a complete stop. The movement was largely spontaneous, but it acquired some organization through a "Soviet," or council, of trade-union representatives, among whom was young Leon Trotsky.

Creation of the Duma. In the face of irresistible popular pressure, the government had to give way. Nicholas issued a manifesto (30 October 1905) promising to guarantee civil liberties and to hold elections for a legislative body, the Duma, whose consent would be required for all laws. Manhood suffrage was established; the cabinet remained responsible to the Czar. Russia, it appeared, had at last started on the road to constitutionalism, but that assumption foundered on Nicholas's duplicity. The Czar had yielded to necessity with no intention of keeping his word once the immediate crisis had passed.

The first Duma, which met in 1906, was composed principally of representatives who wished to carry the reforming process further, but its efforts were persistently blocked by the Czar, and after a short session it was dissolved for "refusal to cooperate with the government." About half of the members retired to Viborg in Finland, where they issued a manifesto calling on the people to support them by refusing to pay taxes or obey the conscription laws. The response was disappointing, but a second Duma proved to be even more radical than the first, in spite of strenuous efforts on the part of the government to have "official" candidates elected. The liberal Count Witte, who had been made Prime Minister in 1905, was replaced by the more conservative Stolypin, who tried, as we have seen, to win peasant support by promising additional land reforms. The new Duma, nevertheless, turned out to be preponderantly socialist, whereas its predecessor had been controlled by the Constitutional Democrats, or Cadets, whose ambitions were limited to the establishment of parliamentary government on the British model. The second Duma's career was also brief and stormy, and after its dissolution Nicholas revised the franchise so as to give greater weight to the upper classes. This expedient at last gave Nicholas an assembly that suited him, but it did nothing to eradicate the causes of popular unrest. The government, it is true, did not revert to the blind reaction of Alexander III. Nicholas II cast himself in the role of "enlightened despot," but his good intentions were invariably nullified by his own lack of will power and the incompetence and corruption of Russian officialdom.

ITALY, SPAIN, AND THE DUAL MONARCHY

Although the social problems with which Europe had to contend can best be studied in the four major powers, some others have played an important enough part in modern world politics to make an understanding of their internal history desirable. Italy, like Germany, was a conspicuous product of nineteenth-century nationalism, but the new Italian kingdom failed to match the phenomenal growth of the German Empire. Italy lacked the material resources to be a really great power, industrial or military, and in that fact lay the explanation for most of Italy's troubles. The country tried too hard to "keep up with the Joneses." While a flourishing industrial society developed in the north, in Piedmont and Lombardy, the agrarian south was impoverished and plagued by lawlessness, the heritage of the Bourbon misrule. Conditions were so bad that millions of Italian peasants emigrated, most of them to the United States and South America.

The "Prisoner of the Vatican." Curiously enough, in overwhelmingly Catholic Italy relations between church and state were worse than in any other European country. When the Italians occupied Rome in 1870, Pius IX immured himself in the Vatican and refused to recognize the legality of the Kingdom of Italy, a policy continued by his successors. The government's offer of a cash indemnity for the annexation of the Papal States and a guarantee of the inviolability of the Vatican was rejected, and Catholics were forbidden to vote or hold office under the Italian crown. This ban on political activity was subsequently modified in the early years of the twentieth century, when the spread of socialism and syndicalism among the industrial workers of northern Italy reached such alarming proportions that it seemed advisable for the church to give some support to the established authorities. Officially, however, nonrecognition remained in effect and the pope continued to be the "prisoner of the Vatican."

Despite these problems, Italy was much better off than her Mediterranean neighbor, Spain. There, the restoration of the Bourbons after the fall of Napoleon I precipitated a bitter conflict between liberalism and conservatism which plunged Spain into a long cycle of civil wars and revolutions. Finally, in 1868, the country was left without any acceptable government, and the search for a king to restore stability led to the incident that provoked the Franco-Prussian War. After the failure to secure a Hohenzollern prince, the Spaniards turned to a young son of Victor Emmanuel, Amadeo of Savoy, who became king in 1871. The hostility of the church to the House of Savoy was so great, however, that Amadeo abdicated after a reign of two years. A republic followed, but it collapsed in 1875 after a turbulent career, and the Bourbon dynasty was restored, with a constitution providing for a legislature (Cortes) and a responsible ministry.

Spain then enjoyed a long period of internal peace, although not of complete content. As in the rest of the world, industrialism appeared with its customary manifestation of social unrest. The middle class objected to the power of the aristocracy and the clergy, while the industrial workers turned to the revolutionary doctrines of anarchism and syndicalism. Separatist movements among the Catalans of the northeast and the Basques of the northwest were also a disturbing element. Finally, Spaniards could hardly be expected to find satisfaction in their country's lowly position as a world power, a status dramatized by the loss of its last American possessions in the Spanish-American War.

The Hapsburg Empire. A state which was rated as a major power was the Dual Monarchy of Austria-Hungary, in spite of internal pressures that constantly threatened disintegration. Nationalism, a unifying force in most other European countries, was an insoluble problem for the Hapsburg Empire. The *Ausgleich* of 1867 was reasonably satisfactory to the Germans of Austria and the Magyars of Hungary, but it offered nothing to the other racial groups scattered throughout the monarchy. Particularly disappointed were the Czechs of Bohemia and Moravia, who felt themselves to be economically and culturally the equals of their German neighbors. Czech proposals for "trialism"—a German-Czech-Magyar combination—instead of "dualism" were ignored. Besides the Czechs, the monarchy had minority groups of Slovaks, Poles, Ruthenians, Italians, Jews, Rumanians, Croats, Slovenes, and Serbs. All not only resented the domination of the Germans and Magyars but as a rule were unfriendly to each other, a situation which the imperial authorities found exceedingly useful, as it enabled them to play off the rival racial groups against each other.

The two halves of the Empire were quite dissimilar in their development. Austria became industrialized and moderately liberal; in fact, concessions late in the nineteenth century so incensed the Germans that rioting broke out, beginning when German and Czech members of the legislature, the *Reichsrat,* chose to express their feelings by throwing inkstands at each other. Manhood suffrage was adopted in 1907, partly in the hope that an extension of democracy would weaken racial antagonism, which it did not. Hungary remained an agrarian society, with a mass of peasants dominated by an incredibly reactionary landed aristocracy. The right to vote was narrowly restricted so as to maintain Magyar supremacy.

Ramshackle and torn by dissension as it was, the Dual Monarchy gave Central Europe a degree of stability that has been sadly lacking since the Hapsburg dominions fell apart in 1918. The two sections, the industrial west and the agricultural east, complemented each other economically, and the existence of a central government for the whole region kept the discordant races in some semblance of order. The collapse of the Hapsburg Empire was perhaps inevitable in an era of fanatical nationalism, but it is unfortunate that no substitute was found for the political unity it represented.

27

The Progressive Movement
in the United States

The reaction to the problems of industrialization in the United States had its own distinctive characteristics. For one thing, it was slower to develop than in Europe. Until the closing decade of the nineteenth century, the physical expansion of the country absorbed the energies of the American people so completely that little attention was given to the effects of the process on American life in general. The initial outbursts of discontent among farmers and industrial laborers were sporadic, disappearing readily in the face of improved economic conditions; there was no constant pressure from below such as existed in Europe. Then, when progressivism rose as a potent reform movement, its direction was governed by the strongly individualistic pattern of American thought. Socialism attracted so slight a following in the United States as to be inconsequential, and the progressives displayed little interest in social security legislation of the type adopted in Germany and Great Britain. Their program was based on the premise that the curtailment of monopoly and special privilege and the strengthening of direct control of government by the people would enable the individual to take care of himself.

THE CURRENCY AND THE TARIFF

American politics during most of the quarter century following the Civil War showed little surface evidence of being affected by the vast changes that were taking place in American life. Elections were a monotonous repetition of artificial emotions. The Republicans harped end-

431

lessly on the Civil War; the Democrats retorted with charges of corruption in public office. Both parties sedulously avoided controversial issues as much as possible.

Nevertheless, the pressures of economic change had a disconcerting habit of making themselves felt. The unrest among the farmers was a political force that could hardly be ignored. The antirailroad crusade of the Grangers was confined to legislation by a few states and did not become a national issue until the late 1880's; the agrarian demand for expansion of the currency was, however, a different matter. It began immediately after the Civil War, when a decision had to be reached regarding the $450,000,0000 of greenbacks issued by Congress during the war. The business community favored their gradual retirement from circulation, or at least their redemption in gold, while the farmers, on the other hand, wanted further issues of legal-tender paper money in order to raise prices.

The Greenback Issue. The question was first raised when Senator George Pendleton of Ohio, a Democrat, proposed that the Civil War debt be paid in greenbacks, but this "Ohio idea" was killed by the victory of the "sound-money" Republicans in 1868. Even the Republicans, however were startled by a decision of the Supreme Court in 1870 (*Hepburn v. Griswold*), questioning the right of Congress to issue unsecured legal-tender currency, because, if the greenbacks were unconstitutional, the sudden contraction of the volume of money in circulation was going to have a disastrous effect on prices. Two opportune vacancies on the Supreme Court relieved the situation; the men appointed by President Grant to fill these posts had more lenient views on greenbacks than their predecessors, and in 1871 the Court reversed itself (*Knox v. Lee*) to rule that the issuance of the greenbacks had been a proper exercise of Congress's war powers.[1]

The status of the greenbacks was settled by the Resumption Act of 1875, which provided for the redemption of all United States currency in specie by 1 January 1879. The "cheap-money" school, arguing that an expanding country needed more money rather than less, fought back, and a Greenback party displayed considerable strength in the congressional elections of 1878. Resumption, however, took place on schedule, materially assisted by heavy exports of American grain to Europe which caused a flow of gold into the United States and bolstered the country's reserves of specie. It was small consolation to the Greenbackers that some $340,-000,000 of the legal-tender notes were kept in circulation.

---

[1] In 1884 the matter was finally settled in *Julliard v. Greenman,* in which the Court took what would appear to be the obvious position—that its constitutional authority to regulate the currency gave Congress the power to issue legal-tender money at any time.

Greenback agitation died out after 1878, partly because of a temporary rise in farm prices, but mainly because interest in expansion of the currency turned to the silver question. Until 1870 most nations of the world had been on a bimetallic monetary standard of gold and silver, the principal exception being Great Britain, which had adopted a gold standard in 1815. The great disadvantage of bimetallism is that gold and silver are not only standards of monetary value but commodities whose value fluctuates, so that periodic readjustment of the specie content of the currency is necessary if the two are to be kept in equilibrium. With the increasing complexity of economic life in the nineteenth century, a monometallic standard appeared to offer greater stability. Germany went on a gold basis in 1871; France and Italy followed suit a year later, along with several smaller states; and the United States dropped silver from its coinage in 1873. This act, which passed Congress unnoticed and without discussion, merely recognized an existing situation. For the previous twenty years the legal ratio making sixteen ounces of silver (to be exact, 15.988 ounces) the equivalent of one ounce of gold for coinage purposes had been less than the market value of silver as bullion, and the metal had accordingly disappeared from circulation.

The Free-silver Agitation. But, just at the time when the demand for silver was thus diminishing, tremendous new deposits were being discovered in the American West. The result, of course, was a sharp decline in the price of silver, until by 1875 its market value was below the 16 to 1 ratio. Too late, the silver miners awoke to the implications of the coinage law of 1873, which they proceeded to denounce as the "Crime of '73," a conspiracy on the part of unspecified financial interests to enrich themselves at the expense of the masses. Their demand for the restoration of bimetallism was supported by all who favored cheap money, since the remonetization of silver offered an attractive method of achieving their desires. A silver currency would avoid the risks inherent in issues of unsecured paper money; yet because the metal was now so abundant, its unlimited coinage at the former 16 to 1 ratio would permit almost indefinite expansion of the currency.

The new gospel of "free silver" as a cure for economic ills spread amazingly fast. In 1878 it had acquired enough strength to push the Bland-Allison Act through Congress over the veto of President Hayes, requiring the Treasury to purchase from two to four million dollars' worth of silver a month and coin it. The act was a compromise which satisfied no one. For the silverites, it was not enough; for the champions of the gold standard, it was too much; and the amount of silver added to the currency was too small to have any effect on prices. In 1889 the admission of six new Western states (North and South Dakota, Montana, Washington, Idaho, and Wyoming) strengthened the silver forces in Congress, and in the following year the Sherman Silver Purchase Act was passed. Eastern Republicans swallowed their distaste for the measure and voted for it because they needed the support of their Western colleagues for the McKinley tariff bill. The Silver Purchase Act required the Treasury to purchase 4,500,000 ounces of silver each month at the market price and pay for it with notes, redeemable in either gold or silver.

The sole effect of this act was to create uncertainty about the financial policy of the United States government. When depression came in 1893, the hoarding of gold by timid individuals resulted in a severe drain on the Treasury's gold reserve, since silver certificates were presented in quantities for redemption in gold. President Cleveland, to whom the gold standard was an unalterable article of faith, immediately called a special session of Congress to repeal the Silver Purchase Act. Hard times, however, had intensified the demand of the West and South for cheap money, and repeal was carried only after a bitter fight in which party lines split. To Cleveland's disappointment, the Treasury's gold reserve continued to dwindle, and he resorted to selling bonds for gold on the New York money market. This expedient was something less than satisfactory. The bankers took the bonds on favorable terms and procured the gold with which to buy them by withdrawing it from the Treasury in exchange for greenbacks and silver certificates, so that while the government's indebtedness increased, its gold supply did not. After two bond issues had turned out in this way, the assistance of J. P. Morgan was invoked to float a third, with an agreement that half the gold should be imported from Europe and none withdrawn from the Treasury. This step, and a fourth bond issue sold directly to the public in 1895, raised the gold reserve to what was considered the safe level of $100,000,000.

The free-silver advocates thoroughly disapproved of these proceedings. They insisted that a much simpler remedy for the crisis, and one which would benefit the mass of the people rather than the bankers of Wall Street, was the removal of all restrictions on the coining of silver and its use as a specie reserve in place of gold. Within the President's own party revolt was open and widespread, and the "silver Democrats," led by "Silver Dick" Bland of Missouri and young William Jennings Bryan of Nebraska, served notice that the issue would be fought out in the next presidential campaign. The Republicans were also split, but the party's strong ties with Eastern business interests made silver sentiment in its ranks less pronounced.

The Tariff Problem. The economic battle lines formed over the currency issue also marked a widening cleavage on the tariff question. The high tariff rates imposed during the Civil War were avowedly protectionist in intent, but they were accepted at least in part on the ground that they were needed to increase the revenue of the government. When the war ended, however, the industrialists were in the saddle and there was no lowering of duties. As time passed, it became increasingly evident that the high tariff fostered monopoly by shutting out foreign competition, but efforts to reduce it were fruitless.

Finally, in 1884 the long Republican ascendancy was broken by the election of Grover Cleveland to the presidency, after a shoddy campaign in which the principal issues were the dubious political integrity of the Republican candidate, James G. Blaine, and the fact that Cleveland was the father of an illegitimate child. Many prominent Republicans, the "mugwumps," bolted to Cleveland rather than support a man they re-

"The TARIFF ?"   PUCK, Mch. 7, '88.

A HYDRA THAT MUST BE CRUSHED — AND THE SOONER THE BETTER.

This cartoon, coming shortly after President Cleveland's famous tariff message, reflects the view that the tariff was the "mother of trusts."

garded as corrupt, but the deciding factor was a last-minute blunder by Blaine, when he permitted an overardent clergyman to characterize the Democratic party as the party of "Rum, Romanism, and Rebellion." The remark alienated the Irish vote in New York and gave the state to Cleveland by a narrow margin.

Cleveland objected to the existing level of tariff duties not only because it encouraged trusts and raised prices artificially, but because it produced revenue in excess of the government's current needs and thereby opened the way for extravagance in the form of "pork-barrel" legislation and special pension laws for Civil War veterans, deserving and undeserving. When Congress failed to act, the President dramatized the problem by devoting his entire annual message in 1887 to a plea for tariff reduction. A bill for this purpose passed the House but was blocked in the

Senate by Nelson W. Aldrich of Rhode Island, a staunch devotee of extreme protection.

The election of 1888 was then fought on the tariff issue, without a clear decision being reached. Cleveland secured a larger popular vote than the Republican Benjamin Harrison but lost the critical state of New York, and with it the presidency, through a blunder on the part of the British Minister in Washington. An individual purporting to be a naturalized Englishman wrote to the Minister, Sir Lionel Sackville-West, asking for advice on how to vote, and because negotiations over the perennial Newfoundland fishery problem were then in progress, Sir Lionel recommended that Cleveland be kept in office. Publication of his reply enabled the Republicans to attach a pro-British label to Cleveland, particularly damaging at a time when Irish-Americans were stirred up by the defeat of Gladstone's Home Rule bill. The Republicans chose to interpret their victory as a mandate to raise the tariff, which they accomplished by the McKinley tariff of 1890.

The assumption that the people as a whole wanted a higher tariff proved to be unfounded; the unpopularity of the McKinley bill was a major factor in returning Cleveland to the White House in 1892. He again pressed for tariff reduction, but ran into the complication that Democrats from industrial districts were just as sensitive to local pressure as Republicans, and the number of Democrats in this category was being steadily increased by the industrial expansion of the South. By the time the special interests had finished with it, the Wilson-Gorman tariff of 1894 differed from its predecessor only in detail, and not at all in principle. President Cleveland regarded the Wilson-Gorman bill as a violation of his party's campaign pledges but allowed it to become law without his signature.

THE ELECTION OF 1896

In the early 1890's the various currents of unrest in the United States began to swell to torrential proportions. An astonishing collection of grievances accumulated within a period of less than ten years. Farm discontent was raised to an angry pitch by the rejection of agrarian demands for cheap money; organized labor was smarting under its defeats in the Homestead and Pullman strikes, for which it was disposed to blame intervention by public authority on the side of management; hopes that big business could be curbed were frustrated by the ineffectiveness of the Interstate Commerce and Sherman Antitrust Acts. The performance on the tariff question indicated that Congress was more responsive to special interests than to the voice of the people, with the Senate as the chief offender. When public opinion did succeed in bringing Congress into line, privilege found a refuge in the courts. It was judicial interpretation that emasculated the Interstate Commerce and Antitrust laws, and in 1895 the Supreme Court gave reformers another issue by declaring unconstitutional the Federal income tax provided for in the Wilson-Gorman tariff (*Pollock v. Farmers' Loan and Trust Company*). This tax, amounting to 2 per cent on incomes above $4,000, had been adopted primarily because customs revenues were expected to decline rather than as a restraint on great concentrations of wealth, but the five justices who voted against it—one of them had changed his mind at the last minute—made it evident that their attitude was determined less by constitutional theory than by their belief that a tax on incomes was an assault on the rights of property.

Populism. The rising discontent found its earliest political outlet in the People's party, better known as the Populist party, which has been identified previously as the product of the Farmers' Alliance movement. The party campaigned locally, and with some success, in the congressional elections of 1890, but its formal appearance as a national organization came in 1892. Its platform, written by Ignatius Donnelly, demanded first and foremost the free and unlimited coinage of silver; its other demands included government ownership of the railroads, a graduated income tax, a postal-savings system, the restriction of immigration, an eight-hour day in industry, and direct popular election of United States senators.

Although the Populists polled over a million votes in 1892 and carried four states (Kansas, Colorado, Nevada, and Idaho), their effective strength as an organized group was restricted to the Great Plains and Rocky Mountain areas. The gospel of "white supremacy" kept the white farmers of the South safely inside the Democratic party, and the colored farmers did not count politically. Industrial labor in the North was not attracted to a predominantly agrarian movement. The influence of Populism, however, was not confined to the party organization. With the coming of depression in 1893, the clamor for reform became too loud to be ignored by the major parties. Southern farmers might vote Democratic, but they thought Populist, and under leaders of the stamp of Ben Tillman they temporarily dethroned the "Bourbon" control of the Democracy in their section. In the West, the "silver Democrats" and the Populists were indistinguishable. The Republicans had no Southern wing to be similarly affected, but they too were feeling the pressure of silver sentiment in the West.

Thus, when the national conventions met in 1896, the stage appeared set for a showdown on economic issues. The Republican organization fell under the control of Marcus Alonzo Hanna, a shrewd and capable Cleveland businessman who had for some time been grooming his friend William McKinley for the presidency. McKinley was nominated on the first ballot, with a platform which tried to avoid the controversial silver issue by stressing the desirability of a high tariff to restore prosperity. His campaign slogan was "the full dinner pail," suggesting that protection meant high wages for labor. On the money question, the Republicans recommended maintenance of the gold standard until bimetallism could be established on a world-wide basis by international agreement, a prospect which everyone knew was too remote to be considered seriously. Hanna's deft management steered the party in the direction he wanted it to go, with only one note of discord when Senator Henry M. Teller of Colorado led a small band of silver Republicans out of the convention hall.

The "Cross of Gold." The Democratic convention was a more turbulent affair. Cleveland and his followers made a hopeless, last-ditch fight for the gold standard; the silverites captured the party organization, adopted a platform calling unequivocally for free silver and incorporating other features of the Populist program, and then turned to the choice of a suitable candidate. Bland and Bryan both had considerable support, and Altgeld would have been strongly in the running, as a candidate with a powerful appeal to labor, if he had not been ineligible because of his German birth—his parents brought him to the United States when he was six months old. Bryan's success was ensured by his immortal "Cross of Gold" speech, which roused the delegates to hysterical enthusiasm by its eloquent championship of the plain people against big business and its stirring peroration, "You shall not press down upon the brow of labor this crown of thorns, you shall not crucify mankind upon a cross of gold." Populist endorsement of Bryan marked the virtual absorption of that party by the Democrats. The silver Republicans also supported Bryan, while the gold Democrats ran a candidate of their own.

The campaign that followed was fiercely contested. The Bryan candidacy had all the emotional fervor of a great crusade. Bryan himself, unquestionably the finest orator of his day, stumped the country in a tremendous single-handed effort. On the other side, Hanna made no attempt to have McKinley compete with Bryan. The Republican campaign was a matter of careful, detailed planning and lavish expenditure, the money being raised by assessments on big corporations.

The event showed that the time was not yet ripe for a full-scale reform movement. Bryan carried the South and much of the West, but the solid backing of the industrial Northeast gave McKinley the election. The popular vote was close: 7,000,000 to 6,500,000. Bryan's failure in the industrial states can be attributed to the fact that labor was as convinced of the merits of protection as capital, and it could see no remedy for its own grievances in free silver. On the contrary, the industrial laborers in general were apprehensive about the effects of currency depreciation, and their fears were exploited to the utmost by Republican spokesmen.

The excitement died out with remarkable speed after the election was over. A general improvement in economic conditions in the last half of the decade reduced internal unrest to a minimum, and public attention was diverted to other matters by the Spanish-American War. The Republicans credited the return of prosperity to the Dingley tariff of 1897, which raised rates to a new high level, but the evidence shows that recovery began at least as early as the summer of 1896 and was, indeed, a factor in Bryan's defeat. A more potent stimulus was provided by the fresh supplies of gold from the Klondike and South Africa. The influx of gold also enabled the Republicans to pass the Gold Standard Act of 1900, which placed all United States currency on a gold basis and settled the money question for the time being.

In the long run the outcome of the election of 1896 did more good than harm to the cause of political and economic reform. The free-silver issue was essentially superficial. The experience of the entire world in recent years has demonstrated that there is nothing sacred about the gold standard but, on the other hand, that juggling the currency does not provide a remedy for economic ills. Yet in 1896 the question had become so highly charged emotionally that it had to be settled one way or the other before proper consideration could be given to more fundamental problems.

THE RISE OF THE PROGRESSIVES

The defeat of Bryan merely staved off one threat to the reign of big business; it did nothing to remove the underlying causes of discontent. With the turn of the century, after the first enthusiasm over the country's venture into imperialism had worn off, domestic reform again assumed a prominent place in the American scene. The progressive movement of this era inherited many of the ideas of the earlier reformers, but it was broader in scope than its predecessors and rather more realistic in its approach to the problems of industrial civilization. Progressivism cannot be classified as either a labor or an agrarian movement, although it drew adherents from both sources. It was preeminently a manifestation of middle-class liberalism and humanitarianism, very similar to the New Liberalism in contemporary Britain. It ignored party lines; both major parties were subjected to a vigorous internal struggle between progressives and conservatives.

The Muckrakers. The evils that the progressives hoped to remedy were described for the American public with pitiless clarity by the group of writers whom Theodore Roosevelt characterized as the "muckrakers."

The implication that they were engaged in nothing more than a species of sensational journalism was misleading. The great bulk of the muckraking literature was based on careful investigation, and if it was sensational, it was because the subject matter made it so. Political corruption and the business practices of the trusts scarcely required embellishment.

The muckraking school began with the publication of Henry Demarest Lloyd's *Wealth against Commonwealth* (1894), a vehement attack on the trusts. His lead was followed by contributors to popular magazines such as Ida M. Tarbell, whose *History of the Standard Oil Company* is still a classic, and Lincoln Steffens, who exposed the sorry condition of state and local governments; and novelists like Frank Norris, whose works *The Pit* and *The Octopus* showed how the farmer was at the mercy of speculators and railroad corporations, and Upton Sinclair, whose description of the meat-packing industry in *The Jungle* led to the passage of the Pure Food and Drug Act in 1906 and the hasty quarantining of American meat products by several European countries. Public opinion was also aroused by books of the type of Jacob Riis' *How the Other Half Lives,* a shocking description of slum conditions in New York, and Gustavus Myers' *History of the Great American Fortunes,* whose thesis was that many of the great fortunes had been accumulated at the expense of society as a whole. A philosophy for attacking the concentration of wealth was provided by Thorstein Veblen in the *Theory of the Leisure Class* and the *Theory of Business Enterprise,* at least for those who were capable of understanding him. The cataloguing of the literature of protest could be continued indefinitely; it was impressive in both volume and quality, and it was a major factor in winning public support for the progressives.

The Progressive Philosophy. The progressives were reformers and not revolutionaries. They had no intention of altering the framework of American society; they merely wanted to remove some cankerous growths from it. They had a profound faith in democracy. Indeed, their diagnosis of the nation's troubles was fundamentally that the control of government —national, state, and local—had passed into the hands of privileged interests, and their primary remedy was to restore political power to the people. They were, therefore, acutely interested in methods of strengthening the democratic process, and it is to the progressives that the United States owes the adoption of such techniques as the direct primary, the initiative, and the referendum. Through the Seventeenth Amendment to the Constitution, adopted in 1913, they carried out the old Populist demand for direct election of United States senators. It may be noted that both British and American democracy had to face the problem of a predominantly conservative upper house at this time, but where the

British Liberals curtailed the powers of their upper chamber, the American progressives chose to make theirs more responsible to the people.

Civil service reform did not originate with the progressives, but they promoted it aggressively as the best means of improving public administration. Abolition of the spoils system was first vigorously urged in the 1860's by Congressman Thomas A. Jenckes of Rhode Island, who wanted to adopt a merit system patterned on the British civil service, and because the idea was supported by Carl Schurz, Charles Sumner, and other influential Republicans, it was given a brief and farcical trial during the Grant administration. Patronage was too valuable a political tool to be given up easily. When, however, President Garfield was killed by a disappointed office seeker, public sentiment was sufficiently aroused to compel passage of the Pendleton Act in 1882, requiring competitive examinations for about a tenth of the appointive positions in the national government and establishing a Civil Service Commission to administer the act. The President was authorized to extend the merit system at his discretion, and both Cleveland and Theodore Roosevelt did so on a a large scale. The progressives were also influential in having civil service adopted by states and municipalities.

State and Local Government. Their achievements in the field of state and municipal government were perhaps the most striking accomplishment of the progressives. It is easy to arouse public interest in national issues but difficult to focus attention on local matters. Yet the progressives were able to break the power of entrenched privilege in state after state. Among the men who rose to prominence as reform governors were Theodore Roosevelt and Charles Evans Hughes in New York, Robert M. LaFollette in Wisconsin, Hiram Johnson in California, and Woodrow Wilson in New Jersey. Municipal government, accurately characterized by Lord Bryce in the 1880's as the most conspicuous failure of American democracy, underwent a similar overhauling at the hands of such men as Tom Johnson of Cleveland and "Golden Rule" Jones of Toledo. Much of this work, it is true, was undone later; having voted a reform administration into office, people too frequently assumed that the job was finished, and left the way clear for the political machines to come back. Party organizations experienced little trouble in getting control of primaries because the public was generally indifferent. Nevertheless, substantial gains were made, and if the machinery set up by the progressives was too often unused, it was at least available when the occasion arose.

Progressivism and the Judiciary. Social reform moved at a rather slower pace than political reform, largely because of the unsympathetic attitude of the courts. This phase of the progressive program was in a bewildering constitutional position. Unless interstate commerce was directly involved, the regulation of economic activity was regarded as a state and not a Federal function, and the states appeared to have ample authority in their "police power"—their right to protect public health, safety, and morals. In the exercise of their police power, however, the states found themselves restricted by judicial interpretation of the due-process clause in the Fourteenth Amendment, and the progressives discovered, to their intense irritation, that in economic matters judges were disposed to apply due process to the preservation of *laissez faire* in its most extreme form.

The apex of judicial conservatism was reached in the case of *Lochner v. New York* (1905), in which the United States Supreme Court ruled unconstitutional a New York law establishing a ten-hour day in bakeries. The court held that such legislation was not a valid exercise of the police power for the safeguarding of public health, since it could not be shown that there was any relationship between the hours of labor and the quality of bread, and that it violated the due process because it interfered with the right of the workers to contract freely for their own services—or, to quote the majority opinion, "Statutes of the nature of that under review, limiting the hours in which grown and intelligent men may labor to earn their living, are mere meddlesome interference with the rights of the individual." Justice Holmes, dissenting, pointed out that the Fourteenth Amendment did not enact Mr. Herbert Spencer's *Social Statics* and added, "the accident of our finding certain opinions natural and familiar, or novel, and even shocking, ought not to conclude our judgment on whether statutes embodying them conflict with the Constitution of the United States."

The Lochner decision was modified soon afterwards in *Muller v. Oregon* (1908), in which the Court affirmed the right of a state to regulate hours of labor for women, and most states thereupon followed the lead of those few which had already adopted legislation for the protection of women and minors. Laws aimed at preventing industrial accidents and providing compensation in case of injury also began to meet with judicial approval after 1910. The doctrine of liberty of contract nevertheless died hard. As late as 1923 it was restated in all its original vigor to invalidate a Federal law establishing minimum wages for women in the District of Columbia (*Adkins v. Children's Hospital*), the majority on the Supreme Court declaring that it saw no connection between wage scales and either health or morality. Justice Holmes dissented from this decision also.

Prohibition. Progressivism had a strong moral tinge, exemplified in a number of ways: private ventures into humanitarianism and social welfare, of which the settlement houses such as Jane Addams' Hull House in Chicago were conspicuous examples; the evolution of a "social gospel" among both Protestant and Catholic clergymen, resembling the Christian

Socialist movements in Europe; legislative attacks on gambling and vice; and, above all, agitation to control the liquor traffic, or outlaw it altogether. Prohibition by state or local action was widespread in the United States during the early years of the twentieth century, and in 1913 Congress passed the Webb-Kenyon Act to prevent the shipment of liquor from "wet" to "dry" areas. These measures proving ineffective, a demand for national prohibition arose, which was unexpectedly aided by the First World War, when Congress, to promote national economy and efficiency, forbade the manufacture and sale of intoxicating beverages. The Eighteenth, or Prohibition, Amendment to the Constitution followed in 1919, although a progressive President, Woodrow Wilson, disapproved of it as going too far.

Immigration. The restriction of immigration was an important issue of the progressive era, but it was not in itself an integral part of progressive doctrine. In fact, the alignment on this question found normally antagonistic elements working on the same side. Industry and labor took positions on straightforward economic lines, one favoring and the other opposing free immigration because it represented a constant supply of cheap and unorganized labor, but about 1900 the noneconomic aspects of the problem began to appear even more important. The sources of immigration by then had shifted perceptibly from northern to southern and eastern Europe—that is, from Great Britain, Germany, and the Scandinavian countries, to Italy, Austria-Hungary, Russia, and the Balkans. On the Pacific coast, the Chinese and Japanese provided an additional complication. The bewildering variety of racial and linguistic groups caused grave doubts as to whether these new immigrants could be assimilated without altering the character of American life and American institutions. The result was that trade-unionists and liberals who feared the effects of this mass of uneducated immigrants on democracy found themselves in the same camp with exponents of "native Americanism" and "Nordic supremacy," while other liberals who wanted the United States to continue its historic role as an asylum for oppressed peoples joined hands with the industrialists.

The weight of public opinion was for restriction. In the 1880's Congress began the enactment of a long series of laws prohibiting the admission of criminals, revolutionaries, the physically or mentally unfit, and those likely to become public charges. Attempts to impose a literacy test were blocked by presidential veto until 1917, when a measure to this effect was passed over President Wilson's objection that literacy was a test of opportunity rather than fitness. Racial groups as such were not discriminated against, with the exception of Orientals. Because of pressure from the Pacific coast states, Chinese immigration was stopped in 1882. Agitation for the application of a similar policy to the Japanese had a very unfortunate effect on Japanese-American relations. Theodore Roosevelt tried to appease the domestic clamor without offending Japan by negotiating a "gentleman's agreement" in 1907 whereby the Japanese government consented to discourage emigration of its laboring classes to the United States, but neither he nor his successors could check the enactment of anti-Japanese legislation by the Western states. Japanese exclusion finally became law in 1924. At the same time Congress, by acts of 1921 and 1924, adopted a quota system for immigration in general. It was weighted in favor of northern European countries and did not apply to the nations of the Western Hemisphere. This step was unquestionably necessary on economic grounds, but it should be pointed out that, on the basis of the best available evidence, the apprehensions about the recent immigrants proving unassimilable or constituting a menace to American democracy were unfounded.

THE ADMINISTRATION OF THEODORE ROOSEVELT

The path of the progressive movement in national politics would have been far more difficult if it had not been given aggressive and colorful leadership by the accession of Theodore Roosevelt to the presidency in consequence of the assassination of McKinley by an anarchist in 1901. The new President brought to his office a remarkable variety of experiences in public life: a member of the New York State Assembly, Civil Service Commissioner under Harrison and Cleveland, Police Commissioner of New York City, Assistant Secretary of the Navy at the beginning of the McKinley administration, organizer and leader of the Rough Riders in the Spanish-American War, and Governor of New York. His activities in this last post "won" for him the Republican vice-presidential nomination in 1900, a move engineered by the party machine in New York to get Roosevelt out of the state and, it was hoped, push him into permanent obscurity.

The extent of Roosevelt's progressivism has occasionally been challenged. It is true that, during his term of office at any rate, it was frequently difficult to tell just where he stood. He could denounce "malefactors of great wealth" and "muckrakers" with equal vehemence, or wax enthusiastic about "trust busting" while carefully distinguishing between "good" and "bad" trusts. Yet he was a crusader by temperament, with a genuine sympathy for the underdog and all the acute Roosevelt sense of what the people wanted. If he consulted the reactionaries of his own party, Aldrich and "Uncle Joe" Cannon, the Speaker of the House, it was less because of sympathy for their ideas than because he needed the support of the party organization for his own measures. The Republican "old guard" certainly did not consider Roosevelt as one of their number. Mark Hanna's grief at the death of his friend McKinley was overshadowed by his consternation over its political consequences. "Now look," he said, "that damned cowboy is President of the United States."

Trust Busting. The best known of Theodore Roosevelt's activities is his campaign against the trusts. After the E. C. Knight decision, the Sherman Act had become a dead letter as far as business was concerned, and the trend to combination became more pronounced about 1900. Roosevelt himself was not opposed to bigness as such, but merely to abuse of economic power, and he would have preferred Federal regulation of corporations to "trust busting." Since, however, he could not get Congress to enact regulatory legislation, he had to turn to reviving the Sherman Act.

His first notable success was the dissolution of the Northern Securities Company, a holding company formed in 1901 as the result of a clash between the Hill-Morgan combination controlling the Great Northern and Northern Pacific Railroads and E. H. Harriman, who had rehabilitated the Union Pacific. Both parties wanted the Chicago, Burlington and Quincy as a bridge line to give their respective systems a secure connection with the eastern railways at Chicago. When Hill and Morgan won the race to buy the Burlington, Harriman countered by trying to wrest control of the Northern Pacific from them. The resulting battle precipitated a stock-market crisis, with the result that the combatants decided to come to terms and pool their interests by means of the holding company. To their amazement and indignation, Roosevelt promptly ordered the Attorney General to institute suit against the Northern Securities Company for violation of the Sherman Act, and to their further dismay, the Supreme Court in 1904 ordered the company dissolved.

The victory in the Northern Securities case was followed by vigorous assaults on other trusts. In addition to judicial action, a Department of Commerce and Labor was established in 1903, containing a Bureau of Corporations whose specific function was to investigate corporate practices. Yet the gains of the trust-busting crusade were more apparent than real. More combinations came into existence than were dissolved, and devices such as interlocking directorates and "community-of-interest" agreements enabled monopolistic practices to be continued without openly violating the law.

The Hepburn Act. More tangible results were achieved in the field of railway regulation. Like the Sherman Act, the Interstate Commerce Act had lapsed into desuetude, and railroad malpractices continued unabated. The granting of rebates, indeed, had been carried to such an extreme that by 1903 the railroads themselves were appealing to the government for relief. Congress responded with the Elkins Act, which made it illegal for shippers to accept rebates as well as for carriers to give them. Then, at the insistent urging of the President, Congress in 1906 passed the Hepburn Act, which marks the beginning of effective regulation of railroads in the United States. The act gave the Interstate Commerce Commission power to prescribe maximum rates, subject to judicial review but with the responsibility for appealing to the courts placed on the railroads and not on the Commission. The Commission's authority was expanded to include storage and terminal facilities, sleeping-car and express companies, and pipe lines. Free passes were prohibited, except for railroad employees, and the "commodities clause" attempted, not too successfully, to exclude the railroads from ownership of such enterprises as mines, timber lands, and steamship lines. The Commission's jurisdiction was extended by the Mann-Elkins Act in 1910 to telephone and telegraph companies, and it was given the right to suspend rate increases pending investigation of their reasonableness. This act also created a commerce court to expedite the adjudication of appeals from the Commission's rulings, but progressive members of Congress soon afterward became convinced that this court was too friendly to the railroads and abolished it by refusing to vote its appropriations.

Conservation. Roosevelt's greatest personal accomplishment in domestic policy was the stimulation he gave to the conservation of natural resources. Until 1890 little attention was given to this problem. A casual assumption that the country's resources were inexhaustible was reflected in the public-land system, which permitted the disposal of valuable timber and mineral land at absurdly low prices, and in general indifference to appallingly wasteful methods of exploitation. Agitation by a few enlightened individuals gradually produced an awareness that there were limits to the supply of natural resources, and in 1891 Congress passed the Forest Reserve Act, permitting the President to establish forest reserves on the public domain by executive order. In the next ten years some 45,000,000 acres were thus set aside. Then Theodore Roosevelt, with his crusading temperament and a bolder conception of presidential power, added a further 150,000,000 acres to the total, besides withdrawing from public entry some 85,000,000 more in both the continental United States and Alaska until their mineral and water-power resources could be investigated.

Public interest in conservation was further aroused by Roosevelt's appointment of an Inland Waterways Commission in 1907 to study the whole question of water transportation and the relationship of forest and soil conservation to stream flow. Support for this step came partly from the hope that improved waterways might help to control the railroads. In the same year the President called a national conservation conference at the White House, to which were invited all the state governors, members of the cabinet, Justices of the Supreme Court, and prominent figures in science and education. The conference made sweeping recommendations which were not adopted at the time because the Western states were becoming alarmed at what they considered Roosevelt's interference with their development.

Important as Roosevelt's achievements were, they constituted little more than a start on the whole problem of conservation. Soil erosion and the waste of mineral resources remained untouched problems. Something was done to protect wild life, but not enough. The omissions were not Roosevelt's fault; he went as far as public opinion would let him. He could take satisfaction in having placed forest conservation on a firm foundation and in arousing an interest in the preservation of natural resources which would make possible advances in the future.

THE PROGRESSIVE REVOLT

In 1908 Theodore Roosevelt could have had another term as President for the asking. He was only fifty years old, and he was securely established in the affections of the common people. However, after his easy victory over Alton B. Parker in 1904, "Teddy" had announced that he would not run again, so that in 1908 he confined his efforts to the choice of a suitable successor. Secretary of State Elihu Root, the ablest man in the cabinet, was passed over because his previous career as a corporation lawyer made him unacceptable to progressive opinion, and the Roosevelt mantle fell on the Secretary of War, William Howard Taft. The Democrats, after their unfortunate venture into conservatism in 1904, turned again to Bryan, with no more success than before. Taft was duly elected, whereupon Roosevelt, to avoid embarrassing the new President, departed on a big-game hunting expedition, speeded on his way by J. P. Morgan's wish that the first lion he met in Africa would do its duty.

There is no doubt that Taft honestly intended to continue Roosevelt's policies, at least in accordance with his understanding of them. He prosecuted trusts zealously and made some valuable additions to the conservation program. Yet within a few months Taft and the Republican progressives were at loggerheads, for reasons that were not entirely Taft's fault. Any man who had to succeed Theodore Roosevelt in the White House was bound to suffer by comparison, and Taft's characteristics contrasted sharply with his colorful predecessor's. Where Roosevelt was impulsive, Taft was cautious. Roosevelt interpreted the powers of the presidency generously; Taft regarded his authority as limited to what was expressly specified in the Constitution. In addition, Taft was fundamentally conservative in his outlook, with no real sympathy for or comprehension of progressive ideals.

The Payne-Aldrich Tariff. The first and most important breach occurred over the tariff question. Roosevelt had carefully avoided it as likely to split the party, but by 1908 the tariff was again under fire as the "mother of trusts" and the Republicans pledged themselves to "revision," a term defined by Taft himself as meaning reduction. However, when he called a special session of Congress in 1909 to redeem this pledge, the protectionists got the upper hand, and the Payne-Aldrich Tariff raised the duties on all the really important commodities. The Republican progressives resisted the bill tenaciously, but they were given no encouragement from the White House. Then, after Taft had signed the bill, when he might have followed Cleveland's example in the case of the Wilson-Gorman Tariff, he delivered a speech at Winona, Minnesota, right in the region where progressive sentiment was strongest, in which he praised the Payne-Aldrich Act as the best tariff the Republican party had ever passed.

Other irritants presently made their appearance, among them a quarrel between Taft's Secretary of the Interior, Richard A. Ballinger, and Gifford Pinchot, Chief of the Forest Service and an intimate friend of Theodore Roosevelt's. Pinchot accused Ballinger of conniving to obtain for the Guggenheim interests reserved coal lands in Alaska. Taft upheld Ballinger and dismissed Pinchot. Subsequent investigation has largely disproved Pinchot's charges, but at the time the incident disturbed the conservationists and was an important factor in opening a rift between Taft and Roosevelt.

Return of Roosevelt. The administration's loss of popularity was clearly revealed when the Democrats won control of the House in the congressional elections in 1910. Shortly afterward Taft's prestige suffered another blow in the shape of a disastrous defeat for one of his cherished policies, tariff reciprocity. An agreement with Canada seemed assured of ratification until Champ Clark, the new Democratic Speaker, blunderingly hailed it as the first step toward the annexation of Canada. The Canadian reaction was immediate and vehement; the government which had conducted the negotiations was thrown out of office. By this time Taft's opponents within the Republican party had founded the National Progressive Republican League for the purpose of securing the nomination of a progressive, presumably LaFollette, as the next Republican presidential candidate. Meanwhile, Theodore Roosevelt had returned to the United States. After viewing the political scene for some time and finding the role of elder statesman unsuited to his abundant energy, he threw in his lot with the progressives by his "New Nationalism" address at Osawatomie, Kansas, 31 August 1910. At first he was ostensibly supporting the LaFollette candidacy, but it was not in his nature to be content with a secondary part, and before long he had superseded the Wisconsin senator as the hope of the progressives.

The "Bull Moose" Campaign. In the battle for delegates, Roosevelt carried most of the states that had presidential primaries, but there were not enough of them to give him a majority and the party organization held the others firmly in line for Taft. When the Republican convention met, several delegations were in dispute. The conservatives won a strategic point by electing Elihu Root as temporary chairman, and most of the contests were settled in favor of Taft, who was then renominated. The Roosevelt men thereupon walked out, formed the Progressive party, and nominated their idol in a spirit of evangelical fervor. At the Progressive convention the delegates sang "Onward, Christian Soldiers" as they voted and Roosevelt proclaimed, "We stand at Armageddon and we battle for the Lord." His statement that he felt like a "Bull Moose" gave the new party its insignia and the campaign its nickname.

The immediate consequence of the Republican schism was to guarantee a Democratic victory, provided the Democrats did not lose their own progressive voters by nominating a conservative. There was a bitter fight in the Democratic convention between Champ Clark, representing the conservatives, and Governor Woodrow Wilson of New Jersey, who had the influential support of Bryan. Finally, after forty-six ballots, the progressive Democrats were able to nominate Wilson. He was a comparative newcomer to active politics, although he had long been known in intellectual circles as a student of government and had attracted nationwide attention as president of Princeton University by his efforts to democratize that institution. Elected Governor of New Jersey in 1910 by a Democratic machine which needed a respectable "front," he displayed a surprising flair for practical politics by breaking the grip of the machine and enacting a program of progressive legislation. His presidential aspirations were nurtured by the Texas politician who became his alter ego, Colonel Edward M. House.

With the Republicans split, Wilson was able to win an overwhelming majority in the electoral college with a little over forty per cent of the popular vote. Roosevelt finished second in both electoral and popular votes; Taft carried two states—Vermont and Utah. Besides the presidency, the Democrats carried both Houses of Congress. The subsequent fate of the Progressive party can be related briefly. It had high hopes for 1916, but when the time came the First World War overshadowed domestic issues, and Roosevelt's hatred of Wilson led him to return to the Republican party and advise his followers to do the same. Most of them did, although a few chose to go over to the Democrats; in any event, the Progressive party was extinct.

THE NEW FREEDOM

When Woodrow Wilson became President of the United States, he had little interest in foreign affairs and certainly no inkling of what the future held for him. His interest was focused on domestic reform, and in the brief period given him before the outbreak of world conflagration, his achievements were nothing short of astounding. His program, the "New Freedom" was in its essentials indistinguishable from Roosevelt's "New Nationalism." Wilson accepted big business as inevitable and in many ways a beneficial economic development, but he believed that its social consequences imposed on government the duty of protecting the rights and dignity of the individual.

As his first step, Wilson not only tackled the problem of tariff reduction; he succeeded where Cleveland and Taft had failed. The Underwood-Simmons Tariff of 1913 lowered the average level of duties from 37 to 27 per cent. It was still a protective measure, but it represented a genuine attempt to equalize domestic and foreign costs of production and thereby preserve competition. The special interests that had made a farce of previous gestures at tariff reform were checked by Wilson's leadership, especially by his success in appealing to the people to hold their representatives to their promises. Attached to this measure was a new provision for a Federal income tax, now fully constitutional under the Sixteenth Amendment, which had been adopted in 1913.

Antitrust Legislation. To deal with the trusts, two important pieces of legislation were enacted in 1914. The Federal Trade Commission Act transferred the functions of the Bureau of Corporations to a bipartisan commission, declared unfair methods of competition to be illegal, and empowered the commission to issue "cease-and-desist" orders to any corporation that it found to be violating the law. The Clayton Act attempted to put teeth into the antitrust legislation by defining what constituted restraint of trade, the list of forbidden practices including price discriminations which tended to foster monopoly, interlocking directorates, and the ownership by corporations of stock in competing companies. Labor and farm organizations were excluded from the scope of the act, and the use of injunctions in labor disputes was forbidden except to prevent "irreparable injury to property."

Despite its explicit terminology, the Clayton Act did not realize the expectation of its sponsors. When its provisions were tested in the courts, the results were discouraging. Moreover, when the United States went to war, the antitrust laws were held in abeyance because of the greater need to coordinate industry for wartime production, and afterward the administrations of Presidents Harding, Coolidge, and Hoover showed little disposition to revive them.

The Federal Reserve System. The greatest and most lasting accomplishment of the New Freedom was its reform of banking and credit through the creation of the Federal Reserve System. That something needed to be done was acknowledged by conservatives and progressives alike. There had been no centralized control of banking in the United States, at least by any legally recognized authority, since the days of Andrew Jackson. The National Bank Acts of the Civil War period merely provided for a sound banknote currency, and even in that they proved to have a serious defect. The national banknotes were sound enough, but they lacked the flexibility to provide a satisfactory paper currency, since the amount in circulation was restricted by the legal requirement that the issuing banks own government bonds amounting to 90 per cent of the value of the notes. As a result, business operations suffered from periodic shortages of banknote currency.

Banking reform, in other words, involved an aspect of the currency question which had not been settled by the decision of 1896 and which had been with the American people since colonial days. There was not enough "hard money" for the country's economic needs. There was still a substantial outward movement of specie. Until the beginning of the twentieth century the physical expansion of the United States outran its industrial capacity, so that there were continuous heavy imports from Europe in spite of the high tariffs; in addition, interest had to be paid on the European capital which had financed much of the industrial development of the United States. Quite apart from these factors, American economy had become much too complex for such a cumbersome procedure as the use of specie in everyday business transactions. What was needed was a circulating medium whose volume could be readily expanded or contracted as conditions required.

In the absence of an authorized central banking system, control over banking and credit gravitated naturally to the center of the nation's financial strength, the great banking houses of New York. This concentration of financial power possessed two admittedly undesirable features: (1) small banks deposited their reserves in larger banks and so up the ladder until there was an unhealthy accumulation of funds in the New York money market, so that a disturbance there could lead to a constriction of credit throughout the country; (2) it seemed unsound public policy to have control over the nation's credit resources exercised by a few individuals responsible to no one but themselves.

The first remedy proposed, sponsored by Senator Aldrich, was to create what would in effect have been a Third Bank of the United States, modeled on its predecessors of a century before and on the central banks of Europe and financed and managed chiefly by private capital. This scheme, however, was totally unacceptable to a Democratic party whose distrust of "money monopoly" was a tradition extending from Andrew Jackson to William Jennings Bryan, still an influential figure as Wilson's Secretary of State. The solution was the Federal Reserve Act of 1913, which established twelve regional banks in the principal financial centers of the United States. Each Federal Reserve Bank is owned by the member banks in its district and deals primarily with them, functioning as a depository for their reserves, rediscounting their loans, and acting as issuing agent for Federal Reserve notes. These notes were provided for in the act to create a banknote currency with the desired flexibility; they are issued with a backing of 40 per cent of their value in gold and the rest in commercial paper. A Federal Reserve Board appointed by the President supervises the entire system. All national banks were required to become members, and all others were invited to do so. The Federal Reserve Act was a conspicuous success; it has required only minor changes in later years, and those have been in the direction of extending and strengthening the system as the most effective method of maintaining sound banking.

Decline of Progressivism. The reforming zeal of the Wilson administration was not exhausted by these achievements. The LaFollette Merchant Seamen's Act of 1915 and the Adamson Act of 1916 have been described previously. The Federal Farm Loan Act in 1916 set up a structure similar to the Federal Reserve System for the purpose of making credit more easily available to agriculture. Two attempts were made to restrict child labor, once in 1916 by an act prohibiting the shipment of products of child labor in interstate commerce, and again in 1919 by discriminatory taxation of such products. Both laws, however, were declared unconstitutional.

By 1916 internal problems were being pushed into the background by war. The question of foreign policy split the ranks of conservatives and liberals alike, and when the United States entered the war, reform was suspended for the duration; when a conservative reaction followed the war, the progressive movement passed into history. Thus, the New Freedom, like the New Deal later, had its career terminated by the onset of a world conflict in which the United States found its own interests inextricably involved. Yet, if progressivism itself disappeared, the forces which created it did not; they would presently emerge again in a somewhat different form.

PART SEVEN

The New Imperialism

Capitalizing on the new weapons of military and economic conquest given them by their advanced industrial and commercial development, the major European nations began about 1870 a competition in empire building which resulted by 1914 in the domination of more than half the land surface of the world and more than a billion persons by a few imperialist states.

This extraordinary expansion was the product of the interaction of many causes. Political rivalry and national prestige and security were fully as important as causes as were the economic factors; and by many of its proponents imperialism was explained and justified as a Christianizing and civilizing mission.

In an evaluation of the consequences of imperialism, the cultural and material benefits afforded backward lands and the economic and patriotic stimulation enjoyed by the Great Powers appear to be outweighed by the record of exploitation of subject peoples, of intensification of nationalism, and of diplomatic crises and major and minor wars attributable to imperialism. The treaty makers of Versailles sought in vain to put a term to imperialism, and the resurgence of empire building in the 1930's ranks high among the causes of the recent war.

American imperialism did not equal, either in ardor or in extent of territory, that of the principal European states. Aside from the 600,000 square miles of Alaska, the United States added only 135,000 square miles of dependencies with some 12,000,000 people, while its Caribbean area of economic influence included 200,000 square miles and 9,000,000 inhabitants. But the taking of parcels of colonial territory, however modest, in the Caribbean and the Pacific, was the prime factor responsible for thrusting the United States into world politics, elevating the country to the status, replete with hazards and responsibilities, of a world power.

28

The Rise of Modern Imperialism: The Partition of Africa

To some of the Great Powers, the economic advantages of imperialism had a powerful appeal. There was a growing demand for raw materials, particularly tropical products, which could be turned into finished products in the factories of the leading industrial powers. The increased manufacture of goods frequently led to surpluses which acted to intensify a search for new markets. Locating new (real or fancied) markets served to provide additional opportunities for those engaged in the export business and further acted as an incentive to the investment of surplus capital. The ever-growing ease of communication and transportation combined to make colonies more desirable than formerly. Then, too, there were countries, such as Italy for example, which advanced the argument of surplus population in order to justify imperialistic tendencies.

But the economic motive had assistance in selling the attractions of imperialism to the people at home. A very convincing companion argument was the claim that national pride and prestige demanded for one's state "a place in the sun." Great Britain constantly sought a stronger position throughout the world, as she seemed to enjoy greater prosperity as a result of adding colonies, protectorates, and spheres of influence to her imperial crown. France, smarting under her resounding defeat in the Franco-Prussian War and aware that the time was not yet ripe for *revanche*, eagerly turned to the subject of a revived and expanded colonial empire after the war. In this activity, she was given plenty of encouragement by Bismarck, who was himself convinced that no colony was "worth the bones of a single Pomeranian grenadier" and who was delighted at any chance to sanction French wastage of lives and treasure. Once colonies were obtained, he was convinced they would represent a constant drain. Thus weakened, France would lessen her chances of regaining Alsace and Lorraine and squaring accounts with Germany.

Despite Bismarck's aversion to colonies, he was reluctantly forced by popular pressure to put his approval upon the acquisition of colonial territory by Germany in the later stages of his regime. The enthusiasm for colonies shown by the Germans can be traced to the channeling into imperialist expansion of some of the nationalism born of unification.

As far as the other major powers are concerned, Russia and Austria concentrated their energies on the domination of nearby lands rather than expansion overseas, while Italy actively (and belatedly) entered the race for empire in order to assure herself great-power status.

Still another cause of imperialism was the civilizing mission which the major powers were all prone to stress. Missionary and colonial societies in the various countries were encouraged by the foreign offices, who saw in their activities nothing but grist for their mills. The public was converted everywhere by the facile pens of historians and publicists who urged the extension of the superior national culture enjoyed by their fellow countrymen and with it the acceptance of the "white man's burden."

THE PRINCIPAL ADVOCATES OF IMPERIALISM

Many classes in every imperialistic state lent their enthusiastic support to the impetus given the revival of empire in the period after 1870 because they were confident of economic rewards for themselves. Industrialists, shipping magnates, armament makers, and bankers were to be found in this group.

Then, too, there were the statesmen and other public officials whose awareness of the trends of the time prompted them to espouse imperialism as a vital necessity for the well being of their particular country. Examples are numerous and the following will suffice: Disraeli, Joseph Chamberlain, and the Marquis of Salisbury in England; Jules Ferry and Théophile Delcassé in France; Kaiser Wilhelm II and Admiral von Tirpitz in Germany; and Theodore Roosevelt, Senator Beveridge, and Admiral A. T. Mahan in the United States. Additional champions were recruited from such diverse ranks as explorers, adventurers, missionaries, and literary men. Here we find the names of Stanley, Rhodes, Livingstone, Karl Peters, Kipling, Sir Charles Dilke, Rider Haggard, Josiah Strong, and others. The net result of the work of these men was to bring about strong public acceptance of the idea of imperialism in most countries.

Despite their support, the public was, on the whole, none too willing to leave home to take up life again in one of the colonies. Those who did were motivated by a variety of reasons. In the first place, there was an ever-present land hunger which could hardly be satisfied at home. In Europe, ownership of the land was traditionally reserved for certain classes. Thus, the dominant love of the soil which is natural to man had to seek outlet somewhere else. Furthermore, wages tended to be higher in the new country where help was scarce. Then, too, there were those attracted by the hopes of political liberty. Others were motivated by a desire for social equality, and still others sought real religious liberty. Adventure beckoned its fair share and accounts for many of the rogues and scoundrels who became intimately connected with the quest for empire in the nineteenth and twentieth centuries. Yet another element was that comprising the younger sons of aristocratic families. Particularly was this true of Great Britain, where primogeniture was in vogue. It is a readily demonstrable fact that many of England's greatest colonial administrators have been younger sons. Finally, there were those whose reasons were altruistic, especially the heroic Christian missionaries who dedicated their lives to spreading the gospel among the pagan peoples of the world.

THE BRITISH IN SOUTH AFRICA

The first theater of this new imperialistic action was Africa, which until the nineteenth century was really a "dark continent." Europeans knew only a little about the northern part and something less about the river mouths along the coast, but the interior was unknown, hence the name "dark continent" in the sense of mysterious and unexplored.

In modern times, South Africa is one of the best known parts of Africa, and so we shall use it as a beginning point for our study. The Cape of Good Hope region was colonized by the Dutch in the middle of the seventeenth century as a convenient way station on the route to the Indies. The original Dutch settlers were later joined by a body of French Huguenots, and these two groups merged to create the stock called the Boers, with a language of its own, now called Afrikaans.

During the early Napoleonic Wars the British conquered the Boers as a precautionary measure for the protection of India. By the Treaty of Amiens (1802), the Cape was returned to the Dutch, but at the Congress of Vienna the British received Cape Colony, which was added to the British Empire. Differences, especially in regard to treatment of the natives, tended to create friction between the British and the Boers. The Boers decided to leave, and by 1840 most of them had gone north, driving the natives away. This hegira is known as the Great Trek and resulted in the foundation of the Orange River Free State, a republic with the Bible as its constitution. The discovery of better land beyond the Vaal River caused the settlement of Transvaal to be made.

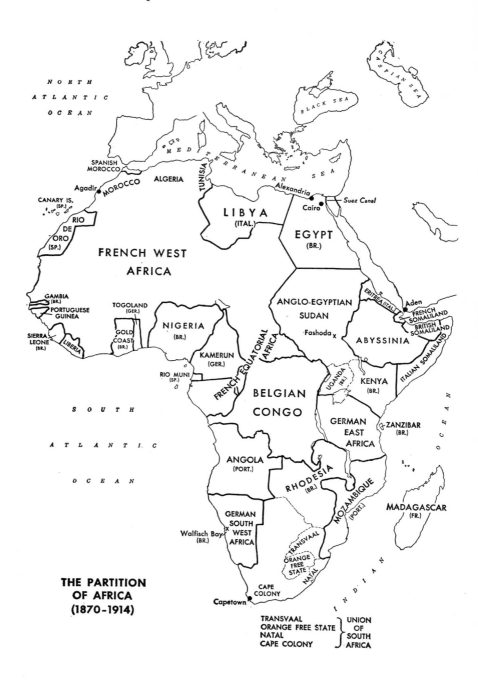

NORTH
ATLANTIC
OCEAN

CASPIAN SEA

BLACK SEA

MED ITE RRA NEA N SEA

SPANISH
MOROCCO

Agadir

CANARY IS.
(SP.)

RIO
DE
ORO
(SP.)

MOROCCO   ALGERIA

TUNISIA

LIBYA
(ITAL.)

Alexandria

Cairo   Suez Canal

EGYPT
(BR.)

FRENCH WEST
AFRICA

GAMBIA
(BR.)
PORTUGUESE
GUINEA

SIERRA
LEONE
(BR.)

LIBERIA

TOGOLAND
(GER.)

GOLD
COAST
(BR.)

NIGERIA
(BR.)

KAMERUN
(GER.)

RIO MUNI
(SP.)

FRENCH EQUATORIAL AFRICA

ANGLO-EGYPTIAN
SUDAN

Fashoda x

ERITREA (ITAL.)

R.

Aden

FRENCH
SOMALILAND
BRITISH
SOMALILAND

ABYSSINIA

ITALIAN SOMALILAND

BELGIAN
CONGO

UGANDA
(BR.)

KENYA
(BR.)

SOUTH

ATLANTIC

OCEAN

ANGOLA
(PORT.)

GERMAN
EAST
AFRICA

ZANZIBAR
(BR.)

INDIAN

OCEAN

RHODESIA
(BR.)

MOZAMBIQUE
(PORT.)

MADAGASCAR
(FR.)

GERMAN
SOUTH
WEST
AFRICA

Walfisch Bay
(BR.)

TRANSVAAL

ORANGE
FREE
STATE

NATAL

CAPE
COLONY

Capetown

**THE PARTITION
OF AFRICA
(1870-1914)**

TRANSVAAL
ORANGE FREE STATE
NATAL
CAPE COLONY

} UNION
OF
SOUTH
AFRICA

In 1856, the British founded Natal colony (named originally by Diaz on Christmas Day, 1497) in order to prevent the Boers from spilling over into the region with its splendid harbor later known as Durban. Thus, there were now four political units in South Africa evenly divided between the Boers and the British. All could survive comfortably if there were not too rapid a development and if the natives could be kept in hand. The Boers were determined to live alone and be left alone, but this proved impossible for at least three reasons. In the first place, British missionaries entered their lands. Secondly, pioneers from Natal and the Cape Colony were guilty of interloping. Finally, the Boer states turned out to be rich in diamonds and gold.

In addition, the British began the establishment of a system of protectorates effected through the simple medium of giving presents to the native leaders.

Cecil Rhodes. In 1889 the British South Africa Company, chartered to operate between the Transvaal and the Congo, made its appearance. Destined to be one of the greatest colonial and trading companies ever formed, it was primarily the work of one man, Cecil Rhodes, who had won fame by getting control of the diamond fields and eliminating all competition. He founded the famous De Beers Mining Company and later became prime minister of Cape Colony. A man who would use questionable methods if necessary, he was nonetheless an idealist. He was particularly enamored of the British Empire and hoped to see a Cape-to-Cairo railroad which would mean British control of Africa.

By the late 1880's, matters had become quite complicated because of the discovery of gold on the Witwatersrand in the Transvaal. This precipitated a wild gold rush during which the city of Johannesburg was founded, and myriad foreigners poured over Transvaal like locusts. The new President, Oom Paul Kruger, who hated the Uitlanders (foreigners), did all he could to make life unpleasant for them. To protect themselves, the foreigners formed the Transvaal National Union and arranged with Prime Minister Rhodes of the Cape Colony to stage a revolt against Kruger which Rhodes financed. It was planned for Christmas Day, 1895, and when the Uitlanders had established control one Dr. Jameson would come in from Natal and take charge. The planned revolt did not materialize, but Jameson and five hundred armed men invaded Transvaal, on 29 January 1896. Since most of them were inebriated they were quite handily captured by Kruger, whose people won the support of the world as a result of this foolish and aggressive Jameson raid. The German Kaiser, Wilhelm II, sent a somewhat tactless telegram of congratulations to "Oom Paul" which infuriated the British.

For his part in the raid, Rhodes had to resign both his posts as prime minister and as managing director of the South Africa Company and was tried in England by a committee of Parliament. In less than a year, he was as influential as ever in South Africa, since his visit home had been almost turned into a monster reception for a conquering hero.

The Boer War. Kruger, however, refused to have anything to do with the British, who sent one of their greatest imperial enthusiasts, Sir Alfred Milner, to see him. It was Sir Alfred's opinion, he stated to Joseph Chamberlain, Colonial Secretary, that the only solution lay in war. Kruger obliged the British by sending them ultimata in October, 1899, which they could not accept. So within two days war broke out between Great Britain and the Boers.

At first the Boers, who introduced barbed-wire entanglements to modern warfare and whose uniforms blended with the country where the war was waged, scored a number of victories.[1] The British soldiers made perfect targets until Kitchener changed their uniforms to khaki. Moreover, the Boers, although unable to raise an army of more than 40,000, had the advantage of men trained to live an outdoor life, expert marksmen and riders, to add to the fact that they believed almost fanatically in their cause and so gave "the old college try." But their cause was hopeless from the first, since the British had in the field by the end of the war an army over twice the entire Boer population. Within six months, the tide began to turn, and, by the end of the first year, the Boers were reduced to waging guerrilla warfare, which they did with great effectiveness through the agency of commandos, which they originated.

On 31 May 1902 the Treaty of Vereeniging was signed, granting self-government to the Boers plus several other guarantees together with £3,000,000 compensation to make good for the farm losses suffered. Just a few weeks previously, Rhodes had died and so did not see an old wish actually fulfilled. Thus ended a war which advertised British weakness to the world and revealed to the British the startling fact that their policy of "splendid isolation," while far from "splendid," had certainly left them isolated. It had also gone a long way to worsen Anglo-German relations, since the Kaiser had made it a somewhat embarrassing practice to send his condolences to his uncle, the British king, whenever Britain suffered reverses during the war. In 1910, the British combined their four South African possessions into the Union of South Africa which later achieved dominion status.

THE BRITISH OCCUPATION OF EGYPT

Egypt, always a prize, has been ruled throughout most of her long history by non-Egyptians; Persians, Greeks, Romans, Arabs, and the Ot-

---

[1] Among British prisoners of war was a young man named Winston Churchill whose captor was Louis Botha, later prime minister of the Union of South Africa.

toman Turks—who assumed control in 1517—played the conqueror's role. The Sultan at Constantinople was the nominal ruler, but his viceroy or pasha was actually in charge. In the eighteenth century, the country suddenly assumed new importance because of its location relative to India. Much of Britain's trade with India was carried across the Isthmus of Suez. In 1798, Napoleon had sought in vain to conquer Egypt, but had performed an invaluable service to the world through the discovery of the Rosetta Stone by one of the scientists he brought with him, Professor Champollion. This discovery unlocked Egypt's past.

The Isthmus of Suez is a very low stretch only a few feet above water. In ancient times, there had been a canal from the Red Sea to the Mediterranean, but it gradually had become clogged up by about 200 B.C. European commerce by the last half of the nineteenth century needed a canal, since the cost of land portage and transshipment of goods was extremely high. The result was that the French engineer Ferdinand de Lesseps, a close friend of the Khedive of Egypt, Ismail, succeeded in 1869 in constructing the Suez Canal with the financial assistance of the Khedive, who received majority control of the stock.

Ismail was a notorious spendthrift and endeavored to modernize Egypt through such expensive projects as the construction of beautiful public buildings, the erection of telegraph wires, the building of railroads, and Africa's finest harbor, Alexandria. His dealings with European bankers were none too happy and, in 1875, owing to the refusal of the French to loan him the money he wanted, he turned to Disraeli, then British prime minister, and sold his interest in the canal. Britain, through Disraeli's brilliance in expediting the deal (he borrowed the money privately), now had control of this vitally important waterway.

In 1876, again in financial difficulties, Ismail agreed to a system of dual control whereby an Englishman collected Egypt's revenues and a Frenchman controlled expenditures. In 1879, the Khedive Ismail was ousted because of his efforts to abolish this system, and the British and French replaced him with his son Tewfik, who accepted dual control, under which a healthy share of Egypt's national revenues was earmarked for foreign bondholders. Some of his subjects were resentful and a revolt broke out in 1882, led by a commoner named Ahmed Arabi, an army officer. The British proposed punishing the rebels but the French prime minister, Gambetta, refused. Therefore, the British alone employed force and occupied the country. On 13 September 1882, Arabi was defeated at the Battle of Tel-el-Kebir and exiled to Ceylon, where he became a prosperous tea grower.

From 1882 to 1914, Egypt was technically part of the Turkish Empire but actually was under British military rule and became a British protectorate in 1914. The British Agent and Consul-General was the actual ruler of the country. From 1883 to 1907, this office was held by one of Britain's greatest imperial servants, Lord Cromer (Evelyn Baring).

OTHER BRITISH AFRICAN HOLDINGS

Through an Anglo-German Convention of 1890, the British won control over Zanzibar together with that part of Africa north of the equator up to Abyssinia and Italian Somaliland. In the Anglo-Congolese Convention of May, 1894, they rented a strip of territory twenty-five miles wide from upper Lake Tanganyika to British East Africa together with the right to build a railroad there and certain steamship rights on Lake Tanganyika. This arrangement facilitated the "all-red route" which Rhodes envisaged. The British then divided their holdings into Uganda and British East Africa, both of which were made crown colonies. Uganda attracted some colonists, since it is capable of settlement by Europeans. The area proved attractive also to Hindus, who numbered about fifty thousand by 1914, mostly in Kenya, which became the new name for British East Africa.

In the 1890's, Rhodesia and Nyasaland were developed chiefly by Rhodes' British South Africa Company, and in central Africa other British holdings were acquired and strengthened. These included Gambia, Sierra Leone (Lion Mountain), the Gold Coast, Nigeria, and British Somaliland.

Completing the picture is the Anglo-Egyptian Sudan, where the British had to quell the revolt of el Mahdi in the eighties. The "prophet" slaughtered the old hero of the Taiping Rebellion in China, General "Chinese" Gordon, and his entire command at Khartoum. Not until September, 1898, were the Sudanese conquered. The British victor was General Kitchener, who defeated them in the Battle of Omdurman, following which a condominium between Great Britain and Egypt was established.

Kitchener then advanced to Fashoda at the headwaters of the Nile, where he met a French force under Captain Marchand. The two forces, encamped under their rival flags, stood firm and hostilities appeared inevitable. With both countries willing to fight, the new French Foreign Minister, Théophile Delcassé, although an aggressive imperialist himself, decided to yield and ordered Marchand's forces to abandon Fashoda. This action paved the way for an Anglo-French treaty in 1899 which bettered France's position in West Africa and gave England uncontested supremacy in the Nile valley.

THE FRENCH IN AFRICA

Despite the prominence of British activities in Africa, it was the French who actually commenced the partition of the continent in the nineteenth century. Charles X, the French ruler, finding himself in difficulties at home, decided upon the expedient of foreign war in an effort to strengthen his faltering position. He decided that the Bey of Algeria was obnoxious and needed to be punished. Charles and his advisers had no intention of acquiring territory. They merely wished to wage and win a war "on the cheap," so they went to war against the Algerians in 1830. On the same day that Algiers fell to the French, Charles X was driven into exile. His successor Louis Philippe turned the adventure into a war which pinned down French forces for eighteen years, took tens of thousands of French lives, and cost the French taxpayers millions of dollars.[2] Ironically enough, the French conquest coincided with the fall of Louis Philippe in 1848. With a colony on their hands which they had not sought, the French decided to settle the land by an attractive homestead policy which, however, attracted numerous Italians and Spaniards. By 1914, Algeria was successful and prosperous and was governed as an integral part of France with representation in the French Chamber of Deputies.

By 1914, there were five parts of Africa under French control. These were: Morocco, Algeria, and Tunisia in the North; French West Africa (Afrique Occidentale Française); French Equatorial Africa (Afrique Equatoriale Française); French Somaliland; and the island colonies of Madagascar, the Comoros, and Réunion.

The Tunisian story is an interesting illustration of the part imperialism played in European diplomacy in the days leading up to the First World War. By 1880, there were about twenty thousand Italians living there. The business houses and shipping lines were mostly in their hands, and had it not been for Bismarck the Italians probably would have taken over possession of the country. The Iron Chancellor had a dread of the possibility of the two Latin races coming together to form an amicable understanding. Such an alignment would strengthen Germany's old enemy and conversely would be harmful to Germany. Therefore, at the Congress of Berlin in 1878, Bismarck privately suggested to the Italian representative the advisability of Italian acquisition of Tunisia and assured him such a step would win German approval. To the French, he repeated this maneuver and promised German acquiescence should the French annex Tunisia.

In 1881, the imperial-minded Jules Ferry came into power in France. Determined to rehabilitate French prestige, he put into operation a plan for gaining Tunisia which resulted in the winning of a French protectorate through the Treaty of Bardo, in 1882. This arrangement guaranteed the position of the reigning house but provided for French domination. Italy's resentment over losing drove her into the arms of Bismarck and resulted in the formation of the Triple Alliance in 1882.

[2] It was during this war that the French Foreign Legion came into being.

GERMANY AND THE DARK CONTINENT

At this point, it is advisable to turn to Germany's interests in this great continent, since they were destined to worsen relations between her and Great Britain and France.

While France sought compensation for the loss of Alsace and Lorraine largely through a revival and expansion of her colonial interests, Germany stood pat in the period from 1870 to 1884. During this time about six million Germans left the country, but Bismarck was not interested in gaining colonies to attract them nor for that matter was he particularly concerned about building a fleet. He even went so far as to encourage both the British and the French in their colonial enterprises, since he felt both would lose far more than they could gain from such activity and the net result would be beneficial to Germany's position. He was essentially a "little German," satisfied with the unification of Germany and eager to maintain the European *status quo,* which was favorable to Germany. But the spectacle of young Germans going forth to other lands which were not under the German flag caused a feeling of unrest among German bankers, manufacturers, and educators. These groups now forced Bismarck into expansion against his wishes.

From the late 1600's to the early 1700's, Germany had played a role in Africa. Frederick the Great had founded the Brandenburg-Africa Company, which established a number of slave-trading posts along the African coast and which had leased some West Indian islands from Denmark for selling these slaves. The business eventually collapsed, but the point is that there actually existed a tradition of German enterprise overseas.

Many German traders and missionaries began to visit Africa as early as a generation before unification but were hampered by not having a strong national government behind them similar to that of England and France. It was largely through her businessmen that Germany acquired a colonial empire. The argument that Germany was becoming so highly industrialized and so needed colonies for raw materials and surplus products proved a strong one, as did the prestige propaganda. The latter stressed the point that Germany's leading rivals, the great nations of Britain and France, had empires, and if Germany, too, were to be truly great she ought to acquire these attributes of greatness—colonies. Then, too, there was the point that her young people would not be lost to other countries if Germany offered them a place to go.

While all of these arguments were lost on Bismarck, the manufacturing, shipping, and banking interests so shaped public opinion that he was forced to capitulate. The German Colonial Society was formed to influence the public, and, by 1878, it selected the site of the first colony. This was to be German Southwest Africa, which had a good harbor, Walfisch

Bay. But that very year, Great Britain annexed Walfisch Bay while the Germans were talking about it—a fact which greatly excited German public opinion.

German Acquisitions. Several years later, 1882, a German merchant bought a harbor near Walfisch Bay from the native ruler for a few dollars, and some beer, rum, and whisky. The harbor, Angra Pequena, was a poor one but it was the only other one in the region. The British protested against this entrance of Germany into the African scramble and got the Portuguese to do likewise. Bismarck, faced with an aroused domestic opinion, had to establish a German protectorate over South-West Africa. By the acquisition of territory in three other parts of Africa and in eastern waters, Germany set up a colonial empire.

Togoland on the west coast was the next spot taken. In the summer of 1884, Herr Nachtigal, German consul-general in West Africa, made a series of treaties with local chieftains who accepted German control. He now went out to secure all the territory between the Niger and Congo Rivers, but the French and the British preempted the French Congo and Nigeria. Nachtigal did manage to purchase Kamerun, and, in late 1884, Bismarck had to ratify this holding.

In East Africa, the German most active was Dr. Karl Peters, consul-general of East Africa, who had made over one hundred treaties and had gained Zanzibar by February, 1885. This German activity alarmed the British and from 1884 to 1890 relations between the two countries deteriorated somewhat. The British formed an East Africa Company and from 1888 to 1890 serious consequences seemed imminent. But in 1890 an agreement was reached between the two countries. Great Britain received Zanzibar, Germany got the island of Helgoland in the North Sea, and East Africa was divided. It might be noted in passing that this proved to be one of the most disastrous deals Britain every signed, since Helgoland became a deadly menace to her security in two world wars.

THE ITALIANS IN AFRICA

Like Germany, Italy was a belated entrant in the colonial race. But Italy possessed one of the greatest heritages in this field of any of the powers. She was the child of both the Roman Empire and the great trading centers of the Italian city states.

In 1870, several Italian trading houses banded together and bought the port of Assab on the Red Sea from the Emperor of Abyssinia, who freely agreed to the sale because he felt it would facilitate the import of European goods into his country. From the beginning, the merchants tried to get the government to take over the port, and in 1882 they succeeded. The Italian government of that period had just missed out on Tunisia and in the same year lost a golden opportunity to join with the British in the occupation of Egypt. They had refused the British invitation because of lack of foresight and also inertia. They were very dilatory in getting around to taking over control of Assab, as can be seen from the above.

Having joined the Triple Alliance largely as a result of the French annexation of Tunisia, the Italian government underwent a marked change. The popular clamor for empire could no longer be resisted and, in 1885, the government began to undertake a definitely imperialistic policy. Until 1896, Francesco Crispi, sometimes called the Italian Disraeli, sounded the note of imperialism.

In 1885, the port of Massawah on the Red Sea was occupied. Italy now gradually took over the territory between Assab and Massawah and, in 1887, announced the formation of the colony of Eritrea. Crispi now went after the independent kingdom of Abyssinia (Ethiopia). In 1889, a deal was consummated whereby the native ruler, Menelik II, ceded his coastal territories to Italy. England and France managed to horn in at the right moment, and the result was the creation of British and French Somaliland. By 1889, Abyssinia had no coastline, and Italy had the colonies of Eritrea and Italian Somaliland, two extremely hot, thinly populated regions.

Not satisfied, the Italians, who feared further interference by the British and French, began to make plans for the acquisition of Abyssinia by trickery. War broke out and culminated in the massacre of an Italian army at Adowa. Crispi was forced out of office, and Italy made peace and promised to respect the independence of doughty Abyssinia.

By 1905, Italy's imperialistic dreams were revived as a strong demand for an empire where young Italians might emigrate was raised. In fact, from this time forward in the twentieth century, the cardinal point of Italy's foreign policy was the acquisition of colonies.

Conquest of Libya. At the Algeciras Conference in 1906, France informally recognized Italy's right to help herself to any possessions in North Africa not already staked out by another European power. The *quid pro quo* here was an Italian green light for French designs on Morocco. Great Britain made a similar arrangement in return for Italian recognition of her position in Egypt. Thus, Italy was turning toward the rivals of her Triple Alliance partners, Germany and Austria-Hungary. Having cleared the way with Britain and France and fearful lest their German ally might act first, the Italians suddenly moved in an effort to secure the last remaining North Africa possessions not held by a European power—Tripoli and Cyrenaica. On 26 September 1911, Italy demanded that Turkey turn over to her these two provinces or go to war. When no answer was forthcoming from the Turks, Italy declared war. By October, 1912, the then effete Turkish government was forced to capitulate in the Treaty of Lausanne. In addition to the former Turkish tributary provinces of Tripoli and Cyrenaica in North Africa, which the Italians now renamed Libya, the victors annexed the Dodecanese Islands in the Mediterranean. A young socialist journalist named Benito Mussolini got into difficulties with his government for attacking the Libyan adventure in his newspaper, but the conquest was generally well received by the Italian people, who felt their victory gave them much needed prestige in the eyes of the world.

Thus, by 1914, Italy had obtained possession of a modest colonial empire which had very little to recommend it. The colonies proved somewhat of a drain but were written off as worth the expense, since they were "exhibit A" for the claim that Italy was a "great power."

THE LESSER POWERS IN AFRICA

The great powers were not alone in their partition of Africa, since such lesser European states as Belgium, Portugal, and Spain also carved out possessions in the dark continent at the expense of the natives.

One of the most intriguing regions in all Africa was the dreaded Congo. In the period between 1850 and 1870 this great heart of Africa was made known largely through the work of David Livingstone, a Scots missionary, and Henry Stanley, a Welsh-American newspaperman and explorer. Livingstone's discovery of the titanic Victoria Falls and his stories of the African heartland won for him the position of British consul for South Africa. News that he was missing in 1872 aroused world-wide attention and resulted in a search for him led by the American newspaperman, Stanley.

Stanley accomplished his mission when he came to the shores of Lake Tanganyika, where he discovered his quarry living happily among the natives. Livingstone refused to return to civilization and stayed content until his death. His remains were shipped to England and buried in Westminster Abbey. Meanwhile, Stanley became world-famous through this exploit and wrote a book entitled *How I Found Livingstone in Africa,* which sold millions of copies and was translated into many languages. Now an explorer on his own account, he was sent on an expedition in 1874 by the New York *Herald* and the London *Daily Telegram.* He crossed the continent from west to east and discovered the Congo River and the Stanley Falls. Returning to civilization in 1878, he wrote another book, *Through the Dark Continent.*

The work of these two explorers attracted great attention in Europe, particularly in Belgium, where Leopold II conceived the idea of erecting a vast private domain for investment. He founded a group called the International Association. When Stanley returned, Leopold made him head of an expedition to go to the Congo valley country. On this junket, Stanley made agreements with the natives to accept the overlordship of Leopold.

The French, not to be outdone, rushed an expedition down and seized French Equatorial Africa. The Portuguese grabbed Angola, and the British moved into the interior to the west and beyond the Boers. It became evident that something would have to be done, and so at the suggestion of Portugal the Berlin Congress of 1884–1885 was called. The American minister to Germany acted as an official observer, and nearly all the European nations sent delegations.

The Belgian Congo. On the eve of the Congress the wily Leopold got the jump by announcing the creation of the Congo Free State under his sovereignty. The powers, faced with a *fait accompli,* recognized Leopold's action but whittled down his holdings along the seacoast. The powers instituted free trade in the Congo basin together with equality of commercial opportunity and laid down the rule that nations wishing a part of Africa must announce their intention to the world, back their declaration by effective occupation, and be willing to settle disputes by arbitration.

The Congo Free State was bound to Belgium by personal union and was not strictly a colony. Leopold sank a great fortune in the region to little avail and was bitterly disappointed over the turn of events. True to his promise, he allowed the foundation of numerous concession companies, which, for the most part, employed harsh and repressive methods in dealing with native labor. Early in the 1900's the truth of the Congo brutalities leaked out when Sir Roger Casement, a British consul in Africa and later a prominent figure in the Irish Easter Week Rebellion of 1916, reported what he had heard about conditions. The British sent Lord Cromer down from Egypt to investigate, and he verified the reports. The great uproar which followed resulted in adverse world opinion, later reflected by the American poet, Vachel Lindsay, who penned his scathing *The Congo* (1914), containing the expression "Leopold in hell." In 1909, the monarch turned the Congo over to Belgium as a colony, and, by 1914, on the eve of the war, King Albert had commenced a real house cleaning there.

Spain in Africa. Spain, the world's leading power in the fifteenth and early sixteenth centuries, had been the first power to possess an empire on which "the sun never set." But she had retrogressed to a fourth-rate power by the time of her defeat by the United States in 1898. In 1900, she set out determinedly to begin the road back by attempting to develop her scraps of empire.

She owned Ceuta and Melilla in Morocco and fell in with the French designs on Morocco in return for a promise of getting the back country to these two cities. In 1912, she established, with the backing of England

and the approval of France, the protectorate of Spanish Morocco, which represented an extension of her holdings. What had been a foothold along the Gold River was developed into the colony of Rio de Oro, 1898–1914, when the four Spanish holdings there were consolidated. This colony's value was largely strategic and the German, Graf Zeppelin, once remarked it would be worth Germany's acquiring since it made a good take-off place for planes to South America.

Thus, all things considered, Spain had built up a tidy little colonial empire in Africa by the outbreak of the First World War and had done a great deal to regain its self-respect. The chief drawback was that the only place it could secure capital for development was from the Germans, who laid out railroads, provided regular steamship service, and built plantations. Hence, by 1914, economically the Spanish colonies were dominated by Germany.

Portuguese Possessions. The last of the European African powers to be mentioned is Portugal. The Portuguese interests in Africa went back to the late fifteenth century when she picked up two islands in the Gulf of Guinea—Sao Thome and Principe. After slaving had run its once lucrative course there, these possessions sank into insignificance, but nonetheless Portugal retained title to them.

By drawing on various claims, Portugal was able in the 1880's and 90's to bring the desirable colonies of Angola and Mozambique into her colonial empire. At the Congress of Berlin, 1884–1885, the English and French, anxious to keep Germany in check and also not to allow Leopold II to get too much territory, managed to draw very generous boundaries for Angola.

In the 1890's the British made possible Portugal's acquisition of Mozambique. Portugal was England's oldest ally and since the eighteenth century had also become economically dependent upon Britain. Thus, Britain could exploit Angola and Mozambique indirectly and, by 1914, had these colonies economically well in hand. Yet in 1898 Germany and Great Britain had worked out a plan to split Angola and Mozambique should Portugal ever go bankrupt, an event the British never allowed to happen. In 1913 and 1914, the German ambassador to England, Prince Lichnowsky, took the matter up again with Sir Edward Grey in the British Foreign Office. A deal was initialed but not signed when the war broke out.

29

European Imperialism in Asia and the Pacific

Asia, a continent with a population many times that of Africa and possessed of several great ancient civilizations, was an early object of modern European imperialism. The attractions of the Indies had lured Columbus and the intrepid Portuguese navigators before and after him. It was the Portuguese who were first destined to establish great imperial holdings in Asia, but their power yielded before the greater drive of the more brusque Dutch, who in turn were forced to share hegemony in the Far East with the French and the British. Less spectacular, perhaps, but nonetheless as convincing was the steady advance over the adjacent Asiatic land mass of the Russian steam roller, which had reached the Pacific as early as the seventeenth century.

THE OPENING OF CHINA

Greatest among the indigenous powers in the Far East was China, the sleeping giant which appeared oblivious to the encroachments of European imperialism but which was made to feel its effects most strongly in the nineteenth century. Inordinately proud and completely static, China lived on much as she had for centuries past. Her emperor bore the august title of the Son of Heaven, a position which since 1644 had been the property of the Manchus, a once virile race of conquerors from the north.

The first Europeans to secure a precarious foothold in China were the Portuguese, who had established a trading station at Macao near Canton

470

in 1557. Others who later carried on trade on a strictly limited scale with Chinese merchants were chiefly British and Americans. But the only power whose relations were dignified by treaty status was the Russians (1689).

The Manchu dynasty looked with disfavor on trade with the West and sought strenuously to limit it. Yet the Western insistence upon more trade, together with the removal of the hampering restrictions governing this relationship, grew increasingly in the early years of the nineteenth century. To appreciate how unsatisfactory the conditions were from the point of view of the West, a brief description is in order. Canton was the only port open to trade, and Europeans doing business there were stringently restricted in the matter of residence. Trade could be carried on only with the monopolistic Co-Hong, a guild of Chinese merchants who were the only natives permitted to engage in trading with foreigners. Since the Manchu government would not deign to treat the European governments as equals, the latter had no diplomatic or consular officials in China, a fact which hurt foreigners trading there who might have grievances which demanded redress.

The Opium Wars. The opium question brought to a head this unsatisfactory condition. Until the appearance in the China trade of this drug produced in India by the British East India Company, the balance of trade heavily favored the Chinese, who demanded payment in silver for Chinese goods. Opium, however, tipped the balance in favor of the British (and Americans, too), but the Chinese government decided to put a stop to this trade because of the deleterious effects of the drug upon its subjects. The result was the Opium War, 1839–1842.

In fairness to the British, it must be said that opium was not the only cause of the war. Rather China's general irritating attitude toward foreigners, together with the harshness of the conditions of trade and the inequalities of Chinese law as it affected foreigners, was the basic cause. The ease with which the British decisively defeated China revealed to the world the weakness of the Manchus and also the vast superiority of Western arms and military methods. By the terms of the Treaty of Nanking (1842), several new ports, including Shanghai, were thrown open to trade with residential rights guaranteed, the monopoly of the Co-Hongs was broken, and China agreed to recognize European consuls. In addition, the Chinese paid an indemnity to the British and ceded outright the island of Hong Kong, which became a British crown colony. Furthermore, a regular tariff was established which could not be altered except by mutual agreement. Nothing was said about the opium traffic and so by tacit consent it was allowed to flourish without curb. The following year, the General Regulations of 1843 granted foreigners the right of extraterritoriality, which removed them from the jurisdiction of Chinese law and permitted them to be tried by their own officials and under their own law.

The privileges granted the British were accorded all foreigners by the Chinese government. Determined to secure a formal guarantee, the United States rushed over to China a crack diplomatic negotiator, Caleb Cushing, who signed with the Manchus the Treaty of Wanghia (1844) granting all these concessions, including extraterritoriality, to Americans. The French also made sure the privileges were theirs by the Treaty of Whampoa (1844). Thus, the Opium War paved the way for the opening of China to Western exploitation, which began in earnest in the latter part of the nineteenth century.

Meanwhile, the Chinese officials continued to show hostility to the "foreign devils," and so the Second Opium War broke out in 1856. This time the British were joined by the French, who used the pretext of the murder of a missionary as a cause. Together, they thoroughly whipped the pitifully equipped Chinese. The conduct of the conquerors left a bitter taste because in their exuberance they burned the emperor's summer palace at Peking and bombarded and sacked the capital. The Treaty of Peking (1860) provided another indemnity together with further concessions. These included permission for the establishment of foreign embassies in Peking, the right of foreign missionaries to seek converts unmolested and with the protection of the government, the privilege of free travel into all parts of China, and the placing of China's customs under foreign supervision. Similar treaties were accorded the United States and Russia as well.

Taiping Rebellion. The hapless Manchus were plagued by a domestic uprising during the Second Opium War. This was the Taiping Rebellion, 1850–1864, a revolt against the Manchus by the Chinese people which resulted in terrible destruction of land and property and took a toll of millions of lives before it was finally quelled. The Taipings were disgusted with the weakness shown by the government in the original Opium War and were affected by the impact of the West. They had adopted a form of Christianity which was a combination of the teachings of Christ and their own ancestor worship. The fact that they were so favorably impressed by Christianity alienated the educated class, who remained loyal to the Manchus. The Manchus, after years of failure to end the uprising, hired foreign mercenaries and adventurers such as General Frederick Townsend Ward of Salem, Massachusetts, to lead the "Ever-victorious Army" which in the end proved too much for the Taipings. Ward was mortally wounded in one of the engagements, and Major Charles Gordon, a Britisher, then took command. Gordon was nicknamed "Chinese," owing to his fondness for dressing in Mandarin costume.

THE EMERGENCE OF JAPAN

While the nineteenth century advertised the weakness of China, it also brought into the spotlight of world attention a non-Western power which was destined to cut quite a swath in the field of imperialism. Contrary to once prevalent belief, Japan was not a completely closed country prior to 1853. In the sixteenth and early seventeenth century, the Japanese proved receptive to foreigners. The government, however, became alarmed over the great inroads the Catholic missionaries who came in the wake of St. Francis Xavier had made and decided to wipe out Christianity. Following the slaughter of thousands of native converts, the survivors were driven into secret practice of their religion, since open profession of their faith constituted a capital crime. The Tokugawa family in 1603 captured the shogunate, the office of military dictator, and closed the country to foreign intercourse in 1638. Foreigners were not allowed to enter Japan nor natives to leave. Outside of a few Chinese junks, the sole exception to this rule was the permission given the Dutch to land one shipload of goods annually at Nagasaki. In this way, the Japanese officials kept informed of what was transpiring in the outer world. Through its military power, efficient administrative system, and tight financial controls, the Tokugawa shogunate unified Japan and completely divested the hereditary emperor of all real power.

The increased opportunities afforded the West in China after 1842 focused attention on Japan. It was reasoned that the island empire ought to be reopened by force if necessary since it would serve the two-fold purpose of an additional trade market and a convenient coal and water station en route to China. Owing to the preoccupation of the European powers with the aftermath of the revolutions of 1848 and the Crimean War, it remained for the United States to win the distinction of reopening Japan.

The fact that the expansion of the United States had reached the Pacific coast together with the increase in its maritime commerce combined to influence the American government to accede to the memorials of its merchants that something be done about Japan. Through a combination of native tact and a display of force which overawed the Japanese, Commodore Matthew C. Perry, USN, succeeded in winning from the Japanese a treaty, on 31 March 1854, which accorded the United States most-favored-nation status,[1] opened two ports for the fueling and provisioning of American ships, and promised to correct the barbaric treatment previously accorded shipwrecked American sailors. Further-

[1] The United States would automatically be granted any concessions given any other power.

more, the treaty provided that the United States could open a consular office at Shimoda. Perry's treaty was followed by the work of Townsend Harris, the first American consul in Japan, who won a commercial treaty in 1858 which opened four more ports, provided reciprocal diplomatic representations, fixed Japanese customs charges, and granted extraterritoriality to Americans.

The Meiji Restoration. The result of this Western impact was a series of changes which brought about the resignation of the shogun in 1867. The following year ushered in the Meiji restoration, wherein the emperor now took over control of the government. His advisers were convinced that the only way in which Dai Nippon could win equality with the Western powers was to adopt their methods. The results were phenomenal. In a little over two generations (1867–1937), the Japanese changed from an agricultural economy and a feudal system into an efficient industrial society. From an almost complete economic isolationism, they became extremely active internationally. True to their goal, they borrowed heavily from the experience of others, but their methods were highly specialized and were adapted to their peculiar needs. Their slogan can be well summed up in the words: "adopt, adapt, and invent." The population more than doubled in this period and so did the standard of living.

The modernization and industrialization of the country were so advanced that between 1894 and 1899 she was able to put an end to extraterritoriality and the so-called "unequal" treaties which interfered with her customs and the regulation of her financial affairs. Perhaps the chief factor enabling Japan to win the desired treaty revision was her smashing victory over China in the Sino-Japanese War, 1894–1895. This conflict arose over the status of Korea, a Chinese vassal. The modern Japanese army (German trained) and her efficient navy (English trained) completely routed their Chinese adversaries in a war which the world felt would end in the extinction of the Japanese "ant" by the Chinese "elephant." By the terms of the Treaty of Shimonoseki (1895), the independence of Korea was granted by China, which also paid an indemnity and ceded Formosa, the Pescadores, and the valuable Liaotung peninsula to Japan. This latter transfer so upset the designs of the Russians that they secured the backing of France and Germany and forced the victors to return Liaotung to China in return for a further indemnity.

THE SCRAMBLE FOR CONCESSIONS IN CHINA

There now commenced a wholesale scramble for leaseholds in China. The Russians inaugurated the rush by securing a ninety-nine year lease over the selfsame Liaotung peninsula in southern Manchuria which they had forced Japan to return. This action by Russia so enraged the Japanese that they began to plan a war of revenge. Russia also won the right to build railroads (the Chinese Eastern and the South Manchurian) in Manchuria to tie up with the Trans-Siberian Railroad.

The murder of two German missionaries in Shantung province enabled the Kaiser to secure a ninety-nine year lease over the rich Shantung peninsula, long eyed covetously by Germany, together with the right

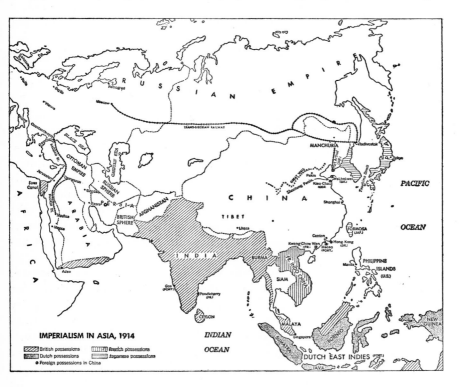

IMPERIALISM IN ASIA, 1914

British possessions · French possessions · Dutch possessions · Japanese possessions · Foreign possessions in China

of building railroads there and exploiting the coal mines for the benefit of German industry. The city of Kiaochow also went to the Germans for the usual long-term lease in 1897. The English secured Wei-hai-wei for as long a period as the Russians should occupy Port Arthur (at the tip of Liaotung), and the French took over Kwang-Chowan, an island off the southeast coast of China. Italy suffered the humiliation of being refused a lease on Sanmen Bay because China knew that the Italians were not then in a position to enforce their request.

China was thus by the end of the nineteenth century cut into spheres of influence. Great Britain was in control of the basin of the Yangtze; Germany had the Shantung peninsula; Russia was paramount in Manchuria; France in south China; and Japan controlled the region opposite Formosa.

At this point, the United States, through its Secretary of State, John Hay, who feared for the future of American trade in China, now took a hand. On 1 September 1899, Hay sent a note to the interested powers seeking a promise of equality of commercial opportunity for all in China. A second note contained a request that the sovereignty of China and its future territorial integrity be pledged. These actions constituted the policy of the "Open Door." The evasive replies of the powers were made public by Hay in such fashion that it was believed all had agreed.

The Boxer Rebellion. All of this aggression by foreigners at China's expense coupled with the dislocations suffered in the native industries in the face of the manufactured goods and articles of the West fanned the flames of resentment and produced the Boxer Rebellion in 1900. The Boxers were poverty-stricken peasants and workers who belonged to an organization called the Society of Harmonious Fists (*Ilochuan*) or the Fists of Righteous Harmony, badly translated by foreigners as "Boxers." Originally anti-Manchu like the earlier Taipings because of the government's helplessness in the face of the nation's adversaries, they were cleverly turned against the West by agents of the Manchus. Ostensibly an athletic organization, they were trained to resist the "foreign devils" and at their meetings were given good stiff doses of nationalistic propaganda. The Dowager Empress, Tzu-hsi, was most active in supplying needed assistance to the cause.

An international army commanded by a German, Count Waldersee, was formed to defeat the Boxers, but other foreign troops arrived first and ended the uprising. China was required to pay a heavy indemnity and to promise suppression of all antiforeign societies. The United States was awarded a share of the indemnity, but President Theodore Roosevelt returned almost half of it and President Coolidge later gave back another 25 per cent. A grateful China used this money to establish a fund to send students annually to American universities. Not the Open Door but the jealousy of the European powers toward one another served to end the seizure of Chinese territory. It is probable that collective action would have been taken against any individual power that sought to extend its holdings.

THE RUSSO-JAPANESE WAR

In 1902, for reasons which will be made clear below, Great Britain entered into an alliance with Japan. The agreement provided that one would remain neutral should the other go to war against a single power, but that each would aid the other should it be involved in war with more than one power. The alliance was in reality directed against Russia and paved the way for the outbreak of the Russo-Japanese War in 1904.

Russia's action in securing the Liaotung peninsula at Japan's expense and the former's designs on Korea prompted Japan to commence war with Russia by an unannounced attack on the Russian Far Eastern fleet based on Port Arthur. The other notable engagements, both Japanese victories, were the naval battle of Tsushima and the land battle of Mukden. The war resulted in Japan's second straight victory over a major opponent and was especially significant in that it marked the first defeat in modern times of a Western power by an Asiatic. Japan's victory had important repercussions throughout the Orient, especially in the lands under the domination of Western imperialism, where it caused a strong spirit of nationalism to emerge. The war was noteworthy also in the fact that it marked the turning point in Japanese-American relations, which up to that point had been quite cordial on the whole. The Japanese blamed the American government for their failure to win an indemnity and to gain greater territorial booty, whereas the United States, whose bankers had largely financed the Japanese war effort, now saw a new threat to the Open Door policy in the place of the one (Russia) removed.

The peace negotiations were held and the treaty signed in the Portsmouth, New Hampshire, Navy Yard in September, 1905. President Theodore Roosevelt acted as mediator and won the Nobel Peace Prize for his work. The Treaty of Portsmouth recognized Japanese hegemony in Korea (which she annexed in 1910), and transferred Russia's lease of the Liaotung peninsula together with her railroad and mining rights to Japan. In addition, Russia ceded the southern half of the island of Sakhalin.

INDIA

Sometimes considered part of the Far East but usually looked upon as a separate area and virtually a continent in proportions is India, home of approximately one-fifth of the human race, and, like China, mother of an ancient civilization. A highly desirable prize, it was destined to become practically the sole property of one power—Great Britain. Long famous for the excellence of its handicraft goods, it began to attract European traders who settled there in the sixteenth century following the discovery of an all-water route by the Portuguese Vasco da Gama. In addition to the pioneer Portuguese, the traders were chiefly British, French, and Dutch. In fact, there was formed in each one of these countries in the early seventeenth century an East India Company possessed of a government charter and monopolistic trade privileges.

It can justly be said that the term India came to be purely a geographical expression. It did not denote unity either politically,[2] since it was divided into hundreds of states, or racially (there was over a score of races) or linguistically (over a hundred different languages with thousands of dialects) or religiously (Hindus, Mohammedans, Buddhists, Christians, Sikhs, Parsees, Animists, *et al.*). Thus its hopeless division created a golden opportunity for the European, who could employ a policy of *divide et impera* with great success. In the struggle which ensued, the British East India Company was victorious. France was left as a result with only a few trading stations flying the French flag. Portugal, the only other European state with possessions in India, was allowed to retain its modest holdings.

For the next one hundred years, the government of India from the British point of view was the exclusive prerogative of the Company and represented a very gradual extension of power. Its officials often became fabulously wealthy. It was quite common for a fashionable young man to go out to India in the service of the Company, amass a personal fortune, and return home and buy a landed estate and a seat in Commons. Such men were called the "nabobs," a term contemptuously given them by their detractors. During this period, the Company extended its control over more and more parts of India.

The Mutiny. This was a situation which was so annoying to many of the natives that they awaited only the proper opportunity to arise against the interlopers. Such an occasion was provided by the Sepoy Mutiny in 1857.[3] The widespread conflagration which resulted from the uprising of native soldiers almost overthrew the British raj. It did put an end to rule by the Company owing to the domestic dissatisfaction over its control in England. Its prerogatives were now assumed by the crown, and the cabinet was increased by the addition of a Secretary for India. Disraeli's flair for the dramatic was given a chance to exhibit itself, when in 1877, he was able to proclaim Queen Victoria to be Empress of India. The subcontinent had indeed become the "jewel of greatest value in the crown of empire."

Until the retirement of Lord Curzon as Viceroy in 1905, little of importance had taken place in India since the Sepoy Mutiny. But the times demanded concessions to still the mounting native dissatisfaction, and so the British government passed the Morley-Minto Reforms in 1909, a series of innocuous changes which provided a mild form of native representation on the Viceroy's council and that of the Secretary of State for India and made provincial chambers partly elective.

By the eve of the First World War, Great Britain could look with

[2] Not long after da Gama's visit, India did manage to achieve a temporary political unity in the Mogul Empire (1526–1761) founded by Babar.

[3] Sepoy was a generic term for the native soldiery employed by the Company.

some pride on her accomplishments in India, where she had corrected numerous barbaric practices, ended tribal warfare, codified law, improved transportation and communication, and made agriculture more productive. Such, however, is the nature of the human race that the good was easily overlooked and the evils of British rule exaggerated by native elements, desirous of home rule, and by foreign meddlers, jealous of British success.

SOUTHEAST ASIA

Imperialistic activity was also quite marked in the regions of Southeast Asia and the East Indies. Here, the foremost powers proved to be Great Britain, France, the Netherlands, and the United States. The latter's experiences will be treated in the following chapter.

The British succeeded in annexing Burma, a country with an area only slightly less than the American state of Texas, in a series of campaigns begun in the 1860's and culminating in 1885. On 1 January 1886, Burma became a British possession, and was administered until 1937 as a province of India, into which it was incorporated by the British despite the mutual antagonism of the Burmese and the Hindus. Long dissatisfaction with its lot won for Burma the title of the "Ireland of the Far East," a none too accurate designation since Burma is usually not considered part of the Far East, an expression reserved for China, Japan, and Korea.

In addition to Burma, the British assumed valuable holdings in Malaya, including Singapore, a crown colony originally acquired by Sir Thomas Stamford Raffles, one of Britain's most famous colonial figures.

Indo-China. While the British were busy in Burma, the French were equally active in Indo-China, the name given a heterogenous collection composed of Annam, Tonkin, Cambodia, Cochin-China, and Laos. French interest dated back to the seventeenth century, but it was under the Second Empire that real activity commenced. By 1863, French conquests in Cochin-China were recognized by the Annamite emperor in a formal treaty and France won title over several provinces. By 1893, French control over what came to be known as French Indo-China was complete but French rule was never too popular. Perhaps the sole distinction won by the French was that they produced in Indo-China proportionately the greatest number of Christian converts to be found in any important Asiatic possession of a European power.

The Netherlands Indies. First to appear in the vast region lying to the south and southeast of continental Asia were the Portuguese in the fifteenth century, but they were gradually ousted from their most important holdings by the Dutch until today Portugal retains only Timor and a few smaller nearby islands.

The successful Dutch were faced with English rivalry in the seventeenth and eighteenth centuries through the activities of the British East India Company, which managed to retain a portion of Sumatra until the period after the Napoleonic Wars. As a matter of fact, during that world upheaval the British seized control of the Dutch East Indies for the period from 1811 to 1818 for fear they might fall into the hands of Napoleon, who had already overrun the mother country of Holland itself. The postwar settlement resulted in Britain's relinquishing the East Indies to the Netherlands in return for the latter's promise to give Britain a free hand in Malaya.

In the years that followed, the East Indies developed into what was probably the most lucrative of all colonial possessions. At first this result was achieved by ruthless exploitation of the native population, but in time public opinion in the Netherlands forced the abolition of these abuses. By the end of the nineteenth century the Dutch were following a policy based on the premise that the continued prosperity of Indonesia depended on promoting the welfare of the inhabitants of the islands. Nevertheless, nationalism grew in spite of the efforts of the Dutch to check it. The success of the Japanese by 1905 encouraged Indonesian native leaders to seek equality with Europeans. Their failure to secure such treatment (they noted that the Japanese were treated as equals in the Indies by the whites) enraged them. There now sprang up a revival of Javanese culture through the foundation of the High Endeavour Society (Budi Utomo) together with Sarekat Islam, an Islamic Indonesian agitation group. By the outbreak of the First World War in 1914, native dissatisfaction, despite the benefits bestowed by Dutch rule, was pronounced.

PENETRATION INTO CENTRAL ASIA

In the region of Central Asia from about 1850, Russia and Great Britain became rivals. The southward advance of the Russians in their persistent quest for warm-water ports alarmed the British, who saw in this march a menace to the security of India. Following the Russian conquest of the Pamir plateau in the 1890's, their nearness to India was such that it seemed as if nothing stood in the way and that a new raj would rule India.

Three spheres of rivalry between the countries developed—Persia, Afghanistan, and Tibet. Britain felt that her influence must be paramount in these countries in order to set up buffers for the protection of India. Her first step was the annexation of Baluchistan and the pacification of the Punjab. Following these actions she commenced to interfere in the internal affairs of Persia, Afghanistan, and Tibet.

Persia. Looking first at Persia, we find that it was but a remnant of one of the great states of antiquity but it was by no means a small country. Its mineral resources were known to be important, but transportation was such an acute problem that little had been done. The British by the 1890's were anxious to uphold the country's sovereignty or, if that proved impossible, to get control of it themselves. Otherwise, the Russians would be down on the Persian Gulf and out on the Arabian Sea, a development not to be relished. Russia was as keenly aware as Britain of the importance of Persia, and so Teheran, the Persian capital, became a hotbed of intrigue.

After both sides had made headway through the agency of loans to the spendthrift native ruler, the shah, to the extent that Persian indebtedness threatened the country's independence, a patriotic uprising in 1906 of the Young Persians, a nationalist organization, brought the country almost to chaos. Because of changed world conditions in 1907, Great Britain and Russia settled their differences amicably, as will be shown below. Persian resistance to foreign pressure soon collapsed, and Persia became independent in name only.

Afghanistan. Lying to the east of Persia is Afghanistan, a little-known land of mountains and bloody tribal feuds. Most of its citizens were nomadic tribesmen. Two groups of rival nobles were subsidized by the Russians and the British, respectively. British troops, however, invaded the wild country and set up a native ruler of their own choice. Undaunted, the Russians succeeded in reaching Afghanistan's northern border. Actually, there was nothing in this country but trouble, and both Russia and Britain had plenty of that. Strategically, however, it was tremendously important as it controlled the Khyber and Bolan passes into India.

Tibet. Third of the regions attracting the rivals was Tibet, which lies above northeastern India. This huge land of lofty mountains (it is twice the size of Texas) contains some of the most difficult terrain in the world. Traditionally isolated from the world, it was technically a part of the Chinese Empire, although China's control was only nominal. Its ruler was the Dalai Lama and most of its inhabitants were also Buddhist monks. The capital city, Lhasa, was forbidden territory for Europeans. Despite the problems inherent in making entry, the Russians first succeeded in 1901 in opening relations. When the British got wind of this, they sent a military mission from India under Colonel Younghusband to make a treaty with the Tibetans in 1904, giving the British the equivalent of a protectorate over the land of mountains and valleys.

With affairs at this stage in the three regions in 1907, the British and the Russians got together and their foreign ministers signed a treaty. Fear of Germany was the main reason to account for this development, but

Russia had also met a setback at the hands of Japan in the Russo-Japanese War and was accordingly in a more conciliatory mood. Furthermore, the fact that France had allied herself separately with both countries was an important factor. The treaty divided Persia into three strips; the northern part of the country was to be a Russian sphere of influence and the southern British, with the middle zone left open to both but ostensibly for the Persians. Both agreed to get out of Tibet, which was to revert to the status of a Chinese vassal. Finally, in Afghanistan, the Russians recognized British control.

TURKEY AND THE BAGDAD RAILWAY

Vexing as these matters had been for Great Britain, the menace of Germany in the Levant (Near East) was equally pressing. This region had long been the special property of Turkey, but the Sublime Porte was a dying power. Accordingly, by the end of the nineteenth century, several important European powers had spheres of influence in the Levant. Russia had her eye on the southeastern part of Turkey; Great Britain herself had set her sights on Palestine; the French wanted Syria; Italy had marked out Adalia (the southwestern quarter of Asia Minor) as very attractive; Greece desired the area around Smyrna; and Germany hoped to acquire the northern half of Asia Minor and as much more as she could get. By all appearances, Asiatic Turkey was destined to be cut to pieces by European imperialism.

The Berlin-to-Bagdad Railway plans of the Germans served to create great excitement over the entire region. It was a very rich area and seemingly possessed unlimited mineral wealth. Its oil made it particularly enticing. Furthermore, it contained considerable rich land which only Turkish misrule had caused to lose its natural productiveness. The Germans appear to have been the first to sense its great potentialities. From 1875 to 1914, there was considerable German literature claiming that the northern half of Asia Minor might be had if Turkey were befriended by Germany and stressing the importance of a German *Drang nach Osten*.

The young Kaiser, William II, did his part. In 1889, he made a visit to the region and became convinced of its worth as a place for German investment. In 1898, he made another trip there and even included Palestine on his agenda. One of his activities was to place a wreath on the tomb of Saladin, the great Saracen conqueror. His words suited his actions because he announced that, if Islam needed a friend, it could count on Germany. This was not good listening for British ears, since the Empire contained millions of Moslems.

Building the Railway. The railway project began with the construction between 1888 and 1892 of a line from Haider Pasha, opposite

Constantinople, to Angora. Then, however, it ran into serious difficulties. Since the British regarded a German-controlled railway to Bagdad and the Persian Gulf as a menace to India, they closed the London money market to the promoters, and the resources available to the German company proved insufficient for the formidable task of crossing the Taurus Mountains. After prolonged haggling, the Germans undertook to raise funds by building a branch line to tap the Moslem pilgrim traffic to Mecca and Medina. It was completed from Aleppo through the Holy Land to Medina in 1908 and was immediately profitable.

Soon afterward Great Britain decided that further opposition would be fruitless, and in 1914 an agreement was reached whereby Britain would permit funds to be raised in London and in return would receive one less than half the memberships on the board of directors. In addition, Britain would build the extension from Bagdad to Basra. The outbreak of the First World War prevented this arrangement from materializing, and the result of the conflict brought the whole line under British control. It was ultimately completed in 1937.

30

American Imperialism

At the end of the Civil War the expansionist fervor of the era of Manifest Destiny had apparently disappeared. Absorbed with the problems of reuniting their country, with the settlement of the West, and with their stupendous industrial expansion, the American people were fully enough occupied at home and had little incentive to concern themselves with what was going on outside their borders. This attitude was destined to endure for a quarter of a century. It first revealed itself in the convincing rejection by the Senate of a treaty in 1869 which provided for the purchase of the Danish West Indies and cropped up again the following year when another treaty was rejected which called for the annexation of Santo Domingo. Not even the outbreak in 1868 of the Ten Years' War between Cuba and Spain could revive enough expansionist sentiment to capitalize on this situation by acquiring Cuba.

There was one significant exception to this failure of American expansionism at this time. Alaska was purchased in 1867 from the Russian government for the paltry sum of $7,200,000. The man most responsible for this priceless addition to the territory of the United States was Secretary of State Seward. His "extravagance" was roundly deplored in the United States, and Alaska was popularly referred to as "Seward's Folly" or "Seward's Icebox." The wisdom displayed by Mr. Seward in this instance needs no elaboration to a generation acquainted with the importance of Alaska in the realm of aviation. The purchase price has been refunded many times over through the gold alone taken from its land and streams during the colorful Klondike era at the end of the century.

THE UNITED STATES AND LATIN AMERICA

During the latter part of the nineteenth century, Latin America became increasingly more important from the point of view of the United

States. The history of Central and South America during this period re-veals several points worthy of mention. In the first place, there was a marked unevenness of growth within their ranks. The so-called ABC powers (Argentina, Brazil, and Chile), had far outstripped their smaller neighbors (with the possible exception of Mexico) in population, wealth, and material advancement. While there are undoubtedly many reasons to explain this fact, perhaps the most important is that the ABC states were favored by a far greater influx of European immigrants than the others. An exception to this general rule might be noted in that Uruguay actually gained more in this respect than did Chile but, on the whole, the gen-eralization holds true. The latter nineteenth century was an era of consid-erable influx and the years before the First World War were to witness a sharp acceleration in this process. These three countries were also the re-cipients of a great deal of foreign investments which naturally aided their development.

Secondly, frequent revolutions characterized nineteenth- and, for that matter, twentieth-century Latin America. The dreary repetition of these upheavals demonstrated some lack of political maturity. This weakness has, however, been offset to some extent by the ability shown by Latin Americans in the field of jurisprudence, where they today have become recognized throughout the world for their achievements in in-ternational law and organization.

A third factor to be taken into consideration when discussing Latin America in the nineteenth century is the not unnatural widespread mis-trust of the United States which persisted throughout her sister republics to the south. Since the activities of the United States here are shortly to be chronicled below, suffice it to say at this point that the reputation en-joyed by the "colossus of the North" was none too healthy.

Finally, a lively rivalry existed between the United States and Great Britain for commercial and other preeminence in this region which was handily won by the British. The latter were far more astute and circum-spect in their dealings with Latin America and were furnished with ample propaganda material by the rather clumsy attitude shown by the Americans in most matters dealing with Central and South America. Time and time again the United States revealed scant appreciation of the manners and customs of its neighbors, only to learn to its surprise that these proud people were offended.

The United States and the Isthmian Canal. When William Maxwell Evarts became American Secretary of State under President Hayes, 1877–1881, the United States manifested a renewed interest in the affairs of Latin America and particularly in the idea of an isthmian canal under American control. The news that the aged Ferdinand de Lesseps of Suez Canal fame was planning to build such a canal with European backing produced quite a flurry in the American press. There was even talk in congressional circles of a violation of the Monroe Doctrine. Accordingly in 1880, Evarts compiled a paper on what he felt an isthmian canal should be. His feeling can be summed up in the expression "an American canal under American auspices." This statement proved so impressive to the French government that the French ambassador in Washington agreed to commit to writing a statement to the effect that his government had no interest in the De Lesseps project.

Regarding Latin America, Evarts felt that the United States should do what it could to maintain peace there and should attempt to mediate if Latin-American states went to war against one another. After a few minor successes in his policy of "good will and interests," Evarts and his successors proved unable to stop the War of the Pacific, 1879–1883, between Chile and the combination of Peru and Bolivia. This rebuff was not very complimentary to the United States.

Blaine and Pan-Americanism. Despite Evarts' failures in this part of his program, his successor, James G. Blaine, sought to carry on his mediation program and also his canal policy. Blaine's Latin-American policy really had two objects: (1) to bring about peace in Latin America and prevent future wars; (2) to encourage American trade there. In the canal matter, both Blaine, who remained in office only while Garfield was President, and his successor, F. T. Frelinghuysen, were rebuffed by the British, who reminded them that the Clayton-Bulwer Treaty had never been abrogated and that the interest of Great Britain in a canal was not subordinate to the United States. This setback did not deter Blaine from seeking the fruition of his other plans, *i.e.,* peace and trade. He conceived the idea of a Pan-American Congress for this purpose but left office before he had a chance to hold the projected meeting. The new administration was cool to it, and it lay dormant until Blaine again became Secretary of State in 1889. The Second Pan-American Conference opened in Washington in October, 1889. Following the introductory ceremonies, the delegates of the eighteen nations present were whisked off on a tiresome junket whose object was to impress the visitors with the greatness and wealth of the United States. Blaine's efforts to establish an Inter-American Customs Union wherein tariffs would be reduced and European trade cut and to create machinery for the arbitration of disputes were fruitless. His work was not entirely barren, because out of it came the Pan-American Union in Washington, an organization dedicated to the promotion of good inter-American relations.

Blaine's efforts at friendliness toward Latin America were not aided by the *Baltimore* incident. Two American sailors attached to the U.S.S. *Baltimore* were killed by a Chilean mob in Valparaiso and several others injured in 1891. Harrison's annual message to Congress that year was quite strong about this incident. Blaine secured full satisfaction from Chile, but the attitude of the American press and public had not been very peaceful.

The Venezuela Boundary Dispute. This sort of thing, coupled with American failures in its canal policy and in its Latin-American arbitration hopes, did not win for the powerful young state much respect in the world of statesmen. However, in 1895, President Grover Cleveland risked a war with Great Britain by announcing that, since the latter had refused to arbitrate a boundary dispute with Venezuela, the United States would investigate the situation and establish a line! Fortunately, Britain's problems were so serious in other respects that she quickly agreed to arbitrate, and the affair was satisfactorily closed. One of the most remarkable features of the whole episode was Secretary of State Olney's pronouncement that the United States was practically sovereign in North and South America and its fiat was law. Known as "Olney's twenty-inch gun," it was a rather presumptuous statement, which indicated a return to a position closely approximating the bumptious 1840's and 1850's.

BACKGROUND OF THE SPANISH-AMERICAN WAR

When considering this question, it is well to remember that the 1890's was a period of intense nationalism, as witness the *Baltimore* incident and the Venezuelan affair cited above. Three terms widely used in the United States during that decade were the Monroe Doctrine, the Panama Canal, and a Big Navy. The latter was necessary to support the nationalistic spirit and build it up. The pitiful condition of the American Navy after the Civil War made necessary an increase in its strength. As the navy grew in the 1890's, the United States was in a better position to demand a canal, defend the Monroe Doctrine, and seek naval bases. Along with this went a certain emotional development. The Civil War was now only a memory, and there was a feeling that the time was at hand for another war. William James wrote his *A Moral Equivalent for War,* in which he pointed out the zest and excitement for war. He said people needed this excitement and would have war unless something better could be found to replace it. Historical novels and romances were quite popular. Emotionalism led quite naturally to a revival of Manifest Destiny.

To support this attitude Darwin's theory of natural selection and the survival of the fittest came in quite handy. John Fiske, American philosopher and historian, took over the Darwinian theory and pointed out the superior characteristics of Anglo-Saxons, their language, customs, and people. The Reverend Josiah Strong, a Congregationalist, said the Anglo-Saxon was divinely commissioned to be his brother's keeper. Professor John W. Burgess of Columbia University announced that the United States had a world mission to perform. He advocated a strong colonial policy in order to help backward peoples. Captain Alfred Thayer Mahan, USN, put his emphasis on sea power. Without a navy no people could attain their highest stature. He pointed out the advantages of an increased navy, an increased world trade, and colonies. Equally enthusiastic with the foregoing were such political figures as Theodore Roosevelt and Henry Cabot Lodge.

Long before the war with Spain commenced, American publications were trained in the imperialistic outlook. Propaganda was plentiful. The business interests and Wall Street did not have to finance it and, as a matter of fact, were opposed in the early 1890's to war but had become converted to the cause by 1898. News of Dewey's victory at Manila sent stocks up, since the victory was so complete it seemed as if the war would be short and would bring in its wake considerable Oriental trade.

COURSE OF THE WAR

In 1895, Cuba once more revolted against Spanish rule. The Spaniards sent General Weyler to crush the uprising. His efforts, which included the establishment of a military dictatorship featuring the *reconcentrado* system of concentrating the population around military camps, earned for him the name of "Butcher." The Cubans, desirous of winning American sympathy, painted the Spaniards as murderers and artfully glossed over their own seamy conduct. American citizens had investments of about $50,000,000 in Cuba, and not only their property but also their lives were in jeopardy.

Probably the chief factor in involving the United States in war was not the sympathy for Cuba nor the American investment there but the role of the American "yellow press." W. R. Hearst's New York *Journal* was engaged in a battle with Joseph Pulitzer's New York *World* for circulation. They both featured the atrocity angle of the Cuban War. While conditions in the war were certainly bad, these papers exaggerated them considerably. Their success was ample proof that this was what the public wanted, and their influence became national in scope as imitators arose to cash in on public sentiment.

In the election of 1896, William McKinley had been victorious on the Republican platform, which called for Cuban independence. He favored a policy of watchful waiting, but in June, 1897, his Secretary of State, the venerable John Sherman, sent a sharp diplomatic note to Spain chiding the Spanish for the methods they employed in the war. The Spanish rejoinder declared that these methods were copied from those of a General W. T. Sherman, USA, in his march through Georgia (Secretary Sherman's brother).

The act which produced the immediate cause for an American declaration of war was the blowing up of the American battleship *Maine* in Havana harbor, 15 February, 1898, with the loss of 268 lives. The cause of the explosion is still undetermined, but the Spaniards were immediately blamed by the American press and public. The news of the sinking electrified the country and the slogan "Remember the *Maine!* To hell with Spain" swept the land. Congress rushed through a bill appropriating $50,000,000 for defense, and McKinley sent a sharp note to Spain. The Spaniards became alarmed and began to make some redress. They revoked their concentration-camp policy in Cuba and started a move to have the pope arbitrate the conflict. On 9 April 1898, the Spanish government yielded to the American demands, and the American minister to Spain cabled Washington that, if the United States did not humble Spain any further, the whole affair would be satisfactorily resolved. A strong executive could have done this, but McKinley lacked the courage to oppose the popular clamor and sent Congress a war message on 11 April. Two weeks later war was declared. Thus began an unnecessary conflict between two unevenly matched contestants.

Conduct of the War. The two navies were nearly equal in the number of ships and guns, but the newer American ships and better trained crews had a great advantage and displayed overpowering superiority. The United States Army possessed only a small number of regulars but quickly added hastily trained volunteers and militia so that the total force amounted to about 200,000. Behind them stood an estimated one million volunteers ready if needed. The Spaniards, on the other hand, had about 200,000 in scattered garrisons in Cuba and their other possessions but were unable to reinforce these men or supply them adequately because the United States Navy controlled the sea.

As one-sided and ridiculous in many respects as the war was, there was a great wave of panic along the Atlantic coast of the United States for a time, when it was feared that the missing squadron of Admiral Cervera was planning to bombard the big eastern seaboard cities. On 13 May his ships were finally sighted in the West Indies, where they headed harmlessly for Santiago, Cuba.

Of the war's campaigns only one involved sharp fighting or produced serious American losses. This was the action around Santiago at El Caney and San Juan Hill, where Lieutenant Colonel Theodore Roosevelt and his "Rough Riders" achieved fame. Here the Americans were victorious, but the Spanish distinguished themselves by their courage and ability. The others, all smashing American triumphs, were: Manila Bay, where Admiral Dewey annihilated the Spanish fleet without the loss of a single American life; the destruction of Cervera's fleet off Santiago; and the conquest of Puerto Rico. At Manila, Dewey was unable to capture the city until troops could come from the United States. In the interim, the ships of several nations had arrived to watch the proceedings and to afford protection to the lives and property of their nationals. Of these foreign ships the Germans managed to send the most imposing array. Their ships outnumbered those of the British, who had a greater financial interest there than the Germans and were even more than a match for Dewey's force.

Actually, the Germans, who now eagerly desired colonies, had an eye on the Philippines. They felt that the United States had no wish to annex the islands and seem to have been strengthened in this belief by a group of American anti-imperialists. Dewey was patently upset by the presence of the Germans, under Vice Admiral von Diederichs, in such strength. Furthermore, he was annoyed at their refusal to respect the blockade regulations he had established. On one occasion, he lost his temper and practically hurled a challenge at von Diederichs. Actually, Dewey had been somewhat remiss in his failure to give the specific blockade limits. On 13 August, the day of Manila's capture by the American forces, an incident took place. While the United States fleet was preparing to shell the Spanish shore batteries, Captain Chichester, the British commander, worked his ships between Dewey's and the Germans. His purpose was simply to get a better view of the action, but it was interpreted as a gesture of friendship toward the Americans if the Germans should demonstrate hostility.

RESULTS OF THE WAR

The events of August had proved the final straw for Spain, and hostilities were ended. Representatives of the two powers met at Paris, on 1 October 1898, to sign the treaty of peace. By the terms of the Treaty of Paris, signed 10 December 1898, the United States acquired from Spain title over the Philippines, Puerto Rico, and Guam.[1] Twenty million dollars was paid Spain to get her to agree to relinquishing the Philippines. She was also forced to recognize the independence of Cuba.

At this point, there commenced in the United States one of the most spirited battles over the ratification of a treaty that the country has ever witnessed. In the Senate, the forces of the anti-imperialists were led by Senator George Frisbie Hoar of Massachusetts. Prominent among the

[1] In the light of future history, an unfortunate event was the failure of the United States to acquire Spain's remaining Pacific possessions, the Marshall, Caroline, and Marianas groups. These were subsequently purchased by Germany, conquered during the First World War by Japan, and became Japanese mandates.

anti-imperialists throughout the country were such important figures as President Eliot of Harvard, Grover Cleveland, William Jennings Bryan, Samuel Gompers, Andrew Carnegie, William James, Jane Addams, and Mark Twain. They argued that: (1) government without the consent of the governed was un-American; (2) the United States would require a larger army and navy and would become involved in Far Eastern problems which could easily lead to war; (3) the cost of administration would greatly exceed any returns from such holdings; and (4) the Constitution did not permit the acquisition of extraterritorial areas.

Despite the formidable opposition to the treaty, it managed to pass the Senate by the narrow margin of two votes, 6 February 1899, very largely through the influence of Bryan, who swung enough Democrats over to the Republican adminstration to guarantee ratification. He had undergone a change of mind, which was formerly explained on the belief that he did it in the hope of hanging a millstone around the Republican necks. The more recent theory is that he did not plan to conduct the election of 1900 on the issue of imperialism but rather on free silver. Furthermore, he argued that it was expedient to get the Philippines away from Germany and Japan, both of which coveted the archipelago, for the time being, and then free them later.

The Philippine Insurrection. When the Filipinos learned that they were not going to secure their independence, they inaugurated the sanguinary Philippine Insurrection, 4 February 1899. It became necessary, before the natives could be subdued, for the United States Army to employ a force of 70,000 men and to consume two years in ferocious fighting which added little to the luster of the United States. The uprising was finally broken with the capture of the native leader, Emilio Aguinaldo. The whole episode need never have occurred had the administration been willing to back a resolution promising ultimate independence to the islands. This proposal was defeated on 14 February 1899, when Vice-President Hobart exercised the rarely used privilege of voting to break a tie.

A far more important result of the war, especially in the light of the future, was the change in Anglo-American relations. The American action in declaring war against Spain was favorably received by both the British government and press—much to the surprise of the Americans. Britain's action was not motivated primarily by love or altruism. Instead it was a hardheaded conclusion based on a painstaking analysis of the world situation. Her South African problems were rapidly heading for war with the Boers, and her relations with both France and Russia were so delicate that the possibility of war with either or both was not remote. Furthermore, there was the growing menace of Germany's rapid rise to world power to be considered. It is little wonder then that Britain's policy makers saw in the United States at least the hope of a benevolent neutral or possibly even an ally if England were to reverse her previous position toward that country. Reverse it she did from 1898 onward, with few minor exceptions, down to the First World War. In fact, the British even went so far as to take the side of the United States in the latter's dispute with Canada over the Alaskan boundary in 1903 and ruled for the Americans against Newfoundland in 1905 in the fisheries controversy.

THE ANNEXATION OF HAWAII

The interest of the United States in the Hawaiian Islands dates back to the early part of the nineteenth century, when American whaling vessels began to stop there and American missionaries, mostly from New England, began to go to the island in search of converts. In time, many Americans came to be engaged in the business of operating sugar plantations. In 1875, a reciprocity treaty was signed between the United States and Hawaii. Under the terms of the treaty each country admitted free the principal products of the other. This agreement continued until 1887 when it was renewed and the United States was granted the privilege of utilizing the Pearl River harbor for coaling and naval purposes. During these years sugar production increased enormously. The American planters became quite prominent and began to express a lack of sympathy with conditions in the islands. In 1887 they succeeded in getting the native king to agree to a constitution which made the government parliamentary and provided the American property owners with considerable power.

In 1891, upon the king's death, his sister came to the throne as Queen Liliuokalani. Within two years, Queen "Lil," who disliked the Americans in the islands, decided that she would proclaim a new constitution which would in effect undo the work of 1887. Afraid for their lives and property, the Americans tooks steps to organize a revolution and a provisional government which requested the American Minister, John L. Stevens, for military aid. This dignitary promptly arranged for the landing of some 150 bluejackets and 10 officers together with two cannon from the U.S.S. *Boston* in order "to protect American life and property." When this action was followed by a request from the provisional government for American recognition, Stevens complied immediately. Two weeks later, he announced that Hawaii was now a protectorate of the United States and personally raised the American flag, which soon flew over all public buildings. This result was made possible because the queen yielded not to the provisional authoritites but to the United States government.

In February, 1893, a treaty of annexation was drawn up. Although approved by the Senate Committee on Foreign Relations, the session of Congress ended before action could be taken. In the meantime, a new administration under Grover Cleveland took office. The President decided to examine the treaty and reopened the affair by sending to Honolulu a James Blount to investigate. Mr. Blount was then made American Minister, replacing Stevens. The new American representative's findings were nearly all in favor of Liliuokalani, whom he found the bulk of the population desired back on the throne. This report influenced Cleveland to aid the queen, but the President put one restriction on his help. The queen must promise to grant amnesty to all the people involved in the revolution. Upon her announcement that she not only refused this request but would see to it that they lost their lives and property, Cleveland washed his hands of the whole matter by turning it over to Congress. The Senate concluded that Liliuokalani ought not to be restored, and that there should be no tampering with the provisional government for the time being.

President McKinley's first year of office in 1897 saw a treaty of annexation fail to secure the necessary two-thirds approval in the Senate. But the following year, under the stress of Dewey's position in Manila, Hawaii was annexed by the United States through the medium of a congressional joint resolution, a move designed to circumvent the two-thirds rule in the Senate, since this device requires only a mere majority of the membership of both houses.

THE PANAMA CANAL

The results of the Spanish-American War, which saw the American people in possession of important Pacific territories, convinced many that the time had come to build an American canal connecting the Atlantic and the Pacific. During the war itself, the strategic necessity for such a canal was dramatized by the voyage of the U.S.S. *Oregon,* which had to sail all the way around Cape Horn from San Francisco in order to join the fleet in the Caribbean.

A big question at the turn of the nineteenth century was whether the canal would be built in Nicaragua or Panama. In 1899 the Walker Commission spent one million dollars to make a survey of all possible routes. At this juncture, the representatives of the New Panama Canal Company (this was the French group which had failed) began lobbying in Washington in an effort to get the United States to build in Panama. Active in the attempt to unload the French holdings were the former chief engineer of the company, Philippe Bunau-Varilla, and the company's American lawyer, William Cromwell. Meanwhile, a group known as the Maritime Canal Company worked with equal fervor on behalf of a Nicaraguan route. Still a third interest, the transcontinental railroads, labored feverishly against both.

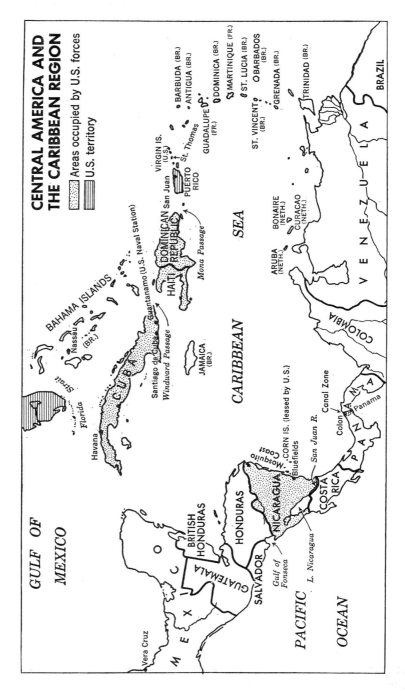

CENTRAL AMERICA AND
THE CARIBBEAN REGION

Areas occupied by U.S. forces

U.S. territory

494

In 1902, the House of Representatives passed the Hepburn bill, which favored a Nicaraguan canal. Even before the measure could reach the Senate, the French interests announced that they would sell for $40,000,000, which was represented as a great bargain. The Spooner Amendment then gave the President of the United States authority to acquire the rights of the French company for a sum not to exceed $40,000,000, declared that the United States should acquire from the Republic of Colombia a strip of land wide enough to construct the canal, and further stipulated that if these two conditions were not met within a reasonable time, a Nicaraguan canal should be built.

Diplomatic Preliminaries. Previously, the United States had managed successfully to rid itself of the Clayton-Bulwer Treaty through an arrangement known as the Hay-Pauncefote Treaty (1901) which gave the United States the exclusive right to construct, control, and fortify an isthmian canal. This concession on Britain's part was in line with her recently altered American policy.

Then in 1903 the United States and Colombia drew up the Hay-Herran Convention, but this agreement proved distasteful to the Colombian senate, which refused to ratify it. Colombia's action was ill advised in the light of the fact that a revolution was brewing in the province of Panama. Aiding and abetting the revolutionaries were Bunau-Varilla and Cromwell of the French company. When President Theodore Roosevelt let it be known that while the United States could not stoop to aid such a revolt, a *fait accompli* would delight him, the success of the revolution was practically assured.

The Panama Revolution. The uprising was planned for 3 November 1903. The commandant of the Colombian troops in Panama was bribed and his men were all assured of fifty dollars apiece. At this point, the leader of the Panamanian revolutionaries, a Dr. Amador, cabled Bunau-Varilla in New York that the Colombian authorities had learned all the details of the plot. Bunau-Varilla made a hasty trip to Washington, where he learned that the U.S.S. *Dixie* and *Nashville* had been sent to Panama already. The revolution then went ahead as scheduled. Dr. Amador was moved to make a speech in which he declared that he and his men were heroes and concluded with the announcement that Theodore Roosevelt "had made good." The following day the *Nashville* landed troops, thus preventing the Colombians from sending forces to defeat the *coup d'état*. On the sixth, the United States officially recognized Panama and an American army officer personally hoisted the Panamanian flag. A treaty was quickly concluded between the Republic of Panama, represented by Bunau-Varilla, and the United States wherein the latter was given all the rights it sought in the Canal Zone. In 1913, the administration of Woodrow Wilson suggested the payment of $25,000,000 to Colombia to soothe her injured feelings, which was finally done during the presidency of Warren G. Harding in 1921.

While the United States did not instigate the revolution in Panama, it did everything it could to ensure its success. This unneutral action was boastingly referred to by Roosevelt in a public speech some years later when he declared that "I took Panama and let Congress debate." The blighting effect of this performance on inter-American relations was serious and prolonged. The one redeeming feature was that the United States government did go vigorously to work. First of all, benefiting from research done on malaria under the supervision of Dr. Walter Reed of the Army Medical Corps, which had identified the mosquito as the carrier of the disease, the conditions which had caused a terrible death toll among the French company's workers in Panama were eliminated in an energetic clean-up campaign conducted by Dr. William C. Gorgas. Then, under the direction of Colonel George Washington Goethals of the Corps of Engineers, the canal itself was taken in hand and opened to traffic in 1914.

OTHER AMERICAN POSSESSIONS

The Samoan archipelago, strategically located on the sea lanes of the South Pacific, attracted American attention as early as 1838, but serious interest did not develop until the 1870's. Finally in 1878 the United States secured the right to maintain a naval station at Pago Pago on the island of Tutuila. This step resulted in a three-cornered contest for domination in Samoa between the United States, Germany, and Great Britain, which reached a climax early in 1889 when seven warships— three American, three German, and one British—lay in the roadstead of Apia with guns loaded while their respective governments arranged a conference at Berlin to try to prevent an open clash. At this juncture a hurricane took a hand in the proceedings. On 16 March 1889 a storm of tremendous violence wrecked all the American and German vessels at Samoa with appalling loss of life. As the British ship fought her way to the safety of the open sea, she was cheered by the crew of a doomed American vessel.

Chastened by the catastrophe, the three powers temporarily settled their differences and established a joint protectorate over Samoa, a clumsy arrangement that worked as badly as might have been predicted. Finally, in 1899, after the Spanish war had left the American people more favorably disposed toward outright annexation of overseas territory, Samoa was divided between the United States and Germany, the former retaining Tutuila and the latter getting the rest of the archipelago. Great Britain took its compensation in the form of a clear title to the Gilbert and Solomon Islands.

Other Pacific holdings acquired by the United States are the small islands of Wake, Midway, Jarvis, Baker, Howland, Canton, and Enderbury. Originally of negligible value, they have been made very important by the development of aviation. Rounding out the American empire are the Virgin Islands in the Caribbean, purchased from Denmark in 1916 in order to forestall possible acquisition by Germany.

THE EVOLUTION OF A COLONIAL POLICY

The acquisition of noncontiguous territory by the United States proved, as was foreseen by the anti-imperialists, a problem in government. It became the practice, beginning in 1900, to divide American territories into "incorporated" and "unincorporated." The latter were considered not parts of the United States in the same sense in which the former were. Such territories as Alaska, Oklahoma, New Mexico, and Arizona were considered "incorporated," whereas Hawaii, the Philippines, and Puerto Rico were placed in the "unincorporated" category as a result of the so-called Insular Cases before the Supreme Court which evolved this distinction. In brief, it may be said that inhabitants of both classes possess the fundamental rights of Americans, but the residents of the "unincorporated" territories lack certain formal privileges. The Supreme Court retains for itself the right to decide which parts of the Constitution are fundamental and which formal. It has ruled, however, that inhabitants of areas annexed by the United States are not *ipso facto* citizens of the United States—citizenship can be attained only by the express grant of Congress.

The Philippines. In 1901, following the termination of the Insurrection, the American Congress permitted the establishment of a civil government in the Philippines. In 1902, an organic act was passed launching the inhabitants toward eventual self-government. In 1916, the Jones Act set up a bicameral legislature and increased the number of voters. It lasted until 1935 when it was replaced by the Philippine Commonwealth, which came about as a result of American legislation in 1933 and 1934.

The Hare-Hawes-Cutting Act became law in January, 1933, and provided for Philippine independence after a ten-year period of transition. However, it was not to take effect unless the Filipinos ratified it within one year. Their decision to reject the measure led to the substitution of the Tydings-McDuffie Act in 1934, which proved acceptable to the Filipinos. 15 November 1935 saw the Commonwealth of the Philippines formally inaugurated. At the expiration of a ten-year period, the Islands were to be given their complete independence. Despite the intervention of the war in 1941, which saw the Japanese occupation of the archipelago, the United

States was able to keep its promise, and 4 July 1946 the Republic of the Philippines became a reality.

Cuba and the Platt Amendment. At the outset of the Spanish-American War, the Teller Resolution had declared that the United States would leave Cuba to govern itself. With the conclusion of hostilities, the island was in a shambles. General Leonard Wood, United States Military Governor, did exceptional work in cleaning up the mess—an indefatigable worker, he founded schools, improved transportation and communication facilities, and reestablished municipal functions and courts. Wood also summoned a constitutional convention which modeled itself on the United States but neglected to insert any mention of future relations between Cuba and her liberator. Accordingly, the United States took action, and Congress passed the Platt Amendment to the Treaty of 1901 between the United States and Cuba. It was destined to endure until 1934 and included among its provisions the following: (1) Cuba must enter no pact with a foreign power which might jeopardize her independence; (2) Cuba must keep down her public debt; (3) Cuba must permit the United States to intervene to preserve Cuban independence and to aid the Cuban government when the situation demanded such action; (4) all acts of the United States during the military occupation after the war were to be ratified by Cuba; (5) Cuba was to carry on the work of sanitation begun by the United States; and (6) Cuba must sell or lease to the United States certain lands necessary for coaling or naval stations. The Cubans opposed the third provision strenuously, and it took considerable persuasion to get them to accept it. In 1902, the first Cuban president was installed under his own flag, and American troops were withdrawn.

The Foraker Amendment (1899) covered the economic side of Cuban-American relations. It prohibited the granting of any economic concessions whatsoever during the American occupation. The idea of reciprocity proved attractive to many, but the beet-sugar interests in the United States were in strong opposition. However, in 1903, thanks to the ardent support of President Theodore Roosevelt, a treaty of reciprocity was passed which revitalized the Cuban sugar industry.

Puerto Rico. For a period after the war, Puerto Rico had a military government, but in 1900 provision was made for civil government with an elective assembly and an executive council appointed by the President.

A second measure passed in 1917 bestowed American citizenship upon residents of the island. The voters choose a resident commissioner every four years. This official represents them in the House of Representatives in Washington, but he does not possess a vote. The local executive is a governor, appointed by the United States Senate until 1947, when the office was made elective. A bicameral legislature consisting of a senate and a house of representatives is elected by popular vote. Furthermore, there is an adequate judiciary composed of two sets of courts, Federal and territorial. Although this arrangement has been acceptable to most of the people of Puerto Rico, some of them have agitated for statehood, while a very small but extremely fanatical Nationalist party has demanded complete independence. This latter group was responsible for an attempt to assassinate President Truman in 1950, and three of its number fired a fusillade of shots into the chamber of the House of Representatives in Washington in March, 1954, injuring five of the members.

REASSERTION AND ENLARGEMENT OF THE MONROE DOCTRINE

In 1902, Venezuela again came into the spotlight, and Theodore Roosevelt became worried over what he considered were German designs in the Caribbean. His annual message of 1901 had said that the United States did not guarantee any country against punishment if it was guilty of misconduct. Such punishment, however, must not take the form of the acquisition of power or territory by any non-American power at the expense of an American country. The specific point to which he had reference was a dispute over debts involving Venezuela. Cipriano Castro had become dictator of that country in 1899, and shortly thereafter Venezuela defaulted on its international obligations. The three countries principally affected were Germany, Great Britain, and Italy. A German offer in 1901 to submit the dispute to the Hague Tribunal was rejected peremptorily by Castro. Accordingly, the three powers which suffered from Venezuela's breach sent an ultimatum to the offending government on 7 December 1902 threatening her with a blockade of her ports if she did not make amends. This action was acceptable to Roosevelt and his Secretary of State John Hay, who reasoned that the Monroe Doctrine did not apply.

When Germany sank two Venezuelan gunboats, and the three powers made a formal proclamation of blockade, Castro became alarmed and suggested that the United States act as arbitrator of the dispute. This pleased Roosevelt immensely, but Hay dissuaded him and recommended that the Hague Tribunal review the case. Ultimately, a tribunal of ten commissioners under the auspices of the Hague found for the three allied powers, and the case was settled. The significance of the dispute was great, for never before had the powers paid the United States and its Monroe Doctrine such deference. Furthermore, it marked the first time that any Latin-American state had asked the President of the United States to arbitrate a dispute.

Scarcely had this affair come under control when a similar difficulty cropped up in Santo Domingo. The dictator of that island country had been assassinated in 1899, following which matters became quite complicated. European creditors grew angry, and several of their governments threatened to intervene. On 17 October 1903, Belgium proposed to the United States a plan of joint action. The two powers would seize all customhouses and arrange for the governing of the island by an international commission of the largest creditors. This suggestion was politely refused by the United States.

The Roosevelt Corollary. At this point, a new strong man came into power. This man, General Morales, was friendly to the United States and said he was willing to have the United States take over and administer the Dominican customs. Roosevelt was willing, but since the election of 1904 was at hand he had to proceed with caution. Nonetheless in the spring of 1904 a number of periodicals came out with articles on Santo Domingo! On 20 May 1904 the President wrote a letter to Elihu Root which the latter read at a banquet in honor of the second anniversary of Cuban independence. This was the beginning of the famous Roosevelt corollary to the Monroe Doctrine. It declared that the United States desired to see its neighbors stable, orderly, and prosperous, but they must act with decency, keep their obligations, and maintain order. If there is brutal wrongdoing or weakness in a country, disorder is the inevitable result. This requires intervention by some civilized power. In the Western Hemisphere, the United States must be this "civilized power." Originally designed by the United States to prevent others from intervention, the Monroe Doctrine was now to be employed to justify intervention by the United States!

A commission met in July, 1904, and reported on Santo Domingo's debt to the United States. It recommended that if the former defaulted, the United States should appoint a financial agent for the Dominican customs, a pair of developments which quickly materialized. Roosevelt's victory in the election of 1904 meant that he could now come out and fight for his corollary, and his annual message of 1904 indicated that he would do just this. It used language which was virtually identical with that of his letter to Root. In January, 1905, two American naval vessels were sent to Santo Domingo, and in February a protocol between the two countries was ready. This understanding paid glowing tribute to the "new" Monroe Doctrine and declared that American intervention was only civil and not military. The United States pledged itself to respect the territory of Santo Domingo and arranged to divide the latter's customs receipts so that 45 per cent went to the Dominican government and 55 per cent would be used to meet the debt owed foreign governments. The United States Senate viewed the agreement askance and refused to ratify it, but Roosevelt was undismayed and proceeded on a temporary basis. He appointed collectors of customs, an arrangement which lasted for two years and proved eminently successful. The Dominican government, receiving only 45 per cent of its customs income, actually was provided with more funds than under the old regime. In the end, the President's persistence won and a permanent treaty was negotiated 25 February 1907. It might be noted that, with typical Roosevelt forcefulness, T. R. had maintained American warships in Dominican waters during the whole time. As he put it, they were needed to do good work.

In general, the American public and the increasingly friendly British government approved of the Roosevelt corollary. Latin America was for the most part also sympathetic at the outset, although in later years these states came to detest the corollary, which was used to justify frequent American military intervention in their affairs.

Intervention in Cuba. Meanwhile, American relations with Cuba were being governed by the Platt Amendment. Although there was little difference between Cuba's principal political parties, the Liberals and the Moderates, a revolution broke out in 1906 against President Estrado Palma. This official hastily requested Roosevelt to dispatch two American warships to aid his regime. It so happened that T. R. was disgusted with the Cubans and was chary of intervening. Added to his sentiments was the fact that his Secretary of State Root was then on a good-will tour of Latin America, so it was thought unwise to interfere. Instead, Roosevelt wrote the Cubans an open letter in which he called upon them to settle their differences. When this action had less than no effect, he sent Secretary of War Taft and Assistant Secretary of State Bacon down to the troubled island. The arrival of this mission caused all semblance of government to disintegrate, so, in September, 1906, Taft took over the government temporarily, assisted by a Marine detachment which eventually reached 8,600 men.

Taft gave way as Governor of Cuba to another American, Charles Edward Magoon, whose administration sought to hold an honest election in accordance with the will of the majority of Cubans. This event took place in 1908 and resulted in the election of the popular Gomez. The Magoon administration came to an end now that a Cuban was ready to assume the direction of affairs. By January, 1909, the last of the Americans got out, an action which surprised the world.

Under the presidency of Woodrow Wilson, American meddling in Cuban affairs became quite patent. Secretary of State Bryan went so far as to cable the Cuban president, General Menocal, that the American government did not approve an amnesty bill passed by the Cuban legislature and therefore the Cuban executive must veto it, which he did.

Trouble cropped up during the election of 1916. Menocal was re-elected but owing to a slight oversight there were more votes cast than there were voters. Recognizing that it was essential for him to secure the backing of the United States, Menocal declared all his enemies were pro-German, a device which accomplished his purpose. One day after the American declaration of war in April, 1917, he recognized a state of war between his country and Germany. His second administration, which began in May, 1917, was marked by great prosperity.

The calm which descended on Santo Domingo following the American control of the country's customs was rudely shattered in 1911 with the assassination of President Caceres. His successor, General Victoria, dissipated the former surplus in ten months and even added $1,500,000 to the public debt. This extravagance prompted the United States Department of State to feel that the Convention of 1907 had been violated and so 750 American marines were sent to explore the situation. In August, 1914, President Woodrow Wilson sent two commissioners to insist upon peace. Upon the election of a new chief executive in Santo Domingo, the United States declared that he must agree to put the collection of internal revenue in the hands of the United States as well as the customs or there would be no recognition.

Political conditions remained poor and in the spring of 1916 some 1,800 American marines were landed. The United States refused to pay the Dominican authorities anything at all unless the latter would agree to do the bidding of the Americans. The upshot of it all was that in November, 1916, the United States declared Santo Domingo to be under the military protection of the United States. This state of affairs endured until 1924, when a new convention was signed providing the American president with the power of appointing a collector of customs.

Intervention in Haiti. On the other half of the island of Santo Domingo, the foreign relations of the Republic of Haiti became quite involved in the period between 1910 and 1914. An American company had been given a concession to build a railroad in Haiti, but construction was stopped owing to the persistence of revolutions whose participants could not be constrained by the mere presence of the railroad. Since progress on the road was stopped, the Haitian government refused to pay.

The election of a new president in 1914 seemed a good time for the United States to speak its piece relative to Haiti. Secretary of State Bryan bluntly informed the Haitian president that the American government would accord his adminstration recognition only if it would accept these stipulations: (1) an American customs receivership, (2) settlement of the problem of the American railroad, and (3) the promise of Haiti never to lease any part of its land to a foreign nation.

The new president took office, but in 1915 was succeeded by President Sam, who jailed a number of his political enemies and then ordered the massacre of the majority of them. This action did not appeal to the citizenry, who went after Sam and literally tore him to pieces. American forces thereupon occupied the capital and let it be known that the United States would view with favor only a president who would be content to do American bidding. Such a person being found and duly installed in office, martial law was declared, and the United States took over the customs. A treaty in February, 1916, officially made the United States Haitian customs receiver. Haiti promised not to increase its public debt without American approval and agreed not to part with any of its territory to any foreign power. This treaty lasted until 1934, when the administration of Franklin Roosevelt put an end to it.

Nicaragua. The Central American republic of Nicaragua fell under the grip of a dictator in 1893. This individual, José Zelaya, held not only the United States but also the European powers of Great Britain and Germany in very low esteem. His increasing tyranny caused foreign economic interests great unhappiness, and in 1909 a number of foreign merchants doing business in the country advanced funds to a group of revolutionaries who aspired to oust Zelaya. Contrary to its usual procedure in such matters the United States supported the revolutionaries because Zelaya had permitted two Americans to be murdered. The American attitude assured the revolution's success, since the United States paid no attention to the Zelaya government's blockade, and American ships sailed blithely into blockaded ports with supplies for the revolutionaries.

Since finances were at the bottom of the whole thing, the United States arranged the Knox-Castrillo Convention (1911) whereby American bankers floated a loan for Nicaragua on the security of the Nicaraguan customs, which were to be administered by the United States. Although this agreement proved too bold for the American Senate, which refused to ratify it, the bankers went ahead under a slightly different guise. Despite opposition in Nicaragua, the loan was arranged largely through the instrumentality of the convenient presence of an American warship in Nicaraguan waters while the negotiations were in progress.

In late 1911 an American became collector-general of the Nicaraguan customs through the approval of the Nicaraguan government. This was only the beginning of a series of American interventions in Nicaraguan affairs. On several occasions in years to come, American marines were landed in that country for the sole purpose of protecting American investments.

"DOLLAR DIPLOMACY"

The foregoing material demonstrates the fact that American interests in the Caribbean area grew steadily after 1900, with resultant twisting of smaller nations by the "colossus of the North" to its own desires. The procedure was simple. American financiers made investments and insisted that their government protect them if they became jeopardized. When the State Department assented to this request, "Dollar Diplomacy" was the result.

Under Philander C. Knox, American Secretary of State, 1909–1913, this policy was highly developed. Mr. Knox felt that the government ought to back up its business interests in the Caribbean. This would help to remove British interests, investments, and influence and pave the way for their replacement by American. Dollar Diplomacy utilized the Monroe Doctrine's new meaning, which bestowed upon the United States a sort of international police power. It led quite naturally to the expansion of the United States Navy in order to protect American interests, including the Panama Canal.

Techniques of United States Control. To pursue such a policy, in general, the United States had to develop devices to assist governments it wished to favor. In the first place, the power to refuse recognition to a revolutionary faction grew to be quite an important one, since it became patent that if the United States acted in this fashion it would go hard on the revolutionaries. Thus, the question logically presented itself: how was it possible for a revolutionary government to win the favor of the United States? The answer seemed to be to get the various faction chiefs to hold an election under the supervision of the United States and to have all sides agree to respect its outcome. Yet this proposition has had varied results. For example, in 1913 General Huerta in Mexico was asked to hold an election, but the United States refused to allow him to run. The safest way to insure recognition was for a new government to grant political and economic concessions to the United States. In such case, Washington usually decided that the government was then unobjectionable.

Another way in which American interests could be served was for the United States to throw its influence directly on one side by granting the chosen faction arms and munitions and refusing them to the opposition. It had been American policy to allow freedom in this respect, but this practice was altered. An example was Santo Domingo in 1905, when the United States announced that no arms could go to the rebels, who thereupon obligingly gave up. In 1912, Congress passed a joint resolution stating that in the case of domestic violence in any Caribbean country it would be a violation to export arms except at the discretion of the President of the United States.

Should both the foregoing methods fail, there was always a third way for the United States to make sure its wishes would be respected. This was a resort to direct force. Various alternatives presented themselves under this option. Patrols might be established along the coasts of the country in question. American interests were frequently aided by the appearance of naval units. Another possibility was the declaration of a neutral zone, in a disturbed region where American interests were threatened. A good instance of this procedure is Nicaragua in 1910. There the rebels who held the city of Bluefields were losing, so the American naval commander declared the city to be a neutral zone and prohibited the government forces from bombardment. Should either of these means fail or not appear sufficiently attractive at the moment, the marines could always be landed. To cite an instance where the leathernecks put the situation in hand, Nicaragua is again convenient. In 1912, when Adolpho Diaz was president of that country, a revolt led by General Mena was staged against the administration. The United States dispatched a fleet of eight vessels and landed 2,600 men with the result that the luckless Mena surrendered. Following this episode, the United States maintained a force of men in Nicaragua until 1925, resulting in over a decade of orderly government (from the American point of view). It is interesting to note that exactly three months after the marines departed, a revolution took place! Of course should the American policy makers become squeamish about using too much force, they could resort to a system whereby native troops would serve under American officers as a sort of constabulary. This was done in Haiti in 1915.

However, it was financial supervision which had the greatest appeal. This policy can be said to have been the American adaptation of imperialism. In general, this would involve financiers demanding some kind of a guarantee for debts, which usually was assured by American control of the customs in the particular country where the investments or interests might be in danger.

WOODROW WILSON AND LATIN AMERICA

When Thomas Woodrow Wilson became President in March, 1913, he decided to adopt a new procedure in the Latin-American policy of the United States, which he hoped would overthrow Dollar Diplomacy. There was to be no more exploitation of Latin-American countries by the United States under the cover of the Monroe Doctrine. American businessmen must be made to recognize the risk attached to their investments and not expect American military support if their interests were placed in jeopardy. In fact, the countries of Latin America should be associated in a common policy and be placed on a par with the United States. This theme was brought out strongly in a speech at Mobile, Alabama, on 27 October 1913. Furthermore, he asserted the United States would not seek further territory by conquest.

The United States and Mexico. The first real test of Wilson's good intentions was to come in Mexico. There President Diaz had been in power from 1876 until he met some formidable opposition in the election of 1910 from Francisco Madero, an idealistic type of individual and author of a book which strongly criticized Diaz. The latter clamped his opponent in prison and, of course, proved victorious in the "election." Madero upon his release started a revolution. He demanded effective suffrage, land redistribution, and pledged that one term in office would satisfy him. In 1911, the revolution proved a success, and Madero was installed as president but had the misfortune to be assassinated in 1913 by Victoriano Huerta, a former general who now became a dictator. All eyes were turned toward Washington to see whether the United States would recognize Huerta. William Howard Taft, the outgoing Chief Executive, decided to let the Wilson administration handle the problem. Wilson and his Secretary of State Bryan agreed to refuse recognition, although both sincerely felt that Madero had been misguided. But by saying that they would never recognize Huerta they in reality gave him great leeway to do as he pleased, for Mexico was no tiny Caribbean republic but a proud country which had once gone to war with the United States and still retained unpleasant memories of the "gringo."

It so happened that the British Minister to Mexico, Sir Lionel Cardin, was of the opinion that His Majesty's Government ought to recognize Huerta in order to secure oil concessions. At this juncture, the Panama Canal entered the picture. By the terms of the Hay-Pauncefote Treaty of 1901 all ships of all nations were placed on an equal footing in the use of the waterway. During the last year of the Taft administration, Congress passed the Panama Canal Tolls Act exempting American vessels in the coastwise trade from tolls. To the British, this action was an infraction of the Hay-Pauncefote Treaty and they were quite angry about it. The differences were amicably ironed out through a series of talks, and an informal understanding was reached by 13 November 1913, according to which Wilson was to press for repeal of the tolls legislation and the British Foreign Office was to inform Sir Lionel in Mexico to cease his interference with Wilson's policy toward Huerta. Everything seemed to proceed smoothly. Wilson carried the day with Congress, and Cardin was hushed.

Wilson now tried in earnest to eliminate Huerta and establish a government with clean hands. He sent a mission to gather together the various Mexican leaders and tell them that he would arrange a loan for Mexico from American bankers. Huerta, who was omitted from the parleys, naturally opposed the plan, so Wilson resorted to arms control. He sent arms and munitions to Huerta's rivals and permitted none to go to Huerta from American sources. For good measure, an American naval vessel was stationed off Vera Cruz as a sort of blockade.

The Tampico Incident. An incident occurred at Tampico which threatened the already strained relations between the United States and Mexico. A party of uniformed American bluejackets were arrested by

Mexican authorities at Tampico but were quickly released. The American commandant, Admiral Mayo, took it upon himself to demand a salute by way of reparations. Huerta shrewdly refused because he knew that, if the United States employed punitive measures, all factions in Mexico would make common cause with him. In the United States there was a touch of war fever. Wilson successfully requested the permission of Congress to use forceful intervention to secure redress, and the next day after it was granted, 21 April 1914, Admiral Mayo shelled Vera Cruz and took over the city and the customs. A full-dress war appeared imminent when the ABC powers (Argentina, Brazil, and Chile) fortuitously offered to act as mediators.

The dispute was arbitrated at Niagara Falls, New York, in May and June, 1914. Shortly thereafter Huerta went into exile and was succeeded by Venustiano Carranza, a strong-minded individual. Upon the recommendation of and in conjunction with the leading Latin-American states, the United States recognized Carranza in 1915. Relations, nonetheless, continued bad, with resultant losses in American life and property in Mexico. Meanwhile, Carranza's failure to remove reform from the realm of theory into reality provoked another revolutionary movement led by a desperado named Pancho Villa, who possessed great popularity among the downtrodden Mexican peasants. This fanatic massacred some sixteen American citizens in Mexico in cold blood and had the further temerity to conduct a raid on Columbus, New Mexico, in January, 1916. This action, which resulted in the death of seventeen Americans, was not permitted to go without retaliation, as General Pershing was sent by Wilson to capture the bandit leader dead or alive. For the sake of the record, Carranza was cajoled into approval of the expedition, although he was most reluctant to do so. By February of 1917, despite a rather deep penetration of Mexican territory by Pershing's forces, the will-o'-the-wisp Villa went uncaptured. The futility of further fruitless chasing led Wilson to order the return of the soldiers. The imminence of war between the United States and Germany was an additional factor.

PART EIGHT

The First World War and the
Peace Settlement

Under the stress of new social forces, the uncertain stabilization achieved by the "concert of Europe" weakened. The emergence of the German and Italian nations cast the problem of the European balance of power in new terms; no longer was British sea power and diplomacy sufficient to impose an uneasy peace. Rival alliances of great powers took form. International relations were embittered by clashes over imperialistic booty, while military establishments grew to proportions that made their very existence a menace. Certain cooperative tendencies were not lacking in the world, but they proved weaker than these potent forces. Following a long series of nerve-wracking crises, the lid blew off with a deafening bang in 1914, and the so-called "Hundred Years' Peace"[1] was shattered.

The conflict of 1914–1918 revealed the possibilities of warfare under modern conditions created by nationalism and the industrial revolution. This war, destined in its turn to pale insignificance in comparison with that of 1939–1945, nonetheless dwarfed previous ones in extent, destructiveness, and intensity. Yet the increase in intensity of combat failed to increase the speed with which a decision could be reached as between adversaries roughly equal. The exhaustion of the combatants might have produced a compromise peace had not the entry of the United States brought vast new resources to the side of the Allies.

When at last the time to make peace came, hatreds and fears overshadowed a determination on the part of many to make this an occasion

[1] The term is misleading since numerous sanguinary conflicts raged in the period from 1815 to 1914. It is based on the fact that no all-embracing conflict like the Wars of Napoleon or the First and Second World Wars took place.

for establishing world-wide justice and erecting effective barriers against war. The armed truce which resulted satisfied the cravings of few and contained the seeds of unrest that soon again disrupted the peace of the world.

For the United States the war represented a major step in the evolution of its position as a world power. Although American participation was of relatively short duration, the United States, both as a neutral and as a belligerent, exerted a tremendous influence on the course of the struggle and emerged at the end as incomparably the wealthiest and potentially the strongest nation in the world. The opportunity to assume world leadership was, however, allowed to go by default, partly because of disillusionment over the peace settlement reached at Versailles and partly because partisan politics at home resulted in the repudiation of Woodrow Wilson's idealistic hopes.

31

The Coming of the War

The underlying factors responsible for this catastrophe were nationalism, imperialism, power politics and the alliance system, militarism, and the absence of any effective international machinery to prevent war.

Nationalism, the dominant force of the nineteenth and twentieth centuries, was so powerful that it overrode such forces as liberalism and democracy whenever a clash took place. Its beginnings were in patriotism. People were indoctrinated with a love of their country which could easily be turned into an equally violent hatred of rival countries. It was marked by extreme national pride and recognized no higher law than national interest, leading thereby to international anarchy and imperialism. For many who lacked any semblance of religion, it provided a suitable substitute. An extreme form of this virus was chauvinism, which took the position of "right or wrong, my country." In fact, by 1914, to be considered a bona fide "patriot" one had to espouse this far-fetched view.

The various world powers had their nationalistic ambitions in the years from 1870 to 1914 which were frequently at variance with those of a rival power and so tended to produce conflicts of national interest that were war breeders. Great Britain was determined to maintain her commercial, colonial, and maritime supremacy against all challengers. France had set her heart upon securing revenge on Germany for the humiliation of the Franco-Prussian War and especially dreamed of recovering the lost provinces of Alsace and Lorraine. The government of the Third Republic carefully cultivated the hope of *revanche* among its citizens by every means at its disposal. Furthermore, France's ambitions included the extension of her new colonial empire. The newly unified German Empire's nationalism was traceable to such factors as her recent arrival in the ranks of the well-to-do through her great upsurge in the Industrial Revolution. It is evident that her new riches partly turned her head. Moreover, she came to look upon herself as the historic champion of Europe against the Slavs. This national pride lent itself, not universally, of course, to a belief that the Germans were the descendants of a pure race, the Nordic, which had surpassed all others in desirable qualities. Even Germany could stand improvement, which was possible through scientific breeding to produce better Nordic specimens (tall, blond, blue-eyed). This specious theory was advanced by the writings of Count Henry de Gobineau and Houston Stuart Chamberlain. Curiously enough, the former was a Frenchman and the latter an Englishman, son-in-law of Richard Wagner, the famous composer. These various beliefs coalesced in a movement known as Pan-Germanism which recommended the union of all Germanic peoples, who would thereby enchance the glory of the great Nordic race. Germany sought for herself a "place in the sun" through the building up of trade, colonies, and sea power. In this connection, Germany came to resent the older colonial powers, who had acquired the choicest holdings before Germany had had a chance to make her bid. Austria-Hungary desired to hold together her polyglot empire and expand in the Balkans for greater strength and security. Russia sought the realization of her "historic dream," Constantinople and control of the straits leading from the Black Sea into the Mediterranean. She was further very active in the promotion of Pan-Slavism, a movement which sought close ties among Slavic peoples under the tutelage of Russia. Italy, like Germany only newly united, clamored for colonies, the recovery of *Italia irredenta* (the Trentino, Trieste, and Istria), and the prestige of a world power. Further, she hoped to supplant Austria as arbiter of the Adriatic. The only non-Western power in the group of leading powers afflicted with nationalism was Japan, which sought leadership and empire in east Asia.

POWER POLITICS AND THE ALLIANCE SYSTEM

Power politics, of which it has been said with a good deal of truth that there can be no politics without power, involved frequent shifting of the balance of power in Europe. It was practiced by combinations or alliances of nations which came about through the realization that it was often expedient to enlist the aid of other powers in order to achieve objectives. It involved a certain amount of adjustment and compensation in the matter of national ambitions. The desired objectives were pursued, often ruthlessly, through diplomatic maneuvers, which were usually secret and which were backed by the threat of force.

In the hectic years between 1870 and 1914, a system of alliances was created which ultimately divided Europe into two hostile armed camps awaiting only the moment judged most propitious for a final show-down based on force. The originator of this system was Bismarck, who realized that Germany needed time to consolidate the gains accruing from three victorious wars in the short space of six years. His other objective in formulating alliances was to isolate France so that she could not secure allies in order to gain vengeance on Germany for her defeat in 1870–1871 and thereby regain Alsace and Lorraine.

Bismarck's Alliances. Bismarck's first arrangement was the *Drei-kaiserbund* or League of the Three Emperors (Germany, Austria, and Russia) in 1873. The signatories merely promised to aid each other in maintaining the status quo. It foundered as a result of the Congress of Berlin (1878), which was called to settle a European crisis resulting from the Russo-Turkish War of 1877. Russia's victory in this conflict raised the hopes of the Pan-Slavists to a feverish pitch, but Austria took alarm at the prospect of Russian domination of the Balkans, and Great Britain threat-ened war to prevent the Russian Bear from taking possession of the Bosphorus and the Dardanelles and thereby establishing himself on the flank of Britain's "life line" through the Mediterranean.[1] Faced with this opposition, Russia reluctantly disgorged some of its gains and consented to a strengthening of Austria's position in the Balkans. Russia's resentment against the Dual Monarchy was intense, and some of it was directed at Germany as well, since the Russians felt that Bismarck had ignored their just claims at the Congress and had favored the Austrians, although Bis-marck himself insisted that he had merely played the part of an "honest broker." Realizing Russia's bitterness, Bismarck set to work to consolidate Austro-German relations by arranging the Dual Alliance in 1879. This achievement softened Russia's attitude, and Bismarck was quick to exploit the opening thus presented by securing a renewal of the League of the Three Emperors in 1881. This time the signatories agreed to remain neu-tral should any one of their number be attacked by a fourth power.

The clashing Balkan ambitions of Russia and Austria-Hungary again proved irreconcilable, and the League smashed up a few years later. How-ever, Bismarck, while managing to keep intact the Dual Alliance, suc-ceeded in 1887 in signing the so-called "Reinsurance Treaty" with Russia. Destined to last for three years and subject to extension at the expiration of that time, this agreement provided that the other would remain neutral should either go to war with a third power unless it happened to be a war against Austria or France in which case the provision was void. Finally, Germany agreed to recognize "rights historically acquired by Russia in the Balkans" (whatever that might mean). In 1882, as we have seen, the

[1] A British music-hall ditty of this period: "We don't want to fight, But by Jingo if we do, We've got the ships, we've got the men, We've got the money too," gave the term "jingoism" to the English language.

Dual Alliance added a third member, Italy, and became the Triple Alliance.

The Franco-Russian Alliance. At this point, the poor relations between the new German Kaiser William II and his Chancellor led to Bismarck's resignation in 1890. The headstrong young Kaiser surrounded himself with other advisers and when the question of a renewal of the Reinsurance Treaty with Russia came up, Germany rejected it. This development presented France with her golden opportunity to secure an ally at last. Russia sorely needed someone to provide her with financial assistance, since her finances were in a state of chronic embarrassment. Furthermore, neither France nor Russia then enjoyed particularly good relations with England. A temporary Franco-Russian agreement in 1891 gave way in 1894 to a full military alliance between the two powers.

Thus, two armed camps, consisting of Germany, Austria-Hungary, and Italy on the one side, and Russia and France on the other, were established. Only England of the major European powers remained aloof. Her "splendid isolation" now became a thing of the past, as the events of the Boer War demonstrated her lack of friends. Were Britain to join either line-up, as seemed likely in the early years of the twentieth century, most observers would doubtless have selected the Triple Alliance as being the one. The reasons for this were that her relations with France had been historically poor, while with Russia she had long been at odds over Turkey and more recently had come to fear the Bear's ambitions in the Far East and toward India. In fact, her uneasiness was so great that she concluded an alliance with Japan in 1902 which was patently directed against Russia. The facts which militated successfully against England's joining the German group included Britain's dislike of Germany's commercial and industrial progress, the quixotic character of the Kaiser, and the fear of Germany's growing naval strength. Even at that, there might have been an understanding reached had Germany not acted so cavalierly toward England, whom the Germans underestimated by considering her a decadent power which would be eternally grateful to Germany for condescending to ally herself with the supposed suppliant.

The Triple Entente. The task of winning England over to his side was undertaken by the able French Foreign Minister, Théophile Delcassé. This astute diplomat was no lover of Britain, but his dislike of Germany was even greater. Seeing that an agreement with England possessed many advantages for France and determined to cash in on the mounting Germanophobia in Britain, Delcassé made overtures to the British Foreign Office which resulted in 1904 in agreement between the two powers. The Entente Cordiale, as it was called, provided that France recognize the priority of England in Egypt in return for a similar acknowledgment by England of France's rights in Morocco. Secretly, each gave the other a green light in the specified country should she decide to alter the existing situation. The Entente was quickly followed by secret military and naval agreements between the two countries.

Then in 1907, to the surprise of the Germans, France's two partners came together in the Anglo-Russian Entente, which thereby completed the division of the powers into two rather evenly matched camps—the Triple Alliance and the Triple Entente. The 1907 accord, as we have seen, settled disputes between England and Russia in Asia.

MILITARISM

It will be remembered that it was during the course of the French Revolution that the doctrine of the "nation in arms" had been originated. The practice of universal military training was next taken up by the Prussians following their defeat by Napoleon at Jena. The great successes of Prussia in the years between 1864 and 1870 convinced all the major European powers—with the exception of Great Britain—that universal service was a *sine qua non* for national defense, and by 1875 it was widely adopted. The argument used everywhere to convince doubters was essentially the same—a country that is well prepared for war need not fear aggression.

War itself came to be exalted and philosophies glorifying strength and force were widespread.[2] Uniforms were to be seen everywhere in the years before 1914 as the influence of the militarists spread, until in some countries the primacy of the army was clearly recognized. Wherever this condition existed, there was a distinct tendency to subordinate everything to military preparedness. All other national interests became secondary. Artful propaganda was employed to win popular support for the military. Even the classroom was invaded as Neo-Darwinian theories were dreamed up to fit the clamor for preparedness, and war was depicted as a "biological necessity."

The standing armies (which, of course, excluded the hordes of reservists) of Russia, France, and Germany on the eve of the war in 1914 numbered, respectively, 1,600,000, 910,000, and 870,000, and the expensive new military equipment necessary to arm them increased military budgets to enormous sums. Although there was naturally some grumbling, the citizens of the respective countries felt it was their duty to submit to this heavy taxation because "their country" and "their flag" must never be permitted to risk defeat simply because the people were unpatriotic.

[2] Helpful toward this end were the writings of such as the following: Treitschke and Bernhardi in Germany; Maurice Barrès, Paul Leroy-Beaulieu and Paul Deroulède in France; Rudyard Kipling and Professor Cramb in England; Homer Lea in the United States; and Gabriele d'Annunzio in Italy.

Their continued success with the people affected the military leaders like heady wine. These men, sold on the theory that war was not only inevitable but virile, began in some cases to overreach themselves and become even more arrogant than usual. Their overzealousness resulted in their adopting a passion for secret military plans which were sometimes not shared with the foreign offices.

Anglo-German Naval Rivalry. The race to build armies was matched by a naval rivalry between Great Britain and Germany. In 1889 the British passed a Naval Defense Act which proclaimed that England must possess a navy that equalled the combined power of any other two navies. The reasons for this feeling are obvious if one considers England's insular position. In 1896, Germany inaugurated a policy designed to increase her naval strength. New navy bills followed in 1898 and 1900 which clearly indicated that Germany meant business, a realization which alarmed England. The Kaiser had a dream of establishing Germany as a great naval power, an accomplishment he believed would rank him with Germany's immortals. He was aided in his ambitions by the head of the German Admiralty, Admiral Alfred von Tirpitz.

In 1906, the German fleet was again augmented. During the previous year the British began the construction of a new type of battleship, H.M.S. *Dreadnought,* whose name came to signify any ship of her kind in the future. The cost of a dreadnought was twice what the older battleships had required, making such ships an expensive proposition. Since they made all predecessors obsolete, Germany now had a golden chance to begin construction of these ships on virtually equal terms with Britain. Biennially, in 1908, 1910, and 1912, efforts were made to reach a naval holiday between the two countries over the naval race. Germany, however, was unable to match England in production since, among other things, she was primarily a land power and her finances could not stand the dual strain.

THE ABSENCE OF INTERNATIONAL MACHINERY TO PREVENT WAR

There had been some talk of ending war, or at least minimizing its possibility, through the instrumentality of an international arms-limitation agreement. With such a view in mind (ostensibly at any rate), Czar Nicholas II of Russia took the lead in summoning an international peace conference at The Hague in 1899. Present were some twenty-six nations, including the United States. The American delegation was especially interested in the questions of arbitration and a world court and did a yeoman service toward these goals but with limited success. A court of arbitration was established but without compulsory jurisdiction. Other achievements of the conference included agreements to codify international law and to limit the use of certain lethal weapons in warfare. The Second Hague Conference was called in 1907 with the Czar again sending out the invitations. This time a potent force in the preliminaries which led to the call was President Theodore Roosevelt. Forty-four nations, including almost all the American republics, attended the sessions. Once again the sum total of accomplishments left much to be desired. The provisions accepted by the Conference dealt exclusively with methods of warfare: restrictions on the use of weapons, *e.g.,* dum-dum bullets; the setting up of an international prize court; the requirement of a formal declaration of war before the commencement of belligerent actions; and the Porter Resolution, which stated that the powers would not have recourse to armed strength to recover contract debts. It was also agreed that future conferences would be held regularly over the space of the years.[3]

The student will note that no general agreement on arms limitation was reached at either of the Hague Conferences. Nor was there even any real effort made to root out the causes of war. The great Russian statesman Count Witte actually admitted later that Russia's proposals were not meant seriously. And notwithstanding President Roosevelt's activity prior to the 1907 Conference, the United States Senate in voting to ratify the Second Hague Convention added a reservation to the effect that the traditional policy of the United States was abstention from the affairs of Europe. In 1909, the London Conference was held to establish the rules of naval warfare, but British opposition toward attempts to realize the goals of the conference was too powerful for anything to be accomplished.

Despite the failure to set up international machinery to prevent war, there were many peace movements in the pre-1914 years which at least tried to combat the mounting waves of nationalism and militarism that threatened to engulf civilization in a devastating war. International congresses of pacifists were held annually from the last years of the nineteenth century right down to 1914. Christianity naturally was in the forefront of the opposition to the danger of war, and international socialism called upon its brethren to work for the overthrow of the imperialists who sought war which could only hurt the working class. Yet when the test came in 1914, the great majority of the socialists chose to heed their own country's call. Nationalism was too strong an opponent for internationalism!

CRISES CAUSED BY NATIONALISTIC AND IMPERIALISTIC CLASHES

The First Moroccan Crisis. France for some time had been busily engaged in paving the way for the establishment of a French protectorate over Morocco. *Quid pro quo* agreements with Italy (1900), Great

[3] The Third Hague Conference was to have met in 1915.

Britain (1904), and Spain (1905) had secured the blessing of those possible objectors to such a step, and the future of the plan looked indeed promising. The German Chancellor von Bülow had other ideas, however, and in March, 1905, arranged to have the Kaiser pay a visit to the Sultan of Morocco. In a speech at Tangier meant for French ears, the Kaiser referred to the Sultan as an independent ruler who could count on the friendship of Germany.

The upshot of this incident was that Delcassé resigned his post in the French Foreign Office, and the French government agreed to a German demand that an international conference on Morocco take place. Theodore Roosevelt took a hand in this decision by using his influence to get the French to consent to attend such a conference. Unfortunately for Germany, Britain stood squarely behind France at the Algeciras Conference (1906) on Morocco. The conference agreed to the establishment of an international bank to untangle the Moroccan financial muddle and also voted that France and Spain should train and officer the Moroccan police. Once again, Roosevelt intervened and urged Germany to accept this settlement. Although Germany had won the opening round by getting rid of Delcassé and having the conference, she was the loser in the end, as France won a clear-cut victory.

The Annexation of Bosnia and Herzegovina. Intense as the rivalry between France and Germany may have been in Morocco, the duel between Austria-Hungary and Russia in the Balkans was even keener. Here too, Germany was by no means an idle spectator. In the previous section mention was made of the German *Drang nach Osten,* which aimed at a German corridor all the way to Bagdad and the Persian Gulf. Once allied with the Dual Monarchy, Germany cooperated with her partner in southeastern Europe. One facet of their joint policy was the strengthening of Turkey, while another was a drive to reduce the position of both Great Britain and Russia in the area.

The Russians did not like in the least this turn of events but decided to resort to a diplomatic deal in order to achieve their historic dream of controlling the Straits (the narrow bodies of water which connect the Black Sea with the Mediterranean). The Russian Foreign Minister, Isvolsky, succeeded in reaching an agreement at Buchlau in 1908 with Aerenthal, the Austrian Foreign Minister, whereby Austria-Hungary would raise no objection to use of the Straits by Russian ships of war. In return, Russia gave consent to Austrian annexation of the former Turkish provinces of Bosnia and Herzegovina in the Balkans, which the Dual Monarchy had been administering since 1878, following the Congress of Berlin. Scarcely had the agreement been reached when Austria annexed Bosnia and Herzegovina, but Great Britain's objections nullified Russia's hopes of realizing her part of the bargain. Instead of berating Great

Britain for her action, Isvolsky elected to put the blame on Austria and even claimed that he knew nothing of any agreement.

A crisis now arose because the Balkan states of Serbia and Montenegro protested Austria's action. Bosnia and Herzegovina were Serb-speaking provinces, and Serbia had earmarked them for future annexation as part of her plan for a united Slav state. Russia as the protector of the Slavs was appealed to for help against the "aggression" of Austria, but when Germany announced that she would back Austria-Hungary to the hilt, the Slavs had to withdraw their objections. Russia, which had just recently been defeated in the war with Japan and which had also undergone a serious domestic revolt in 1905, was in no position to act at this time, so she had to counsel the Serbs to accept the *fait accompli*.

The Bosnia-Herzegovina crisis in 1908 had been a most serious one. At the same time, it was quite revealing of the tactics which great powers would employ to gain their ends. Russia had shown herself perfectly willing to ignore the plans of her fellow Slavs—Serbia and Montenegro—if her own schemes could materialize. When they did not, Russia became very righteous in her denunciation of Austria, ostensibly on behalf of her small Slavic friends.

The Moroccan Crisis of 1911. The honors were even between the Alliance and the Entente in the first two great crises which might have led to war. In 1911 came a third threat. As a result of internal complications in Morocco, the French occupied the capital city of Fez early that year. This action upset the Germans, who saw in it the prelude to French annexation of the country. When diplomacy availed them nothing, the Germans ordered the gunboat *Panther* to "protect" German interests in the port of Agadir.

This "Agadir incident" caused France to adopt an attitude toward Germany in the Moroccan matter which can be described as at least receptive. The French were now prepared to talk the matter over with their rivals, who hoped to consummate a bargain by getting the French Congo in exchange for giving France the right of way in Morocco. At this point in the negotiations, England entered the picture and demanded an explanation from Germany for her action in employing the gunboat. While Germany was preparing her reply, the British Chancellor of the Exchequer, Lloyd George, delivered a saber-rattling speech which indicated how serious the crisis was in the minds of the leading actors. Britain's firm support of France helped reduce the chances of immediate trouble, since the Germans were not anxious for war. In the end, the affair was resolved through the reaching of an agreement between France and Germany whereby France gave Germany some 100,000 square miles of worthless French Congo territory in return for a recognition that she might establish a protectorate in Morocco.

The chief significance of this affair is the willingness—almost eagerness—to fight demonstrated by Great Britain. Second in importance was the additional strength given to Franco-British relations. Finally, there were domestic consequences in France. Poincaré replaced Caillaux as the French Premier. A fire-eater had taken over from a pacifist—a most important factor from the point of view of Russia in 1914.

THE BALKAN WARS, 1912-1913

In 1911, the same year as the second Moroccan crisis, Italy and Turkey became engaged in a war which had serious repercussions. From the Russian point of view, anything which weakened the position of Turkey was good, but from the standpoint of the other leading parties in the recent Near Eastern crisis of 1908, Germany and Austria-Hungary, this development was not pleasing. It indicated that all was not exactly well within the framework of the Triple Alliance and conversely that Italy's interests might actually be closer to those of the Triple Entente. Furthermore, the weakness revealed by Turkey in her conflict with Italy touched off the Balkan Wars of 1912–1913.

Bulgaria, Greece, Serbia, and Montenegro saw a golden opportunity for themselves to secure gains at the expense of fast-weakening Turkey. Accordingly, they banded together to demand a series of reforms from Turkey in Macedonia. On 8 October 1912, tough little Montenegro declared war all alone against Turkey but within a week was followed by the others. The allies, led by Bulgaria, scored a series of resounding triumphs over the once mighty Turkish armies, and on 26 March 1913, despite the fact that the most virile political group in Turkey was in power, the Turks had no alternative but to sue for peace. In the Treaty of London (1913) Turkey was stripped of nearly all of her European possessions.

Out of the war there emerged a new state, Albania, whose creation, largely a result of the machinations of Austria and Italy, helped to precipitate the Second Balkan War (1913). This found Bulgaria alone against her former allies and also Rumania, which had remained aloof from the first fracas. Just to show that there were no hard feelings, the Turks also jumped in on the side of the allies, their former enemies. Bulgaria was able to withstand this kind of opposition for only a few weeks before capitulating. By the terms of the Treaty of Bucharest, the Bulgars had to disgorge most of their gains from the first war. Thus, all the participants in the two wars gained territory with the exception of Turkey, which did manage to recoup a portion of its losses.

The important results of the wars were: the increase in the ill feelings between Austria and Russia and between Austria and Serbia; the augmented military preparations in both the Alliance and the Entente; and the increased confidence gained by France because French arms had appeared to show themselves superior to the products of the Germans in this laboratory of Mars.

WAR BETWEEN TRIPLE ALLIANCE AND TRIPLE ENTENTE

The Balkans were destined to provide the incident which ignited the fuse blowing the world into the maelstrom of the First World War. More particularly, it was the Serbs who produced the crisis. Serbia had never forgiven Austria for the annexation of Bosnia and Herzegovina. Although she had given a pledge that she would not tolerate any anti-Austrian propaganda within her borders, the country actually seethed with it. As a result of the Bosnian crisis, there had been formed in Serbia a nationalistic society known as the Narodna Odbrana (National Defense), whose activities were extremely bellicose toward Austria.

In 1911 another Serb society came into existence, which pledged itself to form a union between Serbia and all other Serb-speaking peoples. This group, the Union or Death, was more commonly known as the Black Hand and had members throughout the Serb lands in the Balkans. Its membership was drawn from the ranks of the army, the government, the police, and the University of Belgrade, and included many who also belonged to the slightly less bloodthirsty Narodna Odbrana.

The Sarajevo Murder. These fanatical nationalists hit upon a plan early in 1914 to assassinate the Archduke Francis Ferdinand, heir to the throne of Austria-Hungary. It was known that the Archduke was to be in Sarajevo, the capital of Bosnia, in June for the army maneuvers, so plans were made to murder him in the hope of precipitating a war between Austria and Serbia which would draw Russia in to aid the Serbs. The youths who were to do the job of murder were Bosnians and so Austrian subjects, but they were trained for their task in Serbia by fellow members of the Black Hand who were officers in the Serb army. The Prime Minister of Serbia himself had advance knowledge of the plot, yet did not issue any warning to the Austrian government. The closest approach to such a warning was the offhand remark of a Serbian diplomat to an Austrian, to the effect that Bosnia was a dangerous place where guns were sometimes known to go off and that it might be advisable for the Archduke not to make the visit.

The Archduke and his wife drove through the streets of Sarajevo on 28 June 1914, a Sunday and the great Serb holiday, Vidov-Dan (St. Vitus' Day). Stationed at intervals in the crowd were the three teen-aged Bosnians who were to assassinate Francis Ferdinand. The first attempt failed when one of them missed aim with a bomb which succeeded only in delaying the official entourage slightly. The Archduke insisted on continuing, and so his car reached the spot where the second youth, Princip, was able to fire the bullets which fatally wounded both Francis Ferdinand and his wife. These were indeed shots "heard round the world."[4] Great revulsion was felt in most quarters when the news arrived.

Austria immediately conducted an investigation by an able lawyer whose findings in the main supported the suspicion that Serbia was guilty. This, however, should not obscure the fact that Austria for some time had been eager to deal with Serbia because of the latter's threat to the unity of the empire. Despite the Austrian investigation, the Austrian Foreign Minister, Count Berchtold, lacked much of the information we now possess about the crime. Nonetheless, he was anxious to punish Serbia. Although the Prime Minister of Hungary, Count Tisza, did not approve, Berchtold won over the old Emperor Francis Joseph, who agreed to inform Germany that it was his wish to punish Serbia. The consent of Germany having been obtained, the government of the Dual Monarchy now presented Serbia with an ultimatum on 23 July. The prior approval of Austria's ally, Germany, seems to have been based on the rather naïve belief that, should Austria and Serbia go to war, it would only be a localized conflict.

The Austrian Ultimatum. The ultimatum was certainly a strong one. Serbia was given exactly forty-eight hours to accept it or face the consequences. One of the demands was that Austrian officials would be allowed to operate on Serbian soil in connection with both the fulfillment of some of the demands and in the trial of those connected with the murders. Shortly before the expiration of the time limit, Serbia made its response to the Austrian minister in Belgrade. The Serbs agreed to the terms except where their independence would be jeopardized. In this case, they expressed a willingness to submit to arbitration at The Hague or before some other international group. The Austrian minister claimed that the reply was unsatisfactory, broke off diplomatic negotiations, and left the country immediately. At the same time, mobilization was ordered in Austria-Hungary.

As for the other powers that might be involved in the imminent war, Germany insisted upon localization of the Austro-Serb dispute; Russia had clearly warned Austria even in advance of the ultimatum that it would permit no abuse of Serbia; France, through its President, Raymond Poincaré, who made an official visit to St. Petersburg 20–23 July,

---

[4] The Archduke's death was a particular tragedy in that he had worked out a plan whereby the principal minorities would be accorded autonomy within the empire under a federal parliament headed by the monarchy. It is interesting to speculate what the subsequent history of this region might have been had the plan had a chance to go into operation.

stood firmly behind Russia come what may; while Great Britain bent its efforts to effect mediation.

Russian Mobilization. On 26 July a conference of representatives of Great Britain, Germany, France, and Italy was proposed by the British Foreign Secretary, Sir Edward Grey, and rejected only by Germany, chary about such meetings owing to past experience. On 27 July Germany cooperated with Britain in an effort to induce Austria to talk things over with Russia and also to mediate with Serbia. Despite rejecting Grey's proposed conference on the previous day, Germany had agreed to this step because she seems to have felt that Serbia's reply to the Austrian ultimatum had been satisfactory. But Austria was determined to punish Serbia and would have no part of mediation. She thereupon declared war against Serbia on 28 July. For three days, despite this declaration, Germany sought to get Austria to mediate, which she finally promised to do on 31 July—too late because Russia had already mobilized, a step then tantamount to a declaration of war. Germany sought, in the period following the Austrian announcement that a state of hostilities existed with Serbia, to restrain her ally because she now knew for certain that the war could not be localized. The Russian Czar was so impressed with a telegram from his "Cousin Willy" that he consented to change the Russian mobilization from "general" to "partial." His advisers were able to prevent this change from taking effect by finally securing the vacillating Czar's consent once more to "general" mobilization on 30 July.

Russian mobilization resulted in an ultimatum from Germany on 31 July giving Russia half a day to demobilize. Her failure to agree led Germany to declare war on Russia that very day. At the same time as Germany sent the ultimatum to Russia, she dispatched one to France with a slightly longer (six hours) time limit, demanding France's promise to be neutral. France's reply was that she "would consult her interests," which she did by commencing to mobilize on 1 August, whereupon Germany declared war against her on 3 August.

The Invasion of Belgium. Italy claimed that the terms of her agreement with Germany and Austria-Hungary were defensive and that the action of her allies could not be so construed and so proclaimed her neutrality. Great Britain, the sole member of the Triple Entente not yet in the war, made her entry by declaring war on Germany on 4 August because of Germany's indefensible violation of the neutrality of Belgium, a neutrality guaranteed by Germany itself, Great Britain, France, and Austria-Hungary. Although the invasion of Belgium was, as we shall see, an integral part of Germany's war plans, the Germans demanded free passage through the little country on the flimsy pretext that they had information of French intentions to march into Belgium. The Belgian reply is best summed up in King Albert's expression, "Belgium is a nation, not a thoroughfare." Germany's action resolved a serious dispute in the British Cabinet about the country's proper course and served to unify public opinion, but Britain could hardly have remained neutral in any case. Apart from the fact that secret military and naval agreements with France existed, particularly a naval accord of 1912 which Grey recognized as obligating the British fleet to protect the French Channel and Atlantic coasts, Britain could not, as a matter of plain self-interest, have allowed France to be crushed and Germany to become master of Europe. When the British ultimatum demanding the withdrawal of German troops from Belgium arrived in Berlin, Chancellor von Bethmann-Hollweg committed another of Germany's historic blunders by referring to the Belgian neutrality treaty as "a scrap of paper."

32

The First World War

When the last frantic efforts of the diplomats failed and the armies began to march in the summer of 1914, the world was launched on four years of warfare such as it had never seen before. Beginning as a European quarrel, the war eventually drew in all the great powers of the world and many of the smaller ones. It saw the belligerents mobilize their man power and organize their economies on a scale that would hitherto have been considered impossible. The resources of modern science and technology were exploited to the utmost, to introduce, among other things, airplanes, tanks, submarines, and poison gas as full-fledged weapons of war. The long, exhausting struggle gravely weakened the structure of Western civilization; by the time it ended, four great empires—the Russian, German, Austrian, and Ottoman—had collapsed in revolution, much of the rest of Europe was threatened with social disintegration, and colonial peoples throughout the world were seething with unrest. It was not the first war to be world-wide in scope, but it was the first general conflict of modern times in which non-European states played a significant part, and the title "First World War" has been generally accepted for it.

The basic strategic position of the contestants was fixed by the pattern of European alliances which determined the initial alignment, and it was not substantially affected by the spread of the war. Germany and Austria-Hungary were joined by Turkey (November, 1914) and Bulgaria (October, 1915) to form the combination known as the Central Powers. The Entente states, generally termed the Allies after the war began, had the support of Belgium and Serbia at the outset and eventually of a majority of the nations of the world. The significant accessions of strength, as far as the actual course of hostilities was concerned, were

Japan (August, 1914), Italy (May, 1915), Rumania (August, 1916), and the United States (April, 1917).

The principal asset of the Central Powers was their interior position, which enabled them to concentrate their forces readily against individual opponents. They also enjoyed a considerable unity of command, since Germany was so much the strongest member of the coalition that she could easily dominate it. This situation, however, also revealed an element of weakness; Germany's partners proved to be increasingly burdensome liabilities. The Allies were widely scattered geographically, Russia in particular being virtually isolated. Coordination of their military efforts was almost nonexistent until the final year of the war. Even on the Western Front, where British and French armies fought side by side, there was no unified command until 1918. On the other hand, the Allies had the greater potential resources. Their naval superiority enabled them to draw on the entire world for supplies and at the same time to impose a stringent blockade on their enemies which eventually produced critical shortages of food and raw materials. To summarize the situation: the Central Powers' best chance of winning the war lay in a quick, decisive military stroke; for a prolonged endurance contest the Allies had the better staying qualities.

THE OPENING CAMPAIGNS

When hostilities began, the plans that military staffs had been formulating and elaborating for years were put into operation, and of these, none was more fateful in its consequences than Germany's Schlieffen Plan. Since the conclusion of the Franco-Russian Alliance, German strategists had taken it for granted that they would have to fight France and Russia simultaneously. Count von Schlieffen, Chief of the General Staff from 1890 to 1906, organized the mobilization of the German armies on the premise that the Russians, with their poor internal communications, would be slow to get into action and that there would accordingly be a brief interval during which Germany could safely concentrate on a sudden, overwhelming blow against France. Because time would not permit the reduction of the French frontier fortresses, Schlieffen proposed to mass the German armies for a drive through Holland and Belgium, to cross the Seine west of Paris and trap the French armies by a vast encircling movement. When he died in 1906, his last words reputedly being "keep the right wing strong," he was succeeded by General von Moltke, a nephew of the great Prussian commander. Moltke altered Schlieffen's arrangement by dropping the invasion of Holland and strengthening the German left in Alsace and Lorraine.

The existence of the Schlieffen Plan placed an impossible burden on

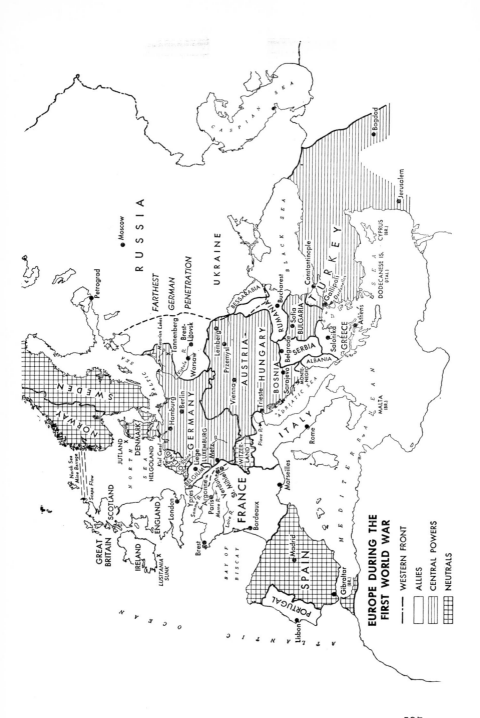

EUROPE DURING THE
FIRST WORLD WAR

- - - WESTERN FRONT

ALLIES

CENTRAL POWERS

NEUTRALS

RUSSIA

Moscow

Petrograd

FARTHEST
GERMAN
PENETRATION

UKRAINE

BESSARABIA

CASPIAN SEA

BLACK SEA

TURKEY

Bagdad

Jerusalem

CYPRUS
(BR.)

Constantinople

Gallipoli

Dardanelles

DODECANESE IS.
(ITAL.)

Bucharest

RUMANIA

Sofia

BULGARIA

SERBIA

Belgrade

Sarajevo

BOSNIA

MONTE-
NEGRO

ALBANIA

Salonika

GREECE

Athens

Masurian Lakes

Tannenberg

Brest-
Litovsk

Warsaw

Vistula R.

Lemberg

Przemysl

AUSTRIA-HUNGARY

Vienna

Trieste

ADRIATIC SEA

Piave R.

ITALY

Rome

MEDITERRANEAN SEA

MALTA
(BR.)

SWEDEN

NORWAY

BALTIC SEA

Berlin

Hamburg

GERMANY

DENMARK

JUTLAND

HELGOLAND

Kiel Canal

North Sea
Mine Barrage

Scapa Flow

SCOTLAND

GREAT
BRITAIN

IRELAND

LUSITANIA
SUNK

ENGLAND

London

BELGIUM

Liège

LUXEMBURG

Metz

SWITZER-
LAND

St. Mihiel

Verdun

Argonne

Marne R.

Ypres

Somme R.

Paris

FRANCE

Loire R.

Brest

BAY OF
BISCAY

Bordeaux

Marseilles

SPAIN

Madrid

PORTUGAL

Lisbon

Gibraltar
(BR.)

ATLANTIC OCEAN

German diplomacy. It meant that as soon as the Russian order of general mobilization became known, the German armies had to start marching westward, away from the only obvious threat, because the high command had staked everything on knocking out France before the sluggish Russian Bear could bestir himself. The attack on France and still more on unoffending Belgium not only insured Great Britain's entry into the war; it stamped Germany as the aggressor in the eyes of world public opinion. The Kaiser himself recoiled from the abyss that his generals had opened and appealed to Moltke for a change of plan so as to concentrate against Russia. Moltke, however, replied that it could not be done, since mobilization was already in progress and the elaborate logistic arrangements could not be upset without creating irremediable confusion.

The "Miracle of the Marne." The Schlieffen Plan, therefore, was allowed to proceed, and it almost worked. The invasion of Belgium was foreseen by the French high command, but its strength was greatly underestimated, with the result that the main French forces went plunging into Alsace while the Germans swept through Belgium and northern France to the Marne in the face of spirited but outnumbered Belgian, British, and French resistance. Then, however, Moltke's redistribution of the German forces began to take effect. The French offensive in Alsace was stopped and the participants driven back behind their own frontier defenses, where they could be conveniently regrouped to meet the threat from the north. Meanwhile, the truncated German right could not envelop Paris but had to cut eastward of the city, exposing its flank to a sortie from the Parisian fortifications, which materialized in the form of the famous "taxicab army," rushed out of the city in commandeered vehicles. This attack on 5 September 1914 opened the Battle of the Marne, and after several days of confused fighting the Germans were compelled to retreat from the immediate vicinity of the French capital, their hopes for a quick victory over France shattered.

Both sides then engaged in what was termed the "race to the sea," a series of attempts to outflank each other, which culminated in a furious German assault in Flanders, aimed at disrupting communications between France and Britain by capturing the French ports on the English Channel. A stubborn Allied defense frustrated this scheme also, and by the end of 1914 the rival combatants on the Western Front had dug themselves in from the North Sea to Switzerland, in positions which did not substantially change for the next three years.

Tannenberg. While their western offensive was at its height, the Germans had to face an unexpected crisis in the east. Well ahead of the German high command's anticipations, two Russian armies invaded East Prussia, one north and the other south of the Masurian Lakes. The German commander on the spot became panic-stricken and appealed to

Moltke for reinforcements and permission to evacuate the whole province. Moltke promptly removed him, replacing him with Paul von Hindenburg, an elderly general already on the retired list, who was thoroughly familiar with the topography of East Prussia. A young general who had distinguished himself in Belgium, Erich von Ludendorff, was assigned to Hindenburg as his Chief of Staff. Furthermore, Moltke decided that the campaign in the west was going so well (this was in August) that two army corps could safely be transferred from Belgium to East Prussia. At the crisis of the Marne, therefore, these troops were on their way eastward; by the time they reached their destination the "Russian steam roller" had already been thrown into reverse by the decisive German victory at Tannenberg (26–31 August 1914), a triumph which made national heroes of Hindenburg and Ludendorff.

Simultaneously, however, the Dual Monarchy's weakness was being made distressingly evident. The Austrians entangled part of their uncertain strength in an ill-advised effort to overrun Serbia before they dealt with the Russians. The Serbs threw the invaders out, and in the meantime the remaining Austro-Hungarian armies suffered a series of crushing defeats at the hands of the Russians, from which, indeed, the forces of the Dual Monarchy never recovered.

THE MILITARY DEADLOCK

The years 1915 and 1916 saw the Allies and the Central Powers fight each other to a standstill. On the Western Front stagnation developed very early, because neither the weapons nor the tactics of the period were suited to breaking through the elaborate trench systems that were created. Offensive operations required a tremendous artillery barrage to pulverize the opposing defenses, but if the bombardment was at all adequate, it necessarily tore up the ground too badly for the attacking troops to advance either rapidly or far, and if it was not, the attacking infantry was certain to be mowed down by machine-gun fire before it could cross "no man's land." To overcome these difficulties, the Germans introduced poison gas in 1915 and the British the tank in 1916, but both weakened the effect of their new weapons by using them prematurely and with insufficient preparation.

The futility and costliness of trench warfare resulted in both sides giving consideration to the possibility of seeking a decision elsewhere. Early in 1915 the Allies embarked on a project, promoted enthusiastically by Britain's First Lord of the Admiralty, Winston Churchill, for forcing the Dardanelles and capturing Constantinople. Since Bulgaria was not yet in the war, Turkey was isolated from her partners, and the scheme, if successful, would eliminate her and at the same time open a good supply line from the western Allies to Russia. It was, in addition, an operation which would permit the Allies to utilize their naval superiority. In spite of these attractions, the proposal met with a divided reception. The French military men were naturally preoccupied with the task of evicting the Germans from France, and their attitude was shared by many influential people in Britain. Russia, which was intended to be principal beneficiary of the scheme, was cool to it because the Russians disliked the idea of anyone but themselves capturing Constantinople; in fact, Russian pressure was responsible for the rejection of an offer of support from Greece, support which in all probability would have made the difference between success and failure.

The Dardanelles Expedition. Largely because of these disagreements, the Dardanelles campaign evolved as a mass of compromises and half measures, atrociously bungled in execution. At first a purely naval attack was tried (March, 1915), to be abandoned when three elderly battleships ran into a mine field. Evidence brought to light after the war revealed that, when the naval attack was broken off, the Turks were dangerously short of ammunition.

Then, because Allied prestige was now too deeply involved to permit withdrawal, a military expedition was reluctantly organized to seize the Gallipoli peninsula and open the vital straits. The troops, among whom the Anzacs (Australia and New Zealand Army Corps) especially distinguished themselves, succeeded in establishing beachheads on Gallipoli, but that was as far as they ever got. At the end of 1915 the Allied governments confessed failure and abandoned the enterprise, the evacuation being the only well-conducted part of the whole operation. Blame for the disaster fell, somewhat unjustly, on Churchill, who had to retire temporarily from public life.

The Dardanelles expedition had important consequences. The Allied show of strength in the Mediterranean helped to persuade Italy to join them in May, 1915. Italy had spent the period since the war broke out in bargaining with both sides and felt that the terms offered by the Allies in the secret Treaty of London (1915) were more attractive than those dangled before her by her erstwhile partners. The manifest failure of the Gallipoli campaign encouraged Bulgaria to declare for the Central Powers in October, a step which doomed Serbia to temporary extinction as German, Austrian, and Bulgarian armies converged on it.

The remnants of the Serbian army, after retreating across Albania to the Adriatic, were reorganized and transported to Salonika in Greece, where, along with British and French troops, they constituted one of the subsidiary theaters of war referred to as "side shows" by devotees of concentration on the Western Front. Other "side shows" were the operations against the Turks in Mesopotamia and Palestine, with progress in both areas negligible until 1917, and the occupation of Germany's overseas colonies, which was completed by the early part of 1915, although German forces remained active in East Africa until after the Armistice. The colonies in Africa were taken by the British (including South African forces) and French; in China and the Pacific, by the Japanese, except for some islands south of the equator that were occupied by Australians and New Zealanders.

Assault on Russia. Germany also turned to the east in 1915, partly from the same motive as the Allies, to seek a decision in a more promising field, and partly from necessity, because Austria-Hungary was in desperate straits and was likely to collapse altogether unless German aid was forthcoming immediately. In May a tremendous offensive was unleashed against the Russians; by the end of the year the Germans had not only recovered all the territory the Dual Monarchy had lost but had swept over Poland and bitten deeply into western Russia. Yet they had not secured their decision. The Russian armies, badly battered as they were, with losses of 1,500,000 in this year alone, nevertheless remained intact. Faced with an adversary immensely superior in equipment and leadership, they avoided destruction by the traditional technique of withdrawing into the vast spaces of their own country. Eventually the strain was to prove too much for the Czarist regime, but for the moment all the Germans achieved was to extend the Eastern Front without eliminating it and to enhance the reputation of Hindenburg and Ludendorff as men who won victories.

Verdun. In 1916 the emphasis swung back to the west, beginning with the German attack in February against the historic fortress of Verdun. Their original intention was not to capture the place. They calculated that the French, as a matter of pride, would make every effort to hold Verdun, and since the battle lines were so located that the defense would necessarily be confined to a narrow area, the Germans planned a "mincing machine," whereby French troops crowded in front of Verdun would be systematically pounded to pieces by massed artillery. There was one curious blind spot in the thinking of the German strategists; they failed completely to foresee that, once the battle was joined, German prestige would be as much involved in capturing Verdun as French prestige in holding it. The result was a grim combat in which all the long-standing enmity between Frenchman and German seemed to come to a head. The defense of Verdun was entrusted by French Commander in Chief Joffre to General Henri Pétain, and Pétain's troops, with the slogan *"On ne passera pas,"* succeeded after heavy fighting in bringing the German drive to a halt.

The attack on Verdun anticipated a series of offensives by the principal Allied powers, who had at last seen the necessity of at least trying to coordinate their operations. The plan was to launch simultaneous attacks in the middle of the summer, but events forced a rearrangement of schedules. In response to an appeal from Italy, whose forces were being hard pressed by the Austrians, Russian armies under General Brusilov struck at the southern end of their long battle front and achieved a startling initial success. Although Brusilov's offensive was presently stopped by exhaustion of its materials and the arrival of German reinforcements, it served its immediate purpose. The Italians were able to throw back the Austrians and embark on a drive of their own. They made a good start but then were halted in rugged mountain country.

Meanwhile, on 1 July 1916, British and French armies began a ponderous assault on the German position in the valley of the Somme. After four months of fighting, featured by the first employment of tanks in battle, the maximum advance was only seven miles and Allied casualties exceeded 600,000. Nevertheless the Germans, in order to hold their lines here, had to abandon their attack on Verdun, and the pressure on them was sufficiently strong to induce them to withdraw this sector of their front some twenty miles to the Hindenburg Line in the spring of 1917.

The Naval War. Thus, at the end of 1916 the great efforts made by both sides to break the stalemate on land had been completely unavailing. At sea also, the war appeared to be at a standstill. The pressure of the Allied blockade was undiminished, but it had not as yet visibly affected the ability of the Central Powers to wage war. Germany's countermeasure, the submarine blockade of the British Isles, begun on 4 February 1915, had been a blunder. The idea of striking at Great Britain's most vulnerable point, her maritime communications, was sound enough, but the time was poorly chosen, since the German U-boat fleet in 1915 was too small to strike decisively at Britain's supply lines. The material damage inflicted by the submarines was far outweighed by their influence in turning neutral opinion against Germany. The greatest naval engagement of the war, the Battle of Jutland (31 May 1916), was a spectacular but indecisive encounter which left the naval situation precisely as it had been before.

Momentous events—the collapse of Russia and the intervention of the United States—were just over the horizon, but at this midway point in the war there was little indication of any relief from the prolonged deadlock. Dissatisfaction with this condition took two forms. Great Britain and Germany reorganized their governments to invigorate prosecution of the war. In the former, the Asquith government was replaced by a coalition cabinet headed by the energetic Lloyd George; in the latter, Hindenburg and Ludendorff were brought from their local command on the Eastern Front to assume the supreme direction of the German armies. In addition, the Central Powers suggested, in December, 1916, that peace negotiations were in order. It was a logical move for them, because, while they were in possession of large areas of Allied territory, they had reached the peak of their military strength. The Allies, on the other hand, still had undeveloped resources of men and material and could reasonably anticipate that their military position would soon become more favorable. They were, moreover, suspicious of the good faith of their opponents, since the Central Powers had not specified the terms on which a settlement might be arranged. The "peace offensive" thus came to nothing, as did a peace move initiated at the same time by President Wilson. At this point neither side was capable of imposing its will on the other and neither was prepared to offer peace on conditions that the other could accept.

ORGANIZATION FOR TOTAL WAR

When the war began, opinion among belligerents and neutrals alike almost unanimously agreed that it would be short. It was, indeed, widely believed that no nation could stand the financial strain of a modern war for more than six months, or perhaps a year in very favorable circumstances. It was assumed also that hostilities would be confined to the organized military forces and that civilians, except in actual combat areas, would be left undisturbed in their normal pursuits.

No one, consequently, was prepared for the type of war that developed. Realization of the true nature of the struggle came gradually, and with it a slow and occasionally painful reorganization of national life in each of the belligerent countries in the direction of total mobilization of all their resources. The munitions problem was the first to become acute, since the massive offensives and prolonged fighting of trench warfare called for guns and shells beyond anything in previous experience. France and Britain found their operations in 1915 seriously hampered by a lack of munitions. Great Britain abandoned "business as usual" with the appointment of Lloyd George to the new post of Minister of Munitions in 1915, while France, although gravely handicapped by German occupation of her principal industrial area, undertook a program which effectively converted her economy to war production.

Governmental intervention to control the production of munitions was merely the initial step to the extension of control over every phase of national life. The list of materials needed for war soon went far beyond weapons and ammunition, labor supply became an acute problem with the drafting of millions of men for military service, and the expenditure of money reached levels far above the wildest of prewar estimates. The programs adopted were all fairly similar. Industrial production was carefully regulated to supply military needs and at the same time provide at least the minimum required to keep the home fronts functioning. Food rationing began in Germany in 1916 and in France and Great Britain a year later. Labor was found by employing women in occupations previously regarded as suitable only for men; Germany eked out its labor supply by conscripting workers in the occupied countries. The financial demands of the war were met largely by borrowing. The Allies floated huge loans in the United States (a billion and a half dollars by 1917) as well as among their own people; the Central Powers, less popular among the neutrals, had to rely mainly on their own internal resources.

The Allied Blockade. The widening economic ramifications of the war appeared in the increasing complexity and stringency of the Allied blockade. As the conflict intensified, the list of goods classified as contraband grew steadily longer, and with reason, because there are few raw materials or manufactured commodities that are not important to the prosecution of modern warfare. Not only was direct trade with the Central Powers cut off, but every effort was made to prevent shipments from reaching them through adjoining neutral countries by elaborating the "continuous-voyage" doctrine of the American Civil War. The blockade involved the Allies, especially Great Britain, in repeated controversies with the United States; but after the United States entered the war the blockade was stiffened still more. Since it was seldom possible to determine accurately whether goods sent to a European neutral would ultimately reach the Central Powers or not, the neutrals were finally permitted to import only enough to meet the estimated (by the Allies) requirements of their own people. An Allied Shipping Board was created with full authority over all Allied shipping. It also, through charters and control of coal supplies, supervised most of the neutral tonnage that existed.

Not only did civilians find themselves subjected to elaborate controls in the interest of the war effort; in some cases they found themselves to be the objects of direct hostile attack. German naval forces bombarded English coastal towns, and German aircraft attacked London, Paris, and other cities. These air raids were puny in comparison with their successors of the Second World War, but they made a profound impression at the time because of their novelty. At first the Germans employed Zeppelins, but they proved too vulnerable, and after 1916 the raids were carried out by airplanes almost exclusively. In 1917 and 1918 the Allies retaliated by bombing the Rhineland.

THE ENTRY OF THE UNITED STATES

When war broke out in 1914, the attitude of most Americans was that this was just another European squabble, with which the United States need have no concern. Yet in such a world-wide conflict there were necessarily pressures, emotional, economic, and political, which made it impossible for American opinion to be strictly impartial. Pro-Ally sentiment was preponderant from the outset. The German invasion of France and Belgium seemed to most Americans to be unprovoked aggression, and their sympathies naturally went to the heroic little nation that was willing to stand up for its rights and to France, the country whose aid had helped to win American independence and which was now fighting bravely to preserve its own. In the case of Great Britain, community of language, the strong English heritage in American civilization, and the close and friendly relationship between the United States and Canada were all factors predisposing the American people to see the British cause in a favorable light. Nor was the point overlooked that Britain and France were democracies while Germany and Austria were autocracies, although the presence of Russia on the Allied side rather weakened the argument. Interest in the fortunes of the Allies was strengthened as the war progressed by the fact that thousands of Americans enlisted in the British and French forces, the most conspicuous group being the celebrated "Lafayette Escadrille" in the French Air Force. The Central Powers were championed mainly by German-Americans, but not by any means all of them, and some rabid Irish-Americans whose hatred for England overshadowed everything else.

Propaganda. This marked preference for the Allies needs to be borne in mind in approaching the much-discussed subject of propaganda. It is quite true that Allied propaganda in the United States was skillful and extremely effective, but it owed its effectiveness in large measure to the receptiveness of the audience. It is also true that the Allies controlled most of the cables and other channels through which news reached the United States, but enough remained to give the Germans ample facilities for presenting their case. That they failed to take advantage of their opportunities was due to their own incredible obtuseness. Assertions of the righteousness of Germany's cause were likely to be rendered unconvincing by the torpedoing of another passenger liner or the deportation of more Belgian civilians for forced labor in Germany. The Germans, moreover, persisted in the senseless practice of trying to quiet American indignation at such incidents by publishing long, dull, legalistic arguments to prove that they had a technical right to do what they had done.

The activities of their agents in the United States did nothing to enhance the standing of the Central Powers in American opinion. Plots to stir up labor unrest and sabotage munitions plants were traced to the German and Austrian diplomatic corps. In September, 1915, the Austrian ambassador, Dr. Constantine Dumba, went home at the request of the United States government, and shortly afterward the German military and naval attachés followed him. The naval attaché, Captain Boy-Ed, disappeared into obscurity, but his military colleague, Captain Franz von Papen, was just at the beginning of a long and lurid career.

Economic Factors. Besides these largely emotional factors, the war generated economic influences that had an important bearing on American policy. At first there was a sharp decline in American exports when trade with the Central Powers was cut off, but by 1915 the rapidly mounting volume of Allied purchases had launched the United States on a business boom. The fact that American materials went almost exclusively to the Allies was not a matter of bias or preference on the part of the United States government or people; it was simply the natural consequence of Allied sea power. By the end of 1915 Allied buying had reached such proportions that it was exhausting the dollar credits of the Allied governments and had to be financed by loans floated in the American money market. The United States thus acquired a substantial economic and financial interest in the Allied cause.

Neutral Rights. As the most important of the neutrals during the first two years of the war, the United States found itself involved in disputes with both belligerents over the historic question of freedom of the seas. With the Allies there were prolonged controveries over definition of contraband and interference with American commerce. Shortly after the outbreak of hostilities the United States tried to get both sides to accept the unratified Declaration of London of 1909, but since the provisions of this document favored the weaker naval power, the Allies naturally declined to surrender one of their principal assets. In other circumstances the United States might have resorted to drastic measures to enforce its desires; the Allies would have relaxed their blockade rather than face an embargo on American munitions. The Wilson administration, however, shared the prevalent American partiality toward the Allies and was unwilling to push matters to the point of hampering their war effort, especially in view of the fact that no real damage was being done to American trade. Confiscated cargoes were frequently paid for, and claims for such loss of property as was incurred could always be settled after the war. The Allied blockade did not result in the loss of American lives; the German submarine campaign did; and this distinction was fundamental for the American government and people.

The German decision to establish a "counterblockade" with submarines has been mentioned previously. In an era which has seen far more drastic methods of warfare freely employed, it is perhaps difficult to understand the horror with which the use of submarines against merchant ships was viewed in the First World War. The novelty of the weapon had much to do with it; there was a similar reaction to the German introduction of poison gas at Ypres in April, 1915, and to their **air** raids on England. The U-boat affected neutral opinion especially strongly because, by its very nature, it could not conform to the accepted usages of warfare at sea. It could not put a prize crew aboard a captured vessel, it could not remove passengers and crew to a place of safety before sinking its victim, and, because of its extreme vulnerability on the surface, it had to attack without warning if there was any suspicion that its victim might be armed. German submarine commanders, moreover, were inclined to be careless about distinguishing between belligerent and neutral ships. Their excuse was that Allied merchantmen frequently sailed under neutral colors, which was true enough, but the underlying cause for these instances of mistaken identity was that the Germans wanted to destroy any shipping that might be of use to their opponents.

The Lusitania **Incident.** When the submarine attack on commerce was initiated, President Wilson promptly warned the German government that it would be held to "strict accountability" for American lives and property. Incidents, nevertheless, began to accumulate early. An American citizen was lost with the British liner *Falaba* on 28 March 1915, and the American tanker *Gulflight* was torpedoed a month later. Then, on 7 May 1915, a U-boat sank the Cunard liner *Lusitania* off the coast of Ireland with a loss of over eleven hundred lives, of whom 128 were American citizens. If Wilson had been trying to maneuver the United States into war, he could have had his way there and then; Theodore Roosevelt and other prominent figures were clamoring for immediate action. But the President wanted peace and believed that the majority of the American people, shocked and angry as they were, agreed with him. Consequently he contented himself with vigorous and stinging protests, strong enough to cause the resignation of isolationist Secretary of State Bryan.

The German replies to Wilson's notes were evasive and procrastinating. The only valid argument that could be offered was that the *Lusitania* was a legitimate target because she was carrying munitions for the Allies. Technically this contention was correct, since the vessel was carrying a quantity of small-arms ammunition, but for the German government to advance this as an excuse for the sinking was a clumsy effort to explain away a stupid blunder. German statesmanship was in a sorry plight if it felt that the destruction of a few hundred cases of rifle cartridges justified antagonizing the United States and stamping German methods of warfare as ruthless and inhuman in the eyes of most of the world.

The Sussex Pledge. While the *Lusitania* controversy was still raging, two Americans were lost when the White Star liner *Arabic* was sunk, on 19 August 1915. Since the vessel was westbound at the time, it could hardly be alleged that she was carrying munitions. American indignation reached such a height that the German government hastily promised to refrain from torpedoing passenger liners without warning. Tension then subsided until on 24 March 1916 the French cross-channel steamer *Sussex* was torpedoed. Several Americans aboard were injured, although none were killed. The German government promptly disclaimed responsibility, asserting that no U-boat was in the vicinity at the time, but unfortunately for Bethmann-Hollweg's veracity, the *Sussex* did not sink. She reached port with fragments of unmistakably German torpedo embedded in her hull. This time Wilson threatened to break off diplomatic relations, whereupon the German government gave the United States the so-called "Sussex Pledge" on 4 May 1916, promising that submarines would not attack merchantmen without warning.

Submarine depredations were reduced by the Sussex Pledge, and for some months German-American relations were comparatively quiet. The American public was absorbed in the presidential election, in which, although foreign policy was the major issue, there was anything but a clear-cut expression of opinion. The Republicans attacked Wilson for being unduly lukewarm toward the Allies and at the same time, with an eye to the German-American vote, for being unneutral—a contradiction which their candidate, Charles Evans Hughes, found to be an awkward handicap. Wilson, for all his marked pro-Ally leanings, was reelected because "he kept us out of war." The race was close; Hughes, indeed, had the disconcerting experience of going to bed on election night believing that he was the next President of the United States and waking up the next morning to discover that he was not. A narrow Democratic victory in California gave Wilson just enough electoral votes to win.

Preoccupation with the election did not, however, shut out the din of war altogether. During this year an isolationist group in Congress sponsored the Gore-McLemore Resolutions, which would have refused passports to American citizens who proposed to travel on belligerent vessels, but this move was blocked by Wilson because he felt that to surrender to Germany on one point of principle would fatally weaken America's whole position on neutral rights. The summer of 1916 witnessed the passage of laws authorizing substantial increases in the army and navy, certainly a reasonable precaution in the existing state of the world but indicative also of a growing conviction, felt rather than clearly expressed, that a German victory in Europe would endanger the security of the Western Hemisphere. For a century American foreign policy had been able to assume a relatively stable balance of power in Europe and the presence of a normally friendly British navy to support the Monroe Doctrine. Now the United States was faced with the possible domination of Europe and the extinction of British sea power by an aggressive and militaristic Germany, and it viewed this prospect with misgiving.

Efforts to Mediate. Concurrently with preparations for war went peace moves. Early in 1916 Wilson sent Colonel House to Europe to sound out the belligerents on holding a peace conference, but nothing came of the mission. Then in December of the same year, with the election safely out of the way, he renewed his efforts by appealing to both sides for a statement of war aims.

The timing, however, was unfortunate, because the American proposal came only a few days after the "peace offensive" of the Central Powers and seemed to the Allies to be abetting what they regarded as a Teutonic trick. The replies made it obvious that no immediate peace was likely, but Wilson used the opportunity to formulate his conditions of peace. In an address to Congress on 22 January 1917 he laid down the general principles which were elaborated a year later into the Fourteen Points and called for "peace without victory."

Unknown to Wilson, the decision which would involve the United States in the war had already been made. In the fall of 1916 the new German high command took stock of its position. What it saw was not wholly satisfactory. The armies of the Central Powers had won battles and conquered territory, but they had not won the war and there was no indication that they were likely to. Not one of the principal Allied powers had been knocked out; all, indeed, were at that moment striking back vigorously. Hindenburg and Ludendorff, like everyone else, were fatefully unaware that in another six months the whole military picture would be drastically changed by Russia's collapse into revolution; as they viewed the situation in September, 1916, it offered no prospect of a quick and decisive German victory on land.

Yet a quick and decisive victory of some sort Germany had to have. While Allied strength was still growing, that of the Central Powers faced steady but inevitable decline. The blockade was causing shortages of food and raw materials that would become progressively more acute, and the strain of the war as a whole was finding expression in internal unrest, not so much in Germany as yet as among her partners. The heterogeneous nationalities of the Austrian Empire were fast losing what little sense of unity they possessed; during Brusilov's offensive Czechoslovak troops deserted to the Russians by regiments. Turkey was having its troubles in the form of an Arab revolt, fostered, of course, by the Allies and led by the colorful and almost legendary Lawrence of Arabia.

The German Challenge. The only visible prospect of securing a quick decision was in resuming unrestricted submarine warfare. The German naval authorities calculated that, with over 100 U-boats now at their disposal, they could destroy enough shipping in six months to force Great Britain out of the war, provided the restraints on submarine activities were removed. With Britain defeated, the rest of Germany's enemies would have little choice but to abandon the struggle. The object of the U-boats, it should be emphasized, would be to sink ships, regardless of nationality or cargo. If the total amount of Allied and neutral shipping could be reduced by a million tons a month, the Germans estimated that in six months there would not be enough cargo space in existence to carry the necessary food supply for the population of the British Isles, let alone enable Britain to prosecute a war. The sole drawback to the plan was that, barring an unlikely yielding on the part of Woodrow Wilson, the repudiation of the Sussex Pledge and the resumption of unrestricted U-boat operations would almost certainly provoke the United States into war, but the German warlords decided to accept the risk. They assumed that the United States would be slow to organize for war and would be unable to intervene before the German victory had been won. The Kaiser himself vetoed a German admiralty suggestion that the U-boats might "overlook" American ships.

While the decision was made in September, 1916, and communicated secretly to the Reichstag on 7 October, it was not until 31 January 1917 that Ambassador Bernstorff informed the United States government that, beginning the following day, all ships within a prescribed war zone covering the British Isles, the coast of France, and the Mediterranean would be sunk on sight and without warning. As a special concession, an American ship would be permitted to sail to Falmouth, England, once a week, provided it carried distinctive markings and followed a course designated by the German admiralty. Diplomatic relations were immediately broken off. Wilson, still hoping to avoid open conflict, proposed to arm American ships. A filibuster in Congress blocked him, but after the adjournment of the session on 4 March he found the necessary authority in a forgotten law of 1797.

Declaration of War. At this juncture, with the United States still hesitating, the German Foreign Office pushed matters along a little more. It sent a message, signed by Undersecretary Zimmerman, to the German ambassador in Mexico, instructing him to propose an alliance between Germany and Mexico against the United States, Mexico's reward to be recovery of the territory taken by the United States in 1848. Mexico was also to try to induce Japan to abandon the Allies and join the anti-American combination. The Zimmerman Note was intercepted and decoded by the British, and then turned over to the United States government. Its effect on American public opinion can readily be imagined. Mexico, it may be added, understandably refused to have anything to do with the proposal, which in effect invited her to tackle the United States single-handed until such time as Germany might be clear enough of her European complications to offer assistance. Faced with this evidence of

German meddling in the Western Hemisphere and a rising toll of American ships sunk by U-boats, Wilson decided that war could no longer be avoided. He asked Congress for a declaration of war on 2 April 1917, and four days later it became effective.

American Organization for War. Once committed to the struggle, the United States plunged energetically into the task of winning it. Allowing for some confusion and mismanagement, the mobilization of the nation's man power and economic resources was carried out far more efficiently and intelligently than in any previous American war. In May, 1917, Congress passed a Selective Service Act, under whose provisions some two million men were inducted into the army. Between the draft and voluntary enlistment, which continued in operation, over four million men were recruited for the armed services altogether. Command of the expeditionary force to be sent to France was given to General John J. Pershing, who had recently demonstrated his capabilities on the Mexican border, but the force itself would not be trained and organized in time to get into action before 1918.

Industrial mobilization was in the hands of the War Industries Board, headed by Bernard Baruch. Through a system of priorities, and the power, never used, to take over or shut down any plant refusing to comply with its regulations, the Board achieved a coordination of production which drew reluctant admiration from the Germans, themselves supposedly masters of organization. The food supply was placed under the supervision of Herbert Hoover, distinguished by his administration of Belgian relief. His task was to provide enough food not only for the American people but for the Allies also. There was no rationing, but a program of voluntary conservation worked fairly well.

The cost of the war, including loans to the Allies amounting to ten billion dollars, was met by increased taxation, which produced about a third of the needed funds, and such devices as the sale of Liberty Bonds. The United States Shipping Board, created in 1916, and the Emergency Fleet Corporation built a "bridge to France" by constructing ships in unprecedented quantity—4,000,000 tons in 1918. One step which was not repeated in the Second World War was the taking over of the railroads by the government. The strain of wartime traffic threatened to break down internal transportation and made it necessary for the government to operate the entire railway network as a single unit, under the direction of the Secretary of the Treasury, William G. McAdoo. The results were satisfactory as far as moving the traffic was concerned, but the government lost $700,000,000 in the process.

The task of marshaling public opinion was vested in a Committee on Public Information, headed by a newspaperman, George Creel. It was a many-sided organization, having control of censorship and American propaganda abroad as well as of selling the war to the American people. This last function, as Creel himself ruefully admitted afterward, it performed rather too well. A wave of anti-German hysteria swept the country. People who had German names, or otherwise failed to meet the standards of superheated patriots, were persecuted. German music was not played in public, and schools and colleges dropped German from their curricula—although one would suppose that a knowledge of the enemy's language would be a military asset. Even sauerkraut had to be rechristened "Liberty cabbage." Supplementing the activities of the committee were the Espionage Act of 1917 and the Sedition Act of 1918, which curtailed civil liberties to an extent previously unknown in the United States.

THE END OF THE WAR

The intervention of the United States came at a critically important time. Without it, indeed, the Allies would have lost the war. American military participation was admittedly limited in extent compared to the efforts of the European powers, but the torrent of American materials poured across the Atlantic was a decisive contribution to the defeat of the Central Powers, and, above all, the support of the United States was of incalculable value to Allied morale at a time when Allied prospects of victory seemed extremely dark.

The year 1917 began with hopes that the limited coordination of the previous summer could be improved upon and the war brought to an end, but the Allied position deteriorated rapidly and unexpectedly. The abdication of Nicholas II of Russia in March and the organization of a provisional government with democratic tendencies were hailed at first as removing the taint of autocracy from the Allied cause; by midsummer, however, it was obvious that Russia was disintegrating into chaos and could no longer be counted on as a military factor. War-weariness and defeatism arose among the western Allies. After a costly and futile offensive in the spring of 1917, the French army was shaken by mutinies, and it took General Pétain, hastily appointed commander in chief when disaffection appeared, the rest of the year to straighten matters out. There was also a drastic reorganization of the French government, which made the eighty-year-old Clemenceau, the "Tiger of France," Prime Minister. War-weariness was also a factor in the Italian disaster at Caporetto in November of that year. Except for Germany, the Central Powers were scarcely better off; in fact, the Emperor Charles of Austria, who had succeeded the aged Franz Joseph in 1916, was caught, much to his embarrassment, trying to open private peace negotiations.

The Crisis of 1917. The burden of Allied military operations in 1917 was necessarily thrown on the British. They spent four months in a dreary offensive in the mud of Flanders, which gained them a few square miles of quagmire at a cost of almost half a million casualties. A tank attack at Cambrai in November suggested the technique for ending the stagnation of trench warfare, but the British were unable to follow up their initial advantage. Two of the "side shows" provided rather more encouragement. In March, 1917, a British force captured Bagdad, and in December General Allenby's army took Jerusalem—both good for morale but remote from the decisive theater of action in France.

At sea the Allies had to surmount an acute crisis. In the month of April, 1917, submarine sinkings approached the million-ton mark, and it appeared that the German gamble would succeed. Admiral Sims, sent over from the United States to investigate the naval situation, was told frankly that Britain could not stay in the war much longer unless the U-boats were brought under control. Eventually, after a hard struggle, the danger was mastered. Sinkings were reduced by the general adoption of convoys for merchant ships, and the invention of the depth charge provided an efficient method of attacking submarines. American naval assistance helped to supply the needed escorts, and the American shipbuilding program upset German estimates of replacement capacity. By 1918 the submarine was a nuisance rather than a menace. Geography also handicapped the Germans. The Straits of Dover were fairly effectively closed, forcing the U-boats to make the long trip through the North Sea to reach their cruising grounds, and this route was made hazardous late in 1918 by the laying of a mine barrage from Scotland to Norway, largely an American achievement.

There was, however, still another serious threat to be faced. The collapse of Russia proceeded at a steadily accelerating pace, until in November, 1917, the Bolsheviks were able to seize power with a program calling, among other things, for immediate peace. Negotiations were not actually completed until March, 1918, when the Treaty of Brest-Litovsk was signed, a victor's peace whereby Germany annexed, or placed under German-controlled puppet governments, all of Poland, the eastern coast of the Baltic, and most of the Ukraine. The disappearance of the Eastern Front released millions of German troops for service elsewhere, and it was perfectly obvious that Germany would make a great effort to win the war before the United States could tip the balance again in favor of the Allies.

The lull during the winter of 1917–1918 was marked by the announcement of Woodrow Wilson's peace program, the Fourteen Points (8 January 1918).[1] This program was more than an intellectual exercise on Wilson's part. He was the recognized spokesman for the Allies, and his peace plan gave the Allied peoples something concrete to fight for. It also conveyed to many of the people of the Central Powers a very power-

[1] The Fourteen Points are itemized in the next chapter.

ful suggestion that they would be just as well off if the Allies won—a suggestion incorporated also in Wilson's repeated assertions that the war was being waged against militaristic governments and not against their presumably unwilling subjects.

The Last German Offensive. For the time being, Germany preferred to take its chance on a final mighty drive to win a decision on the Western Front before the Americans could appear in force. The storm broke on 21 March 1918, the area selected being the junction point of the French and British armies. The Germans had devised new tactics of infiltration, whereby picked units of "storm troops" exploited weak spots in the defense, leaving the strong points to be dealt with by what can best be described as the second team. They were also aided by a heavy fog, which blinded the defenders during the first crucial days and curtailed the operations of the Allied air forces—a situation curiously resembling their last desperate offensive in the Ardennes in 1944.

German hopes seemed on the way to fruition when their armies penetrated the Allied lines to a depth of thirty-five miles. The Allies, however, with defeat staring them in the face, finally did what they should have done long before and appointed a supreme commander for the Western Front, the choice falling on the French general, Ferdinand Foch, who had distinguished himself at the Marne and Ypres early in the war and had later been French chief of staff.

Ludendorff had anticipated that this first offensive would lose its momentum and had planned subsidiary drives to draw off the Allied reserves. The first of these, launched in the Ypres area in April, enjoyed an early success but failed to reach any decisive point. The second was unleashed on the French front along the Aisne in May. It came as a complete surprise, and within a month the Germans were once more on the Marne. Again, however, the Allies held, this time, ominously for the Germans, with the aid of American troops, who fought capably at Château Thierry and Belleau Wood.

By the end of June the German assaults had spent their force. A final effort to break through on the Marne, begun on Bastille Day, 14 July 1918, failed completely, and four days later the passing of the initiative to the Allies was signalized by a Franco-American counteroffensive on the Marne which was the beginning of a general onslaught on the whole German position in France. The arrival of American troops in greater numbers and at a more rapid pace than had been anticipated gave Foch assurance of ample reserves and made possible operations on a scale that would have been out of the question with the depleted British and French armies.

American Military Operations. During the crisis of the spring, such American units as were available were thrown into action wherever they were needed, but Pershing never abandoned his desire to have a separate American army with its own sector of front and independent of British or French command—subject, of course, to Foch's over-all authority. His wishes were finally realized in September, when American forces took over the front in the neighborhood of Verdun. Their first operation was a well-planned and neatly executed flattening of the St. Mihiel salient, begun 12 September and finished in two days. The Germans had decided to evacuate the salient to conserve man power, but the American attack caught them before they were ready. The Americans then swung north into the Argonne Forest to form the right arm of a pincer, the left to be provided by a British attack on the Hindenburg Line, whereby Foch hoped to trap the Germans in northern France. The objective of the American attack was the historic French city of Sedan, which was reached on 6 November after hard fighting in the rugged Meuse-Argonne country by over a million American troops. While the German armies were not trapped, their lines crumbled under the impact of continuous Allied attacks.

Collapse of the Central Powers. The general collapse of the Central Powers started with the surrender of Bulgaria on 30 September, after an Allied offensive on the long-neglected Salonika front. Simultaneously, Turkish resistance in Palestine and Syria went to pieces, and Turkey gave up on 30 October. Austria-Hungary simply disintegrated; when its forces laid down their arms on 3 November, Austria and Hungary were about to part company and the Republic of Czechoslovakia had already been proclaimed.

Meanwhile, in Germany the specter of defeat provoked internal unrest. The Kaiser desperately tried to save his throne by last-minute reforms, but it was too late. In October the long-inactive German fleet was ordered to sea, in the hope that a naval success might improve Germany's bargaining position. The crews of some of the battleships, however, mutinied, and, when it appeared that most of the fleet was infected with the same spirit, the operation was cancelled. This incident touched off outbursts of discontent throughout the country, until finally the Kaiser fled to Holland on 9 November and a provisional government was formed, composed chiefly of Social Democrats and Centrists. This collapse of the home front was not, as the Nazis later alleged, a "stab in the back" by a few traitors; it represented the cumulative effect of hunger, the strain of the long war, the shattering of morale caused by military defeat, and the infiltration of Bolshevist propaganda into Germany after the peace of Brest-Litovsk.

Negotiations for an armistice were begun by a hastily appointed liberal Chancellor, Prince Max of Baden, early in October and were completed before the Kaiser's flight. The document was signed 11 November at a meeting in a railway car in the forest of Compiègne, and at 11 A.M. on that day the guns at last fell silent. The terms of the armistice were designed to guarantee that Germany would not resume hostilities if peace negotiations broke down. The German armies were to evacuate all occupied territory, as well as the entire left bank of the Rhine and bridgeheads at Mainz, Coblenz, and Cologne. Tanks, heavy guns, and aircraft were to be destroyed. All submarines and the best part of the surface fleet were to be interned under Allied control, pending agreement on their future disposition. Subsequently, most of the surface vessels were scuttled by their crews in Scapa Flow.

Obviously, there could be no renewal of the conflict once these provisions were carried out, and Germany would have no option but to accept whatever peace terms the Allies chose to offer. The war was over; its four years of fighting had cost the combatants some thirty million casualties, of whom almost a third were dead. The toll among civilian populations from starvation, disease, and massacre cannot be accurately estimated, but it was at least as great and probably greater.

33

The Postwar Peace Settlements

Early in 1919 the Allied and Associated Powers gathered at Paris to lay down specific terms of peace to the beaten Central Powers. Unfortunately, the Paris Peace Conference got off to a poor start merely by meeting in "the city of light." It immersed the delegates in an atmosphere of hatred which could scarcely do otherwise than communicate its venom to the peacemakers—many of whom were already steeped in hate. Had the conference been held in Geneva, Lausanne, or The Hague, it would have at least eliminated this bad feature. Each one of these cities possessed adequate facilities, together with an atmosphere more conducive to successful settlement than Paris. It was the French who insisted on their capital city. The French sense of poetic justice is extremely acute, and they were determined to avenge themselves on Germany for the humiliation they had been forced to swallow in 1871, when the German Empire was born on French soil in the Hall of Mirrors at the Palace of Versailles. When the question first arose about 1915 as to where the Allies could hold a peace conference in the event of victory, the British had agreed to Paris, and so the French simply took it for granted. France had suffered so during the war she felt anyway that she needed the profits attendant to the conference. Prices rose sharply, and shopkeepers and hotels profiteered.

THE VERSAILLES CONFERENCE

Since it was customary for the heads of governments and their staffs to attend such a meeting and since in Europe the head of the state was a prime minister or premier, there were approximately a dozen of these

547

powerful figures present along with another dozen or so foreign ministers. In the United States, the question arose as to who should represent the nation—the President or someone chosen by him with the advice of Congress. President Wilson himself decided to lead the American delegation, although this would shatter precedent. He was warned that his personal inexperience in diplomacy might prove a detriment, but he considered it an asset rather than a liability and refused to alter his determination to go.

The Chief Personalities. This exceedingly individualistic and straightforward man was too much of an idealist for the rough, tough tasks facing him. Moreover, although he had been both a university professor and president, he could neither speak nor understand French or German. To assist him in the negotiations, he took Robert Lansing, the successor to Bryan as Secretary of State, and Henry White, a former American Ambassador to France and the American representative at the Algeciras Conference. The latter was an extremely mild Republican whose selection did nothing to convince the G.O.P. that Wilson was at all bipartisan. Far more acceptable Republicans would have been Elihu Root, former President Taft, or Senator Henry Cabot Lodge, chairman of the Senate Committee on Foreign Relations. Rounding out the top-level Americans were two individuals already in Europe, General Tasker M. Bliss and Colonel House. The student will observe the absence of a bona fide representative either of the Republican party or of the United States Senate.

At the head of the British delegation was the astute politico, David Lloyd George. Unlike Wilson, who had suffered a stinging rebuff in the American congressional elections of 1918 in answer to his bold request to the American people that they choose a Democratic Congress, Lloyd George had scored a tremendous victory in the "khaki election" of December, 1918. Employing artful slogans designed to take advantage both of the unpopularity of Germany and the gratitude of the victorious British people, Lloyd George had in his pocket the full backing of the electorate, which sent him to Paris with a *carte blanche*. Again in contrast to his American opposite number, the British prime minister brought with him the Conservative chieftain, Andrew Bonar Law.

The host was the cynical veteran of long years in the opposition ranks of French politicians, Georges Clemenceau. The French premier, variously styled "the modern Talleyrand," "the Tiger," and "the Father of Victory," was not only cynical but very cocky. He believed himself to be the greatest man present but as a rule behaved quite suavely. He knew the English language perfectly, being married to a lady from Wisconsin and having served as a French newspaper correspondent during the American Civil War. He was the only leading personality at the conference who had an accurate knowledge of geography, a rather handy accomplishment when the map was being redrawn.[1]

The Italians were represented by the premier, Vittorio Orlando, an able diplomat, likeable, and quite expressive except that he could not speak English. Despite his accomplishments, he and his chief assistant, Sidney Sonnino, were minor figures. Their inability to win for Italy the fulfillment of the promises made her caused their withdrawal from the gathering and their replacement by the almost equally unsuccessful Francesco Nitti and Tomaso Tittoni.

Other personalities present but not as important as the foregoing included Kimmochi Saionji and Nobuaki Makino of Japan, Roman Dmowski of Poland (he was replaced by the celebrated pianist and great Polish nationalist Ignace Paderewski), Eleutherios Venizelos, the Cretan revolutionary, from Greece, Eduard Beneš of Czechoslovakia, Pasic and Trumbich of the kingdom of Serbs, Croats, and Slovenes (hereafter referred to as Yugoslavia, the name officially adopted in 1929), John Bratianu of Rumania, and Jan Christian Smuts and Louis Botha of the Union of South Africa.

In addition to the top-ranking representatives, there were various experts attached to each delegation. Great Britain, for example, had some 2,500 financiers, bankers, jurists, cartographers, etc., who required the facilities of a number of hotels to house them.

Conduct of the Conference. The impossibility of conducting sessions with such a huge official registration resulted in plenary sessions being held only six times. The big powers ran things to suit themselves, and there was little the lesser states could do about it. To expedite matters, a Supreme Peace Council composed of the two principal delegates from each of the "Big Five" was established. But from March, 1919, on, the work was performed by the "Big Four," the heads of the American, British, French, and Italian delegations, an arrangement acceptable to the Japanese except where a matter involving the interests of Japan was at stake. When Orlando became huffy in April and took his departure, it was the "Big Three" of Wilson, Lloyd George, and Clemenceau who really wrote the treaty with Germany.

The architects of peace were beset with numerous difficulties as they set out to draft the Treaty of Versailles, of which the most embarrassing was the matter of reconciling the promises the Allies had made one another in their various secret agreements with Wilson's pledge of "a peace without victory" concretely expressed in his Fourteen Points, which the

---

[1] Lloyd George once blurted out in perplexity, "Where is Transylvania?" Indeed it was remarked by the Australian prime minister that the Conference revealed "the appalling ignorance of every nation as to the affairs of every other nation —its geographical, racial, historical conditions, or traditions."

Germans had accepted as the basis for peace. This difficulty resulted in a number of sharp clashes which usually saw the idealism of Wilson emerge in second place. Unfortunately, Wilson claimed in 1919, while in the process of making a case for the Treaty of Versailles before a number of American Senators, that he had been in the dark about even the existence of any secret treaties when he had announced the Fourteen Points in January, 1918. The evidence is abundantly clear that this could not be so. Charity dictates that the then highly overwrought President might have forgotten that he knew of these treaties. This concession is the most Wilson is entitled to in this matter, unless it be argued that he simply chose to ignore these treaties in the belief that armed with the strength of righteousness he could thus triumph over the evils of the secret treaties when the test came.

PRINCIPAL PROBLEMS

Meanwhile, as the delegates were deliberating in Paris, Europe was presented with the postwar spectacle of a half-dozen or so conflicts raging in the still smouldering ashes of the devastating war. The eagerness to strengthen one's own borders at the expense of a neighbor precipitated this series of sharp struggles which could, potentially at any rate, erupt into a contest important enough to threaten the success of the peace conference. Disconcerting and dangerous as these brawls may have been, the drafting of the treaty was further complicated by several very difficult points to solve. These included (1) security for France; (2) reparations; (3) the question of the German colonies; (4) the demands of ambitious powers like Italy, Poland, and Japan; (5) the carving up of the Austro-Hungarian and Turkish empires; (6) the question of Russia; (7) and the Covenant of the League of Nations.

France had suffered invasions from Germany twice within the lifetimes of many present at Paris. It was only natural that the French should insist upon guarantees to prevent a future repetition of this Germanic custom. Among other things France hoped to secure the establishment of a self-governing, neutral state under French auspices in the region between the Rhine on the east and the Low Countries on the west. The western boundary of Germany was to be fixed at the Rhine. There was opposition to this scheme by both the United States and Great Britain, with the result that a compromise was reached which provided for an Allied occupation of the region with a progressive withdrawal over a five- to fifteen-year time limit. In addition, an area east of the Rhine was to be demilitarized, *i.e.,* Germany was neither to fortify it nor to be allowed to station troops there. To satisfy the French even further, Wilson and Lloyd George agreed that their countries would come to France's aid at any time in the future when she might be subjected to German aggression. The disappointment of Clemenceau and the French when the United States Senate later refused to ratify this gratuitous promise on the President's part is easily imaginable. To make their bitterness worse, Lloyd George notified the French that Britain's pledge hinged upon American ratification and therefore had to be withdrawn.

To aid France's economic recovery, Germany had to cede the coal mines of the valuable Saar Basin to France for a period of fifteen years, at the expiration of which a plebiscite would be held to determine which country was to have permanent title. In the interim, the region was to be governed by the League of Nations. The problem had its delicate aspects since the French were eager to annex the area, but Wilson was equally determined that they should not since most of its people were German-speaking.

Reparations. The battle over reparations was wearisome—especially to Wilson. It was quickly established that the Germans ought to pay "for all damages done to the civilian population of the Allies and to their property by the aggression of Germany by land, by sea, and from the air." This sum was estimated to be in the neighborhood of ten and one-half billion dollars. It was an amount well within the capacity of Germany to pay, and had this been the price agreed upon a far more equitable treaty would have resulted. Such a sum, however, did not appeal to either the British or the French. The government of Lloyd George had campaigned for reelection in 1918 on a platform which included such demands as "shilling for shilling and ton for ton." These planks in the platform created the impression in Great Britain that a veritable bonanza would be forthcoming from Germany which would prove very helpful to the public, which had been hagridden to meet the war's expenses. The French feeling was that a financial settlement which soaked Germany properly would mean less likelihood of a German comeback, a prospect dreaded by every Frenchman.

Wilson, however, had made it quite clear that the Germans were not to pay the cost of the war but only for the damages they had wrought. It remained for his old correspondent, General Smuts, to win him over to the ingenious plea that Germany be required to pay pensions for all the Allied troops. Smuts argued that such a payment was Germany's responsibility, since Germany had been guilty of causing the war and thus brought about the military service of these men for whom pensions were now in order. This quaint bit of reasoning convinced Wilson, and there now remained the question of the amount Germany should pay. Since no one could figure it out, it was decided that she must sign a blank check which the Allies would later fill in after an Allied commission had determined both how much and in what way Germany ought to pay.

Territorial Demands.   A third of the perplexing problems which caused the peacemakers considerable concern was that of the demands of ambitious powers. Italy, it will be remembered, had entered the war as a result of the secret Treaty of London in 1915, wherein she was promised territory all the way from the Tyrol to Albania, the Dodecanese Islands, and both African and Asiatic possessions. She now insisted upon the fulfillment of these promises and added Fiume and additional Dalmatian coast for good measure. When the Allies gave her less of the Dalmatian territory even than she had been promised in 1915, Orlando and Sonnino left Paris in a great huff. Their replacements were no more fortunate, with the result that the dissatisfaction of Italy continued even after she signed the treaty.

The Poles were equally determined to win territorial concessions. Promised by the Allies restoration as a free and independent country with an outlet to the sea, Poland had to be a party to the violation of the principle of self-determination. To reach the sea, a corridor had to be cut separating East Prussia from the rest of Germany. Although Poland hoped to acquire the corridor's natural seaport, predominantly German Danzig, it was made a free city under the supervision of the League of Nations.

Japan gave Wilson a splitting headache and succeeded in inflicting an outright defeat upon him in the case of Shantung. Shortly after Japan's entrance into the war in 1914, the Japanese captured the various German concessions, including Tsingtao, in Shantung. Subsequently, the Japs signed a treaty with the Allies which ratified Japan's plan to hold these concessions. According to the understanding with China whereby the latter entered the war on the side of the Allies, she was to regain possession of all the German holdings in the country. Thus, the Allies had promised two powers the same thing. When the test came and Wilson tried to help the Chinese, the Japanese threatened to quit the conference. The Allies decided in favor of the side with the greater power, and so China was cheated of her rightful possessions. Wilson comforted the Chinese by offering the scant consolation that eventually the League of Nations would right such patent wrongs, a possibility China declined to accept, because she refused to sign the Treaty of Versailles. Her signature was later affixed to the treaty with Austria and she thus became a bona fide member of the League.

During the war there had been considerable talk among the Allies to the effect that it was a new kind of war. This being the case, the old rule of grab ought not to be permitted. Instead it was decided to punish Germany, not by dividing her colonies among the victors but by turning them over to the League of Nations and then parceling them out to countries which would hold them as trustees. The actual settlement will be described in the following chapter on the League.

Great Britain, France, and Russia had reached agreement on methods for the disposal of the Turkish Empire. The Russian share of the spoils, which included Constantinople and the Straits, could be forgotten since Russia had forfeited her rights by her defection in 1917. France was to get Syria, and Britain's share was Palestine and Mesopotamia. Unfortunately, Britain had made pledges to both the Jews (the Balfour Declaration) and the Arabs relative to Palestine, and had also encouraged the Arabs in the belief that Syria would be a part of a great Arabian state after the war. To settle these conflicting promises and claims proved a perplexing task.

Meanwhile, a former member of the Allies, Russia, was locked in the throes of a desperate domestic battle between the forces of Bolshevism and those who opposed the new movement. In addition, there were Allied expeditionary forces on Russian soil, engaged periodically in skirmishes with Russian forces. The British were at Archangel and in the Caucasus, the French were at Odessa, and in Siberia were to be found Americans, Japanese, and Czechs. Wilson and Lloyd George were both anxious to see the situation remedied and invited representatives of the conflicting Russian parties to meet with the Allies on an island in the Sea of Marmora, a suggestion which was ignored.

The League of Nations. Finally, the problem of the Covenant of the League of Nations was a thorny one. Of the Big Four, only Britain and the United States (as represened by Wilson) showed enthusiasm for the idea. France and Japan were willing providing certain conditions be met. The French finally consented only in the belief that the United States and Great Britain had guaranteed to aid France in the event of future aggression by Germany. The Japanese sought unsuccessfully to have a pledge of racial equality included. Their failure, although because of Great Britain and Australia, which did not wish to see unimpaired Oriental immigration, was blamed by the Japanese on Woodrow Wilson, chairman of the committee which voted adversely to Japan's hopes. Wilson, originally favorable to the proposal, had been cooled off by the British with the result that he did not vote on the issue.

FATE OF THE FOURTEEN POINTS

It will be recalled that the surrender of Germany was signed in the belief that the peace treaty would be formed on the basis of Woodrow Wilson's famous Fourteen Points. They were (1) open covenants of peace, openly arrived at, and in the future no secret diplomacy; (2) freedom of the seas; (3) removal, as far as possible, of all economic barriers to international trade; (4) reduction of armaments among nations; (5) impartial adjustment of all colonial claims, with the interests of the subject populations receiving equal weight with the government seeking title; (6) evacuation of Russia, with Russia free to decide her own future; (7) evacuation and restoration of Belgium; (8) evacuation and restoration of French territory, including Alsace-Lorraine; (9) readjustment of Italian frontiers along clearly recognizable lines of nationality; (10) autonomous development for the peoples of Austria-Hungary; (11) evacuation and restoration of Serbia; (12) independence for the Turkish portions of the Ottoman Empire, autonomy for the non-Turkish peoples, and freedom of shipping through the Straits; (13) establishment of an independent Poland with access to the sea; (14) formation of a general association of nations under specific covenants for the purpose of affording mutual guarantees of political independence and territorial integrity to great and small states alike.

The German surrender witnessed the removal of any reference whatsoever to freedom of the seas, but otherwise the points remained. Subsequent speeches by the President had stressed the right of self-determination of peoples and the claim that reparations would not be punitive. At any rate, it is interesting to examine the fourteen points in an effort to discover what happened to them.

Point one, if it applied to the peace settlement, was a manifest impossibility. There were very few open or plenary sessions of the delegates and what there were occurred only for publicity purposes. Wilson's actions at Paris seem to indicate that what he came to mean by this point was that the sessions of the future League would be of this character. The second point was deleted, as we have seen, while the third had to await postwar developments which proved so hectic that additional barriers were erected instead of those existing being removed. Number four likewise never materialized, although some work was done along the lines of naval disarmament as will be shown below. The fifth point did become a reality in that a system of mandates was established under the League, but the interests of the mandated peoples were never considered. The next point on Russia was achieved after some hesitancy. Seven and eight were satisfactorily implemented.

Number nine was patently violated, since that portion of the Tyrol awarded to Italy was peopled by Germans. Furthermore, the majority of those in Istria and along the Dalmatian coast who were transferred to Italian sovereignty were non-Italians. The tenth point went beyond its original intent. The former subject peoples of Austria and Hungary became for the most part not autonomous but completely independent.

Points eleven, twelve, and thirteen were for the most part satisfactorily achieved, although Poland's restoration with access to the sea had to be obtained at considerable expense to Germany. The latter suffered also at Poland's hands in the matter of the coal mines of Upper Silesia. The fourteenth point, and the most important of all from Wilson's standpoint, saw the creation of the League of Nations, but its chances for success were reduced at the start owing to the American defection and the absence of Russia. The League had been bought at a very dear price by Wilson, since to get it he had to compromise on many of the other points.

THE TREATIES

Following the approval of the proposed treaty with Germany by a secret plenary session of all the Allied and Associated Nations on 6 May, the German delegation was called in the next day and presented with a *fait accompli*. This treaty consisted of over two hundred pages and was designed to reduce Germany and keep her impotent. The German delegates read the treaty with horror. One fainted and others wept. They protested against the terms vehemently but to no avail. The head of the German group, Count von Brockdorff-Rantzau, bitterly assailed the Allies on the grounds of their postarmistice food blockade of his country, which caused the deaths "of thousands of noncombatants." Germany was given three weeks to sign or face the consequences. After a wild period in Germany, the German Constituent Assembly at Weimar voted on the final day of the time limit, 23 June 1919, to accept unconditionally.

Versailles: Germany. Accordingly, on 28 June in the Hall of Mirrors at Versailles, scene of the birth of the German Empire in 1871, and on the anniversary of the assassination of Francis Ferdinand, the Treaty of Versailles was autographed by representatives of Germany and all of those arrayed against her in the war except China.

Territorially, Germany lost Alsace-Lorraine to France, Eupen and Malmedy to Belgium, Northern Schleswig to Denmark (by plebiscite in 1920), most of Posen and the greater part of West Prussia to Poland, Upper Silesia to Poland (by means of a plebiscite), and the cities of Memel and Danzig on the Baltic to the Allies (Memel was turned over to Lithuania in 1923). Overseas, she gave up "all rights, titles and privileges whatever in or over territory which belonged to her or her allies" which meant that Japan secured her leaseholds and concessions in China. The rest of her holdings were distributed as mandates with Japan being awarded the German Pacific islands north of the equator while those south of that line went to Australia and New Zealand. The Union of South Africa secured German Southwest Africa while German East Africa was given to Great Britain. Finally, the Kamerun and Togoland were divided between France and Britain.

Germany agreed to recognize the independence of Belgium and Austria, together with the fact that Luxemburg no longer would belong to the German customs union. Moreover, the Germans gave up all claims under the Treaty of Brest-Litovsk signed with Russia in 1918. Financially, as has been seen, Germany agreed to sign a blank check in the matter of reparations. Until the amount should be decided, she was to pay five billions in gold and materials in kind. The justification for this treatment was her acknowledgement under duress that she and her allies were guilty of having caused the war. This was the famous Article 231. In addition, the former German Emperor was charged with "a supreme offense against international morality and the sanctity of treaties" and was to be tried by an international tribunal. Important German statesmen and generals were to be surrendered for trial, among them cabinet ministers and directors of munitions plants. This part of the treaty, however, was never enforced.

Militarily, the German army was to be limited to 100,000 men and 4,000 officers—all of whom were to be professional soldiers enlisted for long terms. The General Staff was abolished. In order to prevent subterfuge, the number of policemen, coastguardsmen, customs officers, forestry patrols, etc., could not exceed the 1913 total. The manufacture of armaments was strictly limited and most of the munitions plants were to be destroyed. What manufacturing there was to be would be under the supervision of Allied offices with storage under Allied control. Germany had to agree forever to abolish compulsory military training. As a last means of keeping Germany from building an army, athletic organizations were limited. From her powerful prewar naval position, she was to retain only six battleships, six cruisers, and a dozen torpedo boats, but no submarines. There were to be no more than 15,000 men in the navy, all of whom were to be professionals, who could not resign to enter the merchant marine. No military or naval planes, dirigibles, or balloons were permitted. The Kiel Canal was thrown open to the shipping of all nations and the fortifications on Helgoland were demolished.

The net result of these terms was a treaty which was unsatisfactory from any point of view. It was too harsh to allow Germany to recover properly—yet it was not severe enough to crush her if that was what was wanted. Thus, she was left to struggle to her feet in a bitter frame of mind as far as most of her populace was concerned.

St. Germain: Austria. The treaties with the other defeated powers were similar in that they were dictated in the same uncharitable spirit and were just as hard on these powers as Versailles was on Germany. The first one was with Austria, and was signed 10 September 1919. Told to submit their protests in writing, the Austrian delegation made only one protest, viz., that the whole treaty was bad. Especially distressing in the light of their hopes for the future was the clause forbidding union with Germany. The Austrian liberals had created the Republic of German Austria

(*Deutschösterreich*) 12 November 1918—so named because they felt Austria could not live by itself. This union (*Anschluss*) was denied because of French and Italian opposition. The Treaty of St. Germain-en-Laye specifically required Austria to change its name from German Austria. Austria was further obliged to cede territory to Italy, Czechoslovakia, Poland, Rumania, and Yugoslavia. From Hungary she was given the small region known as the Burgenland, largely German speaking. She lost in all approximately three-quarters of her territory and most of her mines and factories. She surrendered her entire navy and was allowed only a few police boats on the Danube, which was now internationalized. Her army was limited, and she too was compelled to sign a blank check in the matter of reparations. From a powerful empire she was reduced to a small land-locked country stripped of four-fifths of her population.

Neuilly: Bulgaria. Bulgaria was brought to book on 27 November 1919 at still another suburb of Paris, Neuilly. Territories were sliced off and awarded to Yugoslavia, Rumania, and Greece. Her only access to the Aegean was taken from her, and she was forced to ship via the Black Sea. Her army was cut and her navy was abolished, except for a few torpedo boats to protect fishing in the Black Sea. She had to turn over much of her livestock to Greece, Yugoslavia, and Rumania and agree to pay an indemnity of $450,000,000 over a period of thirty-seven years. From the strongest of the Balkans, she now became the weakest.

The Trianon: Hungary. The Trianon, a small palace near that of Versailles, was the scene of the treaty with Hungary. It was not signed until 4 June 1920, because of the chaos in that country which saw a sanguinary communist seizure of the government by Bela Kun from March to August, 1919, followed by an invasion of Hungary by the Rumanians, whose behavior left bitter memories. Finally, a conservative government was able to establish some semblance of order and the Hungarians were ready for their turn at the hands of the Allies. Territories were taken from her and awarded to Rumania (Hungary's richest wheatlands—the province of Transylvania), Yugoslavia, Czechoslovakia, and even Austria. Her army was cut to one-fifth its previous size; the navy reduced to river patrols. Her territorial reduction amounted to almost three-quarters, and her population was cut from 20,000,000 to 8,000,000.

Sèvres: Turkey. Turkey was the last of the enemy states to sign a treaty. This was due to splits between Britain, France, Italy, and Greece. Furthermore, a revolution was under way in Turkey which saw the Young Turk nationalists struggling for control against the Sultan. At Sèvres, a Parisian suburb, the Allies, who had come to terms among themselves, secured a treaty from the Sultan's government 10 August 1920. Under its terms, Turkey agreed formally to the loss of the entire Ottoman Empire except upper Asia Minor—about five-sixths of all its territory. An Allied

Financial Commission was appointed to supervise Turkish economic affairs. The Straits—the Dardanelles and the Bosphorus—were demilitarized and internationalized.

Although the Sultan's government had signed the Treaty of Sèvres, the Turkish National Assembly led by Mustapha Kemal refused to ratify it. In September, 1920, Kemal signed an accord with the Bolshevists in Russia. He next turned to forcing the Italians and the French from the achievement of their objectives on Turkish soil and secured from both the concession that they would favor revision of the Treaty of Sèvres. Then, in 1921, war broke out between Greece and Turkey. Following initial minor reverses, the Turks by September, 1922, had driven the Greeks into the sea at Smyrna in a mighty nationalistic surge. Lloyd George backed the Greeks, but the British people were war-weary and would have none of it, while the French and Italians actually supplied Mustapha Kemal with arms. His victory over the Greeks led this doughty individual to turn on the Allied garrisons on the Straits. The withdrawal of the French and Italians left the British alone. The upshot of it all was the scrapping of the Treaty of Sèvres and its replacement by the Treaty of Lausanne, 24 July 1923. The resurgent Turks regained Anatolia, Adalia, Smyrna, Cilicia, and eastern Thrace. The demilitarization and freedom of the Straits were continued, but the other controls imposed by Sèvres were lifted.

WILSON, THE TREATY OF VERSAILLES, AND THE UNITED STATES SENATE

On 12 July 1919, Wilson submitted his treaty to the American Senate. Previously there had been considerable evidence to show that Senator Henry Cabot Lodge of Massachusetts, chairman of the powerful Committee on Foreign Relations and, prior to Wilson's advent to the presidency, known as "the scholar in politics," was going to cause trouble. He did. His committee kept the treaty for two months. Lodge took two weeks to read it aloud, apparently on the assumption that his colleagues were illiterate, and then spent six weeks in public hearings. On 10 September the Foreign Relations Committee reported. It made forty-five amendments and had four reservations designed to protect traditional American policies. The purpose behind this elaborate performance was to delay the vote on ratification until the opposition could muster its strength. The major issue was whether, by ratifying the treaty, the United States should join the League of Nations; while there were some objections to certain of the actual peace provisions, they would not in themselves have stirred up public opinion to any great degree.

When the treaty came before the Senate, about four-fifths of the membership was willing to approve it in some form. Most of the 47 Democrats backed the President in his desire to ratify the treaty as it stood; most of the 49 Republicans wished to include reservations; about a dozen "irreconcilables," led by Senator William E. Borah of Idaho, would have nothing to do with the League on any terms. The forty-five amendments of the Foreign Relations Committee were rejected and replaced by fourteen reservations drafted by Lodge, in obvious imitation of Wilson's Fourteen Points. These reservations included the preservation of the Monroe Doctrine (already provided for in the Covenant), a requirement that Congress must approve in each separate case before the United States was obligated to aid in enforcing League decisions, a stipulation for the right of withdrawal from the League, and a protest against the separate representation given to the British dominions.

It is still uncertain whether Lodge was willing to see the treaty ratified on his terms or whether he deliberately framed his reservations to make them unacceptable to Wilson, so that the President would have to bear the onus of defeating his own treaty. Unwilling to compromise, the President set out on a tour of the country to make a direct appeal to the people, trailed relentlessly from city to city by Borah and other irreconcilables. Wilson's health broke under the strain. On 25 September 1919 he burst into tears in the middle of a speech at Pueblo, Colorado, and was stricken with paralysis that evening. A second stroke followed on 4 October. Wilson eventually recovered, but during the crucial period of the fight over the treaty he was an invalid, out of touch with the political currents on Capitol Hill and querulously insistent that the League Covenant should be accepted without reservation.

The Votes in the Senate. The result was that senators who basically wanted to join the League, and were supported in their stand by the bulk of public opinion, found themselves voting against each other. The treaty with the Lodge reservations was rejected on 19 November 1919, the opposition consisting of a weird coalition of the irreconcilables and the Democrats—in other words of the bitter enemies and the strongest friends of the League. The Democrats voted as they did because they considered themselves obligated to respect Wilson's wishes on the matter of reservations. A second vote on 19 March 1920 saw some defection in the Democratic ranks, but enough remained loyal to the President to prevent the treaty, still with reservations attached,[2] from receiving the requisite two-thirds majority. It may be added that the rejection of the treaty left the United States technically at war with Germany until 2 July 1921, when hostilities were terminated by joint resolution. A peace treaty followed shortly afterward.

[2] There were fifteen this time, one having been added indorsing independence for Ireland.

The defeat of the League was totally unnecessary. Many Republican senators were willing to modify the Lodge reservations, and most of the Democrats would have agreed to a compromise, since it was perfectly obvious that there was not the slightest prospect of the treaty's being ratified without reservations. If Lodge was guilty of partisanship and personal vindictiveness, Wilson was guilty of a stubborn refusal to face the realities of the situation, although his illness must be considered an extenuating circumstance. Part of the President's attitude seems to have been based on an assumption that the people would approve his position in the forthcoming election. By the middle of 1920, however, public interest in the League had cooled off, and it was anything but the key issue of the campaign. Moreover, the ambiguity of the Republican platform and the noncommittal attitude of the Republican candidate, Warren G. Harding, make it impossible even now to determine what the Republican victory signified regarding the League.

34

Liquidating the Peace Settlement

During the First World War there came into being a great feeling of revulsion against war on the part of people throughout the world. There was a widespread feeling that unless war could be outlawed in the future, civilization was in danger of being wiped out. In the past there had been numerous projects devised to end war. In the fourteenth century, Dante in his *De Monarchia* had suggested the unification of all Christendom under one monarch. About the same time, in France, Pierre Dubois, a lawyer, suggested that the rulers of Europe get together for peace and proposed that an international court be organized under the pope.

At a time when religion was a cause of war, Henry IV of France, just before his assassination in 1610, came forward with his "Grand Design," a plan similar to the League of Nations. Then, in 1625, during the Thirty Years' War, Hugo Grotius, "the father of international law," published his first treatise *On the Law of War and Peace*. Grotius held that if international law could be worked out and its principles applied, all would go well.

Following the wars of Louis XIV, there were additional proposals. The Quakers (Society of Friends) sought to prevent war. One of their number, William Penn, was the author of *An Essay toward the Present and Future Peace of Europe,* which envisaged an international parliament. At the same time, a German, Gottfried Leibnitz, the philosopher, proposed a Catholic federation under the Holy Roman Empire and the supervision of the pope.

Hard on the heels of the Seven Years' War, the English philosopher Jeremy Bentham published a plan for universal and perpetual peace which embraced the establishment of an international court of justice and called for the abolition of secret diplomacy. In the midst of the Wars

561

of the French Revolution, another eminent philosopher, Immanuel Kant, brought out a suggestion for perpetual peace which recommended democratic government as the solution. If the people were in control, he argued, there would be no wars. He advocated the association of nations into one large federation and called for the abolition of armies.

These were but a few of the many proposals advanced by sincere champions of peace. Christians have long worked valiantly in the interests of a peaceful world dedicated to Christ, the Prince of Peace. There were others like Napoleon, the architects of the Congress of Vienna, and the framers of the concert of Europe, who believed that peace could be achieved by force. Still others championed peace by conciliation. By 1914 there were well over one hundred peace societies in the Western world, among which were: the American Peace Society, founded in 1816 in the belief that education would turn the trick; the World Peace Foundation, established in Boston by the millionaire pubisher Edward Ginn; and the Carnegie Endowment for International Peace, founded by the steel baron, who believed that education of students was the only way. In 1901, Nobel, the great Swedish armaments manufacturer, set aside an allotment for the cause of peace. The Nobel Peace Prize is still awarded annually to the "person who had most or best promoted the fraternity of nations."

During the First World War, as was noted above, there were strong yearnings expressed for a permanent peace. In the forefront of this group was Pope Benedict XV who, within five days of his coronation in September, 1914, vainly implored the belligerents "to be satisfied with the ruin already wrought." Again, in November, 1914, in his Encyclical *Ad Beatissimi*, he declared: "Surely there are other ways and means [than warfare] whereby violated rights can be rectified." In July, 1915, he once more begged the belligerents to call a truce and replace their fighting with arbitration. Far from winning a favorable response, the pope was destined to be brushed aside in the secret Treaty of London that very year (1915) wherein Italy joined the Allies. A clause in this agreement prohibited "the representatives of the Holy See to undertake any diplomatic steps having for their object the conclusion of peace." In 1917, at what appeared an opportune moment, the pope made his final appeal. This time he addressed a seven-point program to the belligerents which emphasized justice, a virtue easily forgotten in the heat of war. The response was unsatisfactory, and the war continued.

THE LEAGUE OF NATIONS

All efforts to halt the war whether by religious or political leaders failed until Germany finally was forced to agree to an armistice. Notwithstanding these failures, there was a great hope that the world had seen the last of war. Meanwhile, two men occupying key positions had been working independently upon just such a project. One of these men was Woodrow Wilson, President of the United States; the other man was Jan Christian Smuts of the Union of South Africa. He had fought the British in the Boer War but had become reconciled to them afterward and served the British Empire loyally. In 1914, it was his unpleasant duty to aid in putting down an insurrection in South Africa against participating in the war against Germany. He and Wilson both studied numerous projects of the past for peace and were each greatly impressed by Henry IV's "Grand Design." Hearing of each other's work, they corresponded and between them worked out the idea of the League of Nations.[1] Wilson had made "a general association of nations" his fourteenth point. The League became almost a fetish with him, and he insisted that it be made an integral part of the peace treaties.

The members of the League were to be the signatories of the Treaty of Versailles (victors only) together with various specially invited states. The original membership consisted of thirty Allied and Associated Powers plus thirteen selected neutrals. The maximum number of states belonging was sixty-two, which was reached in 1935. The objects which the League sought to realize were four in number, viz., (1) to prevent war; (2) to achieve international peace and security; (3) to carry out the terms of the peace settlement; (4) and to promote international cooperation in humanitarian matters.

Organization. The machinery of the League called for: (1) an Assembly in which all the member states were represented, each with one vote although it could have three representatives; (2) a Council of nine members, five permanent (United States, Great Britain, France, Japan, and Italy) and four nonpermanent. The latter were to rotate among the lesser powers. Ultimately, Germany and Russia were granted permanent seats, while the number of nonpermanent members was gradually increased to ten; and (3) a Secretariat—a permanent body of officials responsible to the Assembly and the Council—whose job it was to carry out the administrative and clerical tasks connected with the League. In addition, a permanent Court of International Justice and an International Labor Office were provided for. The League's headquarters were at Geneva, Switzerland, and the funds for its operations were supplied by a budget with each nation paying according to its ability. Meetings of the Assembly were held annually in Geneva, while the Council was to meet four times a year in Geneva or wherever occasion should arise.

The members pledged themselves to respect the territorial integrity

[1] The ultimate draft was largely the work of the American David Hunter Miller and Sir Cecil Hurst of Great Britain.

and political independence of each of their fellows. They were required to submit their disputes to arbitration or to allow the Council to make an inquiry into them and to promise not to resort to war until three months (a "cooling-off" period) after a decision had been reached by those to whom the dispute had been submitted for arbitration or by the Council. Should arbitration be chosen and should it fail to solve the dispute, the parties were obliged to submit the dispute to the Council. Here the Council had to reach a unanimous decision (parties to the dispute excluded). Inability on the Council's part to reach a unanimous decision meant that the disputants could legally wage war. Civil war and armed rebellion were outside the League's jurisdiction. Here, then, were instances demonstrating the League's inability to outlaw war even on paper. Furthermore, if a member insisted on going to war in violation of those specific prohibitions, the League was in reality armed only with "sanctions," although it could "recommend" military action by its members against the aggressor. "Sanctions" involved the cutting of all trade and financial relations between the League's members and the aggressor state and also called for preventing nationals of the aggressor country from any intercourse with the nationals of all other states (League members or not). Finally, in an effort at preventing war, the League members were expected to work for arms reduction. To aid in the work of making the peace effective, the permanent Court of International Justice (World Court) was established in 1921 with its seat at The Hague. The Court was in permanent session and had a membership of fifteen judges. The latter served for a term of nine years and were appointed by the common action of the Council and Assembly. Its jurisdiction embraced "any dispute of an international character which the parties thereto submit to it." It was empowered to give advisory opinions to the Council and Assembly. Such opinions were not binding, but its decisions when a dispute was submitted to it were. A state which refused to accept such a decision would lose its membership in the League.

Specific Functions. To carry out the terms of the peace settlement, the League had to do such things as conduct several plebiscites, administer Danzig and the Saar, protect the minorities provided for in the various treaties, and keep watch over the powers administering the former German and Turkish possessions as mandates.

Lastly, the League was to perform such tasks as: to give financial assistance to needy countries in emergencies; to aid in the coordination of the work of various health and scientific organizations; to wipe out the traffic in women and children; to curb the production and consumption of opium; to combat slavery; to study labor methods and the cost of living and aid in improving the former and reducing the latter where possible; and to codify international law.

The International Labor Office, attached to the League and since taken over by the United Nations, is a general conference of four delegates from each member state (like the League Assembly) and a governing body (like the League Council) of thirty-two members, eight representing the employees, eight the employers, and sixteen the governments. It has no legislative power but recommends certain policies which have been generally found desirable. Its purpose is to make surveys on labor conditions in different countries. On 20 August 1934 the United States became a member of the I.L.O. on condition that it did not assume "any obligations under the Covenant of the League of Nations."

THE LEAGUE IN OPERATION

The weaknesses of the League of Nations included: (1) the failure of the United States, whose President had been the dominant force in the foundation of the League, to become a member; (2) the absence of Russia, which was undergoing the beginning of the Bolshevist "experiment" and rated as a pariah among the nations; (3) the identification of the League in the eyes of the vanquished with an instrument to enforce the Treaty of Versailles and the other peace treaties; (4) the presence of too much nationalism on the part of the members, which made for selfishness and produced such dangerous splits as that between France and Great Britain, two powers whose cooperation was essential to the success of the League; (5) the lack of an international police force to provide the force necessary to deal with a determined aggressor; (6) the total inadequacy of the Court; and (7) the requirement of a unanimous vote in the Council on all important issues.

The League did manage, however, to achieve certain successes, largely in the field of its humanitarian endeavors, such as its labor and health services and its fight against the drug traffic. Its efforts at mediating disputes were successful in the case of minor quarrels, but not where major powers were involved.

It mediated such conflicts as the Aaland Islands dispute between Sweden and Finland[2] (1920); the Mosul Oil Fields Case involving Iraq and Turkey (1926); and the Greek-Bulgar frontier quarrel (1925). But almost from the start determined powers were able to use force to gain their ends. Poland's seizure of Vilna in 1923 at the expense of Lithuania went unchecked. The same year saw a highhanded Italian attack on the island of Corfu, in complete disregard of the League, because of a dispute between Italy and Greece over the Greek-Albanian frontier. These were minor incidents; it was left for the 1930's to demonstrate tragically how

[2] Although the inhabitants are mostly Swedish, the League awarded the islands to Finland because of their geological structure.

even in a major crisis a well-armed great power could defy the League of Nations with impunity.

THE REPARATIONS PROBLEM

The postwar years witnessed an international inability to solve pressing economic problems whose solutions were vital to peace. Among these was the reparations question. It will be remembered that Germany had signed a "blank check" at Versailles. By 1 May 1921 an Allied Reparations Commission was expected to have decided upon the amount to be required.

The total reparations bill set by the Commission was $32,000,-000, thirty-two times that demanded by Germany from France in 1871 and an amount at least three times that recommended by the British economist John Maynard Keynes at the time of the Paris Peace Conference. This decision was known as "the London Schedule." According to this agreement, Germany would be expected to pay a minimum of one-half billion dollars a year, and interest on the unpaid balance of the reparations bill. At this rate, she might never have been able to pay off the debt. Moreover, to meet the demands made of her, Germany now required a favorable balance of trade so that she could thus acquire foreign credits to pay her reparations. She would either have to cut her imports to the bone, or increase her exports to an extremely high degree, or do both. It was the latter she tried. In her efforts to export her goods, she ran into the barrier of the high postwar tariffs universally erected. She was forced to cut her imports even more—an extreme which was later to prove harmful to the Allies because it meant that Germany now had to institute a painstaking drive for self-sufficiency.

Her efforts to meet reparations were destined to prove impossible under the restrictions she faced. Her only other remedy was borrowing. As long as foreign funds came into Germany, she could try to meet her obligations. Up to 1924, Germany did everything in her power to fulfill those obligations and actually paid a fair sum, but most of it was in the form of materials.

Divisions among Allies. A split developed among the Allies on the reparations question as early as 1922. The British favored reducing Germany's reparations 50 per cent, but France declined. The French now sought to declare Germany deliberately in default and occupy the Ruhr, the heart of German industry. Such action, they reasoned, would force the Germans to pay. Accordingly, in January, 1923, basing their action on a flimsy bit of evidence, the French occupied the Ruhr. The Germans in that area resorted to a general strike. They refused to work and were supported by the rest of the country. The German government deliberately inflated the currency until it reached incredible proportions. Thousands of

Germans were deported from, or voluntarily left, the Ruhr during the occupation and scores were killed or injured. In the winter of 1923–1924, France got Belgium to aid her in an attempt to set up a buffer state in the Rhineland. Flotsam and jetsam from the length and breadth of Germany were brought in and prompted to declare the region independent. The movement collapsed and in February, 1924, France had to drop the idea.

Dawes and Young Plans. The destruction of Germany's monetary system and the widespread economic confusion forced France to reconsider the whole matter. The result was the Dawes Plan (so named because Charles G. Dawes of the United States was the Commission's chairman, although the real work was done largely by Sir Josiah Stamp) which created a central bank of issue in Germany (Reichsbank) with a fifty-year monopoly on the issue of paper money and provided that further reparations should start at approximately a quarter of a billion dollars a year and rise slowly over a four-year period to approximately six hundred and twenty-five million dollars a year. Foreign experts were to supervise several important facets of German economic life, and an immediate loan of $200,000,000 was granted. This arrangement neglected to reduce the total owed by Germany, provided for too elaborate a system of foreign controls, and gave evidence that the bill would never be met, so it was replaced in 1929 by another plan. This was the Young Plan (the chairman was again an American, Owen D. Young of the General Electric Company). Under its terms, the total was reduced to $8,000,000,000, and a definite time period was set in place of the indefinite arrangement which previously prevailed. It further abolished the foreign control and founded the Bank of International Settlements, thereby assuming for the first time that Germany was an "honest" country. It was a case of "the pardon which came too late" because the great crash hit the world in 1929 and plunged it into economic chaos and depression. Between 1924 and 1931 Germany was able to pay as much as she actually did (approximately $2,725,000,000) only because she was able to borrow a sum considerably in excess of this figure from abroad.

By 1931, however, the international financial debacle so affected Germany that she was in a state of near economic collapse. Consequently, President Hoover of the United States successfully proposed a one-year moratorium on all international debt payments. For all practical purposes, the expiration of the holiday marked the end of any further German reparations payments, since Hitler's advent to power in January, 1933, meant the scrapping of the *Diktat* of Versailles in short order.

INTERALLIED DEBTS

Paralleling the German reparations was the problem of interallied war debts. While the First World War was in progress and immediately afterward the United States government loaned a sum in excess of ten billion dollars to about twenty different European nations. The principal recipients were Britain, France, Italy, and Belgium. The bulk of this money was spent in the United States for war material. It was raised largely through the sale of Liberty Bonds purchased by the American people.

In 1922 Congress created the World War Foreign Debt Commission, which ultimately worked out agreements with the debtor nations. These called for the loans to be repaid in annual installments over a sixty-year period, with the rate of interest set according to the individual country's "capacity to pay." This arrangement actually provided for somewhat of a reduction from the terms agreed upon at the time the loans were originally made. In the case of France, she was expected to pay back only 50 per cent of her original debt. Italy was handsomely treated and secured a reduction of almost 75 per cent. Nevertheless, there was a universal spirit of dissatisfaction among the debtors. The United States was termed "Uncle Shylock" for insisting that anything at all be paid, while, on the other hand, the consistent failure of the European states to make good reacted unfavorably on the American people, who resented being "gypped." The net result was that virtually nothing was repaid, the majority of the payments going only to meet the interest.

Although the United States insisted that there was no connection between reparations and intergovernmental debts, the Hoover Moratorium of 1931 seemed to imply that such a connection existed. Furthermore, the Allies acted in a manner calculated to convince the United States that this was their conviction. In July, 1932, they signed the Lausanne Agreement, which reduced Germany's total reparations to a mere $714,000,000 in the form of 5 per cent redeemable bonds which were not to be put on sale by the Bank of International Settlements until 1935, thereby giving Germany three years of grace. Although Britain, France, Italy, and Belgium reached an accord pledging each of them to withhold ratification until the United States reduced the interallied debts, the Lausanne Agreement was tantamount to the end of reparations by allied action.

Debt Defaults. The United States declined to alter its stand, which had been expressed by Calvin Coolidge when he remarked, "They hired the money, didn't they?" and refused to suspend "payments." But by 1934 even those who had been making "token payments" fell by the wayside. Finland alone paid in full and was treated to considerable favorable publicity in the American press, which usually failed to mention the point that Finland was able to pay its debt because it was one of the few countries enjoying a favorable balance of trade with the United States. 15 June 1934 marked the end, to all practical purposes, of the interallied debts, which could only have been repaid in goods and services, the one thing which the United States would not even consider. As a matter of fact, Congress raised the American tariff barriers in 1922 and again in 1930 to the highest levels in American history, thereby ensuring Europe's inability to meet the debts by denying the debtor countries an opportunity to acquire balances.

Feeling ran so high in the United States over Europe's failure to make good that the Congress passed the Johnson Debt Default Act in 1934, which prohibited any country owing the United States money from borrowing any more. It also declared flatly that "token payments" were unsatisfactory. In signing the measure, President Roosevelt described the loans as "vital means for the successful conclusion of a war which involved the national existence of the borrowers, and later for a quicker retoration of their normal life after the war ended."

MULTIPOWER PACTS

Following the setback dealt the postwar settlements by Turkey's successful revision of the Treaty of Sèvres, it was apparent that the League required some auxiliary help. The League, therefore, hit upon the idea of seeking to outlaw war and, in case aggression did occur, to provide assurance to the victims of attack.

First in the series of security plans of a multipower nature was the Geneva Protocol. This was a scheme for the pacific settlement of international disputes, which was adopted by the Fifth Assembly of the League of Nations in October, 1924. Under its terms, the signatories pledged themselves not to go to war against nations which adhered to international obligations. They agreed also to submit any disputes to which they were a party to the World Court and to accept the Court's decision. Refusal to submit its dispute to arbitration would cause a state to be branded an aggressor. If this happened, or if a state refused to abide by the Court's decision, the League Council was empowered to recommend to the other League members whatever economic or military steps were deemed necessary to compel the recalcitrant to comply.

Although most of the League's membership ratified the agreement, its demise was certain when Great Britain refused ratification upon the grounds of her numerous imperial requirements. She proposed, however, that each special need be met by special treaties. Her failure to ratify killed any chances the Geneva Protocol might have had, but it did not close the door to special arrangements. One such was the Locarno Peace Pacts.

Locarno. In October, 1925, France, Great Britain, Germany, Italy, Belgium, Poland, and Czechoslovakia sent delegates to Locarno, Switzerland, where a friendly atmosphere prevailed. The leading personalities present were Sir Austen Chamberlain, Aristide Briand, and Gustav Stresemann, foreign ministers of their respective countries, and Benito Mussolini. The mere fact that the meeting was held at all was a hopeful sign because the number of handicaps which had to be overcome in advance was great. Chief among them was the German insistence upon having the Versailles guilt clause stricken out and the French fear that any German participation in such a meeting was for the purpose of a trick.

There were nine agreements signed at Locarno, the most important of which was the Rhineland Security Pact wherein Britain, France, Germany, and Italy (Belgium ultimately excused herself from participating) signed pledges mutually guaranteeing their borders as fixed by the Treaty of Versailles. Germany promised also to abide by the demilitarization of a special zone in the Rhineland. Other agreements signed included German-Polish and German-Czech arbitration treaties. Ratification of the Pact resulted in Germany's admission to the League in September, 1926, at which time she was given a permanent seat on the League Council. To say that Locarno's effect on Europe was enthusiastic is to put it mildly. It looked indeed as if the millennium had arrived.

The Kellogg-Briand Pact. But the multipower agreement which aroused the highest hopes and was widely celebrated with "fireworks followed by dancing on the green" was the Kellogg-Briand Treaty (1928). Born in the brain of an American citizen, this plan was initiated by Aristide Briand, then French foreign minister. He proposed to Frank B. Kellogg, the American Secretary of State, that the United States and France sign an agreement pledging the two countries never to go to war with each other. Kellogg suggested that other countries be permitted to participate. The result was that fifteen nations including Great Britain, Italy, Japan, the U.S.S.R., and Germany, in addition to France and the United States, signed the Pact of Paris on 27 August. The agreement required the signatories to renounce war forever as an instrument of national policy and to promise to settle their disputes by pacific means. Ultimately over sixty nations signed it.

There were, however, qualifications. The right to go to war in self-defense was expressly recognized, and allowance was made for obligations incurred under the League Covenant or the Locarno Pacts. The United States stipulated that its adherence was not to affect its right to uphold the Monroe Doctrine, while Great Britain made a similar reservation regarding the protection of certain of the frontier areas of the Empire. Moreover, since no provision for enforcement was included, the Kellogg-Briand Pact could hardly be considered anything more than a declaration of good intentions.

DISARMAMENT

Up to this point there has been sketched a list of the more important conferences held and treaties made in the name of security. It should not be imagined that a most obvious way of achieving this desirable goal was neglected. This, of course, was disarmament. Unfortunately, its record is as dreary and discouraging as that of the conferences and treaties which frequently aroused some wide hopes only to result in failure.

The Washington Conference. The first attempt to reach the ultimate objective of world disarmament was the Washington Conference of 1921–1922. It was called by President Harding, who always maintained that it had been his idea right along. Actually, it seems to have originated in the British Foreign Office, and the initiative in the United States was taken by Senator Borah, who introduced a resolution in the Senate requesting the administration to call such a conference. Harding's participation was limited to giving an address of welcome, in which he uttered the platitudes customary for such occasions; the spokesman for the United States when the conference went to work was Secretary of State Charles Evans Hughes.

Naval limitation was the only field in which the powers could expect to reach an agreement, since there was no prospect of immediate military disarmament because of the uncertainties of the postwar era, the fear of Russian communism, and the desire to keep Germany impotent. But it was hoped that the new naval race that was developing between the United States, Great Britain, and Japan could be checked, with resultant benefits to their respective taxpayers. Inasmuch as there were also problems concerning the Far East which needed to be solved and which were closely related to the naval rivalry, it was deemed advisable to undertake this work at the same time. Consequently, in addition to the naval powers present, the United States, Great Britain, Japan, France and Italy (all of whom had possessions or interests in the Far East also), China, Belgium, the Netherlands, and Portugal were invited because of their stake in Far Eastern affairs. The agreements reached in relation to the Far East will be discussed below.

The Washington Naval Treaty declared a ten-year naval holiday during which no new capital ships[3] were to be constructed, except that Great Britain could build two to place the Royal Navy on an equal footing with the United States Navy in postwar vessels. Capital ships could not be replaced until they were twenty years old, the number allowed each signatory was restricted, and they were not to exceed 35,000 tons or

---

[3] A capital ship was defined as a vessel, other than an aircraft carrier, with a displacement over 10,000 tons and guns exceeding 8 inches in caliber.

carry guns larger than 16 inches in caliber. The total capital-ship tonnage was fixed at a ratio of $5:5:3:1.67:1.67$, or 525,000 tons each for the United States and the British Empire, 315,000 tons for Japan, and 175,000 tons each for France and Italy. The total tonnage of aircraft carriers was also restricted, and the unit size of these ships was limited to 27,000 tons, except that each signatory could convert two of the capital ships under construction into "experimental" carriers.

Neither France nor Japan liked the naval treaty, but both finally accepted it. Japan was given a concession in the form of an agreement whereby she, the United States, and the British Empire were not to add to their fortifications over a wide area of the Pacific during the lifetime of the treaty. It proved impossible to impose limitations on cruisers, destroyers, and submarines. The Washington Treaty was to run until 31 December 1936.

Other Naval-limitation Agreements. In 1927 President Coolidge proposed a conference to take up the question of limiting the smaller warships. France and Italy refused because auxiliary vessels were considered vital by both of these powers for their operations in the Mediterranean, and because of their smaller capital-ship tonnage they argued they could not afford any further limitations on their naval strength. Britain and Japan both accepted and the conference was held at Geneva. The meeting ended in flat failure because of the inability of the British and the Americans to agree. The British wished a limitation put upon heavy cruisers, in which the United States predominated, and the United States wished it applied to light cruisers, Britain's specialty. The distinction between the two types was that a heavy cruiser mounted 8-inch guns, the largest permitted to a cruiser under the Washington Treaty, while a light cruiser carried guns of 6-inch caliber or less. The efforts made by Japan to strike a compromise were fruitless, and the conference came to nought.

Following preliminary negotiations by President Hoover and Prime Minister MacDonald, the five naval powers came together again in London in January, 1930. Although national self-interest predominated, some agreements were reached by April. These included a parity arrangement between Britain and the United States, which checked the naval race these powers were having; several limitations on carriers and auxiliary vessels;[4] application of rules of international law to submarines in the case of an attack on a merchant ship with respect to the safety of the passengers and crew; extension of the capital-ship holiday for another five years; and, finally, the "Escalator Clause" to the effect that a power could increase its tonnage of any type if it felt its "national security" was en-

---

[4] Auxiliary vessels covered everything except capital ships and carriers. The ratio fixed for them was $10:10:7$.

dangered, provided the said power gave adequate notice of its intentions to the other signatories. A blow to the success of the conference was the refusal of France and Italy to sign.

The Geneva Disarmament Conference. On 2 February 1932 Geneva played host to over fifty nations assembled for the world's first disarmament conference. It was held at a most inauspicious time since Japan was then busily engaged in overrunning Manchuria at China's expense. Nevertheless, hopes were very high that the meeting would prove a success. The chief obstacles to this goal—French intransigence and German insistence upon equality—produced an intolerable situation. President Hoover's proposal, in June, 1932, that each one of the powers promise to reduce its armies by one-third fell on unreceptive ears, and the conference dragged on. In the spring of 1933 President Roosevelt proposed to the heads of all the states participating that they abolish all offensive weapons and also suggested that they sign a nonaggression pact which would bind them not to send their national armies across anyone else's borders.

Shortly afterward, the American emissary, Norman H. Davis, announced in so many words that the United States would cooperate in any plan designed to bring about effective disarmament. The failure to produce such a plan invalidated this offer and when the conference came to a halt in June, 1933, its achievements were nil. Its resumption in October was violently punctuated by the sudden withdrawal of Germany, who also declared her intention of quitting the League of Nations. Germany's actions were based on a claim that she had been treated too long as an inferior. This move on the part of Germany produced the adjournment of what had been an unprofitable attempt to remedy the situation. A final resumption of the conference in 1934 was equally fruitless, smashing again on the old rock of French "security" and German "equality."

The End of Naval Limitation. The last naval disarmament conference was held in 1935 at London. Present were representatives of the United States, Great Britain, Japan, France, and Italy. The need for such a meeting was imperative since the limits set by the earlier conferences were shortly to expire. Japan and Italy both proved intransigent. The Japanese argued that their security was jeopardized and that they required absolute equality with Britain and the United States, a view these two powers refused to accept, whereupon Japan took her leave of the conference. Italy's peeve was directed against the League of Nations sanctions. She refused to sign any agreements until these were withdrawn and ultimately left the conference in a highly excitable state.

With both Japan and Italy among the missing, the remaining powers felt constrained to reach some kind of agreement in order to salvage whatever scraps of prestige were left to the conference. Even so their accomplishment was decidedly meager. The best they were able to do was to agree to a temporary plan to limit both the size and armaments of heavy cruisers and capital ships and to promise to exchange their naval construction plans annually. When the Washington and London Agreements expired in 1936 a naval race was officially begun. Thus, finis was written to disarmament efforts.

PART NINE

Internal Problems, 1919–1939

The First World War left in its wake serious problems of readjustment: physical damage resulting from military operations, strained economies, and considerable political and social unrest. Few states, large or small, escaped having to face serious internal stresses. Many of them succumbed under this pressure to totalitarianism, a twentieth-century variation of dictatorship characterized by the imposition of a uniform ideology on the people of the state in question, the domination of its government by a single political party, and the forcible suppression of all opposition. Of the great powers, Russia, Germany, Italy, and Japan followed this course. There was nothing fundamentally new about their methods. The same techniques had been employed by dictatorships of the past, but the modern totalitarians enjoyed technological advantages denied to their predecessors for forming and controlling public opinion and for repressing discontent.

Other countries, notably Great Britain, France, and the United States, wrestled with their problems within the framework of democratic government. The first named was faced throughout this period with a continuous economic crisis, and witnessed an important political change in the rise of the Labour Party to major status. The British Empire also underwent significant reorganization. France suffered from acute internal cleavages but managed to preserve its republic until its shattering military defeat in 1940. The United States went through two distinct phases: the first, the extreme conservatism of the 1920's, terminated by the world-wide depression of 1929–1932; the second, the reform era known as the New Deal.

35

Totalitarianism in Europe

For a large part of Europe, the difficulties created by the First World War proved fatal to institutions of self-government, and there was a general recourse to the apparently easy solution of dictatorship in one form or another. Russia, which had never known free government, saw the Czarist regime overthrown while the war was still in progress and eventually came under the control of a faction dedicated to the principles of Marxian communism. Italy, Germany, and some lesser imitators turned to fascism, a philosophy both anticommunist and antidemocratic. All, however, evolved a rather similar pattern of a superstate with absolute authority over its citizens.

THE RUSSIAN REVOLUTION

By 1917 the dwindling confidence of the Russian people in the "Little Father" had reached the vanishing point. Incompetence and corruption might be partially covered up in peacetime, but military disaster and internal chaos could hardly be concealed. Confidence in the Czar was further undermined by the influence acquired at court by the pseudo monk Gregor Rasputin, who dominated the superstitious empress because of his ability, apparently through some sort of hypnotic influence, to handle the Czarevitch (the heir to the throne), a sufferer from hemophilia. Rasputin virtually dictated appointments to high political and military offices until he was assassinated by some young noblemen at the end of 1916, and by then irreparable damage had been done to the prestige of the monarchy.

Disorder broke out in the capital, Petrograd (formerly St. Petersburg and later Leningrad), early in 1917, and, following the example of 1905, a Petrograd Soviet of Workers and Soldiers was organized. It soon became evident that disaffection pervaded every level of Russian society. In the middle of March Nicholas II was persuaded to abdicate and was replaced by a provisional government representing most shades of Russian liberal opinion. Its official head was Prince Lvov, a Constitutional Democrat, but its outstanding member was Alexander Kerensky, leader of the Social Revolutionary party, which, despite its horrendous title, was a peasant party interested primarily in drastic land reform.

The provisional government had an unhappy and ineffectual career. Its component elements were too diversified to be able to agree on a permanent form of government, and on the one point on which they did agree, that Russia should remain in the war, they were directly at variance with the desires of the great majority of the Russian people. The result was a heightening of confusion and chaos and the acquisition of commanding influence by the numerous soviets which were organized on the Petrograd model and were increasingly dominated by the well-disciplined Bolsheviks.

Rise of the Bolsheviks. The Bolshevik leader, Nicolai Lenin, was in Switzerland when the revolution broke out but was given passage to Russia by the Germans in the hope that he would undermine the provisional government and thereby handicap any resumption of Russia's military efforts. His success exceeded anything the Germans expected or desired. The Bolsheviks, although a small minority, attracted more and more popular support by their slogan of "peace, land, bread." Russia's armies disintegrated as the authority of the officers was taken over by soldiers' committees. Finally, on 7 November 1917, a Bolshevik *coup d'état* overthrew the provisional government.[1]

The immediate prospects of the new regime could hardly be considered bright. Its one asset at the moment was that it controlled the only reliable military force in Russia, the Red Army which Leon Trotsky was busily organizing. The Russian people were uncertain about it; at an election for a Constituent Assembly on 25 November they chose a majority of Social Revolutionaries. The assembly was not allowed to meet. The Bolsheviks inherited Russia's war with the Central Powers and at the same time found themselves in conflict with the Allies, who sent expeditions to various points in Russia, ostensibly to keep military supplies from falling into German hands, but also in the hope of encouraging the anti-Communist elements in Russia. Their appearance stimulated the organization of anti-Bolshevik, or "White" armies. In addition, the Finns, Letts, Lithuanians, and Estonians took advantage of Russia's troubles to declare their independence, Rumania seized the province of Bessarabia, and the

[1] Since Russia still used the Julian Calendar, this event took place in October according to Russian reckoning and is therefore termed the "October Revolution."

new state of Poland produced extensive territorial claims which it tried to make good by force. To complicate matters a little more, an army of some 45,000 Czechs was in possession of the Trans-Siberian Railway. These men, mostly deserters from the Austrian armies, had been fighting for the liberation of their homeland and on the outbreak of the Russian Revolution had decided to try to reach the Western Front via Vladivostok.

The survival of the Bolsheviks was due to the able leadership of Lenin and Trotsky and lack of cooperation among their opponents. Peace was purchased from the Central Powers at Brest-Litovsk, admittedly on humiliating terms, but Lenin realized that his government was in no position to bargain. Allied intervention was never very effective; since the Allied peoples were in no mood for further military adventures and felt that the Russians should be left to fight out their own differences, most of the Allied troops were withdrawn by 1920, although the Japanese remained in Siberia until 1922. The Czechs fundamentally desired nothing more than to go home. The independence of Finland and the Baltic states was conceded by 1920 also. Russo-Polish relations created something more of a flurry. In the spring of 1920 Polish forces penetrated as far as Kiev but then were driven back all the way to Warsaw, where the Russians in turn were defeated with the aid of hastily shipped French supplies and a French military mission. The ensuing settlement left Poland in possession of territory which the Russians claimed was rightfully theirs.

Inside Russia, civil war raged, with both sides displaying an appalling ferocity. The Bolsheviks, following a policy reminiscent of the Terror in the French Revolution, mercilessly exterminated all who were suspected of "counterrevolutionary" sympathies, among their victims being the Imperial family, who were shot at Ekaterinburg when White armies approached the town. The Whites were equally ruthless but not as adept at winning popular support. Their noisiest element was the reactionaries, who proclaimed their intention of restoring the estates which the peasants had seized from the nobility, with the result that the peasants, although not enamored of communism, saw the Bolshevik regime as the lesser evil. One by one the White armies were destroyed, until in 1921 the Bolsheviks were at last in control of all Russia.

THE ORGANIZATION OF THE SOVIET STATE

While the new regime was engaged in its life-and-death struggle with its enemies, external and internal, it could not undertake to provide Russia with a permanent government. Authority was exercised through the local soviets, with coordination nominally in the hands of an All-Russian Congress of Soviets. In practice, Lenin was a dictator. With the return of peace, this structure was formalized into a constitution, officially promulgated in 1923. In its broad principles this document expounded the Marxist philosophy of its framers. Russia, or to be accurate, the Union of Soviet Socialist Republics, was declared to be a socialist state, with all natural resources, means of production, and communication the property of the people. It was, in other words, Marx's dictatorship of the proletariat, the transitional stage between the revolution and the emergence of a classless society. When the latter is attained, the political state, according to Marx, should "wither away," but this phenomenon has not yet manifested itself in Russia.

The mechanism of government in the U.S.S.R. is still based on the local soviets, which are chosen by the "productive" classes of society. Under the Constitution of 1923, the town and factory soviets elected delegates directly to the soviets of the various republics in the U.S.S.R. and to the Union Congress of Soviets—the federal legislature—while the rural population had its representation strained through a pyramid of district and regional soviets, the reason being that the urban workers were considered more devoted to communism. This distinction was removed in the Constitution of 1936. Representation is by occupation rather than by geographical districts. The U.S.S.R. is officially a federal union.

The Communist Party. Pervading the whole structure, and far more important than the formal machinery of government, is the Communist party, the only party legally permitted to exist. Membership in this body is restricted to those who are considered to be properly indoctrinated and willing to give unquestioning obedience to the will of the party. In 1939 there were about 2,500,000 party members in a population of almost 200,000,000. Decisions on matters of policy are made by an executive committee, the Politburo, and decisions of the party become automatically policies of the government. All major governmental posts are filled by Communists, and while minor positions are given to outsiders, no one can be elected or appointed without the party's approval. Attendance at religious services means expulsion from the party; in the Soviet state the practice of religion, although permitted, is discouraged. An extension of the Communist organization was the Comintern, or Third International, whose headquarters were at Moscow and whose function was to promote communism and coordinate the activities of Communist parties throughout the world.

The importance of the Communist party is strikingly demonstrated by Stalin's rise to power. When Lenin died in 1924, it was generally assumed that Leon Trotsky would take his place. Yet Trotsky was ousted from office and eventually driven out of the country by Stalin, operating from the advantageous position of Secretary-General of the Communist party, a post which enabled him to fill key offices in the party and the government with his own adherents. Until 1941, when he became prime minister (officially, President of the Council of People's Commissars), Stalin held no official position in the government of the U.S.S.R. He was merely chairman of the Politburo and Secretary-General of the party.

Secret Police. Another agency of commanding importance is the secret police. This organization has gone by a variety of titles (Cheka, OGPU, NKVD) without any noticeable change in character. It functions virtually as a state within a state, with power to arrest and sentence, without recourse to the regular courts, individuals suspected of disloyalty to the regime—a term covering everything from open treason to failure to meet production quotas.

In 1936 and 1937 the outside world was astounded by a series of spectacular and highly publicized treason trials, the first of a type which has since become regrettably familiar. The accused, who included many of the old Bolsheviks of revolutionary days as well as high-ranking army officers and innumerable other officials, "confessed" in court to the most incredible crimes against the Soviet regime and begged to be given rigorous punishment—a request which was invariably granted. While there was doubtless considerable discontent with Stalin's dictatorship, particularly in view of the complete ruthlessness with which the Five-Year Plans had been imposed on the Russian peasantry, the basic reason for the "purge" appears to have been that Stalin at last felt himself strong enough to solidify his position by exterminating all possible rivals.

SOVIET ECONOMIC POLICIES

When the Bolsheviks seized power, they adopted a policy of "war communism," which was a combination of Marxist doctrine and the urgent necessity of keeping Russia's economic machine functioning in extremely difficult circumstances. All factories were taken over by the government, the property of the Orthodox Church and the estates of the nobles were confiscated, and an attempt was made to begin the socializing of agriculture. Crops were requisitioned by the government, partly to destroy the profit motive among the peasantry but mainly because the system of distribution had broken down and famine threatened the cities.

War communism was not a success, for reasons that were not entirely subject to the control of the Soviet regime. Seven years of foreign and civil war had raised havoc with Russia's economic structure, and to the physical task of reconstruction was added the problem of inadequate managerial skill. The factory executives had belonged to the capitalist middle class and had, to a large extent, been destroyed or dispersed by the Revolution. Moreover, the peasants disliked the requisitioning of their crops and were beginning to refuse to plant any more than was necessary for their own subsistence.

The New Economic Policy. Lenin, therefore, decided in 1921 that some deviation from Marxist orthodoxy would have to be accepted in order to get the economic system on its feet again and to attract the foreign capital and technical assistance that Russia had to have. The result was the New Economic Policy, which permitted private enterprise in business concerns employing not over twenty workers, allowed the peasants to sell their crops on the open market and confirmed their acquisition of the aristocracy's estates, and offered special concessions to foreigners who desired to invest their capital in Russia. Heavy industry, transportation, and banking remained in the hands of the state. There were some misgivings about this deviation from Communist principles, but Lenin defended it as a "strategic retreat." The policy was moderately effective in reviving Russian economic life. By 1926 production had returned to the prewar level. In the occupations where private enterprise was permitted, small-scale industry and retail trading, a new capitalist class, the "Nepmen," emerged, although the government actively encouraged competition in the form of cooperatives. In agriculture also, the freedom granted by the N.E.P. resulted in the formation of a class of wealthy peasants, known as "kulaks," who managed to acquire substantial land holdings and to become employers of agricultural labor.

The Five-Year Plans. In 1928 the Soviet regime decided that the time was ripe to resume the advance toward complete socialization, which it undertook to achieve by a series of five-year plans, the assumption being that by systematic planning Russia could in a short space of time match the industrialization of the capitalist nations of the West. The First Five-Year Plan had three primary objectives: to develop "heavy" industry on a mammoth scale; to collectivize agriculture; and to abolish illiteracy.

It was recognized that the industrial phase of the program would temporarily lower the standard of living, since emphasis had to be placed on the production of capital goods rather than consumers' goods. Moreover, because machines and tools would have to be imported in large quantities, Russian credit abroad would have to be bolstered by exporting as much as possible, regardless of internal demand. It was accordingly deemed necessary to "sell" the plan by a vigorous promotional campaign designed to stir up an enthusiasm which would make the people willing to accept the sacrifices imposed on them. The results achieved were considerable, sometimes spectacular, but serious defects nevertheless appeared. Russia's rail and highway system was woefully inadequate for the burdens thrust upon it by rapid industrial expansion, and there was still a severe shortage of trained executives and skilled workers. To stimulate production where it was lagging, the Soviets had to resort to such capitalistic devices as higher wages for workers who exceeded their quotas.

Collective Farms. The socializing of agriculture met with considerable resistance from the peasants, especially the kulaks. In some areas there was not only passive obstruction of the type employed against war communism but actual armed opposition. This time, however, the Soviet regime was securely enough established to make concessions unnecessary. The kulaks were ruthlessly "liquidated"; their hostility, indeed, was an asset to the government, since they could be saddled with the blame for the Five-Year Plan's failures. The disturbed conditions in the grain-producing regions, coupled with bad weather, resulted in a major famine in 1932, whose full effects were never revealed to the outside world. Starvation broke the back of peasant resistance, and by 1933 they were prepared to accept the government's policy.

Collective farms were organized in two ways: the *kolkhoz,* or cooperative farm, which was administered by its own members, subject to the qualification that the supervisory authorities were almost invariably Communists; and the *sovkhoz,* which was virtually a state-owned agricultural factory. Improvements in the efficiency of Russian agriculture followed, but with some limitations. The Russian peasants were unaccustomed to using machinery, and the supply of farm machines was short because the collectivization of agriculture outran the capacity of Russian industry to meet the demand.

A Second Five-Year Plan was inaugurated in 1933 to continue the work of the first and also to stimulate the production of consumers' goods. A third plan followed in 1938, but by that time Russian industrial output was being absorbed increasingly by military requirements. It is impossible at this point to evaluate accurately the achievements of the five-year plans. There can be no doubt that much was accomplished and that Russia's technical efficiency became greatly superior to what it had been under the Czars. Apart from the economic phases of the program, the drive on illiteracy seems to have been fairly successful. On the other hand, the Russian standard of living was not raised to a level comparable with that of Western nations, and the quality of the goods produced was generally inferior, although this defect may be regarded as unavoidable during the early stages of industrialization.

FASCISM IN ITALY

Italy emerged from the First World War as a very dissatisfied victor. Some of her aspirations had been realized but many had not. The aftermath of war found Italian economy in poor condition, and unrest developed to proportions that alarmed conservatives. In the industrial north there was some agitation among the workers to have Italy follow the example of Russia, manifested in severe strikes and occasional seizure of factories by workmen. There was actually nothing in the situation which an ordinary firmness could not have controlled, but the various ministries of this period were faction-ridden and inept, with the result that nationalistic Italians became attracted to the idea of a strong government, capable of maintaining order at home and restoring Italy's prestige abroad.

EUROPE BETWEEN THE FIRST AND SECOND WORLD WARS

Mussolini. At this juncture ex-socialist Benito Mussolini came to the fore. After he had abandoned his former associates to agitate for Italy's entrance into the war on the side of the Allies, he was called up for military service and rose to the rank of corporal before being wounded by the bursting of a trench mortar. At the end of the war he organized groups of disgruntled veterans into *fasci di combattimento,*[2] to resist forcibly the spread of socialism and communism. In some parts of Italy there was virtual civil war, with the government looking on idly and the Fascists

---

[2] The name was derived from the "fasces," the bundle of rods carried by the lictors of ancient Rome as a symbol of authority.

emerging victorious. In 1922 the prestige of the government sank so low that it was easily overthrown by the Fascist "March on Rome" in October. Had King Victor Emmanuel so desired, he could probably have crushed this movement by calling upon the army; it appears, indeed, that Marshal Badoglio urged him to do so. The king, however, wished to avoid bloodshed and so invited Mussolini to become Prime Minister.

The "Duce" moved cautiously at first until his regime could be firmly established. His first step was to secure a new electoral law (the Acerbo) in 1923 whereby the party receiving the greatest number of votes in a national election was given two-thirds of the seats in the Chamber of Deputies. With the aid of a little pressure on the voters, including the dosing of recalcitrants with liberal quantities of castor oil, the Fascists won the necessary majority in 1924. In 1926 the opposition parties were abolished, and Italy, like Russia, became a one-party state.

The Fascist Regime. Fascism derived its philosophy from a variety of sources. Its political thinking rejected democracy and emphasized authority and discipline, with supreme power vested in the Duce and the Fascist Grand Council, a body of twenty-five party leaders chosen by Mussolini. Fundamentally, fascism stressed the idea that the interests of the state were superior to those of its individual members—in other words, it repudiated the doctrine that an individual possessed "inalienable rights." In its economic beliefs, fascism, although ostensibly antisocialist, showed some trace of Mussolini's earlier affiliations and also borrowed heavily from syndicalism. Private capitalism was preserved, but all economic activity was subject to detailed regulation by the government.

It was, in fact, a former syndicalist, Edmondo Rossoni, who evolved the basic features of fascism's principal contribution to the science of government, the corporate state. Rossoni sought to reconcile syndicalism and capitalism by organizing associations of both employers and workers and making these associations the basis of representation in government. In accordance with his ideas, thirteen "Fascist syndicates" were established by law in 1926, six each for employers and employees in the principal branches of Italian industry and one for professional men and intellectuals. They had the exclusive right of collective bargaining; strikes and lockouts were prohibited and labor courts were created with final jurisdiction over industrial disputes.

Then in 1928 the Chamber of Deputies was reorganized. Its membership was made up by having the syndicates and certain other Fascist-approved organizations nominate a total of 1,000 candidates, from whom the Fascist Grand Council chose 400, or the Council could substitute any other names it saw fit. This official list was then submitted to the voters for acceptance or rejection as a whole. Suffrage was restricted to members of syndicates or taxpayers, and women were disfranchised, since the Fascists believed that woman's place was in the home. Subsequently the syndicates were converted into "corporations," twenty-two in number, administered by the government and each representing a separate occupational group and containing both employers and employees. Finally, in 1938 the Chamber of Deputies was abolished and a Chamber of Fasces and Corporations substituted, composed of 700 representatives of the Corporations, the Fascist party, and the state, all named by Mussolini.

The domestic achievements of the Fascist regime were considerable and superficially impressive. Vigorous efforts were made to attain agricultural self-sufficiency through extensive reclamation projects and the promotion of modern methods of farming, and to free Italy from dependence on imported coal by developing its hydroelectric power resources. Awe-struck tourists returned from Italy to report that Mussolini must be a great man because he made the trains run on time. The accomplishments were substantial enough to enable the Italian budget to be balanced in the late 1920's, an unusual feat in the history of modern Italy, but the coming of world-wide depression in 1929 wiped out most of the gains, and Mussolini's subsequent military adventures demonstrated that Italy still lacked the economic strength necessary to be a great power.

The Lateran Accord. The most dramatic and unquestionably the most valuable of Mussolini's internal accomplishments was his settlement of the long-standing controversy between the Italian crown and the papacy by the Lateran Accord of 11 February 1929. Papal recognition was at last given to the Kingdom of Italy; in return, Italy pledged itself to respect the independence of the pope and to permit free access to Vatican City in both peace and war. The Roman Catholic faith was made the religion of the Italian state, although toleration was granted to other creeds, religious instruction was made mandatory in the schools, and Catholic organizations were permitted to function provided they refrained from political activity. In addition, the Church was given some $90,000,000 as compensation for the loss of its territories in 1870.

On the reverse side of the Italian picture were the usual features of totalitarianism: a ubiquitous secret police, suppression of civil liberties and the exile or imprisonment of political opponents, glorification of war and militarism, conversion of the educational system into a propaganda machine, and the organization of the entire youth of the country into Fascist societies. Shortly after the signing of the Lateran Accord, Pope Pius XI spoke out against some features of the Fascist regime, especially the subordination of the family and the church in the training of young people, with the result that relations between the papacy and the Italian state again deteriorated.

A glaring weakness of the Fascist regime was its inefficiency and corruption. The detailed regulation of every phase of Italian life required the creation of a vast bureaucracy, on which there was no check through public opinion or in any other way. Fascist officials took full advantage of their position to enrich themselves by dispensing favors and special privileges for a price. When Italy finally became involved in a major war, it was quickly made evident that the supposed efficiency of dictatorship was nothing more than a veneer.

THE GERMAN REPUBLIC

Defeated Germany was in a sorry plight when the First World War ended in 1918. German economy was crippled, with industrial machinery and railway equipment worn out, millions of demobilized veterans returned home to find that there was no place for them, and politically the country verged on anarchy. The provisional government formed under Friedrich Ebert, a Social Democrat, found itself assailed on both sides: from the Right by conservatives who wanted to restore the monarchy; and from the Left by the Communists, known at the moment as Spartacists because their leader, Karl Liebknecht, used the pen-name "Spartacus," after the gladiator who led a revolt against Rome. The immediate danger of a Communist revolution was removed when the Spartacists were defeated in a week of street fighting in Berlin in January, 1919, and their leaders, Liebknecht and Rosa Luxemburg, killed "trying to escape." A year later an attempted Rightist *coup,* the Kapp *Putsch,* gained possession of the capital, but its leaders were then unable to decide what to do next and a general strike forced them to abandon the enterprise.

The Weimar Constitution. Meanwhile, a popularly elected national assembly met in the city of Weimar, capital of the state where Goethe had once been prime minister, to draft a constitution. Its sessions lasted from February to July, 1919. The parties favoring a republic—the Social Democrats, Centrists, and some smaller groups, later known collectively as the "Weimar parties"—had a substantial majority of the delegates and drafted a very liberal constitution, which nevertheless retained much of the old Imperial constitution. The Reichstag remained as the principal legislative body, with greater power than it had had under the Empire. Its members were chosen by universal suffrage. The upper chamber still represented the German states. It could delay but not reject laws passed by the Reichstag. The head of the state was a president chosen by direct popular vote for a seven-year term. Ordinarily he was a figurehead, with real executive authority vested in a chancellor and cabinet responsible to the Reichstag, but one fateful article of the Weimar Constitution (Article 48) empowered the president, in concurrence with the chancellor, to govern by decree in case of emergency.

The constitution centralized Germany to an extent that would have made Bismarck envious. The national government was given control of railways and waterways, natural resources, labor legislation, and education. As would be expected from the socialist leanings of its sponsors, the document also provided liberally for the regulation of economic life and for social security legislation.

The extent to which the German people supported the republic is not easy to appraise. That a majority of them were willing to give it a trial seems certain; until the coming of the depression in 1929, the Weimar parties were always able to retain control of the government, although sometimes by slender margins. On the other hand, when President Ebert died in 1925, Field Marshal von Hindenburg, a personification of the Empire and the Prussian military caste, was elected to replace him. Hindenburg, however, disappointed his monarchist adherents by remaining faithful to his oath of office, at least until senility caught up with him.

When one considers the handicaps that faced the Weimar Republic, the surprising feature is that it lasted as long as it did. It had to try to govern a defeated and bankrupt nation, and throughout its career it had to face the intractable hostility of powerful groups of both reactionaries and radicals. The principal conservative party during the 1920's was the Nationalists, monarchist in sentiment and backed by the old aristocracy, the army officers, and the big industrialists. The National Socialist party, better known as the Nazis, was still an obscure collection of fanatics, although in 1923 it came briefly into the limelight when Adolf Hitler and General Ludendorff staged an abortive "beer-hall *Putsch*" in Munich. The Communists in Germany were quiescent for some time after the crushing of the Spartacists, but they never forgave the republican government for that act. Above all, the Weimar Republic had to bear the onus of signing the Versailles Treaty. It had no choice in the matter, and it was certainly not responsible for Germany's defeat; nevertheless, its opponents attacked it ceaselessly for weakness and cowardice, and these charges were accepted uncritically by people who needed someone to blame for the injury to their national pride.

Economic Difficulties. Between 1919 and 1923 the republican regime had to cope with economic dislocation as well as political unrest. To the normal difficulties of reconstruction was added the burden of reparations payments. Currency inflation became progressively worse until it got completely out of control when the French occupied the Ruhr in 1923. In that year the mark reached a ratio of four trillion to the dollar. Drastic measures were then adopted to restore financial stability, and with the aid of the Dawes Plan they succeeded. The inflation, however, gravely weakened the German middle class, which ordinarily would have constituted the main stronghold of republicanism.

The next five years were relatively calm. Foreign loans stimulated a moderate degree of economic recovery, and Germany's prestige in international affairs was partially restored through the efforts of the able Dr. Gustav Stresemann, Foreign Minister from 1923 until his death in 1929 and one of the few outstanding statesmen produced by the republic. Given a few more years of progress along these lines, the Weimar Republic might have attained security.

Collapse of the Republic. In 1929, however, depression struck Germany with devastating force. The country's economic recovery depended largely on loans from the United States, and, when the source of supply dried up, Germany was left without any reserves of capital or credit to meet the crisis. Unemployment figures rose to almost 7,000,000 in a population of 65,000,000. Particularly serious because of its political consequences was the heavy incidence of unemployment among university graduates and other middle-class groups. The desperation of the German people was reflected in substantial gains by both the Nazis and the Communists in an election held in 1930, the Nazis becoming the second largest party in the Reichstag. The Social Democrats were still first.

The Weimar parties retained sufficient strength to keep Chancellor Heinrich Brüning, a Centrist, in office for two years more. As the depression deepened, Brüning, unable to secure Reichstag approval for the drastic financial measures he considered necessary, persuaded Hindenburg to invoke Article 48 of the Constitution and govern by decree.

This expedient failed to arrest either the economic decline or the growth of antirepublican sentiment, and Brüning finally resigned in May, 1932. There had been hopes that Hitler's accession to power might be headed off when Hindenburg, who despised the Nazi leader, was reelected President in April of this year, with Hitler as his principal opponent. But the old field marshal was now eighty-five and completely under the influence of Prussian *Junker* advisers. He made Franz von Papen Chancellor, although von Papen's Nationalist party was now an insignificant minority in the Reichstag. Two elections in the last half of 1932 saw further Nazi and Communist gains, whereupon von Papen resigned, and, after an eight-week term of office by General Kurt von Schleicher, Hindenburg invited Adolf Hitler to become Chancellor (28 January 1933).

THE NAZI DICTATORSHIP

The new Chancellor was born a subject of the Dual Monarchy. He tried unsuccessfully to become an artist, ending as a house painter. His extreme Pan-Germanism made him unpopular with his fellow workers, and his failures resulted in his becoming bitterly antisocialist and anti-Jewish. When the First World War broke out, he joined the Bavarian Army and was wounded in action on the Western Front. In 1919 he became the seventh member of the German National Socialist Workers party (Nazi is the abbreviation of its German title), an organization founded by an engineer named Gottfried Feder.

As their sweeping title suggests, the Nazis directed their appeal to a wide range of interests. To the masses they offered a brand of socialism which would be superior to the "international Jewish socialism" of the Marxists. To conservatives they offered the suppression of communism. They appealed to German nationalism by denouncing the "Versailles *Diktat*" and promising the restoration of Germany's military power. They adopted bodily the theories evolved during the nineteenth century which taught that the Germans were a "pure" Aryan, or Nordic, race and therefore superior to all others. Elaborations of their own were added by such figures as Alfred Rosenberg and Julius Streicher. To preserve this racial purity, non-Aryan elements such as the Jews were to be eliminated from German life.

When the "beer-hall *Putsch*" failed, Hitler was imprisoned for six months, which he utilized to write *Mein Kampf,* a verbose but comprehensive exposition of his ideas and intentions. Upon his release he resumed his political activity, and the party grew slowly but steadily, feeding on the discontent of postwar Germany. It was organized on lines similar to the Italian Fascist party, with Hitler as the *Führer*. It had two semimilitary organizations: the "storm troops" (S.A.), or "brownshirts," who were assigned to protect Nazi meetings and break up radical gatherings forcibly; and the "Elite Guards" (S.S.), or "blackshirts,"[3] who were employed for special missions.

Liquidation of Opposition. When Hitler became Chancellor, the Nazis were still a minority of the Reichstag. A new election was called for March, 1933, and in the meantime a campaign of terrorism was launched against the opposition parties. The final touch was the burning of the Reichstag building, which was promptly blamed on the Communists, although evidence produced at the Nuremberg trials in 1946 has proved what was generally suspected all along, that the Nazis set fire to the building themselves. The election gave the Nazis and their nationalist allies a majority, whereupon they promptly abolished all other parties. In July, 1933, the National Socialist party was made the only legal political organization in Germany.

The first and last act of the new Reichstag was to give Hitler complete power to govern by decree. Thereafter it met only to hear, and unanimously approve, statements of policy from the *Führer*. State governments were replaced by administrative officials appointed by Hitler. When Hindenburg died in 1934, Hitler combined the offices of president and chancellor in himself. At the same time he found it necessary to

[3] The Italian Fascists also used the black shirt as their uniform.

assert his mastery over his own party. The storm troopers, who represented the socialist wing of the Nazi party, became discontented with the failure of the government to undertake radical economic changes, and there was also some rivalry between them and the regular army. It is not clear to what extent a conspiracy had developed. Hitler struck first, on 30 June 1934. Ernst Roehm, the leader of the S.A., was summarily executed, charged with sexual perversion as well as treason. (He had previously been one of Hitler's most intimate associates.) Former Chancellor von Schleicher and his wife "resisted arrest." The total number of victims is unknown; there are grounds for believing that the Nazi leaders took advantage of the opportunity to pay off some private scores.

Persecution of the Jews. With their power securely established, the Nazis proceeded to impose on Germany a totalitarianism more comprehensive than that of Italy and more repressive than that of Russia. The Jews were driven out of practically every phase of German life and subjected to systematically organized persecution. In 1935 they were deprived of citizenship, and in 1938 they were virtually pauperized in alleged reprisal for the murder of the third secretary of the German embassy in Paris by a young Jew whose parents had been deported without warning to Poland. This deed also precipitated an especially violent series of attacks on Jews in Germany and their property, the result, according to Propaganda Minister Goebbels, of an outburst of "spontaneous" indignation on the part of the German people. The spontaneity, indeed, was so great that the attacks began at the same moment all over Germany.

All opponents of nazism, ranging from Communists to moderate liberals, were rigorously suppressed. Those who were guilty of disaffection, or even suspected of it, were rounded up into concentration camps, except for those fortunate enough to be able to get out of the country. Civil liberties disappeared. To indoctrinate all Germans with the principles of nazism, cultural life was placed under the control of a Ministry of Propaganda and Public Enlightenment, headed by Paul Josef Goebbels. Loyalty to the regime was enforced by the secret police, the Gestapo, which under Heinrich Himmler acquired an appalling reputation for ruthlessness and cruelty. Nazi youth organizations followed the lines already established in Russia and Italy, *i.e.,* they took precedence over all other young people's activity and even over the family.

Economic Policies. In the economic field the Nazis adopted a policy of "autarchy," designed to make Germany self-sufficient. Industry and commerce were subjected to detailed regulation, although it appears that the regulations rested lightly on certain favored groups like the armament manufacturers. Strenuous and on the whole successful efforts were made to develop synthetic substitutes for critical materials that Germany lacked, such as gasoline and rubber. Responsibility for this industrial program was largely vested in Hermann Goering, the much-uniformed and bemedaled airman who was also Minister-President of Prussia and head of the *Luftwaffe,* the reincarnated German Air Force. The financing of this economic policy was done by weird juggling of the mark, which had different values for various purposes. Because of Germany's unfavorable international economic position, foreign trade was conducted, where possible, by barter.

Labor was brought under Nazi control by dissolving the old trade-unions, confiscating their funds, and organizing a "labor front" to include all German workers. To alleviate unemployment, a vast public-works program was undertaken, most of it with military significance. The *Autobahnen,* or superhighways, built by the Nazis, were noted by foreign observers to be located where they would have a high strategic value.

The Nazis and the Churches. The most persistent opposition to the Nazis came from the churches. While Hitler himself was nominally a Catholic, many prominent Nazis regarded Christianity as a foreign religion and wished to revive the cult of the old Teutonic gods. Since the German people as a whole were not prepared to take such a drastic step, the Nazis tried to bring the churches under their control. Early in 1933 they took steps to consolidate all the German Protestant groups into a single body, headed by a "Reichsbishop" appointed by Hitler. Most congregations joined, with considerable reluctance, but a minority led by the Reverend Martin Niemöller, a former U-boat commander of the First World War, defied the Nazis. Most of the dissident pastors, including Niemöller, landed in concentration camps. There they presumably met the numerous Catholic clergymen who had incurred the displeasure of the Gestapo. The Church of Rome also refused to accept Nazi interference in ecclesiastical matters and, as in Italy, was disturbed by encroachments on Catholic schools and youth organizations. A concordat between the German government and the papacy was signed in 1933, but the callous disregard of the Nazis for their promises made this document worthless. The outstanding German Catholic critic of the Nazis was Cardinal von Faulhaber of Munich.

The German Army. The relations between the Nazis and the German Army were too complex to be discussed in detail here. Suffice it to say that the Nazis needed the support of the army to stay in power and therefore left it alone, while the army (which means the officer class) accepted the Nazi regime as the best prospect of restoring German military strength. While some high-ranking officers disliked Hitler and his policies, foreseeing that he would plunge Germany into a disastrous war, they hesitated to oppose him openly, and in due time the *Führer* was able to make his authority over the army more secure. He required all military personnel to take a personal oath of allegiance to him, and in

1938 he was able to effect the removal of unsympathetic generals from key positions.

Nazi foreign policy will be discussed in connection with the outbreak of the Second World War, but it may be appropriate here to point out that Nazi doctrine considered the fatherland to be entitled to the allegiance of people of German blood in every part of the world. The presence of numerous Germans in adjacent territories—the Saar, Austria, Czechoslovakia, and Poland—in due course provided excuses for aggressive moves against those countries, except in the case of the Saar, which returned to Germany peacefully by plebiscite in 1935. Further afield, the Nazis worked energetically among Germanic groups in the United States and South America. Some of their spokesmen asserted that there were 40,000,000 Germans in the United States who were subjected to persecution and discrimination by the Anglo-Saxon majority.

36

The European Democracies

The European states which lapsed into totalitarianism during the period between the First and Second World Wars were uniformly those in which genuine popular government had either never existed or was of such recent origin as to have secured only a tenuous foothold. Where institutions of self-government had been firmly established, they survived in spite of the strains to which they were subjected. The free peoples of Europe may have been encouraged to adhere to their accustomed way of life by observing that their neighbors who had sacrificed liberty to the hope of attaining economic security had merely lost the first without gaining the second. Of the great powers of Europe, Britain and France remained in the democratic ranks, and it is to them that the major share of attention has to be devoted.

ECONOMIC COMPLICATIONS IN GREAT BRITAIN

When the First World War ended, Great Britain found itself, after a brief flurry of prosperity lasting until 1920, beset with economic difficulties that remained largely unsolved during the ensuing twenty years. The effect of the war was to accentuate the unfavorable features of Britain's position in world economy. Because of the necessary conversion of industry to war production, export markets had been lost to the United States and Japan. One rival, Germany, had been struck down, but Germany had also been Britain's best customer on the continent of Europe. Recovery of the lost ground was impeded by the multitude of new tariff barriers resulting from the creation of new and intensely nationalistic states by the Versailles settlement. The constriction of international trade

594

also hurt Britain's maritime commerce, the decline of shipping reacted adversely on the shipbuilding industry, and that in turn reduced the demand for steel.

The most serious blow to British economy was a catastrophic drop in exports of coal. The competition of oil as an industrial and domestic fuel was to some extent responsible; the market for British coal in Europe was also curtailed by reparations deliveries from Germany to France and Italy. To meet these conditions, British coal mining needed to be organized for the utmost possible efficiency in operation, but it was not. The industry was a conglomeration of independent producers, many of them working deep and narrow seams with high costs of production, and with technological processes inferior to those of the United States and Germany. The textile industry was similarly handicapped; with chaotic organization and obsolescent equipment, it had to compete with the modern factories of Japan and the Southern states of the United States.

The cumulative effect of these factors was to plunge Britain into a prolonged depression for which there was no apparent remedy. Unemployment figures rose to 2,000,000 at the end of 1920 and remained at that level with only occasional variations. The coal-mining regions of South Wales and Scotland, the shipbuilding centers on the Clyde and the Tyne, and the textile centers of Lancashire became what the government euphemistically termed "special areas," where unemployment was chronic and much of the population lived on the "dole," the supplement to unemployment insurance provided by the government for those who had been out of work so long as to exhaust their insurance benefits.

Political Changes. British politics necessarily reflected this disturbing economic situation. In the reshuffling of political forces that followed the First World War, the Liberal party became almost extinct. It was split badly by factional quarrels between the adherents of Lloyd George and those of Asquith; moreover, the left-wing Liberals tended to move over to the Labour party while the right-wingers were driven into the Conservative ranks by their fear of socialism. One result of this disintegration of Liberalism was that Winston Churchill returned to the Conservative fold after an absence of almost twenty years.

The coalition government headed by Lloyd George lasted until 1922, when it was brought to an end by the withdrawal of Conservative support. The Canadian-born Andrew Bonar Law, a Conservative, then became Prime Minister but had to retire after a few months because of ill health. His successor was Stanley Baldwin, who had just achieved prominence by negotiating a settlement of Britain's war debt to the United States. The new administration proposed, as a partial solution for the economic problem, the adoption of "safeguarding" duties for industries especially menaced by foreign competition. However, when this reversal of the nation's long-standing free-trade policy was submitted to the public at an election in 1923, it was repudiated. No one party emerged with a majority in the House of Commons, but the free-trade groups, Liberal and Labour, outnumbered the Conservatives.

This situation gave Great Britain its first Labour government, which took office in January, 1924, with James Ramsay MacDonald as Prime Minister. The Labour program was moderately socialistic, calling for nationalization of the railways, the mines, and certain other key industries, to be achieved by democratic processes, and a "capital levy" on all fortunes in excess of £5,000, a threat which precipitated a flight of capital. Its foreign policy was pacifist, favoring the strengthening of the League of Nations and revision of the Versailles treaties. During his short term of office MacDonald accomplished little except to resume diplomatic relations with Russia. Since his government existed on Liberal sufferance, he was not in a position to undertake any drastic internal reform.

In October, 1924, the Labour government fell when Liberal support was withdrawn because of apprehensions about its relations with Russia. A "Red scare" was precipitated when a Conservative newspaper published the "Zinoviev letter," which purported to be a message to the British workers from the head of the Comintern, announcing that revolution was at hand. Subsequent evidence suggests strongly that the letter was a forgery, but at the time it helped the Conservatives to win an overwhelming victory.

The General Strike. The second Baldwin administration, in which Churchill appeared as Chancellor of the Exchequer, had nothing more to offer in the field of economic policy than a cautious resumption of safeguarding. It broke off diplomatic relations with the Soviet Union and subsequently closed the Soviet trade agency in London, Arcos, on the ground that it was a distributing center for Communist propaganda. Its most spectacular accomplishment was to get itself involved in a conflict with organized labor which culminated in a nine-day general strike in May, 1926. The trouble began with a labor dispute in the coal industry, where mines were closing down and owners were insisting that wages would have to be reduced if they were to stay in business. Conditions were so bad that the government subsidized coal production for nine months while a special committee investigated the situation. The report satisfied no one, and the Trades-Union Congress called the general strike to support the miners. It was not especially effective. Less than half the total union membership struck, and, contrary to what had been expected, there was little violence. In fact, several thousand volunteers had a rather enjoyable time running trains and streetcars. After nine days, the obvious futility of the strike induced the T.U.C. to call it off.

The miners continued their fight for another six months but finally had to return to work on the owners' terms. Since public opinion was now unsympathetic to the unions, the Conservatives were able to pass the Trades Disputes Act of 1927, outlawing general strikes, forbidding picketing, and imposing restrictions on the collection of funds by unions for political purposes. Repeal of the act was one of the first steps taken by the Labour government which came into power in 1945. The only other important item of legislation sponsored by the Baldwin administration was an act of 1928 reducing the voting age for women from thirty to twenty-one, there having been a patent difficulty in the way of getting voters of this sex to admit having reached the age of thirty. Because of this "flapper-vote law," Britain's electorate contained two million more women than men.

Labour and the Depression. Baldwin's failure to improve economic conditions resulted in his defeat at an election held early in 1929. The Labour party for the first time became the largest group in the House of Commons, although it did not have a complete majority, and MacDonald again became Prime Minister. The Liberals, now reduced in number to 59, once more held the balance of power. This situation, as before, made it impossible to enact the more extreme parts of the Labour program, but it does not explain completely the government's dismal record in dealing with internal problems. The attractions of high public office diminished the reforming fervor of MacDonald and some of his colleagues, and MacDonald himself devoted most of his attention to foreign affairs. Most important, the depression of 1929 made conditions in Great Britain so much worse that the government had to concentrate on staving off bankruptcy rather than reorganizing the economic system.

In 1931 unemployment reached the three million mark. Moreover, the British banking system was affected by the financial disasters in central Europe, and loss of confidence in Britain's own financial stability led to withdrawals of gold, until, by the middle of 1931, the Bank of England's gold reserve was in serious danger. Borrowing from the Federal Reserve System and the Bank of France failed to check the withdrawals. To make matters worse, a committee of financial experts, the May Committee, reported that balancing the budget, a step considered necessary to restore confidence, would require drastic reductions in expenditure, including unemployment and old-age benefits. This proposal, needless to say, was politically distasteful to the Labour party. MacDonald and a few others, notably Chancellor of the Exchequer Philip Snowden, favored it, but most of their colleagues refused to accept it.

MacDonald thereupon resigned at the end of August and a day later became head of a National Government composed of the Conservatives, the Liberals, and his few Labourite adherents, dedicated to "saving the pound." The recommendations of the May Committee were adopted, to the accompaniment of much protest from those whose incomes were cut. The drain of gold nevertheless continued and in September, 1931, Great Britain went off the gold standard. The effect was something short of disastrous; if anything, Britain's position in world trade was improved.

The new government then decided to seek a popular mandate and held an election in October with a platform which merely asked the people to give it a "blank check" to do what it considered best. The result was a landslide victory, in which the Conservatives alone won a substantial majority over all other groups in Parliament. The principal step taken to stimulate recovery was the abandonment of free trade and the adoption of protection in 1932. Attempts were also made to promote trade within the empire by encouraging "imperial preference," an idea cherished by the Conservatives since the days of Joseph Chamberlain. This policy, however, ran into the difficulty that the dominions were by now more interested in developing their own industries than in opening their markets to British goods. At the Ottawa Conference in 1932 some tariff concessions were granted, but they were far less than the British had hoped for.

The Abdication of Edward VIII. MacDonald remained in office until 1935, when he retired in favor of his old rival, Stanley Baldwin. Baldwin, reinforced by another victory at the polls in the same year, held the premiership until 1937, when he in turn resigned and was succeeded by Neville Chamberlain. Internally, the third Baldwin administration was featured by the constitutional difficulty which arose when King George V died in 1936. His successor, Edward VIII, presently announced his desire to marry a twice-divorced American woman, Mrs. Wallis Warfield Simpson, and found himself at odds with the Prime Minister, who had the backing of most of the British people and the dominions. Their objection was not to the king marrying an American, but to the two divorces. The king's most prominent sympathizer was Winston Churchill, now at odds with the Conservatives because he insisted on criticizing their laxity in arming against the revived German menace. In the end, Baldwin had his way. Edward abdicated after a reign of ten months, with a moving speech whose language curiously resembles Churchill's. He was given the title of Duke of Windsor and shortly afterward married Mrs. Simpson. His younger brother, the Duke of York, became King as George VI.

With this crisis surmounted, Baldwin gave way to Chamberlain. The new administration, still Conservative (officially National, but most of the non-Conservative members of the government had withdrawn), was faced with the imminent approach of the Second World War and is best known for Prime Minister Chamberlain's well-meant but unfortunate attempt to "appease" the dictators. The internal condition of the country was no longer a matter of acute concern, since the rearmament program, although sluggish and somewhat ineptly managed, was stimulating industrial activity. The coal industry remained a problem child. In 1938 the Chamberlain government passed a Coal Act providing for the purchase of all collieries by the state over a period of four years. The outbreak of war prevented this act from going into operation, but it is interesting to note that the Conservatives themselves had come to the conclusion that nationalization was the only remedy for the ills of British coal mining.

THE COMMONWEALTH OF NATIONS

At the end of the First World War it was evident that relationships between Great Britain and the self-governing dominions had entered a new phase, representing the completion of a process that had been under way for some time. The dominions had become, for all practical purposes, independent states. When the League of Nations was organized, Canada, Australia, New Zealand, South Africa, and India became members in their own right, although India was not a self-governing dominion. Subsequently the Irish Free State was added to the list. In addition, Australia, New Zealand, and South Africa were assigned mandates, independently of Great Britain, and Canada and Australia began to appoint their own diplomatic representatives to the United States and other countries where they had special interests. In 1923 Canada signed a fishery treaty with the United States, the first treaty in its history, or that of any dominion, to be negotiated without British assistance.

Clarification of this altered situation was manifestly desirable but extremely difficult. At the Imperial Conference in London in 1926, Lord Balfour, who had a peculiar genius for phrasing complex ideas in a way that satisfied everybody and committed nobody, defined Great Britain and the dominions as "autonomous communities within the British Empire, equal in status, in no way subordinate one to another in any aspect of their domestic or external affairs, though united by a common allegiance to the Crown, and freely associated as members of the British Commonwealth of Nations." Somewhat more specific terminology was employed in the Statute of Westminister in 1931. This act recognized and gave formal legal sanction to the new status of the dominions by four provisions: (1) the title of the king was changed to read "king . . . of Great Britain, Ireland, and the dominions beyond the seas"; (2) no act of the British Parliament was binding on a dominion without the dominion's consent; (3) no law of a dominion could be annulled on the ground that it conflicted with British law; and (4) appeals could not be taken from dominion courts to the Privy Council without the assent of the dominion government.

The dominions in existence at the time this act was passed were Canada, South Africa, Australia, New Zealand, the Irish Free State, and Newfoundland. The last named surrendered its dominion status in 1934 because of serious financial difficulties which required British help and supervision.[1] Ireland, whose story will be considered below, has ceased to be a member of the Commonwealth.

TROUBLE SPOTS IN THE EMPIRE

Not all of Great Britain's imperial problems were settled as easily and amicably as the question of dominion autonomy. The end of the First World War witnessed an upsurge of nationalism among subject peoples —a phenomenon not by any means confined to the British Empire—and several areas of serious friction developed.

First of all Ireland, restless throughout the war, flared into open violence in 1919. In the "khaki election" of December, 1918, seventy-three members of the Sinn Fein were chosen in Ireland. They refused to sit in the British Parliament; instead they set up their own legislature in Dublin (minus forty-four of their number who were either in prison or hiding) and proclaimed an Irish Republic, with Eamon de Valera, born in Brooklyn of a Spanish father and an Irish mother, as president. Civil war followed between the "Irish Republican Army" and a special constabulary organized by the British and known because of its uniforms as the "Black and Tans."

Late in 1920 Britain attempted to restore peace by a new Home Rule Act, providing separate governments for southern Ireland and Ulster. Ulster accepted, but southern Ireland, bent on complete freedom and disapproving of partition, refused, and so the conflict continued. After another year, however, both parties were wearying of the struggle and becoming convinced that neither could win. On 6 December 1921 Lloyd George and Arthur Griffith, representing the Sinn Fein, signed a treaty creating the Irish Free State, with full dominion status. Britain retained certain naval bases in Ireland, and Ulster, given the option of joining the Free State or retaining its separate government, chose the latter.

A fresh civil war then ensued between the Free Staters and the unreconciled Republicans, led by De Valera. The Free State faction won, but the Republicans carried on underground resistance until 1927, when De Valera, finding that these tactics were alienating the Irish people, abandoned violence in favor of constitutional opposition. In 1932, aided by discontent caused by the effects of the depression in Ireland, his party won control of the Free State government.

[1] In 1948 Newfoundland voted to join the Dominion of Canada.

The Irish Republic. Within the next few years Ireland's relationship to Great Britain changed radically. The oath of allegiance to the
British crown was abolished in 1933. Meanwhile De Valera impounded
annuities owed to British bondholders, representing installments on loans
made under the land-purchase laws of the late nineteenth century. This
action precipitated a tariff war between Great Britain and Ireland in
which Ireland suffered most. The dispute was settled in 1935 by an agreement whereby the Irish government made a lump-sum payment in final
discharge of the obligation and Britain in return surrendered its naval-base
rights.

The culmination of De Valera's policy was the adoption of a new
constitution in 1937, establishing the sovereign and independent state of
Eire. No mention was made in the document of the British crown or Commonwealth, and Ireland's national territory was declared to be the entire
island. Although the constitution affirmed Ireland's devotion to the Catholic Church, the first President of Eire, Dr. Douglas Hyde, was a Protestant. This was done in order to impress Ulster that religious bigotry did
not exist in Eire despite the religious nature of the constitution.

Eire stayed neutral during the Second World War, although one
Irishman is reported to have said, "We know which side we're neutral on."
Thousands of Irishmen served in the British forces, including the celebrated "Paddy" Finucane of the Royal Air Force. When H.M.S. *Prince
of Wales* and *Repulse* were sunk off Malaya in 1941, the Irish newspapers,
unable to refer openly to their fighting countrymen, had to carry numerous
obituaries "by boating accident in the Far East." Nevertheless, Irish
neutrality handicapped the United Nations, since ability to use Irish bases
would have aided antisubmarine operations materially. In 1948 the last
formal tie with the Commonwealth—the accrediting of Irish diplomats
by the British crown—was severed, and Eire became the Republic of
Ireland.

India. Of the parts of the Empire not in the Commonwealth, India
was Great Britain's most serious problem. Although India supported Great
Britain loyally during the First World War, both the National Congress,
predominantly Hindu, and the Moslem League made it clear that further
self-government would have to be granted. Considerable unrest developed in 1919, and anti-British feeling reached dangerous proportions because of the "Amritsar massacre," which occurred when a trigger-happy
general ordered his troops to fire into a large crowd assembled, illegally
but peacefully, in a public square.

The British response to Indian discontent was embodied in the
Montagu-Chelmsford Act of 1919. A legislature, chosen by a limited
franchise, was provided for British India (excluding the semi-independent
states, some 600 in number still governed by their native rulers). The

viceroy retained full control over finances and defense, and could, in emergencies, govern by decree. For the provincial governments, a system termed "dyarchy" was instituted. The governors, appointed by the viceroy, had exclusive power over the police and the administration of law, while elective provincial councils were given jurisdiction over agriculture, education, and public health.

Gandhi. This arrangement did not satisfy the Indian nationalists, and agitation continued. The movement's outstanding leader was Mohandas K. Gandhi, known as the "Mahatma," or holy one. A peculiar combination of politician and mystic, Gandhi had a tremendous hold on the Indian masses. He despised Western industrialism as excessively materialistic and hoped to restore India to a handicraft economy. Since he abhorred violence, his opposition to British rule took the form of passive resistance and civil disobedience—refusal to obey British laws and regulations. His political objectives wavered between dominion status and independence. In the course of time Gandhi withdrew more and more into his mysticism, and active leadership of the National Congress, or Congress party, devolved upon Jawaharlal Nehru, who, like Gandhi, was a product of English education.

One can sympathize with the British feeling that the nationalists were greatly oversimplifying matters in claiming that the removal of the British raj was the only problem that mattered. The complexities of the Indian situation were bewildering. The diversity of castes, races, and religions in the great subcontinent made the attainment of political unity far more difficult than the optimistic assertions of the Congress party implied; indeed, when the party held a national Congress, any delegate who wished to be understood by everyone present had to speak in English. The Moslems, some 70,000,000 in number, or about a fifth of India's population, wanted separate representation and guarantees of their rights, an understandable attitude in a country where Hindu-Moslem riots were chronic. Later the Moslem League, headed by Mohammed Ali Jinnah, formulated a demand for a separate Moslem state. Moreover, the native princes, who controlled a third of India, were largely unsympathetic toward the aims of the Congress party.

In an effort to clarify matters, the British government appointed a special commission in 1927 to investigate the entire Indian problem. By an unfortunate piece of tactlessness, no Indian was placed on this commission, which was thereupon boycotted when it reached India. Then a series of round-table conferences was held in London between 1930 and 1932 to work out an acceptable constitution for a federated India.

Government of India Act. From the round-table conferences emerged a new constitution for India embodied in the Government of India Act of 1935. It enlarged the powers of the provincial assemblies (eleven in all) and increased the number of voters entitled to participate in provincial elections to about 35,000,000. The federal legislature was chosen partly by these provincial assemblies and partly by the princes of the Native States. Safeguards were provided for minority groups, and authority over foreign relations and defense, as well as his former power to govern by decree in emergencies, was reserved to the viceroy. Burma was separated from India and given its own government. This document was greeted with a chorus of disapproval. Indian nationalists and British liberals agreed that it did not go far enough; rabid imperialists, represented by Churchill and the great newspaper publisher Lord Beaverbrook (born in Nova Scotia as Max Aiken) insisted that it went much too far. When it was put into operation, quarrels promptly broke out between the various legislative bodies and the British administrative officials and continued to rage until the outbreak of war, when the constitution was suspended.

Egypt. The other major trouble spots were two regions not officially part of the British Empire—namely, Egypt and Palestine. In the former, made a British protectorate in 1914, a nationalist party, the Wafd, came into being, and serious anti-British outbreaks occurred between 1919 and 1921. Britain was perfectly willing to concede self-government to Egypt, provided her vital strategic interest in the Suez Canal and her substantial economic stake in the Sudan were secured. Officially the protectorate was terminated by a proclamation of 28 February 1922, declaring Egypt to be an independent state but reserving to Great Britain the right to guard the Canal, to protect Egypt from aggression, and to control the Sudan.

The revival of aggressive Italian imperialism in Africa resulted in Egyptian opinion becoming somewhat less hostile to the idea of British protection, and in 1936 an Anglo-Egyptian treaty was signed conceding to Britain the right to defend the Suez Canal and to use Egyptian facilities in time of war, and abolishing "capitulations," extraterritorial privileges for foreigners. A year later Egypt was admitted to the League of Nations. The question of the Sudan remained unsettled.

Palestine. The difficulties in Palestine arose from a conflict of two nationalisms, Jewish and Arab, both of which had been encouraged by the Allies during the First World War. Zionism had become an active force during the latter part of the nineteenth century, and some Jewish colonies had been planted in Palestine prior to 1914, with the consent of the Turkish government. In 1917 Great Britain, in order to gain Jewish support for the Allies and also to pay a debt of gratitude owed to Dr. Chaim Weizmann for critically important research in the production of explosives, issued the Balfour Declaration, pledging support for the establishment of a Jewish "national home" in Palestine, "it being clearly understood that nothing shall be done which may prejudice the civil and religious rights of existing non-Jewish communities." The Declaration was subscribed to by the other Allied and Associated powers (including the United States) and incorporated into the mandate for Palestine awarded to Great Britain in 1921.

Apart from its specific reservation with regard to non-Jewish communities, the Balfour Declaration was ambiguous in that it did not specify whether a "national home" meant a separate state or not. The Arabs later insisted that it did not, since, in return for their support against the Turks, they had been promised political independence, and they interpreted the pledge as extending to all Arab territory, including Palestine. In reality, definite commitments with regard to Palestine were carefully avoided by both parties in the Anglo-Arab negotiations, and it appears that, if Arab nationalism had not been antagonized by the refusal of the Allies to grant complete independence to the rest of the Arab world, it might have been willing to concede Palestine to the Jews. In fact, the Emir Feisal, later king of Syria until he was driven out by the French and afterward king of Iraq, reached an agreement with Dr. Weizmann at the Paris Peace Conference, but it was conditional on the organization of the rest of the territory taken from the Ottoman Empire as a single, independent Arab state. Instead, the Allies cut the area into mandates, closely following the division of spoils arranged in the secret treaties of 1915 and 1916. Palestine, Transjordania, and Iraq went to Great Britain; Syria and Lebanon to France.[2]

Although there were occasional clashes between Arabs and Jews, Palestine was relatively calm during the 1920's, and the activities of the Jewish colonists raised the country's economic standards considerably. In the 1930's, however, the advent of the Hitler regime in Germany and the spread of anti-Semitism led to sharp increase in the number of European Jews desiring to settle in Palestine. Fears that this migration would convert the Arab population into an oppressed minority were carefully worked on by such individuals as the Grand Mufti of Jerusalem, a "spiritual leader" who conducted a terroristic campaign not only against the Jews but against any Arabs who were inclined to conciliation. During the Second World War he became an open adherent of the Axis. Germany and Italy fished in the troubled waters of Palestine by encouraging Arab discontent and providing arms.

There were repeated outbursts of violence between 1936 and 1938. The Zionists accused the British administration of negligence in controlling the Arabs, but inasmuch as the Arabs were simultaneously charging the British with being unduly responsive to Jewish opinion at home, the claims

---

[2] Iraq attained its independence in 1932, subject to the right of Great Britain to maintain certain military and air bases. Syria and Lebanon achieved theirs in 1946.

of both factions should be discounted heavily. Great Britain, in fact, was trying to find an acceptable compromise between Zionism and Arab nationalism. A royal commission appointed to investigate the Palestine problem reported in 1937 in favor of partitioning the country, but this scheme was promptly rejected by the Arabs and received without enthusiasm by the Jews. Two years later Great Britain itself abandoned partition and by a White Paper of 17 May 1939, committed itself to the establishment of an independent Palestine in ten years, with Jews and Arabs on an equal footing. In the interim, land sales and Jewish immigration were to be restricted. The outbreak of war, however, interrupted the execution of this policy.

DOMESTIC PROBLEMS OF THE FRENCH REPUBLIC

In some respects France emerged from the First World War in rather better condition than her neighbor across the Channel. Much of her wealthiest industrial area had been devastated by military operations and German occupation, but her national economy as a whole was better able to return to normal than that of Britain because it was not as exclusively industrial and therefore less subject to fluctuating world conditions. Her worst problems were financial. Most of the heavy cost of the war had been met by borrowing, until the national debt had reached the limit of the country's capacity. Valuable assets in the form of foreign investments had disappeared, since French loans prior to 1914 had been governed by political motives and the largest debtor had been Czarist Russia. The reconstruction of the devastated areas was accomplished with remarkable speed and effectiveness, but it was done without regard to cost, on the assumption that Germany would foot the bills.

Financial Difficulties. Consequently, although France did not have Britain's troubles of unemployment and industrial stagnation, her budgetary woes ranked next to her quest for security as a cause for frequent cabinet upheavals. For a time it appeared that the franc would follow the German mark into uncontrolled inflation. Neither the Bloc National, a coalition of conservative parties exclusive of the royalists which was in power from 1919 to 1924, nor the Cartel des Gauches, a combination of liberal groups excluding the Socialists and Communists, which gained control of the Chamber of Deputies in 1924, could muster enough support to pass any drastic financial reforms, but when insolvency became imminent in 1926, they joined forces in a National Union ministry headed by former President Poincaré. With the assurance of backing from all but the extremist parties, Poincaré was able to increase taxes and reduce government expenditures, steps which previous cabinets had not dared risk. In 1928 the franc was stabilized at a fifth of its prewar value, a move which also relieved France's financial burdens because, in effect, it wiped out four-fifths of her domestic debt. The same year also witnessed the enactment of a comprehensive social security law.

After Poincaré retired because of ill health in 1929, the National Union broke up and France again was plagued with short-lived cabinets. Since these changes seldom involved the replacement of an entire ministry, some individuals were able to remain in office for extended periods. André Maginot, for example, became Minister of War in 1930 and remained in that post through several cabinets to commit France to the construction of the ill-fated Maginot Line. Another prominent figure, Pierre Laval, was Prime Minister throughout 1931, although he had three different cabinets in that time.

When the crash of 1929 struck, it appeared at first that it had missed France altogether. The reaction was merely delayed, however; by 1932 France was in the throes of depression and facing internal unrest. The Communists, of course, exploited the economic distress for all it was worth, and various fascist groups made their appearance—the Croix de Feu, an organization of war veterans, the *Cagoulards,* or "hooded ones," a French version of the Ku Klux Klan, and others.

Discontent came to a head with the Stavisky scandal of 1933. Alexandre Stavisky was a shady figure who had somehow become connected with the municipal pawnshop of Bayonne and had used his position to issue fraudulent bonds. When the scandal broke, Stavisky fled and shortly afterward was found dead. The official report was that he had committed suicide, but, since he had been closely associated with a number of leading politicians, most of the French people were convinced that he had been killed by the police to prevent his talking in court.

The incident gave the opponents of the republic an issue, with the result that three days of rioting occurred in Paris in February, 1934. Royalists, Fascists, Communists, and police battled each other vigorously in the Place de la Concorde. The government of Edouard Daladier resigned and was replaced by a strongly conservative ministry, including Laval and Marshal Pétain, which succeeded in restoring order.

The Popular Front. The threat to the republic, the continuation of the depression, and the unchecked growth of the fascist organizations brought the parties of the Left together in a "Popular Front" to which even the Communists gave their support. (It may be noted that at this time the Soviet Union was pursuing a policy of collective security against fascism). In 1936 the Popular Front gained control of the Chamber of Deputies and the leader of the Socialist party, Léon Blum, became premier, with Daladier second in command. Blum hoped to carry out a program similar to the New Deal in the United States. His major achievement was to increase the government's control over the Bank of France, previously dominated by a self-perpetuating group representing two hundred wealthy families. Legislation was also passed establishing a forty-hour week and guaranteeing the right of collective bargaining.

The full realization of the Popular Front's aims was blocked by unforeseen complications. Its most rabid adherents, the industrial workers, greeted it with an epidemic of "sit-down" strikes, apparently to make it clear that the pledges to labor must be carried out. It was a shortsighted move, because the resulting economic dislocation was a grave handicap to the Blum administration. Financial difficulties were intensified by the fact that French capitalists, disapproving of the government's policies, began to ship their wealth out of the country. The outbreak of the Spanish Civil War added to Blum's troubles. The Popular Front sympathized strongly with the Spanish republicans but diplomatic considerations made it necessary for Blum to follow the British policy of nonintervention.

Blum was forced out of office in June, 1937, and the Popular Front gradually broke up. The growing menace of Germany necessitated a concentration of French effort on building up armaments, and some of the Popular Front's labor legislation had to be repealed. There was some objection from the labor unions, but on the whole the French people accepted the changes as essential. Indeed, the need for coordination of French production was so obvious that when Daladier, again prime minister, asked for power to rule by decree, immediately after the German occupation of Czechoslovakia in March, 1939, his request was granted almost without opposition.

Like Britain, France had to face the rise of nationalism in various parts of her empire. There was unrest in Indo-China, a serious problem with aggressive Japan in the vicinity. In Morocco, the Riff tribesmen who defeated the Spaniards extended their operations to French territory, and prolonged military operations were necessary before they could be subdued and their leader, Abd-el-Krim, exiled to Madagascar.

The worst difficulty, however, was encountered in Syria, where the Arab population bitterly resented the French mandate. Disorders began almost at once, with the result that Feisal, elected king by the Syrians, was evicted by French forces in 1920. Another insurrection in 1925, precipitated by highhanded actions on the part of General Sarrail, the French high commissioner, was featured by a French bombardment of Damascus, which caused heavy casualties.

French policy in Syria followed the "divide and rule" precept by separating predominantly Christian Lebanon from the rest of Syria. Both sections were given republican constitutions by 1930, still under close French supervision. Treaties signed in 1936 provided for independence and the admission of Syria and Lebanon to the League of Nations, reserving to France certain military privileges in both states. These objectives had not been fully attained when the Second World War broke out.

THE SMALLER DEMOCRACIES OF EUROPE

Besides these two great powers, the democratic standard in Europe was upheld by several smaller states: Sweden, Norway, Denmark, Finland, Holland, Belgium, Switzerland, and Czechoslovakia. Most of them by choice stayed out of the turmoil of European politics. They were not, however, isolationist; the League of Nations had no more staunch supporters. In their domestic affairs they were generally successful in avoiding the violent upheavals that convulsed their neighbors. Sweden and Denmark, indeed, offered conspicuous examples of the feasibility of steering a middle course between laissez-faire individualism and socialism.

Czechoslovakia, located in the heart of troubled Central Europe, was beset with problems that made the survival of its democracy a highly creditable and almost miraculous achievement. The basic agreement for the organization of the new state was reached by Czech and Slovak groups in the United States during the war years, and the Republic of Czechoslovakia was formally proclaimed in Paris, 18 October 1918. Following the Armistice a government was established in Prague with Thomas Garrigue Masaryk as President (he took his middle name from his American mother) and Eduard Beneš as Foreign Minister. When Masaryk retired in 1935, Beneš succeeded him.

Economically, Czechoslovakia did very well. It had flourishing industries in Bohemia and Moravia and a fertile agricultural area in Slovakia, and it managed to secure a strong position in world trade. Its troubles were racial and nationalistic. When its boundaries were finally settled, Czechoslovakia included minority groups of Magyars, Ruthenians, and, most important, Germans. These last lived in the Sudeten Mountain region between Bohemia and Germany. They had formerly been subjects of the Austrian Empire, but geography ruled out their inclusion in the Austrian Republic. Their own wishes in 1919 were for union with Germany; however, since the Sudetenland gave Czechoslovakia its best natural defenses against Germany, the Peace Conference of 1919 subordinated self-determination to strategy. Although these minorities were treated with scrupulous fairness, there was a good deal of friction. Furthermore, the two major racial elements did not get along. The Slovaks, agrarian and strongly Catholic, felt that they were subordinated to the Czechs, who were industrial and either Protestant or only nominally Catholic. As long as Czechoslovakia was left to manage its own affairs, these problems were handled without serious difficulty, but when the Nazis began looking for opportunities to stir up trouble, the ingredients were present.

37

Reaction and Depression
in the United States

During the decade that followed the First World War the United States apparently turned its back on the idealism of the previous generation, the idealism which had created the progressive movement and made American participation in the war a crusade to "make the world safe for democracy." Political life, where it was not corrupt, was marked by inertia and a pronounced complacency toward the increasing domination of the nation's economy by big business. A genuine and healthy economic expansion was permitted to develop into a wild speculative boom. This attitude was reflected in the public at large. Exposure of political scandals was greeted with apathy, and the experiment in national prohibition, while perhaps ill advised, was allowed to degenerate into a breeding ground of crime by widespread connivance at violation of the law. The period ended with a spectacular crash, touching off a depression that shook the entire world and in the United States led to far-reaching changes in public policy.

"BACK TO NORMALCY"

The new era was ushered in by the election of 1920. The victorious Republican candidate, Senator Warren G. Harding of Ohio, was an amiable nonentity who could be depended on to heed the wishes of the party organization, and his Democratic opponent, Governor James M. Cox of Ohio, was equally uninspiring. The vice-presidential candidates, in fact, were more interesting. The delegates to the Republican convention, after dutifully nominating Harding at the behest of their leaders, staged a revolt to give second place on the ticket to Governor John Calvin Coolidge of Massachusetts; the Democratic candidate for Vice-President was Franklin D. Roosevelt, who had served capably during the Wilson administration as Assistant Secretary of the Navy. The voters passed judgment, as far as they passed it on anything, on Harding's call for a return to "normalcy." Whether Harding was ever quite sure what this expression meant is questionable, but the American people interpreted it as pledging the end of governmental regulation, of wartime taxes, and of idealistic ventures either at home or abroad.

The "Red Scare." Public opinion at the time was characterized by an unhealthy intolerance, partly an aftereffect of the war and partly stimulated by the triumph of communism in Russia and the resultant fear that the rest of the world would be infected. In 1919 and 1920, Wilson's Attorney General, A. Mitchell Palmer, known as "the fighting Quaker" and later as "the quaking fighter," tried to advance his presidential aspirations by sensational but unproductive mass arrests of suspected alien radicals. Numerous states passed laws restricting freedom of speech and assembly, and the New York legislature expelled five Socialist members in 1920, over the protest of distinguished citizens like Charles E. Hughes and Alfred E. Smith. Strikes, unavoidable in the period of inflation and economic readjustment that followed the war, were attributed to radical agitation; Calvin Coolidge owed his national prominence to his dictum, expressed during the Boston police strike of 1920, that "there is no right to strike against the public safety." The Ku Klux Klan was revived as an anti-Negro, antialien, anti-Catholic, and anti-Semitic organization. The distrust of aliens was an important factor in the impositions of quotas on immigration in 1921 and 1924, which reduced the annual influx from Europe from over a million to 150,000.

The most celebrated incident of the "Red scare" was the trial in Massachusetts of two anarchists, Nicola Sacco and Bartolomeo Vanzetti, on a charge of murder. The evidence against them was debatable, but, after proceedings had dragged along for seven years, the two men were executed in 1927. It may be added that a final investigation of the case, which sustained the verdict of the court, was made by a special committee including Presidents Lowell of Harvard and Stratton of M.I.T.

The Harding administration, however, was not so perturbed by the "Red menace" as to be unable to devote its attention to getting back to the "good old days" and taking care of its friends. The repudiation of progressivism was manifested in the Fordney-McCumber Tariff of 1922, which raised duties to a level somewhat above that of the Payne-Aldrich Tariff of 1909. The Fordney-McCumber Act permitted the President, upon the advice of the Tariff Commission, to raise or lower duties by 50 per cent in order to meet changes in domestic and foreign costs of production. The only reductions made by Harding and Coolidge were on bobwhite quail, phenol, cresylic acid, millfeeds, and paintbrush handles.

Teapot Dome. More direct methods of distributing the spoils of victory produced an orgy of corruption outmatching the Grant administration at its worst. The most spectacular scandal was the Teapot Dome affair. Some years previously, two oil fields, Elk Hills in California and Teapot Dome in Wyoming, had been reserved for the United States Navy. Shortly after Harding took office, these fields were transferred from the Navy Department to the Interior Department, and Secretary of the Interior Albert B. Fall then leased them, without competitive bidding, to a group of oil men headed by Henry F. Sinclair and Edward L. Doheny. Subsequently, Congress became suspicious, and an investigation conducted by Senator Thomas J. Walsh of Montana uncovered the fraud. Fall, it developed, had received bribes totalling $400,000, given to him in cash in a "little black bag," which was handed to him in the lobby of a Washington hotel. After a lengthy process, the leases were cancelled, Fall was sent to jail, and Secretary of the Navy Denby found it expedient to resign. Sinclair received a short prison term for contempt of the Senate, involving refusal to answer questions, and for trying to bribe the jury at his trial, but he and Doheny were acquitted of giving the bribes that Fall was convicted of receiving.

The most astounding feature of these scandals is that so few people were at all shocked by them. Some highly respectable newspapers, in fact, went so far as to suggest that the Walsh investigation into Teapot Dome be discontinued, on the grounds that raking up all this unpleasantness might be bad for business. There was little disposition to hold the party in power responsible. Harding himself might have been too much of a liability for the Republicans to carry, but he died in 1923, just as the misdeeds of his appointees were coming to light, and his successor, Calvin Coolidge, was indisputably honest. In the election of 1924 he won an easy victory over John W. Davis, a conservative Democrat, and Robert M. LaFollette, who made a valiant but futile effort to revive the Progressive party. The business boom of the 1920's was developing visibly at this time, and to most people it was not worthwhile disturbing "Coolidge prosperity" because of a little misconduct in public office.

THE BOOM PERIOD

The return of peace brought to the United States an inflationary rise in prices, terminated by a brief depression in 1921. Then the business cycle started upward again, culminating in the fantastic speculative boom which collapsed in 1929.

Among the factors responsible for the upswing in business, the first in importance was the phenomenal expansion of a group of new industries, with automobiles leading the way. The annual production of automobiles increased from a million and a half in 1921 to almost five million in 1929; by the latter year there was a passenger car for every six persons in the United States. The market for this tremendous output was found by decreasing unit costs through improvement in the techniques of mass production, thereby bringing prices within the reach of the lower income groups, and by a general resort to credit in the form of installment buying. As millions of Americans acquired automobiles, they naturally demanded good roads to drive on, so that a great increase in highway construction accompanied the growth of the automobile industry. Petroleum and rubber were also, of course, major beneficiaries of the automobile boom.

Radio, even more of a newcomer than the automobile, enjoyed an equally striking expansion. Commercial broadcasting began in 1922, and two years later it was possible to broadcast the national conventions of the two major parties and the World Series on nationwide networks (all regarded as sporting events by the great majority of the listening public). The electric-power industry and the manufacture of electrical appliances also made marked advances. Of the older industries, steel more than held its own, a natural consequence of general industrial expansion, and there was a distinct boom in building construction.

A second factor contributing to business expansion was the favorable international economic position of the United States. The nation emerged from the war with its productive capacity not only unimpaired but actually increased, and there was a heavy demand for both American goods and American capital to aid the reconstruction of war-ravaged Europe. In addition, foreign markets which the industrial nations of Europe had had to abandon during the war were largely taken over by the United States. Consequently, exports and foreign loans both increased markedly, the latter stimulated by banking houses which found the flotation of such loans highly profitable. Some cautious economists pointed out that this process of lending foreign buyers the money with which to purchase American goods could not be continued indefinitely and that the return to high tariffs would complicate the problem of repayment, but in the prevailing atmosphere of prosperity and easy credit, the general inclination was to postpone such considerations to an indeterminate future.

Return to Laissez Faire. Finally, the attitude of the government was distinctly favorable to business, especially big business. The economic philosophy of the Republican administrations of the 1920's appears to have been that, if big business were allowed to prosper, the benefits would percolate throughout the national economy. This philosophy governed the fiscal program of Andrew W. Mellon, Secretary of the Treasury from

1921 to 1930 and himself the head of one of the nation's biggest industrial combinations, the Aluminum Company of America. When taxes were lowered from the high levels reached in wartime, the greatest reductions were in the upper income brackets and in taxes on corporations, on the thesis that funds would thereby be released for investment in productive enterprises. To some extent this idea worked, but eventually a saturation point was reached and the excess capital was diverted to speculative purposes.

Enforcement of the antitrust laws, as has been stated, was neglected. Indeed, the Commerce Department, under Secretary Herbert Hoover, openly sponsored the formation of trade associations to eliminate "wasteful" competition. These associations drew up codes of fair practices, some of which were incorporated bodily into the NRA when the New Deal arrived. Of the examples of business combination during this period, the most striking was to be found in the electric-power industry. Theoretically a public utility and therefore subject to regulation, it developed much as it wished during the 1920's. The Federal Water Power Act of 1920 applied only to power plants on navigable waterways or public lands, and state authorities were helpless in the face of complex and far-flung utility structures. The greatest combination was Samuel Insull's Middle Western Utilities, which at its height included approximately 150 holding companies and subsidiaries, so weirdly and confusingly interrelated that Insull himself got lost in their ramifications.

The power problem gave rise to a heated political controversy. A progressive bloc in Congress, led by Senator George W. Norris of Nebraska, fought for public ownership of hydroelectric plants and more effective regulation of the industry as a whole. The center of conflict was the Wilson Dam at Muscle Shoals on the Tennessee River, built during the war to provide power for the manufacture of nitrates. Presidents Harding, Coolidge, and Hoover all favored turning the property over to private interests but were unable to overcome the opposition in Congress; the progressives, on the other hand, lacked the strength to pass their program over presidential vetoes.

Interstate Commerce. The one industry to remain under effective regulation was the railways. When the war ended, the railroads were returned to private ownership, and in effecting the transfer, the Wilson administration took the opportunity to enact a broad restatement of national policy, the Esch-Cummings Act, or Transportation Act of 1920. The declared purpose of this law was to provide an adequate national system of transportation. It extended the power of the Interstate Commerce Commission to include supervision over railway finance as well as operation and authorized it to evaluate railroad property and fix rates that would yield a fair return on the investment. Consolidation in the interests of efficient operation was encouraged, and a "recapture clause" took part of the earnings of the stronger roads to support the weaker ones.

These last provisions did not work in practice. The recapture clause was later repealed, and the railroads themselves have never been able to agree on a plan for consolidation. The chief problem of the railroads, though, was not their relations with the government, but the rise of new and powerful competitors in the field of transportation. By the middle 1920's, highway vehicles were cutting into both the freight and passenger traffic of the railroads, particularly for light loads and short runs. Railway mileage, indeed, began to decline after 1922 as branch lines were abandoned in the face of highway competition. The railroads were handicapped in meeting this threat by the fact that highway traffic, besides having virtually free use of the roads that were built with public money, was not regulated at all by the national government and only indifferently by the states. In 1935, the Motor Carriers Act placed buses and trucks engaged in interstate commerce under the jurisdiction of the Interstate Commerce Commission. The greatest volume even of commercial highway traffic, however, was intrastate, and, in the case of passenger business, no legislation was likely to affect the competition offered by the private automobile.

Another menace to the railroads was the growth of commercial aviation, which was greatly stimulated by the passage of the Air Commerce Act of 1925, providing liberal subsidies in the form of contracts for carrying mail. In contrast to the automobile or bus, whose effects were felt mostly in the short-haul, low-fare passenger business, the airlines competed with the railroads for the long-distance, Pullman-class travelers.

The Speculative Mania. As the boom developed, its speculative features became steadily more pronounced. The American people, in fact, seemed to have become obsessed with a "get-rich-quick" mania. While most of the speculation took place in securities, it had other manifestations also. In the early part of the decade, there was a feverish inflation of Florida real estate values, stimulated initially by the fact that rising incomes made it possible for greater numbers of people to take winter vacations in Florida. At the peak of the craze, thousands of people paid fabulous prices for tracts of land they never saw, many of them to discover later that the lots on which they envisaged future palatial resorts springing up were actually completely submerged. The "Florida bubble" burst in 1925.

The stock-market boom reached its height in 1928 and 1929. The general prosperity of industry caused a natural rise in security prices and created a "bull" market, into which new issues were continually being fed by the organization of additional industrial combinations, the pyramiding of holding-company structures, and the mounting volume of foreign loans.

A new device appeared also, the investment trust, with the ostensible purpose of protecting the small investor by enabling him to buy stock in an organization whose own holdings would be widely diversified. Many of them were owned by banking houses as a convenient means of disposing of security issues which could not readily be floated on the open market. The steady upward trend of stocks from 1922 to 1929 appeared to offer an easy way to riches, until by the latter year several million people were playing the market, many of them in complete ignorance of the nature of the securities they were handling. Much of the buying was done on margin: that is, by putting up 10 to 20 per cent of the purchase price, on the assumption that the rest could be taken care of by the profits from resale of the stock. This practice was facilitated by liberal credit policies on the part of the banks and the Federal Reserve System, which made it easy to obtain funds for speculative purposes.

WEAK POINTS IN THE ECONOMY

The prosperity of the 1920's was very unevenly distributed. Large sections of the population either shared in it only slightly or did not benefit from it at all, and there were notable exceptions to the expansion of industry. Bituminous coal mining, adversely affected by the increasing use of oil and natural gas for fuel, experienced a severe slump, with many of the less efficient mines being forced to close down and wages being cut throughout the industry. Textile manufacturing was another industrial cripple, suffering from changes in clothing styles which demanded less cloth and substituted silk, rayon, and nylon for wool and cotton, as well as from competition in the world market from Japan and China. New England was the principal victim; more and more of its textile plants migrated to the South, leaving ghost towns and unemployed workers behind them. Part of the attraction of the South was the greater accessibility of materials and markets, but the greatest lure was cheap and unorganized labor. A handicap shared by both coal and textiles was that, in an era of combination and consolidation, they continued to operate in thousands of independent producing units, unable to control output or prices as their successful contemporaries were doing.

Labor. Labor as a whole failed to secure a proportionate share of the economic gains of the 1920's. Although wages increased, they did so more slowly than profits or dividends; between 1922 and 1929 wages rose on the average about 10 per cent while corporate profits increased approximately 65 per cent. The result was that the ability of the working masses to consume fell steadily behind the ability of industry to produce. Accentuating this situation was a considerable volume of unemployment, caused largely by technological improvements which made it possible to replace men with machines. Thus, although manufacturing raised its output by 30 per cent between 1920 and 1929, the number of workers engaged in it declined slightly. To some extent this "technological unemployment" was offset by gains in service and "white-collar" occupations, but nonetheless the most reliable estimates indicate that even at the height of the boom there were from one to two million unemployed in the United States. No accurate figures are available, since no attempt was made to collect them. Government and industry alike regarded the phenomenon of unemployment with interest but without concern, since it was assumed that expanding production would solve the problem automatically.

A stronger union movement might have enabled labor to keep pace more closely with industry, but the unions, after a period of prosperity during the First World War, had gone into a decline. They had been weakened by unsuccessful strikes in 1919 and 1920, their leadership was generally inert, and the government was unsympathetic. More important was the fact that the craft structure of the American Federation of Labor was becoming an anachronism in an age of assembly-line production. Individual skills meant little in industries where most operations had been reduced to a simple routine process, capable of being learned in a few days, or frequently a few hours. Yet, with a few exceptions, the member unions of the A.F. of L. were cool to the idea of substituting industrial for craft organization.

Some industries offered their workers alternatives to unionization in the form of employee representation plans, company unions, welfare activities, or opportunities to buy stock in the company; others suppressed union activity by strong-arm methods and the use of labor spies. Such outbursts of labor unrest as occurred were sporadic and futile. Dissatisfaction with the attitude of the government led the unions to support the LaFollette candidacy in 1924, but after the election they returned to their longstanding nonpartisan policy. The most striking evidence of union weakness was the loss of a million members between 1919 and 1929.

The Farm Problem. Worse off than any of these groups were the farmers, whose position in many ways repeated the story of the post-Civil War period. During the First World War, American agriculture enjoyed a tremendous boom, which continued for a year or two afterward while the United States continued to be the principal source of Europe's food supplies. Then the inevitable happened. European agriculture recovered its normal productivity, the end of the wartime shipping shortage reopened the distant agricultural regions (Australia, New Zealand, India, Argentina), and the restoration of internal stability in Russia meant renewed exports of Ukrainian grain, the cumulative result being that by 1921 the American farmer once again found himself in an unrestricted and fiercely competitive world market. Prices fell sharply, and the very considerable number of farmers who had borrowed money during the wartime boom to expand their holdings and purchase machinery found themselves in serious difficulties. In a field as great and as diversified as agriculture, the economic picture was necessarily varied. Specialized operations such as dairy farming and the growing of citrus fruits were generally profitable; the slump was felt most severely in the export staples.

The wasteful methods which had been developed in the days of abundant cheap land now rose to accentuate the farmer's troubles. The high prices of the war period encouraged the utilization of low-quality land and concentration on the maximum production of cash crops, regardless of the risk, indeed the certainty, of accelerated soil erosion. The collapse of farm prices left thousands of farmers stuck on this "submarginal" land, with nothing better to do than keep cultivating it in the hope that prices would rise again, although they were in fact guaranteeing that prices would stay down by continuing to add to the surplus production. When the depression came, many of these farmers, called the "Okies" because large numbers of them came from Oklahoma, abandoned their hopeless struggle and became migratory agricultural laborers. In the case of cotton, the sharecropping system militated against any restriction of output, because of the circumstance mentioned earlier that landlords and creditors of sharecroppers insisted on production of a marketable crop.

Legislative Remedies. It was a serious matter that a group representing almost half the population of the United States[1] should be in economic distress, but the national administration had nothing better to offer than higher tariffs on farm products, a solution that was of course futile for a problem caused by the production of surpluses that had to be exported. The "farm bloc" in Congress, a bipartisan combination, had its own remedy in the form of schemes which would give to agriculture the equivalent of the aid given industry by the tariff. The first of these, embodied in the McNary-Haugen bill, proposed to support domestic prices by having the government buy the surplus and dump it abroad, the loss, represented by the difference between the domestic and the world price, to be met by an equalization fee charged against the farmers. Since about a fifth of the output of staple crops was exported, it was assumed that the fee would be more than offset by the rise in prices at home. This measure was twice vetoed by President Coolidge. Its sponsors then turned to an "export-debenture" plan, whereby exports would be subsidized by issuing debentures redeemable in payment of tariff duties, but this proposal never passed Congress.

[1] A most significant indication of economic change was that the census of 1920 classified a larger part of the population of the United States as urban than as rural, for the first time in the nation's history.

In the election of 1928, the farm problem could hardly be ignored, and Herbert Hoover pledged himself to take action. His first step was to call a special session of Congress to revise the tariff for the benefit of agriculture, but, since the Smoot-Hawley Tariff did nothing at all for the farmer, it can be left for consideration elsewhere. A more promising scheme was the Agricultural Marketing Act of 1929. It created a Federal Farm Board whose function was to stabilize prices by buying and storing surplus crops, with the idea that they could eventually be released when, as it was hoped, agricultural prosperity returned. Unfortunately for the Farm Board, its best efforts were unavailing against the forces of depression, which sent farm prices to catastrophically low levels.

PROHIBITION

Closely intertwined with the economic and political trends of the 1920's was the experiment in national prohibition undertaken by the adoption of the Eighteenth Amendment, which was ratified in 1918 and formally proclaimed in 1920. More accurately perhaps, the "noble experiment" should be dated from the passage of the Volstead Act in 1919, over the veto of President Wilson. This act set up the machinery of enforcement necessary to implement the constitutional ban on the manufacture, transportation, and sale of intoxicating liquors and defined such beverages as those containing more than one-half of one per cent alcohol.

The initial enthusiasm for prohibition was short-lived, lasting just long enough, indeed, for a new liquor industry, illegal but flourishing, to get itself established. Internal sources of supply were developed through the abuse of permits for the medicinal use of liquor (Attorney General Daugherty, who had been implicated in the Teapot Dome scandal, was finally dismissed by Coolidge for conniving at these abuses), the long-standing "moonshining" operations of the Southern mountaineers, and, above all, the production of "home brew" and "bathtub gin." A thriving import business also sprang up, in spite of the efforts of the government to check the flow. Liquor was smuggled across the Canadian and Mexican borders or from such convenient transshipment points as Nassau in the Bahamas and the French islands of St. Pierre and Miquelon, off the coast of Newfoundland. Vessels from Europe frequently anchored in "Rum Row," just outside American territorial waters, and transferred their cargoes there to fast motorboats.

Within the country, attempts to enforce prohibition broke down almost completely under the weight of public indifference or open hostility. Rural areas were overwhelmingly "dry,'" in sentiment if not always in practice, but the industrial regions were unalterably opposed to prohibition and in them state and local authorities made no serious effort to aid the Federal government in the task of enforcement. With people demanding liquor and not disposed to be particular about where and how they got it, a lucrative field was opened for criminal activity. In many a community the "bootlegger" became almost a respectable business figure, and the "speak-easy" replaced the old-time saloon with only a casual pretense of concealment. Rival gangs preyed on each others' supplies, fought for control of the liquor traffic in their territory, and made corrupt alliances with political machines.

Prohibition in Politics. Under these conditions, the question of retaining prohibition soon became a heated political issue, the more so because it was regarded as a moral question by the "drys" and a matter of personal liberty by the "wets." The Republicans, strongly entrenched among the farmers of the West, were generally in favor of keeping the law as it stood. The Democrats, however, were torn between the "dry" South and the "wet" cities of the North, with the result that in 1924 these two factions, supporting William G. McAdoo and Alfred E. Smith respectively, battled through 105 ballots before the exhausted delegates finally turned to a compromise candidate in John W. Davis. Four years later, the popular "Al" Smith won the Democratic nomination, but his antiprohibition views and the fact that he was a Catholic cost him Southern support and resulted in the Republicans carrying four states of the Solid South for the first time in fifty years. Smith, however, had little chance of being elected in any case. With the business boom at its height, people were not disposed to risk a change of administration.

It was obvious, nevertheless, that prohibition was not working satisfactorily. President Hoover's answer to the problem was to appoint a special commission, the Wickersham Commission, to investigate the whole question of law enforcement. The Commission's report, issued in 1931, was a valuable compilation of facts, but its recommendations had no visible relation to those facts. The evidence that prohibition could not be enforced was overwhelming, but the Commission advised that further attempts should be made.

Meanwhile, the depression had arrived, bringing with it an upsurge of "wet" sentiment. With tax revenues declining and relief costs rising, public opinion was no longer willing to spend millions in a hopeless cause, and it was attracted by the prospect of the tax revenues and the possible stimulation of employment that would come from restoring the liquor industry to legality. The Democratic platform of 1932 called for outright repeal of the Eighteenth Amendment. After Franklin D. Roosevelt's victory, a preliminary step was taken late in 1932 by amending the Volstead Act so as to permit the manufacture of beverages containing up to 3.2 per cent alcohol. Then, at the end of 1933, the Twenty-First Amendment to the Constitution repealed the Eighteenth, with a qualifying clause forbidding the transportation of intoxicants into a state or territory whose laws prohibited their use.

THE DEPRESSION

When Calvin Coolidge made the enigmatic announcement, "I do not choose to run for President in 1928," his party took the statement at what appeared to be its face value and selected Herbert Hoover as his successor. Hoover rode easily into the presidency on the crest of the prosperity wave. His campaign slogan was "a chicken in every pot and two cars in every garage." The American people were assured that continuation of the policies of the previous eight years was all that was needed to make the "new economic era" permanent. There was much in the character of the new President to provide grounds for this optimism. A successful engineer and businessman, with a distinguished record of public service, Hoover seemed to be the type of executive who could put prosperity on a lasting foundation. As a reflection of the prevailing mood, stock prices rose to new highs in the spring of 1929; most issues were far above any value warranted by their earning power.

The crash came in October, 1929. During the last two weeks of that month stock prices first began to sag and then fell precipitously as panic struck the millions of small investors who had gambled on a continued rise. At first, the collapse was regarded as a natural deflation of absurd stock prices, but it gradually became evident that it was merely a symptom of grave disorders in both American and world economy. Storm signals, in fact, had been flying for some time, although no one in authority had chosen to look at them. Within the United States, the automobile industry, whose expansion was a basic element of the boom, found that its market was approaching saturation. Similar conditions prevailed with radios, electrical appliances, and residential construction. The stimulation of purchasing power through installment selling had also been carried as far as it could go—if anything, too far for safety.

Causes of the Crash. The bursting of the bubble in the United States was, however, only part of the story. It cannot be too strongly emphasized that this depression was a world-wide phenomenon. Nothing, in fact, illustrates more cogently the economic interdependence of the modern world than the way in which the forces making for economic catastrophe supplemented each other. In Europe there had been no real recovery from the shattering effects of the First World War. European economy had been given an artificial stimulus by the easy flow of American loans, but the saturation point had been reached here also. The shaky condition of foreign investments was a factor in precipitating the stock-market crash, and when the crash in turn cut off the flow of American loans, Europe's economic structure collapsed. The essentials of genuine recovery were lacking. Europe needed a healthy international trade, but the channels of commerce were clogged by reparations and war debts and the tariff barriers which virtually every nation erected after the war.

The tariff policy of the United States did nothing to help matters. The Fordney-McCumber tariff provoked retaliation by other countries, and still more followed the Smoot-Hawley tariff of 1930. This measure, it will be recalled, was intended primarily as an aid to agriculture, but when it.emerged from Congress its schedules on manufactured goods were the highest in American history. Although he was deluged with protests from manufacturers with large export markets, the American Bankers' Association, and over a thousand economists, Hoover signed the bill without demur. The predicted reprisals were not long in appearing; within two years some twenty-five countries imposed higher duties on American goods and American exports fell to a third of their former volume.

Another major contributing cause to the depression was the world-wide overproduction of raw materials, with consequent decline in prices and loss of purchasing power. The plight of the American farmer was one phase of this situation; similar conditions existed among such diverse groups as the coffee growers of Brazil and the rubber producers of the East Indies.

Hoover and the Depression. It took some time for the government and the people of the United States to grasp the seriousness of the depression. The stock market was expected to right itself without disturbing economic activity as a whole, but it did not. Instead, commodity prices dropped, factories began to close, and unemployment rose to alarming proportions. The leaders of government and business were thoroughly bewildered. It was perhaps only natural that this inexplicable phenomenon should be attributed to some sort of demon, who might conceivably be exorcised by incantation. Political and business leaders periodically issued statements such as "prosperity is just around the corner" or "the country is fundamentally sound" and exhorted the public not to "sell America short."

More directly, the President tried to maintain consuming power by getting industry to agree not to reduce employment or wage levels, but these agreements broke down as business conditions became worse. He also attempted to stimulate recovery on a world basis by proposing a one-year moratorium on reparations and international debt payments. Unfortunately, the plan was accepted only after prolonged negotiations, France being the principal stumbling block because she feared that reparations payments, once discontinued, would never be resumed, and, by the time the moratorium went into effect in 1931, it was too late to prevent the economic collapse of Germany and most of the rest of Central Europe.

Beyond these measures Hoover was unwilling to go. A firm believer in what he termed "rugged individualism," he felt that the economic system should be left to remedy its own troubles without intervention on the part of the government, except for expansion of public-works construction. This negative attitude failed to arouse any popular enthusiasm. In the congressional elections of 1930, the Democrats won control of the House and picked up enough Senate seats to give them a working majority in alliance with insurgent Republicans. Thereupon the administration decided to stave off further political disaster by making some concessions to the demand for positive action to halt the continuing downward spiral of depression.

Emergency Measures. The principal Hoover measure for meeting the depression was the Reconstruction Finance Corporation, created in January, 1932, for the purpose of stimulating recovery, or "priming the pump," by lending money to railroads, banks, insurance companies, agricultural-credit agencies, industrial and commercial enterprises, and eventually to local governments. The RFC was of incalculable value in supporting key points of the nation's economy whose collapse might have had catastrophic results, but it still attacked the depression on too narrow a front. It gave no direct aid to the millions of unemployed—the total was estimated at fifteen million in 1932—or to the farmers who were having their mortgages foreclosed. Yet when progressives in Congress urged that needy individuals deserved help from the Federal government as much as tottering corporations, Hoover balked. He believed that relief was a matter for private charity, or at best for state and local authorities, although it was pointed out that private charity was not geared to the needs of the worst depression the United States had experienced and that state and local governments were approaching the end of their resources. The spectacle of unemployed men and women selling apples in the streets offered abundant evidence of the inadequacy of existing relief agencies. Finally, with the presidential election looming up, the administration consented to the allocation of RFC funds for relief purposes.

Other incidents accumulated to enhance the administration's unpopularity. Back in 1924 Congress had passed, over President Coolidge's veto, an act providing a bonus for veterans of the First World War in the form of certificates maturing in twenty years. With the depression a demand arose for immediate payment, on the grounds that it would not only help needy veterans but would facilitate recovery by putting money in circulation. In June, 1931, a "Bonus Army" marched on Washington to present its demands to Congress. It accomplished nothing, but many of its members remained encamped on vacant lots on the outskirts of the city. Clashes occurred between the bonus marchers and the police; finally the President called in the army, and the country was treated to the spectacle of veterans being driven forcibly from the national capital.[2]

[2] The bonus was paid in full in 1936, Congress overriding a veto of President Roosevelt to do so.

On a broader scale, public opinion was disturbed by revelations of misconduct in high financial circles. A Senate investigation into the causes of the stock-market crash brought to light evidence of careless handling of other people's money by leaders of industry and finance, and it also adduced the startling information that some very wealthy individuals had been able to take advantage of loopholes in the revenue laws to avoid payment of income taxes in 1930 and 1931. Additional seamy facts regarding financial manipulation were unearthed with the disintegration of Ivar Krueger's international match monopoly after the Swedish "match king" had committed suicide, and with the spectacular failure of Samuel Insull's utilities empire, which proved to have been built largely on paper values.

The Election of 1932. The election of 1932 was a foregone conclusion. The Republicans renominated Hoover in a spirit of gloomy fatalism and saw their progressive wing desert almost to a man. The Democrats passed over the residual claims of Al Smith to pick Franklin D. Roosevelt, then Governor of New York and described by Walter Lippmann as "an amiable man who, without any important qualifications for the office, would like very much to be President." After running for Vice-President in 1920, Roosevelt had been struck down by infantile paralysis and his career seemed ended. He had, however, overcome his physical handicap; he had even turned it to advantage by using his enforced idleness for study and for correspondence on public issues with Democrats of all degrees of prominence and shades of opinion. He now conducted an aggressive campaign in which he proposed sweeping reform measures and captured the imagination of the people by pledging a "new deal" for the "forgotten man." There was no corresponding appeal in Hoover's prediction that grass would grow in the streets of American cities if the Democrats won. Roosevelt received 23,000,000 votes to Hoover's 16,000,000.

During the four months that elapsed between the election and the inauguration of the new President, the depression became perceptibly worse. Industrial production declined further, unemployment increased, and in the farm belt a condition approaching civil insurrection was reached, with angry farmers forcibly preventing foreclosure sales. Still more serious was the coming of a severe banking crisis, which resulted in the closing of almost every bank in the United States by state authorities in the first days of March, 1933. It has been claimed that this fresh slump was caused by the destruction of business confidence by the outcome of the election, but the evidence for this point of view is unconvincing. A better explanation is that deep-rooted weaknesses in world economy were only now taking effect in the United States.

The banking crisis can be traced back to 1931, when the failure of the Credit Anstalt, the great Rothschild bank in Vienna, caused a general financial debacle in Central Europe. The German banking system was involved in the disaster, and its troubles reacted in turn on Great Britain, whose banks had large European loans outstanding, and contributed to the British gold crisis of September, 1931. By 1932 the general constriction of credit was affecting American banks, some of which were in rather shaky condition. In fact, between 1929 and 1932 some 5,000 banks in the United States had been forced to close.

The virtual four-month interregnum, when one administration was going out of office and its successor had not yet taken over, made effective action impossible. The dangers inherent in this situation hastened the adoption of the Twentieth Amendment, sponsored by Senator Norris, which moved the inauguration date from 4 March to 20 January. It was ratified in 1933, but it did not affect Hoover's term of office. Whether earlier adoption would have lessened the economic crisis is questionable. As matters stood, when Roosevelt was inaugurated, the United States was on the verge of economic paralysis.

THE MATURING OF AMERICAN CULTURE

The period of the Great Depression is so distinctive a landmark in the development of the modern United States that it may be taken as a convenient point at which to survey the principal features of American cultural and intellectual life in the twentieth century. In general, growth in this area reflected the increasing maturity of American society as a whole. Until the close of the nineteenth century Americans who wished to devote themselves to learning or the arts had to rely predominantly on Europe for training and support, but this situation has markedly changed. Western culture, while retaining its essential unity, is no longer centered in the Old World. Europe has retained its primacy in some fields; in others, however, the center of gravity seems clearly to have crossed the Atlantic. One indication of this trend has been the extent to which scholars and students of other nations, particularly in the years after the First World War, have increasingly sought American universities.

Education. Indeed, the progress of education during this period affords one of the most interesting commentaries on the development of American cultural life as a whole. By the time the New Deal came along, a substantial majority of the children of school age in the United States got as far as high school, and about one in six attended college—all in conformity with the American ideal that a democratic society should provide the fullest possible opportunities for education. This enthusiasm for education, however, was not always accompanied by a clear understanding of what education ought to be. Mounting enrollments frequently led to mass-production methods, an astounding proliferation of curriculums, and a tendency on the part of professional educators to stress techniques at the expense of content.

Literature. American literature has been in a vigorous and flourishing condition, with a long and impressive list of first-rate writers—too long, indeed, for more than a sampling to be given here. During the boom period of the 1920's there was a tendency among literary figures to be repelled by the apparent crassness of contemporary American society, and to dwell on the theme of the necessity for individual self-expression. This attitude appeared in novelists such as F. Scott Fitzgerald and John Dos Passos and to some extent in the plays of Eugene O'Neill and Maxwell Anderson. The ablest satire of the American scene in the 1920's was that of Sinclair Lewis, who nevertheless could view his world with more sympathy than some of his contemporaries. "Babbitt" has become immortalized as the personification of the materialistic, orthodox middle-class businessman, but it is clear that Babbitt's creator rather liked him. The South produced a number of important writers at this time, notably Thomas Wolfe and William Faulkner, although the latter's somewhat depressing interpretations of Southern life took some time to achieve recognition.

The depression and the New Deal turned American writers to social and economic problems. The volume of literature thus produced was perhaps more impressive in quantity than in quality. John Steinbeck's novel *The Grapes of Wrath,* a study of the migration of drought-ridden farmers—the "Okies" and "Arkies"—from the Dust Bowl regions of Oklahoma and Arkansas to California, possessed outstanding merit. Robert Penn Warren's *All the King's Men,* which was based on the life of Huey Long, and some of the works of James T. Farrell were also definite contributions to literature, but much of the work that was attempted was too obviously written to propagate left-wing doctrines. This tendency was stimulated by the apparent breakdown of capitalism during the depression and was accentuated by the antipathy of most American intellectuals for fascism—an attitude well demonstrated in Ernest Hemingway's novel of the Spanish Civil War, *For Whom the Bell Tolls.* Yet not all American literature was governed by "social consciousness." One of the most successful novels of the period was Margaret Mitchell's massive work on the Civil War and Reconstruction, *Gone with the Wind,* and few writers showed more craftsmanship and insight than John P. Marquand in his description of New England aristocracy.

The twentieth century also witnessed a revival of American poetry, even though the reading public was not as strongly attracted to poetry as in the days of Longfellow and Whittier. There was a good deal of experimentation with verse forms, some of them bearing little resemblance to what most people were accustomed to regard as poetry. Few laymen could comprehend Ezra Pound and T. S. Eliot; there was more appreciation of such figures as Robert Frost, Edna St. Vincent Millay, and Stephen Vincent Benét, whose *John Brown's Body* comes close to being the great epic poem of American history.

Music and the Arts. The fine arts and classical music continued to be areas of European leadership, although such men as Grant Wood and Thomas Hart Benton maintained the tradition of having some talented American artists produced in each generation, and the WPA art project of the New Deal stimulated more widespread interest in painting than had ever before been aroused. In music, there was a striking development of the native American style variously known as "ragtime," "jazz," or "swing"—one of the noteworthy contributions of the Negro race to American civilization. In the hands of individuals like George Gershwin, Irving Berlin, Cole Porter, and Jerome Kern, this type of music demonstrated that it was capable of achieving greatness.

New Cultural Media. Of profound significance to modern American culture has been the growth of new media—moving pictures, radio, and, after the Second World War, television. As instrumentalities of mass entertainment their influence has been tremendous—and controversial. They have grown into big businesses, dependent on "box-office appeal" and advertising, and they have shown a marked tendency to set their standards at a level calculated to appeal to the greatest possible number. On the other hand they all have at times produced work of definite artistic merit.

All in all, as the twentieth century approached its halfway mark, American culture, like the American economy, may be safely said to have come of age. It is still an integral part of the culture of the Western world, but it is no longer dependent on outside sources of inspiration and support. It can maintain itself. It has become too extensive and complex for more than a brief survey here, but perhaps enough has been said to indicate its general characteristics. One final point needs to be made. While there have been some dissenting voices, the prevalent American attitude has been that educational and cultural opportunities should be made readily available to all. The pursuit of this goal has necessarily produced a cultural atmosphere somewhat different from that of the older societies where such things were limited to the elite. Whether the results are better or worse depends largely on one's point of view on what constitutes culture; the fact that this situation exists, however, must be realized if one is to understand American life.

38

The New Deal

The verdict of history has yet to be passed on the New Deal, if, indeed, a final vedict ever can be reached. When the administration of Franklin D. Roosevelt took office, it proceeded to enact a sweeping reform program, designed to promote recovery, to take steps which would prevent, or at least minimize, a future economic catastrophe, and to eradicate the evils that the depression had unearthed. Part of this program was formulated in advance by the group of advisers whom Roosevelt had gathered about him and who were popularly termed the "brain trust." Part of it, on the other hand, was improvised to meet the emergency situation existing at the time of Roosevelt's inauguration, and the combination produced some contradictions, perhaps unavoidable.

Two points can be made with some degree of certainty. One is that much of the New Deal has been permanently incorporated into American life. The other is that the New Deal was as American in origin as an ice-cream soda. Virtually every important part of its program was drawn from proposals advanced by the Populists and the progressives, from the experience in economic regulation acquired during the First World War, and even, as has been pointed out, from the coordination of industry sponsored by the Department of Commerce under Herbert Hoover.

THE "HUNDRED DAYS"

The spectacle presented to President Roosevelt on the day of his inauguration, 4 March 1933, was scarcely one to make his assumption to office attractive. The banking crisis seemed to presage the imminent collapse of the whole economic structure, and the nation was in the grip of

627

bewilderment and panic. Yet it was a situation made to order for bold leadership. The people wanted immediate action, and Congress, reflecting the popular mood, was prepared to subordinate partisanship and accept, for the moment at least, vigorous executive direction. The President himself, in his Inaugural Address, clearly indicated the course he would follow. Beginning with an appeal for confidence in the words, "The only thing we have to fear is fear itself," he went on to denounce the "unscrupulous money changers" who had brought the United States to the brink of disaster and to characterize the existing state of the nation as an emergency equivalent to war and requiring measures as drastic as those that would be employed to meet a foreign invader.

The most pressing need was to put the banking system into operation again. Roosevelt's first official act was to order a national bank holiday and prohibit the export of gold and silver. On 9 March Congress passed an Emergency Banking Act providing for inspection of the banks by the Treasury Department, the reopening of those found to be solvent, a more liberal issue of Federal Reserve notes, and regulation by the President of transactions in specie and foreign exchange. A few days later it was possible to end the bank holiday, and the restoration of public confidence was demonstrated by the fact that the banks permitted to do so were able to resume business under normal conditions. There was no rush of depositors to withdraw their funds; on the contrary, deposits previously withdrawn and hoarded gold were returned.

Legislative Action. Then followed a spate of legislation dealing with other crucial economic problems. The urgent need for relief was met first by the creation of the Civilian Conservation Corps at the end of March, designed to put unemployed young men to work on useful projects such as reforestation, and the establishment shortly afterward of the Federal Emergency Relief Administration, which granted funds directly to state and local governments for relief purposes. On 12 May the Farm Relief and Inflation Act launched a new agricultural policy based on subsidizing the farmers to curtail production in order to raise prices and increase farm income. Six days later a momentous experiment in conservation and the development of hydroelectric power under government auspices was undertaken by the Muscle Shoals Act, establishing the Tennessee Valley Authority, for the purpose of developing the resources of the Tennessee basin as a coordinated whole.

On 27 May the Truth in Securities Act initiated Federal regulation of stock exchanges, although the law had to be amplified by the Securities Exchange Act of 6 June 1934, which created a Securities and Exchange Commission with extensive powers over the registration of security issues and stock-market operations in general. Then, on 16 June 1933, came two more key pieces of legislation. The Glass-Steagall Act expanded the Federal Reserve System, increased the authority of the Federal Reserve Board. over the issuance of bank credit, required the separation of commercial and investment banking so that banks could no longer siphon their depositors' funds into their own subsidiaries, and organized the Federal Deposit Insurance Corporation to insure deposits up to a maximum of $5,000. The National Industrial Recovery Act provided for adoption of codes of fair competition in industry and by the famous Section 7(a) guaranteed to labor the right to bargain collectively through agents of its own choosing. Title II of the NIRA appropriated over three billion dollars for public works to relieve unemployment, most of this fund being entrusted to a Public Works Administration under Secretary of the Interior Harold L. Ickes.

Thus, within a period of four months, most of the basic elements of the New Deal had been enacted into law, the most important exception being social security. Since it covered so many fields, the only way to follow the program clearly is to trace the fortunes of each part individually.

THE CURRENCY QUESTION AND FOREIGN TRADE

The reforms achieved through the Emergency Banking Act and the Glass-Steagall Act proved sufficient to restore the banking system to stability. Radical critics of the administration grumbled that an opportunity had been lost to transfer control of credit from private hands to the government, an issue stressed by Father Charles E. Coughlin, the Detroit "radio priest," whose "social justice" program was especially emphatic during its early days in denouncing bankers. The public in general, however, was satisfied to have the banks reopened with some guarantee of their stability by the Federal government.

Financial policy could not stop with the rehabilitation of the banks. Late in 1931 Great Britain abandoned the gold standard and was followed by most of the rest of Europe, a development which placed the United States at a disadvantage in competing for world markets. President Roosevelt was willing to modify the gold standard but opposed to unrestrained currency inflation. On the other hand, the depression had revived the monetary ideas of greenback and free-silver days to such an extent that a powerful bloc in Congress was urging liberal issues of legal-tender money or the remonetization of silver at the old 16:1 ratio, which, incidentally, was far above the current market price of silver. Any revision of currency policy, therefore, was not only certain to be opposed by orthodox believers in the gold standard but was liable, unless carefully handled, to get out of control under the pressure of inflationary forces.

The initial step was to continue, by Executive Order of 5 April 1933,

.the prohibition of the free circulation of gold certificates except under license from the Treasury Department, the effect being to abandon the gold standard in practice if not in theory. A further step in this direction was a joint resolution of 5 June annulling the "gold clause" in both public and private bonds. This proviso had been commonly inserted after the free-silver scare of 1896 in order to reassure investors against repayment in depreciated currency. The right of Congress to cancel the gold clause in private securities was sustained by the Supreme Court in 1934(*Norman v. Baltimore and Ohio Railroad*), on the ground that the gold clause infringed upon the power of Congress to regulate currency; where government bonds were concerned, the Court disapproved but held that the plaintiff in question had no grounds for bringing suit because he could not show that he had suffered any loss of property.

Devaluation. The inflationists in Congress wanted to go much further, and it was only with difficulty that the President induced them to settle for the Thomas Amendment to the Farm Relief and Inflation Act, which gave him discretionary authority to adopt any or all of these devices: issuance of legal-tender notes up to three billion dollars; free coinage of silver at a rate to be fixed by him; devaluation of the dollar to 50 per cent of its existing gold content. Only the third option was utilized. During the last few months of 1933 Roosevelt tried to manipulate the value of the dollar so as to keep it in a constant relation to prices, but what Al Smith termed the "baloney dollar" was not a success, and in January the dollar was stabilized at 59.06 per cent of its former gold content.

Since the devaluation of the currency was intended primarily to raise domestic prices, the adoption of this policy had unfortunate consequences on the London Economic Conference, which met in June, 1933, to attempt to promote international economic recovery. The head of the American delegation, Secretary of State Cordell Hull, was an earnest advocate of freer international trade. The President, however, supported by Assistant Secretary of State Raymond Moley, felt that internal recovery should come first. He refused to consider an agreement for international monetary stabilization, and since the remaining gold standard countries, led by France, insisted that the money question must be settled before anything else could be considered, the Conference ended in dismal failure. It was after its adjournment that the "managed dollar" experiment was undertaken.

Reciprocal Trade Agreements. In 1934 the administration turned away from economic nationalism toward Hull's ideas, a change highlighted by the passage of the Reciprocal Trade Agreements Act in June, 1934. It authorized the President, acting through the State Department, to negotiate trade agreements in which tariffs would be lowered as much as 50 per cent, such agreements to be valid without the necessity of being ratified by the Senate. In this way Roosevelt and Hull hoped to avoid the pitfalls of previous attempts at tariff reduction. By 1939 pacts had been negotiated with most of the Latin American states, Canada, France, Sweden, and Great Britain.

One consequence of the New Deal currency policies was the concentration of gold and silver in the hands of the United States government. The devaluation of the dollar was achieved by raising the price of gold, with the result that much of the world supply of the metal flowed to the United States. In all, about 80 per cent of the world's gold came to be deposited in the vaults at Fort Knox, Kentucky. The corresponding silver policy was not of the administration's choice; it was forced upon it by the powerful "silver bloc" in Congress and was a compromise accepted in order to forestall more drastic silver legislation. By the Silver Purchase Act of 19 June 1934 the Treasury was required to buy silver until its holdings reached a third of its gold stock and to issue silver certificates. This specie policy had some stimulating effect on domestic prices, but it had a very damaging influence on the currencies of other countries by draining their specie to the United States.

INDUSTRY

The industrial policy expressed in the National Industrial Recovery Act was superficially the most drastic innovation of the "Hundred Days," in that the Federal government had undertaken to encourage rather than discourage industrial coordination. The act provided for the formulation of codes of fair competition for each industry, which would outlaw such undesirable practices as uncontrolled price-cutting and "sweatshop" labor conditions and would stabilize production. The contradiction between these provisions and the antitrust laws was handled by suspending the antitrust laws for the duration of the NIRA, although "monopolistic practices" were still theoretically forbidden. To administer the act, a National Recovery Administration was established, and pending the drafting of the individual codes, the President promulgated a "blanket code" containing the basic requirements the government wished to have adopted.

For the first few months of its existence the NRA seemed likely to succeed. The cotton textile industry, which stood to benefit considerably from having order and organization imposed on it, completed its code first, and the others gradually fell into line, until some five hundred codes in all were in existence. Public support was drummed up by monster parades and by using the "Blue Eagle" as an emblem for those who complied with the codes. By 1934, however, a marked upswing was taking place in industry. Whether the NRA was responsible or whether the improvement would have come in the natural course of events is still a moot point. At any rate, as the patient began to convalesce, he became irritable. Complaints of excessive regulation arose, and evasion of code provisions by buyers and sellers alike was widespread.

The most telling charge against the NRA was that it fostered monopoly. In the drafting of the separate codes, the larger concerns in each industry naturally had the strongest influence, and investigations demonstrated that they had taken full advantage of their opportunity. Administrative difficulties, moreover, were serious. To staff the profusion of new agencies, the government had to draw heavily on both the academic and business worlds, and in the NRA "dollar-a-year" men were frequently engaged in applying and interpreting code provisions which affected their own companies. This problem might have been solved if the code system had been restricted to the major industries, but the attempt to include every type of business activity in the country, big and little alike, created a situation that rapidly became unmanageable.

The Schechter Case. The NRA, in fact, was approaching administrative breakdown when the Supreme Court unanimously declared it to be unconstitutional in May, 1935, in the Schechter case (*Schechter Poultry Corporation v. United States*). The decision was based on two points: first, following the definition of commerce laid down in the E. C. Knight case of 1895, the Court ruled that the regulation of business and industry exceeded the powers granted to the Federal government; second, it held that the broad authority given to the President to formulate codes was an improper delegation of Congress's legislative power.

An effort was promptly made to retain the benefits of code regulation for the bituminous coal industry by the Guffey-Snyder Coal Act (30 August 1935), which provided for allocation of output, control of prices, and regulation of labor conditions. Compliance was secured by a tax on coal which was refunded to the producers who conformed to the requirements of the act. The Supreme Court, however, threw out the Guffey-Snyder Act also, on the ground that the tax was a misuse of the taxing power for an unconstitutional purpose and that mining coal had nothing to do with interstate commerce. This case (*Carter v. Carter Coal Company*, May, 1936) was decided by the far less conclusive majority of five to four.

Other New Deal measures designed to stimulate industrial recovery were an expansion of the functions of the Reconstruction Finance Corporation and liberal expenditures for heavy construction through the Public Works Administration, established, as previously stated, by Title II of the NIRA, which was not affected by the Schechter decision. PWA funds were used, among other things, to finance a substantial volume of naval construction, including the carriers *Enterprise* and *Yorktown*. Residential building was assisted by the Federal Housing Administration, a function distinct from that of the Home Owners' Loan Corporation, whose purpose was to enable people who already owned homes to keep them by refinancing mortgages.

LABOR

That the New Deal would be friendly to labor was obvious from the nature of the 1932 campaign as well as from F. D. Roosevelt's record as Governor of New York. It was also evident that an essential step toward recovery was to check the steady decline in wages that had come with the depression. The administration's policy was incorporated into the NRA codes through provisions for minimum wages and maximum hours, the prohibition of child labor, and the guarantee of the right of collective bargaining in Section 7(a) of the NIRA.

Unfortunately, Section 7(a) was phrased in such general terms that its practical application gave rise to endless controversies. The National Labor Board which was created to administer this part of the act found itself in the middle of a bitter conflict between industry and the national labor unions over what constituted for labor "representatives of its own choosing." A great many concerns hastened to organize company unions, which they claimed met the requirements of the law. The regular labor organizations insisted that company unions were dominated by management and so could not be free bargaining agencies. Some large firms simply defied the Labor Board's authority altogether. Labor's discontent with this situation, plus the fact that in the recovery of 1934 prices and the cost of living rose more rapidly than wages, resulted in an outbreak of industrial conflict, with major strikes in the automobile and textile industries.

The Wagner Act. The enactment of a more effective labor law was already in progress when the Supreme Court invalidated the NRA, and that event expedited the passage of the Wagner-Connery Labor Relations Act in July, 1935. This act reaffirmed the right of collective bargaining and prohibited employers from pursuing certain practices that were defined as unfair, the list including refusal to bargain collectively, interference with employees in choosing bargaining agents, and discrimination against union members. Company unions were discouraged by forbidding employers to support them financially, and a new National Labor Relations Board was established to enforce the act.

Formation of the CIO. Meanwhile, organized labor was undergoing a drastic internal upheaval. The advent of a friendly national administration sent union membership climbing again but some labor leaders felt that the American Federation of Labor was not taking sufficient advantage of its opportunities. The gains were being registered in the established unions, while great areas of industry, notably steel, automobiles, utilities, and rubber, remained not only unorganized but with no effort being made at organization. These dissidents, led by John L. Lewis of the United Mine Workers, formed the Committee for Industrial Organization early in 1935 to promote more aggressive action and presently left the A.F. of L. altogether. There was some clash of personalities in this split, but the main issue was one of principle. The seceding unions all represented the idea of industrial organization as opposed to the craft organization favored by the A.F. of L.—that is, they believed that all workers in a given industry should belong to the same union. They felt that the craft basis of organization was out of date and in particular that it had nothing to offer semiskilled and unskilled labor.

When the CIO moved into the strongly antiunion steel and automobile industries, full-fledged industrial warfare appeared imminent. The technique of the "sit-down" strike, whereby striking workers remained in the factories, was imported from France to create a novel problem; occupation of automobile plants in Michigan in this manner was barely prevented from flaring into serious violence. An additional complication was the uncertain status of the Wagner Act. An organization known as the American Liberty League, composed mainly of wealthy industrialists, appointed a board of lawyers to study the act; they pronounced it "palpably unconstitutional" and advised employers to ignore it.

The impending crisis, however, was largely dissipated when the United States Steel Corporation reversed its traditional policy to come to terms with the CIO in March, 1937. The decision was in part a reflection of the overwhelming New Deal victory in the election of 1936, but it was rather more a consequence of the sincere desire of the corporation's chairman, Myron S. Taylor, for industrial peace. A month later the Supreme Court upheld the constitutionality of the Wagner Act in a historic opinion which annulled the previous distinction between manufacturing and commerce (*United States v. Jones and Laughlin Steel Corporation*). Shortly afterward General Motors accepted the CIO union as the bargaining agent for its employees, but the Ford Motor Company stubbornly resisted unionization until 1938.

The gains made by the CIO suggested to some observers that it might replace the A.F. of L., just as that organization had superseded the Knights of Labor, but this assumption failed to materialize. The further progress of the CIO was checked by internal quarrels, which in due course led to the secession of the United Mine Workers. In 1938 the CIO changed its title to Congress of Industrial Organizations.

Fair Labor Standards Act. The final item of New Deal labor legislation was the Fair Labor Standards Act, or Wages and Hours Act, passed in June, 1938. Its objectives, which were to be achieved by gradual steps, were a maximum work week of 40 hours and a minimum wage level of 40 cents an hour. Overtime pay was required for work in excess of the prescribed maximum, and child labor was prohibited. Opposition to this act was led by Southerners in Congress who feared that their section would lose its economic advantage of cheap labor. They were successful in writing numerous exceptions into the law, the most important being a wage differential giving Southern workers a slightly lower minimum than Northern.

RELIEF AND SOCIAL SECURITY

The measures designed to achieve recovery and institute reforms in the industrial system represented the long-term aspirations of the New Deal, but they had no immediate effect on the millions of individuals who had been victims of the depression. They had to be cared for on an emergency basis. The creation of the Civilian Conservation Corps and the Federal Emergency Relief Administration has already been described. With the passage of the NIRA, the burden of relief was assumed by the appropriations for public works provided for in Title II of that act. However, the awarding of contracts for heavy construction was a time-consuming operation and even when completed would not absorb all the unemployed. A substantial portion of the funds, therefore, was diverted to a Civil Works Administration, which during the winter of 1933–1934 employed some four million people on "make-work" projects, in accordance with the administration's belief that work relief, while more expensive than direct cash grants, would maintain the morale and preserve the skills of the recipients.

The WPA. A year later the burden was still heavy, and a more sweeping approach to the problem was undertaken. It was evident that a considerable proportion of those on relief would have to be classified as unemployable, on grounds of age or because of other disabilities. Responsibility for their care was returned to the states. For the others, the Works Progress Administration was established in April, 1935, with an appropriation of almost five billion dollars and a gigantic program of relief, vocational rehabilitation, and public works. The size of the program, which was administered by Harry Hopkins, was such that some blunders and a certain amount of confusion were unavoidable. The WPA worker leaning on his shovel provided the public with an endless stock of jokes, and some of the projects inspired the derisive term "boondoggling." Yet the WPA accomplished an impressive volume of constructive work which otherwise would have been left undone. It built highways, bridges, hospitals, and schools; its arts and writers program made substantial contributions to American culture; and through the National Youth Administration it enabled thousands of students to stay in high school and college.

Social Security. The administration preferred to regard these relief measures as temporary expedients until the whole problem of economic security could be placed on a lasting footing. For this purpose the Social Security Act was passed, 14 August 1935. It was a most comprehensive piece of legislation, providing for unemployment insurance, old-age pensions to the needy aged and a system of old-age insurance, and assistance to the blind, to crippled children, and to dependent mothers and children, all to be supervised by a Social Security Board. For constitutional reasons, the insurance features of the law had to operate through the states. The act levied a 1 per cent tax on payrolls, but 90 per cent of the amount collected within each state was refunded to the state if it adopted an unemployment and old-age insurance system that met the standards of the Social Security Board. The remainder was kept by the Federal government for the expenses of central administration. Needless to say, the states promptly complied.

Although systems of this type had been in operation in most European countries for many years, and had been adopted on a small scale by several states, the Social Security Act was a drastic innovation in American practice. That it was accepted without a bitter political battle was due to the pressure of more radical schemes, which made conservatives willing to approve this law as a relatively moderate solution of the problem. Of the other proposals, one was the Townsend Plan, which was a scheme for creating prosperity by giving a pension of $200 a month to everyone over the age of sixty, on the sole condition that the recipient should cease working and should spend all the money. In addition, Huey Long, the "Kingfish" of Louisiana, with a political machine whose methods distinctly suggested the totalitarian states of Europe, was pushing a "share the wealth" campaign whereby every family in the United States was to be guaranteed an income of $5,000 a year.

AGRICULTURE

For the solution of the farm problem, Franklin D. Roosevelt had a wide variety of plans to choose from; virtually every proposal advanced for the relief of agrarian distress since the Civil War had its claims urged on him when he took office. His decision, or rather the decision of his agricultural advisers, was in favor of raising farm prices by restricting production through a scheme for subsidizing the farmers to reduce the acreage under cultivation. The leading figure in the agricultural policy of the New Deal was Henry A. Wallace, who became Secretary of Agriculture, a post held by his father in the Harding Cabinet.

The policy of crop curtailment was put into operation by the Farm Relief Act of 12 May 1933. The act created an Agricultural Adjustment Administration, under the control of the Secretary of Agriculture, with authority to make agreements to pay farmers for the reduction of acreage. The methods of payment for each crop varied in detail but not in basic principle. The farm products initially affected were cotton, wheat, corn, hogs, tobacco, rice, and milk; subsequently others were added to the list. The program was financed by a tax on the processing of these products.

As a means of raising aggregate farm income, the AAA was a conspicuous success. The combination of higher prices and government bounties gave the farmers of the United States as a whole some 20 per cent more income in 1935 than they had had in 1932. There were, of course, spots on the picture. The rise in wheat prices was accelerated by severe droughts in 1934 and 1935, which turned a substantial area of the Great Plains into a "Dust Bowl." Wheat farmers in general profited, but those in the Dust Bowl were worse off than ever. The droughts, indeed, curtailed wheat production so drastically that it was possible to sell the surpluses accumulated by the Federal Farm Board, and in 1935 the United States was even importing wheat. It was also pointed out that where tenant farming was prevalent, especially in the share-cropping areas of the South, the major share of the benefits went to the landowners, who did not need them, rather than to the tenants, who most emphatically did. Another unforeseen complication was that crop yields were not reduced in the same proportion as acreage, since many farmers were stimulated by rising prices to adopt more intensive methods of cultivation.

The Hoosac Mills Case. The AAA was halted in mid-career by the verdict of the Supreme Court in *United States v. Butler* (6 January 1936). The defendant, receiver of the Hoosac Mills in Massachusetts, challenged the constitutionality of the processing tax and was upheld in a 6 to 3 verdict. The majority ruling asserted that the tax was not a revenue measure but a method of enabling the Federal government to exercise a power not granted to it by the Constitution—namely, the regulation of agriculture. It then proceeded to annul the entire AAA program on the ground that it was "coercion by economic pressure." Justice Stone, with Justices Brandeis and Cardozo concurring, filed a dissenting opinion in which he rather bluntly accused his colleagues of engaging in judicial legislation. The decision was an expensive one, since all the processing taxes had to be refunded, while the government was still obligated to complete its contracts with the farmers.

The administration was somewhat staggered by the inclusiveness of the Butler decision, but it found a way out in the form of the Soil Conservation and Domestic Allotment Act of 1936, which was an extension of an act of the previous year appropriating funds to combat soil erosion. Under the 1936 law farmers were to be compensated for adopting soil-conserving practices, including reduced planting of soil-depleting crops. These soil-depleting crops were wheat, corn, cotton, tobacco, etc.

The Second AAA. This plan was not too satisfactory and was regarded by the administration as at best a temporary expedient. In February, 1938, when both the personnel and the attitude of the Supreme Court had undergone a marked change, a new Agricultural Adjustment Act was passed. It was a very comprehensive piece of legislation. It restored the crop-control features of the original AAA provided two-thirds of the farmers concerned approved, and retained the basic elements of the Soil Conservation Act. In addition, it guaranteed "parity payments" for staple crops, to keep farm prices at what was regarded as an equitable relationship to commodity prices in general. Surplus crops were to be stored, in accordance with Secretary Wallace's plan for an "ever normal granary," a scheme which fundamentally contemplated the duplication of Joseph's arrangements for saving the surplus of fat years in order to provide for lean years. Finally, the new AAA established a system of crop insurance to protect victims of droughts and other natural disasters.

The AAA was the most important but not by any means the only phase of New Deal farm policy. Liberal credit facilities were provided for agriculture through the Farm Credit Administration, which was a consolidation of existing loan agencies, and the Commodity Credit Corporation, a subsidiary of the RFC. In 1935, the Resettlement Administration was formed, under a prominent "brain truster," Rexford G. Tugwell, for the purpose of assisting farmers on submarginal land to move to better locations and rehabilitating poverty-stricken farmers. It enjoyed a limited success, and in 1937 its functions were transferred to a new Farm Security Administration. In the same year (1937) the Bankhead-Jones Act provided funds to assist tenant farmers to become owners. As part of the New Deal's power policy, the Rural Electrification Administration increased both the efficiency and the attractiveness of rural life by facilitating the use of electricity on farms.

CONSERVATION AND ELECTRIC POWER

Franklin D. Roosevelt inherited all his namesake's enthusiasm for the conservation of natural resources, and he moved promptly to institute a series of measures for this purpose. Much work was done under the Soil Erosion Act of 1935 and its successors. The droughts and dust storms of 1934 and 1935 were responsible for a project, derided at the time by "practical" individuals, for planting shelter belts of trees to break the force of windstorms on the Great Plains; it was successfully completed in 1940. The Taylor Grazing Acts of 1934 and 1936 provided for controlling grazing on 136,000,000 acres of public range land. These acts, apart from their influence on conservation, had a historic significance in that they marked the end of free public land in the continental United States.

The TVA. The conservation program was closely related to the administration's policy on electric power, since Roosevelt not only accepted the belief that sources of hydroelectric power should remain under public ownership, but also felt that their development should be integrated with flood control, the improvement of navigation, and the preservation of soil and forests. It was this philosophy which inspired the creation of the Tennessee Valley Authority, whereby the original Muscle Shoals project was expanded into a novel experiment in regional planning. The TVA was given broad powers to coordinate the improvement of the Tennessee River and its tributaries, including, of course, the hydroelectric plants, with conservation and general economic reconstruction in the entire Tennessee basin, an area extending into seven states.

The TVA built twelve dams in the Tennessee Valley, with the original Wilson Dam at Muscle Shoals making a thirteenth. One of the new dams and the town which was located near it were called Norris in honor of Senator George W. Norris, whose long fight to keep Muscle Shoals in public hands was now victoriously concluded. The full scope of TVA activities cannot be given in detail here, but it can be safely stated that they were enormously beneficial to the residents of the Tennessee Valley. Soil erosion was checked, submarginal land was withdrawn from cultivation, and cheap power was made easily available, not only directly through the TVA but through reductions made by private utility companies to meet TVA competition. The result of lowering rates was a great increase in the consumption of electricity throughout the region.

The power companies, nevertheless, fought the TVA bitterly. The Commonwealth and Southern Corporation, the holding company which controlled most of the private utilities in the area, led the attack, its president, Wendell L. Willkie, thereby emerging as a prominent figure in public life. Inevitably, the constitutionality of the experiment was challenged, but in February, 1936, the Supreme Court ruled that the TVA was covered by the Federal government's jurisdiction over navigable rivers. Although there were some loose ends in the decision, it was sufficient, together with the result of the 1936 election, to convince Commonwealth and Southern that it was fighting a losing battle, and in 1938 it sold its properties in the Tennessee Valley to the government.

Other Power Projects. Large-scale power developments were also undertaken with the construction of the Grand Coulee and Bonneville dams on the Columbia River, both of which were, in addition, to provide water for the irrigation of extensive areas. A scheme for using the tides of the Bay of Fundy to generate electricity was begun at Passamaquoddy, Maine, but abandoned because of opposition in Congress.

One function of these projects was to provide "yardsticks" by which the rate structures of privately owned utility companies could be measured. The demand for more effective regulation of these companies, voiced by Norris and others during the 1920's and intensified by the Insull fiasco, resulted in the Public Utility Act of 1935. It increased the authority of the Federal Power Commission over private power developments on navigable waterways and the interstate transmission of electric power, and by the "death-sentence" clause gave the Securities and Exchange Commission the duty of simplifying holding-company structures.

POLITICS AND THE JUDICIARY

The congressional elections of 1934, the first test of public reaction to the New Deal in operation, resulted in a striking endorsement of the administration. Contrary to the usual pattern of American politics, the party in power increased its majorities in both House and Senate. Yet as the end of "F.D.R.'s" first term approached, the opposition became more vehement, if not more numerous. Its more rabid spokesmen insisted vociferously that free enterprise was being destroyed and replaced by socialism; in private conversation they seldom referred to the President by any more complimentary title than "That Man in the White House." The critics were not confined to the Republican party. In 1936 several prominent Democrats accompanied Alfred E. Smith when he "took a walk" rather than support Roosevelt's reelection.

The Republicans were in a quandary. The wing of the party with the most money wanted to abolish the New Deal and all its works; on the other hand, the progressive wing, which was likely to attract the most votes, was openly sympathetic to much of the New Deal. The party's candidate, Governor Alfred M. Landon of Kansas, represented a choice acceptable to both these elements, while the platform sternly denounced the New Deal and simultaneously promised to carry out all its major objectives more effectively. The Democrats were in no such dilemma about either their candidate or their platform. The only striking feature about the Democratic Convention was the abrogation of the two-thirds rule imposed on the party by Andrew Jackson a hundred years before. Of the election itself nothing need be said beyond the fact that Landon carried two states, Maine and Vermont.

This overwhelming endorsement was interpreted by Roosevelt as a mandate to continue with the program of reform. He had, however, come to the conclusion that further progress was impossible until something had been done about the normally unfriendly attitude of the Supreme Court. Of the principal New Deal measures enacted during this first term, only two, the monetary legislation and the TVA, had met with judicial approval. The NRA, the AAA, the Bituminous Coal Act, and several others had been invalidated, and the status of the Wagner and Social Security acts was still in doubt. Moreover, in *New York v. Morehead* (1936) the Court had disallowed minimum wage legislation by the states, thereby creating what the President called a "twilight zone" in which neither national nor state authority could be exercised. The decision was based on the Adkins case of 1923, with the peculiar qualification, to a layman, that although several members of the Court questioned the correctness of the majority opinion in the Adkins case, they had to regard it as the governing precedent because they had not been asked to review it. The personnel of the Court had not changed since Roosevelt took office.

The "Court-packing" Plan. Roosevelt's remedy for this situation was based on the assumption that the trouble lay solely in the obtuseness of individual justices and not in the fundamental relationship of the judiciary to the rest of the government. In a special message to Congress on 5 February 1937, he asked for reforms in the lower Federal courts, most of which were enacted without argument, and for the right to appoint an additional judge for every Federal judge who had passed the age of seventy and had not retired. On the Supreme Court the maximum number of such appointments would be six.

This proposal touched off a furious controversy. The idea of "packing" the Supreme Court was distasteful to many who were otherwise staunch supporters of the New Deal, and the chronic Roosevelt-haters found themselves in unaccustomed company. The opposition in Congress was led by Senator Burton K. Wheeler of Montana, long classed as a liberal and the vice-presidential candidate on the LaFollette ticket in 1924. As the battle dragged on into the summer, it became evident that public opinion was against tampering with the Supreme Court, a striking tribute to the prestige of the institution, and the President's plan was finally rejected by the Senate Judiciary Committee.

If the Court had remained obdurate on the matter of popular legislation, it might have dissipated its support, but it proceeded to exemplify Mr. Dooley's dictum that "the Supreme Court follows th'iliction returns." The year 1937 witnessed a startling alteration in its attitude. The sustaining of the Wagner Act has been noted; shortly afterward the Social Security Act was upheld in a series of decisions interpreting generously the power of Congress to "promote the general welfare." The right of the states to regulate wages was established and the Adkins case reversed in *West Coast Hotel Company v. Parrish,* which involved a law passed by the State of Washington. This change of heart contributed heavily to the defeat of the "packing" plan.

Moreover, at the height of the controversy, Congress passed an act permitting Federal judges to retire on full salary upon reaching the age of seventy, with the result that in the next few years the Supreme Court was almost entirely reconstituted. The Roosevelt appointees have never been unanimous[1] but, as could be expected, the trend of opinions favorable to the New Deal was continued.

Administrative Reorganization. While the Supreme Court controversy was still reverberating, the President asked Congress for broad powers to reorganize the executive branch of the Federal government. That something needed to be done could scarcely be questioned. The steady expansion of governmental functions during the preceding half-century had been accompanied by an increase in the number of administrative agencies, until in 1937 well over a hundred independent agencies existed, over and above the ten cabinet departments. The whole structure had grown up without order or plan; new organizations were piled upon old, and attempts by various Presidents from Theodore Roosevelt on to introduce system and efficiency into the national administration had been largely futile. The sudden extension of governmental activity under the New Deal made for still greater confusion, a situation for which Franklin D. Roosevelt himself was largely responsible, since administration was not his strong point.

The proposal submitted to Congress in 1937 envisaged the coordination of all the administrative agencies into twelve departments and the creation of what amounted to an administrative General Staff to assist the President. While some of the details were open to criticism, the plan as a whole was reasonable enough. It would appear obvious that if the President is to carry out his duties as Chief Executive properly, he must have adequate control over his administrative organizations. Nevertheless, Congress, still suspicious and irritated over the attack on the judiciary and acutely sensitive on the subject of presidential "dictatorship," rejected the plan. In 1939, when tempers had had time to cool, a modified reorganization bill was passed. Some improvements resulted, but the coming of the war interrupted any comprehensive overhauling of the government's administrative machinery.

[1] It has seldom been possible to assume that a justice of the Supreme Court would reflect the ideas of the President who appointed him. McReynolds, the principal conservative spokesman between 1933 and 1937, was appointed by Woodrow Wilson, while Stone, the leader of the liberals, was appointed by Calvin Coolidge. Stone, a Republican, was promoted to the chief justiceship when Hughes retired in 1941.

NEW DEAL FOREIGN POLICY

During the early days of the New Deal the pressing domestic crisis necessarily overshadowed questions of foreign policy, and Franklin D. Roosevelt showed no disposition to initiate major changes. His restoration of diplomatic relations between the United States and Russia was a step long overdue. He refused to revive the League of Nations issue. He followed his predecessors in urging that the United States join the World Court but when, like them, he was blocked by the Senate, he dropped the matter. The "Good Neighbor" policy toward Latin America was an inheritance from Coolidge and Hoover.

The fostering of genuine inter-American harmony must be ranked nonetheless as one of the greatest successes of the New Deal. The 1920's had been for Latin America a period of prosperity and political stability. The Great Depression, however, was felt as severely in Latin America as elsewhere, and discontent took the accustomed form of outbursts of violence. So intense was the unrest that even the ABC powers saw their governments overthrown by military coups in 1930 and 1931. Chile shortly afterward returned to constitutional government and even came under the control of a Popular Front later in the decade; Brazil became a dictatorship under Getulio Vargas; and Argentina fell under the control of a conservative oligarchy, whose leanings toward fascist ideas reached their climax with the seizure of power by Juan Peron in 1943. The smaller states were similarly affected, and Paraguay and Bolivia in 1933 became involved in the bloody and costly Gran Chaco War.[2]

The End of Intervention. There were manifest potentialities of trouble in this situation. During the 1930's the Latin-American states were assiduously wooed by the Axis powers, who had a strong lever in the numerous Germans and Italians who had settled in Argentina, Brazil, Chile, and Uruguay, and it would have been easy for discontent to focus on "Yankee imperialism." It was fortunate that the United States had already taken two important steps to cultivate the good will of its neighbors. One was to terminate the long-standing friction between the United States and Mexico. The latter country had achieved political stability under a constitution drafted in 1917 which made elaborate provision for social reform, including the virtual confiscation of foreign-owned oil properties. The new regime also proved to be anticlerical. On both counts there was strong dissatisfaction in the United States, but the differences between the two countries were peacefully and amicably resolved by Ambassador Dwight W. Morrow in 1927, and friendly relations have since been main-

---

[2] Fought over an area of unexplored jungle claimed by both parties. The League of Nations proved unable to settle this dispute, but hostilities were finally terminated through the combined efforts of the American republics.

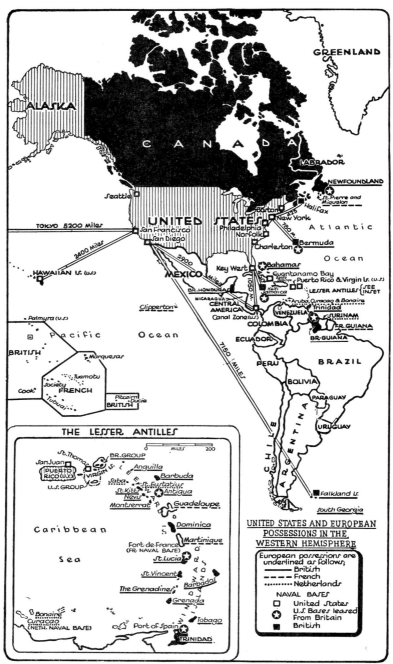

Reproduced by courtesy of *The New York Times*.

tained. The second major step was the termination of armed intervention in the Caribbean area. Beginning with Santo Domingo in 1924, the marines were gradually withdrawn until the last detachment left Nicaragua at the end of the Hoover administration. In addition, by the Clark Memorandum of 1930, the United States expressly renounced the right of intervention.

Nevertheless, suspicion of the "colossus of the North" died hard. At the Pan-American Conference in Havana in 1928 it was patent that Latin America still regarded the United States as a threat, and this residual suspicion had to be dissipated. A good-will trip to South America by Franklin D. Roosevelt shortly after his election and the extremely tactful conduct of Secretary of State Hull at the Montevideo Conference in 1933 contributed much to the attainment of this objective. A more tangible opportunity was provided in 1933 when a Cuban revolution overthrew the dictator Machado. The United States not only kept its hands off but by treaty in the following year abrogated the Platt Amendment.

The results were seen when at Lima in 1938 resolutions of inter-American solidarity were adopted in the face of a good deal of Axis intrigue. Argentina, it may be said, went along grudgingly. Unsatisfactory trade relations were partly responsible, since the United States and Argentina were competitive producers of beef and grain; the pro-Axis leanings of the Argentine ruling class were also a factor; but the main reason was one of prestige—Argentina resented the assumption by the United States of a leadership in South America which she considered to be properly hers. The conclusive demonstration of the success of the Good Neighbor policy was the cordial support given the United States by Latin America, again with the exception of Argentina, during the Second World War.

The United States and Canada. The other great American nation, Canada, may appropriately be mentioned here. Relations between Canada and the United States were uniformly friendly during this period, and, as the world crisis developed, Canada occupied the peculiarly important position of being intimately associated with the United States and at the same time a member of the British Commonwealth of Nations. Canada's most troublesome internal problem was the rise among the Quebec French of a strong faction marked by intense provincialism (it occasionally mentioned secession from the Dominion), isolationism, and more than a little sympathy for fascism. In Canadian-American relations the most striking development of the 1930's was President Roosevelt's speech at Kingston, Ontario, 18 August 1938, explicitly including Canada in the Monroe Doctrine, although Roosevelt himself insisted that this was not an innovation but merely a reiteration of an accepted principle of American foreign policy. Economic cooperation on a gigantic scale between the United States and Canada was envisaged in the St. Lawrence

Seaway proposal, which would make the Great Lakes accessible to ocean-going vessels of considerable size and would also create new and extensive sources of hydroelectric power, but this scheme failed to meet with congressional approval. A Seaway treaty negotiated in 1932 failed of ratification in the United States Senate two years later.

The Neutrality Acts. The rise of aggressive totalitarianism and the accompanying threat of a new world war gradually focused attention on general questions of foreign policy, and especially on the desirability of clarifying the position the United States would adopt in the event of war. The generally isolationist temper of public opinion was reflected in Congress by the passage of a series of Neutrality Acts between 1935 and 1937, for the avowed purpose of keeping the United States out of any war that might come, regardless of the circumstances or issues involved. The main provisions of these laws were: on the outbreak of war, a mandatory embargo was to be imposed on the shipment of arms and munitions to belligerents; the President was required to designate "war zones," which American ships were forbidden to enter; loans to belligerents were prohibited (they were already effectively barred by the Johnson Act of 1934, closing the American money market to nations that had defaulted on their war debts); and materials other than arms and munitions were to be purchased by belligerents on a "cash-and-carry" basis—*i.e.,* paid for on the spot and transported in their own ships. It may be noted that by this legislation the United States voluntarily surrendered the principles of neutral rights that it had maintained since winning its independence.

The Neutrality Acts were not at all to the liking of President Roosevelt or Secretary of State Hull. Both believed that it was fundamentally wrong for the United States to make no distinction between an aggressor and his victim, and they were convinced that the arms embargo in particular was an open incitement for the well-armed totalitarians to attack their weaker neighbors. Yet appeals for revision found Congress obdurate and the public apathetic. In a speech in Chicago on 5 October 1937, the President sent up a "trial balloon" in the form of a suggestion that collective action be taken to "quarantine" aggressors, but the response was discouraging. He was unwilling to insist more vigorously on his point of view because at this time he was still primarily concerned with his domestic program and was unwilling to jeopardize it by precipitating a quarrel with Congress over foreign policy.[3]

The Japanese invasion of China in 1937 presented further complications. Since neither party formally declared war, Roosevelt did not apply the Neutrality Acts, whose arms embargo would have worked markedly

[3] He did, however, exert pressure on Congress to shelve the proposed "Ludlow amendment" to the Constitution, which would have required a national referendum before declaring war.

to China's disadvantage. The United States protested Japan's violation of American rights in China and the sinking of the U.S.S. *Panay* on the Yangtze River by Japanese aircraft in 1937. The Japanese apology for the destruction of the gunboat arrived with suspicious promptness, but on other matters there was a definite intimation that the Open Door was now shut.

The forces and events which led to the outbreak of the Second World War will be discussed in the next section. For the present chapter, it is sufficient to say that the coming of the war brought the New Deal to an end. Quite apart from the inevitable diversion of public interest from domestic issues, the war imposed two specific barriers to any further advance of the New Deal. First, in view of a growing reluctance in Congress to enact additional reform measures, Franklin D. Roosevelt alone could have mustered the popular support needed to keep his program moving, and his energies were necessarily absorbed by the international crisis. Second, there was a sharp division of opinion on whether the United States should aid the democracies, as Roosevelt and Hull desired, or withdraw still more into its isolationist shell, and the strongest congressional support for the President's foreign policy came from those same Southern Democrats who were among the most determined opponents of the New Deal. For the second time in a quarter of a century, therefore, internal reform in the United States was pushed aside by the exigencies of world conflict.

39

The Far East between World Wars

As a result of the First World War, the countries of East Asia came to the attention of the peoples of the Western world to a greater degree than ever before. In these Oriental lands the forces of nationalism had become quite strong and made their powers a source of annoyance to the Westerners who were living in East Asia for one reason or another. But there was more to it than a reaction against the interference of the West in their lands. There developed in addition to the anti-Western uprisings a fierce clash between Japanese and Chinese nationalisms. In order to appreciate the impact of this struggle, it is necessary to discuss its background briefly.

THE CHINESE REVOLUTION

In 1911–1912 there had taken place in China a revolution against the corrupt and effete Manchu dynasty which had ruled since 1644. The gradual spread of new ideas had been responsible for this uprising against the old ways of life. The modern educated youth of the land had become disgusted with the Manchus, and their ideas had managed to make an impression on the uneducated masses. Another group seeking change were those whom the Manchus had driven into exile on account of their radical activities. Chief among them was Dr. Sun Yat-sen, who had spent many years abroad and had earned an M.D. in Hong Kong, where he was instrumental in founding a Chinese revolutionary society, the "Dare to Dies."

The revolution to oust the Manchus commenced in October, 1911. So weak were the Manchu defenses and so eager for change were the people that South China was completely in the hands of the rebels within a few weeks. By December, Sun was back in the country. He had been in the United States, where he had fallen under the spell of Henry George's ideas, when the revolution began. On 1 January 1912 he was elected Provisional President of the young Chinese Republic but agreed to sacrifice himself in the interests of strengthening the government and allowed General Yüan Shih-kai, who had vainly tried to save the Manchus, to replace him. Sun then formed the Kuomintang (National People's party).

Yüan Shih-kai temporarily overthrew the Republic in 1915 and tried to proclaim himself Emperor but a revolution by Sun's Southern Republicans dislodged him early in 1916 and he died shortly afterwards of "heart failure." The restored Republic was subjected to another brief *coup d'état* in the summer of 1917 when a Manchu in the person of the "Boy Emperor" (later Henry Pu-yi of Manchukuo notoriety) was put on the throne. This interlude lasted only two weeks, and the Republic was back to stay this time. But the South Chinese did not care for the new government and declared themselves independent. Sun was generalissimo of the Southern forces, and hostilities soon broke out. A temporary peace was achieved in February, 1919, with the result that the two governments (Peking and Canton) combined to send a peace delegation to Versailles.

Japan and China. During the war Japan had taken advantage of the preoccupation of the Allies in Europe and the weakness of China to force upon the latter the infamous Twenty-one Demands. China skillfully managed to block the political demands which would have made her practically a Japanese colony but had to grant a number of important economic concessions in the face of Japan's superior force. The United States alone of the powers took heed of China's plight. William Jennings Bryan, who was then Secretary of State, warned the Japanese that his government refused "to recognize any agreement or undertaking . . . impairing the treaty rights of the United States and its citizens in China, the political or territorial integrity of the Republic of China, or the international policy relative to China, commonly known as the Open Door policy." But this admirable step was later vitiated by the Lansing-Ishii Agreement in 1917, which saw the United States acknowledge that Japan had "special interests" in China.

Japan emerged from the First World War in possession of both valuable concessions from China and the former German possessions there which she had conquered during the war and which she was awarded at Versailles. At this juncture China's new nationalism asserted itself magnificently. Led by the student class, the Chinese waged such a successful economic boycott of Japanese goods that the Japanese were forced to come to terms with China at the Washington Conference.

THE WASHINGTON CONFERENCE, 1921–1922

The naval aspects of this conference were discussed above. It was also the scene of a settlement of several important Far Eastern problems. The Nine-Power Treaty (United States, Great Britain, France, Italy, Japan, China, Belgium, The Netherlands, and Portugal) produced an agreement whereby the signatories promised to respect the sovereignty, the independence, and the territorial and administrative integrity of China and to uphold the principle of the Open Door.

Shantung was restored to China and a commission was authorized to study the possibility of granting China power over her own tariffs. The Four-Power Treaty (United States, Great Britain, France, and Japan) was a promise to respect the others' Pacific possessions. Its creation canceled the Anglo-Japanese Alliance and thus tended to relieve American fears of a possible hostile combination against her. It is interesting to note that the Dominion of Canada, America's good neighbor to the north, was very active in helping to end this alignment of the mother country and Japan.

CHINA'S CIVIL WAR

Turning back to events in China, one finds that in the north various war lords were engaged in a steady struggle for control of the Peking government, while in the south, Sun Yat-sen had risen to the top of the Canton government as President in 1921. At this time he proclaimed his government to be the Republic of China and sought the aid of the powers. Only Soviet Russia heeded his plea, and in 1923 Comrade Joffe arrived in Canton and paved the way for the later arrival of Comrade Borodin, who brought Sun financial assistance.

The Kuomintang now underwent a reorganization and Chinese Communists were admitted to its ranks. The Communist party in China had been founded in 1921, and it added anti-imperialism, anti-capitalism, and even anti-Christianity to the now potent nationalistic movement. The Russian advisers assisted in helping the Cantonese establish the Whampoa Military Academy and also aided in training an improved army.

The death of Sun Yat-sen in 1925 changed things. A Central Executive Committee took his place, and Chiang Kai-shek (Sun's posthumous brother-in-law) was recognized as the military chief. The Kuomintang party utilized the Three People's Principles of the dead leader for propaganda purposes. These were: nationalism, democracy, and social justice. The Central Executive Committee now announced that Sun's will had stated what the job was to make China truly independent: to throw off all shackles of foreign control and privilege.

Meanwhile, a struggle for control raged within the ranks of the Kuomintang, which was divided into left- and right-wing sections. In the former were the Communists, agrarian elements, and urban workers; in the latter were to be found the landlord class, the industrialists, the financial interests and many army officers. Despite the cleavage it was decided to undertake the Northern Campaign, or "March to Peking," in 1926, which commenced with great success. At Hankow the triumphal forces established temporary headquarters, but progress continued unabated as Shanghai and Nanking fell. In the latter city, Chiang decided to call a halt long enough to unify his forces. He threw in his lot with the right wing in 1927 and in no uncertain terms dealt with the left. The Communists were expelled from the party and the Russian advisers sent home. The following year (1928) Chiang became head of the Kuomintang as well as the army and was accorded foreign support.

By June of 1928, Chiang was in possession of Peking and the country was temporarily unified. The Nationalist government was now organized under the primacy of the Kuomintang party, and it became a monopoly for the party members. True to the plan of Dr. Sun Yat-sen the government was divided into five principal departments (executive, legislative, judicial, examination, and control).

The Chinese Communists. From 1928 to 1936, the Chinese Nationalists devoted themselves to solidifying their position by trying to introduce reforms. Meanwhile, a vigilant fight was carried on against their old partners in the Kuomintang, the Communists. The latter had grown quite strong after 1929 in the rural areas of south-central China and had formed their own armies under the leadership of such able persons as Mao Tse-tung, Chu Teh, and P'eng Teh-huai. By 1931, the strength of the Communists had grown so that they were able to establish a government of their own. The Nationalist armies captured their capital in 1934, and the Communists were forced to flee. This was the beginning of the famous "long march" in the course of which the Red Army retreated all the way to North China. Near the end of 1936 they established their new capital at Yenan in Shensi Province.

The Communists had found haven in a region of China where a peasant revolt had been taking place for some time, and they simply assumed leadership. The movement now spread into a number of nearby provinces. It stressed the need for agrarian reform and so proved popular with the peasants who had long been victimized by their landlords. The Communists based their political organization directly upon the Russian system and their leaders took orders from Moscow, with which they had long been on the most intimate of terms. For a long while they posed as agrarian reformers, and their apologists in the West were fond of claiming that "they really weren't Communists at all." The "agrarian reformer" guise was a most natural one, since China had so little industry it would have been futile to don the garb of the "proletariat."

JAPAN

Meanwhile, China's insular neighbor, Japan, had come out of the First World War in first-rate condition. She had profited from her participation, which had been at little real cost to her, and had acquired, besides Shantung and the other former German holdings in China, the German North Pacific islands (Marianas, Carolines, and Marshalls). She had also strengthened and extended her already strong position in Manchuria.

A change in domestic leadership, however, took place in Japan in 1922 and lasted until 1931. The liberals who assumed control of Japan at that time were able to set the country's policy on a basis which was extremely moderate. The causes of this transformation from an aggressive military expansionist policy to that espoused by the liberals were many and need not concern us here. Its manifestations were numerous and prove the point that policy had altered. As examples, we may cite Japan's pledges in 1921–1922 at the Washington Conference; moreover, she was a party to the Kellogg-Briand Pact (1928), and under Baron Shidehara pursued a reasonably friendly policy toward strife-torn China.

But from 1927 on, Japan began to toughen up again. The growth of communism within the country led the government to pursue vigorous tactics in repressing this movement. By 1931 the stage was set for a return to power by the militarists, a comeback which introduced a new program of expansion.

THE MANCHURIAN "INCIDENT"

Japan was guilty of an attack on the Chinese province of Manchuria in September, 1931, because her military men and industrialists were disgusted with the tactics of the liberals and felt that, if Japan were ever to become the dominant nation in Asia, now was the time. Two conditions indicated that it was now or perhaps never. In the first place, China had made such strides toward unification (despite the Communists and the remaining war lords) that, if Japan waited too long, she would never be able to control her gigantic neighbor. In the second place, the Western world was caught in the iron grip of the greatest depression the world had ever seen and was beset with domestic problems.

On 18 September 1931, with no advance warning, the Japanese armies in Manchuria (where Japan owned and had the privilege of defending the South Manchurian Railroad) launched an attack on the Chinese garrisons at Mukden and Changchun, as well as other key spots, and took them completely by surprise. The "incident" which touched off this onslaught was an alleged explosion of a section of track of the South Manchurian Railway, supposedly blown up by Chinese soldiers. Few realized the full import of what happened that day in far-off Manchuria.

China, of course, was in no position to resist effectively and so ap-

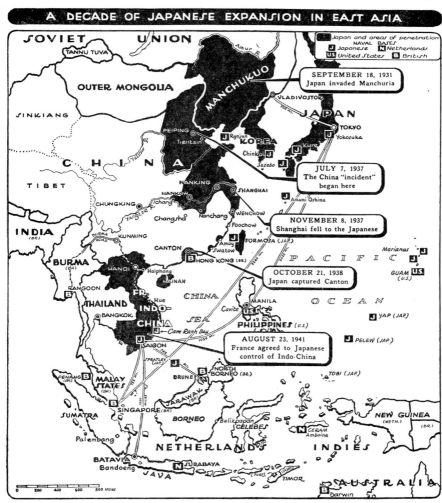

A DECADE OF JAPANESE EXPANSION IN EAST ASIA

SEPTEMBER 18, 1931
Japan invaded Manchuria

JULY 7, 1937
The China "incident"
began here

NOVEMBER 8, 1937
Shanghai fell to the Japanese

OCTOBER 21, 1938
Japan captured Canton

AUGUST 23, 1941
France agreed to Japanese
control of Indo-China

Reproduced by courtesy of *The New York Times*.

pealed to its fellow members in the League of Nations. The Japanese temporarily pooh-poohed the seriousness of the situation to the League Council, and so that collection of worthies adjourned until the middle of October. Meanwhile, the United States protested to Japan that her actions were in violation of her pledged word. Secretary of State Stimson also notified the League that an American was authorized to consult with the

Council on the situation. It was not until near the end of October that the Council began to sense the danger and ordered the Japanese to withdraw their troops, a suggestion the Japanese neglected to follow. Further palavering followed, and Japan suggested the sending of a League commission of inquiry to Manchuria to investigate. In the meantime, it goes without saying that the Japanese were slaughtering Chinese and overrunning Manchuria, a task which was completed by January.

The Lytton Commission, including the American appointed to consult with the League Council, went on a leisurely junket to Manchuria, China, and Japan by way of the United States and finally made a unanimous report in September, 1932, which stated that Japan's actions were not in self-defense, although it admitted that the Japanese had a real problem on their hands in protecting their life and property in Manchuria. The League accepted this report unanimously, but it was scant solace to China, which had been deprived of Manchuria.

The "Stimson Doctrine." The United States had issued a strong proclamation, the "Stimson Doctrine," on 7 January 1932, in which Mr. Hoover's Secretary of State informed China and Japan that the American government would not recognize any change in the territorial *status quo* brought about by the use of force. For good measure, he declared that the United States frowned upon any violation of the Open Door principle. Great Britain refused Mr. Stimson's suggestion that it take a similar action, a refusal which could not do other than comfort the Japanese. In fairness to England, it must be said that Mr. Stimson's policy existed only on paper and that the United States had no intention of employing force to make its wishes respected, a fact well known to the Japanese.

Japan acted as if fully convinced that she had nothing to fear from either Britain or America. Ostensibly to secure revenge for the violent treatment of some Japanese nationals by a Shanghai mob but in reality to punish the city for its effective boycott of Japanese merchants and goods, the Japanese bombed the Chapei district of the Chinese Greater Municipality of Shanghai (religiously avoiding the International Settlement and the French Concession) on 29 January with deadly effect. The carnage was horrible and was followed by the landing of Japanese bluejackets and troops. The attack continued unabated from all directions until the heroic Chinese defenders (the radical Nineteenth Route Army) were finally forced to yield after holding out for six weeks against vastly superior odds. Their object accomplished at considerable cost, the Japanese consented to withdraw their troops.

While this was going on, the Japanese managed to get a group of puppets in Manchuria to declare their independence from China on 18 February 1932. From this action there ultimately emerged the "sovereign" state of Manchukuo, just two weeks before the Lytton Commission made its report. As "regent" of the new state the Japanese appointed Henry Pu-yi, last Manchu emperor of China. He had served in this capacity for a few days before he was ten years old. In 1934, he was promoted to emperor and took the name Kang-teh.

The Lytton Report. Following the issuance of the Lytton report, the Japanese consumed some time in taking exception to those parts of it which did not please them. But as the Irish delegation to the League Assembly put it: "Let there be no mistake—if the moral force of the League is broken on this issue, then the League as at present constituted cannot survive. . . ." Great Britain and her dominions, however, cognizant of Britain's stake in the Far East and at the same time fully aware of her weakened imperial position, took a view which amounted to appeasement. As was said above, she did so in the full confidence that the stand adopted by the United States existed in reality only on paper. France strove manfully to assert the authority of the League but to no real avail.

While the League continued to ponder, the Japanese continued to act and in January, 1933, invaded the rich North China province of Jehol, an important source of opium poppies and a springboard to Outer Mongolia. The League ultimately adopted, in February, 1933, by a unanimous vote of those participating, a report which by inference at any rate was a blow against Japan. It could not recommend sanctions since no declaration of war had been made by either party to the "incident." The result was Japan's withdrawal from the League and the extension of her military operations to the point where China accepted an armistice 31 May which was tantamount to giving Japan a free hand in Manchuria (Manchukuo), although China adamantly refused to recognize the new puppet state.

The significance of the entire episode, of course, is patent. The League had failed to meet the real test thrown up to her by a determined great power. The lack of cohesion on the part of the League's chief powers combined with the absence from the League of the United States—which contented itself with mouthing a pious phrase about nonrecognition of what was a *fait accompli*—and Russia—which refused a League invitation to consult on the matter—proved too great an obstacle to surmount. Henceforward, other aggressors could more readily visualize a green light for their nefarious schemes.

THE SINO-JAPANESE CONFLICT

Generalissimo Chiang Kai-shek had shown little interest in trying to check Japan's aggression by meeting force with force in the period of the

Manchurian "incident." Nor had his government been especially vigilant in respect to the subsequent events. He concentrated his efforts instead on an anti-Communist campaign and defended his domestic alacrity and his foreign apathy by saying that China's first task was unity. With this achieved, she would then be in a position to turn to the task of facing Japan more resolutely.

Chiang's repeated indifference to the inroads Japan was making resulted in his kidnapping at Sian in December, 1936, by the "Young Marshal," Chang Hsueh-liang, who was commander in chief of China's Northwestern Army. Chang had once performed Chiang an invaluable service, and in gratitude the latter had rewarded him with high military and civil posts. It seems, however, that, instead of fighting the Communists of the Northwest as he had been instructed to do, the "Young Marshal" had become too friendly with them. Chiang had gone to Sian to see for himself whether this was true and was thereupon kidnapped by Marshal Chang in the hope that he would agree to end the anti-Communist activity and concentrate all of China's energy to defeat the Japanese. Ransomed by his wife, Chiang flew back to Nanking with her and the now penitent Chang. There he agreed of his own volition to form a United Front of all Chinese (Communists included) against Japan. The Communists were delighted because Moscow was worried about Japan's successes in Manchuria and North China, which the Russians interpreted as the beginning of a war against them which would have the blessing of the West.

Chiang Kai-shek was now about ready to act, but so were the Japanese, who contrived to create another incident. They claimed that a Japanese soldier had been killed by the Chinese at the celebrated Marco Polo Bridge near Peiping and in retaliation launched a full-scale attack on the city, which fell to them. On the date 7 July 1937 a war began which was to last eight years and ultimately to involve the entire world although, of course, none could foresee it at the time. By 1939, the Japanese had occupied the China coast, all her major cities and railroads, and had become allied with Germany and Italy. But the setbacks dealt Japan's Kwantung Army by Russia's crack Red Banner Army, a skirmish to be described below, combined with the signing of the Russo-German Nonaggression Pact in the summer of 1939, served as a check upon Japan for the time being and saw China settle down to protracted resistance. Her government had been forced to retreat to West China where a new capital, Chungking, was established.

SOVIET RUSSIA AND THE FAR EAST

Long interested in the Far East, Russia had played an important role in that region prior to the First World War. The setback administered her by Japan in 1904–1905 merely checked her aspirations, and she later reached an agreement with the Japanese clearly marking out spheres of influence. Russia was to have Northern Manchuria, Outer Mongolia, and Sinkiang (Chinese Turkestan). During the latter part of the First World War, Siberia was occupied by an Allied Expeditionary Force which included some 70,000 Japanese whose object was the acquisition of Siberia. As a result of the Washington Conference, the Japanese finally agreed to leave Siberia in 1922, but they stayed on in the northern half of Sakhalin until 1925, at which time the U.S.S.R. gave them valuable economic concessions including fishing rights. In return, Japan recognized the Soviet government.

Meanwhile, the Russians had taken an interest in China. In 1917 the Bolsheviks renounced all the "unequal treaties" to which the Czarist government had been a party in the Far East. This action was an earnest of their good faith in opposing imperialism. And as previously indicated, the Soviets closely cooperated with Sun Yat-sen and the Kuomintang in China until Chiang Kai-shek's expulsion of the Communists and his severance of relations with Russia in 1927.

All during the period, 1931–1945, the Soviets succeeded in pursuing a tortuous course with both Japan and China. With the latter, diplomatic relations were officially restored in 1932, an event which annoyed the Japanese. However, the Japanese were soon to be mollified when Russia in 1935 sold the Chinese Eastern Railway (which cuts across Manchuria to Vladivostok and thus reduces the distance required by the Trans-Siberian) to Manchukuo. This action was prompted quite clearly by Japan's military success at China's expense and also by the League's failure to check Japan's aggression. But trouble cropped up in the relations of the two powers once again. In 1935 border incidents began to occur around Outer Mongolia, an autonomous region of China long friendly to the U.S.S.R. Technically, the disputes were between the "countries" of Manchukuo and the Mongol People's Republic. The powers themselves were having trouble over fisheries but ultimately would come together and temporarily reach agreement, thus postponing any showdown on their differences. When Japan signed the Anti-Comintern Pact in 1936, Russia was deeply angered and refused to sign a renewal of the fisheries agreement. Moreover, it actively encouraged the formation of a united front in China. It is conceivable that the kidnapping of Chiang at Sian in December, 1936, had its background in the fact that Japan had joined Germany in a pact directed against Russia.

Russo-Japanese Relations. From the time of Japan's second attack on China, beginning in 1937, Russo-Japanese relations grew worse. For one thing, there was the customary acrimony over the border problems and the usual wrangling over extending the fisheries agreement. But a new factor was the help being given China by Russia. The Soviets despised Chiang Kai-shek but did not let this interfere with their assistance, which, of course, was in their own interest. The following year (1938) witnessed a sharp conflict at Changkufeng near the junction of Manchukuo, Korea, and the Maritime Province of Russia. Fighting began 31 July between the Red Banner Army and the Kwantung Army Group, two of the finest units of their respective countries, and it continued for nearly two weeks. The evidence seems to indicate that Japan was given a rude surprise and that if any winner can be declared it was the Soviets. Not convinced, the Japanese elected to try again and fighting was renewed in May, 1939, along the border between Manchukuo and Outer Mongolia in a region called Nomohan. This was no skirmish but a full-dress engagement which saw large numbers of planes and armor employed on both sides. An agreement to cease hostilities was signed in September, and when the fighting did end the crack Kwantung Army had failed to dislodge the Russians.

From 1939 to 1941 the two nations faced one another along the world's longest armed frontier and were reported to have armies of approximately 1,000,000 men apiece. Suddenly, in 1941, Japan and Russia concluded a pact of nonaggression which came not long after the Rome-Berlin-Tokyo military alliance in the fall of 1940. The Japanese were the instigators of the pact, but the Russians were pleased to sign it, for it meant that each could now turn to its other concerns.

PART TEN

The Second World War and After

In general it may be asserted that the origin of the most devastating war the world has ever experienced was a result basically of the same set of causes which produced the war of 1914–1918. It is not for nothing that the 1919–1939 period is often referred to as the "Twenty Years' Armistice." It will be remembered that the First World War was ascribed to nationalism, imperialism, power politics and the alliance system, militarism, and the absence of any effective international machinery to prevent war. The last factor differed this time in that there actually was a League of Nations designed to make good this deficiency. Unfortunately, this attempt at collective security proved a failure, and so its lack of success may be listed as a major cause of the war. As in 1914, American isolationism played its part. By contrast with the earlier war when this point was somewhat negligible, albeit present, in 1939 it was a highly significant consideration.

The war itself raged through every part of the world and left no nation, even those that remained aloof, unaffected. At its end, fascism had gone down to defeat, and the forces of democracy and communism, thrown into involuntary partnership during the conflict, were left to work out the future of the world between themselves. This time there was on the part of the government and people of the United States recognition and acceptance of the responsibilities implicit in their country's unquestioned position of world leadership. Full support was given to the creation of a new international organization, the United Nations.

40

The Causes of the
Second World War

Treating the causes here briefly, it may be said that nationalism was extremely potent as a roadblock to peace. Following the Treaty of Versailles, France, fearful for her security, was determined to keep her old rival Germany impotent. Germany, for its part, seems to have nurtured a desire to gain revenge as soon as the opportunity presented itself. Certainly, Hitler clearly revealed his insistence upon full retaliation for the humiliation suffered by Germany. All the other victor states were determined to hold steadfast to their gains with the exception of Italy, who felt that she had been short-changed at the peace table and so lent herself to a movement led primarily by Germany for a revision of the postwar treaties. Hungary was another active, if somewhat diminutive, state espousing revision, while Austria was not exactly silent in this respect. The so-called "Succession States," *e.g.,* Czechoslovakia and Yugoslavia, were equally insistent upon measures to maintain the *status quo.*

Imperialism entered the picture through such events as the natural desire of the colonial powers to hold on to what they had in the matter of real estate and the equally natural insistence of the "have not" powers led by Germany, Italy, and Japan. This "Unholy Three" clamored loudly that as first-rate powers they were entitled to a better division of the spoils of empire, especially since they either lacked completely or had inadequate resources of coal, iron, oil, rubber, and cotton, to mention only the most important items in which they were deficient. Failing to secure redress of what they maintained were their grievances, they each

661

resorted to the only weapon which they were convinced would entitle them to what they sought. This was the use of force.

The abortive attempts at disarmament have been discussed previously. Suffice it to say here that militarism was reasserted on a previously unknown scale in the thirties. Germany, Italy, Japan, and Soviet Russia armed themselves to the teeth while France feverishly sought to bolster her allies. The totalitarian powers invented specious theories to justify to their people their disproportionate emphasis on force and, by the time the war had broken out (and Russia was then allied with Germany), the issue had patently become one wherein democracy was gripped in a life-and-death struggle with totalitarianism.

THE REVIVAL OF THE ALLIANCE SYSTEM

One of the most conspicuous symptoms of the world's lack of faith in its mechanism for preserving peace was the scramble for military allies which began almost before the ink was dry on the Versailles peace settlements and went on with increasing intensity as a new holocaust approached. The first steps in this direction were taken by France, which was worried about the prospect of a German comeback as a military power and placed little confidence in the efficacy of the League of Nations—particularly after the refusal of the United States to join.

France reached a military agreement with Belgium on 7 September 1920. In accordance with the Covenant the League was notified but the military aspects of the treaty were kept secret. Then came a Franco-Polish treaty in 1922 wherein each agreed to protect the other against Germany. For France this new ally was a replacement for her old Russian alliance. Since Poland was impecunious, France had to loan her money for war supplies and experts for her army. In 1920 France had helped Poland with men, money, and munitions to drive the Red army out of the country.

The Little Entente. A French attempt to secure a new alliance with Britain in 1921 was declined by Lloyd George; thus, France had to seek new allies to replace the old Entente Cordiale. She sought these recruits among the members of what came to be known as the Little Entente (Czechoslovakia, Rumania, and Yugoslavia). These powers were signed in the above order in 1924, 1926, and 1927. By 1927, France felt that she was well protected although the cost was excessive. French bankers loaned huge sums to members of the Little Entente and to Poland, but it was considered good national insurance.

The hegemony of France was one of the chief causes for the creation of two other similar systems by the U.S.S.R. and Italy respectively. Russia felt that she would be subjected to attack if she lacked allies since she was viewed askance by the Western world on account of her violent revolution, her economic structure, and her backing of the Comintern. She sought for and achieved a series of nonaggression pacts in 1925 and 1926 with Turkey, Germany, Afghanistan, Latvia, and Lithuania.

Italy, engaged in a contest with France for control of the western Mediterranean, felt her position precarious and engineered a series of treaties of friendship and neutrality in the period from 1924 to 1927 with the Little Entente members, Albania, Spain, and Hungary. In 1927 she broadened her arrangement with Albania into a twenty-year defensive alliance.

Thus, by 1927 there had come into existence three sets of European alliances in the place of the two which had existed prior to 1914. The French system was the most dangerous because it saw France obliged to defend five countries, all of whom were second-rate powers beset with enemies.

The coming of the Nazis into power in Germany projected a new force onto the scene in 1933, which brought about alterations in the alliance systems. The likelihood that Germany would rearm resulted in feverish activity in many quarters. Soviet Russia in the months of June and July, 1933, made a series of nonaggression pacts with all her western neighbors in the hope of protecting her borders in the West in case Japan in the East might take advantage of her. The Little Entente strengthened its arrangements (1933), and the Balkans (with the exception of Albania and Bulgaria) concluded the Balkan Entente in 1934, while the Baltic states in that year did the same thing by agreeing to cooperate in defense matters. Rounding out this busy year, Britain, France, and Italy had issued a joint proclamation affirming their intention to maintain the integrity of Austria. France proceeded to reach an accord with Italy shortly afterward in which the French made several minor colonial concessions in return for Italy's apparent promise to side with her against Germany. Then in 1935 France and Russia reached a mutual assistance pact, and Russia followed it with a similar one with Czechoslovakia.

The Axis Powers. Germany was losing no time in her newly revived strength. In 1934 she won a nonaggression pact with Poland, an achievement which represented a sharp setback for French foreign policy. In 1936 Germany enjoyed even greater success. On 11 July 1936 an Austro-German treaty was signed, easing relations between the two countries, which had been tense since 1934. The real significance of the event, however, was that it was achieved with the approval of Mussolini, thereby indicating his shift from the stand he had previously taken on the side of the democracies against Nazi machinations in Austria. The new Italo-German friendship ripened in October, 1936, into the understanding which came to be known as the Rome-Berlin Axis. Its ostensible reason for existence was the common hatred of the two fascist powers for communism. The month following, Japan signed the Anti-Comintern Pact with Germany, which was broadened a year later by the addition of Italy, thus forming the Rome-Berlin-Tokyo Axis.

As the tension mounted in the wild scrambling which took place, England and France came together again in 1938 in the face of common necessity and commenced efforts to attract the U.S.S.R. The latter, angry over the Munich crisis, which will be described below, refused and in the summer of 1939 startled the world by signing a nonaggression treaty with Germany.

THE CIVIL WAR IN AUSTRIA

The tiny remnant which was once Austria had existed since 1918 in a very precarious condition. Its parliament was split into various parties, chief among which at this time were the Christian Socialists, a Catholic party; the Social Democrats, whose stronghold was Vienna; and the National Socialists. Each had armed forces upon which it could call. The rural regions were the home of various armed groups which were rather loosely connected under the name of *Heimwehr*. In Vienna, which accounted for about one-third of the country's population, the Socialists had an army which was known as the *Schutzbund*. The Nazis had no name for their armed groups as such but they had a forceful organization which was spoiling for a fight.

In May, 1932, a Christian Socialist, Engelbert Dollfuss, became chancellor and within less than a year dismissed parliament because of the hopeless deadlock which existed there. The press was censored and the right to assembly abridged. In addition to the Socialists, the Nazis became the targets of the government, which demonstrated an increasingly friendly attitude toward Mussolini.

Fighting broke out in February, 1934, on the heels of the French riots of that month. In a three days' battle the government broke the Socialist force, the *Schutzbund,* and during the fighting in Vienna bombarded the famous workers' apartment house, the Karl Marx Hof, said to be the largest building of its kind in the world. On 1 May 1934 a new constitution setting up a corporate state was promulgated.

The Nazis, who had watched the Christian Socialist government and the Social Democrats do battle, elected to stage a *coup d'état* on 25 July 1934. On that date with ridiculous ease they succeeded in capturing Chancellor Dollfuss and murdering him in cold blood in the chancellery. The malefactors were quickly rounded up, and the conspiracy failed. Since it appeared as if the Nazis of Germany were involved (actually the plot was of Austrian Nazi origin), Mussolini rushed troops to the border and announced his intention of defending Austria should Hitler move. The crisis was soon passed without war and the late "Millimetternich," Dollfuss, was succeeded by Kurt von Schuschnigg. Thus, an event which might have led to a general European war was quietly liquidated for the time being.

THE ASSASSINATION OF KING ALEXANDER OF YUGOSLAVIA

The year 1934 was not to end without another sanguinary threat to peace. The unstable succession state of Yugoslavia had been going through a series of very violent and painful growing pains which resulted largely from the incompatibility existing between the Serbs and Croats, the leading races among the dozen or so which made up the country. The situation deteriorated to the point where King Alexander had undertaken a personal dictatorship. From abroad, the French and Italians were engaged in a struggle for ascendant influence over this turbulent land. In 1934, Yugoslavia joined the Balkan Pact aimed against revisionist Hungary. This step was a victory for France and was so interpreted by Italian diplomacy. On 9 October King Alexander was in France cementing ties when he was assassinated by a member of the Croat terrorist organization, the Ustashi, which had refuge on both Hungarian and Italian soil. Alexander's companion at Marseilles, the French Foreign Minister, Louis Barthou, was also murdered by the assassin.

So much excitement was engendered by the twin murders that it was brought before the League, where Yugoslovia accused Hungary of complicity in the deed. The Italians vigorously defended the Hungarians. The British and French, who had enough problems of their own without adding to them, applied the brakes to Yugoslavia, and the crisis harmlessly dissipated. That it could have led to war goes without saying. What it did to the already jittery international situation is also patent.

THE REARMAMENT OF GERMANY

Disgusted with their inability to secure arms equality, the Nazis withdrew in 1933 from the Geneva Disarmament Conference and simultaneously announced their departure from the League on 14 October 1933. This action was followed by resignation also from the International Labor Office and the World Court, steps which constituted Germany's complete severance from the international peace movement.

These moves paved the way for the unilateral achievement of arms parity by the Nazis. On 16 March 1935, Hitler proudly announced that

Germany's rearmament had commenced, a step which involved the breaking of the military shackles imposed on Germany by the Treaty of Versailles. Conscription was reintroduced and the military forces, including a potent *Luftwaffe,* were strengthened. France sought desperately to block this consummation of a fear she always held. A special meeting of the League Council was hurriedly called and unanimously adopted a French resolution condemning Germany's treaty breaking. The German answer was prompt and unequivocal. It defiantly and insultingly declared that the League ought to mind its own business.

This curt refusal to rescind was shortly followed by the signing of the Anglo-German Naval Pact of 18 June 1935, which was tantamount to renunciation of the military clauses of Versailles by one of its principal architects. The reaction among the other signatories can readily be imagined. Suffice it to say, they took umbrage at Britain's defection.

While Europe and the world were recovering from the shock of this distressing happening, Hitler sent his forces into the Rhineland 7 March 1936. This constituted not only a violation of Versailles but of Locarno as well. Again a terrific hullabaloo ensued. Hitler defended himself on the grounds that the Franco-Russian Alliance of 1935 was itself a repudiation of Locarno and thus Germany was forced to defend itself by remilitarizing the Rhineland. The convening of the Locarno Powers (other than Germany) produced a French demand that German troops be forcibly ejected from their new positions. The League itself passed a resolution condemning Germany's treaty breaking. Consultations developed among the general staffs of Britain, France, and Belgium. Nothing happened, and Hitler had won yet another "bloodless conquest" through the use of what then appeared to be his uncanny sense of timing. The Rhineland crisis, although it provided Germany another triumph in the end, served to heighten an atmosphere that was already charged with electricity. Nor should it be forgotten that the joyous successes of the Nazis shook the entire League structure to its very foundations.

THE ETHIOPIAN ADVENTURE

Meanwhile, a second war[1] had broken out which clearly demonstrated the weakness of the League of Nations to keep the peace in the face of a determined aggressor. Following a series of "border incidents" between Ethiopia and Italian Somaliland which began in December, 1934, at a place called Wal Wal, Mussolini readied his legions to punish the "offenders," *i.e.,* the Ethiopians. The background of this particular situation dated back to the crushing defeat suffered by the Italians at Adowa in 1896. This blot on the Italian escutcheon had to be effaced.

[1] The first was, of course, the Japanese invasion of Manchuria in 1931.

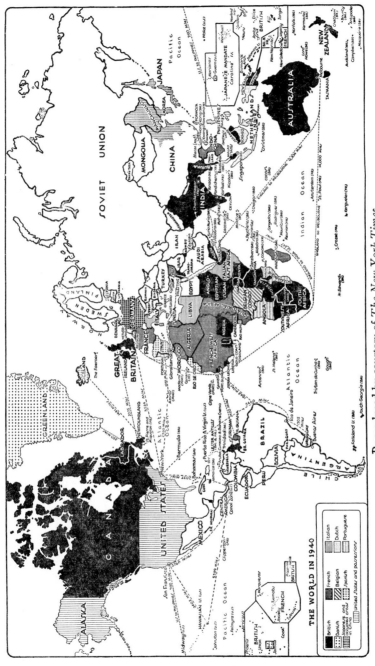

THE WORLD IN 1940

British
Danish
French
Danish
Islands and occupied areas in China
Italian
Belgian
Spanish
Dutch
Portuguese
United States and possessions

Reproduced by courtesy of *The New York Times*.

Furthermore, Ethiopia was one of the two remaining independent countries on the great African continent, a fact which limited land grabs at the expense of the weak by the greedy. Mussolini was determined at all costs to build a great new "Roman Empire." The acquisition of Ethiopia would be a fitting inaugural step. Then, too, it could serve as a convenient springboard from which to launch an attack against the Anglo-Egyptian Sudan, a land whose potentialities made il Duce drool. From the Sudan, Suez could then be threatened. The British "life line of Empire" would then be cut, and Mussolini would have little trouble in defeating the last obstacle to the reestablishment of the North African empire of ancient Rome—decadent France. He would indeed be the new Caesar. To assuage Arab fears, he had already begun to pose as the "Protector of Islam." It was all so simple and inviting on paper!

As the incidents increased in intensity in 1935, the hapless Ethiopians unsuccessfully sought direct negotiations. Mussolini very reluctantly consented to submission of the dispute to the League. A commission of conciliation set up by the League failed to solve the problem, and it went back to the League itself. Thereupon, Mussolini declared that his patience was at an end. On 3 October 1935, Italian troops invaded the semi-barbaric Ethiopia with ridiculous ease just a few days before the League Council summoned up its courage enough to issue a unanimous report condemning Italy's action as a direct violation of the League Covenant. The Assembly shortly ratified this declaration.[2]

League of Nations Sanctions. This action did not deter Mussolini, who understood the necessity the League had for some face-saving gesture. Especially comforting to him was the knowledge that the then French Premier, Pierre Laval, had reached an accord with Italy and would be a redoubtable "ace in the hole" if things really began to grow black.

With the future of the League hanging perilously in the balance, it was now decided to take the unprecedented step of applying sanctions in an effort to halt the Italian war machine. These measures went into effect 18 November 1935 but began to lose force within a matter of four short months. The sanctions called for were fourfold. They followed an arms embargo to Italy (the United States had ceased selling to both the belligerents) and were: (1) the refusal of further loans or credits to Italy; (2) a ban on all imports from Italy or its colonies; (3) a ban on certain exports to Italy and its colonies, *e.g.*, such raw materials as rubber; and, finally, (4) a League promise to offer mutual economic assistance aimed at lessening and minimizing losses to those League members adhering in the application of sanctions.

These sanctions were serious but by no means strong enough to dissuade Italy. As a matter of fact, the British fleet movements in the Medi-

---

[2] The only dissenters were Italy, Austria, and Hungary.

terranean bothered Mussolini more, and he protested to Britain. The British, however, had no taste for war with Italy since they could not count upon France. The French, in turn, were torn between fear of what Germany might do in the event of Franco-British military steps and their newly found friendship with Italy which Laval had established. Thus, Britain and France were effectively hamstrung.

American Policy. Meanwhile, there remained the question of what stand the powerful but strongly isolationist United States would adopt. No answer to this poser ever came, although the State Department did counsel Italian caution. President Roosevelt, indeed, went so far as to remark in the summer of 1935 that the conflict was of no immediate concern to the United States. In candor, it must be noted that this was the prevailing sentiment of the American people. Shortly after the outbreak of hostilities in October, the President officially proclaimed American neutrality by formally recognizing that a state of war existed. Americans were forbidden to ship any matériel of war to either belligerent and were requested not to travel on the ships of either belligerent. If the latter provisions were disregarded, such travel was at the risk of the individuals. The consequences of this stand became quite obvious, judged from the vantage point of hindsight. In brief, aggressors were given encouragement in the belief that the United States was determined to stay out of war come what may. Conversely, it meant that those who looked for ultimate aid from the United States in the event of war had their hopes rudely dashed.

Now that the United States had shown its feelings about checking Italy, there remained the question of whether American firms should continue to trade with Italy. Two days after war broke out, the President declared that persons who did so must realize that it was at their own risk. The Chief Executive's remarks were blithely overlooked, and raw materials, including oil, continued to be shipped merrily to Italian consignees. Meanwhile, in Geneva the League got around to the possibility of an oil embargo by its members. At this juncture, Sir Samuel Hoare, the British Foreign Minister, reached an accord on 8 December 1935 with the French Premier, Pierre Laval. The Hoare-Laval Agreement provided for a redrawing of the Ethiopian border at the considerable expense of that country and further recommended that much of Ethiopia be placed under the Italians as a sort of economic sphere where privileges of settlement would also be allowed. To preserve some semblance of decency, the generous partitioners of Ethiopia were willing to allow the Ethiopians to retain sovereignty over the zone (which embraced about half the country's area). Even here there was a joker in that Ethiopian administration would be subject to League directives. This accord was looked upon by its framers as a recommendation to be given to the belligerents. In the meantime, the schemers hoped that the proposed oil embargo would have to wait on the reaction of the parties to the dispute. Time would be thus consumed to the advantage of the advancing Italians, whose planes and mechanized equipment were already pulverizing the poorly and primitively armed natives.

The Italian Victory. A leak revealed the sorry deal almost instantly, and the storm of indignation which went up everywhere (including British and French public opinion) resulted in its abandonment and the forced resignation of both Hoare and Laval. Despite the celerity with which this proposal was jettisoned, it had the effect of further confusing the League and resulted in the additional loss of precious time. The Duce took advantage of the woeful indecision to lay down the gauntlet. He announced through his controlled press that the invocation of an oil embargo meant war as far as Italy was concerned and would be so construed by his government. While the confused League powers continued to fuss and fume in their indecision, Herr Hitler seized upon his golden opportunity and remilitarized the Rhineland, 7 March 1936. This action hurled a bombshell into the League and took immediate precedence over the Ethiopian question. On 5 May Addis Ababa, capital of Ethiopia, was captured. On 16 July the League accepted a *fait accompli* and removed the sanctions which had already been voted.

Thus ended a most melancholy revelation of the weakness of the League. Indecision, confusion, and trickery had aided the aggressor. Nor was the role played by the United States in the least an edifying one. When the League wavered, no moral assistance worthy of the name ever came from Washington. This episode has been dwelt upon at some length in order that the student might have at least one case study of the rapid deterioration which was besetting the ideal of world cooperation and hurtling the world toward the abyss of another world war.

THE SPANISH CIVIL WAR

Few events in the twentieth century have attracted so much attention as the Spanish Civil War, and few have left in their wake such a heritage of bitterness and recrimination. There are several factors which help to account for the outbreak of this vicious struggle. In the first place, Spain had suffered acute dislocation as a result of the changes brought about in Spanish society during and after the First World War. Spain enjoyed the advantages which accrued to the few European neutrals during that conflict. With numerous orders to fill, her agricultural produce was profitably marketed. However, it was in the field of manufacture where the greatest changes occurred. Thousands flocked from the rural areas into the new factory centers, found employment at wages which seemed unbelievable, and enjoyed the social features of life in the city as compared with the drabber aspects of rural existence. The boom ended almost as suddenly as it began, and unemployment mounted dangerously. People refused to return to the land, and conditions in the urban centers became quite unsatisfactory. The new proletariat began to vent its resentment on the government and was an attractive target itself for radical doctrines spread by native agitators and Comintern agents.

Second, the Spanish army, whose hold on the people had long been extremely powerful, continued its senseless policy of pouring Spanish lives and treasure down the drain that was Spanish Morocco. Since the Spanish had acquired an enlarged colony in Morocco in 1912, the loss of lives in the seemingly endless battle to pacify the natives had reached the staggering total of over 130,000. When the Riffs made the mistake of attacking the French as well, Spain was ultimately rescued. Even then the combined allies required many months (1925–1927) to subdue the valiant Abd-el-Krim.

Thirdly, although the monarch himself retained popularity, the monarchy had lost much of its glamour, and there developed a rather widespread feeling of opposition to it, based on the patent corruption of several persons close to the throne.

Finally, the Catholic Church had become a target for anticlericals and persons who had become desperate owing to their straitened economic circumstances. The Church's land holdings became an object of envy and served conveniently to equip foreign agitators, as well as domestic, with a potent weapon of propaganda.

As early as 1923, those elements which feared that the force of the gathering storm might sweep away so much that was vital to their way of life were able to unite behind General Primo de Rivera, who established a dictatorship of the right. Because he was too conservative to suit the radicals and too liberal to please the extremists of the right, his regime was under constant fire. Unable to check the advances of the former despite the adoption of the extraordinary measures, de Rivera's government fell in 1930, and he fled to France where he later died in penurious exile. So convincing was the antimonarchist sentiment revealed in the elections of 12 April 1931 which ensued that Alfonso XIII abdicated and went into exile.

The Spanish Republic. The Spanish republic which followed was founded in a spirit of idealism perhaps somewhat remote from the realities of Spanish life. Its constitution, among other things, formally recognized Spain's obligations to the League of Nations. The republicans embarked on an ambitious program of curtailing the privileges of the nobility, the army, and the Church but were unable to implement it properly, thereby irritating their opponents without weakening them. The radicals, for their part, became impatient with the slow progress of moderate reform and turned to direct action, including murderous attack on churchmen which resulted only in alienating many of the republic's supporters. Therefore, in the elections of November, 1933, parties of the right and the middle of the road won control of the state. This state of affairs was as displeasing to the leftists as their policies had been to their opponents, and they resorted to the weapons of strikes and violence to cripple the new regime. By February of 1936, after a series of bloody incidents had taken place, the conservatives were ousted by a union of leftists, the Popular Front led by Manuel Azaña.

Outbreak of War. In an effort to conciliate its more radical supporters, the new government decreed a sweeping political amnesty which released thousands from jail and attracted others who had fled to their ideological haven, Russia, to return. This action, produced further violence. Battles began to take place between opposing bands. Strikes and riots were commonplace. Finally, on 17 July 1936, the Civil War officially began with the revolt of the Spanish Foreign Legion in Morocco. The original leader, General Sanjurjo, was killed in a plane crash at the outset of the uprising, and leadership fell to General Francisco Franco, who quickly crossed over to the mainland to take command. Ranged on the side of the government (Loyalists) were the Communists, socialists, radical republicans, syndicalists, anarchists, the industrial workers, and the Catalonian separatists. Supporting the insurgents (Rebels) were the army, monarchists, most of the churchmen, many moderate republicans, and the fascists.

International Complications. From the very beginning the conflict achieved international proportions. Italy and Germany were pro-Rebel whereas Russia and France (to a lesser degree) were pro-Loyalist. In the United States and Great Britain there was a division of opinion, with that favoring the Loyalists undoubtedly much stronger owing to the dislike of Hitler and Mussolini. The ideological aspects of this war were not lost on a large number of people throughout the world who clearly saw what the stakes were. Aid began to flow in the form of "volunteers" and supplies from Russia to the Loyalists and from Germany and Italy to the Rebels. Franco was officially recognized in November, 1936, by the two fascist powers, while in August Great Britain and France had imposed an arms embargo on both the Spanish belligerents, a position bitterly assailed by British and French leftists. One of the many paradoxes which characterized the whole question of the war was the establishment of the twenty-seven-nation nonintervention agreement, which numbered among others such interested nations as Germany, Italy, Portugal, and Russia—a development which was characterized by continued repetition of charges of unneutrality by one group of sympathizers or other. Britain and Italy reached a separate "gentleman's agreement" in January, 1937, which amounted to a pledge to allow each other free passage in the Mediterranean.

In the actual fighting done by foreigners in Spain, the greatest contribution was made by Italy. In addition to the part played by the nationals of the countries mentioned, American Loyalist sympathizers formed the Abraham Lincoln Brigade, a unit whose casualties were extremely high. The policy of the American government was at first confused since the neutrality legislation did not as yet apply to a civil war. Efforts were made to deter (by recommendation only) the shipment of arms to either side. This went unheeded and resulted in a congressional resolution at President Roosevelt's behest which officially prohibited the export of arms, 8 January 1937. Later, on 1 May 1937, a new law was passed which put civil wars under the neutrality provisions applying to international war.

On 13 March 1937, the Non-Intervention Committee established a naval patrol to police the Spanish coast. An incident which could have had even graver consequences resulted from the bombing of fascist patrol boats by Loyalist fliers. The German pocket battleship, the _Deutschland,_ was hit 29 May. In retaliation, a German squadron bombarded the Loyalist port of Almeria, 31 May, with heavy damage.

By late 1938 the steady progress of the Rebels, whose command of the skies was employed to good advantage in bombing cities—then considered a shocking practice—had coupled with such events as the Ethiopian venture and the German absorption of Austria and Czechoslovakia to reduce interest in the Spanish crisis. In early 1939 the war ended as success after success crowned the efforts of Franco's forces. Madrid was captured 28 March and shortly thereafter all of Spain was under the control of the Nationalists, as the Rebels preferred to be called.

Once again an event which seemed certain to bring about a general war had been concluded without such a realization, but the extent of foreign involvement and the ideological issues at stake pointed up clearly the imminence of such a conflict. The generally unsatisfactory performance given in the name of peace did little to reassure people that peace could be maintained.

ANSCHLUSS

It will be recalled that in 1934 during the crisis precipitated by the murder of the Austrian Chancellor Dollfuss by native Nazis, Hitler's Germany had acted swiftly to disavow either its connection with or its interest in such an act. The speedy action of Mussolini in rushing troops to the Brenner Pass undoubtedly had much to do with this stand. But in the meantime conditions had changed radically. Italy and Germany had become allied in the Anti-Comintern Pact, and, while Mussolini had not yet become the firm's junior partner, his running mate was progressing at a rapid rate. Furthermore, Italy, essentially a poor country, had made a considerable sacrifice in both the Ethiopian and Spanish adventures.

Nazi pressure upon Austria was exerted by 1938, and on 12 February of that year Hitler "invited" Chancellor Kurt von Schuschnigg to visit him at Berchtesgaden. This visit resulted in the appointment of the Austrian Nazi Arthur Seyss-Inquart (executed at Nuremberg in 1946) as Minister of the Interior. In this post, Seyss-Inquart had control of the country's police. The cabinet was also rearranged to suit the *Führer,* numerous political prisoners were released, and the activities of the Nazi party in Austria were now to be looked upon officially with more favor.

Schuschnigg announced on 9 March that a plebiscite would be held the following Sunday (13 March) to test the will of the people on the issue of independence against *Anschluss* (union) with Germany. There can be little doubt as to what the outcome would have been had the plebiscite ever taken place. The majority of Austrian people cherished their independence enough by this time to have lost their early postwar enthusiasm for union. Hitler, of course, knew this. On 11 March he sent an ultimatum to Schuschnigg demanding postponement of the voting. Less than two hours later that same day came a second German ultimatum, to the effect that the Chancellor resign in favor of Seyss-Inquart and insisting that the majority of cabinet seats be given to Nazis, together with other demands. Schuschnigg thereupon went on the radio as the new ultimatum expired and announced to the people that he was resigning in the hope of saving Austria. Almost immediately he was followed by Seyss-Inquart, who brought the news that German troops were already on their way to Austria. The frontier was actually crossed in a matter of a few hours, and the next day there were German troops in Vienna. Hitler himself was on Austrian soil the night of 12 March. Following the obviously planned and very scientific absorption of the country, the *Führer* was ready for a plebiscite on the question of *Anschluss*. It was held 10 April, but the voting was not confined to Austria alone. Instead it was universal throughout the Reich. The announced verdict was a mere 99.77 per cent *Ja*. By this bloodless conquest, Hitler had added greatly to Germany's strength and had become senior partner in the firm of Hitler and Mussolini.

"WHO HOLDS BOHEMIA IS MASTER OF EUROPE"

Everywhere it became increasingly obvious that Czechoslovakia was next on the German timetable. Great Britain and France felt such a move was a grave possibility, and they concluded an alliance in April, 1938, pledging the preservation of Czech independence. The presence of some three and a half million Germans in Czechoslovakia, the majority of whom were in the Sudetenland in Bohemia, provided an attractive target for the Nazis. As the summer of 1938 passed, excitement became intense. The Germans began menacing preparations, and their press poured forth a flood of vituperation.

The Sudeten Crisis. Taking cognizance of the growing danger, the British government dispatched a special emissary to Prague, Lord Runciman. Meanwhile, the so-called Sudeten Germans had made a series of demands on the Czech government which President Beneš answered on 6 September with a reasonable plan designed to satisfy the Sudetens. Beneš's plan received Lord Runciman's approval but apparently not that of the Sudetens since incidents began almost immediately. By 12 September the violence had intensified so that Runciman announced his mission was concluded and left for home.

Suddenly, on the 15th, Prime Minister Chamberlain flew to Berchtesgaden to see Hitler. This visit was then followed by an Anglo-French conference in London between Chamberlain and Daladier, the French premier. Their conversations produced an agreement to propose that all districts in Czechoslovakia having a population of over 50 per cent German be transferred without any plebiscites to Germany. Czechoslovakia's borders would then be guaranteed against attack. These proposals were given to the Czechs on 18 September, and they were told to reply by the 21st. The affirmative reply to this Anglo-French proposition was immediately followed by the resignation of the Czech government and the formation of a new one.

Munich. At this juncture, Hungary and Poland came forward and requested Hitler to support their territorial claims against Czechoslovakia. This development produced another visit from Chamberlain to Hitler at Godesberg. The harassed prime minister learned for his pains that Germany's price had now increased. The new German demands, which included the Hungarian and Polish claims, proved completely unacceptable to the Czechs and were even distressing to Chamberlain. The conference, therefore, collapsed, and the prime minister returned to England, where preparations for war reluctantly were commenced. It was now Hitler's turn to offer concessions. Modifying his demands somewhat, he suggested a four-power conference (Great Britain, France, Germany, and Italy) at Munich on 29 September. This proposal was accepted and agreement reached the very first day. The Munich Pact permitted the Germans a gradual military occupation of the Sudetenland by 10 October. A commission of the four powers plus Czechoslovakia would fix the limits of the German occupation. In several other areas, plebiscites would be held, and, finally, people could elect to enter or leave transferred territories. Hitler, on his part, assured the world that Germany's territorial claims on Europe were complete.

Returning to London, Chamberlain was accorded a tremendous reception because it appeared as if war had been prevented and "peace in our time" achieved. Despite this sentiment, Great Britain and France began to make belated military preparations to strengthen themselves. An ominous note to the whole affair was the exclusion of Russia, which has ever since represented Munich as Allied appeasement of Hitler in the vain hope that he would live up to earlier promises and turn east to deal with the Soviet.

Hitler followed up the addition of Sudetenland to the Reich by taking over the rest of the country, 15 March 1939, under the pretext that the maintenance of order made it necessary, Bohemia and Moravia were made "protectorates"; Slovakia became an "independent" republic under German auspices; and the Carpatho-Ukraine (Sub-Carpathian Ruthenia) was awarded to Poland and Hungary. The latter action had the virtue of lulling the Poles into believing Hitler was their friend. It also solidified existing ties between Germany and Admiral Horthy's Hungary.

THE OUTBREAK OF WAR

Hitler lost no time in moving toward his next objective, Poland. On 21 March 1939 a German ultimatum was handed to Lithuania demanding the return of the former German city of Memel. The Lithuanians, having no alternative, yielded. Before a week had elapsed, the straws were in the wind when Poland received and rejected a formal demand from Germany that the latter be permitted to build its own railroad and motor highway across the Polish Corridor.

By this time the British government had belatedly discovered that Hitler's word was meaningless. Sensing the threat to Poland, the Chamberlain government went on record on 31 March as guaranteeing Poland, an offer which was accepted by the Poles. While these events were taking place, the junior member of the firm specializing in assorted aggressions had reached the conclusion that Herr Hitler had been enjoying the spotlight a little too frequently. Accordingly, on 7 April 1939 (Good Friday), Albania was invaded by Italy in violation of existing treaties. Despite strong opposition which embarrassed the legions of the "New Rome," the doughty Albanians were crushed and their ruling monarchs forced to flee. Albania was then made part of the Italian empire under Victor Emmanuel, who ruled the country as king.

The Nazi-Soviet Pact. On 16 April 1939 the United States attempted to arrest the dangerous decline toward war when President

Roosevelt personally requested Hitler and Mussolini to promise they would refrain from attacking any other country for at least ten years. In the interim, of course, it was hoped that the causes of war might be permanently corrected. The response of the dictators was, as may be suspected, most uncooperative. Hitler's campaign against Poland intensified with Danzig and the Polish Corridor as the special targets. Feverish diplomatic activity throughout Europe characterized the summer of 1939. Among the most inviting prospects for an alliance now that war appeared imminent was Russia. In the warm summer months a combined Franco-British delegation was in Moscow seeking to reach some kind of accord. The Russians subjected the visitors to the worst kind of delaying and evasive tactics. In the midst of protracted negotiations, it was suddenly announced on 23 August 1939 that formal ratification of a Russo-German Non-aggression Pact had just taken place in Moscow. The way was now open for Germany to proceed against Poland. Russia had indeed flashed a green light, and Poland and the Western democracies were in mortal peril.

Two days after the formal announcement of the pact's ratification, Great Britain reaffirmed its Polish ties. There followed vain appeals to Hitler to desist from plunging the world into war. Poland's refusal to cede Danzig and the Corridor caused German forces to cross her borders early on the morning of 1 September although no war declaration was issued. On 3 September Britain and then France made declarations of war on Germany. Italy remained a benevolent neutral, a fact which satisfied German diplomacy. Britain's dominions, with the exception of Eire, all declared war by 10 September, Canada being the last. Thus began history's most terrible conflict.

In conclusion, Hitler's contemptuous remarks on the causes of the war in a speech to the German generals on 22 August 1939 are worth quoting: "I shall give a propagandist cause for starting the war; never mind whether it be true or not. The victor shall not be asked later whether we tell the truth or not. In starting and making a war, not the right is what matters but the victory—the strongest has the right."

41

The Second World War:
European Phase

The war which began with the German invasion of Poland was in some respects a continuation of the First World War on a larger scale. The alignment was somewhat changed, with Italy and Japan fighting against their former allies, but the forces of nationalism and imperialism were as powerfully present, and the weapons introduced in the first war —aircraft, tanks, and submarines—played a major role in the second. The Second World War, however, was more than a simple renewal of the earlier struggle. Besides the clash of national interests, it involved bitter ideological conflicts which occasionally transcended national lines. Aggressive fascism threatened both democracy and communism with extermination, and both had to join forces to survive.

THE EARLY BLITZKRIEGS

The German attack on Poland revealed to the world the tactics of the "blitzkrieg," an overwhelming and well-coordinated assault by aerial and mechanized forces. Against it the Poles had little to offer but courage. No aid came from their Western allies. Britain and France had worked out plans for coordinating their forces, with France to have the supreme command on land and Britain at sea, but their strategy was entirely defensive. The last act in the Polish tragedy, a bitter but hopeless defense of Warsaw, ended on 27 September. Ten days earlier Soviet troops had marched into eastern Poland to occupy territory claimed by the Russians since 1920, and by a second Treaty of Brest-Litovsk between Russia and Germany, the Fourth Partition of Poland was agreed on.

678

The "Phony War." The war then settled down for the winter into a phase known as the "sitzkrieg" or the "phony war." Allied and German armies sat inactive behind the Maginot and Siegfried Lines respectively. In the air, both sides confined themselves to minor raids on strictly military targets. Operations at sea were somewhat more lively but far from decisive. German submarines achieved some success; they were not at this period, however, a serious threat. On the other hand, the pocket battleship *Admiral Graf Spee,* one of a type from which much had been expected as commerce raiders, was chased into Montevideo by three smaller British warships on 13 December and then scuttled on direct orders from Hitler.

Meanwhile, other powers were considering their position. Italy took a stand defined by Mussolini as "nonbelligerent" rather than neutral. Italy, in other words, was going to await developments before committing itself. In the United States, public opinion was strongly anti-German and at the same time anxious to avoid involvement in the war. Upon the outbreak of hostilities President Roosevelt invoked the Neutrality Acts, but, as he had previously announced he would do, he summoned a special session of Congress shortly afterward and asked for repeal of the arms embargo. After a vigorous debate, the first stage of a controversy over national policy which would grow in intensity for the next two years, the embargo was lifted on 4 November 1939. The other provisions of the act, notably "cash and carry," remained in effect, but it was hoped that access to American war materials would give Britain and France sufficient aid to enable them to cope with Hitler. At the same time the American republics met in conference at Panama and established a "neutrality zone" around the Western Hemisphere. The purpose to be served was not quite clear, except that it would give the United States Navy, which would have to do the bulk of the patrolling, an opportunity to keep an eye on operations in the Atlantic.

Russia's Attack on Finland. The Russians were much more active. The diplomatic rapprochment between Germany and the Soviet Union extended far beyond a mere pledge of mutual nonaggression. In a striking parallel to the Treaty of Tilsit between Napoleon and Alexander I, Hitler and Stalin had negotiated, or were in process of negotiating, a group of pacts dividing Europe between themselves. Russia agreed to make available much-needed raw materials and food supplies to Germany, and the Soviets also gave the Germans base facilities at Murmansk which helped them to by-pass the Anglo-French blockade. Yet neither party really trusted the other, and Russia's moves in the fall of 1939 can be interpreted only as precaution against a future German attack. After the occupation of eastern Poland, the Soviets demanded and secured the right to establish military bases in Estonia, Latvia, and Lithuania. Similar demands on Finland, plus one for changes in the frontier so as to push the Finnish border back from Leningrad and the Leningrad-Murmansk railway, were rejected, however, with the result that on 30 November 1939 the Soviets attacked their little neighbor.

The Russians appear to have underestimated the opposition, although it is possible that they deliberately started their second team in order to mislead the rest of the world regarding their military strength. For four months the Finns won the admiration of the world by a brilliant defense. The admiration, however, was not accompanied by much in the way of tangible support. Great Britain, France, and Sweden sent war materials, and many Swedish volunteers joined the Finnish forces. Mussolini, who could not shed his anti-Communist leanings as casually as his Axis partner, tried to send Italian aircraft to Finland, but they were held up in transit by the Germans. The United States extended credit to Finland for the purchase of nonmilitary supplies. And for what it was worth, the League of Nations solemnly expelled the Soviet Union. None of these steps was sufficient to maintain the Finns against the overwhelming might of Russia, and in March, 1940, they had to give up.

The Invasion of Norway and Denmark. In April, 1940, the "sitzkrieg" came to a dramatic end. On the 9th of that month German troops invaded Denmark and Norway, on the pretext that they had to protect these unoffending neutrals from the nefarious designs of the British. Documentary evidence of such designs was obligingly produced by Dr. Goebbels. The real motives appear to have been principally to secure Germany's access to the iron-ore deposits of northern Sweden, the route to which, in winter, lay through the Norwegian port of Narvik, and also to acquire submarine bases that could not readily be sealed off.

As a military operation, apart from ethical considerations, the German invasion was well planned and executed. Denmark was overrun with almost no resistance; even with ample warning, there was little the Danes could have done. In Norway, German land, air, and naval forces were skillfully coordinated with German agents inside the country. Norwegian defense forces were confused by faked orders, and "peaceful" German merchant ships lying in Norwegian ports suddenly disgorged cargoes of troops. The Norwegians fought back valiantly, but they were disorganized by the suddenness of the German onslaught. Every important Norwegian city was captured on the first day, which meant that the Germans had in their hands the centers of communication, the principal military installations, and the airfields.

The British and French were equally taken by surprise. They had some warning of an impending German move, enough for the British fleet to put to sea on 7 April, but no clear idea of what was coming. Although some clashes occurred, bad weather enabled the German fleet to escape interception and carry out its part of the campaign. Not until a week after the German invasion did the first units of a hastily improvised Anglo-French expedition land in Norway, by which time the Germans had made their foothold secure.

The principal Allied effort was directed against the city of Trondheim, since, of the ports on the west coast of Norway, it offered the easiest access into the interior. The force that was sent over was inadequately trained and equipped, the only ports available to it were little more than fishing villages with poor facilities for unloading supplies, and nothing could be done about the absolute German control of the air, the result of their getting to Norway's airfields first. After two weeks of fighting, the position of the Allied troops in the Trondheim area was so hopeless that they were withdrawn. Farther north, British, French, and Norwegian forces succeeded in retaking Narvik, but the catastrophe in France necessitated the abandonment of this enterprise also.

By the middle of June the Germans were in complete possession of Norway. King Haakon and his government escaped to London, where they continued to direct Norwegian resistance. The Germans set up a puppet government under Vidkun Quisling, whose name gave the world a new synonym for traitor. Their gains in strategic position and access to important materials were considerable; for the Allies, the only consolation was that they came into possession of Norway's excellent merchant fleet, the fourth largest in the world. An additional consequence of the Norwegian campaign was the fall of Neville Chamberlain. When the Trondheim fiasco turned a large part of his own Conservative party against him, he resigned and was succeeded by Winston Churchill.

THE FALL OF FRANCE

The best that Churchill could offer the British people was "blood, toil, tears, and sweat," because in the week he took office, Hitler launched his main offensive in the west. At dawn on 10 May 1940, German armies crossed the frontiers of Holland, Belgium, and Luxembourg. The move was not unexpected; during the "sitzkrieg" there had been occasional alarms of a new version of the Schlieffen Plan. Yet the defenders were singularly ill prepared to meet it. The combined French, British, Belgian, and Dutch armies were approximately equal to the Germans by actual numerical count, but they were fatally inferior in organization and technique, particularly in the employment of mechanized forces. In the air, Britain's Royal Air Force was qualitatively superior to the *Luftwaffe* but sadly deficient in numbers; the French Air Force was a joke, and most of the Dutch and Belgian aircraft were destroyed on the ground on the first day.

Worse still was the lack of any coordinated arrangements for meeting the German onslaught, although it had been known that such an attack was a reasonable possibility. Holland and Belgium, anxious to preserve their neutrality by ostentatiously avoiding any step that might be regarded as provocation by the Nazis, had refused to discuss joint defense plans either with the British and French or with each other. The British and French were in the awkward position of being unable to make detailed preparations for aiding two countries whom they would be morally obligated to help when the crisis came.

The Breakthrough. Resistance in Holland lasted only five days. The traditional Dutch water barriers were no impediment to an enemy who could fly over them, and there were fifth columnists to paralyze the defenders. While German infantry poured over the frontier, airborne troops seized the airport at Rotterdam. The city itself was bombed mercilessly, the attack lasting for some time after it had surrendered. Meanwhile, a still greater catastrophe was developing in Flanders. The French high command calculated that the major German offensive would follow substantially the route taken by Moltke's armies in 1914; the possibility of a serious threat through the rugged Ardennes country, just beyond the northern terminus of the Maginot Line, was discounted. It was here, nevertheless, that the German armored divisions were concentrated, and on 14 May they reached the Meuse at Sedan, a name of ill omen for French arms. Seven days later the German spearhead reached the English Channel at Abbeville, driving a wedge between the Belgian, British, and French forces in Flanders and the main French armies to the south.

To make matters worse, on 28 May King Leopold of Belgium, against the wishes of his cabinet, ordered his troops to lay down their arms. While the French and British governments had some advance warning of Leopold's intentions, they had reasonable grounds for indignation in that, after the breakthrough on the Meuse, they had kept their armies in Flanders only at Leopold's urgent request.

Dunkirk. In the circumstances the exultant Nazis seemed fully justified in proclaiming to the world the impending annihilation of the trapped French and British armies, but they were wrong. Inundations and a heroic rear guard stopped the tanks, R.A.F. planes operating from England checked the *Luftwaffe,* considerably aided by a two-day fog, and between 29 May and 4 June a hastily assembled mass of small craft evacuated 335,000 men from the beaches of Dunkirk. Magnificent as the achievement was, it was still, as Churchill pointed out at the time, a major defeat. The rescued men were exhausted and disorganized; their artillery, tanks, and transport had been completely lost.

The Germans then turned on the remaining French armies, most of which had been deployed on an improvised line along the Somme. Total

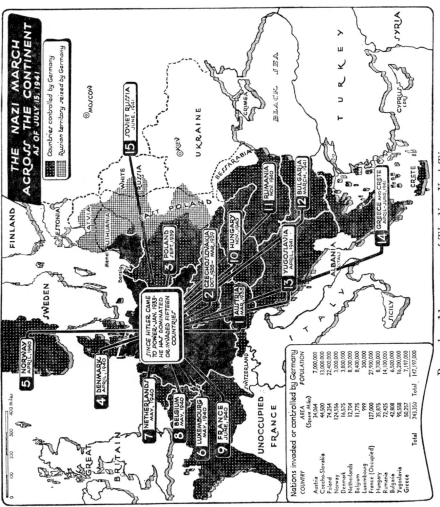

Reproduced by courtesy of *The New York Times*.

collapse followed rapidly. Paris was declared an open city and abandoned without a struggle; the Maginot Line, on which France had expended so much money and effort, was taken from the rear; and on 16 June Premier Reynaud resigned and was succeeded by Marshal Pétain, who immediately asked Hitler for an armistice. Prior to his fall, Reynaud had made a despairing appeal to Roosevelt for aid which the American President was in no position to give, both because the "clouds of aeroplanes" requested by Reynaud did not exist and because, as the President pointed out, only Congress could commit the United States to active intervention. To Reynaud also fell the unpleasant task of asking Great Britain to release France from its promise not to conclude a separate peace. The British countered with a proposal to unite the two countries, but when it was rejected they reluctantly assented to the French appeal, on condition that the French fleet be sent to British ports.

In the midst of these events Italy's entry into the war on 10 June was almost ludicrous. Mussolini decided that he had better join in and claim his share of the spoils before it was all over. His intervention was not noteworthy.

Hitler's attitude toward his victory was symbolized by his conducting the armistice negotiations in Foch's railway car[1] in the Forest of Compiègne, in the precise spot where the armistice of 1918 had been signed. The terms, which became effective on 25 June, were severe in the extreme. France was disarmed, and the country as far south as the Loire, plus the entire Biscayan coast, was placed under German occupation, the costs to be paid by France.

The Vichy Regime. The surrender involved a drastic change in France's internal structure. The constitution of the Third Republic was scrapped, and Pétain, with the title of Chief of State, became head of an authoritarian regime with its capital at Vichy. Pétain himself seems to have attempted to preserve as much independence for France as he could, but his profound distrust for democracy and his anti-British feelings inclined him to the belief that France's future lay in cooperating with the "New Order" in Europe. His right-hand man at the beginning was Pierre Laval, an open advocate of full collaboration with Germany. In the fall of 1940 Pétain and Laval quarreled, and the latter was replaced by Admiral Jean Darlan. Some Frenchmen refused to accept either defeat or the Vichy government. Led by General Charles de Gaulle, they established a Free French committee in London for the purpose of continuing their country's struggle.

Unattractive as it was, the Vichy regime was far from negligible. It controlled the bulk of the vast French empire—mainly, it would appear, because Hitler preferred not to goad France into further resistance by

[1] Later destroyed by the Nazis in their defeat.

pressing extensive colonial claims at the moment. French Equatorial Africa and later New Caledonia declared for De Gaulle; in the Far East Japan took advantage of French weakness to assume the "protection" of Indo-China. Allowing for these exceptions, Vichy remained in possession of substantial resources. Since Pétain was on bad terms with the British, the United States took on the task of maintaining good relations with him, in the hope of stiffening his resistance to German demands and preventing France from openly joining the Axis.

THE BATTLE OF BRITAIN

The position of Great Britain after the fall of France was distinctly unenviable. The victorious Germans were poised across the Channel, presenting Britain with a graver threat than she had faced in centuries. Her crowded island was within easy striking distance of German air bases in France and Belgium; her sea lanes were equally accessible to German aircraft and to submarines operating from French ports. The danger of invasion was still more menacing. The British could make such an attempt extremely costly, but it was by no means certain that they could stop it. Elsewhere in the world the outlook was equally gloomy. The collapse of France and the appearance of Italy jeopardized the British position in the Mediterranean. Spain was a potential enemy. In fact, Spain would probably have joined the Axis except that the devastation of her own civil war made it impossible for her to undertake a new conflict without substantial material aid, which Hitler was unwilling to give because he believed the war in the west to be virtually over. Japan was unfriendly to Britain, and Russia was still pursuing its policy of cooperation with Germany. The United States, although sympathetic, was torn by conflicts of opinion on the proper course to follow. The utmost the United States government could do at the moment was to make available to the British a quantity of surplus military equipment, most of it left over from the First World War.

The British faced this situation resolutely. Churchill's government, organized on a coalition basis, was given sweeping powers to mobilize all the nation's resources; Britain, indeed, eventually achieved a more thorough and total mobilization than Germany, where the personal ambitions and rivalries of the Nazi leaders sometimes interfered with the war effort. Yet in the days after Dunkirk is was an open question whether Britain would have time to make up for years of neglect and muddling.

The French Fleet. One problem that required immediate attention was the threat to the British naval position implicit in the uncertain status of the French fleet. At the time of France's surrender, many of the smaller units of the French Navy and a few of the heavy ships were in

British ports, but a powerful force lay at Oran in Algeria. On 3 July 1940 the British acted. They took possession of the French ships in their own ports. A strong British force appeared off Oran and presented the French admiral there with an ultimatum giving him the option of joining the British, interning his ships at a neutral, preferably American, port, or having them sunk. When no reply was forthcoming, the British waited for two hours beyond the time limit given and then opened fire. Most of the French ships in the harbor were sunk or put out of action. In the light of subsequent events this drastic action against a former ally was perhaps needless, since French naval men appear to have been sincere in their determination not to allow their ships to fall into Axis hands. Under the conditions of 1940, however, the British can hardly be censured for deciding that they could not afford to take a chance.

Air Attack on Britain. If the Germans had followed their victory over France with an immediate stroke at Britain, they might have won the war there and then. Instead, the British were given a priceless two months to prepare for the coming blow. The reason was that the German high command itself was surprised by the sudden collapse of France and was simply not ready for a new major operation. It needed time to formulate plans, to redeploy its forces, and to assemble the materials and equipment that would be needed. Consequently, the first phase of the German attack did not begin until the middle of August. It took the form of large-scale daylight air raids, concentrating on London but striking also at airfields, military bases, and industrial plants. The Germans undoubtedly hoped that Britain's will to resist might be broken by the bombings, but they did not really expect it. Their primary objective was to gain control of the air by forcing the Royal Air Force to expend itself in constant fighting. Then, and only then, a cross-Channel invasion would be feasible. The odds were in their favor. The *Luftwaffe* outnumbered the R.A.F. by about three to one, and while neutral observers conceded the qualitative superiority of British aircraft, few of them believed that this would offset the numerical disparity.

The conflict, one of the decisive battles of history and the first to be fought in the air, raged with mounting fury until mid-September. The damage inflicted by the Germans was severe but not crippling. The Air Raid Precautions services worked satisfactorily and the toll of civilian casualties, while substantial, proved to be lower than had been anticipated. In aircraft losses the figures were lopsidedly in favor of the British. The Stukas, tremendously effective against ground forces without aerial protection of their own, were unsuited for "strategic" bombing and were extremely vulnerable to fighter attack. Britain was also aided by early development in radar, which reduced the strain on R.A.F. pilots by making it unnecessary to keep patrols constantly in the air. Nor was the battle entirely defensive on the British side. The bomber command of the R.A.F. struck back vigorously at industrial and military targets in Germany and German-controlled territory and at the "invasion" ports on the European side of the Channel. By mid-September Nazi losses were becoming unsupportable. The tempo of their daylight raids began to slacken and in October they switched to night bombing, tacitly acknowledging the defeat of their attempt to win mastery of the air. The invasion was indefinitely postponed.

The Battle of the Atlantic. Despite this startling victory, Britain was far from out of the woods. The night bombings were destructive and no adequate defense against them existed. Worse still was the acute danger to Britain's vital overseas supply lines represented by the German conquest of Europe's Atlantic coast. German submarines and surface raiders had far easier access to the ocean trade routes than they had enjoyed in the First World War, and they were now supplemented by aircraft, which not only attacked shipping directly but also functioned as scouts for U-boats.

The principal defending force, the Royal Navy, had been deficient in destroyers and escort vessels when the war started, and subsequent events had not improved matters. The small warships suffered most in the operations off Norway and Flanders; moreover, the fall of France necessitated the diversion of British destroyers to the Mediterranean to perform the tasks previously assigned to the French Navy. This situation gradually improved. Among other factors, the growth of the Canadian Navy and the acquisition of fifty destroyers from the United States in September, 1940, under circumstances to be discussed below, helped to relieve the strain. Nevertheless, the winter of 1940–1941 witnessed a grim struggle in the North Atlantic, with the British holding on by a critically slender margin.

A dramatic interlude in this phase of the war was provided by the newly commissioned German battleship *Bismarck* late in May, 1941. In a brief but spectacular cruise she succeeded in destroying H.M.S. *Hood,* then the world's largest warship, but was in turn run down by air and naval forces and sunk only 400 miles from the safety of Brest.

The Battle of Britain may be said to have ended with the German invasion of Russia. The necessary transfer of Nazi air strength to the east brought a sharp diminution of raids on Britain and in fact transferred the aerial initiative in the west to the rapidly growing R.A.F. The U-boat war continued to rage unabated. This particular menace would not be overcome until the final years of the war. But by the summer of 1941 countermeasures, including increasingly active assistance from the United States, had produced sufficient improvement for Britain to be no longer fighting for mere survival.

THE MEDITERRANEAN AND THE BALKANS

While the Battle of Britain was raging in full force the war was spreading to southeastern Europe and across the Mediterranean to Africa. This development was in part a consequence of Italy's intervention; it was also, in part, because of a renewal of Germany's *Drang nach Osten*. With his hold on western Europe apparently secure, Hitler felt free to pursue his dreams of eastern conquest. Here German and Russian aspirations began to come into conflict, as they had done so often in the same region in the past. In anticipation of German moves, the Russians occupied the Rumanian province of Bessarabia (until 1919 part of the Russian Empire) in June, 1940. Beyond that, for the moment, the Kremlin was not prepared to go. It stood aside while Hungary and Rumania were converted into German satellites during the summer of 1940, with the *Führer* himself "mediating" their long-standing dispute over the possession of Transylvania. When Bulgaria was garnered into the Axis fold in March, 1941, the Russians were obviously disturbed, but they still did nothing.

Meanwhile, Mussolini was having his troubles in duplicating the victorious career of his Axis partner. Control of the Mediterranean should have passed into his hands with the fall of France, but it did not. Even the island of Malta, situated on Italy's doorstep and squarely in the middle of "Mare Nostrum," remained firmly in British hands; Malta, indeed, was destined to stage an epic resistance to Axis attacks and win for itself the title of "the most bombed spot on earth." The Italian military machine, except for its brief campaign against France after the latter was already beaten, did not move until September, 1940, when Marshal Rodolfo Graziani advanced some seventy miles into Egypt.

Italy's Invasion of Greece. The Duce then decided that the formula for conquest was to be found in picking a weak opponent, and on 28 October 1940 he launched what was planned as a blitzkrieg on Greece. The Greeks unfortunately refused to cooperate. Less than two weeks later the invaders were streaming back into Albania, avidly pursued by their intended victims. This repulse was only the beginning of Mussolini's troubles. On the night of 11 November British naval aircraft raided the great naval base at Taranto and crippled three of Italy's six battleships. A month later Graziani's army in Egypt was completely surprised by a British attack. By the first week of February, 1941, the Italians had been driven out of Cyrenaica, shedding 130,000 prisoners on the way.

Italian Reverses. The victors then turned on the Italian empire in East Africa. The Italian defenders, isolated from any hope of reinforcement, were subjected to a series of concentric attacks. On 5 April 1941, Addis Ababa, the capital of Ethiopia, was taken, and Haile Selassie returned to the throne from which Mussolini had driven him five years before. To cap the tale of disaster, on 28 March 1941 the remainder of the Italian battle fleet, putting to sea for reasons that still are not clear, fell afoul of the British Mediterranean fleet off Cape Matapan in Greece and suffered a stinging defeat.

Matapan represented the last Allied success in the Mediterranean area for a long time to come. Hitler had disliked Mussolini's invasion of Greece, since there was a good prospect that all southeastern Europe would succumb to the methods employed in Hungary and Rumania, but it was manifestly not to Germany's interest for Italy to drop out of the war altogether, something the majority of the Italian people would have been only too glad to do. Nazi military units moved into Italy in January, 1941, to prop up Mussolini's shaky regime, making Italy, as some of its inhabitants bitterly observed, one of the "occupied countries." German airmen made passage of the Sicilian channel hazardous for British convoys, and in North Africa the *Afrika Korps,* commanded by General Erwin Rommel, was able by the end of March to recover all of Cyrenaica except the fortress of Tobruk.

The reason for this sudden reversal was that a substantial part of the British army had been sent to Greece, where all signs pointed to an early German attack. The regent of Yugoslavia, Prince Paul, signed a pact with Hitler on 24 March providing for economic cooperation and allowing Germany the right to send military materials through Yugoslavian territory. This, however, was more than the people would accept. With the Serbs leading the way, they staged a bloodless *coup d'état,* expelled Paul, and repudiated the treaty. For a few days the German position in the Balkans appeared to be seriously jeopardized.

German Intervention. Hitler, however, gave his opponents no time to consolidate and combine. On 6 April 1941 the Germans struck with the same devastating force that Poland and western Europe had already witnessed. The Yugoslav armies were dissolved in five days, although partisan bands, led by Draha Mihailovich and later by the Russian-sponsored Tito, maintained a resistance that the Germans were never able to put down. The Greeks and the British fought stubbornly but hopelessly for three weeks, driven from one position to another by the weight of German aerial and mechanized power. After a brief lull while they digested their gains on the mainland, the Germans took the island of Crete in May by a spectacular airborne invasion.

This victory, coupled with Rommel's drive to the Egyptian frontier, left the allies with poor prospects of holding the Near East if the Germans chose to press on. Their apparent invincibility emboldened a pro-Axis faction in Iraq to seize control of that country. The Germans, however, had other plans. Their Balkan campaign, indeed, had been an unwelcome diversion for them, since the necessity of undertaking it forced them to postpone their attack on Russia. The Nazis did send some aid to their Iraq adherents, transporting it through Syria with the connivance of the Vichy governor, but it was not enough to prevent the British from suppressing the revolt. Then, because the incident had focused attention on the danger of Axis domination of Syria, British and Free French troops occupied that country in June.

THE INVASION OF RUSSIA

The friendly relations established between Nazi Germany and the Soviet Union in August, 1939, could not in the nature of things have lasted indefinitely. Fundamental conflicts of philosophy and interest would eventually have resulted in a breach between the two. Russia could hardly feel secure with an aggressive Germany in control of the rest of Europe, and Hitler still cherished his dreams of *"Lebensraum"* in the east. Specific causes of friction began to appear with the German penetration into the Balkans, where the Soviets inherited the ambitions of Imperial Russia. It appears, moreover, that the Germans were irritated by the failure of the Soviets to deliver promised supplies and that the Nazi strategists felt themselves handicapped by uncertainty regarding Russia's intentions. Stalin, as a matter of fact, was too cautious to force a showdown while the Nazis were at the height of their power; nevertheless, in the fall of 1940 Hitler ordered plans to be drafted for an attack on the Soviet Union in the following spring.

As these preparations neared completion, a weird attempt was made to enlist Britain on the Nazi side. Rudolf Hess, next after Goering in the line of succession to Hitler, landed by parachute in Scotland on 10 May 1941. His mission apparently was to get in touch with some of the prominent Britons who had been sympathetic toward the Nazis during the 1930's and through their influence either persuade or compel the government to abandon the war against Germany. All he accomplished was to break his leg in landing and get himself interned as a prisoner of war.

The assault on Russia began on 22 June 1941. Germany was joined by Hungary, Rumania, and Finland, and supported by an Italian army and "volunteers" from Spain and Vichy France. The pope, however, refused to recognize the Nazis as the champions of Christian civilization. One interesting result was that Communist parties throughout the world, including the United States, performed an intellectual somersault overnight. A war which until this point had been "capitalistic and imperialistic" now became a momentous struggle for human freedom.

The magnitude of this new conflict makes description impossible. The Germans and their allies are estimated to have deployed nine million men for their initial assault, on a battle front extending from Finland to the Black Sea. Since their mobilization was still incomplete, the Russians were probably inferior in numbers at the outset. In the first week the Axis tide swept over most of the territory acquired by the Soviets since 1939 and on into Russia itself.[2]

The German Objectives. There were three main German attacks: toward Leningrad in the north, toward Moscow in the center, and into the Ukraine in the south. The drive on Leningrad reached the outskirts of the city early in September, where it joined another force coming from Finland. Leningrad was surrounded, but it was never captured. The offensive against Moscow, which represented the major German effort, was held up for almost two months by bitter fighting around Smolensk. In the Ukraine the going was somewhat easier; by the end of November the Germans had overrun almost the entire territory, penetrating as far as Rostov on the Don.

Thus, as winter approached, the Germans had made immense gains but had not broken Russian resistance. In October they made a great effort to reach a decision by taking Moscow; in fact, at the end of that month the *Führer* himself announced that the last Soviet armies had been destroyed. He was apparently misinformed. Russian reinforcements and bad weather halted the Nazis at the gates of the capital, and on 4 December the German high command announced the suspension of further offensive operations. At almost the same time the Russians recaptured Rostov. The significance of these events was somewhat obscured at the time by the dramatic outbreak of war in the Pacific, but it was nonetheless substantial. Nazi hopes for a blitz victory over the Soviet Union had been frustrated.

Aid to Russia. As soon as Russia was attacked, Winston Churchill, although a long-standing foe of communism, pledged the wholehearted support of Great Britain in the common struggle against nazism. Material aid was given to the limit of Britain's capacity, and the United States government extended Lend-Lease to include the Soviet Union. As in the First World War, the great difficulty was the problem of getting supplies to Russia. The most direct route was to Murmansk and Archangel, but it was exposed to attack by German air and naval forces based in northern Norway. Subsequently, an alternative route was opened through Iran, relatively free from attack but requiring a long voyage around Africa and then transportation over a very inadequate rail and highway system. Despite these handicaps, supplies were delivered, at a heavy cost in men

[2] In many of these regions the German troops were greeted as liberators, but most of this good will was quickly dissipated by the brutality and racial fanaticism of the Nazis.

and ships in the case of the "Murmansk run." This contribution to the Russian war effort was given a very grudging acknowledgment by the Soviet government.

THE UNITED STATES AND THE WAR

The reaction of the United States to the outbreak of war in 1939 has already been described. The ensuing winter brought no new developments. Public opinion was beginning to divide between those who wished to give "all aid short of war" to the Allies and those who advocated strict isolationism, but for the moment the lull in the war made it appear that the repeal of the arms embargo would be as far as the United States needed to go. In January, 1940, President Roosevelt sent Sumner Welles to Europe to explore the possibilities of making peace, on the sound assumption that the best and indeed the only way to keep the conflict from spreading was to terminate it. The mission was futile; Welles himself concluded that American efforts in this direction would have no effect on Hitler unless they were backed by a threat to enter the war.

The Foreign-policy Debate. The events of the spring of 1940, culminating with the fall of France, came as a profound shock to the people of the United States. With France gone and Britain's future in doubt, they were faced with the unpleasant prospect of having to live in a world of aggressive and well-armed dictatorships, with a German-dominated Europe on one side of them and a Japanese-dominated Orient on the other. That a bitter and angry debate on American policy ensued is not surprising. The majority of the people agreed with President Roosevelt and Secretary of State Hull that the proper course for the United States was to give all possible aid to the countries still resisting the Axis and at the same time to arm the nation against future eventualities, but a substantial minority clung to isolationism. The dispute transcended party lines. While the Republicans in Congress were generally isolationist, an outstanding Republican editor, William Allen White, was the organizer of the Committee to Defend America by Aiding the Allies. Moreover, in June, 1940, two "interventionist" Republicans, Henry L. Stimson, Hoover's Secretary of State, and Frank Knox, Landon's running mate in 1936, entered the Roosevelt Cabinet as Secretary of War and Secretary of the Navy respectively.

On the other side the principal isolationist organization, the America First Committee, counted both the Democratic Senator Wheeler of Montana and the Republican Senator Nye of North Dakota among its chief spokesmen, along with such nonpolitical figures as Charles A. Lindbergh and the committee's chairman, Robert E. Wood, president of Sears, Roebuck. Although most of the isolationists were sincere and patriotic individuals, the verdict of history is likely to be that they were tragically blind to the facts of life. Under conditions as they existed in 1940 and 1941, for the United States to remain completely aloof from the war was to ensure an Axis victory, a fact of which the Axis powers themselves and their sympathizers in the United States were fully aware. The America First Committee soon found itself in embarrassing association with native fascist groups like Father Coughlin's social justice organization and with openly pro-Axis bodies like the German-American Bund.

Preliminary Defense Measures. Under the pressure of emergency Congress adopted a far-reaching program for building up American military strength. The two-ocean navy bill of May, 1940, authorized a 70 per cent increase in the fleet, and substantial appropriations were made to increase aircraft production. The army presented a more controversial problem, since the only effective way of raising the necessary man power was by conscription. It required a prolonged debate before Congress passed the Burke-Wadsworth Act on 16 September 1940, providing for the first peacetime draft in American history. The proponents of the measure had to make two concessions to get it accepted; the term of service was limited to twelve months and the number of men drafted in any one year was not to exceed 900,000.

Since these measures would take time to complete, the administration was faced with the problem of bolstering resistance to the Axis by whatever expedients were available until the United States could mobilize its resources and make up its mind what to do with them. One distinctly encouraging factor was the staunch support given by the other American republics. The possibility that Germany might lay claim to French or Dutch possessions in the Caribbean was blocked by the Act of Havana (27 July 1940) in which the American republics jointly forbade the transfer of territory in the Western Hemisphere without their consent. In effect, the Monroe Doctrine became a multilateral rather than a unilateral policy. Then, on 3 September 1940, President Roosevelt and Prime Minister Churchill negotiated an executive agreement whereby the United States transferred fifty of its First World War destroyers to the British and Canadian navies in exchange for leases on a chain of bases from Labrador to British Guiana.

As the American position slowly clarified, the Axis powers resorted to the only weapon they understood—intimidation. On 27 September 1940 Germany, Italy, and Japan signed the Tripartite Pact, pledging mutual support if any of the signatories were to be attacked by a major power "not at present involved in the European war or the Sino-Japanese conflict." The pact expressly stated that this definition did not mean the Soviet Union. The American rejoinder was to embargo the shipment of aviation gasoline and scrap iron and steel to Japan. A more drastic embargo had long been advocated by friends of China in the United States, but the administration had held off in the hope that Japanese-American relations would improve. The only step so far taken had been to abrogate the existing commercial treaty between the two countries. Now, however, with Japan definitely aligned in a hostile combination, the time had come to begin applying pressure.

The presidential election of 1940 can scarcely be said to have settled the issue of foreign policy. Because of the world crisis, President Roosevelt shattered precedent by running for a third term. His opponent was Wendell L. Willkie, who stampeded the Republican convention in a whirlwind campaign. Willkie was as ardent an advocate of aid to the Allies as Roosevelt. There was, therefore, no clear-cut expression of opinion, and the war issue was complicated by the purely internal considerations of the desirability of breaking the two-term tradition and the still active controversy over the New Deal. Willkie made a spirited race; his defeat appears to have been due mainly to the isolationist record of his party and the feeling that in this period of crisis an experienced hand was needed at the helm.[3]

Lend-Lease. With the election over, Roosevelt was free to give more positive direction to American policy. It was obvious that the United States would have to extend assistance on a much larger scale if the war was not to go to the Axis by default. In Europe, the British were holding out stubbornly, but to continue to do so they would need a continuous flow of American supplies, food, and raw materials as well as arms and munitions, and their financial resources were approaching exhaustion. In the Far East, Japan was in Indo-China and was pressing hard on the Chinese, whose sole life line for outside aid was the tortuous Burma Road. Nor were these the only claims on American support. The possibility of a victorious Axis turning in the direction of South America was not to be ignored, and Japan was known to be casting covetous eyes on the tremendous resources of the Netherland Indies.

The President's solution to this problem was the Lend-Lease Act, introduced into Congress in January, 1941, and given the symbolic number H.R. 1776. By its provisions the President was authorized to make available American material of all kinds to any nation whose defense was vital to the security of the United States. The debate over this measure was prolonged and heated, but it finally passed on 11 March 1941, by a two-to-one majority in both Houses of Congress, the vote representing fairly accurately the division of public opinion.

Passing a law, however, would not by itself stop the ·march of Axis aggression. Shortly after the enactment of Lend-Lease Wendell Willkie

---

[3] The popular vote was: Roosevelt, 27,243,466; Willkie, 22,304,755. The electoral vote was 449 to 82.

and others began calling for use of the navy to escort Lend-Lease shipments to their destinations on the ground that materials lying on the bottom of the ocean were contributing nothing to the security of the United States. The administration's response was to increase the activity of the neutrality patrol in the North Atlantic. Subsequently, when American forces occupied Iceland in August,[4] the United States Navy assumed responsibility for keeping the sea lanes safe that far.

Undeclared Naval War. By this time the United States and Germany were waging an undeclared naval war. In May a U-boat sank the American freighter *Robin Moor* while the vessel was on a voyage to Capetown, carrying a nonmilitary cargo and well outside any declared war zone. Clashes between American and German warships followed during the summer, with the Americans under instructions to fight only if attacked, until 11 September, when the President issued his "shoot-on-sight" order.

Meanwhile, as a natural corollary, the United States and Great Britain were drawing closer together. Their military staffs were drawing up plans for concerted action in the event that the United States became involved in the war, and on 14 August 1941 Roosevelt and Churchill met in Placentia Bay, Newfoundland, and issued the Atlantic Charter, an eight-point peace program substantially reaffirming Woodrow Wilson's Fourteen Points. There was no official commitment on the part of the United States to enter the war. There could be none, because the American people were still uncertain about their course; they wanted to see the Axis beaten but they also wanted to remain at peace. As late as November, 1941, a bill to extend the term of service under the draft act passed the House of Representatives by a vote of 203 to 202.

Pearl Harbor. In the end it was Japan that resolved the doubts of the American public. To the Japanese militarists the events of 1941 offered a glorious opportunity. With Russia and Britain both waging a struggle for existence in Europe, with the United States just beginning to arm and—as the Japanese saw it—torn by internal dissension, Dai Nippon could take whatever steps were necessary to complete its "Greater East Asia Coprosperity Sphere." The replacement of the moderately fascist Prince Konoye as premier in October, 1941, by the fanatical General Tojo indicated the direction of Japanese intentions. Until the moment to strike arrived, the United States could be lulled by peace negotiations, the more so as the American government was earnestly trying to find some way of ending the tension in the Pacific. Ambassador Nomura was joined in Washington by a special envoy, Saburu Kurusu, and the two exchanged

---

[4] The British had sent troops to Iceland following the German occupation of Denmark, but their ability to hold it against a determined German attack at this time was questionable.

views with Secretary of State Hull. There was no meeting of minds. The Japanese demanded resumption of trade relations and the withdrawal of American recognition of and aid to the Chiang Kai-shek government in China; Hull asked for the restitution of Japanese conquests and a non-aggression pact among the Pacific states. On 6 December 1941, President Roosevelt sent a personal appeal for peace to the Emperor Hirohito, but it was never delivered. On the following afternoon, while Nomura and Kurusu were again conferring with Hull, news arrived of the Japanese attack on Pearl Harbor.

It appears that high officials of the American government were aware that a Japanese stroke of some sort was impending, but they placed it in the Far East rather than in Hawaii. Consequently, the Japanese blow was, in a material sense, highly successful. The Americans were caught completely off guard, partly because of faulty coordination between the military and naval authorities. Of the eight American battleships in the harbor, two were destroyed and the other six were damaged. Most of the defending aircraft were caught on the ground. Fortunately the carriers of the Pacific Fleet were all away on various missions and so escaped, but the extent of the disaster ruled out any effective American counter-stroke against the Japanese for many months to come.

In the larger sense, however, the attack on Pearl Harbor can be adjudged one of the great blunders of history. It unified the American people as nothing else could have done. On the next day an angry Congress declared war on Japan with only one dissenting vote (Congress-woman Rankin of Montana). When, three days later, Hitler and Musso-lini declared war on the United States, Congress accepted this challenge also. The Second World War thus entered a new phase of terrifying magnitude.

42

The Second World War:
Global Conflict

The clouds of smoke rising from the burning battleships in Pearl Harbor heralded the expansion of the Second World War into a truly global conflict, whose termination would be marked by other clouds of smoke—the mushrooming columns sent up by the atom bombs at Hiroshima and Nagasaki. Between these points lay almost four years of war on a scale dwarfing everything that had gone before. While the struggle grew in intensity on the existing battle fronts, it also engulfed areas that had previously been remote from it, and men fought and died in places of whose existence they had been completely unaware. The combatants marshaled all their resources of science, technology, industry, and man power to meet the constant fresh demands of total war. For an anxious year after Pearl Harbor it appeared that the advantage gained by the Axis powers through their earlier preparation and surprise tactics would carry them to victory before their opponents—who may now properly be termed the United Nations—could mobilize their potentially greater strength. But by the end of 1942 the tide had turned, and the remainder of the war saw the United Nations slowly but conclusively pound the Axis to irretrievable destruction.

MOBILIZING AMERICA FOR WAR

When the United States found itself actively involved in the war, the role that it would have to play was clearly indicated. It would not only have to make a tremendous military effort, but it would have to super-

697

impose that effort on the task it had already undertaken, that of becoming the "Arsenal of Democracy." It was all to the good that several important preliminary steps had been taken. Orders from the Allied countries, America's own rearmament, and Lend-Lease had initiated the conversion of industry to war production, and a directing agency, the Office of Production Management, had come into existence. In January, 1942, the OPM became the War Production Board, headed by Donald M. Nelson. Under its auspices American industry was effectively geared for war. Mistakes, it is true, were made; examples of mismanagement and waste were not too difficult to find, and there was the inevitable war profiteering and occasional corruption. It would have been miraculous if a program of this size, carried out under the pressure of war, had been flawless, and the over-all results were so breath-taking as to make the defects negligible. In three years the United States produced some 300,000 aircraft, beginning with 50,000 in 1942. In that year American shipyards turned out 8,000,000 tons of merchant shipping, twice the figure for 1918, and in addition were constructing an entirely new navy. The automobile industry, besides producing tanks, poured out a torrent of trucks and jeeps, tractors and bulldozers, all as essential to victory as the combat vehicles. The list could be continued indefinitely, but these examples should suffice to indicate the extent of the industrial achievement.

Organizing the Home Front. The coming of open hostilities complicated the problem of economic conversion not only by increasing the demands on American production but also by curtailing supplies of some very essential materials. The Japanese conquests of 1942 shut off the existing sources of rubber, tin, and quinine. The destruction of tankers by U-boats and the necessity of using the available tanker tonnage for military purposes led to shortages of gasoline and fuel oil in the northeastern states. A special program for stimulating the manufacture of synthetic rubber had to be instituted, and gasoline and oil were rationed. Other commodities which became scarce because of wartime conditions were rationed also, although Americans suffered nothing like the drastic curtailment of living standards that the people of the other belligerents had to endure. The rationing system was operated by the Office of Price Administration, which also had the necessary but unpopular task of keeping the nation's economy stable against the inflationary pressure caused by the decline in the production of civilian goods while buying power was increasing under the stimulus of the "war boom."

The function of meeting the requirements of the armed forces for man power and also of filling the demands of the expanding war industries was performed by the War Manpower Commission. The selective service system worked, on the whole, satisfactorily, but the WMC lacked the authority to allocate labor to the industries where it was most needed. Some maladjustments developed, but it does not appear that essential production was seriously impeded. Labor disputes were mediated by a War Labor Board. While both the A.F. of L. and the CIO gave "no-strike" pledges and did their best to live up to them, the great acceleration of industrial production provided ample opportunities for friction. The marshaling of scientific and technical skill was done by the Office of Scientific Research and Development. Of its long list of achievements the most spectacular was, of course, the atomic bomb, a joint production of scientists of several nations, including some who had been driven from Germany by Nazi intolerance.

The Office of War Information had the dual task of keeping the public informed on the course and issues of the war and of attempting to present the ideals of the United Nations to the Axis peoples. There was also an Office of Censorship, although censorship at home was largely a matter of voluntary cooperation by the press and radio. The Office of Strategic Services secured information from enemy and neutral countries, while the Board of Economic Warfare worked to keep critical materials out of Axis hands.

Many of these agencies, it will be observed, had counterparts in the First World War. There was, however, one important step of the earlier conflict which was not repeated. The railroads remained under their own management, although supervised by the Office of Defense Transportation. This arrangement proved adequate to meet the heavy demands placed on the railways—heavier than could have been foreseen, because the acute shortage of shipping meant that much of the former coastwise commerce had to go by rail.

Strategic Planning. The administration of the American military effort fell to General George C. Marshall, Chief of Staff, and Admiral Ernest W. King, commander in chief of the Fleet. The basic pattern of American strategy was clearly determined by fairly obvious factors. The war against Japan was primarily a naval and aerial war. There would be no opportunity in the Pacific for the United States to employ major land forces until an invasion of Japan itself became feasible. A land front in China was out of the question; the Burma Road could not supply the Chinese armies, let alone a large-scale American expedition as well.

In Europe, on the other hand, the island of Britain was available as a base for an invasion of the Continent, and operations there would concentrate the principal armies of the United Nations, the American, British, and Russian, against the strongest of the Axis powers, Germany. For Britain and Russia this concentration was not a matter of choice. Britain was at war with Japan, but she could hardly divert much of her strength to the Far East while she was engaged in a life-and-death struggle at home in

Europe. Russia was not at war with Japan and would certainly avoid taking on any additional enemies while German armies occupied much of her territory. Moreover, the shortage of shipping caused by U-boat depredations made it much more economical to use the available tonnage for the relatively short haul to Europe rather than in the enormous distances of the Pacific. Thus, the most profitable course for the United States was to contain Japan while the bulk of the American armies assisted in destroying the European end of the Axis.

Prompt measures were taken to secure maximum cooperation between the United States and its allies. On 2 January 1942 twenty-six nations signed the United Nations Agreement at Washington, pledging mutual support until victory had been won. Lend-Lease was extended and elaborated to become an international arrangement with each participating country contributing to the best of its ability. With the exception of Argentina all the American republics either joined in the war or severed diplomatic relations with the Axis. Brazil, which formally entered the war on 22 August 1942, provided bases of inestimable value in controlling the South Atlantic and in functioning as links in the air route to West Africa, and Brazilian troops eventually fought in Italy. Military coordination among the Western powers was secured through a Joint Chiefs of Staff council in Washington. It was never possible to include the Soviet Union in this arrangement.

THE HIGH TIDE OF THE AXIS

For some time after Pearl Harbor it appeared that the war would be lost before the United States could bring its enormous resources to bear. The Japanese swept over the southwest Pacific area in a manner reminiscent of Hitler's blitzkriegs, and the Germans in 1942 expanded their conquests to the farthest points they were to reach.

In the Far East the Japanese followed up the blow at Pearl Harbor by striking simultaneously at Malaya, the Philippines, Hong Kong, Guam, and Wake. The last three, isolated by Japanese naval and air power, succumbed rapidly, all being in Japanese hands by Christmas Day, 1941. It early became evident that the Japanese had been underrated by their opponents, especially in the matter of aerial strength. The Zero fighter, in particular, was faster and more maneuverable than anything the United Nations could put in the air against it until late in 1942. Japan, moreover, was in a position to make replacements easily, while American or British fighter planes had to be carried on a long ocean voyage to reach the theater of combat. Ships were lacking for this purpose, and the supply of aircraft late in 1941 was woefully inadequate to meet the demands on it. Thus, the Japanese enjoyed almost complete mastery of the air during their opening campaigns.

Landings at various points in the Philippines were made on 8 December and gradually expanded until at the end of the month the outnumbered defenders, under the command of General Douglas MacArthur, withdrew into the rocky peninsula of Bataan. The one encouraging feature was that the Filipinos fought stubbornly and courageously against the invaders. In contrast, other colonial populations, in Malaya, Burma, and Indonesia, remained more or less indifferent spectators of the conflict.

Japanese Conquests. The main Japanese effort was directed at Malaya and the great British fortress of Singapore. There the tale of disaster was unrelieved. Thailand (Siam) capitulated to Japanese forces from Indo-China after one day's resistance. Then, on 10 December, United Nations naval strength in the Pacific, already weakened by the damage at Pearl Harbor, suffered another shattering blow when the two British capital ships based on Singapore, H.M.S. *Prince of Wales* and *Repulse,* were caught and sunk by Japanese aircraft while they were endeavoring to check landings on the Malayan peninsula. The defenders of Malaya, lacking both aerial and naval support, were inexorably driven southward into Singapore itself, and finally the city had to be surrendered on 15 February 1942.

At the same time, the Japanese were pushing into the Netherlands Indies, where they were opposed by determined but outnumbered Dutch forces and odds and ends of American, British, and Australian units. Because of their slender resources the defenders had to abandon the outlying islands and concentrate on trying to hold Java, the wealthiest and most populous of the Dutch Indies. But, although several telling blows were struck at the Japanese, Java could not be saved.

From Malaya and Thailand the Japanese pressed on into Burma, where they met both British and Chinese troops, the latter under the command of an American general, Joseph W. Stilwell. Neither Stilwell nor the British commander, Sir Harold Alexander, could do anything more than effect a masterly retreat; by the end of April the Japanese had closed the Burma Road and reached the borders of India. At the same time, they were able to allot larger forces to deal with the American-Filipino resistance on Bataan. The epic stand on Bataan ended on 9 April, when the defenders, weakened by exhaustion and lack of food, were finally overwhelmed. The fortress of Corregidor held out for another month. The commander of this last stand was General Jonathan Wainwright, since MacArthur had earlier been transferred to Australia to organize and lead the coming United Nations counteroffensive.

The Battle of Midway. The first three months of 1942, therefore, saw the Japanese gain possession of vast territories and reach positions threatening both Australia and India. At this point, however, they were stopped. They managed to occupy the Solomon Islands, but their further progress was arrested by the American naval victory in the Coral Sea, 4–7

May. A month later the Japanese suffered a still more serious check when they sent a powerful expedition against the Island of Midway. Although the forces engaged were small in comparison to those used later in the Pacific war, the Battle of Midway was one of the decisive sea fights of history. On the critical day, 4 June 1942, four Japanese aircraft carriers were sunk, at the cost of one American carrier, the U.S.S. *Yorktown*. From then on the initiative in the Pacific was in American hands, albeit somewhat precariously for the rest of 1942. A subsidiary Japanese move against Alaska gained them possession of the islands of Kiska and Attu, from which they were evicted a year later.

Farthest German Advances. In Europe, the winter of 1941–1942 saw the British again on the offensive in Libya and the Russians pushing the Germans back from some of their gains. Both, however, soon found themselves in worse straits than before. In June, 1942, the Eighth Army suffered a serious defeat which drove it back to El Alamein in Egypt, only 70 miles from Alexandria. There the Germans were held, although the Axis was so confident of victory that Mussolini in person crossed over to Africa in order to lead the triumphal entry into Cairo.

In Russia, meanwhile, the Germans made what was destined to be their last great offensive effort. With the coming of spring they brought the deliberate Russian winter advance to a halt and switched over to a massive onslaught of their own in the Ukraine, always a focus of Nazi ambitions. The Russian lines crumpled under the initial impact. By the end of summer the Germans had reached the Volga at Stalingrad and were pushing toward the oil fields of the Caucasus. The Russian retreat, however, had been anything but a rout. Stalingrad held firmly against a terrific battering by aircraft and artillery and against infantry assaults that produced hand-to-hand fighting not merely from house to house but from room to room. Once again, as so often happened in both the First and Second World Wars, German armies reached the one-yard line and then were unable to make the rest of the distance. When it became evident that Stalingrad could not be taken, the German generals pleaded with Hitler to withdraw the attacking troops from their exposed position, but the *Führer* refused to abandon an inch of ground.

To complicate the problems of the United Nations during this critical summer, German U-boat activities reached new heights of destructiveness. The entry of the United States into the war gave the submarines an opportunity to turn from the relatively well-guarded Atlantic convoys to the unprotected shipping along the American coast and in the Caribbean, and for some months they enjoyed rich pickings. For a time the losses outran even the accelerated shipbuilding production of the United States, and the decline in shipping tonnage threatened to cripple the entire United Nations war effort. Eventually the situation was brought under control by vigorous measures, including the building of hundreds of escort vessels and the provision of more adequate air cover.

THE UNITED NATIONS COUNTEROFFENSIVE

The first indication that the Axis was beginning to rotate in reverse was the landing of American marines on Guadalcanal, 7 August 1942. Guadalcanal, at the southern end of the Solomons chain, offered a site for an airfield which, in conjunction with the fine adjacent harbor of Tulagi, would give the Japanese a base dangerously close to the sea route between the United States and Australia. They had occupied the island at the time of the Battle of the Coral Sea, and work on the airfield was in progress. It was primarily to deny them this position that the American attack was staged; with most of its available resources earmarked for forthcoming operations in Europe, the United States could not contemplate a major stroke against Japan. But, like many "limited-liability" operations, the Guadalcanal campaign grew into something much larger than the original estimates.

Guadalcanal. The landing took the Japanese by surprise. The airfield, renamed Henderson Field,[1] was secured without difficulty, although there was hard fighting at Tulagi. Then came near-catastrophe. On the night of 10 August a Japanese naval force arrived undetected off Savo Island, a little island about halfway between Guadalcanal and Tulagi, and sank one Australian and three American cruisers. The blow was severe enough to necessitate the withdrawal of the transports that were carrying supplies for the marines, so that it was impossible for them to clear the rest of Guadalcanal, and the Japanese were given time to send reinforcements.

For the next four months the situation was precarious, sometimes desperately so. The marines hung grimly on to Henderson Field in the face of "banzai" attacks by fanatical Japanese, naval and aerial bombardments, malaria, and fatigue, while both sides struggled to establish the control of the surrounding waters that would mean the difference between victory and defeat. The intensity of the fighting may be judged by the fact that six major naval battles were fought around Guadalcanal, and the body of water between Guadalcanal and Tulagi was dubbed, with excellent reason, "Iron Bottom Bay."

The balance began to swing to the United States at the end of October. On the 26th of that month the Battle of Santa Cruz resulted in the crippling of Japanese carrier strength, although the United States lost the U.S.S. *Hornet,* which in the previous April had carried General Doo-

---

[1] In memory of Major Lofton Henderson, who was killed leading a squadron of marine dive bombers at Midway.

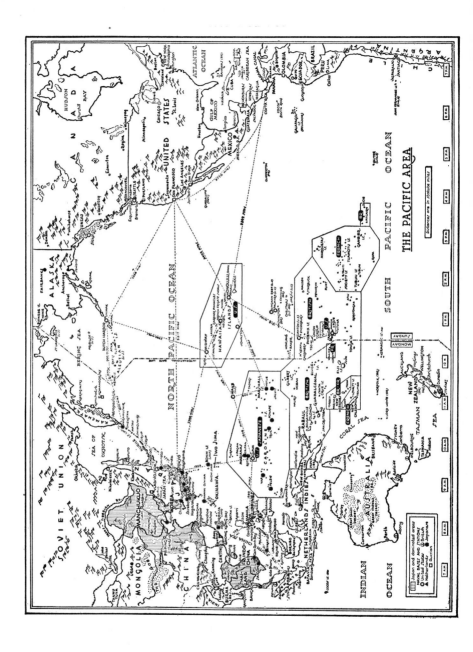

704

little's B-25's on their dramatic raid on Tokyo. In mid-November the Japanese made another great effort, this time to meet a crushing defeat. After that Guadalcanal was written off by the Imperial high command, although fighting continued until January, 1943.

New Guinea and Bougainville. Concurrently with the Guadalcanal campaign, Australian and American troops under the command of General MacArthur first of all checked a Japanese drive on Port Moresby in New Guinea and then took the offensive themselves, an effort of appalling difficulty involving the crossing of the 14,000-foot Owen Stanley Mountains and fighting through some of the world's most primitive jungle. Not until the end of January, 1943, were positions on the northern coast of New Guinea secured.

This dual pressure on the Japanese continued through 1943. While MacArthur worked his way along the New Guinea coast, Admiral William F. Halsey's forces "climbed up the ladder" of the Solomons, taking Munda on New Georgia Island in August and establishing themselves at Empress Augusta Bay on Bougainville early in November. Viewed against the whole picture of the war, these achievements seemed minor. Only a few points on the periphery of Japan's conquests had been recovered, and each had witnessed a long and stubborn fight. Yet more had been achieved than appeared on the surface. The damage to Japan's naval and aerial strength was severe, and the experience gained in these early assaults went far to guarantee the success of the later major invasions.

North Africa. The real weight of the growing United Nations military strength was falling upon the Axis in Europe. On 23 October 1942 the British Eighth Army, reorganized under General Sir Bernard Montgomery, unleashed a tremendous onslaught at El Alamein. Once again the British overran Cyrenaica, but this time they kept on going. As Rommel retreated, a new threat to him appeared at the other end of North Africa when American and British troops landed in Morocco and Algeria on 8 November 1942.

The North African invasion was a scheme accepted by President Roosevelt, somewhat reluctantly, as a substitute for an immediate "second front" in Europe, which the Russians were demanding but for which the British felt they were not ready. The enterprise, which was commanded by General Dwight D. Eisenhower, involved delicate political and military considerations—in other words, the reaction of the French was uncertain. General de Gaulle, whose relations with the United States government were not cordial, was ruled out of the picture on the ground that he would be unacceptable to French officials in Africa, and hopes were placed on General Henri Giraud, who had been smuggled out of France after escaping from a German prison camp.

Landings took place at Casablanca, Oran, and Algiers and were resisted at all three points. By a fortuitous circumstance, however, Admiral Darlan was in Algiers and decided to change sides, with the result that on 11 November he ordered resistance to cease and was recognized by the Americans and British as the supreme French authority in North Africa. His sudden conversion was of unquestioned military value. It greatly facilitated the occupation of Algeria and Morocco by forces which were at best somewhat slender (the Anglo-American expedition numbered about 100,000), and it gave the United Nations possession of the strategic port of Dakar without a struggle. Politically Darlan was an embarrassment because of his previous record. He conveniently disappeared from the scene when a young Frenchman assassinated him on 24 December, but bickering continued in North Africa between the partisans of Giraud and De Gaulle.

The immediate German response to the North African invasion was to occupy Vichy France. There was no opposition, except that the French fleet in Toulon was scuttled by its crews. German and Italian forces were also rushed to Tunisia. It had been hoped on the United Nations' side that this province could be secured too, but men and materials were lacking to effect a landing there simultaneously with those farther west. As soon as Algeria was under control, troops were sent into Tunisia. The proximity of Sicily, however, gave the Axis a decided edge in building up strength in this area, and several of Eisenhower's divisions, moreover, had to be held on the border of Spanish Morocco until Franco's attitude clarified.[2] Consequently, although British troops drove to within a few miles of Tunis, they were unable to take the city, and winter weather compelled the suspension of further operations.

The Casablanca Conference. During this period of deadlock Roosevelt and Churchill met at Casablanca for a conference. Stalin declined an invitation to attend, and no Chinese representative was included because the discussions were primarily concerned with Europe. In addition to formulating plans for the immediate future, the Casablanca Conference announced that no terms short of unconditional surrender would be granted the Axis. As a war measure, this attitude was expected to solidify the United Nations, principally by offering the suspicious Russians a guarantee of the good faith of their allies; whether it offered a satisfactory basis for peacemaking was another matter.

Meanwhile, Rommel was wending his way across Tripolitania with Montgomery hard on his heels. The desert armies arrived in Tunisia at the end of January, and the last phase of the North African campaign began. Attacks by Rommel on American and French positions in southern Tunisia gained some initial successes but then were repulsed. About this

[2] Franco took the eminently prudent course of avoiding commitments until it was clear which side was going to win.

time Rommel was recalled to Germany, since he had become a great hero to the German people and it would be a severe blow to their morale if he were involved in a surrender. By 6 May 1943 the allied armies were battering the last Axis positions. Both Tunis and Bizerte fell two days later, and the remaining Axis troops were penned into the narrow peninsula of Cape Bon. United Nations' sea and air power eliminated any possibility of an Axis "Dunkirk." So, despite personal orders from the *Führer* to fight to the end, the Aryan supermen threw in the towel.

Overthrow of Mussolini. The victors had no intention of resting on their laurels. Just two months later American and British forces landed on Sicily and Italian resistance collapsed. Important Fascist leaders, including his son-in-law, Count Ciano, turned against Mussolini, and on 25 July King Victor Emmanuel dismissed him and placed him under arrest. His successor, Marshal Badoglio, opened peace negotiations, but unfortunate delays prevented the Italian surrender from becoming official until 8 September, the day on which American and British forces landed at Salerno.

The delay enabled the Germans to find out what was going on and take countermeasures which the weak Badoglio government could not prevent. They rescued Mussolini and set him up as head of an "Italian Fascist Republic," secured themselves in central and northern Italy, and almost repulsed the Salerno landing. The beachhead was made good after a furious struggle, and the subsequent northward advance resulted in the capture of Naples. Then a deadlock developed in rugged mountain country between Naples and Rome. If it was disappointing that the Germans still held most of Italy, yet the United Nations had made substantial gains. The Italian armed forces were out of the war, except for the few partisans of Mussolini. What was perhaps more important, the surrender of the Italian Navy and the occupation of Sicily and southern Italy reopened the Mediterranean to United Nations traffic, as well as releasing Anglo-American naval units for service elsewhere.

The Stalingrad Disaster. Although the Nazis had staved off an immediate catastrophe in Italy, their troubles were mounting ominously. A month after Montgomery's attack at El Alamein opened, the Russians launched a tremendous drive in the Stalingrad area. The German Sixth Army in front of Stalingrad could not withdraw in time; it was encircled and completely destroyed.

The home front was also a discouraging prospect for the Germans. American and British air power was subjecting the Reich to an increasingly intensive round-the-clock bombing. This constant battering put a heavy strain on Germany's productive capacity, which was also suffering from accumulating shortages of man power and materials. The manpower problem was alleviated by forced labor from the occupied countries, but nothing could be done about materials. Moreover, as the prospect of a United Nations victory grew brighter, the people of the occupied countries became more and more restive. Underground movements were scarcely checked by the ruthlessness of the Gestapo; indeed, as German repression grew more severe, the hostility of the conquered peoples became fiercer.

THE INVASION YEAR

Since 1942 American troops and supplies had been flowing into Britain in an uninterrupted stream to prepare for the invasion of western Europe that would come in due time. Late in 1943 General Eisenhower was recalled from the Mediterranean to take command of this larger undertaking, along with General Montgomery, who was to command the ground forces. The campaign in Italy was entrusted to General Alexander, whose task was to divert German attention as much as possible to this subsidiary theater. It was a thankless assignment. All through the winter American troops battled vainly for the mountain stronghold of Cassino, which barred the road to Rome. A landing at Anzio, just south of Rome, on 22 January 1944, failed to break the deadlock for the moment, but a new general offensive in May resulted in the capture of the Eternal City just before the great invasion struck in France.

The Invasion of Normandy. D Day was 6 June 1944. American, British, and Canadian troops, escorted by a tremendous armada of warships and covered by 11,000 aircraft, went ashore on the bay of the Seine, between the mouth of the river and the Cotentin Peninsula. The Germans were harassed by French partisans, now formally organized as the French Forces of the Interior, and their communications were so thoroughly smashed by aerial bombardment that they had difficulty moving their reserves to the combat area. Moreover, during the first critical days of the invasion, the German high command, apprehensive that a second landing might take place north of the Seine, kept an entire army out of action.

The first stage of the invasion was completed when American troops captured Cherbourg on 27 June. Then followed a dogged, yard-by-yard advance through the hedgerows of Normandy until on 26 July American forces crashed through the German defenses at St. Lô and broke into open country. A general German retreat then followed, accelerated by a fresh American landing on the French Mediterranean coast on 15 August. French and American troops entered Paris on the 25th and swept on to the German border. The British and Canadians, who had had the task of containing the bulk of the German forces at their end of the Normandy beachhead, raced along the Channel coast into Belgium, taking the great port of Antwerp intact. On their way they overran the sites from which the Germans had been launching "robot" bombs, or "V-bombs," at England.

The advance came to a halt in front of the Siegfried Line, mainly because Eisenhower's troops had outrun their supplies. This was a factor on which the Germans had counted. They assumed that no invasion could succeed without gaining possession of a major port; accordingly, they held on to most of the French ports and demolished those they had to give up. They failed, however, to foresee that the allies would bring two prefabricated ports along with them (one was destroyed in a gale, but the other remained in service until the end of the war) or lay pipe lines across the Channel. The lack of port facilities was nevertheless a serious handicap, not overcome until Antwerp was opened. An unsuccessful effort was made in September to end the war in the west quickly by landing airborne troops in Holland to turn the northern end of the Siegfried Line.

Russian Advances. If the Germans had gained a respite, their outlook was still gloomy, with both frontiers of the fatherland being assailed at the same time. On the eastern front there was no interruption in the Russian advance that had begun in the summer of 1943. Shortly after the Normandy landing a series of massive assaults drove the Germans across the 1939 borders of the Soviet Union. Soviet armies then poured into both the Balkan and Baltic states, to knock Germany's satellites out of the war by the end of the year. In the center of the front a regrettable incident occurred. When Russian troops reached the Vistula opposite Warsaw on 1 August 1944, the Polish underground in the city promptly rose, only to be left to fight a hopeless battle by itself for the next six weeks. Recriminations naturally followed. The Russians claimed that they had to bring up supplies and reinforcements before they could undertake an assault on the city, while the Poles insisted that they had risen on the strength of Russian assurances of support. It was interesting that while the Western powers tried to supply the Poles by air from Italy, the Russians on the other side of the Vistula made no corresponding effort.

However ominous this incident might be for the future, it gave little comfort to the Germans. The declining fortunes of the Reich were sharply outlined when an attempt was made to assassinate Hitler on 20 July 1944. Although the plot miscarried and was immediately suppressed, it gave evidence of a stronger current of anti-Nazi opinion than had been believed to exist. Among the conspirators were many high-ranking generals, including Rommel. At the time of the plot he was hospitalized because of injuries received during an air attack. He later committed suicide at the suggestion of the Gestapo.

The Central Pacific. No more vivid illustration of the rapid expansion of United Nations military strength can be offered than the fact that it was possible to strike devastating blows at Japan while the invasion of Europe was in progress. Beginning with the sanguinary conquest of Tarawa in the Gilbert Islands in November, 1943, American forces under the general command of Admiral Chester W. Nimitz began to move westward through the Japanese islands in the central Pacific. This direct route was now practicable because the United States Navy had been built up to the point where its strength relative to its Japanese opponent was overwhelming. Supplementing Nimitz's drive were MacArthur's steady advance along the coast of New Guinea, bombing of the Japanese homeland by giant B-29's—flying from bases in China and later from Pacific islands as they were taken over by the United States—and extremely damaging attacks on Japanese shipping by American submarines.

Early in 1944 the principal bases in the Marshall Islands fell into American hands. The next jump was to Saipan in the Marianas, which was attacked on 15 June and taken after three weeks of fanatical resistance. Nearby Guam was recovered shortly afterward. An attempt by the Japanese fleet to intervene resulted only in defeat at the hands of American forces commanded by Admiral Raymond Spruance, the victor of Midway.

The Return to the Philippines. Current plans then contemplated attacks by the Nimitz forces on Yap and the Palau Islands while MacArthur effected a landing on Mindanao, after which the two would combine for a landing on Leyte. During a cruise off the Philippines in September, however, Admiral Halsey became convinced that Japanese air strength in the Philippines and Formosa was much less than had been estimated and recommended that the intermediate steps be dropped and the Leyte invasion moved up. His suggestion was accepted both by MacArthur and by the Joint Chiefs of Staff, who happened to be attending a Roosevelt-Churchill conference in Quebec at the time. The Palau expedition was on its way and was allowed to proceed, but the others were canceled and the Leyte invasion began on 20 October 1944, fulfilling MacArthur's pledge to the Filipinos that he would return.

The Japanese, now desperate, threw all their remaining naval strength into a bold but badly coordinated effort to repel the invasion. Three fleets converged on Leyte Gulf. The first, coming through Surigao Strait, was annihilated by the American Seventh Fleet, five of whose six battleships had been victims of the attack on Pearl Harbor. The second, approaching from north of Luzon, was smashed up by Halsey. The third and most powerful Japanese force managed to get through the San Bernardino Strait and fight a weird battle with a force of American escort carriers. For a time disaster threatened the Americans, but the Japanese broke off the action and withdrew. After the Battle of Leyte Gulf, the Japanese Navy ceased to be a factor in the war.

The Japanese in the Philippines were in the same position as the

Americans had been in three years before. Deprived of naval and aerial support, their eventual destruction was assured. Leyte was in MacArthur's hands by the end of 1944; on 9 January 1945 his troops landed at Lingayen Gulf, and a month later they entered Manila. Bataan and Corregidor were taken soon afterward. What remained then was the somewhat protracted process of mopping up isolated Japanese units.

The invasion year was an election year for the United States, but the political campaign was noteworthy only in that Franklin D. Roosevelt was elected for the fourth time. His Republican opponent, Governor Thomas E. Dewey of New York, failed to convince the voters that a change of administration in wartime was desirable. Roosevelt was not destined to see the final victory of the United Nations. On 12 April 1945 he died of a cerebral hemorrhage. On his running mate of 1944, Harry S. Truman, devolved the burden of ending the war and restoring peace.

THE END OF THE WAR

The last days of Nazi Germany began with a desperate gamble to dislocate the western front before the onrushing Soviets crossed the eastern frontiers of the Reich. Taking advantage of poor flying weather, which screened them from aerial observation, the Germans mustered their last mobile reserves for a stroke through the Ardennes, the scene of their great triumph of 1940. This sector was thinly held by the allies in order to concentrate troops for attacks elsewhere. The German objective was to reach the Meuse and if possible Antwerp.

The offensive, which was launched on 16 December 1944, came as a complete surprise. In a few days the German armored divisions drove a bulge 50 miles deep into the American First Army. But it was a bulge and not a breach; 1944 was not 1940. American units, although isolated and frequently surrounded, fought back stubbornly and were able to delay the German advance sufficiently for effective countermeasures to be organized. The key highway center of St. Vith was held for several critical days before the defenders finally withdrew, and the equally important town of Bastogne remained firmly in American hands. To a demand for the surrender of Bastogne, the American commander, General McAuliffe, replied with the single word, "Nuts." The Battle of the Bulge faded out in January, 1945, with the Germans hastily abandoning all their gains. The effort had cost the Nazis heavily. Their losses in men and equipment were irreplaceable, and they were left weaker than ever to face the heavy blows that were about to fall.

Victory in Europe. The Battle of the Bulge, was scarcely over before the Allied advance was resumed. A concerted drive eliminated all German resistance west of the Rhine by 10 March 1945, and an unexpected windfall put American troops across the river at one point. A patrol found the Ludendorff Bridge at Remagen still intact and promptly secured it before the Germans could touch off the demolition charges. A substantial bridgehead was established, although the bridge itself was so damaged by German artillery fire that it fell into the river ten days later. While the Western armies were deploying along the Rhine, the Russians were massing on the Oder after overrunning the German defenses in Poland and East Prussia.

At the end of March the line of the Rhine was forced in a brilliant operation and the Allied forces swept over western Germany. Simultaneously the Russians crossed the Oder to reach Berlin, which they took on 2 May after twelve days of savage street fighting. Just before the end came, both Hitler and Goebbels committed suicide. Meanwhile, on 25 April, American and Russian patrols had met on the Elbe at Torgau, and to the great disappointment of the Nazis greeted each other cordially. In Italy also the long grueling campaign finally terminated as the British Eighth and American Fifth Armies broke down the last German defenses. A formal surrender was effected on 2 May. Mussolini attempted to flee to Switzerland but was caught by Italian guerillas and executed.

When Hitler's death was revealed, Admiral Karl Doenitz proclaimed himself the *Führer's* designated successor. He tried to play off the Western powers against the Soviets in negotiations for an armistice, but, receiving no encouragement and with his forces laying down their arms piecemeal, he signed a formal surrender at Rheims on 7 May 1945. A day later the ceremony was repeated in Berlin.

Closing in on Japan. These events left Japan alone in an unfriendly world. The neutrals whose sympathies had inclined toward the Axis—Spain and Argentina—were now demonstrating ostentatious friendship for the United Nations; Argentina went so far as to declare war, not to indulge in any fighting but to gain admission to the San Francisco Conference scheduled for April, 1945. Moreover, although the Japanese were still unaware of it, a conference between Roosevelt, Churchill, and Stalin at Yalta in the Crimea (3–11 February 1945) had produced, among other things, a pledge from the Russian dictator to enter the war in the Far East three months after the termination of hostilities in Europe.

As it was, Japan's existing opponents were closing in relentlessly. Late in February, 1945, United States forces landed on Iwo Jima in the Bonins, 750 miles from Tokyo and the site of airfields from which fighter planes could escort bombers to Japan. It took a month of savage fighting to put down Japanese resistance, since the defenders held out in caves and pillboxes with a fanatical obstinacy which might have been admirable if it had not been so completely futile. The same story was repeated at Okinawa in the Ryukyu Islands. Here the initial landing on 1

April was almost unopposed; yet the final subjugation of the island was not completed until 21 June. The naval units engaged in this campaign and supporting operations suffered heavily from attacks by kamikazes, or suicide planes.

Nevertheless, by summer positions had been secured from which a constant torrent of bombs could be rained on the cities of Japan. At the same time Japan's stolen empire was falling apart. While the Iwo and Okinawa campaigns were in progress, the British recovered Burma and began, in cooperation with the Dutch, to work on Indonesia. The Chinese, after eight weary years of harrying by a better equipped foe, at last saw the Japanese begin to relax their hold.

The Atomic Bomb. A stunning climax was reached in August. On the 8th Russia declared war on Japan, and Soviet forces were able to overrun Manchuria against little more than token opposition. Two days earlier the first atomic bomb was dropped on Hiroshima, and on the 9th a second fell on Nagasaki. The effects of this new weapon, produced by years of research and an expenditure of two billion dollars, were appalling. Indeed, the scientists who had devised it were more dismayed than gratified; they announced to the world that warfare must hereafter be abolished, or the human race would face destruction.

Japanese peace feelers had already been sent out but were still indefinite. On 10 August, however, an offer to surrender was made, provided the Emperor was allowed to retain his throne. The United Nations accepted the Japanese offer, subject to the qualification that the Emperor would exercise his authority under the supervision of the commander of the occupation forces, a post for which General MacArthur was designated. On 2 September 1945 the capitulation was signed aboard the battleship *Missouri* in Tokyo Bay.

The end of the war was greeted with hysterical rejoicing all over the world. Americans littered their streets with gasoline coupons and ration cards. Then they settled down to the sobering task of rehabilitation and peacemaking. The cost of the conflict has still to be calculated, if, indeed, it can ever be done. The loss of life in combat was in the neighborhood of fifteen million, with Germany and Russia contributing over two-thirds of the total. Total American casualties were about 1,000,000, of whom some 300,000 were dead or missing. The total loss of noncombatant lives will probably never be known. The toll of aerial bombardments was a relatively minor part of the figure. The Nazis slaughtered at least 12,000,000 people by their systematic exterminations of Jews, Poles, and others. Other millions were uprooted and left as a homeless, destitute mass. The destruction of property and the expenditure of money can only be approximated in astronomical figures.

43

International Cooperation

THE UNITED NATIONS

Even before the United States had formally entered the war, its administration began to concern itself with the problem of insuring a "better future for the world." On 14 August 1941 the United States and Great Britain dedicated themselves to this task in the Atlantic Charter, a collection of eight principles to which were subsequently added the "Four Freedoms," viz., freedom of religion, freedom of speech, freedom from want, and freedom from fear.

Early in 1943 an international conference on food and agriculture convened at Hot Springs, Virginia, and proposed the creation of a Food and Agriculture Organization of the United Nations. Such an agency, it was agreed, would go a long way toward improving conditions and averting war through prevention of famine. Late that fall in the White House forty-four nations signed an agreement for a United Nations Relief and Rehabilitation Administration, which as its name suggests was designed to go into action at the end of the war in an effort to minimize the dislocation caused by war by providing on-the-spot assistance to war-devastated countries. Shortly afterward, on 28 March 1944, President Roosevelt signed a congressional joint resolution calling for American participation in UNRRA with authorization for appropriations up to $1,350,000,000.[1]

Meanwhile, the United States, the United Kingdom, the Union of Soviet Socialist Republics, and China had issued the Moscow Declaration, 1 November 1943, a statement recognizing the necessity of an inter-

---

[1] UNRRA spent some four billions, mostly supplied by the United States, before it expired on 1 January 1947.

national organization for the maintenance of international peace and security.

Congressional Action. This step had been both preceded and followed by American congressional action. On 21 September 1943 the House of Representatives had passed the Fulbright Resolution, an expression of congressional intention to support the idea of American membership in such an organization, by a vote of 360 to 29, with some 40 members not voting. On the other side of Capitol Hill, the Senate had witnessed numerous resolutions designed to express American interest in a better world. Among them was the celebrated "B_2 H_2 Resolution" introduced by Senators Ball, Burton, Hatch, and Hill. The final result was the Connally Resolution, which incorporated a portion of the Moscow Declaration, advanced by the chairman of the Senate Foreign Relations Committee. This resolution carried by a vote of 85 to 5.

Preliminary Conferences. The vital questions of food, agriculture, relief, and rehabilitation having already received preliminary attention, the problem of international finance was tackled at the United Nations Monetary and Financial Conference at Bretton Woods, New Hampshire, in July, 1944. These sessions produced the International Monetary Fund and the International Bank for Reconstruction and Development. The Fund's purposes included the promotion of international monetary cooperation, the expansion and growth of international trade, and exchange stability. The Bank's objectives included the offering of assistance in the reconstruction and development of the territories of the members and help in trying to facilitate the transition from wartime to peacetime economies. A somewhat ominous note was struck by Russia's refusal to participate in either the Fund or the Bank although a quota had been set for her and an important place made ready.

With the United States once more in the role of host, the Dumbarton Oaks conversations were held in Washington from 21 August to 7 October 1944. These meetings were attended by representatives of the major powers excepting France, which was somewhat piqued at being omitted. Since Russia and Japan were still at peace, the Americans and British met first with the Russians and then later with the Chinese separately. Preliminary draft proposals outlining the structure and powers of an international organization for the maintenance of peace and security resulted, known as the Dumbarton Oaks Plan. These proposals were widely discussed, and in the United States at least citizens had an opportunity to express their views on the subject. They were then submitted to the various governments to serve as a basis for discussion at a full United Nations Conference to be called to prepare a Charter for the world organization. Membership was declared open to "all peace-loving states."

Rounding out the year, an International Civil Aviation Conference, held at Chicago, was attended by fifty-two nations. Once again the Soviet Union elected to be the sole prominent dissenter. The Provisional Organization set up at Chicago came into force in June, 1945, when the twenty-sixth nation ratified the agreement.

The Yalta Conference produced, among other things to be mentioned later, an agreement on the method of voting in the projected international organization formulated by President Roosevelt. An apparent impasse had previously been reached owing to the fact that Dumbarton Oaks had not settled the question of just how far the five big powers holding permanent seats on the Security Council of the projected world organization were to be allowed to go in the exercise of their right to defeat proposals not to their liking. This special privilege given to the great powers was justified on the grounds that responsibility for the maintenance of peace rested ultimately on their shoulders. It was the contention of the Soviet that this veto should embrace all matters of substance. The position taken by the United States favored this exclusive big-power privilege but opposed the idea that it could apply in cases where a state was a party to a dispute. Roosevelt's compromise was to the effect that on procedural or routine matters the Security Council's decisions would be based on the votes of any seven of the eleven members. On all other matters, seven votes including the concurring votes of the five permanent members would be required. If the question involved "pacific settlement of disputes," parties to the dispute were to abstain from voting. The effectiveness of this qualification was ruined, however, by the fact that action to enforce the decision taken in a question involving "pacific settlement of disputes" was left subject to the veto without any qualification whatsoever.

THE SAN FRANCISCO CONFERENCE

The United Nations Conference on International Organization opened at San Francisco, 25 April 1945, to draft the Charter of the United Nations. In accordance with a pledge made at Yalta by Roosevelt and Churchill, the Russian republics of the Ukraine and Byelorussia were granted membership. Argentina won admission over the strenuous objections of the Soviet. The bitter fight which took place in this instance was almost matched by the great-power split over the questions of the veto and the powers of the General Assembly. The big-power wrangling at a time when the war was not yet over did not augur well for the future. It revealed to trained eyes the gratuitous assumption on which the Charter was to be based, viz., that three great powers,[2] one of whom possessed a

[2] France was by courtesy ranked in the Big Five as was China, but it is clear that at the time neither had *de facto* achieved such eminence.

radically different outlook and philosophy from the others, could agree without the necessity of yielding any important measure of their sovereignty to a commonly accepted and binding international law.

The members signed the Charter 26 June, and it was approved by the United States Senate a few weeks later by an overwhelming majority. Following an interval of about a month, the Charter together with the Statute of the International Court of Justice was ratified by President Truman. On 24 October it was pronounced in effect since the other members of the big five and the requisite majority of the lesser states had accepted it.

The UN Organization. The machinery of the Charter bore a strong resemblance to that of the League of Nations. It consists of the following principal organs:

1. A General Assembly of all nations, each with a single vote although it may have up to five representatives. This is the policy-making body of UN and is required to meet at least once a year and more often if necessary. Voting on important questions is by a two-thirds vote, and by a majority vote on all other questions. The Assembly possesses supervisory power in that all organs of UN must report to it on their work. It is also the agency which sets the costs paid by the members and has control of the budget. This body, sometimes called the "town meeting of the world," can consider and make recommendations on any question of international import provided that the Security Council is not studying the matter. It should be noted, too, that its recommendations are not mandatory. The Assembly does have the power of electing the nonpermanent members of the Council.

2. A Security Council of eleven members in continuous session. The five great powers possess permanent seats, with the remaining six held for two-year terms. Each member of the Council has one vote, and decisions on routine matters, *i.e.,* procedure, are by a majority of any seven. As demonstrated above in this chapter, on matters of substance the majority of seven must include the votes of the Big Five.

3. An Economic and Social Council of eighteen members elected by the General Assembly to promote the welfare of the people of the world together with respect for human rights and fundamental freedoms. Various specialized agencies have been established to work out the objectives of the Council. These bodies work to a great extent as independent agencies but are coordinated by the Council. To mention a few, there are the Food and Agriculture Organization (FAO); United Nations Educational, Scientific, and Cultural Organization (UNESCO); the Economic Commission for Europe (ECE); the Economic Commission for Asia and the Far East (ECAFE); the Human Rights Commission; the Commission on the Status of Women; the World Health Organization (WHO);

the International Refugee Organization (IRO); and surviving League of Nations agencies such as the International Labor Organization.

4. An International Court of Justice with its seat at The Hague. Its fifteen judges are elected by the General Assembly and the Security Council. No two justices can be citizens of the same state. Although not selected on a basis of nationality, attention is given to insure that the principal legal systems of the world are all represented. The judges' term of office is nine years, and they are eligible for reelection. Being a court of law, it deals only with legal disputes, not political. The states concerned can refer to it any case they wish, or the Security Council may refer a legal dispute to it. Moreover, any UN organ may ask the Court for an advisory opinion on any legal matter.

The Court's jurisdiction is voluntary in that a case comes before it only with the consent of the parties concerned. The states themselves have the power to decide over what cases the Court is to have compulsory jurisdiction. This may be done either through separate agreement or by signing the "optional clause" of the Court Statute. In the latter case, the Court's authority is compulsory in all cases involving such matters as the interpretation of a treaty, the breach of an international obligation, or any question of international law. The United States has indicated its willingness to strengthen the Court by having been among the first to sign this clause.

5. A Trusteeship Council composed of the states administering trust territories, the permanent members of the Security Council, and members elected by the General Assembly for a three-year term. The number of the latter is flexible in that it is designed to make equal the number of states not holding trusteeships on this Council with those administering such territories.

6. A Secretariat headed by the Secretary-General aided by eight Assistant Secretaries-General. This important organ is designed to perform the daily routine work of the organization. Its personnel is drawn from the entire nation membership and is paid out of the budget set by the General Assembly. The staff is appointed by the Secretary-General under regulations established by the General Assembly.

THE UNITED NATIONS IN OPERATION

Despite the occasional great-power bickering which accompanied its birth, the United Nations began its existence under far more favorable auspices than its predecessor. Both the United States and the Soviet Union were members, and both were ostensibly committed to whole-hearted support of the organization. Moreover, most of the peoples of the world were sufficiently chastened by the experience they had just un-

ORGANS OF THE UNITED NATIONS

PRINCIPAL ORGANS AND SUBSIDIARY BODIES

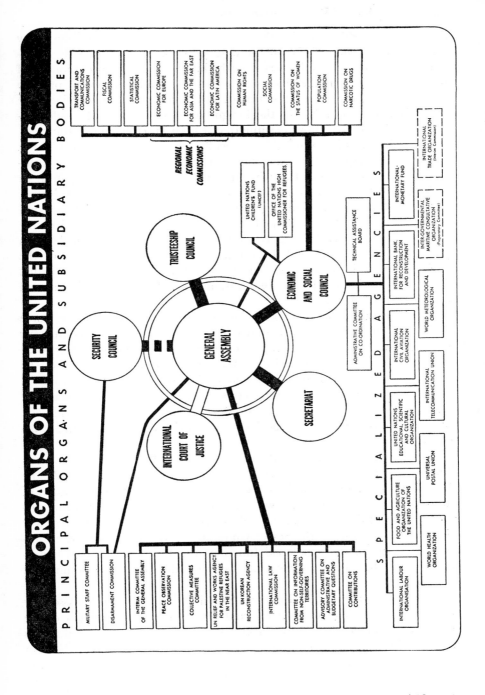

dergone to be willing to give this experiment in international order every opportunity to succeed. In the ensuing years the UN admittedly disappointed many of its admirers—partly because their expectations had been exaggerated in the first place. There was a tendency to put too much faith in the mere existence of the Charter and to overlook the harsh fact that the UN, like the League of Nations before it, could succeed only if the great powers supported it both in letter and in spirit.

Achievements. Viewed realistically, the United Nations had a record of accomplishment during its first few years that was far from inconsiderable. It secured the withdrawal of Soviet forces from Iran in 1946, assisted in the organization of independent governments in Korea, Libya, and Indonesia, and negotiated an armistice between Israel and the Arab states—the last-named achieved at the cost of the life of the UN mediator, Count Folke Bernadotte of Sweden, who was murdered in Jerusalem by an outlawed Jewish terrorist group. The action of the United Nations in Korea was of historic significance in that it was the first time that an international organization had offered collective armed opposition to aggression.

In the economic and social sphere United Nations agencies have done much useful work, particularly in cooperation with the Point Four program of the United States. UN commissions also drafted a Genocide Convention, which attempted to prohibit by treaty any repetition of the mass slaughter of Jews and others practiced by the Nazis, and a Universal Declaration of Human Rights, a verbose and loosely worded document which nevertheless represented a praiseworthy effort to give world-wide recognition to the status of the individual human being in a highly organized civilization.

Weaknesses. On the other hand, the weaknesses of the United Nations have been painfully evident. Some of them were structural: the UN, like the League of Nations before it, was created as an association of independent, sovereign states who retained in their own hands the ultimate power of decision; and the right of veto given the great powers was susceptible of abuse, as the Soviet Union amply demonstrated. More important perhaps, in its political functions the UN was seriously handicapped by the persistent cleavage between the free and Communist worlds.

As early as 1948 the Interim Committee of the General Assembly proposed the calling of a general conference to consider revision of the Charter, as provided in Article 109. At first opposed, the United States changed its mind by 1954. Suggested revisions covered a substantial area of the operations of the UN; of special importance to the United States was the abandonment of the veto in cases involving the pacific settlement of international disputes and the admission of new members.

POLICY MAKING THROUGH CONFERENCES

As the Allied fortunes of war began to mount, President Roosevelt revealed further principles of peacemaking to buttress the United Nations Declaration. On 7 January 1943 he declared before Congress that Germany and Japan must be disarmed and kept disarmed and that they must abandon the philosophy of fascism.

During the Casablanca Conference, 14–26 January 1943, he proclaimed that the United Nations would adhere to a policy of unconditional surrender by their enemies. This was followed up, 25 August 1943, by a letter to Congress in which Mr. Roosevelt said the people of the Axis countries need not fear unconditional surrender but that their leaders would be punished.

Thus the first principles of peacemaking were set, including: (1) the points stated in the Atlantic Charter; (2) the UN declaration of complete victory and no separate armistice or peace; (3) disarmament, denazification, unconditional surrender, and no punitive peace for the people.

The Moscow Conference. At Moscow, 19–30 October 1943, the foreign ministers of the United States, the United Kingdom, and the Union of Soviet Socialist Republics (Cordell Hull, Anthony Eden, and Vyacheslav M. Molotov) together with high-ranking military leaders of the three countries gathered in an epochal meeting which marked the first three-power conference of the war.

The powers issued a joint communiqué at the end of their conversations, which stated that measures to be taken to shorten the war against Germany and her satellites in Europe were discussed, *i.e.,* the "second front," and that all three were pledged "to continue the present close collaboration and cooperation in the conduct of the war into the period following the end of hostilities, and that only in this way could peace be maintained and the political, economic, and social welfare of their peoples fully promoted."

Separate declarations were issued on General Security, Italy, and Austria. The first of these was mentioned above. In the Declaration Regarding Italy, the three governments agreed that "Allied policy towards Italy must be based upon the fundamental principle that Fascism and all its evil influences and emanations shall be utterly destroyed and that the Italian people shall be given every opportunity to establish governmental and other institutions based upon democratic principles. . . . Freedom of speech, of religious worship, of political belief, of the press and of public meeting shall be restored in full measure to the Italian people. . . ."

The Declaration on Austria stated that "They regard the annexation imposed upon Austria by Germany on March 15th, 1938, as null and void. . . . They declare that they wish to see reestablished a free and independent Austria, and thereby to open the way for the Austrian people themselves, as well as those neighboring states which will be faced with similar problems, to find that political and economic security which is the only basis for lasting peace."

The Cairo Conference. Since China had not been represented at Moscow, except to have the Chinese Ambassador to Russia sign the Moscow Declaration envisaging a future world organization, President Roosevelt and Prime Minister Churchill, who were then both en route to Teheran to meet Stalin, decided that a separate conference with Chiang Kai-shek on problems of the Far Eastern war and the future was in order. At Cairo, 22–26 November 1943, these three chiefs of state together with political and military advisers conferred, marking the first time that the Anglo-American leaders had gone over the complex situation in the Far East with Chiang personally.

The military aspects of the problem were carefully explored, and the three powers promised to leave no stone unturned in a relentless effort to crush Japan. They asserted in the Cairo Declaration that they coveted "no gain for themselves and have no thought of territorial expansion." Continuing further, the Declaration stated that "Japan shall be stripped of all the islands in the Pacific which she has seized or occupied since the beginning of the First World War in 1914, and that all the territories Japan has stolen from the Chinese, such as Manchuria, Formosa, and the Pescadores, shall be restored to the Republic of China. Japan will also be expelled from all other territories which she has taken by violence and greed." "Mindful of the enslavement of Korea" the three powers were "determined that in due course Korea shall become free and independent."

The Teheran Conference (1943). Up to this point the wartime conferences had been productive of satisfactory results and mutual cooperation, but from Teheran on they reveal a number of things which are justifiably open to doubt. For one thing, the heads of three states undertook to make effective decisions involving the lives of millions of people in lands which did not belong to these statesmen. Secondly, these conferences were singularly one-sided. In every instance, Russia received territory and concessions without offering much in return. While many may claim that she was getting back what was once hers anyway, this argument is far from conclusive. If the former owners were to be restored everywhere in this world, the resulting situation would be chaos.

On the other hand, one realizes what motives prompted this generosity on the part of the Anglo-American leaders. It was clearly a case of the paralyzing fear that Russia would make a separate peace with Germany despite her pledged word not to do so. Should this happen, the added cost in Anglo-American lives would, of course, be terrible. Again, in fairness to the diplomacy of the President and the Prime Minister, it is indisputably true that Russia was in a fair position to take these territories anyway. However, it needs to be remembered that there is a vast degree of difference between stealing territories and having them awarded to you by the generosity of your allies. Finally, it is extremely difficult to reconcile these territorial acquisitions either with the Atlantic Charter, which Russia recognized, or the repeated statements made by the Russians that they sought no territorial gains but wished only to drive the "German fascist beasts" from their soil.

The practice of awarding territory to Russia commenced at Teheran in the case of eastern Poland. This transfer was effected by the Big Three without the trouble of consulting the wishes of the Polish people involved, although the second point of the Atlantic Charter states that there are to be "no territorial changes that do not accord with the freely expressed wishes of the peoples concerned."

The actual Three Power Declaration issued at Teheran was innocuous enough and contained platitudinous statements relative to the complete unity existing and the common desire to fight through together to final victory and of "a world family of Democratic Nations."

In a radio address to the American people upon his return the President paid glowing tribute to Marshal Stalin with whom he said "to use an American and ungrammatical colloquialism, I may say that I 'got along fine.'" Stalin was further pictured as "a man who combines a tremendous, relentless determination with a stalwart good humor. I believe he is truly representative of the heart and soul of Russia; and I believe that we are going to get along well with him and the Russian people—very well indeed."

The Yalta Conference. On 3–11 February 1945, Roosevelt, Churchill, and Stalin together with their foreign secretaries met at Yalta in the Crimea in what was to be their last meeting and one characterized by secret and personal diplomacy hard to justify in a democracy. Final acceptance was made by the Anglo-American partners of the cession of eastern Poland to Russia. In return it was agreed that Poland would be compensated in the west at the expense of Germany. Poland's eastern boundary would become the Curzon Line, drawn in 1919. The terms of unconditional surrender were reemphasized along with the announcement of various political agreements.

Among the latter was the statement that "democratic means" would be employed to assist Europe's liberated peoples. The three big powers agreed to act jointly to help the said liberated peoples create democratic institutions of their own choice.

This was the extent to which the agreements made at Yalta were revealed at the time. There were, however, at least four others which were kept secret. That dealing with the Far East was made public on the occasion of the first anniversary of Yalta, 11 February 1946. The holding back of this agreement was justified by explaining that at that particular time Russia was not at war with Japan and to have published the pact might easily have had deleterious effects on allied military strategy. At any rate, Russia was awarded the Kurile Islands in return for her promise to enter the war against Japan and was granted privileged rights in the Chinese cities of Port Arthur and Dairen (Dalny) from which she had been expelled by Japan in 1905. China was not even extended the courtesy of being a party to this arrangement. To save face and in return for a recognition of the Nationalist government as the only legitimate government of China together with a promise of material help (never kept) from Russia, China legitimized this highhanded action in the Soong-Stalin Treaty of August, 1945.

Of the other secret deals made at Yalta, two had to do with the proposed United Nations Organization. In one of them, it was agreed that the Ukraine and Byelorussia would be granted full and equal membership in UN. In the other arrangement, the United States was to get three votes in the Assembly of UN in order to match Russia's three and Britain's several (since it was assumed by the assembled diplomatists that the dominions would add some votes to Britain). This agreement leaked out before Mr. Roosevelt's death, and the unfavorable impression it created on the American people caused it to be abolished.

Potsdam. On 17 July–2 August the Potsdam Conference took place with a rather different personnel. Only Stalin was a holdover from the leaders who had been at Yalta. Harry S. Truman succeeded the late President Roosevelt, and midway during the sessions Clement Attlee replaced Winston Churchill as a result of the first national elections held in Britain since 1935. At the next level, there were also changes. James F. Byrnes was the new American Secretary of State, and Ernest Bevin succeeded Anthony Eden. Molotov provided the sole direct link with Yalta.

Since the war in the Far East was still in progress with Russia as yet a nonbelligerent, decisions with respect to this area were announced by the United States, the United Kingdom, and China in a separate proclamation on 26 July defining their terms for the surrender of Japan. Japan was warned that failure to accept this invitation would result in its "utter destruction." There then followed the promises that Japan would not be destroyed, that it would be made democratic, and that it would have a chance to trade peacefully in the future with the rest of the world.

With the Far Eastern aspects thus disposed of in this manner, the Big Three turned to the pressing problem of the future of defeated Germany. Agreement was announced relative to "uniformity of treatment" of the Germans within the country, to the fact that "the administration of affairs in Germany should be directed toward the decentralization of the political structure and the development of local responsibility," and to the point that "for the time being no central German government shall be established."

In the economic field, agreements were also reached that central German agencies in finance, transport, communications, foreign trade, and industry should be created. It was further agreed: (1) "At the earliest practicable date, the German economy shall be decentralized for the purpose of eliminating the present excessive concentration of economic power as exemplified in particular by cartels, syndicates, trusts, and other monopolistic arrangements." (2) "In organizing the German economy, primary emphasis shall be given to the development of agriculture and peaceful domestic industries."

Reparations. On the matter of reparations, it had previously been agreed at Yalta that Germany pay "to the greatest extent possible" for damages it had caused. The Russians favored a figure of $20,000,000,000 in capital equipment, foreign assets, current production, and labor. Russia's share was to be half of this total. The British felt that no exact figure should be set. Instead they proposed dividing what Germany should supply on a percentage basis. At Potsdam it was decided that Germany should pay with whatever industrial equipment was deemed unnecessary for her peacetime economy. German foreign holdings were to be taken in their entirety. Russia and Poland were to take their reparations from the Soviet zone of occupation, while the Western powers (the United States, the United Kingdom, and France) would take theirs out of their own zones. In addition, Russia was awarded 25 per cent of the total taken from the three Western zones, but she was to pay for 15 per cent of these additional reparations in such things as food, coal, and oil. The problem of Germany's external assets was somewhat simplified, on paper at least, by Russia's renouncing claims in all other lands except in eastern Europe and her own zone in Austria in return for a pledge by the three Western powers to do the same in the reparations regions thus awarded to the Soviet. The Germans were to be left with sufficient domestic resources to enable them to live on a standard of living not exceeding the average for Europe, excluding Russia and Britain.

Since other countries obviously had claims against Germany, a Paris Conference on Reparation was held in the fall of 1945 at which eighteen nations were present. Their claims had to be assessed against the Western zones excluding Russia's 25 per cent there. The British thesis that no amounts be fixed, only percentages, prevailed. This meeting produced the Inter-allied Reparations Agency with its headquarters to be located at Brussels.

It was also agreed that Germany should be disarmed and deprived of some of its territory. In addition to the arrangements previously made at Yalta, the United States and the United Kingdom promised, when the time came to conclude a treaty of peace, to support a proposal that Koenigsberg and the surrounding area be ceded to the U.S.S.R. Poland was granted the temporary right, likewise subject to final settlement in a treaty, to administer Upper and Lower Silesia, and parts of East Prussia, Brandenburg, and Pomerania.

The Nuremberg Trials. The three powers at Potsdam discussed the question of how German war criminals would be tried and punished, and a few days after the Conference concluded they reached agreement. They set up an International Military Tribunal with France as a full member and by August, 1945, had listed the first batch of defendants. Three months later the Nuremberg trials began with twenty-four top Nazis on trial. Twelve were sentenced to death, and of these ten executions were carried out, since Goering managed to commit suicide in dramatic fashion and Bormann had been tried and condemned *in absentia*. Several, including Hess and Raeder, were imprisoned for life, while Von Papen and Horace Greeley Hjalmar Schacht were set free. The process of trying war criminals continued until the spring of 1948 when the job was declared completed.

Finally, it was determined at Potsdam to establish a Council of Foreign Ministers representing the five principal powers (China was added) to meet periodically in the future. Its first assignment was "to draw up with a view to their submission to the United Nations, treaties of peace with Italy, Rumania, Bulgaria, Hungary, and Finland, and to propose settlements of territorial questions outstanding on the termination of the war in Europe." It should be noted that the Council was not to replace the meetings of the Big Three's foreign secretaries, which continued well into the postwar period.

LIQUIDATING THE WAR

Germany. Quarrels over the Potsdam Agreement began practically with the termination of the conference. The Allied Control Council which had been set up for Germany produced remarkably little in the way of cooperation, and the reparations settlement proved to be extremely unsatisfactory. The cleavage between the Soviet Union and the Western powers made it impossible to treat Germany as an economic unit, and the Russians were more than casual about their obligation to ship materials in part payment for their share of Western-zone reparations.

On the other hand the Western powers were able to work harmoniously with each other and with the Germans in their part of the country —an achievement for which much credit must go to the high caliber of the men who have served as American High Commissioners: General Lucius D. Clay, John J. McCloy, and Dr. James B. Conant, former president of Harvard University. By 1948 the French, British, and American zones had been combined into a single administrative unit, and a year later most of the responsibilities of government in Western Germany were turned over to the German Federal Republic. The new state's relations with the occupying powers were regulated by an Occupation Statute, replaced in 1953 by the Bonn Convention.

Under this agreement the German Federal Republic was given full authority over its internal and external affairs. Relations between Bonn and the Western powers were henceforth carried on through the latter's ambassadors. The powers maintained the rights to station armed forces in Germany and to control West Berlin. They also reserved rights relating to the ultimate unification of Germany and a definitive peace treaty.

Japan. Japan was completely disarmed and demilitarized following the end of the Second World War. It even agreed in its new constitution to outlaw war by pledging itself to give up an army, navy, and air force for all time.

The world situation would not allow this self-abnegation by the Japanese to endure for long, since in the 1951 Security Treaty signed between the United States and Japan, the latter undertook "to assume responsibility for its own defense" in time. Accordingly, Japan embarked once again upon a program of rearmament and made some progress toward the creation of the Japanese Defense Forces. The United States then undertook to help its former enemy by providing major items of land, sea, and air equipment.

The rearmament program described above followed, of course, the signing of the Japanese Peace Treaty. From 1945 until 1951 Japan was occupied by Allied forces under the command of General Douglas MacArthur, Supreme Commander of the Allied Powers (SCAP) and head of the Allied Council. Technically, MacArthur received directives from the Far Eastern Commission, which had its headquarters in Washington, but in reality occupation leadership was pretty much of a one-man show as long as MacArthur was on the scene. There was also an Allied Council for Japan (United States, U.S.S.R., Britain, and China) which did very little apart from endeavoring to criticize "the General," an activity which the American member of the Council opposed.

Negotiations for a Japanese Peace Treaty. On 17 March 1947, General MacArthur, with the apparent consent of the State Department, made the surprising announcement in Tokyo that all had gone so well during the occupation that it was time for a treaty of peace, after which the United Nations could assume the responsibility for keeping watch on Japan. He did admit that there were economic problems remaining unsolved. In this he was quite correct since, as former Premier Yoshida pointed out back in 1946, Japan had to support 70 per cent of her former population with only 56 per cent of her former territory. The territorial loss stripped her of a considerable source of raw materials, which now had to be imported and paid for by manufactures. Then, too, her population had been growing at a rapid pace since the war's end.

Undoubtedly, the Supreme Commander's statement was in the nature of a trial balloon. At any rate, the State Department proposed in July, 1947, to the other members of FEC that a conference be held to discuss the Japanese treaty in August. Whoever was responsible for selecting this particular time was blissfully unaware that a British Commonwealth of Nations Conference on the same subject had already been scheduled for Canberra in August. Therefore, Britain and her dominions requested a postponement but agreed to the idea of such a meeting in the immediate future. Russia alone of the FEC nations demurred. Instead, the Russians after blasting the American proposal suggested a meeting of the Council of Foreign Ministers for the same purpose. This procedure would, of course, by-pass the smaller powers and contravene the American desire to have them participate on the same basis as the Great Powers.

Thus an impasse resulted, with the United States and the other members of the Far Eastern Commission on one side and Russia on the other. It lasted until 1950 at which time the United States, disgusted with the intransigence of the Soviet Union, decided to give up the conference method of making a Japanese peace treaty and to substitute for this approach the use of diplomatic processes. This method had the advantage of preventing any one nation from blocking a treaty.

The actual negotiations began at the end of the summer of 1950 at the United Nations General Assembly in New York. Consultations, conferences, and written exchanges of views took place, following which a United States presidential mission led by John Foster Dulles visited the capitals of the ten other nations, excepting Russia, most concerned with the projected treaty.

In January, 1951, the United States drafted the principles agreed upon by that time and circulated the draft among some twenty interested countries for study and recommendations. Meanwhile, the British had held a Commonwealth conference of their own at which certain conclusions were reached. They thereupon circulated their draft. In June the efforts of the United States and the Commonwealth of Nations were combined in a third draft text.

While these preliminary drafts were making the rounds, the Soviet Union adopted a most critical attitude. Despite this, the Soviet accepted an invitation from the United States and the United Kingdom, as co-sponsors, to a conference to be held in the San Francisco Opera House for the purpose of concluding the Japanese peace treaty. Russia's acceptance was based upon the vain hope of so disrupting the proceedings that no treaty could be concluded. The efforts made to accomplish this end proved unavailing, so Gromyko and his colleagues walked out of the conference in a huff. Of the fifty-one nations which put in an appearance only the U.S.S.R., Czechoslovakia, and Poland failed to sign the treaty.

The Peace Settlement with Japan. By its terms Japan was reduced to her four main islands and a few minor ones and promised to agree to an American trusteeship under the United Nations of the Bonin and Ryukyu Islands, including Okinawa.

Japanese rearmament was permitted although the Japanese constitution still outlawed armed forces and renounced war. The portion of the treaty dealing with security made possible the retention of American troops in Japan. To obviate any problems in this connection the United States and Japan signed a separate agreement at San Francisco which authorized the United States to maintain its forces in Japan for an indefinite period. To allay the fears of some of the signers of the peace treaty over a revival of Japanese aggression, the United States then concluded defense pacts with the Philippines, Australia, and New Zealand.

In the matter of reparations the peace treaty recognized that Japan should pay for the damages and suffering it caused during the war. However, it was stated that Japan's resources could not then stand such a drain if its economy were to be viable. Therefore, it was suggested that nations having just claims on Japan might send raw materials to Japan and receive in return consumers' goods and industrial equipment.

Austria. Austrian independence was pledged at the Moscow Conference in 1943, but following the termination of the war the hapless country was split into four zones (France receiving a zone) with armies of occupation in each of them and an Allied Control Council in Vienna, which was under joint occupation. This arrangement was to endure until such time as a treaty with Austria would be signed.

Russia unsuccessfully sought recognition of an Austrian government under its auspices and controlled by native Communists not long after the war's end. A compromise was reached in 1946, however, allowing the creation of an Austrian provisional national government, which was set up following free elections and which received the recognition of all the occupational powers. The occupation saw fit to limit the effectiveness of this government by reserving the right to veto any action taken by it upon a unanimous vote of the four powers. The Allied Council consisting of four high commissioners assumed an advisory role to the new government.

The story of the efforts by the three Western powers to secure a treaty with Austria which would end the occupation by all the powers, including Russia, is a dreary one which reveals a string of broken promises made by the Russians. If any doubts were entertained regarding the Soviets' plans to keep troops in Austria indefinitely, they were effectively removed by the Berlin Conference in 1954.

Two sources of disagreement between the West and the Soviet Union in the matter of Austria have been the question of what constitutes German assets in Austria (and would therefore be subject to Russian confiscation) and Yugoslav reparations demands against Austria.

In the latter case Russia used Yugoslav claims for bargaining purposes and would have quickly dropped them in return for Allied acceptance of Russia's definition of what constituted German assets in Austria. Actually, the Yugoslav claims were based on damages caused by Hitler's armies and should have been against Germany and not Austria. In addition to reparations the Yugoslavs called for the cession of a considerable part of the Austrian province of Carinthia and smaller portions of Styria and Burgenland. Following Tito's break with Moscow in 1948, the Soviets lost interest in this matter.

In the question of German assets the Russians have maintained a most lively interest. The Soviets seized over three hundred enterprises in their zone and demanded that they be given permanent possession. If their demands were granted, they would be left in control of two-thirds of Austria's entire oil production, all of its oil reserves, and about three-fourths of the refineries; the Danube Shipping Company; three hundred industrial plants; and the country's leading banks and most of its insurance companies. The bulk of this property was classifiable as German only by ignoring the fact that it had been stolen by the Nazis after the *Anschluss.*

As the occupation dragged on with no apparent termination in sight, it was no wonder that Austria's most popular motion picture in 1954 was one which predicted that the occupation would still be in effect in the twenty-first century.

Italy and the Satellites. Early in 1946 the Council of Foreign Ministers met in Paris to draft peace treaties for Italy, Rumania, Hungary, Finland, and Bulgaria. The result of their labors was submitted for consideration to a general conference, also held in Paris, of representatives of the Big Five and sixteen other states which had participated actively in the war against the European members of the Axis. The Paris Conference cleared the way for final work on the treaties by the Council of Foreign Ministers which met in New York from 4 November to 12 December 1946. Here Molotov for a long time acted as if he had no intention of facilitating settlement of any of the outstanding problems. Ultimately, however, he made a number of concessions, as did the others.

Territorially, the following changes were made: Italy ceded the Dodecanese Islands to Greece, eastern Venezia Giulia to Yugoslavia, Trieste and its hinterland to the newly established Free Territory of Trieste, and several small Alpine regions to France; Finland yielded the Karelian Isthmus, Salla Sector to the U.S.S.R. as well as Petsamo; Rumania turned over northern Bucovina and Bessarabia to the Soviets and southern Dobruja to Bulgaria; and lastly Hungary gave Bratislava to Czechoslovakia.

Militarily, the defeated nations were proscribed from the possession of a number of kinds of armaments, and their air forces were strictly limited as well as their naval strength in the case of those which had navies. Financially, Italy's reparations figure was set at $360,000,000 to be divided among Yugoslavia ($125,000,000), Greece ($105,000,000), Russia ($100,000,000), Ethiopia ($25,000,000), and Albania ($5,-000,000). Bulgaria was assessed $7,000,000, of which Greece was to get $45,000,000 and Yugoslavia $25,000,000. No reparations were exacted from the others.

Trieste and the Italian Colonies. The questions of Trieste and the Italian colonies in Africa remained unsettled since no agreement could then be secured on these points. Temporarily, Great Britain undertook to administer the former Italian colonies.

In 1949 the General Assembly of the United Nations secured an agreement whereby the former Italian colony of Libya would become independent by 1 January 1952. Helped both by Britain and the United States, which included it in the Point Four program, the infant nation was launched on schedule with its own king and government. Somaliland was placed under Italian administration on behalf of the United Nations for a ten-year period as a trust territory during which its political, economic, and social preparation for independence was to be furthered. Eritrea was granted a federated status with Ethiopia under which the former would control its own domestic affairs, but its finance, defense, and foreign affairs would be in the latter's hands.

The question of Trieste proved more durable and thorny than that of the colonies. In March, 1948, preliminary steps were taken by the Americans, British, and French to return Trieste and its hinterland to Italy, but they failed to materialize. Yugoslavia's offer to trade Venezia Giulia for Trieste was rejected by Italy, and the impasse continued unbroken until 1954, when Italy and Yugoslavia came to an amicable agreement for division of the disputed territory.

44

The World since the War

Every great war has been followed by a period of uncertainty and instability, and the Second World War was no exception. In fact, the far-ranging scope of the conflict and the appalling devastation that it left in its wake made the problems of reconstruction and readjustment unprecedentedly severe. While the Western world struggled to recover from the shattering ordeal it had passed through, intense nationalism shook both Asia and Africa, and over all hung the shadow of conflict between democracy and communism. International and internal issues in this period are so closely related that it is difficult to distinguish between them, but as a matter of convenience the former will be dealt with in the next chapter. Our concern here is primarily with the principal internal developments in the major nations and regions.

THE IRON CURTAIN

The Soviet Union emerged from the Second World War as one of the world's two great super-powers. Its armies occupied practically all of Central and Eastern Europe as well as Manchuria and northern Korea in the Far East, Communist parties throughout the world gave unquestioning obedience to every nod from the Kremlin, and in the first exultation of victory the people of the West were more than willing to do whatever they could within reason to continue the wartime partnership in peaceful cooperation during the difficult years that lay ahead. On the other hand, Russia's position had serious elements of weakness. Millions of lives had been lost in the struggle with the Nazis, and much of European Russia, the most productive section of the U.S.S.R., was completely devastated.

732

The response of the Soviet regime to this situation was to combine a more rigorous dictatorship at home with the aggressive promotion of communism abroad. Not only Russia but the whole Soviet-dominated world came under the shadow of a grim tyranny, based on a godless materialism, impervious to human values and recognizing no moral law except its own preservation. The reconstruction of Russia was promoted by a ruthless looting of occupied countries, and labor for the rebuilding of the Soviet state—where the world was to see how communism liberated the exploited masses from capitalist oppression—was found by instituting a new form of human slavery. Millions of people, both in Russia and the satellites, were arrested by the secret police on flimsy charges and herded, with or without trial, into forced-labor camps. In the occupied countries victims were especially sought among the propertied classes, the businessmen, and the professional groups—lawyers, educators, scientists—with the calculated purpose of eliminating any potential nucleus of anti-Communist leadership. In addition, prisoners of war were kept in indefinite captivity, sometimes conveniently identified as "war criminals" if inquiry became too pressing.

Along with the secret police, the Communist-party organization tightened the bonds of its discipline. The Comintern, theoretically abolished during the war as a sop to Western opinion, was revived under the title of the Cominform, and rigorous steps were instituted to suppress heresy or "deviationism" of any kind. Not even the arts and sciences were immune. Soviet biologists, for example, were compelled to accept the genetic doctrines of Lysenko, who asserted that acquired characteristics could be transmitted, and writers and artists like the great composer Shostakovich were repeatedly called on the carpet and compelled to recant imitation of "decadent bourgeois" models.

Techniques of Communist Expansion. For the Russian people this state of affairs could be regarded simply as intensification of the sort of thing they were accustomed to, but it represented unrelieved tragedy for the inhabitants of Russia's neighbors, who in the past had experienced at least some measure of freedom. The techniques by which one country after another was brought within the "Iron Curtain"—a phrase coined by Winston Churchill in a speech at Westminster College, Fulton, Missouri, in 1946—were depressingly similar. At the end of the war coalition governments were established in the "liberated" states of Eastern Europe, including representatives of the local Communist parties. The Communists were careful to occupy key cabinet posts, such as the Ministries of Justice and Interior, which controlled the courts and the police. From these vantage points they then proceeded to rid themselves of their opponents on one pretext or another. Russian military power was not used —it was too obviously there to require comment.

Once in power, the Communists set up Soviet states on the Russian model, complete with Five-Year Plans, secret police, forced-labor camps, and spectacular trials at which the accused invariably "confessed" to innumerable crimes, usually as an agent of "Anglo-American capitalist imperialism." Religion was a favorite target of these regimes, as the trial and imprisonment of Cardinal Mindzenty in Hungary and Archbishop Stepinac in Yugoslavia testified. The only trouble with this process was that it seemed to feed on itself, so that after the non-Communists had been duly purged, the Communists invariably proceeded to work on each other.

Czechoslovakia. The Communist stroke which particularly shocked the rest of the world was the seizure of Czechoslovakia in February, 1948. Both the veteran President Beneš and Foreign Minister Jan Masaryk, son of the founder of the Czech state, had made every effort to maintain a democratic government and friendly relations with the Soviets at the same time, but to no avail. At the time of the coup Masaryk was alleged to have committed suicide, and Beneš did not long survive him. In one case, however, the Soviets apparently overreached themselves. Marshal Tito of Yugoslavia, although asserting his devotion to Communist principles, insisted on being his own boss and was in the happy position of having enough military strength and a geographical location sufficiently accessible to the West to enable him to defy the Kremlin. The breach occurred in 1948.

Information regarding conditions behind the Iron Curtain has been no more than fragmentary, owing to the fact that the "People's Democracies" were unwilling to risk having their citizens contaminated by contact with the free world and thus made every effort to restrict communication to closely supervised official channels. Indeed, to restrain those misguided souls who might wish to see for themselves, they closed their frontiers with armed guards, electrified fences, and bloodhounds. Nevertheless, an unending stream of refugees made its way to the West, frequently in the face of unbelievable danger and hardship, to bear testimony to the fact that tyranny remains tyranny under whatever name it may be called.

Death of Stalin. The death of Joseph Stalin early in 1953 produced little mourning but widespread speculation over what changes might ensue in the Communist world. The immediate repercussions were minor, but still interesting. Stalin was succeeded by a triumvirate composed of Georgi Malenkov, who had risen through the ranks of the Communist party much as Stalin himself had done; Lavrenti Beria, head of the MVD; and Foreign Minister Molotov. A few months later Beria was suddenly arrested, executed, and tried (this appears to have been the order of procedure) on the familiar charge that he had really been an agent of capitalists all along. The new regime permitted some relaxation of the rigors of Stalin's dictatorship by ordering the release of a number of political prisoners, permitting slightly more freedom of expression, and announcing that more emphasis would be placed on the production of consumers' goods. While these steps were indicative of considerable discontent behind the Iron Curtain, there was no evidence of any fundamental change in Communist policy.

WESTERN EUROPE

For most of the nations of Western Europe, the return of peace marked the beginning of a long and difficult struggle to restore both economic and political stability. Some made encouraging progress; others did not. Since they were facing similar problems, including the threat

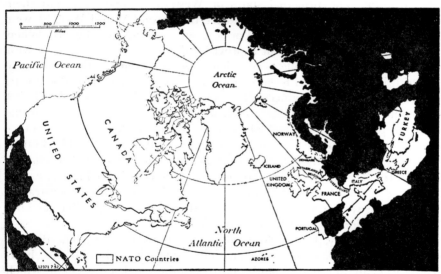

From Department of State Publication 4630, 1952. This map is intended to show *only* the countries which belong to the North Atlantic Treaty Organization. The fact that others are shaded in black indicates merely that they are nonmembers, not that they belong to an opposing group.

of communism both internally and externally, these countries made some tentative steps in the direction of European union. This movement was given a powerful stimulus by the American Marshall Plan, but there was also a considerable initiative shown in Western Europe itself. European leadership was directly responsible for (1) Benelux, the customs union of Belgium, the Netherlands, and Luxembourg, formed 1 January 1948. (2) The Brussels Pact, signed 17 March 1948 between the Benelux countries, Great Britain, and France. Soon to be superseded by the North Atlantic Pact, it was nevertheless the initial step toward the organization of the European Defense Community. (3) The creation in 1949 of the Council of Europe, a body composed of representatives of the parliaments of the member nations, with its seat in Strasbourg. While its functions have been purely advisory, it has had some unifying influence. (4) The Schuman Plan for the integration of Western Europe's coal and steel industries. Proposed in 1950 to the Council of Europe by Robert Schuman, French Foreign Minister, it suggested the erection of a supranational authority to control these industries. Although Great Britain refused to join, the plan was accepted in 1951 by France, Western Germany, Italy, and the Benelux countries and was put into operation two years later.

France. The principal states of Western Europe have had their own special problems in the years since the Second World War. Slowest of all to return to either political or economic stability was France. When the Germans were driven out a provisional government was set up with General Charles de Gaulle as president, and at the end of the war a new constitution was drafted to launch the Fourth Republic. This document, which essentially reproduced the political organization of the Third Republic, was unacceptable to General de Gaulle, who resigned his office in protest over the lack of authority vested in the executive. Subsequently developments suggested that the general was right. The Fourth Republic displayed the same interminable cabinet crises that had characterized the Third. There was no lack of statesmanship in France, as her initiative in the Council of Europe and the Schuman Plan demonstrated. The trouble was in a political structure that made it impossible for anyone to give direction and leadership consistently.

Economically, France suffered from various ailments. The dislocation of the war was, of course, an important factor. Beyond this, however, was an antiquated and poorly administered tax system which distributed the burden inequitably and made tax evasion even more respectable in France than it is elsewhere. The resultant financial weakness produced a steady inflation which still further demoralized French society. To make matters worse, Communist domination of the principal labor unions posed a constant threat of deliberate attempts to wreck the French economy, as was evidenced by the great strikes of 1947 and 1948 which tried to stop France from receiving Marshall Plan aid.

Yet the Fourth Republic showed some of the same resiliency which had carried the Third through seventy shaky years. The government remained consistently in the hands of middle-of-the-road groups built around the MRP (Mouvement Républicaine Populaire), which was led by such figures as Schuman and Georges Bidault. These groups, despite their own internal dissensions, kept the Communist threat under control and at the same time staved off an attempted comeback by de Gaulle as the leader of the right-wing RPF (Rassemblement du Peuple Français).

Italy. War-torn, impoverished, and shorn of her overseas possessions, Italy's plight in 1945 was far worse than France's, and the fact that she recovered at all was little short of miraculous. The Italian people worked vigorously to rebuild their shattered country and reorganize its political system. The House of Savoy turned out to be one of the casualties of war. Victor Emmanuel, whose reign had been tainted by association with Mussolini, abdicated in favor of his son Umberto, but the latter occupied the throne only a short time. In 1947 a plebiscite voted to convert Italy into a republic.

Much of Italy's progress along the road to rehabilitation was due to the able leadership of Alcide de Gasperi, a Christian Socialist who managed to remain at the head of a coalition of moderate parties until 1953. In 1947 and 1948 de Gasperi successfully met a Communist challenge similar to that encountered by France. As in France, Marshall Plan aid was an important element in this crisis, and the influence of the Vatican was also an asset to De Gasperi.

However, Italy's problems were far from solved. The basic difficulty was overpopulation in a country poorly provided for by nature. Added to this was the presence of the largest Communist party outside the Iron Curtain, some revival of fascism, and the same partisan irresponsibility which has been the curse of French politics. De Gasperi attempted to improve matters by pushing through an electoral law which would provide stable working majorities to any group getting over 50 per cent of the vote, but while the law passed, it generated enough opposition to bring about the fall of De Gasperi in 1953.

Germany. Defeated Germany had to begin its comeback from a position of complete political and economic chaos. The collapse of the Nazi regime left behind it nothing resembling authority except the occupying armies. Most of Germany's cities had suffered severe bomb damage, and some areas had seen bitter fighting; in addition, Western Germany was flooded with millions of refugees who had been uprooted by the Soviet advance.

Under these conditions the economic recovery of Western Germany was phenomenal. By 1953 industrial productivity was 50 per cent higher than it had been in 1938, and German goods were again becoming a factor on the world market. There was still serious unemployment in the overcrowded country and a desperate shortage of housing; nevertheless, the Germans were able to get along with fewer controls and restrictions than the British. The political development of Western Germany was also encouraging. The provisional government set up at the end of the war was controlled. by a moderate group under Chancellor Konrad Adenauer, whose Christian Democratic party carried on the tradition of the Center party of the Empire and the Weimar Republic. This regime was gradually given increased authority until in 1949 it was formally incorporated as the German Federal Republic with a constitution drafted at Bonn and ratified by the people of Western Germany. Despite left-wing attacks on Adenauer for his policy of friendship with the West and some survivals of Nazi sentiment, he retained his hold on the government and was convincingly vindicated at the polls in 1953.

In Eastern Germany the Soviets established a "People's Democracy" on the now familiar model. Its constitution, also drafted in 1949, purportedly applied to the whole of Germany and was duly approved by the people of the Soviet zone, although one-third of them voted against it in spite of all the pressure that Communist tactics could bring to bear. The popularity of this regime was revealed to the whole world in June, 1953, when protests against low wages, poor food, overwork, and constant repression resulted in outbreaks that had to be put down by Russian troops.

The prospect of reuniting Germany became increasingly remote as the "cold war" intensified. The Big Four foreign ministers met twice in 1947, again in 1949, and again in 1954 in fruitless efforts to agree on a German peace treaty. At the height of the Soviet pressure on the West in 1948, the Russians attempted to force the other occupying powers out of Berlin by establishing a blockade of the land routes to the city. The Western democracies, however, stood firm and circumvented the blockade by a mammoth airlift, with the result that the Russians eventually gave way. The democracies stayed in Berlin, their prestige in Germany and indeed throughout Europe much enhanced, but the solution of the German problem remained as far away as ever. Nor would a settlement between Russia and the West automatically remove all difficulties, since in German eyes there was still a glaring injustice in the transfer of traditionally German territory to Poland that had been so blithely agreed on at Yalta and Potsdam.

Great Britain. For Great Britain the end of the Second World War brought economic crisis and an experiment in socialism. Immediately after the German surrender, Parliament was dissolved to permit the British people to hold their first general election in ten years. To everyone's surprise, including the victors, the Labour party won in a landslide and for the first time in its history had a clear, indeed overwhelming majority in the House of Commons. The new government, with Clement Attlee as Prime Minister, undertook an extensive program of socialization which envisaged the eventual state ownership of about a fourth of Britain's industries. In the six years after 1945 the Bank of England, the coal mines, all transportation, and the iron and steel industry were nationalized. In addition, a National Health Insurance system was put into operation to provide free medical care for all, with results that have not been conclusively determined.

The development of the Labour program was handicapped by the economic complications which the Second World War left behind. Great Britain's need to import had not diminished in the slightest—if anything it had become greater, since population had increased—but her ability to pay for these imports had been seriously impaired. The surplus wealth accumulated through the long years of industrial preeminence had been drained away and the "invisible exports" such as shipping and financial services had been sharply curtailed by the war. Britain was thus under the stern necessity of stimulating exports and limiting imports in order to get its economy back into balance. For the British people, this situation meant the prolongation and even intensification of rationing, and living under what was termed an "austerity" program.

These conditions made it somewhat difficult to demonstrate the virtues of socialization, particularly when one makes allowance for the inevitable blundering that accompanies any such large-scale operation. In 1950 the Attlee government was retained in office with a majority of six—hardly an enthusiastic endorsement—and a year later the Conservatives returned to power with Churchill (shortly to become Sir Winston Churchill) again at the helm. There was no drastic reversal of policy. The new regime moved to restore truck transportation and steel to private ownership, revealing in the process that it is much easier to nationalize than to denationalize. Improvement in Britain's economic position also made it possible to relax some of the controls.

In foreign policy both the Labour and Conservative governments cooperated closely with the United States, despite some grumbling from left-wing Labourites like Aneurin Bevan, and despite also some differences of opinion regarding policies to be followed with regard to the Communist world. Great Britain has looked more favorably than the United States on trade relations with Iron Curtain countries, and it recognized the Communist government in China in 1949. This step, however, failed to save Britain's substantial investments in China.

The death of the popular George VI in 1952 brought to the throne his daughter Elizabeth, whose coronation the following year provided a colorful spectacle for a nation that had had a long term of drabness. It is not to be wondered at that Britons in general chose to see in the name of the young queen a happy omen, perhaps presaging for them the glories of another Elizabethan Era.

ASIA

The predominant feature of the Asian world in the years following the war was the tremendous upsurge of nationalism which swept from one end of the continent to the other. One of the manifestations of this feeling was hostility to the few vestiges of Western colonialism that remained, and this hostility was exploited to the utmost by the Communists, who sought to absorb and utilize Asian nationalism.

The Far East. The greatest Communist success was won in China, which fell completely under Communist control in 1949. With the international implications of this event we shall deal later; for China itself it may be worth observing that, in spite of their triumph, the new rulers of the Middle Kingdom had formidable obstacles to overcome. The Nationalists had made some halfhearted and ineffectual attempts to reform China's land system, and their failure here had been a major factor in their loss of popular support. Whether the Communists could satisfy China's peasant millions remained to be seen. The new regime was also committed to intensive industrialization, a goal which could scarcely be achieved without some headaches.

Elsewhere in eastern Asia the nationalists managed to get along by themselves. Japan, under the supervision of Allied occupation forces commanded by General Douglas MacArthur, established a reasonably democratic government. The Philippine Republic had trouble for some years with the Hukbalahaps, a group which originated as a resistance movement during the Japanese occupation. When the Huks remained in arms because of the failure of the government to carry out land reforms, they were joined by the local Communists, and a full-scale revolt developed. However, Defense Minister Ramón Magsaysay broke the back of the Huk organization by a combination of firmness plus an offer of amnesty and a grant of land to those who laid down their arms. For this achievement Magsaysay was rewarded by being elected President of the Philippine Republic in 1953. In Indonesia nationalist forces resisted the return of the Dutch. After fruitless efforts to arrive at a compromise whereby Indonesia would enjoy equal status with the Netherlands in a commonwealth relationship, the Dutch finally withdrew and the Republic of Indonesia was established in 1949.

India and Pakistan. The British empire in India was another casualty of war. As the result of negotiations begun in 1942, India was partitioned into Hindu and Moslem states, which on 1 January 1947 became the dominions of India and Pakistan, with the right to withdraw from the Commonwealth if they so desired. At the same time Burma was given its independence, and Ceylon was granted dominion status. Relations between India and Pakistan have not been cordial. Minority groups on each side were massacred during the process of partition, and India's forcible seizure of Kashmir in 1947 and Hyderabad in 1948 almost led to open conflict. Fanaticism reached such a height that Gandhi was assassinated in 1948 by one of his own people for preaching moderation. Both India and Pakistan succeeded in establishing free governments with reasonable promise of stability.

The Middle East. In the Middle East the states of the Arab world all achieved independence by 1946, but nationalistic fervor still caused disturbances. The end of the Second World War brought a three-cornered conflict in Palestine between British, Jews, and Arabs, until the British finally threw up their mandate and turned the whole problem over to the United Nations. The consequences will be discussed in the next chapter.

Iran, strategically located and rich in oil, suffered from internal unrest. In 1951 the country came under the control of Mohammed Mossadegh, who had the support of a terrorist organization and whose claim to statesmanship otherwise consisted of an unfailing ability to faint in moments of political crisis. Mossadegh proceeded to nationalize (expropriate) the properties of the Anglo-Iranian Oil Company, whereupon the country's greatest industry ceased to function and its principal source of revenue dried up. Discontent of course increased, and it appeared that Iran was merely stepping out of the British frying pan into the Russian fire. However, when Mossadegh drove the Shah into exile in 1953 he touched off a reaction which in an amazingly short time brought the exiled monarch back and drove Mossadegh from power.

AFRICA

Africa, like Asia, found the aftermath of world conflict disturbing, although the less highly developed social system of much of Africa made its stirrings somewhat less intense than those of Asia. In North Africa nationalist movements had a familiar stamp. Egypt continued to agitate for the departure of the British, a step the latter finally took in 1954. The overthrow of the Egyptian monarchy in 1953 and subsequent political disorders suggest that the main sources of discontent in Egypt were internal. France also had its troubles with restlessness in Morocco and Tunisia—indeed, the French had to depose the reigning Sultan of Morocco in 1953 for trafficking with nationalist elements.

At the other end of the continent a most unpleasant situation developed. The Union of South Africa came under the control of a faction of fanatical Boer nationalists headed by Daniel Malan, whose ideas on race relationships made the most extreme examples of American Jim Crowism look moderate and tolerant by comparison. A few years of Malan had the white population of South Africa split badly on his racial policies and his threats to withdraw from the Commonwealth, while serious tension existed between the whites, the Negroes, and the substantial Hindu population.

Elsewhere in Africa the relations between the native peoples and the colonial powers were mixed. In such British possessions as Nigeria and the Gold Coast and in the Belgian Congo, there was real progress without the necessity of violence. In East Africa, however, racial antagonism brought bloodshed in the form of the indiscriminate terrorism of the Mau Maus in Kenya.

THE AMERICAN REPUBLICS

The nations of Latin America emerged from the Second World War without the physical damage that others had suffered, but they did face the problem of readjusting their economies to peacetime conditions after some years of "war boom." That this process should have been accompanied by occasional revolutionary outbreaks was scarcely foreign to Latin-American tradition, provided they were kept in the family. As elsewhere, however, there was in Latin America the ever-present danger that unrest and discontent would provide an attractive opening for the Communists. In addition, there was some apprehension that Perón's dictatorship in Argentina might turn into an aggressive militarism. Perón solidified his position in 1946 by winning an election in which the old issue of "Yankee imperialism" was dredged up to serve the Argentinian regime, and for some years thereafter he was intensely hostile to the United States.

This, however, can be regarded as Perón's high-water mark. He had nothing constructive to offer for Argentina's problems of readjustment to the postwar era; on the contrary, the extravagance of a dictatorship trying to purchase popularity had a less than healthy effect on the Argentinian economy. Consequently, as the 1950's arrived, it seems to have become increasingly clear to Perón that it was foolish to antagonize the one source of economic assistance. The change of administration in the United States gave him a convenient opportunity to change his policy, so that after the inauguration of President Eisenhower the Argentinian attitude toward the United States became, outwardly at least, far more friendly.

The Communist Problem. As this potential danger to hemispheric peace receded, the much greater menace of communism increased. A Communist bid for power had to be suppressed forcibly in both Colombia and Costa Rica in 1948, Guatemala came under the control of a Communist-dominated government from 1950 to 1954, and a

Communist "People's party" caused so much trouble in British Guiana that Britain was forced to suspend the colony's constitution in 1953. These were minor threats, and on the whole Latin America was unreceptive to Soviet blandishments. Nevertheless there was clear warning of potential trouble if the economic and social development of Latin America should be seriously retarded.

Canada. Canada had played a vitally important part in the Second World War, not only militarily but also diplomatically as a connecting link between the United States and Great Britain. Wartime developments, in addition, launched an industrial boom in Canada which continued after the return of peace, so that the dominion became a major power in its own right. There was, however, no significant change in Canada's internal politics or its relationship to either Great Britain or the United States. The Liberal party, in power since 1935, maintained its hold on the Canadian electorate without serious challenge, the only noteworthy incident being the retirement in 1948 of the veteran Prime Minister William Lyon Mackenzie King and his replacement by Louis St. Laurent.[1] When the United States continued hesitant about the St. Lawrence Seaway, Canada undertook to do the job by itself and made substantial progress. This demonstration that the seaway was likely to be built in any event assisted its American proponents to get an act through Congress in 1954 authorizing the United States to participate.

Like everyone else, Canada had its Communist problem. Indeed, the first step in unveiling the Red espionage network in the Western Hemisphere occurred when a clerk of the Russian Embassy in Ottawa, Igor Gouzenko, got tired of abusing Canadian hospitality and went to the "Mounties" with a large and embarrassing assortment of documents. The Canadians handled this situation efficiently, but with none of the sound and fury that accompanied similar exposures in their neighbor to the southward.

THE UNITED STATES

The restoration of peace found the United States with a new President, Harry S. Truman, who had made a good record as Senator from Missouri but was untested in the responsibilities so unexpectedly thrust upon him. To complicate matters further, his support in Congress was uncertain. On questions of foreign policy he was fairly secure, since the leaders of both parties were anxious to maintain unity on the international front as far as possible. Domestic politics were another matter. The administration was frequently opposed by a combination of Re-

---

[1] King died in 1950. He had been Prime Minister from 1921 to 1926, 1926 to 1930, and 1935 to 1948.

publicans and Southern Democrats, and in 1946 the Republicans gained a majority in both Houses of Congress for the first time since 1930.

Demobilization. The first task to be performed after V-J Day was the dismantling of the great war machine. The rationing system was scrapped virtually overnight, and price controls, while continued for a year longer, became progressively less effective. The abrupt termination of Lend-Lease after the Japanese surrender came as a shock to the other United Nations, who had expected a more gradual liquidation of the program. The demobilization of the armed forces was carried out at a pace which gravely disturbed the military authorities. The eagerness of most of the twelve million men inducted into the services to return home and of their families to get them back created pressures that could not be ignored, with the result that the personnel of the armed forces sank to a dangerously low figure. To bolster the nation's defenses the administration came forward with a proposal for universal military training, whereby young men would be subject to a year of training on reaching the age of eighteen. Opinion on this question was so sharply divided that nothing was done until June, 1948, when Congress enacted a limited revival of selective service.

The Atomic Energy Act. An equally pressing problem bequeathed by the war, the control of atomic energy, was settled by the Atomic Energy Act of 1946. This piece of legislation, largely the work of Senator Brien McMahon of Connecticut, was designed to guarantee civilian control of the development of this new and terrifying source of power, while at the same time preserving for the military authorities a voice in determining what restrictions should be imposed in the interest of national defense and security. The first chairman of the Atomic Energy Commission created by this act was David E. Lilienthal, previously the head of the TVA.

Labor Unrest. While the reconversion of industry to peacetime production was carried out more smoothly than had been anticipated, the United States did not escape the industrial unrest which habitually comes in the wake of war. Organized labor moved promptly to secure wage increases as compensation for the ending of the high overtime earnings of the war years. The move had its justification in the fact that prices showed no sign of descending, but the concessions that were made undoubtedly contributed to the inflationary trend of the period. Accentuating labor unrest were the continuing rivalry between the A.F. of L. and the CIO and struggles for control in various unions between Communist and anti-Communist elements.

Recurrent strikes, particularly a short-lived tie-up of rail traffic in the spring of 1947 and the chronic work stoppages of the United Mine Workers while new contracts were being negotiated, generated a public demand for governmental action. The administration revived the injunction as an antistrike weapon, the most interesting result being the imposition of a fine of $3,500,000 on the United Mine Workers in 1947 for contempt of court—later reduced by the Supreme Court to $700,000. The government also used its war powers to take over and operate strike-bound industries. This technique worked well enough during the immediate postwar years; when, however, President Truman tried to seize the steel industry early in 1952 he was sharply reminded by the Supreme Court that the powers he was invoking were not inherent in his office but had been granted by legislation which had expired some time before.

When the Republicans gained control of Congress, they offered as their remedy for the labor problem the Taft-Hartley Act of 1947. This measure, which replaced the New Deal's Wagner Act, reaffirmed the right of collective bargaining but imposed some restrictions on union activity. It required a secret vote before a strike could be called, outlawed jurisdictional strikes, abolished the closed shop, prohibited Communists from holding office in labor unions, and restricted the employment of union funds for political purposes. This act was bitterly attacked by the unions, less, it would appear, because it affected the status of the individual worker than because it threatened their institutional power. At any rate, they were not successful in appealing to public opinion. When Senator Robert A. Taft, son of the former President, ran for reelection in Ohio in 1950, he carried the state by the largest majority he had ever received in spite of a concerted effort by organized labor to unseat him.

Subversive Activities and Civil Rights. More far-reaching and disturbing in its effects on American life was the question of subversive activities by Communist sympathizers. That there was an unmistakable threat of this kind was made abundantly evident by the unearthing of a well-organized espionage ring which had transmitted atomic secrets to the Soviet Union and the disclosure that a few highly placed public officials had, to say the least, dubious affiliations. The most spectacular incident was the conviction of Alger Hiss, who had held responsible posts in the State Department, on charges of perjury connected with the transmission of official documents to Soviet agents. On the other hand, the prospect of a "witch hunt" attracted demagogues and publicity-seekers, including several self-confessed ex-Communists, and raised the danger of creating a climate of opinion in which dissent would be identified with sedition. Of the participants in this anti-Communist campaign, the one who attracted most attention was Senator Joseph H. McCarthy of Wisconsin.

The most tangible result of this activity was the Internal Security Act of 1950, an elaborate piece of legislation designed to provide more rigorous surveillance and control of subversive individuals and groups and to restrict the dissemination of subversive doctrines. This law, of course, had to face the problem of where to draw the line between sedition and mere unorthodoxy, and it was severely criticized—in fact, it had to be passed over President Truman's veto—on the ground that it created a serious and unnecessary menace to ordinary civil liberties. Its sponsor, Senator McCarran of Nevada, also helped to produce the McCarran-Walter Immigration Act of 1952, a needed codification of existing immigration law which came under heavy fire because it preserved a quota system for immigration based on the idea of "Nordic" supremacy.

If signs of intolerance were distressingly numerous in these post-war years, there was, to offset them to some extent, a vigorous championship of civil rights for minority religious and racial groups. During the war a Fair Employment Practices Committee combated economic discrimination with some success, but Southern hostility prevented its continuation. Early in 1948 a presidential commission issued an exhaustive report on civil rights, which was made the basis of a recommendation by President Truman for Federal legislation, again blocked by Southern opposition. However, the airing of the subject was all to the good, and some states passed Fair Employment Practices Acts of their own. In addition, several important decisions of the Supreme Court opened the way to greater equality of opportunity in education.

The 1948 Election. All these issues were active in the 1948 presidential campaign, in addition to questions of foreign policy. The Democratic party seemed to be in a sorry plight. On one side, conservative Southerners, outraged by President Truman's program of civil rights and unable to prevent his nomination, organized their own "Dixiecrat" ticket. On the other side, the radical element, especially those who disapproved of the administration's strong policy toward the Soviet Union, seceded under the leadership of Henry Wallace and formed a new Progressive party, a development received with cries of joy by the Communists. The Republicans, scenting victory after sixteen lean years, managed to keep their own internal conflicts under better control as they nominated Governor Thomas E. Dewey of New York for the second time.

The election proved to be the most astonishing upset in American political history. With two schisms in his party, either of which should have been fatal to his prospects, and in the fact of public-opinion polls and "expert" forecasts which predicted an overwhelming Dewey victory, President Truman was reelected in a race which remained in doubt almost until the last ballots were counted.[2] Overconfidence on the Repub-

[2] The result was:

	Popular vote	*Electoral vote*
Truman	24,105,812	303
Dewey	21,970,065	189
Thurmond (Dixiecrat)	1,169,021	39
Wallace	1,157,172	0

lican side and admiration for Truman's courageous fight in an apparently hopeless cause contributed to the result. In addition, the vagueness of the Republican campaign made it possible for Truman to stimulate apprehension, particularly among the farmers, that a Republican victory would mean loss of their government benefits.

The Fair Deal. As President in his own right, Truman presented to Congress in January, 1949, a comprehensive program which he termed the "Fair Deal." Essentially a compilation of measures he had already advocated, it called for an extension of the social-security system, a national health-insurance program (denounced by the American Medical Association as "socialized medicine"), and the assumption of greater responsibility by the national government for guaranteeing full employment and an economy running constantly at full speed—in what direction was not specified.

This "welfare state" failed to attract congressional support. The only important part of the program to receive legislative approval was a revision of the Social Security Act in 1950 to enlarge the number covered by its old-age-retirement provisions and to raise the benefits paid in order to meet the increased cost of living. Congress also extended the existing farm-price-support system in 1949, so that farmers continued to be guaranteed 90 per cent of parity for the crops included in the system. The effect was to maintain both farm income and food prices at extremely high levels and to accumulate in the hands of the government enormous surpluses whose ultimate disposal became an increasingly insoluble problem. In the same year (1949) Congress passed legislation designed to implement the findings of an advisory commission under former President Hoover regarding reorganization of the executive branch of the government.

Even if the Korean War had not intervened, it is doubtful if any more of the Fair Deal program could have been pushed through a reluctant Congress, especially in view of the fact that no great public enthusiasm for it was ever manifested. In addition, within the administration itself there was a noticeable slackening of reforming zeal in favor of enjoyment of the pleasures of office. Embarrassing scandals cropped up in the Bureau of Internal Revenue and the Reconstruction Finance Corporation, and the air was rife with well-founded charges of "influence peddling" and the acceptance by public officials of gifts of mink coats and deep freezers from individuals doing business with the government—one official testified that he would regard the presentation of a ham weighing less than 12 pounds as a friendly gesture, more than that as a bribe.

The Election of Eisenhower. Thus when the 1952 campaign came along, public discontent with "communism, corruption, and Korea" offered the Republicans a favorable prospect of gaining the victory that had so unaccountably eluded them four years before. A strenuous contest for the Republican nomination ensued between General Dwight D. Eisenhower, representing the moderate, internationally minded wing of the party, and Senator Robert A. Taft, who had become his party's undisputed leader in Congress and was known as "Mr. Republican." Taft's support came from the right-wing, isolationist elements, although Taft's own views were more moderate in general than those of his backers. After a rather acrimonious convention battle over disputed delegations, the popular "Ike" won out. On the Democratic side, after President Truman had eliminated himself as a candidate, the nomination finally went to Governor Adlai E. Stevenson of Illinois. The fact that he was relatively unknown while Eisenhower was a national hero was unquestionably a serious handicap to Stevenson in the ensuing race, but it is doubtful if any Democrat could have made headway against the deep-seated feeling of "It's time for a change."

Eisenhower won by 33,936,252 to 27,314,992 and an electoral vote of 442 to 89, carrying several Southern states in the process. His party did not fare quite as well. It emerged with a slight majority in the House and exactly half the seats in the Senate, and it became a minority in the latter chamber when Senator Taft died in 1953 and was replaced by a Democrat. Taft's death was an even more severe blow to the new administration in that he was the one man in the Republican party who could keep the reactionary wing of the organization reasonably under control.

Policies and Problems. In view of its shaky congressional support, it was just as well that the new administration contemplated no drastic changes of policy. It moved circumspectly, seeking, where it disapproved of what its predecessors had been doing, to modify rather than reverse. The national budget was cut, a step materially aided by the end of active fighting in Korea, and there was less disposition to assume that any problem could be handled better by the Federal government than by local authorities or private enterprise. Legislation was enacted to give jurisdiction over the "tidelands" oil areas—oil fields lying offshore—to the states. This issue had come up a few years earlier and had run into Supreme Court decisions that, in the absence of legislation to the contrary, the Federal government alone had jurisdiction over mineral deposits beyond the low-water mark. A farm program with flexible price supports was projected.

The principal shadows in the outlook of this first Republican administration in twenty years were the threat of economic depression as the post–Second World War boom faded away and the inflationary effect of the Korean War disappeared, and the apparent inability of the Republican party to resolve the factional differences which had caused so much ill feeling at the 1952 convention. President Eisenhower had to use all his influence to defeat the constitutional amendment proposed by Senator Bricker of Ohio, which would have seriously restricted the ability of the executive to conduct international relations. The fact that at Yalta and Potsdam rather extensive commitments had been made in behalf of the American people but without their knowledge or consent gave the Bricker Amendment more support than it might otherwise have had, and there was considerable sympathy for the idea of requiring that treaties must conform to the Constitution to be valid—a point not made clear in the original document. What the administration objected to was a provision requiring not only congressional approval of international agreements but in some cases state approval as well. As President Eisenhower pointed out, this was a return to the Articles of Confederation. More serious was the open rift between the Administration and Senator McCarthy, which culminated in an unedifying public exchange of charges and countercharges between McCarthy and the Department of the Army —with, as an undercurrent, a conflict over the basic question of the proper limits of legislative and executive authority.

While this constitutional issue was being thrashed out before the television cameras, an equally important one was being passed on in the calm of the Supreme Court. In the spring of 1954 the Court held, by unanimous vote, that racial segregation in public schools was unconstitutional.

The verdict of the electorate on this record, as expressed in the midterm elections of 1954, was distinctly uncertain. The Democrats gained control of both Houses of Congress, but by such slender margins that the result could hardly be interpreted as a clear-cut repudiation of the administration. As far as it could be interpreted at all, it indicated that the great majority of American voters preferred middle-of-the-road courses in both domestic and foreign policy. The same distaste for extremes was reflected in the action of the Senate in passing a vote of censure on McCarthy after a special committee had reported adversely on the Wisconsin Senator's conduct.

45

The Cold War

During the Second World War the fact that the Western Powers and the U.S.S.R. were fighting a common enemy produced an alliance of sorts. For its part the United States was quite sincerely dedicated to the proposition that communism and democracy could live at peace in the world following the war. Unfortunately, by 1947 it had become lucidly clear to even the most obtuse that, despite occasional protestations to the contrary, the Soviet Union labored under no such delusion. Reluctantly facing the challenge now made manifest, the United States launched a program aimed first at the containment of the Soviet Union but which gradually reached the stage of threats of "massive retaliation" should the Soviet or its satellites commit any further acts of aggression. This is the basis of the Cold War. It began with the Truman Doctrine, which will be discussed later in this chapter, and was followed by the Marshall Plan.

THE MARSHALL PLAN

Western Europe had been left so exhausted and devastated by the war that outside assistance was necessary if its peoples were to survive. The United Nations Relief and Rehabilitation Administration (UNRRA), spearheaded by the United States, did fine work in the matter of providing food and other assistance to the uprooted, but clearly something more was necessary.

In a speech delivered at the Harvard University commencement on 5 June 1947, Secretary of State George C. Marshall extended an invitation to the nations of Europe to cooperate in formulating a plan for com-

750

plete recovery and promised that the United States would provide the aid necessary to implement such a plan.

The result was the establishment in the United States of the Economic Cooperation Administration (ECA) and in Europe of the Organization for European Economic Cooperation (OEEC) with headquarters in Paris. Hence the free countries of Europe together with the United States commenced upon a joint enterprise for European economic recovery as a *sine qua non* for the creation and maintenance of conditions necessary for freedom and peace all over the world.

Soviet Opposition. Although Russia and her satellites were invited to participate in this cooperative enterprise, Russia refused to allow any of the members of the Soviet orbit to do so. Thus the Marshall Plan became a step in the Cold War. Russia's response to the European Recovery Program was the creation of the Communist Information Bureau (Cominform), which supplemented the work of the revived Comintern. The Cominform came into existence at a meeting in Warsaw in the fall of 1947 presided over by Commissar Zhdanov of the Russian Politburo. Headquarters of the new organization were established initially at Belgrade, and its main task was to defeat the European Recovery Program.

Despite the formidable opposition arrayed against it, the Marshall Plan achieved a great measure of success before it was terminated. In the four years of its existence it received over 11 billion dollars from the United States and helped to protect Europe both from economic collapse and Communist domination.

Trade and Aid. As impressive as the achievements of the Marshall plan proved to be, it was clear that something more than aid would be necessary if free Europe were to continue to make progress. In 1952 the phrase "trade, not aid" became popular. The theory here was that if the United States would lower its tariff barriers more European goods could be sold, thereby enabling Europe to strengthen its economic position. While there was much truth in this position, it was equally true that Europe had some house cleaning to do itself. European barriers also existed and called for reduction or removal.

That Europe was aware of its own responsibilities might be seen from such indigenous steps as Benelux, the Brussels Pact, the Council of Europe, and the Schuman Plan.

THE NORTH ATLANTIC TREATY ORGANIZATION (NATO)

Since economic measures alone would not guarantee the defense of free Europe from the Communist threat, military steps were also required. As a result of the necessary ratifications of the North Atlantic

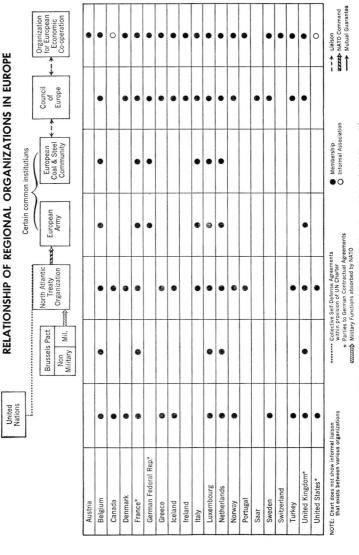

RELATIONSHIP OF REGIONAL ORGANIZATIONS IN EUROPE

From U.S. Department of State Publication 4944 (1953, p. 2).

752

Treaty, the North Atlantic Treaty Organization (NATO) was established in November, 1949, to safeguard peace and security through the combined efforts of the member countries.

NATO was an outgrowth of Western Union, the integration of the military and naval resources of the United Kingdom, France, and the Benelux countries which had been formed in 1948. The United States Senate adopted a resolution by Senator Arthur H. Vandenberg on 11 June 1948 favoring the development of regional and other collective arrangements for individual and collective self-defense and recommending the association of the United States with such arrangements based on "continuous and effective self-help and mutual aid." With the way thus paved for American membership in a military treaty organization, conversations were commenced in Washington between the United States, Canada, and the Western Union nations for a treaty of mutual assistance for the North Atlantic area within the framework of Article 51 of the Charter of the United Nations. Norway, Denmark, Italy, Iceland, and Portugal joined by the time the treaty was signed in 1949, and in 1951 Greece and Turkey became members.

Terms of the Treaty. The mutual-assistance provisions of the treaty provided that they should be applied to an area which included the territory of any of the signatories in Europe, North America, and the Algerian departments of France; and to the occupational forces of any signatory in Europe as well as the Atlantic Ocean north of the Tropic of Cancer. The area would be enlarged as other states joined the agreement.

The North Atlantic Treaty contains no time limit but provides that after ten years, or at any time thereafter, the parties may consult together for the purpose of reviewing it; and that after twenty years any nation may withdraw following a one-year's notice.

The chief body of NATO is the North Atlantic Council, which is in permanent session. The Council, which is assisted by a secretariat, is the civilian branch and is concerned with all matters relating to the implementation of the treaty's provisions.

On the military side is the Military Committee and its subordinate bodies, the Standing Group and the Military Representatives Committee. The Military Committee consists of the chiefs of staff of the NATO members or their representatives. The first two NATO commands to be established were SACEUR, covering the European area, and SACLANT, covering the Atlantic Ocean area. The United States and Canada have their own regional planning group, and others were to be established as the occasion arose. The Supreme Headquarters Allied Powers, Europe (SHAPE), defends continental Europe; and, in the event of war, all land, sea, and air operations in Europe would be under the Supreme Allied Commander, Europe.

THE EUROPEAN DEFENSE COMMUNITY

In an effort to integrate the defense forces of the nations which form the European Coal and Steel Community (Schuman Plan) under one supranational authority, a treaty to establish the European Defense Community was signed at Paris, 27 May 1952.

EDC contained provisions for common political institutions, armed forces, budget, and arms program. The single integrated army was given the name of the European Defense Forces (EDF) in the treaty, and plans were also included for political institutions to supervise EDF and act as the Community's governing body. The same assembly as that of the Coal and Steel Community would act for EDC except that when the Defense Community's affairs were discussed three delegates each from France, Italy, and Western Germany would be added. This plan allotted to the latter three nations eighteen delegates each, ten each to Belgium and the Netherlands, and four to Luxembourg.

The Netherlands and Germany were the first to ratify the treaty. France however proved reluctant to do so. For one thing, even though a French Premier (Pleven) had set in motion the machinery for EDC, France feared a rearmed Germany. Then, too, the miracle of postwar German economic recovery contrasted glaringly with France's own relative slowness to recover.

As a result of France's refusal to ratify the European Defense Community Treaty, a conference was held in London, 28 September to 3 October 1954, in an attempt to find a compromise. Present were the representatives of Belgium, Canada, France, the German Federal Republic, Italy, Luxembourg, the Netherlands, the United Kingdom, and the United States. This conference worked out a system which provided for Western unity within the framework of the Brussels Treaty of 1948. The newly formed Western European Union had the same members as EDC with the significant addition of the United Kingdom, which made a long-term commitment of its military forces to the continent of Europe. The WEU Council was given broad authority, with the power to act in a number of important measures by majority vote, thereby replacing national with international control.

Other agreements reached under the new plan provided for the restoration of (West) German sovereignty. Commencing 4 October 1954, the Allied High Commissioners gave up the exercise of most of their occupation rights. Furthermore, provision was made for Germany to join NATO and thereby to make its contribution to the defense of the West. This was done under a system of armament controls placed upon the Germans.

THE NEAR AND MIDDLE EAST

In this region, an area which has produced three of the chief religions of the world—Judaism, Christianity, and Islam—scarcely a day has gone by since the end of the Second World War that has not produced events of international interest and importance. With its valuable oil fields, and its vital land and sea communications systems, it would be difficult to find an area of greater strategic importance in the contemporary world scene.

The peoples of this region have for the most part only recently secured their independence, a possession they value and wish to maintain and strengthen. Furthermore, a vision of an improved standard of living which would overcome poverty, disease, illiteracy, and their primitive economic systems has been opened up to them.

Iran. In 1945 the Soviet Union not only refused to withdraw the Red Army troops which had entered Iran during the war but helped to establish regimes in Azerbaijan and among the Kurds which were sympathetic toward Russia and its policies. Iran complained to the United Nations and, backed by the United States and the United Kingdom, won the support of the UN, so that the Red troops withdrew in December, 1946.

Since Soviet pressure on Iran continued in other ways, the United States and Iran signed an agreement in 1950 providing for the sending of American arms and munitions to help the Iranian government to combat communism. In addition to this military assistance, Iran received economic help under the American Point Four Program.

Turkey. Czarist Russia's "historic mission" had been to secure control of the straits (the Bosporus and the Dardanelles), but somehow the prize always managed to remain elusive. To the Soviet Union the straits were no less attractive, and even before the war ended in 1945 the Russian government had begun to exert pressure on Turkey. At both Yalta and Potsdam the Russians brought up the question and received American and British assurances that they would back conversations between the three powers and Turkey on the subject of a new agreement covering these strategic passages.

The American government lost little time in proposing in November, 1945, a most equitable revision of the Montreux Convention of 1936 which governed the use and control of the straits. Although both Britain and Turkey agreed to consider the American proposals as the basis for conversations, the Russians declined. They offered a substitute set of proposals in August, 1946, which would not only have placed the straits in their hands but would also have jeopardized Turkish independence.

The United States attempted to heal the breach by suggesting that Turkey should be primarily responsible for the defense of the straits but that should they be threatened or actually attacked it would then become a matter for action by the Security Council of the United Nations.

Russia remained adamant and declined to enter into conversations but at the same time continued its pressure on Turkey and let it be known that Russo-Turkish relations would improve if Turkey should cede some territory in eastern Anatolia.

The Truman Doctrine. Because the Russian threat to Turkey mounted rather than decreased and was joined with outright interference by the Soviet in Greece, the United States felt impelled to retaliate with the so-called Truman Doctrine, which was announced by President Harry S. Truman before Congress on 12 March 1947. It was based upon the security of the United States and upon the precedent established by Franklin Roosevelt that the United States would always aid "free peoples to maintain their free institutions and their national integrity against aggressive movements that seek to impose on them totalitarian regimes." Against the charge that this action by-passed the United Nations, the administration later pointed out the obvious impossibility of getting help to Greece and Turkey so long as Russia continued to abuse her veto power in the Security Council. It was further demonstrated that the need for action was imperative and that the United Nations, assuming it could aid these beleaguered countries, was not in a position to move swiftly enough to block the impending disaster. The Congress finally approved the recommendation of the President and voted an appropriation of $400,000,000. The measure called for loans or grants to Greece and Turkey and also the sending of both military and civilian missions to supervise the aid sent. Furthermore, should either government so desire, its aid would immediately be withdrawn. To satisfy the persistent feeling in some quarters that the UN had been by-passed, Senator Vandenberg inserted a proviso that the program should be terminated if the UN found its continuance to be either needless or undesirable.

By 1950 a total of some $700,000,000 in aid was spent by the United States to help Greece and Turkey defend themselves against the Soviet threat. Important as this program of Greek-Turkish aid was in itself, it proved to have wider significance in that it marked the beginning of the development of an American foreign policy of containment aimed at checking Soviet expansion. This policy of containment was to cover such important facets of American foreign policy as the Marshall Plan, the North Atlantic Treaty, and Point Four.

There can be no doubt that the American aid program saved the independence of Turkey, which then proceeded to advance along the road of democracy with most pleasing results. Government by one party came voluntarily to an end, and in 1950 Turkey's first free election was held. In this historic election the new opposition party, the Democratic party, headed by Celal Bayar, defeated the powerful Republican People's party, which since its foundation by Kemal Atatürk in 1923 had controlled the government.

The Turks have done well in the United Nations, where they have taken their role very seriously and were one of the first countries to respond to the United Nations' call for troops in Korea. In the Korean fighting the Turkish soldiers achieved a remarkable record for bravery.

Greece. Iran and Turkey were both fortunate enough to be spared the horrors of a Communist war, an experience which fell to the lot of Greece in the years 1946–1949. In the course of this terrible civil war in which the Communists sought by force to seize control of the Greek government, 75,000 people lost their lives, 700,000 were unrooted and became refugees, 25,000 children were kidnapped and lost without a trace, and the already war-weakened Greek economy was almost ruined.

The British forces which had been in Greece since the end of the Second World War were unable to cope with the demands put upon them by the civil war, and the Attlee government announced their withdrawal in February, 1947. This step combined with the Russian pressure on Turkey led to the announcement of the Truman Doctrine in March.

American military and economic help enabled the free Greeks to defeat the Communist guerrillas, many of whom were non-Greeks from Bulgaria and Albania, by 1949. Once peace was restored to the shattered country, American aid was used to rebuild the economy and to strengthen the Greek military arm. Greece showed its appreciation of this assistance and its comprehension of the Soviet threat to other lands as well as Greece by sending troops to fight against the Communists in Korea.

In addition to its membership in NATO, Greece signed a five-year friendship and mutual-security pact with its neighbors Turkey and Yugoslavia on 28 February 1953.

The Arab States and Israel. When the British announced their intention of terminating their mandate over Palestine, Zionist elements proclaimed the new state of Israel. The General Assembly of the United Nations sought to partition Palestine in a resolution passed on 29 November 1947. What this partition envisaged was a division of Palestine into separate Arab and Jewish states which would, however, combine in an economic union. Jerusalem, under this plan, would be an international enclave administered by the United Nations.

As the British withdrew, the Arabs endeavored by force of arms to prevent partition from occurring and to block the creation of Israel. In the ensuing war in 1948 between the Israelis and the Arab League,[1] not only were the Arabs soundly defeated but the Israelis were left in possession of more territory than the UN partition plan had allotted them. An armistice achieved by the United Nations gave Israel control of most of Palestine except for portions held by Jordan and Egypt. Jerusalem's status as a result of the war differed from the original UN plan since Israel held the New City and Jordan the Old City.

Israel and her enemies remained on terms of armed truce. Complicating the effective solution of the problem further were the conflicting interests of the American, Russian, and British governments. The United States, nevertheless, sought to do its best to promote a truly peaceful settlement between Israel and the Arab states.

SOUTH ASIA

Afghanistan. In 1949 a dispute took place between Pakistan and Afghanistan over some Moslem tribesmen in the Northwest Frontier Province of the former nation. Afghanistan claimed sovereignty over these Pathans and encouraged them to set up an autonomous state, but for the most part they sided with Pakistan. Pakistani retaliation brought fishing in these troubled waters by outsiders. Adopting the attitude that the United States and the United Kingdom were on Pakistan's side, the Afghans opened trade negotiations with the U.S.S.R. and put to work some Russian technicians. At this point the United States announced that the Export-Import Bank was prepared to grant a credit of $21,000,000 to Afghanistan for the development of a river valley in that country.

The reason for this brief mention of this remote land is that historically in recent times it had been a source of friction in Russo-British relations. Here, as in so many other cases, the United States had taken the place vacated by Britain's withdrawal.

Pakistan. The disputes between India and Pakistan over Kashmir and Hyderabad have already been mentioned, and we shall merely note here that in the Cold War Pakistan revealed herself as a loyal and hardworking member of the United Nations. Her interests were more closely allied with those of the United States than with the U.S.S.R., and so she was the recipient of American aid and in 1953 signed a military-assistance pact with the United States for which both were roundly condemned by India. The latter also took umbrage at the military alliance reached in 1954 between Pakistan and Turkey.

In addition to the military pact, the United States and Pakistan reached agreements calling for technical cooperation under which the

[1] Formed in 1945, the members included Egypt, Trans-Jordan (name changed in 1949 to Jordan), Saudi Arabia, Iraq, Syria, Lebanon, and Yemen.

United States provided funds for technical development in agriculture and industry.

India. Since the achievement of her independence, India has pursued a foreign policy which has attracted a great deal of world notice. The reactions to this policy have been somewhat mixed, however. To understand India's "dynamic neutrality" one has to appreciate (1) the continuing influence which the late Mahatma Gandhi's program of non-violence has exerted over his country and (2) the harsh memories India still retains of imperialism which have led her to wish to see it ended everywhere. This combination of forces has produced a policy of "non-alignment" whereby India refuses to join either of what Indians call "two competing blocs," one led by the United States and the other by the Soviet Union.

Despite political differences which at times have produced some acrid comments on both sides, the United States has been most laudatory of India's efforts to establish herself as a viable democracy. Should India succeed in this attempt, then all the peoples of Asia would have before them the example of a home-bred alternative to communism. For this reason the United States saw fit to overlook occasional Indian criticisms of American foreign policy and included India in the Point Four program.

THE FAR EAST AND SOUTHEAST ASIA

In the Far East and in Southeast Asia hundreds of millions of people have either fallen under Communist role since 1945 or are being subjected to pressures designed to accomplish this objective. American policy in the so-called Cold War has been put to severe tests in this heavily populated and resource-rich area.

The Struggle for China. When victory over Japan was achieved, a race to seize control of China was begun by the Chinese Nationalists and the Communists. The United States helped Nationalist armies to occupy certain strategic centers and took the position in a policy statement at the end of 1945 that it recognized the Nationalist government but urged an end to the civil war then going on and called for a conference between representatives of major political elements in China. General George C. Marshall was appointed as a special American envoy with instructions to work for a united China. Despite Marshall's efforts unification was not achieved, and he returned to the United States early in 1947.

There can be little doubt that American policy in China from 1944 to the failure of the Marshall mission was far from impressive, but to place the blame for the Nationalist collapse at the American doorstep is a gross oversimplification. That American blunders contributed unintentionally to the Communist victory is evident, but fundamentally the reasons for the Communist triumph were largely Chinese. The Kuomintang was simply incapable of winning a military victory and in the attempt to do so collapsed.

By the end of 1947 the Communists, who employed a mobile and less costly type of warfare than the Nationalists, were in control of most of Manchuria, where the Russians had turned over to them vast supplies of captured Japanese matériel; controlled an increasing area of North China; and had begun to head toward the Yangtze and mastery over Central China.

The Communist Triumph. Early in 1949 the Nationalists were driven to move their capital south to Canton. From then on it was just a question of time. Canton fell in October, and the Nationalists tried to return to Chungking in the west, where they had weathered the war with Japan. By the end of November Chungking too had fallen so that the Nationalists now abandoned the mainland and fled to Formosa.

The Communists announced their new regime, the Chinese People's Republic, on 1 October 1949. Mao Tse-tung was chosen President, and Chou En-lai Premier. Peiping rather than Nanking, the old capital of the Nationalists, became the new government headquarters.

Whether destined to remain a Soviet satellite or to become the number-one power of Asia in its own right, the new China had become a force of considerable magnitude in world affairs as its military accomplishments against the United States in the Korean War (1950–1953) should indicate, together with its ability to maintain order domestically, supply the Communist forces in Southeast Asia, and occupy Tibet as the first step in a seemingly planned expansion.

Conscious of its strength and increasing importance, Communist China began to clamor to replace the Nationalists as China's representatives in the United Nations, but found the United States consistently blocking the way. As the pressure began to mount for a recognition of Red China, its admittance to UN, and the opening of trade relations, it was a question of how long the United States could continue to offer resistance to these moves since so many American allies favored these steps despite American opposition.

Korea. At the Cairo Conference in 1943 between the United States, the United Kingdom, and Nationalist China, the three powers had pledged that Korea should become free and independent. At Yalta in February, 1945, it was decided that Russia should occupy the northern half of Korea and the United States the southern portion. This unfortunate decision resulted in a division of the country which ultimately led to war.

Despite UN efforts to bring about Korean unification by peaceful means, the Soviets refused to cooperate and even blocked the holding of elections under UN auspices in North Korea in 1948. The United Nations Temporary Commission on Korea went ahead in South Korea, and as a result of a free election a constitution was drawn up and a government based on democratic processes was established. This led the Russians to retaliate by establishing the puppet Democratic People's Republic of Korea.

It now remained for the occupational forces to withdraw. Russia jumped the gun by suddenly announcing its complete withdrawal on 25 December 1948, but the North Korean puppet government refused to permit the United Nations Commission on Korea to verify this claim. The United States shortly afterward announced that its forces would depart by 30 June 1949 with the exception of a few officers and men of a military advisory group which would stay to help train the army of the Republic of Korea.

The Korean War. Suddenly, without warning, early on the morning of 25 June 1950 armed forces of North Koreans crossed the 38th parallel into South Korea and commenced an attack calculated to unify Korea by force. An immediate UN resolution calling for the end of hostilities at once was ignored by the North Koreans.

The United States then undertook to support by military means the effort of the Council of the United Nations "to terminate this serious breach of the peace." General Douglas MacArthur was authorized to employ American units to aid the South Koreans, and on 7 July 1950 he was appointed commanding general of the forces operating in Korea and was directed to use the flag of the United Nations.

The war raged back and forth, and in November, 1950, Chinese Communist troops entered the contest on the side of the North Koreans. The entrance of the Chinese almost brought about the defeat of United Nations forces under MacArthur, but ultimately a stalemate ensued. MacArthur was forbidden to attack Manchuria for fear of broadening the war by bringing in the Russians. Because he chafed so under the restrictions put upon him, MacArthur was removed from his command by President Truman on 11 April 1951 and replaced by General Matthew B. Ridgway. The military stalemate which continued in the neighborhood of the 38th parallel was enlivened by history's first air battles between fleets of jet planes. In these battles the superiority of the American planes and pilots over the Russian jets flown by Chinese, Koreans, and an occasional Russian pilot was surprisingly great.

Although the American forces and casualties were by far the greatest on the United Nations side exclusive of those of the Republic of Korea, a total of forty-six nations made some kind of contribution, eco-

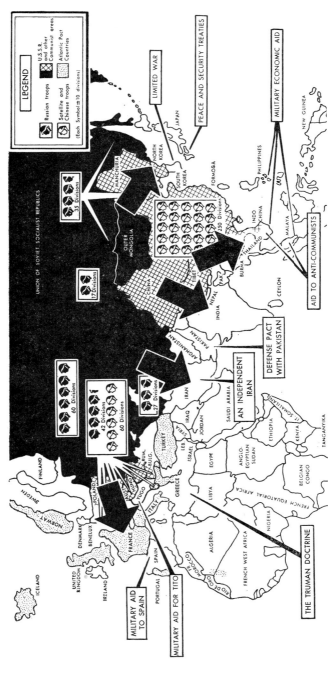

The Cold War: Soviet Pressures and Free World Defenses. Adapted from Department of State Publication 4443, General Foreign Policy Series 67 (November, 1952, pp. 76–77).

nomic or military, although only sixteen of them supplied armed forces.

Diplomatically, the UN invoked sanctions against North Korea and in the same action called upon its members to repel the armed attack on South Korea, later placed its forces under a unified command headed by the United States, branded Red China an aggressor but failed to invoke sanctions against this aggressor, and sought consistently to bring an end to hostilities.

Truce Negotiations. Truce talks were commenced in the summer of 1951 at Kaesong, were switched to Panmunjon, and lasted two years before an uneasy armistice was concluded and a cease-fire achieved. The stumbling block for months in the peace talks was the question of repatriation of prisoners. The position taken by the United States and the United Nations was the right of prisoners to enjoy political asylum if they so desired. The Communists demanded that prisoners and deserters should be forcibly returned. The principle of political asylum finally triumphed, and no prisoners were forcibly returned by either side. The twenty-odd Americans who elected not to be restored to their homeland contrasted markedly with the tens of thousands of Chinese and North Koreans who refused to go home.

The United States and the fifteen other members of the United Nations issued a declaration that, if the armistice should be broken by unprovoked Communist aggression, they would immediately resist and would not promise "to confine hostilities within the frontiers of Korea." In other words, no longer would the Communists be permitted the luxury of their "privileged sanctuary" beyond the Yalu which the United Nations' commanders were not permitted to attack during the duration of the Korean War.

The armistice was, of course, only a temporary affair with a definitive settlement reserved for a political conference. The United States let it be clear in advance that it would not tolerate a repetition of the delaying tactics in such a conference that had marked the long months of truce negotiations. Thus a terminal point for the political conference was set in advance as was the American objective in the conference: the achievement of a "united Korea for free Koreans."

The initial cost of such a united Korea included the lives of over 25,000 Americans together with another 125,000 American casualties; the total Communist casualties are estimated at about 2,000,000.

Indo-China. In a war that began in 1946 and seemed interminable France was engaged in defending Indo-China against communism. The three Associated States of Indo-China, viz., Viet-Nam, Cambodia, and Laos, also actively engaged in this war in order to maintain their independence. Arrayed against France and her allies were the Viet Minh

Communists led by Ho Chi Minh, a career Communist of over thirty years of experience, largely gained outside of Indo-China. The Viet Minh forces were supplied, trained, and advised by Communist China.

The United States took an increasingly lively interest in this long-protracted and fiercely fought war by supplying the French and their allies with a large proportion of their military equipment and supplies together with an impressive amount of economic aid.

Early in 1954 the French position deteriorated sharply, a development highlighted by the fall of the fortified post of Dienbienphu after a protracted siege. At this juncture the United States considered direct intervention in concert with other non-Communist powers but found little enthusiasm for such a step either at home or abroad.

The problem was finally solved by the Geneva Conference (1954), which resulted in the termination of hostilities. France's former colony was partitioned into the free and independent states of Laos and Cambodia, and Viet-Nam was divided into North Viet-Nam (Communist) and South Viet-Nam (free). Provision was made for the maintenance of the France Expeditionary Corps in South Viet-Nam until after the free elections scheduled for 1956.

Malaya. Although not on the scale of the military operations in either Korea or Indo-China, the Communists took up arms in another valuable part of East Asia, Malaya. There at the end of the Second World War the Reds first endeavored to weaken the economy of the Malayan Union by a series of crippling strikes, after which they went into the dense jungle to wage guerrilla warfare. The mobility of the armed Communist bands and the difficult nature of the countryside have combined to give the British a great deal of trouble in their efforts to smash the terrorists.

SEATO

The Geneva Conference revealed the need for unity among the free nations interested in Southeast Asia. Accordingly, in September, 1954, a number of them came together in Manila to negotiate the Southeast Asia Treaty Organization. Included were Australia, France, New Zealand, Pakistan, the Philippines, Thailand, the United Kingdom, and the United States. The result was SEATO, which provides that, in the case of aggression by armed attack, each of the countries will act to meet the common danger. A SEATO Council was established for consultation in military and other planning. Furthermore, the treaty provides that if any party to it believes that the integrity of the treaty area is menaced by other than armed attack, the parties shall consult immediately to agree on common measures.

AFRICA

While not as actively involved as Europe and Asia, the Dark Continent found itself caught up in the current of world affairs to an increasing degree. As nationalism began to assert itself in many parts of Africa, the colonial powers in an effort to retain their positions sought to make their subjects more satisfied through a series of development projects which would at the same time ease the mother country's situation economically as well as politically. But by the middle of the twentieth century the dissatisfaction of so many of the people of Africa with their lot made it appear increasingly unlikely that they would ever again play a subordinate role to the colonial powers.

Space does not permit the kind of attention the rise of Africa calls for and therefore only the most summary mention may be made of developments of immediate concern to the United States. The unrest in French North Africa achieved such proportions that the United States was unable to remain aloof as rioting and political turmoil grew. For example, the attempts made by such Moslem states as Egypt and Pakistan to place the Moroccan situation on the agenda of the UN assembly in 1951 saw the United States loath to incur the antipathy of France, and thereby America aroused the ire of many Moslems, as it did again that year by refraining from voting to allow the Security Council to explore the Tunisian situation in a full-dress debate.

As far as the Anglo-Egyptian quarrel was concerned, the United States kept its hands off. It was made clear that America's interest lay in having the parties arrive at an amicable settlement which would clear the way for the formation of a Middle East defense organization as a barrier to Soviet expansion in that area.

Thus the Cold War had touched Africa relatively lightly by the middle 1950's. Nevertheless there was abundant evidence that Communist agitators were fishing industriously in the troubled waters of anti-colonialism, and that African developments were likely to become matters of increasing concern for the United States.

LATIN AMERICA

With a few minor exceptions imperialism was nonexistent in the Latin-American countries in the middle of the twentieth century; yet the peoples of this continent and their governments revealed themselves to be quite sympathetic toward those peoples of the world who were in opposition to the imperialist nations. This attitude, combined with some growth in the ranks of Latin-American Communists, proved cause for concern on the part of the United States in the Cold War, with the result that increasing attention was paid by the State Department to Latin-American affairs.

Politically, the ties between the United States and its neighbors to the south have been recognized by the development of the inter-American system which preceded the United Nations. The Inter-American Conference at Chapultepec, Mexico, produced the Act of Chapultepec, calling for an inter-American treaty of mutual assistance. This proposal was implemented two years later at the Rio Conference (which actually met at Quitandinha, a suburb of Rio). Argentina tried unsuccessfully to have each signatory given the right of veto over common action against an aggressor, but as a concession to Argentinian susceptibilities, the Rio Pact made special provision for handling conflicts between American states.

The Organization of American States. The treaty also recognized the possibility of disturbance of the peace of the Americas by causes other than conflicts between nations. That this danger was somewhat more than academic was sharply underlined when the next inter-American conference met at Bogotá, Colombia, in 1948. The sessions were held to the accompaniment of gunfire, as Colombian troops battled through the city to suppress a Communist-inspired uprising. In spite of this disturbance the Bogotá Conference drafted a charter for an Organization of American States, which gave permanent institutional form to the structure of inter-American cooperation which had been built up over the preceding two generations. Under this charter the Organization is to function within the framework of the United Nations. It was given a governing council consisting of one representative of each of the member states, and the Pan American Union in Washington was designated as its secretariat. The mutual-security provisions of the Rio Pact were extended to include specifically not only acts of aggression but "any other fact or situation that might endanger the peace of America."

This warning, obviously directed against the sort of thing the delegates were witnessing in Bogotá, was followed by the adoption, at the Caracas Conference in 1954, of an innocuous anti-Communist resolution, along with one denouncing colonialism. The Latin-American states were unwilling to commit themselves further, because of a fear that a stronger policy might afford a pretext for future intervention in their internal affairs.

THE POINT FOUR PROGRAM

Realizing that military assistance and abstract notions of democracy were not in themselves enough to guarantee the containment of communism and that people everywhere, particularly in the underdeveloped areas of the world, required help to develop their resources, President

Truman in the fourth point of his inaugural address in January, 1949, called for action to aid the peoples of such areas:

> We must embark on a bold new program for making the benefits of our scientific advances and industrial progress available for the improvement and growth of underdeveloped areas . . . we should make available to peace-loving peoples the benefits of our store of technical knowledge in order to help them realize their aspirations for a better life. And, in cooperation with other free nations, we should foster capital investment in areas needing development . . .
>
> Our aim should be to help the free peoples of the world, through their own efforts, to produce more food, more clothing, more materials for housing, and more mechanical power to lighten their burdens.

As in the case of the Marshall Plan, the people involved were themselves expected to make the greatest effort of which they were capable to help themselves. The technical aid offered under Point Four included measures to better food production, health, education, and productive skills; the financial assistance was planned to improve transportation, communications, water control and power, and productive industries. The whole program involved a long-range undertaking and required the expenditure of large sums of money but was looked upon as time and money well spent—as an investment in the security of the United States and the rest of the free world.

Point Four was officially inaugurated in June, 1950, by the Act for International Development and soon became part of an international movement on the part of the free world. A portion of Point Four funds went to the support of expanded technical-assistance programs by the United Nations and the Organization of American States. Also cooperating were members of the Commonwealth of Nations through the Colombo Plan, a program relating to South and Southeast Asia which was broadened in 1954 to include the United States and Japan.

THE PROBLEM OF THE ATOM

Important as the subjects are which have been treated in this chapter to this point, they become relatively insignificant in the face of the problem of the atom, control over which will go a long way toward deciding whether the Cold War will ultimately be resolved peacefully or by military means.

The Baruch Plan. The first General Assembly of the UN created an Atomic Energy Commission which was instructed to formulate a plan of effective international control. A few months later the United States placed before the UN Atomic Energy Commission the so-called Baruch Proposals whereby the United States offered to give up its monopoly of atomic weapons and turn over its technical knowledge to the Commission in return for an effective international system of control. When such a system of control had been approved and had come into effect, the United States would terminate the manufacture of atomic bombs and its stockpile of bombs would be disposed of by agreement. The UN would then possess all information relative to atomic-energy production for peaceful and military purposes.

On 4 November 1948 the UN General Assembly overwhelmingly approved what was substantially the Baruch Plan. The only opposition came from Russia and its satellites. Under the plan approved at this time, an international atomic-energy cooperative would be established, to which nations would turn over all their atomic materials to be held in trust by an international control agency. All facilities for the making of atomic materials would also be turned over. The agency would then issue licenses for peaceful use of atomic materials. However, the international agency would retain the right to make inspections and surveys anywhere in the world (1) to locate new deposits of ores, and (2) to detect and prevent illegal activities. Although no area of the world would be exempt from inspection, safeguards against abuse of this power would be guaranteed. Finally, the work of the control agency would not be subject to veto by any nation, nor could a violator of the treaty's terms be protected from the consequences by any legal right, veto or otherwise.

The Soviet rejected this plan and countered with its own, which called for the nations to own, operate, and manage all atomic-energy facilities of their own. There would be an international control body with powers only of periodic inspection of declared facilities alone. Furthermore, the control body proposed in the Soviet plan was limited merely to making recommendations to nations and to the Security Council, a body in which the veto could still be exercised.

With matters continuing at an impasse the United States, the United Kingdom, and France in late 1951 presented a disarmament plan embracing all armed forces and armaments, including atomic weapons, to the General Assembly. This plan involved the employment of international inspectors who would be free to investigate anywhere, and so the Soviet Union opposed it. At first the Russian delegate, Mr. Vyshinsky, attempted to heap ridicule on the proposal but later got around to offering a substitute plan which, however, contained no safeguards. By way of compromise the General Assembly on 11 January 1952 adopted the proposal of the three Western powers with some modifications and established a Disarmament Commission which the Soviet agreed to join only to hamstring effectively through its familiar tactics.

The Eisenhower Program. No progress having been made by 1953, President Dwight D. Eisenhower in an address before the UN

General Assembly on 8 December offered his plan to put atomic energy to peaceful uses. Mr. Eisenhower proposed the establishment of an International Atomic Energy Agency under the United Nations which would receive joint contributions from the nations' stockpiles of "normal uranium and fissionable materials." The agency would be responsible for the impounding, storage, and protection of these materials. It would also be expected to devise methods whereby this fissionable material would be put to peaceful usages. Experts would be mobilized to apply atomic energy to the needs of agriculture, medicine, and other peaceful activities. For example, abundant electrical energy would be released to those areas of the world most in need of it.

While those most concerned were being given an opportunity to consider the Eisenhower proposals, the United States dramatically confirmed suspicions that it had perfected an even more terrible engine of destruction than the atomic bomb. In March, 1954, two hydrogen bombs were detonated in the Pacific area with such startling results that a great proportion of humanity was terrified.

The Hydrogen Bomb. It was revealed that the explosive force of a single hydrogen bomb at this time was some 600 to 700 times as great as that of the atomic bombs dropped on Japan and that each of these new bombs was equal in destructive power to millions of tons of TNT.

Even before the American tests in the Marshall Islands, the Russians had boasted of having built and perfected similar thermonuclear weapons. Since their great physicist, Kapitza, and a number of German scientists in Russian employ were known for their special competence in the field of technical problems relating to the hydrogen bomb, there seemed no reason to doubt the Russian claim.

As Bernard M. Baruch said when he put forth the American plan for control of atomic energy in 1946:

> We are here to make a choice between the quick and the dead. That is our business . . . If we fail, then we have damned every man to be the slave of fear. Let us not deceive ourselves: We must elect world peace or world destruction.

The Declaration of Independence

IN CONGRESS, JULY 4, 1776, THE UNANIMOUS DECLARATION OF THE THIRTEEN UNITED STATES OF AMERICA

When in the Course of human events, it becomes necessary for one people to dissolve the political bands which have connected them with another, and to assume among the Powers of the earth, the separate and equal station to which the Laws of Nature and of Nature's God entitle them, a decent respect to the opinions of mankind requires that they should declare the causes which impel them to the separation.

We hold these truths to be self-evident, that all men are created equal, that they are endowed by their Creator with certain unalienable rights, that among these are Life, Liberty, and the pursuit of Happiness. That to secure these rights, Governments are instituted among Men, deriving their just powers from the consent of the governed. That whenever any Form of Government becomes destructive of these ends, it is the Right of the People to alter or to abolish it, and to institute new Government, laying its foundation on such principles and organizing its powers in such form, as to them shall seem most likely to effect their Safety and Happiness. Prudence, indeed, will dictate that Governments long established should not be changed for light and transient causes; and accordingly all experience hath shown, that mankind are more disposed to suffer, while evils are sufferable, than to right themselves by abolishing the forms to which they are accustomed. But when a long train of abuses and usurpations, pursuing invariably the same Object evinces a design to reduce them under absolute Despotism, it is their right, it is their duty, to throw off such Government, and to provide new Guards for their future security.—Such has been the patient sufferance of these Colonies; and such is now the necessity which constrains them to alter their former Systems of Government. The history of the present King of Great Britain is a history of repeated injuries and usurpations, all having in direct object the establishment of an absolute Tyranny over these States. To prove this, let Facts be submitted to a candid world.

He has refused his Assent to Laws, the most wholesome and necessary for the public good.

He has forbidden his Governors to pass Laws of immediate and pressing importance, unless suspended in their operation till his Assent should be obtained; and when so suspended, he has utterly neglected to attend to them.

He has refused to pass other Laws for the accommodation of large districts of people, unless those people would relinquish the right of Representation in the Legislature, a right inestimable to them and formidable to tyrants only.

He has called together legislative bodies at places unusual, uncomfortable, and distant from the depository of their public Records, for the sole purpose of fatiguing them into compliance with his measures.

He has dissolved Representative Houses repeatedly, for opposing with manly firmness his invasions on the rights of the people.

He has refused for a long time, after such dissolutions, to cause others to be elected; whereby the Legislative powers, incapable of Annihilation, have returned to the People at large for their exercise; the State remaining in the mean time exposed to all the dangers of invasion from without, and convulsions within.

He has endeavoured to prevent the population of these States; for that purpose obstructing the Laws of Naturalization of Foreigners; refusing to pass others to encourage their migrations hither, and raising the conditions of new Appropriations of Lands.

He has obstructed the Administration of Justice, by refusing his Assent to Laws for establishing Judiciary powers.

He has made Judges dependent on his Will alone, for the tenure of their offices, and the amount and payment of their salaries.

He has erected a multitude of New Offices, and sent hither swarms of Officers to harass our People, and eat out their substance.

He has kept among us, in times of peace, Standing Armies without the Consent of our legislature.

He has affected to render the Military independent of and superior to the Civil Power.

He has combined with others to subject us to a jurisdiction foreign to our constitution, and unacknowledged by our laws; giving his Assent to their Acts of pretended Legislation:

For quartering large bodies of armed troops among us:

For protecting them, by a mock Trial, from Punishment for any Murders which they should commit on the Inhabitants of these States:

For cutting off our Trade with all parts of the world:

For imposing taxes on us without our Consent:

For depriving us in many cases, of the benefit of Trial by jury:

For transporting us beyond Seas to be tried for pretended offences:

For abolishing the free System of English Laws in a neighbouring Province, establishing therein an Arbitrary government, and enlarging its Boundaries so as to render it at once an example and fit instrument for introducing the same absolute rule into these Colonies:

For taking away our Charters, abolishing our most valuable Laws, and altering fundamentally the Forms of our Governments:

For suspending our own Legislature, and declaring themselves invested with Power to legislate for us in all cases whatsoever.

He has abdicated Government here, by declaring us out of his Protection and waging War against us.

He has plundered our seas, ravaged our Coasts, burnt our towns, and destroyed the lives of our people.

He is at this time transporting large armies of foreign mercenaries to compleat the works of death, desolation, and tyranny, already begun with circumstances of Cruelty & perfidy scarcely paralleled in the most barbarous ages, and totally unworthy the Head of a civilized nation.

He has constrained our fellow Citizens taken Captive on the high Seas to bear Arms against their Country, to become the executioners of their friends and Brethren, or to fall themselves by their Hands.

He has excited domestic insurrections amongst us, and has endeavoured to bring on the inhabitants of our frontiers, the merciless Indian Savages, whose known rule of warfare, is an undistinguished destruction of all ages, sexes, and conditions.

In every stage of these Oppressions We have Petitioned for Redress in the most humble terms: Our repeated Petitions have been answered only by repeated injury. A Prince, whose character is thus marked by every act which may define a Tyrant, is unfit to be the ruler of a free people.

Nor have We been wanting in attentions to our British brethren. We have warned them from time to time of attempts by their legislature to extend an unwarrantable jurisdiction over us. We have reminded them of the circumstances of our emigration and settlement here. We have appealed to their native justice and magnanimity, and we have conjured them by the ties of our common kindred to disavow these usurpations, which, would inevitably interrupt our connections and correspondence. They too must have been deaf to the voice of justice and of consanguinity. We must, therefore, acquiesce in the necessity, which denounces our Separation, and hold them, as we hold the rest of mankind, Enemies in War, in Peace Friends.

WE, THEREFORE, the Representatives of the UNITED STATES OF AMERICA, in General Congress, Assembled, appealing to the Supreme Judge of the world for the rectitude of our intentions, do, in the Name, and by Authority of the good People of these Colonies, solemnly publish and declare, That these United Colonies are, and of Right ought to be FREE AND INDEPENDENT STATES; that they are Absolved from all Allegiance to the British Crown, and that all political connection between them and the State of Great Britain, is and ought to be totally dissolved; and that as Free and Independent States, they have full Power to levy War, conclude Peace, contract Alliances, establish Commerce, and to do all other Acts and Things which Independent States may of right do. And for the support of this Declaration, with a firm reliance on the Protection of Divine Providence, we mutually pledge to each other our Lives, our Fortunes, and our sacred Honor.

JOHN HANCOCK

JOSIAH BARTLETT
Wm WHIPPLE
SAM^l ADAMS
JOHN ADAMS
ROB^t TREAT PAINE
ELBRIDGE GERRY
STEP. HOPKINS
WILLIAM ELLERY
ROGER SHERMAN
SAM^el HUNTINGTON
Wm WILLIAMS
OLIVER WOLCOTT
MATTHEW THORNTON
Wm FLOYD
PHIL. LIVINGSTON
FRAN^s LEWIS
LEWIS MORRIS
RICH^d STOCKTON
J N^o WITHERSPOON

FRA^s HOPKINSON
JOHN HART
ABRA CLARK
ROB^t MORRIS
BENJAMIN RUSH
BENJ^a FRANKLIN
JOHN MORTON
GEO CLYMER
JA^s SMITH
GEO. TAYLOR
JAMES WILSON
GEO. ROSS
CAESAR RODNEY
GEO READ
THO M:KEAN
SAMUEL CHASE
Wm PACA
THO^s STONE

CHARLES CARROLL of
   Carrollton
GEORGE WYTHE
RICHARD HENRY LEE
TH JEFFERSON
BENJ^a HARRISON
THO^s NELSON jr.
FRANCIS LIGHTFOOT LEE
CARTER BRAXTON
Wm HOOPER
JOSEPH HEWES
JOHN PENN
EDWARD RUTLEDGE
THO^s HEYWARD Junr
THOMAS LYNCH Junr
ARTHUR MIDDLETON
BUTTON GWINNETT
LYMAN HALL
GEO WALTON

Constitution of the United States

We the people of the United States, in order to form a more perfect union, establish justice, insure domestic tranquillity, provide for the common defence, promote the general welfare, and secure the blessings of liberty to ourselves and our posterity, do ordain and establish this Constitution for the United States of America.

ARTICLE I

Section 1. All legislative powers herein granted shall be vested in a Congress of the United States, which shall consist of a Senate and a House of Representatives.

Section 2. (1) The House of Representatives shall be composed of members chosen every second year by the people of the several States, and the electors in each State shall have the qualifications requisite for electors of the most numerous branch of the State legislature.

(2) No person shall be a Representative who shall not have attained to the age of twenty-five years, and been seven years a citizen of the United States, and who shall not, when elected, be an inhabitant of that State in which he shall be chosen.

(3) Representatives and direct taxes shall be apportioned among the several States which may be included within this union, according to their respective numbers, [which shall be determined by adding to the whole number of free persons,][1] including those bound to service for a term of years, and excluding Indians not taxed, [three fifths of all other persons].[2] The actual enumeration shall be made within three years after the first meeting of the Congress of the United States, and within every subsequent term of ten years, in such manner as they shall by law direct. The number of Representatives shall not exceed one for every thirty thousand, but each State shall have at least one Representative; [and until such enumeration shall be made, the State of New Hampshire shall be entitled to chuse three, Massachusetts eight, Rhode Island and Providence Plantations one,

[1] Modified by Fourteenth Amendment.
[2] Superseded by Fourteenth Amendment.

Connecticut five, New York six, New Jersey four, Pennsylvania eight, Delaware one, Maryland six, Virginia ten, North Carolina five, South Carolina five, and Georgia three].[3]

(4) When vacancies happen in the representation from any State, the executive authority thereof shall issue writs of election to fill such vacancies.

(5) The House of Representatives shall choose their Speaker and other officers; and shall have the sole power of impeachment.

Section 3. [(1) The Senate of the United States shall be composed of two Senators from each State, chosen by the legislature thereof, for six years; and each Senator shall have one vote.][4]

(2) Immediately after they shall be assembled in consequence of the first election, they shall be divided as equally as may be into three classes. The seats of the Senators of the first class shall be vacated at the expiration of the second year, of the second class at the expiration of the fourth year, and of the third class at the expiration of the sixth year, so that one third may be chosen every second year; [and if vacancies happen by resignation, or otherwise, during the recess of the legislature of any State, the executive thereof may make temporary appointments until the next meeting of the legislature, which shall then fill such vacancies.][5]

(3) No person shall be a Senator who shall not have attained to the age of thirty years, and been nine years a citizen of the United States, and who shall not, when elected, be an inhabitant of that State for which he shall be chosen.

(4) The Vice President of the United States shall be President of the Senate, but shall have no vote, unless they be equally divided.

(5) The Senate shall choose their other officers, and also a president pro tempore, in the absence of the Vice President, or when he shall exercise the office of President of the United States.

(6) The Senate shall have the sole power to try all impeachments. When sitting for that purpose, they shall be on oath or affirmation. When the President of the United States is tried, the Chief Justice shall preside: and no person shall be convicted without the concurrence of two thirds of the Members present.

(7) Judgment in cases of impeachment shall not extend further than to removal from office, and disqualification to hold and enjoy any office of honor, trust, or profit under the United States: but the party convicted shall nevertheless be liable and subject to indictment, trial, judgment, and punishment, according to law.

Section 4. (1) The times, places, and manner of holding elections for Senators and Representatives, shall be prescribed in each State by the legislature thereof; but the Congress may at any time by law make or alter such regulations, except as to places of choosing Senators. [(2) The Congress shall assemble at least once in every year, and such meeting shall be on the first Monday in December, unless they shall by law appoint a different day.][6]

Section 5. (1) Each House shall be the judge of the elections, returns, and qualifications of its own members, and a majority of each shall constitute a quorum

---

[3] Temporary provision.
[4] Superseded by Seventeenth Amendment.
[5] Modified by Seventeenth Amendment.
[6] Superseded by Twentieth Amendment.

to do business; but a smaller number may adjourn from day to day, and may be authorized to compel the attendance of absent members, in such manner, and under such penalties, as each House may provide.

(2) Each House may determine the rules of its proceedings, punish its members for disorderly behavior, and, with the concurrence of two thirds, expel a member.

(3) Each House shall keep a journal of its proceedings, and from time to time publish the same, excepting such parts as may in their judgment require secrecy; and the yeas and nays of the members of either House on any question shall, at the desire of one fifth of those present, be entered on the journal.

(4) Neither House, during the session of Congress, shall, without the consent of the other, adjourn for more than three days, nor to any other place than that in which the two Houses shall be sitting.

Section 6. (1) The Senators and Representatives shall receive a compensation for their services, to be ascertained by law, and paid out of the Treasury of the United States. They shall in all cases, except treason, felony, and breach of the peace, be privileged from arrest during their attendance at the session of their respective Houses, and in going to and returning from the same; and for any speech or debate in either House, they shall not be questioned in any other place.

(2) No Senator or Representative shall, during the time for which he was elected, be appointed to any civil office under the authority of the United States, which shall have been created, or the emoluments whereof shall have been encreased, during such time; and no person holding any office under the United States shall be a member of either House during his continuance in office.

Section 7. (1) All bills for raising revenue shall originate in the House of Representatives; but the Senate may propose or concur with amendments as on other bills.

(2) Every bill which shall have passed the House of Representatives and the Senate, shall, before it become a law, be presented to the President of the United States; if he approve he shall sign it, but if not he shall return it, with his objections to that House in which it shall have originated, who shall enter the objections at large on their journal, and proceed to reconsider it. If after such reconsideration two thirds of that House shall agree to pass the Bill, it shall be sent, together with the objections, to the other House, by which it shall likewise be reconsidered, and if approved by two thirds of that House, it shall become a law. But in all such cases the votes of both Houses shall be determined by yeas and nays, and the names of the persons voting for and against the bill shall be entered on the journal of each House respectively. If any bill shall not be returned by the President within ten days (Sundays excepted) after it shall have been presented to him, the same shall be a law, in like manner as if he had signed it, unless the Congress by their adjournment prevent its return, in which case it shall not be a law.

(3) Every order, resolution, or vote to which the concurrence of the Senate and House of Representatives may be necessary (except on a question of adjournment) shall be presented to the President of the United States; and before the same shall take effect, shall be approved by him, or being disapproved by him, shall

be repassed by two thirds of the Senate and House of Representatives, according to the rules and limitations prescribed in the case of a bill.

Section 8. (1) The Congress shall have power to lay and collect taxes, duties, imposts, and excises, to pay the debts and provide for the common defence and general welfare of the United States; but all duties, imposts, and excises shall be uniform throughout the United States;

(2) To borrow money on the credit of the United States;

(3) To regulate commerce with foreign nations, and among the several States, and with the Indian tribes;

(4) To establish an uniform rule of naturalization, and uniform laws on the subject of bankruptcies throughout the United States;

(5) To coin money, regulate the value thereof, and of foreign coin, and fix the standard of weights and measures;

(6) To provide for the punishment of counterfeiting the securities and current coin of the United States;

(7) To establish post offices and post roads;

(8) To promote the progress of science and useful arts, by securing for limited times to authors and inventors the exclusive right to their respective writings and discoveries;

(9) To constitute tribunals inferior to the Supreme Court;

(10) To define and punish piracies and felonies committed on the high seas, and offences against the law of nations;

(11) To declare war, grant letters of marque and reprisal, and make rules concerning captures on land and water;

(12) To raise and support armies, but no appropriation of money to that use shall be for a longer term than two years;

(13) To provide and maintain a navy;

(14) To make rules for the government and regulation of the land and naval forces;

(15) To provide for calling forth the militia to execute the laws of the union, suppress insurrections and repel invasions;

(16) To provide for organizing, arming, and disciplining the militia, and for governing such part of them as may be employed in the service of the United States, reserving to the States respectively the appointment of the officers, and the authority of training the militia according to the discipline prescribed by Congress;

(17) To exercise exclusive legislation in all cases whatsoever, over such district (not exceeding ten miles square) as may, by cession of particular States, and the acceptance of Congress, become the seat of the government of the United States, and to exercise like authority over all places purchased by the consent of the legislature of the State in which the same shall be, for the erection of forts, magazines, arsenals, dock-yards, and other needful buildings; and

(18) To make all laws which shall be necessary and proper for carrying into execution the foregoing powers, and all other powers vested by this Constitution in the government of the United States, or in any department or officer thereof.

Section 9. [(1) The migration or importation of such persons as any of the States now existing shall think proper to admit, shall not be prohibited by the

Congress prior to the Year one thousand eight hundred and eight, but a tax or duty may be imposed on such importation, not exceeding ten dollars for each person.]⁷

(2) The privilege of the writ of habeas corpus shall not be suspended, unless when in cases of rebellion or invasion the public safety may require it.

(3) No bill of attainder or ex post facto law shall be passed.

[(4) No capitation, or other direct, tax shall be laid, unless in proportion to the census or enumeration hereinbefore directed to be taken.]⁸

(5) No tax or duty shall be laid on articles exported from any State.

(6) No preference shall be given by any regulation of commerce or revenue to the ports of one State over those of another: nor shall vessels bound to, or from, one State, be obliged to enter, clear, or pay duties in another.

(7) No money shall be drawn from the Treasury, but in consequence of appropriations made by law; and a regular statement and account of the receipts and expenditures of all public money shall be published from time to time.

(8) No title of nobility shall be granted by the United States: and no person holding any office of profit or trust under them, shall, without the consent of the Congress, accept of any present, emolument, office, or title, of any kind whatever, from any king, prince, or foreign State.

Section 10. (1) No State shall enter into any treaty, alliance, or confederation; grant letters of marque and reprisal; coin money; emit bills of credit; make anything but gold and silver coin a tender in payment of debts; pass any bill of attainder, ex post facto law, or law impairing the obligation of contracts, or grant any title of nobility.

(2) No State shall, without the consent of the Congress, lay any imposts or duties on imports or exports, except what may be absolutely necessary for executing its inspection laws: and the net produce of all duties and imposts, laid by any State on imports or exports, shall be for the use of the Treasury of the United States; and all such laws shall be subject to the revision and control of the Congress.

(3) No State shall, without the consent of Congress, lay any duty of tonnage, keep troops, or ships of war in time of peace, enter into any agreement or compact with another State, or with a foreign power, or engage in war, unless actually invaded, or in such imminent danger as will not admit of delay.

ARTICLE II

Section 1. (1) The executive power shall be invested in a President of the United States of America. He shall hold his office during the term of four years, and, together with the Vice President, chosen for the same term, be elected, as follows:

(2) Each State shall appoint, in such manner as the legislature thereof may direct, a number of electors, equal to the whole number of Senators and Representatives to which the State may be entitled in the Congress: but no Senator or

⁷ Temporary provision.
⁸ Modified by Sixteenth Amendment.

Representative, or person holding an office of trust or profit under the United States, shall be appointed an elector.

[The electors shall meet in their respective States, and vote by ballot for two persons, of whom one at least shall not be an inhabitant of the same State with themselves. And they shall make a list of all the persons voted for, and of the number of votes for each; which list they shall sign and certify, and transmit sealed to the seat of the government of the United States, directed to the president of the Senate. The president of the Senate shall, in the presence of the Senate and House of Representatives, open all the certificates, and the votes shall then be counted. The person having the greatest number of votes shall be the President, if such number be a majority of the whole number of electors appointed; and if there be more than one who have such majority, and have an equal number of votes, then the House of Representatives shall immediately choose by ballot one of them for President; and if no person have a majority, then from the five highest on the list the said House shall in like manner choose the President. But in choosing the President, the votes shall be taken by States, the representation from each State having one vote; a quorum for this purpose shall consist of a member or members from two thirds of the States, and a majority of all the States shall be necessary to a choice. In every case, after the choice of the President, the person having the greatest number of votes of the electors shall be the Vice President. But if there should remain two or more who have equal votes, the Senate shall choose from them by Ballot the Vice President.][9]

(3) The Congress may determine the time of choosing the electors, and the day on which they shall give their votes; which day shall be the same throughout the United States.

(4) No person except a natural-born citizen, or a citizen of the United States, at the time of the adoption of this Constitution, shall be eligible to the office of President; neither shall any person be eligible to that office who shall not have attained to the age of thirty-five years, and been fourteen years a resident within the United States.

(5) In case of the removal of the President from office, or of his death, resignation, or inability to discharge the powers and duties of said office, the same shall devolve on the Vice President, and the Congress may by law provide for the case of removal, death, resignation, or inability, both of the President and the Vice President, declaring what officer shall then act as President and such officer shall act accordingly, until the disability be removed, or a President shall be elected.

(6) The President shall, at stated times, receive for his services, a compensation, which shall neither be increased nor diminished during the period for which he shall have been elected, and he shall not receive within that period any other emolument from the United States, or any of them.

(7) Before he enter on the execution of his office, he shall take the following oath or affirmation: "I do solemnly swear (or affirm) that I will faithfully execute the office of President of the United States and will to the best of my ability, preserve, protect, and defend the Constitution of the United States."

[9] This paragraph superseded by Twelfth Amendment, which, in turn, is modified by Twentieth Amendment.

Section 2. (1) The President shall be commander in chief of the army and navy of the United States, and of the militia of the several States, when called into the actual service of the United States; he may require the opinion, in writing, of the principal officer in each of the executive departments, upon any subject relating to the duties of their respective offices, and he shall have power to grant reprieves and pardons for offenses against the United States, except in cases of impeachment.

(2) He shall have power, by and with the advice and consent of the Senate, to make treaties, provided two thirds of the Senators present concur; and he shall nominate, and by and with the advice and consent of the Senate, shall appoint ambassadors, other public ministers and consuls, judges of the Supreme Court, and all other officers of the United States, whose appointments are not herein otherwise provided for, and which shall be established by law: but the Congress may by law vest the appointment of such inferior officers, as they think proper, in the President alone, in the courts of law, or in the heads of departments.

(3) The President shall have power to fill up all vacancies that may happen during the recess of the Senate, by granting commissions which shall expire at the end of their next session.

Section 3. (1) He shall from time to time give to the Congress information of the state of the Union, and recommend to their consideration such measures as he shall judge necessary and expedient; he may, on extraordinary occasions, convene both Houses, or either of them, and, in case of disagreement between them, with respect to the time of adjournment, he may adjourn them to such time as he shall think proper; he shall receive ambassadors and other public ministers; he shall take care that the laws be faithfully executed, and shall commission all the officers of the United States.

Section 4. The President, Vice President, and all civil officers of the United States shall be removed from office on impeachment for, and conviction of, treason, bribery, or other high crimes and misdemeanors.

ARTICLE III

Section 1. The judicial power of the United States, shall be vested in one Supreme Court, and in such inferior courts as the Congress may from time to time ordain and establish. The judges, both of the Supreme and inferior courts, shall hold their offices during good behaviour, and shall, at stated times, receive for their services, a compensation, which shall not be diminished during their continuance in office.

Section 2. (1) The judicial power shall extend to all cases, in law and equity, arising under this Constitution, the laws of the United States, and treaties made, or which shall be made, under their authority;—to all cases affecting ambassadors, other public ministers, and consuls;—to all cases of admiralty and maritime jurisdiction;—to controversies to which the United States shall be a party;—to controversies between two or more States;[—between a State and citizens of another State;][10]—between citizens of different States;—between citizens of the same State

---

[10] Limited by Eleventh Amendment.

claiming lands under grants of different States, and between a State, or the citizens thereof, and foreign States, citizens, or subjects.

(2) In all cases affecting ambassadors, other public ministers, and consuls, and those in which a State shall be party, the Supreme Court shall have original jurisdiction. In all the other cases before mentioned, the Supreme Court shall have appellate jurisdiction, both as to law and fact, with such exceptions, and under such regulations as the Congress shall make.

(3) The trial of all crimes, except in cases of impeachment, shall be by jury; and such trial shall be held in the State where the said crimes shall have been committed; but when not committed within any State, the trial shall be at such place or places as the Congress may by law have directed.

Section 3. (1) Treason against the United States shall consist only in levying war against them, or in adhering to their enemies, giving them aid and comfort. No person shall be convicted of treason unless on the testimony of two witnesses to the same overt act, or on confession in open court.

(2) The Congress shall have power to declare the punishment of treason, but no attainder of treason shall work corruption of blood, or forfeiture except during the life of the person attainted.

ARTICLE IV

Section 1. Full faith and credit shall be given in each State to the public acts, records, and judicial proceedings of every other State. And the Congress may by general laws prescribe the manner in which such acts, records, and proceedings shall be proved, and the effect thereof.

Section 2. (1) The citizens of each State shall be entitled to all privileges and immunities of citizens in the several States.

(2) A person charged in any State with treason, felony, or other crime, who shall flee from justice, and be found in another State, shall on demand of the executive authority of the State from which he fled, be delivered up to be removed to the State having jurisdiction of the crime.

[(3) No person held to service or labour in one State, under the laws thereof, escaping into another, shall, in consequence of any law or regulation therein, be discharged from such services or labour, but shall be delivered up on claim of the party to whom such service or labour may be due.][11]

Section 3. (1) New States may be admitted by the Congress into this Union; but no new State shall be formed or erected within the jurisdiction of any other State; nor any State be formed by the junction of two or more States, or parts of States, without the consent of the legislatures of the States concerned as well as of the Congress.

(2) The Congress shall have power to dispose of and make all needful rules and regulations respecting the territory or other property belonging to the United States; and nothing in this Constitution shall be so construed as to prejudice any claims of the United States, or of any particular State.

[11] Superseded by Thirteenth Amendment so far as it relates to slaves.

Section 4. The United States shall guarantee to every State in this Union a republican form of government, and shall protect each of them against invasion; and, on application of the legislature, or of the executive (when the legislature cannot be convened), against domestic violence.

ARTICLE V

The Congress, whenever two thirds of both Houses shall deem it necessary, shall propose amendments to this Constitution, or, on the application of the legislatures of two thirds of the several States, shall call a convention for proposing amendments, which, in either case, shall be valid to all intents and purposes, as part of this Constitution, when ratified by the legislature of three fourths of the several States, or by conventions in three fourths thereof, as the one or the other mode of ratification may be proposed by the Congress; provided [that no amendment which may be made prior to the year one thousand eight hundred and eight shall in any manner affect the first and fourth clauses in the ninth section of the first article; and][12] that no State, without its consent, shall be deprived of its equal suffrage in the Senate.

ARTICLE VI

(1) All debts contracted and engagements entered into, before the adoption of this Constitution, shall be as valid against the United States under this Constitution, as under the Confederation.

(2) This Constitution, and the laws of the United States which shall be made in pursuance thereof; and all treaties made, or which shall be made, under the authority of the United States, shall be the supreme law of the land; and the judges in every State shall be bound thereby, anything in the constitution or laws of any State to the contrary notwithstanding.

(3) The Senators and Representatives before mentioned, and the members of the several State legislatures, and all executive and judicial officers, both of the United States and of the several States, shall be bound by oath or affirmation, to support this Constitution; but no religious test shall ever be required as a qualification to any office or public trust under the United States.

ARTICLE VII

The ratification of the conventions of nine States shall be sufficient for the establishment of this Constitution between the States so ratifying the same.

Done in convention by the unanimous consent of the States present the seventeenth day of September in the year of our Lord one thousand seven hundred and eighty-seven, and of the independence of the United States of America the twelfth. In witness whereof, we have hereunto subscribed our names.

[12] Temporary provision.

Articles in Addition to, and Amendment of, the Constitution of the United States of America, Proposed by Congress, and Ratified by the Several States Pursuant to the Fifth Article of the Original Constitution

ARTICLE I

(The first ten Articles, in force December 15, 1791)

Congress shall make no law respecting an establishment of religion, or prohibiting the free exercise thereof; or abridging the freedom of speech, or of the press; or the right of the people peaceably to assemble, and to petition the government for a redress of grievances.

ARTICLE II

A well regulated militia, being necessary to the security of a free State, the right of the people to keep and bear arms, shall not be infringed.

ARTICLE III

No soldier shall, in time of peace, be quartered in any house, without the consent of the owner, nor in time of war, but in a manner to be prescribed by law.

ARTICLE IV

The right of the people to be secure in their persons, houses, papers, and effects, against unreasonable searches and seizures, shall not be violated, and no warrants shall issue, but upon probable cause, supported by oath or affirmation, and particularly describing the place to be searched, and the persons or things to be seized.

ARTICLE V

No person shall be held to answer for a capital, or otherwise infamous crime, unless on a presentment or indictment of a grand jury, except in cases arising in the land or naval forces, or in the militia, when in actual service in time of war or public danger; nor shall any person be subject for the same offence to be twice put in jeopardy of life or limb; nor shall be compelled in any criminal case to be a witness against himself, nor be deprived of life, liberty, or property, without due process of law; nor shall private property be taken for public use, without just compensation.

ARTICLE VI

In all criminal prosecutions, the accused shall enjoy the right to a speedy and public trial, by an impartial jury of the State and district wherein the crime shall have been committed, which district shall have been previously ascertained by law, and to be informed of the nature and cause of the accusation; to be confronted with the witnesses against him; to have compulsory process for obtaining witnesses in his favor, and to have the assistance of counsel for his defence.

ARTICLE VII

In suits at common law, where the value in controversy shall exceed twenty dollars, the right of trial by jury shall be preserved, and no fact tried by a jury shall be otherwise re-examined in any court of the United States, than according to the rules of the common law.

ARTICLE VIII

Excessive bail shall not be required, nor excessive fines imposed, nor cruel and unusual punishment inflicted.

ARTICLE IX

The enumeration in the Constitution of certain rights, shall not be construed to deny or disparage others retained by the people.

ARTICLE X

The powers not delegated to the United States by the Constitution, nor prohibited by it to the States, are reserved to the States respectively, or to the people.

ARTICLE XI

(January 8, 1798)

The judicial power of the United States shall not be construed to extend to any suit in law or equity, commenced or prosecuted against one of the United States by citizens of another State, or by citizens or subjects of any foreign State.

ARTICLE XII

(September 25, 1804)

The electors shall meet in their respective states, and vote by ballot for President and Vice President, one of whom, at least, shall not be an inhabitant of the same state with themselves; they shall name in their ballots the person voted for as President, and in distinct ballots the person voted for as Vice President, and they shall make distinct lists of all persons voted for as President, and of all persons voted for as Vice President, and of the number of votes for each, which lists they shall sign and certify, and transmit sealed to the seat of the government of the United States, directed to the president of the Senate;—the president of the Senate shall, in the presence of the Senate and House of Representatives, open all the certificates and the votes shall then be counted;—the person having the greatest number of votes for President, shall be the President, if such number be a majority of the whole number of electors appointed; and if no person have such majority, then from the persons having the highest numbers not exceeding three on the list of those voted for as President, the House of Representatives shall choose immediately, by ballot, the President. But in choosing the President, the votes shall be taken by States, the representation from each State having one vote; a quorum for this purpose shall consist of a member or members from two-thirds of the States, and a majority of all the States shall be necessary to a choice. And if the House of Representatives shall not choose a President whenever the right of choice shall devolve upon them, before the fourth day of March next following, then the Vice President shall act as President, as in the case of the death or other constitutional disability of the President. The person having the greatest number of votes as Vice President, shall be the Vice President, if such number be a majority of the whole number of electors appointed, and if no person have a majority, then from the two highest numbers on the list, the Senate shall choose the Vice President; a quorum for the purpose shall consist of two-thirds of the whole number of Senators, and a majority of the whole number shall be necessary to a choice. But no person constitutionally ineligible to the office of President shall be eligible to that of Vice President of the United States.

ARTICLE XIII

(December 18, 1865)

Section 1. Neither slavery nor involuntary servitude, except as a punishment for crime whereof the party shall have been duly convicted, shall exist within the United States, or any place subject to their jurisdiction.

Section 2. Congress shall have power to enforce this article by appropriate legislation.

ARTICLE XIV

(July 28, 1868)

Section 1. All persons born or naturalized in the United States, and subject to the jurisdiction thereof, are citizens of the United States and of the State wherein they reside. No State shall make or enforce any law which shall abridge the privileges or immunities of citizens of the United States; nor shall any State deprive any person of life, liberty, or property, without due process of law; nor deny to any person within its jurisdiction the equal protection of the laws.

Section 2. Representatives shall be apportioned among the several States according to their respective numbers, counting the whole number of persons in each State, excluding Indians not taxed. But when the right to vote at any given election for the choice of electors for President and Vice President of the United States, Representatives in Congress, the executive and judicial officers of a State, or the members of the legislature thereof, is denied to any of the male inhabitants of such State, being twenty-one years of age, and citizens of the United States, or in any way abridged, except for participation in rebellion, or other crime, the basis of representation therein shall be reduced in the proportion which the number of such male citizens shall bear to the whole number of male citizens twenty-one years of age in such State.

Section 3. No person shall be a Senator or Representative in Congress, or elector of President and Vice President, or hold any office, civil, or military, under the United States, or under any State, who, having previously taken an oath, as a member of Congress, or as an officer of the United States, or as a member of any State legislature, or as an executive or judicial officer of any State, to support the Constitution of the United States, shall have engaged in insurrection or rebellion against the same, or given aid or comfort to the enemies thereof. But Congress may by a vote of two thirds of each House, remove suuch disability.

Section 4. The validity of the public debt of the United States, authorized by law, including debts incurred for payment of pensions and bounties for services in suppressing insurrection or rebellion, shall not be questioned. But neither the United States nor any State shall assume or pay any debt or obligation incurred in aid of insurrection or rebellion against the United States, or any claim for the loss or emancipation of any slave; but all such debts, obligations, and claims shall be held illegal and void.

Section 5. The Congress shall have power to enforce, by appropriate legislation, the provisions of this article.

ARTICLE XV

(March 30, 1870)

Section 1. The right of citizens of the United States to vote shall not be denied or abridged by the United States or by any State on account of race, color, or previous condition of servitude.

Section 2. The Congress shall have power to enforce this article by appropriate legislation.

ARTICLE XVI

(February 25, 1913)

The Congress shall have power to lay and collect taxes on incomes, from whatever source derived, without apportionment among the several States, and without regard to any census or enumeration.

ARTICLE XVII

(May 31, 1913)

The Senate of the United States shall be composed of two Senators from each State, elected by the people thereof, for six years; and each Senator shall have one vote. The electors in each State shall have the qualifications requisite for electors of the most numerous branch of the State legislature.

When vacancies happen in the representation of any State in the Senate, the executive authority of such State shall issue writs of election to fill such vacancies: PROVIDED, That the legislature of any State may empower the executive thereof to make temporary appointments until the people fill the vacancies by election as the legislature may direct.

This amendment shall not be so construed as to affect the election or term of any Senator chosen before it becomes valid as part of the Constitution.

ARTICLE XVIII[13]

(January 29, 1919)

Section 1. After one year from the ratification of this article, the manufacture, sale, or transportation of intoxicating liquors within, the importation thereof into, or the exportation thereof from the United States and all territory subject to the jurisdiction thereof for beverage purposes is hereby prohibited.

Section 2. The Congress and the several States shall have concurrent power to enforce this article by appropriate legislation.

Section 3. This article shall be inoperative unless it shall have been ratified as an amendment to the Constitution by the legislatures of the several States, as provided in the Constitution, within seven years from the date of the submission hereof to the States by the Congress.

ARTICLE XIX

(August 26, 1920)

(1) The right of citizens of the United States to vote shall not be denied or abridged by the United States or by any States on account of sex.

(2) The Congress shall have power by appropriate legislation to enforce the provisions of this article.

ARTICLE XX

(February 6, 1933)

Section 1. The terms of the President and Vice President shall end at noon on the 20th day of January, and the terms of Senators and Representatives at noon

[13] Repealed by Twenty-first Amendment.

on the 3rd day of January, of the years in which such terms would have ended if this article had not been ratified; and the terms of their successors shall then begin.

Section 2. The Congress shall assemble at least once in every year, and such meeting shall begin at noon on the 3rd day of January, unless they shall by law appoint a different day.

Section 3. If, at the time fixed for the beginning of the term of the President, the President elect shall have died, the Vice President elect shall become President. If a President shall not have been chosen before the time fixed for the beginning of his term, or if the President elect shall have failed to qualify, then the Vice President elect shall act as President until a President shall have been qualified; and the Congress may by law provide for the case wherein neither a President elect nor a Vice President elect shall have qualified, declaring who shall then act as President, or the manner in which one who is to act shall be selected, and such person shall act accordingly until a President or Vice President shall have qualified.

Section 4. The Congress may by law provide for the case of the death of any of the persons from whom the House of Representatives may choose a President whenever the right of choice shall have devolved upon them, and for the case of the death of any of the persons from whom the Senate may choose a Vice President whenever the right of choice shall have devolved upon them.

Section 5. Sections 1 and 2 shall take effect on the 15th day of October following the ratification of this article.

Section 6. This article shall be inoperative unless it shall have been ratified as an amendment to the Constitution by the legislatures of three fourths of the several States within seven years from the date of its submission.

ARTICLE XXI

(December 5, 1933)

Section 1. The eighteenth article of amendment to the Constitution of the United States is hereby repealed.

Section 2. The transportation or importation into any State, territory, or possession of the United States for delivery or use therein of intoxicating liquors, in violation of the laws thereof, is hereby prohibited.

Section 3. This article shall be inoperative unless it shall have been ratified as an amendment to the Constitution by conventions in the several States, as provided in the Constitution, within seven years from the date of the submission hereof to the States by the Congress.

ARTICLE XXII

(February 26, 1951)

Section 1. No person shall be elected to the office of the President more than twice, and no person who has held the office of President, or acted as President, for more than two years of a term for which some other person was elected President shall be elected to the office of the President more than once. But this article shall not apply to any person holding the office of President when this article was proposed by the Congress, and shall not prevent any person who may be holding the office of President, or acting as President, during the term within which this article becomes operative from holding the office of President or acting as President during the remainder of such term.

Section 2. This article shall be inoperative unless it shall have been ratified as an amendment to the Constitution by the legislatures of three fourths of the several States within seven years from the date of its submission to the States by the Congress.[14]

[14] Five amendments have been proposed but not ratified. The first and second were proposed on Sept. 25, 1789, along with ten others which became the Bill of Rights. The first of these dealt with the apportionment of members of the House of Representatives. It was ratified by ten states, eleven being the necessary three fourths. The second provided that "No law, varying the compensation for the services of the Senators and Representatives, shall take effect, until an election of Representatives shall have intervened." It was ratified by six states, eleven being necessary. A third was proposed on May 1, 1810, which would have abrogated the citizenship of any persons accepting foreign titles or honors. It was ratified by twelve states, fourteen being necessary. A fourth was proposed on Mar. 4, 1861, which prohibited the adoption of any amendment "to abolish or interfere, within any state, with the domestic institution thereof, including that of persons held to labor or service by the laws of that state." This was approved by three states. The fifth, the proposed child-labor amendment, was proposed on June 2, 1924. It provides:

Section 1. The Congress shall have power to limit, regulate, and prohibit the labor of persons under eighteen years of age.

Section 2. The power of the several States is unimpaired by this article except that the operation of State laws shall be suspended to the extent necessary to give effect to legislation enacted by Congress.

This has been ratified by twenty-eight states and rejected in eleven. The approval of thirty-six states is necessary to complete ratification.

BIBLIOGRAPHY

The following references are intended to provide suggestions for further reading that will be readily available and useful to the student. For the most part, works of interest primarily to the specialist have been intentionally omitted.

Collections of documents and other source materials are indispensable adjuncts to any history text. The authors have found the following especially useful: Columbia University, *Contemporary Civilization* (2 vols.); H. S. Commager, *Documents of American History;* Thorpe, Curti, and Baker, *American Issues* (2 vols.); and Rae, Morse, and Foster, *Readings on the American Way.*

PART ONE: THE EMERGENCE OF THE MODERN WORLD

Chapter 1: Economic Life

Good topical surveys of European economic development during this period can be found in Herbert Heaton, *Economic History of Europe* (1936). Bowden, Karpovich, and Usher, *Economic History of Europe since 1750* (1937), is difficult to read but has much factual information. L. B. Packard, *The Commercial Revolution* (*Berkshire Studies*, 1927), is an excellent concise study. On agricultural change Lord Ernle, *English Farming, Past and Present* (1922), is the most lucid analysis. W. R. Scott, *The Constitution and Finance of English, Scottish, and Irish Joint-stock Companies to 1720* (1912), is the standard authority on the evolution of this type of business organization. On mercantilism and colonial policy there are several good references: for Great Britain, G. L. Beer, *The Origins of the British Colonial System* (1908), and *The Old Colonial System* (1912), and E. Lipson, *Economic History of England* (Vols. 3 and 4, 1931); for France, C. W. Cole, *Colbert and a Century of French Mercantilism* (1939); for Spain, C. H. Haring, *Trade and Navigation between Spain and the Indies* (1918), and *The Spanish Empire in America* (1947). E. F. Heckscher, *Mercantilism* (1935), is a convenient survey.

Chapter 2: Intellectual Progress

J. H. Randall, *The Making of the Modern Mind* (1926), is an excellent comprehensive survey. The best general study of the Reformation is Preserved Smith, *The Age of the Reformation* (1920). C. J. H. Hayes, *Political and Cultural His-*

791

tory of Modern Europe (rev. ed., 1939), gives good summaries of both the Renaissance and the Reformation. R. H. Tawney, *Religion and the Rise of Capitalism* (1926), is worth reading, but the point of view should be accepted with caution.

The rise of science can be studied in Preserved Smith, *History of Modern Culture* (1930), and W. C. Dampier, *History of Science* (1932). L. T. More, *Isaac Newton* (1937), is extremely valuable. For the influence of science on thought, W. E. H. Lecky, *History of Rationalism* (2 vols., 1914), and Carl Becker, *The Heavenly City of the Eighteenth-century Philosophers* (1932), make good reading. Carl Van Doren, *Benjamin Franklin* (1938), is a brilliant study of perhaps the most representative figure of the Age of Reason. Geoffrey Bruun, *The Enlightened Despots* (*Berkshire Studies,* 1929), covers this topic admirably.

Chapter 3: Government and Society

Good summaries of the social structure of the Old Regime in France and of the development of the French monarchy can be found in Leo Gershoy, *The French Revolution and Napoleon* (1933), and Louis Gottschalk, *The Era of the French Revolution* (1929). L. B. Packard, *The Age of Louis XIV* (*Berkshire Studies,* 1929), is succinct and clear.

For the evolution of constitutional government in England, H. A. Innes, *England under the Tudors* (1905), and G. M. Trevelyan, *England under the Stuarts* (1904), present a coherent and understandable narrative. Recommended biographies are A. F. Pollard, *Henry VIII* (1905), J. E. Neale, *Queen Elizabeth* (1934), John Buchan, *Cromwell* (1934), and Arthur Bryant, *Charles II* (1934). The somewhat complex constitutional developments of the eighteenth century are thoroughly treated in L. B. Namier, *The Structure of British Politics at the Accession of George III* (1929).

Chapter 4: The Evolution of the European State System

C. V. Wedgwood, *The Thirty Years War* (1939), is the most up-to-date account of this conflict and the Westphalian peace settlement. The rise of Prussia is well covered in S. B. Fay, *The Rise of Brandenburg-Prussia* (*Berkshire Studies,* 1937), and the longer J. A. Marriott and C. G. Robertson, *The Evolution of Prussia* (3d ed., 1937). The rise of Russia can be studied conveniently in George Vernadsky, *History of Russia* (1929), and Bernard Pares, *History of Russia* (1926).

The world wars of the eighteenth century are adequately summarized in A. H. Buffinton, *The Second Hundred Years' War* (*Berkshire Studies,* 1929). A more detailed study of the mid-century wars is W. A. Dorn, *Competition for Empire, 1740–1763* (*Rise of Modern Europe,* Vol. IX, 1940). Highly recommended are W. S. Churchill, *Marlborough: His Life and Times* (6 vols., 1933–1938), and Basil Williams, *Life of Pitt* (1913).

Chapter 5: The American Colonies

C. H. Haring, *The Spanish Empire in America* (1947), is a modern and thorough description of the Spanish imperial system. H. E. Bolton, *The Spanish*

Borderlands (*Chronicles of America,* 1921), and V. W. Crane, *The Southern Frontier* (1932), are useful for Spanish settlement in the future territory of the United States.

For the British colonies, C. M. Andrews, *The Colonial Period of American History* (4 vols., 1934–1938), is the standard authority. Colonial government and imperial relationships are well covered in L. W. Labaree, *Royal Government in America* (1930), and O. M. Dickerson, *American Colonial Government, 1696–1765* (1912). Also of great value are the six volumes of L. H. Gipson, *The British Empire before the American Revolution.* Colonial economy and social organization are comprehensively and attractively described in two volumes of the *History of American Life* series: T. J. Wertenbaker, *The First Americans* (1927), and J. T. Adams, *Provincial Society* (1928). L. B. Wright, *The Atlantic Frontier* (1947), is a compact and well-written study of the same topics. Carl Bridenbaugh, *Cities in the Wilderness* (1938), is a notable contribution to the study of colonial society.

S. H. Brockunier, *Roger Williams* (1940), and the works of Francis Parkman should appear on any reading list dealing with colonial America.

PART TWO: THE AMERICAN REVOLUTION AND THE ORGANIZATION OF A NEW NATION

Chapter 6: Immediate Causes of the Revolution

Carl Becker, *The Eve of the Revolution* (*Chronicles of America,* 1921), is a well-written and penetrating analysis of the forces that led to the Revolution; the same ground is covered with more detail and less literary merit in John C. Miller, *The Origins of the American Revolution* (1934). C. M. Andrews, *The Colonial Background of the American Revolution* (1924), is a collection of four stimulating essays. L. B. Namier, *England in the Age of the American Revolution* (1930), provides needed information on the British political situation. C. W. Alvord, *The Mississippi Valley in British Politics* (2 vols., 1917), and T. P. Abernethy, *Western Lands and the American Revolution* (1937), say all that needs to be said on the influence of the Western problem. The constitutional issue between Great Britain and the colonies is discussed, from opposing points of view, in C. H. McIlwain, *The American Revolution* (1923), and R. L. Schuyler, *Parliament and the British Empire* (1925). The methods of the radicals in swinging public opinion to their side are well treated in J. C. Miller, *Sam Adams* (1936).

Chapter 7: The Revolutionary War

The most satisfactory general account of the Revolutionary War is J. H. Alden, *The American Revolution* (1954). H. E. Egerton, *The American Revolution* (1923), is an excellent brief study by an English historian. The military side of the story is concisely and clearly described in W. M. Wallace, *Appeal to Arms* (1951). Students should become acquainted with D. S. Freeman, *George Washington* (5 vols., 1948–1952). The international aspects of the war can best be studied in S. F. Bemis, *Diplomacy of the American Revolution* (1935). Carl Van Doren, *Secret History of the American Revolution* (1941), has some illuminating evidence on the career of Benedict Arnold.

Chapter 8: The Aftermath of the American Revolution

The peace settlement is well covered in Bemis's book cited above and also in T. A. Bailey, *Diplomatic History of the American People,* a book with vivacity of style. Reference to the effects of the American Revolution in Great Britain can be found in R. B. Mowat and P. W. Slosson, *History of the English-speaking People* (1943).

The problems of the Confederation are brilliantly described in E. C. Burnett, *The Continental Congress* (1941), and Merrill Jensen, *The New Nation* (1950). Max Farrand, *The Fathers of the Constitution* (*Chronicles of America,* 1921), is an excellent short account with a good chapter on the Northwest Ordinance.

Chapter 9: The Constitution

The clearest account of the work of the Federal Convention is Max Farrand, *The Framing of the Constitution* (1913). Carl Van Doren, *The Great Rehearsal* (1948), is colorful and attempts to draw the analogy between American federalism and the problem of international organization. C. A. Beard, *An Economic Interpretation of the Constitution* (1912), has a point of view that should be studied but not necessarily accepted. Irving Brant, *James Madison, Father of the Constitution* (1949), is the best biography of the key figure of the convention.

Nathan Schachner, *Alexander Hamilton* (1946), N. W. Stephenson and W. H. Dunn, *George Washington* (1940), and S. K. Padover, *Jefferson* (1942), are adequate biographies of the three leading figures of the period. *The Journal of William Maclay* (C. A. Beard, ed., 1927) is an illuminating contemporary account of the working of Congress.

The classic work on John Marshall is A. J. Beveridge, *Life of John Marshall* (1916–1919), Vols. 3 and 4 being especially well done. The subject of judicial interpretation is discussed in E. S. Corwin, *John Marshall and the Constitution* (*Chronicles of America,* 1919), and *The Doctrine of Judicial Review* (1914), somewhat critical of Marshall and the courts; a more favorable interpretation is given in Charles Warren, *The Supreme Court in United States History* (1923).

PART THREE: THE ERA OF THE FRENCH REVOLUTION AND NAPOLEON

Chapter 10: The French Revolution

Crane Brinton, *A Decade of Revolution, 1789–1799* (*Rise of Modern Europe,* Vol. XII, 1934), is the best one-volume interpretation, with Leo Gershoy, *The French Revolution, 1789–1799* (*Berkshire Studies,* 1932), a good second. Few French historians have been able to avoid intense partisanship, but Georges Lefebvre, *The Coming of the French Revolution* (1947), is a fresh analysis of the causes and early stages of the Revolution. Good appraisals of both the National

Assembly and the Directory can be found in Crane Brinton, *The Lives of Talley-rand* (1936). J. M. Thompson, *Leaders of the French Revolution* (1929) and *Robespierre* (1936), offer convenient studies of prominent figures.

Chapter 11: America's Foreign Relations, 1789–1800

The diplomatic history by Bailey previously cited is the best general account of foreign relations in this period. Two excellent studies of particular problems are S. F. Bemis, *Jay's Treaty* (1923), and *Pinckney's Treaty* (1926).

Gilbert Chinard, *Honest John Adams* (1933), gives a satisfactory picture of foreign affairs during the Adams administration, which can be supplemented by G. W. Allen, *Our Naval War with France* (1909).

Chapter 12: Napoleon

Of the innumerable biographies of Napoleon, A. Fournier, *Napoleon the First* (trans. by E. G. Bourne, 1903), J. H. Rose, *The Life of Napoleon I* (1913), and H. A. L. Fisher, *Napoleon* (1924) are the best one-volume accounts. An indispensable addition is A. L. Guérard, *Reflections on the Napoleonic Legend* (1924).

Good general studies of the Napoleonic period are Geoffrey Bruun, *Europe and the French Imperium (Rise of Modern Europe,* Vol. XIII, 1938), Leo Gershoy, *The French Revolution and Napoleon* (1933), and Louis Gottschalk, *The Era of the French Revolution* (1929).

Recommended books on special topics are: A. T. Mahan, *The Influence of Sea Power on the French Revolution and Empire* (2 vols., 1919), a classic study of the struggle between Great Britain and France; F. H. Hecksher, *The Continental System* (1922), for Napoleon's economic warfare; Eugene Tarlé, *Napoleon's Invasion of Russia* (1941), a study by a Russian historian; and Philip Guedalla, *Wellington* (1932), the authoritative biography of the victor of Waterloo. Tolstoy, *War and Peace,* should be included in any reading list of the Napoleonic period.

Chapter 13: Neutral Rights and the War of 1812

Henry Adams, *History of the United States, 1801–1817* (reprinted, 4 vols., 1930), is one of the great pieces of American historical writing. Allen Johnson, *Jefferson and his Colleagues (Chronicles of America,* 1916), is an excellent summary of the whole period. Irving Brant, *James Madison, Secretary of State* (1953), gives a thorough account of the Louisiana Purchase and the struggle to maintain neutral rights.

The war with the Barbary pirate is adequately described in G. W. Allen, *Our Navy and the Barbary Corsairs* (1905). The background of the War of 1812 is thoroughly presented in Bernard Mayo, *Henry Clay: Spokesman of the New West* (1937), and J. W. Pratt, *The Expansionists of 1812* (1925). A. T. Mahan, *Sea Power in its Relation to the War of 1812* (2 vols., 1905), is by the greatest of naval historians.

Chapter 14: The Congress of Vienna and Its Aftermath

The standard authority on the Congress is C. K. Webster, *The Congress of Vienna* (1919). To it should be added Harold Nicolson, *The Congress of Vienna*

(1946), a reappraisal of the work of the statesmen of 1815 in the light of later peace conferences, by a British diplomat who attended the Paris Conference of 1919. W. P. Cresson, *The Holy Alliance* (1922), analyzes Alexander's brain child.

C. K. Webster, *The Foreign Policy of Castlereagh* (1925), brings out the British attitude toward the concert of Europe. Dexter Perkins, *The Monroe Doctrine, 1823–1826* (1927), is the most detailed study of this topic. *Hands Off: A History of the Monroe Doctrine* (1941), by the same author, is briefer but more readable. The British background is well presented in H. W. V. Temperley, *The Foreign Policy of Canning* (1925). A. P. Whitaker, *The United States and the Independence of Latin America* (1938), presents essential material. W. P. Cresson, *James Monroe* (1946), is an outstanding biography, as is S. F. Bemis, *John Quincy Adams and the Foundations of American Foreign Policy* (1949).

PART FOUR: THE INDUSTRIAL REVOLUTION

Good general surveys are E. L. Bogart, *Economic History of Europe* (1942), and Herbert Heaton, *Economic History of Europe* (1936).

Chapter 15: The Revolution in Production

An excellent brief study of the Industrial Revolution in England is T. S. Ashton, *The Industrial Revolution* (1948). The spread of industrialism is treated thoroughly in H. E. Barnes, *Economic History of the Western World* (1935). A. P. Usher, *History of Mechanical Inventions* (rev. ed., 1954), is a useful reference. For American industrialism E. C. Kirkland, *History of American Economic Life* (1939), is the most readable of the standard works.

Good histories of particular industries are: for Great Britain, T. S. Ashton, *Iron and Steel in the Industrial Revolution* (1924), J. H. Clapham, *The Woollen and Worsted Industries* (1907), and J. U. Nef, *The Rise of the British Coal Industry* (2 vols., 1933); for the United States, A. C. Cole, *The American Wool Manufacture* (2 vols., 1926), and Hannah Josephson, *The Golden Threads* (1949). Allan Nevins, *Abram S. Hewitt* (1940), has interesting information on the iron and steel industry before the Civil War. There is a good description of Francis C. Lowell in F. Greenslet, *The Lowells and Their Seven Worlds* (1946). Jeanette Mirsky and Allen Nevins, *The World of Eli Whitney* (1952), is the best available work on this vital figure.

The political and social effects of industrialism in Great Britain are well treated in G. D. H. Cole and R. Postgate, *The British Common People* (1946); C. R. Fay, *Great Britain from Adam Smith to the Present* (1928); and Gilbert Slater, *Growth of Modern England* (1932).

F. T. Carlton, *History and Problems of Organized Labor* (1920), and J. R. Commons, *History of Labor in the United States,* Vol. I (1918), cover the American labor story for this period adequately.

Chapter 16: The Revolution in Transportation

The general economic histories cited for the previous chapter apply to this chapter also.

E. A. Pratt, *A History of Inland Transport and Communication in England* (1914), is comprehensive and detailed. J. H. Clapham, *Economic History of Modern Britain* (Vol. 1, *The Early Railway Age,* 1930), is especially good on the origins and growth of railways.

A highly readable account of American canal building is A. F. Harlow, *Old Towpaths* (1926). A. B. Hulbert, *Paths of Inland Commerce (Chronicles of America,* 1920), is a good concise survey of early inland transportation. Of the mass of books of early railroading, A. F. Harlow, *Steelways of New England* (1946), E. H. Hungerford, *The Story of the Baltimore and Ohio Railroad* (1928), and *Men and Iron: The Story of the New York Central* (1938), are written with popular appeal. For early Western railroading and a study of the land-grant policy P. W. Gates, *The Illinois Central Railroad and Its Colonization Work* (1934), is recommended.

C. G. Jackson, *The Ship under Steam* (1928), is a good introduction to the history of the steamship. F. C. Bowen, *A Century of Atlantic Travel* (1930), is also a convenient summary. J. P. Baxter, *The Introduction of the Ironclad Warship* (1933), should be read for the discussion of technological problems. The clippers have been well written up in A. H. Clark, *The Clipper Ship Era* (1910), and S. E. Morison, *Maritime History of Massachusetts* (1921).

Chapter 17: New Economic Doctrines

Charles Gide and Charles Rist, *History of Economic Doctrines* (1913), and L. H. Haney, *History of Economic Thought* (1922), are excellent surveys. D. O. Wagner, *Social Reformers* (1935), has excerpts from many of the nineteenth-century economic thinkers. Joseph Dorfman, *The Economic Mind in American Civilization* (1946), and V. L. Parrington, *Main Currents of American Thought* (3 vols., 1927–1930), are comprehensive on economic ideas in the United States. G. D. H. Cole, *Robert Owen* (1925), and R. W. Leopold, *Robert Dale Owen* (1940), both give good pictures of the interrelationship between European and American utopianism.

PART FIVE: LIBERALISM AND NATIONALISM IN EUROPE AND AMERICA

Chapter 18: Liberalism and Nationalism in Europe

Arthur May, *The Age of Metternich (Berkshire Studies,* 1933), and F. B. Artz, *Reaction and Revolution, 1814–1832 (Rise of Modern Europe,* Vol. XIV, 1934), are good surveys. Satisfactory histories of individual countries are: G. M. Trevelyan, *British History in the Nineteenth Century* (1938); G. L. Dickinson, *Revolution and Reaction in Modern France* (1892); and Michael Karpovich, *Imperial Russia (Berkshire Studies,* 1932).

A dramatic description of one phase of the Revolution of 1848 is G. M. Trevelyan, *Garibaldi's Defense of the Roman Republic* (1907). *Lord Grey and the Reform Bill* (1920), by the same author, and M. Hovell, *The Chartist Movement* (1918), are illuminating studies of British political movements.

Chapter 19: Liberalism and Nationalism in the United States

Jackson and Jacksonian Democracy are described in Marquis James, *Andrew Jackson* (1937), and A. M. Schlesinger, Jr., *The Age of Jackson* (1946). A brilliant analysis of this whole period is George Dangerfield, *The Era of Good Feeling* (1952). The conflict between Jackson and the Bank is thoroughly discussed in R. C. H. Catterall, *The Second Bank of the United States* (1903).

The democratic influences of American society are well covered in C. R. Fish, *The Rise of the Common Man* (*History of American Life*, 1927), and F. J. Turner, *The United States, 1830–1850* (1935). M. E. Curti, *The American Peace Crusade* (1929), is a good study of humanitarianism, and D. L. Dumond, *The Antislavery Origins of the Civil War* (1939), is probably the most impartial study of abolitionism.

Every student of American history should read F. J. Turner, *The Significance of the Frontier in American History* (rev. ed., 1920). The standard treatise on the West and the frontier is R. A. Billington and J. B. Hedges, *Westward Expansion* (1949). R. M. Robbins, *Our Landed Heritage: A History of the Public Domain* (1941), is the most convenient reference on public land policy.

A. K. Weinberg, *Manifest Destiny* (1935), is a comprehensive survey. N. W. Stephenson, *Texas and the Mexican War* (*Chronicles of America*) (1920), is compact and balanced. Bernard DeVoto, *The Year of Decision: 1846* (1940), is a brilliant study of American expansionism.

Good biographies of the prominent figures of the period are G. G. Van Deusen, *Henry Clay* (1937); C. M. Fuess, *Daniel Webster* (1930); and C. G. Wiltse, *John C. Calhoun* (3 vols., 1944–1951).

Chapter 20: The Second Empire and the Unification of Germany and Italy

R. C. Binkley, *Realism and Nationalism, 1852–1871* (*Rise of Modern Europe*, Vol. XVI, 1935), provides a good general survey. Philip Guedalla, *The Second Empire* (1922), is interestingly written. F. A. Simpson, *Louis Napoleon and the Recovery of France* (1923), presents a favorable picture of the Second Empire.

W. R. Thayer, *Life and Times of Cavour* (1911), is a fairly adequate work on Italian unification. More lively reading are G. M. Trevelyan, *Garibaldi and the Making of Italy* (1912), and *Garibaldi and the Thousand* (1912).

For German unification, two excellent special studies are R. H. Lord, *The Origins of the War of 1870* (1924), and H. Oncken, *Napoleon III and the Rhine* (1928). C. G. Robertson, *Bismarck* (1918), is a more dependable biography than Emil Ludwig, *Bismarck* (1928).

Chapter 21: Nationalism and Sectionalism in the United States

The references given for Chapter 19 are useful for this topic also. Southern sectionalism has been studied intensively. Of the numerous books available, W. E. Dodd, *The Cotton Kingdom* (*Chronicles of America*, 1919), is a compact and brilliant analysis of the Old South. More detail is given in U. B. Phillips, *American Negro Slavery* (1918), and *Life and Labor in the Old South* (1929). F. W. Taussig, *Tariff History of the United States,* is the standard reference on this aspect of sectional controversy.

Allan Nevins, *The Ordeal of the Union* (2 vols., 1947) and *The Emergence of Lincoln* (2 vols., 1950) are authoritative and comprehensive on the Compromise of 1850 and the coming of the Civil War. G. F. Milton, *The Eve of Conflict: Stephen A. Douglas and the Needless War* (1934), is well written and informative on the politics of the period. A. J. Beveridge, *Abraham Lincoln, 1809–1858* (2 vols., 1928) is excellent. C. B. Swisher, *Roger B. Taney* (1935), covers admirably the position of the Supreme Court in the slavery controversy. Other useful works on the politics of the 1850's are R. A. Billington, *The Protestant Crusade* (1938), for the Know-Nothings, and G. G. Van Deusen, *Thurlow Weed* (1947), for the beginning of the Republican party.

The coming of secession and the attempts to prevent it are brilliantly handled in D. M. Potter, *Lincoln and His Party in the Secession Crisis* (1942).

Chapter 22: The Civil War

Good general narratives are C. R. Fish, *The American Civil War* (1937), and G. F. Milton, *Conflict: The American Civil War* (1941).

Lincoln has been the subject of much biographical study. Recommended short works are Lord Charnwood, *Abraham Lincoln* (1917), and B. P. Thomas, *Abraham Lincoln* (1952). H. J. Eckenrode, *Jefferson Davis, President of the South* (1923), is the most satisfactory life of Davis. B. J. Hendrick, *Statesmen of the Lost Cause* (1939) and *Lincoln's War Cabinet* (1946), are valuable political studies. No student of the Civil War can ignore Allan Nevins, *The Statesmanship of the Civil War* (1953).

Of the innumerable military studies, D. S. Freeman, *Robert E. Lee* (4 vols., 1935) and *Lee's Lieutenants* (3 vols., 1937–1939), are classics, now matched on the Union side by K. P. Williams, *Lincoln Finds a General* (3 vols., 1949–1952). T. H. Williams, *Lincoln and His Generals* (1952), is compact and well written.

The diplomacy of the Civil War is thoroughly covered in E. D. Adams, *Great Britain and the American Civil War* (1925), and F. L. Owsley, *King Cotton Diplomacy* (1931). E. M. Coulter, *The Confederate States of America* (*History of the South,* Vol. VII, 1950), gives a comprehensive picture of Southern life during the war. J. G. Randall, *Constitutional Problems under Lincoln* (1926), is illuminating on the methods used to maintain the Northern war effort.

Reconstruction is well summarized in P. H. Buck, *The Road to Reunion* (1937), and C. V. Woodward, *Reunion and Reaction* (1951).

PART SIX: MODERN TECHNOLOGY AND ITS PROBLEMS

Chapter 23: The Expansion of Industrialism

Recommended general accounts of industrial expansion in the United States are E. C. Kirkland, *History of American Economic Life* (rev. ed., 1939); and Broadus and L. P. Mitchell, *American Economic History* (1947). A. A. Berle and G. C. Means, *The Modern Corporation and Private Property* (1932), is an excellent analysis of the corporation in present-day business organization. Eliot Jones, *The Trust Problem in the United States* (1921), is clear and readable.

There is much interesting material in biographies of industrial leaders, of which the best are B. J. Hendrick, *Life of Andrew Carnegie* (2 vols., 1932); Lewis Corey, *The House of Morgan* (1930); and Allan Nevins, *Study in Power: John D. Rockefeller* (2 vols., 1953) and *Ford, the Man, the Times, the Company* (1954). Matthew Josephson, *The Robber Barons* (1934), is fascinating but should be read with caution.

Railroad histories exist in quantity but vary widely in quality. Stuart Daggett, *Chapters in the History of the Southern Pacific* (1922), and Nelson Trottman, *History of the Union Pacific* (1923), are the best accounts of the transcontinentals. Daggett's work should be supplemented by Oscar Lewis, *The Big Four* (1938). C. F. Adams, *A Chapter of Erie* (1886), is a vivid description of financial manipulation by an informed contemporary. The most exhaustive study of railroad regulation is I. L. Sharfman, *The Interstate Commerce Commission* (4 vols., 1931–1937).

For Europe, besides the economic histories of Heaton and Bowden, Karpovich, and Usher previously referred to, J. H. Clapham, *The Economic Development of France and Germany* (1921), is detailed but readable. W. H. Dawson, *The Evolution of Modern Germany* (1919), is good on economic development. Fay, *Great Britain from Adam Smith to the Present,* and Slater, *Growth of Modern England,* continue to be very useful.

Chapter 24: Industrial Society

Two volumes of the *History of American Life* series, Allan Nevins, *The Emergence of Modern America* (1927), and A. M. Schlesinger, *The Rise of the City* (1933), give an excellent picture of the growth of urban society in the United States. An excellent study of the same phenomenon in Europe is C. J. H. Hayes, *A Generation of Materialism* (*Rise of Modern Europe,* Vol. XVII, 1941).

Most of the references on the labor movement given in Chapter 15 may be used for this chapter. In addition, L. L. Lorwin, *The American Federation of Labor* (1933), and Leo Wolman, *The Growth of American Trade Unions* (1923), deal directly with the period under consideration. N. J. Ware, *The Labor Movement in the United States, 1860–1895,* is informative on the Knights of Labor. Ray Ginger, *The Bending Cross* (1949), is a first-rate life of Debs.

Chapter 25: The Industrializing of Agriculture

The best analysis of the problems involved in the last phase of the westward movement is W. P. Webb, *The Great Plains* (1931). Everett Dick, *The Sodhouse Frontier* (1938), is a good social history of the farming frontier, while E. E. Dale, *The Range Cattle Industry* (1930), and Louis Pelzer, *The Cattleman's Frontier* (1936), deal adequately with the cattle kingdom. G. D. Bradley, *The Story of the Santa Fe* (1920), and R. H. Overton, *Burlington West* (1940), are very useful on the work of the railroads as colonizing agencies.

Agrarian unrest in the United States is thoroughly covered in S. J. Buck, *The Granger Movement* (1913), and J. D. Hicks, *The Populist Revolt* (1931). S. J. Buck, *The Agrarian Crusade* (*Chronicles of America,* 1920), is a good summary. E. L. Bogart, *Economic History of Europe, 1760–1939* (1942), does a satisfactory condensation of the changes in European agriculture resulting from overseas competition.

Chapter 26: Political and Social Trends in Europe, 1870–1914

R. C. K. Ensor, *England, 1870–1914* (1936), provides the best general treatment of British history during this period. The late nineteenth century can be particularly well studied in three biographies: J. L. Garvin, *Life of Joseph Chamberlain* (3 vols., 1932–1934); W. F. Monypenny and G. E. Buckle, *Life of Benjamin Disraeli* (6 vols., 1910–1920); and John Morley, *Life of Gladstone* (1903). The rise of the Labour party is adequately described in R. H. Tawney, *The British Movement* (1920). D. C. Somervell, *The Reign of King George V* (1935), has a good account of the political controversies of this period.

W. H. Dawson, *The German Empire* (2 vols., 1919), is by far the most satisfactory survey of Germany. Gustav Stolper, *German Economy, 1870–1940* (1940), illustrates the dominant position of the state. D. W. Brogan, *France under the Republic* (1940), is completely adequate for French internal history in this period. Karpovich, *Imperial Russia,* summarizes Russian affairs competently.

Chapter 27: The Progressive Movement in the United States

Earlier references on agrarian unrest are useful for this chapter. The currency problem is clearly presented in D. R. Dewey, *Financial History of the United States* (12th ed., 1935). Taussig, *Tariff History of the United States,* previously cited, covers this topic, and the political implications of both issues should be studied in Allan Nevins, *Grover Cleveland* (1932).

For the election of 1896, Herbert Croly, *Marcus A. Hanna* (1912), Paxton Hibben, *The Peerless Leader: William Jennings Bryan* (1929), and M. R. Werner, *Bryan* (1929), are all informative.

H. U. Faulkner, *The Quest for Social Justice (History of American Life,* 1931), is a comprehensive survey of the Progressive era. Lincoln Steffens, *Autobiography* (2 vols., 1931), gives the story of an active muckraker. The relationship of the judiciary to social reform is treated in Warren, *The Supreme Court in United States History,* and C. D. Bowen, *Yankee from Olympus* (1942), a study of Justice Holmes which is better on his personal qualities than his judicial philosophy. M. A. Hansen, *The Atlantic Migration* (1941), is the most readable study of immigration.

H. F. Pringle, *Theodore Roosevelt* (1931), and *Life and Times of William H. Taft* (2 vols., 1939), are balanced and complete. They can be supplemented by J. M. Blum, *The Republican Roosevelt* (1954), and N. W. Stephenson, *Nelson W. Aldrich* (1930), a good biography of the outstanding conservative. G. E. Mowry, *Roosevelt and the Progressive Movement* (1946), is a reappraisal of the Republican schism in 1912. C. R. Van Hise and L. Havemeyer, *The Conservation of Our Natural Resources* (1930), is the most complete survey of this subject.

Of the numerous biographies of Wilson, W. E. Dodd, *Woodrow Wilson and His Work* (1921), is the most satisfactory single volume. A. S. Link, *Wilson: The Road to the White House* (1947) and *Woodrow Wilson and the Progressive Era* (1954), are definitive.

PART SEVEN: THE NEW IMPERIALISM

Chapter 28: The Rise of Modern Imperialism: The Partition of Africa

P. T. Moon, *Imperialism and World Politics* (1926), is an outstanding general analysis of imperialism. Somewhat different weight is given to the forces making for imperialism in C. J. H. Hayes, *A Generation of Materialism* (*Rise of Modern Europe*, Vol. XVI, 1941).

H. L. Hoskins, *European Imperialism in Africa* (*Berkshire Studies*, 1930), is brief and clear. More detail can be found in C. P. Lucas, *The Partition and Colonization of Africa* (1922). There are two good biographies of Cecil Rhodes, by S. G. Millin (1933) and Basil Williams (1921).

Chapter 29: European Imperialism in Asia and the Pacific

D. E. Owen, *Imperialism and Nationalism in the Far East* (*Berkshire Studies,* 1929), and H. M. Vinacke, *History of the Far East in Modern Times* (1942), provide satisfactory surveys. Mahoney, Cameron, and McReynolds, *China, Japan, and the Powers,* (1952), is thorough and comprehensive. E. M. Earle, *Turkey, the Great Powers, and the Bagdad Railway* (1923), deals comprehensively with imperialism in the Middle East; and W. M. Shuster, *The Strangling of Persia* (1912), is a detailed case study by a highly qualified observer. Two other very useful works are Amry Vandenbosch, *The Dutch East Indies* (1934), and W. T. Wallbank, *India* (*Berkshire Studies*, 1948).

Chapter 30: American Imperialism

Dexter Perkins, *Hands Off* (1940), A. K. Weinberg, *Manifest Destiny* (1935), and B. H. Williams, *Economic Foreign Policy of the United States* (1929), cover the general topic satisfactorily.

Walter Millis, *The Martial Spirit* (1931), is a readable study of the background and course of the Spanish-American War, but it should be balanced by J. W. Pratt, *The Expansionists of 1898* (1936).

American expansion in the Pacific is thoroughly dealt with in Tyler Dennett, *Americans in Eastern Asia* (1922), and A. W. Griswold, *The Far Eastern Policy of the United States* (1938). The relations of the United States and Latin America are well analyzed in H. C. Hill, *Roosevelt and the Caribbean* (1927), and J. F. Rippy, *Latin America in World Politics* (1938).

Excellent biographies for this subject are Tyler Dennett, *John Hay* (1933), and P. C. Jessup, *Elihu Root* (2 vols., 1938).

PART EIGHT: THE FIRST WORLD WAR AND THE PEACE SETTLEMENT

Chapter 31: The Coming of the War

The literature on the origins of the First World War is voluminous and much of it is intensely controversial. S. B. Fay, *The Origins of the World War* (2 vols.,

1930), and B. E. Schmidt, *The Coming of the War* (2 vols., 1930), are both authoritative but disagree on assessing responsibility. G. L. Dickinson, *The International Anarchy, 1904–1914* (1926), is informative and well written. B. E. Schmidt, *Triple Alliance and Triple Entente (Berkshire Studies,* 1934), is an excellent brief study of the alliance system. It should be supplemented by W. L. Langer, *European Alliances and Alignments* (1931). G. M. Trevelyan, *Grey of Fallodon* (1937), is a magnificent biography of one of the principal figures.

Chapter 32: The First World War

B. H. Liddell Hart, *The Real War, 1916–1918* (1930), is a summary of military operations, critical of Allied generalship. W. S. Churchill, *The World Crisis* (4 vols., 1923–1927) and *The Unknown War* (1931), are written with the author's customary command of English, the first being a personal account and the second a history of the war on the Eastern front. Erich Ludendorff, *My War Memoirs* (2 vols., 1919), is revealing on German military strategy and operations. Memoirs of virtually every important figure of the war have been published. The war at sea is covered in detail in J. S. Corbett and H. Newbolt, *Naval Operations* (4 vols., 1920–1925), the British official history, but it should be checked against H. H. Frost, *The Battle of Jutland* (1935). Other works of special interest are T. E. Lawrence, *Seven Pillars of Wisdom* (1926), or its abridgment, *Revolt in the Desert* (1927).

The problems of American neutrality are well discussed in the diplomatic histories of T. A. Bailey and S. F. Bemis. A. M. Morrissey, *The American Defense of Neutral Rights* (1939), embodies the latest research on the subject.

T. G. Frothingham, *The American Reinforcement in the World War* (1927) is the best survey of American military participation. There is valuable information in P. C. March, *The Nation at War* (1932), a book by the wartime Chief of Staff, and J. J. Pershing, *My Experiences in the World War* (2 vols., 1931). The naval contribution of the United States is well described in E. E. Morison, *Admiral Sims and the New American Navy* (1942). F. R. Palmer, *Newton D. Baker* (2 vols., 1931), gives a good picture of mobilization in the United States.

Chapter 33: The Postwar Peace Settlements

Paul Birdsall, *Versailles Twenty Years After* (1941), and Harold Nicolson, *Peacemaking, 1919* (1933), are excellent analyses of the Peace Conference. T. A. Bailey, *Woodrow Wilson and the Lost Peace* (1944), is a very readable study of Wilson's tactics and the influence of American domestic politics on the Peace Conference. E. M. House and Charles Seymour, eds., *What Really Happened at Paris* (1921), is a useful collection of contemporary accounts. J. M. Keynes, *The Economic Consequences of the Peace* (1920) is a criticism which proved to be remarkably accurate.

The American rejection of the Versailles Treaty is colorfully described in T. A. Bailey, *Woodrow Wilson and the Great Betrayal* (1945). A more detailed account, somewhat more favorable to Wilson, is D. F. Fleming, *The United States and the League of Nations* (1932).

Chapter 34: Liquidating the Peace Settlement

Complete descriptions of the League of Nations can be found in Charles Howard-Ellis, *The Origin, Structure and Working of the League of Nations* (1928), and Felix Morley, *The Society of Nations* (1932). D. H. Miller, *The Drafting of the Covenant* (1928), is an account by one of the principal architects of the League.

The problem of reparations and war debts is carefully analyzed in H. G. Moulton and Leo Pasvolsky, *War Debts and World Prosperity* (1932). International politics in the 1920's are comprehensively discussed in R. J. Sontag, *European Diplomatic History, 1871–1932* (1933). The optimistic mood of the period is reflected in R. L. Buell, *International Relations* (1928), and D. H. Miller, *The Peace Pact of Paris* (1928).

The best description of the Washington Conference is H. H. and M. Sprout, *Toward a New Order of Sea Power* (1940). D. W. Knox, *History of the United States Navy* (1937) is critical of the naval limitation treaties. A profound study of the disarmament problem as a whole is S. de Madariaga, *Disarmament* (1929).

PART NINE: INTERNAL PROBLEMS, 1919–1939

Chapter 35: Totalitarianism in Europe

George Vernadsky, *The Russian Revolution* (*Berkshire Studies*, 1932) is a readable summary of events from 1917 to 1931. The same author's *Lenin* (1931) is probably the most dependable biography of the founder of the Soviet state. M. G. Hindus, *The Great Offensive* (1933), is a somewhat dramatic portrayal of the first Five-year Plan. W. H. Chamberlin, *Russia's Iron Age* (1934), is more substantial. Walter Duranty, *I Write as I Please* (1935), is a book by a well-informed correspondent. F. L. Schuman, *Soviet Politics at Home and Abroad* (1946), is a comprehensive survey, sympathetic to the Russians.

G. Salvemini, *The Fascist Dictatorship in Italy* (1927), and *Under the Axe of Fascism* (1939), cover domestic developments in Italy satisfactorily. A good supplement is C. T. Schmidt, *The Corporate State in Action* (1939).

For Germany, F. L. Schuman, *Germany since 1918* (1937), gives a readable summary of the Weimar Republic. The organization and internal policies of the Nazi dictatorship are lucidly analyzed in S. H. Roberts, *The House That Hitler Built* (1938). Konrad Heiden, *Der Fuehrer* (1943), is a judicious interpretation of Hitler.

Chapter 36: The European Democracies

Britain's internal problems during the 1920's have been exhaustively analyzed in Wilhelm Dibelius, *England* (1930), and André Siegfried, *England's Crisis* (1931). The depression in Great Britain and the dominions is ably studied in Herbert Heaton, *The British Way to Recovery* (1934). Viscount Samuel, *Grooves of Change* (1946), provides a thoughtful commentary on the whole period by a prominent Liberal statesman. W. Y. Elliot, *The New British Empire* (1932), and R. G. Trotter, *The British Empire—Commonwealth* (*Berkshire Studies*, 1932), are clear discussions of changes in the imperial structure. J. Nehru, *Toward Freedom* (1932), is an excellent exposition of Indian nationalism.

D. W. Brogan, *France under the Republic* (1940), covers the ground thoroughly. Briefer but equally informative are André Maurois, *Tragedy in France* (1942); and Alexander Werth, *The Twilight of France* (1942).

Chapter 37: Reaction and Depression in the United States

F. L. Allen, *Only Yesterday* (1931), is a picturesque description of the United States in the 1920's. Mark Sullivan, *Our Times* (6 vols., 1926–1935), does the same thing in greater detail. George Soule, *Prosperity Decade* (*Economic History of the United States,* Vol. VIII, 1947), is a definitive study of the economy of the boom period. Two cooperative research projects, *Recent Economic Changes* (2 vols., 1929) and *Recent Social Trends* (1933), are packed with facts.

M. E. Ravage, *The Story of Teapot Dome* (1924), is illustrative of the Harding administration; and W. A. White, *A Puritan in Babylon* (1939), is a lucid description of Calvin Coolidge. The best place to study prohibition is the Wickersham Committee, *Report on the Enforcement of the Prohibition Laws of the United States* (1931).

A succinct analysis of the causes and course of the depression can be found in a study by the Brookings Institution, *The Recovery Problem in the United States* (1936). C. R. and M. Beard, *America in Midpassage* (1939), is a well-balanced account. W. S. Myers and W. H. Newton, *The Hoover Administration* (1936), presents the case in favor of Hoover.

Chapter 38: The New Deal

There are good comprehensive accounts in Dixon Wecter, *The Age of the Great Depression* (1948), and D. W. Brogan, *The Era of Franklin D. Roosevelt* (*Chronicles of America,* 1950). Broadus Mitchell, *Depression Decade* (*Economic History of the United States,* Vol. IX, 1948), has much material on economic problems.

Among the mass of special studies, those which can be particularly recommended are the Brookings Institution, *The National Recovery Administration* (1935); E. G. Nourse, J. S. Davis, and J. D. Black, *Three Years of the AAA* (1937); R. R. Brooks, *Unions of Their Own Choosing* (1938); and Benjamin Stollberg, *The Story of the CIO* (1939). D. E. Lilienthal, *The TVA: Democracy on the March* (1944), is an excellent piece of work.

Chapter 39: The Far East between World Wars

The references on the Far East given in Chapter 29 can be used for this chapter also.

PART TEN: THE SECOND WORLD WAR AND AFTER

Chapter 40: The Causes of the Second World War

D. E. Lee, *Ten Years* (1942), is a magnificent description of the drift toward war in the 1930's. W. S. Churchill, *The Gathering Storm* (Vol. 1, 1948), has the high literary quality of the author's other works and contains information not previously available.

E. A. Peers, *The Spanish Tragedy* (1936) and *Spain in Eclipse* (1943), are first-class accounts of the revolution and civil war in Spain. The reorientation of American foreign policy is well treated in W. L. Langer and S. E. Gleason, *The Challenge to Isolation* (1952).

Chapters 41 and 42: The Second World War

There is a massive and increasing volume of literature on the Second World War. The following are especially recommended as good reading: W. S. Churchill, *The Second World War* (5 vols. to date); D. D. Eisenhower, *Crusade in Europe* (1948); S. E. Morison, *History of United States Naval Operations in World War II* (8 vols. to date).

The entry of the United States should be studied in Herbert Feis, *The Road to Pearl Harbor* (1950); Basil Rauch, *Roosevelt: Munich to Pearl Harbor* (1950); Langer and Gleason, *The Undeclared War* (1953); and C. C. Tansill, *Back Door to War* (1952), very anti-Roosevelt.

Two good books on the mobilization of the home front in the United States are D. M. Nelson, *Arsenal of Democracy* (1946), by the chairman of the War Production Board, and E. R. Stettinius, *Lend-Lease: Weapon for Victory* (1944), by the Lend-Lease Administrator. The story of the atomic bomb is told in J. P. Baxter, *Scientists against Time* (1946). H. L. Stimson and McG. Bundy, *On Active Service in Peace and War* (1948), is exceptional in quality.

Chapter 43: International Cooperation

Excellent references on the organization of the United Nations are Louis Dolivet, *The United Nations* (1948); L. M. Goodrich and Carl Hambro, *The Charter of the United Nations* (1947); and A. Boyd, ed., *United Nations Handbook* (1946). H. V. Evatt, *The Task of Nations* (1949), presents a distinguished Australian's reflections. The work of the organization is presented in E. P. Chase, *The United Nations in Action* (1950), and A. Vandenbosch and W. N. Hogan, *The United Nations: Background, Organization, Functions, and Activities* (1952). N. Bentwich and A. Martin, *A Commentary on the Charter of the United Nations* (1950), points out the cleavage between theory and practice.

Chapter 44: The World since the War

Of the innumerable books on Russia and the Iron Curtain countries, the following can be particularly recommended: Sir John Maynard, *Russia in Flux* (1948); R. H. Seton-Watson, *From Lenin to Malenkov* (1953); W. W. Rostow and A. Levin, *The Dynamics of Soviet Society* (1953); and Massimo Salvadori, *The Rise of Modern Communism (Berkshire Studies,* 1952). For Western Europe: E. J. Knaplund, *France since Versailles (Berkshire Studies,* 1952); G. F. O. Clarke, *Britain Today* (1951); J. P. Warburg, *Germany: Key to Peace* (1953); and General L. D. Clay, *Decision in Germany* (1950). Paul McGuire, *Experiment in World Order* (1948), is a provocative analysis of the British Commonwealth.

The Asiatic world may be studied in Werner Levi, *Free India in Asia;* L. A.

Mills, *The New World of Southeast Asia* (1949); and H. V. Cooke, *Challenge and Response in the Middle East* (1952). For Africa, see P. E. James, *Africa: A Study in Tropical Development* (1950); and Leo Marquand, *The Peoples and Policies of South Africa* (1952). Modern Latin America can be studied in P. E. James, *Latin America* (1950); and S. G. Hanson, *The Economic Development of Latin America* (1951).

Works on the postwar United States are more numerous than dependable. The appropriate chapters in F. L. Allen, *The Big Change* (1952), and G. W. Johnson, *Incredible Tale* (1952), are written with a sense of historical perspective.

Chapter 45: The Cold War

The literature dealing with the subjects covered in this chapter is voluminous, but much of it is ephemeral. Following is a selective list.

The Council on Foreign Relations annual survey, *The United States in World Affairs*, which was resumed after the war is indispensable.

For the Marshall Plan see William Diebold, Jr., *Trade and Payments in Western Europe: A Study in Economic Cooperation, 1947–1951* (1952); Robert Marjolin, *Europe and the United States in the World Economy* (1953); OEEC, *Europe—The Way Ahead* (1952).

For NATO and EDC see Sir William E. Beckett, *The North Atlantic Treaty, the Brussels Treaty and the Charter of the United Nations* (1950); Drew Middleton, *The Defense of Western Europe* (1952); *The NATO Handbook* (1952); A. C. Turner, *Bulwark of the West* (1953); U.S. State Department, *NATO—North Atlantic Treaty Organization: Its Development and Significance* (1952).

For the Near and Middle East, see the following: Clare Hollingworth, *The Arabs and the West* (1952); J. C. Hurewitz, *Middle East Dilemmas: The Background of United States Policy* (1953); George Lenczowski, *The Middle East in World Affairs* (1952).

India and Pakistan can be studied in W. N. Brown, *The United States and India and Pakistan* (1952); K. P. Karunakaran, *India in World Affairs, August 1947–January 1950* (1952).

The Far East and Southeast Asia are covered by M. E. Cameron, T. H. D. Mahoney, and G. E. McReynolds, *China, Japan and the Powers* (1952); Max Beloff, *Soviet Policy in the Far East, 1944–1951* (1953): W. Thayer, ed., *Southeast Asia in the Coming World* (1953); C. Brandt, B. Schwartz, and J. K. Fairbank, eds., *A Documentary History of Chinese Communism* (1952); E. O. Reischauer, *Japan, Past and Present* (2d ed., 1952).

For Africa see Vernon Bartlett, *Struggle for Africa* (1953); and H. R. Isaacs and E. Ross, *Africa: New Crises in the Making* (1952).

For Latin America see Harry Bernstein, *Modern and Contemporary Latin America* (1952); and German Arciniegas, *The State of Latin America* (1952).

For Point Four see W. A. Brown, Jr., and Redvers Opie, *American Foreign Assistance* (1953); and U.S. State Department, *Point Four* (1950).

The control of atomic energy is covered in U.S. State Department, *International Control of Atomic Energy and the Prohibition of Atomic Weapons* (1949); and *Atomic Power for Peace* (1954).

INDEX

ABC powers, 485, 507, 643
Abolitionists, 298, 299
Abyssinia, 465, 466
   (*See also* Ethiopia)
Act of Union, 51
Adams, Charles Francis, 356
Adams, John, 102, 110, 113, 137
   as peace commissioner, 123–125
   as President, 140, 148, 149, 189, 190
Adams, John Quincy, 217, 299
   and Monroe Doctrine, 228, 229
   as President, 291, 292
Adams, Samuel, 101, 102, 142
Adamson Act, 400, 452
Addams, Jane, 442, 491
Adenauer, Konrad, 738
Adkins v. Children's Hospital, 442, 641, 642
Adowa, 466, 666
Afghanistan, 481, 758
Agadir incident, 519
Agassiz, Louis, 309
Agricultural Adjustment Administration (AAA), 637, 638
Agricultural Marketing Act, 618
Agricultural Revolution, 5
Agriculture, scientific, 5, 403, 404
Aguinaldo, Emilio, 491
Air Commerce Act, 614
Alabama, 354, 356
Alamein, El, 702, 705
Alaska, 68, 228, 492
   purchase of, 484
   Japanese attack on, 702
Albania, 520, 663, 676
Albany Congress of 1754, 82
   Plan of Union, 82
Albert, King of Belgium, 523
Aldrich, Nelson W., 436, 444, 451
Alexander I of Russia, 198, 199, 200, 202, 277

Alexander I of Russia, at Congress of Vienna, 220, 221
   and Holy Alliance, 226
Alexander II (Russia), 357, 365, 414, 426
Alexander III (Russia), 426
Alexander of Yugoslavia, 665
Alexander, Sir Harold, 701, 708
Algeciras Conference, 466, 518
Algeria, 463, 705, 706
Algiers, 207, 208
Alien and Sedition Acts, 148, 149, 190
Allenby, General, 543
Allgemeine Elektrizitäts Gesellschaft, 382
Allied Control Council, 726
Alsace, 322, 511, 528
Altgeld, John P., 396, 398
Amalgamated Association of Iron and Steel Workers, 397, 398
America First Committee, 692, 693
American Federation of Labor (A. F. of L.), 396, 397, 616, 633, 634, 744
American Liberty League, 634
American Peace Society, 562
American Railway Union, 398
Amherst, Jeffrey, 64
Amiens, Peace of, 195, 196
Anderson, Maxwell, 625
Andros, Sir Edmund, 81
Annapolis Convention, 136
Anne, queen of England, 51, 52
Anschluss, 557, 673, 674
Anti-Comintern Pact, 657, 664
Anti-Corn-Law League, 264
Anti-Masonic party, 296
Antietam, Battle of, 348
Antwerp, 709
Anzacs, 530
Appleby, John F., 404
Appomattox Court House, 352
Arab League, 758

Ardennes, 682, 711
Argentina, 232
  and Good Neighbor policy, 643, 645
  in Second World War, 700, 712
  in UN, 716
  after Second World War, 742, 766
Argonne Forest, 545
Arkwright, Richard, 238, 243
Armada, 10
Armed Neutrality, League of, 119, 195
Arms embargo, 646, 692
Arnold, Benedict, 111, 114, 115, 120
Articles of Confederation, 130, 132, 138
Ashburton, Lord, 124
Assignats, 166
Associations Law of 1901, 426
Assumption bill, 145
Atchison, Topeka, and Santa Fe Railroad, 378
Atlanta, 351
Atlantic Charter, 695, 714
Atomic bomb, 713
Atomic energy, 767–769
Atomic Energy Act, 744
Atomic Energy Commission, 744
Attlee, Clement, 724, 738
Audiencias, 69
Audubon, John James, 309
Augsburg, League of, 51, 62
Austerlitz, Battle of, 196
Austin, Stephen, 303
Australia, 599, 701, 705, 764
  Commonwealth of, 421
Austria, 56
  in Napoleonic Wars, 195–198, 200, 201, 204–206
  at Congress of Vienna, 219–221
  and unification of Italy and Germany, 276, 317–321
  Republic of, 556, 557, 661, 664, 665, 673, 674
  after Second World War, 729, 730
Austria-Hungary, 320, 429, 430
  in alliance system, 513, 518–521
  and outbreak of First World War, 521–523, 525
  in First World War, 529, 531, 532, 539, 545
Austrian Succession, War of, 60, 63
Ayacucho, Battle of, 232
Aztecs, 68

Bacon, Nathaniel, 86
Bacon's Rebellion, 86
Badoglio, Marshal, 585, 707
Bagdad, 543

Bagdad Railway, 482, 483
Bainbridge, Captain William, 208, 215
Bakewell, Robert, 5
Bakunin, Michael, 271
Baldwin, Stanley, 595–598
Balfour, Arthur, 599
Balfour Declaration, 553, 603, 604
Ballinger, Richard A., 448
"Baloney dollar," 630
Baltimore, 216
Baltimore and Ohio Railroad, 257, 379
Bank of Amsterdam, 13, 15
Bank of England, 14, 263, 597, 739
Bank of France, 193, 597, 606, 607
Bank of International Settlements, 567, 568
Bank of the United States, First, 144–146, 154
  Second, 154, 155, 290–291, 293–295
Bankhead-Jones Act, 638
Barbary pirates, 207, 208
Baruch, Bernard, 541, 769
Baruch Plan, 767, 768
Bastille, 163, 164
Bastogne, 711
Bataan, 701, 711
Bavaria, 196, 198, 321
Bayard, James A., 217
Beaumarchais, Pierre Caron de, 110
Beccaria, 36
Beecher, Henry W., 335
Belgium, 38, 175, 223, 225, 281
  in First World War, 523, 524, 528
  industrialism in, 240, 385
  in Second World War, 681, 682
Bell, Alexander Graham, 368
Bell, Henry, 258
Bell, John, 340
Bellamy, Edward, 391
Belleau Wood, 544
Benedict XV, 562
Benelux, 735, 736
Beneš, Eduard, 549, 608, 734
Benét, Stephen Vincent, 626
Bennington, Battle of, 115
Bentham, Jeremy, 261, 262, 561
Benton, Senator Thomas H., 300, 306
Benton, Thomas Hart, 626
Berchtold, Count, 522
Beria, Lavrenti, 734
Berlin, Irving, 626
Berlin, 198, 712
  Congress of, 1878, 463, 513
    1884, 468, 469
Berlin blockade, 738
Berlin Conference of 1954, 730
Berlin Decree, 199

Bernadotte, Count Folke, 720
Bernadotte, Marshal, 202, 223
Bessarabia, 222, 578, 688
Bessemer, Henry, 240
Bethmann-Hollweg, Chancellor von, 524
Bevan, Aneurin, 739
"B₂ H₂ Resolution," 715
Biddle, Nicholas, 293
Bill of Rights, English, 51
 United States, 143
Bimetallism, 433, 434, 438
Bismarck, Otto von, 318–322
 domestic program in German Empire, 383, 421–423
 and imperialism, 455, 456, 463, 464
 alliance system of, 513
Bismarck, 687
Blaine, James G., 435, 486
Blanc, Louis, 268, 286
Bland-Allison Act, 433
Blenheim, Battle of, 46
Bliss, General Tasker M., 548
Blount, James, 493
Blum, Léon, 606, 607
Board of Trade and Plantations, 87
Boer War, 460
Boers, 457–460
Bogotá Conference, 766
Bolívar, Simón, 228, 232, 292
Bolivia, 643
Bolsheviks, 391, 543, 578, 579
Bonaparte, Joseph, 200, 205
Bonaparte, Josephine, 196, 201
Bonaparte, Louis, 201
Bonaparte, Louis Napoleon (*see* Napoleon III)
Bonaparte, Lucien, 193
Bonaparte, Napoleon (*see* Napoleon I)
Bonn Convention, 727
Bonneville, Benjamin, 304
Bonus Army, 622
Borah, William E., 559, 571
Borodino, Battle of, 203
Bosnia, 518, 519, 521
Boston, siege of, 111
Boston and Albany Railroad, 256
"Boston Massacre," 102
Boston Tea Party, 104
Botha, Louis, 421, 549
Bougainville, 705
Boulanger, General, 424, 425
Boulton, Matthew, 237
Boxer Rebellion, 476
Boyle, Robert, 33
Braddock, General Edward, 64
Bradford, Governor William, 75
Bragg, Braxton, 349, 350

Brahe, Tycho, 32
"Brain trust," 627
Brandenburg, 56
Brazil, 10, 67*n.*, 232, 643, 700
 discovery of, 10*n.*
Breckinridge, John C., 339, 340
Brest-Litovsk, Treaty of, 543, 556, 579
 second, 678
Bretton Woods Conference, 715
Briand, Aristide, 394, 570
Bricker Amendment, 749
Bright, John, 264
Brisbane, Albert, 267
British North America Act, 358
British South Africa Company, 459, 462
Brock, Isaac, 214
Brockdorff-Rantzau, Count von, 555
"Broken voyage," 211
Brook Farm, 268
Brooks, Preston, 336
Brotherhood of Locomotive Engineers, 395
Brown, Jacob, 215
Brown, John, 339
Brüning, Heinrich, 589
Brussels Pact, 736, 754
Bryan, William Jennings, 434, 438, 439
 and imperialism, 491
 as Secretary of State, 501, 502, 537, 649
Buchanan, James, 336, 338
Buell, Don Carlos, 349
Bulgaria, 520
 in First World War, 525, 530, 545
 peace settlement with, 557
 in Second World War, 688
 after Second World War, 730, 731
Bulge, Battle of the, 711
"Bull Moose," 449
Bull Run, First Battle of, 346
 Second Battle of, 348
Bullfinch, Charles, 309
Bunau-Varilla, Philippe, 493, 495
Bunker Hill, Battle of, 111
Burgoyne, General John, 114–116
Burke, Edmund, 170
Burke-Wadsworth Act (Selective Service Act of 1940), 693
Burma, 479, 603, 701, 740
Burma Road, 694
Burnside, Ambrose, 348
Burr, Aaron, 140, 146, 149, 150
Burritt, Elihu, 298
Burschenschaften, 276, 287
Byelorussia, 724
Byrnes, James F., 724

Cahiers, 162
Cairo Conference, 722
Calhoun, John C., 253, 254, 290, 291*n.*
    in Jackson administration, 296
    and sectionalism, 325, 329, 330
California, 10, 68, 304
    annexation of, 306, 307
    admission of, 332, 333
Calvert, Cecilius, 77
Calvert, Sir George, Lord Baltimore, 48, 77
Calvin, John, 26
Calvinism, 26, 27, 30
Cambrai, Battle of, 543
Camden, Battle of, 120
Campo Formio, Treaty of, 175
Canada, settlement of, 10
    colonial system in, 19
    British conquest of, 64, 65
    in American Revolution, 111, 114
    in War of 1812, 214–216
    Dominion of, created, 357, 358
    as member of Commonwealth of Nations, 599, 600
    and Good Neighbor policy, 645, 646
    declares war on Germany, 677
    in Second World War, 687
    after Second World War, 743
Canadian National Railway, 379
Canadian Pacific Railway, 378
Canals, 250–253
Canning, George, 228–230
Cannon, Joseph, 423
Cape Colony, 457, 459
Cape of Good Hope, 8, 457
Caporetto, 542
Caracas Conference, 766
Carbonari, 314
Cardin, Sir Lionel, 506
Carey, Henry, 266
Carey, Matthew, 266
Carey Act, 409
Carleton, Sir Guy (Lord Dorchester), 114, 183
Carlsbad (Karlsbad) Decrees, 276
Carnegie, Andrew, 371, 372, 491
    "gospel of wealth," 390
Carnegie Endowment for International Peace, 562
Carnegie Steel Company, 371, 380
Carnot, Lazare, 172
Carondelet, Governor, 185
Carpet-bag governments, 362
Carranza, Venustiano, 507
Carroll, John, Bishop of Baltimore, 128
Cartier, Jacques, 71
Casa de Contratación, 18, 69

Casablanca, 705
    Conference at, 706, 721
Casas, Bartolomé de las, 70
Casement, Sir Roger, 468
Cass, Lewis, 332
Castlereagh, Lord, 217, 220, 226
Castro, Cipriano, 499
Catherine the Great, 37, 58, 119
Catholic Emancipation Act (1829), 279
Cattle kingdom, 405–407
Cavaignac, General, 286, 311
Cavaliers, 49
Cavour, Conte di, 314–316
Central Pacific Railroad, 359, 375, 376
Central Powers, 525, 526, 532–536, 539, 542
    collapse of, 545, 546
    in Russian Revolution, 578, 579
Cervera, Admiral, 489, 490
Ceylon, 740
Chamberlain, Sir Austen, 570
Chamberlain, Houston Stuart, 512
Chamberlain, Joseph, 413, 419, 456
Chamberlain, Neville, 598, 675, 676, 681
Champlain, Samuel de, 71
Chancellorsville, Battle of, 348
Chapultepec, 307
    Act of, 766
Charles I of England, 47, 48
Charles II of England, 14, 50, 78
Charles X of France, 277, 278, 280, 281, 463
Charles XII of Sweden, 58
Charles, Archduke of Austria, 200, 201
Charles Albert of Sardinia-Piedmont, 287, 314
Charleston, South Carolina, 120, 339, 344
Chartered companies, 12
Chartism, 246, 284, 285
Chase, Salmon P., 346
Chateau Thierry, 544
Chattanooga, 347, 350
Cherokees, 185
Chesapeake-Leopard Affair, 212
Chesapeake and Ohio Canal, 252
Chiang Kai-shek, 650, 651, 655, 656, 722
Chicago, 241
Chicago, Milwaukee, and St. Paul v. Minnesota, 381
Chickamauga, Battle of, 350
Chile, 232, 486, 643
Chinese Eastern Railway, 384, 475, 657
Chinese Exclusion Act, 395, 443
Chisholm Trail, 407
Chou En-lai, 760
Christian socialists, 268, 442, 443

Church of England, 27, 47, 87
Churchill, John, Duke of Marlborough, 46
Churchill, Winston, 419
    in First World War, 529, 530
    between wars, 595, 596
    in Second World War, 681, 682, 691, 693, 706
    in peacemaking conferences, 722–724
    electoral defeat of, 724
    returns to power, 739
Civil Constitution of the Clergy, 166
Civil rights, 361, 745–746
Civil Service Commission, 441
Civilian Conservation Corps (CCC), 628
Clark, Champ, 448, 449
Clark, George Rogers, 124, 181
Clark Memorandum, 645
Clausewitz, Karl von, 204
Clay, Henry, 210, 217, 228
    "American system" of, 254, 329
    and nationalism in United States, 290, 291
    and Whig party, 293
    in election of 1844, 305
    in nullification controversy, 330
    and Compromise of 1850, 332, 333
Clay, General Lucius D., 727
Clayton Act, 400, 450
Clayton-Bulwer Treaty, 307, 486, 495
Clemenceau, Georges, 425, 548, 549
Cleveland, Grover, 398, 434–436, 491
    and Venezuela boundary, 487
    and annexation of Hawaii, 493
Clinton, De Witt, 214, 252
Clinton, George, 146
Clinton, Sir Henry, 115, 119, 121
Clipper ships, 258, 259
Clive, Robert, 64
Coats, J. and P., 384
Cobden, Richard, 264
Code Napoleon, 193
Coercive Acts (Intolerable Acts), 104
Cohens v. Virginia, 152
Co-Hong, 471
Coke, Robert, 5
Colbert, Jean Baptiste, 17, 18, 41, 250
Colombia, 232, 495, 496, 742
Colombo Plan, 767
Columbus, Christopher, 8
Combinations Law, 245, 392
Cominform, 733, 751
Comintern, 580
Committee for Industrial Organization (*see* Congress of Industrial Organizations)

Committee on Public Information, 541
Committee of Public Safety, 171
Committees of Correspondence, 102, 105
Common Sense, 112
Commons, House of, 47, 52, 282–284, 419, 420
Commonwealth v. Hunt, 248
Commonwealth of Nations, 127, 599, 600
Communist Manifesto, 269
Compact theory, 149, 218
Compromise of 1850, 331–334
Comstock lode, 405
Conant, James B., 727
Concert of Europe, 225–227, 509
Concord, Battle of, 106
Concordat of 1801, 194, 426
Confederate States of America, 343, 344
    Constitution of, 343
Confédération Générale du Travail, 394
Confederation of the Rhine, 198
Congo, 467, 468, 742
Congo Free State, 468
Congregational Church, 76, 128
Congress of Industrial Organizations (CIO), 633, 634, 744
Connecticut, 12, 76, 127
Conquistadores, 68, 69
Conservation, 446, 447
Constantine, Grand Duke, 277
Constantinople, 512, 529
Constitution, 215
Constitutional Union party, 340
Consulate, 192–196
Continental system, 199, 200–202, 212
"Continuous voyage," 353, 534
Cooke, Jay, 374
Coolidge, John Calvin, 572, 610, 611, 620
Cooper, James Fenimore, 308
Copernicus, Nicholas, 31, 32
"Copperheads," 359
Coral Sea, Battle of, 701, **703**
Coram, Thomas, 79
Corn laws, 264
Cornwallis, Lord, 120, 121
Corporate state, 586
Corporation, 369, 370
Cort, Henry, 240
Cortes, Hernando, 69, **307**
Costa Rica, 742
Cotton gin, 238
Coughlin, Charles E., 629, **693**
Council of Europe, 736
Council of the Indies, 68
Council of Trent, 28
Counter Reformation, 28

Court of International Justice, 563, 564, 643
Credit Anstalt, 623
Crédit Mobilier, 376
Creek Indians, 185
Creel, George, 541, 542
"Crime of '73," 433
Crimean War, 312, 313
Crispi, Francesco, 466
Crittenden, John J., 343
Crittenden Compromise, 343
Cromer, Lord, 462, 468
Crompton, Samuel, 238
Cromwell, Oliver, 28, 49, 50
Cromwell, William, 493, 495
"Cross of Gold" speech, 438
Cuba, 232, 308, 484
  and Spanish-American War, 488–490
  and United States imperialism, 498, 501, 502
  and Good Neighbor policy, 645
Cumberland Road (National Road), 251
Cunard Line, 258
Curtiss, Glenn, 368
Cushing, Caleb, 472
Custer, General George, 409
Cutler, Reverend Manasseh, 133
Cyrenaica, 466, 467, 688, 689, 705
Czechoslovakia, 545, 608
  in Little Entente, 661, 662
  dismemberment of, 674–676
  Communist coup in, 734

Daladier, Edouard, 606, 607, 675
Danbury Hatters' Case, 399
Dane, Nathan, 133
Dante, 561
Danton, G. J., 170–173
Danzig, 222, 552, 555, 677
Dardanelles, 513, 529, 530, 558
Darlan, Jean, 684, 706
Dartmouth College v. Woodward, 153
Darwin, Charles, 389
Darwinism, 389, 400, 401, 487, 488, 515
da Vinci, Leonardo, 31
Davis, Jefferson, 343, 345–346, 350, 351, 363
Dawes, Charles G., 567
Dawes Act, 409
Dawes Plan, 567, 588
Dearborn, General Henry, 215
De Beers Mining Company, 459
Debs, Eugene V., 398
Decatur, Stephen, 208, 215
"Decembrists," 277

Declaration of Independence, 35, 108, 112, 113
Declaration of the Rights of Man and the Citizen, 165
Declaratory Act, 97
Deere, John, 241
de Gasperi, Alcide, 737
de Gaulle, Charles, 684, 685, 705, 706
  in Fourth Republic, 736, 737
De Grasse, Admiral, 120–122
Deism, 34
Delaware, 79
Delcassé, Théophile, 456, 462, 514, 518
De Leon, Daniel, 391
de Lesseps, Ferdinand, 259, 313, 424, 461, 485, 486
Democratic party, 292
  and convention system, 296
  and Manifest Destiny, 305
  and Kansas-Nebraska Act, 335, 336
  in election, of 1860, 339, 340
    of 1876, 363
  and free silver, 434, 437, 438
  in election of 1912, 449
  and League of Nations, 559, 560
  and prohibition issue, 619
  in election, of 1936, 640
    of 1948, 746
Denmark, 25, 56, 608, 753
  in Napoleonic Wars, 195
  and Schleswig-Holstein, 319
  in Second World War, 680
Derne, 208
Descartes, R., 33, 34
Desert Lands Act, 409
Detroit, 183
De Valera, Eamon, 600, 601
Dewey, Admiral George, 489, 490
Dewey, John, 401
Dewey, Thomas E., 711, 746
Diaz, Porfirio, 505, 506
Dickinson, John, 98, 113
  drafts Articles of Confederation, 130
  at Federal Convention, 137
Diderot, Denis, 161
Diederichs, Vice-Admiral von, 490
Dienbienphu, 764
Dingley Tariff, 439
Disraeli, Benjamin, 417, 456, 461, 478
Dissenters, 279
Dix, Dorothea Lynde, 298
Dixiecrats, 746
Dollfuss, Engelbert, 664, 665
"Domestic" system, 7
Donnelly, Ignatius, 411, 437
Doolittle, General James, 703, **705**

Dorchester, Lord (Sir Guy Carleton), 114, 183
Dos Passos, John, 625
Douglas, Stephen A., 257, 332–334, 338–340
Drake, Edwin L., 372
Drang nach Osten, 482, 518, 688
Dreadnought, 516
Dred Scott case, 336, 337
Dreikaiserbund, 513
Drew, Daniel, 379
Dreyfus affair, 425
Dual monarchy (*see* Austria-Hungary)
Due process, 369, 442
Dulany, Daniel, 99
Dulles, John Foster, 728
Duma, 427
Dumbarton Oaks Conference, 715, 716
Dumouriez, C. F., 168, 169, 171
Dunkirk, 682
Dupleix, François, 63
Du Pont de Nemours, E. I., 36
Durham, Lord, 127
Durham Report, 127

Eakins, Thomas, 402
East India Company, British, 11, 63, 103, 104, 477, 478
    Dutch, 15
    French, 63
Easter Rebellion of 1916, 421
Eaton, Peggy, 296
Eaton, William, 208
Ebert, Friedrich, 587
Ecuador, 232
Eden, Anthony, 721, 724
Edict of Nantes, 29, 45
Edison, Thomas A., 368
Edward VIII, 598
Égalité, Philippe, 170, 172
Egypt, 176, 460–462
    nationalism in, 603
    in Second World War, 688, 689
    after Second World War, 741
Eighteenth Amendment, 443, 618, 619
Eire, 601
Eisenhower, Dwight D., 705, 706
    and invasion of Europe, 708, 709
    elected President, 748
    international atomic-energy program, 768, 769
El Alamein, 702, 705
Elba, 205, 206
Electoral college, 140
Electoral Commission, 363
Eleventh Amendment, 152

Eliot, Charles W., 401, 491
Eliot, T. S., 626
Elizabeth I of England, 27, 47
Elizabeth II of England, 739
Elkins Act, 445
Emancipation Proclamation, 348
Embargo, 212, 213
Emergency Banking Act, 628
Emergency Fleet Corporation, 541
Emerson, Ralph Waldo, 308
Ems Dispatch, 321, 322
Enclosures, 6, 235
Engels, Friedrich, 269
Enghien, Duc d', 196
Enlightened Despotism, 37, 38
Enlightenment, 37, 38
Entente Cordiale, 514, 515
"Enumerated goods," 20
Erasmus, 25
Ericsson, John, 255, 259
Erie Canal, 251, 252
Erie Railroad, 257, 379
Eritrea, 466, 731
Espionage Act of 1917, 542
Estonia, 679
Ethiopia, 666–670, 688, 731
    (*See also* Abyssinia)
Eugene of Savoy, 46
European Coal and Steel Community (Schuman Plan), 736, 754
European Defense Community (EDC), 736, 754
European Recovery Program (ERP), 751
Evans, George Henry, 248
Evarts, William Maxwell, 485, 486

Fabian Society, 391
Factory Act of 1833, 246
Fair Deal, 747
Fair Employment Practices Act, 746
Fair Labor Standards Act, 634, 635
Fall, Albert B., 611
Fallen Timbers, Battle of, 183
Family Compact of 1761, 118
Far Eastern Commission, 727, 728
Farm Credit Administration, 638
Farm Relief Act, 628, 630, 637
Farm Security Administration, 638
Farmers' Alliance, 411, 412
Farragut, David G., 350, 352
Farrell, James T., 625
Fascist Grand Council, 585
Fashoda, 462
Faulkner, William, 625
Federal Deposit Insurance Corporation, 629

Federal Emergency Relief Administration, 628
Federal Farm Board, 618, 637
Federal Farm Loan Act, 452
Federal Housing Administration (FHA), 632
Federal Reserve Act, 452
Federal Reserve Board, 452, 629
Federal Reserve System, 451, 452, 597, 615, 629
Federal Trade Commission Act, 450
Federal Water Power Act, 613
Federalist papers, 142
Federalist party, 142–150, 217, 218, 290
Ferry, Jules, 424, 456, 463
Feudalism, 39
Feuillants, 167
Fichte, Johann G., 204
Field, Cyrus W., 260
Fifteenth Amendment, 361, 362
Fillmore, Millard, 332
Finland, 200, 568, 579
    in Second World War, 679–680, 690, 730, 731
First Continental Congress, 105
Fisk, Jim, 379
Fiske, John, 487
Fitch, John, 258
Fitzgerald, F. Scott, 625
Five Civilized Tribes of Oklahoma, 409
Five-Year Plans, 582, 583
Fletcher v. Peck, 152
Fleury, Cardinal, 63
Florida, 10, 65, 108, 123, 125, 210, 614
    purchase of, 228
Foch, Ferdinand, 544, 545
Foraker Amendment, 498
Force bill, 330
Ford, Henry, 373
Ford Motor Company, 374, 634
Fordney-McCumber Tariff, 610, 621
Forest Reserve Act, 446
Formosa, 474, 760
Forster Education Act, 417
Fort Donelson, 349
Fort Duquesne, 64
Fort Henry, 349
Fort McHenry, 216
Fort Sumter, 344
Foster, Stephen, 309
Four-Power Treaty, 650
Fourier, François Charles, 266, 267
Fourteen Points, 543, 544, 549, 550, 553–555
Fourteenth Amendment, 361, 362, 369, 442
Fourth Republic, 737

Fox, Charles James, 122
"Fox's Blockade," 199, 212
Francis Ferdinand, Archduke of Austria, 521, 522
Francis Joseph I of Austria, 288, 522
Franco, Francisco, 672, 673
Franco-Prussian War, 316
Frankfurt Assembly, 287–289, 317
Franklin, Benjamin, 64, 82
    Minister to France, 116, 118
    as peace commissioner, 123, 125
    at Federal Convention, 137
Frederick the Great, 13, 37, 64
    and rise of Prussia, 59–61
Frederick William, "Great Elector," 59
Fredericksburg, Battle of, 348
Freedmen's Bureau, 361
Freeport Doctrine, 338
"Free ships, free goods," 182, 187
Free-Soil party, 332
Frémont, John C., 306, 336
French, Daniel C., 402
French alliance, 118, 180, 187
    abrogated, 188
French and Indian War (Seven Years' War), 316, 319–320
Frick, Henry Clay, 371, 397
Frontenac, Comte de, 62
Frost, Robert, 626
Fugger family, 13
Fugitive Slave law, 333, 336
Fulbright Resolution, 715
Fulton, Robert, 153, 258

Gadsden Purchase, 307
Galileo, 32
Gallatin, Albert, 148, 217, 253, 254
Gallipoli, 530
Galloway, Joseph, 105
Gama, Vasco da, 8
Gambetta, Leon, 323, 461
Gandhi, Mohandas K., 602, 741
Gapon, Father, 427
Garfield, James A., 441, 486
Garibaldi, Joseph, 316
Garland, Hamlin, 402
Garrison, William Lloyd, 299
Gasperi, Alcide de, 737
Gaspée, 102
Gates, Horatio, 116, 120
Gaulle, Charles de (*see* de Gaulle, Charles)
General Electric Company, 373
General Motors, 373, 634
"General will," 161, 165
Genêt, Edmond Charles, 180, 181

Geneva Conference of 1954, 764
Geneva Disarmament Conference, 573, 665
Geneva Protocol, 569
Genoa, 316
George I of Great Britain, 52
George III, 5, 53, 94, 104, 126
George IV, 279
George V, 598
George VI, 598, 739
George, Henry, 391, 392
Georgia, 79, 351
Germain, Lord George, 109, 114
German Federal Republic, 727, 737, 738
Germanic Confederation, 222, 276, 317, 318
Gerry, Elbridge, 188, 189
Gershwin, George, 626
Gestapo, 591
Gettysburg, Battle of, 348, 349
Ghent, Treaty of, 217
Gibbons v. Ogden, 153
Gibraltar, 62, 118, 122, 123
Gilman, Daniel C., 401
Ginn, Edward, 562
Girondins, 167, 168
Gladstone, William E., 417, 418
Glass-Steagall Act, 628, 629
Glidden, Joshua, 404
Glorious Revolution, 50, 51
Gneisenau, A. N., 204
Gobineau, Count Henry de, 512
Goebbels, Paul Joseph, 591
Goering, Hermann, 592
Goethals, George Washington, 496
Gold clause, 630
Gold Standard Act of 1900, 439
Gompers, Samuel, 396, 491
Gompers v. Buck Stove and Range Company, 399
Good Neighbor policy, 643, 645
Goodyear, Charles, 368
Gordon, General Charles, 462, 472
Gore-McLemore Resolutions, 538
Gorgas, William C., 496
Gorges, Sir Ferdinando, 77
Gould, Jay, 379
Government of India Act, 602, 603
Gran Chaco War, 643
Grand National Trades Union, 245
Granger cases, 381
Grangers, 380, 381, 411
Grant, Ulysses S., 348–352
  as President, 362
Grattan, Henry, 126
Gray, Asa, 309
Great Awakening, 85

Great Northern Railroad, 378
Great Plains, 300, 406, 407, 637, 639
Greece, 226, 520, 558
  independence of, 279, 280
  in Second World War, 688, 689
  after Second World War, 753, 756, 757
Greeley, Horace, 248, 267, 300
Greenbacks, 359, 432
Greene, Nathaniel, 120
Grenville, George, 96, 97
Grey, Earl, 283, 284
Grey, Sir Edward, 419, 469, 523
Grotius, Hugo, 561
Guadalcanal, 703, 705
Guadeloupe, 65
Guadeloupe-Hidalgo, Treaty of, 307
Guam, 490, 700, 710
Guatemala, 742
Guericke, Otto von, 32
Guffey-Snyder Coal Act, 632
Guiana, British, 743
Guizot, François, 285, 286
Gustavus Adolphus of Sweden, 29
Gustavus III, 38

Hague Conferences, 516, 517
Hague Tribunal, 499
Haiti, 190, 231, 502–503
Halleck, Henry W., 349
Halsey, William F., 705, 710
Hamilton, Alexander, 14
  and framing of Constitution, 136, 137
  as Secretary of Treasury, 143–146
  in election of 1800, 150
  and foreign relations, 179–183
  economic thought of, 266
Hamilton, Andrew, 80
Hammond, George, 179, 181
Hampden, John, 48, 49
Hampton Roads, 120, 354
Hancock, John, 100, 102, 142
Hanna, Marcus A., 437, 438
Hapsburgs, 29, 46, 56, 276, 429, 430
Hardenberg, Prince von, 204, 220
Harding, Warren G., 560, 571, 609–611
Hare-Hawes-Cutting Act, 497
Hargreaves, James, 238
Harmsworth, Alfred (Lord Northcliffe), 389
Harpers Ferry, 339
Harriman, E. H., 445
Harris, Townsend, 474
Harrison, Benjamin, 436
Harrison, William Henry, 210, 215, 297
Hartford Convention, 217, 218

Harvey, William, 33
Hatch Act, 404
Havana, 18, 65, **489**
  Act of, 693
  conference at, 1928, 645
Hawaii, 304, 492, 493
Hawthorne, Nathaniel, 309
Hay, John, 476, 499
Hay-Herran Convention, 495
Hay-Pauncefote Treaty, 495, 506
Hayes, Rutherford B., 363, 433
Haymarket affair, 396
Hayne, Robert Y., 330
Hearst, William Randolph, 389, 488
Helgoland, 465, 556
Helper, Hinton Rowan, 336
Hemingway, Ernest, 625
Henry IV of France, 29, 44, 561
Henry VIII of England, 27, 47
Henry, Joseph, 309, 310
Henry, Patrick, 99, 142
Hepburn v. Griswold, 432
Hepburn Act, 446
Herzegovina, 518, **519**
Hess, Rudolph, 690
Hill, James J., 378, 379, 445
Hill, Rowland, 260
Himmler, Heinrich, 591
Hindenburg, Paul von, 529, 531, 532, 539
  as president of German Republic, 588,
    589
Hindenburg Line, 532, 545
Hirohito, Emperor, 696, 713
Hiroshima, 697, 713
Hiss, Alger, 745
Hitler, Adolf, rise of, 588, 589
  Nazi regime of, 590–592
  diplomacy of, 661
  rearmament of Germany, 665, 666
  annexation of Austria, 673, 674
  annexation of Czechoslovakia, 675, 676
  and outbreak of Second World War,
    676, 677
  in Second World War, 679, 684, 685,
    688–691, 702
  attempted assassination of, 709
  death of, 712
Hoar, George F., 490
Hoare, Sir Samuel, 669, 670
Hohenzollern, House of, 59, 321
Holding company, 370
Holland, 10, 17, 45, 56
  Calvinism in, 26
  religious freedom in, 30
  in American Revolution, 119, 125
  in Second World War, 681, 682
  (*See also* Netherlands)

Holmes, Justice O. W., 442
Holy Alliance, 226
Holy Roman Empire, 56, 198
Home Owners Loan Corporation
  (HOLC), 633
Homer, Winslow, 402
Homestead Act, 300, 301, 359
Homestead strike, 371, 397
Hong Kong, 471, 700
Hood, Admiral, 121, 171
Hood, John B., 351, 352
Hooker, Joseph E., 348
Hooker, Reverend Thomas, 76
Hoover, Herbert, 541, 567, 568, 572, 573
  as Secretary of Commerce, 613
  as President, 618, 620–624
  and government reorganization, 747
Hoover moratorium, 567, 568, 621
Hopkins, Harry, 635
House, Edward M., 449, 539, 548
Houston, Sam, 304
Howard, John, 36
Howe, Admiral Lord, 111, 112
Howe, Elias, 238
Howe, Samuel Gridley, 298
Howe, Sir William, 111, 112, 114, 115
Howells, William D., 402
Hudson's Bay Company, 11, 304
Huerta, Victoriano, 504, 506, 507
Hughes, Charles Evans, 441, 538, 571,
    610, 642*n.*
Hugo, Victor, 203
Huguenots, 17, 19, 29, 44
Hull, Cordell, 630, 631, 645–647, 692,
    696, 721
Hull, Isaac, 215
Hungary, 38, 56, 287, 288
  in Versailles peace settlement, 557
  and background of Second World
    War, 661, 665, 675, 676
  in Second World War, 688, 690
  after Second World War, 730, 731
Huntington, Collis P., 376
Huss, John, 23
Hussey, Obed, 241
Hutchinson, Anne, **77**
Hyderabad, 741

Iceland, 695, 753
Ickes, Harold L., 629
Illinois Central Railroad, 257
Immigration, 84, 85, 247, 299, 369
  restriction of, 395, 443, 444
"Implied powers," 146, 154
Impressment, 184, 211, 212, **217**
Incas, **68**

Indentured servants, 74, 85
Independent Treasury, 295
India, 63, 477–479
  nationalism in, 601–603
  independence of, 740–741, 759
Indo-China, 479, 763, 764
Indonesia, 740
  (*See also* Netherlands East Indies)
Industrial Workers of the World
  (I.W.W.), 391, 397
Injunctions, 398, 399, 450, 745
Inland Waterways Commission, 446
Inquisition, 28, 32
Insular Cases, 497
Insull, Samuel, 613, 623
Intendants, 44, 69
"Internal improvements," 253, 254
Internal Security Act of 1950, 745, 746
International Bank for Reconstruction,
  715
International Court of Justice, 717, 718
International Labor Office, 563, 565, 718
International Monetary Fund, 715
Interstate Commerce Act, 381, 436
Interstate Commerce Commission, 381,
  446, 614
Intolerable Acts, 104
Iran, 691, 741, 755
Iraq, 604, 689, 690
Ireland, 126, 264, 265
  Home Rule controversy, 417, 418, 420,
    421
  separation from Britain, 600, 601
Irish Free State, 599, 600
Irish Land League, 417
"Iron Law of Wages," 263, 269
Iroquois Confederacy, 71, 84
Irving, Washington, 308
Ismail, Khedive, 461
Israel, 757, 758
Iturbide, Augustin, 232
Ivan the Terrible, 57
Iwo Jima, 712

Jackson, Andrew, 216, 247, 254, 291
  as President, 292–296
  and nullification, 330
Jackson, Thomas J., 346–348
Jacobins, 169, 170*n.*, 171
Jacquard loom, 240
James I of England, 47
James II of England, 50, 78
James, Henry, 401
James, William, 401, 487, 491
Jameson Raid, 459
Jamestown, 72

Japanese Peace Treaty, 729
Jay, John, 123, 125, 137, 183, 184
Jay's Treaty, 183, 184
Jefferson, Thomas, 113, 137
  and Northwest Territory, 129
  opposition to Hamilton, 145, 146
  in election of 1796, 140, 148
  elected President, 149, 150
  as Secretary of State, 177–183
  and Barbary pirates, 207, 208
  and purchase of Louisiana, 209
  and Monroe Doctrine, 228
  and Missouri Compromise, 328
Jena, Battle of, 198
Jenckes, Thomas A., 441
Jenkins' Ear, War of, 63
Jenner, Edward, 33
Jerusalem, 543, 757, 758
Jervis, John B., 257
Jesuits (Society of Jesus), 28, 31, 71
Johnson, Andrew, 360, 362
Johnson, Hiram, 441
Johnson Debt Default Act, 569, 646
Johnston, Albert Sidney, 349
Johnston, Joseph E., 346, 350–352
Jones Act, 497
Joseph II, Holy Roman Emperor, 37, 38
Juarez, Benito, 356
Judicial review, 140, 150–152
Judiciary Act, 144
Julliard v. Greenman, 432*n.*
July Monarchy, 281, 285
July Ordinances, 281
July Revolution, 281, 285
Jutland, Battle of, 532

Kamerun, 465
Kansas, 334–336
Kansas-Nebraska bill, 335
Kant, Immanuel, 38, 562
Karlsbad Decrees, 276
Kashmir, 741
Kay, James, 237
Kearny, Colonel Stephen, 305
Kelley, Oliver Hudson, 411
Kellogg, Frank B., 570
Kellogg-Briand Pact, 570
Kelly, William, 240
Kemal, Mustapha, 558
Kentucky, 132
Kenya, 462, 742
Kepler, Johannes, 32
Kerensky, Alexander, 578
Kern, Jerome, 626
Key, Francis Scott, 216
Keynes, John Maynard, 566

Kiel Canal, 319, 383, 556
King, Ernest W., 699
King, Rufus, 133
King, W. L. Mackenzie, 743
King Philip's War, 81
King William's War, 62
Kipling, Rudyard, 456
Kitchener, General, 462
Knights of Labor, 395, 396
Knights of St. Crispin, 395
"Know-nothing" party, 335, 336
Knox, Philander C., 504
Knox v. Lee, 432
Knox-Castrillo Convention, 503
Koch, Robert, 387
Königgratz (Sadowa), Battle of, 320
Korea, 474, 477, 720
Korean War, 760–763
Kosciusko, Thaddeus, 59, 116
Kossuth, Louis, 288, 298
Krueger, Ivar, 623
Kruger, "Oom Paul," 459, 460
Krupp Works, 241
Ku Klux Klan, 361, 610
Kulaks, 582, 583
Kulturkampf, 422
Kuomintang, 649–651, 760
Kurusu, Saburu, 695, 696

Labour party, 391, 392, 393, 419
    in office in 1920's, 595–597
    victory of, in 1945, 738, 739
Ladd, William, 298
La Farge, John, 402
Lafayette, Marquis de, 110, 119, 120, 126
    in French Revolution, 165
    and July Monarchy, 281
La Follette, Robert M., 441, 448, 449, 611
La Follette Merchant Seamen's Act, 400, 452
Land Act of 1820, 300
Land grants, 254, 257, 376–378
Land Ordinance of 1785, 133
Landon, Alfred M., 640
Langley, Samuel P., 368
Languedoc Canal, 250
Lansing, Robert, 548
Lansing-Ishii Agreement, 649
La Plata, 69, 232
Larkhall Victualling Society, 267n.
Lateran Accord, 586
Latvia, 679
Laud, Archbishop William, 48

Lausanne, Treaty of, 558
Lausanne Agreement, 568
Laval, Pierre, 606, 668–670, 684
Lavoisier, Antoine, 33
Law, Andrew Bonar, 548, 595
Law, John, 15
League of Nations, founding of, 550, 553, 643
    rejection of, by United States, 558, 559
    Covenant of, 562–565
    weaknesses of, 565, 566
    in Manchurian affair, 653–655
    decline of, 666–670
Lease, Mary, 411
Lebanon, 604, 607
Lecompton Constitution, 338
Lee, Richard Henry, 113, 142
Lee, Robert E., 346–349, 363
Legislative Assembly, 167, 168
Leibnitz, Gottfried, 32, 561
Leipzig, Battle of, 205
Leisler, Jacob, 86
Lend-Lease Act, 691, 694, 695
Lend-lease program, 700, 744
Lenin, Nicolai, 391, 578–582
Leningrad, 577, 680, 691
Leo XIII, 422, 425
Leopold II of Belgium, 467, 468
Leopold III of Belgium, 682
Lewis, John L., 634
Lewis, Sinclair, 625
Lexington, Battle of, 106
Leyte, 710, 711
Liaotung peninsula, 474, 475, 477
Liberia, 298
Liberty party, 305
Libya, 466, 467, 702, 731
Lichnowsky, Prince, 469
Liebig, Baron von, 403
Lilienthal, David E., 744
Liliuokalani, Queen, 492, 493
Lima Conference, 645
Lincoln, Abraham, in slavery controversy, 338
    election of, 340
    and outbreak of Civil War, 343, 344
    as Civil War President, 346
    issues Emancipation Proclamation, 348
    relations with Europe, 355–357
    Reconstruction policy of, 360, 361
Lindbergh, Charles A., 692
Lindsay, Vachel, 468
List, Friedrich, 265
Lithuania, 676, 679
Little Entente, 662

Liverpool and Manchester Railway, 255, 256
Livingston, Robert R., 209
Livingstone, David, 456, 467
Lloyd, Henry Demarest, 440
Lloyd George, David, 418, 419, 519
  in First World War, 532, 533
  at Versailles Conference, 548–551, 558
  in political changes of 1920's, 595
  and Irish Free State, 600
Locarno Peace Pacts, 569, 570, 666
Lochner v. New York, 442
Locke, John, 35, 78
Lodge, Henry Cabot, 488, 548, 558, 559
Logan, Dr. George, 189
Logan Act, 189
Lombardy, 222, 315
London, Declaration of, 536
  Treaty of (1915), 552, 562
London Economic Conference, 630
Long, Crawford, 310
Long, Huey, 625, 636
Long Island, Battle of, 112
Long Parliament, 48, 49
Longfellow, Henry W., 309
Longstreet, Augustus, 308
Lords, House of, 52, 282–284
  limitation of powers of, 419, 420
Lorraine, 322, 381, 511
Louis XIV, 17, 18, 44, 46, 50, 62, 159
Louis XVI, 118, 126, 163, 168–170
Louis XVIII, 205, 277, 278
Louis Philippe, 281, 285, 286, 463
Louisburg, 63, 64
Louisiana, 15, 62, 65
  Napoleon I's plans for, 194, 195
  purchase of, 209
  state of, admitted, 328
Lowell, Francis Cabot, 239, 243, 247
Lowell, James R., 309
Loyalists in United States, 108, 125
  emigration of, 127
Loyola, Ignatius, 28
Ludendorff, Erich von, 529, 531, 532, 539, 544, 588
Luftwaffe, 592, 681, 682, 686
Lundy, Benjamin, 299
Lundy's Lane, 215
Lunéville, Treaty of, 195
Lusitania, 537
Luther, Martin, 23, 25
Lutheranism, 23
Luxembourg, 681
Lvov, Prince, 578
Lysenko, 733
Lytton Commission, 654, 655

MacAdam, John, 250
McAdoo, William G., 541, 619
MacArthur, Douglas, 701, 705, 710, 711
  receives Japanese surrender, 713
  as commander of occupation forces, 727, 728, 740
  in Korean War, 761
McCarran, Senator Patrick, 746
McCarran-Walter Immigration Act, 746
McCarthy, Senator Joseph, 745, 749
McClellan, George B., 345, 347, 348, 360
McCloy, John J., 727
McCormick, Cyrus, 241, 243
McCulloch v. Maryland, 154, 155
MacDonald, James Ramsay, 572, 595–598
MacDonough, Thomas, 215
McGillivray, Alexander, 185
McKinley, William, 438, 493
  and Spanish-American War, 488–489
McKinley Tariff, 434, 436
McLane, Louis, 294
McMahon, Senator Brien, 744
MacMahon, Patrice Maurice, 322, 424
McNary-Haugen bill, 617
Macon's Bill Number 2, 213
Madero, Francesco, 505, 506
Madison, James, 136, 137, 142, 145
  as President, 213, 214, 254
  and Monroe Doctrine, 228
Madras, 63
Maginot Line, 606, 679, 682, 684
Magoon, Charles Edward, 501
Magsaysay, Ramón, 740
Mahan, A. T., 456, 488
Maine, 489
Maine, 77, 328
Malan, Daniel, 741, 742
Malaya, 479, 700, 701
Malenkov, Georgi, 734
Malpighi, Marcello, 33
Malta, 201, 223, 688
Malthus, Thomas R., 262, 263
Manchester School, 262, 264
Manchu dynasty, 470, 471, 648, 649
Manchukuo, 655, 657
Manchuria, 384, 385, 713
  Japanese invasion of, 652–655
Mandates, 564
Manifest Destiny, 274, 303–308, 331
  decline of, 484
  revival of, 487
Manila, 65, 490, 711
Manila Bay, Battle of, 489, 490
Mann, Horace, 297, 298
Mann-Elkins Act, 446
Manor, 4

Mao Tse-tung, 651, 760
Marat, Jean P., 170, 171
Marbury v. Madison, 151, 152
Marconi, Guglielmo, 388
Marcy, William L., 306, 313
Marengo, Battle of, 195
Maria Theresa, 58, 60
Mariana Islands, 490n., 652, 710
Marie Antoinette, 165
Marlborough, Duke of (John Churchill), 46
Marne, Battle of, 528
    battles in 1918, 544
Marquand, John P., 625
Marshall, George C., 699, 750, 759
Marshall, John, Chief Justice, 142, 150–155
    in XYZ affair, 188, 189
Marshall Islands, 490n., 652, 710
Marshall Plan, 735–737, 750–751
Martinique, 65
Marx, Karl, 269, 270, 390
Marxism, 268–270
    and revisionism, 390, 391
    in U.S.S.R., 580
Maryland, 48, 77
    prohibits slave trade, 129
    and western land claims, 130, 132
    and Bank of United States, 154
    in Civil War, 348
Masaryk, Jan, 734
Masaryk, Thomas G., 608
Mason, James, 355
Mason, Captain John, 77
Mason and Dixon Line, 128
Massachusetts, 12, 75, 76
    financial policy of, 129
    ratifies Constitution, 142
    labor legislation in, 248
Massachusetts Bay Company, 12, 75
Matapan, Battle of Cape, 689
Maury, Mathew F., 310
Max, Prince, of Baden, 545
Maximilian of Hapsburg, 356, 357
May Committee, 597
Mayflower, 74
Mayflower Compact, 75
Mayo, Admiral, 507
Maysville Road bill, 254
Mazzini, Giuseppe, 314
Meade, George G., 349
Medici family, 13
Meiji Restoration, 365, 474
Melanchthon, Philip, 25
Mellon, Andrew, 612, 613
Melville, Herman, 308, 309
Menocal, General, 501, 502

Mergenthaler, Ottmar, 368
Merrimac, 354
Methodism, 38, 246
Metternich, 201, 204, 205
    at Congress of Vienna, 220–222
    and Concert of Europe, 226, 227
    domination of central Europe by, 276
    in Revolution of 1848, 286, 287
Mexico, 232
    and independence of Texas, 303, 304
    war with United States, 305–307
    French invasion of, 356, 357
    and Wilson administration, 505–507
    in First World War, 540
    and Good Neighbor policy, 643, 645
Midway, island of, 497
    Battle of, 702
Milan Decree, 200
Mill, John Stuart, 262, 263, 388
Millay, Edna St. Vincent, 626
Milton, John, 28
Mindzenty, Cardinal, 734
Mines Act of 1842, 246
Miranda, Francisco, 231
"Mississippi Bubble," 15
Mississippi River, 65, 94, 186, 258
    in Civil War, 347, 350
Missouri, 713
Missouri Compromise, 328, 329, 335
Mitchell, John, 399
Mitchell, Margaret, 625
Mobile Bay, 352
Mogul Empire, 478n.
Molasses Act, 20, 96
"Molly Maguires," 395
Molotov, V. M., 721, 724, 734
Moltke, Helmuth von, 319–320, 322
Monitor, 354
Monmouth, Battle of, 119
Monroe, James, 142, 182, 209
    and Monroe Doctrine, 228–230
    opposes internal improvements, 251
Monroe Doctrine, 227–230, 487
    invoked against Napoleon III, 356
    extension of, by T. Roosevelt, 499–501
    and League of Nations, 559
    and Kellogg Pact, 570
    Canada included in, 645
    and Act of Havana, 693
Montagu-Chelmsford Act, 601, 602
Montenegro, 520
Montesquieu, 160
Montevideo Conference, 645
Montgomery, Sir Bernard, 705, 706, 708
Montgomery, Richard, 111
Morgan, J. P., 371, 374, 379, 434, 445
Morley, John, 419

Morley-Minto Reforms, 478
Mormons, 301, 303
Morocco, 207, 208
  crises in, 517–519
  Spanish, 468, 469, 671
  revolt in, 607
  American landing in, 705, 706
  after Second World War, 741, 765
Morrill Act, 298, 404
Morris, Gouverneur, 178
Morris, Robert, 107, 108, 137
Morrow, Dwight W., 643
Morse, Samuel F. B., 260
Morton, William, 310
Moscow, 203, 691
Moscow Conference, 721, 722
Moscow Declaration, 715
Mossadegh, Mohammed, 741
Motor Carriers Act, 614
Mott, Lucretia, 298
Muckrakers, 439, 440
"Mugwumps," 435
Mukden, 477
Muller v. Oregon, 442
Munich Conference, 675, 676
Murat, Marshal, 200, 206
Murmansk, 679, 691
Muscle Shoals, 613, 639
Muscle Shoals Act, 628
Muscovy Company, 11
Mussolini, Benito, 467, 570
  Fascist regime of, 584–586
  diplomatic policy of, 663
  attack on Ethiopia, 666–670
  in Second World War, 679, 684, 688,
    689, 702
  fall of, 707, 712
Mutiny Act, 51
Myers, Gustavus, 440

Nachtigal, Consul-General, 465
Nagasaki, 473, 697, 713
Napier, John, 33
Napoleon I, 173, 174
  as First Consul, 176, 191–196
  becomes Emperor, 196
  and Continental System, 199–202
  invasion of Russia, 202–203
  final defeat, 206
Napoleon III, 285, 311, 312
  Second Empire of, 312–314
  and unification, of Italy, 314–316
    of Germany, 318, 321, 322
  intervention in Mexico, 356, 357
Nashville, 352
Natal Colony, 459

National Bank Acts, 359, 451
National Convention, 169–174
National Industrial Recovery Act
  (NIRA), 629, 631–633
National Insurance Act, 420
National Labor Relations Board, 633
National Labor Union, 395
National Progressive Republican League,
  448
National Recovery Administration
  (NRA), 631–633
National Road (Cumberland Road), 251
National Socialist party, 588–593
National Typographical Union, 248
National Youth Administration, 636
Natural Law, 34, 35
Naval Limitation Agreements, 571–574
Navarino Bay, Battle of, 280
Navigation Acts, 19–21, 127, 178
  repeal of, 259, 265
Necker, Jaques, 41, 163, 164
Nehru, J., 602
Nelson, Admiral Lord, 176, 195, 196
Netherlands, 62, 175, 571
  Kingdom of, 223, 225
  (*See also* Holland)
Netherlands East Indies, 10, 480, 701
  (*See also* Indonesia)
Neutrality Act (1794), 181
Neutrality Acts (1935–1937), 646, 647,
  669, 679
New Brunswick, 127
New Economic Policy, 582
New England, 12, 74
  Dominion of, 53, 81
  maritime commerce of, 83, 84
  in War of 1812, 214, 217–218
  industry in, 239
New England Confederation, 81
New England Emigrant Aid Society, 335
New France, 62
"New Freedom," 449–452
New Georgia, 705
New Granada, 69, 307
New Guinea, 705, 710
New Hampshire, 77
New Haven, 76, 241
New Jersey, 78
New Jersey Plan, 137, 138
New Mexico, 10, 305–307, 333
"New Nationalism," 448
New Netherlands, 11, 78
New Orleans, 71, 186, 350, 352
  Battle of, 216
New Panama Canal Company, 493
New York, city of, 84, 111, 252
  state of, 78, 142

New York v. Morehead, 641
New York Central Railroad, 257, 379
New Zealand, 421, 599, 764
Newcomen, Thomas, 236
Newcomen engine, 236
Newfoundland, 600
  fisheries, 83, 124, 218, 436, 492
Newlands Act, 409
Newport, 84, 119, 120
Newton, Isaac, 32, 33
Nicaragua, 307, 493, 495
  intervention in, 503, 505
  end of, 645
Nicholas I of Russia, 277, 288, 312, 313
Nicholas II of Russia, 426, 427, 516,
  542, 578
Niemöller, Martin, 592
Nigeria, 462, 742
Nightingale, Florence, 313
Nile, Battle of, 176
Nimitz, Chester W., 710
Nine-Power Treaty, 650
Nineteenth Amendment, 388
Nobel, Alfred, 562
Nobel Peace Prize, 562
Nonintercourse Act, 213
Non-Intervention Committee, 673
Nootka Sound controversy, 178
Norman v. Baltimore and Ohio Railroad,
  630
Norris, Frank, 440
Norris, George W., 613, 624, 639
Norris–La Guardia Act, 398
North, Lord, 104, 116, 122
North Atlantic Treaty, 736, 751, 753
North Atlantic Treaty Organization
  (NATO), 753
North Carolina, 78, 142
North German Confederation, 320, 321,
  357
North Sea mine barrage, 543
Northern Pacific Railroad, 374, 376–378
Northern Securities Company, 445
Northern War, 58
Northwest Ordinance, 133, 134, 297, 300
Northwest Territory, 124, 133, 134
Norway, 56, 223, 225, 680, 681, 753
Nova Scotia, 19, 62, 71, 79
Nullification, 149, 329–331
  Ordinance of, 330
Nuremberg trials, 590, 726

Office of Defense Transportation, 699
Office of Price Administration (OPA),
  698

Office of Scientific Research and De-
  velopment, 699
Office of Strategic Services (OSS), 699
Office of War Information (OWI), 699
Oglethorpe, General James, 79
O'Higgins, Bernardo, 228, 232
Ohio Company, 133
Okinawa, 712, 713, 729
Oklahoma, 617
Olney, Richard S., 398, 487
Omdurman, Battle of, 462
"Omnibus Bill," 333
O'Neill, Eugene, 625
Ontario, settlement of, 127
"Open Door" policy, 476, 649
Opium Wars, 471, 472
Oran, 686
Orange River Free State, 457
Orders in Council, 199, 200, 212, 214
Ordinance of Nullification, 330
Ordinance of Secession, 340
Oregon, 493
Oregon, 228, 303–305
Oregon Trail, 304
Organization of American States, 766
Oriskany, Battle of, 115
Orlando, Vittorio, 549, 552
Orleanists, 281, 323
Osborne judgment, 393
Ostend Manifesto, 308
Otis, James, 96, 99
Ottawa Conference, 598
Ottoman Empire, 57, 557
  (*See also* Turkey)
Owen, Robert, 245, 267

Pacific Railway Act, 359, 375
Paine, Thomas, 112, 170
Pakistan, 740, 741, 758, 764
Palestine, 545, 553, 603–605, 741, 757,
  758
Palmer, A. Mitchell, 610
Pan-American Union, 486, 766
Pan-Germanism, 512
Pan-Slavism, 512, 513
Panama, 232
Panama Canal, 485, 486, 493–496
Panama Canal Tolls Act, 506
Panama Canal Zone, 495, 496
Panama Conference, 679
Panama Congress, 291, 292
Panama scandal, 424
Panay, 647
Papen, Franz von, 536, 589, **726**
Paraguay, 232, 643
Paris, Congress of (1856), 313

Paris, Declaration of, 313
  Treaty of, 1763, 93
    1783, 123–125
Paris Commune, 323
Parkman, Francis, 309
Parliament Act, 419, 420
Parnell, Charles Stewart, 417, 418
Pasteur, Louis, 387
Paterson, William, and Bank of England, 14
Paterson, William, of New Jersey, 137
Patrons of Husbandry (Grangers), 380, 381, 411
Patroons, 78, 83
Payne-Aldrich Tariff, 448
Pearl Harbor, 492, 696, 697
Peasants' War, 42
Pedro, Dom, 232
Peel, Sir Robert, 265
Peiping (*see* Peking)
Peking, 472, 651, 656
Pemberton, John C., 350
Pendleton, Senator George, 432
Pendleton Act, 441
Penn, William, 78, 79, 561
Pennsylvania, settlement of, 78, 79
  ratifies Constitution, 141, 142
  industrialism in, 241, 248
Pennsylvania Railroad, 253, 257, 379
Pensacola, 216
"People's budget," 419
Perón, Juan, 643, 742
Perry, Matthew C., 308, 473
Perry, Oliver Hazard, 215
Pershing, John J., 507, 541, 545
Persia, 481
  (*See also* Iran)
Peru, 69, 232
"Pet banks," 294
Pétain, Henri, 531, 542, 684, 685
Peter the Great, 57, 58
Peters, Karl, 456, 465
Petersburg, 351
Petition of Right, 48
Phalanges, 267, 268
Philadelphia, 208
Philadelphia, 84, 115, 120, 252
Philadelphia and Lancaster Turnpike, 251
Philippine Commonwealth, 497
Philippine Insurrection, 491
Philippine Islands, 490, 491, 497
  discovery of, 10
  in Second World War, 700, 701, 710, 711
Philippine Republic, 740, 764
Philosophes, 37, 159, 160

Physiocrats, 36, 261
Pickering, Timothy, 187, 188
Picquart, Colonel, 425
Piedmont-Sardinia (*see* Sardinia)
Pierce, Franklin, 335
Pietism, 38
Pilgrims, 74
Pillnitz, Declaration of, 168
Pinchot, Gifford, 448
Pinckney, C. C., 150, 187, 188
Pinckney, Thomas, 185, 186
Pinckney's Treaty, 185, 186
Pitt, William, 64, 65, 89, 94
Pitt, William, the younger, 178
Pittsburgh, 241, 371
Pius VII, 194, 196
Pius IX, 287, 422, 428
Pius XI, 586
Pizarro, Francisco, 69
Place, Francis, 245
Platt Amendment, 498, 645
Plattsburg, Battle of, 215
Plehve, Count, 426
Plymouth, 75
Pocahontas, 74
Pocket boroughs, 283, 284
Poe, Edgar Allan, 308
Poincaré, Raymond, 520, 605, 606
Point Four Program, 720, 731, 766, 767
  in India, 759
Poland, 56, 221, 281
  partitions of, 58
  in Versailles peace settlement, 552
  in post–First World War diplomacy, 662, 663
  war with Russia, 579
  and outbreak of Second World War, 675–677
  in Second World War, 678, 679, 709
"Police power," 153, 381, 442
Polignac, Prince de, 230, 280
Polignac memorandum, 230
Polish Corridor, 60, 677
Politburo, 580, 581
Politiques, 44
Polk, James K., 305–307, 331
Pollock v. Farmers Loan and Trust Company, 437
Poltava, Battle of, 58
Pontiac's War, 95
Pope, General John, 348
Popular Front, France, 606, 607
  Spain, 672
Popular sovereignty, 332, 333
Populist party, 412, 437
Port Arthur, 384, 475, 477, 724
Porter, Cole, 626

Portsmouth, Treaty of, 477
Portugal, 8, 200, 753
    possessions of, 469, 479
Potomac, Army of, 348
Potomac River, 136, 252
Potsdam Conference, 724–726
Pound, Ezra, 626
Powderly, Terence V., 395
Power loom, 239, 240
Pragmatic Sanction, 60
Pragmatism, 401
Preble, Edward, 208
Preemption Act, 300
Presbyterians, 48, 49
Pressburg, Treaty of, 196
Princeton, Battle of, 112
Princip, 522
Privy Council, 87, 88
Proclamation of Neutrality, 180
Proclamation Line, 95
Progressive party, 449, 611, 746
Prohibition, 442, 443, 618, 619
Promontory, Utah, 376
Proprietary colonies, 77
Protestant Episcopal Church, 128
Proudhon, Pierre Joseph, 270
Prussia, 17, 59–61
    in Napoleonic Wars, 198, 199, 203–206
    at Congress of Vienna, 219–222
    in Revolution of 1848, 287–288
    and unification of Germany, 317–323
Public Utility Act of 1935, 640
Public Works Administration (PWA), 629, 632
Puerto Rico, 232, 490, 498, 499
Pulitzer, Joseph, 388, 389, 488
Pullman strike, 398
Pure Food and Drug Act, 440
Puritanism, 27, 47
Puritans, 27, 28, 48, **75**
Pym, John, 49

Quadruple Alliance, 225, 226
Quakers, 27, 30, 79, 298, 561
Quartering Act, 96, 98
Quebec, 64, 71, 104, 111, 645
Quebec Act, 104
Queen Anne's War, 62
Quesnay, Dr. François, 36
Quisling, Vidkun, 681

Radetzky, General, 288
Randolph, Edmund, 142, **184**
Randolph, John, 329

Rasputin, Gregor, **577**
Rationalism, 35, 36
Reciprocal Trade Agreements Act, 630, 631
Reclamation Act (Newlands Act), 409
Reconstruction Acts, 361
Reconstruction Finance Corporation (RFC), 622, 632, 747
Redemption payments, 415
Reed, Walter, 496
Reform Bill, of 1832, 284
    of 1867, 245, 357, 392, 417
Regulators, 86, 100
Reinsurance Treaty, 513
Remagen bridge, 712
Remington, Frederick, 402
Renaissance, 22, 23
Reparations, 551, 566–568
    in Second World War, 725, 726, 729
Republic of Virtue, 173, 174
Republican party, 146, 147
    founding of, 336
    in election of 1860, 340
    Radicals, 345, 361, 362
    in Civil War, 358, 359
    Reconstruction policies of, 360–362
    in election of 1876, 363
    and currency problem, 437–439
    progressivism in, 447–449
    and League of Nations, 559, 560
    and prohibition issue, 619
    and New Deal, 640
    and Eisenhower administration, 747–749
Resumption Act, 432
Revere, Paul, 84
Reynaud, Paul, 684
Rhineland, after First World War, 550, 551, 566, 567
    remilitarization of, 666
Rhode Island, 12, 30
    settlement of, 76, 77
    in Confederation, 127, 129
    and Constitution, 141
    manhood suffrage in, 295
Rhodes, Cecil, 456, 459
Rhodesia, 462
Ricardo, David, 263
Richelieu, 29, 44
Richmond, 347, 348, 352
Right of deposit, 186
Riis, Jacob, 440
Rio Conference, 766
Risorgimento, 287
Rivera, Primo de, 671
Robespierre, 170–174
Rochambeau, Comte de, 120, 121

Rochdale Pioneers, 267
Rockefeller, John D., 372, 373, 390
Rodney, Admiral George, 119, 121, 122
Rolfe, John, 74
Romanticism, 38
Rome-Berlin Axis, 664
Rome-Berlin-Tokyo Axis, 658, 664
Rommel, Erwin, 689, 706, 707, 709
Roosevelt, Franklin D., 573, 610, 619, 623, 624
   and New Deal, 627–642
   and Supreme Court, 641, 642
   foreign policy of, 643–647, 669, 677
   in Second World War, 679, 684, 691–696, 705, 706, 711
   in peacemaking, 716, 721–724
Roosevelt, Theodore, 373, 375
   in coal strike, 399
   as President, 444–447
   in Progressive party, 448, 449
   and imperialism, 477, 488, 495, 496, 499–501
   in Spanish-American War, 489
   and Panama Canal, 495, 496
   and Hague Conferences, 517
   in Moroccan crisis, 518
Roosevelt Corollary, 500, 501
Root, Elihu, 447, 449, 500, 548
Rosecrans, W. S., 349
Rosetta Stone, 461
Rossoni, Edmondo, 585
Rotten boroughs, 283, 284
Rotterdam, 682
Roundheads, 49
Rousseau, Jean Jacques, 38, 160, 161
Royal colonies, 81
Ruhr, 566, 567
Rule of Reason, 375
Rule of 1756, 182, 211
Rumania, 280, 520, 578
   in First World War, 526
   after First World War, 662
   in Second World War, 688, 690
   peace treaty with, 730, 731
Rumsey, James, 258
Rural Electrification Administration, 638
Rush, Richard, 228
Rush-Bagot Agreement, 218
Russell, Lord John, 355, 356
Russell, Jonathan, 217
Russo-German Nonagression Pact, 656, 677
Russo-Japanese War, 426, 427, 476, 477

Saar Basin, 551, 593
Sacco-Vanzetti case, 610

Sadowa (Königgratz), 320
St. Clair, General, 183
St. Eustatius, 119
Saint Gaudens, Augustus, 402
St. Germain-en-Laye, 556, 557
St. Lawrence River, 19, 71
St. Lawrence Seaway, 645, 646, 743
St. Mary's Canal ("Soo"), 253
St. Mihiel, 545
Saint-Simon, Count Henri de, 266
Saipan, 710
Sakhalin Island, 477, 657
Salerno, 707
Salonika, 530
Samoa, 496
San Francisco, 68
San Francisco Conference, 716, **717**
San Ildefonso, Treaty of, 209
San Jacinto, Battle of, 303
San Juan Hill, 489
San Martin, 228, 232
Sanctions, 668, 669
Santa Anna, 303
Santa Fe Trail, 300, 378
Santiago, 489, 490
Santo Domingo, 195, 231
   United States intervention in, **500**–502
   withdrawal of marines from, 645
Sarajevo, 521
Saratoga, 116
Sardinia, 223, 289
   in unification of Italy, 314–**316**
Sargent, John Singer, 401
Savannah, 120, 351, 352
Saxony, 56, 221
Scharnhorst, G. J. D. von, 204
Schechter Poultry Corporation v. United States, 632
Schleswig-Holstein, 319
Schlieffen Plan, 526, 528, 681
Schmalkalden, League of, 28
Schuman, Robert, 736, 737
Schuman Plan, 736, 754
Schurz, Carl, 288
Schuschnigg, Kurt von, 665, 674
Scioto Company, 133
Scotland, 48, 51
Scott, Winfield, 215, 306, 307, 346
Sebastopol, 313
Second Continental Congress, 106, 107, 130
Second Reform Bill (1867), 245, 357, 392, 417
Second Republic, 311, 312
Securities Exchange Act, 628

Securities and Exchange Commission
(SEC), 628, 640
Security Council, 716–718
Sedan, 322, 682
Sedition Act of 1918, 542
Segregation, Court decision on, 749
Selective Service Act, of 1917, 541
    of 1940, 693
    of 1948, 744
Senior, Nassau, 263
Separatists, 28, 74
Sepoy Mutiny, 478
September Massacres, 169
Serbia, 279, 519–522
    in First World War, 529, 530
Seven Days' Battles, 347
Seven Weeks' War, 316, 319–320
Seven Years' War, 60, 64, 89, 93
Seventeenth Amendment, 440
Sèvres, Treaty of, 557, 558
Seward, William H., 333, 340
    as Secretary of State in Civil War,
        346, 356, 357
    purchase of Alaska by, 484
Seyss-Inquart, Arthur, 674
Shaftesbury, Earl of, 246
Shanghai, 471, 651, 654
Shantung, 475, 552, 652
Sharecropping, 405
Shays, Daniel, 135
Shays' Rebellion, 134, 135
Shelburne, Lord, 95, 122, 124
Shenandoah Valley, 347
Sherman, John, 488
Sherman, William T., 351, 352
Sherman Antitrust Act, 373–375, 436
    and labor unions, 398, 399
    enforcement of, by T. Roosevelt, 445
Sherman Silver Purchase Act, 434
Shiloh, Battle of, 349
Shimonoseki, Treaty of, 474
Shogunate, 473, 474
Shostakovich, Dimitri, 733
Siam (Thailand), 701, 764
Sicily, 201, 316, 707
Siegfried Line, 679, 709
Siemens-Martin process, 368
Sieyès, Abbé, 162, 170, 176, 192
Silesia, 60
Silliman, Benjamin, 310
Simcoe, Governor, 183
Simms, William Gilmore, 308
Sims, William S., 543
Sinclair, Upton, 440
Singapore, 479, 701
Sinn Fein, 418, 421, 600
Sino-Japanese War, 474

Six Acts of 1819, 278
Sixteenth Amendment, 450
Slater, Samuel, 238, 243
Slavery, 86, 129, 223
    and sectional conflict, 327–329, 331–
        340
    abolition of, in United States, 359
Slidell, John, 305, 355
Small Holdings and Allotments Act, 413
Smith, Adam, 36, 261
Smith, Alfred E., 610, 619, 630, 640
Smith, Captain John, 74
Smith, Joseph, 301, 303
Smith-Lever Act, 404
Smithson, James, 309
Smithsonian Institution, 309
Smoot-Hawley Tariff, 618, 621
Smuts, Jan Christian, 421, 549, 563
Smyth v. Ames, 381
"Social contract," 35
Social Democratic party (Germany),
    393, 422, 423, 589
Social Insurance laws (German), 423
Social Security Act, 636, 641, 747
Socialism, 266–270, 390, 391
Society of Jesus (Jesuits), 28, 31, 71
Soil Conservation Act, 638
Solferino, Battle of, 315
Solomon Islands, 496, 701
Somaliland, British, 462, 466
    French, 463, 466
    Italian, 462, 466
Somme, Battle of, 532
Sons of Liberty, 101
"Soo" Canal (St. Mary's Canal), 253
Sorel, Georges, 271
South Africa, 457–460, 599
    Union of, 421, 460
    political change in, after Second
        World War, 741, 742
South Carolina, 78
    nullification movement in, 329, 330
    secession of, 340, 341
South Improvement Company, 372
South Manchurian Railway, 475, 652,
    653
South Sea Company, 15
Southeast Asia Treaty Organization, 764
Southern Pacific Railroad, 376
"Southern Rights" faction, 331, 339
Spain, expansion of, 8, 10
    colonial system of, 18, 67–70
    decline of, 61
    in American Revolution, 118, 122,
        123, 125
    invasion of, by Napoleon, 200
    revolution in, 226, 227, 231, 232

Spain, in Franco-Prussian War, 321, 322
  revival of empire, 468, 469
  in Second World War, 685, 690, 706
Spanish-American War, 488–490
Spanish Civil War, 670–673
Spanish Succession, War of, 46, 62
Spartacists, 587
Specie Circular, 295
Spencer, Herbert, 389
Spinning jenny, 238
Spinoza, 34
Spruance, Raymond, 710
Stalin, Joseph, 580, 581
  in Second World War, 690
  in peacemaking conferences, 722–724
  death of, 734, 735
Stalingrad, 702, 707
Stamp Act, 96, 97
Stamp Act Congress, 97, 101
Standard Oil Company, 372, 380
  of New Jersey, 373
Standard Oil Trust, 372, 373
Stanford, Leland, 376
Stanley, Henry M., 456, 467
Stanton, Edwin M., 349, 362
Stanton, Elizabeth Cady, 298
States General, 39, 44, 126, 162
States rights, 145
Statute of Westminster, 599
Statuto, 289
Stavisky, Alexandre, 606
Steffens, Lincoln, 440
Stein, Baron vom, 204, 220
Steinbeck, John, 625
Stephens, Alexander H., 335
Stephens, Uriah S., 395
Stephenson, George, 255
Stepinac, Archbishop, 734
Steuben, Baron von, 110
Stevens, John L., 492
Stevens, Robert L., 257
Stevens, Thaddeus, 361
Stevenson, Adlai E., 748
Stilwell, Joseph W., 701
Stimson, Henry L., 653–655, 692
Stock Raising Homestead Act, 407
Stolypin, Pëtr A., 415, 427
Stone, Harlan F., 637, 642n.
Story, Joseph, 151
Stowe, Harriet Beecher, 336
Stresemann, Gustav, 570, 589
Strong, Josiah, 456, 487
Stuart, Gilbert, 309
Stuart dynasty, 47
Sudan, 462, 603
Sudetenland, 608, 675

Suez Canal, 259, 313, 461, 603
Suffolk Resolves, 105
Sugar Act, 96
Sully, Duc de, 44, 250
Sumner, Charles, 336
Sumner, William Graham, 389
Sun Yat-sen, 648–650
Sussex Pledge, 537, 538
Sweden, 25, 56
  in Napoleonic Wars, 199, 200, 202
  at Congress of Vienna, 223, 225
  industrialism in, 385
  democracy in, 608
  in Russo-Finnish War, 680
Switzerland, 26, 56
Syllabus of Errors, 422
Sylvis, William H., 395
Symington, William, 258
Syria, 545, 553, 604, 607, 690

Taff Vale decision, 392
Taft, Robert A., 745, 748
Taft, William Howard, 447–449, 501
Taft-Hartley Act, 745
Taiping Rebellion, 472
Talleyrand, 166, 188, 189
  as Napoleon's foreign minister, 194,
    203, 209
  at Congress of Vienna, 220–222
  and July Monarchy, 281
Tallmadge, James, 328
Taney, Roger B., 294, 337
Tannenberg, Battle of, 529
Tarawa, 710
Tarbell, Ida M., 440
"Tariff of Abominations," 329
Taylor, Zachary, 306, 332
Taylor Grazing Acts, 407, 639
Teapot Dome, 611
Tecumseh, 210, 215
Teheran Conference, 722, 723
Telford, Thomas, 250
Teller, Henry M., 438
Teller Resolution, 498
Ten Hours law, 247
Tennessee, state of, 132
  in Civil War, 349, 352
Tennessee River, 349, 613, 639
Tennessee Valley Authority (TVA), 628,
  639
"Tennis Court Oath," 163
Tenure of Office Act, 362
Test and Corporation Act, 279
Texas, 10, 303–305, 333
Texas v. White, 361
Thailand, 701, 764

Thiers, Adolphe, 323
Third Estate, 41, 126, 162
Third Reform Bill, 417
Third Republic, 365, 424–426
Thirteenth Amendment, 359
Thirty Years War, 28, 29, 54, 56
Thomas, George H., 350–352
Three Emperors, League of (*Dreikaiser-bund*), 513
Tibet, 481
Ticonderoga, 111, 115
Tilden, Samuel J., 363
Tillman, Ben, 411, 437
Tilsit, Treaty of, 198, 199
Tippecanoe, Battle of, 210
Tirpitz, Admiral von, 456, 516
Tito, Marshal, 689, 734
Togoland, 465
Tojo, General, 695
Toleration Act, in England, 51
in Maryland, 78
Tolstoy, Count, 271
Toombs, Robert Y., 335
Toronto, 215
Torricelli, 32
Toulon, 171–173, 706
Toussaint L'Ouverture, 190, 195
Townsend Plan, 636
Townshend, Charles, 98
Townshend, "Turnip," 5
Townshend Acts, 98, 99, 101
Trade Union Act of 1871, 392
Trades Disputes Act, 1906, 393
1927, 597
Trades Union Congress, 392, 596
Trafalgar, Battle of, 196
Trans-Siberian Railway, 384, 475
Transcendentalism, 308
Transportation Act of 1920, 613, 614
Transvaal, 457, 459
Trent affair, 355
Trenton, 112
Trevithick, Richard, 255
"Triangular trade," 20
Trieste, 731
Tripartite Pact, 693
Triple Alliance, 463, 514, 515, 520
Triple Entente, 514, 515, 520
Tripoli, 207, 208, 466, 467
Trist, Nicholas P., 307
Trondheim, 681
Trotsky, Leon, 427, 578–580
Truman, Harry S., 711, 743, 745
at Potsdam Conference, 724
and Truman Doctrine, 750
civil-rights program of, 746
reelection of, 746

Truman, Harry S., and Fair Deal program, 747
Truman Doctrine, 750, 756, 757
Trumbull, John, 309
Trusteeship Council, 718
Tsushima, Battle of, 477
Tudor dynasty, 47
Tulagi, 703
Tull, Jethro, 5
Tunis, 207, 208, 707
Tunisia, 463, 706, 707, 741
Turco-Italian War, 466, 467
Turenne, 45, 46
Turgot, A. R. J., 36, 41
Turkey, 312, 482, 520, 753
in First World War, 529, 530, 545
peace settlement with, 553, 557, 558
and Truman Doctrine, 755, 756
Turnpike roads, 250
Twain, Mark, 401, 491
Twelfth Amendment, 140
Twentieth Amendment, 624
Twenty-first Amendment, 619
Twenty-one Demands, 649
Twenty-second Amendment, 139n.
Tydings-McDuffie Act, 497
Tyler, John, 297, 305

Uganda, 462
Ukraine, 543, 691
in UN, 716, 724
Ulster, 418, 421, 600
"Underground Railroad," 336
Underwood-Simmons Tariff, 450
Union Pacific Railroad, 359, 375, 376
United Mine Workers, 396, 399, 634, 744, 745
United Nations, in Second World War, 697, 700, 705, 706
Charter of, 717, 718
organization of, 714–716
in operation, 718–720
and Palestine problem, 741, 757, 758
and Truman Doctrine, 756
and Korean War, 760–763
and atomic energy, 767–769
United Nations Agreement, 700
United Nations Relief and Rehabilitation Administration (UNRRA), 714
United States v. Butler, 637
United States v. E. C. Knight Company, 374, 375
United States v. Jones and Laughlin Steel Corporation, 634
United States Steel Corporation, 372, 634

Universal Declaration of Human Rights, 720
Uruguay, 232, 643
Utah, 303
Utilitarianism, 261, 262
Utrecht, Treaty of, 62

Valcour Island, 114
Vallandigham, Clement L., 359
Valley Forge, 108
Valmy, Battle of, 169
Van Buren, Martin, 248, 292, 295, 296
  in election of 1844, 305
  and Free-Soil party, 332
Vandenberg, Arthur H., 753, 756
Vanderbilt, Cornelius, 379
Vargas, Getulio, 643
Veblen, Thorstein, 440
Vendée, 171, 175
Venetia, 222, 315, 316
Venezuela, 231, 232, 487, 499
Vera Cruz, 307, 506, 507
Verdun, 531, 532
Vereeniging, Treaty of, 460
Vergennes, Comte de, 110, 116, 118, 122, 123
Versailles, Treaty of, 549, 550, 555, 556
  rejection of, by United States, 558, 559
  and Weimar Republic, 588
  repudiation of, by Nazis, 666
Vesalius, Andreas, 33
Vichy France, 684, 685, 706
Vicksburg, 347, 350
Victor Emmanuel II, 314–316
Victor Emmanuel III, 585, 707, 737
Victoria, Queen, 284, 478
Viet Minh, 764
Viet-Nam, 764
Villa, Pancho, 507
Villafranca, 315
Virgin Islands, 497
Virginia, 72, 120
  prohibits slave trade, 129
  western land claims of, 130, 132
  ratifies Constitution, 142
  joins Confederacy, 344
  in Civil War, 347–349
Virginia Company, 12, 72
"Virginia dynasty," 291
Virginia and Kentucky Resolutions, 148, 149, 152
Virginia Plan, 137
Volstead Act, 618, 619
Voltaire, 160

Wabash case, 381
Wade, Senator Ben, 362
Wade-Davis bill, 361
Wade-Davis Manifesto, 361
Wagner Act, 633, 634, 641, 745
Wagram, Battle of, 201
Wainwright, Jonathan, 701
Wake Island, 497, 700
Walker Tariff, 265
Wallace, Henry A., 637, 638, 746
Walpole, Sir Robert, 52, 63
Walsh, Thomas J., 611
Wanghia, Treaty of, 472
War Hawks, 210, 214
War Industries Board, 541
War Manpower Commission, 698, 699
War Production Board (WPB), 698
Ward, Frederick Townsend, 472
Warren, Robert Penn, 625
Warsaw, 579, 709
  Grand Duchy of, 199, 220, 221
Washington, George, 64
  in Revolutionary War, 110, 115, 120, 121
  at Federal Convention, 136
  as President, 142, 146–148, 177
  Farewell Address of, 186, 187
  canal project of, 251, 252
Washington, city of, 216, 347
  Treaty of, 354
Washington Conference, 571, 572, 650
Washington Naval Treaty, 571, 572
Water frame, 238
Waterloo, Battle of, 206
Watt, James, 237, 243
Wayne, "Mad Anthony," 183
Webb-Kenyon Act, 443
Webster, Daniel, 124, 293, 304
  Reply to Hayne, 325, 330
  and Compromise of 1850, 332, 333
Webster-Ashburton Treaty, 124n.
Weimar Constitution, 587, 588
Weizmann, Chaim, 603, 604
Weld, Theodore, 299
Wellington, Duke of, 200, 205, 285
  at Waterloo, 206
  and War of 1812, 216
  at Congress of Vienna, 220
  and repeal of Corn Laws, 265
  and First Reform Bill, 283, 284
Wesley, Charles, 246
Wesley, John, 246
West Coast Hotel Company v. Parrish, 642
West Indies, 20, 129, 178
West Virginia, 344, 345
Western European Union, 754

Westinghouse, George, 258, 373
Westphalia, Treaties of, 54
Weyler, General, 488
Wheeler, Burton K., 641, 692
Whig party (U.S.), 293, 297, 305, 335
Whisky Rebellion, 148
Whistler, G. W., 256
Whistler, James McNeill, 401
White, William Allen, 692
Whitman, Walt, 309
Whitney, Eli, 238, 241, 368
Whittier, John G., 309
Wickersham Commission, 619
"Wilderness," 351
Wilkinson, John, 237
William I, German emperor, 318, 321–323, 423
William II, German emperor, 423, 456, 482
and coming of First World War, 514, 516, 518
abdication of, 545
William IV of England, 282–284
William of Orange, 50, 52
and Mary, 51
Williams, Roger, 28, 30, 76, 77
Willkie, Wendell L., 639, 694
Wilmot, David, 331
Wilmot Proviso, 331
Wilson, James, 137
Wilson, Thomas Woodrow, 400, 449–452
Latin-American policy, 501, 502, 505–507
in First World War, 536–644
in Peace Settlement, 548–559
growth of concept of League of Nations, 563
Wilson-Gorman Tariff, 436, 437
Windischgrätz, General, 287, 288
Winthrop, John, 28, 75, 76
Winthrop, John, Jr., 76
Witte, Count, 384, 426

Wolfe, James, 64
Wolfe, Thomas, 625
Woman suffrage, 298, 387, 388
Wood, Grant, 626
Wood, Leonard, 498
Works Progress Administration (WPA), 635, 636
World Peace Foundation, 562
World War Foreign Debt Commission, 568
Wright brothers, 368
Writs of assistance, 96
Württemberg, 196, 198, 321
Wycliffe, John, 23
Wyndham Act, 418

Xavier, St. Francis, 473
XYZ Affair, 188, 189

Yalta, 712, 716, 723, 724
Yancey, William Lowndes, 339
Yangtze, 647
Yorktown, 120, 121
Young, Brigham, 303
Young, Owen D., 567
Young Plan, 567
Ypres, 536, 544
Yugoslavia, 661, 662, 665
in Second World War, 689
in Peace settlement, 731

Zanzibar, 462, 465
Zenger, John Peter, 80
Zimmerman Note, 540, 541
Zionism, 603–605, 757
Zola, Émile, 425
Zollverein, 265, 286, 314, 317
Zwingli, Ulrich, 25, 26